Literature Criticism from 1400 to 1800

Guide to Gale Literary Criticism Series

When you need to review criticism of literary works, these are the Gale series to use:

If the author's death date is:	You should turn to:
After Dec. 31, 1959 (or author is still living)	***Contemporary Literary Criticism*** for example: Jorge Luis Borges, Anthony Burgess, William Faulkner, Mary Gordon, Ernest Hemingway, Iris Murdoch
1900 through 1959	***Twentieth-Century Literary Criticism*** for example: Willa Cather, F. Scott Fitzgerald, Henry James, Mark Twain, Virginia Woolf
1800 through 1899	***Nineteenth-Century Literature Criticism*** for example: Fedor Dostoevski, Nathaniel Hawthorne, George Sand, William Wordsworth
1400 through 1799	***Literature Criticism From 1400 to 1800 (excluding Shakespeare)*** for example: Anne Bradstreet, Daniel Defoe, Alexander Pope, François Rabelais, Jonathan Swift, Phillis Wheatley
	Shakespearean Criticism Shakespeare's plays and poetry
Antiquity through 1399	***Classical and Medieval Literature Criticism*** for example: Dante, Homer, Plato, Sophocles, Vergil, the Beowulf Poet

---

Gale also publishes related criticism series:

Children's Literature Review

This series covers authors of all eras who have written for the preschool through high school audience.

Short Story Criticism

This series covers the major short fiction writers of all nationalities and periods of literary history.

Poetry Criticism

This series covers poets of all nationalities and periods of literary history.

ISSN 0740-2880

Volume 16

Literature Criticism from 1400 to 1800

Excerpts from Criticism of the Works of Fifteenth-, Sixteenth-, Seventeenth-, and Eighteenth-Century Novelists, Poets, Playwrights, Philosophers, and Other Creative Writers, from the First Published Critical Appraisals to Current Evaluations

James E. Person, Jr.
Editor

Gale Research Inc. • DETROIT • LONDON

STAFF

James E. Person, Jr., *Editor*

Tina N. Grant, Zoran Minderovic, Joseph C. Tardiff,
Allyson J. Wylie, *Assistant Editors*

Jeanne A. Gough, *Permissions and Production Manager*

Linda M. Pugliese, *Production Supervisor*
L. Mpho Mabunda, Maureen A. Puhl, Jennifer VanSickle,
Editorial Associates
Donna Craft, Paul Lewon, Camille Robinson, Sheila Walencewicz,
Editorial Assistants

Maureen Richards, *Research Supervisor*
Paula Cutcher-Jackson, H. Nelson Fields, Judy L. Gale,
Mary Beth McElmeel, *Editorial Associates*
Robin Lupa, Tamara C. Nott, *Editorial Assistants*

Sandra C. Davis, *Text Permissions Supervisor*
Josephine M. Keene, Denise Singleton, Kimberly F. Smilay,
Permissions Associates
Maria L. Franklin, Michele M. Lonoconus
Shalice Shah, Nancy K. Sheridan, Rebecca A. Stanko,
Permissions Assistants

Patricia A. Seefelt, *Permissions Supervisor (Pictures)*
Margaret A. Chamberlain, Pamela A. Hayes, *Permissions Associates*
Keith Reed, *Permissions Assistant*

Mary Beth Trimper, *Production Manager*
Mary Winterhalter, *External Production Assistant*

Arthur Chartow, *Art Director*
C. J. Jonik, *Keyliner*

The paper used in this publication meets the minimum requirements of American National Standard for Information Sciences—Permanence Paper for Printed Library Materials, ANSI Z39.48-1984.

835 Penobscot Bldg.
Detroit, MI 48226-4094

Library of Congress Catalog Card Number 84-643570
ISBN 0-8103-6115-9
ISSN 0740-2880

Printed in the United States of America

Published simultaneously in the United Kingdom
by Gale Research International
(An affiliated company of Gale Research Inc.)

Contents

Preface

Literature Criticism from 1400 to 1800 (LC) presents criticism of world authors of the fifteenth through eighteenth centuries. The literature of this period reflects a turbulent time of radical change that saw the rise of drama equal in stature to that of classical Greece, the birth of the novel and personal essay forms, the emergence of newspapers and periodicals, and major achievements in poetry and philosophy. Much of modern literature reflects the influence of these centuries. Thus the literature treated in *LC* provides insight into the universal nature of human experience, as well as into the life and thought of the past.

Scope of the Series

LC is designed to serve as an introduction to authors of the fifteenth through eighteenth centuries and to the most significant interpretations of these authors' works. The great poets, dramatists, novelists, essayists, and philosophers of this period are considered classics in every secondary school and college or university curriculum. Because criticism of this literature spans nearly six hundred years, an overwhelming amount of critical material confronts the student. *LC* therefore organizes and reprints the most noteworthy published criticism of authors of these centuries. Readers should note that there is a separate Gale reference series devoted to Shakespearean studies. For though belonging properly to the period covered in *LC,* William Shakespeare has inspired such a tremendous and ever-growing corpus of secondary material that the editors have deemed it best to give his works extensive coverage in a separate series, *Shakespearean Criticism.*

Each author entry in *LC* attempts to present a historical survey of critical response to the author's works. Early criticism is offered to indicate initial responses, later selections document any rise or decline in literary reputations, and retrospective analyses provide students with modern views. The size of each author entry is intended to reflect the author's critical reception in English or foreign criticism in translation. Articles and books that have not been translated into English are therefore excluded. Every attempt has been made to identify and include the seminal essays on each author's work and to include recent commentary providing modern perspectives.

The need for *LC* among students and teachers of literature was suggested by the proven usefulness of Gale's *Contemporary Literary Criticism (CLC), Twentieth-Century Literary Criticism (TCLC),* and *Nineteenth-Century Literature Criticism (NCLC),* which excerpt criticism of works by nineteenth- and twentieth-century authors. Because of the different time periods covered, there is no duplication of authors or critical material in any of these literary criticism series. An author may appear more than once in the series because of the great quantity of critical material available and because of the aesthetic demands of the series's *thematic organization.*

Thematic Approach

Beginning with Volume 12, roughly half the authors in each volume of *LC* are organized in a thematic scheme. Such themes include literary movements, literary reaction to political and historical events, significant eras in literary history, and the literature of cultures often overlooked by English-speaking readers. The present volume, for example, focuses upon the cultural significance of Northern Humanism. Future volumes of *LC* will devote substantial space to authors of Fifteenth-Century English Literature, the English Metaphysical poets, and the Spanish Golden Age, among many others. The rest of each volume will be devoted to criticism of the works of authors not aligned with the selected thematic authors and chosen from a variety of nationalities.

Organization of the Book

Each entry consists of the following elements: author or thematic heading, introduction, list of principal works (in author entries only), annotated works of criticism (each followed by a bibliographical citation), and a bibliography of further reading. Also, most author entries contain author portraits and other illustrations.

- The **author heading** consists of the author's full name, followed by birth and death dates. If an author wrote consistently under a pseudonym, the pseudonym is used in the author heading, with the real name given in parentheses on the first line of the biographical and critical introduction. Also located here are any name variations under which an author wrote, including transliterated forms for authors whose native languages use nonroman alphabets. Uncertain birth or death dates are indicated by question marks. The **thematic heading** simply states the subject of the entry.

- The **biographical and critical introduction** contains background information designed to introduce the reader to an author and to critical discussion of his or her work. Parenthetical material following many of the introductions provides references to biographical and critical reference series published by Gale in which additional material about the author may be found. The **thematic introduction** briefly defines the subject of the entry and provides social and historical background important to understanding the criticism.

- Most *LC* author entries include **portraits** of the author. Many entries also contain illustrations of materials pertinent to an author's career, including author holographs, title pages, letters, or representations of important people, places, and events in an author's life.

- The **list of principal works** is chronological by date of first book publication and identifies the genre of each work. In the case of foreign authors whose works have been translated into English, the title and date of the first English-language edition are given in brackets beneath the foreign-language listing. Unless otherwise indicated, dramas are dated by first performance, not first publication.

- **Criticism** is arranged chronologically in each author entry to provide a useful perspective on changes in critical evaluation over the years. For the purpose of easy identification, the critic's name and the composition or publication date of the critical work are given at the beginning of each piece of criticism. Unsigned criticism is preceded by the title of the source in which it appeared. All titles by the author featured in the critical entry are printed in boldface type. Publication information (such as publisher names and book prices) and parenthetical numerical references (such as footnotes or page and line references to specific editions of works) have been deleted at the editors' discretion to provide smoother reading of the text.

- Critical essays are prefaced by **annotations** as an additional aid to students using *LC*. These explanatory notes may provide several types of useful information, including: the reputation of a critic, the importance of a work of criticism, the commentator's individual approach to literary criticism, the intent of the criticism, and the growth of critical controversy or changes in critical trends regarding an author's work. In some cases, these notes cross-reference the work of critics within the entry who agree or disagree with each other.

- A complete **bibliographical citation** of the original essay or book follows each piece of criticism.

- An annotated bibliography of **further reading** appears at the end of each entry and suggests resources for additional study of authors and themes. It also includes essays for which the editors could not obtain reprint rights.

Cumulative Indexes

Each volume of *LC* includes a cumulative **author index** listing all the authors that have appeared in *Contemporary Literary Criticism, Twentieth-Century Literary Criticism, Nineteenth-Century Literature Criticism, Literature Criticism from 1400 to 1800,* and *Classical and Medieval Literature Criticism,* along with cross-references to the Gale series *Short Story Criticism, Poetry Criticism, Children's Literature Review, Authors in the News, Contemporary Authors, Contemporary Authors Autobiography Series, Contemporary Authors Bibliographical Series, Dictionary of Literary Biography, Concise Dictionary of Literary Biography, Something about the Author, Something about the Author Autobiography Series,* and *Yesterday's Authors of Books for Children.* Readers will welcome this cumulative author index as a useful tool for locating an author within the various series. The index, which includes authors' birth and death dates, is particularly valuable for those authors who are identified with a certain period but whose death dates cause them to be placed in another, or for those authors whose careers span two periods. For example, F. Scott Fitzgerald is found in *TCLC,* yet a writer often associated with him, Ernest Hemingway, is found in *CLC.*

Beginning with Volume 12, *LC* includes a cumulative **topic index** that lists all literary themes and topics treated in *LC, NCLC* Topics volumes, *TCLC* Topics volumes, and the *CLC* Yearbook. Each volume of *LC* also includes a cumulative **nationality index** in which authors' names are arranged alphabetically under their respective nationalities and followed by the numbers of the volumes in which they appear.

Each volume of *LC* also includes a cumulative **title index,** an alphabetical listing of the literary works discussed in the series since its inception. Each title listing includes the corresponding volume and page numbers where criticism may be located. Foreign-language titles that have been translated are followed by the titles of the translations—for example, *El ingenioso hidalgo Don Quixote de la Mancha (Don Quixote).* Page numbers following these translated titles refer to all pages on which any form of the titles, either foreign-language or translated, appear. Titles of novels, dramas, nonfiction books, and poetry, short story, or essay collections are printed in italics, while individual poems, short stories, and essays are printed in roman type within quotation marks.

A Note to the Reader

When writing papers, students who quote directly from any volume in the Literary Criticism Series may use the following general forms to footnote reprinted criticism. The first example pertains to material drawn from periodicals, the second to material reprinted from books.

T. S. Eliot, "John Donne," *The Nation and the Athenaeum,* 33 (9 June 1923), 321-32; excerpted and reprinted in *Literature Criticism from 1400 to 1800,* Vol. 10, ed. James E. Person, Jr. (Detroit: Gale Research, 1989), pp. 28-9.

Clara G. Stillman, *Samuel Butler: A Mid-Victorian Modern* (Viking Press, 1932); excerpted and reprinted in *Twentieth-Century Literary Criticism,* Vol. 33, ed. Paula Kepos (Detroit: Gale Research, 1989), pp. 43-5.

Suggestions Are Welcome

In response to various suggestions, several features have been added to *LC* since the series began, including a nationality index, a Literary Criticism Series topic index, thematic entries, a descriptive table of contents, and more extensive illustrations.

Readers who wish to suggest new features, themes, or authors to appear in future volumes, or who have other suggestions, are cordially invited to write to the editor.

Acknowledgments

The editors wish to thank the copyright holders of the excerpted criticism included in this volume, the permissions managers of many book and magazine publishing companies for assisting us in securing reprint rights, and Anthony Bogucki for assistance with copyright research. We are also grateful to the staffs of the Detroit Public Library, Wayne State University Purdy/Kresge Library Complex, and the University of Michigan Libraries for making their resources available to us. Following is a list of the copyright holders who have granted us permission to reprint material in this volume of *LC*. Every effort has been made to trace copyright, but if omissions have been made, please let us know.

COPYRIGHTED EXCERPTS IN *LC*, VOLUME 16, WERE REPRINTED FROM THE FOLLOWING PERIODICALS:

African Literature Today, n. 5, 1971. Copyright 1971 by Heinemann Educational Books Ltd. All rights reserved. Reprinted by permission of Africana Publishing Corporation, New York, NY.—***The American Scholar,*** v. 56, Summer, 1987 for "Portrait of Justus Lipsius" by Anthony Grafton. Copyright © 1987 by the author. Reprinted by permission of the publishers.—***Black American Literature Forum,*** v. 19, Summer, 1985 for "Disguised Voice in 'The Interesting Narrative of Olaudah Equiano, or Gustavus Vassa, the African' " by Wilfred D. Samuels. Copyright © 1985 Indiana State University. Reprinted by permission of Indiana State University and the author.—***English Literary Renaissance,*** v. 12, Autumn, 1982. Copyright © 1982 by *English Literary Renaissance.* Reprinted by permission of the publisher.—***Journal of the History of Ideas,*** v. XXXVI, January-March, 1975. Copyright 1975, Journal of the History of Ideas, Inc. Reprinted by permission of the publisher. v. XI, October, 1950; v. XV, October, 1954. Copyright 1950, renewed 1977; copyright 1954, renewed 1982, Journal of the History of Ideas, Inc. Both reprinted by permission of the publisher.—***Journal of the Warburg and Courtauld Institutes,*** v. 26, 1963. © 1963, The Warburg Institute. Reprinted by permission of the publisher.—***Kyushu American Literature,*** n. 20, June 1979 for "Olaudah Equiano: The Prototypal Christian Abolitionist Transfigured from an African Heathen" by Sekio Koike. Reprinted by permission of the publisher and the author.—***Negro History Bulletin,*** v. 46, October-December, 1983. Reprinted by permission of The Association for the Study of Afro-American Life and History, Inc.—***Past and Present: A Journal of Historical Studies,*** n. 45, November, 1969. © World Copyright: The Past and Present Society, 175 Banbury Road, Oxford, England. Reprinted by permission of the publisher.—***PHYLON: The Atlanta University Review of Race and Culture,*** v. 45, June, 1984. Copyright, 1984, by Atlanta University. Reprinted by permission of *PHYLON.*—***Renaissance and Reformation,*** n.s. v. V, 1981. Reprinted by permission of the publisher.—***Research in African Literatures,*** v. 13, Spring, 1982. Copyright © 1982 by the University of Texas Press. Reprinted by permission of Indiana University Press.—***Studies in Philology,*** v. LXXX, Summer, 1983 for "In Praise of Wisdom and the Will of God: Erasmus' 'Praise of Folly' and Swift's 'A Tale of a Tub' " by Eugene R. Hammond. © 1983 by The University of North Carolina Press. Reprinted by permission of the publisher and the author.—***The Times Literary Supplement,*** n. 3557, April 30, 1970. © Times Newspapers Ltd. (London) 1970. Reproduced from *The Times Literary Supplement* by permission.

COPYRIGHTED EXCERPTS IN *LC*, VOLUME 16, WERE REPRINTED FROM THE FOLLOWING BOOKS:

Adams, Robert P. From ***The Better Part of Valor: More, Erasmus, Colet, and Vives, on Humanism, War, and Peace, 1496-1635.*** University of Washington Press, 1962. Copyright © 1962 by the University of Washington Press. Reprinted by permission of the publisher.—Agrawal, R. R. From ***Tradition and Experiment in the Poetry of James Thomson (1700-1748).*** Institut für Anglistik und Amerikanistik Universität Salzburg, 1981. Reprinted by permission of the publisher.—Aston, Margaret E. From "The Northern Renaissance," in ***The Meaning of the Renaissance and Reformation.*** Edited by Richard L. DeMolen. Houghton Mifflin, 1973. Copyright © 1974 by Houghton Mifflin Company. All rights reserved. Reprinted by permission of Houghton Mifflin Company.—Bainton, Roland H. From ***Erasmus of Christendom.*** Charles Scribner's Sons, 1969. Copyright © 1969 Roland H. Bainton. All rights reserved. Reprinted with the permission of Charles Scribner's Sons, an imprint of Macmillan Publishing Company.—Baker, Houston A., Jr. From ***The Journey Back: Issues in Black Literature and Criticism.*** The University of Chicago Press, 1980. © 1980 by The University of Chicago. All rights reserved. Reprinted by permission of the publisher and the author.—Bernstein, Eckhard. From ***German Humanism.*** Twayne, 1983. Copyright 1983 by Twayne Publishers. All rights reserved. Reprinted with the permission of Twayne Publishers, a division of G. K. Hall & Co., Boston.—Best, Thomas W. From *The Humanist Ulrich Von Hutten: A Reappraisal of His Humor.* The University of North Carolina Press, 1969. Reprinted by permission of the publisher and the author.—Bloom, Edward A. and

Lillian D. Bloom. From ***Satire's Persuasive Voice.*** Cornell University Press, 1979. Copyright © 1979 by Cornell University. All rights reserved. Used by permission of the publisher, Cornell University Press.—Butler, Pierce. From ***The Origin of Printing in Europe.*** The University of Chicago Press, 1940. Copyright 1940 by The University of Chicago. Renewed 1967 by Mrs. Pierce Butler. All rights reserved. Reprinted by permission of the publisher.—Cameron, James K. From "Humanism in the Low Countries," in ***The Impact of Humanism on Western Europe.*** Edited by Anthony Goodman and Angus MacKay. Longman, 1990. © Longman Group UK Limited 1990. All rights reserved. Reprinted by permission of the publisher.—Cazamian, Louis. From ***A History of English Literature: Modern Times (1660-1914), Vol. 2.*** Translated by W. D. MacInnes and Louis Cazamian. Macmillan, 1927. Copyright, 1927, by Macmillan Publishing Company. Renewed 1955 by Louis Cazamian. All rights reserved. Reprinted with permission of the publisher.—Colet, John. From a letter in ***The Correspondence of Erasmus: 1514-1516.*** By Desiderius Erasmus, translated by R. A. B. Mynors and D. F. S. Thomson. University of Toronto Press, 1976. © University of Toronto Press 1976. Reprinted by permission of the publisher.—Costanzo, Angelo. From ***Surprizing Narrative: Olaudah Equiano and the Beginnings of Black Autobiography.*** Greenwood Press, 1987. Copyright © 1987 by Angelo Costanzo. All rights reserved. Reprinted by permission of Greenwood Publishing Group, Inc., Westport, CT.—Daiches, David. From ***A Critical History of English Literature, Vol. II.*** The Ronald Press Company, 1960. Copyright © 1960 by the Ronald Press Company. Renewed 1988 by David Daiches. All rights reserved. Reprinted by permission of David Higham Associates.—DeMolen, Richard L. From "The Age of Renaissance and Reformation," in ***The Meaning of the Renaissance and Reformation.*** Edited by Richard L. DeMolen. Houghton Mifflin, 1973. Copyright © 1974 by Houghton Mifflin Company. All right reserved. Reprinted by permission of Houghton Mifflin Company.—Dorp, Maarten van. From a letter in ***The Correspondence of Erasmus: 1514-1516.*** By Desiderius Erasmus, translated by R. A. B. Mynors and D. F. S. Thomson. University of Toronto Press, 1976. © University of Toronto Press 1976. Reprinted by permission of the publishers.—Douglas, A. E. From "Erasmus as a Satirist," in ***Erasmus.*** Edited by T. A. Dorey. Routledge & K. Paul, 1970. © T. A. Dorey, 1970. Reprinted by permission of the publisher.—Edwards, Paul. From "Three West African Writers of the 1780's," in ***The Slave's Narrative.*** Edited by Charles T. Davis and Henry Louis Gates, Jr. Oxford University Press, 1985. Copyright © 1985 by Oxford University Press, Inc. All rights reserved. Reprinted by permission of the author.—Erasmus, Desiderius. From a letter in ***The Correspondence of Erasmus: 1501-1514.*** By Desiderius Erasmus, translated by R. A. B. Mynors and D. F. S. Thomson. University of Toronto Press, 1975. © University of Toronto Press 1975. Reprinted by permission of the publisher.—Erasmus, Desiderius. From a letter in ***The Correspondence of Erasmus: 1514-1516.*** By Desiderius Erasmus, translated by R. A. B. Mynors and D. F. S. Thomson. University of Toronto Press, 1976. © University of Toronto Press 1976. Reprinted by permission of the publisher.—Gates, Henry Louis, Jr. From ***The Signifying Monkey: A Theory of Afro-American Literary Criticism.*** Oxford University Press, 1988. Copyright © 1988 by Henry Louis Gates, Jr. All rights reserved. Reprinted by permission of Oxford University Press, Inc.—Gilmore, Myron P. From ***The World of Humanism, 1453-1517.*** Harper & Brothers Publishers, 1952. Copyright, 1952, by Harper & Row, Publishers, Inc. Renewed 1980 by Sheila Gilmore. All rights reserved. Reprinted by permission of HarperCollins Publishers, Inc.—Grendler, Paul F. From "Printing and Censorship," in ***The Cambridge History of Renaissance Philosophy.*** Edited by Charles B. Schmitt, Quentin Skinner, Eckhard Kessler and Jill Kraye. Cambridge at the University Press, 1988. © Cambridge University Press 1988. Reprinted with the permission of the publisher and the author.—Henkel-Hobbs, Julia S. From "School Organizational Patterns of the Brethren of the Common Life," in ***The Dawn of Modern Civilization: Studies in Renaissance, Reformation and Other Topics Presented to Honor Albert Hyma.*** Edited by Kenneth A. Strand. Ann Arbor Publishers, 1962. Copyright, 1962, 1964 by Ann Arbor Publishers. Reprinted by permission of the editor.—Holborn, Hajo. From an introduction to ***On the Eve of the Reformation: "Letters of Obscure Men."*** By Ulrich Von Hutten, edited and translated by Francis Griffin Stokes. Harper Torchbooks, 1964. Introduction to the Torchbook edition copyright © 1964 by Hajo Holborn. Reprinted by permission of HarperCollins Publishers, Inc.—Hyma, Albert. From ***The Brethren of the Common Life.*** Eerdmans, 1950. Copyright, 1950, by Wm. B. Eerdmans Publishing Company. Renewed 1978 by Albert Hyma. All rights reserved. Reprinted by permission of the Literary Estate of Albert Hyma.—Hyma, Albert. From ***The Youth of Erasmus.*** University of Michigan Press, 1930. Copyright, 1931, by Graduate School, University of Michigan. Renewed 1959 by Albert Hyma. Reprinted by permission of the publisher.—IJseqijn, Jozef. From "Humanism in the Low Countries," in ***Renaissance Humanism: Foundations, Forms, and Legacy, Vol. 2.*** Edited by Albert Rabil, Jr. University of Pennsyvlania Press, 1988. Copyright © 1988 by the University of Pennsylvania Press. All rights reserved. Reprinted by permission of the publisher.—Kaiser, Walter. From ***Praisers of Folly: Erasmus, Rabelais, Shakespeare.*** Cambridge, Mass.: Harvard University Press, 1963. Copyright © 1963 by the President and Fellows of Harvard College. All rights reserved. Excerpted by permission of the publishers and the author.—Lipsius, Justus. From ***Two Bookes of Constancie.*** Translated by Sir John Stradling, edited by Rudolf Kirk. Rutgers University Press, 1939. Copyright, 1939, by The Trustees of Rutgers College. Renewed 1967 by Rudolf Kirk. Reprinted by permission of the publisher.—Loggins, Vernon. From ***The Negro Author: His Development in American to 1900.*** Columbia University Press, 1931. Copyright 1931 Columbia University Press. Renewed 1959 by Vernon Loggins. Reprinted by permission of the Literary Estate of Vernon Loggins.—McGrath, Alister E. From ***Reformation Thought: An Introduction.*** Basil Blackwell, 1988. Copyright © Alister E. McGrath 1988. All rights reserved. Reprinted by permission of Basil Blackwell Limited.—Nicolson, Marjorie Hope. From ***Newton Demands the Muse: Newton's "Opticks" and the Eighteenth Century Poets.*** Princeton University Press, 1946. Copyright 1946 by Princeton University Press. Renewed 1973 by Marjorie Hope Nicholson. Reprinted with permission of the publisher.—Nussbaum, Felicity A. From ***The Brink of All We Hate: English Satires on Women, 1660-1750.*** University Press of Kentucky, 1984. Copyright © 1984 by The University Press of Kentucky. Reprinted by permission of the publisher.—Olin, John C. From an introduction to ***Christian Humanism and the Reformation: Selected Writings of Erasmus, with the Life of Erasmus.*** By Beatus Rhenanus, edited by John C. Olin. Revised edition. Fordham University Press, 1975. © copyright 1975 by Fordham University Press. All rights reserved. Reprinted by permission of the publisher.—Pace, Richard. From a letter in ***The Correspondence of Erasmus: 1518-1519.*** By Desiderius Erasmus, translated by R. A. B. Mynors and D. F. S. Thomson. University of Toronto Press, 1982. © University of Toronto Press 1982. Reprinted by permission of the publisher.—Phillips, Margaret Mann. From "Ways with Adages," in ***Essays on the Works of Erasmus.*** Edited by Richard L. DeMolen. Yale University Press, 1978. Copyright © 1978 by Yale University. All rights reserved. Reprinted by permission of the publisher. Post, R. R. From ***The Modern Devotion: Confrontation with Reformation and Humanism.*** Brill, 1968. Copyright 1968 E. J. Brill, Leiden, Netherlands. All rights reserved. Reprinted by permission of the publisher.—Richards, Edward Ames. From ***Hudibras in the Burlesque Tradition.*** Columbia University Press, 1937. Copyright 1937, renewed 1965 Columbia University Press, New York. Used by permission of the publisher.—Rowse, A. L. From ***The English Spirit: Essays in Literature and History.*** Revised edition. Funk & Wagnalls, 1966. © A. L. Rowse 1966. Reprinted by permission of Curtis Brown Ltd.—Sandiford, Keith A. From ***Measuring the Moment: Strategies of Protest in Eighteenth-Century Afro-English Writing.*** Associated University Presses, 1988. © 1988 by Associated University Presses, Inc. Reprinted by permission of the publisher.—Schrijvers, P. H. From "Literary and Philosophical Aspects of Lipsius's 'De Constania in Publicis Malis'." in ***Acta Conventus Neo-Latini Sanctandreani.*** Edited by I. D. McFarlane. Medieval & Renaissance Texts & Studies, v. 38, Binghamton, NY, 1986. © copyright 1986 Center for Medieval and Early Renaissance Studies. Reprinted by permission of the publisher.—Scott, Mary Jane W. From ***James Thomson: Anglo-Scot.*** The University of Georgia Press, 1988. © 1988 by the University of Georgia Press. All rights reserved. Used by permission of the publisher and the author.—Smith, Preserved. From ***The Age of Reformation.*** Holt, 1920. Copyright, 1920 by Henry Holt and Company. Renewed 1948 by Preserved Smith.—Sowards, J. Kelley. From ***Desiderius Erasmus.*** Twayne, 1975. Copyright 1975 by Twayne Publishers. All rights reserved. Reprinted with the permission of Twayne Publishers, a division of G. K. Hall & Co., Boston.—Spitz, Lewis W. From ***The Religious Renaissance of the German Humanists.*** Cambridge, Mass.: Harvard University Press, 1963. Copyright © 1963 by the President and Fellows of Harvard College. All rights reserved. Excerpted by permission of the publishers and the author.—Stradling, Sir John. From "The Epistle to the Reader," in ***Two Bookes of Constancie.*** By Justus Lipsius, edited by Rudolf Kirk, translated by Sir John Stradling. Rutgers University Press, 1939. Copyright, 1939, by The Trustees of Rutgers College. Renewed 1967 by Rudolf Kirk. Reprinted by permission of the publisher.—Strand, Kenneth A. From "The Brethren of the Common Life and Fifteenth-Century Printing: A Brief Survey," in ***The Dawn of Modern Civilization: Studies in Renaissance, Reformation and Other Topics Presented to Honor Albert Hyma.*** Edited by Kenneth A. Strand. Ann Arbor Publisher, 1962. Copyright, 1962, 1964 by Ann Arbor Publishers. Reprinted by permission of the editor.—Sutherland, W. O. S., Jr. From ***The Art of the Satirist: Essays on the Satire of Augustan England.*** The University of Texas, 1965. © 1965 The University of Texas. Reprinted by permission of the publisher.—Thompson, Craig R. From an introduction to ***Ten Colloquies of Erasmus.*** By Desiderius Erasmus, translated by Craig R. Thompson. The Liberal Arts Press, 1957. Copyright ©, 1957 The Liberal Arts Press, Inc. Renewed 1985 by Craig Ringwalt Thompson. Copyright © 1986 by Macmillan Publishing Company. Reprinted with permission of Macmillan Publishing Company.—Thompson, Sister Geraldine. From ***Under Pretext of Praise: Satiric Mode in Erasmus' Fiction.*** University of Toronto Press, 1973. © University of Toronto Press 1973. Reprinted by permission of the publisher.—Tracy, James D. From "Erasmus the Humanist," in ***Erasmus of Rotterdam.*** Edited by Richard L. DeMolen. Twayne, 1971. Copyright 1971 by Twayne Publishers. All rights reserved. Reprinted with the permission of Twayne Publishers, Inc., a division of G. K. Hall & Co., Boston.—Wasserman, George. From ***Samuel "Hudibras" Butler.*** Twayne, 1989. Copyright 1989 by Twayne Publishers. All rights reserved. Reprinted with the permission of Twayne Publishers, a division of G. K. Hall & Co., Boston.—Wheelis, Sam. From "Ulrich Von Hutten: Representative of Patriotic Humanism," in ***The Renaissance and Reformation in Germany: An Introduction.*** Edited by Gerhart Hoffmeister. Frederick Ungar Publishing Co., 1977. Copyright © 1977 by The Ungar Publishing Company. Reprinted by permission of the publisher.—Wilders, John. From an introduction to ***Hudibras.*** By Samuel Butler, edited by John Wilders. Oxford at the Clarendon Press, 1967. © Oxford University Press, 1967. Reprinted by permission of the publisher.

PHOTOGRAPHS AND ILLUSTRATIONS APPEARING IN *LC*, VOLUME 16, WERE RECEIVED FROM THE FOLLOWING SOURCES:

Courtesy of Maison d'Erasme, Anderlecht, Belgium: **p. 315;** The Bettmann Archive: **p. 326.**

Samuel Butler

1612-1680

English poet and prose writer.

Butler was one of Restoration England's most popular satirists and is best remembered for *Hudibras,* a mock epic poem in which the author attacks the perceived hypocrisy of the Puritans who had ruled his country from 1642 to 1660. Influenced by Miguel de Cervantes's *Don Quixote* (1605), Butler related the comic adventures of the Puritan knight errant Sir Hudibras and his squire Ralpho. Butler's use in *Hudibras* of an eight-syllable line commonly reserved for "heroic" works and his unconventional rhymes comprise a distinctive and often-imitated poetic style that came to be known as "hudibrastic" verse. Although its popularity as a work of literature has declined, *Hudibras* is still considered valuable commentary on the religious and political thought of seventeenth-century England and is admired for incisive, biting wit.

Little documentation on Butler's life exists. The son of Samuel Butler, Sr., a landowner and parish clerk, Butler was baptized in 1613 at Strensham, Worcester. Commentators conjecture that he received some formal education, after which he was employed as secretary for various public officials and noble families. During the late 1620s, while in the service of Elizabeth Grey, Countess of Kent, Butler likely became acquainted with the jurist and antiquarian John Selden; many critics discern Selden's influence in the religious and political views expressed in Butler's writings. Little is known of the poet's activities during the next two decades. Until the twentieth century, biographers believed that Butler spent most of the 1630s and 1640s in the service of Sir Samuel Luke, a Presbyterian member of Parliament who scholars long believed served as a model for the character of Sir Hudibras. Letters by and about Butler discovered by Ricardo Quintana in 1933, however, place him in London's Holbourne district at the time and indicate that he may have pursued a career in law at Gray's Inn. These documents also reveal the true source of Hudibras's character to be Sir Henry Rosewell, a member of Parliament with whom the poet became acquainted in Holbourne. During this period, in which civil war broke out in England and Charles I was executed, Butler may have written several unsigned political pamphlets in defence of the monarchy.

Some commentators date the composition of *Hudibras* as early as 1645, and others believe he began writing the mock epic during the late 1650s. When *Hudibras, The First Part* was published in 1662, the monarchy had been restored in England and Butler was employed by Carbery, Lord President of Wales, as the steward at Ludlow Castle. The poem was a popular success that prompted five reprintings and several unauthorized editions within the year; the second and third parts of the poem, published in 1663 and 1677, were equally successful. Butler was hailed as England's foremost satirist, and many of the poem's witticisms became popular adages. In addition to *Hudibras,* Butler wrote nearly two hundred character sketches examining a variety of personalities and professions, but these remained unpublished until after his death. Butler reportedly was insolvent in his later years, possibly as a consequence of having several editions of *Hudibras* pirated, which deprived the poet of income. Critics also speculate that Butler mismanaged his finances; and, though awarded an annual stipend from Charles II, he may have never received it. Butler died in London in 1680.

Hudibras depicts three days in the adventures of self-righteous, hypocritical Sir Hudibras and the unprincipled, foolish Ralpho in the former's attempt to marry the Lady and secure her fortune. The friendship between the knight and his squire is repeatedly tested by their diverging religious beliefs; although each is a Puritan, Hudibras supports the Presbyterian faction in favor of reform and an established hierarchy in the church, while Ralpho follows the more liberal, self-governing Independents. Butler satirizes both beliefs by presenting lengthy debates between the two in which each abuses logic to gain advantage. Butler similarly ridicules the principles of the secular characters Hudibras and Ralpho encounter, which include scientists, politicians, and lawyers. The poem concludes with the rejection of Hudibras by the Lady, who subjects her suitor to a discourse on the superior intelligence of women in matters of politics and religion.

The hudibrastic verse form features octosyllabic couplets, of deliberately awkward rhythm, and unconventional rhymes (such as "ecclesiastic" and "instead of a stick"), a style intended by Butler to produce a comic effect. Early critics, including John Dryden and Joseph Addison, however, disparaged the verse form of *Hudibras* as doggerel. While subsequent criticism has tended to focus on the content, rather than the style, of the poem, twentieth-century commentators John Wilders and Ian Jack have maintained that Butler's cacaphonous style aptly reflects the discord between the poet's views and those of his age, as well as his intent to mock literary as well as social conventions.

Critics have posited various people and ideas as the objects of Butler's satire. In 1715, a "key" to *Hudibras,* attributed to Sir Roger L'Estrange, was published as part of Butler's *Posthumous Works.* This guide, which identifies each character with the historical counterpart L'Estrange believed Butler had intended to satirize, was generally accepted among critics until 1933, when Quintana's discovery of Butler's letters prompted renewed speculation on the identity of Butler's targets. In an examination of *Hudibras* as political allegory, Hardin Craig suggested that in the scene in which Hudibras and Ralpho attack a group of spectators at a bearbaiting, the bearbaiters recall specific members of the English Parliament, and the beleaguered bear Bruin is analogous to Charles I. Joseph T. Curtiss assigned satirical significance to the astrologer Sidrophel, with whom Hudibras consults. Curtiss maintained that Butler twice revised the character of Sidrophel, a miscreant and a fraud, to ridicule the professional ethics and personalities of his contemporaries, William Lilly and Sir Paul Neile.

Critics have also debated the specifics of Butler's religious and political convictions, several commenting that Butler's writings reveal a pronounced skepticism and a disdain for humanity. Butler's views are often compared with those of the philosopher Thomas Hobbes, whose treatise on human nature and government, *Leviathan* (1651), emphasizes the responsibility of the individual for civil stability and progress. Although *Hudibras* treats similar concerns, Butler presents a distinctly pessimistic view of the ability of men and women to shape their circumstances. Describing Butler as a "thoroughgoing misanthrope," Earl Miner has discussed *Hudibras* as a persuasive case for the inherent depravity of human nature. According to Miner, the cynicism couched in the farcical plot elements and comic rhetoric of *Hudibras* produces "a terrible, terrible, great poem."

Much like *Hudibras,* Butler's prose "Characters," written between 1665 and 1669 and published in *The Genuine Remains* in 1759, satirically examine the moral values and manners of various characters and personality types. George Wasserman has suggested that Butler's "Characters" portray both "man's need to deceive himself and his ingenuity in the use of reason to devise means of deceiving others" and are therefore, like *Hudibras,* "firmly rooted in the moral assumptions of their author."

Many critics suggest that the people and ideas in Butler's works, and the contempt he displayed toward them, were largely inspired by the contentious period in which the author lived. Thus rooted in the particularities of an increasingly distant age, Butler's works have often been regarded as possessing diminishing appeal. *Hudibras,* however, retains the esteem of literary historians, both as a contribution to the development of satire and as a commentary on political and religious issues during the seventeenth century.

PRINCIPAL WORKS

Hudibras. The First Part (poetry) 1663
Hudibras. The Second Part (poetry) 1664
Hudibras. The Third and Last Part (poetry) 1678
The Genuine Remains in Verse and Prose (poetry and prose) 1759
Characters and Passages from Note-Books (prose) 1908
Satires, and Miscellaneous Poetry and Prose (poetry and prose) 1928
Samuel Butler: Prose Observations (prose) 1979

John Dryden (essay date 1693)

[*Regarded by many scholars as the father of modern English poetry and literary criticism, Dryden was a prominent figure in England during the last four decades of the seventeenth century. By deliberately and comprehensively refining the language of Elizabethan England in all his works, he developed an expressive, universal diction that has had immense impact on the development of speech and writing in Great Britain and North America. Although recognized as a prolific and accomplished Restoration dramatist, Dryden wrote satirical poems and critical essays which are acknowledged as his greatest literary achievements. In the excerpt below, he praises* Hudibras *as well written and morally instructive, but objects to the meter and rhyme scheme of burlesque poetry in general.*]

The sort of Verse which is call'd *Burlesque,* consisting of Eight Syllables, or Four Feet, is that which our excellent ***Hudibras*** has chosen. . . . The Worth of his Poem is too well known to need my Commendation, and he is above my Censure: His Satire is of the *Varronian* kind, tho' unmix'd with Prose. The Choice of his Numbers is suitable enough to his Design, as he has manag'd it: But in any other Hand, the shortness of his Verse, and the quick returns of Rhyme, had debas'd the Dignity of Stile. And besides, the double Rhyme, (a necessary Companion of Burlesque Writing) is not so proper for Manly Satire, for it turns Earnest too much to Jest, and gives us a Boyish kind of Pleasure. It tickles aukwardly with a kind of pain, to the best sort of Readers; we are pleas'd ungratefully, and, if I may say so, against our liking. We thank him not for giving us that unseasonable Delight, when we know he cou'd have given us a better, and more solid. He might have left that Task to others, who not being able to put in Thought, can only make us grin with the Excrescence of a Word of two or three Syllables in the Close. 'Tis, indeed, below so great Master to make use of such a little Instrument. But his good Sence is perpetually shining through all he writes; it affords us not the time of finding Faults: We pass through the Levity of his Rhyme, and are immediately carri'd into some admirable useful Thought. After all, he has chosen this kind of Verse; and has written the best in it: And had he taken another, he wou'd always have excell'd. As we say of a Court-Favourite, that whatsoever his Office be, he still makes it uppermost, and most beneficial to himself. (pp. lxxxi-lxxxii)

John Dryden, "The Dedication," in The Satire of Decimus Junius Juvenalis *translated by John Dryden and others, Jacob Tonson, 1693, pp. i-xc.*

John Dennis (essay date 1693)

[*An English dramatist, critic, and poet, Dennis was one of the leading literary theorists of Restoration England. As a member of a circle of fashionable writers that included John Dryden and William Congreve, he was an important contributor to many of the literary debates of his time. Dennis remains best known for his critical works* The Advancement and Reformation of Modern Poetry *(1701) and* An Essay on the Genius and Writings of Shakespeare *(1712). In the following excerpt from his Preface to* Miscellanies in Verse and Prose *(1693), he defends the legitimacy of burlesque as a literary style, citing Butler's* Hudibras *as its finest example.*]

[Since] Burlesque, at present, lies under the disadvantage of having two great Authorities against it, viz. Boileau's, and Mr. Dryden's [see Dryden excerpt dated 1693]: I think my self oblig'd not only upon that account, but upon consideration too of that wonderful pleasure which I have so often receiv'd from Butler, to vindicate Burlesque from the scandal that is brought upon it, by the Censures of two such extraordinary Men.

The charge of Boileau is in his *Art of Poetry,* Chant premier, in these Lines.

> Quoyque vous ecriviez, evitez la bassesse
> Le style, le moins noble, a pourtant sa noblesse,
> Au mepris du bon sens le Burlesque effronté
> Trompa les yeux d'abord, pleut par sa noveaute,
> On ne vid plus en vers que pointes triviales;
> Le Parnasse parla le language des Hales.

Which in *English* paraphrastick Prose, is thus: Whatever you write, let a Gentleman's manner appear in it; The lowest stile of the man, who knows how to write, will still have a noble Air with it. But rightly to observe this rule, you must be sure to decline Burlesque, which not long since insolently appear'd in contempt of Reason, and pleas'd at the expence of good Sense: it pleas'd indeed a while, but pleas'd only as it was a fantastick novelty: It debas'd the dignity of Verse by its trivial Points, and taught Parnassus a Billingsgate Dialect.

This indeed is a violent charge, and may hold very good against Scaron, and the French Burlesque; but there is not one Article of it but what will fall to the Ground, if it comes to be apply'd to Butler. Scaron's Burlesque has nothing of a Gentleman in it, little of good Sense, and consequently little of true Wit. (pp. 6-7)

But the contrary of whatever has been said of Scaron, is certainly true of Butler: There is seen much of a Gentleman in his Burlesque; There is so much Wit and Good sense to be found in him, and so much true observation on mankind, that I do not believe there is more, take Volume for Volume, in any one Author we have, the *Plain-Dealer* only excepted; Besides, there is a vivacity and purity in his Language, whereever it was fit it should be pure, that could proceed from nothing but from a generous Education, and from a happy Nature. And further Butler's Burlesque was certainly writ with a just design, which was to expose Hypocrisie. Scaron's Burlesque, was writ either with no design, or but with a very scurvy one. For the only design that can be imagin'd of his *Virgil Travesty,* was to ridicule Heroick Poetry, which is the noblest invention of human Wit. Since then, Butler excell'd in so many things in which Scaron is defective, we may very well conclude, That Boileau's accusation reaches not our English Poet. Which Sir William Soames saw very well, when he translated this *Art of Poetry,* for he was so far from declaring against Burlesque, that he ventur'd, tho it was foreign from his Author, to propound Butler as a model to those who had a mind to write it. The late Lord Rochester, who was very well acquainted with Boileau, and who defer'd very much to his Judgment, did not at all believe that the censure of Boileau extended to Butler: For if he had, he would never have follow'd his fashion in several of his masterly Copies. Nor would a noble Wit, who is a living Honour to his Country, and the English Court, have condescended to write Burlesque, if he had not discern'd that there was in Butler's manner something extreamly fine, as well as something extreamly sensible in very many of his Thoughts.

I now come to examine Mr. Dryden's objections to Butler, which I shall do with all the submission and deference that is due to the judgment of that extraordinary Man. And therefore I have reason to hope that I shall give no offence to him nor to any Man, by undertaking my own defence. For to plead the Cause of Butler is at present to maintain my own. For if he who is so admirable an Original, is rightly reprehended for writing in Burlesque: I who am but his follower, and can never pretend to come near his excellence, ought much more severely to be censur'd. I must confess that in Mr. Dryden's accusation of Burlesque, there are no such murdering Articles, as there are in that of Boileau against Scaron; For Mr. Dryden allows Butler to have shewn a great deal of good Sense in that way of writing; so that we have here gain'd one considerable Point, which Boileau seem'd not to allow us, which is that good Sense is consistent with Burlesque. Mr. Dryden's quarrel is to the numbers of Butler: he says that he might have chosen a better sort, affirming that he would equally have excell'd in all.

Whether he would have practised all sorts of Numbers

with equal felicity, is what I have not now time to examine. But granting that, it is more than probable that he chose aright. For I would fain ask any man one question; Whether he thinks Nature had given Butler a Talent to treat of the adventures of ***Hudibras***? For if any one grants that she had given him such a Talent, I will not stick to affirm that it could not fail to suggest to him the properest means for the carrying on his design. (pp. 7-8)

Before I take my leave of Burlesque and Butler, I think fit to say something of the latter, which has not so direct a reference to his way of writing (tho that too is indirectly commended by it) as to the incomparable genius of the Man. It is this that if any one would set the Common places of Tassone and Boileau's *Lutrin* against those of Butler, it would appear for the Honour of England, that neither the French man nor Italian could stand before us. The most diverting thing in all the *Lutrin* is the "Battle at Barbin's Shop." Chant. 5. Yet that, if it is compar'd with the Battle in the second Canto of the first part of ***Hudibras,*** tho it is so diverting when we read it alone, will appear to be perfectly insipid. (p. 10)

John Dennis, "Preface to 'Miscellanies in Verse and Prose'," in The Critical Works of John Dennis: 1692-1711, Vol. I, *edited by Edward Niles Hooker, The Johns Hopkins Press, 1939, pp. 6-10.*

Joseph Addison (essay date 1711)

[*A prominent English statesman and man of letters, Addison, along with Richard Steele, is considered one of the most important essayists of the early eighteenth century. With Steele, he founded the* Spectator, *a daily journal designed to improve the morals and manners of the day. Among Addison's best essays are those in which he adopted the persona of the fictional country squire Sir Roger de Coverley, providing incisive observations on life, literature, and society. Didactic and moralizing, yet witty and ironic, Addison's style epitomizes the ideals of neoclassical lucidity and moderation; Samuel Johnson remarked that Addison's work is characterized by "an English style familiar but not coarse, elegant but not ostentatious." Here, in a discussion of the characteristics of comedy and burlesque, he defines* Hudibras *as burlesque poetry written in doggerel, rather than heroic style. This essay was first published in the December 15, 1711 issue of the* Spectator.]

The two great Branches of Ridicule in Writing are Comedy and Burlesque. The first ridicules Persons by drawing them in their proper Characters, the other by drawing them quite unlike themselves. Burlesque is therefore of two kinds, the first represents mean Persons in the Accoutrements of Heroes; the other describes great Persons acting and speaking, like the basest among the People. *Don Quixote* is an Instance of the first, and Lucian's Gods of the second. It is a Dispute among the Criticks, whether Burlesque Poetry runs best in Heroic Verse, like that of *The Dispensary,* or in Doggerel, like that of ***Hudibras.*** I think where the low Character is to be raised the Heroic is the proper Measure, but when an Hero is to be pulled down and degraded, it is done best in Doggerel.

If ***Hudibras*** had been set out with as much Wit and Humour in Heroic Verse as he is in Doggerel, he would have made a much more agreeable Figure than he does; tho' the generality of his Readers are so wonderfully pleased with the double Rhimes, that I do not expect many will be of my Opinion in this Particular. (pp. 238-39)

Joseph Addison, in an excerpt in The Spectator, Vol. II, *edited by Gregory Smith, 1907. Reprint by J. M. Dent & Sons Ltd, 1963, pp. 237-40.*

William Warburton (letter date 1759)

[*Warburton was an English theologian, historian, essayist, and literary critic who is best remembered as the first person to collect and publish the works of Alexander Pope. In the following excerpt from a letter to Richard Hurd, Bishop of Worcester, he condemns Butler's narrative technique and characterization while admiring his wit.*]

As to these ***Remains*** of Butler they are certainly his: but they would not strike the publick, if that publick was honest. But the publick is a malicious monster, which cares not what it affords to dead merit, so it can but depress the living. There was something singular in this same Butler. Besides an infinite deal of wit, he had great sense and penetration, both in the sciences and the world. Yet with all this, he could never plan a work, nor tell a story well. The first appears from his ***Hudibras,*** the other from his **"Elephant in the Moon."** He evidently appears to have been dissatisfied with it, by turning it into *long* verse: from whence, you perceive, he thought the fault lay in the doggerel verse, but that was his *forte;* the fault lay in the *manner of telling.* Not but he might have another reason for trying his talents at heroic verse—emulation. Dryden had burst out in a surprising manner; and in such a case, the poetic world (as we have seen by a later instance) is always full of imitators. But Butler's heroics are poor stuff; indeed only doggerel, made languid by heavy expletives. This attempt in the change of his measure was the sillier, not only as he had acquired a mastery in the short measure, but as that measure, somehow or other, suits best with his sort of wit. His characters are full of cold puerilities, though intermixed with abundance of wit, and with a great deal of good sense. He is sometimes wonderfully fine both in his sentiment and expression; as where he defines the proud man to be *a fool in fermentation;* and where, speaking of the Antiquary, he says, *he has a great veneration for words that are stricken in years, and are grown so aged that they have out-lived their employments.* But the greatest fault in these characters is, that they are a bad and false species of composition. (pp. 286-88)

William Warburton, in a letter to Richard Hurd on July 8, 1759, in his Letters from a Late Eminent Prelate to One of His Friends, second edition, *T. Cadell and W. Davies, Strand, 1809, pp. 286-90.*

Samuel Johnson (essay date 1779)

[*Johnson is one of the outstanding figures in English literature and a leader in the history of textual and aesthetic criticism. Popularly known in his own day as the "Great Cham of Literature," Johnson was a prolific lexicographer, essayist, poet, and critic whose lucid and extensively illustrated* Dictionary of the English Language *(1755) and* Prefaces, Biographical and Critical, to the Works of the English Poets *(10 vols., 1779-81; reissued in 1783 as* The Lives of the Most Eminent English Poets) *were new departures in lexicography and biographical criticism, respectively. As a literary critic he was neither a rigid theorist nor a strict follower of neoclassical rules, tending instead to rely on common sense and empirical knowledge. In the following excerpt from his essay on Butler's life and works, Johnson assesses the strengths and weaknesses of* Hudibras.]

The poem of ***Hudibras*** is one of those compositions of which a nation may justly boast; as the images which it exhibits are domestick, the sentiments unborrowed and unexpected, and the strain of diction original and peculiar. We must not, however, suffer the pride, which we assume as the countrymen of Butler, to make any encroachment upon justice, nor appropriate those honours which others have a right to share. The poem of ***Hudibras*** is not wholly English; the original idea is to be found in the *History of Don Quixote;* a book to which a mind of the greatest powers may be indebted without disgrace.

Cervantes shews a man, who having, by the incessant perusal of incredible tales, subjected his understanding to his imagination, and familiarized his mind by pertinacious meditation to trains of incredible events and scenes of impossible existence, goes out in the pride of knighthood, to redress wrongs, and defend virgins, to rescue captive princesses, and tumble usurpers from their thrones; attended by a squire, whose cunning, too low for the suspicion of a generous mind, enables him often to cheat his master.

The hero of Butler is a Presbyterian Justice, who, in the confidence of legal authority, and the rage of zealous ignorance, ranges the country to repress superstition and correct abuses, accompanied by an Independent Clerk, disputatious and obstinate, with whom he often debates, but never conquers him.

Cervantes had so much kindness for Don Quixote, that, however he embarrasses him with absurd distresses, he gives him so much sense and virtue as may preserve our esteem: wherever he is, or whatever he does, he is made by matchless dexterity commonly ridiculous, but never contemptible.

But for poor Hudibras, his poet had no tenderness: he chuses not that any pity should be shewn or respect paid him: he gives him up at once to laughter and contempt, without any quality that can dignify or protect him.

In forming the character of Hudibras, and describing his person and habiliments, the author seems to labour with a tumultuous confusion of dissimilar ideas. He had read the history of the mock knights-errant; he knew the notions and manners of a presbyterian magistrate, and tried to unite the absurdities of both, however distant, in one personage. Thus he gives him that pedantick ostentation of knowledge which has no relation to chivalry, and loads him with martial encumbrances that can add nothing to his civil dignity. He sends him out a *colonelling,* and yet never brings him within sight of war.

If Hudibras be considered as the representative of the presbyterians, it is not easy to say why his weapons should be represented as ridiculous or useless; for, whatever judgement might be passed upon their knowledge or their arguments, experience had sufficiently shewn that their swords were not to be despised.

The hero, thus compounded of swaggerer and pedant, of knight and justice, is led forth to action, with his squire Ralpho, an Independent enthusiast.

Of the contexture of events planned by the author, which is called the action of the poem, since it is left imperfect, no judgement can be made. It is probable, that the hero was to be led through many luckless adventures, which would give occasion, like his attack upon the *bear and fiddle,* to express the ridiculous rigour of the sectaries; like his encounter with Sidrophel and Whacum, to make superstition and credulity contemptible; or, like his recourse to the low retailer of the law, discover the fraudulent practices of different professions.

What series of events he would have formed, or in what manner he would have rewarded or punished his hero, it is now vain to conjecture. His work must have had, as it seems, the defect which Dryden imputes to Spenser; the action could not have been one; there could only have been a succession of incidents, each of which might have happened without the rest, and which could not all co-operate to any single conclusion.

The discontinuity of the action might however have been easily forgiven, if there had been action enough; but I believe every reader regrets the paucity of events, and complains that in the poem of ***Hudibras,*** as in the history of Thucydides, there is more said than done. The scenes are too seldom changed, and the attention is tired with long conversation.

It is indeed much more easy to form dialogues than to contrive adventures. Every position makes way for an argument, and every objection dictates an answer. When two disputants are engaged upon a complicated and extensive question, the difficulty is not to continue, but to end the controversy. But whether it be that we comprehend but few of the possibilities of life, or that life itself affords little variety, every man who has tried knows how much labour it will cost to form such a combination of circumstances, as shall have at once the grace of novelty and credibility, and delight fancy without violence to reason.

Perhaps the Dialogue of this poem is not perfect. Some power of engaging the attention might have been added to it, by quicker reciprocation, by seasonable interruptions, by sudden questions, and by a nearer approach to dramatick spriteliness; without which, fictitious speeches will always tire, however sparkling with sentences, and however variegated with allusions.

The great source of pleasure is variety. Uniformity must

tire at last, though it be uniformity of excellence. We love to expect; and, when expectation is disappointed or gratified, we want to be again expecting. For this impatience of the present, whoever would please, must make provision. The skilful writer *irritat, mulcet,* makes a due distribution of the still and animated parts. It is for want of this artful intertexture, and those necessary changes, that the whole of a book may be tedious, though all the parts are praised.

If inexhaustible wit could give perpetual pleasure, no eye would ever leave half-read the work of Butler; for what poet has ever brought so many remote images so happily together? It is scarcely possible to peruse a page without finding some association of images that was never found before. By the first paragraph the reader is amused, by the next he is delighted, and by a few more strained to astonishment; but astonishment is a toilsome pleasure; he is soon weary of wondering, and longs to be diverted.

> Omnia vult belle, Matho, dicere: dic aliquando
> Et bene, dic neutrum, dic aliquando male.

Imagination is useless without knowledge: nature gives in vain the power of combination, unless study and observation supply materials to be combined. Butler's treasures of knowledge appear proportioned to his expence: whatever topick employs his mind, he shews himself qualified to expand and illustrate it with all the accessories that books can furnish: he is found not only to have travelled the beaten road, but the bye-paths of literature; not only to have taken general surveys, but to have examined particulars with minute inspection.

If the French boast the learning of Rabelais, we need not be afraid of confronting them with Butler.

But the most valuable parts of his performance are those which retired study and native wit cannot supply. He that merely makes a book from books may be useful, but can scarcely be great. Butler had not suffered life to glide beside him unseen or unobserved. He had watched with great diligence the operations of human nature, and traced the effects of opinion, humour, interest, and passion. From such remarks proceeded that great number of sententious distichs which have passed into conversation, and are added as proverbial axioms to the general stock of practical knowledge.

When any work has been viewed and admired, the first question of intelligent curiosity is, how was it performed? ***Hudibras*** was not a hasty effusion; it was not produced by a sudden tumult of imagination, or a short paroxysm of violent labour. To accumulate such a mass of sentiments at the call of accidental desire, or of sudden necessity, is beyond the reach and power of the most active and comprehensive mind. I am informed by Mr. Thyer of Manchester, the excellent editor of this author's reliques, that he could shew something like ***Hudibras*** in prose. He has in his possession the common-place book, in which Butler reposited, not such events or precepts as are gathered by reading; but such remarks, similitudes, allusions, assemblages, or inferences, as occasion prompted, or meditation produced; those thoughts that were generated in his own mind, and might be usefully applied to some future purpose. Such is the labour of those who write for immortality.

But human works are not easily found without a perishable part. Of the ancient poets every reader feels the mythology tedious and oppressive. Of ***Hudibras,*** the manners, being founded on opinions, are temporary and local, and therefore become every day less intelligible, and less striking. What Cicero says of philosophy is true likewise of wit and humour, that 'time effaces the fictions of opinion, and confirms the determinations of Nature.' Such manners as depend upon standing relations and general passions are co-extended with the race of man; but those modifications of life, and peculiarities of practice, which are the progeny of error and perverseness, or at best of some accidental influence or transient persuasion, must perish with their parents.

Much therefore of that humour which transported the last century with merriment is lost to us, who do not know the sour solemnity, the sullen superstition, the gloomy moroseness, and the stubborn scruples of the ancient Puritans; or, if we know them, derive our information only from books, or from tradition, have never had them before our eyes, and cannot but by recollection and study understand the lines in which they are satirized. Our grandfathers knew the picture from the life; we judge of the life by contemplating the picture.

It is scarcely possible, in the regularity and composure of the present time, to image the tumult of absurdity, and clamour of contradiction, which perplexed doctrine, disordered practice, and disturbed both publick and private quiet, in that age, when subordination was broken, and awe was hissed away; when any unsettled innovator who could hatch a half-formed notion produced it to the publick; when every man might become a preacher, and almost every preacher could collect a congregation.

The wisdom of the nation is very reasonably supposed to reside in the parliament. What can be concluded of the lower classes of the people, when in one of the parliaments summoned by Cromwell it was seriously proposed, that all the records in the Tower should be burnt, that all memory of things past should be effaced, and that the whole system of life should commence anew?

We have never been witnesses of animosities excited by the use of minced pies and plumb porridge; nor seen with what abhorrence those who could eat them at all other times of the year would shrink from them in December. An old Puritan, who was alive in my childhood, being at one of the feasts of the church invited by a neighbour to partake his cheer, told him, that, if he would treat him at an alehouse with beer, brewed for all times and seasons, he should accept his kindness, but would have none of his superstitious meats or drinks.

One of the puritanical tenets was the illegality of all games of chance; and he that reads Gataker upon Lots, may see how much learning and reason one of the first scholars of his age thought necessary, to prove that it was no crime to throw a die, or play at cards, or to hide a shilling for the reckoning.

Astrology, however, against which so much of the satire is directed, was not more the folly of the Puritans than of others. It had in that time a very extensive dominion. Its predictions raised hopes and fears in minds which ought to have rejected it with contempt. In hazardous undertakings, care was taken to begin under the influence of a propitious planet; and when the king was prisoner in Carisbrook Castle, an astrologer was consulted what hour would be found most favourable to an escape.

What effect this poem had upon the publick, whether it shamed imposture or reclaimed credulity, is not easily determined. Cheats can seldom stand long against laughter. It is certain that the credit of planetary intelligence wore fast away; though some men of knowledge, and Dryden among them, continued to believe that conjunctions and oppositions had a great part in the distribution of good or evil, and in the government of sublunary things.

Poetical action ought to be probable upon certain suppositions, and such probability as burlesque requires is here violated only by one incident. Nothing can shew more plainly the necessity of doing something, and the difficulty of finding something to do, than that Butler was reduced to transfer to his hero the flagellation of Sancho, not the most agreeable fiction of Cervantes; very suitable indeed to the manners of that age and nation, which ascribed wonderful efficacy to voluntary penances; but so remote from the practice and opinions of the Hudibrastick time, that judgement and imagination are alike offended.

The diction of this poem is grossly familiar, and the numbers purposely neglected, except in a few places where the thoughts by their native excellence secure themselves from violation, being such as mean language cannot express. The mode of versification has been blamed by Dryden, who regrets that the heroick measure was not rather chosen. To the critical sentence of Dryden the highest reverence would be due, were not his decisions often precipitate, and his opinions immature. When he wished to change the measure, he probably would have been willing to change more. If he intended that, when the numbers were heroick, the diction should still remain vulgar, he planned a very heterogeneous and unnatural composition. If he preferred a general stateliness both of sound and words, he can be only understood to wish that Butler had undertaken a different work.

The measure is quick, spritely, and colloquial, suitable to the vulgarity of the words and the levity of the sentiments. But such numbers and such diction can gain regard only when they are used by a writer whose vigour of fancy and copiousness of knowledge entitle him to contempt of ornaments, and who, in confidence of the novelty and justness of his conceptions, can afford to throw metaphors and epithets away. To another that conveys common thoughts in careless versification, it will only be said, 'Pauper videri Cinna vult, & est pauper." The meaning and diction will be worthy of each other, and criticism may justly doom them to perish together.

Nor even though another Butler should arise, would another ***Hudibras*** obtain the same regard. Burlesque consists in a disproportion between the style and the sentiments, or between the adventitious sentiments and the fundamental subject. It therefore, like all bodies compounded of heterogeneous parts, contains in it a principle of corruption. All disproportion is unnatural; and from what is unnatural we can derive only the pleasure which novelty produces. We admire it awhile as a strange thing; but, when it is no longer strange, we perceive its deformity. It is a kind of artifice, which by frequent repetition detects itself; and the reader, learning in time what he is to expect, lays down his book, as the spectator turns away from a second exhibition of those tricks, of which the only use is to shew that they can be played. (pp. 140-47)

Samuel Johnson, "Butler," in his Lives of the English Poets Vol. I, *Oxford University Press, 1906, pp. 135-47.*

William Hazlitt (essay date 1819)

[*An English essayist, Hazlitt was one of the most important critics of the Romantic age. He was a deft stylist, a master of the familiar essay, and a leader in what was later termed "impressionist criticism": a form of personal analysis directly opposed to the universal standards of critical judgment accepted by many eighteenth-century critics. Hazlitt popularized the critical techniques of evocation, metaphor, aphorism, and personal reference and, acutely aware of the abstract nature of literature as well as the limitations of his audience in understanding questions of aesthetics and style, he strove to produce palatable literary criticism. In the excerpt below from* Lectures on the English Comic Writers *(1819), Hazlitt praises Butler's originality and wit, but finds* Hudibras *to be flawed by poor characterization and overemphasis on political issues.*]

The greatest single production of wit of [the Restoration], I might say of this country, is Butler's ***Hudibras.*** It contains specimens of every variety of drollery and satire, and those specimens crowded together into almost every page. The proof of this is, that nearly one half of his lines are got by heart, and quoted for mottos. In giving instances of different sorts of wit, or trying to recollect good things of this kind, they are the first which stand ready in the memory; and they are those which furnish the best tests and most striking illustrations of what we want. Dr. Campbell, in his *Philosophy of Rhetoric,* when treating of the subject of wit, which he has done very neatly and sensibly, has constant recourse to two authors, Pope and Butler, the one for ornament, the other more for use. Butler is equally in the hands of the learned and the vulgar; for the sense is generally as solid, as the images are amusing and grotesque. Whigs and Tories join in his praise. He could not, in spite of himself,

> —narrow his mind,
> And to party give up what was meant for mankind.

Though his subject was local and temporary, his fame was not circumscribed within his own age. He was admired by Charles II. and has been rewarded by posterity. It is the poet's fate! It is not, perhaps, to be wondered at, that arbitrary and worthless monarchs like Charles II. should neglect those who pay court to them. The idol (if it had sense) would despise its worshippers. Indeed, Butler hardly merited any thing on the score of loyalty to the house of Stuart. True wit is not a parasite plant. The strokes which it aims at folly and knavery on one side of a question, tell equally home on the other. Dr. Zachary Grey, who added notes to the poem, and abused the leaders of Cromwell's party by name, would be more likely to have gained a pension for his services than Butler, who was above such petty work. A poem like ***Hudibras*** could not be made to order of a court. Charles might very well have reproached the author with wanting to shew his own wit and sense rather than to favour a tottering cause; and he has even been suspected, in parts of his poem, of glancing at majesty itself. He in general ridicules not persons, but things, not a party, but their principles, which may belong, as time and occasion serve, to one set of solemn pretenders or another. This he has done most effectually, in every possible way, and from every possible source, learned or unlearned. He has exhausted the moods and figures of satire and sophistry. It would be possible to deduce the different forms of syllogism in Aristotle, from the different violations or mock-imitations of them in Butler. . . . Butler makes you laugh or smile by comparing the high to the low, or by pretending to raise the low to the lofty; he succeeds equally in the familiarity of his illustrations, or their incredible extravagance, by comparing things that are alike or not alike. He surprises equally by his coincidences or contradictions, by spinning out a long-winded flimsy excuse, or by turning short upon you with the point-blank truth. His rhymes are as witty as his reasons, equally remote from what common custom would suggest; and he startles you sometimes by an empty sound like a blow upon a drum-head, by a pun upon one word, and by splitting another in two at the end of a verse, with the same alertness and power over the odd and unaccountable in the combinations of sounds as of images.

There are as many shrewd aphorisms in his works, clenched by as many quaint and individual allusions, as perhaps in any author whatever. He makes none but palpable hits, that may be said to give one's understanding a rap on the knuckles. He is, indeed, sometimes too prolific, and spins his antithetical sentences out, one after another, till the reader, not the author, is wearied. He is, however, very seldom guilty of repetitions or wordy paraphrases of himself; but he sometimes comes rather too near it; and interrupts the thread of his argument (for narrative he has none) by a tissue of epigrams, and the tagging of points and conundrums without end. The fault, or original sin of his genius, is, that from too much leaven it ferments and runs over; and there is, unfortunately, nothing in his subject to restrain and keep it within compass. He has no story good for any thing; and his characters are good for very little. They are too low and mechanical, or too much one thing; personifications, as it were, of nicknames, and bugbears of popular prejudice and vulgar cant, unredeemed by any virtue, or difference or variety of disposition. There is no relaxation or shifting of the parts; and the impression in some degree fails of its effect, and becomes questionable from its being always the same. The satire looks, in length, almost like special-pleading: it has nothing to confirm it at the apparent good humour or impartiality of the writer. It is something revolting to see an author persecute his characters, the cherished offspring of his brain, in this manner, without mercy. Hudibras and Ralpho have immortalised Butler; and what has he done for them in return, but set them up to be 'pilloried on infamy's high and lasting stage?' This is ungrateful!

The rest of the characters have, in general, little more than their names and professions to distinguish them. We scarcely know one from another, Cerdon, or Orsin, or Crowdero, and are often obliged to turn back, to connect their several adventures together. In fact, Butler drives only at a set of obnoxious opinions, and runs into general declamations. His poem in its essence is a satire, or didactic poem. It is not virtually dramatic, or narrative. It is composed of digressions by the author. He instantly breaks off in the middle of a story, or incident, to comment upon and turn it into ridicule. He does not give characters but topics, which would do just as well in his own mouth without agents, or machinery of any kind. The long digression in Part III. in which no mention is made of the hero, is just as good and as much an integrant part of the poem as the rest. The conclusion is lame and impotent, but that is saying nothing; the beginning and middle are equally so as to historical merit. There is no keeping in his characters, as in *Don Quixote;* nor any enjoyment of the ludicrousness of their situations, as in [the illustrations of William] Hogarth. Indeed, it requires a considerable degree of sympathy to enter into and describe to the life even the ludicrous eccentricities of others, and there is no appearance of sympathy or liking to his subject in Butler. His humour is to his wit, 'as one grain of wheat in a bushel of chaff: you shall search all day, and when you find it, it is not worth the trouble.' Yet there are exceptions. The most decisive is, I think, the description of the battle between Bruin and his foes, Part I. Canto iii., and again of the triumphal procession in Part II. Canto ii. of which the principal features are copied in Hogarth's election print, the Chairing of the successful candidate. The account of Sidrophel and Whackum is another instance, and there are some few others, but rarely sprinkled up and down.

The widow, the termagant heroine of the poem, is still more disagreeable than her lover; and her sarcastic account of the passion of love, as consisting entirely in an attachment to land and houses, goods and chattels, which is enforced with all the rhetoric the author is master of, and hunted down through endless similes, is evidently false. The vulgarity and meanness of sentiment which Butler complains of in the Presbyterians, seems at last from long familiarity and close contemplation to have tainted his own mind. Their worst vices appear to have taken root in his imagination. Nothing but what was selfish and groveling sunk into his memory, in the depression of a menial situation under his supposed hero. He has, indeed, carried his private grudge too far into his general speculations. He even makes out the rebels to be cowards and well beaten, which does not accord with the history of the times. In an excess of zeal for church and state, he is too much disposed to treat religion as a cheat, and liberty as a farce. It was the cant of that day (from which he is not free) to cry down sanctity and sobriety as marks of disaffection, as it is the cant of this, to hold them up as proofs of loyalty and staunch monarchical principles. Religion and morality are, in either case, equally made subservient to the spirit of party, and a stalking-horse to the love of power. Finally, there is a want of pathos and humour, but no want of interest in ***Hudibras.*** It is difficult to lay it down. One thought is inserted into another; the links in the chain of reasoning are so closely rivetted, that the attention seldom flags, but is kept alive (without any other assistance) by the mere force of writing. There are occasional indications of poetical fancy, and an eye for natural beauty; but these are kept under or soon discarded, judiciously enough, but it should seem, not for lack of power, for they are certainly as masterly as they are rare. Such are the burlesque description of the stocks, or allegorical prison, in which first Crowdero, and then Hudibras, is confined: the passage beginning—

> As when an owl that's in a barn,
> Sees a mouse creeping in the corn,
> Sits still and shuts his round blue eyes,
> As if he slept, &c.

And the description of the moon going down in the early morning, which is as pure, original, and picturesque as possible:—

> The queen of night, whose large command
> Rules all the sea and half the land,
> And over moist and crazy brains
> In high spring-tides at midnight reigns,
> Was now declining to the west,
> To go to bed and take her rest.

Butler is sometimes scholastic, but he makes his learning tell to good account; and for the purposes of burlesque, nothing can be better fitted than the scholastic style. (pp. 62-7)

William Hazlitt, "Lecture III: On Cowley, Butler, Suckling, Etherege, etc.," in his Lectures on the English Comic Writers and Fugitive Writings, *J. M. Dent & Sons Ltd., 1963, pp. 49-69.*

H. A. Taine (essay date 1863-64)

[*Taine was a French critic and founder of the sociological school of literary criticism. Although out of favor among critics today. Taine's work has had a profound influence on the development of Marxist critical thought in the twentieth century. In the following excerpt from a work originally published in French in 1863-64, he contends that* Hudibras *is poorly conceived and written, thereby reflecting the particularly uncivilized period in English history in which it was composed.*]

When we scratch the covering of [a late seventeenth-century] Englishman's morality, the brute appears in its violence and its deformity. One of the English statesmen said that with the French an unchained mob could be led by words of humanity and honour, but that in England it was necessary, in order to appease them, to throw to them raw flesh. Insults, blood, orgie, that is the food on which the mob of noblemen, under Charles II., precipitated itself. All that excuses a carnival was absent; and, in particular, wit. Three years after the return of the king, Butler published his ***Hudibras;*** and with what *éclat* his contemporaries only could tell, while the echo of applause is kept up even to our own days. How low is the wit, with what awkwardness and dulness he dilutes his revengeful satire. Here and there lurks a happy picture, the remnant of a poetry which has just perished; but the whole work reminds one of a Scarron, as unworthy as the other, and more malignant. It is written, people say, on the model of *Don Quixote;* Hudibras is a Puritan knight, who goes about, like his antitype, redressing wrongs, and pocketing beatings. It would be truer to say that it resembles the wretched imitation of [Fernández de] Avellaneda. The short metre, well suited to buffoonery, hobbles along without rest and limpingly, floundering in the mud which it delights in, as foul and as dull as that of [Scarron's] *Enéide Travestie.* The description of Hudibras and his horse occupies the best part of a canto; forty lines are taken up by describing his beard, forty more by describing his breeches. Endless scholastic discussions, arguments as long as those of the Puritans, spread their wastes and briars over half the poem. No action, no simplicity, all is would-be satire and gross caricature; there is neither art, nor harmony, nor good taste to be found in it; the Puritan style is converted into an absurd gibberish; and the engalled rancour, missing its aim by its mere excess, spoils the portrait it wishes to draw. Would you believe that such a writer gives himself airs, wishes to enliven us, pretends to be funny? What delicate raillery is there in this picture of Hudibras' beard!

> His tawny beard was th' equal grace
> Both of his wisdom and his face;
> In cut and die so like a tile,
> A sudden view it would beguile:
> The upper part whereof was whey,
> The nether orange, mix'd with grey.
> This hairy meteor did denounce
> The fall of sceptres and of crowns:
> With grisly type did represent
> Declining age of government,
> And tell with hieroglyphic spade
> Its own grave and the state's were made.

Butler is so well satisfied with his insipid fun, that he prolongs it for a good many lines:

> Like Samson's heart-breakers, it grew
> In time to make a nation rue;
> Tho' it contributed its own fall,
> To wait upon the public downfall. . . .
> 'Twas bound to suffer persecution
> And martyrdom with resolution;
> T' oppose itself against the hate
> And vengeance of the incens'd state,
> In whose defiance it was worn,
> Still ready to be pull'd and torn,
> With red-hot irons to be tortur'd,
> Revil'd, and spit upon, and martyr'd.
> Maugre all which, 'twas to stand fast
> As long as monarchy should last;
> But when the state should hap to reel,
> 'Twas to submit to fatal steel,
> And fall, as it was consecrate,
> A sacrifice to fall of state,
> Whose thread of life the fatal sisters
> Did twist together with its whiskers,
> And twine so close, that time should never,
> In life or death, their fortunes sever;
> But with his rusty sickle mow

Both down together at a blow.

The nonsense increases as we go on. Could any one have taken pleasure in humour such as this?—

> This sword a dagger had, his page,
> That was but little for his age;
> And therefore waited on him so
> As dwarfs upon knights-errant do. . . .
> When it had stabb'd, or broke a head,
> It would scrape trenchers, or chip bread. . . .
> 'Twould make clean shoes, and in the earth
> Set leeks and onions, and so forth.

Everything becomes trivial; if any beauty presents itself, it is spoiled by burlesque. To read those long details of the kitchen, those servile and crude jokes, people might fancy themselves in the company of a common buffoon in the market-place; it is the talk of the quacks on the bridges, adapting their imagination and language to the manners of the beer-shop and the hovel. There is filth to be met with there; indeed, the rabble will laugh when the mountebank alludes to the disgusting acts of private life. Such is the grotesque stuff in which the courtiers of the Restoration delighted; their spite and their coarseness took a pleasure in the spectacle of these bawling puppets; even now, after two centuries, we hear the ribald laughter of this audience of lackeys. (pp. 328-32)

H. A. Taine, "The Restoration," in his History of English Literature, *translated by H. Van Laun, 1889. Reprint by Henry Holt and Company, 1904, pp. 320-70.*

Reginald Brimley Johnson (essay date 1893)

[*In the following excerpt from his preface to* The Poetical Works of Samuel Butler, *Johnson offers an appreciation of Butler's literary talent.*]

[What] are the distinguishing characteristics of ***Hudibras***? The popularity it attained just after the Restoration affords no testimony to its merits, for a very inferior work, with the same object, might then have been equally successful. To-day it is not read, and to a large extent would not be understood. Yet it is living still, for it was the work of an original genius. Its phrases have passed into the language, and everyone is familiar with certain passages from it. The term Hudibrastic has a recognized meaning, though it is obvious that Butler borrowed much from Cervantes, and though it appears that the peculiar jingle of his rhythm and rhyme was not, strictly speaking, original.

"The Hudibrastic" it was stated long ago, in the *Grub Street Journal,* No. 39,

> is to differ from the Epic, as comedy does from tragedy. It must be narrative, like the Epic; it must, like that species of Poem, have its fable, its variety of characters, and its proper style; but all these in such a manner as to move, not terror or compassion, as in tragedy, but laughter, as in comedy. The Fable must be formed by the narration of one, entire, ridiculous action; the characters must be such as either occur in low life or are in their own nature odd and ridiculous; and these in as great variety as possible; and the style or language must be contrived so as to heighten the ridiculousness of the representation.

In one word the Hudibrastic is a mock-Epic, and the above definition gives due emphasis to the important point that *everything* therein must be subservient to the main object of ridicule. The irregularity of the rhythm, the uncouth language, and the startling rhymes are directed towards this end, while even the too frequent coarseness of the allusions may be said to heighten the desired effect. Butler seems to gather up his whole energy to the overburdening of each sentence with point, and as Hume declares [in his *History of England* (1754)], "though scarcely any author was ever able to express his thoughts in so few words, he often employs too many thoughts on one subject, and thereby becomes prolix after an unusual manner." He has moreover debased his own wit and learning to lessen the dignity of his hero.

Hudibras himself is the personification of humbug. Save for his accompanying squire and steed, his attributes and adventures bear little or no resemblance to those of his prototype Don Quixote. He starts upon a crusade of reform, but pursues it after a fashion that would inspire us with the strongest digust if it were meant to be taken seriously.

He is at once a fool and a knave, a brag and a coward, a preacher of unclean life, and a magistrate without any conception of justice, pledged to restrain all licenses but his own. He is a whining Pharisee and a fat-paunched Justice, the slave of a stupid passion for a widow's jointure, the dupe of soothsayers and lawyers, a knight-errant with the capacities of a tin-soldier. He harangues his enemies on the battle-field after the manner of a Homeric hero, and garnishes his speech with volumes of misapplied erudition. He will chop logic till he is hoarse, and refine upon a definition till it vanishes under his touch. The Squire Ralph has none of the faithfulness or shrewdness of Sancho, and differs from his master in nothing but theological opinions. They are dressed in the guise of Puritans, but the blindest prejudice could scarcely have failed to recognize the intentional exaggeration.

Butler's power is in hard-hitting, and he does not much care what elements he introduces to strengthen the blow. He never misses absurdities, but carefully separating them from any sincerity or good feelings with which, in real individuals, they may have been combined, flings them all pell-mell upon the shoulders of his creations, who are thus little more than pegs for his satire. As Hallam frankly put it [in his *Literature of Europe* (1854)]:

> In the fiction of ***Hudibras*** there was never much to divert the reader, and there is still less left at present. But what has been censured as a fault, the length of the dialogue, which puts the fiction out of sight, is in fact the source of all the pleasure that the work affords. The sense of Butler is masculine, his wit inexhaustible, and it is supplied from every source of reading and observation. But these sources are often so unknown to the reader that the wit loses its effect through the obscurity of its allusions, and he yields to the bane of wit, a purblind mole-like pedantry.

The mention of Butler's obscure allusions reminds us of the additional difficulty which has been ingeniously thrown in the way of their interpretation, by supposing that every passage in ***Hudibras*** has an allegorical bearing. But surely the direct satire is sufficiently comprehensive. Here are burlesques upon the poetic intervention of gods and goddesses, the rhymester's trick of an echo, the bombast of conventional dedications, and the artificiality of a "rustic muse." Lawyers, doctors, and men of science fare no better than preachers and politicians. Every foible of humanity is laid under requisition. Only the honest man, if he exist, is spared, and no sneer has passed the poet's lips against religion or morality.

There may be evidence in ***Hudibras*** and ***The Remains*** that Butler could have written tender or dignified poetry, but it is folly to suppose that in the composition of his great burlesque his genius was not at home. Yet, it may be asked, can ***Hudibras*** be worthy of our admiration, for it struck at those that were down, and was not tempered with justice or mercy? The question involves a misconception of Butler's aims and methods, which were literary and not moral. We call him great, because of the unflagging diligence and faithfulness with which he carried them out, his respect for good work, and his belief in himself.

If we knew nothing of his Commonplace Books with their endless copyings and recopyings, if we were unable to trace his revisions in the second edition of ***Hudibras,*** the poem itself would bear witness to his patience and thoroughness. While the cares of State and the claims of Religion were driving art and literature out of men's minds, there remained one who, in the midst of wars and rumours of wars, turned not his hand from the plough, but with singleness of eye, and tenacity of hold, kept his mind upon the acquirement of knowledge and the perfection of style. Surrounded by men of action, he clung to thought. Without burying himself among books he spent his life in their service, and courted the muse on the battle-field or in the meeting-house.

And in later years, when a portion of his work was before the world, when he had been first applauded and then forgotten, the craftsman did not neglect his workshop, but strove still upon his task. The inattention and ingratitude of men could not move him, and for himself, as for us, the labour was not in vain. (pp. xvii-xxii)

Reginald Brimley Johnson, "Memoir," in The Poetical Works of Samuel Butler, *Vol. 1, George Bell & Sons, 1893, pp. ix-xxii.*

Edmund Blunden (essay date 1928)

[*Blunden was associated with the Georgians, early twentieth-century English poets who reacted against the prevalent contemporary mood of disillusionment and the rise of artistic modernism by seeking to return to the pastoral, nineteenth-century poetic traditions associated with William Wordsworth. In this regard, much of Blunden's poetry reflects his love of the sights, sounds, and ways of rural England. In the following excerpt, he argues that Butler was a poet whose genius is obscured by the eccentricities of* Hudibras.]

Topical success is doomed to be followed by shadows and mortality, no matter how brightly it blazes to the astonishment of multitudes; and there is so great an amount of ephemeral allusion in ***Hudibras*** that, although once it was possible for a man to have inscribed on his tombstone "He knew immortal ***Hudibras*** by heart," it would be difficult to-day to find anyone who could repeat six lines of it. Some of its famous expressions are still from time to time misquoted, and that is almost all that ***Hudibras*** is to the modern reader. We can no longer be particularly moved to pursue the satirist's meaning through the ins and outs of ancient sectarian disputation, nor excited if it is suspected that the original of Butler's pseudo-Quixotic knight was none other than Sir Samuel Luke. The strokes of the lash fall on worthies or unworthies who died long enough ago without leaving even their names to the reference-books. A hundred and fifty years have passed since Dr. Johnson, with his usual sympathy for the ordinary reader, admitted the inevitable passing of the intention of ***Hudibras*** [see excerpt dated 1779]. "Of the ancient poets," he remarked, "every reader feels the mythology tedious and oppressive. Of ***Hudibras,*** the manners, being founded on opinions, are temporary and local, and therefore become every day less intelligible, and less striking." This said, Johnson proceeded to explain to the public the national experiences which had enabled and impelled their great-grandfathers to read ***Hudibras*** from end to end.

Perhaps there are some imaginative spirits left, who can summon up the history of England in the seventeenth century so realistically as to enjoy, or at any rate to feel with intensity, the portraits, politics and religious criticism of Butler. The rest of us would be not a little obliged for a skilful selection of his permanent wit and poetry—whatever deserves to be disentangled, so far as may be possible, from the litter of knockabout comedy and now almost meaningless preparation. If something of the kind is not done, Butler's genius will be forgotten, and several masterpieces of expression lost to view. Already we may say without diminishing his glory that it is a pity he wrote ***Hudibras***—almost his life-work, apparently—at all, and entrusted his intellectual jewels to that brilliant-looking vessel, so little calculated to weather the ever-changing seas of human interest; we may wish (however vainly) that a general allegory like Cervantes' or Bunyan's had captured his energetic mind. Rarely can there have been a poet more abounding in the materials for a vast picture of humanity.

Some sort of index to Butler's mental wealth, his observation and concentration of many-coloured life, his profound acquaintance with the workings of nature, may be quickly found in almost any page of ***Hudibras*** if we look only at his metaphors and comparisons. He seems to have been one of God's spies. Illustration jostles illustration with cinematographic rapidity. Consider, for instance, the describing of Hudibras in love but afraid to own it:

> Like caitiff vile, that for misdeed
> Rides with his face to rump of steed;
> Or rowing scull, he's fain to love,
> Look one way and another move;
> Or like a tumbler that does play
> His game, and looks another way,

Until he seize upon the coney;
Just so does he by matrimony.

Or this:

Doubtless the pleasure is as great
Of being cheated, as to cheat;
As lookers-on feel most delight,
That least perceive a juggler's sleight,
And still the less they understand,
The more they admire the sleight of hand.
Some with a noise, and greasy light
Are snapt, as men catch larks by night,
Ensnar'd and hamper'd by the soul,
As nooses by the legs catch fowl.
Some with a med'cine and receipt
Are drawn to nibble at the bait;
And though it be a two-foot trout
'Tis with a single hair drawn out.

Such is his method, and he has the ordered experience which can inexhaustibly supply it, surprising us probably with even the first ingenious aptitude and then adding others against all expectation with the prodigality of an original.

His images from nature are exceedingly vivid, and display the inborn intelligence of many Englishmen for the animal world. In days when there is a literary affectation of this intelligence in the air, one hails such a countryman as Butler with delight; and his casual observations disclose a familiarity with nature which, after the oppression of modern pretence, is a perfect restoration. A few words by him communicate an insight based only upon life's training. He speaks in original proverbs. Your noncountryman cannot catch up, when it comes to simplicities like this:

They from so formidable a soldier
Had fled like crows when they smell powder.

or this:

They scorn and hate them worse
Then dogs and cats do sow-gelders;

Or this with its artful comment, proper to be repeated even in these enlightened times:

As a fox with hot pursuit
Chas'd through a warren, casts about
To save his credit, and among
Dead vermine on a gallows hung,
And while the dogs run underneath,
Escap'd (by counterfeiting death)
Not out of cunning, but a train
Of atoms justling in his brain,
As learn'd philosophers give out.

One more of these truly rural instances—the well-known picture of the owl, which in its place is considerably amusing as it is applied to Hudibras in his amorous indecision:

And as an owl, that in a barn
Sees a mouse creeping in the corn,
Sits still, and shuts his round blue eyes,
As if he slept, until he spies
The little beast within his reach,
Then starts, and seizes on the wretch;
So from his couch the Knight did start
To seize upon the widow's heart . . .

The fierce controversialist who was so prominent a figure in Butler's composition seems to have hampered the poet in him, not only by involving him in a mass of transiencies but as well in narrowing down his moods and tones. ***Hudibras*** is too remorseless. The severity of the argument is scarcely ever relaxed, unless for the admission of the mere burlesque. Butler keeps up his succession of "Apostolic blows and knocks" with marvellous zeal, but we looked for more refreshment by the way. It is probable that he could have produced many other cadences of feeling, (though to be sure he hardly seems to have the gift of musical variety), had he not loved invective and sarcasm more. Indeed he is once or twice visited by an emotional tenderness, balm as mild and blessed as any poet's. Of that cool and sweet quality (greatly enhanced by the surrounding aridities) comes the long beloved nightpiece:

The sun grew low and left the skies,
Put down (some write) by ladies' eyes.
The moon pull'd off her veil of light,
That hides her face by day from sight,
(Mysterious veil, of brightness made,
That's both her lustre and her shade) . . .

This is the cheering source whence still flows the noble assurance that

Loyalty is still the same
Whether it win or lose the game;
True as the dial to the sun,
Altho' it be not shined upon.

And though Sir Hudibras is the most belaboured, dingy and ludicrous hero that ever author chose, and the most unlikely lover, Butler cannot utterly quell the music of delight and romance from his long sermonizings about love. The parodist sometimes, overcome by "a sovran shame", steals away and leaves not the asinine knight but the poet addressing the lady. Nonsense is enraptured into idealism:

I'll carve your name on bark of trees,
With true-love-knots and flourishes
That shall infuse eternal spring,
And everlasting flourishing;
Drink every letter on't in stum,
And make it brisk Champaign become.
Where'er you tread, your foot shall set
The primrose and the violet;
All spices, perfumes and sweet powders
Shall borrow from your breath their odours;
Nature her charter shall renew,
And take all lives of things from you;
The world depend upon your eye,
And when you frown upon it, die:
Only our loves shall still survive,
New worlds and Nature's to outlive,
And like to heralds' moons remain,
All crescents, without change or wane.

Freed wholly of the manner of hyperbole, Hudibras' opinion on love eventually arrives at a glistening blossom-like beauty comparable with Marvell, to whom perhaps Butler is near akin in poetic appetite:

And what security's too strong
To guard that gentle heart from wrong,
That to its friend is glad to pass
Itself away, and all it has,

Frontispiece for an edition of Hudibras *illustrated by William Hogarth.*

And, like an anchorite, gives over
This world for the heaven of a lover?

I shall gather here one more expression in which with the utmost simplicity and significance Butler swiftly rises from his picaresque foolery to the sublimity of love and pity for the race of men:

His horse had been of those
That fed on man's flesh, as fame goes:
Strange food for horse! and yet, alas!
It may be true, for flesh is grass.

The heraldic simile at the end of one of the Hudibrastic love-passages just now cited is a detail of Butler's characteristic, his enjoyment and mastery of the chimerical and the odd. This vein of his poetry ranges from the stupidly material to the completely legendary, and reminds us that he belongs to the age of "Halloo, my Fancy, whither wilt thou go?" He is extremely happy when he has the opportunity to pour out his treasury of paradoxes and Gothamite inventions, as in the picturing of Sidrophel the astronomer, who "made an instrument" to prove that the moon was not made of green cheese, and could "fire a mine in China here With sympathetic gunpowder." That is the lower track of his whimsicality, and sometimes he rises into the sphere of caprice for its own sake, the region of the undeniable basilisk and the phoenix and turtle. To what grandeur this willing suspension of disbelief may lead so richly stored a mind as Butler's, one spectacular outburst in his satire may be chosen once more to demonstrate:

Like Indian widows, gone to bed,
In flaming curtains, to the dead;

a few lines below which occurs the strange metaphysic rendering of love as

an ague that's reverst,
Whose hot fit takes the patient first,
That after burns with cold as much
As iron in Greenland does the touch;
Melts in the furnace of desire,
Like glass, that's but the ice of fire,
And when his heat of fancy's over,
Becomes as hard and frail a lover.

But that is a scientific kind of crystallization, and aside from the exotic and fabulous eccentricity which shed its timeless and gay-tinted light on so much of Butler's phrase. He owed more to the "Lapland Magi" and "Rosicrucian virtuosis" in his poetical evolution than he realized or pretends to realize. His vocabulary shows it, being fruitful in terms which at first acquaintance effuse a remoteness and a subtlety,

> Discover sea and land, Columbus
> And Magellan, cou'd never compass.

In that *Terra Incognita* he should have walked more freely and frequently, but for the demands of satire; we should have enjoyed more preternatural history such as that of the object which the astrologer Sidrophel mistook for a comet:

> A boy one night
> Did fly his tarsel of a kite,
> The strangest long-wing'd hawk that flies,
> That, like a bird of Paradise,
> Or herald's marlet, has no legs,
> Nor hatches young ones, nor lays eggs.

We should in the acquiescence of fancy tremble to more

> fears
> That spring, like fern, that insect weed,
> Equivocally, without seed.

And surely we should have more such jubilant ancestors of the Walrus and Carpenter than only

> th' Emperor Caligula,
> That triumph'd o'er the British sea,
> Took crabs and oysters prisoners,
> And lobsters, 'stead of cuirassiers;
> Engag'd his legions in fierce bustles
> With periwinkles, prawns and muscles,
> And led his troops with furious gallops
> To charge whole regiments of scallops;
> Not like their ancient way of war,
> To wait on his triumphal car;
> But when he went to dine or sup,
> More bravely ate his captives up . . .

To the above slight reflections on a poet who exhibits the characteristics of genius in glorious profusion, but who by the nature of his principal poetical undertaking is in a manner concealed from general realization, I wish that some more comprehensive appreciator would succeed with a fuller account and selection; not omitting to see and show what a poetic family sprang from ***Hudibras*** in the eighteenth century; meanwhile, a word for Butler's great technical achievement—his witty rhymes. The habit of writing immaculate rhyme, since regrettably developed in England, has robbed us to some extent of the capacity to produce bold and cheerful satirical verse. I am not sure that there has not been a great deal of artistic hypocrisy concerned in this affair of purified rhyming. Particularly, of course, this suspicion is formed by the verse of Browning and Swinburne, by whom the more exacting problems of rhyme are solved always so brilliantly and glibly. The reader presently recoils from these hollow and specious perfections of letter, so often made possible by amputations of spirit. When "floweret", "blossom," "safer" are matched with "embower it," "embosom," and "chafer," and "perorate" evokes "zero rate" or "apostle" falls in with "throstle" and "jostle," and such things occur all through large volumes, it begins to look as if there were more tricks in the world than Ophelia recognized. Old Butler calls us away from this cant of versifying with his hit or miss rhymes, either completely commanded by and answering to the sense, or else obviously presenting themselves as mere witticisms of technique—never as inspired poetry. To conclude in a manner suitable to that affirmation:

> But I shall take a fit occasion
> T'evince these by ratiocination,
> Some other time, in place more proper
> Than this we're in; therefore let's stop here.

(pp. 172-77)

Edmund Blunden, "Some Remarks on 'Hudibras'," in The London Mercury, *Vol. XVIII, No. 104, June, 1928, pp. 172-77.*

Edward Ames Richards (essay date 1937)

[*In the excerpt below, Richards discusses the ways in which romance and fantasy contribute to the verse and characterization in* Hudibras *and examines the poem's influence in the field of political satire.*]

In the author of ***Hudibras*** we meet a man who claims our curiosity and respect rather than any warmth or excitement or allegiance. He owns less pity for the race than scorn, less humor than wit, less hope than stoicism. He has gained himself and his own mind, and that is much, but he has gained no one else. He is cautious, even secretive. He cannot lend himself to people or to causes, and he watches them pass him by while he is considering how little there is that is true. None the less, he cannot enjoy the consolations of philosophy, or religion, or of animal spirits. He speaks no more than a few lonely words about beauty. His consolation would appear to be very largely an extraordinary gift of words and the labor of arranging them and rearranging them in a poem that he calls a romance, while he considers the madness and unreason of the years through which he and his mind have passed. When he writes satire, therefore, he chooses as a center, or norm, not England as a whole, nor the Anglican Church, nor the court of Charles II; he chooses above all his own mind and his own sense of the fitness of things. War, the pretended authority of texts, the strenuous pamphleteers, the vagaries of the New Light, the venal Anglicans, the immoral Charles, are all signs of defective intelligence. He is a partisan of intelligence. "Men fell out," he wrote; "they knew not why." No other single phrase, I believe, contains so much of the meaning of Butler's satire.

[***Hudibras***] was classed by its author as a romance, and since, as is clear from the context, he meant a romance in burlesque, there is no need to quarrel with so weighty an authority. The romantic classification can cause no difficulty since the story provides a lover, a lady, and the attempt of the first to win the second. The definition of what constitutes a burlesque poem, whether romantic or not, entails more difficulty. Without pausing to sort out and discuss the definitions that have previously been offered, I shall say, merely, that burlesque consists primarily, in one line of its development, in realizing an obviously and admittedly improbable action. This means that if the action is improbable it is immediately accepted by the reader without demur or debate for what it is; and it carries characters, scenes, and incidental properties equally improbable which are just as immediately accepted. Hence, burlesque is more like fantasy, or fairy stories, than it is like any other literary kind; Butler defined his poem sufficiently when he called it a romance, since to him the term meant a sequence of improbable actions.

But if ***Hudibras*** is a romance, it is many things besides. For one thing it is travesty; for another, it is satire; for a third, it is burlesque, a term which we must retain for the sake of our own convenience. The author's literary originality lies not so much in the sustained use of the verse form, excellently as he adapted that to his purpose, as it does in the balance which he keeps between the real and the fantastic, or burlesque, elements in his design; between the identification of historical social forces that he was satirizing and the never-never land traversed by his characters. Either one of these tasks is sufficiently difficult to challenge the ability of any first-rate writer. Swift and Byron, in achieving a union of these diverse elements, used more definite and extensive patterns of travel and adventure than did Butler, one creating entire lands and peoples for his fantasy, the other being content with a less fantastic travelogue. The ground trod by Hudibras and Ralpho, on the other hand, is far less easily identified than either Lilliput or the Cyclades. The action of the poem is assumed to take place in England, though Butler never says that it does; the setting is vague; the properties only those of immediate use in the action. One can, indeed, say that Butler is too fond of the abstract to be able to create a rich fictional setting for his fable. But it seems more to the point to say that if ***Hudibras*** is first of all a romance and a fantasy, the misty background, the properties which are at hand as if by magic, are precisely appropriate to that kind of poem. In the same way, it may be true to say that ***Hudibras*** is structurally weak and wandering; but it is perhaps more enlightening to say that structural vagary is one of the most usual characteristics of romance. Against this indeterminate landscape we see the perfectly determinate characters; our minds are diverted, our attention is held by them. They are not real; we meet them not as people who persuade us that they have a meaning. Real people could not live and breathe and act in the hazy atmosphere of this myth; and it does not matter that they could not do so; for the author is presenting us not with single characters, but with the composite and monstrous characteristics of a period and some of its dominant attitudes.

Perhaps enough has been said to suggest what seems to me the chief determining quality of ***Hudibras*** as a whole—the quality of the myth, or the fantasy, or the fairy tale. Someone is sure to protest at once, however, that this unreal atmosphere cannot possibly be the most important literary quality of ***Hudibras.*** How can this poem be a fantasy, I imagine the questioning protest to run, when everybody knows that it is above everything else a markedly sharp and witty and timely piece of writing? Have you not yourself been at some pains to show that Butler was an intellectualist, a skeptic, a cool reasoner? And is not his best-known poem an early monument to the age of prose and reason? The main answer to such questions is a simple "yes," suggesting anew why ***Hudibras*** is, in the complication of its effects, one of the most amazing works ever written. It may be added, however, that Butler as a conscious literary artist, knew quite well what he was about in choosing a traditionally romantic structure to satirize both that structure and those contemporary aspects of life which seemed to him dangerously nonsensical.

Concerning the style in which the poem is built, we may find that no very fruitful discussion is possible; at the same time, so much has been written about "burlesque" verse, and the subject is of so much importance to Butler's imitators, that we cannot avoid a brief discussion of the verse form of ***Hudibras.*** That form is, of course, the octosyllabic or four-stress riming couplet. The form was not new; it is, in fact, one of the oldest forms of modern, as opposed to classical, poetry. I suspect that the extent to which it was the vehicle of medieval French romance formed one of the reasons why Butler was glad to adapt it to satirical uses. I imagine that his dislike of romances was owing partly to the circumstance that they were romances and partly to the unfortunate fact that so many of them were French. The verse form came across the Channel in Chaucer's time and enjoyed some popularity in English, though not predominantly for satirical purposes. In the seventeenth century, indeed, it is particularly pastoral and lyrical in mood and accent, as in William Browne and in Milton. The satirical couplets scattered through Elizabethan and Jacobean plays, the rough verse prefacing so many Civil War pamphlets, the poems of Cleaveland and those in the Musae Deliciarum, are insufficient to deprive Butler of the credit of having made this kind of verse a telling satirical instrument.

What is the difference between Milton's couplets

> With wanton heed and giddy cunning
> The melting voice in mazes running
> Untwisting all the chains that tie
> The hidden soul of harmony;

and those in which Butler's Sidrophel could tell

> How many Dukes, and Earls, and Peers,
> Are in the Planetary Spheres,
> Their Airy Empire: and command
> Their sev'ral strengths by Sea and Land;
> What factions th'have, and what they drive at
> In public Vogue, and what in private.

Both deal hyperbolically with matters beyond the ordinary range of events, with improbabilities, using rhetorical devices that are both elaborate and condensed. Milton's verse, however, attempts to suggest to the reader or listener another kind of sensuous and lyrical experience. It is at once emotionally soothing and emotionally disturbing. Butler on the other hand never makes the lyricist's attempt to engross the entire personality of his readers; he is active and logical rather than sensuously suggestive; impersonal rather than personal; remote rather than immediate; amusing rather than appealing. In this instance, at least, the difference between the two kinds of verse is not primarily one of the choice of words, or of movement, or even of the artistic purpose of the author. The difference is primarily a difference in men. One is capable of feeling sensuous delight and of believing that it is a good thing; he takes pleasure in that complex association of memories and of habits of observation which contributes to the sense of beauty; and he tries to satisfy his own sense of beauty by his own poetry. The other poet pays no attention to what we ordinarily mean by a sense of beauty; it does not occur to him that it is important; he feels no need to induce it in others. He takes no pains to distinguish between the beautiful and the unbeautiful, or between the moral and the immoral; he is scornfully cognizant of the thousand differences between the rational and the irrational, and he carries in stock an even greater number of modern instances of human imbecility. Given these temperamental differences in the poets, the differences in diction and in rhythm between lyrical and unlyrical octosyllabics follow simply enough and examples can easily be gathered by anyone in search of diversion.

It is necessary to distinguish the verse of ***Hudibras*** not only from lyrical verse but from other burlesque verse in the same meter, chiefly that of Scarron and his translators and imitators in English, and of travesty in general such as travesties of Virgil and Ovid. We have seen that ***Hudibras*** is itself a travesty in part, in so far as it satirizes the romantic conventions of form and content. If this were all that it did it would deserve no unique place in literary history such as it actually holds.

We can find no marked difference in verse form between, let us say, Cotton's *Virgil Travestie* and ***Hudibras;*** but the difference in scope and in meaning is at once apparent. The travesty is almost entirely a literary tidbit, concocted for the pleasure of educated readers thoroughly familiar with the originals. It may bear a relation to contemporary life or to a satirical presentation of it, but as we shall see in a later instance, the satirist who tries to present in a consistent way both the travesty of a classical pattern and a social satire as well, has his hands full. The travesty in ***Hudibras*** is an unobtrusive and incidental element; it appears as merely a part of, or as another example of, unreason and unreality. Hence, in examining the poems written after the publication of ***Hudibras*** and of *Scarronides,* we should be put to it to find the proper point of reference if we regarded only the form of the verse. We shall need rather to examine the content and the main drift of the later works.

The hudibrastic couplet met a formidable competitor in the heroic couplet. The former was extremely popular and was considerably imitated for well over a century. But in its own day it failed to have so general a vogue as the couplet of Dryden. I suspect that it did not because it was not used by the dramatists, and further, that the dramatists eschewed it because of the difficulties which it puts in the way of the actor. In short passages the hudibrastic couplet is a better vehicle for pointed epigram than is the heroic. But in longer passages, both sense and sound are too often interrupted by the rime, and the temptation to parenthesis also becomes very strong. The effects of this temptation are easily seen when this verse form goes to pieces in the hands of Churchill. Furthermore, the fashionable poetic literature of the Restoration was required to be either elegant or august. ***Hudibras*** was neither. At its best it possesses a leanness and a hardness which comparatively few heroics achieve, and Butler did not neglect to illustrate the incurable tendency to heroic inflation in his second version of **"The Elephant in the Moon."**

Nevertheless, the octosyllabic couplet is an exceedingly difficult form to control. Limited in the first place to nondramatic uses, it is further limited by its tendency to change mood in the course of a few lines. At first sight this may appear to be a very desirable quality, suggesting the possibility of adaptation to many uses. In practice, however, dependability is just as great an asset as adaptability, and the octosyllabic couplet has shown great capacity for getting those who write it off the track. If the couplets are closed, they are exceedingly irritating in their monotony; if they are open, they are likely to be equally irritating in diffuseness and inconsequence. Butler's own jesting comment on one line for sense and one for rime is a fair indication of the dangers of the medium. For good heroics, an easy length is desirable; for hudibrastics, a hard, sensible brevity. The apparent easiness of the form has misled many writers into attempting it, who have proved that to produce even one good couplet is a hard task indeed, while to achieve a broad pattern is beyond them entirely.

Butler thought that a good style is like truth: it contains nothing but what is plain, open, and easy to come at both for writer and reader. This perhaps sounds like strange doctrine from a poet whose fame rests partly on a supposed faculty for bringing out-of-the-way comparisons and other figures of speech into his work. They may have been startling to the author; they may seem startling to us. The point is, however, that they seemed apt to him, and most of them strike us in the very same way.

When we apply the word "hudibrastic" to other works than ***Hudibras,*** we cannot limit the meaning of it to the form of the verse. Apparently the term has meaning only in the field of satire. It may refer to the nature of the thing attacked, to the content of the story or fable, to the point of view of the satirist, to the form of the verse, or to a mixture of two or more of these elements. Although "hudibrastic" is applied almost universally to poems written in the verse form of ***Hudibras,*** without respect to the other qualities of the poem to which it may be applied, and without respect to the other early satirists in this form, it will not be possible to confine the inquiry to such simple limits in discussing the imitators of Butler.

What does a writer do when he sets out to imitate ***Hudibras***? Obviously, imitation does not mean duplication, for duplication is as undesirable to a writer as it is impossible to a personality. It means that one man's way of thinking has seemed to another to be so convenient and attractive that he thinks of himself as being in some sense a disciple; it may mean also that aside from a sort of spiritual kinship, the follower finds his master's method of expression so apt that he takes as much of it as he can assimilate for his own use. The accent, the superficial symbols of a style, are the easiest to imitate, without any intellectual connection necessarily existing between the original author and his imitator. Hence it comes about that people so diverse as Matthew Prior, the diplomatic errand boy, and Thomas Fessenden, the New England editor and Jack-of-all-trades, both claim to write, and do write, hudibrastic verse, though underneath this common claim is a world of diversity.

When we read ***Hudibras*** in connection with the rest of Butler's work, we are struck by the way in which his general views of society and human nature transcend the limits of his best poem, and we conclude that the author was not temperamentally or intellectually a very good or very useful partisan. His view of humanity was too consistently somber to allow him to go all the way in condemning any part of it. There seems little doubt, however, that to his contemporaries, and to those who immediately followed him, he appeared to be predominantly and especially the satirist of Dissent. His literary fame rested then, as it rests now, on what he had to say in retrospect about the forces commonly held responsible for the Civil War. None of his contemporaries praises the sinuous debates between Hudibras and the Widow, or the burlesque meeting of the Rump, or the satire on romance. But many were no doubt glad to have a lampoon on the excesses of a troublesome part of the population and to have gained thereby a convenient point of literary reference for attacking these same forces or other forces which could be shown, fairly or not, to have gained their strength from '41 and their shame from '49. ***Hudibras*** was assumed to be for all practical purposes an expression of High Anglicanism and of absolute royalty, and is therefore the source of, and in a sense the authority for, a great deal of intensely partisan verse by men who enjoyed no part of Butler's comparatively broad and impersonal view of the principles involved.

We can therefore distinguish several types among the imitators of ***Hudibras.*** First, there are those who were amused by the verse form and who experimented with it themselves, often, apparently, on the assumption that the form was easy to handle or that it would be effective even though mishandled. The second class took over the verse form, more or less of the hudibrastic machinery, and also what they conceived to be Butler's political point of view. A third class were interested not so much in the obvious marks of hudibrastic verse, or in the fable, or in the politics of Butler, as they were in the subtler qualities of his mind, such as his precision, his polish, his playfulness, and his witty and agnostic movement through the field of familiar notions.

Among the imitators those authors with the freshest and most inventive minds naturally produced the most creditable imitations. ***Hudibras,*** indeed, has marked shortcomings as the source and beginning of a satiric school. In the first place, it is too thorough, too complete; little is left to be said about the main defects of the Dissenting temper after Butler has gone over them.

In the next place, the poem can be said to have closed rather than to have inaugurated a period. In a sense, Butler wrote extensive, and learned, and amusing footnotes to the history of the Civil Wars and of the experiments in government that followed them. The years from 1640 to 1660 were to him a bloody, confused, and meaningless interlude; or, if the blood and confusion had any meaning, it was a warning against allowing an ignorant and passionate theocracy, an ignorant and passionate democracy, to have any part in the matters of state. Nasty and crooked as the course of government must be, that course must be shaped by sensible and shrewd men of this world, not by men claiming authority in both this world and the next. Men may be immoral, but they need not be unintelligent. Butler's prose notes show that he felt almost as strongly in opposition to the Roman power in England, but he never got to the point of working his ideas into verse. The satirical current flowed on without him. He made no pretense to prophecy; one reads him in vain to find out what he thought would happen or what ought to happen in England. He records only his interpretation of what he has seen. To him, it is a farce so fantastic that only a burlesque can do it justice.

In other ways, too, Butler may be regarded as one who looked backward rather than forward in time. He lashes scholastic philosophy, but his allusions to Descartes and Hobbes are by no means complimentary; he spends hundreds of lines in ridiculing soothsaying and astrology, but he finds little to choose between them and the new experimental science; he decries worship of the classics and the imitation of contemporary foreign literatures, but his allusions to his own English contemporaries are few and frosty. His cultural indignations are very largely reserved for former cultures, while he feels little generosity for movements of his own day. It is as though he felt that all things had come to an end in his time. In any event, he could not turn himself into a literary handy man for any party, and that was the requirement of the age for a man of letters who wanted to get ahead.

Those among his literary followers who took over chiefly the political tendency of ***Hudibras*** as their satirical guide found themselves beating a dead horse. And the more they took over, the worse off they were. It is true that the "jealousies and fears" which occasioned the Civil Wars, and which the wars in turn occasioned, lived for a very long time in the national memory, as such fears will. But it seems equally true that there was no real political danger from the Independents and the Presbyterians, as such, in England after the Restoration. The members became more secular in attitude and their interests came to be identified with those of the trading and manufacturing classes. They fought for toleration, indeed, but in relation to this issue showed power only in conjunction with the Catholic interest, as in the Revolution of '88; of themselves they were not sufficiently numerous or sufficiently united on religious issues to constitute a political danger. For this reason those satires directed against religious Dissent give the impression of boxing with the shadows of ghosts. The intellectual content of ***Hudibras*** became attenuated to the thin cries of Tory pamphleteers who could interpret the opposition as bearing with it the seeds of '41 and of the Good Old Cause. The chief points of political satire in ***Hudibras*** were true enough, and well enough known, to become telling political commonplaces in a fearful and restless society. (pp. 24-35)

Edward Ames Richards, "A Discussion of Hudibras," in his Hudibras in the Burlesque Tradition, *Columbia University Press, 1937, pp. 24-35.*

Ian Jack (essay date 1952)

[*Jack is a Scottish educator and literary scholar who, in his several full-length critical works, has examined English poetry from the Augustan era through the late nineteenth century. In the following excerpt, he examines the verse form, rhetoric, diction, and imagery of* Hudibras, *characterizing the poem as an example of "low" satire rather than burlesque.*]

Butler took the name of his hero from Spenser, and [***Hudibras***] cannot be understood without glancing back to [Spenser's] *The Faerie Queene.* In Book II, which is concerned with Temperaunce, Sir Guyon reaches a castle inhabited by three sisters. The youngest loves pleasure, the second moderation, while the third is a sour hater of all delights. Sir Hudibras, who is contrasted with Sans-loy, the wooer of the youngest sister, makes his suit to the eldest. In a stanza which throws a great deal of light on ***Hudibras,*** he is described as

> . . . an hardy man;
> Yet not so good of deedes, as great of name,
> Which he by many rash aduentures wan,
> Since errant armes to sew he first began;
> More huge in strength, then wise in workes he was,
> And reason with foole-hardize ouer ran;
> Sterne melancholy did his courage pas,
> And was for terrour more, all armd in shyning bras.

'It is not unpleasant to observe', Butler once remarked [in his ***Characters and Passages from Note-Books***], ' . . . how all Sorts of men doe not only act but say things cleane Contrary to what they pretend and meane.' For the reader who remembers his Spenser, this is the element of contradiction and inconsistency which the name Hudibras brings to mind. Butler's Hudibras resembles Spenser's in being more famous than he deserves, in having more strength than wisdom, and in being inspired less by true courage than by 'melancholy' (in this context, madness). But by giving his hero this name Butler does not only indicate the main traits of his character: he also states his own attitude to the civil wars and the discontents which led up to them. The suggestion is that the Royalists, or the more extreme among them, bear an affinity to the youngest daughter Perissa and her lover Sans-loy; that the Parliamentary Party may be similarly compared to the eldest daughter and her wooer Hudibras; while the poet himself, and all moderate men, support the 'great rule of Temp'raunce'.

The title is not the only thing about ***Hudibras*** which reminds one of *The Faerie Queene.* In its whole conception and organization Butler's poem has marked affinities with Spenser's. The parallel between the adventures of Sir Hudibras and those of the hero of each of the Books of *The Faerie Queene* must have been deliberate. Like one of Spenser's knights Butler's hero is involved in continual disputes and adventures, and woos a lady. But in all his endeavours he is an un-Spenserian failure.

The fact that Butler was familiar with the Renaissance doctrine of the heroic poem has a bearing on ***Hudibras*** which is frequently overlooked. Butler knew as well as Spenser or Milton that an allegorical meaning was expected in any long poem.

> Betweene [error], and Truth [he wrote], ly's the Proper Sphere of wit, which though it seeme to incline to falshood, do's it only to give Intelligence to Truth. . . . Wit by a certaine slight of the Minde, deliver's things otherwise then they are in Nature. . . . But when it imploys those things which it borrows of Falshood, to the Benefit and advantage of Truth, as in Allegories, Fables, and Apologues, it is of excellent use, as making a Deeper impression into the mindes of Men then if the same Truths were plainely deliver'd.

Hudibras has something of the same complexity as *The Faerie Queene.* The strong element of the *roman à clef* has always been recognized; and there is no doubt that the poem was intended to embody a complicated allegory. As each of Spenser's knights represents one of the cardinal virtues, or the striving for that virtue, so Sir Hudibras represents one of the basic vices. Dennis suggested that ***Hudibras*** is a satire on hypocrisy [see excerpt dated 1693]: Sir Hudibras is Hypocrisy embodied. Near the beginning of the poem the reader is told that 'Hipocrisie and Nonsence' are in control of Sir Hudibras's conscience; hypocrisy is satirized with particular intensity throughout; and in the brilliant passage, parodying the confessional dialogues and self-communings of the Dissenters, in which Ralpho scares Hudibras into thinking him a supernatural 'Voice', he asks him point-blank:

> Why didst thou chuse that cursed Sin,
> Hypocrisie, to set up in?

To which the knight replies, without demur:

> Because it is the thriving'st Calling,
> The onely Saints-Bell that rings all in.

Throughout ***Hudibras*** great emphasis is laid on the difference between profession and performance, outer seeming and inner reality. It would hardly be an exaggeration to say that in this poem every species of human folly and crime is represented as a species of hypocrisy.

Although political satire is the most obvious 'end' of ***Hudibras,*** therefore, Hazlitt [see excerpt dated 1819] was right when he remarked that Butler 'could not, in spite of himself,

> narrow his mind
> And to party give up what was meant for mankind.

There are many passages where Butler makes no pretence to be limiting his satire to a political party, but attacks lawyers, women, the Royal Society, and pedantry of every kind. If ***Hudibras*** had been completed it seems likely that every type represented in Butler's prose **'Characters'** would have found its niche in a comprehensive 'Anatomy of Melancholy'.

In giving his satire this wide scope Butler was following the tradition of such works as Barclay's *Ship of Fools* and the *Encomium Moriae* of Erasmus. Satire is like a shot fired at sea: when it hits its target it causes a series of rings to radiate outwards towards all other follies and vices whatever. And so one finds in ***Hudibras*** strokes of general satire that have a very wide application:

> . . . Most Men carry things so even
> Between this World, and Hell and Heaven,
> Without the least offence to either,
> They freely deal in all together.

Butler had a great admiration for Ben Jonson, and in some respects he was his pupil. As in *Volpone* and *The Alchemist* Jonson's main satire against greed is accompanied and enriched by incidental attacks on other species of folly and sin, so in ***Hudibras*** hypocrisy is only the principal target. '[Butler] in general ridicules not persons, but things', said Hazlitt, 'not a party, but their principles, which may belong, as time and occasion serve, to one set of solemn pretenders or another.' Because Butler was a man of genius what began as a political burlesque ended as what Dennis truly called a very just satire.

. . . . .

No passage in ***Hudibras*** is more familiar than that in which Butler ridicules his hero's addiction to rhetoric:

> For *Rhetorick* he could not ope
> His mouth, but out there flew a Trope:
> And when he hapned to break off
> I'th'middle of his speech, or cough,
> H'had hard words, ready to shew why,
> And tell what Rules he did it by.

Such satire was thoroughly conventional: one has only to turn to Erasmus to find all the charges that Butler brings against rhetorical pedantry brilliantly deployed by the greatest of all the humanists. What is satirized is not rhetoric itself but the pedantic affectation of rhetoric, fine words and elaborate figures out of season. It would be a serious mistake to suppose that Butler is here rebelling against old attitudes; and it would be equally false to imagine, from his satire on rhetoric, that he himself had no use for it. What Butler wrote of Sprat—'The Historian of Gresham Colledge, Indevors to Cry down Oratory and Declamation, while He uses nothing else'—is equally true of himself. The point is important because the modern reader, knowing little of decorum and the kinds, has a natural tendency to regard ***Hudibras*** as inspired doggerel and its author as a literary jester who knew no other way of writing. Nothing could be farther from the truth. Butler's other works make it clear that Sir William Temple's description of Rabelais as 'a Man of Excellent and Universal Learning as well as Wit' is no less applicable to him.

It follows that Butler's choice of verse and style was perfectly deliberate. The limited value of metrical notations appears in the fact that the same name must be given to the metre of ***Hudibras*** as to that of Marvell's *To his Coy Mistress* and *The Garden,* as well as many parts of *L'Allegro* and *Il Penseroso.* Like the iambic pentameter, the tetrameter is endlessly adaptable: it is the use that Butler makes of it, the tune that he plays on it, that is significant. His verse 'stands indeed upon Four Feet', as an anonymous critic [in the Advertisement to *Pendragon; or, the Carpet Knight His Kalender*] remarked in 1698;

> but its Liberties and Priveleges are unbounded; and those Four Feet are, I think, by no means oblig'd to be but Eight Syllables; for in place of the Last, it is a part of its Excellency sometimes to have Two, Three, or Four Syllables (like so many Claws) crowded into the Time of One Foot. . . . It is wonderful to traverse its Arbitrary Power, how it proceeds without regard to *Periods, Colons,* or *Comma*'s: How sometimes it will change *Accents* for the sake of *Rhyme,* and, according to the most vulgar and careless Pronunciation, leave out what *Consonants* it pleases. . . .

What is particularly remarkable is the rushing vigour of ***Hudibras,*** the unfailing energy of the verse.

In reflective and sententious passages, which are among the most brilliant parts of the poem, Butler often confines the sense to couplets for twenty or thirty lines at a time. On such occasions the affinity of his verse to familiar proverbs is particularly evident. But the 'numbers' of the poem, as Johnson pointed out, are 'purposely neglected' [see excerpt dated 1779]. There are examples enough to show that 'harmonious verse' was well within Butler's reach; but he seldom wanted it. Instead there are frequent harsh enjambements.

The effect of these enjambements is often enhanced by the rhymes. Rhyme fulfils different functions in the hands of different poets. In Pope, very often, it perfects the epigram: in Tennyson it serves most characteristically as an addition to the orchestral resources: in Butler, as Dennis understood, it is frequently part of the satire. 'A Rime alone is very often a Jest', he remarked, 'as all who are acquainted with ***Hudibras*** very well know.' For example,

> He us'd to lay about and stickle,
> Like *Ram* or *Bull,* at *Conventicle;*

or again:

> Madam, *I do, as is my Duty,*
> *Honour the Shadow of your Shoe-tye.*

Perhaps the odd rhymes have too often distracted attention from the more solid wit of ***Hudibras,*** as Addison thought [see excerpt dated 1711]. They are certainly less numerous than is commonly supposed.

'Il est vif & serré, & dit en peu de vers, ce qu'ils (his imitators) étendroient en une longue Kirielle de rimes.' This praise of Scarron may be allowed to draw attention to one of the sovereign merits of Butler's use of the tetrameter, his power of gaining effects of remarkable brevity. Sometimes he takes pleasure in spinning out a far-fetched thought; but when he wants to be concise he cuts language to the bone.

The question of Butler's forerunners and models is not very important. Some such use of the tetrameter as his must always have been common in lampoons and other popular sorts of verse, such as the vulgar ballad. It may be found here and there in the Middle Ages, as in the satirical parts of *Le Roman de la Rose.* Scarron, with whose work Butler's shares 'une trompeuse facilité', must have been familiar to him; and he may well have taken a hint from the authors of certain of the poems in *Musarum Deliciæ* and *Wit Restor'd,* two witty miscellanies published in 1656 and 1658. But no earlier poet of genius had specialized in the satirical use of this metre.

Butler's metre cannot usefully be considered in isolation from the other aspects of his idiom, for there is a perfect partnership between his versification and his diction. Even if the verse itself were what is misleadingly termed 'heroic' (iambic pentameters rhyming in pairs), any serious attempt at the 'harmonious numbers' appropriate to heroic verse in the full sense would be ludicrously out of place as an accompaniment to the prosaic diction which is Butler's chosen medium. For this reason Dryden's censure of the metre of ***Hudibras*** must be read rather as a reflection of his own choice of a suitable metre for satire than as impartial literary criticism [see Dryden excerpt dated 1693].

As is natural in a poem of such length—there is a greater number of lines in ***Hudibras*** than in *Paradise Lost*—the style varies considerably from passage to passage; but the staple of the idiom is a personal development of the least elevated of the three styles distinguished by Renaissance and Augustan rhetoricians, the 'low' style appropriate to the base sort of satire. Occasionally, indeed, Butler satirizes by describing his butts sarcastically in elevated language:

> 'Mong these the fierce *Magnano* was,
> And *Talgol* foe to *Hudibras;*
> *Cerdon* and *Colon,* Warriors stout
> And resolute as ever fought:
> Whom furious *Orsin* thus bespoke.

And sometimes Butler reminds the reader of Dryden's description of *La Secchia Rapita,* alternating with lines which seem 'majestical and severe' afterthoughts which 'turn them all into a pleasant ridicule':

> Next march'd brave *Orsin,* famous for
> Wise Conduct, and success in War:
> A skilful Leader, stout, severe,
> *Now Marshal to the Champion Bear.*
> With Truncheon tip'd with Iron head,
> The Warrior to the Lists [he] led;
> With solemn march and stately pace,
> *But far more grave and solemn face.*

But although tetrameters were occasionally used with a heroic idiom, the metre of ***Hudibras*** is not well suited to ironical solemnity. The sustained irony of the mock-heroic was not Butler's goal. Whenever he essays it, one senses his natural bent to downright ridicule impatiently waiting for its chance.

The characteristic mode of satire in ***Hudibras*** is the opposite of the mock-heroic, that of describing everything in the most undignified manner possible [Jack's italics]:

> When civil fury first grew high,
> And men *fell out* they knew not why,
> When hard Words, Jealousies, and Fears,
> *Set* Folks together *by the Ears,*
> And made them *fight, like mad or drunk,*
> For *Dame* Religion *as for Punk,*
> Whose honesty they all durst *swear for,*
> Though *not a man of them knew wherefore.*

Satire and the sympathetic feelings are absolutely incompatible. Butler's object in these lines, the essential satirist's object, is to kill any sympathy which the reader may feel for the subject of his satire, moving him instead to amusement and contempt. Nor is there anything indirect in the working of the satire. The method is that of straightforward 'diminution': the reader is told that the quarrels which led to the civil war were of no more account than a brawl for a whore, and his acceptance of this view is made inevitable (at least temporarily) by the fact that the whole affair is described in an idiom which ridicules everything it touches. Butler's subject is as different as possible from that of the romantic epic poet. Instead of Ariosto's

> Le donne, i cavallier, l'arme, gli amori,
> Le cortesie, l'audaci imprese,

he is concerned with light wenches and prudish viragos, costermongers and fanatics, rudeness in every sense and of every kind. And his style is equally remote from that of heroic verse. The elementary principle on which he works is that while many people might sympathize with a *crowd,* no one cares to take sides with a *rout.* The essence of low satire could not be more simple.

The nature of Butler's low style is nowhere more evident than in the *sententiae.* Following the rhetorical precept of the time, Butler made considerable use of this figure, particularly at such points as the beginning and end of a canto; but while sententious passages are often written in a high style, those in ***Hudibras*** are in the most colloquial language:

> Ay me! what perils do environ
> The Man that meddles with cold Iron!
> What plaguy mischiefs and mishaps
> Do dog him still with after-claps!
> For though Dame Fortune seem to smile
> And leer upon him for a while;
> She'll after shew him, in the nick
> Of all his Glories, a Dog-trick.

The contrast between these lines and the opening couplet of [Dryden's] *MacFlecknoe,* which is equally sententious, affords a vivid example of the difference between the low style and the heroic:

> All humane things are subject to decay,
> And, when Fate summons, Monarchs must
> obey.

While it could hardly be more different in style, ***Hudibras*** like *MacFlecknoe* belongs to the class of satires which Dryden named Varronian. The basis of the poem is narrative. To call it a 'burlesque' is to invite confusion. If the essence of burlesque consists in describing dignified characters and actions (which are usually not of the poet's invention) in a ludicrous manner, then the parts of ***Hudibras*** which deal directly with the wars may be so described. But the poem as a whole is the result of an act of the creative imagination. Only in the sense that the whole world of ***Hudibras*** symbolizes the civil wars can its heart be said to consist in a discrepancy between subject and style. Sir Hudibras and the adventures he meets with as he rides 'a Colonelling' are extremely undignified. When they are described in a low style the result is not incongruity but rather a perfect aptness: the style matches the characters and action. The result is that it can only be misleading to compare ***Hudibras*** with such burlesques as Cotton's *Virgil Travestie.*

. . . . .

All has not been said of the 'original and peculiar' diction of ***Hudibras*** when it has been assigned to the category of low style. It is remarkably varied. The second paragraph of the poem, for example, introduces a new element, that of parody:

> A *Wight* he was, whose very sight wou'd
> Entitle him *Mirror of Knighthood;*
> That never bent *his stubborn knee*
> To any thing but *Chivalry.*

This element of literary satire demands modifications of style which enhance the variety of the poem.

The critical attitude which inspires the parodies in ***Hudibras*** is precisely that which one would expect of Butler, an Augustan conservatism looking back to classical models and suspicious of innovation. The principal targets are such writers of 'romantic' epics as Ariosto, Spenser, and Davenant. Other unclassical genres which are parodied include the ballad, the metrical romance of the Middle Ages, which survived among humble readers during the seventeenth century, and the prose heroic romances so popular in France and England during Butler's lifetime. Although Butler has his fling at modern translators, the great classical epics themselves are parodied comparatively seldom.

The literary satire which finds expression in perpetual 'allusions' thoughout ***Hudibras*** is only one aspect of a comprehensive critique of the uses and abuses of the English language. No less than Rabelais or James Joyce, Butler was a fascinated student of language. Odd words interested him as much as odd ideas. It would not be hard to imagine him spending an evening with Robert Burton listening to the swearing of the bargees at Folly Bridge. It may be that he had no need to go out of his way to find freaks of language. If there is any truth in the tradition that he was at one time secretary to Sir Samuel Luke, he must have had every opportunity of hearing the latest in cant terms. Perhaps he used some of his numerous notebooks for recording the words he heard. With an intense satiric mastery he culled the language of sectarians and pedants of every sort. ***Hudibras*** became the receptacle of this wealth of strange words; as a result it has a greater variety of idiom than any other poem in the language.

Yet it would be quite wrong to think of Butler simply as an enthusiast for 'stunning words'—however different his criterion from Rossetti's. He lived in an age of linguistic flux when the native genius of 'the finest of the vernacular tongues' seemed to many good judges to be in peril. Sprat complained [in his *History of the Royal-Society* (1667)] that the language had 'receiv'd many fantastical terms, which were introduced by our *Religious Sects* . . . and *Translators'.* Dryden returned to this subject time and time again. 'I have endeavoured to write English', he wrote in his first considerable critical essay [*Epistle Dedicatory of The Rival Ladies* (1664)], which appeared in the same year as the Second Part of ***Hudibras,*** 'as near as I could distinguish it from the tongue of pedants, and that of affected travellers. Only I am sorry, that (speaking so noble a language as we do) we have not a more certain measure of it, as they have in France'. In this revival of the Renaissance zeal for ennobling the vernacular Butler played his own part. 'That Barbarous Canting which those use who do not understand the sense and Propriety of a Language' is continually a target of his satire.

> All the abilities of our moderne Guifted men consist in fantastique Senseles expressions, and silly affected Phrases [he complained in one of his notebooks] just in such a Stile as the great Turke, and the Persian Sophy use to write, which they believe to be the true Propriety of the Spirit, and highest perfection of all Sanctity . . . Like a Spell or charme, [Cant] has a wonderful operation [on] the Rabble, for they Naturally admire any unusuall words which they do not understand, but would gladly seeme to do, as believing all wisdome as these men do all holines to consist in words. They call their Gifts Dispensations, because they believe God do's dispence with them for any wickednes which [they] can Commit.

'This Canting runs through all Professions and Sorts of men', Butler added, 'from the Judge on the Bench to the Begger in the Stocks'; and he laid all these sources under contribution for his great satire. Sidrophel, with his lore of Paracelsus, 'Behmen' and 'the dog of Cacodemon', has at his tongue's end all the cant of his kind:

> Quoth *Whachum, Venus* you retriv'd,
> In opposition with *Mars,*
> And no benigne friendly Stars
> T'allay th'effect. Quoth *Wizard,* So!
> In *Virgo?* Ha! quoth *Whachum,* No.
> Has *Saturn* nothing to do in't?
> One tenth of 's *Circle* to a minute.

Butler's use of the special vocabularies of trades and professions may be regarded as a satirical footnote to the dispute about 'terms of art' which raged so fiercely from the early Renaissance onwards. 'The Tearms of all Arts are generally Nonsense', he wrote, 'that signify nothing, or very improperly what they are Meant to do, and are more Difficult to be learn'd then the things they are designd to teach.' The cant of lawyers he found even more objectionable than that of astrologers; it is satirized in the language of the practitioner whom Sir Hudibras consults about his complicated affairs. He says that he can find his client plenty of 'Knights of the Post', ne'er-do-wells who live

> [By] letting out to hire, their Ears,
> To Affidavit-Customers:
> At inconsiderable values,
> To serve for Jury-men, or Tales,
> Although retain'd in th' hardest matters,
> Of Trustees, and Administrators.

The affectation of legal terms by the half-educated so common among the Roundheads is unsparingly parodied in the speeches of Sir Hudibras, who delights to give authority to his pronouncements by a judicious smattering of the 'Barbarous French' and Latin of the law:

And therefore being inform'd by bruit,
That *Dog* and *Bear* are to dispute;
For so of late men fighting name,
Because they often prove the same;
(For where the first does hap to be
The last does *coincidere*)
Quantum in nobis, have thought good,
To save th'expence of Christian blood,
And try if we by Mediation
Of Treaty and accomodation
Can end the quarrel.

Sir Hudibras's verbal habits are precisely those which John Eachard censured [in *The Grounds, & Occasions of the Contempt of the Clergy and Religion Enquired into* (1883)] when he described 'a sort of Divines, who, if they but happen of an unlucky hard word all the week, . . . think themselves not careful of their flock, if they lay it not up till Sunday, and bestow it amongst them, in their next preachment'. Like Eachard's preacher, the Knight disdains words 'such as the constable uses' as much as matter 'such as comes to the common market'.

Another form of pedantry common among the Dissenters and parodied in ***Hudibras*** is the affected use of terms from formal logic. 'It would be possible', said Hazlitt, 'to deduce the different forms of syllogism in Aristotle, from the different violations or mock imitations of them in Butler.' Such passages show that in Butler parody of a man's idiom is inseparable from satire on the cast of his mind. He particularly rejoices in 'metaphysical' arguments which prove that black is white or deal in matters completely unrelated to the realities of life:

The Question then, to state it first,
Is which is *better,* or which *worst,*
Synods or *Bears?*

A choice example of this sort of dialectic parodies the species of elegant sophistry of which Lovelace's *To Althea from Prison* is the best-known example:

. . . Th'one half of Man, his Mind
Is *Sui juris* unconfin'd,
And cannot be laid by the heels,
What e'er the other moiety feels.
'Tis not Restraint or Liberty
That makes Men prisoners or free;
But perturbations that possess
The Mind or Æquanimities.

Equally masterly is Butler's exposition of the problem of pain. In such passages he directs against the sects precisely the charges which Reformation satirists had so frequently hurled against the Catholic Church. The Lady explicitly

Sir Hudibras (left) and his squire, Ralpho, by Hogarth.

compares Sir Hudibras's skill in argument with that of the most subtle of the Catholic orders:

> You have provided well, *quoth She,*
> (I thank you) for your self and me;
> And shewn your *Presbyterian* wits
> Jump punctual with the *Jesuits.*

. . . . .

While the diction of ***Hudibras*** is remarkably varied, it is the astonishing profusion of witty images that distinguishes it most sharply from the common run of burlesques. It is clear from the 'character' of **"A Small Poet"** and from numerous prose jottings that Butler was keenly interested in the analogical uses of language. Like Bacon's, indeed, his was 'a mind keenly sensitive to all analogies and affinities . . . spreading as it were tentacles on all sides in quest of chance prey' [R. W. Church, in his *Bacon* (1884)]. If ever a man was haunted by 'the demon of analogy', it was he.

As one would expect, a very large number of the images in ***Hudibras*** are of the 'diminishing' sort characteristic of direct satire. Fat bawds are

> All Guts and Belly like a Crab.

Clever people

> . . . [keep] their *Consciences* in Cases,
> As *Fidlers* do their *Crowds* and *Bases,*
> Ne'er to be us'd but when they're bent
> To play a fit for *Argument.*

'Many Heads'

> obstruct Intrigues,
> As slowest Insects have most Legs.

The realistic bent of Butler's mind led him to fill his satire with imagery from the most commonplace objects of daily use, 'Out-of-fashion'd Cloaths', bowls, watches that go 'sometime too fast, sometime too slow', 'a Candle in the Socket', and beer 'by Thunder turn'd to Vineger'. He takes his choice from the familiar things of the farmyard and kitchen-hearth, children's games and men's employments. Images from animals are particularly common. Mahomet

> Had Lights where better Eyes were blind,
> As Pigs are said to see the Wind.

The Rump Parliament

> With new Reversions of nine Lives,
> Starts up, and, like a Cat, revives.

We Dissenters—says one of them—have friends who

> Are only Tools to our Intrigues,
> And sit like Geese to hatch our Eggs.

Again,

> . . . All Religions flock together,
> Like Tame, and Wild-Fowl of a Feather.

These are only a few of the animal-images from a single canto: to quote more would be tedious. What is remarkable is the effect that Butler achieves. By crowding his poem with similes from animals of 'low' associations like dogs, cats, pigs, and mice ('Valor's a Mouse-trap, Wit a Gin, Which Women oft are taken in') he gains an effect of homely caricature. The reader feels that no more is needed to demonstrate the folly of Butler's targets than reference to the store of common sense summed up in the nation's proverbs and homely sayings.

In a poem as long as ***Hudibras*** it is natural that a poet with a passion for images should have drawn on many aspects of life for his analogies. It is unnecessary to give examples of similes from law, low life, politics, religion, and the rest: they may be found on every page. The prevalent tone, however, remains that given by the 'low' comparisons which are so numerous. This is not least clear when Butler is dealing with abstractions:

> He'd extract numbers out of matter,
> And keep them in a Glass, like water.

. . . .

> By help of these (as he profest)
> He had *First Matter* seen undrest:
> He took her naked all alone,
> Before one Rag of *Form* was on.

Or again:

> Honour is, like a Widow, won
> With brisk Attempt and putting on;
> With ent'ring manfully, and urging;
> Not slow approaches, like a Virgin.

Butler was remarkably skilled in this art of finding a concrete image for an abstract idea. Such images parody one of the commonest habits of the Dissenting preachers, many of whom had a passion for the more abstruse reaches of theology for which they were ill fitted by education.

Decorum and common sense alike required that there should be more images in some parts of the poem than in others. 'The Nature of a Narrative', Butler noted, 'require's nothing but a Plaine, and Methodicall Accompt of Matter of Fact Without Reflictions, and witty observations on the by, which are more Proper for Discourses, and Repartees.' That is not true of the kind of satirical narrative that one finds in ***Hudibras.*** Yet it is very noticeable that the speeches contain far more metaphors and similes than the rest of the poem; it is because the speeches together make up a large part of the whole that Butler was able to indulge so fully his passion for fantastic figures.

In creating this profusion of imagery Butler was again adapting to the purposes of his own satire a common practice of the Dissenters, who were accused, with justice, of being 'indiscreet and horrid Metaphor-mongers'. 'As for the common sort of people that are addicted to this sort of expression in their discourses', Eachard complained in 1670, 'away presently to both the Indies! rake heaven and earth! down to the bottom of the sea! then tumble over all Arts and Sciences! ransack all shops and warehouses! spare neither camp nor city, but that they will have them!' Sir Hudibras's proud principle, never to speak 'to Man or Beast, In notions vulgarly exprest', inspires the speeches of many of Butler's characters: in nothing is its meaning more clearly illustrated than in their imagery:

> For, as in Bodies Natural,
> The Rump's the Fundament of all;

So, in a Commonwealth, or Realm,
The Government is call'd the Helm:
With which, like Vessels under Sail,
Th'are turn'd and winded by the Tail.
The Tail, which Birds and Fishes steer
Their Courses with, through Sea and Air;
To whom the Rudder of the Rump is
The same thing With the Stern and Compass.
This shews, how perfectly the Rump
And Commonwealth in Nature jump.
For, as a Fly, that goes to Bed,
Rests with his Tail above his Head;
So in this Mungril State of ours,
The Rabble are the Supreme Powers.
That Hors'd us on their Backs to show us
A Jadish trick at last, and throw us.

Again:

For as the *Persian Magi* once
Upon their *Mothers* got their *Sons,*
Who were incapable t'injoy
That Empire any other way:
So *Presbyter* begot the other
Upon the *Good Old Cause,* his Mother,
That bore them like the Devil's Dam,
Whose *Son* and *Husband* are the same.

As might be expected, it is not only the Dissenters whose verbal habits are parodied in the imagery of ***Hudibras.*** A connoisseur of folly in all its forms, Butler was equally amused by the extravagances of the poets of his day, and satirized their commonplace images:

Some with *Arabian Spices* strive
To embalm her cruelly alive;
Or *season* her, as *French* Cooks use
Their *Haut-gusts, Buollies,* or *Ragusts;*
Use her so barbarously ill,
To grind her Lips upon a *Mill,*
Until the *Facet Doublet* doth
Fit their *Rhimes* rather than her mouth;
Her mouth compar'd t' an *Oyster's,* with
A row of *Pearl* in't, stead of *Teeth.*

Of the prevalent fashions none interested Butler more than the different varieties of the Metaphysical idiom, now (in spite of numerous late appearances) past its heyday. As he turned the pages of such poets as Donne and Cowley and his friends Davenant and Cleveland there was nothing that drew his attention more frequently than their bold juxtapositions of ideas. His own relation to the Metaphysical poets is never more evident than in some of his images:

His Body, that stupendious Frame,
Of all the World the Anagram,
Is of two equal parts compact
In Shape and Symmetry exact.
Of which the Left and Female side
Is to the Manly Right a Bride.

The satirical tendency implicit in Metaphysical poetry from the first is very marked in the work of Cleveland; in Butler, it might be said, this tendency becomes fully developed. The truth is rather that Butler was the first comic poet to invade the territory of Metaphysical verse and use with genius the spoils that he found there. More brilliantly than any previous poet, he used 'wit' for the purposes of low satire. As a result he occupies a distinctive place in the evolution of the idioms of English poetry in the later seventeenth century. ***Hudibras*** was one of the principal channels by which the 'wit' of the earlier part of the century was transmitted to the greatest of the Augustans.

Yet it would be a mistake to think of Butler too narrowly as a satirist. Dennis found 'a vivacity and purity in his Language, *wherever it was fit it should be pure,* that could proceed from nothing but from a generous Education, and from a happy Nature'. Such a passage as this illustrates what Dennis meant:

For though out-number'd, overthrown,
And by the Fate of War run down;
Their Duty never was defeated,
Nor from their Oaths and Faith retreated.
For Loyalty is still the same,
Whether it win or lose the Game;
True as a Dial to the Sun,
Although it be not shin'd upon.

This is not 'high style', which would be out of place; but there are no cant terms in these lines, the diction is pure, and the image is handled with a remarkable felicity. The same is true of the **"Heroical Epistle of Hudibras to his Lady,"** which is not the work of a man completely unskilled in the mode of writing which it parodies. The man who could write like this:

The *Sun* grew low, and left the Skies,
Put down (some write) by *Ladies* eyes.
The *Moon* pull'd off her veil of Light,
That hides her face by day from sight,
(Mysterious Veil, of brightness made,
That's both her lustre, and her shade).

was no *mere* burlesque-writer. And indeed ***Hudibras*** contains a number of passages that would lend distinction to any lyric of the age:

For as we see th'eclipsed Sun
By mortals is more gaz'd upon,
Than when adorn'd with all his light
He shines in Serene Sky most bright:
So Valor in a low estate
Is most admir'd and wonder'd at.

No 'Caroline lyrist' could do better than this:

To bid me not to *love,*
Is to forbid my *Pulse* to move,

or excel this image, perhaps the finest of all:

Like *Indian*-Widows, gone to Bed
In Flaming Curtains to the Dead.

Such a simile reminds one for a moment that Butler was a younger contemporary of Henry King. Occasionally in reading him one hears the rhythms of the Caroline lyric resonant beneath the surface of the verse. A gift for epigram was not the only thing he had in common with Andrew Marvell.

In spite of the 'kinds' there was in the seventeenth century no such hard and fast distinction between 'poetry' (conceived of as a serious and indeed solemn thing) and 'light verse' as became a commonplace in the nineteenth century. As many of the love poems of the time make clear, verse was a much subtler instrument then than it was later to become. A poet could modulate from one level of seriousness to another in a couplet, or within a single line. Satire and elegy, burlesque and 'the lyric note' were not always mutually exclusive. The best Augustan poetry retains something of this subtlety of tone.

. . . . .

When ***Hudibras*** is regarded simply as a long satiric or comic poem Butler's mastery in many of the traditional branches of the poet's art becomes evident. Since he commonly receives less than his due and has been the subject of remarkably little criticism of late, I wish to conclude this chapter with some examples of his skill.

Many passages from the speeches which are among the most remarkable features of the poem have already been quoted. One more must suffice. It is made by a messenger who rushes up to Hudibras and his friends 'pale as Death', to gasp out his story 'by fits':

> That beastly Rabble,—that came down
> From all the Garrets—in the Town,
> And Stalls, and Shop-boards,—in vast Swarms,
> With new-chalk'd Bills,—and rusty Arms,
> To cry the Cause—up, heretofore,
> And bawl the Bishops—out of Door;
> Are now drawn up,—in greater Shoals,
> To Roast—and Boil us on the Coals:
> And all the Grandees—of our Members
> Are Carbonading on—the Embers;
> Knights, Citizens and Burgesses—
> Held forth by Rumps—of Pigs and Geese.
> That serve for Characters—and Badges,
> To represent their Personages.

Examples of Butler's skill as a narrative and descriptive poet are equally numerous:

> And now the cause of all their *fear,*
> By slow degrees approach'd so near,
> They might distinguish diff'rent noise
> Of *Horns,* and *Pans,* and *Dogs,* and *Boys,*
> And *Kettle Drums,* whose sullen *Dub*
> Sounds like the hooping of a *Tub:*
> But when the Sight appear'd in view,
> They found it was an antique Show:
>
> . . . .
>
> And follow'd with a world of *Tall* Lads,
> That merry *Ditties* trol'd, and *Ballads;*
> Did ride, with many a good morrow,
> Crying, *hey for our Town* through the *Burrough.*

No English poet has written with more zest than Butler, or more vividly:

> When *Tinkers* bawl'd aloud, to settle
> *Church Discipline,* for patching *Kettle.*
> No *Sow-gelder* did blow his Horn
> To geld a Cat, but cry'd *Reform.*
> The *Oyster-wom[e]n* lock'd their Fish up,
> And trudg'd away to cry *No Bishop.*
> The *Mouse-trap* men laid *Save-alls* by,
> And 'gainst *Ev'l Counsellors* did cry.

The category of 'burlesque' does not throw any light on such a passage. One is reminded, rather, that Butler has no serious rival between Jonson and Crabbe as a realistic poet of low life. To match his description of the astrologer's zany—

> His bus'ness was to pump and wheedle,
> And Men with their own keys unriddle.
> To make them to themselves give answers,
> For which they pay the *Necromancers.*
> To fetch and carry *Intelligence,*
> Of whom, and what, and where, and whence.
>
> . . . .
>
> Draw *Figures, Schemes,* and *Horoscopes,*
> Of *Newgate, Bridewell, Brokers* Shops.
> Of Thieves *ascendent* in the *Cart,*
> And find out all by rules of *Art.*
> Which way a Serving-man that's run
> With Cloaths or Mony away, is gone:
> Who pick'd a *Fob,* at *Holding-forth,*
> And where a *Watch,* for half the worth,
> May be redeem'd; or Stolen Plate
> Restor'd, at Conscionable rate;

—to match this one must go to Defoe's descriptions of rogues and vagabonds.

Although the set 'character' is less prominent in Butler's satire than in that of Dryden or Pope, it plays no unimportant part; as we should expect of the man who wrote such witty prose 'characters', these portraits in verse are brilliantly done:

> Fast Friend he was to *Reformation,*
> Until 'twas worn quite out of fashion.
> Next Rectifier of Wry *Law,*
> And would make three, to cure one flaw.
> Learned he was, and could take note,
> Transcribe, Collect, Translate and Quote.
> But *Preaching* was his chiefest Talent,
> Or Argument, in which b'ing valiant,
> He us'd to lay about and stickle,
> Like *Ram* or *Bull,* at *Conventicle:*
> For Disputants like *Rams* and *Bulls,*
> Do fight with *Arms* that spring from *Skulls.*

There is no doubt that Butler was one of Dryden's principal masters in the art of satire. 'The worth of his poem is too well known to need my commendation', Dryden remarked, 'and he is above my censure.' It is interesting to compare the 'character' of Shaftesbury in ***Hudibras*** with the well-known sketch in *Absalom and Achitophel:*

> 'Mong these there was a *Politician,*
> With more Heads then a *Beast in Vision,*
> And more Intrigues in ev'ry one
> Then all the *Whores of Babylon;*
> So politick, as if one eye
> Upon the other were a Spy;
>
> . . . .
>
> Could turn his Word, and Oath, and Faith,
> As many ways as in a Lath;
> By turning, wriggle, like a Screw
> Int' highest Trust, and out for New.

Butler's 'character' is in the 'low' style, as against Dryden's heroic portraiture; he makes no pretence of impartiality; his aim is frankly that of the caricaturist. Butler's 'character' of the Presbyterians, finally, is particularly reminiscent of Dryden:

> A Sect, whose chief Devotion lies
> In odd perverse Antipathies;
> In falling out with that or this,
> And finding somewhat still amiss.
>
> . . . .
>
> Still so perverse and opposite,
> As if they worshipp'd God for spight,
> The self-same thing they will abhor
> One way, and long another for.

One is reminded of the apostrophe to the 'Almighty crowd' that shortens all dispute in *The Medal.* Butler resembled Dryden in despising the crowd, and fearing it. 'I do not remember in all History', he wrote in one of his notebooks, 'any one good thing that ever was don by the People, in any government, but millions of bad ones.' Butler's satire on Dissent is inspired by fear of the mob. This 'anti-democratic' note came to be almost a constant characteristic of the best in Augustan satire.

Butler's distinction is twofold. He took over a traditional manner of 'low' writing and used it with a brilliance and variety of effect which were new things, and which led Dennis to call him 'a whole Species of Poets in one'. And, secondly, he differed from earlier burlesque writers in using this amazing idiom 'with a just design, which was to expose Hypocrisie'. So doing, Butler was true to his own ideal of satire: 'A Satyr', he wrote, 'is a kinde of Knight Errant that goe's upon Adventures, to Relieve the Distressed Damsel Virtue, and Redeeme Honour out of Inchanted Castles, And opprest Truth, and Reason out of the Captivity of Gyants or Magitians.' By adapting burlesque to the fundamental requirement of decorum, a worthy and unifying 'end', Butler was able to write one of the greatest comic poems in the language. (pp. 15-42)

Ian Jack, "Low Satire: 'Hudibras'," in his Augustan Satire: Intention and Idiom in English Poetry 1660-1750, *1952. Reprint by Oxford at the Clarendon Press, 1966, pp. 15-42.*

Ellen Douglass Leyburn (essay date 1953)

[*In the excerpt below, Leyburn examines elements in* Hudibras *typical of satirical allegory.*]

The game of identifying particular individuals in ***Hudibras*** has exercised such fascination for scholars that their investigation of the poem has largely been an exploring of possible models for Butler's characters. Literary critics, on the other hand, have been so bewitched by the brilliance of the couplets that one [E. Blunden, in the *London Mercury* XVIII] even suggests discarding the bulk of the poem in order to display its units, feeling apparently that the whole is less than the sum of its parts. Professor Ricardo Quintana has the distinction of presenting the large philosophic perspective from which the poem is conceived and its clear moral purpose; but he does not analyze it as a work of art [see the first Quintana entry in Further Reading]. E. A. Richards, who does so consider it, confines himself to a study of it as burlesque [see excerpt dated 1937]. These writers are enlightening; but ***Hudibras*** still demands consideration as satiric allegory. Such a consideration throws light on the virtues and defects of the poem which have been fairly consistently pointed out at least since Johnson's Life of Butler [see excerpt dated 1779]. Furthermore, it can reasonably be suggested that such a treatment conforms to Butler's own view of ***Hudibras.***

Butler's pondering over the use of allegory is repeatedly revealed in his **"Characters"** and ***Miscellaneous Observations.*** The wide scattering of his comments makes them the more emphatic testimony to his preoccupation with the purpose of indirection in art. He says concerning Books and Authors:

> Men take so much Delight in lying that Truth is sometimes forcd to disguise herself in the habit of Falshood to get entertainment as in Fables and Apologues frequently usd by the Ancients, and in this she is not at all unjust, for Falshood do's very commonly usurp her Person.

In discoursing of Reason, he had already projected the same view of fiction:

> Betweene this [Falshood], and Truth, ly's the Proper Sphere of wit, which though it seeme to incline to falshood, do's it only to give Intelligence to Truth. For as there is a Trick in Arithmetique, By giving a False Number, to finde out a True one: So wit by a certaine slight of the Minde, deliver's things otherwise than they are in Nature, by rendring them greater or lesse then they really are (which is cal'd Hyperbole) or by putting them into some other condition then Nature ever did . . . But when it imploys those things which it borrows of Falshood, to the Benefit and advantage of Truth, as in Allegories, Fables, and Apologues, it is of excellent use, as making a Deeper impression into the mindes of Men then if the same Truths were plainely deliver'd. So likewise it becomes as pernicious, when it take's that from Truth which it use's in the service of Error and Falshood; as when it wrest's things from their right meaning to a sense that was never intended.

He clings to the old conception of fiction as falsehood in a comment in which, though he thrusts it into the character of **"A Player"** in a thoroughly offhand manner, he seems almost to define for himself the province of the art of representation:

> It is not strange that the world is so delighted with fiction, and so averse to truth, since the mere imitation of a thing is more pleasant than the thing it self, as a good picture of a bad face is a better object than the face itself.

The inadequacy, even the perversity, of human reason, which forms the basis of Butler's view of the purpose of fable, is succinctly put in his observations on Books and Authors:

> He that would write obscure to the People neede's write nothing but plaine Reason, and Sense, then which Nothing can be more Mysterious to them. *For those to whom Mysterious things are plaine, plain Things must be mysterious.*

This same human predilection for the lie is expressed in ***Hudibras*** itself:

> The World is nat'rally averse
> To all the Truth, it sees or hears
> But swallows Nonsense, and a Lie,
> With Greediness and Gluttony.

Butler is clear-cut and implacable about the moral function of allegory:

> Allegories are only usefull when they serve as Instances, to illustrate Some obscure Truth: But when a Truth, Plaine enough, is forcd to serve an Allegory, it is a prepostorous mistake of the end of it; which is to make obscure things Plaine, not Plaine things obscure; and is *no less foolish, then if wee should looke upon things that ly before us with a Perspective, which is so far from assisting the sight, that it utterly obstructs it* beside the Prepostorous Difficulty of forcing things against their Naturall inclinations, which at the best do's but discover how much wit a man may have to no purpose; there being no such Argument of a slight minde as an elaborate Triffle.

His conception of the moral purpose of satire is just as clear in a little conceit which is itself an allegorical satire in small:

> A Satyr is a kinde of Knight Errant that goe's upon Adventures, to Relieve the Distressed Damsel Virtue, and Redeeme Honor out of Inchanted Castles, And opprest Truth, and Reason out of the Captivity of Gyants or Magitians: and though his meaning be very honest, yet some believe he is no wiser then those wandring Heros usd to be, though his Performances and Atchievements be ever so Renownd and Heroicall. And as those worthys if they Livd in our Days, would hardly be able to Defend themselves against the Laws against vagabonds, So our modern Satyr has enough to do to secure himselfe against the Penaltys of Scandalum Magnatum, and Libells.

It is hard to believe that in such comments Butler does not have his own principal work in mind. At least he is shaping the creed by which it is written.

. . . . .

Since, as Quintana makes clear, the object of mockery in the satire was to be the misuse of the mind, all the extravagances of unreason, Butler chose the strongest illustration available to him in the religious bickerings of the mid-century. In the quarrels of the Saints he saw illustrated the human faults that most repelled him: argumentativeness and a manipulation of reason for the rationalization of false arguments, together with a setting aside of reason to trust individual, irrational manifestations of so-called truth. Combined with and accentuating these defects of intellect were those of spirit: avarice as a motive, self-righteous arrogance, hypocrisy about virtue of behavior, and dishonor regarding oaths. Such was Butler's view of the Puritans as it is directly set forth in one biting portrait after another in his **"Characters."** The characters and miscellaneous writings not only clarify the habit of mind and total philosophic attitude manifest in ***Hudibras,*** but even depict with straightforward scorn the very traits Butler is ridiculing in the poem. Philosophically they are illuminating as to the basic ideas, the fundamental judgments, in terms of which ***Hudibras*** is conceived. Furthermore, **"A Quarreler," "An Obstinate Man," "An Hypocrite,"** and many more give positive help in interpreting particular characters in the poem. But artistically they are even more illuminating in a negative way, for they are written without the help of any fiction; and biting as their directness is, they do not take hold of the imagination as the poem does. Because of the allegorical representation, ***Hudibras*** makes "a Deeper impression into the mindes of Men then if the same Truths were plainely deliver'd." The characters are the same people, observed by the same keen, skeptical intelligence; but we see the truth more clearly in ***Hudibras*** because, in keeping with his artistic theory, Butler is there giving us the help of a lie. Even in the **"Characters,"** with all their definiteness, Butler is dealing with universal human weaknesses. Especially in the ones depicting modern types, we are conscious that the general and the particular are closely related. The sharpness of the criticism comes from the positive set of values in terms of which Butler is viewing the follies which are defections from it. The character of **"A Fifth-Monarchy Man"** and **"An Anabaptist"** owe something to that of **"A Fanatic."**

In ***Hudibras*** the standard of values is the same. So is the choice of illustrations, though its range is more limited, for in the **"Characters,"** Roman Catholics draw as much of Butler's fire as do Dissenters, whereas the poem concentrates on Presbyterians, Independents, and other sectaries. But there is still the feeling that Butler is saying something about human traits in terms of particular human beings. The **"Late Wars"** afford the amplest illustrations of the points he wants to make. This time, however, instead of writing directly about the figures of the day who illustrate his views, he is using the wit which "by a certaine slight of the Minde, deliver's things otherwise then they are in Nature, . . . [employing] those things which it borrows of Falshood, to the Benefit and advantage of Truth, as in Allegories, Fables, and Apologues." The poem is a convincing demonstration of the claim which he makes for such imaginative indirection that "it is of excellent use, as making a Deeper impression into the mindes of Men then if the same Truths were plainely deliver'd."

By choosing to couch his satire in allegory, he creates for himself the problems of conceiving appropriate fictional characters to embody his meaning and of involving them in appropriate action to sustain his point. Of all the varieties of fable open to Butler, he chooses perhaps the most difficult: simply a set of adventures of a mock hero in a real world. He gives himself none of the help of the writer of animal allegory or the creator of fantastic worlds, for whom the levels of the apparent story and the real story are so obviously distinct that once he leads us into making the initial adjustment, he can write almost straightforwardly and trust that the vehicle and the tenor of the metaphor will be grasped almost simultaneously. Butler's characters, while they may be freaks, are still human beings; and their actions, while they may be fantastic, must be possible for human beings. Yet their distinctness from the world of fact must be preserved. The proximity of the planes of reality and representation is what makes the neatness and the difficulty of the problem. The world in which the creatures of Butler's imagination function is the English world in which bear baitings and skimmingtons and the rogueries of astrologers and lawyers took place. The world of the surface narrative is part of the same world which Presbyterians and Independents would inhabit if they were being portrayed directly. Thus in both character and action Butler is dealing with the familiar and the actual, simply out of focus. It is a peculiarly complicated mode of indirection which he employs, a peculiarly intellectual one, involving constant adjustments of judgment as well as of imagination. Butler is not wholly successful in sustaining it; but it is a brilliant choice of imaginative framework for what he wishes to communicate. Hudibras is a burlesque, a caricature of a proper human being, just as the traits which he represents are in reality distortions of the proper mind of man. The actions in which he is involved are fantastic, just as the behavior of real people in its baseness and irrationality is a travesty of behavior appropriate to man.

In order to establish the impression of Hudibras, Butler gives us first a survey of the confusion of his mental traits. His stoutness is mentioned early; but it is not until page nine of Waller's edition that we have any extended description of his person. This makes the object of Butler's satire unmistakably clear in the very beginning; but it is also unmistakable that the intention is mockery through distortion, not straightforward analysis and condemnation. Each trait in turn is held up to the refracting mirror of Butler's mind. Hudibras is "shy of using" his wit; he displays tags of learning inappropriately; he corrupts logic for hair splitting; he uses geometry for measuring food and drink; by divination he can tell

> Whether the Serpent, at the fall
> Had cloven Feet, or none at all;

he proves his religion by contentiousness. The couplet:

> A Sect, whose chief Devotion lies
> In odd perverse Antipathies,

might be taken for the summarizing of his mind. Perversity in the use of his powers, misapplication of what talents he has, make him already a caricature of a person. So far Hudibras might be one of the **"Characters,"** or a combination of **"An Hypocritical Nonconformist"** and **"An Hermetic Philosopher."** Only after establishing the impression of his temperament does Butler make use of physical description. The oddity of the knight's mind has prepared us for the craziness of his appearance. Butler is reversing the common practice of the satiric allegorist of alluring our imagination first through sense impressions in order to spring his trap. But the use of physical detail when it does come is deft. Butler uses it to complete the winning of poetic faith in his knight as hero of a fictitious action rather than of a character essay. Once we have seen the knight's beard, with its upper part of whey and its "nether orange mixed with grey" as a "hairy meteor," we are convinced of his artistic existence. But the physical is the enforcement of the mental image. Hudibras wears his beard unshorn until the king shall be overthrown; and such a bizarre use of his beard fits the description of his mind. Butler proceeds in exactly the same way in the description of his figure. He barely pauses to make us see the hunched back and huge paunch before he uses the size of the paunch as a point of departure to speak of the gluttony of his hero, a subject which is continued in the description of his breeches. Such physical details as there are, are all extravagant; but they simply enforce the impression of the mind "perverse and opposite." His physical actions, too, come now as the expression and accompaniment of a mind we know already as ridiculous. The lack of physical coördination suggests that of his mental motions.

> But first with nimble active Force
> He got on th'Outside of his *Horse,*
> For having but one Stirrup ty'd
> T'his Saddle, on the further Side,
> It was so short, h'had much ado
> To reach it with his desp'rate Toe.
> But after many Strains and Heaves,
> He got up to the Saddle-Eaves.
> From whence he vaulted into th'Seat,
> With so much Vigour, Strength and Heat,
> That he had almost tumbled over
> With his own Weight, but did recover,
> By laying hold on Tail and Main;
> Which oft he us'd instead of Rein.

We cannot see this picture of bodily awkwardness without feeling that it betokens mental absurdity. At least we cannot do so reading it in context, for Butler has begun by convincing us of the absurdity of the mind of Hudibras. This impression is sustained whenever Butler uses physical representation. Oddly enough, it is only when Hudibras speaks, as he does repeatedly and at length, that we occasionally lose the impression. But when we see him falling on the bear, or running from the skimmington, or picking Sidrophel's pockets, we are convinced that we have to do with part knave and part the tool "that Knaves do work with, call'd a Fool."

In the description of Ralph, the procedure is curious. There is not a single detail of his appearance; what is being mocked is first the low social status of the Independents and second their pretension to "Gifts" and "New-light." But there is such a wealth of physical detail in the imagery that we have the impression of seeing Ralph. The crosslegged knights that give us at once an image of Templars and of tailors, the "*Dark-Lanthorn* of the Spirit, Which none see by but those that bear it" with its property of leading men to dip themselves in dirty ponds, and playing upon "The Nose of Saint, like Bag-pipe Drone"—all this wealth of sense impression gives us the feeling of seeing Ralph, when actually all we have before us is his mind, ignorant and misled by fancied inspiration.

The company of grotesques who make up the bear-baiting group are much more briefly dealt with, the presentation of the whole group comprising fewer lines than the description of Hudibras. But the procedure is much the same. We are presented with a quarrelsome crew; and the few physical details sharpen the impression of roughness. Crowdero is most completely described with his warped ear, grisly beard, and leg of oak; Orsin is stout, but the description concentrates on his stoutness of mind, and more space is given to his pouch of quack medicines than to his person. Bruin's visage is formidably grim; and Trulla is simply a lusty virago. The treatment of Talgol is taken up with a mock heroic presentation of his exploits of butchering cows and sheep, that of Magnano with the same sort of suggestion of his tinker's calling, and the one of Cerdon with references to his cobbler's trade. Finally Colon, the hostler, is presented in terms of equestrian exploits. The object is to present them as a group of low combatants. But the presentation has been so vigorous, so full of lively detail that we have the impression of seeing them, of experiencing both physically and intellectually an angry crowd. Professor Hardin Craig's identification of them as Parliamentary leaders is ingenious [see Further Reading] and not out of keeping with Butler's own comment:

> [I] am content (since I cannot helpe it) yt everyman should make what applications he pleases of it, either to himselfe or others, Butt I Assure you my cheife designe was onely to give ye world a Just Acco[un]t of ye Ridiculous folly & Knavery of ye Presbiterian & Independent Factions then in power.

However the antagonists of Hudibras and Ralph are particularly identified, the point of the bickering among dissenting groups is roundly made. The hilarious rough and tumble of the fight is perfectly suited to these common folk, whether Butler means the extra implication to be a slur upon the lowly origins of the upstart sectaries or a slur upon the temper of mind that makes important people act like hoodlums. Their coarse violence is exposed in any case, and through it the contentiousness of the Puritans and of man. The episode is one of the funniest low comedy scenes in the poem. The quality of the actors, the kind of action, and the mocking point to be made—all concur to produce the desired effect. It is a perfect little allegorical satire in itself with its point completely digested into the imaginative scheme and yet completely made.

Hudibras himself is steadily absurd in his behavior as the figure in the fable; but the overweening, dictatorial temper of the Presbyterians, and of a certain sort of human beings exemplified in them, is never far from our minds. Though the way Hudibras conducts himself is ludicrous, it is not entirely cowardly. Indeed, he often displays a reckless daring, what Butler calls a "high, outrageous Mettle," from his first rant, preaching peace among the saints by surveying their past combativeness, to his last misguided blow against Trulla. In this connection, perhaps Johnson's criticism should be met:

> If Hudibras be considered as the representative of the presbyterians it is not easy to say why his weapons should be represented as ridiculous or useless, for, whatever judgment might be passed upon their knowledge or their arguments, experience had sufficiently shewn that their swords were not to be despised.

To be sure the pistol of Hudibras is made ridiculous:

> But *Pallas* came in Shape of Rust,
> And 'twixt the Spring and Hammer thrust
> Her *Gorgon* Shield.

But Hudibras comes off victorious in the first battle; and the shot he lets fly at random in the second does considerable damage. It is true that he is afraid at the approach of the skimmington which creates the center of action in Part II; but he rebukes the procession as boldly as he had done the bear baiters. In Canto III of Part II he attacks Sidrophel with violence, though he does flee, supposedly leaving Ralph to take the blame when he thinks Sidrophel dead. He is afraid to give himself the whipping penance prescribed by the widow and is fearful of the devils' drubbing he receives at her house. Yet Butler does not make him wholly a coward. His alternations of fear and rash boldness show the perversity and inconsistency which is his only consistency. Butler uses both the fear, which makes him betray his promise to the widow, and his flight from her house as opportunities for the mordantly satiric passages of rationalization about the setting aside of oaths and of the mock philosophy of war ending with the description of Caligula:

> That triumph'd o'er the *British* Sea
> Took Crabs and Oysters Prisoners,
> And Lobsters, 'stead of Cuirasiers;
> Engag'd his Legions in fierce Bustles,
> With Periwinckles, Prawns, and Muscles;
> And led his Troops with furious Gallops,
> To charge whole Regiments of Scallops;
> Not like their ancient Way of War,
> To wait on his triumphal Carr:
> But when he went to dine or sup,
> More bravely eat his Captives up;
> And left all War, by his Example,
> Reduc'd to vict'ling of a Camp well.

Hudibras is rather irrational and hypocritical than cowardly.

But Johnson's objection raises the whole question of Butler's fairness in his portrayal, for as Root suggests, "To be completely successful, the satiric portrait must be drawn with at least the appearance of fairness" [*The Poetical Career of Alexander Pope* (1938)]. Veldkamp in his study of Butler [*Samuel Butler: The Author of Hudibras* (1923)] begins a section entitled "Faults and abuses of the time imputed to Puritanism" by saying, "Yet many other things are ridiculed in Hudibras which had nothing to do with Puritanism, but which Butler ridicules in the doings and sayings of the Presbyterian Knight. This is of course not quite fair even in an author whose set aim is ridicule, burlesque, satire." Veldkamp especially objects to the mockery of Presbyterians as believers in astrology and witchcraft; but actually Hudibras has little faith in astrology. He is hostile to Sidrophel, and his whole conversation with him is an expression of disbelief. It is Ralpho who urges consulting the astrologer, saying:

> Do not our great *Reformers* use
> This *Sidrophel* to forbode *News.*

Certainly William Lilly, who was at least one of the models for Sidrophel, was consulted by Parliament. Veldkamp himself really acknowledges the charge of witchcraft; and Hopkins, the notorious witch hunter, was a Puritan. Veldkamp further objects to Butler's attributing licentiousness to the Puritans. Yet in point of morality, what Butler is mocking is clearly not the special immorality of the Puritans, but their claim to sainthood, the sins which "*Saints* have title to."

For *Saints* may do the same Things by
The *Spirit,* in Sincerity,
Which other Men are tempted to,
And at the devil's Instance do.

In any case, the love story of Hudibras is a story of the love of wealth. Cupid takes his stand "upon a Widow's Jointure land." Hudibras is perfectly frank about this:

Let me your Fortune but possess,
And settle your Person how you please.

The lady is equally candid:

'Tis not those *Orient Pearls,* our Teeth,
That you are so transported with;
But those we wear about our Necks,
Produce those amorous Effects.
Nor is't those *Threads* of *Gold,* our *Hair,*
The *Perriwigs you make us wear;*
But those bright *Guineas* in our Chests
That light the Wild-fire in your Breasts.
("The Lady's Answer")

The avarice of the knight is what Butler is ridiculing. Veldkamp's final charge against Butler is that he satirizes "the perverted chivalry of the time . . . in the person of 'the Presbyter Knight'." Chivalry is not one of the objects of satire at all, but an external part of the scheme for presenting the satire. Butler is not writing another *Don Quixote,* but merely using Cervantes' scheme of action to give a framework for his allegory. The perverted chivalry of Hudibras is part of the disguise, the "falshood," which Butler is using to present his truth. To consider this part of the device for conveying the point as being itself one of the objects of satire is to this extent to miss the sense of the fable. The very obviousness with which Butler thrusts references to Romance into the narrative, as for instance at the beginning of Part I, Canto II, suggests that he feels the need of a reminder that he has employed the terms of chivalry for his framework. All of Veldkamp's charges can be dismissed if we subscribe to the view of Butler's central purpose set forth above.

But the comparison with Cervantes suggests a score on which the fairness of ***Hudibras*** may be challenged: whether Butler seems to be dealing justly with the kind of folly he castigates. When Root declares that the satiric portrait must be drawn with the appearance of fairness, he is setting up an artistic rather than a moral criterion. It is the feeling of fairness to be communicated to the reader which concerns him in judging Pope and which properly concerns the critic of ***Hudibras*** as well. Butler's artistic point of view is perfectly consistent. It is an angle of vision that creates steady distortion and persistently reveals the perverted human mind that he scorns. But it is exactly his unmitigated scorn which prevents the final success of his point of view. The reader is likely to share Johnson's feeling: "But for poor Hudibras, his poet had no tenderness; he chuses not that any pity should be shewn or respect paid him: he gives him up at once to laughter and contempt, without any quality that can dignify or protect him." Butler has fallen into the difficulty inherent in the kind of representation he has chosen. If distortion is his medium, consistency of distortion should be a virtue, but the excess of the virtue here makes a defect. The portrait is so full of vitality that we are scarcely conscious of any lack as we read. But if it leaves us artistically disturbed rather than satisfied, the reason for uneasiness may be Butler's excess of zeal in heaping opprobrium on his creature. What is important is not so much whether the Presbyterians had each particular folly displayed by Hudibras, but whether he is a satisfying symbol of human extravagance of mind. His not quite being so is what keeps him from supreme artistic fitness. We cannot entirely equate the knight with what he stands for. The portrait seems overdrawn so that our reception of Hudibras as an artistic creation is jarred by the question of whether the human mind is as distempered as this image of it.

Though probability, once "certain suppositions" have been made, is the important artistic consideration, the questions just considered lead to the constantly teasing one of whether the characters stand for persons who actually existed. Grey in the preface to his edition [1744] makes it part of his praise "that the greatest part of the Poem contains a *Series* of Adventures that did really happen: all the real Persons shadow'd under fictitious Characters will be brought to view from Sir *Roger L'Estrange,* who being personally acquainted with the *Poet,* undoubtedly received the Secret from him." The key attributed to L'Estrange was published with Butler's ***Posthumous Works*** in 1715; and perhaps the game of identifying the actors in Butler's drama had begun before that, as a demand for a key would imply. Scholars in our own century suggest a key quite different from that of L'Estrange. One of the most detailed studies of identity [see Joseph Toy Curtiss entry in Further Reading] analyzes the change in the model for Sidrophel, which Grey had already pointed out. Another [see the second Quintana entry in Further Reading] shifts the weight of evidence from Sir Samuel Luke to Sir Henry Rosewel in the controversy over the prototype for Hudibras, without making the point that Butler might have used both men in forming his fictitious character. It is perfectly conceivable, and indeed in keeping with the mode of composition suggested by his commonplace books, that he noted traits from a great number of sources and then put them together as they fitted his purposes. The characters are dramatized representations of general types that may be drawn from as wide a variety of sources as the pictures of **"A Modern Politician"** and **"A Dunce"** in the **"Characters."** It is possible, and indeed likely, that Butler's intention is to make them stand only for habits of mind as do the inhabitants of Brobdingnag, rather than for individuals as do Flimnap and Reldresal and other figures in Lilliput. In any case, it is their vitality in displaying persistent follies which gives them their enduring interest. The excitement of linking them with particular people who did live in history comes from the fact that they do live in art, not the other way around.

. . . . .

The other part of Grey's sentence, "that the greatest part of the Poem contains a *Series* of Adventures that did really happen," brings us to a consideration of the action in which the characters are involved. Grey seems to mean no more than that bear baitings, for instance, did take place and were subjects of controversy. He observes in a note signed Mr. B. (called in the Preface "the worthy and ingenious Mr. Christopher Byron") "that we have the exact characters of the usual Attendants at a *Bear-bating.*" Such praise seems curiously misplaced. Literal realism, where it exists at all, is obviously the least of Butler's concerns. Just as we know from the beginning that the knight is more than a knight, so we know that his adventures are more than attempts to stop a bear baiting and a skimmington, more than courtship of a widow and consultation with an astrologer and a lawyer. But again, as in judging the characters, we wonder if the episodes prefigure actual events or simply a kind of event that the civil wars had made familiar. Butler's own statement: "Butt I Assure you my cheife designe was onely to give ye world a Just Acco[un]t of ye Ridiculous folly & Knavery of ye Presbiterian & Independent Factions then in power," gives us no help, for he could have been just in using either sort of allegorical representation. It is a temptation to see particular historical events in the episodes; but any close analogy breaks down. Professor Craig has made a clever suggestion about the bear episode, but there are difficulties in his interpretation, as he himself points out. Any attempt to make the events of the story yield their secret drives us to the conclusion that they simply have nothing to conceal in specific historical event. What they hold is the "Truth in Person" like "Words congeal'd in Northern Air," but it is a truth about the kind of mad action Butler had witnessed during the period of the wars, not about the particular events of those wars.

For Butler's purpose this was a wise choice. In the first place, it fits the conception of his characters. They are absurdly distorted actors representing absurd distortions of human intellect as especially manifest in "the Late Wars." The action in which they are involved is appropriate to them in the mode in which they exist. These grotesques are engaged in grotesque adventures. For Hudibras to have eggs thrown at his beard and devils pummel him fits the world of fantastic horseplay that he inhabits. A comparison with Book I of *Gulliver* is again illuminating. Since Swift is using a realistic mode with reduction of size as the only means of sharpening the effect of the Lilliputians as human beings, he can best make his point by involving them in adventures that exactly parallel real historical events, letting the absurdity of the small people come out in the pettiness of their actions. Since Butler's artistic mode is distortion, he would have to distort history to fit a scheme of exact correspondence and precisely in so doing the exact correspondence would break down. Furthermore, the wars were already a travesty of what history should be. The artist can better represent this general travesty by using a farcical representation of human actions of individuals for his allegory than by making a one-to-one equation of his metaphorical action with particular events.

The organization of the poem has been criticized often for lack of necessary connection between the episodes. But Butler forestalls this objection by choosing the framework of romance for his allegory. The adventures are all the adventures of the same mock hero except the straight historical drama in Part III, Canto II, which is frankly a digression. ***Hudibras*** is as unified as *Don Quixote,* from which its scheme of organization comes, or as the picaresque novels with which it has inherent affinity. A more important artistic consideration is whether the loose structure is allegorically sound. To this test it measures up admirably. Butler suggests that confusion and inconsequence of events are the inevitable result of the unsound principles of the participants in the events. The attempt to suppress the bear baiting and the love of the widow's jointure, which are juxtaposed in the poem, have no more to do with each other than have rigid, domineering self-righteousness and avarice, which were juxtaposed in the mind of the Puritan as Butler conceived him. The odd, perverse antipathies of the protagonists produce the inconsequence of the action.

If then the action is allegorically right in the buffoonery of the episodes and right in the rambling quality of the structure, what are its faults? There are two important ones. The poem is too long. However much we should like to know what further action Butler had in mind for his hero, we cannot really wish ***Hudibras*** longer than it is. A more serious defect is linked with the first. Part of the length of the poem is due to the length of the conversations. Much of the best wit is contained in the speeches of the characters so that it would be rash to wish them away; but they do not get wholly digested into the allegorical framework and so make a confusion of artistic effect. The conversation between Hudibras and Ralph in the first canto seems perfectly in character and in keeping with the metaphorical scheme that has been established. The jargon of Privilege, Fundamental Laws, thorough Reformation, etc., with which Ralph's speech is larded seems just part of his distorted view of bear baiting, and a legitimate reminder to us of what is being mocked. The conversation purports to be a discussion of bear baiting *per se;* any further meaning is conveyed entirely by implication. But with the harangue of Hudibras to the rabble, we move into a different imaginative mode. Butler is giving the history of actual events from 1638 to 1643. The old covenant, the Bishops' Wars, the *et cetera oath,* the "*Six Members* quarrel", the Solemn League and Covenant, and making war for the king against himself are all used as arguments to break up the bear baiting, the controversy over which must now be linked with these actual historical events as a quarrel among the saints. The only indirection in the rant of Hudibras is that Butler's own scorn of the Puritans is steadily revealed to the reader through Hudibras's honorific survey of their actions. The speech is extremely funny in itself and very pointed satire. But it departs from the allegorical world into which we have been projected in the presentations of the characters and into which we are again thrust when they begin to act. From that point on, we are never sure in which world the characters are going to speak. Ralpho congratulates Hudibras after the first encounter as a self-denying conqueror; and we wonder for a moment if we have been concerned with the battle of Naseby. The rest of Ralph's speech is much better digested into the allegorical framework. His talk of revelation and Perfection-Truths has no special reference, it fits his character, which is altogether more consistent than that of Hudibras, and is a perfectly possible comment from such a person on the actual situation in the poem. But after the second round of the battle when Ralpho and Hudibras are in the stocks, we are again removed from the sphere of the allegorical representation of the foolish controversies of the saints to direct discussion of them. Again the shift is suddenly made. Hudibras, like the foolish knight originally presented to us, is comforting himself with ends of verse and philosophical tags, bolstering his self-esteem by saying:

> If he, that in the Field is slain,
> Be in the *Bed of Honour* lain;
> He that is beaten may be sed
> To lie in Honour's *Truckle-Bed*

when Ralpho speaks directly of Presbyterian zeal and wit; and from there on the quarrel is directly about synods as "mystical *Bear-Gardens*". Again it is extremely clever satire in itself and succeeds in making both Presbyterians and Independents ridiculous. The gallimaufry of terms in Ralpho's speech: Gospel-Light, Dispensations, Gifts, Grace, Spiritual Calling, Regeneration, and a dozen more, make skilful mockery of the vocabulary which seemed to Butler pure cant. But the debate over "*Synods* or *Bears*" repeatedly jerks us back and forth in the two modes of conception.

In Part II some of the speeches have the same effect. The harangue of Hudibras to the skimmington crowd, like that to the bear baiters, deals with straight history: the support of women to the Cause. The discussions of Hudibras and Ralpho on breaking oaths and on going to Sidrophel, since saints may do what they please, present without allegory what Butler took to be Puritan attitudes. The discussion of oaths is perhaps the most mordant satire in the poem. But this discussion is full of reference to actual history which fits confusedly with the issue of whether Hudibras can swear with impunity that he has received the whipping and with the horseplay at the end when he attempts to give Ralph the whipping as his proxy.

The point of view in the poem is further confused by the fact that the conversations with the widow and with the lawyer are kept entirely away from history. The mockery of motive in them is general and is entirely wrought into the story of the knight as such. On the other hand in the second canto of Part III, after the section of narrative of historical events (which seems almost the straight telling of what has been allegorically presented), we have two speeches which also use historical events to make their points and are supposedly really uttered in the Rump, not in the imagined world of Hudibras and Ralph at all. Therefore the feeling of unwarranted confusion in the poem comes not from disorganization in the action, which fits the total conception, but from the shifts in focus in the speeches from allegory to straight satire and back again. Thus the consideration of the poem as allegory throws light on the prevailing feeling among literary critics that it is a collection of brilliant sections rather than a coherent work of art. (pp. 141-60)

Ellen Douglass Leyburn, " 'Hudibras' Considered as Satiric Allegory," in The Huntington Library Quarterly, *Vol. XVI, No. 2, February, 1953, pp. 141-60.*

W. O. S. Sutherland, Jr. (essay date 1965)

[In the following excerpt, Sutherland focuses attention on each of the three parts of Hudibras, *discussing their relevance to Butler's theories on the nature of humanity.]*

In ***Hudibras*** Butler has created a major poem which is not so much a comment on life as an expression by the poet of his conception of the nature of man and of the relation between man and man and between man and woman. The undue concern of many critics with the "objects" of Butler's satire has led them into a misreading of the poem and to a most unfortunate underreading as well. The common assumption that it is not a violence to Butler's purpose to discuss his language and wit without reference to the central purposes of the poem is a good example of underreading. ***Hudibras*** deserves the respect due any work of art: to be examined for itself rather than for its relation to historical events, literary history, the history of ideas, or the history of the author's thought. (p. 54)

Before discussing ***Hudibras,*** some answer should be made to the question, "What is the poem?" It was first published in three parts, and most critics regard all three parts together as "the poem." This is, of course, a legitimate way of looking at the work. It has, as a matter of record, the support of the *New English Dictionary.* However, it is also a matter of record that this way of looking at the poem has been unfruitful as far as form is concerned. Dr. Johnson, to cite the most eminent example, regarded the poem as incomplete and thought that even if it had been finished "there could only have been a succession of incidents, each of which might have happened without the rest, and which could not all co-operate to any single conclusion" [see excerpt dated 1779]. It seems wise, therefore, to try another approach that might yield more to the reader.

The position of most writers on the relation of the three parts is not stated explicitly, but it is nonetheless clear. They regard ***Hudibras*** as a long, continuously unfolding series of adventures. But this view obscures the way Butler published the poem. Part I is dated 1663; Part II, 1664; and Part III, 1678. Pepys purchased a copy on December 26, 1662. It read ***"Hudibras, the first part."*** The crux is in the meaning of the word *part.* If it means an uncompleted portion, the breaks between the three parts can safely be ignored. But this is not the conception of the poem adopted here. The breaks between Parts I and II and between II and III are not arbitrary; rather they reflect a significant change in Hudibras the character and the values he holds and represents. The evidence for this conception will develop as the work itself is discussed. The chief critical result of the old view of "the whole poem" has been to encourage critics to make generalizations about Parts I, II, and III from observations made in Part I. Such generalizations have obscured the real nature of the development of ***Hudibras.***

. . . . .

The constant emphasis upon the anti-Puritanism of ***Hudibras,*** the necessity for explaining contemporary allusions, and the trying and detailed efforts to identify real people in the poem have all tended to emphasize the contemporaneousness and the immediate apparent satiric objectives of Part I. It has been decoded, dated, and annotated, all of which is certainly the legitimate province of the literary historian. Such activity tends, however, to give a warped conception of the poem as a product of the imagination, for it leaves the impression that once the political situation has been explained the work of art has somehow been made clear. So few critics have worked with the poem itself that a number of crucial questions remain unanswered. One stands out above all others: What is the significance of the mock epic or mock romance of ***Hudibras***? Why is Hudibras *Sir* Hudibras? What is the justification for mixing the anti-heroic and the anti-Puritan?

That Hudibras is both a Presbyterian and a knight errant should have aroused a great deal of comment. The usual explanation seems tacit. Hudibras was based upon Sir Henry Rosewell or Sir Samuel Luke; he must therefore be a knight. Since he is a knight, it is logical for him to engage in chivalric episodes. But such an answer should satisfy no one who has respect for Butler as an artist. A serious critic of the poem should comment, for a Presbyterian hero of romance requires admiration if nothing more.

The anti-heroic applied to the Presbyterians makes sense only as they are reformers, as they are the church militant. In that respect there is a grain of truth in the Presbyterian knight. But the hero of romance—and Sir Hudibras is that—has accepted a personal, heroic ideal which separates him from the religious "fanatic." Only one group in Butler's culture did accept the heroic ideal. The Cavaliers, not the Presbyterians, read the French romances. The Cavaliers, not the Presbyterians, held to the ideal of personal honor. They were the dashing heroes of the Civil Wars. Yet in spite of these ideals many of their number were corrupt, selfish, and cynical. And their heroism was futile and meaningless when measured practically. None of the Cavaliers saw himself in ***Hudibras,*** but then the Cavaliers were as serenely self-deceived as Hudibras himself.

It would be crude to say that the Cavaliers are an object of satire in the poem. This very denial is a measure of the way ***Hudibras*** has been warped by an historical interpretation. If the poem is looked at as an expression in poetic form of some sort of value or meaning which the author feels or has experienced, we will no longer be confronted by the black beasts of literalness and historicity. Looked at as an imaginative creation made out of the author's experience, Sir Hudibras can be seen as possessing characteristics of groups on both sides of the great social struggle. On this level he is not a representative of either group, for he is not an allegory. He expresses something that is not exclusive to either group but can be identified with both. Hudibras, whether the author is making the conscious effort or not, is able to express a feeling about man and society that is appropriate for all groups. If Hudibras has his birth partly as a result of this feeling, he is no longer inexplicable, for he is an anomaly only so long as we insist upon one "object" for Butler's satire, the Presbyterians.

Butler's ability to bring together disparate elements consciously can be illustrated on a less spectacular scale in the description of Hudibras. Hudibras does not cut his beard since he has vowed to let it grow until monarchy falls.

> But when the State shall hap to reel,
> 'Twas to submit to fatal Steel,
> And fall, as it was consecrate,
> A Sacrifice to Fall of State.

Hudibras is a Presbyterian, but Butler has borrowed the beard and oath from Phillip Nye, one of the dissenting brethren who opposed Presbyterian doctrines in the Assembly of Divines. In religious fanaticism, Butler sees there are no important differences between the sects. Hudibras is an object of religious satire, but Butler makes him something more than that, giving the character and the poem meaning and relevance for man and society as well as for one segment of that society. Hudibras has wider and more general significance than Butler has been given credit for. The anti-heroic is plot and fun, but what it signifies is also an essential part of the poem's accomplishment.

The anti-heroicism of ***Hudibras*** is almost always discussed in terms of the mocking of epical conventions and cliches as well as in terms of the "low" language and distorted rimes. Such discussions from this point of view must inevitably be inadequate, for they assume that the language of ***Hudibras*** is a device imposed from the outside. It is a good deal more than that. It is a symptom and essential technique which depends entirely upon the assumptions of the poem. These assumptions grow out of the values which the poet is giving expression to. This poem is no mere literary exercise like John Philip's Miltonic parody, the *Splendid Shilling.* Though we cannot say at any point that this is what Butler thought—or thought he thought—we can say that the poet has created a man and society that has consistency and satiric validity. The assumption of the anti-heroic is basic in that creation.

Although the poet's point of view is consistently anti-heroic, he must adjust his technique to his materials. Material which the heroic point of view would regard as "low" is treated ironically.

> The upright *Cerdon* next advanc't
> Of all his Race the Valiant'st;
> *Cerdon* the Great, renown'd in Song,
> Like Herc'les for repair of wrong.

Matters that the heroic point of view would regard as highly valuable may be associated with material the heroic point of view looks down on

> In *Mathematicks* he was greater
> Than *Tycho Brahe,* or *Erra Pater:*
> For he, by *Geometrick* scale,
> Could take the size of *Pots* of *Ale.*

Sometimes Butler relies on straight realism

> He thrust his Hand into his Hose,
> And found both by his Eyes and Nose,
> 'Twas only Choler, and not Bloud,
> That from his wounded Body flow'd.

The basic irony of Part I is the interplay between the points of view of author and character.

But what does the anti-heroic lead to in the poem? Profes-

"Hudibras Triumphant": Sir Hudibras and Ralpho prepare the public stocks for the bearbaiter Crowdero, in an illustration by Hogarth.

sors Quintana and Leyburn subsume Hudibras' anti-heroic actions under the term *grotesque,* and regard that quality as functional in the poem. Quintana calls the grotesque "a conceptual device by means of which the ordered world of reason, where all illusions have been dispelled by the intellect, is affirmed" [see Further Reading]. Miss Leyburn says: "Butler's artistic point of view is perfectly consistent: it is an angle of vision that creates steady distortion and persistently reveals the perverted human mind that he scorns" [see excerpt dated 1953].

The grotesque does perform a philosophical and at the same time aesthetic function in the poem, but the reader cannot assume that the criterion against which it must be judged is a proper, attainable norm of human behavior. At the risk of oversimplifying, the critical problem which the grotesque presents can be reduced to alternative questions: Is Butler implying that Hudibras has deviated from a code of conduct which—though perhaps not attainable in its ideal form—can and ought to be followed by all men? or Is ***Hudibras*** a poem which by satiric exaggeration emphasizes that ideals of human conduct are mere pretense, having no relationship to man's actual nature, which is foolish, selfish, and immoral?

Butler's technique obscures the answer somewhat. In most satires the false view is represented by the satirized object, and the poet, by one means or another, states or implies the "right" view. This right view is almost always a simple, moral assumption that is easily accepted: All men should act reasonably, for example. But Butler does not soothe his readers with a platitude. ***Hudibras*** has two points of view, the author's and Hudibras'. In Part I, at least, Hudibras' view is consistently heroic. His basic assumptions are probably very close to most of the readers', though his eccentricities tend to make his heroic values more obvious than they are in most people. He has personal, religious, and social ideals which he is willing to act upon. His belief in human reason is complete. When he cannot live up to his ideals, he rationalizes rather than abandon them.

The point of view of the author, on the other hand, is just as consistently anti-heroic. Hudibras is denigrated—with increasing bitterness as the poem progresses—and the poet gives no hint that anyone in the poem might live up to any sort of heroic ideal. There are no "good" characters, and the poem emphasizes the discrepancy between what Hudibras is and what he thinks he is or pretends to be. The reader may believe it possible for man to live by heroic values, but there is no evidence in the poem that its author thinks so.

Author and reader condemn the values of Hudibras, but those who look from the poem to a world of ordered reason take one more step than the work itself justifies. They assume that Butler is using Hudibras as an extreme example and that it is the extravagance of his heroic assumptions rather than the assumptions themselves that Butler is emphasizing. From this assumption it inevitably follows that Butler would be willing to accept the ideals of Hudibras if they were not stated in an extreme form. Neither this assumption nor its consequence can be shown to be valid for the poem. The fact that the poet gives no such authorization is in itself significant; so is the fact that this assumption is more typical of one who holds Hudibras' point of view than one who agrees with the poet. Since this notion leads to a perversion of the presented values of the poem, it ought to be rejected. The anti-heroic is basic in the poet's conception, not just a technique. The contrast in values is between what Hudibras thinks he is and what the poet shows him to be, not between what Hudibras is and the proper mind of man.

Butler's anti-heroic assumptions are nowhere clearer than in his language. It has, of course, always been quoted approvingly, but often without a demonstration of a full understanding of its greatness. Anyone who can analyze the language without reference to the purpose of the poem sees through the glass darkly. The notion that this is mere rollicking doggerel is, as most would agree generally, utterly false. The poem could have been written, as Dr. Johnson pointed out, only by a man of great learning and great observation. The language shows the highest degree of sophistication, which in a work of art should not be equated to elegance. One of the very interesting points to be noted in examining the language is how much relatively is devoted to demolishing the heroic assumptions of the character and how little, in comparison to the widespread impression, to religious fanaticism.

Some of Butler's language is direct denunciation, as his lines on the *New Light* are.

> 'Tis a *Dark-Lanthorn* of the Spirit,
> Which none see by but those that bear it.
> A Light that falls down from on high,
> For Spiritual Trades to couzen by:
> An *Ignis Fatuus* that bewitches,
> And leads Men into Pools and Ditches,
> To make them *dip* themselves, and sound
> For Christendom [in] dirty Pond;
> To dive like Wild-foul for Salvation,
> And fish to catch Regeneration.

This passage is characteristic of Butler. The three brilliant figures of light give an impression almost of improvisation. But they are not random. The first figure—*"Dark-Lanthorn"*—carries the implication of theft, the second—"to couzen by"—a direct statement of knavery following an ironic reference to the self-designated saints. The third reference—to false fire—ties the falseness and knavery to the Anabaptists' religious practices, at the same time making an ironic reference to the sectarians as fishers, though instead of fishers of men Butler calls them *Wild-foul.* Seen as a pun, this term fits physically and morally as a description of men who have been led into pools and ditches. This is a splendid passage, and surely the humor and jingle in it are only contributing qualities.

Usually, however, Butler depends upon indirection rather than straightforward denunciation. The homely term is a frequent means of attacking the heroic. It is, of course, a device that usually produces humor.

> This said, the high outrageous mettle
> Of *Knight* began to cool and settle.

Puns are used the same way:

> The trenchant blade, *Toledo* trusty,
> For want of fighting was grown rusty,
> And eat into it self, for lack
> Of some body to hew and hack.

The figurative use of eat takes on a literal meaning in the midst of vittles and eating. This literal hunger of the sword is brought out in the rest of the passage:

> The peaceful Scabbard where it dwelt,
> The Rancor of its Edge had felt:
> For of the lower end two handful,
> It had devoured 'twas so manful.

The scabbard is even measured in handfuls.

Though this does not pretend to the sort of analysis Butler's language has so long deserved, two more anti-heroic strategies should be especially noted. One is Butler's trick of turning an abstract quality, sometimes a spiritual one, into something tangible and concrete. This is the philosopher's stone with a vengeance, for it turns pure gold to lead.

> By help of these (as he profest)
> He had *First Matter* seen undrest:
> He took her naked all alone,
> Before one Rag of *Form* was on.

Or

> He could raise Scruples dark and nice,
> And after solve 'em in a trice:
> As if Divinity had catch'd
> The Itch, of purpose to be scratch'd.

The effect of these is to indicate the inadequacy of Ralph's understanding and the lack, in Hudibras, of a serious intellectual or emotional purpose.

The other use of language is the allusion. This is a thorny subject because the kinds of allusions, the frequency, and the application vary from one canto to another. The sort that is of particular interest here is that in which the allusion has its heroic qualities reduced by being compared to an obviously unheroic situation in ***Hudibras.*** The tendency of many of these is not to emphasize the difference between a low situation in ***Hudibras*** and a heroic one outside the poem. The tendency is to degrade the heroic allusion itself by showing how it is like the low thing or situation in the poem.

> Sturdy he was, and no less able
> Than *Hercules* to cleanse a stable. . . .
>
> For as *Achilles* dipt in Pond,

Was *Anabaptized* free from wound. . . .

When *Orsin* first let fly a stone
At *Ralpho;* not so huge a one
As that which *Diomed* did maul
Aeneas on the Bum withal.

These allusions and others like them attack the heroic beyond the limits of ***Hudibras.*** In effect, Butler is putting the heroes of antiquity into the same category with Hudibras. He shows here not a mere trick of language, but a philosophical assumption.

But what of the language of Hudibras himself. With some reservations it can be called rather consistently heroic. (The speech to the rabble in Canto II of Part I is exceptional on several counts.) It reflects rather accurately what Hudibras feels, and Hudibras feels like a hero. If this were a normal mock heroic, the poet would "elevate" a "low" subject, which is what Butler does with the bear baiters. For the most part Hudibras retains his own heroic outlook and the irony lies in the discrepancies between his point of view and the poet's.

The rimes of ***Hudibras*** grow out of the same assumptions, but there is so little factual information on the rimes that it would be futile to discuss them in detail unless they had been examined with care. Many of the easy generalities about Butler's twisted rimes are obviously wrong. Most of his riming is true, though the sounds were based on actual pronunciation—sometimes variant pronunciations—rather than on spelling. Dryden's work is so available that he may well represent our concept of the late seventeenth-century standard. But Dryden's insistence upon agreement of spelling as well as pronunciation—his "correctness"—is rather uncommon. Butler should rather be compared to John Oldham, who is also misjudged in this respect. Without digressing to offer linguistic evidence, one might suggest that Butler's strained rimes depend upon a slight shift in stress and juncture rather than upon mispronunciation of sounds.

For Butler language is a great and subtle instrument through which he presents a conception of man. Like any poetic language its effectiveness depends upon an integral relation with the material presented and the author's assumptions. And it should be examined like any other poetic language, not as an interminable series of jabs and stabs or anti-Puritan thumps.

Satiric narrative usually has more symbolic than literal meaning. Considered as an entity, the first part has demonstrable and adequate narrative coherence. Canto I contains the descriptions of Hudibras and Ralph, their sighting of the crowd, and their consequent discussion of bear baiting, which is interrupted. Canto II has the descriptions of the enemy heroes and heroine and the account of the first battle, which ends in the defeat of Hudibras' enemies and the imprisonment of Crowdero. Canto III contains the rallying of the crowd; the second battle, which ends in the defeat of Hudibras and Ralph by Trulla; the imprisonment of Hudibras and Ralph; and, finally, the resumed discussion between the two in which Ralph tries to prove that synods are mystical bear gardens.

The action comes after the description of the main characters—D'Avenant used the same procedure in *Gondibert*—and once it has begun it unfolds as single, complete, and of a certain magnitude. The plot itself is ironic, for the conventional lines of plot development have been reversed. If Hudibras were a normal hero he would arouse the fears of his readers by facing almost certain defeat, then vindicate their heroic assumptions about him by utterly defeating the enemy in a second engagement. But Hudibras suffers from his alliance with an unsympathetic poet. Instead of losing the first battle, Hudibras wins. The second battle, which he should win, he loses. These battles, it should be said, are notable more for their realism than for their more widely reputed exaggeration or distortion, though the language in which they are described, especially in the second canto, is often heightened.

The Gun went off: and as it was
Still fatal to stout *Hudibras,*
In all his feats of Arms, when least
He dreamt of it to prosper best;
So now he far'd, the shot let fly
At randome 'mong the Enemy,
Pierc'd *Talgol*'s Gabberdine, and grazing
Upon his Shoulder, in the passing
Lodg'd in *Magnano*'s brass Habergeon,
Who straight *a Surgeon* cry'd, *a Surgeon.*
He tumbled down, and as he fell,
Did *Murther, murther, murther* yell.
This startled their whole Body so,
That if the *Knight* had not let go
His Arms, but been in warlike plight,
H' had won (the second time the fight.)
As if the *Squire* had but fal'n on,
He had inevitably done:
But he diverted with the care
Of *Hudibras* his wound forbare
To press th' advantage of his fortune,
While danger did the rest dishearten.

But even in defeat Hudibras cannot be a sympathetic character. The final scene of Hudibras and Ralph in the stocks debating the proposition that synods are mystical bear gardens furnishes the ironic plot with a resounding anticlimax. The end is a trailing off rather than a conclusion.

Any broader view of ***Hudibras*** has implications for the character Ralph. He is, of course, a prime part of the propagandistic function of the poem. But even after he has been called an Independent, a good deal remains to be said. Ralph has two great interests—logic and religion—which he manages to combine. These are not mean interests as such. Most of Butler's contemporaries would probably have agreed that religion and reason were God's greatest gifts to man. Why, then, is Ralph a humorous, unsympathetic character?

Ralph appears in three different lights in the poem: (1) in the description of Canto I; (2) in the battles of Cantos II and III; and (3) in the debates of Cantos I and III. In the description of Canto I, the poet deals most unsympathetically with Ralph's "Gifts" and sectarianism. He is treated with scorn as both short-witted and superstitious. Over half the description is devoted to Ralph's "mystick Learning," though it is not used at all later in the poem. This description is sharply at variance with Ralph as we see him in the battles. He is humorous, it is true, but he also gives Hudibras wise advice. In the battles he is thoroughly sympathetic.

> Quoth *Ralph,* How great I do not know
> We may by being beaten grow;
> But none that see how here we sit
> Will judge us overgrown with Wit.

The description of Canto I is also at variance with Ralph the debater, for Ralph is brilliant in argument, at least if one accepts Biblical proofs. The proposition which he defends is not orthodox divinity: all synods are mystical bear gardens. It is, however, exactly right for Butler's purposes. If Ralph proves it, Butler makes a point. But the proposition is bizarre enough to give the whole serious proceeding an air of insanity. The atmosphere, however, should not obscure Ralph's excellent arguments. His analogy between Presbyterianism and Roman Catholicism can hardly be called nonsense by those who nod approvingly over Milton's "new presbyter is old priest writ large."

> *Presbytery* does but translate
> The Papacy to a *Free State,*
> A *Commonwealth of Popery,*
> Where ev'ry Village is a *See*
> As well as *Rome,* and must maintain
> A *Tithe Pig Metropolitane:*
> Where ev'ry *Presbyter* and *Deacon*
> Commands the *Keys* for Cheese and Bacon;
> And ev'ry Hamlet's governed
> By's *Holiness,* the *Church's Head,*
> More haughty and severe in's place
> Than *Gregory* and *Boniface.*

Ralph as the poet describes him and Ralph as the poet presents him is not wholly consistent.

The discrepancy can be looked upon as proof of a failure on the part of the poet to create a consistent character. Possibly this explanation would be accepted as the poet's conscious intent. But it avoids the crux, which is explaining why Butler would allow this inconsistency to exist, for it is, after all, difficult to maintain that Butler would write something he did not think made sense. A more logical position is that the description of Ralph and the actions of Ralph are both of them views held by Butler.

Butler's attitude toward Ralph, as we see it in the poem, is ambivalent. The fact that the views are apparently contradictory does not mean that each cannot have validity, for of course each can. But what is it in Ralph that the poet admires and scorns? It is certainly not the humane nature of Ralph's religion, for the characters in the poem regard religion as a series of tenets rather than a way of life. It is not Ralph's Independency, for this sect is ridiculed. The place Ralph is treated gentlest is in the exercise of reason. By seventeenth century standards his attack on synods was well handled. Though Ralph defends *Light* and *Gifts,* he does not depend on them. After Hudibras offers his thin and ironically self defeating arguments, Ralph is given the lines attacking learning.

> Quoth *Ralpho,* Nothing but th'abuse
> Of *Humane Learning* you produce;
> *Learning* that Cobweb of the Brain,
> *Profane,* erronius, and vain;
> A trade of knowledge as repleat
> As others are with fraud and cheat;
> An Art t'encumber *Gifts* and *Wit,*
> And render both for nothing fit; . . .
>
> For nothing goes for *Sense* or *Light*
> That will not with old rules jump right.
> As if Rules were not in the Schools
> Deriv'd from Truth, but Truth from Rules.
>
> This *Pagan, Heathenish* invention
> Is good for nothing but Contention.
> For as in Sword-and-Buckler Fight,
> All blows do on the Target light:
> So when Men argue, the great'st part
> O' the Contest falls on terms of Art,
> Until the Fustian stuff be spent,
> And then they fall to the' Argument.

This is not altogether fool. But since Ralph's technique of argument is the same as Hudibras'—it is just a better argument—this comment leads to distrust of all argument. The ambivalence, then, would seem to lie in a favorable attitude toward reason, an attitude which could be deduced from the well-made argument presented sympathetically, and an unfavorable attitude toward that same process of reason as shown in Ralph's attack on learning. The man himself is described as a short-witted, superstitious near-knave. This attitude toward Ralph refutes the notion that Butler is attacking only the abuse of reason. Of course he is attacking the extreme. But in drawing Ralph as he has, he seems to be directing his distrust at reason itself. Admittedly there is something to be said on both sides, but whichever side is taken Ralph must no longer be looked upon as merely a ridiculous representative of a Puritan sect. He has become a means by which Butler has expressed his value of the rational process. In addition, the ambivalence of Butler's attitude toward this character helps show that he is not a simple counter moved about in jest.

Hudibras is composed of the Puritan and the heroic, qualities that would adequately symbolize completeness at the time ***Hudibras*** was written. He is a man obsessed by religion and by a point of view. He rationalizes, and his love for the widow is not untainted by self-interest, but he should not be called a rogue. Though he poet presents Ralph as something of a cheat, his emphasis with Hudibras is chiefly on the anti-heroic. Perhaps this is why ***Hudibras,*** Part I, is innocent rather than bitter. Hudibras' misconception grows out of naïveté rather than evil. The laughter is still devastating, though neither Ralph nor Hudibras is made obnoxious morally. But of course Hudibras' misconception of himself is so fundamental that it antedates morals.

. . . . .

The second part is not a mere extension of the first, though the two are joined by continuation of action and characters. The subject is different, the characters show a new conception, and the poet's technique has changed. The time of the poem shifts from the early days of the Civil Wars to a period at least as late as the Commonwealth. Although Hudibras is not through with battle, he is no longer primarily a soldier, and in dropping this role he drops many of the heroic attitudes of the first part. The main subject of the first two cantos is love; the whole action depends upon it. Unlike Hudibras' earlier obsessions, this one is selfish; his attitude is cynical. Part II is not pleasant and light; it is peopled by knaves.

The moral character of Hudibras degenerates as Part II proceeds. In Canto I his love for the widow is shown to be a feigned passion motivated by selfish, material motives.

> I do confess, with Goods and Land,
> I'd have a Wife, at second hand;
> And such you are: nor is't your person,
> My stomach's set so *sharp*, and fierce on,
> But 'tis (your better part) your *Riches*,
> That my enamour'd heart bewitches.

His lack of moral fiber is further revealed in Canto II as he and Ralph decide to swear that he has been whipped even though he has not. Finally, at the end of Canto III he acts the part of thief, coward, and treacherous friend.

This change in Hudibras has important consequences. It means an end of a sustained attempt at the mock heroic, for there is no longer an heroic character to mock. Although the poet's assumptions in the second part may not be essentially different from those of the first, there are elements of bitterness and misanthropy which are new. Whether Part II should be called cynical or realistic depends largely upon the reader's own assumptions about man, but the world Butler presents is a world of knavery and broken faith. Love is in great part his topic, and a writer's attitude toward love can be used as an indication of his assumptions about man. Love before marriage can be seen in Hudibras and the widow; love after marriage in the skimmington ride. Although neither state conforms to a romantic conception of ideal love, Butler may have regarded them as more accurate statements of actual human values. The parody of romantic debates on love is very likely an expression of Butler's digust with the pretense of the romantic ideal.

Butler's use of love as the key issue of Part II allows Hudibras to retain a universality. Religion, as it did in Part I, demonstrates qualities of mind. Love is used to demonstrate Hudibras' point of view, no longer naively heroic but now meanly selfish. If Hudibras is only a vehicle for religious satire, he is grossly eccentric and amusing. But if we take him as Butler's way of saying something about man, he becomes serious; indeed he becomes at the same time funny and profoundly discouraging. Butler's use of Sidrophel raises a number of interesting artistic problems. It is enough here to say that as it does deal with the supernatural, astrology is an obvious field to harbor fraud and pretense. In the poem it serves as a parallel to, perhaps substitute for, religion.

The change apparent in Hudibras also leads to a significant change in technique. No longer do we have the parallel, conflicting points of view with Hudibras supporting the heroic and the poet the anti-heroic. Hudibras is no longer capable of heroic assumptions. He is a fraud and cheat, and he recognizes it. There is, then, but one point of view toward Hudibras and, by extension, toward the way men act. This shift away from the heroic has its effect upon the language of this part. There is very little discrepancy between the language of the poet and that of the characters, for they all look at life in the same way. There seem to be fewer allusions to the great men of antiquity, and probably fewer altogether, though the occurrence of allusions varies from place to place.

The change in Hudibras also leads to an end to innocent laughter. The new Hudibras is a conscious villain, and even as we laugh there is a tinge of disillusion or disappointment. The reader with heroic impulses no longer has anything in common with the "hero." This new-found discouragement carries with it the feeling that there is no moral hope for Hudibras. Insofar as ***Hudibras*** can be generalized, this world created by Butler is one without real hope of moral improvement. The kind of degradation imposed on Ralph makes this point neatly. In Part I Ralph was in places given gentle treatment. Butler did have some admiration, however reluctant and temporary, for the power of reason. In Part II, the assumption is different. Man is selfish, willing to follow his own advantage. Reason is corruptible, ready to prove whatever the will of man wishes. What Hudibras desires, Ralph can prove.

If we take the pattern of characterization of this part as something more than merely perfunctory, we can only say that it seems to reflect not so much a sense of the anti-heroic as a recognition of the pretense of human conduct. Hudibras is the winner at the end of Part II, but he wins at the expense of all moral principle. The debates that take place in each canto can have no issue in truth for the debaters themselves are frauds and cheats. This part is notable for insincere debate and self-defeating action. While it may be true that the action of Part II would be inadequate for an epic or romance, it is more appropriate for this poem if it is considered symbolically. Hudibras wins twice during the three cantos. His first triumph is an intellectual one in which he (as he thinks) outwits the widow by finding a way out of his whipping. This first victory is a fraudulent self-deception gained at the expense of personal intellectual honesty. The second victory, over Sidrophel and Whachum, is one from which he flees in fear, leaving his squire Ralph to take the blame. This latter victory demonstrates his lack of honor and integrity. Both actions grow out of the same qualities in Hudibras, but they are complementary in that the first is shown by the poet as primarily a failure of personal integrity; the second is more obviously social in that it shows his failure to fulfill what he owes to Ralph.

Part II shows a bitter change. The feelings that dominate the characters are mean, selfish, and dishonest. Nor is this represented as a deviation from normal, human conduct, for the poet agrees that this is human nature.

. . . . .

The change from Part I to Part II was sharp, but the transition from II to III is much easier. The third and last part is tied to the preceding canto by similarities in technique, language, conception of the characters, and action. Only in form, in the inclusion of a middle canto on a topic outside the "plot" of ***Hudibras,*** is there striking change.

Part III is the degradation of Hudibras. He is a thieving,

lying, canting, superstitious fool. He is contemptible, and the laughter which he inspires is altogether unsympathetic. The subject of love is concluded in Canto I as the widow and Hudibras debate the condition of marriage. The widow argues that the woman's fortune is the only object of love.

> To that alone the Bridegroom's wedded,
> The Bride a Flam that's superseded.
> To that their Faith is still made good,
> And all the Oaths to us they vow'd.
> For when we once resign our Pow'rs,
> W' have nothing left we can call ours.
> Our Money's now become the Miss,
> Of all your Lives and Services;
> And we forsaken, and Post-pon'd,
> But Bawds to what before we own'd.
> Which as it made y' at first Gallant us,
> So now hires others to supplant us.

Hudibras' arguments are either obviously false or self-defeating. Not much is made of Hudibras' religion in the first canto, though it is made the basis of the baffled knight's final, degrading confession. The "spirit" questions him for almost fifty lines.

> What's Orthodox and true Believing
> Against a Conscience?—A good Living.
> What makes Rebelling against Kings
> A Good Old Cause? Administrings.
> What makes all Doctrines plain and clear?
> About Two hundred pounds a year.
> And that which was prov'd true before,
> Prove false again? Two hundred more.

If there were any justice in Hudibras' position, the satire on the law in Canto III would lose a good deal of its bite. ***Hudibras*** has been called unfinished, but that is because the critics have looked only at the action. The title page indicates this is the last part. It is. But the finality lies in the character of Hudibras rather than in the accumulation of incident. The heroic point of view has been degraded and discredited. There remains nothing new for Hudibras to do. The poet has made his point.

Canto II is a digression from the adventures of Hudibras. Although it raises a number of interesting questions, none of them are germane to this discussion.

The third canto of Part III, the canto on the law, closing with the epistles of Hudibras and the widow, is more conventional in its subject matter and more obviously not directed toward the Puritans. It is significant to an interpretation of the poem in that it adds law and the courts to the other objects of satire. The counsellor is a villain of the same stamp as Hudibras. Once again we cannot conclude that because he is evil he is an example of a deviation from some human norm. Indeed, appearance is in favor of taking the lawyer as satirically representative of actual human values. The poet's description of justice implies there are no others.

Butler concludes this third and last part with two verse epistles, **"An Heroical Epistle of Hudibras to his Lady"** and **"The Lady's Answer To The Knight."** The subject is love, and they give the final view of Hudibras. It is an ugly, repulsive view of a man who is selfish, deceitful, and stupid.

Viewed in its three successive parts, ***Hudibras*** is a poem about the nothingness of human ideals. They are pretenses to which human conduct gives the lie. Those who see the poem as merely anti-Puritan satire strip it of its greatest achievement, for its greatness lies in what it says about man. To state the values of the poem is to judge them, for they can be formulated only in terms of the values as religion, love, honor, self-knowledge, friendship, reason, cynical despair. To others it may be an honest satiric appraisal of the state of man, unflinching in the courage of its realism. Dealing as it does with a fundamental view of life, touching as themes such values as religion, love, honor, self knowledge, friendship, reason, superstition, and justice, this great poem reaches to the heart of the human condition. It is hard to believe that some critics are merely amused. (pp. 54-71)

W. O. S. Sutherland, Jr., "Object to Symbol," in his The Art of the Satirist: Essays on the Satire of Augustan England, *The University of Texas, 1965, pp. 25-82.*

John Wilders (essay date 1967)

[*In the following excerpt, Wilders offers a general discussion of the content and form of* Hudibras.]

For personal reasons on which it would be fruitless to speculate from the slight evidence available, Butler's outlook was unsettled, sceptical, and pessimistic. He found it impossible to sympathize with any of the religious or political factions of his time. One cause was no doubt the nature of the age itself, which was a period of violent political unrest and one in which men's ways of thinking underwent a fundamental change. Long-established beliefs, many of them inherited from classical times, were being shown to be false, and truths derived from theological premises were being replaced by truths based upon empirical observation. This intellectual revolution, of which Bacon was the major prophet, was effected by Hobbes, Locke, and others, and, by the end of the century, its foundations were complete. ***Hudibras*** is a product of the transitional period. This is clear from the fact that, while Butler's outlook is in some ways very modern, his knowledge was derived from the Middle Ages and beyond. Its sources can be found in such writers as Aristotle, Pliny, and the Roman historians. The period was, moreover, peculiarly favourable to the writing of satire, since the ideas of former ages were being criticized by the standards of the new. Whatever may have been the psychological causes of Butler's scepticism, the age itself induced in him the distinctive tensions of the satirist: a sense of the opposition between the ideal and the actual, between what ought to be and what is. Hence he was impelled, like most satirists, to reveal the reality which he believed to lie behind traditional opinion and popular superstition. In ***Hudibras*** he attempted to show that scholarship was often no more than futile pedantry, that religion was commonly a pretext for the acquisition of power or wealth, that romantic love was generally a cover for self-interest, and that military honour was the reward for barbarism. The range of his satire is extremely wide, but his point of view is generally consistent both within the poem and with his other writings, particularly the commonplace books. He applies to the objects of his satire the same sceptical attitude which pervades the notebooks, and tests them by the same principles of practical, empirical common sense.

The first of the three parts is undoubtedly the most successful. The action is more complete than that of the other two parts, the wit is more concentrated, and the whole piece is animated by an energy and inventiveness which Butler failed to sustain into the later cantos. It also tackles delusion in a more fundamental way, by examining the basic principles by which men judge the truth, and attacking false kinds of knowledge at their roots. Although the two protagonists, Hudibras and Ralpho, belong to different churches, and although the cause of their frequent arguments is theological, their essential difference lies in the ways in which they believe truth to be ascertainable. The interest of this part, like that of much of Butler's work, is philosophical as well as moral.

The knight is an Aristotelian, 'profoundly skill'd in Analytick', who can examine and dispute any proposition according to the rules of logic. He is well versed in Latin, Greek, and Hebrew, knows all the rules of rhetoric, and is learned in the scholastic philosophy. Yet for practical purposes his intellectual achievements are useless. They either enable him clumsily to discover the obvious or prevent him from seeing things which are apparent to common sense. His logic teaches him what everyone knows—for example, that committee-men are 'rooks'—his mathematical skill induces him to calculate the time by algebra, and his philosophical training has filled his mind with false and useless information. When, in the Second Part, he meets a village procession, he thinks it is a Roman triumph. Whereas Hudibras is encumbered by excessive scholarship, Ralpho prides himself upon his ignorance, his freedom from that carnal knowledge which he sees as an impediment to divine inspiration,

> A Liberal Art, that costs no pains
> Of Study, Industry, or Brains.

He is also a neo-Platonist, a follower of the Hermetic philosophers, and a disciple of Thomas Vaughan. He claims to be divinely inspired and to know things beyond the scope of empirical experience. He is, however, shrewder than his master, for he does not take his own prophetic claims seriously. He keeps up the pretence of inspiration for his own ends: the light that inspires him is a light 'for Spiritual Trades to cousen by'. The fundamental differences between the two men are revealed in the great disputation at the end of the First Part. The immediate cause of their quarrel is theological: Ralpho asserts that Presbyterian synods are nothing more than bear-gardens, while Hudibras is roused to defend his own church against the Squire's attack. But, when called upon to defend his accusation, Ralpho follows his inclination to mysticism and describes a synod as a 'type' or emblem of a bear-garden, ingeniously accumulating parallels between the two. Hudibras, a '*Presbyterian* true blew', is anxious to refute Ralpho's arguments, but cannot do so by simple common sense. Instead, he grapples with them by the cumbersome methods of formal logic:

> That both are *Animalia,*
> I grant, but not *Rationalia:*
> For though they do agree in kind,
> Specifick difference we find.

The knight's reply prompts Ralpho to criticize his master, not for his Presbyterian convictions, but for his use of Aristotelian logic, which, to him, is

> An Art t'incumber *Gifts* and wit,
> And render both for nothing fit.

The two now confront each other not as representatives of two opposing religious sects but as a logician and a mystic; and, as Hudibras realizes, the ground for their disagreement is no longer a question of church government but of something more fundamental:

> But to the former opposite,
> And *contrary as black to white;*
> Mere *Disparata,* that concerning
> *Presbyterie,* this, *Humane Learning.*

At this point the discussion stops, both parties having exhausted themselves without convincing their opponents, but having demonstrated to the reader the futility both of formal logic and of mystical delusion. Both men are blinded by sectarian prejudice, and, while the squire is led by his imagination into making ridiculous statements, the knight is prevented by his scholarship from exposing their absurdity.

With the appearance of Sidrophel, in the Second Part, Butler returns to the theme of intellectual delusion, this time with reference to astrology, astronomy, and experimental science. Sidrophel, like Hudibras, is a learned man who has 'been long t'wards *Mathematicks, Opticks, Philosophy,* and *Staticks*'. But his learning is, like all theoretical knowledge, useless and deceptive. Seeing a boy's kite through his telescope, he mistakes it for a comet and is struck with terror at the prospect of some universal disaster. Burdened with excessive scholarship, he has failed to make any progress towards the discovery of truth. Butler compares him to a dog turning a spit, who exerts all his energy in the hope of moving forward but is kept by his own weight in the same place.

> So in the *Circle* of the *Arts,*
> Did he advance his nat'rall Parts;
> Till falling back still, for retreat,
> He fell to *Juggle, Cant,* and *Cheat.*

He has therefore resorted to charlatanism, and has become an astrologer in order to earn a living, selling amulets and charms or drawing up horoscopes for his credulous clients. Butler's criticism of astrology is that, like Ralpho's mysticism, it has no foundation in experience and admits of no empirical proof. The knight demonstrates at length how the astrologers have disagreed amongst themselves over such fundamental questions as the exact location of the stars and the extent of their influence on the affairs of the world. Moreover, besides encouraging delusion, astrology is of no practical value:

> So when your Speculations tend

Above their just and useful end,
Although they promise strange and great
Discoveries of things far fet,
They are but idle *Dreams* and *Fancies.*

Sidrophel attempts to answer the knight's criticisms and to convince him that the art he practises is intellectually sound, but, failing to do so and finally exposed as a charlatan, he resorts to violence in order to defend his reputation. This is not the only occasion in the poem when a character turns to violence in order to protect his beliefs or pretensions. Talgol, accused of betraying the Puritan cause, comes to blows with Hudibras, while the Saints themselves are accused of deciding all controversies by 'Infallible *Artillery*'. Butler believed that one of the logical effects of error and delusion was often bloodshed—a result which he had no doubt observed in the controversies of his own age—and that 'when [a man] is possest with an opinion, the less he understand's of it, the more confident and obstinate he is in asserting it'.

Closely related to his attacks on self-deception is Butler's satire on hypocrisy, the art of deceiving others. He is especially critical of religious and political hypocrisy, believing that men in power can justify practically any crime by appealing to the will of God or the welfare of the nation. As he remarked in his commonplace book, 'When Absolom had resolvd to Rebel against the King his Father, he had no way so proper to put his Designe in execution, as that of pretending to pay a vow which he had made to the Lord.' In his discussion of the sanctity of oaths, in the Second Part, Ralpho looks back on the events of recent history and finds in them a series of vows all broken on some moral or political pretext. The King had been attacked on the pretext of his own safety, the House of Lords, which the Commons had sworn to preserve, had been abolished as 'dangerous and unuseful', and Cromwell, pledged to protect the Commons, had used his own army to destroy it. The real motive behind political and religious idealism is, according to Butler, self-interest:

To domineer and to controul
Both o're the body and the soul,
Is the most perfect *discipline*
Of Church-rule, and by *right divine.*

Concerned in the dark and terrified of what he believes to be a devil, Hudibras is forced to confess that his pretensions of sanctity are a cover for avarice, and that 'what makes all Doctrines Plain and Clear' is 'about two Hundred Pounds a Year'.

. . . . .

The mode of Butler's attack is extremely varied, ranging from irony to simple invective, and including caricature, mock-disputation, and farce. Parts of ***Hudibras*** are set loosely in the form of a mock-heroic poem, which, like all works of that kind, depends for its effect on the violent contrast between subject and treatment. In adopting this form Butler was influenced by Cervantes, to whom he alludes several times, and who had created a comic discrepancy between the outmoded ideals of his hero and the reality of the world in which he found himself. Scarron, Butler's near-contemporary, created a more crudely comic antithesis between the stature of his epic heroes and the 'Billingsgate' language in which he described them. In England the wits Sir John Mennis and James Smith had used octosyllabic couplets for comic purposes, and had written short travesties of the epic in their miscellanies *Musarum Deliciae* (1655) and *Wit Restor'd* (1658). Butler may have been influenced by them and certainly adapted several features from *Don Quixote* and the *Virgile Travesti,* but none of these influences was radical: he created a new form, in which several sources may be recognized but which was essentially original. His originality lies partly in the fact that he composed a satire that was simultaneously a criticism of contemporary public morality and outmoded ways of thinking and a parody of what, in common with Hobbes and Davenant, he regarded as an outmoded literary form. For him both the knight's attempts to discover truth by Aristotelian logic and the conventional trappings of heroic poetry, with its chivalric heroes and magic castles, were relics of a superstitious past. Both kinds of satire, the philosophical and the literary, were effected simultaneously by the ingenious device of presenting figures like Hudibras, Ralpho, and Sidrophel within the framework of a mock-heroic poem. Whereas earlier parodies of the epic, like Scarron's *Virgile Travesti* or James Smith's *Innovation of Ulysses and Penelope,* had been no more than literary *jeux d'esprit,* Butler adapts their mode, the literary travesty, for more serious critical purposes. His was thus the first poem in a new tradition that was later to include *MacFlecknoe* and *The Dunciad,* where the conventions of epic are used for purposes of satire which is both literary and moral.

Hudibras has none of the sustained and detailed ingenuity of *The Dunciad,* where Pope consistently parodies both the general structure and the very phrases of the epic. In ***Hudibras*** both epic and romance are parodied indiscriminately, and the literary device itself is frequently abandoned in favour of other comic modes, such as the mock-disputation or farce. The poem itself is divided into books and cantos, each canto headed by its appropriate 'argument', in the manner of *The Faerie Queene.* The sudden turns of fortune which occur in the narrative, such as the arrival of the Skimmington in the Second Part, or the burning of the rumps in the Third, are a feature adapted from Italian romance like the *Orlando Furioso,* which Spenser had also used. Mock-heroic elements occur most frequently in the First Part, which, in accordance with convention, plunges *in medias res* with the description of the two chief characters before setting the scene 'in Western Clime' half-way through the first canto. The hero, whose name is taken from *The Faerie Queene,* is presented as a knight-errant setting out on horseback to remedy wrongs. He addresses the rabble in words taken from Lucan and later courts his mistress in phrases adapted from Lucretius. Athene and Mars intervene in the brawl, as they had intervened in the Trojan War (the former assuming the more earthy form of 'rust'), and Orsin laments the loss of his bear, as Hercules had lamented the loss of Hylas in the *Argonautica.* The village stocks are described like an enchanted fortress of romance, and Sidrophel is the comic equivalent of Archimago or Merlin. The most sustained mock-heroic passage is, however, the description of the rabble in the second canto, which parallels the list of epic combatants. Each member is given a suitably high-sounding name appropriate to his trade: the fiddler is called Crowdero, the bearwarden Orsin, the butcher Talgol, and the farmer Colon. They are also ironically compared to classical heroes—Crowdero is compared to Chiron, Talgol to Ajax, Colon to Hercules, and Trulla to Camilla. The effect of these literary allusions is by no means simple. At times they emphasize the meanness of the characters in comparison with their epic trappings—and Butler may well have seen himself as living in a mock-heroic age, when tailors claimed divine inspiration and the sons of brewers commanded regiments. But the antithesis between form and subject also acts in the opposite direction, the presence of coarse characters and 'low' actions within a heroic framework reflecting critically upon the literary conventions themselves.

From the notebooks it appears that Butler objected to heroic poetry on the grounds that it 'handle's the slightest, and most Impertinent Follys in the world in a formall Serious and unnaturall way'. In other words, he disliked the style and conventions of such poetry because they were artificial, but also rejected its ideals as trivial and foolish. In ***Hudibras*** he satirizes both the conventions of heroic poetry and its ideals. He shows up the artificiality of its style by applying its conventions to a crowd of unruly tradesmen. But his criticism is more than literary: one of the themes of ***Hudibras*** is the foolishness of the ideals of epic and romance when judged by practical, realistic standards.

The two virtues primarily upheld by heroic poetry are those of military valour and chivalric love. That this was Butler's view is shown in the opening to the second canto:

> There was an ancient sage *Philosopher,*
> That had read *Alexander Ross* over,
> And swore the world, as he could prove,
> Was made of *Fighting* and of *Love:*
> Just so *Romances* are, for what else
> Is in them all, but *Love* and *Battels?*

Far from being virtues, however, Butler believed them to be illusory and, in performance, absurd, 'for if any man should but imitate what these Heroical Authors write in the Practice of his life and Conversation, he would become the most Ridiculous Person in the world'. This criticism is implicit throughout much of the First Part, where the high exploits of the Greeks and Trojans are reduced to—and identified with—a common brawl, where the knight's protestations of love are shown to be a cover for the appropriation of his lady's dowry, and the 'noble trade' of the demi-gods and heroes is dismissed as 'slaughter and knocking on the head'. In the Second Part the criticism becomes more explicit, for the conversation between Hudibras and the widow centres chiefly on the subjects of military prowess and romantic love, in which the knight's apparent idealism is rebuked by the widow's realistic common sense. Hudibras, soundly beaten by Trulla and thrown into the stocks, attempts to convince himself that defeat is actually victory, partly by citing the Stoic view of pain and also by claiming that, by chivalric standards, suffering is a virtue:

> For what's more honorable then *scarrs,*
> Or skin to tatters rent in *Warrs?*

—an opinion which is contradicted by his own ridiculous situation in the stocks and by the colloquial realism with which he expresses it. The widow, however, pretends to take the statement literally, and suggests that he should accumulate even greater honours by suffering a whipping:

> But if a *beating* seem so brave,
> What *Glories* must *a Whipping* have?

Hence the knight's heroic ideals are put to the test and he finds himself pledged to thrash his own backside for the sake of honour.

The conversation proceeds to a lengthy debate on the subject of love, in which Hudibras voices the conventionally romantic view, whereas the widow, seeing through his schemes to lay hands on her fortune, attacks the whole notion of love as it is expressed in romantic literature. The knight woos her in the exaggerated manner of contemporary lyric poets:

> The *Sun* and *Day* shall sooner part,
> Then *love,* or you, shake off my heart.
> The *Sun* that shall no more dispence
> His own, but *your* bright influence;
> I'l carve your name on *Barks* of *Trees,*
> With *true-loves knots,* and *flourishes;*
> That shall infuse eternal *spring,*
> And ever-lasting flourishing.

The widow, however, realizes that these words have no relation to the knight's real feelings:

> For you will find it a hard *Chapter,*
> To catch me with *Poetique Rapture,*
> In which your *Mastery* of *Art*
> Doth shew it self, and not your *Heart.*

Finally, the conversation passes to other matters, and the knight leaves his lady, still protesting love and vowing to keep his pledge of whipping, while actually scheming to lay hands on her money and determined to evade his promise. The conventional attitudes of heroic poetry have been shown to be false; the conventional values have been put to the test and found ridiculous.

. . . . .

It appears from Butler's letter to Sir George Oxenden that, on its first appearance, the characters in the First Part were identified by its readers with certain prominent personalities living at the time. Butler's own comment on this interpretation is that, although the characters of Hudibras and his squire were inspired by an actual knight and his clerk (whom many people recognized in the poem), the rest were not modelled on specific people and were not designed to be identified as such: 'the other Psons as Orsin a Beareward, Talgol a Butcher, Magnano a Tinker, Cerdon a Cobler, Colon a Clowne &c: are such as Commonly make up Bearebaitings', and 'though some curious witts heere pretend to discover ceartaine Psons of Quallity w th whome they say those Characters agree', no such resemblance was intended.

Hardin Craig [see Further Reading] has also suggested that the characters in the First Part stand for 'ceartaine persons of quallity', and that the action is an allegorical representation of certain political events. His theory—put forward before the discovery of the letter to Oxenden—is that 'the brave resistance of the bear, his flight and establishment in a place of at least temporary comfort' may 'represent the flight of King Charles from Hampton Court to Carisbrook', and that the knight's defeat by the rabble 'may represent the defeat of the Presbyterians and their overthrow by the leaders of the army'. If this is so, then the bear stands for Charles I, Hudibras for the Presbyterians, and the mob for the Independent party. The ruthless Colon may be Cromwell, Talgol the butcher may be Fairfax, Magnano may be the 'magnanimous' Skippon, and Cerdon may be Ireton 'the scholar of the rebellion'.

It is true that the First Part, like the rest of ***Hudibras,*** is full of political allusion, and that the action appears to take place during a particular phase of the Civil War. The inclusion of political allegory would also be in keeping with Butler's intention to write a parody of heroic poetry, since other poems in that tradition, notably *The Faerie Queene,* invite such an interpretation. Whether or not he intended specific political implications to be seen in the poem can, perhaps, never be known for certain, but the question depends upon the external evidence and upon the extent to which the poem itself is intelligible without recourse to allegorical interpretation. The external evidence of Butler's letter suggests that there is no such allegory: the figures in the second canto are consistent only with his purpose in writing a mock-heroic poem. They are not public figures, but 'a Beareward, a Butcher, a Tinker, a Cobler, a Clowne', placed ironically in the context of an epic. It is, of course, possible that Butler's explanation is itself ironical, but the poem itself makes consistent good sense simply as a parody of heroic poetry in which no sustained allegorical significance need be recognized. The bear-baiting and the subsequent brawl are the comic equivalent of an epic battle, and the knight's duel with Trulla is a parody of encounters with such warlike women as Ariosto's Bradamante and Spenser's Radigund. The description of the rabble in the second canto is the equivalent of the epic rollcall in which, according to convention, the appearance, character, and skill of each warrior is described in turn, and, though the manner is heroic, the meaning relates to the distinctive attributes of the different tradesmen. Talgol, for example, is a butcher (his name means, literally, 'cut-throat') and he wears the 'Gantlet blew and Bases white'—the blue sleeves and white apron—of his profession. He has, we are told, slaughtered many beasts with his 'keen blade' and, like Don Quixote, has killed many a flock of sheep. Colon is 'right expert in Command of horse', not necessarily because he is a soldier or represents Cromwell, but because he is a farmer (Latin *colonus*) and can both plough a field and 'clense a Stable'. The other characters are likewise presented in heroic terms ironically adapted to their trades.

This does not prevent Butler from making incidental thrusts against contemporary figures from time to time, for it was a fact of seventeenth-century public life that several political and military leaders came from humble origins, as the authors of popular ballads and lampoons were quick to point out. The figure of Cerdon, the cobbler, for example, is used as part of Butler's attempt to deflate the reputation of the epic heroes, but may at the same time have given him the opportunity for a casual allusion to one of Cromwell's officers, Hewson, who had once been a cobbler in Westminster. Colon may have been intended to remind the reader of Desborough who, as the anti-Puritan lampoonists eagerly insisted, was originally a farmer. Such incidental allusions are, however, very different from the full-scale political allegory envisaged by Craig, in which each character is an allegorical figure and in which the narrative parallels actual political events. Both the poem itself and Butler's other writings show that his interests were not primarily political, but that he was much more concerned with the moral and philosophical principles that lie beyond politics. Like most satirists, he attacked human weaknesses in the forms in which his own age presented them to him. Politicians did not interest him, nor did political parties, except in so far as they were guilty of human ambition or self-deception, to which he was always sensitive.

. . . . .

The mock-heroic is only one, and one of the least frequent, of the modes through which Butler reveals the pretensions and triviality of man. His greatest satirical weapon is his style, with its earthy, colloquial language, intentionally clumsy rhythms, and comic rhymes, which debase everything they describe. His language ranges from the coarse to the elevated and the pedantic. He can ridicule the idea of divine inspiration, for example, by describing it in homely images and coarsely realistic terms:

> This Light inspires, and playes upon
> The nose of Saint, like Bag-pipe-drone,
> And speaks through hollow empty soul,
> As through a Trunk, or whisp'ring hole,
> Such language as no mortall ear
> But spiritual Eaves-droppers can hear.

The plain colloquialism of Butler's language is a vehicle for his practical, realistic outlook. It is one way by which he tests human behaviour and shows it to be foolish or hypocritical. At other times he attacks pretension by using the very language by which it is perpetuated. Butler is well versed in the cant and professional terms employed by the kind of people he attacks—the Puritans, the politicians, and the scientists. The use of 'hard words' was, he says, one of the incitements which led to the outbreak of war. The poem contains plenty of examples of the political jargon of the day, including such terms as 'Malignants', 'Delinquents', 'the well-affected', and Butler can make his characters speak the characteristic language of the Puritans. Hudibras is said to know more than forty philosophers 'as far as words and termes could go', and he sprinkles his conversation with Latin tags, philosophical terms, and the language of the law. Sidrophel, too, and the lawyer use their own professional jargon, the speciousness of which Butler reveals by exposing it as a cover for ignorance and self-interest.

The imagery of ***Hudibras,*** like its language, is generally of two kinds. It is either so homely and commonplace that it deflates its subject or so fantastically learned and pedantic that it mocks itself by its own excess. It has been pointed out [see Ian Jack excerpt dated 1952] that the 'lowering' metaphors are often grotesque images of animals:

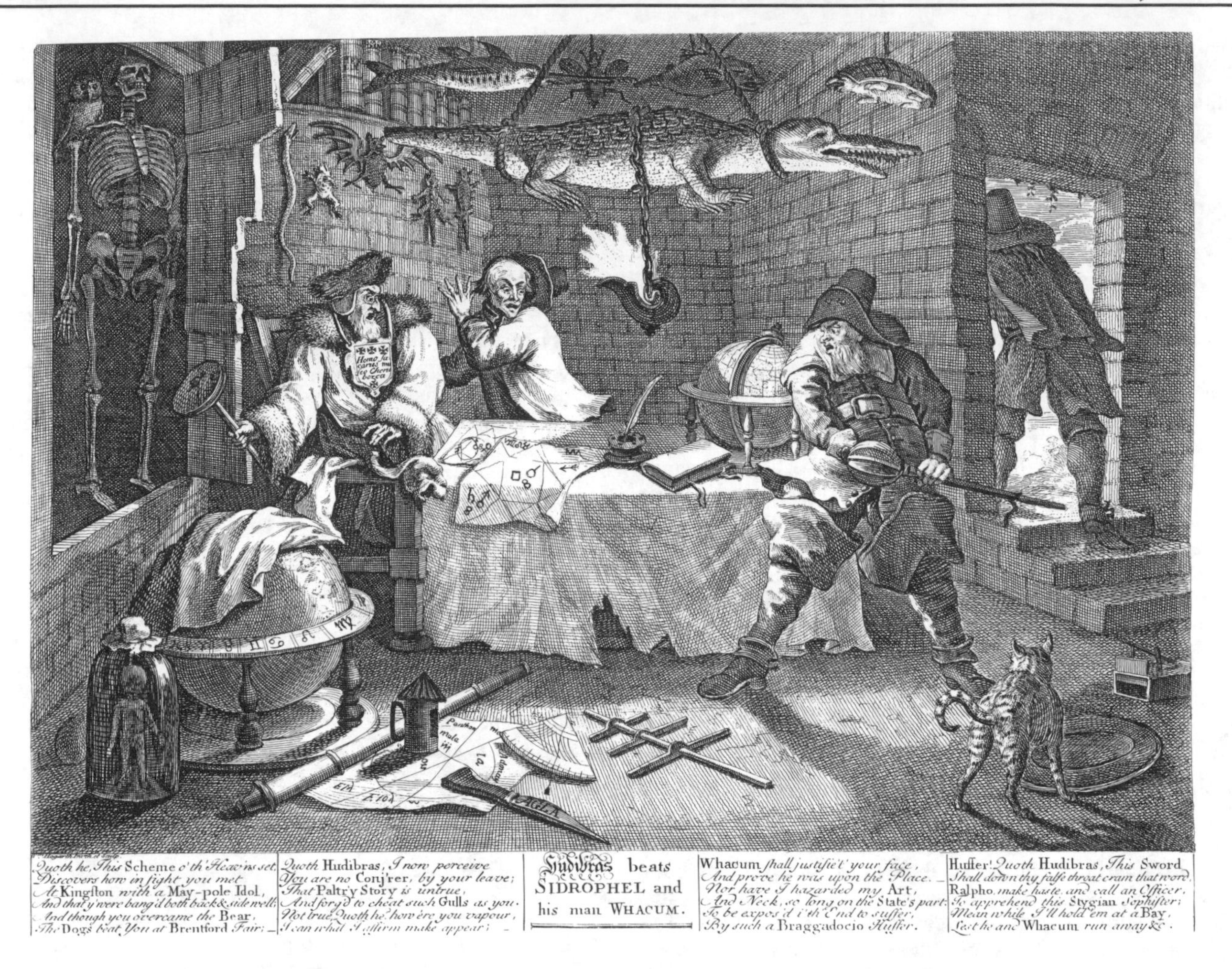

Sir Hudibras draws his sword against the astrologer Sidrophel.

> Mighty he was at both of these,
> And styl'd of *War* as well as *Peace.*
> (So some Rats of amphibious nature,
> Are either for the Land or Water) . . . .
>
> Beside 'tis known he could speak *Greek,*
> As naturally as Pigs squeek:
> That *Latin* was no more difficile,
> Then to a Blackbird 'tis to whistle.

The rural, animal imagery of ***Hudibras*** is one of the few evidences of Butler's early experiences as a boy in Worcestershire, but it is also a means of expressing the unpretentious, realistic outlook he may have acquired there, from which he judged the public world that he encountered later.

The peculiarly learned imagery of the poem was no doubt derived from Butler's reading in the libraries of his aristocratic employers. The copiousness and obscurity of its allusions is, in fact, one of the most distinctive and celebrated features of ***Hudibras.*** There are references to philosophy, theology, science, astrology, witchcraft, alchemy, medicine, the classics, history, and foreign travel. Indeed Butler has acquired a reputation not unlike Burton's as a purveyor of recondite information. He generally alludes to such things, however, in order to discredit them. The poem abounds with references to 'authors', 'histories', and 'antiquaries', both real and imaginary, who are credited with patently absurd opinions—that a Saxon duke, for example, was unwittingly consumed by mice, that the Prince of Cambay feeds on basilisks and kisses his wives to death, or that the Median emperor

> dreamt, his Daughter
> Had pist all *Asia* under water,
> And that a *Vine,* sprung from her *hanches,*
> O'erspread his *Empire,* with its branches;
> And did not *Southsayers* expound it,
> As after by th'event he found it?

'There is no certaine Knowledg', wrote Butler, 'without Demonstration', and his repeated gibes against learned authorities are yet another way in which he shows the difference between practical reality and popular delusion.

Irony, exaggeration, innuendo, the mock-heroic, the use of incongruous language and imagery are among the many indirect means by which Butler carries out his satirical purposes. Some of the most impressive passages in ***Hudibras,*** however, consist of simple, violent invective. The knight's first speech, in which he inquires the cause why

'*Dog* and *Bear* are to dispute', starts as a parody of pedantic and political argument, but moves imperceptibly into an attack on the predatory nature of man, in which the poet seems to be expressing his own convictions:

> But no Beast ever was so slight,
> For man, as for his God, to fight.
> They have more wit, alas! and know
> Themselves and us better then so.
> But we, we onely do infuse
> The Rage in them like *Boute-feus.*
> 'Tis our example that instills
> In them th'infection of our ills.
> For, as some late Philosophers
> Have well observ'd, Beasts that converse
> With Man, take after him, as Hogs
> Get Pigs all th'year, and Bitches Dogs.
> Just so by our example Cattel
> Learn to give one another Battel.

Hudibras is in many ways an unsatisfactory poem. Butler's use of rhythm for comic effect precludes much metrical subtlety or variety. As Ian Jack has pointed out, the metre is scarcely recognizable as that of 'Il Penseroso' or Marvell's 'The Garden'. The comic invention which enlivens the first two parts appears only intermittently in the third, which is also verbose and has little of the terseness of expression of the earlier parts. Moreover, the poem has no coherent form and reaches no satisfactory conclusion. Its greatest qualities are the vigour of Butler's expression and the fertility of his wit. These appear at their best not so much in single, unexpected strokes of ingenuity as in extended speeches and character-sketches where the images are copious and the poet's power of invention rises vigorously to its height. Like Swift, Butler engaged in a kind of desperate intellectual ingenuity as an antidote for his prevailing pessimism. If the total effect of his satire is largely destructive, it is probably because he could see little in his age but partisan violence and delusion. Hence he was incapable of sympathizing even with the constructive movements of his time and was compelled to remain an uncommitted but troubled spectator. (pp. xxviii-xliii)

John Wilders, in an introduction to Hudibras, *by Samuel Butler, edited by John Wilders, Oxford at the Clarendon Press, 1967, pp. xiii-xliii.*

Edward A. Bloom and Lillian D. Bloom (essay date 1979)

[*In the following excerpt, the Blooms examine* Hudibras *as a religious satire.*]

In [***Hudibras***], which pays more attention to dialogue than to action, ridicule imparts a distinction to the wit interwoven with many strands of irony, hyperbole, and parody. These have all been combined to produce a semblance of joviality, but Butler's light touch deceives; his satire often disguises the cruelty of debasement and innuendo. The poem is nevertheless rich in laughter that helps to soften incipient rancor. This ambivalence becomes especially apparent as the Knight prepares for action against bear-baiting, but not until—still mounted—he makes a speech from his Presbyterian perspective. In a comic oration reminiscent of upstart aspirations in a tatterdemalion time,

> When tinkers bawl'd aloud, to settle
> Church discipline, for patching kettle.
> No sow-gelder did blow horn
> To geld a cat, but cried *Reform.*
> The oyster-women lock'd their fish up,
> And trudg'd away, to cry *No Bishop.*

Dissent, in this hudibrastic vision, is served shabbily by "a Gospel-preaching-ministry" who are more partial to the old clothes they hawk than to canonical vestments. The grotesque Knight's run-on peroration makes his appeal to religious principle as ludicrous as the jingles of a music-hall routine.

He is Butler's persona for antiheroic diminution through whom everything is leveled. For "poor Hudibras, his poet had no tenderness: he chooses not that any pity should be shown or respect paid him: he gives him up at once to laughter and contempt, without any quality that can dignify or protect him" [see Samuel Johnson excerpt dated 1779]. When Butler allows his mock hero interludes of lofty or seemingly reflective discourse they sound so affected that they emphasize and reemphasize the *faux dévot.* These same harangues also magnify other qualities—for instance, a bumbling, amorous vulgarity—that the poet wishes remembered about the Knight as a parody of the courtly suitor:

> Quoth he, to bid me not to love,
> Is to forbid my pulse to move,
> My beard to grow, my ears to prick up,
> Or (when I'm in a fit) to hickup;
> Command me to piss out the moon,
> And 'twill as easily be done.

Although the lover swaggers as ineptly as the preacher, Hudibras has—if nothing else—mastered the use of the low metaphor. The language of chivalry and religion alike remain beyond his capacity to articulate.

From the precepts of Renaissance and later rhetoric, Butler derived several principles of *elocutio* to which ***Hudibras*** owes its comic intensity. Low words are thematically important; they bring the Presbyterian hero down to gutter level. And so likewise is his absurd oratory, its very excess abusive of all meaning:

> For rhetoric, he could not ope
> His mouth, but out there flew a trope.

The rhetorician becomes analogous to the courtier and bigot as an object of scorn. With usual obtuseness about his own failures of comparison, thus, Hudibras warns Ralpho against the dangers of comparison:

> Thou canst at best but overstrain
> A paradox, and th' own hot brain.
> For what can Synods have at all
> With bears that's analogical?
> Or what relation has debating
> Of Church affairs with bear-baiting?
> A just comparison still is,
> Of things *ejusdem generis.*

Jog-trot rhythms, antic uninhibited rhymes, "unpoetic" diction, and an unabashedly pedantic and redundant closing couplet—all these make Hudibras his own unwitting judge, as prone to incriminate himself through self-revelation as Dogberry was.

Moreover, insect and animal imagery both complements and stretches the possibilities of human denigration beyond Hudibras the individual. Allusions that evoke disgust—"maggots bred in rotten cheese" and gin-drinking rats—graphically symbolize everything that is squalid in experience and contrary to religious expectation. The man steeped in theological error not only corrupts his own kind, according to Butler, but actually infects animals with his vices:

> For, as some late philosophers
> Have well observ'd, beasts that converse
> With man, take after him, as hogs
> Get pigs all th' year, and bitches dogs.
> Just so by our example cattle
> Learn to give one another battle.
> We read in Nero's time, the heathen,
> When they destroy'd the Christian brethren,
> They sow'd them in the skins of bears,
> And then set dogs about their ears:
> From whence, no doubt, th' invention came
> Of this lewd, Antichristian game.

The "Antichristian game" is bear-baiting, which provides through the recurrent imagery of dogs and bears the likeness of religious division. Equally symptomatic of faulty religious observances is the willingness to be taken in by superstition. To make his point, the poet created Sidrophel, a trickster who substitutes the pseudofindings of astrology for Christian miracles. Parodic of episodes in Homer and Virgil, the satirist has the protean Sidrophel transform himself first into a bear and then, when the courageous Hudibras is too much for the sorcerer, into a goose who escapes by diving below the pond's surface. A dealer in magic and transference for the amazement of the gullible, Sidrophel spins out what appears to be a mockery of the immersionists. In any event, the metamorphosis violates both reason and Christian belief. Butler uses it for a tacit attack upon the vulgar acceptance of play-acting ritual and pseudoprophecy.

The satire on Puritanism dominates, but the poem encompasses other failures equatable with religion's inadequacy, chief of which is dissimulation or fraud. In the sixty-odd years following publication of ***Hudibras,*** in Dennis's judgment, nothing could approximate it as "a very just [satire] on hypocrisy" [*Critical Works* (1720)]. Looked at from a viewpoint that posited the oneness of church and state, truthfulness—political and religious—in characters like Sir Hudibras and his squire exudes mere expedience at best. Ralpho feels no shame in the premise that "oaths are but words, and words but wind, / Too feeble implements to bind." "Reformado Saints" (figuratively, leaders without followers), typified by the Knight, contract obligations under vows and yet "know little of their privilege." Honor, says Ralpho with Falstaffian candor, stays "but a word / To swear by only." Even in love the standard of hypocrisy prevails: "'tis not what we do, but say."

The poet himself brands the hero's consummate duplicity: "As if hypocrisy and non-sense / Had got the advowson of his conscience." Like Spenser's Huddibras in *The Faerie Queene,* Sir Hudibras proves "not so good of deedes, as great of name." And in a provocatively analogous sense, he too is "all arm'd in shyning brass." Derivatively, then, the name describes one who seems at first glance worthier than he is in fact: the surface appearance covers an unattractive reality. The possible Spenserian connotations of "hubris" and "brazen" are, perhaps, relevant to an interpretation of the Knight's role in the later poem. But another dyslogistic echo here should be underscored. "Hudibras" readily becomes "hue of brass" (suggestive in tone if not in meaning of *hue de bras* or even *Hugh de Bras*), a mocking nonce-word that, hinting at Anglo-French courtliness, endorses the hero's chivalric calling. By extension, the name implies a brassy coloration that could be mistaken for gold and thus allow the false or hypocritical to triumph. And brass, in the scriptural epithet, is "sounding," the echo of emptiness and deceit.

As a trait of the religious pretender, militancy irritated Butler, who deplored the violence of sectarian zeal. Palpably scornful, he denounced the "true-blue" Presbyterian as one of the "Errant Saints" of the "Church Militant." The poet rose up in feigned horror that faith should be built upon "the holy text of pike and gun," that there were those who would

> Decide all controversies by
> Infallible artillery;
> And prove their doctrine orthodox
> By apostolic blows and knocks;
>
> . . . . .
>
> More peevish, cross, and splenetic,
> Than dog distract, or monkey sick.

And the "infallible" Independent Ralpho—as much a hybrid as his master—is equally prepared "to fit himself for martial deed." An amateur warrior, he glibly mouths professional terms, "van, main battle, rear." Punning is shamelessly explicit:

> Both kinds of mettle he prepar'd,
> Either to give blows, or to ward,
> Courage within, and steel without,
> To give, or to receive a rout.
> His death-charg'd pistols he did fit well,
> Drawn out from his life-preserving vittle.

Whatever their religious differences—and they are many—this oddly mated quixotic pair share a belligerence of spirit and rhetoric.

As Johnson describes them: "The hero . . . is a Presbyterian Justice who, in the confidence of legal authority and the rage of zealous ignorance, ranges the country to repress superstition and correct abuses, accompanied by an Independent Clerk, disputatious and obstinate, with whom he often debates, but never conquers him." Each in his own way is an ineffectual clod through whom Butler satirizes the follies of religious zealotry, pretense, and aspirations built upon inadequate substance. Sir Hudibras, for example, with his hairsplitting incompetence was a makeshift logician who could confute himself or, indebted to Aristotle, prove finally that "a man's no horse." An addlepated philosopher, he could twist a tough "rope of sand." His squire Ralpho stands forth a memorable caricature, the most amusing and satirized features of his personality being compressed into religious idiosyncrasies. He parades as a mystic guided by inspiration, his "dark lantern of the spirit." His inner light comes to him from on high. It is

> An *ignis fatuus,* that bewitches,
> And leads men into pools and ditches,
> To make them dip themselves, and sound
> For Christendom in dirty pond.

Butler's mockery of the Dissenters' ritual of baptism reduces immersion to absurdity:

> To dive like wild fowl for salvation,
> And fish to catch regeneration.

Little less profane than the diving scene in Book II of *The Dunciad,* this one exemplifies in all the brilliance of belittlement the satirist's antagonism to Christian zeal.

Borrowing from the imagery and idiom of chivalric romance, he defined his moral purpose. Satire, he wrote, is "a kind of Knight Errant that goes upon adventures, to relieve the distressed damsel Virtue, and redeem honor out of enchanted castles, and oppressed truth, and reason out of the captivity of giants or magicians." Moved by the spirit of his own poem and theory, he wrote satire because he felt driven to it by a gloomy distrust of man's religious institutions. In the act of writing he assumed that he created something positive, perhaps even spiritually and humanely restorative. If he thought of himself as a knight errant, he was closer to Don Quixote than to Lancelot, and like the good mad knight—although he never lost touch with experience—transfigured dull reality into the shimmer of make-believe. We must concede Butler's special brand of pessimism, one ameliorated by *humanitas,* enough of which shines through to affirm his regard for man's possible worth. (pp. 175-81)

Edward A. Bloom and Lillian D. Bloom, " 'Sacramentum Militiae': Religious Satire," in their Satire's Persuasive Voice, *Cornell University Press, 1979, pp. 160-201.*

Felicity A. Nussbaum (essay date 1984)

[*In the excerpt below, Nussbaum examines* Hudibras *in the context of the Amazonian myth, which features women as aggressive and authoritarian figures.*]

In seventeenth- and eighteenth-century literature the male presentation of powerful and frightening female societies in men's imaginations often focuses on the myth of the Amazon women, who represent, as the "imagined fiend" and the "unsexed lady," women's ability to form a Utopian society in which men are unnecessary for procreation or protection. In the myth of Amazonian societies, the women of necessity evolve a government by and for women because they have been deserted, marooned, or widowed. Women alone discover they do not require men's protection or domination, and they develop their talents at martial arts, especially archery. They dress in military costume to signify the importance of war in the maintenance of their society, even amputating their right breasts in order to improve their marksmanship. The women procreate annually by venturing to their borders to mate with male partners, but without love or passion. In one eighteenth-century version, Samuel Johnson's translation of the Abbé de Guyon's *Dissertation on the Amazons* (*Histoire des Amazones Anciennes et Modernes,* Paris, 1740), virgins were required to kill three men before mating in order to insure that they would not become enamored of the sex. Male offspring born to Amazons were mutilated, killed, or cast off, while young girls were immediately adopted into the female community and trained to hunt. Thus women usurped the authority men once had over their lives, and the function of the male sex was denigrated to an annual sexual servicing. (pp. 44-5)

Samuel Butler employs the Amazonian myth in his satire ***Hudibras*** (Part I published in 1663, Part II in 1674, and Part III in 1678) and, in fact, provides a prototype of the Amazonian woman in Trulla, who appears throughout the eighteenth century in literature and art, including Hogarth's series of engravings of ***Hudibras.*** In a short satire entitled **"Women,"** Butler unflinchingly assaults women's foibles and invents a phrase that is constantly repeated in eighteenth-century satires against the sex—that women, following Aristotle's argument, have no souls at all:

> A Parsons Wife, some Critiques use to Recon
> Half-way in Orders, like a Foemall Deacon
> That by their Husbands Copys, are ordaind,
> And made their Vicars, at the Second Hand;
> And by their Spirituall Callings, have their Shares
> In ordering the Parishes Affairs.
> And chang the Nature of their Sex, betwixt
> The Clergy, and the Layety Commixt.
> The one half of the world have been begot
> Against the other Parts Designe and Plot.
> The Soules of women are so small
> That some believe th'have none at all;
> Or, if they have, like Cripples, still
> Th'ave but one Facu[l]ty, the Will;
> The other two are quite layd by
> To make up one great Tyranny:

In his various thoughts on women written during the course of his life, Butler delights in satirizing women for their naturally timorous nature, their bedevilment of men at the Creation and after, and their personification of the ancient Furies. He reserves violent language for profligate women, yet he stuns us with his perceptions of the similarities between pornography and romance: "There are more Baudy Pictures made of Lucrece, the Martyr of chastity, than ever were of all the Common Prostitutes of all Ages and Nations in the whole world." He defends the double standard, yet he deplores confining virtue in women to a negative quality—to nothing but chastity—"As if that Sex were capable of no other morality, but a mere Negative Continence." Elsewhere he expresses a similar sentiment: "And yett virtue in Women in the ordinary Sence of the world signifies nothing else but Chastity; and vice the Contrary; as if they were Capable of neither good nor Bad above the Middle." Thus we have to tread very carefully in assuming that the satire on **"Women"** indicates Butler's unequivocal condemnation of the sex as his considered personal view. He argues with equal vehemence for female governance in his random prose observations:

> The Governments of women are commonly more Masculine then those of men: For women delight in the Conversation and Practices of men; and men of women. This appeare's by the management of State Affayrs in the Reigns of Queen Elizabeth, Catharine De Medices Regent of France, and the Princes (Princess) of Parma in the Low Cuntrys, compard with the best of any other Christian Princes of those times.

At first the passage seems to be a feminist defense of female rulers, but with more precise attention to the language, we see that Butler is using pallid words to restate John Knox's charge in *First Blast of the Trumpet Against the Monstrous Regiment of Women*—that a ruling woman is a "monstre in nature." A female government can only succeed if the women imitate male rules, and yet that means the women are monsters who contradict their nature. According to Knox, women are not natural rulers, though some women may seem to possess wit and reason that is superior to the wit and reason of some men.

Filled with references to the interchangeable nature of sex roles, Butler's long satire presents a foolish Puritan knight, Hudibras, whom women overpower in physical combat, tests of wit, struggles for governance, and the use of the romantic conventions of love. Hudibras is the dupe of the belligerent warrior Trulla, the unfaithful wife (who is called both a whore and an Amazon), and the learned and crafty Widow. Earl Miner has argued that "the advocacy of female superiority by Butler is so extraordinary and so persistent in the poem that it must be considered a central theme" [see excerpt dated 1974]. While I agree that sex roles and sexual ambiguity are central to ***Hudibras,*** I do not think the poem is, finally, feminist, for Butler's persona seems to argue that women, in order to be superior, must be something other than themselves—Amazons, goddesses, angels, or masculine rulers.

Trulla, who overpowers Hudibras physically, makes her first appearance among the bear-baiters in Part I. In love with Magnano, the tinker, she stands beside him in battle. "A bold *Virago,* stout and tall / As *Joan* of *France* or *English Mall.*" She puts aside her modesty, runs "a-tilt at men," and demonstrates that government by women may bring "pernicious consequence" to men. Butler makes her an enthusiastic warrior. When a reconciliation between the debating Ralph and Hudibras seems imminent, Trulla revives the fight. She charges Hudibras from behind in an imitation of the manner in which Hudibras planned to take the Lady: "He that gets her by heart must say her / The back-way, like a Witche's prayer." Trulla is a triumphant victor: "With home-made thrust the heavy swing, / She laid him flat upon his side, / And mounting on his trunk astride, / Quoth she, I told thee what would come / Of all thy vapouring, base Scum." Trulla then uses her female power to manipulate men and to turn the law (in this case military law) against them. As a governing power the belligerent Trulla arranges for Hudibras to take the place of the imprisoned character Crowdero. Butler thus suggests that the only pernicious consequence women like Trulla bring to government is a justice unfavorable to fools. In a satiric reversal of our expectation that men possess reason, Butler makes reason feminine, and yet women, as the agents of rationality, create strife among men. When Trulla conquers Hudibras she demeans him by requiring him to wear her mantle. They metaphorically trade sex—she becoming the powerful male, he the defeated female.

Women use their sexual power to make foolish men weak and feminine, just as Trulla employs her physical power. Butler reverses the romance conventions of the heroic male and the passive female to make the female heroic and the male a captive of his own stupidity. Love, Hudibras argues, makes men into the conventional females, passive servants:

> 'Twas he, that brought upon his knees
> The *Hect'ring* Kill-Cow *Hercules;*
> Reduc'd his *Leager-lions* skin
> T'a *Petticoat,* and made him spin:
> Seiz'd on his *Club,* and made it dwindle
> T'a feeble *Distaff,* and a *Spindle.*

Hudibras maintains that when women marry men without loving them, it is the equivalent of rape: "A *Rape,* that is the more inhumane, / For being acted by a *Woman.* / Why are you *fair,* but to entice us / To *love* you, that you may despise us?"

Similarly, the unfaithful wife of the Skimmington procession (a public mockery of an adulterous wife and her cuckolded husband) creates domestic strife, usurps her husband's authority, and makes her defeated husband feminine. The "*Amazon* triumphant" is preceded by her petticoat hung high as a banner:

> Bestrid her *Beast,* and on the *Rump* on't
> Sate *Face* to *Tayl,* and *Bum* to *Bum,*
> The *Warrier* whilome overcome;
> Arm'd with a *Spindle* and a *Distaff,*
> Which as he rod, she made him twist off;
> And when he loyter'd, o're her shoulder,
> Chastiz'd the *Reformado* Souldier.

Hudibras, whose view we know is suspect, sees the victorious show as pagan and anti-Christian; and after some mild disagreement from Ralph, they agree that the only just occasion for public mockery is when the husband has retreated without concern for his honor:

> But to turn *Tayl,* or run away,
> And without blows give up the Day;
> Or to surrender e're the *Assault,*
> That's no mans fortune but his fault:
> And renders men of *Honor* less,
> Then all th' *Adversity* of Success.
> And only unto such, this Shew
> Of *Horns* and *Petticoats* is due.

But as Hudibras works himself into a frenzy of battle against the procession, he defends the female sex against scandal:

> *Women,* that were our first *Apostles,*
> Without whose aid w'had all been lost else,
> *Women,* that left no stone unturn'd,
> In which the *Cause* might by concern'd:
> From *Ladies* down to *Oyster-wenches,*
> Labour'd like *Pioners* in Trenches.

A flying egg interrupts Hudibras's defense of the sex, and

the procession turns into a brawl. Hudibras and Ralph retreat—the very act they have most condemned—but they defend their behavior as a bold adventure in the *"Sexe's honor,"* which ought to impress the widow Hudibras is trying to woo.

Hudibras, then, is not idealizing women. Hudibras, who defends the sex in spite of the treachery of the Skimmington whore, sees the procession as an expedient way to woo the Widow. He employs feminism in the cause of romance. In the [**"Heroical Epistle of Hudibras to his Lady"**], Hudibras cites the tradition of the Romans taking the chaste Sabine women by force to prove that men have a right to any woman. It is natural for men to rape women, he argues, and consequently natural for men to exert power over their wives:

> For Women first were made for Men,
> Not Men for them.—It follows then,
> That Men have right to every one,
> And they no freedom of their own:
> And therefore Men have pow'r to chuse,
> But they no Charter to refuse:

The entire **"Heroical Epistle"** assaults the sex and asserts masculine supremacy, though Hudibras finally denies, of course, that his words have specific application to the Widow. The satire unveils the antifeminist logic of such men as Hudibras, Ralph, and Sidrophel, and the reader begins to believe that they deserve to be ruled, fooled, and even tortured by the tyrannical beings, women. In contrast to the greedy and beastly male sex, women use the art and wit men lack to gain power, while men cower in fear. The rule of women, while not to be desired, seems to be more acceptable than the rule of a Hudibras, Ralph, or Sidrophel.

The generally accepted Puritan view was that women are not equipped to exercise political authority, but there are occasional God-ordained exceptions. Though the genuine views of Calvin and "the Geneva group" were quite complex, the Anglicans believed that they argued against government by women without exception, and the Calvinists were often labeled antifeminists. The antifeminist aspects of Puritans in popular lore must have led Butler to allow those implications to be at play in the antifeminist sentiments voiced by Presbyterian Hudibras and Independent Ralph.

The Widow demonstrates the enormous power of women in a variety of ways, but female power exists because men fail to grasp the intricacies of romance conventions. Butler grants women power, but he mocks the conditions under which that power is established and perpetuated. The shrew and Trulla are, after all, whores who understand more about power than the men. To provoke love in men, to make men love them, affords them authority. The Widow demands plain-speaking, something Hudibras cannot sustain for long. She demystifies and deromanticizes love with her wise and cynical eye. She reports, for example, that in addition to romance, love also creates bestial perversions such as Pasiphaie's love for a bull and Semiramis' passion for horses. She persuasively argues that romantic love is not associated with marriage. Marriage is unnatural, an exchange of sex roles between men and women.

In the strongly feminist **"The Ladies Answer to the Knight"** the widowed Lady mocks Hudibras's **"Heroical Epistle"** and wittily reasserts the power of women over men. She takes up her pen as a learned writing lady who fulfills men's greatest fears by encouraging domestic discord. Simultaneously she represents that feared Amazon, the unruly ruling woman who ought to be subject to romantic wooing but who refuses to succumb to male romantic subterfuge. She satirizes the defeat of Hudibras's "sword" by Trulla, and reminds him that in breaking his vow to the Lady he has acted in the way women are accused of acting. She exposes his desire for her money, and then uses antifeminist texts to insist on female power: "For if you all were *Solomons,* / And *Wise* and *Great* as he was once, / You'l find Th'are able to subdue, / (*As they did him*) and baffle you." Because men are attracted by artifice (ruby red lips, eyes like diamonds), she continues, men force women to create more artifice, to pretend to perfection and grace. Women were first made for men, she concedes, but then, in an inversion of the Fall, Mary, a woman, restored men to life: "Since all the *Priviledge* you *Boast,* / And Falsly *usurp'd,* or *vainly lost:* / Is now our Right, to *whose Creation,* / You ow your *Happy Restoration.*"

The Widow calls on men to acknowledge that women rule everything and that any power men believe they have is an illusion. The marketplace, public meetings, the seas, the home, and posterity all fall under women's rule. Every church, every country, every war is a women's province:

> We Manage things of Greatest weight,
> In all the world's *Affairs of State.*
> Are Ministers in War, and Peace,
> That sway *all Nations* how we Please,
> We rule *all Churches,* and *their Flocks,*
> *Heretical, and Orthodox.*

The voice of the Lady is so sure, so wise, so strong, that the reader easily accepts her voice as the satirist's, and we share her desire to deflate Hudibras's rhetoric and to expose his arrogance. But Samuel Butler is suspicious of extremes, no matter how righteous his proponent of excess may seem. In his **"Thoughts Upon Various Subjects,"** Butler writes, "The greatest Drunkards are the worst Judges of Wine—the most Insatiable Leachers the most Ignorant Criticks in Women, and the Greediest Appetites, of the best Cookery of Meats—for Those that use *Excess* in any Thing never understand the Truth of it, which always lies in *the Mean.*" The Widow's excessive claims typify, of course, men's most irrational fantasies. If men are distressed with this status, she concludes, let them give place and submit; or if they must, let them seize the unjust power: "Let Men usurp Th'unjust Dominion, / As if they were *the Better Women.*" **"The Ladies Answer"** attacks conventional attitudes as displayed in heroic poetry. The Lady turns away from domestic duties and from the male sex. She refuses the natural functions of a woman, and she usurps male prerogatives. She refuses to fall in love and to succumb to men's power. Truly an unruly monster who terrorizes men and mocks them, she becomes a satiric fiction of the woman who does not need men.

Hudibras relies on debate rather than action, and each canto and section of the poem fails to reach resolution. The ambiguity in the poem contributes to the sense that the battle for power between the sexes will also remain unresolved. Clearly ***Hudibras*** indicates that the rule of women, while superior to that of men, is not much to be preferred. The myth of the Amazon—the ruling woman or the masculinized woman who exemplifies man's fear of uselessness—is defused by creating the counter romantic fiction that love will lead independent women to relinquish their autonomous state. ***Hudibras*** plays with those expectations and turns them upside down. Butler exuberantly challenges the assumptions of the myth of the Amazon and forces the reader to reread antifeminist texts. Butler's Widow refuses to come into the domestic fold, to acknowledge her inferiority, or to support and nurture men; with powerful irony, she challenges men to dare to prove they are as capable as ruling women. Such women who refuse to exist solely for and through men give the lie to the romantic expectation that they must solicit masculine approval in order to give meaning to their lives. Butler successfully demystifies the autonomous woman, gives her a rational (if strident) voice, and allows her to mock the Puritan sects who feared her threat to patriarchal authority. The frightful female monster, the Amazon, would resurface to haunt men's imaginations throughout the eighteenth century and beyond. (pp. 48-56)

Felicity A. Nussbaum, "The Better Women: The Amazon Myth and 'Hudibras'," in her The Brink of All We Hate: English Satires on Women 1660-1750, *University Press of Kentucky, 1984, pp. 43-56.*

George Wasserman (essay date 1989)

[*In the following excerpt, Wasserman examines Butler's views on human nature, politics, and religion as they inform the sketches in his "Characters."*]

Although none of Butler's prose **"Characters"** was published in his lifetime, Robert Thyer, who first published 121 of them in ***The Genuine Remains*** (1759), surmised from the state of the author's manuscripts that some had been prepared for the press. In 1908, A. R. Waller reprinted Thyer's collection along with sixty-six additional Characters which Thyer had also transcribed from Butler's manuscripts. Eleven more have since come to light. Eight of these found their way into some numbers of the *London Magazine* (1825-26), and another (**"Schoolmaster"**) turned up in William Longueville's commonplace book. Two more Characters, **"War"** and **"A Covetous Man"** (said to be an early version of **"The Miser"**), have been uncovered in the holograph British Museum manuscript material by Hugh de Quehen and are published, for the first time as Characters, in his edition of the ***Prose Observations.*** This brings the total of Butler's **"Characters"** to 198, not counting fragments, the largest production of any English writer of the form. (p. 113)

Taken as a body . . . Butler's **"Characters"** appear to present a conflict of intention in the author: on the one hand, they reveal the essential, hidden perversity of human nature (Butler has left us no Character of a virtuous subject); on the other, they depict the infinite variety through which that perversity manifests itself. Butler seems compelled to name these varieties or "professions," to undo the conspiracy of silence in our social institutions that he alludes to in his Character of **"A Cheat":** "all the greater Sort of Cheats being allowed by Authority, have lost their Names (as *Judges,* when they are called to the Bench, are no more stiled *Lawyers*) and left the title to the meaner only, and the unallowed." Butler is therefore also interested in what he terms the "Callings," the inherent aptitudes or ruling passions of his subjects. Specifically, he focuses upon the discrepancy between "calling" and "profession," for this difference constitutes the satiric situation of his **"Characters."** The Character of **"A Cheat,"** for example, makes clear the close interdependence that Butler finds among his subjects: the Cheat "is a Freeman of all Trades, and all Trades of his," it begins; and later: "He can do no Feats without the cooperating Assistance of the Chowse (Gull), whose Credulity commonly meets the Imposter half Way, otherwise nothing is done; for all the Craft is not in the Catching (as the Proverb says) but the better half at least in being catched." Often, two Characters represent merely two views of the same deception, as **"A Popish Priest"** and **"A Proselite," "A Lawyer"** and **"A Litigious Man," "A Mountebank"** and **"A Medicine-Taker."** Butler is able to name the character even of a subject that has no "calling," a characterless-Character, as it were. **"A Cully,"** or Dupe—a nonentity himself—is described entirely in terms of the actions of those who work upon him: he "is a gibbet for all manner of cheats and rogues to hang upon; a Bridewel (a prison), where pickpockets and rooks are set on work and kept . . . Gamesters knap him with a whore . . . and rooks build in him like a tree."

Other Characters illustrate Butler's conviction that all extremes are ultimately identities—as **"A Popish Priest"** and **"A (Puritan) Fanatic,"** or **"A Philosopher"** and **"A Mathematician"** (the mathematician beginning "in Nonsense . . . ends in Sense, and the other (the philosopher) quite contrary begins in Sense and ends in Nonsense). Of particular interest in this connection are the unexpected relationships that Butler reveals as existing between the subjects of quite different Characters, professional disparities that are wittily brought into focus as a single image. Thus, "An Hermetic Philosopher . . . is a Kind of Hector in Learning, that thinks to maintain himself in Reputation by picking Quarrels with his gentle Readers"; **"A Modern Critic"** is "a Mountebank, that is always quacking of the infirm and diseased Parts of Books, to shew his Skill"; the alcohol in a **"Sot"** is like the inner light of a Quaker; **"A Virtuoso"** is compared to (of all things) a "Country-gentleman" (compare Butler's **"Bumpkin or Country Squire"**): as the squires "talk of Dogs to those that hate Hunting, because they love it themselves; so will he of his Arts and Sciences to those that neither know, nor care to know any Thing of them."

This practice of interchanging character types provided Butler with a special rhetoric, a secondary language of "professions" designed to articulate the especially elusive "callings," and furthermore enabling him to reuse apt witticisms without the effect of repetition. The **"Republican,"** for example, "is a civil Fanatic . . . and as all Fanatics cheat themselves with Words, mistaking them for Things; so does he with the false Sense of Liberty." The **"Virtuoso"** "differs from a Pedant, as *Things* do from *Words;* for he uses the same Affectation in his Operations and Experiments, as the other does in Language." Butler's metaphorical vehicles are self-generating, spreading like ripples in wider, more inclusive rings: "A Pimp Is a *Solicitor* of Love, a Whore's *Broker, Procurator* of the most serene Commonwealth of Sinners, and *Agent* for the Flesh and the Devil" (italics added). Such figures, demonstrating the essential unity of the various forms of human folly and villainy, suggest that Butler's penchant for analogy—"If ever a man was haunted by 'the demon of analogy,' it was he," writes Ian Jack [see excerpt dated 1952]—was in fact the natural consequence of his peculiar view of the nature of life. John Wilders [in his Introduction to ***Hudibras***] and Hugh de Quehen see this instinct for analogy as evidence of Butler's commitment to an older, analogical worldview that celebrated universal order. Would it not be more reasonable, though, to understand the analogical language of the **"Characters"** as a burlesque of that view of order, or to find the source of this language in that paradox . . . : that, whereas the singleness of truth is the most difficult achievement in the world, the devising of passable alternatives to truth (that is, falsehoods) is the easiest. Falsehood, Butler observed in the prose observations, "has change of faces and every one proof against all impression." Like a modern psychologist, he, too, recognized that human beings assume roles for social or personal reasons; but he regarded this phenomenon as a cause for laughter or rebuke, rather than for understanding or sympathy. To Butler, the danger of such behavior lay not in any violation of individual integrity (though, of course, the deceived is always at the mercy of the deceiver), but in the undermining of any surviving trace of order in human society. The man who assumes the name, but not the virtues, of learning, piety, nobility, or justice creates a confusion that makes these virtues—rare enough to begin with—all the more inaccessible.

In pointing out this deception, Butler's **"Characters"** seem to make only a negative claim to truth: Justice is *not* this magistrate or that attorney, they say; this **"Huffing Courtier"** is *not* a picture of nobility. Nevertheless, a positive value shines through this apparently destructive outlook; for, if we are brought to see that Justice is merely a judge's "profession," it is likely that we shall be on our guard in the future against his true "calling," amassing wealth. "As other mens harmes make us cautious, so the Miscarriages of others may make us wise," Butler remarked in the prose observations. "He that see's another in a wrong way, is so much nearer to the right himself."

"The Generall Temper of Mankind," Butler observed, "is nothing but a Mixture of Cheat and Folly." Let us, therefore, consider his **"Characters"** as portraits of deceivers and the victims of deception (their own or another's). The victims, Butler's fools, . . . misunderstand their true natures because they either lack reason (the madmen and proper or "natural" fools) or because they misuse it (the ignorant or "artificial" fools); and, as a consequence of both causes, they bear a closer resemblance to animals or machines than to men. I have explained the general category of folly using Butler's assertion that "Men without Reason (and men who misuse it) . . . fall short of that which give's them their Being . . . ." Such a man, we read in the Character of **"A Fool,"** is "not actuated by any inward principle of his own, but by something without him, like an engine; for he is nothing, but as he is wound up, and set a going by others"—by others, or by the fluctuating pressures of his own passions or "humours": but in neither case does he remain himself. The result, viewed from the outside, is usually ridiculous: the **"Affected (Man),"** for example, "is a Piece of Clockwork, that moves only as it is wound up and set, and not like a voluntary Agent"; and the **"Sot"** has washed down his soul and pist it out . . . has swallowed his Humanity and drunk himself into a Beast, as if he had pledged *Madam Circe* . . . He governs all his Actions by the Drink within him . . . (and having) a different humour for every Nick his Drink rises to . . . proceeds from Ribaldry to Bawdery to Politics, Religion, and Quarreling . . . ." Or here is the **"Fantastic,"** the seventeenth-century dandy who exists merely to embody the changing modes of fashion: "His Brain is like Quicksilver, apt to receive any Impression, but retain none. . . . He is a Cormorant, that . . . devours every Thing greedily, but it runs through him immediately." This wild instability of character, which is typical of natural folly or madness, contrasts, as we shall see, with the obsessive behavior exhibited in many types of artificial folly.

Except, perhaps, for those natural fools who seem compelled to be other than themselves (the **"Affected (Man),"** the **"Sot,"** and the **"Fantastic"**), playing a role is presented as, generally, a pleasurable experience; and this pleasure bears out the truth of Butler's belief that men are happiest when devising tricks that keep them from thinking about their own miseries and weaknesses—happiness as "a perpetual Possession of being well Deceived," in Swift's later formulation. It is only to the objective observer that unnatural behavior is painful, for it appears to him as destructive to individual integrity as innovation is to national integrity. In the Character of the **"Affected (Man),"** Butler conveys this view, the sheer difficulty of the unnatural, through the use of an analogy of organic growth:

> All his Affections are forced and stolen from others, and though they become some particular Persons where they grow naturally, as a Flower does on its Stalk, he thinks they will do so by him, when they are pulled and dead. He puts Words and Language out of its ordinary Pace, and breaks it to his own Fancy, which makes it go so uneasy in a Shuffle, which it has not been used to. He delivers himself in a forced Way like one that sings with a feigned Voice beyond his natural Compass.

This behavior, of course, is a form of social affectation, adopting the clothes and mannerisms of a social station higher than one's own. More interesting to Butler was what we might call professional affectation, the dabbling in some rather prestigious occupation for which one has no aptitude. But the motivation for both forms of pretense is identical: "All the Business of this World is but *Diversion,*" the devising of "tricks" by which men manage to ignore their own shortcomings. Even the most humble occupation should be self-fulfilling, and, to the degree that it is, its product has a value. But men literally lose themselves in their occupations, with the result that their labors are fruitless. Butler's Character of **"An Officer"** (no more precise title will fit him) is the clearest statement of the idea: "Nature meant him for a man, but his office intervening put her out, and made him another thing; and as he loses his name in his authority, so he does his nature. The most predominant part in him is that in which he is something beside himself."

The Character of **"An Officer"** explains the fatal attraction of those persuits that Pope later satirized as "dullness," and that Butler analyzed more particularly in the Characters of **"A Curious Man," "A Virtuoso," "An Hermetic Philosopher,"** and **"A Pedant."** Before becoming "An Officer," we read, the subject "was nothing of himself, but had a great ambition to be something, and so got an office, which he stands more upon than if he had been more of himself; for having no intrinsic value he has nothing to trust to but the stamp that is set upon him, and so is necessitated to make as much of that as he can." Pedantry in any profession justifies itself in the same way. Butler's **"Pedant"** happens to be a physician, but could be a member of any profession: "he gives his Patients sound hard words for their Money, as cheap as he can afford; for they cost him Money and Study too, before he came by them, and he has Reason to make as much of them as he can." The *little* that such pretenders make much of is their capacity to engage in "the ordinary Bus'nes, and Drudgery of the world," the office for which nature originally designed them, endowing them with qualities like patience and industriousness, which then become comically inappropriate to the roles they tend to assume, and cause them to succeed only in perverting their usefulness in the world. Created for slavery, such men turn whatever occupation they pretend to into drudgery. Thus the **"Virtuoso,"** or dilettante, having "nothing of Nature but an Inclination . . . strives to improve (it) with Industry," which would itself be admirable "if it did not attempt (only) the greatest Difficulties . . . for he commonly slights any Thing that is plain and easy . . . and bends all his Forces against the hardest and most improbable."

It is only a step from such comic forms of self-delusion (costing the pretender only an occasional embarrassment) to much more troublesome forms of deception. In fact, the only thing preventing our taking a sterner view of the fools whom we have thus far considered is Butler's assurance of their total innocence or irrationality. But the moment the **"Virtuoso"** (for instance) embarks upon an impossible pursuit—because it is impossible and because it permits him to say or do whatever he pleases (since no man may say he is wrong)—he deceives not only himself (or more likely not himself at all), but another. We then have what Butler (adopting the new scientific interest in motion to explain the processes of deception) called the "Mechanics of Cheat" and the "mathematical Magic of Imposture," the science of which he is perhaps the most perceptive analyst in English.

We might, in fact, regard Butler's **"Characters"** as a much more comprehensive and much more subtle Restoration version of the old Elizabethan coney-catching books, those collections of admonitory fictions exposing the techniques of thieves and confidence men. How does **"A Ranter,"** one of a wild sect of religious libertines who openly defamed the scriptures, the church, and all its conventions, practice deception? Or in what sense can the charge of deception be levelled at **"A Latitudinarian,"** a seventeenth-century church liberal who was all for dissolving those narrow denominational differences that offered a sort of orthodox sanction for religious hypocrisy? Butler's answers to such questions in the **"Characters"** illustrate his extraordinary interest in knavery as a conscious mental process (*signification,* we would call it today), an interest that recognized that appearances and statements exert predictable and adaptable forces. For Butler, deception was a problem in mechanics, not semiotics. The **"Knave"** is "an Engineer of Treachery, Fraud, and Perfidiousness," who knows "how to manage Matters of great Weight with very little Force, by the Advantage of his trepanning Screws." Butler's portraits of knavery trace the progress of this science. The **"Ranter,"** for example, has "found out by a very strange Way of new Light, how to transform all the *Devils* into *Angels of Light.*" When a society as sophisticated as Restoration England has come to recognize saintliness as the mask of true wickedness, may not an unsaintly manner carry the force of virtue? In his **"Satyr upon the Licentious Age of Charles the 2D,"** Butler explained the change from Commonwealth to Restoration mores in just this way:

> For those, who heretofore sought private Holes,
> Securely in the Dark to damn their Souls,
> Wore Vizards of Hypocrisy, to steal
> And slink away, in Masquerade, to *Hell,*
> Now bring their Crimes into the open *Sun,*
> For all Mankind to gaze their worst upon.

Thus the **"Ranter"** "puts off the *old Man,* but puts it on again upon the *new one* . . . He is but an *Hypocrite* turned the wrong Side outward; for, as the one wears his Vices within, and the other without, so when they are counterchanged the *Ranter* becomes an *Hypocrite,* and the *Hypocrite* an able *Ranter.*" On the other hand, the **"Latitudinarian"** is simply "a Kind of modest Ranter": he maintains that "*Christian* Liberty and *natural* Liberty may very well consist together"; and, in the event of a conflict between the two, he is prepared to give the latter ("being of the elder House") the "Precedency."

Often the line between a subject's ignorance of his motivations and his deliberate self-misrepresentation is difficult to draw. Butler's **"Fanatic,"** for example, seems willing to endure persecution in order to conceal his unwillingness to channel his energies toward a more effective end. "He is all for suffering for Religion, but nothing for acting; for he accounts *good Works* no better than Encroachments upon the Merits of *free believing.* . . . " Yet this Character begins with Butler's observation that "the *Fanatics* of out times are mad with too little (learning)"; and Butler concludes by calling him "a Puppet Saint" whose "Ignorance is the dull leaden Weight that puts all his Parts in Motion." Although there is remarkable logical consistency of opinion in the **"Characters,"** it is difficult to generalize from them to what could confidently be regarded as Butler's attitude toward his subjects. If his view of the **"Fanatic"** seems strangely ambivalent, his judgments upon similar faults in the **"Sceptic"** and the **"Zealot"** (a second version of the **"Fanatic"**) are not: in "undervaluing that, which he cannot attain to," the **"Sceptic"** would make his Necessity appear a Virtue . . . "; and of the **"Zealot"** we are told "his Zeal is never so vehement, as when it concurs with his Interest. . . . He is very severe to other Men's Sins, that his own may pass unsuspected. . . . "

We know from a statement in his notebook that Butler, like Dante, took a graver view of fraud than of violence: "a Cheat is worse than a Thiefe," he wrote; for the former "do's not only Rob a man of his Goodes (as a thiefe do's) but his Reputation also, and makes him Combine and take Part against himself: Steale's and convey's him, out of his Reason, and Senses. . . . " In general, the **"Characters"** can be read as a demonstration of this Aristotelian view of wrongdoing. Nevertheless, Butler's moral bias should not allow us to forget his relationship to the Overburian writers and, in particular, to their conversion of the traditional moral Character into an occasion for witty improvisation. Butler continued this tradition by employing the Character as an intellectual exercise, a "diversion," according to Earl Miner [see excerpt dated 1974], rather than a form of moral exhortation—organizing large parts of a particular portrait around a central image, creating an entire sketch out of contrasting conceits, or testing the limits of ironic perspective.

Butler would have taken little satisfaction as an artist in repeating, for example, the hackneyed anti-Catholic prejudices that he no doubt shared as an English Protestant. He therefore begins his Character of **"A Popish Priest"** by taking for granted certain contemporary assumptions about the subject—about the priest's "profession." Specifically, he assumes that every man, at least, knows that the Catholic priest's chief duty in England is to infiltrate the family in order to proselytize its women, and so "his Profession is to disguise himself, which he does in Sheep's-Cloathing, that is, a Lay Habit." There is, in other words, no question about the essentially deceptive nature of priesthood; nor is there, for once, any mystery about the discrepancy between the subject's "profession" and his true "calling." Or is there? The "great Question," Butler goes on to say, is whether the "Sheep's-Cloathing" of the priest covers a "Wolf, a Thief, or a Shepherd." Interestingly, in Milton's *Lycidas,* the thief and the wolf are combined in a figure that blurs the distinction between Anglican and Roman clergy: while the Christian flocks "rot inwardly" in the care of Episcopacy, the idle and greedy clergymen "for their bellies' sake, / Creep and intrude and climb into the fold," while "the grim wolf (understood as a Catholic) with privy paw / Daily devours apace, and nothing said." The good shepherd, Lycidas, or those who weep for him, remain to represent the reformed churches. The flocks in Butler's Character are also "rotten"—though "with Hypocrisy"—and the Popish priest is clearly a thief: "only this is certain, that he had rather have one Sheep out of another Man's fold, than two out of his own." But he is more a thieving shepherd than a wolf: he "keeps his Flock always in Hurdles . . . (and) . . . he tars their Consciences with Confession and Penance, but always keeps the Wool, that he pulls from the Sore, to himself." Butler makes no distinction between the priest and Milton's shepherd: "He gathers his Church as Fanatics do." The reader may answer the "great Question" as he pleases; the author, we might believe, considered it a purely rhetorical one. For Butler, this Character was primarily a form of witty play, testing the validity of the cliché.

Often Butler's play is pure invention, the exercise of the imagination upon only one or two features of the subject. In the following allusions to the "Anabaptist's" affinity for water, for example, we notice how self-contained—how much a part of the witty allusions themselves—is the polemical force of the Character:

> [He is] a Water-saint, that like a Crocodile, sees clearly in the Water, but dully on Land.
> [He lives] in two Elements like a Goose.
> He is contrary to a Fisher of Men; for instead of pulling them out of the water, he dips them in it.
> He is a Landerer of Souls, and tries them, as Men do Witches, by Water, He dips them all under Water, but their Hands, which he holds them up by—those do still continue *Pagan.*
> His dipping makes him more obstinate and stiff in his Opinions, like a Piece of hot Iron, that grows hard by being quenched in cold Water.
> He does not like the use of Water in his Baptism, as it falls from Heaven in Drops, but as it runs out of the Bowels of the Earth, or stands putrefying in a dirty Pond.
> He chuses the coldest Time in the Year to be dipped in, to shew the Heat of his Zeal, and this renders him the more obstinate.
> His Church is under the watry Government of the Moon, when she was in *Aquarius.*
> He finds out Sloughs and Ditches, that are aptest for launching of an Anabaptist; for he does not christen, but launch his Vessel.

The same procedure is employed in the Characters of **"A Huffing Courtier,"** who is defined in terms of clothing, and of **"An Haranguer,"** which was probably inspired by William Prynne, the Puritan pamphleteer whose libelous tongue cost him both ears in the pillory. Throughout **"An Haranguer"** Butler plays upon both details ("His Ears have catched the Itch of his Tongue"), and the result is something closer to caricature than portraiture.

I suspect that Butler composed such pieces at great speed, dashing off the images as they came, with one suggesting another. The **"Horse-Courser"** and the **"Churchwarden,"** we know, were composed on the same day, an association that defies explanation until we reach the final sentence of the **"Horse-Courser,"** who, like a Puritan "Saint," is "a strict observer of Saints Days," when fairs were held, and "where all Sorts of Trades are most used; and always where a Saint has a Fair he has a Church too." Butler paid little attention to repetition, sequence, or consistency (**"A**

Rabble," for example, is described as a flock of sheep, a herd of swine, and the "most savage Beast in the whole World"); he cared only whether he pressed his imagination to its limit and thoroughly exhausted it on a subject. Rather than expunge or revise, Butler used superfluous imagery to prime his imagination on some new aspect of the subject.

The various imperfections in the Character of **"An Undeserving Favourite"** permit us to form some idea of his working method. Because a "favorite" is literally defined by the favors he receives from his king, Butler's chief emphasis in this Character is upon the contrast between these favors and the undeservingness of the subject. Accordingly, the opening clause defines the type as a coin, but one of "base Metal," a counterfeit, and its sole authenticity is the impression of the king's face that it bears: "An Undeserving Favourite / Is a Piece of base Metal with the King's Stamp upon it"—adding, as if at the suggestion of the color of the base metal or the shape of the coin, this appositive: "(he is) a Fog raised by the Sun, to obscure his own Brightness." This implied concern for the moral reputation of the king ("the Sun") is uncharacteristic of Butler, so much so that we wonder if he has not failed to make his intended point. A similar difficulty appears in the next sentence. "He came to Preferment by unworthy Offices, like one that rises with his Bum forwards, which the Rabble hold to be fortunate." Again the point is obscure; but, rather than delete or revise it, Butler makes another attempt to state it more clearly: "He got up to Preferment on the wrong Side, and sits as untoward in it." And then, as if still unsatisfied with his expression of the idea, he gives us yet another explanation. The favorite is not comfortable in his seat of favor; since he does not deserve his place, he does not become it. Based upon something other than worth, his elevation is merely superficial; it fails to distinguish him above his peers: "He is raised rather above himself than others," Butler writes, "or as base Metals are by the Test of Lead, while Gold and Silver continue still unmoved." Though the last figure picks up the metal imagery of the counterfeit coin, we might well feel that "the Test of Lead" is somewhat incorrectly applied in this context since heavy or "base Metals" would be precipitated rather than "raised" from mixtures containing gold or silver (as Butler more nearly suggests with the same figure in the Character of **"An Ignorant Man."**)

But this figure may also have brought to a more conscious level in Butler's mind several other notions only faintly suggested thus far in the Character. One of these is the juxtaposition, from the very first sentence, of images suggesting both sinking and rising. It is of course in the nature of a favorite to rise, and we may suppose too that he is *light* insofar as he lacks substantial value; but the type is also, for Butler, essentially heavy, dull, leaden, endowed with the qualities of ignorance rather than with intelligence and wit. This paradoxical nature of the favorite now emerges in the alchemical figure as an actual confusion in the author's mind. Furthermore, the figure suggests a new focus of interest in the subject. In order to show that the undeserving favorite is a counterfeit creation, Butler observes that "he is raised rather above himself than others." Although this statement indicates that undeserved favoritism does not alter the essential nature of the favored, it also suggests that it has no effect upon the unfavored, an implication that Butler, as a case of unrecognized merit himself, would probably have rejected. In describing metaphorically the relative effect of favors, Butler suggests, however, the essential injustice of the situation: "Gold and Silver continue still unmoved"—that is, true worth goes unrecognized. We may see now that Butler seems to have been moving toward this idea from the very beginning (we notice, for instance, the increasingly distinct echoes of Shakespeare's thirty-second sonnet); but we only gradually became conscious of it. Not until the fifth sentence is it fully articulated: "He is born like a Cloud on the Air of the Prince's Favour, and keeps his Light from the rest of his People."

Butler's range of metaphorical reference in the **"Characters"** is much wider than the preceding passage from **"An Undeserving Favourite"** indicates. Indeed, it is difficult to think of a field of learning, an activity, or a human experience that does not contribute some image or allusion to his **"Characters."** Much of this material is learned in nature, the product of reading, study, or attention to the complex affairs of contemporary politics, religion, and philosophy. The portrait of **"A Fifth-Monarchy-Man,"** for instance, includes references to Perkin Warbec and Lambert Simnel, political pretenders of earlier English history; the Anabaptist leader, John of Leyden; Romulus, one of the legendary founders of Rome; the abortive insurrection and punishment of Thomas Venner and his Fifth-Monarchy-Men (1660-61); the fairy-land monarchy of King Oberon; Aeneas's visions of the Roman Empire; Mahommed; and King Arthur. Among the philosophers mentioned in the **"Characters,"** we find such expected names as Plato, Aristotle, Hobbes, Descartes, Bacon, and More, as well as a number of lesser-known writers on more esoteric branches of the subject, such as Agrippa, Cardon, Charlton, Raymond Lully, Conrad Gesner, Jacob Boehme, and Alexander Ross.

Butler may employ a scholastic distinction in a secular context—like that which compares the conversation of **"An Amorist"** to the intuition of an angel—or draw upon recent scientific investigation to develop a remark on religion or morality, as when he observes that ritual increases the force of religion in the Catholic much as a magnet draws a greater weight through a piece of iron, or compares the Sot's way of renewing his childhood with "the *Virtuoso's* Way of making old Dogs young again," that is, by transfusion. Even Butler's puns tend to be learned—typographical, like the identification of the "Cuckhold's" head with Pythagoras's letter (both are "troubled with a forked Distinction"); etymological, like the "Undeserving Favourite's *honor*" (it is to be understood in its "original Sense . . . which among the Ancients (*Gellius* says) signified Injury"); or grammatical (**"A Pimp"** is "a Conjunction copulative, that joins different Cases, Genders, and Persons"). Scriptural allusions (though rather common ones) are frequent, as are also references to the Greek classics and the Roman satirists. But, outside of an obviously literary subject like **"A Small Poet,"** allusions to later literary figures are rare. In the last-named Character, Butler refers to Ben Jonson and Edward Benlowes, the emblem poets, William Prynne, and perhaps Sir William Davenant. Elsewhere, the important French critic Julius Scaliger is several times mentioned, and there are references to Sylvester's translation of Du Bartas, to Chaucer's pilgrims, and to occasional recollections of characters from the plays of Jonson, Marlowe, and Shakespeare.

In marked contrast to this learned material are the allusions to popular legend, fable, and proverb, the imagery of everyday life, and commonsense truth that Butler uses in the **"Characters."** Some of this material may have been recalled from his rural youth and early career at various country estates: glimpses of the wretched roads of the North Country, which appear as an analogy for the tiresome discourse of the **"Tedious Man",** references to rustic drinking customs, and to the special knowledge of farmers, hunters, and fishermen. Here, too, is the expertise of popular games—bowls, dice, tennis, *L'Ombre,* and "Inn and Inn"—reference to the forms of popular festivity, and the sights and sounds of the city: the "link-boy" who lights the dark ways (a metaphor for the self-illuminated Quaker); the watchman with his blunt bill speciously "chalk'd" to appear sharp (an analogy of false wit); street names like "Ram-alley" and "Lewkner's Lane"; and shop-signs like the "Turks Head," where Harrington's Rota Club met, and the vintner's "bush."

For the modern reader, this witty application of the commonplace is probably the most memorable feature of Butler's **"Characters:"** the "Haranguer's" tongue, always in motion, though to little purpose, is "like a Barber's Scissors, which are always snipping, as well when they do not cut, as when they do." The clothes-conscious "fantastic," "sure to be earliest in the Fashion, lays out for it like the first Pease and Cherries"; on the other hand, the **"Knave"** "grows rich by the Ruin of his Neighbors, like Grass in the Streets in a great Sickness." One of the few generalizations we can make about such figures—aside from the obvious fact that each presents a fresh impression of Butler's actual world—is that they tend to be one-dimensional: they are merely witty illustrations rather than expressions of insight. True, the image of a luxuriant growth of grass in the street of a plague-infested city is actually quite complex; it may express desertedness, the triumph of the natural over the artificial, or the irrepressibility of the life force. For Butler, however, the value of the image is drastically restricted: he means only that the Knave and the grass are alike in that both flourish at the expense of men. Butler's figures collapse under any greater interpretive pressure. They are to be enjoyed simply as unexpected similitudes, wondered at, perhaps, for their perspicuity, but then dropped for the next in turn; and since the peripheral overtones of these images are nonfunctional, we find little sense of poetic coherence in the **"Characters."** Unity is a feature not of individual Characters, but of the entire collection and is due chiefly to Butler's tendency to repeat images (animals, machinery, clothes). The significant patterns emerge only in broad perspective. Man is a beast—or worse—the **"Characters"** say collectively; or man, the rational animal, is a flattering fiction—in reality, he is an automaton; or men are never what they appear to be—all practice some form of deception. These images, and their implications in Butler's thought have been mentioned in earlier chapters. But one other class of repeated imagery may yet be mentioned, that of buying and selling, the making and spending of money, and the production and consumption of commodities.

In many cases, of course, the language and imagery of commerce is called for by the middle-class subjects of the **"Characters"** (**"A Shopkeeper," "A Vintner," "A Banker"**), and Butler is quite adept at employing the special vocabularies of the professions and trades he describes. But I am thinking now of commerce as a metaphor: the **"Small Poet"** as "Haberdasher . . . with a very small Stock, and no Credit"; the **"Lawyer"** as "Retailer of Justice, that uses false Lights, false Weights, and false Measures"; and the **"Astrologer"** as "Retailer of Destiny, and pretty Chapman to the Planets." It is probably a mistake to take such imagery too seriously, or to suggest, as Norma Bentley does [in her Ph.D. dissertation "Hudibras Butler" (1944)], that Butler aspired to membership in the leisure class and hence was contemptuous of the middle class he wished to, but could not, rise above. Indeed, there is a touch of this sentiment in his Character of **"A Shopkeeper"**: "Country Gentlemen," he wrote, "always design the least hopeful of their Children to Trades, and out of that Stock the City is supplied with that sottish Ignorance, which we see it perpetually abound with." It is also true that the middle-class moneymakers of Butler's day were usually Puritans, and of course Butler was critical of the Puritans. But his criticism was directed at the spiritual pretenses of Puritanism, not at its economic philosophy—or, indirectly, at the latter only if it revealed pretense, as in this passage from the long polemical Character of **"A Hypocritical Nonconformist":**

> The Wealth of his Party . . . is no mean Motive to enflame his Zeal, and encourage him to use the Means, and provoke all Dangers, where such large Returns may infallibly be expected. . . . For so many and great have been the Advantages of this thriving Persecution, that the Constancy and Blood of the primitive Martyrs did not propagate the Church more, than the Money and good Creatures earned by these profitable Sufferings have done the Discipline of the modern Brethren.

The brand of commerce was for Butler not a social, but an ethical, stigma. "Many excellent Persons have been born and lived in the City," he says in the Character of **"A City-Wit,"** but "there are very few such that have been bred there, though they come from all Parts and Families of the Nation; for Wit is not the Practice of the Place and a London Student is like an *University* Merchant." Butler's **"Characters"** suggest that the men of commerce were themselves aware of what they had done to trade. The **"Shopkeeper,"** for example cannot call his occupation a "profession," and he is ashamed to regard it as a "calling": he speaks of it, therefore, as a *"Mystery";* Butler adds, however, that "rightly interpreted (this mystery) signifies only this—That as all *Turks* are Tradesmen, even so all Tradesmen are Turks." (pp. 115-29)

George Wasserman, in his Samuel "Hudibras" Butler, *Twayne Publishers, 1989, 163 p.*

Hudibras is tormented by "devils" sent by The Lady, in an etching by Hogarth.

FURTHER READING

Bruun, Sv. "Who's Who in Samuel Butler's 'The Elephant in the Moon'?" *English Studies* 50 (1969): 381-89.

Speculates on the identities of the historical figures on whom Butler based the principal characters in his satirical poem "The Elephant in the Moon."

Craig, Hardin. "*Hudibras,* Part I, and the Politics of 1647." *The Manly Anniversary Studies in Language and Literature,* edited by John M. Manly, pp. 145-55. Chicago: University of Chicago Press, 1923.

Seeks to ascertain the composition date of *Hudibras* through an examination of the political milieu in England as represented in the poem.

Curtiss, Joseph Toy. "Butler's Sidrophel." *PMLA* XLIV, No. 4 (December 1929): 1066-78.

Suggests that Butler based the character of Sidrophel in *Hudibras* on the astrologer William Lilly and that he later revised the character in "An Heroic Epistle of Hudibras to Sidrophel" to satirize Royal Society founder Sir Paul Neile.

Dowden, Edward. "Samuel Butler." In his *Puritan and Anglican: Studies in Literature,* pp. 279-310. London: Kegan Paul, Trench, Trübner & Co., 1900.

Overview of Butler's life and works, contending that much of Butler's satire is the product of his "remorseless intelligence."

Edwards, Thomas R. "The Hero Emasculated: *Hudibras* and Mock-Epic." In his *Imagination and Power: A Study of Poetry on Public Themes,* pp. 39-46. New York: Oxford University Press, 1971.

Study of poetry containing political or "public" themes that focuses on *Hudibras* as an unconventional portrayal of the epic hero.

Farley-Hills, David. "Hudibras." In his *The Benevolence of Laughter: Comic Poetry of the Commonwealth and Restoration,* pp. 46-71. Totowa, N. J.: Rowman and Littlefield, 1974.

Analyzes the strengths and weaknesses of *Hudibras,* citing the poem as one of the finest examples of burlesque in the Restoration period.

Gibson, Dan, Jr. "Samuel Butler." In *Seventeenth Century*

Studies, edited by Robert Shafer, pp. 277-335. Princeton: Princeton University Press, 1933.

Examines Butler's views on the Church, the State, the study of science, and literary criticism as reflected in his poetry and notebook entries.

Hill, Christopher. "Samuel Butler (1613-80)." In his *The Collected Essays of Christopher Hill, Volume One: Writing and Revolution in 17th Century England,* pp. 277-97. Sussex, England: Harvester Press, 1985.

Regards Butler as a progressive thinker among his contemporaries in an examination of the convictions expressed in *Hudibras* concerning science, religion, and politics.

Horne, William C. "Butler's Use of the *Rump* in *Hudibras.*" *The Library Chronicle* XXXVII, No. 2 (Spring 1971): 126-35.

Examines the Royalist satiric verse anthologized in *Rump* (1662) as an influence on the narrative and characterization of Butler's *Hudibras.*

———. "Hard Words in *Hudibras.*" *Durham University Journal* n.s. LXXV, No. 2 (June 1983): 31-43.

Analyzes Butler's use of "hard words"—slang, political or religious doublespeak, and esoteric academic language—for satiric purposes in *Hudibras,* claiming that "for Butler abuse of language is . . . a cause of violence, a symptom of violence, and violence in itself."

Ker, W. P. "Samuel Butler." In his *On Modern Literature: Lectures and Addresses,* pp. 1-12. 1955. Reprint. St. Clair Shores, Mich.: Scholarly Press, 1971.

Comments on Butler in terms of his contemporaries, discovering a paradox in Butler's work. Ker maintains that while Butler's "spirit and temper" anticipate those of the "unenthusiastic" eighteenth century, his "methods of expression are in his own time already rather antiquated."

Korshin, Paul J. "Typology and Satire." In his *Typologies in England, 1650-1820,* pp. 269-327. Princeton: Princeton University Press, 1982.

Includes discussion of *Hudibras* in a study of "typologies" in the literature of the English Englightenment.

Miner, Earl. Review of *Hudibras,* by Samuel Butler, edited by John Wilders. *Philological Quarterly* XLVIII, No. 3 (July 1969): 340-42.

Favorable review of both a 1967 edition of *Hudibras* and its introduction by John Wilders (see excerpt dated 1967).

———. "Butler: Hating Our Physician." In his *The Restoration Mode from Milton to Dryden,* pp. 158-97. Princeton: Princeton University Press, 1974.

Examines Butler's pessimistic attitude toward humanity as represented in *Hudibras.* Focusing in particular upon Butler's portrayal of female characters, Miner suggests parallels between Butler's views and those of the seventeenth-century philosopher Thomas Hobbes.

Quintana, Ricardo. "The Butler-Oxenden Correspondence." *Modern Language Notes* 48, No. 1 (January 1933): 1-11.

Attempts to discern the year in which Butler began the composition of *Hudibras, Part I,* through the use of recently discovered correspondence between the poet and Sir George Oxenden.

———. "Samuel Butler: A Restoration Figure in a Modern Light." *ELH: A Journal of Literary History* 18, No. 1 (March 1951): 7-31.

Argues that "as a Restoration figure in the narrow sense Butler's significance may seem to lie primarily in his commentary as a moral philosopher. But it was as satirist that he came closest to embodying the spirit of the age then beginning—the age of Swift and Hogarth."

Richards, Gertrude R. B. "Butler's *Hudibras.*" *More Books: The Bulletin of the Boston Public Library* XVIII, No. 9 (November 1943): 407-10.

Examines the historical facts surrounding the composition and publication of *Hudibras.*

Seidel, Michael A. "Patterns of Anarchy and Oppression in Samuel Butler's *Hudibras.*" *Eighteenth-Century Studies* 5, No. 2 (Winter 1971-72): 294-314.

Explores the "extremes of civil and domestic anarchy and tyrannic oppression" in *Hudibras.*

Staves, Susan. "Oaths and Vows." In her *Players' Scepters: Fictions of Authority in the Restoration,* pp. 191-252. Lincoln: University of Nebraska Press, 1979.

Includes analysis of Butler's *Hudibras* in a discussion of the nature of vows made by men and women in both religious and judiciary contexts.

Totten, Charles F. "Hypocrisy and Corruption in Four Characters of Samuel Butler." *Essays in Literature* 11, No. 2 (Fall 1975): 164-70.

Discusses "contrapuntal motifs of hypocrisy and corruption which inform the satire of [Butler's] entire book of *Characters,*" focusing on four of that volume's best known sketches.

Walker, Hugh. "From the Eclipse of Satire to Butler." In his *English Satire and Satirists,* pp. 120-44. London: J. M. Dent & Sons, 1925.

Describes Butler's works as representative of the rebirth of satirical literature during the reign of Charles I.

Wilding, Michael. "The Last of the Epics: The Rejection of the Heroic in *Hudibras* and *Paradise Lost.*" In his *Dragons Teeth: Literature in the English Revolution,* pp. 173-204. Oxford: Clarendon Press, 1987.

Regards *Hudibras* and *Paradise Lost* as rejections of traditional epic values in literature, concluding that "for both Milton and Butler, happiness came to be seen as residing not in military glory, noisy public splendor: nor in literary 'retirement'; but in the *everyday,* the domestic."

Olaudah Equiano

1745?-1797

(Also known as Gustavus Vassa) Beninese-born Anglo-African autobiographer and poet.

Equiano is widely regarded as the most influential English-speaking black writer of the eighteenth century. His autobiography, *The Interesting Narrative of the Life of Olaudah Equiano, or Gustavus Vassa, the African,* figured prominently as a catalyst of the abolitionist movement in England during the 1790s. Today, it remains a seminal document of black history—particularly in the development of slave narrative literature—admired both for its candid portrayal of the vicissitudes of its author's life and as a lively and observant travel narrative. Sidney Kaplan termed Equiano's narrative "a classic of its genre, . . . recounting the evolution of a bewildered, exiled slave into a statesman of his people" which "surely ranks with the autobiographies of Benjamin Franklin and Frederick Douglass."

Though scholars frequently dispute the exactness of Equiano's childhood memories in his narrative, most agree that he was born around 1745 in the village of Esseka, somewhere in the interior of modern-day eastern Nigeria. It is believed that his father held tribal positions of power and prestige—positions Equiano had been destined to inherit. Kidnapped by local tribesmen when he was about eleven years old, Equiano was sold into slavery along with his sister and traded among African natives for nearly six months. When he was finally delivered to white slavers on the coast, he was loaded onto a slave ship bound for Barbados. Once there, he was purchased by a Virginia planter, who later sold him to Michael Henry Pascal, the captain of a slave-trader ship and a lieutenant in the Royal Navy. Pascal transported Equiano to England and renamed him Gustavus Vassa after the sixteenth-century Swedish king Gustavus Vasa.

During the first half of 1757 Equiano sailed in and out of various ports around the British Isles, visited Holland twice, and witnessed naval engagements off the coast of France—all the while acclimating himself to European manners and customs and learning the English language. Within a year he had served Pascal aboard a number of ships, eventually accompanying the captain to North America where the Seven Years' War between France and England was in progress. Returning to England in 1759, Equiano was placed by Pascal under the tutelage of the latter's relations in London, the Misses Guerin, who taught him to read and write and educated him in Christian dogma; they eventually persuaded Pascal to have Equiano baptized. A few months later, however, Pascal set sail for the Mediterranean. Equiano was made ship steward on this voyage and gained the friendship of Pascal's personal attendant, Daniel Queen, a sailor in his forties. He taught Equiano how to read the Bible and how to dress hair; perhaps more importantly, he instilled in young Equiano a sense of human dignity and personal freedom. Equiano later wrote of Queen: "He was like a father to me. . . . Indeed I almost loved him with the affection of a son." Equiano returned to England in early 1761 for a brief stay and then accompanied Pascal on an expedition that included naval engagements off the Breton coast. This was Equiano's last voyage with Pascal. Upon their return to London in late 1762, Pascal falsely accused Equiano of planning to escape and immediately sold him to Captain Doran, who, upon their arrival in Montserrat in early 1763, sold Equiano to Robert King, a Philadelphia Quaker and merchant. Equiano further improved his seamanship and education and learned the commercial arts while in service aboard King's ships, which plied the American coast to the Caribbean. A devoted Quaker, King insisted that Equiano purchased his freedom through earned money and permitted him to conduct his own trading. Finally, in 1766, Equiano, at age twenty-one, received his manumission papers for £40, but he continued to work aboard King's ships as a freeman. Equiano observed that he had been more fortunate than most American and West Indian slaves, who often suffered brutal cruelty at the hands of savage masters. Thus his dream of abolition was ignited, and, in early 1767, he left King to sail for England.

When he arrived in London, Equiano called upon the Guerin sisters, who found him employment as a hairdresser to a gentleman, Captain O'Hara. Equiano worked for O'Hara until early 1768, then hired himself out as hairdresser to Dr. Charles Irving, a scientist noted for his desalination experiments. During this period Equiano converted to Methodism, while his wanderlust for seafaring adventure grew stronger. In 1773 he accompanied explorer Constantine Phipps on a scientific expedition to the Arctic in search of the North Pole. In 1775 he rejoined Irving, this time as his partner in a short-lived venture to establish a plantation on the Mosquito Shore of Central America. Some years later, Equiano attempted to direct English philanthropist Granville Sharp's attention to the massacre of over 130 slaves aboard the HMS *Zong* off the West African coast in 1783. This disclosure prompted a storm of parliamentary debates over the slave trade. In the meantime Equiano returned to the seas and briefly stopped at Philadelphia, his "favorite old town." In 1787 he was appointed Commissary for Stores for a British expedition of freed slaves who were settling in Sierra Leone. In 1788, undaunted by the abrupt dismissal from his appointment, Equiano petitioned the Queen of England "that . . . a period may now be put to [the slaves's] misery." This event marks the conclusion of Equiano's autobiography, and relatively little is known about the rest of his life. Upon completion of *The Interesting Narrative* in 1789, he traveled throughout the British Isles, selling copies of his book and speaking out against the slave trade. In 1792 he married an Englishwoman, Susanna Cullen. He may have had children, but no conclusive evidence survives. Equiano died on 31 March 1797.

Equiano concluded his narrative by asking his readers to bear in mind that the work "was written by one who was as unwilling as unable to adorn the plainness of truth by the colouring of imagination." Yet the *Interesting Narrative* became immediately popular upon publication in 1789; within three years it ran through eight English editions, one of which included the poetry of the black American poet Phillis Wheatley, and an American one. Early reviews were generally favorable, though some critics questioned whether Equiano himself actually wrote the whole book. *The Monthly Review* of June 1789 posited that "it is not improbable that some English writer has assisted him in the compilement, or at least the correction of his book, for it is sufficiently well written." Nonetheless, critics generally acknowledge the presence of Equiano's hand throughout his autobiography; one eighteenth-century reviewer reasoned in *The General Magazine and Impartial Review* that only Equiano could have written the *Interesting Narrative,* since it is "a round unvarnished tale . . . written with much truth and simplicity." However, some recent critics have strongly questioned the truthfulness and authenticity of Equiano's recollections of his native Africa, noting striking similarities between descriptive passages in the *Interesting Narrative* and those of contemporary European travel narratives. According to S. E. Ogude, the first chapter of Equiano's *Interesting Narrative* is "the work of a very competent collector of tales. . . . The most interesting part of his story is the least reliable as a historical document." One of the most debated issues concerning the *Interesting Narrative* involves the matters of genre and canon. Most scholars tend to view slave narrative as an almost exclusively American literary phenomenon; hence, Equiano perhaps may not deserve recognition in the "American canon." According to some commentators, since Equiano spent only a negligible amount of his life in America and identified himself with the abolitionist movement in England, he more correctly "belongs" to Anglo-African letters. Still others accord his work a place in the development of the literature of spiritual conversion. Wilfred D. Samuels noted that "the crux of his narrative is related more to his spiritual freedom than his physical freedom. . . . An eighteenth-century reader would have realized at once that Equiano's focus was his effort to make straight 'the crooked paths' of a 'sinful' life."

Equiano's *Interesting Narrative* is recognized as a classic by merit of its lasting popularity and its shaping role in the development of slave narrative literature. Critics on both sides of the Atlantic continue to consider Equiano's *Interesting Narrative* an extremely valuable account of eighteenth-century black life. Ogude noted that Equiano initiated "for the African the image of the achiever. For *Interesting Narrative,* in spite of its occasional display of spiritual humility, is perhaps the first deliberate attempt to celebrate black achievement in print."

(For further information about Equiano's life and works, see *Dictionary of Literary Biography,* Vols. 37, 50.)

PRINCIPAL WORKS

**The Interesting Narrative of the Life of Olaudah Equiano, or Gustavas Vassa, The African.* 2 vols. (autobiography and poetry) 1789; also published as *The Life and Adventures of Olaudah Equiano; or Gustavus, the African. From an Account Written By Himself* [abridged edition], 1829; also published as *Equiano's Travels* [abridged edition], 1967; also published as *The Life of Olaudah Equiano or Gustavus Vassa, The African, 1789.* 2 vols., 1969

*The first edition of this work contains an appendix entitled "Miscellaneous Verses, or Reflections on the State of My Mind during My First Convictions; of the Necessity of Believing Truth, and Experiencing the Inestimable Benefits of Christianity."

The Monthly Review, London (essay date 1789)

[*In the following excerpt, the anonymous critic favorably appraises "the sable author" and his* Interesting Narrative.]

We entertain no doubt of the general authenticity of this very intelligent African's interesting story; though it is not improbable that some English writer has assisted him in the compilement, or, at least, the correction of his book:

for it is sufficiently well written. The narrative wears an honest face: and we have conceived a good opinion of the man, from the artless manner in which he has detailed the variety of adventures and vicissitudes which have fallen to his lot. His publication appears very seasonably, at a time when negroe-slavery is the subject of public investigation; and it seems calculated to increase the odium that hath been excited against the West-India planters, on account of the cruelties that some of them are said to have exercised on their slaves; many instances of which are here detailed.

The sable author of these volumes appears to be a very sensible man; and he is, surely, not the less worthy of credit from being a convert to Christianity. He is a Methodist; and has filled many pages, toward the end of his work, with accounts of his dreams, visions, and divine impulses; but all this, supposing him to have been under any delusive influence, only serves to convince us that he is guided by principle; and that he is not one of those poor converts who, having undergone the ceremony of baptism, have remained content with that portion, only, of the Christian Religion: instances of which are said to be almost innumerable in America, and the West-Indies; Gustavus Vassa appears to possess a very different character; and, therefore, we heartily wish success to his publication, which we are glad to see has been encouraged by a very respectable subscription. (pp. 551-52)

A review of "The Interesting Narrative of the Life of Olaudah Equiano," in The Monthly Review, *London, Vol. LXXX, 1789, pp. 551-52.*

Vernon Loggins (essay date 1931)

[*Loggins was an American educator, editor, essayist, and biographer. Among his works are* The Hawthornes: The Story of Seven Generations of an American Family *(1951) and* The Negro Author *(1931). In the following excerpt from the latter, he comments on the literary significance of Equiano's* Interesting Narrative.]

[Perhaps] the most powerful direct protest against the system for which an eighteenth-century Negro was in any way responsible came in one of the most important books attributed to American Negro authorship. That book is the autobiography, ***The Interesting Narrative of the Life of Olaudah Equiano, or Gustavus Vassa, the African.*** With the exception of his folk songs, the Negro's most valuable contributions to American literature have been in the form of personal memoirs. The social history of the African in America has been such that until the race produces a Pushkin or a Dumas, a creator whose work is of such excellence that his own personality is entirely overshadowed by it, there is going to be more interest in how a Negro has achieved a certain accomplishment than in the accomplishment itself. The life of practically every American Negro who has attained distinction in any field of activity has been an evolution filled with drama. He has in most cases sprung from slavery, or the most humble social position. His climb has demanded a struggle of adventure, involving often the strange, exciting, and thrilling. It is not surprising that Booker T. Washington's *Up from Slavery* is counted among the more widely read American books, and that Frederick Douglass was called upon to revise his memoirs until they grew from a thin booklet to a massive volume. From the point of view of American literary history, Gustavus Vassa's ***Life*** is of greater significance than either of these. At the time it was published, in 1789, few books had been produced in America which afford such vivid, concrete, and picturesque narrative.

Because of the fullness of his autobiography, we have perhaps a more complete picture of Gustavus Vassa than of any other eighteenth-century Negro. . . . His one big contribution to the cause of abolition was his autobiography, completed in 1788 and already in the eighth edition by 1794. According to the dedicatory remarks in a 1790 issue of the ***Life,*** he in that year presented to Parliament a petition for the suppression of the slave trade. The anonymous author of an 1815 edition of the ***Life,*** who stated that he had been unable to determine where Vassa died, suggested 1801 as the probable date of his death.

Since Vassa lived so little of his life in the United States, any place accorded him in American Negro literature might be questioned. However, England, where he spent most of his years when he was not on the sea, has not claimed him. The custom, at least with book cataloguers, has been to group him with the American writers; and, after all, America was as much his home as any other country except Africa. While he was in slavery, one of his masters, according to his ***Narrative,*** was a Virginia planter and another was a Pennsylvania Quaker. During his many years on the sea, he seems to have passed much time in the American Atlantic coast towns, from New York to Savannah. Besides, his book, although originally published in England and popular there in antislavery circles during the first ten years of its life, has been many times reprinted in America. In the stressful abolition period, it shared a place of prominence with Phillis Wheatley's poems and Benjamin Banneker's almanacs among the works most often pointed to as examples of what the Negro mind could accomplish.

It is the naturalness of the style which gives the book its strength. Unlike Williams, Sancho, Phillis Wheatley, and "Othello," Vassa did not imitate. His details are, as Henri Grégoire claimed, the impressions of a child of nature, and he recorded them without art. There is almost continuous narrative in the book, of the spontaneous variety which one associates with Bunyan or Defoe. Whenever there is explanation, as in the chapters on his religious experiences and conversion, it is enlivened by concrete pictures. Vassa remained the African, gifted with an imagination which foreign environment could not destroy. His temperament was not made over again by the civilization with which he came in contact, and which he seems always to have evaluated according to his native African standards. One feels in his pages the Negro's mysticism, his unquestioning acceptance of the strange, his genius for adapting himself, his almost uncanny common-sense insight into the characters of those around him, his spirit of laughing resignation when in adversity, and his fully awake sensitiveness to the concreteness of life.

The idealized pictures of Africa, especially in the chapters in which Vassa recounts his memories of his childhood, make up perhaps the most valuable section of the book. Of all the Negro slaves who wrote of their lives, Cugoano and Vassa are unique in having distinct recollections of their childhood days in Africa. Cugoano's style is chaotic, and his brief description of his early life is vague. Vassa, on the contrary, retained clearly in his mind the little things; his pictures of his life in the "kingdom of Benin" are definite and realistic and full of a simple charm. He tells about how the gods are worshipped, how justice is administered, how marriages are celebrated, how wars are planned and fought, and how crops are grown and harvested and bartered. And there is never a note of condemnation for the customs of his native country. One statement shows his general attitude when comparing life in Africa with that in Europe: "Our manner of living is entirely plain; for as yet the natives are unaccustomed with those refinements in cookery which debauch the taste." Although his recollections of his childhood impressions are too sentimentalized to be of value to the sociologist devoted to a study of African habits, they are indeed an interesting unconscious contribution to the literature of the simple life, the literature of the "noble savage," already popular in Europe at the time Vassa wrote.

He also fits interestingly into the program of the rising romanticists of his day in stressing with a calm *naïveté* the unusual, the marvelous, the supernatural. In relating the experiences of his kidnapping, he does not emphasize so much his misfortunes as his wonder in seeing new places and new people. When after months of travelling with different African masters he finds himself in chains on a ship, he casually concludes that the white men whom he views for the first time are spirits. When he is settled on a plantation in Virginia, he is sent one day to fan his master, who is sleeping.

> The first object which engaged my attention was a watch which hung on the chimney, and was going. I was quite surprised at the noise it made, and was afraid it would tell the gentleman anything I might do amiss: and when I immediately after observed a picture hanging in the room, which appeared constantly to look at me, I was still more frightened, having never seen such things before.

When he witnesses a snowfall for the first time, he is convinced that the heavens are raining down salt. He never gave up his African superstitions. The following was written long after he had become Christianized, after he had planned to go back to Africa as a missionary to his people:

> We have serpents of different kinds, some of which are esteemed ominous when they appear in homes, and these we never molest. I remember two of these ominous snakes, each of which was as thick as the calf of a man's leg, and in color resembling a dolphin in water, crept at different times into my mother's night-house, where I always lay with her, and coiled themselves into folds, and each time they crowed like a cock.

His temperament responded with enthusiasm to the Christian belief in divine providences. The phenomenon of an earthquake in Montserrat is explained as the destructive visitation of a God wrathful over the evils of slavery. Profanity is one of the sins which he has difficulty in renouncing when he is undergoing his conversion to Methodism. With a crushing fear in his heart, he observes a curse of God on one of his fellow sailors:

> One morning a young man was looking up to the foretop and in a wicked tone, common on shipboard, d—d his eye about something. Just at that moment some small particle of dust fell into his left eye, and by the evening it was much inflamed. The next day it grew worse, and within six or seven days he lost it.

On a trading voyage from Montserrat, the cargo is composed of bullocks and turkeys, the latter of which belong to Vassa. The bullocks all die before an American port is reached, but the turkeys live and are sold at a good profit. In this fateful kindness Vassa sees the hand of a democratic God favoring the lowly. His spirit of credulity, perhaps the main source of his charm, is not confined to religious marvels. Off the coast of Greenland he sees one morning "vast quantities of sea-horses, which neighed exactly like any other horses." A comment on social conditions in New York in 1784 is given with absolute belief:

> While we lay here, a circumstance happened which I thought extremely irregular. One day a malefactor was to be executed on the gallows; but with a condition that if any woman, having nothing on but her shift, married the man under the gallows, his life was to be saved. This extraordinary privilege was claimed; a woman presented herself; and the marriage ceremony was performed.

In writing his book Vassa certainly did not know that he was following any new fashions in literature. But he did know that he was fighting slavery. Several chapters are devoted exclusively to arguments for abolition; and whether he is dealing with African customs, his superstitions, his conversion, or his experiences as a sailor, the subject of slavery is likely to be dragged in. That his dominating aim in writing was to attack slavery is constantly before the reader. And he put his protest into such a readable narrative that it is perhaps not an exaggeration to say that he did more than any other Negro before Frederick Douglass to stir up antislavery feeling.

It is certain that the ***Life*** underwent editing before it was submitted to the public. The opening pages, in which there is the conventional apology for writing an autobiography, do not exhibit that simplicity and artlessness which characterize the style after Vassa gets into the story of his life. The very first sentence manifests an eighteenth-century formality which is totally different from the Bunyan-like simplicity found in the narrative which follows: "I believe it is difficult for those who publish their own memoirs to escape the imputation of vanity; nor is this the only disadvantage under which I labor: it is also their misfortune, that what is uncommon is rarely, if ever, believed, and what is obvious we are apt to turn from with disgust, and to charge the writer with impertinence." The formal arguments against slavery in the concluding chapters contain similar evidences of an affected style. Fortunately, these evident emendations are few. The book as a whole is written with the ingenuousness of a naïve and candid soul. And it is that ingenuousness which makes ***The Interesting Narrative of the Life of Olaudah Equiano, or Gustavus Vassa*** a memorable book, a work which is one of the chief adornments of American Negro literature. The estimate of a 1789 commentator still holds as valuable:

> We entertain no doubt of the general authenticity of this very intelligent African's interesting story. . . . The narrative wears an honest face: and we have conceived a good opinion of the man from the artless manner in which he has detailed the variety of adventures and vicissitudes which have fallen to his lot [see excerpt dated 1789].

(pp. 40-7)

Vernon Loggins, "The Beginnings of Negro Authorship, 1760-1790," in his The Negro Author: His Development in America to 1900, *1931. Reprint by Kennikat Press, Inc., 1964, pp. 1-47.*

Paul Edwards (essay date 1971)

[*Edwards is an English educator, essayist, and author. He has translated several Icelandic romances and legends and has written on West African literature. In the following excerpt, Edwards perceives conscious artistic efforts in Equiano's* Interesting Narrative, *a work usually admired for its simple "unvarnished" style.*]

A contemporary review of Equiano's ***Interesting Narrative*** speaks of it as a 'round unvarnished tale' . . . with much truth and simplicity and indeed it is this very quality which is likely to convince the reader of the book's authenticity. Equiano's friend, Ottobah Cugoano, a Fante who worked as manservant to the court painter Cosway in London, had published in 1787 his book 'Thoughts and Sentiments on the Evil of Slavery'; this was so rhetorical in style that many readers have expressed doubts about whether it could have been written by Cugoano at all. A comparison of the surviving manuscript letters of Cugoano with the text of his book leaves no doubt that it must have been extensively revised and in many places entirely rewritten—there is some evidence pointing to Equiano himself as reviser. In the case of Equiano's ***Narrative,*** the one existing manuscript letter indicates that Equiano would have been perfectly capable of writing his book, which is less elaborate than Cugoano's both in style and argument. But a question I want to raise here is whether Equiano's style is quite as simple and 'unvarnished' as it might at first appear.

Equiano made no claim to be a literary artist, only a man telling the story of his life; and so it would be unreasonable to make close comparisons between his book and the works of the major writers of fiction and biography at that time. All the same, the situation of Equiano has a touch of both Robinson Crusoe and Gulliver: from one point of view, his is a story of economic and moral survival on the bleak rock of slavery, a study in initiative and adaptability not entirely unlike Robinson Crusoe's; and from another, it is a tale, like Gulliver's, of new perspectives gained by physical alienation, in this case of the black man in a white world. An important difference, of course, is that Crusoe, Gulliver, and their adventures, emerge largely from their creators' imaginations and have the distinctive marks of conscious creative artistry about them, whereas Equiano is apparently doing no more than trying to tell the direct truth about his own experience. At the same time, he has many of the qualities of the more interesting eighteenth century literary heroes, particularly those of Defoe, revealing himself in the narrative in a wholly convincing way and never resorting to affectation or self-display merely in an effort to sentimentalise and to conceal his true nature. At times he presents himself as entirely ignorant, confused and vulnerable, at others as boastful or self-seeking, and is always prepared to mock his own weaknesses. . . .

[While] the author deliberately reveals himself in these instances in a comical or grotesque light, this is balanced by our recognition that self-mockery implies self-knowledge; tensions are set up in our response to the narrator, so that even his devotion to writing his journal gives to the comic a touch of the heroic. Self-revelation through self-mockery is a persistent feature of the ***Narrative***—see for instance the episode of the grampuses or the wild ride on horseback. The comic possibilities are never avoided in an effort to adopt heroic or pathetic postures, and in consequence the author's character as narrator of his own tale is seen in deeper perspective.

Still more interesting are the ambivalent feelings which Equiano displays from time to time for those who help him, particularly in chapters nine and ten, where there is considerable tension between the affection he feels for Captain Farmer, and the nagging irritation of his subordinate place in life: what becomes apparent is Equiano's need to release himself not only from his enemies, but also from his friends. This whole section offers a remarkable example of the psychology of subordination, as regret for Farmer's death mingles inextricably with the pleasure Equiano feels (and is prepared to reveal as having its boastful and complacent side) about the opportunity which Farmer's death has given him to display his own skills as a navigator and leader of men. . . . There are a number of reversal situations like this in the narrative. For instance, the former slave who has been saved by the paternalistic attentions of others, dreams that his master's ship was 'wrecked amidst the surfs and rocks, and that I was the means of saving every one on board.' The dream comes true. As in the previous chapter, Equiano again takes over from the ship's captain, and remarks with some satisfaction on the superior conduct of the 'three black men and a Dutch creole sailor' to that of the white men. Significantly, when the Captain orders the hatches to be nailed down on the slaves in the hold, Equiano the former slave takes over from him and the hatches are not nailed down. Of course, this is not to say that the racial attitudes taken up by Equiano are simple ones for the white men of his experience form a very mixed company, and for this reason his responses to the world into which he has been thrown at the age of eleven are bound to be complex, as the episode of the death of Captain Farmer shows. But the emancipation of the slave Equiano is brought about by more than the mere payment of forty pounds sterling: he also has to act out roles of dominance through which he can shed his past.

It might be unwise to make much of the rhetorical passages in the ***Narrative*** in view of the doubts that have been expressed about whether these might not have been added by another hand, but there is really no good reason why Equiano, an avid reader of eighteenth-century religious tracts as well as the Bible and (bearing in mind his frequent quotations) at least the first two books of *Paradise Lost,* should not have written with some degree of expansive eloquence. But these passages are in a way less interesting than the plainer ones. One reason for thinking them to be additions by another author might be their occurrence alongside episodes described in a very much plainer language, and nowhere is this more marked than in Chapter 2, which begins in the plain style and ends with a fine rhetorical flourish. But if we look closely at this chapter it becomes clear that these two manners of writing are being used deliberately and appropriately, and that the plain style is in a sense the subtler of the two. This style occurs in its most naïve form when Equiano is describing his initial fear and perplexity at the ways of the white men:

> One white man in particular I saw, when we were permitted to be on deck, flogged so unmercifully with a large rope near the foremast, that he died in consequence of it; and they tossed him over the side as they would have done a brute. This made me fear these people the more; and I expected nothing less than to be treated in the same manner. I could not help expressing my fears and apprehensions to some of my countrymen; I asked them if these people had no country, but lived in this hollow place? (the ship): they told me they did not, but came from a distant one. 'Then,' said I, 'how comes it in all our country we never heard of them?' They told me because they lived so very far off. I then asked where were their women? had they any like themselves? I was told they had. 'And why,' said I, 'do we not see them?' They answered, because they were left behind. I asked how the vessel could go? they told me they could not tell; but that there was cloth put upon the masts by the help of the ropes I saw, and then the vessel went on; and the white men had some spell or magic they put in the water when they liked, in order to stop the vessel. I was exceedingly amazed at this account, and really thought they were spirits. I therefore wished much to be from amongst them for I expected they would sacrifice me; but my wishes were vain—for we were so quartered that it was impossible for any of us to make our escape.

What is distinctive here is Equiano's skill in creating a dramatic language, not merely to describe in literal terms, but to recreate the very sense of the speakers' childhood simplicity and incomprehension and to distinguish this from an articulate and informed 'present'. Thus objects are described in naïve terms—the ship is 'this hollow place', the sails 'cloth put upon the mast' and the anchor becomes 'some spell or magic they put upon the water, when they liked, to stop the vessel.' Equiano does not merely write about his perplexity; his language becomes, dramatically, that of the perplexed boy he once was. This is true of the whole dialogue, in the naïve assumption behind 'how comes it in all our country we never heard of them?', the implied ignorance of the more 'knowledgeable' people who are replying to the boy's questions, and the very simplicity of the sentences in which question and response are formed, itself suggesting an innocent, untutored view of life.

Many of the best effects of the ***Narrative,*** in fact, are gained by this kind of dramatic or ironic simplicity—the episode of the dying man on board the ship already referred to, the account of Equiano's petty trading and the theft of the bags of fruit or of yet another reversal situation, where the Indians are the perplexed innocents and Equiano is now in the position of authority and wisdom. Notice in particular how a complex sentence structure and a literary vocabulary are suddenly and dramatically discarded for particular effect. Equiano is describing the conduct of the drunken Indian Governor who,

> getting quite drunk, grew very unruly and struck one of our most friendly chiefs, who was our nearest neighbour, and also took his gold-laced hat from him. At this a great commotion took place, and the Doctor interfered to make peace as we could all understand one another, but to no purpose; and at last they became so outrageous that the Doctor, fearing he might get into trouble, left the house and made the best of his way to the nearest wood, leaving me to do as well as I could among them, I was so enraged with the Governor that I could have wished to have seen him tied fast to a tree and flogged for his behaviour, but I had not people enough to cope with his party. I therefore thought of a strategem to appease the riot. Recollecting a passage I had read in the life of Columbus when he was amongst the Indians in Mexico or Peru, where on some occasion he frightened them by telling them of certain events in the heavens, I had recourse to the same expedient, and it succeeded beyond my most sanguine expectations. When I had formed my determination I went in the midst of them, and, taking hold of the Governor, I pointed up to the heavens. I menaced him and the rest: I told them God lived there, and that he was angry with them, and they must not quarrel so; that they were all brothers, and if they did not leave off and go away quietly, I would take the book (pointing to the Bible), read, and *tell* God to make them dead. This was something like magic. The clamour immediately ceased and I gave them some rum and a few other things, after which they went away peaceably, and the Governor afterwards gave our neighbour, who was called Captain Plasmyah, his hat again. When the Doctor returned he was exceedingly glad at my success in thus getting rid of our troublesome guests.

It is worth noting that up to this point, the Indians have been established as at least moderately noble savages, with many of the virtues of Equiano's 'Eboes' of the opening chapters, and capable of being compared advantageously to the Europeans. But it is at this moment that the drunken Indian Governor appears to disrupt the happy proceedings, the situation being saved by the trickery of the original white adventurer Columbus, the doctrines of European Christianity, and the sharp wit of an African ex-slave, who adds, characteristically, a note on Dr Irving's reliance on him to settle the situation. The effects gained by Equiano in his narrative are often, it seems to me, conscious artistic effects; they may at times be unconscious; but one thing must be clear, that his simplicities are really not quite so simple. (pp. 12-19)

Paul Edwards, "Equiano's Round Unvarnished Tale," in African Literature Today, *No. 5, 1971, pp. 12-20.*

Sekio Koike (essay date 1979)

[In the following excerpt, Koike illuminates Equiano's integration of abolitionist and religious elements in his Interesting Narrative, *noting that "the two elements . . . do not contradict, but supplement each other."]*

The Interesting Narrative of Olaudah Equiano is one of the best American slave narratives. Vernon Loggins says: " . . . [it] is of greater significance than either of these [autobiographies by Frederick Douglass and Booker T. Washington]. At the time it was published, in 1789, few books had been produced in America which afford such vivid, concrete, and picturesque narrative" [see excerpt dated 1931]. Paul Edwards points out: " . . . he has many of the qualities of the more interesting 18th century literary heroes, particularly those of Defoe, revealing himself in the narrative in a wholly convincing way and never resorting to affectation or self-display merely in an effort to sentimentalize and to conceal his true nature" [see excerpt dated 1971]. The book was also instrumental in advancing the cause of abolitionism. Loggins says: " . . . He did more than any other Negro before Frederick Douglass to stir up antislavery feeling." John Hope Franklin, a historian, esteems him to be representative of "the growing independence of spirit which the Negro was manifesting at the end of the eighteenth century."

From one point of view, the ***Narrative*** is a work of protest literature that tells of an African's vicissitudes that involve as its essential parts his confrontation with the higher civilization, his enslavement, and his liberation. From another point of view, it is a history of the transfiguration of an African who, apparently forced to emerge out of the darkness, moves on to become a Christian saved and bathed by God's love. How it came to pass for an African heathen to grow to be saved by grace is the tenor of this autobiography, as well as most of the slave narratives whose heroes are African born. It is also the tenor of a greater part of slave literature where American-born slaves tell of the ways they gained their freedom. The two elements, abolitionist and religious, do not contradict, but supplement each other. Equiano's narrative takes an important place as the first work in prose in the history of American slave literature that fused the two elements into a highly readable autobiography, the prototype of slave narratives that were to be produced in plenty in the nineteenth century.

Equiano tells us that in writing his narrative he was "actuated by the hope of becoming an instrument towards the relief of his suffering countrymen." Beginning with a citation from Isaiah on the title page, "Behold, God is my salvation. . . . " he ends the two-volume narrative, contemplating:

> I early accustomed myself to look for the hand of God in the minutest occurrence, and to learn from it a lesson of morality and religion, and in this light every circumstance I have related was to me of importance. After all, what makes any event important, unless, by its observation we become better and wiser, and learn 'to do justly, to love mercy, and to walk humbly before God?'

It may not be too erroneous to infer that the simplicity, the freedom from affectation in an effort to conceal his true nature, the quality which critics find praiseworthy in his writing, sprang from the humility with which he asked to walk before God.

The concepts in the religion with which he lived his early life in Africa were far from those of Christianity; yet he was surprised to find some strong analogies between the customs of his countrymen and those of the Jews, particularly of the patriarchs in the pastoral state described in Genesis, such as circumcision and the manner in which offerings and feasts were made on that occasion. It led him to think that both were sprung from one people, as Dr. Gill deduced in his commentary on Genesis "the pedigree of the Africans from Afer and Afra, the descendants of Abraham by Keturah." Those all together corroborated his belief in the truth given in the Bible: "God hath made of one blood all nations of men for to dwell on all the face of the earth."

When Captain Pascal sold him away, contrary to Equiano's presumption that he would not be re-sold into slavery since it would be sinful of his master to commit an act of deception, a sin the terrible consequences of which he used to be told by his master to keep away from, he was naturally so shocked that he wished for death. He protested against Pascal and Captain Doran, who was to take him to the West Indies, that because he had been baptized his master could not sell him by the law of the land.

His baptism, the base on which he claimed his human rights, had taken place in February, 1759, in St. Margaret's Church, Westminster. The Guerin sisters, whom he had been sent by his master to wait upon while in London, treated him kindly, sending him to school and persuading his master to let him be baptized, when he expressed his wish for admittance into Heaven through baptism. Whether or not a baptized slave remained a slave had been discussed in Britain, and such judicial decisions that a slave remained a slave whether or not he had been baptized were being sharply criticized by British abolitionists with strong currents of opinion favorable to slaves prevailing.

However, his protest was quite in vain, and he sank deep in his agony, at whose bottom he collected himself and reflected that he must have done something to displease the Lord that he thus punished him.

> I, therefore, acknowledged my transgression to God . . . I besought him not to abandon me in my distress, not cast me from his mercy for ever. . . .

Sure enough, it was God who permitted it to come to pass in order to teach him resignation and submission so that he might be a better instrument in his hand. His prayer was soon answered.

In the West Indies he soon won the great favor of two important men by virtue of diligence and abilities. His new master, Robert King, never treated Equiano like a common slave, but rather like a free man, and manumitted him on July 10, 1766, when he was able to hand him the sum for the manumission proposed by King. More helpful than King was Captain Farmer, who was in charge of one of King's ships and so much liked Equiano working on his ship that he helped him earn his ransom in as many ways as he could. In fact Equiano was so able a hand that he became the captain's right-hand man, and Captain Farmer was so tenderly held by his black friend that when the captain died at sea he was called a friend and a father to him.

The freedom he earned, however, set him in a state in which he found himself in the clutch of another kind of slavery. Sin took hold of him, making him uneasy and uncertain of his eternal state, the concern over which had especially been aroused by dangers he met during the voyage to the Arctic. Determined that he would be sure of his entrance into Heaven, he set out to make himself "a first-rate Christian," by keeping the ten commandments, but in spite of his exertion, he was never happily assured. He tried churches of various denominations including those of Roman Catholicism, the Quakers, and Judaism, but none of them gave him peace of mind. Providence, however, led him to meet with some humble people who were so sure of going to Heaven as to make him envious and wondering and so friendly to each other as to remind him of the earliest followers of Christ. Through their influence, though not until he had gone through agonies in which he even wished for death, he was brought to understand that salvation comes not by works but only by faith in Christ. He came to know that it was God who had everything happen to him to lead him to God. Now the meaning of every occurrence in his life was revealed to him.

> . . . the Lord was pleased to break in upon my soul . . . I saw clearly with the eye of faith the crucified Saviour bleeding on the cross on mount Calvary: the condemned criminal under the law . . . Now every leading providential circumstance that happened to me, from the day I was taken from my parents to that hour, was then in my view, as if it had just then occurred. I was sensible of the invisible hand of God, which guided and protected me when in truth I knew it not: still the Lord pursued me although I slighted and disregarded it; this mercy melted me down.

He passed the examination given at Westminster Chapel and was received into church fellowship. He knew now what it was like to be re-born, to pass from the old man, sinful and perishable, into the new man. In 1779 at the suggestion of Governor MacNamara, in whose service he was, he applied to the Bishop of London to get ordained to spread the gospel in Africa. This wish of his to help Africans as a missionary was fruitless, and his second chance to return to Africa with a view to helping his countrymen offered by the colonization plan of Sierra Leone was again abortive. Still he continued his activities against slavery in Britain. His involvement in the abolitionist movement is said to have been brought about only a few years after his settling in England that took place in the late 1770's. In 1783, he called on Granville Sharp, a leading abolitionist, about the *Zong* incident. The case of brutal treatment of slaves being thrown overboard for the sake of insurance money apparently brought Equiano into association with abolitionists Sharp and General Oglethorpe. One of those who experienced the terror of the slave trade, Equiano fought against it, traveling round Britain speaking against it and selling copies of his book. He was one of co-signers of a letter to Granville Sharpe, written on December 15th, 1787 and entitled "The Address of Thanks of the Sons of Africa to the Honourable Granville Sharp, Esq." He wrote a letter of thanks to the Committee for the Abolition of the Slave Trade published in 1789. In the same year a letter of his addressed to Lord Hawkesbury was published, in which he emphasized: "A commercial intercourse with Africa opens an inexhaustible Source of Wealth to the manufacturing Interest of Great Britain; and to all which the Slave Trade is a physical Obstruction." The same point of view concerning the reciprocal prosperity of Britain and Africa is set forth in the ***Narrative,*** along with his comments on the economic folly which cruel slave owners were daily committing without knowing that kindness pays.

His ***Narrative*** may be said to have had no less, probably much more, influence than his lectures and letters on the advancement of the abolitionist cause. The list of subscribers which begins with the names of the Prince of Wales and the Duke of York, indicates that it had supporters from influential classes of the society, and as Paul Edwards reminds us, it must have had brisk sales, 1,900 copies selling in the Dublin 4th edition alone. Equiano was, as Edwards cites Thomas Diggs as saying, "a principal instrument in bringing about the motion for a repeal of the Slave-act."

Equiano, a Christian abolitionist transfigured from an African heathen with his narrative published, is the prototype of the successive 19th century black abolitionists, and his life shows that he had the two qualities essential to those who wish to live to liberate the oppressed, namely, humility and interest in the oppressed, both of which are in truth one that is love enlivened in man by God's grace. (pp. 8-13)

Sekio Koike, "Olaudah Equiano: The Prototypal Christian Abolitionist Transfigured from an African Heathen," in Kyushu American Literature, *No. 20, June, 1979, pp. 8-13.*

Houston A. Baker, Jr. (essay date 1980)

[*Baker is an American educator, editor, critic, author and poet. Focusing on black culture and the aesthetics of the black literary tradition, his works include* Long Black Song: Essays in Black American Literature and Culture *(1972),* Singers at Daybreak: Studies in Black American Literature *(1974), and* Modernism and the Harlem Renaissance *(1987). In the following excerpt, Baker shows that Equiano's narrative not only promotes humanitarian values, but also provides "an enthralling narration of terms for order that subsequent African writers in American have adopted."*]

The Africanness, the Christian import, and the creative self-consciousness that combine to form a discernible pattern in Wheatley's canon are more than matched in the work of Gustavus Vassa. To judge by the time span between Hammon's "An Evening Thought" and ***The Life of Olaudah Equiano,*** early black American literature developed with amazing rapidity, leaving behind the devout otherworldliness of its first published author and in just thirty years bringing forth an assured, at times brilliant, treatment of the secular problems of Africans in an alien world. Gustavus Vassa's narrative begins with a description of Essaka, a village in Benin (now Nigeria), where the author was born in 1745. Life in the village, where all men and women are chaste and free, serves as a referent for the author throughout his account. Against Essaka's seemly backdrop are set the brutality of the European slave trade, the horrors of West Indian slavery, the changing fortunes of the Seven Years' War between England and France, the cunning mechanics of the eighteenth-century industrial revolution, and the various competing theologies of a world in transition. As one might gather from the foregoing, the narrator sets forth myriad experiences, but he always remains the "African" specified by the work's title, one upon whom "all the adversity and variety of fortune . . . served only to rivet and record" the manner and customs of his homeland.

It is not Vassa's love of country alone that provided a unifying cast for the work. There is a subtlety in the ***Life*** that defies the single view. For it contains certain collocations of words, or "foregroundings," that do not easily yield their meanings to the casual reader. The Russian formalists were the first to introduce the concept of "foregrounding" to describe an instance in literary works where an unusual grouping of words calls attention to itself. In more recent years, Geoffrey Leech has employed the concept in interpreting Dylan Thomas and has also used the phrase, "cohesion of foregrounding," to describe the repetition of certain foregroundings within a single text. What I am suggesting in the case of Vassa is that foregroundings and their cohesion provide a certain force of meaning in the narrative.

The deeper semantic aspects of the book are seen in the narrator's progressive ease in the company of his "new" countrymen (the British), his omnipresent urge to enjoy the rights and privileges of a free man, his growing comprehension of the industrial revolution, and his expanding awareness of the true path to Christian salvation. What one has is a sophisticated developmental autobiography. The only way to take it as the episodic rambling of an exotic primitive is to fail to provide an adequate code to contain the work's elusive possibilities. For only at a very primitive level of literary understanding could one interpret Vassa's assertions of the "unbounded credulity and superstition" of his fellow Essakans and his descriptions of the indigenous purity of Africa's interior as testimony from the school of noble savagery.

A consideration of one of the ***Life***'s more striking foregroundings lends support to a claim for the work as a carefully crafted aesthetic text. Vassa says of his long journey with his kidnapers to the west coast of Africa: "I saw no mechanics whatever in all the way. . . . The chief employment in all these countries was agriculture, and both the males and females, as with us, were brought up to it, and trained in the arts of war." His first encounter with machine culture is aboard the *African Snow,* the slave ship that carried him to the West Indies. On board, he is amazed by the quadrant and by all other aspects of navigation. But in one of those vivid verbal structures so prevalent in the ***Life,*** Vassa—who is almost the only black on a Virginia plantation—captures one of the most significant implications of the European industrial revolution:

> I was one day sent for to his [the master's] dwelling house to fan him; when I came into the room where he was I was very much affrighted at some things I saw, and the more so as I had seen a black woman slave as I came through the house, who was cooking the dinner, and the poor creature was cruelly loaded with various kinds of iron machines; she had one particularly on her head, which locked her mouth so fast that she could scarcely speak and could not eat or drink. I was astonished and shocked at this contrivance, which I afterwards learned was called the iron muzzle.

Not only has he arrived in a land moving toward a new mechanical order (one in which the African is muzzled and cut off from nourishment), but also he has come face to face with a culture where objects of manufacture are put to cruel and inhumane use.

These conclusions are hinted in the first chapter of the ***Life*** when the author notes that the Africans' desire for products of industry (e.g., firearms) often occasioned intertribal wars designed to procure slaves as objects of barter in the transatlantic slave trade. The narrator's final response, however, is not to advocate casting out technology. Instead, he urges the conversion of technology to a more salutary end. Near the conclusion of his narrative, he asserts that various articles of "usefulness" are the "pleasing substitutes for the *torturing thumbscrew,* and the *galling chain.*" Those who will welcome such a shift are none other than British industralists. It is they who recognize the desirability of ending the slave trade and engaging Africa as a source of raw materials and a market for commerce.

From a bemused, frightened child overwhelmed by machines, the narrator moves to a stance as a prophet for a new commercial-industrial utopia in which England and Africa play complementary roles. Of course, such a projection and the way in which it is reached in the ***Life*** do not simply manifest Vassa's skill at foregrounding. They also reveal a stunning awareness of eighteenth-century economic and political currents. British industrialists did, finally, exert a large influence in the abolition of the slave trade, and they certainly had very fixed notions about the "civilizing" effects of commerce on the peoples of the world.

There are other unusual groupings of words and episodes that illustrate the depth and complexity of the ***Life.*** They surround the narrator's experiences with the sea, mercantilism, and religion as ordering constructs in a variegated existence. By careful juxtapositions (e.g., Christian baptism and a nearly fatal plunge into the Thames), seemingly naive disclaimers, and an artful blend of simple narration and forceful exposition, Vassa shows that it is possible for an African to become a complete, gentle Christian and a learned abolitionist. For if there is a public voice in the ***Life,*** it is one that ceaselessly condemns the abuses of slavery and seeks to justify the equality of Africans, while revealing, at the same instant, the author's own personal sense of salvation and freedom in a manifold world. In sum, the work amply satisfies the expectations set forth by its demurring author: "If, then, the following narrative does not appear sufficiently interesting to engage general attention, let my motive be some excuse for its publication. . . . If it affords any satisfaction to my numerous friends, at whose request it has been written, or in the smallest degree promotes the interest of humanity, the ends for which it was undertaken will be fully attained, and every wish of my heart gratified." Not only did Vassa promote the interests of humanity, but he also provided an enthralling narration of terms for order that subsequent African writers in America have adopted. His adamant call for black liberation and his repeated speculations that Africans are the chosen people of the Lord combine to give the ***Life*** a peculiarly modern tenor. It stands well in a line of accomplished successors. (pp. 15-18)

Houston A. Baker, Jr., "Terms for Order: Acculturation, Meaning, and the Early Record of the Journey," in his The Journey Back: Issues in Black Literature and Criticism, *The University of Chicago Press, 1980, pp. 1-26.*

S. E. Ogude (essay date 1982)

[*In the following excerpt, Ogude seeks to demonstrate that Equiano's* Interesting Narrative *is largely fictional, claiming that Equiano heavily borrowed from European travel literature and African legend.*]

There is a strong tendency to ignore the literary quality of Olaudah Equiano's ***Interesting Narrative,*** but as I shall demonstrate, the book has definite literary pretensions. For one thing Equiano's ***Interesting Narrative*** is presented in a popular eighteenth century literary form: the voyage. In the second place, Equiano's narrative is to a large extent fictional. Let us observe here that Equiano the narrator and Equiano the commentator are two different characters who perform different roles in the overall conception of the book. The narrator tends to be fictional in his accounts, while the commentator shows evidence of the historical man. The fictional content of Equiano's narrative may be illustrated from the early part of the ***Interesting Narrative.***

The first chapter of Equiano's ***Narrative*** is the work of a very competent collector of tales. It fuses together two disparate sets of experience: the wide range of tales about Africa that were generally retailed in travel literature and the body of legends about Africa that naturally developed among the African slaves. It is also natural that these legends should romanticize Africa and, for his immediate purposes, Equiano definitely had cause to paint a brighter picture of what was to be called the Dark Continent.

Equiano's account of his early life cannot bear close scrutiny and it is to his credit that genuine and serious attempts have been made to locate his exact home in the Ibo country. If he were kidnapped at a little over ten in 1755, it is unlikely that he would remember so much about his home at the age of 45. If we accept his surname as an anglicized version of some Ibo name, his first name, however, is not immediately recognizably Ibo. I am not myself clear why Equiano's people refer to some mahogany-colored people as "Oye Eboe," an expression that Equiano interprets as "red men living at a distance." It is possible, of course, that Essaka and Timnah, the only two African towns specifically mentioned in the ***Interesting Narrative*** may have disappeared from the face of the earth. The sort of analysis in which G. I. Jones indulges in his "Olaudah Equiano of the Niger Ibo" [see Further Reading] is based on the assumption that Equiano's account is historically and ethnographically reliable. Equiano's achievement, however, lies in his talent as a compelling narrator rather than in the authenticity of his narrative. The most interesting part of his story is the least reliable as a historical document.

For Equiano's story of his early life in Africa is an imaginative reorganization of a wide variety of tales about Africa from an equally wide range of sources. We should always bear in mind that Equiano was only ten or so when he was captured and that he was recollecting his early experience some thirty years later. Even with the best of memory there were bound to be real problems. The tenderness of his age would naturally limit the range of his experience, but Equiano's narrative suggests that he was well acquainted with every aspect of his society. The only obvious conclusion is that in his narrative, Equiano relied less on the memory of his experience and more on other sources. I would further suggest that these sources include various published accounts of travels on the Guinea Coast, accounts of fellow slaves, and, not least, Equiano's considerable narrative power that successfully blended these divergent sources into one imaginative reconstruction of what his African society might have been in the middle of the eighteenth century.

There is evidence to show that Equiano was conversant with a wide range of travel literature and that he drew heavily on these often lopsided views of Africa. A classic case is Equiano's attempt to define Guinea. He must have drawn his information from a number of sources. One obvious source is William Snelgrave's *A New Account of Some Parts of Guinea and the Slave Trade* (1734): "Guinea extends from Cape de Verde to Angola, the River Kongo being the farthest place where the English carry-on their trade." Another example from Snelgrave occurs in a general definition that combines a number of other definitions: "Guinea or Ghinney is a large extent of coast, reaching from River Sanaga to Cape Lope Gonsalvo." Equiano's definition:

> That part of Africa known by the name of Guinea to which the trade for slaves is carried on extends along the coast above 3,400 miles, from the Senegal to Angola, and includes a variety of kingdoms.

In spite of his attempt to be precise, Equiano's definition definitely derives from the same source as the two already given. Indeed, as the passage piles on information, we discover that Equiano had telescoped a number of "facts" that were available in the travel literature of the eighteenth century. For instance, when he characterized the kingdom of Benin as "The most considerable . . . both as to extent and wealth, the richness and cultivation of the soil, the power of its king and the number and warlike disposition of the inhabitants," he was obviously using non-African sources. He continues:

> It is situated nearly under the Line and extends along the coast about 170 miles, but runs back into the interior part of Africa to a distance hitherto I believe, unexplored by any traveller; and seems only terminated at length by the Empire of Abyssinia, near 1500 miles from its beginning.

First, let us compare the above vaguely worded (in spite of the deceptive attempt to play with figures) description of the limits of Benin with Thomas Astley's abstract from the literature of early eighteenth century: "The kingdom of Benin, Binnin, Binni or Benni (for so it is variously written by authors) is a country whose bounds are not well-known to travellers, or defined by geographers."

After examining various configurations of the exact position of Benin in relation to other kingdoms, including "the countries of Awerri [Warri] and Kalbari or Kallabar," Astley concludes: "We cannot pretend to vouch, much less can we ascertain its due dimension" and then adds significantly, "further than that it may extend along the coast, from Cape Lagoa, or Lagos, to Rio Forcados about an hundred or sixty, or an hundred and seventy miles." The point is not that Equiano copied Astley who was himself a mere collector of other people's accounts; the point is that Equiano's geography is directly derived from eighteenth century geography of Africa as it was then conceived by European writers. As a rule, Astley either used his sources directly or used material that occurs in several authors and, therefore, commands a degree of relative accuracy. Indeed, Equiano's assertions about the military strength of the king of Benin appear to derive originally from Dapper whom Astley credits with the story that "the king of Benin is reported able to raise in one day, twenty thousand men, and in time of need, eighty or an hundred thousand: so that he is formidable to all his neighbours. . . ."

Even in those areas where we expect Equiano's account to have an authentic stamp of originality, we discover, much to our disappointment, that his reliance on European sources is extensive. So much so that we begin to suspect that Equiano's life in his beautiful village named Essaka is quintessentially inspired by travel literature. As I shall demonstrate, much of what is authentic in ***Interesting Narrative*** has behind it the authority of travel literature. Whenever he departs from this primary source, Equiano's attempt to reconstruct his early experience from memory almost ends in disaster. We realize of course that he was considerably hampered in his effort by the necessity to adapt Ibo sounds to English sound pattern and then represent them in English orthography. The result of Equiano's experience has been nearly disastrous to his claim to a reliable memory, producing such minor riddles as *Olaudah, Timnah,* and *Essaka.* I am aware that Chinua Achebe has argued that Equiano was from "Isieke in Ihiala division" and has explained in a footnote:

> There is more than a mere hunch in my choice of Isieke (pronounced Iseke) for Equiano's Essaka. If one puts together the evidence of Igbo words in Equiano's book (including Equiano's name itself); the dialect suggested by the words; the house-building technique etc. described by Equiano, one would be led inevitably, I think, to Isieke.

The matter, however, is not as simple as that. In spite of his appeal to his memory, or his slender recollection, Equiano was conscious of his sources of information. His extraordinary personality has misled many to accept his narrative at its face value. Yet it is clear from his comment on the Igbo community of Essaka that he knew a lot more than was credibly probable, knowing fully well that traditional African societies were organized on a system of age groups with their respective taboos. His comments on the organization of his village society, on such taboo subjects as adultery and what Astley referred to as "the monthly disorder of women" are incompatible with his tender age. Few European travellers and writers of travel books failed to comment on the severity with which adultery was punished in African societies. It is part of the myth of the libidinous nature of the African character and his destructive jealousy so cruelly dramatized in Shakespeare's *Othello.* Thus we learn that even among the Hottentots, adultery "is always punished with death." Astley, citing both Jobson and Barbot, writes:

> In case of adultery, both the offenders . . . are sold out of the country without redemption; . . . the Negroes are very jealous; and if they can surprise their wives in any act of infidelity, the husband will kill the adulterer, and repudiate the wife. . . .

We may profitably compare the above quotations with Equiano's version:

> Adultery, however, was sometimes punished with slavery or death, a punishment which I believe is inflicted on it throughout most of the nations of Africa, so sacred among them is the honour of the marriage bed and so jealous are they of the fidelity of their wives. . . .

Almost all the information in the above passage is derived from the accounts of the travellers. Indeed, Equiano's extension of his comments "to most of the nations of Africa"

THE
INTERESTING NARRATIVE
OF
THE LIFE
OF
OLAUDAH EQUIANO,
OR
GUSTAVUS VASSA,
THE AFRICAN.
WRITTEN BY HIMSELF.

VOL I.

Behold, God is my salvation: I will trust and not be afraid, for the Lord Jehovah is my strength and my song: he also is become my salvation. And in that day shall ye say, Praise the Lord, call upon his name, declare his doings among the people. Isaiah xii. 2, 4.

FIRST AMERICAN EDITION.

NEW-YORK:
Printed and Sold by W. DURELL, *at his Book-Store and Printing-Office,* No. 19, Q. Street.
M,DCC,XCI.

Frontispiece and title page for the first American edition of Equiano's autobiography.

is a veiled acknowledgement of his debt to these Europeans who delighted in retailing salacious information about Africa.

It comes as a shock to discover that Equiano's proud assertions about the industry of his people, their cleanliness, their humanity, and their religious institutions were probably derived from these foreign sources. His observations on certain African traditional beliefs and practice and their similarity to Jewish tradition would, at first, appear original. Again, much of the observation may have been derived from contemporary accounts of travellers. Take the following passage from Equiano, for instance:

> I have before remarked that the natives of this part of Africa are extremely cleanly. This necessary habit of decency was with us a part of religion, and therefore we had many purifications and washings; indeed almost as many and used on the same occasions, if my recollection does not fail me, as the Jews. Those that touched the dead at any time were obliged to wash and purify themselves before they could enter a dwelling house. Every woman too, at certain times, was forbidden to come into a dwelling-house or touch any person or anything we ate.

Now compare with the above passage, the following from Astley, taking note of the context of both passages:

> the Whidah Negroes seem to have borrowed from the Jews the law of separation from their wives at certain seasons. On these occasions the women are obliged, on pain of death, to quit the husbands or parents' house as soon as they find themselves ill, and to forsake all correspondence with any person as long as their disorder continues. According to the number of women in a family, there is one or several houses at the end of the inclosure, where they remain under the care of some old women who tend them, and take care to wash and purify them before they return to their families.

Thus where it is verifiable, the evidence presented by Equiano almost always leads to a European source. The conclusive evidence of nearly total dependence on other sources for what he claimed to be his personal experience strengthens, in a curious way, the personality of Equiano. It also gives ***Interesting Narrative*** a literary quality that it shares with the fiction of Defoe and Swift. Equiano's talent as a narrator and his ability to impose his personality on a whole range of experiences and dominate every bit of them with confidence and conviction is evident throughout ***Interesting Narrative.*** In Equiano, credibility becomes an aspect of character rather than of the tale. He tells every story from his standpoint and always with considerable advantage to himself. If Constantine Phipps (Lord Mulgrave) had not published the account of his voyage to the North Pole, we would have had to conclude from Equiano's account of that nearly disastrous voyage that Equiano played a much more important part than that of the personal servant of a scientist. Indeed, from the way Equiano introduced the subject of the voyage in his ***Interesting Narrative,*** one would think that he was one of the principal actors in the undertaking:

> Thus I went on [purifying the briny element and making it fresh] till May 1773, when I was roused by the sound of fame to seek new adventures, and find, towards the North Pole what our Creator never intended we should, a passage to India.

It is easy to demonstrate that the ensuing narrative could have been different if Lord Mulgrave never published his *Voyage Towards the North Pole.* Similarly, much of the last section of the ***Interesting Narrative*** was not particularly original and, although suggestions for alternative commodities to slaves in the trade between England and Africa were common, Equiano's ideas appear closest to those of Clarkson in *The Impolicy of the African Slave Trade.*

Yet in spite of these apparently alarming revelations, the integrity of Equiano's primary purpose remains unimpaired. We might almost say that it was essential for the realization of his purpose, that Equiano did what he did: create for the African the image of the achiever. For ***Interesting Narrative,*** in spite of its occasional display of spiritual humility, is perhaps the first deliberate attempt to celebrate black achievement in print. Equiano must have had at the back of his mind the ideas of Hume, later eminently reechoed by Thomas Jefferson, about the inferiority of the black race. He refutes these ideas, first by creating the fiction of beautiful Essaka and second by realizing in himself the portrait of the supreme black achiever. He elevates his meanest act to the highest level of heroism. He definitely was not a prince, but he was high born and was destined to receive the highest title in his society. He was a born man of action and was, if we believe him, definitely acquainted with all the horrors of war before he was ten. Equiano expects us to suspend our disbelief as we watch him watching a battle at the village common from a tree top. He has a charmed life. Nothing really hurts him, not even poisonous snakes, and at the battle front in foreign lands and in navel engagements far away from the beautiful plains of Essaka, the bullets were to fly about him without as much as grazing him. He was even more successful as a sailor who in moments of extreme danger always took charge of the situation when his superior white officers had lost their nerve. What is more he saw his achievement as a divine gift that he held in trust for his fellow men. His own comments on his role in the Bahamas shipwreck sufficiently underscore his sense of his own importance:

> I could not help thinking, that if any of these people had been lost God would charge me with their lives, which perhaps was one cause of my labouring so hard for their preservation, and indeed every one of them afterwards seemed so sensible of the service I had rendered them, and while we were on the key I was a kind of chieftain amongst them.

Always, Equiano sees and presents himself as first among men, be they black or white. Even in matters of religion he occupied the pride of place among all comers and so great was his zeal for the Christian life that an Indian prince on board the ship bound for South America was compelled to ask: "How comes it that all the white men on board who can read and write, and observe the sun, and know all things, yet swear, lie, and get drunk, only excepting yourself?" It is true that the Indian, wisely or foolishly, chose to go to hell with the white men, but Equiano has made his point; that is what really matters. Above all, Equiano is the great achiever who bought his own liberty and, in spite of all odds, maintained a respectable position in a hostile world.

Because of the insistent note of self-dramatization and self-approval in the characterization of the central actor-character of the ***Interesting Narrative*** we tend to forget that the book is built on a solid fictional base. Indeed, it follows the traditions of the travelogue and the adventure tale that were popular throughout the eighteenth century. In many respects Equiano emerges as a typical Defoe character whose strength lies in his wide experience as a traveller and his survival instincts even in the most hopeless situation. Equiano was, by any standard, a well-traveled man. His experience spans the continents of Africa, America, Europe, and part of Asia. ***Interesting Narrative*** belongs in some respects to the tradition of the *voyage imaginaire* and shares some of the characteristic traits of the tradition. Equiano has and shows all the weaknesses of great travellers—a love of exaggeration, a respect for lies about distant places, and an open display of prejudice in order to conceal ignorance. The voyage form was therefore a splendid vehicle for the propagation of the new ideas about Africa. Always Equiano was aware of his self-imposed duty of giving Africa a new image among Europeans and thus constantly opposed black values to European ideals. He seems to have seen himself as a typical Ibo man and the Ibo people as typical Africans. His record of achievement is thus the record of black achievement. According to Equiano the Ibo people combine hardiness, intelligence, zeal, and integrity with perfection of form and physical fitness. In his naive idealization of his people, and in utter disregard for the European idea of the Ibo, Equiano proudly declares: "Deformity is indeed unknown amongst us. . . . Numbers of the natives of Eboe now in London might be brought in support of this assertion, for in regard to complexion, ideas of beauty are wholly relative." This history is worse than false, for Equiano definitely knew that only physically healthy blacks were ever allowed to cross the Atlantic. Besides, the idea that blacks were generally physically perfect was fairly commonplace. It was part of the noble savage cult that endowed the Indian, the African, and later the Polynesian with remarkable physical vitality and perfection of parts; hence black characters in English and French fiction were generally "well proportioned," for it was believed that physical and moral degeneration was a concomitant of civilization. James Grainger, in his *Essay on the More Common West India Diseases,* observed that black women rarely had deformed children and offered his medical opinion:

> Deformity in children would seem to be owing to swathing the infants too tight, and by the preposterous use of stays and straight clothing—Negro children are not thus encombered; and never deformed except by accidents. . . .

Grainger's explanation has all the marks of primitivistic adoration of the natural man with his dark heroic frame. It is a different matter when ethnic groups are described.

Bryan Edwards, whose account of the various ethnic groups of Africa in British West Indies is generally accurate, describes the Ibos as cowardly. When James Grainger, in *The Sugar Cane* describes the various ethnic groups of African slaves in the West Indies, the portrait of the Ibos that emerges is far from heroic. The Ibos are not like the Kormantyns who formed the cream of the Maroons and the dread of every West Indian Planter. These must not be bought, because they are "of breed too generous for the servile field," the slaves from the Guinea coast were chronic suicides, and those from Cape Coast were stubborn. Then he comments on the ravages leashed on the plantations by cane rats and advises the planter to cherish the cat and spare the snake for obvious reasons. Then he adds: "Thy foes, the teeth-filled Ibbos also love / Nor thou their wayward appetite restrain." His explanatory note on the above lines adds an entirely new angle to the Ibo image:

> Teethfil'd Ibbos or Ebbos, as they are more commonly called are a numerous nation. Many of them have their teeth filed and are blackened in an extra-ordinary manner. They make good slaves when bought young, but are in general foul feeders.

Dr. James Grainger had varied medical experience, having served as an army surgeon before establishing a private practice in London. He then went to St. Kitts in 1759 as a physician. He had links with the literary circle of London and was well known to Samuel Johnson, Dr. Thomas Percy, and the landscape enthusiast and poet William Shenstone. Grainger's ode on solitude had appeared in 1755, and, according to Boswell, Johnson had characterized the first stanza of the poem as "very noble." Grainger showed evidence of great learning in *The Sugar Cane,* which combines considerable literary quality with fairly reliable information not only on sugar cane culture and the white planter, but also on the ethnography of the slave population in the West Indies. Indeed, his *Essay on the More Common West India Diseases* contained "hints on the management of negroes." His note on the Ibos here is also far from flattering and, although it was obviously erroneous, it would appear to have been the general opinion about the Ibos in the West Indies and to a large extent agrees with his explanatory note:

> In Ibbo country, the women chiefly work; they therefore are to be preferred to the men of the same country at a Negro sale; And yet there is a great risk in buying women; for from their scantiness of clothing in their country, not to mention other reasons, they often labour under incurable obstructions of the menses, whence proceed barrenness and many disorders.

Grainger's pseudomedical explanation is sheer fiction, but it is hardly worse than Equiano's romanticized recollections of his early childhood. To judge by his own account, Equiano's Africa is a veritable paradise where man is at one with man and nature rewards with prodigious yield the labor of man. Indeed the slave raider merely underscores the essential goodness of this natural society where the harshest words of reproach are "may you rot" or "may you swell" or "may a beast take you." That was part of Equiano's deliberate purpose, though unstated, of reversing the contemporary European image of Africa as a land of barbarous hordes of savages, the type of image which slave traders and plantation owners paraded in the popular press. In the process, Equiano had to romanticize a past that he never knew, and it is to the credit of his creative commonsense that not only his contemporaries, but even modern commentators have willingly accepted his portrait of his "Igbo heritage" as faithfully if somewhat nostalgically presented. The fact, of course, is that the first chapter of Equiano's book is a synthesis of aspects of a wide range of African societies as represented in travel literature as well as in romantic tales about Africa that sustained the spirit of the slaves in their forced and unbearably harsh exile. (pp. 31-40)

S. E. Ogude, "Facts into Fiction: Equiano's Narrative Reconsidered," in Research in African Literatures, *Vol. 13, No. 1, Spring, 1982, pp. 31-43.*

Wilfred D. Samuels (essay date 1983)

[*Samuels is a Costa Rican-born American educator, literary critic, and editor whose work includes* Five Afro-Caribbean Voices in American Culture, 1917-1929 *(1979). In the following excerpt, he claims that the themes and styles introduced in the* Interesting Narrative *continue to dominate black literary traditions, particularly Equiano's successful creation of the "prototypical Black hero" who appears through the merging of the narrative voice and the narrator's fictional self.*]

For the most part, the recent literature concerning Black Slave narrative/autobiographical texts continues to overlook the significant role that Olaudah Equiano and his narrative, ***The Interesting Narrative of the Life of Olaudah Equiano, or Gustavus Vassa, The African, Written by himself*** (1789), play in the development of the Black literary tradition. Although several historians have identified his seminal role as an eighteenth century abolitionist, and although a few literary scholars have suggested the central place his narrative should occupy among the works published by the cadre of Black writers who were in the vanguard, most omit this luminary writer of Black life or fail to explore the relation of his work to modern Black fiction. Yet, it is impossible not to agree with Arna Bontemps that Equiano's narrative is perhaps "the first truly notable book in the genre. In fact, it is not in any way farfetched to perceive it as the mold from which successive narratives were cast, and even more importantly to see it as an important prototype of the Black novel. This is particularly true when one takes into consideration the fact that Olaudah Equiano was one of the first Black writers to record the African *and* the diaspora experiences of slavery, which he knew first-hand while a slave in Africa, the Caribbean, the North American Colonies, and England. It becomes even more convincing when one takes careful assessment of the thematics and characterizations of the narrative, for like the modern hero in Black fictions, Equiano remains, above all in his narrative, an exile in a manner that differs very little from Bigger Thomas in Wright's *Native Son* (1940), Ellison's protagonist in *Invisible Man* (1952), Milkman Dead in Morrison's *Song of Solomon* (1978), or Okonkwo in Chinua Achebe's *Things Fall Apart* (1959). Suffering for the most part from a sense of socio-cultural liminality and ontological void, he is engulfed throughout his work with a sense of nothingness which results, to a degree, either from circumstances over which he has no control, or from the conscious decisions which he makes. In his response to life, Equiano epitomizes the Black fictional character whose research is for wholeness and meaning in a world that often does not offer incorporation or fulfillment.

An Igbo born in what is perhaps now eastern Nigeria, Equiano was kidnapped, along with his sister, into slavery at the age of eleven. In his narrative, he recapitulates his severance from his African homeland, the horror of the journey through the "Middle Passages," and his multifarious experiences as a slave in Barbados, Virginia, Philadelphia, and England, his adopted home. Equiano begins his twelve-chapter, two-volume work with an introduction to the manners and customs of his Essakan community, which includes descriptions of the social, political, and economic systems of eighteenth century traditional Igboan life. He seems careful to emphasize his belief that though his culture was built on simple manners and few luxuries, and though it was one in which slavery was practiced and polygamy was a way of life, it was judicious. Adultery was condemned, and slaves were often considered members of the community.

Because Equiano's announced purpose is to promote the abolitionist's cause, he uses both volumes to call the attention of his audience to the real nature of slavery. After carefully delineating, with the most vivid images possible, the perilous path traveled by the slave vessels, the decadent behavior of the slavers, the effort of those taken to commit suicide by jumping overboard, the galling of chains, and excruciating cries of the women and the dying, Equiano turns his attention to what to him was the most unpardonable aspect of the experience: the separation of family members. He declares:

> O ye nominal Christians! might not an African ask you—Learned you this from your God, who says unto you, Do unto all men as you would men should do unto you? Must every tender feeling be likewise sacrificed to your avarice? . . . Why are parents to lose their children, brother their sisters, or husbands their wives? Surely, this is a new refinement in cruelty, which, while it has no advantage to atone for it, thus aggravate distress and adds fresh horrors even to the wretchedness of slavery.

Although the frightening experiences that he either witnessed or experienced directly during ten years of enslavement led him to wish for his death on several occasions, Equiano succeeded, through his own business ventures, shrewdness, and perseverance, to amass the necessary amount to purchase his freedom. Never returning to Africa, although he traveled as commissary of provisions in the first party of emigrants who set out to settle Sierra Leone, Equiano spent the remainder of his life in England working to abolish slavery.

The polemical nature of his narrative obscures the fact that the then forty-four year-old Igboan wanted to do more than graphically describe the horrors and atrocities of slavery. In the spirit of his high maritime adventures which took him half way around the world and on an expedition to the Arctic, Equiano seems to venture beyond the limits of the extant slave narratives into the unchartered waters of the developmental stages of this genre. Consequently, in the process of recreating his historical self, Equiano succeeds in creating a narrative voice and a fictional self that emerge at the end of the second volume to form a prototypical Black hero and introduce themes and styles that continue to dominate the Black literary tradition. His practice of combining and ordering words (a form of masking) to pull out of them a wide variety of meaning allows us to see in the introduction to Chapter Two yet another and perhaps more important reason for writing his narrative, for here Equiano confesses that he still looks "back with pleasure on the first scenes of (his) life, though that pleasure has been for the most part mingled with sorrows."

Equiano, who had explained earlier that art in his community focused on "some interesting scene of life," carefully designs episodic chapters for his narrative, and he uses them as vehicles to transport him retrospectively to the earliest stages of his life, the formative years which were spent in Africa, to better understand the development, discovery, and creation of an identity which for him remained salient and which is to be found in his identification of himself as THE AFRICAN. The narrative, then, allows him to vicariously travel the labyrinthian path that had led him from his *axis mundi* and had left him, the son of a village elder, a slave—an identity which stood in direct contrast to his perception of himself. Incorporated into his pronouncements, then, is the crux of the conflicts which result from his idealized African self, which Equiano accepts as his legacy, and the harsh reality that, having served as a slave in a foreign culture, he had not been able to fully realize this self. Thus, Equiano is not merely concerned with historical truth or abolitionist propaganda: him he is fundamentally interested in his private experiences which he presents through his creation of a single self. This results more in autobiography than in history, and it allows us to look at "the self as the container of meaning."

What can be perceived as Equiano's interest in presenting a single self is firmly embedded in the frontispiece with which he begins the narrative. An engraved portrait, the frontispiece features an individual who, precisionly adorned in both frock and waist coats, ruffled shirt, and cravat, bears the appearance of eighteenth century gentility: he presents an image of an individual of excellent character, sincerity, humility, integrity, and confidence. Although this dress might cause one to associate him with the elegantly dressed and indulgently treated Black slave-servant of the likes of Dr. Johnson's Francis, Equiano's self-portraiture throughout the narrative reveals that the self which he attempts to depict in the frontispiece must not be divorced from the name that appears beneath it: OLAUDAH EQUIANO, THE AFRICAN. Although he dons for his portrait, then, the most conventional clothing of British aristocracy, he does not do so solely to reflect the social order of his Georgian world or the formulaic role which is his. His clothing serves in fact to disguise and introduce from the outset the fundamental metaphor of self which he will amplify throughout the narrative: Africa(n), a metaphor for rebirth and rejuvenation, also signifies dignity, honor and perhaps the wholeness which he seeks. Its name, like his image, must be associated with the highest values, morals, and qualities one might seek.

Without a doubt, then, Equiano's portrait, an iconic signifier, projects the idea that he is a paragon of African virtues. His dark oval face frames a luminously dignified smile, and his high, intelligent forehead gives way to noble eyes that sparkle with honesty and integrity, a broad, African nose and heavy but sturdy lips. Crowned by a crop of carefully manicured hair that cascades naturally like a pharoah's khat down the back of his unwigged head, his elliptical visage resembles a ritual mask that is imperviously pedestaled to his broad shoulders. Instead of a former slave or a pampered servant, Equiano, in dress and aire, bears a *mark of grandeur and distinction*—one which might be considered commensurate with British aristocracy, but also one which, when we are mindful of the fact that he was born into the Essakan aristocracy and that he believed himself *destined* to be titled like his father and brother, must not only bear ties to his African self but fundamentally to the metaphor of self that Equiano wished to develop. When one further considers that Equiano published his own narrative without the introductory authenticating documents that later became important instruments of verification in the slave narrative, the significance of this powerful portrait and the meaning he intends it to convey reveal his complexity as a creative writer and his effort to use symbols competently in his narrative. He is, from the outset, a master masker.

To be sure, the unique and powerful aspects of Equiano's narrative are to be found in the narrator's voice and eyes, which present the gamut of the Black experience in Africa, the Caribbean, North American Colonies, and England during the late eighteenth century. Equally important, however, is the masterful manner in which Equiano successfully masks his intention of developing and maintaining a metaphor of self from the frontispiece to the very last page of his narrative, suggesting in the process the intricate foundation of the Black literary tradition. (pp. 99-100)

Wilfred D. Samuels, "Retrospective Glance: The Interesting Narrative of the Life of Olaudah Equiano Reconsidered," in Negro History Bulletin, *Vol. 46, No. 4, October-December, 1983, pp. 99-100.*

Victor C. D. Mtubani (essay date 1984)

[*In the following excerpt, Mtubani examines contemporary black participation in and reaction to late eighteenth-century abolitionist efforts, focusing on the impact and influence of Equiano's autobiography and letters.*]

The most articulate spokesman for the African cause, and by far the most widely travelled African living in England in the second half of the eighteenth century, was Olaudah Equiano (1745-1797), sometimes known as Gustavus Vassa, the African. Unlike [Ignatius] Sancho, Equiano had experience of Africa, having been born of Igbo stock in Nigeria. He was ten years old when he was captured and sold into slavery. He did not regain his freedom till 1766, when he was twenty-one years old. During that time he had travelled widely and had served two masters, Captain Pascal and Mr. Robert King. He had served Pascal during the campaigns of General Wolfe in Canada and Admiral Boscawen in the Mediterranean, during the Seven Years' War with France. He had made numerous voyages between America and the West Indies in the service of Robert King. He had visited England also several times while still Pascal's slave and even had been sent to school by Pascal's cousins, the Misses Guerin. After obtaining his freedom he had toured the Mediterranean, had been to the polar region on an expedition and had spent some time among the Mosquito Indians of South America as an assistant to an English doctor. The main concern of this paper is with Equiano as a spokesman for the African cause.

Equiano finally settled in England in the 1770s. By the 1780s he had become deeply involved in the politics of the black people, championing their cause and fighting for the abolition of the slave trade. In his role as the black spokesman, he made contacts with such influential and sympathetic whites as Granville Sharp. It was Equiano, for example, who informed Sharp about the *Zong* murders. Sharp recorded on March 19, 1783, that "Gustavus Vassa, a negro called on me, with an account of 130 negroes being thrown alive into the sea." That Equiano played the most important part in bringing the *Zong* murders to the public eye there can be no doubt. Sharp says that Equiano not only told him about the murders, but also pleaded with him to do something to bring the culprits to justice. As he says, he finally took the case to court "having been earnestly solicited and called upon by a poor negro for my assistance to avenge the blood of his slaughtered countrymen." Here then, we see an African actively involved in securing justice for his people. The fact that in the end, he did not succeed in getting the offenders convicted and punished is not the issue here. What is important is that Equiano acted in the *Zong* affair and, in conjunction with Sharp, General James Oglethorpe and other sympathizers, brought this shocking case before the court and the public.

By the late 1780s Equiano had become the recognized leader of the black community in Britain, in succession to Sancho. In 1785 he and other Africans addressed a letter to the Quakers, thanking them for their campaign against slavery and the slave trade. This action again shows Equiano's wide contacts with people and organizations sympathetic to the African cause. In 1786 Equiano's qualities of leadership were recognized by the British Government which appointed him His Majesty's Commissary for Stores for the Black Poor going to Sierra Leone. This appointment, however, was terminated in March 1787, before the expedition left Plymouth for Sierra Leone. The fact that he was dismissed because of his outspoken defence of the black people against the high-handed actions of Joseph Irwin, the Agent, is particularly significant, for it shows his unwillingness to be an instrument of his own people's exploitation. He clearly took seriously his responsibilities as Commissary and as a black man. By protesting loudly and vigorously against Irwin and by openly accusing him of callousness and high-handedness in his dealings with the prospective settlers, he was giving notice that he was no Uncle Tom. He was prepared to risk challenging the establishment itself in order to obtain justice.

The attack on Equiano that followed his dismissal as Commissary illustrates clearly that certain sections of white, even pro-abolitionist, society would not tolerate what they considered insubordination. For example, Equiano was accused of stirring discontent and rebellion among the black people. And on April 14, 1787, the *Public Advertiser* published a vicious, racist letter which accused Equiano of, among other things, "advancing falsehoods as deeply black as his jetty face." Equiano, to his credit, was unrepentant, and, as it turned out, his criticisms of the expedition and especially of Irwin were soon proved correct.

On his return to London from Plymouth, Equiano continued his call for significant changes in the condition of the blacks and to campaign for the abolition of slavery and the slave trade. He was especially scathing in his attack on some of the supporters of slavery. In 1785 James Tobin had published his *Cursory Remarks upon the Rev. Mr. Ramsay's Essay on the Treatment and Conversion of African Slaves in the British Sugar Colonies* in which he had attacked Ramsay, a strong supporter of abolition. Equiano replied to Tobin with an open letter, published in the *Public Advertiser* of 28 January, 1788, in which he argued that no person "less ferocious than a tiger or wolf" would try to justify West Indian slavery and its attendant cruelties. Angrily he told him:

> I confess my cheek changes colour with resentment against your unrelenting barbarity, and wish you from my soul to run the gauntlet of Lex Talionis at this time; for as you are so fond of flogging others; it is no bad proof of your deserving a flagellation on yourself.

These are more powerful lines than those of Sancho. Yet Equiano also cannot free himself completely from the conventions of white society. The statement, "my cheek changes colour," coming from a black man, is merely a white cliché. Equiano can do better than that.

Equiano was uncompromising in his attacks on racism and prejudice. For example, he tells Tobin, who had expressed strong opposition to interracial marriages: "A more foolish prejudice than this never warped a cultivated mind—for as no contamination of the virtues of the heart would result from the union, the mixture of colour would be of no consequence."

The theme is not new, but as the personal expression of a former black slave the letter is significant; and in conjunction with Equiano's biography to be published the following year, it marks the growth of a more forceful body of opinion by a black than is to be found in the Sancho letters two decades earlier, or indeed in the effusions of some of the white abolitionist writers.

Tobin was not the only pro-slavery writer whom Equiano attacked publicly. In 1786 Gordon Turnbull had published his *An Apology for Negro Slavery: or the West India Planters Vindicated from the Charge of Inhumanity.* As a reply to the advocate of "this infamous traffic," Equiano published a letter in the *Public Advertiser* of 5 February, 1788. In it he strongly defended Dr. Ramsay, whom Turnbull had attacked viciously: "But we trust that inspite of your *hissing* zeal and impotent malevolence against Mr. Ramsay, his noble purpose of philanthropy will be productive of much good to many and . . . be a means of bringing about the abolition of slavery."

To Turnbull's assertion that slaves were well treated, Equiano's reply was uncompromising. It was, he retorted, "A glaring falsehood!" In this letter, as in that to Tobin, the reader can easily identify with Equiano. The style is lively and direct and the feeling is intense. There are not the cumbersome and self-conscious devices that one often finds in Sancho's letters.

In his campaign against slavery, Equiano appealed to all sections of British society. On March 21, 1788, for instance, he even wrote to the Queen, imploring "your Majesty's compassion for millions of my African countrymen, who groan under the lash of tyranny in the West Indies." One might wonder whether Equiano really believed that the Queen could do anything about slavery. It would be wrong, however, to see this letter as a misguided effort. While the Queen had no power to interfere with slavery, she could help in an indirect way. For example, she could put pressure on members of the Royal Family to end their close association with the West Indian planters. If the Queen set an example, it would be easier to put pressure on the public to follow her action. In any case, such a letter should be seen as a part of a larger propaganda campaign to influence opinion and encourage the friends of abolition.

Equiano worked in close association with other Africans in London such as Cugoano. In 1788 they wrote the "Letters of Sons of Africa" which they sent to various public figures, including such politicians as Sir William Dolben, Pitt and Fox. It is the letter addressed to Sharp, however, that is most moving. In it the Africans expressed their appreciation for the part which the abolitionist was playing on their behalf: "We are those who were considered as slaves, even in England itself, till your aid and exertions set us free." They tell Sharp: "Sir, you may allow us to believe that the name of GRANVILLE SHARP, our constant and generous friend, will be drawn forth by our more enlightened posterity, and distinguishingly marked in future times for gratitude and praise."

This letter is particularly significant when we consider that after Equiano's dismissal from the job of Commissary for Stores, even Sharp had wrongly believed the story told about him by Irwin and the English press. The fact that Equiano remained a great admirer of Sharp shows that he always put the interests of the black people before his own. In all these letters one sees clearly the hand of Equiano. Similarly, it was he who sent a letter of thanks to the Committee of the newly formed Society for the Abolition of the Slave Trade. And in 1789 his letter to Lord Hawkesbury was published in the evidence of the Committee investigating the slave trade. These letters by Equiano alone and by Equiano and other "Sons of Africa" show clearly that Africans in Britain were not just passive observers of the debate on their fate, but active participants in it.

In 1789 Equiano published his autobiography, ***The Interesting Narrative of Olaudah Equiano or Gustavus Vassa, the African,*** as a contribution to the anti-slavery campaign. The book proved popular, going, before 1800, into eight editions in Britain alone, as well as being translated into Dutch and German. Equiano himself travelled widely in England, Scotland and Ireland, selling his book and speaking against slavery.

The ***Narrative*** gives details of Equiano's travels as a slave and as a freeman, campaigning with Wolfe's army in Canada and Boscawen's fleet in the Mediterranean, as a merchant seaman in the West Indies and as a Surgeon's mate in the Phipps Expedition to the Arctic in 1772. However, it is much more than a catalogue of places and events, although these are interesting in themselves. At a deeper level the book shows Equiano's attitude to important issues of the day as they affected a black man and a slave. Take, as an example, his account of his impotence against force oppressing him. In the winter of 1762-63 he is re-sold and sent back into slavery. When he tells Captain Doran, his new master, that Captain Pascal could not have sold him, the reply which he gets is simple, but shattering:

> "Why," said he, "did not your master buy you?" I confessed he did. "But I have served him," said I, "many years, and he has taken all my wages and prize-money . . . besides this I have been baptized; and by the laws of the land no man has a right to sell me." And I added, that I had heard a lawyer and others . . . tell my master so. They both said that those people who told me so were not my friends.

When Equiano continues protesting against his slavery, "Captain Doran said I talked too much English; and if I did not behave myself well, and be quiet, he had a method on board to make me." Equiano is no fool. He knows that he is beaten: "I was too well convinced of his power over me to doubt what he said." Here then, we see, in no uncertain terms, the issue of authority or power as it was exercised over the black slaves. In these few lines is expressed the totality of that power.

Equiano was baptized at St. Margaret's, Westminster in 1758. In 1768 he visited Turkey, a Moslem country. At this time Christians did not consider Islam to be anything other than a "heathen" practice. So here we see Equiano, a devout Christian and a Calvinist, visiting a "heathen" country. The treatment which he receives there goes against all expectations:

> The natives . . . treated me always with great civility. In general I believe they are fond of black people; and several of them gave me pressing invitations to stay amongst them . . .

When he visited Turkey again in 1769 he was no less impressed: "I always found the Turks very honest in their dealings." The impression which Equiano obtains of Turkey contrasts sharply with the view which he has of so-called Christian countries. He, a Christian, had been denied freedom and humanity by fellow-Christians. Yet in a non-Christian country like Turkey he had been considered a brother. It is not surprising, therefore, that in his attitude in contrasting Islam with Christianity he is sometimes bitter.

In Turkey, Equiano is impressed by the respect given to women. By contrast, he is shocked and disgusted by the barbarities practiced on black, women slaves by so-called Christians. As he says, "it was almost a constant practice with our clerks, and other whites, to commit violent depredations on the chastity of the female slaves."

> I have known our mates to commit these acts most shamefully, to the disgrace, not of Christians only, but of men. I have even known them to gratify their brutal passion with females not ten years old. . . . And yet in Montserrat I have seen a negro man staked to the ground, and cut most shockingly, and then his ears cut off bit by bit, because he had been connected with a white woman who was a common prostitute.

It is in the light of his disillusion with the shocking and immoral practices of the so-called Christians that he tells Captain Hughes: "I had been twice among the Turks, yet had never seen any such usage with them, and much less could I have expected anything of this kind amongst Christians."

It is not just that Equiano, having once been a slave, reacts so strongly against the inhumane and oppressive practices of the whites. Rather it is also that he is genuinely ashamed of these people whose religion he shares. He has judged them by the strict, humane standards of their religion and found their actions woefully inadequate. It is against this background that we must view his statement contrasting slavery in Africa with that in the West Indies: "Those prisoners who were not sold or redeemed we kept as slaves: but how different was their condition from that of the slaves in the West Indies!"

Similarly, we must view as an expression of disgust and disappointment his statement that after "finding those who in general termed themselves Christians not so honest or so good in their morals as the Turks, I really thought the Turks were in a safer way of salvation than my neighbours." Equiano's indictment of false or nominal Christians contrasts, in its combination of passionate pleading and grim realism, with much of the sentimental writing of the period.

Nevertheless, Equiano's behaviour was sometimes ambiguous. This is understandable when his alienation in the white world is considered. For example, throughout his travels he is always longing "to return to Old England." He longs to see "those pleasing scenes I left behind, where fair Liberty in bright array / Makes darkness bright, and e'en illumines day." Could it be that he has forgotten that the bright liberty which he talks about does not really shine for slaves in "Old England?" I do not think so. Despite these warm sentiments, Equiano was still an outsider, as all blacks were. If he had not been, he would not have campaigned as he did for the rights of black people. Also, when he finally settled in Old England he always designated himself as "the African." In other words, as an outsider in English society. Edwards puts it well when he says that Equiano, as an outsider "never ceases to be aware of himself (nor does the world let him) as a negro, a former slave, a member of a despised and maltreated race." We saw how, as Commissary for Stores, he came face to face with the sad reality of a black man in a white society. We saw how certain sections of the public in Old England attacked him in crude, racist tones. While there is no doubt about Equiano's love for England and its comparative freedom, there is equally no doubt about his awareness of the precarious position of a black man in it. This heightens the ambivalence in the book.

Ambivalence also exists elsewhere in the ***Narrative.*** For example, how should a slave react to a good master when, as in Equiano's case, he knows that slavery is in itself a bad thing? In the ***Narrative,*** as Edwards points out, the very whites who befriend Equiano are also involved in buying and selling his people. Because of this awareness, one is not sure what to think of the gratitude which Equiano expressed to Robert King for allowing him his freedom. It is possible to argue that King was a good man to allow him freedom at all, when other masters did not often do so. Yet it is no less true that it was freedom which Equiano bought by paying the full amount that King originally purchased him with. Such indeed is the high price, despite Farmer's telling King that "Gustavus has earned you more than a hundred a-year, and will still save you money, as he will not leave you." What is clear is that black men were vulnerable to all the whims and caprices of the slave owner. The ambivalence in Equiano is just an indication of that insecurity and confusion.

There is even greater ambiguity when Captain Farmer dies and Equiano takes charge of the ship. Farmer's death means the loss of one of Equiano's best benefactors, but it also gives him the opportunity to display his skill as a navigator and his qualities as a leader. He himself puts it thus:

> I now obtained a new appellation and was called Captain. This elated me not a little and it was flattering to my vanity to be thus styled by as high a title as any man in this place possessed.

And in another episode, as a result of the incompetence of one of his Captains, Equiano takes charge of the ship, rather ironic for a former slave. And there are indications in the text that Equiano is not unaware of the irony.

As a black man in a white world and as a slave or ex-slave, Equiano had to keep adapting to new and sometimes contrary experiences. It was these experiences, perspectives of, and insights into white society which prepared him well for the leadership of the black community. As Walvin says, "In his great range of occupations, as slave, sailor, domestic, commissary, princely African and black Englishman and friend to the new 'popular' London radicals, Equiano was able to speak with greater authority and assurance than Sancho, whose life had been, in black terms, relatively sheltered."

This was a fact recognized by the Society for the Abolition of the Slave Trade. In a manuscript letter of 1792, Equiano wrote about his role in the campaign against slavery and the slave trade: "I trust that my going about has been of much use in the Cause of the accu(r)sed Slave Trade—a Gentleman of the Committee the Rev. Dr. Baker has said that I am more use to the Cause than half the people in the Country—I wish to God I could be so."

His writings and activities clearly suggest that abolition was the most important cause of his life in England. He did everything he could to further the black cause. (pp. 90-7)

Victor C. D. Mtubani, "The Black Voice in Eighteenth-Century Britain: African Writers against Slavery and the Slave Trade," in PHYLON: The Atlanta University Review of Race and Culture, *Vol. 45, No. 2, June, 1984, pp. 85-97.*

Wilfred D. Samuels (essay date 1985)

[*In the following excerpt, Samuels demonstrates that in* The Interesting Narrative, *Equiano fused the historicity of his adventures with allusions to the self that had been denied realization because of slavery, fashioning thereby an image of himself to veil his "covert intentions."*]

The author of the slave narrative confronted the difficult task of reporting his lived experiences during slavery to an audience which did not recognize him as a member of its society and, in fact, viewed him "as an alien whose assertion of common humanity and civil rights conflicted with some of its basic beliefs," including the institutionalization of theories of the racial superiority of whites and the inferiority of African slaves. This difficulty was further compounded in certain cases by the former slave, who addressed the question of abolishing slavery, an institution to which members of his audience were often inextricably bound, because, economically speaking, their prosperity was ensured by the slave trade. Consequently, although the narrator often sought, on the one hand, to garner support and sympathy for the abolition of slavery, he recognized, on the other hand, that the very act of writing his narrative or the simplest error on his part could not only be viewed as insolence, but could alienate the very audience that he needed if he were to accomplish his goal.

The already difficult task of not alienating the audience became especially complex for Olaudah Equiano, an Ibo who, after being kidnapped at age eleven and experiencing ten years of slavery, published his two-volume narrative ***The Interesting Narrative of the Life of Olaudah Equiano, or Gustavus Vassa, the African, Written by Himself*** in 1789. To be sure, the condescending tone of the review which appeared in *The Gentleman's Magazine* reveals the dilemma of the slave narrator in general and specifically of Equiano. According to the reviewer, "These memoirs, written in very unequal style, place the writer on a par with the general mass of men in the *subordinate stations of civilized society,* and so prove that there is no general rule without an exception."

That Equiano had in the foreground of his interest the objective of attracting an audience whose power and voice could, if it decided to act, strike a meaningful blow against the slave trade and slavery is, I believe, suggested in the overtly stated purpose which Equiano couches in the humblest language and tone at the beginning of Chapter I:

> I am not so foolishly vain as to expect from it [his narrative] either immortality or literary reputation. If it affords any satisfaction to my numerous friends, at whose request it has been written, or in the smallest degree promotes the interest of humanity, the ends for which it was undertaken will be fully attained, and every wish of my heart gratified.

Equiano further reveals his anticipation of some negative response as well as his awareness of the importance of audience when he declares that, in order to avoid censure, he has chosen not to "aspire to praise." In fact, Equiano, one might argue, purposely designs a narrative that is as much about travel in the Mediterranean as it is about slavery in the New World to assure his audience that his purpose throughout is not to offend or alienate.

Yet a common error is made by the critic who, taking Equiano's announced purpose at face value, fails to see his creation of a self whose muted voice veils covert intentions that lie hidden behind the facade—the mask, with which he disguises himself from the very opening lines of the work. For example, Frances Foster Smith incorrectly concludes that "Equiano rarely alters the dispassionate and modest tone of his prefatory remarks. . . . His denial of personal involvement beyond the desire to please friends and to make a small contribution to 'the interest of humanity' is in accordance with accepted standards of gentlemanly humanitarianism."

Although it is indeed correct that Equiano was interested in "gentlemanly humanitarianism," it can be argued that Equiano's posture here allows us to see the control that he seeks to establish over his narrative from the beginning, for as Robert Stepto tells us, the letters, introductions, prefaces, appendices, and other such documents that formed authenticating auxiliary voices in the slave narratives dictated who, in the final analysis, had control: the former slave or his white guarantor.

Thus, more important than Equiano's announced purpose in Chapter I, one might argue, is the significance of an introductory document, in the form of a letter written by him, which begins the narrative. In it, Equiano's voice emerges, cogently though humbly, to address "the Lords Spiritual and Temporal, the Commons of the Parliament of Great Britain":

> *My Lords and Gentlemen,*
>
> Permit me, with the greatest deference and respect to lay at your feet the following genuine Narrative; the chief design of which is to excite in your august assemblies a sense of compassion for the miseries which the Slave-Trade has entailed on my unfortunate countrymen. By the horrors of that trade was I first torn away from all the tender connexions that were naturally dear to my heart; but these, through the mysterious ways of Providence, I ought regard as infinitely more than compensated by the introduction I have thence obtained to the knowledge of the Christian religion, and of a nation which, by its liberal sentiments, its humanity, the glorious freedom of its government, and its proficiency in arts and sciences, has exalted the dignity of human nature.
>
> I am sensible I ought to entreat your pardon for addressing to you a work so wholly devoid of literary merit; but, as the production of an unlettered African, who is actuated by the hope of becoming an instrument towards the relief of his suffering countrymen, I trust that *such a man,* pleading in *such a cause,* will be acquitted of boldness and presumption.
>
> May the God of heaven inspire your heart with peculiar benevolence on that important day when the question of Abolition is to be discussed, when thousands in consequence of your Determination, are to look for Happiness or Misery!
>
> I am,
My Lords and Gentlemen,
Your most obedient,
And devoted humble Servant,
OLAUDAH EQUIANO
or
GUSTAVUS VASSA

Clearly, Equiano, in his introductory letter, takes an overt posture that someone interested in operating from a basic logic of humility would assume. He accomplishes this with such carefully chosen phrases as "greatest deference," "respect," and "august assemblies"; and by his flattering description of Great Britain as "liberal" and humane and as a nation whose government knew "glorious freedom." Although the "chief design" of his narrative might not be obvious, the result is; for with this stance, Equiano—a Black and a former slave, by definition a pariah to some of his eighteenth-century readers—captures the attention of his white audience. He succeeds in establishing what Mary Louis Pratt calls an "affective relation" with his audience, one that reduces hostility and gets attention without being offensive. Simultaneously, he gains the upper hand, and from the beginning he succeeds in establishing a power relation in which he takes control. Like a champion chess player who, after making certain instrumental moves, castles his king for safeguarding while he uses his queen to wreak havoc on his opponent, Equiano, by assuming this position, is able to race across the pages of his narrative like a powerful monarch in a "game" that sees him overtly genuflecting and groveling but covertly, and primarily through language, slashing away at his oppressors. Indeed, his use of irony in his opening letter reveals this, for how can a nation known for its liberal sentiments, humanity, and the glorious freedom of its government directly or indirectly justify its involvement in a slave trade that, in its horror, would tear an individual, especially a child, "from all the tender connexions that were naturally dear to [his] heart"?

Equiano's letter, coupled with a frontispiece that features him poised with Bible in hand, pages of errata, and a table of contents, listing exciting chapter-by-chapter captions of the author's adventures, served to present the author's point of view as that of an inoffensive African who wishes to describe his "interesting" experiences to his reading audience. Moreover, his inclusion of an impressive list of subscribers—headed by the Prince of Wales and the Duke of York, but also including the names of England's top dignitaries, Members of Parliament, esquires, barristers, and clergymen, from the Duke of Bedford and the Bishop of Banghor to the Duke of Northumberland and Lord Mulgrave, Granville Sharp, Esq., and the Reverend Mr. John Wesley—serve only to crystalize this idea for his audience. Also, by publishing his narrative on August first, the "Queen's Birthday," Equiano enhances this perception, for the sacred manner with which her subjects view the Queen would have led them to see the ***Narrative***'s appearance as an activity in her honor. Finally, that Equiano's portrait was engraved by Daniel Orme, who, as Historical Engraver to the Prince of Wales, was responsible for engraving the chief heroes of the time, only served to further reduce any possibly negative perception by his audience.

Thus, from the beginning, Equiano's intentions are enhanced by his disguises. With his posture, Equiano catches the interest and imagination of the populace; and with an impressive list of subscribers, which not only suggested that these individuals contributed financially by purchasing copies (some as many as six), but also that they supported and approved of the work, he is able to ensure himself of an audience. Equiano's success in this regard is suggested in the review his narrative received in the prestigious *Monthly Review; or, Literary Journal,* in which, ironically, the reviewer claims that "the narrative wears an honest face."

In presenting these images of himself, Equiano reminds us of the African folk trickster hero Anansi. For like Anansi, who, though small, is able to outwit and overpower the larger animals, often leading to their destruction, Equiano, the powerless former slave, outsmarts, with his tricks, his British audience. By donning the mask of the docile slave, he outwits his audience and simultaneously reveals that its members are unscrupulous and uncaring.

What remains important, however, is that each factor comes together to solidify the control which Equiano maintains from the beginning over his two-volume work: There are no auxiliary voices, no mitigating voices stealing the thrust of his words. Equiano organizes, coordinates, lays out, writes, and publishes his narrative, regardless of who else might assist. What we are left with, then, is what for Pierre Macherey is a "literary production," for we can see that Equiano is conscious of his purpose and the power of the written word.

Because we are able to find in the narrative's structure the author's strong association with Africa, both suggested and stated, it is possible to argue that Equiano's muted voice camouflages what one might deem the single most important purpose of his narrative: the recreation of a "single self" which is related to an idealized African identity that Equiano wishes to claim as his legacy.

In the light of my contention, Equiano's narrative can be best understood if we make a distinction between the actual sequence of events of the text (*l'histoire*) and the presentation of these events (*recit*). I don't mean to suggest here, of course, that Equiano, at forty-five years of age, was not interested in historicity, in the events that identified his outer self. His interest in the dynamics of his early life in Africa, ten years of slavery in the New World, maritime experiences which included participation in the Seven Years' War and travel to the Arctic, involvement in British culture during the eighteenth century, in the Abolitionist Movement and the colonization of Sierra Leone—historical events in which he participated actively or inactively—is clear. However, it becomes equally clear that what concerns him more than *what* he has done is who he has or has not become as a result of these events. In short, his feelings and thoughts, the "inner man," remain salient to him. In what must be viewed as his careful self-study, Equiano in his ***Interesting Narrative of the Life*** seems anxious to know, in the words of Carlyle: "In God's name, what *art* thou?" Consequently, what ultimately concerns us here is related to a question of intentionality: What, in the final analysis, did Equiano intend?

It is in the interpretation or "the construction of textual meaning," to borrow a phrase from E. D. Hirsch, that one might find deeper insights into the meaning of Equiano's text. For Hirsch the critic's first task is the construction of textual meaning: One must interpret the text correctly. This is to be done, he further argues, by identifying the "Intentional Object" of the narrator's awareness as well as the "Intentional Act," the mode by which the narrator becomes aware of the object. Through these, the critic can ascertain the verbal meaning of the text and gain insight into its explicit meaning, which is shared by all. Furthermore, to distinguish what a text implies from what it does not imply, Hirsch argues, the critic must posit, insofar as it is possible, the "horizon" of the text, or "a system of typical expectations and probabilities," to unravel its total meaning. And to specify horizon, the interpreter must familiarize him- or herself with the "typical meaning of the author's mental and experiential world." In spite of what must be clearly designated the inaccessibility of the author's intention, Hirsch's argument is particularly useful.

From what I have suggested thus far, it is possible to conclude that Equiano's narrative is the "intentional act" through which he becomes aware of his intentional object: slavery. However, in the prefatory remarks of Chapter II,

Equiano lists an implied and perhaps more important intentional object, one that—because he wishes to avoid censure, as he tells us at the beginning of Chapter I—he subverts with the question of slavery. Apologizing for what some might have considered boldness on his part in sharing with his readers in Chapter I an account of the manners and customs of his African community, Equiano declares that " . . . whether the love of one[']s country be real or imaginary, or a lesson of reason, or an instinct of nature, *I still look back with pleasure on the first scenes of my life, though that pleasure has been for the most part mingled with sorrow*" (my emphasis). Equiano's use of the present tense here is important, for it connotes a contemporaneous act; there is, in other words, a sense of "nowness" to his act of "looking back with pleasure" over his earlier life; and there are further implications that the desire to do so is continuous. In the present tense verb *look* is found Equiano's point of view, which embodies implications and irony, for his discourse conceals his simultaneous activity: He will not only be relating his experiences in slavery, whose abolition would enhance, as he says, "the interest of humanity," but concurrently recalling a past life which remains, without a doubt, more meaningful to him with each passing day.

We can better understand the development, discovery, and creation of identity, which for Equiano remains salient, as well as come to grips with his experiences as a slave, which came in direct conflict with this identity, by adopting Hirsch's hermeneutics, which would lead us to unravel the meaning of the text in what we might call the "horizon" of Equiano's experiences. Interestingly enough, the very images that lead us to perceive Equiano as a subservient and passive former slave also embody the very complex characterization of him that we find in the narrative. Perhaps no other image offers a clearer example than the one that emerges from his treatment of his participation in the Seven Years' War. (pp. 64-6)

Ironically, in this very war that was fought to gain dominance over a part of West Africa that was not very far from his own homeland, and to control such "commodities" as sugar, tobacco, indigo, and Black African slaves, Equiano found an avenue for rising above the "blood-stained gates of slavery," to find meaning, dignity, and honor while still enslaved. Equiano wants his readers to believe that he was able to find in the Seven Years' War an avenue for regaining the power, valor, honor, and respect—in short, the humanity—of which he had been robbed by his abduction into slavery.

In the same manner that his documentations throughout the narrative are more than random inclusions of unrelated voices, the lengthy descriptions of Equiano's experiences at sea contain more than scattered and isolated incidents for the sake of rambling. They, too, reveal an Equiano who in his own tale successfully fashions himself as a protagonist who, in his traditional African experiences, could easily have risen to heroic stature. If, as he seems to suggest throughout his narrative, traditional African communal life must be associated with that which is heroic and ideal, then the Equiano we see in his implied characterization epitomizes the traditional African man, who would manifestly have been the great traditional warrior and title bearer. Consequently, the enigma that characterizes his narrative must be carefully examined when found in his tales about his experiences at sea with his master, Captain Pascal of the Royal Navy, especially those involving Pascal's service under Admiral Boscawen during the Seven Years' War.

On the surface, in his narration of the war Equiano serves as an eyewitness—as an on-the-scene correspondent, reporting with precision the land and sea engagements between the British and the French. But he seems especially aware of those battles in which Boscawen's gallant feats were accomplished when the *Namur,* the vessel on which Equiano along with his master-captain is sailing, is Boscawen's flagship. Perhaps no battle was more important to Boscawen (and, indeed, to Equiano) than the one at Gibraltar in August 1759. A firsthand eyewitness and participant, Equiano carefully details the events of the encounter. He dramatically and suspensefully reports the August battle:

> The engagement now commenced with great fury on both sides. The *Ocean* immediately returned our fire, and we continued engaged with each other for some time; during which I was frequently stunned with the thundering of the great guns, whose dreadful contents hurried many of my companions into awful eternity. At last the French line was entirely broken, and we obtained the victory, which was immediately proclaimed with loud huzzas and acclamations. We took three prizes, *La Modeste,* of sixty-four guns, and *Le Temeraire* and *Centair,* of seventy-four guns each. The rest of the French ships took to flight with all the sail they could crowd.

To be sure, Equiano, by creating an image of the war, is able to catch the unique moment in history and to reproduce it for his British audience, who must have been dazzled by the former slave's careful and detailed reporting, his enviable knowledge of naval vessels, and his apparent sense of nationalism.

Although his tale of the engagement ends, Equiano continues by explaining to the reader his assigned role during the battle, making it clear that his role as active participant cannot be gainsaid. Indeed, unlike Robinson Crusoe's Friday or the servant in the plantation literature of Thomas Page, who goes to war with his master to polish his boots and care for his horse, Equiano reveals that he functioned as more than a personal servant during the engagement. He was a fighter:

> My station during the engagement was on the middle deck, where I was quartered with another boy, to bring powder to the aftermost gun; and here I was witness of the dreadful fate of many of my companions, who, in the twinkling of an eye, were dashed in pieces, and launched into eternity. Happily I escaped unhurt, though the shot and splinters flew thick about me during the whole fight. Towards the latter part of it, my master was wounded, and I saw him carried down to the surgeon; but though I was much alarmed for him, and wished to assist him, I dared not leave my post. At this station, my gun-

> mate (a partner in bringing powder for the same gun) and I ran a very risk, for more than half an hour, of blowing up the ship. For, when we had taken the cartridges out of the boxes, the bottoms of many of them proving rotten, the powder ran all about the deck, near the match tub; we scarcely had water enough at the last to throw on it. We were also, from our employment, very much exposed to the enemy's shots; for we had to go through nearly the whole length of the ship to bring the powder. I expected, therefore, every minute to be my last especially when I saw our men fall so thick about me; but, wishing to guard as much against the dangers as possible, at first I thought would be safest not to go for the powder till the Frenchmen had fired their broadside. . . . But immediately afterwards I thought this caution was fruitless; and cheering myself with the reflection that there was time allotted for me to die, as well as to be born, I instantly cast off all fear or thought whatever of death, and went through the whole of my duty with alacrity.

Here Equiano again resembles the African folk trickster Anansi, who is sometimes caught in the traps that he sets for others, for although he undoubtedly is aware of the possibly indignant reaction of his audience to his work were they to conclude that he had overstepped the bounds of his assured social role, Equiano can be found unmasked for a brief moment when we peer behind the facade. We find in the above passage not the subservient or passive slave, but instead an Equiano who has covertly assumed the role of the chivalrous warrior from the very beginning. And, again, we are made aware that Equiano is saying more in his discourse than what immediately stands before us.

Unlike Admiral Byng, whose retreat jeopardized Great Britain's safety and cost him his life, Equiano, a man of action, "casts off all fear" and rises to the occasion. Though his human instincts cause him to be slow in reacting at first, he, responding with bravery, answers the call of duty nevertheless. Indeed, by telling us that he fearlessly carried the gun powder that was used to send the solid cannon balls splitting over the vast ocean, in spite of the immediate danger, Equiano, one might even be led to conclude, wants his reader to believe that this historical battle could not have been won without the brave Ibo's role and the chivalrous manner in which he met his duties during these pre-armored-warship days when Britain's wooden naval vessels gained control of the ocean.

One cannot help but notice that the humility with which Equiano generally garbs himself seems to have been completely stripped away here, as he calls attention to his heroic performance, and the shift from the observing eye in the "I" of the narration to the "I" of the action becomes important because it moves the focus inward, taking Equiano beyond the explicit meaning that his activities may have conveyed to his British audience. Equiano is in fact saying, I believe: This is not only a world that I objectively experienced, but one that I, through my intrepid acts, helped to create.

To be sure, through his exciting narration and careful choice of words of action and through his functional use of the first-person plural "we," he allows his British readers to participate in the battle, and he gives them a reason for celebration. Here in his narrative they could find yet another record of their undaunting strength and power; here they could find yet another testimony to the masterful skills of their beloved Admiral Boscawen; and here they had evidence of their ability to overcome the enemy, France. Thus, at the explicit level of his narrative, he succeeds in giving his audience both the romance and the drama that it might have associated with naval battle and encounter, a fact that was undoubtedly heightened by the knowledge that this was "Pitt's War," and he boosted their pride in their maritime war for maritime empire, providing rejuvenation after the universal disgrace they had suffered with Byng's defeat.

Equally important, however, is what might be perceived as Equiano's effort to guide his readers' response towards his abolitionist concerns, for with his description and powerful rhetoric he indirectly forces his audience to confront the question of the injustice of slavery and, indeed, to find validation in his argument against this inhuman system that had enslaved an individual of his caliber, one whose personal qualities, dignity, and values represented the highest ideals of British culture. His audience, one might even believe, might somehow have become infuriated by their own participation, direct or indirect, in this heinous system, and with Equiano, they might have concluded that slavery "depresses the mind and extinguishes all its fire and every noble sentiment." Equiano's success in capturing and controlling his audience, and his personal account of one of England's finest hours, undoubtedly contributed to the popularity of his narrative, which was to undergo more than fifteen editions.

What remains of paramount importance, however, are the implications of Equiano's text, because throughout his reported acts he places himself firmly in the middle of this "world wide struggle in which the main lines of the British Empire were finally laid down." Rather than hide, escape, or skirt responsibilities, although armorless, Equiano, the African, girds his loins and resolves to meet head on his task, no matter what the required sacrifice, danger, or outcome. A mere lad of fourteen at the time of the battle, he here assumes, he wants us to believe, the role of leader. Overcoming his initial fears and showing tremendous discipline, Equiano in the final analysis emerges as one who had risen to the status that would have been his in Essaka, where the male youth's self-understanding was firmly grounded in the conceptual metaphor "man is warrior" and "warrior is a person of honour, action, and bravery." Consequently, the horizon of Equiano's experience, the conscious and unconscious meanings that are present in his discourse, must be unraveled before the full meaning of his text can be ascertained. The horizon would inevitably include his African past.

The son of a village elder, Equiano retrospectively views his childhood in Africa as his "former happy state," during which he basked in the warmth of his mother's love, was cradled in an awareness of his aristocratic father's wealth and prestige, and was nourished by the knowledge

The "Racehorse" and the "Carcass" in the Arctic, 1773. Equiano sailed on these ships as part of Constantine Phipps's Arctic expedition.

that his parents were committed to securing for him a place within their community through which he, too, would gain the mark of grandeur and distinction that was borne by his father and brother. In preparing him for his *destined* role as a communal leader, Equiano's mother, unaware, of course, of the tragic future that awaited her favorite child, dressed him "with the emblems, after the manner of our greatest warrior." He tells us that, before being kidnapped, he was "trained up in the earliest years in the art of war: my daily exercise was shooting and throwing javelins."

Implied in Equiano's text here is the suggestion that the personal history of a pariah, which had been carved out in the wasteland of Western slavery and culture, is not his sole interest. Present also is the notion that the Ibo wants to confront questions related to the loss of personal legacy that this history has wrought. He tells us that slavery did not divert him from the course on which he had been set by a mother who dressed him after the manner of the great Ibo warriors. In fact, in his own traditional world, he would have crossed the threshold into manhood after such dauntless actions, and, indeed, he could have danced to the drum beat reserved for the great warriors.

Finding no warrior's circle in which to dance proudly, finding no marketplace in which to display his war trophies, although he had brought home the "enemies' " head in the form of the ships taken as prizes, Equiano finds, in his narrative-autobiography, not only an avenue for celebrating his valorous act, but also a means of claiming the achievement of his identity and thereby assuming the social role that was rightfully his as an Ibo, Essakan, and African. Equiano thus weaves into his narrative an important "metaphor of self," which, as James Olney tells us, is used by the autobiographer to grasp and understand the unique self that he is—"to grasp the unknown for the known." Equiano's "metaphor of self" is one that makes him the African traditional warrior-man.

Given Hume's contention that the mind is a theater which "parades a variety of posture and situation," one finds it difficult not to agree with Sir Victor Pritchett, who claimed that what the autobiographer is faced with in the final analysis is a decision of "what play [he is] putting on, what its theme is and what postures fit into it." Pritchett tells us: "The play is not '*the* truth' but '*a* truth' of '*our* truth.' " In other words, it is possible to argue that the historicity and veracity of Equiano's tale about his role in the Seven Years' War is, in a sense, unimportant. What ultimately *is* important is the metaphor of self that he has chosen in relating the events. Thus, although the explicit "posture" he assumes for his audience, that of the abolitionist, is one that we continuously see, it is the implicit posture, grounded in the signification of warriorhood to his traditional African community, that eventually presents the represented self that he has chosen to amplify in the hidden purpose of his narrative.

Consequently, although he succeeds through narration and description in recreating for his readers a sense of the slave trade during the eighteenth century, Equiano ends up recreating what Roy Pascal, in a related context, terms "a part of [his] life in the actual circumstance in which it was lived." In the final analysis, what we get is closer to autobiography, in which, as Pascal tells us, "The centre of interest is the self, not the outside world, though necessarily the outside world must appear so that the personality can find its particular shape."

What we learn from Equiano's autobiographical acts, I believe, is that he can only find in his retrospective assessment of slavery an excruciating severance and senseless extirpation: As he came to realize, slavery meant physical separation from the community and culture which offered reciprocity during the first eleven years of his life. Whereas Essaka meant bonding, security, and aggregation, slavery meant separation, alienation, and liminality. It was for him a void to be transcended, an overpowering force that threatened to dash him into a world of eternal meaninglessness, an experience from which, through the narrative, he would seek a sense of wholeness and being.

Deeply embedded in Equiano's discourse, specifically in its ironies and implications, is the conflict which resulted from conflict between the idealized African self, which he as a member of his Essakan community and as an Ibo accepts as his legacy, and the harsh reality that, having served as a slave in a foreign land, away from family and culture, he had not been able fully to realize this self. The act of writing the narrative becomes not only a process, then, of taking a retrospective glance over the primary experiences that served to form Equiano's historical self, but perhaps more importantly, it functions as praxis, for it allows him to explore his life and at the same time create, develop, and extract from it the meaning which to him remains important. Equiano's self-portraiture contains ironic and metaphoric values which upon examination reveal the dual nature of the thematics and characterization of his narrative. Fundamentally, it reveals that in his efforts to build subjectivity in a world of reification, Equiano reclaims his voice by masking and disguising it. Indirectly, he teaches us to not only listen to the explicit voice of Gustavus Vassa, the person created by the Western enslavers who gave him this name, but also to the voice of Olaudah Equiano, the would-be warrior, whose name means 'fortunate' and 'favored.' (pp. 67-9)

Wilfred D. Samuels, "Disguised Voice in 'The Interesting Narrative of Olaudah Equiano, or Gustavus Vassa, the African'," in Black American Literature Forum, *Vol. 19, No. 2, Summer, 1985, pp. 64-9.*

Paul Edwards (essay date 1985)

[In the following excerpt, Edwards discusses negative aspects of white European society which Equiano attempted to come to terms with in his autobiography.]

In 1789, Equiano published his autobiography, combining a remarkable account of personal economic and moral survival with a unique attack on slavery and the slave trade—unique because he was the only African of his age to record in detail what it was like to undergo the experience.

Equiano never forgot his African childhood. His account of the isolated Ibo community in which he spent the first ten or so years of his life draws a picture which is strikingly similar in almost all respects to descriptions of Ibo village life in the first half of the present century, and it is to the values underlying Ibo custom that his mind continues to return:

> I hope the reader will not think I have trespassed on his patience in introducing myself to him with some account of the manners and customs of my country. They had been implanted in me with great care, and made an impression on my mind, which time could not erase, and which all the adversity and variety of fortune I have since experienced served only to rivet and record; for, whether the love of one's country be real or imaginary, or a lesson of reason, or an instinct of nature, I still look back with pleasure on the first scenes of my life, though that pleasure has been for the most part mingled with sorrow.

Thus at several points in the ***Narrative*** Equiano draws comparisons between non-Christian and Christian societies to the disadvantage of the latter. He likes the Amerindians because their customs and conduct remind him of "Eboe"—plurality of wives combined with propriety of married life, joint labour "exactly like the Africans," modesty of diet, the absence of swearing, their fondness for body-painting:

> I never saw any mode of worship among them; but in this they are not worse than their European brethren or neighbours: for I am sorry to say that there was not one white person in our dwelling, nor any where else that I saw in different places I was at on the shore, that was better or more pious than those unenlightened Indians.

Parallels also occur in Equiano's account of his experiences with the Turks; he constantly finds on his visits to Smyrna echoes of his homeland, and his general conclusion is that he believed "those who in general termed themselves Christians not so honest or so good in their morals as the Turks," with the result that "I really thought the Turks were in a safer way of salvation than my neighbours."

But there are pressures working in other directions. His first impression of white men was that they were monsters and he questioned "if we were not to be eaten by those white men with horrible looks, red faces, and loose hair." But after the Atlantic crossing he was bought by a British naval officer, and befriended on the journey to England by a white boy named Dick Baker, who looked after him and gave him his earliest English lessons. He and Dick were at first lodged with a family at Falmouth where the woman of the house "behaved to me with great kindness and attention; and taught me every thing in the same manner as she did her own child, and indeed in every respect treated me as such." The growth of personal affections coincided with the excitement of learning:

> I have often reflected with surprise that I never felt half the alarm at any of the numerous dangers I have been in, that I was filled with at the first sight of the Europeans, and at every act of

> theirs, even the most trifling, when I first came among them, and for some time afterwards. That fear, however, which was the effect of my ignorance, wore away as I began to know them. I could now speak English tolerably well, and I perfectly understood every thing that was said. I now not only felt myself quite easy with these new countrymen, but relished their society and manners. I no longer looked upon them as spirits, but as men superior to us; and therefore I had the stronger desire to resemble them; to imbibe their spirit, and imitate their manners; I therefore embraced every occasion of improvement; and every new thing that I observed I treasured up in my memory. I had long wished to be able to read and write; and for this purpose I took every opportunity to gain instruction, but had made as yet very little progress. However, when I went to London with my master, I had soon an opportunity of improving myself, which I gladly embraced. Shortly after my arrival, he sent me to wait upon the Miss Guerins, who had treated me with much kindness when I was there before; and they sent me to school.

Even aboard British men-of-war, he continued to get an education. By the age of fourteen he could read, and had begun to learn to write:

> I had leisure [on the *Ætna*] to improve myself in reading and writing. The latter I had learned a little of before I left the *Namur,* as there was a school on board.

The period on the *Ætna* was a happy one, leading to great expectations, but again we find that in the very process of discovering his new world, he turns to his origins, "wonderfully surprised to see the laws and rules of my country written almost exactly here" (i.e. in the Bible):

> I thought now of nothing but being freed, and working for myself, and thereby getting money to enable me to get a good education; for I always had a great desire to be able at least to read and write; and while I was on ship-board I had endeavoured to improve myself in both. While I was in the Ætna particularly, the captain's clerk taught me to write, and gave me a smattering of arithmetic as far as the rule of three. There was also one Daniel Queen, about forty years of age, a man very well educated, who messed with me on board this ship, and he likewise dressed and attended the captain. Fortunately this man soon became very much attached to me, and took very great pains to instruct me in many things. He taught me to shave and dress hair a little, and also to read in the Bible, explaining many passages to me, which I did not comprehend. I was wonderfully surprised to see the laws and rules of my country written almost exactly here; a circumstance which I believe tended to impress our manners and customs more deeply on my memory. I used to tell him of this resemblance; and many a time we have sat up the whole night together at this employment. In short, he was like a father to me; and some even used to call me after his name; they also styled me the black Christian. Indeed I almost loved him with the affection of a son.

Had Equiano endured only the cruelty and barbarism of the slave trade he might have lived out his life in a state of inarticulate hatred, or sullen, unrelieved despair. But consequent upon the very nature of his experience of slavery, ambivalent feelings towards white people and white society were established which emerge in his attitudes towards authority even when it might seem benevolent, in conflicts more intense than those we have seen in Sancho.

In the passage just quoted, Equiano is hoping to buy back his freedom with the prize money being shared among the crew as a result of their capture of a French ship. It is at this very moment of hope, excitement, and emotional release that the blow falls. Not only does Equiano's owner, Captain Pascal, whom he had begun to see as a benefactor, refuse him any share in the prize money, he resells Equiano back to American slavery. Refusing him permission to take even his books and chest of clothes, Pascal has Equiano carried aboard a waiting ship:

> . . . just as we had got a little below Gravesend, we came alongside of a ship which was going away the next tide for the West Indies; her name was the Charming Sally, Captain James Doran; and my master went on board and agreed with him for me; and in a little time I was sent for into the cabin. When I came there Captain Doran asked me if I knew him; I answered that I did not; 'Then,' said he 'you are now my slave.' I told him my master could not sell me to him, nor to any one else. 'Why,' said he, 'did not your master buy you?' I confessed he did. 'But I have served him,' said I, 'many years, and he has taken all my wages and prize-money, for I only got one sixpence during the war; besides this I have been baptized; and by the laws of the land no man has a right to sell me:' And I added, that I had heard a lawyer and others at different times tell my master so. They both then said that those people who told me so were not my friends; but I replied—it was very extraordinary that other people did not know the law as well as they. Upon this Captain Doran said I talked too much English; and if I did not behave myself well, and be quiet, he had a method on board to make me. I was too well convinced of his power over me to doubt what he said; and my former sufferings in the slave ship presenting themselves to my mind, the recollection of them made me shudder. However, before I retired I told them that as I could not get any right among men here I hoped I should hereafter in Heaven; and I immediately left the cabin, filled with resentment and sorrow. The only coat I had with me my master took away with him, and said if my prize-money had been £10,000 he had a right to it all, and would have taken it.

During Equiano's subsequent years as slave to a Quaker, Mr. King, England offers him a recurring vision of safety and security—his constant wish, he tells us, was "to return to old England;" or again, "I was determined that the year following, if it pleased God, I would see old England once more." At the same time, he never ceases to be aware of himself (nor does the world allow it) as a Negro, a former slave, a member of a despised and maltreated race. His voyages in the West Indies and on the American coast, even after he had his freedom, show him to be profoundly vulnerable in a society where the white man's word was always taken against the black man's and where the black man's property, even his life, was subject to the whims and arbitrary violence of a white slave-owning society. The crucial ambivalence lies perhaps in the idea of a *good* slave-owner. If slavery is evil—and Equiano knows well enough that it is—how should he respond to what the world would call a *good* master? The very white men who aid and befriend him, in fact, are also playing their part in the appalling system which has enslaved and brutalized him and his people. Without the power to act for himself, he is forced to seek the aid of slave-owners, such as Robert King, in order to get his rights against the white barbarians. The trouble is that, in his situation, he has little choice but to make the best of things and think himself lucky not to be a plantation slave. All the same, the rage he has to crush emerges in unexpected ways, in ironies and contradictions which may or may not be conscious. Equiano's response to "generous" treatment is ambivalent:

> Many . . . used to find fault with my master for feeding his slaves so well as he did; although I often went hungry, and an Englishman might think my fare very indifferent; but he used to tell them that he always would do it, because the slaves thereby looked better and did more work.

What begins as a compliment to King's humaneness is suddenly qualified by a rather bitter comparison with English diet, and then virtually reversed as Equiano redirects attention to the underlying self-interest of his owner. He writes of his transports of gratitude and delight when King grants him his freedom, but at the same time enables the reader to see the mean and grudging side of King's behaviour: first, King tries to go back on his promise to release Equiano and has to be persuaded by Captain Farmer; then King insists on full repayment even though as Captain Farmer says, "Gustavus has earned you more than a hundred a year." Equiano continued throughout his life to use the name Gustavus Vassa given him by Pascal, along with his African name. He stresses in this episode that had it not been for the support of Captain Farmer, King might well not have released him at all. And the reader must judge for himself the significance of this comment by Equiano on King:

> I have often seen slaves, particularly those who were meagre, in different islands, put into scales and weighed, and then sold from three pence to six pence or nine pence a pound. My master, however, whose humanity was shocked at this mode, used to sell such by the lump.

When Equiano, a few pages later, declares his wish to return to England and see Captain Pascal—the man who had arbitrarily resold him at the very moment Equiano was anticipating his freedom—from motives of affection, it is clear that his real motive is to show Pascal that he has survived in spite of Pascal's callous treatment of him. As it turns out, their meeting is comically acrimonious:

> When he saw me he appeared a good deal surprised, and asked me how I came back? I answered, 'In a ship'. To which he replied drily 'I suppose you did not walk back to London on the water.'

But perhaps the most striking example of Equiano's ambivalent relationships with whites is with Captain Farmer, the very man who helped him get his freedom, and consequently the man to whom he feels morally indebted. Significantly, Equiano signs up for a voyage with Captain Farmer only to repay this debt, and is burdened by it:

> Here gratitude bowed me down; and none but the generous mind can judge of my feelings, struggling between inclination and duty.

It is in this frame of mind that he begins his last voyage with Farmer, and immediately they quarrel over whether or not he is to be allowed to transport some bullocks of his own—the ship is carrying a cargo of bullocks. Farmer will only let him take turkeys, but the journey is rough, the bullocks all die, the turkeys survive, and Equiano remarks, "I could not help looking on this, otherwise trifling circumstance, as a particular providence of God." Farmer is butted by a bullock, falls mortally ill, and asks on his deathbed for reassurance that he has never harmed Equiano. Equiano pays lip-service to pious convention on Farmer's death, but his real feelings are more complex, as the final paragraph indicates. Equiano takes over the ship and steers it into port at Antigua:

> Many were surprised when they heard of my conducting the sloop into the port, and I now obtained a new appellation, and was called Captain. This elated me not a little, and it was quite flattering to my vanity to be thus styled by as high a title as any free man in this place possessed. When the death of the captain became known, he was much regretted by all who knew him; for he was universally respected. At the same time, the sable captain lost no fame; for the success I had met with increased the affection of my friends in no small measure.

What is apparent is that Equiano needs release not simply from subjection to his enemies, but from indebtedness to his friends. This whole section is a revealing demonstration of the effects of paternalism and subordination, as regret for Farmer's death is assimilated into the pleasure Equiano feels—and seems prepared to reveal as having its touch of vanity—that Farmer's death has given him a way to display his own skills as a navigator and leader.

The very next section of his book describes yet another sea journey, this time aboard, of all vessels, a slave ship, which he takes over from a white captain. The former slave who has been "saved" by the paternalistic kindness of others, dreams that his master's ship "was wrecked amidst the surfs and rocks, and I was the means of saving every one on board." The dream comes true and Equiano takes over from the cowardly and incompetent white captain. The captain orders the hatches to be nailed down on the slaves in the hold. Equiano countermands the order and the hatches are not nailed down. The slaves, however, are still delivered to their destination.

Clearly the emancipation of the slave Equiano is not to be brought about by the mere payment of forty pounds sterling; he has also to act out roles of dominance through which he can shed his slave past. Yet it may seem ironical, though not consciously so perhaps, that the new role involves him in assuming the title of Captain (the rank of the man who first bought him as a slave, as well as of the man who helped to free him) and acting out that role as master of a slave ship.

After gaining his freedom, Equiano worked as surgeon's mate to Dr. Irving on expeditions to the Arctic in 1772 and to the Indians of Central America in 1775, and as gentleman's valet on a grand tour of the Mediterranean. In 1786 his status among the black people of Britain was acknowledged in his appointment as Commissary for Stores to the Sierra Leone expedition. But even in this he found his authority undermined not only by the enemies of abolition, who continued to attack him in the press, but also by men who should have been his friends and colleagues. Shortly after taking up his appointment, he was at loggerheads with several of the leaders of the expedition, notably the Agent in charge, Irwin, and the Chaplain, the Rev. Fraser. Equiano accused Irwin of misappropriating equipment and foodstuffs and gained himself a reputation of troublemaker. Captain Thompson, who commanded the expedition, acknowledged, "I do not find Mr. Irwin the least calculated to conduct this business: as I have never observed any wish of his to facilitate the sailing of the ships, or any steps taken by him which might indicate that he had the welfare of the people the least at heart." But he writes in the same letter criticizing "the conduct of Mr. Gustavus Vasa, which has been, since he held the Commissary, turbulent and discontented, taking every means to actuate the minds of the Blacks to discord." Fraser complained that the black members of the expedition had, under Equiano's influence, absented themselves from divine service and public prayers "for no other reason whatever than that I am *white,*" and even Granville Sharp was to write to his brother that "all the jealousies and animosities between the Whites and the Blacks had subsided, and that they had been very orderly since Mr. Vasa and two or three other discontented persons had been left on shore at Plymouth." Whatever rift there might have been between Equiano and Sharp seems to have been healed, however; Equiano continues to have nothing but praise for him, and Sharp was at Equiano's deathbed. "He was a sober, honest man—and I went to see him when he lay upon his death bed, and had lost his voice so that he could only whisper," wrote Sharp to his niece many years later.

The evidence indicates that Equiano was doing no more than his duty in drawing attention to the neglect of his fellows. Those in charge appear to have been often complacent or condescending, at worst downright dishonest, but as a black man, Equiano was virtually bound to experience conflicts, both within himself and outwardly, in his relations with even a benevolent white authority. Black people were expected to be acted upon rather than take the lead themselves, and for some of the supporters of abolition, charity could be an act of self-gratification, the pleasures of which were not so palatable when seasoned with the aggressive, uncompromising, and no doubt irritating rectitude of Equiano and his like. Even from his abolitionist friends, then, Equiano might sometimes experience wounding behavior, and one such slight is the subject of a letter written to him by a Susannah Atkinson in March 1791. "Suffer yourself not to be hurt with triffles (*sic*) since you must in this transitory and deceitful world meet with many unpleasing changes," she writes; "I was sorry we should be so unfortunate as to recommend you to any who would in the least slight you . . . . " That the activities of Equiano on behalf of his fellow Africans could arouse racist feelings even in the heart of an abolitionist can be seen in a letter to the *Public Advertiser* responding to his criticisms of the Sierra Leone preparations. He is accused of "advancing falsehoods as deeply black as his jetty face," and the author of the letter adds a cluster of puns on Equiano's "black reports" and "dark transactions of a Black." So Equiano never returned to Africa, but left the expedition at Plymouth and came back to London, where he wrote his autobiography during the next two years. Perhaps we should be glad of his dismissal from his post of Commissary, for it left him free to carry out a task which many would consider more important, the writing of his autobiography. Equiano's ***Interesting Narrative*** is not only a unique document for the modern reader; in its own day, it was distributed so widely by its itinerant author and sold so many copies that he was said by one of his contemporaries to be "a principal instrument in bringing about the motion for a repeal of the Slave-act." (pp. 188-96)

Paul Edwards, "Three West African Writers of the 1780's," in The Slave's Narrative, *edited by Charles T. Davis and Henry Louis Gates, Jr., Oxford University Press, 1985, pp. 175-98.*

Angelo Costanzo (essay date 1987)

[*Costanzo is an American educator, author, and editor. In the following excerpt, he suggests that the structure of Equiano's* Interesting Narrative *illuminates important themes in early black autobiography in general and specifically provides "an artistic framework" for tracing Equiano's personal and spiritual growth.*]

[Equiano's narrative] . . . Became the forerunner of the numerous black autobiographies known as the fugitive slave narratives that emerged in the nineteenth century. Equiano's narrative established the form and character of a new genre in literature, the autobiographical slave narrative. An important element of this form of narrative included an exposition of inhumanity in the cruelties of the institution of slavery practiced by nominal Christians who disobeyed almost every Christian precept.

The black narrators revealed that the slaves desired their physical, mental, and spiritual freedoms. Many sought to escape, but few were as fortunate as Equiano, who was permitted to earn his freedom. In the eighteenth century, escape meant getting away to England. This is where Equiano and his fellow blacks fled in order to avoid being dragged back into slavery.

A vital part of Equiano's narrative is the winning of his freedom; he becomes a new man as he is reborn into a society where he can operate on a free plane of existence. His physical and spiritual liberations enable him to complete himself as a human being. He assumes new and commanding roles, such as taking over as captain of a ship in time of emergency, serving as a minister in order to bury a child, and ultimately becoming a leader of the abolitionist movement in England.

One critic has stated about Equiano that by "defining himself as a bicultural man, he found the means to imagine his relationship to the world in terms that did not require his becoming either totally co-opted by or totally alienated from the Western socio-cultural order." Equiano immersed himself in eighteenth-century Western literary culture and resorted to many of its literary traditions when he wrote his narrative. One tradition Equiano used was that of the young individual picaresque hero or anti-hero, a popular subject in the eighteenth century. This hero or rogue journeys from place to place in search of experience that contributes to his growing awareness of the world and to his sense of maturity. The picaresque tradition can be traced from the Spaniards of the sixteenth century, to the Elizabethan prose writers, and to the eighteenth-century novelists that included Swift, Defoe, Smollett, and Fielding.

Equiano's use of the picaresque tradition helped to fix the role of the picaro type of character in slave narrative writings. His accomplishment widely permeated later slave literature. [In his essay "Binary Oppositions in Chapter One of *Narrative of the Life of Frederick Douglass, an American Slave, Written by Himself*" (1978)] Henry Louis Gates, Jr. has pointed out the affinities that exist between the picaresque and the slave narrative writings: "There is in the narration of both a profusion of objects and detail. Both the picaro and the slave, as outsiders, comment on if not parody collective social institutions. Moreover, both, in their odysseys, move horizontally through space and vertically through society." Gates credits much of the success of the slave narrative in large measure to the popular appeals of the picaresque narrative convention.

Equiano's figure of the picaro is in the portrayal of himself as a young and innocent African who, after being kidnapped and sold into slavery, journeys all over the world, thereby gaining knowledge and education that make possible the great work of his life: the writing of his autobiography. At times, he satirizes his own weaknesses when he presents himself as a naive and ignorant youth. We can observe his use of ironic humor in the account of the dying silversmith from whom Equiano and Captain Farmer hope to inherit a fortune, but instead they are duped by him. Another time Equiano admits his stupidity in taking a lighted candle and holding it in a barrel of gunpowder. On a voyage to the North Pole, while writing in his journal one night, a spark from his candle sets the storeroom on fire, and Equiano is nearly burned to death. During his first trip to England, he thinks the grampuses are responsible for stopping the ship when the wind dies down. He also describes his gullibility in the episode relating his fear that the whites are preparing to eat him and his friend Dick Baker. One morning upon awakening, he sees his first snow and thinks "somebody in the night had thrown salt all over the deck." In Virginia, he is under the impression that a watch and a picture hanging in a room are spying on him as he fans a sleeping gentleman. Equiano thinks people carry on conversations with books when he sees crew members reading, and he movingly describes his foolish attempts to learn from books by talking to them. Once while riding a runaway horse, he nearly is killed and expresses his determination not to be "so foolhardy again in a hurry." A humorous and ironic situation takes place when Equiano attends a religious love feast expecting a banquet of food but instead is "astonished to see the place filled with people, and no signs of eating and drinking." In his attempts to free a slave, Equiano tries to serve a writ of habeas corpus on a gentleman from whose house he is barred. Equiano comically relates how he fools the people in the gentleman's house: "My being known to them occasioned me to use the following deception: I whitened my face, that they might not know me, and this had its desired effect."

In writing about the picaro in the slave narrative [in a 1982 issue of *American Literature*], Raymond Hedrin states that the early narrative figures were picaresque because their lives were picaresque. In the later narratives, however, the survival techniques of the picaro became important to the slave, but he had to depict himself as being righteous in the cause of freedom. As a result, the slave narrators attempted to "purify the picaro." While it is true that many of the picaresque happenings in Equiano's story are told simply for their humor, the incidents demonstrate Equiano's use of the picaro behavior for survival purposes. In addition, Equiano portrays himself as a justified picaro fighting for the abolition of slavery. Contrary to what Hedrin says, we need not wait for the later narratives to reveal the higher type of character, for Equiano created the "purified picaro" and probably influenced the use of this character in the later narratives.

This claim can be reinforced by the careful observation that what is notable about Equiano's adaptation of the picaresque figure is that he makes his hero an instrument of social purpose in the antislavery crusade of the eighteenth century. Up to that time, picaresque heroes were depicted primarily for their entertainment value or for the religious propaganda that showed the wayward person finally seeing the light by converting and freeing himself from sin and subsequently dedicating his life to God. Equiano delights readers with the account of his naive, youthful self journeying through new lands and over strange seas, all the while having perilous but thrilling experiences. Later he undergoes a religious conversion and devotes his life to serving the Lord, but Equiano adds to this the depiction of himself as the now mature young man dedicating his life to social and humanitarian principles in the fight against slavery.

The influence of eighteenth-century primitivism on the slave narratives was strong. Several of the autobiographers, such as Gronniosaw, Cugoano, Equiano, and Smith, recalled their memories of idyllic days that ceased when European influence spread over Africa. These writers knew of the powerful sentimental attraction that such ideas as primitivism and the noble savage had on the eighteenth-century Western world, and thus the narrators described their memories of Africa according to the prevailing primitivist notions popularized by the numerous travel books written by autobiographers and historians. These included books by the Quaker antislavery writer Anthony Benezet, whose works on Africa and the slave trade were widely read in the 1770s and 1780s. Equiano and Cugoano mentioned Benezet in their narratives and borrowed information from him.

The eighteenth century saw a great deal of primitivist travel literature—fictional and nonfictional—written as personal narrative. The outstanding examples in the nonfictional realm are such works as Captain Cook's *Voyages* and John Green's *New General Collection of Voyages and Travels, the World Display'd.* Of more significance are the fictional writings of Defoe, to which Equiano's narrative is closely allied. In Equiano's work, there is close attention to specific circumstantial detail and to the sense of verisimilitude that we see in *Robinson Crusoe,* and Equiano also shares with Defoe the delineation of the protagonist's sense of discovery of strange and awesome objects and of people in hitherto unknown lands. The fictional and nonfictional travel literature stresses the physical journey or voyage over strange areas of the globe as being also a journey of awakening consciousness to life on this earth. Implicit in some of the narratives is the concern also for spiritual awareness and development that a physical journey of education allows the traveler to undergo. (pp. 45-9)

Equiano's and Defoe's works must be seen in relation to the whole tradition of spiritual autobiography in Western literature. Such sects as the Puritans, Quakers, and Wesleyan Methodists were the foremost groups to come under the general inspiration of spiritual autobiographical writing stemming from St. Augustine. A close examination of life was encouraged by the Puritans, who produced their personal histories of exemplary lives for the direct purpose of having a moral effect upon their fellowman. The Quakers also urged their members to keep journals and diaries and to write autobiographies in order to evaluate themselves in their spiritual development. John Woolman and the great Quaker leader George Fox wrote journals to probe their inner states of moral and spiritual enlightenment because their concern was always to arrive at the inner light of experience with God. John Wesley, the great Methodist figure (who read Equiano's book), encouraged his brethren to write their autobiographies as means to moral self-evaluation and spiritual improvement. As a result, Methodists wrote thousands of conversion narratives. The lives portrayed in these works served as models for others to emulate in their struggles for spiritual salvation.

Equiano's narrative follows in this tradition and genre of spiritual autobiography. In it, Equiano looks back on his life and describes his personal struggles for freedom and identity and religious salvation. He evaluates his life and judges it as a good example to serve for others who would seek their freedom and spiritual development. Although his story deals with his freedom from physical slavery, an important point of his narrative is that spiritual freedom cannot be attained until a person's physical being is free. Like other spiritual autobiographies, the first half of Equiano's book is taken up with the sinner's ways and the latter part with the converted man acting virtuously. Equiano's narrative in the first part portrays him as suffering at the hands of white sinners and thus being denied the possibility of leading a life devoted to God's precepts. After he wins his physical freedom, the former slave is able to follow God's teaching and to dedicate his life to helping others. Equiano uses the form of spiritual autobiography for portraying the evils of slavery. He incorporates the story of his religious development, salvation, and personal identity into the narrative of his life under slavery and his emergence out of it to freedom.

In the eighteenth century, a change occurred in the writing of spiritual autobiography. The growing secularization of society, with its emphasis on material acquisition by means of the Protestant work ethic, turned people's interest to the rags-to-riches stories that depicted strong individualistic characters in the land of opportunity. The prototype of this kind of story is probably Benjamin Franklin's *Autobiography* in which Franklin describes himself as a naive and innocent youth who arrives in Philadelphia as a penniless boy and is laughed at by a girl as he eats his loaves of bread in the street. Later, Franklin shows himself attaining wealth and fame as he succeeds in society by means of hard work and native ability. He becomes prosperous and prominent and, ironically, marries the girl who laughed at him in his youth. Franklin's autobiography is secular in that its main concern is material and personal success; however, one of its important concerns is the spiritual self-improvement of its writer's life. Franklin keeps lists of practical moral virtues, which he attempts to follow faithfully. Although Franklin conducts no deep inquisition of the soul, he does employ the techniques of spiritual autobiography. His narrative is a self-scrutiny that reveals insights derived from a life of personal discovery. Franklin is a pilgrim; however, he is not on a religious quest but on one leading to character building for material achievement and service to humanity. His depictions of how far he comes from his early stage of poverty resemble the before-and-after conversion accounts of the spiritual writers. And also like them, Franklin writes his story in order to instruct.

Equiano's work belongs in part to the Franklin tradition of autobiography. A large part of Equiano's life is spent in working hard in order to purchase his freedom. He does this by employing himself after his regular slave duties are over. He eventually saves enough to buy his manumission paper, and afterward he continues to work earnestly for himself and for the benefit of others. His freedom and material success are arrived at through hard labor and the use of his ability and intellect.

Much of Equiano's narrative is written in a vivid, flowing, plain style. He relates the story of his life chronologically and tries to capture the feelings and thoughts of his young, curious mind as he journeyed from freedom in Africa to slavery in the West Indies. In the early parts of the narrative, his retrospective comments are few and unobtrusive to the narrative flow. As he amasses his strong evidence against slavery, he becomes more polemical, in the style of Cugoano, until finally he closes the book with antislavery letters and resolutions.

The narrative has a three-part structure. The first part deals with Equiano's capture in Africa and with his subsequent bondage as he is transported over Africa to the coast and then through the Middle Passage to the West Indies. The picture is one of a young boy journeying from freedom in a happy, pastoral Africa to slavery in a cruel, materialistic Western world. As such, it is a journey of education from innocence to experience. The young Equiano is amazed by the wonders of the outside world, but he then also sees the evils of white society. He is quick to learn the ways of this new life, and soon he comes to an understanding that hard work and money are the gods of the white world. Thus, through industry and economic means, Equiano obtains his freedom by earning enough money in working each day after his slave duties are over.

The second part deals with the purchase of his freedom, the turning point in his life. He publishes his manumission paper in the center of his narrative, and from that point on, his character changes, and so does the tone and the style of the book. This pivotal point in the work marks Equiano as a reborn man. He obtains a strength of character that allows him to fulfill many roles in a free world of possibility, and his physical freedom allows him to practice faithfully his newfound Christian religion. He was converted while a slave, but now that he is free, he can develop himself along spiritual and humanitarian lines. Thus, in the third part of the narrative, he becomes more religious, and he fights hard in the antislavery crusade in England. This part of his book is written in a highly moralistic and pious tone, which follows logically from the development of Equiano's character and from the thesis of the book. It shares the limitation of most other spiritual autobiographies in which the first parts dealing with the sinful ways of people are always more interesting to read than the latter parts dealing with moral amendment of character and spiritual instruction.

[In his book *The Examined Self*] Robert F. Sayre has defined autobiography as a whole life that is seen as a complete and unified work: "Autobiography is an examination of the self as both a sovereign integrity and a member of society. In fact, the self is at all times both these things, and autobiography is an endless stream of demonstrations of their inseparability." Equiano from the onset conceived of his personal story as a complete picture and study of his life in the world of people and nations, and he saw it as a means of instruction to society on the evils of slavery and the practice of Christian principles.

When Equiano wrote his narrative, he was a middle-aged black living a free and relatively comfortable existence in London. His chief interests were in religious matters and antislavery crusades. As a result, there are two major themes in his autobiography: the black person's cause and the Christian religion. In the first chapter, Equiano writes: "Does not slavery itself depress the mind, and extinguish all its fire and every noble sentiment?" and in the beginning of that first chapter, he states: "I regard myself as a *particular favourite of Heaven,* and acknowledge the mercies of Providence in every occurrence of my life." Throughout the book, but especially in the latter parts, he dwells on the opposing institutions of slavery and Christianity, and thus much of what he relates about his early adventures is presented as supporting evidence for his thesis.

Equiano's quick-moving autobiography is written in a prose style marked by balanced sentence structure and a well-organized chronological order. His paragraphs are arranged in an arbitrary fashion as different narrative incidents come one after another without many paragraph breaks and without much transition between events and paragraphs. He begins his narrative with a typical eighteenth-century introduction that is full of modesty and humility on his undertaking such a task. He calls himself a "private and obscure individual" and solicits the "indulgent attention of the public."

Much of Equiano's prose style exhibits the kind of parallelism and balance made famous by Samuel Johnson. The narrative combines an expansive kind of rhetoric with passages written in the plain style, which are used deliberately and appropriately. Paul Edwards points out in his introduction to Equiano's book that what is distinctive about the plainer prose is "Equiano's skill in creating a dramatic language, not merely to describe in literal terms, but to recreate the very sense of the speaker's past simplicity and incomprehension and to distinguish this from an articulate and informed 'present' " [see Further Reading]. For example, Equiano describes the slave ship on which he is taken aboard "in naive terms—the ship is 'this hollow place', the sails 'cloth put upon the masts' and the anchor becomes 'some spell or magic they put upon the water, when they liked, to stop the vessel'. Equiano does not merely write about his perplexity, his language becomes, dramatically, that of the perplexed boy that he once was."

At times, however, Equiano uses his other voice when he breaks his narrative in order to moralize, point out, and instruct readers on the significance of the various events. In these passages, Equiano seems almost like a preacher when he sermonizes against the evils of slavery and when his religious fervor impels him to see God's will in everything that happens to him. This strident voice comes from the exhortative language of social protest devised by Cugoano. It is a voice in sharp contrast to that of the plain narrative parts where literary conventions required a balanced, matter-of-fact style. Equiano's double voice can be heard in many of the future slave narratives. For example, in Frederick Douglass's narrative, the two voices are exhibited clearly. [In his essay "Identity and Art in Frederick Douglass' *Narrative*" (1973)] Albert E. Stone points out that the "dominant one is the unassuming prose narrator who can set a scene, describe an action, or portray a person with forceful economy." Douglass's other voice is that of the "rich periods of the pulpit and platform, which sound so inflated and indulgent to modern ears."

The accounts of Equiano's youth in Africa and his kidnapping there form the most absorbing parts of his narrative. He was born in 1745 in the interior part of the kingdom of Benin, in present-day Nigeria. He carefully describes the African landscape and the customs of the people who till the soil in a fruitful land. It is doubtful that Equiano was able to know or remember all the geographical and cultural details about Africa that he touches upon in ordering and classifying the topographical and agricultural aspects of the country. Several passages in his first chapter are borrowed closely from Anthony Benezet's *Some Historical Account of Guinea,* which he credits in two footnotes. He must have been impressed greatly by Benezet's antislavery writings, which were published in the 1770s and 1780s. Benezet was one of the many Quakers who wrote against slavery in the eighteenth century. His histories of Africa and the slave trade enlightened many whites who had been unaware of the inhumanities of slavery and who had thought of Africa as a dark, crocodile-infested jungle. (pp. 49-55)

Benezet's account stresses the idea that the natives are goodnatured, while Equiano emphasizes the "warlike disposition of the inhabitants." Equiano was trying to paint a picture of the African as a noble savage of heroic dignity, while Benezet perhaps was describing the African from the viewpoint of Quaker virtue. Equiano also borrowed many other facts and ideas, such as the order of government in Benin, the strict penalties for theft, murder, and adultery, the ways in which kings kidnapped slaves in wartime, and the nature of the African religion. Benezet's work is moderate in its treatment of slavery. Unlike most other antislavery writers, who created sentimental romances and idealistic depictions of the Africans, Benezet fought for the abolition of slavery in a more realistic manner by describing exactly what he witnessed of the horrors of the slave trade and by presenting reasoned argument for its termination. By choosing Benezet as an important source, Equiano gave his work a credibility that could be accepted by white readers.

In the first chapter, Equiano depends heavily on Benezet to supply him with information about the land and customs of Africa, but in the second chapter, he relies more on his memory, for he relates his youthful days in Africa in a vivid and fascinating way. Equiano's graphic accounts of his capture and his journey into slavery are recollections of his own experience. Even here, however, Equiano re-creates his African days with ideas he read about and with the knowledge he acquired from a lifetime of experiences. Equiano describes his childhood in the context of Africa as an edenic place where even the snakes are harmless, but he shows that evil snakes exist who are the whites—mainly the Europeans—who have entered Africa to corrupt and pollute, resulting in the fall and enslavement of the noble savage.

Young Equiano is his mother's favorite child, and he lives an idyllic life in his father's house. His father is a wealthy chief. Although he owns many slaves, they are all treated with kindness, as indeed are all of the other slaves held by Equiano's people. These advanced Africans resemble the chosen race of the Jews because they practice circumcision and make "offerings and feasts on that occasion." They name the children for some "fancied forboding at the time of their birth." Equiano's first name, Olaudah, signifies "vicissitude or fortune also, one favoured, and having a loud voice and well spoken." He leads a joyful existence in which he is trained to be a happy warrior: "My daily exercise was shooting and throwing javelins; and my mother adorned me with emblems, after the manner of our greatest warriors." All this comes to an end when he is eleven years old. He and his sister are kidnapped by their tribe's enemies, and after being separated and then briefly reunited, they are parted forever, and he is sold into slavery. Equiano describes how he was sold from one master to another during a span of six or seven months that took him always toward the Atlantic coast. As he is "carried to the left of the sun's rising, through many different countries, and a number of large woods," he begins to observe the corrupting influence of the Europeans on the Africans. His first master is a smith who owns a bellows for working gold. Later, as he nears the coast, Equiano sees the mechanized instruments of industry and warfare. (pp. 56-7)

In delineating his African experience, Equiano wisely introduces the thesis that Western technology is being used to produce ill effects on people. Equiano's images of Africa are mainly his own as he ladens the primitivistic scene with realities that he directs toward the larger thematic concerns of his autobiography. It is true, then, what Houston A. Baker, Jr., says in his remarks about Equiano's work: "Only at a very primitive level of literary understanding could one interpret Vassa's assertions of the 'unbounded credulity and superstition' of his fellow Essakans and his descriptions of the indigenous purity of Africa's interior as testimony from the school of noble savagery" [see excerpt dated 1980].

The rest of Equiano's narrative deals with his adventures in the West Indies, England, the Mediterranean, the Arctic—indeed almost all over the world—as he serves his various masters, who are usually merchants or naval captains. The young man learns quickly as he exercises his curiosity and wonders over everything he witnesses and experiences. He has a small boy's wonder and a sense of the marvelous about everything he sees. He watches ships start and stop, looks through a quadrant, examines brick houses, hears a watch ticking, and sees a picture hanging in a room. He thinks he is in another world and that everything about him is magic.

This magical charm soon gives way to the harsh realities of civilization. Equiano undergoes the wretched plight of the slave condition. He sees blacks treated as animals everywhere he goes, especially in Georgia and in the West Indies. He himself often fares badly; however, most of his masters are kind to him, although they sometimes make his life miserable. Equiano also experiences firsthand some of the other evil aspects of civilization. While serving under British Captain Pascal, he is involved in several naval battles with the French, and many times he is the subject of deceptions and frauds practiced upon him by whites. Sometimes he is used for the sport of white gentlemen. On a ship from Holland to England, he and the white boys are paired with one another and made to fight for the diversion of the passengers on board. The boys are encouraged to bloody each other by being given a few shillings. (pp. 58-9)

What is remarkable about Equiano's cruel journey from innocence to experience is that he never becomes bitter or cynical after undergoing and witnessing all forms of intolerance and ruthlessness. He keeps himself alive in buoyant spirits, and he has a strong belief that God will always take care of him. Sometimes he can even laugh at his misfortunes. While still a slave, Equiano and his friend, Captain Farmer, take care of a dying silversmith in Georgia, who promises to bequeath them his huge fortune if they minister to his needs. They attend him day and night until he dies, and then they discover that the dead man has left one dollar and a half in his trunk. They hurriedly leave the corpse, and Equiano humorously remarks: "We went away greatly mortified, and left the deceased to do as well as he could for himself, as we had taken so good care of him when alive for nothing." The ironic humor is increased if Equiano intended a pun on the word *mortified.*

In the first half of the book, Equiano is interested in dreams, magic, and superstitious tales. When he arrives in Philadelphia for the first time, he visits a fortune teller, who propitiously informs him he will not be a slave for long. Here he is unlike the young Franklin who bought loaves of bread to munch on while walking down Market Street. Equiano is more interested in the spiritual quality of life. In the early part of the book, this is seen in his concern for religion, whether it is the African variety of his homeland where God lives in the sun and genially smokes a pipe or his early Christian religion mixed with his African notions of dream and magic.

As he proceeds with his slave duties, Equiano takes his newfound faith to heart, and now when he thinks of escape, he calls upon God to deliver him. He recalls the golden rule and states: "I trust it has ever been my ruling principle, that honesty is the best policy." This maxim from *Poor Richard's Almanack* reminds us of the story of Franklin's rise to success. In fact, Franklin is very much in our minds when we read of how Equiano earns enough money to buy his freedom by working hard in various enterprises he conducts after his regular working hours. He vividly and carefully describes his first business ventures:

> After I had been sailing for some time with this captain [Farmer], at length I endeavoured to try my luck and commence merchant. I had but a very small capital to begin with; for one single half bit, which is equal to three pence in England, made up my whole stock. However I trusted to the Lord to be with me; and at one of our trips to St. Eustatia, a Dutch island, I bought a glass tumbler with my half bit, and when I came to Montserrat I sold it for a bit, or sixpence. Luckily we made several successive trips to St. Eustatia (which was a general mart for the West Indies, about twenty leagues from Montserrat); and in our next, finding my tumbler so profitable with this one bit I bought two tumblers more; and when I came back I sold them for two bits, equal to a shilling sterling. When we went again I bought with these two bits four more of these glasses, which I sold for four bits on our return to Montserrat: and in our next voyage to St. Eustatia I bought a jug of Geneva, nearly about three pints in measure. When we came to Montserrat I sold the gin for eight bits, and the tumblers for two, so that my capital now amounted in all to a dollar, well husbanded and acquired in the space of a month or six weeks, when I blessed the Lord that I was so rich.

Equiano is fascinated by his ability to compound his money. He is intensely absorbed in his increase of wealth through his own efforts; however, at the same time he is mindful that his material success is an act of Providence.

Houston A. Baker, Jr., has written about Equiano's work that the "structure of the text of the narrative seems to reflect the author's conviction that it is absolutely necessary for the slave to negotiate the economics of slavery if he would be free" [see Further Reading]. We see that this is a belief held deeply by Equiano as he directs his efforts to their ultimate end: the purchase of his liberation.

The young slave gains his freedom on July 10, 1766. Equiano includes his manumission form in its entirety in the middle of his narrative. Up to that point, he has depicted himself as a kind of picaresque hero whose main interest is in his survival by his wit and cunning in a world of nets and snares. He is a young black captured from his African home who quickly catches on to the ways of the world of experience and thus prepares himself for survival and deliverance through his industry and his clever intelligence. He appeals to his Quaker master by way of the friendly Captain Farmer, and he offers his master a good business deal and a free Quaker conscience at the same time.

Once Equiano gains his freedom and presents his manumission form, the style, tone, and character of the narrative change. The last half of the book is concerned mainly with his newfound freedom that transforms him into a lofty figure. His freedom from the bondage of slavery permits him to function in a world as a new man in his outward dealings and in his inward concerns for salvation. He escapes perils at sea, his business ventures succeed while those of others around him fail, and he gains fame as the "sable captain" when he safely conducts a ship to port after Captain Farmer dies. On another ship, he dreams three times of a wreck; when it happens, he is responsible for saving everyone after the captain proves himself to be a stupid coward. When everyone is safe on an island, the grateful Equiano orders limes, oranges, and lemons planted on shore "as a token to any one that might be cast away hereafter."

Captain Farmer's death aboard ship soon after Equiano achieves his legal freedom gives the former slave mixed feelings. Paul Edwards writes that "regret for Farmer's death mingles inextricably with the pleasure Equiano feels (and is prepared to reveal as having its boastful and complacent side) about the opportunity which Farmer's death has given him to display his own skills as a navigator and leader of men." After he gains his freeman status, it is clear that Equiano does not immediately feel himself a free man, for when he signs up to work as an able-bodied sailor, he says, "I consented to slave on as before." It is not until Captain Farmer dies and Equiano takes command of the vessel that he comes into his own. The captain's death gives him responsibility that allows him to become psychologically as well as legally free:

> The whole care of the vessel rested, therefore, upon me, and I was obliged to direct her by my former experience, not being able to work a traverse. . . . Many were surprised when they heard of my conducting the sloop into the port, and I now obtained a new appellation, and was

called Captain. This elated me not a little, and it was quite flattering to my vanity to be thus styled by as high a title as any free man in this place possessed. When the death of the captain became known, he was much regretted by all who knew him; for he was a man universally respected. At the same time the sable captain lost no fame; for the success I had met with increased the affection of my friends in no small measure.

Equiano's freedom allows him to assume a protean character. He can do almost anything and succeed at it. In Georgia, he is asked to officiate as a parson at a funeral. Later he signs up for a remarkable expedition to the North Pole, which gets closer to the pole than any other excursion up to this time. He returns to England and settles down as a hairdresser. Like John Marrant, he plays the French horn, and he lives his life his own way, picking himself up whenever the spirit of the sea moves him to sail on a voyage to the Mediterranean or to some other part of the globe. He spends his time in antislavery work and even petitions the queen for the abolition of slavery. In this case, he displays his cogency because his plea for ending the slave trade is based mainly on economic arguments. He argues that England's manufacturing interests would benefit greatly if the trade in humans were ended and trade and commerce in material goods were carried on between England and the vast, emerging continent of Africa.

The most important benefit that Equiano's freedom gives to him is the development of his religious and spiritual life. In the latter part of the narrative, he relates his growing experiences in the Christian faith. In London, he attends religious "soul feasts" among dissenters and is taught that salvation is freely given by God because people are unworthy of attaining it on their own. He keeps the commandments and tries to improve himself morally and spiritually. The blasphemous language of the sailors on ship now troubles him, and he decides to associate "with those whom the scripture calls the excellent of the earth." The language of the narrative becomes biblical: "I saw the blessed Redeemer to be the fountain of life, and the well of salvation. I experienced him all in all; he had brought me by way that I knew not, and he had made crooked paths straight." Equiano sees God's providence in all of his life—from his kidnapping in "pagan" Africa to his salvation in Christianity. When the polar expedition fails to find a northeast passage to India, it is because of God's will: "I was roused by the sound of fame, to seek new adventures, and to find, towards the north pole, what our Creator never intended we should, a passage to India." In Philadelphia, he studies the Quakers' gentle ways and applauds their free schooling for blacks.

The most significant change in the latter part of the autobiography is Equiano's inward probing of his spiritual life. According to him, his entire life has been a steady working of God's providence in leading the young Equiano from the primitive creed in Africa to a true Christian religion in the Western world. Earlier in his narrative, he compares the African religious customs to the Jewish practices. He does this so he can suggest now that the African creed is not an entirely alien belief but that it resembles the Jewish faith in being a developing step on the stairway to Christian truth. In typological fashion, Equiano finds he has been involved in a reenactment of a biblical pattern in that his life has shown a spiritual progress from the old law to the new. In Africa, he was born in a culture that he now equates with the Hebrew one; in a way, his conversion is a fulfillment, not an extreme turn from "paganism" to Christianity. (pp. 59-64)

Angelo Costanzo, "The Spiritual Autobiography and Slave Narrative of Olaudah Equiano," in his Surprizing Narrative: Olaudah Equiano and the Beginnings of Black Autobiography, *Greenwood Press, 1987, pp. 41-90.*

Keith A. Sandiford (essay date 1988)

[*Sandiford is a Barbadian-born Canadian educator. In the following excerpt, he shows how Equiano's* Interesting Narrative *bolstered the abolitionist cause in eighteenth-century England, emphasizing Equiano's politically evocative presentation of his experiences before, during, and after his enslavement.*]

With the appearance in 1789 of Olaudah Equiano's two-volume autobiography, the revolution of racial and political consciousness in Black literature of eighteenth-century England reached its highest form and effectiveness. Published during the climactic phase of abolitionist agitation, ***The Interesting Narrative of the Life of Olaudah Equiano, or Gustavus Vassa, the African*** was supported by the British Anti-Slavery Trade Society and was proposed to the British public as an authentic document to bolster the abolitionist case and to win the sympathy of Parliament, which was then beginning active formal debate on measures to end the slave trade. Although Equiano was no stranger to antislavery partisans (he had made several political representations on his African brothers and sisters' behalf during the preceding fifteen years), this literary event gave to the world a permanent and inspiring record of a Black man's experience under slavery. It offered a persuasive account of the actual conditions of that economic system which exploited the free labor of Blacks for the material prosperity of whites and of a social system which dehumanized members of the African race through laws and practices that were hostile, discriminatory, and oppressive.

Both Equiano's personal life as depicted in the ***Life*** and his public activities as attested by independent sources corroborate the thesis that the Africans themselves were a major force in the struggle for and eventual achievement of respect for their human dignity and value. If committed, imaginative leadership consists in using the tools of wide personal experience to seize and transform the circumstances of a given historical moment, Equiano's performance wins that citation deservedly. Many experiences helped to shape his colorful career as an abolitionist and political activist: the rigors and hazards he endured as a seafarer; the resourcefulness he acquired as a small trader; and the spiritual intensity he experienced as a convert to Calvinism. This extraordinary accretion of practical abilities and moral endowments fitted him well for the challenge of verbalizing more explicitly those issues of race and status which [Ignatius] Sancho was forced to equivocate about and which [Ottobah] Cugoano had inveighed against in a more heavy-handed polemical style. As the third figure in the triumvirate of eighteenth-century Black writers, Equiano joins the moderating impulses of religion and humanitarianism to the sterner techniques of politics and activism to epitomize in himself all that was most ennobling and heroic in the anti-slavery struggle. (pp. 118-19)

[Equiano's life] bespeaks a life defined by rapid change, where crucial choices were externally imposed and where adjustment to them had to be as quick as present fortune was variable. Even before he left Africa, Equiano was faced with these uncertainties and had begun to feel their profound psychological effects. He was sold repeatedly in the different communities that lay between his native village and the slave coast. Even though he was treated with affectionate indulgence by some of his masters, the wrenching pangs of loss and the terror of things unknown left him heartsick and distraught. Every youthful dream of happiness and permanence was frustrated by a fresh shift in circumstance: he had become a victim of the inexorable laws of trade in the commodity of human flesh. Equiano thus recalls his distress on being passed from the control of a people whose customs were similar to his own to that of a people whose customs were strange and repugnant:

> At the very moment I dreamed of the greatest happiness, I found myself most miserable; and it seemed as if fortune wished to give me this state of joy, only to render the reverse more poignant. The change I now experienced was as painful as it was sudden and unexpected . . . but I came at length to a country the inhabitants of which differed from us in all particulars [manners, customs, and language]. I was very much struck with this difference, especially when I came among a people who did not circumcise, and ate without washing their hands.

But if Equiano's encounter with different tribes of his own race evoked from him responses of prejudice and distrust, his initiation into the culture of the Europeans occasioned him even greater trauma. The long hair and strange language of the white men on board the slave ship intimidated him and intensified his sense of total dissociation from this strange, new world: "I was now persuaded that I had gotten into a world of bad spirits, and that they were going to kill me." The sounds and sights of human misery among the African captives, the unhealthy stench of crowded quarters, and the brutal floggings inflicted on them by the white men all filled him constantly with a fear of his own death.

The manners of the whites and the mechanics of their world were to remain continual sources of fear and puzzlement with Equiano for a long time to come: "I could not help expressing my fears and apprehensions to some of my countrymen: I asked them if these people had no country, but lived in this hollow place [the ship]: they told me they did not, but came from a distant one. 'Then,' said I, 'how comes it in all our country we never heard of them?' They told me because they lived so very far off." He was convinced that his new masters must be a race of evil sorcerers to invent and operate something as marvelous to him as a sailing ship, and he relates his confused astonishment in terms of striking self-humour and naivete: "I asked how the vessel could go? They told me they could not tell; but that there were cloths upon the masts by the help of the ropes I saw, and then the vessel went; and the white men had some spell or magic they put in the water when they liked in order to stop the vessel. I was exceedingly amazed at this account and really thought they were spirits."

Other symbols of Western culture were to stir Equiano's imagination further. On the high seas, he was fascinated by the use of the quadrant; in Campbell's Virginia plantation house, the ticking of the clock on the wall raised in his unsophisticated mind the fear "that it would tell the gentlemen anything I might do amiss"; and on Pascal's ships he conceived the notion, from watching his close friend Dick Baker read, that white people literally conversed with books: "I have often taken up a book, and talked to it, and then put my ears to it, when alone, in hopes it would answer; and I have been very much concerned when I found it remained silent."

The relation of incidents such as these carry plural significance. First, it shows that although Equiano was, by the time of writing, a man widely traveled in and knowledgeable about the white man's world, he does not disdain that earlier image of himself as the archetypal innocent, the primitive stricken by fear and amazement at the wonders of an alien world. Then, we are forced to ponder what must have been the heavy emotional costs, not only to Equiano individually, but to all African slaves collectively, of sudden propulsion from their cultural matrix into a vastly different civilization. It is clear that Equiano's confusion was aggravated by his initial inability to communicate in English. After leaving the slave ship, he had met no one who spoke his native tongue, and after less than two years, he was to lose the companionship of Dick Baker to the vagaries of navy life.

As if friendlessness and language difficulties were not enough, Equiano had to suffer the constant humiliation of being called by a different name, according to the whims of successive masters. On the slave ship he was called Michael; in Virginia they called him Jacob; and in England Pascal renamed him Gustavus Vassa. Evidently, Equiano disliked this last appellation and resisted it spiritedly for a time. On the other hand, he took great pride in Olaudah, his African name, and retained a lasting respect for his people's native tradition of naming children purposefully—as he explains it, "from some event, some circumstance, or fancied foreboding at the time of their birth."

All these changes and chances threatened the integrity of his ego and the survival of his personal cultural inheritance. And although age and maturity would eventually reconfirm his faith in Africa, in her people and their traditions, during these early years among the Europeans, he found himself doubting his own identity and loathing his physical features. From his first observations of the Europeans' manners on the slave ship, Equiano had acquired the notion that they would surely eat him. This notion was unwittingly reinforced by the playful taunts of crew members and, in later years, by his master Pascal and by other

The wreck of the slave ship "Nancy" on the Bahama Banks, 1767. This engraving served as the frontispiece for volume II of the American edition of Equiano's Narrative.

sailors in the navy. The possibility that this childish fantasy could transform itself into an annihilating reality seemed to increase in direct proportion to his contacts with white people during his early months in England. Again, it is instructive to attempt a speculative analysis of Equiano's psychic state. It illuminates both his individual behavior and the collective behavior of all the slaves under the shock of cultural displacement. We may see Equiano's fear of being cannibalized by the whites as his apprehension of the white master's ultimate prerogative over the Black slave. We may see it further as a death wish through which he hoped to find a speedy issue out of present affliction. But perhaps more revealingly, we may perceive in the coincidence of self-loathing emotions with the fear of cannibalism the logical extremes to which white dominance over Blacks must have driven the slave in those times: just as food, eaten and digested, in time becomes an integral part of the eating organism, so in this fantasy we may perceive an unconscious succumbing to that assimilation which was the fate of the New World slave.

That Equiano's primary self-concept, forged in the security of his African homeland, was beginning to quail under assault from the powerful images of the new world around him is even more vividly illustrated in another recollection. In it, he recalls his despondency about the difference in complexion between himself and a little female playmate he met at Guernsey: "I had often observed that when her mother washed her face it looked very rosy; but when she washed mine it did not look so; I therefore tried oftentimes myself if I could not by washing make my face the same colour as my little playmate (Mary), but it was all in vain." As his fluency in English improved, Equiano began to feel easier among the English and to repudiate his irrational fears. Greater understanding of English manners and customs, however, only had the adverse effect of depreciating those he had been socialized to in Africa. He strove to remake himself in the white man's image in order to become more acceptable in his society: "I soon grew a stranger to terror of every kind, and was, in that respect at least, almost an Englishman. . . . I now not only felt myself quite easy with my new countrymen, but relished their society and manners. I no longer looked upon them as spirits, but as men superior to us; and therefore I had the stronger desire to resemble them; and to imbibe their spirit and to imitate their manners." Temporarily, at least, we may see in Equiano's fond attachment to Pascal, to Daniel Queen, and to Robert King in particular an orphaned youth's search for a surrogate father. His readiness to embrace English culture may likewise be viewed as the adaptive reorganization of a culturally displaced person's ego-identity to meet the demands of a new life.

Unlike Cugoano's *Thoughts,* Equiano's ***Life*** poses no significant questions of authorship. The story agrees closely enough with other slaves' accounts of slavery conditions and with the record of independent history. It is written with a simplicity that is the mark of honest truth and with a moral earnestness that is usually lacking, or at best only contrived, in ghostwritten slave narratives. By the time he came to write his narrative, Equiano had received considerable tuition in reading and writing: on the ships from his young teacher, Richard Baker, and from the father figure, Daniel Queen; and in London from the Misses Guerin and from a tutor at the Reverend Gregory's academy. His irresistible curiosity about books is illustrated elsewhere in this chapter. Besides, he makes numerous references to reading the Bible and other devotional books.

In addition to these conscious sources of intellectual stimulation, one must also take into account the unconscious education he derived from his association with Evangelical mentors; from abolitionists like Granville Sharp, Thomas Clarkson, and Peter Peckard; and from prominent persons like Governor MacNamara (whom he served for some months in 1779), Dr. Charles Irving, and Constantine Phipps, the explorer.

Despite the weight of all this evidence for independent authorship, there have been a few hints, even from reviewers persuaded of Equiano's ability, that he was assisted in writing. Even a reviewer as appreciative as the writer in the *Monthly Review,* who praised Equiano's artlessness profusely and accepted the authenticity of the ***Life*** ("the narrative wears an honest face," he wrote), still guardedly conceded that he may have been assisted, if only in the proofing [see excerpt dated 1789]. Of course, this is to cavil rather triflingly, for even the work of eminent established writers undergoes some proofing and emendation at the hands of others. A number of grammatical and mechanical errors have been remarked, but in the main they are either identical with those found in other eighteenth-century native English writers or are non-native features common in West African English. There is, then, no serious doubt that Equiano wrote his autobiography on his own: the evidence of personal letters and the testimony of reliable contemporaries establish him as the indisputable and sole author of the ***Life.***

The success of Equiano's book was largely due to the timeliness of its publication, the topicality of its subject matter, and the popularity of its literary form. When it appeared in 1789, Parliament was inquiring into the operations of the slave trade. Up to that time, much of the evidence about that traffic was supplied by prejudiced observers and vested interests. Now, the availability to the lawmakers of an ex-slave's authentic account of the indignities he suffered was bound to weigh heavily against abolition's foes. Furthermore, the active promotion of the book by the Abolition Committee soon established it as an authoritative document from which antislavery advocates in Parliament quoted regularly.

Both the volume of the subscription list and the quality of persons whose names appeared on it showed the extent to which all social classes had been sensitized to abolitionist activities. The publication of an eighth edition only five years after the first is proof of the continued interest in Equiano's character and in his point of view on slavery. Nor was the book's appeal confined to metropolitan London. In the decade between 1789 and 1799, Equiano traveled extensively throughout Great Britain speaking on behalf of the Abolition Committee and promoting his book. He was in Birmingham in 1789; Manchester, Nottingham, and Cambridge the next year; Belfast on Christmas Day, 1791; Dublin and Hull in 1792; and at Bath and Devizes, in the west of England, in 1793. In Ireland alone the book sold nineteen hundred copies in an eight-and-a-half month period.

Like Sancho and Cugoano before him, Equiano wrote his autobiography with a clear conception of the readers it would appeal to. In a general sense, also, the identity of his audience was much the same as theirs: readers whose support for broad humanitarian causes encompassed a sympathy for the plight of the African. Yet Equiano's work did not thrive solely on inherited fortune. Certain important distinctions in the character of his narrative and in the quality of his life served to enrich the African literary heritage and expand the audience for these productions. Sancho's *Letters* was likely to attract mainly the aficionados of sentimentalism and good-natured drollery after the manner of Sterne. Cugoano's *Thoughts,* on account of its more formal rhetorical features, could, by and large, sustain the interest of only the most literate, even erudite, readers. But Equiano's choice of an engaging human story, told in a consistently lucid style, makes the ***Life*** the most permanently interesting of the three works. What is more, the wider range of experiences he relates and the strategic emphases he places on certain categories of experience gave him a wider scope for audience appeal than either of his forerunners.

Besides profiting from widening popular support for the African cause, Equiano's book also participated in certain important developments favoring the genre of autobiographical writing. The Methodist Revival in religion encouraged converts to give form and validity to their lives by recording their experiences in spiritual memoirs. A marked tendency towards openness about personal feelings (the inevitable result, no doubt, of a corresponding interest in self-analysis) made the interior truth of individual lives a fit subject for conventional literature. And if all these developments point to a concern for depth rather than surface, a preoccupation with essence rather than appearance, it is not hard to see why the African, who suffered so much from prejudice against his external features, should now be rescued from eternal nonentity by a literary form eminently suited to reveal his full humanity to European readers. Shumaker's comments about general autobiography are applicable here: "The truth about character, men began to realize, could not always be observed in outward behaviour."

Equiano was compelled by his troubling self-consciousness in the presence of white people to search deeper within himself to rediscover the meaning of blackness, both in the narrow political terms of eighteenth-century slavery and in the broader terms of his relation to the human race. Autobiography provided a medium through which to recreate that identity which his early encounter with the Europeans had threatened to efface. Also, through the peculiar rhetoric of this literary form, he was able to confront his readers with the proposition that the African was capable of spiritual and emotional sensations which slavery might deny but could not destroy. While his day-to-day life was marked by constant flux, self-doubt, hardship, and change, the intellectual process of transforming these realities into a single object of literary art afforded him a new vision of himself and a new valuation of his people. Any such observation necessarily defines a difference between how an individual perceives the raw materials of daily existence as life hands them to him and how he perceives them after they have been tempered in the forge of recollected experiences.

This difference manifests itself in Equiano's work as two contrastive prose styles. When he wants to recapture the bewilderment and ignorance of young Olaudah, the kidnapped victim, his narrative style is naïve, the language plain, almost studiedly simplistic. (pp. 121-26)

On the other hand, when he wants to show that maturity had taught him to value himself and his cultural heritage, the style is confident and self-affirming. It is strategically significant that those qualities characterize the better part of chapter 1 and a small portion of chapter 2, where he outlines the circumstances of his upbringing and the manners of his people. . . . In this way, Equiano achieves two vital ends: the necessary imperative of self-discovery and the greater end of establishing the human truth about his race.

Although Equiano shuns the confrontational polemics of Cugoano by giving more space to spiritualized reflection than to political rhetoric, he still challenges directly certain widely published views of Africa and some of the most common misconceptions about her people. Typically, he does this in calm, declarative statements. In the following simple declaration, he answers, without naming his opposition, those detractors of African character who painted Africans as constitutionally prone to indolence and shiftlessness: "Agriculture is our chief employment; and every one, even the children and women, are engaged in it. Thus we are all habituated to labour from our earliest years. Every one contributes to the common stock; and as we are unacquainted with idleness, we have no beggars." The high incidence of mendicancy and vagrancy in eighteenth-century England makes the last sentence tellingly sarcastic. To those racial chauvinists who associated physical beauty and intellectual power with fair skins, blue eyes, and blond hair, Equiano, again unobtrusively, proposes these sobering thoughts:

> The West India planters prefer the slaves of Benin or Eboe to those of any other part of Guinea, for their hardiness, intelligence, integrity, and zeal. Those benefits are felt by us in a general healthiness of people, and in their vigour and activity. I might have added too in their comeliness. Deformity is indeed unknown amongst us, I mean that of shape. Numbers of natives of Eboe now in London might be brought in support of this assertion: for in regard to complexion, ideas of beauty are wholly relative.

Now writing as the abolitionist of 1789, Equiano has supplanted the naïve self-depreciation of the boy of 1757 with a mature apprehension of the nature of things.

Equiano's life as a slave and seafarer eloquently attested the native virtues of his people. Jostling daily among men given to drunkenness, swearing, and bloodthirsty threats, he stood out as a model of virtue and industry, sparing no effort to perform his duties diligently and winning for himself his masters' respect and his captains' trust. To Robert King he became an indispensable factotum:

> There was scarcely any part of his business or household affairs, in which I was not occasionally engaged. I often supplied the place of clerk, in receiving and delivering cargoes to the ships, in tending horses and delivering goods: and, besides this, I used to shave and dress my master when convenient, and take care of his horse, and when it was necessary, which was very often, I worked likewise on board of different vessels of his.

To Thomas Farmer, a captain on one of King's vessels, he proved equally trustworthy: "better to him on board than any three white men he had." Under pressure of many perilous situations at sea, Equiano's fortitude and self-possession that saved the crew from total disaster, the captain's navigation having proved inept and the crew having abandoned themselves to drunken desperation: "I could not help thinking that if any of these people had been lost, God would charge me with their lives, which perhaps, was one cause of my labouring so hard for their preservation, and indeed every one of them afterwards seemed so sensible of the service I had rendered them; and while we were on the key I was a kind of chieftain among them."

The diligent reader will detect a generous measure of boastful exaggeration and personal aggrandizement in this passage (note the last eight words) and others. Also, although the calamity described in the first two lines occurred before his conversion, the manner of his remembering it is strongly informed by the religious self-consciousness of his maturer years. Narrative invention notwithstanding, to an abolitionist audience these solid demonstrations of individual integrity affirmed the African's human capabilities and gave point to antislavery agitation for the end of the dehumanizing trade. They gave even greater urgency to proposals for the establishment of a social order that would recognize the Africans' intrinsic dignity and replace the plantation ethos.

So Equiano wrung from the autobiographical mode a positive image of his own personal worth, expressed in terms of his capacity for work. He rediscovered and redefined the self in affirmative images, while implicitly repudiating the slanders of the slavocrats. Although not scored in a strident rhetorical key, such indirect statements are equally effective as protest. Mary Williams Burger calls them "positive protest"—a protest that creates as it eliminates and deals with the opposition's ugliness by concentrating on its own beauty."

Just as Equiano reinterpreted slave labor, which was otherwise only drudgery and a mark of menial status, so that it becomes one of his most sophisticated subversive tools, he used religion (which the colonial establishment used to make slaves passive and obedient) to add greater moral authority to his politics and his writing. That authority was the fruit of long self-searching and of observing an almost unrealistic standard of rectitude in personal conduct.

Equiano endeavored very early in his youth to make a positive protest against slavery, not so much by resisting overtly as by presenting himself as a moral agent in his own right, certainly equal, if not superior, to the whites he worked among. His regular practice of prayer and Bible reading won him the respect of his crew mates. On the *Aetna,* the sailors styled him the "black Christian." In the ***Life,*** he is confident that his piety was the cause of many a narrow escape from death, both for himself and for his fellow sailors. He claims to have had several premonitory dreams about shipwrecks, one of which was realized much as he had dreamed it during the 1767 voyage alluded to above. He ascribes spiritual significance to the most commonplace events and fosters a firm belief in the universal influence of Providence: "I had a mind on which everything uncommon made its full impression, and every event which I considered as marvellous. Every extraordinary escape or signal deliverance, either of myself or others, I looked upon to be effected by the interposition of Providence." G. A. Starr remarks on this tendency in spiritual autobiographers to spiritualize every aspect of their common experience: "Since mere trifles can have the gravest consequences if allowed to pass unheeded, it follows that nothing is beneath the notice of the alert Christian." And the Abbé Gregoire, in specific reference to Equiano, viewed his spiritualizing tendency as a result of the African's peculiar social condition in the world of the eighteenth century: "The effect of adversity is to give more energy to religious sentiments. Man abandoned by his fellow man and unfortunate upon the earth, turns his looks towards heaven, to seek there consolations and a father."

A great majority of the mishaps and emergencies recounted in the narrative precede Equiano's conversion. While the genuineness of his spiritual faith, as it emerges in this situation, is unimpeachable, it is obvious that Equiano was highly self-conscious about the moral leverage which his profound spirituality gave him over the white men. There is noticeable religious conceit in his self-portrait as it appears in the description of the shipwreck off Cadiz in March 1775. He is the image of resignation and self-composure, secure in the knowledge of God's will, while the rest of the crew are thrown into panic and confusion: "Although I could not swim and saw no way of escaping death, I felt no dread in my then situation, having no desire to live. I even rejoiced in spirit, thinking this death would be sudden glory. But the fulness of time was not yet come. The people near to me were much astonished in seeing me thus calm and resigned; but I told them of the peace of God, which through sovereign grace I enjoyed. . . . "

At the start of the narrative, Equiano prefaces his life story with words skillfully chosen from the repertoire of rhetorical convention. He courts the interest of his readers by modestly characterizing himself as a "private and obscure individual, and a stranger too," disclaiming any interest in literary sensationalism ("I offer here the story of neither a saint, a hero, nor a tyrant.") and any desire for personal glory ("I am not so foolishly vain as to expect from it [the narrative] either immortality or literary reputation").

But Equiano displays considerable technical capacity in creating, through these disclaimers, an illusion of artless autobiographical writing while fulfilling the less obvious political designs of his abolitionist sponsors. While it may be assumed that a sympathetic audience and a more reliably informed public would have been willing to generalize on the basis of Equiano's proven capacity for hard work and intense spiritual faith, Equiano did not leave it entirely up to his readers to reshape their received images of Africans solely on the evidence of his exemplary life. He devoted significant space to a deliberate description of Ibo life in particular and to a spirited defence of African culture in particular. (pp. 127-30)

By such strategies of indirection and implied criticism, Equiano debunked the myths of Western European cultural superiority. He corrected some of the impressions white people had about Africa by affirming Africa's authentic cultural validity and by showing that difference or strangeness was not a criterion of value, since ideas of progress and civilization were all relative to time and place. Paul Edwards and Ian Duffield, in a joint article examining in greater depth Equiano's appreciation of Turkey and Africa, assess his achievement thus: "The picture Equiano draws of Ibo society seems a generally accurate one, and without extravagance, but with understandable pride he shows us a society which is, within its own terms, rational, pious, virtuous, frugal, hygienic, industrious. Equiano offers us the earliest defense of African social order to be written by an African and addressed to a white audience.

Equiano's long service as a slave and later as a sailor provided him with a unique narrative context. Slavery involved suffering; it was a living reminder of man's inhumanity to man. Seafaring entailed hazards and adventures, both of which put the traveler's physical and moral strength to the test. Each of these two narrative sources represented an important metaphor for the spiritual life with which eighteenth-century Evangelical readers were familiar. And nothing must have commended Equiano's autobiography more to them than his insistence on spiritualizing even the smallest incidents of his common life. As he writes, Equiano stresses the moral advantages of reflective narrative over the merely factual recording of secular experience. In choosing the reflective mode of autobiography, he identified himself with a revered tradition of converts, and thus the narrative was approved by the generality of Evangelical readers.

For all the mental torture that his enslavement caused him, Equiano still reasoned that such adversity was the will of God. He viewed his passing from the ownership of Mr. Campbell, the Virginian slaveholder, to the ownership of Captain Pascal as an act of providential deliverance, especially since Pascal proved to be the more humane master. He described it as the work of "the kind and unknown hand of the Creator who in very deed leads the blind in a way they know not." (pp. 131-32)

While it is true to say that Equiano-the-writer was a product of slavery, it is also remarkable that the autobiography does not devote greater attention to particularizing the horrors of slavery. Among abolitionist leaders, Equiano was certainly one of the best qualified to render a faithful account of the operations of the trade and of the conditions that existed in slave society. And yet, in spite of his special qualifications (personal experience and firsthand observation), the quantum of explicit antislavery statements is moderate by comparison with the emphases of Cugoano's *Thoughts* or Ramsay's *Essay,* for example. There are good reasons for this. Equiano seemed determined to win support for the cause of his enslaved fellows more by the subtler arts of self-revelation than by the hurly-burly tactics of polemical writing. Besides, he did not perceive his primary audience to be the confirmed enemies of the African (as Cugoano did): he was speaking more to the converted, both as to religious convictions and as to political awareness. Equiano's introductory statements to the ***Life*** show that while he had set his face firmly against romanticizing his life for the sake of popularity, he had also resolved to observe steadfastly the rules of decorum in imaginative art. (pp. 134-35)

What direct addresses Equiano makes to proslavery partisans are sparse, although none the less cogent. Apologists for the European slave trade rationalized it by pointing to the existence of slavery in Africa. Equiano candidly admits that the Ibos and their neighbors kept slaves, but he makes some important distinctions. He insists that his people sold and enslaved only those who were prisoners of war or such as were "convicted of kidnapping, or adultery, and some other crimes, which were esteemed heinous." He affirms that slaves were treated as members of their masters' households, sharing the work thereof with free members, rather than being relegated exclusively to the performance of menial labor or bearing any stigma of social disgrace as a mark of their status. This description agreed with the testimony of Cugoano and others, but stood in manifest opposition to those commentaries that painted West Indian slavery as benign compared to African. Equiano also took to task those publicists who depreciated the slaves' contribution to the colonial economy by depicting them as unskilled drudges whose upkeep outstripped their productivity. With remarkable virtuosity in logical argument, Equiano asked rhetorically why it was that the purveyors of such opinions were also the most stubborn opponents of abolition: "I suppose nine-tenths of the mechanics throughout the West Indies are negro slaves; and I well know the coopers among them earn two dollars a day; the carpenters the same, and oftentimes more; as also the masons, smiths, and fishermen, &c. and I have known many slaves whose masters would not take a thousand pounds current for them."

It was in statements of this kind that Equiano proved his inestimable value to the abolitionists. Hitherto, the proslavery forces challenged antislavery spokesmen on the ground that they criticized the slave system out of emotional sentiment springing mainly from inaccurate information—in short, they tried to discredit them because, for the most part, they had not witnessed slavery firsthand. Equiano had. He was able to make a special contribution to the evidence already supplied by Benezet, Ramsay, and Clarkson, throwing the full weight of his unimpeachable integrity behind that evidence. Proslavery's last refuge was to raise a spurious allegation that he was not born in Africa, as he claimed, but on the Dutch island of Santa Cruz. Equiano was able to lay that charge to rest by invoking the testimony of all those prominent persons who knew him as a slave boy traveling in and out of England on navy ships.

On the whole, these sequences of explicit antislavery discourse in the ***Life*** stand out as examples of honest argument in the interest of noble humanitarian goals. Equiano displays great discipline of mind in keeping humanitarian purposes the single-minded motivation of his narrative. One of his chief impressions was that the slave trade was entirely "a war with the heart of man." With perceptive philosophic insight, he viewed its continuance as a threat to the survival of those liberal institutions on which the progress and prosperity of human civilization rested. In short, he took the position that the degradation of any single race of humans would ultimately touch the whole species, because slavery destroyed those natural affections that distinguish human beings from beasts.

These were strong objections, evidently aimed at the humanitarian sentiments of a British public whose social consciousness had evolved beyond the purely sentimental effusions of Sancho's time to the practical concern for relieving poverty and distress wherever they existed. Always the man of action himself, Equiano found this shifting of emphasis in abolition strategy towards more active political agitation congenial to his temperament. His remarks to Captain Doran . . . indicate that he took an early interest in the words and deeds of abolitionist leaders. The evidence of his acquaintance and cooperation with prominent abolitionists is clear and impressive. While still in the West Indies, he had met Ramsay, and he kept up an association with him throughout his later time in England. Similarly, he had a close working relationship with Clarkson and his professor, Dr. Peckard. (pp. 140-41)

Abolitionists were dogged and persistent in their condemnation of the slave trade, but they possessed enough imagination and flexibility to harness the winds of intellectual change to suit the objectives of their cause. Equiano's campaigning through various parts of Great Britain coincided with the emergence of a new power bloc of capitalist industrialists. This group was beginning to agitate against the traditional mercantilist philosophy, which protected the West Indian sugar interests at the expense of other entrepreneurs and at considerable cost to the British consumer and taxpayer. The group supported a policy of free trade that would open up new markets and spread the benefits of progressive commerce more widely among the British people. In championing a reformed commerce, they natually opposed the West Indian monopoly and unwittingly (at first) supported the abolitionists. The abolitionists quickly grasped this coincidence of interests and lost no time in courting their alliance. Equiano became one of the most intelligent interpreters of the new economic thinking in abolitionist circles.

As early as 1788, Equiano had written a letter to Lord Hawkesbury, president of the Privy Council for Trade, outlining proposals for a new relationship between Britain and Africa, based on conventional trade, commerce, and industrialization. Now, during his travels, he disseminated those same ideas in the industrial towns. It was not mere coincidence that his abolitionist sponsors arranged for him to visit Birmingham, Manchester, Nottingham, and Sheffield and addressed his letters of introduction to some of the leading citizens of these towns. Birmingham gave Equiano an enthusiastic welcome; Sheffield, center of the steel industry, had, by the time of his arrival, started a protest movement in favor of importing rum and sugar from the East Indies. Together, these towns were the strongholds of the cotton manufacturers, the shipowners, and the sugar refiners—all interests that stood to benefit from an expansion of trade with Africa.

Thus, the abolitionists and the free trade forces were able to make common cause against the West Indian plantocracy and coalesce into a stronger force to break the power of the sugar barons. Equiano provided the "friends of humanity" with abundant proof about the undesirability of the slave trade, and the free trade interests awakened the British public to the costliness to them of the sugar monopoly and to its function as a disincentive to progressive enterprise.

The program for reformed trade that Equiano promoted during his campaign was the same one he outlined in the letter to Lord Hawkesbury and essentially that which he included in the closing pages of the ***Life.*** The advocates of commercial and industrial expansion would have found their ideas ably represented in Equiano's proposal, perhaps more persuasively so, since Equiano was an African and genuinely interested in Africa's progress and prosperity. Equiano called on the British to reshape their relations with Africa by substituting trade in human bodies for trade in raw materials and manufactured goods. He understood that the material interests of traders and manufacturers would be aroused to support this scheme, for it was calculated to extend their markets and increase their profits. Africa's rich natural resources would fulfill Britain's industrial needs, and Britain's manufactures would in turn find a lucrative market among Africa's teeming millions: "It is trading upon safe grounds," he coaxed. "A commercial intercourse with Africa opens up an inexhaustible source of wealth to the manufacturing interests of Great Britain, and to all which the slave trade is an objection."

It is indicative of Equiano's remarkable proficiency in abolitionist political and economic thought that he was able to enunciate this policy as eloquently as he did. But he did more than retail what must then have been an orthodox creed among most antislavery leaders. He invested the new ideology with his own patriotism and his firm vision of Africa's future greatness. He perceived that a new relationship, constructively pursued, could potentially give to Africa the best that European civilization had to offer. In concord with other philanthropists of the period, he cherished the optimism that if Europe could pursue peaceful relations with Africa as stubbornly as it prosecuted the slave trade and extend its love of freedom to the Black race, a new era of progress would embrace the whole world. He coupled this vision of secular progress with a vision of Christian messianism, drawing inspiration and expression from the Evangelical idiom describing the First Coming: "May Heaven make the British Senators the dispersers of light, liberty, and science, to the uttermost parts of the earth: then will be Glory to God on the highest, on earth peace, and goodwill to men: Glory, honour, peace, &c. to every soul of man that worketh good, to the Britons first, (because to them the Gospel is preached) and also to the nations."

One reservation may be expressed about Equiano's support for this policy of commercialization. He expressed more enthusiasm for Africans' adopting British manners, fashions, and customs—in effect, cultural imperialism—than might have been prudent. It may not have occurred to him that the "civilizing" benefits of broadened cultural and economic relations with Africa were not a fair exchange for the considerable material profits the Europeans would derive from full-scale colonization. Given the formidable resistance the abolitionists faced in their struggle to end slavery, they either thought that exploitation of material resources was a lesser evil than exploiting human bodies or, in their optimism for a new age of universal equality and harmony, they were not as mindful of consequences as they might have been.

Equiano's personal reputation and the public reception of the ***Life*** can be finally appraised by a sampling of contemporary judgments. Wherever he went during his years of antislavery campaigning (1789-93), he was attended by the good opinions of the "friends of humanity." The testimonial statements contained in the letters of introduction he took with him from town to town show that he had won the respect of prominent humanitarians around England. Both Peter Peckard and Thomas Clarkson commended him highly. The leading philanthropists of the industrial towns in his circuit appeared notably impressed by the force of his personal presence and the integrity of his narrative. Thomas Digges of Belfast adjudged him "an enlightened African of good sense, agreeable manners, and of excellent character." Digges also attested to Equiano's association with Sir William Dolben (the sponsor of the parliamentary bill to limit the number of slaves carried on slave ships), Granville Sharp, and John Wilkes. Digges accorded Equiano the distinction of being a "principal instrument in bringing about the motion for the repeal of the Slave Act." William Eddis of Durham praised Equiano in like terms, alluding appreciatively to his African proposal as "a plan truly conducive to the interests of Religion and Humanity."

For the most part, the ***Life*** drew very favorable critical reviews from the press. Reviewers seem to have been impressed most by its unmistakable authenticity and by the genuine sincerity of its author. William Langworthy, who wrote a letter of credit on Equiano's behalf of William Hughes at Devizes, commented: "The simplicity that runs through his Narrative is singularly beautiful and that beauty is heightened by the idea that it is true. . . . " The reviewer in the *General Magazine* called it "a round unvarnished tale . . . written with much truth and simplicity" and seemed deeply affected by its account of slavery's brutality. He expressed what must have been the common response of sensitive readers: "The reader, unless perchance he is either a West Indian planter or a Liverpool merchant, will find his humanity often severely wounded by the shameless barbarity practised towards the author's hapless countrymen in our colonies."

Only the *Gentleman's Magazine* was niggling in its praise. Its reviewer found the narrative style "very unequal" and the work as a whole "an innocent contrivance to interest national humanity in favour of negro slaves." And, as though to detract from Equiano's achievement, the writer trotted out the well rehearsed "good-for-a-Black" qualifications that have persistently dogged the achievements of so many Black artists: "These memoirs," he insinuated, "place the writer on a par with the general mass of men in the subordinate stations of civilized society, and proves that there is no general rule without an exception."

Equiano's career as a Black abolitionist is nothing short of illustrious. When he retired from seafaring, he had served many masters, had been an independent small trader for four years, and was thoroughly familiar with the operations of slavery. He therefore brought to abolitionist agitation the benefit of credibility born of personal experience. He contributed to anti-slavery a variegated background and an intense personal history not unlike those which Saint Paul brought to his work in the early Christian church. Equiano too had been shipwrecked several times, scourged, arrested, and imprisoned. Not surprisingly, he thought he perceived in all his mixed fortunes the constant hand of Providence preparing him for a great work. (pp. 145-48)

Keith A. Sandiford, "Olaudah Equiano: The Appeal to Humanity and the Political Self," in his Measuring the Moment: Strategies of Protest in Eighteenth-Century Afro-English Writing, *Associated University Presses, 1988, pp. 118-48.*

Henry Louis Gates, Jr. (essay date 1988)

[*Gates is an American educator, author, essayist, and editor. His* Black Literature and Literary Theory *(1984) significantly contributed to the study of black literature. His other works include a PBS television series, "The Image of the Black in the Western Imagination" (1982) as well as the books* Figures in Black: Words, Signs, and the Racial Self *(1987) and* The Signifying Monkey: Towards a Theory of Afro-American Literary Criticism *(1988). In the following excerpt from the last-named book, he probes the ultimate meaning of Equiano's* Interesting Narrative *in terms of the author's "strategies of self-presentation and rhetorical presentation."*]

[In 1789] Cugoano's friend Olaudah Equiano published his slave narrative, ***The Interesting Narrative of the Life of Olaudah Equiano.*** Equiano's ***Narrative*** was so richly structured that it became the prototype of the nineteenth-century slave narrative, best exemplified in the works of Frederick Douglass, William Wells Brown, and Harriet Jacobs. It was Equiano whose text served to create a model that other ex-slaves would imitate. From his subtitle, "Written by Himself" and a signed engraving of the black author holding an open text (the Bible) in his lap, to more subtle rhetorical strategies such as the overlapping of the slave's arduous journey to freedom and his simultaneous journey from orality to literacy, Equiano's strategies of self-presentation and rhetorical representation heavily informed, if not determined, the shape of black narrative before 1865.

Equiano's two-volume work was exceptionally popular. Eight editions were printed in Great Britain during the author's lifetime, and a first American edition appeared in New York in 1791. By 1837, another eight editions had appeared, including an abridgment in 1829. Three of these editions were published together with Phillis Wheatley's *Poems.* Dutch and German translations were published in 1790 and 1791.

Equiano told a good story, and he even gives a believable account of cultural life among the Igbo peoples of what is now Nigeria. The movement of his plot, then, is from African freedom, through European enslavement, to Anglican freedom. Both his remarkable command of narrative devices and his detailed accounts of his stirring adventures no doubt combined to create a readership broader than that enjoyed by any black writer before 1789. When we recall that his adventures include service in the Seven Years War with General Wolfe in Canada and Admiral Boscawen in the Mediterranean, voyages to the Arctic with the 1772-73 Phipps expedition, six months among the Miskito Indians in Central America, and "a grand tour of the Mediterranean as personal servant to an English gentleman," it is clear that this ex-slave was one of the most well-traveled people in the world when he decided to write a story of his life.

Like his friend Cugoano, Equiano was extraordinarily well read, and, like Cugoano, he borrowed freely from other texts, including Constantine Phipps's *A Journal of a Voyage Towards the North Pole* (London, 1774), Anthony Benezet's *Some Historical Account of Guinea* (London, 1771), and Thomas Clarkson's *An Essay on the Slavery and Commerce of the Human Species* (London, 1785). He also paraphrased frequently, especially would-be "direct" quotations from Milton, Pope, and Thomas Day. Nevertheless, Equiano was an impressively self-conscious writer and developed two rhetorical strategies that would come to be utilized extensively in the nineteenth-century slave narratives: the trope of chiasmus, and the use of two distinct voices to distinguish, through rhetorical strategies, the simple wonder with which the young Equiano approached the New World of his captors and a more eloquently articulated voice that he employs to describe the author's narrative present. The interplay of these two voices is only as striking as Equiano's overarching plot-

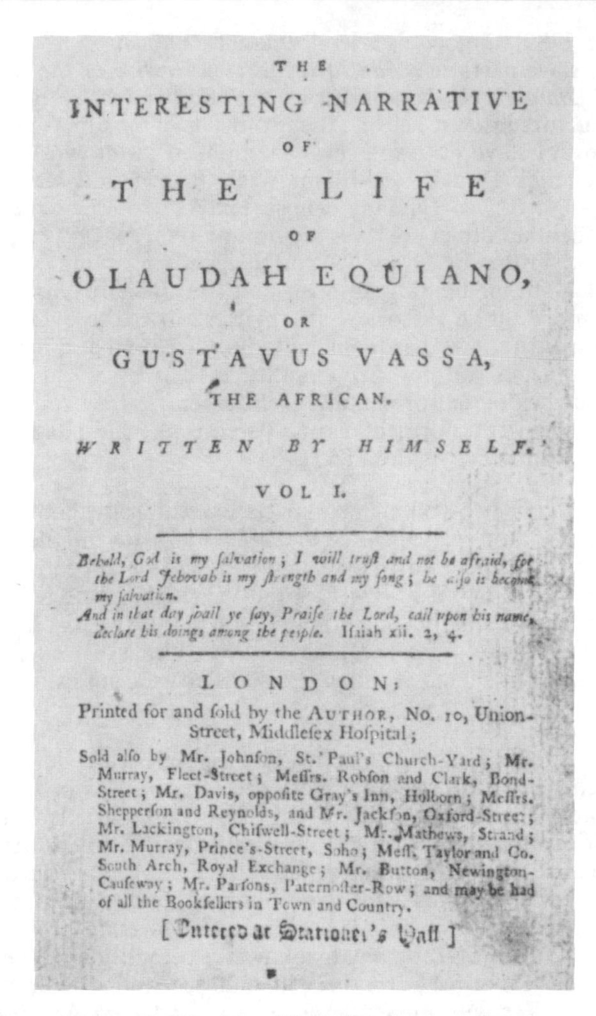

THE

INTERESTING NARRATIVE

OF

THE LIFE

OF

OLAUDAH EQUIANO,

OR

GUSTAVUS VASSA,

THE AFRICAN.

WRITTEN BY HIMSELF.

VOL I.

Behold, God is my salvation; I will trust and not be afraid, for the Lord Jehovah is my strength and my song; he also is become my salvation.
And in that day shall ye say, Praise the Lord, call upon his name, declare his doings among the people. Isaiah xii. 2, 4.

LONDON:

Printed for and sold by the AUTHOR, No. 10, Union-Street, Middlesex Hospital;

Sold also by Mr. Johnson, St. Paul's Church-Yard; Mr. Murray, Fleet-Street; Messrs. Robson and Clark, Bond-Street; Mr. Davis, opposite Gray's Inn, Holborn; Messrs. Shepperson and Reynolds, and Mr. Jackson, Oxford-Street; Mr. Lackington, Chiswell-Street; Mr. Mathews, Strand; Mr. Murray, Prince's-Street, Soho; Mess. Taylor and Co. South Arch, Royal Exchange; Mr. Button, Newington-Causeway; Mr. Parsons, Paternoster-Row; and may be had of all the Booksellers in Town and Country.

[Entered at Stationer's Hall]

Title page of the first edition of Equiano's autobiography.

reversal pattern, within which all sorts of embedded reversal tales occur. Both strategies combine to make Equiano's text a representation of becoming, of a development of a self that not only has a past and a present but which speaks distinct languages at its several stages which culminate in the narrative present. Rarely would a slave narrator match Equiano's mastery of self-representation.

Equiano refers to his literacy training a number of times. Richard Baker, an American boy on board the ship that first took Equiano to England, was, Equiano tells us, his "constant companion and instructor," and "interpreter." At Guernsey, his playmate Mary's mother "behaved to me with great kindness and attention; and taught me every thing in the same manner as she did her own child, and indeed in every way treated me as such." Within a year, he continues,

> I could now speak English tolerably well, and I perfectly understood everything that was said. I not only felt myself quite easy with these new countrymen, but relished their society and manners. I no longer looked upon them as spirits, but as men superior to us; and I therefore had the stronger desire to resemble them, to imbibe their spirit, and imitate their manners. I therefore embraced every occasion of improvement, and every new thing that I observed I treasured up in my memory. I had long wished to be able to read and write; and for this purpose I took every opportunity to gain instruction, but had made as yet very little progress. However, when I went to London with my master, I had soon an opportunity of improving myself, which I gladly embraced. Shortly after my arrival, he sent me to wait upon the Miss Guerins, who had treated me with such kindness when I was there before; and they sent me to school.

Equiano also used the sea as an extension school, as he did on the "Aetna fireship":

> I now became the captain's steward, in such situation I was very happy: for I was extremely well treated by all on board; and I had leisure to improve myself in reading and writing. The latter I had learned a little of before I left the Namur, as there was a school on board.

Equiano, in short, leaves a trail of evidence to prove that he was fully capable of writing his own life's story. Despite these clues, however, at least the reviewer for *The Monthly Review* wondered aloud about the assistance of "some English writer" in the production of his text [see excerpt dated 1789].

Equiano uses the trope of the Talking Book in his third chapter, in which he describes his voyages from Barbados to Virginia and on to England. It is on this voyage that he begins to learn English. Equiano uses the trope as a climax of several examples sprinkled throughout the early pages of this chapter of sublime moments of cross-cultural encounters experienced by the wide-eyed boy. His encounters with a watch and a portrait are among the first items on his list:

> The first object that engaged my attention was a watch which hung on the chimney, and was going. I was quite surprised at the noise it made, and was afraid it would tell the gentleman any thing I might do amiss: and when I immediately after observed a picture hanging in the room, which appeared constantly to look at me, I was still more affrighted, having never seen such things as these before. At one time I thought it was something relative to magic; and not seeing it move I thought it might be some way the whites had to keep their great men when they died, and offer them libations as we used to do our friendly spirits.

When he sees snow for the first time, he thinks it is salt. He concludes just before introducing as a separate paragraph the Talking Book scene, "I was astonished at the wisdom of the white people in all things I saw."

Equiano returns to Gronniosaw's use of the trope for its details and refers to gold only implicitly, in his reference to the "watch which hung on the chimney." The trope is presented in a self-contained paragraph, which does not refer directly either to the paragraph that precedes it or to the one that follows. Nevertheless, the trope culminates the implicit list of wonderments that the young African experiences at the marvels of the West. As Equiano narrates:

> I had often seen my master and Dick employed in reading; and I had a great curiosity to talk to the books, as I thought they did; and so to learn how all things had a beginning: for that purpose I have often taken up a book, and have talked to it, and then put my ears to it, when alone, in hopes it would answer me; and I have been very much concerned when I found it remained silent.

A watch, a portrait, a book that speaks: these are the elements of wonder that the young African encounters on his road to Western culture. These are the very signs through which Equiano represents the difference in subjectivity that separates his, now lost, African world from the New World of "white folks" that has been thrust upon him.

Significantly, Equiano endows each of these objects with his master's subjectivity. The portrait seems to be watching him as he moves through the room. The watch, he fears, can see, hear, and speak, and appears to be quite capable of and willing to report his actions to his sleeping master once he awakes. The watch is his master's surrogate overseer, standing in for the master as an authority figure, even while he sleeps. The painting is also a surrogate figure of the master's authority, following his movements silently as he walks about the room. The book that speaks to "my master and Dick" is a double sign of subjectivity, since Equiano represents its function as one that occurs in dialogue between a human being and its speaking pages. What can we make of these elements that comprise Equiano's list of the salient signs of difference?

While dramatizing rather effectively the sensitive child's naiveté and curiosity, and his ability to interpret the culture of the Europeans from a distinctly African point of reference, Equiano is contrasting his earlier self with the self that narrates his text. This, certainly, is essential to his apparent desire to represent in his autobiography a dynamic self that once was "like that" but is now "like this." His ability to show his readers his own naiveté, rather than merely to tell us about it or to claim it, and to make this earlier self the focus of his readers' sympathy and amusement, are extraordinarily effective rhetorical strategies that serve to heighten our identification with the openly honest subject whose perceptions these were and who has remembered them for us to share. But Equiano is up to much more. Under the guise of the representation of his naive self, he is naming or reading Western culture closely, underlining relationships between subjects and objects that are implicit in commodity cultures. Watches do speak to their masters, in a language that has no other counterpart in this culture, and their language frequently proves to be the determining factor in the master's daily existence. The narrative past and the narrative present through which the narrator's consciousness shifts so freely and tellingly are symbolized by the voice that the young Equiano attributes to the watch. Portraits, moreover, do stare one in the face as one moves about within a room. They are also used as tokens of the immortality of their subjects, commanding of their viewers symbolic "libations," which the young Equiano "thought it might." Portraits are would-be tropes against the subject's mortality, just as Equiano imagined them to be. Books, finally, do speak to Europeans, and not to the Africans of the eighteenth century. The book recognizes "my master and Dick," acknowledging both their voices and their faces by engaging in a dialogue with them; neither the young African's voice nor his face can be recognizable to the text, because his countenance and discourse stand in Western texts as signs of absence, of the null and void. The young Equiano has read these texts closely, and rather tellingly, while the older Equiano represents this reading at a double-voiced level, allowing his readers to engage this series of encounters on both a manifest and a latent level of meaning.

But what can we make of the shift of tenses (from "had" to "have," for example) in Equiano's passage on the Talking Book? One key to reading this shift of tenses within the description itself is Equiano's endowment of these objects of Western culture with the master's subjectivity. Equiano, the slave, enjoys a status identical to that of the watch, the portrait, and the book. He is the master's object, to be used and enjoyed, purchased, sold, or discarded, just like a watch, a portrait, or a book. By law, the slave has no more and no less rights than do the other objects that the master collects and endows with his subjectivity. Of course the book does not speak to him. Only subjects can endow an object with subjectivity; objects, such as a slave, possess no inherent subjectivity of their own. Objects can only reflect the subjectivity of the subject, like a mirror does. When Equiano, the object, attempts to speak to the book, there follows only the deafening silence that obtains between two lifeless objects. Only a subject can speak. Two mirrors can only reflect each other, in an endless pattern of voided repetition. But they cannot speak to each other, at least not in the language of the master. When the master's book looks to see whose face is behind the voice that Equiano speaks, it can only see an absence, the invisibility that dwells in an unattended looking-glass.

Through the act of writing alone, Equiano announces and preserves his newly found status as a subject. It is he who is the master of his text, a text that speaks volumes of experience and subjectivity. If once he too was an object, like a watch, a portrait, or a book, now he has endowed himself with his master's culture's ultimate sign of subjectivity, the presence of a voice which is the signal feature of a face. The shift in verb tenses creates irony, because we, his readers, know full well by this moment within the narrative that Equiano the narrator no longer speaks to texts that cannot see his face or that, therefore, refuse to address him. Equiano the author is a speaking subject, "just like" his master. But he is not "just like" his master and never can be in a culture in which the blackness of his face signifies an absence. Nevertheless, Equiano's use of shifting tenses serves to represent the very movement that he is experiencing (in a Middle Passage, as was Gronniosaw) as he transforms himself from African to Anglo-African, from slave to potential freedman, from an absence to a presence, and indeed from an object to a subject.

If the master's voice endows his objects with reflections of his subjectivity, then the representation, in writing, of the master's voice (and this process of endowment or reflection of subjectivity) serves to enable the object to remake himself into a subject. Equiano's shift in tenses enables his readers to observe him experiencing the silent text, within a narrative present that has been inscribed within a passage from his past; but it also serves, implicitly, to represent the difference between the narrator and this character of his (past) self, a difference marked through verb tense as the difference between object and subject. The process by which the master endows his commodities with the reflection of subjectivity, as figured in the African's readings of the watch, the portrait, and the book, is duplicated by Equiano's narrator's account of his own movement from slave-object to author-subject. The shift of tenses is Equiano's grammatical analogue of this process of becoming—of becoming a human being who reads differently from the child, of becoming a subject by passing a test (the mastery of writing) that no object can pass, and of becoming an author who represents, under the guise of a series of naive readings, an object's "true" nature by demonstrating that he can now read these objects in both ways, as he once did in the Middle Passage but also as he does today. The narrator's character of himself, of course, reads on a latent level of meaning; the first test of subjectivity is to demonstrate the ability to read on a manifest level. By revising the trope of the Talking Book, and by shifting from present to past and back to present, Equiano the author is able to read these objects simultaneously on both levels and to demonstrate his true mastery of the text of Western letters and the text of his verbal representation of his past and present selves. (pp. 152-57)

Henry Louis Gates, Jr., "The Trope of the Talking Book," in his The Signifying Monkey: A Theory of Afro-American Literary Criticism, *Oxford University Press, 1988, pp. 127-69.*

FURTHER READING

Acholonu, Catherine Obianju. "The Home of Olaudah Equiano—A Linguistic and Anthropological Search." *The Journal of Commonwealth Literature* XXII, No. 1 (1987): 5-16.

Provides cultural and anthropological data to support a survey of Equiano's use of English orthography for transcribing the sounds and ideas of Igbo, his native language.

Baker, Houston A., Jr. "Figurations for a New American Literary History." In his *Blues, Ideology, and Afro-American Literature: A Vernacular Theory,* pp. 15-63. Chicago: University of Chicago Press, 1984.

Attempts to identify a different historical subtext that distinguishes Equiano's *Narrative* from "traditional, historical, and literary historical discourse" by exploring the relationship between the *Narrative* and the economics of slavery.

Bontemps, Arna. Introduction to *Great Slave Narratives,* edited by Arna Bontemps, pp. vii-xix. Boston: Beacon Press, 1969.

Ascertains that Equiano's *Narrative* achieves its strength on the basis of "the book's naturalness, its wealth of fascinating detail and narrative events."

Edwards, Paul. Introduction to *Equiano's Travels: The Interesting Narrative of the Life of Olaudah Equiano or Gustavus Vassa the African,* by Olaudah Equiano, edited by Paul Edwards, pp. ix-xviii. New York: Frederick A. Praeger, 1967.

Discusses critical problems surrounding Equiano and his work, particularly the veracity, authenticity, and literary significance of his *Narrative.*

Francis, Elman V. "Olaudah Equiano: A Profile." *Negro History Bulletin* 44, No. 2 (August-June 1981): 31, 43-4.

General biography, concluding that Equiano "is one of the unsung heroes of the unexplored and unnoticed black people who helped to build the European civilization."

Review of *The Interesting Narrative of the Life of Olaudah Equiano,* by Olaudah Equiano. *The Gentleman's Magazine and Historical Chronicle* 59, No. 6 (June 1789): 539.

Brief review of Equiano's *Narrative.* The anonymous critic indicates that the work is "written in a very unequal style."

Jones, G. I. "Olaudah Equiano of the Niger Ibo." In *Africa Remembered,* edited by P. D. Curtin, pp. 60-9. Madison: University of Wisconsin Press, 1967.

Attempts to definitely locate and accurately describe Equiano's ancestral home in the Ibo country of Nigeria.

Kaplan, Sidney. "Olaudah Equiano: The Image of Africa." In his *The Black Presence in the Era of the American Revolution,* pp. 193-206. Greenwich, Conn.: New York Graphic Society, 1973.

Detailed biography, offering a "sketch of his rich life with a few scattered passages, in his own good words, from *The Interesting Narrative.*"

Porter, Dorothy B. "Early American Negro Writings: A Bibliographical Study." *The Papers of the Bibliographical Society of America* 39 (1945): 192-268.

Primary bibliography of writings by eighteenth-century black American authors, with a discussion of the related problems of identification and location.

Southern, Eileen. "An Origin for the Negro Spiritual." *The Black Scholar* 3, No. 10 (Summer 1972): 8-13.

Cites a passage from Equiano's autobiography describing the importance of dance and music in native African culture.

Walvin, James. "The Free Black Voice." In his *Black and White: The Negro and English Society: 1555-1945,* pp. 80-104. London: Allen Lane, 1973.

General biography, highlighting Equiano's religious conversion and abolitionist activities.

Desiderius Erasmus

1469?-1536

(Born Geert Geerts; also known as Gerhard Gerhards; adopted name Desiderius Erasmus Rotterdammensis; also known as Desiderius Erasmus Roterodamus) Dutch essayist and satirist.

The leading figure in northern humanism, Erasmus is recognized as one of the greatest intellectuals of the sixteenth century. Viewing religion as a matter of morality and piety rather than of ceremony and doctrine, Erasmus attempted to syncretize the secular, critical, and rational nature of classical antiquity with devout religiosity. His desire to promote the causes of religious toleration and the elimination of ecclesiastical abuses was impeded by societal inflexibility and distrust of moralistic Christianity. Erasmus's criticism of conditions within the Church and his stress on personal piety led Martin Luther to believe that the humanist would support the Lutherans in their revolt against doctrinal abuses within Catholicism. However, while Erasmus desired the purification of existing dogma and practices, Luther demanded separation from the Church. As one critic notes, "The times did not permit Erasmus to play his role of moderator nor does modernity even now seem ready to agree with Johan Huizinga that 'cultural humanity has cause to hold Erasmus's memory in esteem, if for no other reason than that he was the fervently sincere preacher of that general kindliness which the world still so urgently needs'."

Specific dates and details related to Erasmus's early life are few and fraught with uncertainties, many of them deliberately obscured by the humanist himself. According to a letter Erasmus wrote to Conradus Goclenius, he was the son of Gerard and Margaret, a young couple whose longed-for marriage was successfully blocked by Gerard's parents. Some years later, having entered the priesthood, Gerard discovered that Margaret had borne him a son. Erasmus claimed 1466—a date preceding his father's ordination—as his year of birth, implying that he was not the son of an ordained priest and, therefore, not the product of incest in the eyes of the Church. Most historians doubt the veracity of this account, however, claiming that Erasmus concocted the story in order to prevent future difficulties in obtaining patrons and Church benefices. Most scholars estimate Erasmus's year of birth to be 1469. Erasmus began his education at the Gouda city school, and at the age of nine went with his older brother, Peter, to the St. Lebwin school in Deventer. This institution was run by the Brethren of the Common Life, a religious sect noted for its piety and aversion to dogmatism. The boys remained in Deventer for nine years. Toward the end of his time at Deventer, Erasmus met the humanists Alexander Hegius and Rudolf Agricola. Agricola's enthusiasm for poetry and literature had a great impact on Erasmus's intellectual development.

Their mother having died when the plague struck Deventer in 1484, Erasmus and his brother returned to Gouda to join their father, who likewise succumbed to the plague a short time later. The boys were placed under the guardianship of three men appointed by Gerard and enrolled at the school at 's Hertogenbosch. This facility was also run by the Brethren of the Common Life, but was as yet uninfluenced by humanism. Erasmus gave his impression of the Brethren at this school in his correspondence, noting that their "chief concern, should they chance to see any youth of unusually high spirits and quick disposition, is to break his spirit and to humble him with blows, threats, scoldings and other means, which they call 'breaking in'. . . ." When the plague hit 's Hertogenbosch in 1486, the guardians persuaded the brothers to leave town and enter the monastery at Steyn. There, the asceticism of the Augustinian order repelled Erasmus, but the freedom to use their library pleased him tremendously. Erasmus was ordained a priest in 1492.

The next year, unhappy with life at Steyn, Erasmus accepted an offer to be temporary secretary to the bishop of Cambrai. To avoid returning to Steyn for several years, he convinced the bishop to finance his studies toward a doctorate in theology at the Sorbonne. Erasmus enrolled at the Collège de Montaigu in 1495. The Collège was governed by Jan Standonck, a reformer who had been educated in the devotio moderna by the Brethren of the Common Life. According to Faludy, "Standonck maintained the atmosphere of the devotio at its harshest in his college, a regimen of abstinence and silence. Any student who displayed an interest in humanistic studies was automatically suspect, and the slightest infraction of the rules was punished by flogging." Erasmus left Paris without having obtained his doctorate in 1496, but he returned shortly to tutor students, among them Thomas Grey, Robert Fisher, and William Blount, Lord Mountjoy. It was by the invitation of the last that Erasmus made his first journey to England in 1499. While in England, Erasmus met and thrived upon the intellectual stimulation provided by several of the most prominent humanist intellectuals of the day: Thomas More, John Colet, Thomas Linacre, and William Grocyn. But when he left England for France in early 1500, customs officers at Dover confiscated most of Erasmus's money in compliance with a royal decree that no more than two pounds could be taken from the country by any one person. Penniless by the time he reached Paris, Erasmus quickly compiled and published his first volume of adages, the *Adagiorum collectanea.*

Erasmus spent the next several years traveling between France and the Low Countries visiting patrons, and working on literary projects. In 1504, he visited the Premonstratensian monastery near Louvain, where he found a manuscript of Lorenzo Valla's *Annotationes* on the New Testament. This critique of the Vulgate, corrected with Greek sources, had a great impact on Erasmus, who entertained hopes of someday translating the Greek New Testament into Latin. (This hope was realized with the publication of his *Novum instrumentum* in 1516.) After arranging for the Valla manuscript to be published, in 1505, Erasmus embarked on a year-long second visit to England, during which time he collaborated with More on a translation of Lucian's works.

In 1506, Erasmus went to Italy, where, shortly afterward, he received his master and doctor of divinity degrees from the University of Turin. During the next three years, Erasmus lived for various periods of time in Venice and Padua; he enjoyed Italy tremendously and considered a permanent move to Rome. But when Henry VII died in 1509, however, Mountjoy summoned his protégé back to England, where "the cause of literature was flourishing, the sky was laughing, and tears of joy were flowing from all eyes." Legend has it that while visiting More shortly after his arrival in London, Erasmus suffered an attack of kidney stones; and that to distract himself he composed the satiric oration that is probably his best-known work, the *Moriae encomium* (*The Praise of Folly*)—in seven days. Erasmus lectured on divinity at Cambridge and occupied himself with various literary projects, but England was not as pleasurable as earlier. He departed for the Continent in 1514, and over the next three years traveled several times between England and the Continent in attempts to further his literary career.

In 1517, Erasmus settled in Louvain, a surprising move considering its reputation as a seat of orthodoxy and scholasticism. At about this time, the religious controversy surrounding Luther and the future of the German Church began in earnest. There is much information suggesting that Erasmus approved of Luther's actions in the infancy of the Reformation. Luther wrote to Erasmus in 1519, hoping to garner support for his cause from the renowned humanist, but Erasmus answered that he preferred to remain neutral in the debates, "the better to assist the new flowering of good learning." Erasmus assisted Luther by insisting that the latter's arguments be heard and considered. As disputes between the Church and the Lutherans intensified, Erasmus began to fear its outcome. He struggled to moderate the dispute and avoid an insurmountable schism within the Church. For while Erasmus recognized the need for reform, he also wanted to maintain peace and unity. Harassed by theologians to write a tract denouncing Luther, he left Louvain and settled in Basel in 1521. But in 1524 Erasmus finally attacked Luther in *De libero arbitrio* (*Discourse on Free Will*). Luther responded in 1525 with *De servo arbitrio* (*The Bondage of the Will*). When significant religious disturbances began in Basel in 1529, Erasmus moved to Freiburg. Here he resumed his conciliatory efforts in the continuing controversy while remaining neutral, a position that infuriated the leaders of both factions. Erasmus returned to Basel in 1535, and died there the following year.

Erasmus's literary reputation rests on a small percentage of his works, the first of note being his collection of adages. Originally published in 1500 as *Adagiorum collectanea,* this work is a compilation of more than 800 Latin proverbs taken from classical authors. Erasmus hoped the phrases would be helpful both in teaching students correct Latin construction and refining their literary eloquence. The *Adagiorum* were revised and expanded in a 1508 edition which included well over 3,000 proverbs taken from both Latin and Greek sources. While both editions were very successful, the enlarged edition was particularly praised by scholars and established Erasmus as an intellectual of the first degree. Another edition of the *Adagiorum,* published in 1536, contains over 4,100 aphorisms and commentaries. The book maintained its stature for many years, as its popularity during the Enlightenment shows.

Erasmus continued his literary endeavors with the *Enchiridion militis christiani* (*The manuell of the christen knyght*). Published in 1503, the *Enchiridion* advocates simple Christian piety, rejecting such customary formal rituals of the Catholic church as pilgrimages and ceremonies. The *Enchiridion* also insists on the importance of recognizing the spirit of the Scriptures instead of strictly literal interpretations. The *Enchiridion* is the first manifestation of Erasmus's *philosophia Christi,* a view of Christianity which permeates his later works. Erasmus places the burden of responsible Christianity on the individual, not on the dogma or ceremonies of the Church. "Two fundamental and related ideas run throughout the book," John C. Olin notes. "One is that the great weapon of the Christian is the knowledge of Holy Scripture . . . ; the other is that religion is not primarily a matter of outward signs and devotions but rather of interior disposition and the inward love of God and neighbor." Not as immediately popular as the *Adagiorum,* the *Enchiridion* nonetheless enjoyed a generally favorable critical reception. Some critics believe Erasmus did not sufficiently understand the metaphysics of theology, and that he therefore undercut several of his assertions by straying too far into the mysteries of the Catholic faith. Just slightly more than a decade after its first appearance, however, this work was commonly used in university courses throughout Europe.

Published in 1511, the *Moriae encomium,* or *The Praise of Folly,* is probably Erasmus's most enduring work. Dedicated to Thomas More, *The Praise of Folly* is a mock oration in praise of foolishness. Critics from Erasmus's day forward have recognized the likely influences of Sebastian Brant's *Ship of Fools* and Lucianic satire upon the work. In his *Erasmus* (1972), George Faludy summarizes the main ideas of the mock oration by stating that "First . . . there is an inordinate amount of stupidity, hypocrisy and corruption in the world and in each man; second, that a radical programme based on the teachings of Christ (and Socrates) is the only possible solution to the evil inherent in human nature. The second idea is in effect the underlying motive of the book, the message embodying the whole of Erasmus's goal. It is a plea to resist indifference and satanical cynicism, and a warning that there can be no easy and immediate transformation of man. It is also an optimistic reaffirmation that the aims of humanism will, slowly but surely, prevail." Securing Erasmus's place both as a writer and as the leader of humanism, the work has enjoyed immediate and continuing popular success, as evidenced by its popularity with the leading figures of the Enlightenment and the publication of many editions of it during the twentieth century.

A leading mind of the sixteenth century, Erasmus was a key figure in establishing and disseminating the tenets of humanism throughout Europe. Such works as his enormously successful *Praise of Folly* reveal his knowledge of the corruption and ecclesiastical abuses within the Church and subtly call for their elimination. The *Enchiridion* urges the reader to live the humanistic life of simple Christian morality and piety. Erasmus's steadfastness of purpose in an era of religious and political upheaval has led many scholars through the ages to agree with Colet, who wrote that the "name of Erasmus shall never perish, but [he] will win for [his] name eternal glory. . . . "

PRINCIPAL WORKS

**Adagiorum collectanea* (aphorisms) 1500; also published in revised form as *Adagiorum chiliades tres, ac centuriae fere totidem,* 1508, 1515

Enchiridion militis christiani (prose) 1503

[*A booke called in latyn Enchiridion militis christiani, and in englysshe the manuell of the christen knyght, replenysshed with most holsome preceptes . . . To the whiche is added a newe and mervaylous profytable preface,* 1533]

De ratione studii (prose) 1511

Moriae encomium (satire) 1511

[*The Praise of Folie. Moriae Encomium a booke made in latyne by that great clerke Erasmus Roterodame,* 1549]

De duplici copia verborum, commentarii duo (prose) 1512

Christiani hominis Institutu Erasmi Roterodami (prose) 1515

Institutio principis christiani (prose) 1516

[*Erasmus' 'Institutio Principis Christiani'* (partial translation), 1921]

†*Novum instrumentum* (prose) 1516

‡*Poete Regii libellus, de obitu Pontificis Maximi Anno M.D.XIII.* (prose) 1517

[*The dyaloge bytwene Jullius the seconde, Genius, and saynt Peter,* 1535]

Querela pacis undique gentium ejectae profligataeque (prose) 1517

[*The Complaint of peace,* 1559]

Sileni Alcibiadis (dialogue) 1517

De contemptu mūdi epistola (prose) 1519

[*De Contemptu Mundi,* 1533]

§*Familiorum Colloquiorum Formulae* (dialogues) 1519; also published as *Familiarium colloquiorum opus multis nominibus vtilissimū, nūc postreina cura ab authore* [revised edition], 1527

[*The Colloquies; or, Familiar Discourses of D. Erasmus,* 1671]

Paraclesis (prose) 1519

[*An exhortation to the diligent studye of scripture,* 1529]

Antibarbari (dialogue) 1520

[*The Book Against the Barbarians,* 1930]

Libellus de sonscribendis epistolis (prose) 1522

De libero arbitrio διατριβη, *sive Collatio* (prose) 1524

[*Discourse on Free Will,* 1961]

Christiani matrimonii institutio, per Des. Erasmum Roterodamum, opus nunc primum & natum, & excusum (prose) 1526

Hyperaspistes diatribae adversus Servam Arbitrium M. Luther (prose) 1526-27

Dialogue cui titulus Ciceronianus, siue, De optimo genere dicendi (prose) 1528

De pueris instituendis (prose) 1529

[*That chyldren oughte to be taught and broughte up gētly in vertue and learnynge, and even forthwyth from theyr nativities: a declamacion,* 1550]

De civilitate morum puerilim per D. Erasmum libellus, ab autore recognitus et novis scholiis illustratus (prose) 1530

[*De civilitate morun puerilium . . . Libellus nunc primum & conditus & aeditus. Robert Whitintoni interprete. A lytle booke of good maners for chyldren,* 1532]

Apophthegmata (prose) 1531

[*Apophthegmes,* 1542]

De praeparatione ad mortem (prose) 1534

[*Preparation to Deathe, A boke as deuout as eloquent,* 1538]

Omnia opera D. Erasmi (prose, dialogues, letters) 1540

Desiderii Erasmi Roterodami Opera omnia, emendatiora et avctiora, ad optimas aditiones praecipve qvas ipse Erasmus postremo cvravit svmma fide exacta, stvdio et opera Joannis Clerici, cvm jvsdem et aliorvm notis (prose, dialogues, letters) 1703-06

Opus Epistolarum Des. Erasmi Roterodami. 12 vols. (letters) 1906-58
The Poems of Desiderius Erasmus (poetry) 1956
The Correspondence of Erasmus (letters) 1974

*The 1515 edition contains the first printing of the dialogue *Dulce bellum inexpertis.*

†The preface to this work was the *Paraclesis,* which was published separately in 1519.

‡This work is commonly referred to as the *Julius exclusus.* While it is generally attributed to Erasmus, he neither confirmed nor denied his authorship.

§The original manuscript to this work was written around 1498 and published without Erasmus's permission by Beatus Rhenanus in approximately 1518. The 1519 edition was authorized, revised, and expanded by Erasmus.

Desiderius Erasmus (letter date 1504)

[*In the following excerpt from a letter to John Colet, Erasmus writes of his intent to "address* [*himself*] *to the Scriptures and to spend all the rest of* [*his*] *life upon them."*]

I am now eager, dear Colet, to approach sacred literature full sail, full gallop; I have an extreme distaste for anything that distracts me from it, or even delays me. But the ill will of Fortune, which has ever regarded me with steadfast hostility, is the reason why I have not been able to free myself from these vexations; and so it was in order to shake them off as best I could, even if I proved unable to abolish them altogether, that I withdrew to France. Hereafter I intend to address myself to the Scriptures and to spend all the rest of my life upon them. Three years ago, indeed, I ventured to do something on Paul's Epistle to the Romans, and at one rush, as it were, finished four volumes; and would have gone on, but for certain distractions, of which the most important was that I needed the Greek at every point. Therefore for nearly the past three years I have been wholly absorbed by Greek; and I do not think my efforts have been altogether wasted. I began to take up Hebrew as well, but stopped because I was put off by the strangeness of the language, and at the same time the shortness of life and the limitations of human nature will not allow a man to master too many things at once. I have gone through a good part of Origen's works; under his guidance I think I have achieved worthwhile results, for he reveals some of the well-springs, as it were, and demonstrates some of the basic principles, of the science of theology.

I am sending you a small literary gift, consisting of a few of my minor works, including that same debate on the fear of Christ in which we once confronted each other in England, though it is so much altered that you would hardly recognize it. (I may add that your answers, and my rejoinders, could not be reconstructed.) The ***Enchiridion*** I composed not in order to show off my cleverness or my style, but solely in order to counteract the error of those who make religion in general consist in rituals and observances of an almost more than Jewish formality, but who are astonishingly indifferent to matters that have to do with true goodness. What I have tried to do, in fact, is to teach a method of morals, as it were, in the manner of those who have originated fixed procedures in the various branches of learning; as for all the rest, I wrote them almost against the grain, especially the ***Paean*** and ***Obsecratio;*** this task was discharged in deference to the wishes of my friend Batt and the sentiments of Anna, princess of Veere. I was so reluctant to compose the ***Panegyricus*** that I do not remember ever doing anything more unwillingly; for I saw that this kind of thing could not be handled without some flattery. However I employed a novel strategem; I was completely frank while I flattered and also very flattering in my frankness.

If you would like to have any of your works printed, merely send me the manuscript and for the rest I will see to it that the printed version is quite accurate. Lately I sent a letter, as I believe you recall, about the hundred copies of the ***Adagia*** sent to England at my own expense, and three years ago at that. Grocyn had written to me, saying that he would take the utmost pains to see that they were sold as I wished; and I have no doubt he kept his promise, for he is the most upright, excellent man now living in England. So will you please oblige me by lending me your help in this matter, admonishing and goading into action those by whom you think the business ought to be concluded; for it must be that over such a long period all the books have been sold and the purchase price paid to someone; and it would be more useful to me to have the money now than ever before, since I have somehow to provide myself with several months' complete leisure in order to discharge the commitments I have entered into with respect to secular literature; I hoped it might be possible to do so this winter, and so it would have been had not so many of my prospects proved false. But I can still purchase this liberty not too expensively—for a few months at any rate.

So I beseech you to help me as far as you can in my burning zeal for sacred studies by releasing me from the kind of literature which has now ceased to give me pleasure. I cannot ask my friend the count, William Mountjoy; all the same there would be some point and sense in his action, if of his kindness he were to afford me some help, either because he has always encouraged my studies in this way, or because the subject was one I undertook on his initiative and dedicated to himself, namely the ***Adagia.*** I regret the first edition, both because it is so full of printers' errors that it looks as if it had been deliberately spoiled, and because some people encouraged me to hurry the work, which now begins to seem to me thin and poor, when I have at last read the Greek authors through. I have decided therefore to publish a second edition to repair the printers' mistakes as well as my own, and at the same time to be of service to scholars by treating a most useful theme. Now, though for the present I am concerned with what may be a rather mundane subject, still while I linger within the garden of the Greeks I am gathering by the way many flowers that will be useful for the future, even in sacred studies; for experience teaches me this, at any rate, that we can do nothing in any field of literature without a knowledge of Greek, since it is one thing to guess, another to judge; one thing to trust your own eyes, and another again to trust those of others. See how long my letter has grown! But it is affection, not a fault of character, that makes me so talkative. Farewell, Colet, my learned and good friend. (pp. 86-9)

Desiderius Erasmus, in a letter to John Colet in 1504, in his The Correspondence of Erasmus: 1501-1514, *by Desiderius Erasmus, translated by R. A. B. Mynors and D. F. S. Thomson, University of Toronto Press, 1975, pp. 85-9.*

Desiderius Erasmus (letter date 1511)

[*In the excerpt below from a letter to Thomas More, Erasmus relates the circumstances surrounding the composition of the* Moriae encomium.]

As I was returning lately from Italy to England, in order to avoid squandering upon vulgar and uneducated talk the whole time I had to spend on horseback, I sometimes preferred inwardly to savour some memory, either of the studies you and I shared once, or of the learned and congenial friends whom I had left behind in this country. Of these you were always one of the very first to come to mind. Indeed my delight in the thought of you when you were absent was like the pleasure I used to take in your company; my life upon it if I have ever in my life enjoyed a sweeter experience than that. Well then, since I thought I must at all costs occupy myself somehow, and since that particular time seemed hardly suitable for serious scholarly writing, I decided to compose a trifling thing, ***Moriae encomium.*** You will ask how some Pallas Athene came to put that idea into my head. First, I was inspired by your surname of More, which is as close in form to *Moria* (Folly) as you are in fact remote from folly itself—to which, as all agree, you are a complete stranger. Second, I guessed that this flight of fancy might find especial favour in your eyes since you take immense pleasure in frolics of this kind, by which I mean those that are neither crude, which I hope to be the case, nor altogether devoid of wit, and as a rule you play the part of a kind of Democritus in human life at large. Yet, though as a rule you disagree widely with vulgar opinions because of that singularly penetrating wit of yours, nevertheless your affability and kindness are so extraordinary that you are both able and pleased to play with everyone the part of a man for all seasons. So I beg you to accept this short essay as a souvenir of your comrade, but also to acknowledge and cherish it, inasmuch as it has been dedicated to you and is no longer mine, but yours.

For there will perhaps be some wrangling critics who will falsely assert either that these trifles are too airy to be quite suitable to a theologian's pen, or that they are more sarcastic than suits the modesty of a Christian. They will loudly accuse me of imitating the Old Comedy or some kind of Lucianic satire, and of attacking the whole world with my teeth. Now as for those who find the triviality and humour of the theme offensive, I should like them to reflect that this is no vein of my own invention, but reflects the habitual practice of great writers of the past; inasmuch as Homer, all those centuries ago, wrote in jesting vein his Battle of the Frogs and Mice, Virgil of the Gnat and the *Moretum,* Ovid of the Walnut; in addition encomiums on Busiris were written by Polycrates and his critic Isocrates, on injustice by Glaucon, on Thersites and the quartan ague by Favorinus, on Baldness by Synesius, on the Fly and the Art of Being a Parasite by Lucian; and finally Seneca wrote a playful apotheosis of Claudius the emperor, Plutarch a jesting dialogue of Gryllus with Ulysses, Lucian and Apuleius an 'Ass' apiece, and someone or other the 'Testament of Grunnius Corocotta the piglet,' mentioned also by St Jerome.

So let them make up stories about me if they wish, alleging that I have sometimes played draughts for recreation, or ridden a hobby-horse if they would rather; for, considering that every way of living is permitted its appropriate recreation, it would be monstrously unfair to allow no diversion whatever to those who pursue literary studies, especially if nonsense leads to serious matters and absurd themes are treated in such a way that the reader whose senses are not wholly dulled gains somewhat more profit from these than from some men's severe and showy demonstrations, as when someone delivers a laborious patchwork speech in praise of rhetoric or philosophy, another expatiates on the virtues of some ruler, another recommends opening a crusade against the Turks, another utters predictions about the future, and another coins quibbling questions on some point of goat's wool. For, as there is nothing more frivolous than to handle serious topics in a trifling manner, so also there is nothing more agreeable than to handle trifling matters in such a way that what you have done seems anything but trifling. Others will judge me; but unless my vanity altogether deceives me, I have written a Praise of Folly without being altogether foolish.

Now to reply to the peevish complaint that I am sarcastic. Men's intellects have always been granted freedom to exercise the play of wit upon human life at large, with impunity so long as this freedom does not turn into furious rage. I am therefore the more surprised at those delicate ears which nowadays can scarcely tolerate anything any more except the usual honorific addresses. You can also find some whose notions of religion are so perverse that they could sooner endure the most dreadful abuse of Christ than the very slightest jest which might cast an aspersion on pope or prince, especially if it touches their bread and butter, that is, their income. And yet if someone censures the lives men live in such a way that he does not denounce a single person by name, tell me if he appears to bite and worry mankind, or rather to teach and admonish them? In any case, look at all the points on which I censure myself. Besides, one who leaves no class of human beings unscathed appears angry not with any person in particular but with every kind of vice. So, if anyone arises to cry out that he is hurt, he shows either that his conscience is pricking him or at least that he is afraid. St Jerome let himself go in this way with much greater freedom and incisiveness, sometimes not even sparing names. For myself, apart from the fact that I name no names at all, I have also exercised such restraint of my pen that the intelligent reader will easily realize that my aim was to amuse and not to criticize. Never have I dabbled, after the fashion of Juvenal, in the hidden cesspool of iniquities; and I have taken care to examine practices which are to be laughed at rather than detested. If, again, there are some who cannot be appeased even by these arguments, they should at least remember that it is creditable to be lashed by Folly's tongue; for when I brought her on stage I had to make her speak in character. But why do I say this to you, a lawyer of such eminence at the bar that you can present brilliantly even a case whose brilliance leaves much to be desired? Farewell, eloquent More; and put up a stout defence of *Moria* your kinswoman. (pp. 161-64)

> *Desiderius Erasmus, in a letter to Thomas More in 1511, in his* The Correspondence of Erasmus: 1501-1514, *by Desiderius Erasmus, translated by R. A. B. Mynors and D. F. S. Thomson, University of Toronto Press, 1975, pp. 161-64.*

Maarten van Dorp (letter date 1514)

[*Dorp was a professor of philosophy at the Collège du Lys and a friendly acquaintance of Erasmus's. In the following excerpt from a letter to the great humanist, Dorp mildly chastises Erasmus for the satiric treatment given churchmen in* The Praise of Folly. *Further, he comments upon Erasmus's studies and translations of the New Testament, advising Erasmus to proceed with caution.*]

The first thing you should know is that your ***Folly*** has aroused a good deal of feeling, and that too among your oldest and most faithful supporters. Who would not be a sincere supporter of a man whose mind the Muses have chosen as a favourite haunt, and philosophy and theology the same? Although there were some people, and still are, who made vigorous excuses for it, yet those who approved it at all points were very few indeed. It is all very well, they say; but even if what he says were perfect truth, surely it is madness to wear oneself out with the sole purpose of making oneself unpopular. Surely it would be folly to act a play, however well written, which no one could see without taking offence, and by which many people are very greatly offended? Then take the faculty of theology, for which it is so important to retain the respect of common folk; what good did it do, indeed how much harm it will do, to attack it so bitterly, however much we may grant at the same time that what you said about some individuals is the truth. And then Christ, and the life in Heaven—can the ears of a good Christian endure to hear foolishness ascribed to him, while life in Heaven, it says, is likely to be nothing but a form of lunacy? We know that it is not only what is false that is a stone of stumbling, but anything that may prove a cause of undoing for the weaker brethren for whom, no less than for great wits, Christ laid down his life. Many things of the sort have been condemned in the majority of councils, although in other respects they were perfectly true (as was clear at the Council of Constance); we have the authority of the famous doctor Jean Gerson. For my part, dearest Erasmus, the way I have answered these arguments would take too long to tell; at least I have never held my peace, I have never let things pass, because I thought it in your interests to watch in all prudence, not only what is said of you by people who may not be gifted but are free of malice, but also the outpourings of the lowest class of men, that it might be refuted either by your friends who are here or by you in writing if you are far away. (pp. 18-19)

In the old days everyone admired you, they all read you eagerly, our leading theologians and lawyers longed to have you here in person; and now, lo and behold, this wretched Folly, like Davus, has upset everything. Your style, your fancy, and your wit they like; your mockery they do not like at all, not even those of them who are bred in the humanities. And that is the point, Erasmus my most learned friend: I cannot see what you mean by wishing to please only those who are steeped in humane studies. Is it not better to be approved rather than rejected, even by rustic readers? We like it, surely, if even a dog wags his tail at us as a sign of friendship. But (you will say) that you should be a good man and do what is right—that is within your responsibility; that other men should think well of you and never speak against you is not in your power to secure. And so like Christ you spurn the Pharisees as moved by ill will, the blind leading the blind. I hear you saying that, Erasmus dearest of men. But those who condemn you and your work are only human; they do it from weakness and not wickedness—unless you think nothing but the humanities, not even philosophy or sacred study, can make a good man. They do it for good reason, not a reason they have simply picked up, but one they have been provided with by you, it seems, although it was in your power not to. 'And what, pray,' you will reply, 'am I to do? What's done cannot be undone. I wish I could change my policy, I wish that everyone who once thought well of me should do so once more.' O sweetest Erasmus, if only I could persuade you to think like that and to talk like that! A man of your active mind cannot fail to know what to do; not for me to tell you, like Minerva and the sow. But I hope, so far as I understand it, that the easiest way to put everything right will be to balance your ***Folly*** by writing and publishing a *Praise of Wisdom.* It is a prolific subject, worthy of your genius and your favourite studies, and will be delightful and universally popular; and it will bring you far more popular acclaim and friendship and good repute and (I might add) profit, even if you despise that, than your ***Folly*** which, as it seems, was so ill-judged. Whether you approve this idea or no, at least I am entirely devoted to you, and always shall be.

Now for the rest of what I had to say in this very long letter. I hear you have purged St Jerome's letters of the errors in which they abounded hitherto, killed off the spurious pieces with your critical dagger, and thrown light upon the dark places. This was a task worthy of you, which will earn the gratitude of all theologians, especially those who hope for a marriage between Christian literature and elegance of style. I understand that you have also revised the New Testament and written notes on over a thousand passages, to the great profit of theologians. This raises another point on which I should like in the friendliest possible spirit to issue a warning. In the first place I say nothing of the efforts of Lorenzo Valla and Jacques Lefèvre in the same field, for I do not doubt that you will surpass them in every respect. But what sort of an operation this is, to correct the Scriptures, and in particular to correct the Latin copies by means of the Greek, requires careful thought. If I can show that the Latin version contains no admixture of falsehood or mistake, will not you have to confess that the labours of all those who try to correct it are superfluous, except for pointing out now and again places where the translator might have given the sense more fully? Now I differ from you on this question of truth and integrity, and claim that these are qualities of the Vulgate edition that we have in common use. For it is not reasonable that the whole church, which has always used this edition and still both approves and uses it, should for all these centuries have been wrong. Nor is it probable that all those holy Fathers should have been deceived, and all those saintly men who relied on this version when deciding the most difficult questions in general councils, defending and expounding the faith, and publishing canons to which even kings submitted their civil power. And that councils of this kind duly constituted never err, in so far as they deal with the faith, is generally agreed among both theologians and lawyers. If some new necessity should arise and require a new general council, this beyond doubt is the text it would follow whenever a knotty problem arose touching the faith. We must confess therefore either that the Fathers were ill-advised and will be ill-advised in the future if they follow this text and this version, or that truth and integrity are on its side. In any case, do you believe the Greek copies to be freer from error than the Latin? Had the Greeks any greater concern than the Latins for preserving the Scriptures undamaged, when you think of the blows Christianity has suffered among the Greeks, and how they firmly hold that everything except St John's Gospel contains some error (to say nothing for the moment on other points), while among the Latins the Bride of Christ, the church, has continued always inviolate? And how can you be sure you have lighted on correct copies, assuming that in fact you have found several, however readily I may grant that the Greeks may possess some copies which are correct?

These arguments move me, my dear Erasmus, not to set a very high value on the work of Lorenzo and Lefèvre; for I do not like to condemn outright anything that is not wholly bad. Nor do I see what they have contributed with all that labour, except that, whenever they point out, as I said, that the translator might have given the sense more fully, I gladly accept this also, when they note that the translator is affected by the Greek or has given a barbarous rendering. That the version could have been much more elegant is common knowledge. If however they contend that a sentence as rendered by the Latin translator varies in point of truth from the Greek manuscript, at that point I bid the Greeks goodbye and cleave to the Latins, for I cannot persuade myself that the Greek manuscripts are less corrupted than the Latin ones. (pp. 19-22)

All this has moved me, dearest Erasmus, to beg and beseech you in the name of our mutual friendship, which you preserve when you are far away, and by your natural courtesy and friendly frankness, to emend only those passages in the New Testament where you can retain the sense and substitute something that gives the meaning more fully; or if your note says that the sense simply must be changed, to answer these arguments in your preface. (p. 22)

Maarten van Dorp, in a letter to Desiderius Erasmus in 1514, in The Correspondence of Erasmus: 1514-1516, *by Desiderius Erasmus, translated by R. A. B. Mynors and D. F. S. Thomson, University of Toronto Press, 1976, pp. 17-23.*

Desiderius Erasmus (letter date 1515)

[*In the excerpt below from his response to Dorp's criticisms and requests, Erasmus defends* The Praise of Folly, *declining Dorp's request to write a counterpart to the satire because of the possibility of arousing further anger. He concludes that the controversy surrounding the* Folly *would "be better left to weaken with time."*]

Your letter never reached me, but a copy of it—secured I know not how—was shown me by a friend in Antwerp. You say you regret the somewhat unfortunate publication of my ***Folly,*** you heartily approve my zeal in restoring the text of Jerome, and you discourage me from publishing the New Testament. This letter of yours, my dear Dorp, gave me no offence—far from it. It has made you much more dear to me, though you were dear enough before; your advice is so sincere, your counsel so friendly, your rebuke so affectionate. This is, to be sure, the mark of Christian charity that, even when it gives rein to its indignation, it retains its natural sweetness none the less. Every day I receive many letters from learned men which set me up as the glory of Germany and call me its sun and moon and suchlike grand descriptions as are more onerous than honorific. My life upon it, none ever gave me so much pleasure as my dear Dorp's letter, written to reproach me. How right St Paul was! Charity is never wrong; if she flatters, she flatters in order to do good, and if she is indignant, it is with the same end in view. I wish I could reply at leisure to your letter, and give satisfaction to so dear a friend. For I am truly anxious that whatever I do should be done with your approval, for I have so high an opinion of your almost divine intelligence, your exceptional knowledge, and your keen judgment, that I should value Dorp's single vote in my favour more than a thousand votes of other men. But I still feel the upset of my sea-voyage and the weariness of the riding that followed, and am, besides that, very busy packing; and so I thought it better to write what I could than to leave a friend thinking as you do, whether these thoughts are your own or were slipped into your head by others, who put you up to write that letter that they might use you as a stalking-horse for their own designs.

First then, to be perfectly frank, I am almost sorry myself that I published my ***Folly.*** That small book has earned me not a little reputation, or notoriety if you prefer; but I have no use for reputation coupled with ill will. Although, in heaven's name, what is all this that men call reputation, except a perfectly empty name left over from paganism? Not a few things of the kind have survived entrenched among Christians, when for instance they use 'immortality' for leaving a name to posterity, or call a man interested in any form of literature a 'virtuoso.' In all the books I have published my sole object has always been to do something useful by my exertions or, if that should not be possible, at least to do no harm. We see even great writers misusing their gifts to discharge their own personal feelings—one singing of his foolish loves, another flattering those he has set his cap at, another using his pen as a weapon to avenge some injury, another blowing his own trumpet and in the art of singing his own praises outdoing any Thraso or Pyrgopolinices. So be it; for myself, in spite of my small wit and most exiguous learning, I have always had one end in view, to do good if I can; but if not, to hurt no one. (pp. 111-13)

But I, who in all the volumes I have published have spoken very sincerely of so many men, whose fair name have I ever blackened? On whose reputation have I cast the smallest slur? What people, class, or individual have I criticized by name? If you only knew, my dear Dorp, how often I have been provoked to do so by falsehoods no man could endure! But I have always fought down my resentment, moved more by the thought of what posterity will make of me than by the wish to treat their malignity as it deserves. If the facts had been as well known to others as they were to me, I should have been thought not satirical but fair-minded and even humble and moderate. No, I said to myself, my private feelings are no other man's concern. How can these affairs of mine be within the knowledge either of people at a distance or of posterity? I will maintain my own standard and not sink to theirs. Besides which, no man is so much my enemy that I would not rather, if I could, be on friendly terms with him again. Why should I bar the way to this, why should I now use language of an enemy which I may wish in vain that I had never used when he has become my friend? Why should I award a black mark to a man from whose record it can never be erased, however much he may deserve that it should be? If I must make a mistake, let me praise those who have done little to earn it rather than criticize those who deserve criticism; for if you praise the undeserving, this is ascribed to your open and generous character, while if you paint in his true colours a man who richly deserves to be exposed, this is sometimes thought to be due not to his deserts but to your vicious disposition. I need not mention in passing that the reciprocal exchange of injuries is not seldom the source of some dangerous conflagration, no less surely than reprisals for wrongs suffered on either side sometimes give rise to some enormous war; or that, just as it is unworthy of a Christian to return evil for evil, so it is unworthy of a generous heart to void its resentment in slander as women do.

Reasons like these have convinced me that whatever I write should hurt no one and draw no blood, and that I should never deface it by mentioning any wrongdoer by name. Nor was the end I had in view in my ***Folly*** different in any way from the purpose of my other works, though the means differed. In the ***Enchiridion*** I laid down quite simply the pattern of a Christian life. In my book on the education of a prince I openly expound the subjects in which a prince should be brought up. In my ***Panegyricus***, though under cover of praising a prince, I pursue indirectly the same subject that I pursued openly in the earlier work. And the ***Folly*** is concerned in a playful spirit with the same subject as the ***Enchiridion.*** My purpose was guidance and not satire; to help, not to hurt; to show men how to become better and not to stand in their way. Plato, serious sage that he was, approves the habit of taking wine with a man at drinking-parties on a generous scale, because he thinks some faults can be dissolved under the cheerful influence of wine which severity could not correct. Horace too thinks good advice even when given in jest no less effective than when serious. 'To tell truth with a smile,' he asks, 'does aught forbid?' . . . The Gospel truth slips into our minds more agreeably, and takes root there more decisively, when it has charms of this kind to commend it than if it were produced naked—a theme pursued at length by St Augustine in his *De doctrina christiana.* I saw how the common throng of mortals was corrupted by the most foolish opinions, and that too in every department of life, and it was easier to pray than to hope for a cure. And so I thought I had found a way to insinuate myself in this fashion into minds which are hard to please, and not only cure them but amuse them too. I had often observed that this cheerful and humorous style of putting people right is with many of them most successful.

If you reply that my assumed character is too trivial to provide an excuse for the discussion of serious subjects, this is a criticism I shall perhaps admit. Ill-judged I do not much object to its being called; ill-natured I do object to. Though the first of these charges I could successfully rebut, if in no other way, at least by the precedents of all the eminent authors whom I have listed in my modest preface. What was I to do? I was staying at the time with More on returning from Italy, and was detained indoors for several days by pain in the kidneys. My books had not yet arrived, and if they had, my illness prevented anything more ambitious in the way of serious study. I began to amuse my idle moments with an encomium on Folly, with no thought of publishing it, but to take my mind off my physical discomfort. I showed a specimen of what I had begun to several ordinary friends, in order to enjoy the joke all the more by sharing it. They were highly delighted, and urged me to continue. I did as they said, and spent a week on it more or less which, considering how trivial the subject was, already seemed to me too much. After that the same people who had encouraged me to write it carried it off to France where it was printed, but from an imperfect as well as corrupt copy. What a poor reception it met with is shown, if by nothing else, by the fact that over seven editions were printed in a few months, and those too in different places. I wondered very much myself what anyone could see in it. So if all this, my dear Dorp, is ill-judged, your culprit owns up, or at least puts up no defence. Within these limits and in an idle moment and to please my friends I judged ill, and only once in my whole life. Who can be wise all the time? (pp. 114-16)

You say that the self-same people who disapprove of my subject think well of the wit, the wide reading, and style, but are offended by the freedom of my satire. These critics actually think more highly of me than I could wish. Not that I care a ha'penny for their kind words, especially as I believe them to have no wit, wide reading, or style themselves; and if they were well supplied with these, believe me, my dear Dorp, they would not be so ready to take offence at humour which aspires to be useful rather than either witty or well read. I ask you: in the name of all the Muses, what can they have in the way of eyes and ears and taste who take offence at the biting satire in that small book? To begin with, what satire can there be in something which criticizes no one by name except myself? Why do they not remember what Jerome so often maintains, that the discussion of faults in general carries no criticism of any individual in particular? If anyone does take offence, he has no cause of action against the author; he may, if he pleases, bring an action for slander against himself as his own betrayer, for having made it plain that that criticism applies to him in particular, which was levelled against everyone in such a way that it was levelled at no individual except such as deliberately made the cap fit. Do you not see how all through the work I have refrained from mentioning people's names so carefully that I have been reluctant even to name a whole country in any critical spirit? For where I list the form of self-love peculiar to each nation, I call the Spaniards proud of their military prowess, the Italians of their literary culture, the English of their good dinners and good looks, and allot to each of the rest in the same way faults of such a kind as anyone, hearing them laid at his door, might not be reluctant to accept them, or at least would greet them with a laugh. Besides which, though the subject I had chosen takes me through every class of men and I spend my time criticizing the faults of individuals, where have I ever said anything scurrilous or bitter? Do I ever uncover a sink of iniquity or stir the mud of Camarina that lurks, as we know, beneath the life of man? Everyone knows how much may be said against evil popes, selfish bishops and priests, vicious princes, and, in a word, against any rank of society, if, like Juvenal, I had not been ashamed to record in writing what many men practise without shame. I have merely surveyed the humorous and comic, rather than the scurrilous, aspect of things, but have done this in such a way as sometimes to touch on major topics, and point out things in passing which it is very important they should know.

I know you have no time to spare for the descent into these details, but yet if you ever have the leisure, do look rather more carefully into the ridiculous jests that Folly makes; and you will find them a good deal closer to the teaching of the evangelists and apostles than some men's disputations which their authors think so splendid, so worthy of their professorial eminence. (pp. 117-18)

My ***Folly*** I myself think not worth a straw, so let no one suppose me concerned about that. Is it surprising if men of the sort I have described choose out a few statements from a long work and make some of them out to be scandalous, some irreverent, some wrongly expressed, some impious and smacking of heresy, not because they find these faults there, but because they bring them in themselves? How much more conducive to peace and suitable to a Christian's fairness of mind to be well disposed to scholars and promote their work; and then, if anything ill thought out should escape them, either to overlook it or to give it a friendly interpretation, instead of looking for holes to pick in a hostile spirit and behaving like an informer rather than a theologian. How much more promising to work together in order either to instruct or to be instructed and, to use Jerome's words, to take our exercise in the field of the Scriptures without hurting one another! (p. 130)

Thinking that the one way to reduce my unpopularity with the theologians and recover the good standing I once enjoyed would be to compose an encomium on Wisdom as a sort of recantation of my ***Praise of Folly,*** you beg and beseech me urgently to do so. For my part, my dear Dorp, as a man who despises no one except myself and who would be glad, if it were possible, to live at peace with the whole human race, I would not refuse to undergo this labour, did I not foresee that any small share of ill will I may have incurred from a few prejudiced and ignorant critics, so far from being extinguished, would be made much worse. And so I think it better not to stir up trouble that is not badly placed and to let this Camarina alone. This hydra, if I mistake not, will be better left to weaken with time.

I now come to the second part of your letter. My work on the restoration of Jerome meets with your high approval, and you encourage me to take up other labours of the same sort. You spur a willing horse; though what I need is not so much people to spur me on to this task as helpers, such is its difficulty. But I hope you will never again believe anything I say if you do not find me speaking the truth in this: those friends of yours who take so much offence at my ***Folly*** will not approve my edition of Jerome either. (pp. 131-32)

Then again what you write in the third part about the New Testament makes me wonder what has happened to you, or what has beguiled for the moment your very clear-sighted mind. You would rather I made no changes, unless the Greek gives the meaning more fully, and you say there are no faults in the version we commonly use. You think it wrong to weaken in any way the hold of something accepted by the agreement of so many centuries and so many synods. I ask you, if what you say is true, my most learned Dorp, why do Jerome and Augustine and Ambrose so often cite a different text from the one we use? Why does Jerome find fault with many things, and correct them explicitly, which corrections are still found in our text? What will you do when there is so much agreement, when the Greek copies are different and Jerome cites the same text as theirs, when the very oldest Latin copies concur, and the sense itself runs much better? Do you intend to overlook all this and follow your own copy, though it was perhaps corrupted by a scribe? For no one asserts that there is any falsehood in Holy Scripture (which you also suggested), nor has the whole question on which Jerome came to grips with Augustine anything at all to do with the matter. But one thing the facts cry out, and it can be clear, as they say, even to a blind man, that often through the translator's clumsiness or inattention the Greek has been wrongly rendered; often the true and genuine reading has been corrupted by ignorant scribes, which we see happen every day, or altered by scribes who are half-taught and half-asleep. (pp. 133-34)

You say that in their day the Greek copies were more correct than the Latin ones, but that now it is the opposite, and we cannot trust the texts of men who have separated from the Roman church. I can hardly persuade myself to believe that you meant this seriously. What? We are not to read the books of renegades from the Christian faith; and how pray do they think Aristotle such an authority, who was a pagan and never had any contact with the faith? The whole Jewish nation turned away from Christ; are we to give no weight to the Psalms and the Prophets, which were written in their language? (p. 134)

Nor can there be any danger that everybody will forthwith abandon Christ if the news happens to get out that some passage has been found in Scripture which an ignorant or sleepy scribe has miscopied or some unknown translator has rendered inadequately. There are other reasons to fear this, of which I prudently say nothing here. How much more truly Christian it would be to have done with quarreling and for each man cheerfully to offer what he can to the common stock and to accept with good will what is offered, so that at the same time you learn in humility what you do not know and teach others ungrudgingly what you do know! If some are so ignorant that they cannot rightly teach anything or so conceited that they are unwilling to learn, let us think no more of them (for they are very few) and concentrate on those who are intelligent or at any rate promising. (p. 136)

Desiderius Erasmus, in a letter to Maarten van Dorp in 1515, in his The Correspondence of Erasmus: 1514-1516, *by Desiderius Erasmus, translated by R. A. B. Mynors and D. F. S. Thomson, University of Toronto Press, 1976, pp. 111-39.*

John Colet (letter date 1516)

[*Colet was an English diplomat and theologian who was Dean of St. Paul's for fifteen years. A member of the Oxford Reformers, he is recognized as a leader of the English Renaissance and was a close friend of Erasmus. In the following excerpt, he praises several of Erasmus's works, declaring that "the name of Erasmus shall never perish. . . . "*]

The copies of your new edition [of the New Testament] sell here like hot cakes and are read everywhere, and many approve your labours and marvel at them; some however disapprove and find fault, making the same criticisms that Maarten van Dorp makes in his letter to you [see excerpt dated 1514]. But these are theologians, of the kind you describe with as much truth as wit in your ***Moria*** and elsewhere, to be praised by whom is a discredit, and whose dispraise is praise. Personally I like your work and welcome your new edition, but in a way that rouses mingled feelings. At one time I am sorry that I never learnt Greek, without some skill in which we can get nowhere; and then again I rejoice in the light which is shed by your genius like the sun. In fact, Erasmus, I am astonished at the fertility of your intellect—you conceive so much, have so much in gestation, and bring forth some perfectly finished offspring every day—especially as you have no certain abode, and lack the support of any fixed, substantial endowment. Your Jerome is awaited here; he owes you a great debt, and so do we all, who can henceforth read him corrected and explained by you. You did well to write ***Institutio principis christiani.*** I wish all Christian princes would follow excellent principles. Their madness upsets everything. I want a copy of that book very badly, for I well know that, like everything else of yours, it will be a really finished performance. (p. 311)

You say you long for a peaceful habitation, and I wish you had one both peaceful and prosperous, such as both your age and your learning deserve. I wish too that you might ultimately settle among us, if we were worthy to harbour so great a man, but you have sampled our quality several times already; at least you have here men who are devoted to you. The archbishop of Canterbury, when I was with him recently, spoke much of you, and warmly expressed the wish that you were here. He is now released from all business, and living happily at leisure.

Your remarks about the pursuit of a Christian philosophy are perfectly just. There is no one, I think, in the Christian world of our own day better fitted for this business and profession than yourself, with the wide range of your learning; you do not say so yourself, I say it, because I really mean it. I have read what you have written on the first psalm, and I admire your ***Copia;*** I long to see the result of your work on the Epistle to the Romans. Do not hesitate, my dear Erasmus, but when you have given us the New Testament in better Latin, go on to elucidate it with your explanations, and let us have a really long commentary on the Gospels. Length from you will seem short. In those who love Holy Scripture the appetite can only grow, provided their digestion is sound, as they read what you have written. If you make the meaning clear, which no one will do better than you, you will confer a great benefit on us all, and make your name immortal. Immortal, did I say? The name of Erasmus shall never perish, but you will win for your name eternal glory, and as you toil in Jesus, you will win for yourself eternal life. (p. 312)

John Colet, in a letter to Desiderius Erasmus in 1516, in The Correspondence of Erasmus: 1514-1516, *by Desiderius Erasmus, translated by R. A. B. Mynors and D. F. S. Thomson, University of Toronto Press, 1976, pp. 311-13.*

Richard Pace (letter date 1519)

[*Pace was an English diplomat who succeeded John Colet as Dean of St. Paul's. In the following excerpt from a 1519 letter, Pace praises Erasmus's paraphrase on St. Paul's* Epistles to the Corinthians.]

I have read your paraphrase on the two Epistles to the Corinthians with the greatest care and wish to say that from this labour of yours I have gained so much that at long last (for such a thing never happened to me before) I dare affirm that up to a point (not to rate my own wits too highly) I understand both what St Paul says and what he means. At last that divine spirit in Paul, which used to seem stilted and intermittent, has its full force. At last those divine precepts, which before tasted to me of bitter aloes, are turned to honey. As it is, your paraphrase has made all so clear to me that I shall bid farewell to all the commentaries by modern interpreters of the Apostle, seeing how in so many places they have merely spread darkness over an author who had enough obscurity and to spare of his own already. There is another point of which I strongly approve: you have pitched your style low enough so that the enemies of good writing cannot possibly accuse you of affected language, but have to recognize the simple utterance proper to the church, whose smooth flow exerts a powerful charm over the reader and holds his attention however long he reads. As a result, for all the simplicity of the style, to my taste no element of eloquence is wanting. Were Paul himself alive today, what could he do except prefer his new self to his old?

Keep it up then, my dear Erasmus, I do beg you, and explain the other Pauline Epistles too in the same way. It is a task fully worthy of your genius, your learning, and not least your cloth, and the completion of it will win you great glory not only among men but in the eyes of God himself. I for my part am impelled to urge you to do so by the fact that the reading of what I have seen was so enjoyable and so profitable as to make me wait eagerly for what is yet to come. (p. 293)

Richard Pace, in a letter to Desiderius Erasmus in 1519, in The Correspondence of Erasmus: 1518-1519, *by Desiderius Erasmus, translated by R. A. B. Mynors and D. F. S. Thomson, University of Toronto Press, 1982, pp. 292-94.*

Frederic Seebohm (essay date 1860)

[*In the excerpt below from an originally unsigned article, Seebohm examines the satiric nature of* The Praise of Folly *and the* Colloquies.]

[In the ***Praise of Folly,*** Erasmus] fulfilled his promise to Colet:—"When I have studied a little deeper, and have got courage enough, I will come to your aid." What Colet and he had whispered in the closet at Oxford, in it he proclaimed upon the house top. And let it be remembered, it was no mere obscure pamphlet, cautiously printed, anonymously, till it should be seen how the world would take it; the wounds it made were not inflicted in the dark by an unknown hand, but the barbed arrows of his satire flew openly in the daylight, straight to the mark, and their wounds were none the less keenly felt because they were known to have come from the bow of the world-famed *Erasmus!*

Folly from her rostrum deals with a variety of topics, and finds votaries everywhere. She portrays the "grammarians" or schoolmasters, as despicable tyrants, and their filthy, unswept schools as "houses of correction." She points to the follies of the lawyer, sophist, and astrologer, in turn, and has her hard hit at each. And then passing from smaller to greater and graver fools, she casts her eye upon the schoolmen. . . . (pp. 54-5)

Truly Erasmus has in good earnest joined Colet in his battle against the schoolmen. He has taken Colet's simple view of theology, and has grown bold enough to publish it. And though the ***Praise of Folly,*** being a satire upon existing abuses, does not tell us fully what he wishes to see in their place; yet there is other abundant evidence, that he not only sought to wean men's minds from the works of the schoolmen, that he also sought to lead them to the Bible. He was already preparing for his Greek New Testament, by a patient study of its contents; and already was the truth dawning on his mind, which afterwards found vent in his defence of his Testament, viz. that the Scriptures should be translated into all languages, so that not only all Christians, but that Turks and Saracens might read them. "I would," said he, "that the peasant should sing the truths of the Bible as he follows the plough; that the weaver should tune them to the whirr of his shuttle; that the traveller should beguile with its stories the tediousness of his journey."

From the *doctrines* of the schoolmen and divines, ***Folly*** turns to the *morals* of popes and clergy, their secular pursuits, and the wars which they engage in themselves, and foment among the princes. . . . (p. 56)

Passing from the clergy to those "who vulgarly call themselves 'the Religious,' and 'Monks,' though most of them are as far from religion as they swarm in numbers," the satire rises to a severer tone—a tone, the very seriousness and solemness of which must have made it doubly stinging to its unfortunate victims. . . .

Thus boldly did Erasmus bid defiance to the most powerful rabble upon earth—a rabble that he well knows will take summary vengeance in one way or another.

As to *indulgences and pardons,* without saying that all pardons are wrong, he points out the evil of their abuse. (p. 57)

As to *saint-worship,* without condemning it altogether, Folly asks, "What do men pray for, and thank the saints for, but such things as minister most to their folly? One has escaped from shipwreck; another has lived through a battle; another, while the rest were fighting as bravely and as happily, fled. Another has broken jail; another, against the will of his physician, has recovered from a fever; but nobody thanks the saints for preserving him from Folly!"

Such was the ***Praise of Folly;*** silent upon the use of these things (if such there be) but bitter as gall upon their prevalent abuse.

We turn now to the ***Colloquies*** to ask, first, under what circumstances they were written, and then what views they expressed. Ten years have passed since the former satire was written. (pp. 57-8)

What are these ***Colloquies?***

"This book (said Erasmus) is not a book upon the doctrines of our faith, it treats upon the art of correct speaking."

It begins with simple instructions as to what a polite boy is to say upon this and upon that occasion, so that he may pass for a gentleman, and not for a churl. It teaches what forms of salutation are used by the vulgar, and what approved by the learned; how to greet a friend or a stranger when you meet, and how to bid them farewell at parting. It then proceeds to explain, by example, how a man may show his concern for another who is ill, or congratulate him if he be well. And, as by degrees the sentences and conversations lengthen, they grow into dialogues on various subjects supposed to be instructive to youth. As these advance, they become less and less trivial, and more and more serious, until at last, by insensible degrees, you find yourself under the full force of the severest satire, one thing after another passing under the lash in turn.

As in the ***Praise of Folly,*** so in the ***Colloquies,*** Erasmus takes no pains to conceal his disgust at the utter hollowness and want of principle which marks the tone of general society, or his conviction that monkery has eaten into its very core, and is to be blamed for much of its rottenness.

Take, for instance, the colloquy of the **"False Knight."** It reminds one of Ellesmere's essay on "The Art of Self-Advancement," in the last series of "Friends in Council." It professes to show how a man may cut a respectable figure in the world, though, in fact, he is nothing at all, and has nothing at all—not even a conscience. (p. 60)

Take again the colloquy called **"Charon,"** in which Erasmus represents the old ferryman mourning his wrecked boat, while his overcrowded passengers are paddling among the frogs. Fame brings him word that he may expect a brisk trade; for the furies have shaved their crowns as smooth as an egg. *Strange animals in black, white, and grey habits,* are hovering about the ears of princes, and stirring them up to war. In France they preach that God is on the French side; in England and Spain that the war is not the king's but God's! Add to this, that a new fire of strife has grown up of late in the *variety of opinions* that men have. At these news Charon determines to invest the halfpence, which for the last 3000 years he has been scraping together, all in a new boat. But, alas! he says, if any should start a peace, my gains will be taken away at once! Never mind that. They who preach peace, preach to the deaf. Alas, too, all the Elysian woods having been felled for burning heretics' ghosts, where is his wood to come from? Then who is to row over these multitudes? The ghosts shall row themselves, says Charon, if they have a mind to get over. What if they have never learned to row? Charon has no respect of persons. He will make kings row, and cardinals row, as well as the poorest peasant. Every one with him takes his turn. Meanwhile the banks of the river are already crowded with ghosts. Charon goes after a boat, and the messenger hastens on to hell with the good news! (pp. 61-2)

Has the great Protestant Revolution materially changed his views? Does he, still hating the schoolmen, still look upon the Bible as the fountain-head of the Christian faith? Does he still point to the Apostles' Creed as the line within which the interpretation of that Bible should be unanimous throughout the Christian Church? Is he still willing to admit that, beyond that line, men may well differ in their interpretations, and need not be too anxious to agree? Now that difference of opinion has become more prominent than ever, does he depart from his liberal views; or does he seek to disarm the difference of opinion of its bitterness by calling men to rally round their points of agreement, rather than fight about unessential points of difference? (pp. 63-4)

Clearly and explicitly must these colloquies be admitted to uphold those general views which we have endeavoured to bring out in these pages, as the views that Colet and Erasmus had accepted before the name of Luther was known outside convent walls.

But it may be said, as it has been said a hundred times, "Why, then, did Erasmus attack Luther?" It is no part of our purpose to deny that Erasmus had faults, or to free his character from every charge of inconsistency. Theory is one thing, and practice another. A man may be sectarian in his very denunciation of all sectarianism, if he denounce it in a sectarian spirit. And that that spirit is to be found embittering the words of Erasmus when in controversy with Luther, far be it from us to deny. Few men of that day were free from it. But it is worth our while to remember, that the charge Erasmus made against Luther, in his controversy on the Freedom of the Will, was not only a charge of error in his view of the question itself, but also the very charge which he and Luther had both made against the schoolmen—*"Why encumber Christianity with your philosophies?"*—That the position taken by Erasmus upon that question was, that it *was* one of *philosophy,*—a question which had vexed Pagans before Christ was born, and which was in its nature inexplicable. He thought, therefore, that it was best not too anxiously even to *try* to fathom its unfathomable abyss.

Leaving, then, the faults and weakness of Erasmus, in matters of action and practice, untold and undefended, we have, in conclusion, to ask only whether any alteration in his general views can be traced in his last works and words.

Would that we could throw anything of tragic interest or brightness round his last years. There is something so grand in a great man's life, ending just in its meridian glory—whether the end comes, as in More's case, upon the scaffold, or the pestilence steps in rudely, as in Colet's case, and spares him the trial of faith, and perhaps the pains of martyrdom—that it is painful to dwell instead upon the long dragging out of life through years of sickness—the pale messenger so long in view, but so long in coming, as if the process of dying were as tedious as man's life is short.

Thus it has been usual to hush up the last days of Erasmus. But we want to know, when we hear of his being crippled by disease, and brought night to death's gate, whether he still holds at seventy, and dying, the views learned from Colet at thirty, published in the ***Praise of Folly*** at forty, and confirmed by his Biblical works and ***Colloquies*** between fifty and sixty.

Let us then look at Erasmus, on the verge of seventy, wrapped up in his blankets, writhing with pain, daily dragging his wasted body, as it were, piecemeal to the grave—and mark that he is writing, in his sixty-seventh year, a simple exposition of the *Apostles' Creed,* and a treatise ***Concerning the Unity of the Church in Love.***

It is well to mark, too, how he bears up under the news of the execution of his darling friend, Sir Thomas More—that execution, of which a severe critic has acknowledged that it was the world's wonder, as well for the circumstances under which it was perpetrated, as for the supernatural calmness with which it was borne—a calamity which was to Erasmus like the severing of his joints and marrow, but which was borne by him patiently, under the full and avowed assurance, that very soon he should meet again that friend. "whose bosom was," he said, "altogether whiter than snow."

Nor did his sorrow stop that work which his maladies could not. His grief found vent in the preface of a treatise, which he named ***Ecclesiastes,*** or ***The Method of Preaching.*** The great want of the Church he thinks to be pure and Christian pastors, who should scatter the seed of the Gospel. He asks, Whence the coldness of men's hearts? Whence so much paganism, under the Christian name? And he answers these questions by saying, "When I was in Italy, I found a people willing to be taught; but I did not find the pastors to teach them."

Thus dropping the negative tone of satire, his mind grapples with positive and practical questions, during the months of suffering and sorrow which usher in his seventieth year, and the pale messenger with it.

He has urged with his dying voice the purity of *pastors* to feed the flock. Thirty years ago he declared his opinion in the ***Praise of Folly,*** that the priests and clergy alone did not make up that Church which is the spouse of Christ. Why should he not add the testimony of his dying voice to the purity which the Gospel demands equally of each individual Christian and member of that Church? He takes up, therefore, his pen once again. "Some think," he says, "that Christ is only to be found in the cloister. I think He is to be found, universal as the sun, lighting the world. He is to be found in the palaces of princes, and in the soldier's camp. He is to be found in the trireme of the sailor, and *in every pious heart*. . . . Know then, oh Christian! thy true dignity, not acquired by thy merit, but given thee from heaven. I am speaking to thee, whether thou art a man or a woman, young or old, rich or poor, noble or ignoble, a king, a peasant, or a weaver; and I tell thee, whoever thou art, if thou art born again in Christ, thou art a king! thou art a priest! thou art a saint! thou art the temple of the living God! Dost thou gaze in wonder at a temple of marble shining with gems and gold? Thou art a temple more precious than this! Dost thou regard as sacred the temple that bishops have consecrated? Thou art more sacred still! Thou art not anointed only with sacerdotal oil; thou art anointed with the blood of the immaculate Lamb." . . . "Each in his own temple," Erasmus goes on to say, "we must sacrifice our evil passions and our own wills—offer up our lives and hearts—if we would at last be translated into the heavenly temple, there to reign with Christ, to whom be glory and thanksgiving for ever!" (pp. 65-7)

Thus the last days of Erasmus set a seal to the consistency with which he held the main tenor of his religious views unchanged to the end. (p. 67)

Frederic Seebohm, in an originally unsigned essay titled "Erasmus as a Satirist," in The North British Review, *Vol. XXXII, No. LXIII, February, 1860, pp. 49-67.*

James Hannay (essay date 1867)

[*In the following excerpt from an originally unsigned article, Hannay provides a brief overview of the subject matter of Erasmus's satiric works, especially the* Encomium moriae *and the* Colloquies.]

We do not disparage [Erasmus] by calling him a satirist, for comedy was one of the elements in which he lived; and a thousand jets of playful satire break out through the voluminous pages of his stately folios. His satire is of the Horatian rather than the Juvenalian school; pleasant, mirthful, pungent, rather than ferocious and biting. His predominant idea is to draw a contrast between the simple holiness of primitive Christianity and the corrupt fabric of his own time; and he points the contrast by humorous little delineations of contemporary theologians and monks, and humorous little hits at their pedantry, ignorance, and vices. It is characteristic of Erasmus that he did not write professed satires. He mixed his satire, like a leaven, with serious discussion or apparently harmless comedy. Thus, in the dedication of his edition of Jerome, he says:—"We kiss the old shoes and dirty handkerchiefs of the saints, and we neglect their books, which are the more holy and valuable relics. We lock up their shirts and clothes in cabinets adorned with jewels . . . and leave their writings to mouldiness and vermin." And in the ***Encomium Moriæ,*** or ***Praise of Folly,*** which he wrote in London after his visit to Italy—about 1508—he does not come to ecclesiastical abuses until he has run over many other kinds of human absurdity. It is then, with a very quiet and sly irony—not the irony of a Swift—that he shows at what a disadvantage the Apostles would be for want of scholastic knowledge if brought face to face with the Scotists, Thomists, Albertists, &c. of his time. They piously consecrated the Eucharist, he says, but if interrogated as to the *terminus a quo,* and the *terminus ad quem,* or as to the moment of time when transubstantiation takes place—seeing that the words effecting it are *in fluxu*—they would never be able to answer with the acumen of the Scotists. Paul, he observes, defines faith and charity *parum magistraliter.* He and his brother Apostles care much more for these, and for good works, than for the *opus operans* and the *opus operatum.* Nor do they tell us whether charity be a substance or an accident, a created or an uncreated thing. It would be a good thing, Erasmus thinks, if all these scholastic sects could be put to use—by being sent out to fight the Turks. This branch of his satire is levelled at the old educational system, which was a vital part of the antique state of things, and which he and his friends, such as Budæus in France, and Reuchlin in Germany, were labouring to supersede by the classical literature,—the chief agent in the intellectual work of the Reformation. But he deals with less abstract matters presently, and complains that practical piety is left by the lay rulers of the world to the *plebs.* The *plebs,* he says, hand it over to the clergy as their business; the secular clergy hand it over to the regulars; the laxer regulars to the stricter ones; all of them together to the mendicants; and the mendicants to the Carthusians,—amongst whom alone piety lies buried, and so buried that it is scarcely ever to be seen! A happy illustration of the true Christian humility follows, where Erasmus reminds his readers that the Holy Spirit descended in the form of a dove, and not of an eagle or a kite. Such are a few of the most characteristic touches of the ***Encomium Moriæ,*** written when Erasmus was the guest of More (it is pleasant to remember that his very best friends were Englishmen), and illustrated by the pencil of Holbein with satirical engravings, which are repeated in the great edition of Le Clerc.

The ***Colloquia*** belong to a later period of the scholar's career; and besides their dramatic liveliness and literature, contain many amusing satirical passages,—especially against the monks, who were the favourite butts of the men of letters, or "humanists," of that important age. It was they who hated the new literature with the deadliest hate—a hate which their ignorance of it well matched. It was their declamatory preaching that worked on the superstitious feelings of women and of the rabble. So their greasy gluttony, their brutal illiterateness, their greed for money, their secret riotousness in sin, were fair game for satirists of every kind; and Erasmus loved to handle them with the playful and elegant mockery which Horace had brought to bear on the sham Stoics of the Roman Empire. Opening the ***Colloquia*** at the dialogue **"Funus,"** we find mendicants of four orders assembled round the bed of a dying man. "What," exclaims Marcolphus, hearing this, "so many vultures to one carcass!" The mendicants, however, have a squabble in the hall, while the master of the house is in his last agony; and representatives of a fifth order, the Cruciferi, having come in, they all set upon them unanimously. The superstitious old gentleman is finally laid on ashes in the habit of a Franciscan, and dies with a Dominican shouting consolation into one ear, and a Franciscan into the other. The description is too picturesque as a whole to be capable of being done justice to in such extracts as our limits permit. We wish only to illustrate the character of the satire of Erasmus, which ranged over a wide field of obsolete nuisances,—foolish pilgrimages, hypocritical funeral pomp, the extravagant adornment of saintly shrines, the superstitious locking-up of poor girls in convents, the scandalous brutalities of wars, and many more. Erasmus did not spare the dignitaries of the Church any more than the monks; though among them were found some like our own Archbishop Warham, who were the steadiest friends of learning. "If there is any labour to be undertaken," says he, "they leave it to Peter and Paul who have plenty of leisure; but the splendour and pleasure they take to themselves." One of the liveliest ecclesiastical sarcasms in the ***Colloquia*** occurs in the **"Charon,"** where he makes the old ferryman tell Alastor that the groves in the Elysian Fields have all been used up for burning the shades of the heretics—*exurendis hæreticorum umbris!* "We have been obliged," Charon adds, "to go to the bowels of the earth for coals." The whole dialogue is a happy adaptation of one of the classical traditions to modern ideas. Another and still more exquisite instance of this occurs in the **"Convivium Religiosum,"** where Erasmus says that he can never read such works as the *Phædo* of Plato without longing to say *Sancte Socrates, ora pro nobis!* Few men have owed more to the ancients than the Sage of Rotterdam; but assuredly still fewer have paid them so much back.

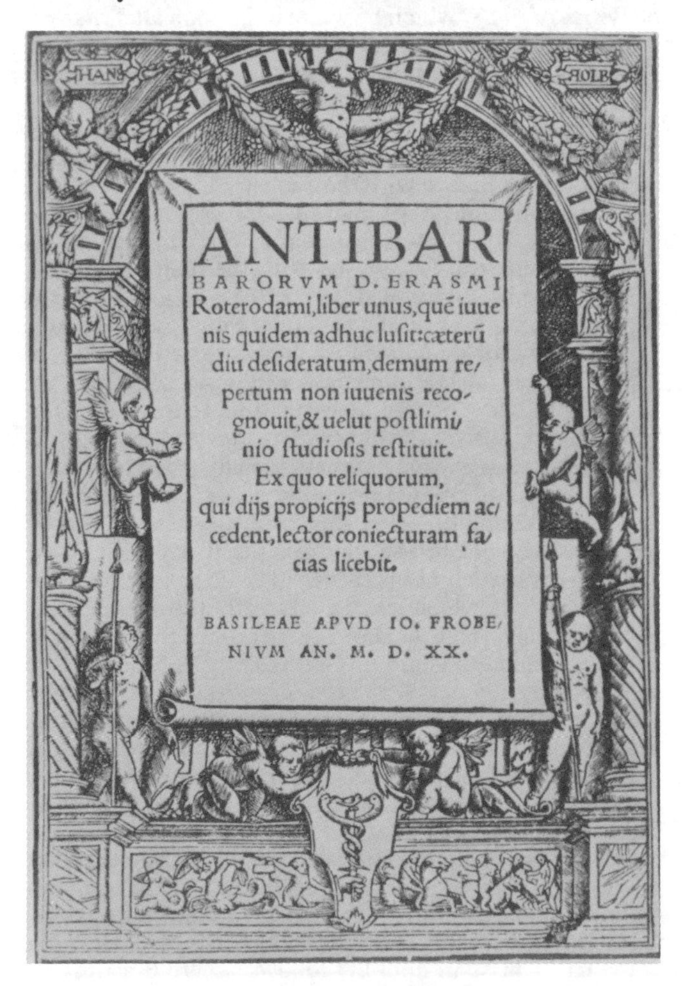
ANTIBAR
BARORVM D. ERASMI
Roterodami, liber unus, quē iuue
nis quidem adhuc lusit: cæterū
diu desideratum, demum re-
pertum non iuuenis reco-
gnouit, & uelut postlimi-
nio studiosis restituit.
Ex quo reliquorum,
qui dijs propicijs propediem ac-
cedent, lector coniecturam fa-
cias licebit.

BASILEAE APVD IO. FROBE-
NIVM AN. M. D. XX.

Title page of the Antibarbari *(1520).*

The wit of Erasmus was not confined to his writings. He shot out many pleasant *bons mots* which flew over Europe; and some of which stuck like barbs in the fat ribs of the bigots. "The fire of Purgatory," said he, "is very useful to these fellows' kitchens." "Luther has done two bad things," he told the Elector Frederick; "he has attacked the crown of the pope and the bellies of the monks." He expressed his wonder that the images did not work miracles when the mobs began to destroy them; they had done so many when there was no need for it. The Lutherans themselves came in for their share of banter from the old humorist, whose care it was to keep an "honest mean," as Pope says, between the parties. It was observed that the first thing an ardent Reformer did on breaking with the Church was to get a wife; so when people were speaking of the movement as "a tragedy," "Nay," said Erasmus, "a comedy,—where the end is generally a wedding." Such were some of the bubbles which rose to the surface of the veteran's favourite burgundy as he sat in his latter years in Basle, looking out on the world with the solid sagacious face, and the large mouth, the delicate lines of which suggest sensibility and humour, so familiar to us all on the canvas of Holbein.

That Erasmus was the greatest of all the satirists of the Reformation, and the one who had most influence on Europe, no competent student of this branch of literature will deny. (pp. 610-13)

James Hannay, in an originally unsigned essay titled "The Satirists of the Reformation," in The Cornhill Magazine, *Vol. XVI, No. 95, November, 1867, pp. 609-28.*

George Bentley (essay date 1873)

[*Bentley was an English publisher and essayist. As editor of* Temple Bar, *he contributed articles on numerous subjects. In the following excerpt, he examines the satire of the* Colloquies, *noting that therein Erasmus indeed acknowledged some positive aspects of the Church and monastic life.*]

The sly covert humour of Erasmus has nothing quite like it in our language. We have other and superior humour; but that mode of sapping by banter which Erasmus undertook, with such success, is a species of humour as distinct in its kind as it is felicitous. In 1511 he published his ***Praise of Folly* (*Encomium Moriæ*),** which was a most lively satire against all sorts of men, from prince to priest, the latter being treated with a severity which any one acquainted with their dense ignorance, their stolid superstition, and their consequent bigotry, knows to be deserved. He tells them that they consider their inability so much as to read to be "a proof of their consummate piety," and adds:

> And when their asinine voices bray out in the churches their psalms, of which they understand the notes, but not the words [*intellectos*], then it is they fancy that the ears of the saints are enraptured with the harmony.

It has been too much the custom to speak of the monks as the preservers of learning, and on that account to regret the abolition of monasteries, the revival of letters just before the Reformation adding very much to this idea; but whatever the monks of earlier days may have been, nothing could surpass their ignorance as a body of men supposed to be educated at the time when Erasmus began to write.

The ***Colloquies,*** published in 1522, are written in an easy lively style, and are full of the result of thought and reading; he composed them originally more for the sake of young people, that they might the more easily learn the Latin language, and partly to act as a counterpoise to the rank superstition of the time. If the former be true, it is a proof how little of a politician Erasmus was, if he could imagine that the monks would suffer such a work to be in the hands of youths. The faculty of theology at Paris at once condemned it; for was not fasting held of less account than charity? was not the invocation of saints derided? and were not the monks made to appear in their true light, as idle, worthless eaters-up of time? To expect the monks to submit to the circulation of such a volume was to expect monasticism to commit suicide.

The ***Colloquies*** consist of a series of Dialogues "*pleasantly* representing several superstitious levities that had crept into the Church of Rome." (pp. 27-8)

The chief result of printing, that which must make its discovery rank also as its chief blessing, is the diffusion of the Bible, and with that the bursting of the bands that swathed religious life and kept it in its cradle. Mere orthodoxy was for a brief but happy period second to truth, just as now by a certain party, and more or less by all parties, truth is postponed to orthodoxy, and pressed into its Chinese shoes. This truth gives a simplicity, a singleness to the minds of that time, and to this may be added as a consequence a greatly increased power. Nothing is more remarkable in the history of the world than the sudden bursting forth in every way—in religion, in literature, in art, in philosophy, in morals—of an extraordinarily gifted race of men. There came upon the world a new youth, giving a beauty, a power, and a truth, to all the thinkers and writers and speakers of the time. It was another Passage of the Red Sea, from the awful and less pardonable darkness of Egyptian Rome to a later Promised Land. Men breathed again, and again drank in inspirations from pure fountains, and our nation was fused into a unity which expressed itself in Shakespeare.

If we speak of these truisms it is because that great period is being decried, because we are getting ashamed of our martyrs, and because with too many the Reformation is no longer a welcome word. Erasmus Roterodamus is one of the most remarkable of those men yielded by the Reformation. Gibbon calls him "the father of rational theology," and to him was chiefly due any moderation that was infused into the controversies of that time. He fancied he saw how at variance with the teaching of the New Testament was the spirit in which the great religious contest of his time was conducted, and he sought to change this.

His beautiful Essay **"The Religious Treat"** has indeed a just claim to its title. In this essay he takes his friends to his garden, and after pointing out its beauties he invites them to a meal within doors, in the course of which three of the Proverbs of Solomon are discussed.

They come afterwards to speak of old age, of Cicero's *De Senectute.* One of the guests, who had joined in the conversation on the Proverbs, says:

> If I did not make a conscience of mingling things profane with sacred, there is something that I would venture to propound to you. I read it this day, with singular delight.
>
> EUSEBIUS. Whatsoever is pious, and conducing to good manners, should not be called profane. The first place must be granted to the authority of the Holy Scriptures; and yet after that, among the Ancients, nay, the Ethnicks, and which is yet more, among the Poets, certain precepts, and sentences, so clean, so sincere, so divine, that I cannot persuade myself but they wrote them by Holy Inspiration, and perhaps the Spirit of Christ diffuses itself farther than we imagine. There are more Saints than we find in our catalogue.

Here is the very spirit of Christianity; the antithesis of the Athanasian spirit, which could calmly propose to a world which had known our Lord to declare that whosoever held not the Athanasian view of the Trinity "without doubt he shall perish everlastingly." The reading of Erasmus should induce some of our modern dogmatists to be more gentle and more modest.

But we come to that part which treats of old age, and of the little desire any one has to live his life again, or for the matter of that to live again in this world at all. Jacob declared his days were few and evil, and Tully puts into the mouth of Cato the following passage, which, beyond its interest as bearing on the question of living twice over, has a sublime foretaste of the future life in it:

> Should God now put it into my power to begin my life again from my very cradle, and once more to run the course over of the years I have lived, I should not upon any terms agree to it. For what's the benefit of life? or rather, how great is the pain! Or if there were none of this, there would be yet undoubtedly in it satiety and trouble; and when I leave this body, 'tis but as an inn, not as a place of abode. For Nature has given us our bodies only to lodge in, not to dwell in. Oh, how glorious will that day be when I will leave the rabble and the trash of this world behind me, to join in council and society with those illustrious spirits that are gone before!

Erasmus remarks, "What could a Christian have said more?" He then says for himself that he would make the same answer as Cato did.

This spirit is not at all alien from the spirit which would cultivate life while possessed. Both Cato and Erasmus would have endorsed Montaigne's faith: "I accept kindly and with acknowledgment what Nature has done for me; am well pleased with it; am proud of it. A man does wrong to the great and potent Giver of all things to refuse, disannul, or disfigure his gift."

But it is when the heat of the day is past, and the sunset of life has come upon us, that we can best appreciate the spirit in which Socrates met death, and most resignedly give up our lives. If we were to live over again, our past experience would be intolerable to us; it would rob the future of all novelty, and fill it with just forebodings of sorrow.

Erasmus proceeds, under the name "Chrysoglottus":

> And 'tis no wonder to find those disordered at their deaths, who have spent their whole lives in the formality of philosophising about ceremonies. I am so far from condemning the Sacraments and Rites of the Church that I have them in high veneration; but there are a wicked, superstitious sort of people (or in good manners I shall call them only simple and unlearned men) that cry up these things as if they were the foundation of our faith and the only duties that make us truly Christians. These I must confess I cannot but infinitely blame.

Erasmus held in advance those opinions entertained by the illustrious band of men in England, commencing with Tillotson. He may be said, as I have before observed, to have laid the foundation of the Broad Church—a church which has been much calumniated, but whose chief characteristic is to insist for themselves and for others for the liberty wherewith Christ has made us free. His manner of introducing the various topics which engage his mind by means of conversations has the great advantage of giving them a humanity, and of removing them out of the pale of abstract reasoning. He is always temperate, occasionally crotchety, seeing far-off meanings where a more obvious one is at his feet, but ever full of thought, of apt illustration, of sly humour, and of grave precept. At times he is lofty in thought and expression, but this is not his ordinary mood, which is rather calm, even, sober and gentle. Of this style is **"The Religious Treat,"** which is a sober entertainment. In its treatment there is no eloquence, but withal it is seasoned with much thought, and flavoured with a certain poetry not usual in his ***Colloquies.*** (pp. 29-32)

"The Rich Beggars" is a return to the humorous mode of treatment used in the **"Religious Pilgrimage."** It is a satire on the Franciscans, who pretend to be the spiritual children of St. Francis, but to whom Pandoches says: "He is a very unlucky *father,* then, for your minds are e'en the worst part of you."

One of the Franciscans is desirous of knowing why Pandoches has such a dislike of their order, and Pandoches, alluding to their habit of quartering themselves, as on this occasion, in the most comfortable quarters for food, says:

> Because you're sure to carry your teeth in your head, and the devil a penny of money in your pockets. If you'd but pay your reckoning I could dispense with your *habits.*
>
> FRANCISCAN. We'll pray for you.
>
> PANDOCHES. And so will I for you, and there's one for t'other.
>
> FRANCISCAN. But there are some people whom you must not take money of.
>
> PANDOCHES. How comes it that you make a conscience of taking any?
>
> FRANCISCAN. Because it does not stand with our profession.
>
> PANDOCHES. And it stands as little with mine to give you your dinner for nothing.
>
> FRANCISCAN. But we are tied up by a rule.
>
> PANDOCHES. So am I, by the clean contrary.
>
> FRANCISCAN. Where shall a body find your rule?
>
> PANDOCHES. In these two verses:
>
> 'Tis the rule of this table, eat as long as you're able,
> But then pay your score; there's no stirring before.

The innkeeper eventually receives the Franciscans, and a most interesting discussion takes place, in which the Franciscan is made to appear in a very favourable light, and Pandoches winds up by saying:

> I have not met with better company. Let me die if I had not rather talk with thee than drink with our pastor.

The same friendly feeling towards monks is shown in **"The Soldier"** and **"The Carthusian,"** and Erasmus takes occasion to show how far preferable is the retired life of the Carthusian to the life of a soldier of fortune. In answer to the reproach of the soldier that his life is a solitary one, the Carthusian says:

> If by solitude you mean only a withdrawing from the crowd, you may reproach with this solitude the ancient prophets, the Ethnick philosophers, and many other persons that have applied themselves to the gaining of a good mind, as well as us; nay, poets, astrologers, and other eminent artists, whensoever they have anything in hand that is extraordinary, do commonly betake themselves to a retreat. But why should this kind of life be called a solitude, when one single friend is a most delightful contradiction to it? I have here almost twenty companions to all sociable and honest purposes, visits more than I desire, and, indeed, more than are expedient. . . . Look you, here are the Four Evangelists. In this book I can confer with Him that accompanied the two disciples in their way to Emmaus, and with His heavenly discourse made them forget the trouble of their journey; with Him that made their hearts burn within them, and inflamed them with a divine ardour of receiving His blessed words. In this little study I converse with Paul, Isaiah, and the rest of the prophets; Chrysostom, Basil, Austin, Jerome, Cyprian, with a world of other learned and eloquent doctors. Where have you such company abroad as this? Or what do you talk of solitude to a man that has always this society?

This is a fine passage, a grand defence of the monastic life. If all monks were as this Carthusian almost one could connive at monasteries. But then, in the **"Colloquy on Funerals,"** he shows us Austin friars, Carmelites, and Dominicans, quarrelling over the deathbed of a rich man, and securing the bulk of his property away from his children. He seems desirous of doing justice to the monkish system, and, foreseeing its downfall and the justice of it, he preserves for after time the few good features which undoubtedly belonged to it. (pp. 32-4)

George Bentley, "An Evening with Erasmus," in Temple Bar, *Vol. XXXVIII, April, 1873, pp. 23-34.*

Percy Ellwood Corbett (essay date 1921)

[*In the excerpt below, Corbett provides a concise introduction to the* Institutio principis Christiani, *focusing on Erasmus's pacifist thought.*]

Throughout the whole of Erasmus' life, 1467-1536, there never was a time when Europe was at peace. In Holland his boyhood witnessed continual struggles between Hoeks and Cabeljaus, intermittent war between the Duke of Gueldres and the Bishop of Utrecht, and the ravages of German bands retained by the oppressive ducal governors. Flanders, Brabant, and Liège were the scenes of repeated revolts against the sovereignty of successive dukes of Burgundy, put down for a time by ruthless massacres of the towns and breaking out afresh at every accession of strength to the Guilds. Further afield were the expeditions of Charles the Bold against France, Alsace and Lorraine, ending in his death at the siege of Nancy in 1477, and resumed by Maximilian after his marriage with Charles' heiress, Mary. In 1494, the year in which Erasmus, by becoming secretary to the Bishop of Cambrai, took his first step into the world, Charles VIII. embarked on his expedition against Naples, thus beginning an ever-shifting series of wars, intrigues and leagues, which was to absorb all the Courts with which the scholar of Rotterdam became familiar in his wandering life. In 1517, Luther nailed his ninety-five theses on the church door at Wittenburg, and the Christian world was thrown into a struggle which, violent as it became during the twenty years left to Erasmus, was destined to involve more bloodshed and destruction than his darkest warnings foreshadowed.

No wonder if, in such a period, men who were able to detach themselves, in the precarious quiet of monastery or university, from the perils of the moment, pondered deeply on the nature and causes of war. This was particularly inevitable in the case of Erasmus, who, through his acquaintance with many courts and princes, temporal and ecclesiastical, had the widest information possible in that day, and who, because he would never bind himself to person or party, could think and speak with complete independence and detachment.

There was already a vast amount of literature on war. In theory, at least, the Church had always been opposed to conflict between the faithful. From the beginning of our era, churchmen had wrangled on the nature of war, some of them, like Clement of Alexandria, Tertullian, Origen, and Lactantius, denying that it could ever be just, while others distinguished between just and unjust war. St. Augustine belongs to the latter school. He admitted all the evils of war, and preached moderation in the profession of arms, but maintained, nevertheless, that to fight in defence of the State and for the general good was no sin. To be just, a war must satisfy three conditions—it must be authorised by a prince (thus St. Augustine excludes private war from the "just" category), it must be undertaken in a good cause, and must be waged with right intention—*i.e.,* to do good or avoid evil. (pp. 7-8)

Of [this] and the numerous other disquisitions on war, the great majority maintained that it was not essentially incompatible with justice. On the other hand, there were out-and-out pacifists, like Wicliffe and the Lollards generally, who condemned it as an unmitigated evil.

Erasmus several times refers to the controversy, though to him the distinction is a matter of entirely secondary interest. He is uncertain, though rather inclined to hold that no war is just, and leaves the question to dwell on the ever-present fact of the horrors of war. He will not concern himself with nice definitions, nor with the scholastic and mystical classifications of war. Even against the Turks he would not rashly take up arms, for he doubts whether Christ would approve of extending his Kingdom by such means. Too often he had seen the pretext of a Crusade used for the purpose of extorting contributions from the peoples. In Europe, as he saw it, war was almost invariably the result of pride, folly and selfish intrigue, and he made it his task to point out how, by proper instruction begun at the earliest age, the Sovereign and his Councillors might be led to abhor what was plainly the worst of all human calamities. (pp. 8-9)

Apart from such general discussions of war, there had been, before the time of Erasmus, various schemes for an organisation of States to secure peace. (p. 10)

With all his efforts to convince Popes and Princes of the iniquity of war, Erasmus devised no scheme for a Confederation of States. Like More's Utopians, he thought many alliances a danger rather than a safeguard for peace. In the ***Institutio Principis Christiani,*** his doctrine is that war is incompatible with reason and morality. The book contains no specific antidote for war; it is rather an attempt to purify the whole system of government, to substitute the principles laid down by the ancient philosophers and the teachings of Christ for that political opportunism which found its most direct expression in an exactly contemporaneous work, Machiavelli's *Prince.*

We find no suggestion, then, in Erasmus' writings, for a Council of Princes or for an International Court. The nearest approach he makes to plans such as those outlined above is in his repeated advocacy of arbitration. But the reference would be not to a previously constituted college of judges, but to popes, abbots, bishops, wise and upright men, summoned *ad hoc.* For such procedure there were ample precedents even in the Middle Ages. As early as 1176 we find a case of detailed provision for arbitration. The conflicting claimants were the Kings of Aragon and of Navarre, and the dispute was referred to Henry II. of England, with pledges for submission to the final verdict, and an arrangement by which the King of France was to be substituted for Henry in the event of the latter's death. Many other cases might be cited when the Sovereigns of the multitudinous kingdoms, principalities and duchies into which the Empire had broken up, called in the Pope, a foreign Prince, a Parlement, or a University to settle questions of title. To quote perhaps the most famous instance, it was in 1498—that is, shortly before Erasmus became secretary to the Bishop of Cambrai—that Pope Alexander VI. made his famous award, adjudging new lands and ocean, to the east and west of a line drawn through the Atlantic, to Portugal and Spain respectively.

Erasmus could only attribute it to the folly, passions or ambitions of Princes that this method of establishing rights between States was not always adopted. Though the arbiters were the most corrupt and incompetent, he says in one passage, yet the result would be less harmful than recourse to arms, for "there can hardly be a peace, however unfair, that is not better than even the most just war." He repeatedly asks how it is that nations calling themselves Christian, united by the blood of Christ, can attack one another on the slightest infringement of a doubtful and negligible right, waging war with a cruelty that might horrify those very Turks whom they profess to despise as infidels and barbarians.

The fault lay not in the people. They knew well, from the poverty and sufferings to which it exposed them, all the vanity and iniquity of war. Those responsible were the rulers, their evil counsellors, and the bands of mercenaries, "dregs of humanity," whom they kept in their pay. And here Erasmus appeals to a political principle which was to be developed in various ways by Althusius and Bodin and Hobbes—princes originated in the choice of the people, government rested on the consent of the governed. How unreasonable, then, that those set up to guard the people's welfare should be the source of their greatest woes!

The ideal form of government, according to Erasmus, is absolute monarchy. But this is only best when the monarch is a man of perfect wisdom and perfect virtue. The State can scarcely hope for such a ruler—must generally, indeed, count itself fortunate in mediocrity. Therefore certain checks are necessary. Even in limited monarchy, however, the King is responsible for a great part of the government, and the best way to secure the common welfare is to train him from childhood, before he comes to the throne, in the real statecraft—truth, justice and wisdom.

Such is the purpose of the ***Institutio Principis Christiani.*** It was dedicated to the Archduke Charles, afterwards the Emperor Charles V., when the latter, already ruler of the Netherlands, had just become King of Spain (1516). A letter of 1517 (to Fabricius Capito) shows the author in high hopes that his dreams of peace are to be realised:—"I am now 51 years old, and may be expected to feel that I have lasted long enough. I am not enamoured of life, but it is worth while to continue a little longer with such a prospect of a golden age. We have a Leo X. for Pope; a French King content to make peace for the sake of religion when he had means to continue the war; a Maximilian for Emperor, old and eager for peace; Henry VIII. King of England, also on the side of peace; the Archduke Charles 'divinæ eujusdam indolis adolescens.' "

The peace was but a lull in the Italian wars, which were soon to break out again, intensified by the conflicts of the Reformation. Writing from Anderlac in 1521, Erasmus records the complete wreck of his hopes: "Oh, what a world! Christendom split in two and committed to a deadly struggle; two young Princes, each fierce and ardent, each bent on the destruction of the other. Immortal God! Where is the Pope? When anything is to be got for the Church he can command angels and devils, but he can do nothing to prevent his children from cutting each other's throats."

Up to his death, in 1536, Erasmus continued counselling peace and moderation in letters addressed to Princes, Pope and Emperor. He has often been accused of indecision, even of cowardice, in his attitude to the Reformation. The question scarcely concerns us here, but it is not surprising that so ardent a lover of peace should have hesitated to identify himself with the violence of either party. Here, as elsewhere, his attitude was perhaps that of a man who exaggerated the effect of reason on human conduct, but it is difficult to dispute his thesis that, of all differences, those relating to religious dogmas are least susceptible of settlement by arms.

The reasons which justify the great efforts for peace being

made in the world to-day are broadly the same as those urged by Erasmus four centuries ago, and there is much in the ***Institutio Principis,*** and in his other utterances on peace, that is neither trite nor of merely historical interest. Modern peace movements take the direction of international organisation, but there is still much to be said for the thesis, which formed the basis of Erasmus' work on the subject, that war can only be finally eliminated by the reform of "human nature." (pp. 12-15)

Percy Ellwood Corbett, in an introduction to Erasmus' "Institutio Principis Christiani": Chapters III-XI, *by Desiderius Erasmus, translated by Percy Ellwood Corbett, Sweet and Maxwell, Ltd., 1921, pp. 7-15.*

Preserved Smith (essay date 1923)

[*Smith was an American historian who wrote what is considered by many critics the authoritative biography of Erasmus. In the following excerpt from that work, he surveys the* Colloquies *and their content, their influence, and their various critics.*]

Of all the works of Erasmus the one in which his own nature and style appeared to the best advantage, that which surpassed all others in originality, in wit, in gentle irony, in exquisitely tempered phrase, and in maturity of thought on religious and social problems, was written as a textbook of Latin style. The ***Familiar Colloquies*** were intended to make easy and pleasant the once thorny path of learning for aspiring youth. They are stories in the form of conversations, always conveying, along with the necessary exercise in Latin, enough instruction and reflection on all sorts of matters to make them profitable reading for thoughtful minds. The author's most important "sources" were, indeed, his own experiences. If he borrowed something from Lucian, a plot from Hroswitha and a tiny bit from Poggio, far more he wove in of his own ripe thought on events in which he had participated.

Like so many of its author's productions, this was a work of many years, each issue being a revision and expansion of the previous one. The first ***Colloquies*** were written at Paris in 1497 for the use of some pupils, among them Augustine Vincent Caminade. The author did not intend them for publication, but, as he wrote later,

> I dictated some trifles or other if anyone wished to chat after dinner and, as Horace says, to sport informally by the fireside. There were some formulas of everyday intercourse and again some convivial conversations. . . . These trifles Augustine Caminade sucked up like an insatiable Laverna, and from them all patched up a book like Æsop's crow; or rather he concocted them just as a cook mixes up many scraps to make a broth. He added titles and names of persons from his own invention, so that the ass in the lion's skin might sometimes betray himself. For it is not as easy to write Latin trifles as some think. . . .
>
> (pp. 286-87)

The earliest colloquies are the easiest and most formal, dealing with such subjects as eating and drinking, games of ball, and matters of everyday life. All manner of proper salutations are catalogued, from the most distant to such affectionate titles as "my life, my delight, my little heart." Such instructions in manners are given as that it is polite to salute people when they sneeze or cough, and to wish them good luck, but not when their bowels rumble or when they are engaged in discharging the duties of nature. The interlocutors are Caminade, James Voecht, a schoolteacher of Schlettstadt named Sapidus, Erasmus, Erasmius Froben, Gaspar, Bernard, and others. The first two names date back to the Paris days; the others were added later. The conversations show that Erasmus joined his pupils in games of tennis, conversed with them on serious topics, and joked them on everything; one pupil, for example, was goodnaturedly ridiculed for having a nose big enough to be used as a bellows, a harpoon, or a candle extinguisher.

In the edition of March, 1522, Erasmus added much, mainly on religion. The tendency of it is all liberal, to emphasize the life of the spirit rather than dependence on ceremonies. In a long ***Religious Symposium,*** an interlocutor called Eusebius says: "I have put Jesus instead of the foul Priapus as protector of my garden." This free manner of speaking, and the juxtaposition of the two names, shocked the conservative. In a later edition, also of 1522, Erasmus added ***An Apotheosis of John Reuchlin,*** who died on June 20, 1522. In this the good man is represented as taken to heaven, whereas an obscurantist, called "the Camel"—probably the Carmelite Egmond—is satirized.

In the next edition, of August, 1523, Erasmus added much, chiefly on love and marriage. One dialogue represents a girl rejecting an infatuated suitor; another shows the young man warning the girl of the dangers of the cloister; and a third exhibits her repentance at having taken the veil. A fourth dialogue sets forth the inconveniences of marriage. Various anecdotes of the writer's friends are inserted, including one of Thomas More's early married life. One of the interlocutors, Xanthippe, perhaps stands for the shrewish second wife of the same man. Nor did Erasmus scruple to add, in this textbook for boys, a realistic dialogue between a youth and a harlot, in which the former tries to convert the girl to a better life, and tells her that he himself has kept pure, even at Rome, by reading the Greek Testament of Erasmus. The author probably took the plot for this story from the tenth-century dramatist and nun, Hroswitha. At any rate it illustrates the freedom with which such matters were then spoken of. Virtue was then supposed to lie not in ignorance, but in knowledge.

Another conversation added at this time contrasts the French and German inns, very much in favor of the former. Still another dialogue, between Antony and Adolph, doubtless Dutch friends of the writer, describes a shipwreck. . . . (pp. 287-89)

This colloquy excellently illustrates the manner in which liberal ideas were instilled into the minds of the readers. One by one the author took up most of the popular abuses in order to hold them up to ridicule. The conversation entitled, "The Inquisition of Faith," minimizes the Church's power of excommunication, showing that only God's fulminations strike the soul and that nothing is necessary to salvation but the Apostles' Creed. A very mild satire on the "poor rich men," *i.e.,* the begging friars, holds up the ideal of men rich only in spiritual gifts. The worship of the saints comes in for constant derision. . . . (p. 293)

Other dialogues ridicule the superstitions of spiritism, or of alchemy, of fasting, or of pilgrimages. It is not surprising that some of them should have given offense to old-fashioned piety. Luther, for instance, though quoted, sided with the conservatives, and, in one of his late, harsh judgments, selects the colloquy on Mariolatry as one that mocks all religion. This censure is, of course, wrong. What Erasmus mocks is not religion, but the false application of it. . . . (pp. 294-95)

But superstition was not the only foible satirized. One colloquy denounced war; another hit off the absurdities of the grammarians; a third was a plea for eugenics, at least to the extent of forbidding the diseased to marry. Others treated of feminism, of horse-cheats, of miserliness, of false nobility, of the love of glory. In fact, every human, or at least every humanistic interest, is taken up, exposed to the free play of mind, and moralized.

Naturally, the free tone of the ***Colloquies,*** and their anti-ecclesiastical tendency, aroused bitter criticism. In the first acknowledged edition, that of March, 1522, Nicholas of Egmond, the conservative of Louvain, detected four passages savoring of heresy, one on vows, one on indulgences, one of confession and pilgrimages, one on fasting. The author had described a man who confessed having made, while drunk, vows to go on pilgrimages to Rome and Compostella and who had carried them out, although he was persuaded that they were foolish and that his wife and children suffered by his absence. Another passage attacked was this: "I hate a snake less than a fish. And I have often wondered why, when the Gospel freed us from the Mosaic law, we believe that God has put this more than Jewish load [of fasting] upon Christian shoulders." In the next edition, of the same year, Erasmus modified these censures, and also deprecated the action about to be taken against him by the university of Paris. This was long delayed, for, though the university drew up a *Determination on the Familiar Colloquies of Erasmus* in May, 1526, it was not published until 1531, the author answering in the following year.

Meantime Erasmus was busy defending his work against other critics. In the edition of June, 1526, he added a ***Letter to the Reader*** "on the utility of the Colloquies," moved thereto by the slander that waxed hot against every man and every book. In his book, he protests, he has for the first time aimed to make the road to learning a pleasant one, for he is convinced that play is the best teacher. Throughout, however, he has pointed morals, for example he has called attention to the evils of pilgrimages, which no one familiar with the disastrous fate of relatives left at home can deny. He has condemned, not indulgences, but the abuse of them. It is nonsense to say that he has ridiculed religion. As for the charge of lasciviousness in the dialogue between the youth and the harlot, he answers that the critics who strain at his gnat swallow the camels of Plautus and Poggio. The obscene word put into the mouth of the shameless girl is said to have been a common one even in the speech of honest matrons. If anyone prefers he may write another word. But save for this the author claims that he has made even the stews chaste.

In like tone Erasmus assured his private friends that his work had in it nothing indecent, impious, or seditious, but that it had, on the contrary, profited many.

To the author the most trying ordeal came not from the camp of his enemies, numerous though these were, but from a probably well-meant attempt to expurgate the offensive matter, in an unauthorized edition by Lambert Campester, a Saxon theologian of Louvain. This gentleman, described as "of squinting eye, but of yet more squinting mind, . . . corrected, that is to say, depraved, some passages about monks, vows, pilgrimages, and indulgences," and changed the names Paris and France to London and England, regardless of the sense; and he also forged an introduction in barbarous Latin, purporting to come from the author. He then published the hateful work at Paris.

But the narrowly religious men in both camps continued to protest against the ***Colloquies.*** Ambrosius Pelargus, a shining light of Freiburg, said that all the youth had been corrupted by that work. Cuthbert Tunstall, Bishop of London, was offended by them. In 1549 one J. Morisotus, did his best to have the ***Colloquies*** superseded by a new work of the same name, written by himself. Dionysius de Zannettinis, Bishop of Milopotamos and delegate to the Council of Trent, described them as very dangerous and as likely to make boys mock all religion. They were censured by a papal commision of cardinals in 1537 and finally put on the Index, with the rest of their writer's works. They were forbidden by the inquisition in Franche-Comté in 1535. The Reformers, too, though they sanctioned the use of the ***Colloquies***—perhaps exscinding some of the freer passages—in their schools in 1528, finally turned against them. "On my deathbed," said Luther, I shall forbid my sons to read Erasmus's ***Colloquies***. . . . He is much worse than Lucian, mocking all things under the guise of holiness." The great Protestant scholar, Joseph Scaliger, thought there were many faults in the Latin of the ***Colloquies.***

All these attacks, however, did not greatly injure the popularity of the work, but rather advertised it. When Vesuvius wrote from France, on February 8, 1527, saying that the censure of the Sorbonne did not alienate the esteem of good men, his opinion was fully borne out by the fact that the mere rumor of the coming condemnation induced a Parisian bookseller to hurry through the press an edition of twenty-four thousand copies. In fact, the sales were enormous, and would be considered so even in modern times. During the eighteen years from their first publication to the author's death about a hundred impressions were called for, and the popularity of the work rather increased than diminished during the next two centuries. This astounding success, which easily broke all previous records and was only surpassed, among contemporary works, by the vernacular Bibles, may be partly accounted for by the international reputation of the author, all civilized countries contributing to swell the sales. Another consideration was that the ***Colloquies*** were used as a text-book, and a successful text-book has always been one of the most vendible forms of writing. There were also many translations, one of the earliest being into Spanish. Separate dialogues were also put into the vernacular: Clement Marot, for example, translating into French verse the dialogues entitled **"The Abbot and the Learned Lady"** and **"The Girl Who Did Not Want to Marry."**

The influence of the Erasmian ***Colloquies*** on the thought of the sixteenth century was proportional to their popularity. Other works, indeed, such as *The Utopia, The Prince, The Revolutions of the Heavenly Spheres,* and *The Babylonian Captivity of the Church,* may have ultimately done more to revolutionize the world's thought, but none of them made such a wide and immediate impression upon the minds of youths at the most impressionable age. The spread of the Reformation in particular, and of ideas still more liberal for that day and generation, was due more to this text-book of style than to any other one volume. Among the Anabaptists and among the Arminians, in Franck and in Acontius, the Erasmian liberalism obtained a full evaluation; in Rabelais and Montaigne it reached a still higher plane of expression.

Among the many educational treatises of all sorts penned by the scholar of Rotterdam, two of the earliest were the ***Method of Study*** and ***The Double Supply of Words and Matter.*** In them the author expressed his preference for the study of language to "that elusive maiden Dialectic," the love of the schoolmen, emphasized the importance of vocabulary, gave examples of how to say the same thing in different ways, and recommended the study of Latin and Greek together for their mutual help.

Other commentaries, text-books, and treatises on pedagogy poured from his pen. Such was his edition of ***The Distichs of Cato,*** some moral couplets which had a great vogue in the Middle Ages, when they were supposed to have been written by Cato the Censor, though believed now to have originated in the third or fourth century. Such was the Greek grammar of Gaza translated by Erasmus in 1516. Such was the Latin grammar, composed jointly by Lyly and Erasmus for Colet's school, which was for centuries the standard Latin grammar, being the one used by Shakespeare, recommended by Doctor Johnson, and the basis of the Eton Latin grammar now in use.

This book made an immediate success; Sapidus, a well-known German schoolmaster, wrote Erasmus how delighted the boys were with his text-book. . . . (pp. 297-302)

Not only to the practical work of writing text-books and grammars, but to the exposition of pedagogical theory, Erasmus contributed much. It is true that he was not very original in method, borrowing largely from Plato, Aristotle, Plutarch, Quintilian, Mapheus Vegius, and the German humanists. With the classical enthusiasm of the age he was thoroughly in sympathy, as he was with the highly aristocratic tendency of the Renaissance. The training of an *élite* was his constant preoccupation and he saw that there was no education like converse with men of character and cultivation. "Live with learned men," he advised, "hear them submissively and with honor, study them, and never think yourself learned." Logically, therefore, the tutorial system was postulated, at least as the ideal. This system, of course, is only open to the wealthy, and it is of the education of these that Erasmus always seems to be thinking. He had no democratic instincts; the immense services rendered to the common-school education of the people by Luther would not have appealed to him. His thoughts were absorbed in excogitating the rational training for a leader, a prince, a prelate, or at least an aristocrat like More or Pirckheimer. The chief, indeed almost the only, subjects to be taught were the classics. This idea, which seems so inadequate to us, was in reality an advance over the mediæval curriculum; the only subjects then taught, except a little barbarous Latin, had been dialectic and Aristotelian philosophy. Compared to this dry course the classics offered real wealth of material. Nevertheless, it is fortunate that Erasmus's plan did not obtain exclusive dominance.

Erasmus saw that the earliest education must come from the mother, and laid down the sound principle that care of the body is the foundation of all. Work should begin by way of play, a tutor (whose qualifications are set almost impossibly high) should be secured when the pupil is five or six. If the boys are sent to school—which, however, is deprecated—lay schools are to be given the preference to religious ones.

The text-books edited by Erasmus allow us to see exactly the method he preferred. A glance at his *De Constructione* (Lyly's grammar of 1515) shows a considerable lack of logical arrangement. This may be partly intended; at any rate, reading was more relied on than formal rules. The first books to be read should be the Proverbs and Gospels in Latin, after them a Latin version of Plutarch's *Apothegms* and *Moralia.* Æsop is to be the first author read in Greek. It is plain that the moral element is preponderant in this choice, the predilection for sententious precepts being especially marked. It is noticeable that Luther shared this taste to the full; Æsop and Dionysius Cato, both edited by Erasmus, being among his favorite books. Following Quintilian, Erasmus then picks out to be read among the Greeks Lucian, Demosthenes, Aristophanes, Homer, and Euripides; among the Latins, Terence, Plautus, Vergil, Horace, Cicero, Cæsar, and Sallust. He excludes mediæval Latin, especially the romances of Arthur and Launcelot.

The author is to be read first for the grammar, then for the style, and finally for the moral instruction. The method followed was that recommended by Milton a century later, the teacher to construe the text to the boys one day and have them repeat it to him on the morrow. Writing was, of course, studied, especially prose, first the oratorical style, then the epistolary, and then the historical. Poetry and Greek composition were also recommended.

It is astonishing to us that so little time is given to anything but language. All other subjects were supposed to be taken in incidentally to philology. History was a by-product of Livy, for example, and natural science of Pliny. Indeed, it sometimes seems as if knowledge of any facts at all was mainly valued for the sake of literary allusion.

Unlike Luther, Erasmus put a very slight value on music. He apparently had little taste for it, sometimes mentioning the congregational singing in the reformed churches as one of their repellent features. Some emphasis was laid on deportment; in 1526 Erasmus wrote a primer of ***Civility for Boys,*** telling them how to carry themselves, how to dress, how to behave at church, at table, in company, at play, and in the dormitory.

In advocating the education of women Erasmus was ahead of most of his contemporaries. He labored to refute the common but erroneous opinion that literature is neither useful to women nor consistent with their reputation and innocence. One of the ***Colloquies*** on the subject shows an abbot, who at first maintained that books took from the weaker sex what little brains they had, finally convinced by a blue-stocking that the learned women of Italy, Spain, England, and Germany had profited mightily by their studies. Both here and elsewhere Erasmus alleged the examples of Sir Thomas More's daughters, and those of Pirckheimer and Blaurer. With More's eldest daughter, Margaret Roper, he was indeed in occasional epistolary correspondence. In her nineteenth year she translated into English one of his tracts under the title ***A Devout Treatise upon the Pater Noster,*** and he repaid the compliment by dedicating to her his ***Commentary on Prudentius' Hymn to the Nativity.***

The influence of Erasmus was doubtless great, but it was not revolutionary, because of the perfect accord between him and the liberal wing of contemporary thought. To distil the lessons of the classics and of the early Christian writings, and then to instil them into the minds of youth, seemed to that and to many subsequent generations the highest wisdom. The principal pedagogical writers of the next generation followed the humanist's recommendations exactly. What do we read in Ascham, and in Ramus, and in Eliot, and in Melanchthon, and in Vives, and in Starkey, but variations upon the tune composed by the scholar of Rotterdam? What new matter did Milton, in the next century, have to recommend? Indeed, the humanistic reform of the sixteenth century formed the basis of all education until the latter part of the nineteenth, when living languages and new sciences began to take the place of the classics. Nowadays the old authors so familiar to our fathers have become little more than ghosts of their former selves; and, like the shades seen by Odysseus in the underworld, they revive to life and warmth only when they drink blood—that of the unappreciative youths and maidens still sacrificed to them in our schools. . . . (pp. 305-08)

"Those who can, do," says Bernard Shaw, "those who can't, teach." This cutting epigram was not true of Erasmus. If he spent his life largely in teaching the art of writing, he was himself one of the greatest masters of that art. As he never sought, so he naturally never attained, the distinctive beauty of the classics: that perfect adaptation of language to thought, that supreme artistry which, sometimes by apparently simple means, sometimes by perceptible elaboration, unfailingly achieved the desired and definite effect. Those who attempted imitation and nothing more fell into an arid, stilted pedantry, alike fatal to all freshness of thought and to all true beauty of form.

But Erasmus, having imbibed, as had few others even in that age of idolatry of the classics, the spirit of the ancients, finally attained a mastery of style at once original and attractive. That Latin was hardly a dead language, but one very much alive both in the mouths and on the quills of scholars, is proved by the perfectly living treatment of the medium by this great master. The very fact that the tongue he wrote was not exactly that of ancient Rome, that it was enriched when necessary with new words, and that it did not even precisely follow the classical usage in the more intricate sequences of moods and tenses, proves not that the writer was careless or ignorant, but that he had a different feeling for the value of words, due to an evolution in human thought itself and, within the narrow limits set by his own taste, perfectly legitimate. Thomas More was occasionally slovenly and obscure, Colet now and then ungrammatical; Luther, a great wielder of his own tongue, was anything but Hellenic or Roman in his thought and manner. But Erasmus, mastering his medium and not mastered by it, fitted modern thoughts into an ancient speech with the ease of a born artist.

Great care, infinite pains, went to the final result. When Erasmus blames "the vice of his nature" for undue haste in precipitating his thoughts, he does himself an injustice. If he wrote rapidly at last, it is because he had toiled painfully at first. His own text-books on composition show the infinite pains he took to acquire a style. Like other masters of language—Pater and Landor, for example—he emphasizes particularly the selection of vocabulary. The words chosen should be apt, elegant, idiomatic, and pure, and like dress should be appropriate to the subject adorned. An unfit style is as awkward as a woman's dress on a man. Mean, unusual, poetic, new, obsolete, foreign, and obscene words should be avoided.

But Erasmus inculcated and practised other excellencies than this. Variety of construction is emphasized and rules given for the proper uses of the copious, and of the concise, manner. But the secret of his own charm is something more elusive and personal than any style acquired by mere study and rote could be. Like all great masters of speech, he invested everything he said with a peculiar and appropriate pungency. By whetting his words to a keen edge, he attained delicate polish and glow of supple beauty. One of the more external and striking elements of his style was the habitual moderation of his statement; the careful guarding against all glares of affirmation or denial. Is a reading in the New Testament ambiguous? No; it is only "slightly ambiguous" (nonnihil ambigo). Does Erasmus reject an argument? Far be such brutal positiveness from him; he "begins to have a glimmering of doubt" (subdubitare coepi). Erasmus thought that Luther wrote excellently well, but all he chooses to assert is that the professor's books are "rather more like Latin than the average" (sermo paulo latinior). Double negatives tone down an otherwise too conspicuous assertion. Except when he is writing to patrons for expected gifts, Erasmus speaks of his friends as "persons not altogether unknown to me." Diminutives play their part in qualifying the brutal shock of things; the writer's person is usually his "poor little body" (corpusculum).

But even as we grasp and press the style, its secret eludes us; the beauty of Erasmus's writings is something more subtle, more difficult, than can be readily indicated by rough analysis. Now and then there is a rapier thrust of perfect epigram; a stab, planted like a wasp's sting, infallibly on the nerve ganglion of the chosen victim. Still more perfect in its way is the repressed irony of the author, never more effective than when most latent, the dry wit that held up to scorn or ridicule an institution or a person, apparently by a simple, matter-of-fact narrative without an abusive, or vulnerable, word in it. It was this that made the persons attacked so furious; they felt that they were being stripped naked and pilloried, while they could not find any weapon of defense. A candid, almost naïve description of a pilgrimage or of an inquisitor makes the reader wonder how anything so silly or so malignant was ever allowed to exist, but what was there in it all tangible enough to strike? A critic, after reading Anatole France's *Île des Pengouins,* a satire much in the Erasmian manner, said that there was nothing left to do but to commit suicide. When the monks read the ***Folly*** and the ***Colloquies*** they felt there was no appropriate comment but to murder the author. (pp. 316-19)

Preserved Smith, in his Erasmus: A Study of His Life, Ideals and Place in History, *Harper & Brothers, 1923, 479 p.*

J. Huizinga (essay date 1924)

[*Huizinga was a Dutch historian. In the excerpt below, from a work originally published in 1924, he examines the content and effectiveness of* The Praise of Folly, *claiming that in it Erasmus "gave something that no one else could have given to the world."*]

[Erasmus] arrived in London, took up his abode in More's house in Bucklersbury, and there, tortured by nephritic pains, he wrote down in a few days, without having his books with him, the perfect work of art that must have been ready in his mind. Stultitia was truly born in the manner of her serious sister Pallas.

As to form and imagery the ***Moria*** is faultless, the product of the inspired moments of creative impulse. The figure of an orator confronting her public is sustained to the last in a masterly way. We see the faces of the auditors light up with glee when Folly appears in the pulpit; we hear the applause interrupting her words. There is a wealth of fancy, coupled with so much soberness of line and colour, such reserve, that the whole presents a perfect instance of that harmony which is the essence of Renaissance expression. There is no exuberance, in spite of the multiplicity of matter and thought, but a temperateness, a smoothness, an airiness and clearness which are as gladdening as they are relaxing. In order perfectly to realize the artistic perfection of Erasmus's book we should compare it with Rabelais.

'Without me', says Folly, 'the world cannot exist for a moment. For is not all that is done at all among mortals, full of folly; is it not performed by fools and for fools?' 'No society, no cohabitation can be pleasant or lasting without folly; so much so, that a people could not stand its prince, nor the master his man, nor the maid her mistress, nor the tutor his pupil, nor the friend his friend, nor the wife her husband for a moment longer, if they did not now and then err together, now flatter each other; now sensibly conniving at things, now smearing themselves with some honey of folly.' In that sentence the summary of the *Laus* is contained. Folly here is worldly wisdom, resignation and lenient judgement.

He who pulls off the masks in the comedy of life is ejected. What is the whole life of mortals but a sort of play in which each actor appears on the boards in his specific mask and acts his part till the stage-manager calls him off? He acts wrongly who does not adapt himself to existing conditions, and demands that the game shall be a game no longer. It is the part of the truly sensible to mix with all people, either conniving readily at their folly, or affably erring like themselves.

And the necessary driving power of all human action is 'Philautia', Folly's own sister: self-love. He who does not please himself effects little. Take away that condiment of life and the word of the orator cools, the poet is laughed at, the artist perishes with his art.

Folly in the garb of pride, of vanity, of vainglory, is the hidden spring of all that is considered high and great in this world. The state with its posts of honour, patriotism and national pride; the stateliness of ceremonies, the delusion of caste and nobility—what is it but folly? War, the most foolish thing of all, is the origin of all heroism. What prompted the Deciuses, what Curtius, to sacrifice themselves? Vainglory. It is this folly which produces states; through her, empires, religion, law-courts, exist.

This is bolder and more chilling than Machiavelli, more detached than Montaigne. But Erasmus will not have it credited to him: it is Folly who speaks. He purposely makes us tread the round of the *circulus vitiosus,* as in the old saw: A Cretan said, all Cretans are liars.

Wisdom is to folly as reason is to passion. And there is much more passion than reason in the world. That which keeps the world going, the fount of life, is folly. For what else is love? Why do people marry, if not out of folly, which sees no objections? All enjoyment and amusement is only a condiment of folly. When a wise man wishes to become a father, he has first to play the fool. For what is more foolish than the game of procreation?

Unperceived the orator has incorporated here with folly all that is vitality and the courage of life. Folly is spontaneous energy that no one can do without. He who is perfectly sensible and serious cannot live. The more people get away from me, Stultitia, the less they live. Why do we kiss and cuddle little children, if not because they are still so delightfully foolish. And what else makes youth so elegant?

Now look at the truly serious and sensible. They are awkward at everything, at meal-time, at a dance, in playing, in social intercourse. If they have to buy, or to contract, things are sure to go wrong. Quintilian says that stage fright bespeaks the intelligent orator, who knows his faults. Right! But does not, then, Quintilian confess openly that wisdom is an impediment to good execution? And has not Stultitia the right to claim prudence for herself, if the wise, out of shame, out of bashfulness, undertake nothing in circumstances where fools pluckily set to work?

Here Erasmus goes to the root of the matter in a psychological sense. Indeed the consciousness of falling short in achievement is the brake clogging action, is the great inertia retarding the progress of the world. Did he know himself for one who is awkward when not bending over his books, but confronting men and affairs?

Folly is gaiety and lightheartedness, indispensable to happiness. The man of mere reason without passion is a stone image, blunt and without any human feeling, a spectre or monster, from whom all fly, deaf to all natural emotions, susceptible neither to love nor compassion. Nothing escapes him, in nothing he errs; he sees through everything, he weighs everything accurately, he forgives nothing, he is only satisfied with himself; he alone is healthy; he alone is king, he alone is free. It is the hideous figure of the doctrinaire which Erasmus is thinking of. Which state, he exclaims, would desire such an absolutely wise man for a magistrate?

He who devotes himself to tasting all the bitterness of life with wise insight would forthwith deprive himself of life. Only folly is a remedy: to err, to be mistaken, to be ignorant is to be human. How much better it is in marriage to be blind to a wife's shortcomings than to make away with oneself out of jealousy and to fill the world with tragedy! Adulation is virtue. There is no cordial devotion without a little adulation. It is the soul of eloquence, of medicine and poetry; it is the honey and the sweetness of all human customs.

Again a series of valuable social qualities is slyly incorporated with folly: benevolence, kindness, inclination to approve and to admire.

But especially to approve of oneself. There is no pleasing others without beginning by flattering ourselves a little and approving of ourselves. What would the world be if everyone was not proud of his standing, his calling, so that no person would change places with another in point of good appearance, of fancy, of good family, of landed property?

Humbug is the right thing. Why should any one desire true erudition? The more incompetent a man, the pleasanter his life is and the more he is admired. Look at professors, poets, orators. Man's mind is so made that he is more impressed by lies than by the truth. Go to church: if the priest deals with serious subjects the whole congregation is dozing, yawning, feeling bored. But when he begins to tell some cock-and-bull story, they awake, sit up, and hang on his lips.

To be deceived, philosophers say, is a misfortune, but not to be deceived is a superlative misfortune. If it is human to err, why should a man be called unhappy because he errs, since he was so born and made, and it is the fate of all? Do we pity a man because he cannot fly or does not walk on four legs? We might as well call the horse unhappy because it does not learn grammar or eat cakes. No creature is unhappy, if it lives according to its nature. The sciences were invented to our utmost destruction; far from conducing to our happiness, they are even in its way, though for its sake they are supposed to have been invented. By the agency of evil demons they have stolen into human life with the other pests. For did not the simple-minded people of the Golden Age live happily, unprovided with any science, only led by nature and instinct? What did they want grammar for, when all spoke the same language? Why have dialectics, when there were no quarrels and no differences of opinion? Why jurisprudence, when there were no bad morals from which good laws sprang? They were too religious to investigate with impious curiosity the secrets of nature, the size, motions, influence of the stars, the hidden cause of things.

It is the old idea, which germinated in antiquity, here lightly touched upon by Erasmus, afterwards proclaimed by Rousseau in bitter earnest: civilization is a plague.

Wisdom is misfortune, but self-conceit is happiness. Grammarians, who wield the sceptre of wisdom—schoolmasters, that is—would be the most wretched of all people if I, Folly, did not mitigate the discomforts of their miserable calling by a sort of sweet frenzy. But what holds good of schoolmasters, also holds good of poets, orators, authors. For them, too, all happiness merely consists in vanity and delusion. The lawyers are no better off and after them come the philosophers. Next there is a numerous procession of clergy: divines, monks, bishops, cardinals, popes, only interrupted by princes and courtiers.

In the chapters which review these offices and callings, satire has shifted its ground a little. Throughout the work two themes are intertwined: that of salutary folly, which is true wisdom, and that of deluded wisdom, which is pure folly. As they are both put into the mouth of Folly, we should have to invert them both to get truth, if Folly . . . were not wisdom. Now it is clear that the first is the principal theme. Erasmus starts from it; and he returns to it. Only in the middle, as he reviews human accomplishments and dignities in their universal foolishness, the second theme predominates and the book becomes an ordinary satire on human folly, of which there are many though few are so delicate. But in the other parts it is something far deeper.

Occasionally the satire runs somewhat off the line, when Stultitia directly censures what Erasmus wishes to censure; for instance, indulgences, silly belief in wonders, selfish worship of the saints; or gamblers whom she, Folly, ought to praise; or the spirit of systematizing and levelling, and the jealousy of the monks.

For contemporary readers the importance of the ***Laus Stultitiae*** was, to a great extent, in the direct satire. Its lasting value is in those passages where we truly grant that folly is wisdom and the reverse. Erasmus knows the aloofness of the ground of all things: all consistent thinking out of the dogmas of faith leads to absurdity. Only look at the theological quiddities of effete scholasticism. The apostles would not have understood them: in the eyes of latter-day divines they would have been fools. Holy Scripture itself sides with folly. 'The foolishness of God is wiser than men,' says Saint Paul. 'But God hath chosen the foolish things of the world.' 'It pleased God by the foolishness (of preaching) to save them that believe.' Christ loved the simple-minded and the ignorant: children, women, poor fishermen, nay, even such animals as are farthest removed from vulpine cunning: the ass which he wished to ride, the dove, the lamb, the sheep.

Here there is a great deal behind the seemingly light jest: 'Christian religion seems in general to have some affinity with a certain sort of folly'. Was it not thought the apostles were full of new wine? And did not the judge say: 'Paul, thou art beside thyself'? When are we beside ourselves? When the spirit breaks its fetters and tries to escape from its prison and aspires to liberty. That is madness, but it is also other-worldliness and the highest wisdom. True happiness is in selflessness, in the furore of lovers, whom Plato calls happiest of all. The more absolute love is, the greater and more rapturous is the frenzy. Heavenly bliss itself is the greatest insanity; truly pious people enjoy its shadow on earth already in their meditations.

Here Stultitia breaks off her discourse, apologizing in a few words in case she may have been too petulant or talkative, and leaves the pulpit. 'So farewell, applaud, live happily, and drink, Moria's illustrious initiates.'

It was an unrivalled feat of art even in these last chapters neither to lose the light comical touch, nor to lapse into undisguised profanation. It was only feasible by veritable dancing on the tight-rope of sophistry. In the ***Moria*** Erasmus is all the time hovering on the brink of profound truths. But what a boon it was—still granted to those times—to be able to treat of all this in a vein of pleasantry. For this should be impressed upon our minds: that the ***Moriae Encomium*** is a true, gay jest. The laugh is more delicate, but no less hearty than Rabelais's. 'Valete, plaudite, vivite, bibite.' 'All common people abound to such a degree, and everywhere, in so many forms of folly that a thousand Democrituses would be insufficient to laugh at them all (and they would require another Democritus to laugh at them).'

How could one take the ***Moria*** too seriously, when even More's *Utopia,* which is a true companion-piece to it and makes such a grave impression on us, is treated by its author and Erasmus as a mere jest? There is a place where the ***Laus*** seems to touch both More and Rabelais; the place where Stultitia speaks of her father, Plutus, the god of wealth, at whose beck all things are turned topsy-turvy, according to whose will all human affairs are regulated—war and peace, government and counsel, justice and treaties. He has begotten her on the nymph Youth, not a senile, purblind Plutus, but a fresh god, warm with youth and nectar, like another Gargantua.

The figure of Folly, of gigantic size, looms large in the period of the Renaissance. She wears a fool's cap and bells. People laughed loudly and with unconcern at all that was foolish, without discriminating between species of folly. It is remarkable that even in the ***Laus,*** delicate as it is, the author does not distinguish between the unwise or the silly, between fools and lunatics. Holbein, illustrating Erasmus, knows but of one representation of a fool: with a staff and ass's ears. Erasmus speaks without clear transition, now of foolish persons and now of real lunatics. They are happiest of all, he makes Stultitia say: they are not frightened by spectres and apparitions; they are not tortured by the fear of impending calamities; everywhere they bring mirth, jests, frolic and laughter. Evidently he here means harmless imbeciles, who, indeed, were often used as jesters. This identification of denseness and insanity is kept up, however, like the confusion of the comic and the simply ridiculous, and all this is well calculated to make us feel how wide the gap has already become that separates us from Erasmus.

In later years he always spoke slightingly of his ***Moria.*** He considered it so unimportant, he says, as to be unworthy of publication, yet no work of his had been received with such applause. It was a trifle and not at all in keeping with his character. More had made him write it, as if a camel were made to dance. But these disparaging utterances were not without a secondary purpose. The ***Moria*** had not brought him only success and pleasure. The exceedingly susceptible age in which he lived had taken the satire in very bad part, where it seemed to glance at offices and orders, although in his preface he had tried to safeguard himself from the reproach of irreverence. His airy play with the texts of Holy Scripture had been too venturesome for many. His friend Martin van Dorp upbraided him with having made a mock of eternal life. Erasmus did what he could to convince evil-thinkers that the purpose of the ***Moria*** was no other than to exhort people to be virtuous. In affirming this he did his work injustice: it was much more than that. But in 1515 he was no longer what he had been in 1509. Repeatedly he had been obliged to defend his most witty work. Had he known that it would offend, he might have kept it back, he writes in 1517 to an acquaintance at Louvain. Even towards the end of his life, he warded off the insinuations of Alberto Pio of Carpi in a lengthy expostulation.

Erasmus made no further ventures in the genre of the ***Praise of Folly.*** One might consider the treatise ***Lingua,*** which he published in 1525, as an attempt to make a companion-piece to the ***Moria.*** The book is called ***Of the Use and Abuse of the Tongue.*** In the opening pages there is something that reminds us of the style of the ***Laus,*** but it lacks all the charm both of form and of thought.

Should one pity Erasmus because, of all his publications, collected in ten folio volumes, only the ***Praise of Folly*** has remained a really popular book? It is, apart from the ***Colloquies,*** perhaps the only one of his works that is still read for its own sake. The rest is now only studied from a historical point of view, for the sake of becoming acquainted with his person or his times. It seems to me that perfect justice has been done in this case. The ***Praise of Folly*** is his best work. He wrote other books, more erudite, some more pious—some perhaps of equal or greater influence on his time. But each has had its day. ***Moriae Encomium*** alone was to be immortal. For only when humour illuminated that mind did it become truly profound. In the

Praise of Folly Erasmus gave something that no one else could have given to the world. (pp. 70-78)

J. Huizinga, "The Praise of Folly," in his Erasmus of Rotterdam, *translated by F. Hopman, Phaidon Press Ltd., 1952, pp. 69-78.*

George Saintsbury (essay date 1928)

[*Saintsbury was a late nineteenth- and early twentieth-century English literary historian and critic. Hugely prolific, he composed histories of English and European literature as well as numerous critical works on individual authors, styles, and periods. In the excerpt below from an essay originally published in 1928 in the* Dial, *he discusses the* Colloquies, *praising Erasmus for writing "engagingly and interestingly about anything from broom-sticks to Grammar."*]

There are no doubt reasons of various kinds which unfit [the ***Colloquies***] now for the school-book it once was: but as there is no intention here of recommending the resumption of it as such, that does not matter. What does matter is that it is a very curious and interesting piece of literature. Indeed it may be questioned whether Erasmus ought not to be honoured and kept in reading more as one of the first modern men of letters than as anything else. His scholarship is, as scholarship is fated to be, rather *hesterna rosa;* his theology was of that kind, perhaps the most dangerous of all kinds in all subjects, which never can make up its mind on which side of the hedge or wall it is coming down. But he was a man of letters in his heart; a man of letters once is a man of letters for ever; and the ***Colloquies*** are at once a proof of this as concerns himself, and a pattern for others. You may almost call Erasmus, long before Montaigne, the first essayist: only the intense *Drang nach* drama in his time induced him to give his things a more or less dramatic form. Sometimes, indeed, as for instance in the Convivium Poeticum where Housekeeper Margaret and the footboy diversify the talk of the bards, bring in beet-root instead of lettuce, et cetera (and when Margaret finally declines to give them anything to eat or drink except mustard), the thing could be made to act with hardly any difficulty at all.

Of the vividness and vigour of his presentations of life and society there can never have been much doubt or question among competent readers: and this quality must have been recognised in itself, though not as his, by hundreds and thousands of persons who never opened the ***Colloquies*** themselves. The description of the inn in *Anne of Geierstein,* one of the liveliest of Scott's later passages, is almost a literal translation, eked with action, from Erasmus: and it would be not quite uninteresting to know how many passages describing escape from wrecks owe royalty in part or in whole, directly or indirectly, to the **"Naufragium."** His account of the experiences of a pilgrim at the shrine of Our Lady of Walsingham might never have been written except for the rather ill-natured ecclesiastical satire which it displays: but it is again vivacious enough, and capable of being made trustworthy by an intelligent reader. The piece which shocks Dr. Mangan and in which a damsel in distinct need of reformation receives it from an old gallant of hers who is himself reformed, is only a transfer into colloquy of one of the liveliest farce-moralities of that most agreeable Dark Age Prioress Hroswitha; but it is at once moral enough and lively enough. This may also be said of the somewhat similar batch dealing with maidens who shrink from or quarrel with marriage. But in all these cases the author is more or less indebted, for better for worse, to his subject.

Now perhaps the great charm of the ***Colloquies*** to a real lover of letters is the way in which their writer shows himself able to write engagingly and interestingly about anything from broom-sticks to Grammar. The book begins with several scores of pages—something like a hundred and fifty in the pocket Tauchnitz edition—of intentionally school-book character, even descending to what in mid-nineteenth century English we used to call 'Ollendorffian' forms of address at meeting people, sketches of probable subjects for conversation; titles of dignity; games; professional manner of things, ending with two long Convivia—one Profanum, one Religiosum—in which things in general that come under the two heads are discussed. And in all this there is nothing silly or caricaturable as there was in the excellent Ollendorff. You can get—if you keep your intelligence awake and have a little precedent knowledge to help you—a much more intimate acquaintance with that all-important time than you are likely to have had before. And if you are shameless enough not to care about learning or profiting by anything, there is plenty merely to delight and amuse you. Sometimes, indeed, he seems to be anticipating a sort of 'Young Novelist's and Dramatist's Guide' as in his lists of possible speeches and replies between Master and Servant and the like.

If, as has perhaps been the case, rather disproportionate attention has been paid, especially in ordinary books of reference, to the religious element in the Life and Works of Erasmus, there is of course considerable excuse for this. The quarrels in which he took part half against his will, were quarrels than which it would be difficult to find any of more importance in the history of the modern world: and they are not 'sopited'—put to sleep with a fair chance of not waking—even yet. Moreover, though this other fact is rather curious, there is hardly any aspect of a literary man upon which it is so difficult to concentrate public attention as his literature. Take the rather interesting colloquy, **"Abbatis et Eurditae,"** in which two persons answering to these descriptions and, further, as at that time they were almost certain to be, 'persons of quality', figure. The abbot is shocked at what he finds in the lady's room. 'Why?' she says, 'Isn't the furniture elegant?' But the offending articles are not exactly furniture but books. 'Why,' she asks again, 'mayn't a *heroina* [the word appears to be used almost in the sense of *"Grande Dame"*, if not even of "lady" in our best or implicit meaning] have books?' Perhaps, if they are French, but not if they're Greek and Latin as these are. Doesn't he himself read? 'French, but not Greek and Latin', and so on. Now it is of course possible to take this as merely an excursion or skirmish in the continual battle against monkery and nunnery: and no doubt also it is this to some extent, perhaps mainly, in original intention. But it has far more interesting possibilities than this. It advises us of what is not the least interesting feature of the Renaissance at large, the prominence of

Albrecht Dürer's engraving of Erasmus.

the 'learned lady' who was not a mere schoolmarm or bluestocking but 'lady' as much as 'learned'. Perhaps the best thing in it comes from the mouth of the unblushingly illiterate and good-for-nothing abbot when he says, 'With immense labour learning is obtained: and then you have to die', which is better still in its native Latin, *'Immensis laboribus comparatur eruditio: ac post moriendum est'*, and which, if not original, remains consummate and unanswerable. But the lady scores fairly often: and the whole thing is alive. Moreover the combination of life and literature is seldom lacking for long in this miniature and colloquial encyclopaedia. Alchemy comes in: they say modern atomic theories may bring that back: and it is only to be hoped—though one fears that there is not much chance of it—that the new Alchemy will be as fortunate in English literature as the old was from Chaucer onwards. Although the queerly titled dialogue, **"Ichthyophagia"** or **"Fish-Eating,"** between a butcher and a saltfish-monger is obviously ecclesiastical in main tenor, all manner of oddments are brought in: and though the stranger Funus (an elaborate account of death-beds and so forth—which follows) might incur charges on the score both of taste and sentiment (Erasmus is vulnerable on both grounds), it has other attractions. He is indeed never exactly kindly—kindliness was not the characteristic of the Renaissance either in the queer fashion which accompanied the occasional savagery of the Middle Ages, or in the homely one which at least our and the German eighteenth century provided.

But, here as elsewhere, he shows that he had many of the gifts which make a first-rate novelist. The famous Inn passage which has been already spoken of and other things of which Charles Reade made use in *The Cloister and the Hearth* show this sufficiently in one sense but quite inadequately in another. The half-hatched novelist, the essayist almost or quite out of the novitiate, appear constantly; and perhaps something else at one time regarded as even less dignified than either—the miscellaneous journalist. Fleet Street when it saw him, which it had plenty of opportunities to do, and which then had or had not for its chief literary association Chaucer's beating or not beating (the beating would have pleased Erasmus much) the Franciscan friar, must have yearned for him with precocious instinct. His interest in things general; his gift of treating them; his almost entire freedom from 'pontifying'—a proceeding sometimes indulged in by journalists and occasionally successful but never so for long—all called him there. Some pontifying itself and other weaknesses of the journalist may be found by the malicious: as for instance in the curious Coronis Apologetica which was written in the month of September of the year 1524. But this only makes him more natural both as an individual and as a forerunner. He maintains the *persona* with his own personality throughout.

And in all this stuff there is, despite its deliberate and formal imitation of the ancients now and then, the distinctly modern 'man of letters' tone. That there are approaches to this in the ancients themselves is of course true. There are passages in Plato and Xenophon which any intelligent editor of a monthly magazine or weekly review would be extremely glad to have to-day. Some people have regarded Cicero as (outside the orations) sometimes at least a model 'contributor' and the Rhetoricians, both Greek and Latin, are even better as such on occasion. But still there is the 'unplumbed, estranging' difference between ancient and modern in all, and Erasmus (though he edited half their extant library and knew the rest) is on our not their side of it. The change in religion is only the most obvious and perhaps the largest constituent of the attraction: many others would take a good deal of trouble and more space than we can afford to single out and characterise. But a good example of the result is the **"Colloquium Senile"**—not in itself one of the most interesting perhaps, but really a specimen. Four old men meet like Oldbuck and Lovel in the beginning of *The Antiquary,* at the starting place of a coach, in this case destined for Antwerp. They turn out to be old friends who have seen little or nothing of each other since their student days in Paris. They agree to engage the whole of the vehicle that they may talk freely: and quite eighteenth or early nineteenth century details are given—such as that if you want a driver who isn't drunk you had better come early to the stand. They take their seats and talk. The first subject is naturally their respective looks: and the widely different ways in which the forty-two years of post-collegiate life have treated them. Then they tell these lives. The first man had taken to business on leaving college; had married a wife with whom he lived happily for years till her death; had accepted public office of some but no great distinction and profit; and in his later years had contented himself with 'retired leisure'. They all agree that it is no wonder he looks young. Next comes Polygamus who looks extraordinarily old, and who for any person acquainted with the Greek language has explained the cause of his senescence already, to at least some extent. *He* had never given up wine, play, et cetera: and though very sorry when any of his numerous wives died, he put things right again by never remaining more than ten days a widower. The third who looks older still, has in part an unhappier lot to tell. He started excellently, furnished by his father with plenty of capital for foreign trade, and engaged to a beautiful girl with a big dowry, but a shipwreck deprives him of all his wealth: and as he is now a beggar the girl's parents break off the match. After debating whether he shall hang himself or join a religious order he decides on the latter course and tries several. As any one who knows anything about Erasmus will expect, the accounts of his experience are not rosy. But at last his father dies; he goes back to trade, marries, and seems fairly satisfied. There remains only Eusebius whose name again tells stories. *He* accepted a prebend early, studied medicine as well as theology that he might better discharge his duties as a secular cleric, and passed a quiet and happy life in doing his duty. The piece ends with a little bit of farce between the drivers.

The thing as was said above is not exceptionally interesting or amazingly clever: but it shows the emergence of literature from certain more or less definite forms with again more or less definite subjects into a stage where the world is all before it to choose what it likes, treat this as it likes, and call itself what it likes. The drama had had this outgate and outlook from fairly early times; the Greek epigram had shared the privilege to some extent in verse and the Rhetoricians had availed themselves of it in prose. In the Dark and Middle Ages the spirit was making way for itself in odd burrowings and short flights such as those of which an admirable account at last exists in Miss Helen Waddell's *Wandering Scholars.* The opening wide of the gate and the multiplication of excursions from it was sure to be one of the chief points of the Renaissance: and the Chief Porter for opening and not barring the gate, the Chief Director not of residence but of excursions, was Erasmus. (pp. 60-5)

George Saintsbury, "The Colloquies of Erasmus," in his A Last Vintage: Essays and Papers, *by George Saintsbury, edited by John W. Oliver, Arthur Melville Clark, and Augustus Muir, Methuen & Co. Ltd., 1950, pp. 60-5.*

Robert P. Adams (essay date 1945)

[*Adams is an American educator and literary scholar. In the following excerpt, he praises both* The Praise of Folly *and Thomas More's* Utopia *as works of satire, deeming Erasmus's work "the finest expression both of the English humanistic optimism at the moment and also of the cosmopolitan conception of European culture shared by More and Colet."*]

Today many who seek more precise critical understanding of the renaissance use of the ancient classics are comparing the humanists' ideas of their own changing culture. For the work of St. Thomas More, Erasmus, and John Colet, during the decade after the accession of Henry VIII, we may ask: how did these men conceive of their own time, of the ages preceding, and of their position in human culture? Especially, how did they use the classics of ancient ethics and history as models for a new social order? (p. 131)

In general, it appears that these three friends—the lawyer, the scholar, and the Dean of St. Paul's—were hopeful in 1509 that they stood on the verge of a splendid new age of cultural growth and religious reconstruction. Yet the achievement of the new order demanded a comprehensive program supported by all friends of learning and justice. One of Erasmus' English patrons, William Blount, Lord Mountjoy, urged the rising Dutch scholar to hasten in serene confidence from war-torn Italy, where his studies had been substantially blocked, to peaceful England. Was not a veritable Augustan age of humane culture to flower under an apparently ideal prince, young Henry VIII? "When you know what a hero (the King) now shows himself," wrote Lord Mountjoy, "how wisely he behaves, what a lover he is of justice and goodness, what affection he bears to the learned . . . you will need no wings to fly to behold this new and auspicious star." Indeed the brave new king had assured Lord Mountjoy personally of his determination to "foster and encourage learned men," declaring nobly that "without them we should scarcely exist at all."

Nevertheless, it is important to observe that during the decade after 1509 More, Erasmus, and Colet thought of this new culture-to-be, not as an isolated English creation, but as an essential part of the loosely unified civilization of all Catholic Europe. If the new Augustan age should come, these humanists at least did not then conceive it as prisoned within the arbitrary boundaries of nations. It would, they eagerly hoped, be as cosmopolitan and as international as the universal Catholic church and as potent an influence for good in all human society. Although later, out of disillusionment, Erasmus sorely regretted leaving Italy—"There one enjoys sweet liberty, rich libraries, the charming friendship of writers and scholars, and the sight of antique monuments," as well as genuine patronage—as he jogged toward London it seemed that at last a true, a Christian Renaissance was to be born.

Erasmus' exuberant ***Praise of Folly*** may be termed therefore the finest expression both of the English humanistic optimism at the moment and also of the cosmopolitan conception of European culture shared by More and Colet. (pp. 131-33)

Moreover, who could justly term the ***Praise of Folly*** to be only a national and English satire, merely because it was written in England? It seems rather to be as characteristic of the renaissance idea at the moment as was the even finer satire in More's *Utopia,* which was partly written in Flanders a few years later, but did not cease thereby to represent English culture. In short, the whole intellectual outlook of More and Erasmus tended then to be, like their wide-ranging correspondence, not national but continental and cosmopolitan in scope. Thus it is not all surprising that both the ***Praise of Folly*** and *Utopia* delighted civilized men, not only in England but throughout Europe. For during the hopeful decade before the Lutheran controversies began, when the new culture seemed possible North of the Alps, these two satires best suggested the grand social optimism of men of good will everywhere on the continent.

To More, Erasmus, and Colet however it was abundantly clear that the development of a better civilization depended upon the cooperative efforts of statesmen and churchmen as well as scholars. Yet if the humanists could provide architectural designs for a new social order, perhaps Henry VIII and Wolsey, with their immense power, might be able to execute the plans. Broadly speaking, one part of the Oxford reformers' grand program—the achievement of peaceful reforms within the established church—lies outside this discussion. Our special interest is concentrated rather upon the humanists' attempts to illustrate their philosophic belief that the power of man's natural reason should be the sovereign authority in all purely human affairs. This daring concept of the latent power of pure reason as a social force was certainly a dominant idea in the social thought of More and Erasmus between 1509 and 1519. Gradually in their essays on reform in society these humanists strove, with the aid especially of certain classics of the later Roman Stoicism, to discover the principles and to picture vividly the major aspects of civilization as it should be if most men, or at least their leaders at the outset, realized in everyday life the latent human power to live strictly "according to reason" for the common welfare—that is, to live according to man's best "nature." In short, More and Erasmus sketched, as a model for their time, a social order in which all men might achieve the utmost good of which men were capable outside the Church.

How can we best account for this intense admiration for the latent power of reason in man?—perhaps the leading characteristic of the renaissance idea at this time in More and Erasmus. For an answer, consider the distinctive view of social problems illustrated in both the ***Praise of Folly*** and in *Utopia.* These satires themselves offer the best proof that, following the lead of John Colet in his Oxford lectures on Romans in 1497, More and Erasmus had greatly broadened the philosophic base on which rested their criticism of society. Many of the most influential medieval social critics had been largely dominated by a desire to perceive, as far as possible, a theological plan in the aspects of human culture. Indeed, the leading medieval tradition, based especially upon the authority of St. Augustine, had tended to consider that major social evils, such as poverty, crime, and war, were punishments visited upon innately sinful mankind by an inscrutable divine Providence.

Beside this Augustinian view, but not excluding it, More and Erasmus in their satires set a contrasting idea of social evils which reveals a significant, a renaissance, expansion in their critical outlook. For during the decade after 1509 these humanists tended increasingly to represent the major social evils as *man-made.* This is not to say that they made a sharp, artificial break with the whole of medieval social criticism; for originally-Stoic political and moral thought, transmitted through writers like Augustine and Ambrose, formed of course an element in the medieval ideas which persisted into the renaissance. When, however, More and Erasmus sought for the natural roots and explanations of social ills in the social environment which man was at least potentially able to modify or even control, they diverged critically from the traditional Augustinian mode of thought which was still strong in their own time. Moreover, inspired with enthusiasm for the New Learning, they turned, for the best ancient ideas on the good life of reason, especially to those classics of the later Roman Stoicism which presented ethics closely harmonious with those of Christ in the Gospels. Plainly the general social optimism which flourished in England for a few years after the accession of Henry VIII stimulated More and Erasmus especially to a renewal of bold Stoic optimism, which is most strikingly seen in this revival of the gallant conception of man as a perfectable creature whose supreme distinction is his natural gift of reason and his capacity for a rational, unified social life.

It should also be observed that in picturing a good life as lived "according to reason" as a model for their age, these humanists anticipated no grave conflict between Christian and natural ethics, between Christian and natural science. On the contrary, they were confident that the authority of natural reason should harmonize with the authority of Christ in the Gospels; there should be no conflict between the provinces of the supernatural and the natural. It was therefore logical that for the ideas of the ancients upon the life of reason, More and Erasmus should have turned particularly to the later Roman Stoicism, and not merely for reasons of availability; for it was agreed that in Stoicism the ancients had come closest to the Christian base ethics. As Professor DeWulf observes regretfully, men like More and Erasmus were not interested in the complete Stoic philosophy, but they had a strong interest in *practical* ethics and in rhetoric. To us it is highly significant that the humanist reformers analyzed intensively, within their limits, the ethical aspects of practical politics and government. In their observations in history, for instance, they patiently sought the causes for the developments, changes, and decay of civilizations. We may observe and agree with Professor Preserved Smith that Erasmus could regard Cicero as inspired and Seneca not far from St. Paul in moral philosophy.

Accordingly, it was first of all upon such writers as Seneca, Plutarch, and particularly Cicero (whose *De finibus* gave the most convenient exposition of Stoicism) that More and Erasmus drew for Stoic ideas of the life of reason, or man's best "nature," to parallel their conceptions of the true Christian way of life. Here are only a few of the more outstanding neo-Stoic arguments which run through the thought on social reform of these humanists between 1509 and 1519. First, man is distinguished from other animals by his natural gift of reason and his capacity for a life ruled by reason, that is by right reason which leads him to seek virtue for its own sake, living, in the Stoic condition of supreme good, according to nature. Man alone, therefore, is equipped to perceive God, or the divine designs, in the form of universal reason evident throughout the cosmos. In the third place, all sane men likewise possess and are ruled by a profound humanitarian social instinct—a sense of a "bond of nature" linking all men as a species—which not only makes human society possible, but also, like a social contract, enjoins all good men to seek the common welfare before that of the individual. Fourth, there is the idea that in all human affairs pure reason or at least rational tradition should rule, while the passions, which are inherently irrational and only too likely to lend a vicious, customary charm to antisocial practices, must be kept in iron discipline under reason's firm authority. Finally, we find the concept that, since the supreme good is to live according to nature, all sane, uncorrupted men will, "by nature," choose to live according to the "natural law," or general principle of social justice, whose most common unwritten form is the *consensus gentium,* or enlightened public opinion. All these basic ideas, which are at the core of the neo-Stoic ruling philosophy in the state of Utopia, may easily be found in the expositions of Stoicism by Cicero, Seneca, and Plutarch which were well known to Erasmus, as to most educated men. Further corroboration was available to the humanists in the views expressed by Ovid, Lucretius, and others on the development and decay of human culture.

Perhaps it may suffice, for the time being, to cite some of the works in which, during this decade, More and Erasmus speculated on the life ruled by pure, uncorrupted reason and in which they applied generally neo-Stoic criticism to what seemed the least rational and most brutish of all widespread human activities, namely war. (pp. 133-39)

Erasmus, at every opportunity to glorify the life of reason as a model for the age, urged the importance of the neo-Stoic ideas which I have summarized, as well as others, in a series of passionate appeals to the leading men of his time. Praise of the life of reason rippled through the ***Praise of Folly*** (1509), which is filled with gay ridicule of the endless absurdities "contrary to reason" in contemporary society. Next, in 1513, the pacifist satire, ***Julius Excluded from Heaven,*** written mostly in England, attacked the irrational and unChristian military ambitions of Pope Julius II. Two years later in the vastly popular edition of the ***Adages,*** now literally expanded into thousands, Erasmus published several new and even more comprehensive attacks upon war as essentially contrary to both natural reason and to Christian ethics. Among these the most notable was an impassioned essay filling fifteen large folio pages, written between 1513 and 1515, developing the theme, "Sweet is war to those who know it not,"—the famous ***Dulce bellum inexpertis,*** which is many vital respects anticipated and paralleled More's thought in *Utopia.* This piece—a sort of farewell to Erasmus' hopes of a scholarly renaissance in England—was Erasmus' fullest neo-Stoic attack upon war as a most ruinous social habit which demands and results in the utter corruption of man's great natural gift of reason and the instinct for social union: moreover, it best expressed his hearty agreement with More and Colet on the question. Furthermore, it had a great vogue throughout literate Europe. Indeed, such publications as this popular little quarto of 1517 really entitle Erasmus to be known as a pioneer in pamphleteering. Before his death in 1536 it ran through thirteen editions, including translations into German and English; while as part of the complete ***Adagiorum chiliades*** it was reprinted on the average every two years throughout the sixteenth century. It must accordingly be reckoned a main channel for the diffusion into the later Renaissance of neo-Stoic humanist ideas on war, peace, and the life of reason. Erasmus quite naturally was highly pleased by the wide sale of the essay and by the interest it aroused in some humanist circles. "These trifles, however slight," he wrote to Guillaume Budé, "I certainly prefer to any of the productions of Darkness." The year of 1516 was, however, the turning point. True, Erasmus, at almost the height of his fame, continued to urge that man's rational "nature" should rule society, in the ***Institute of a Christian Prince*** (1516),—ironically written in the same year as Machiavelli's handbook of power-politics, *Il principe.* A year later came a short piece which is essentially a bitter farewell to his dream of a new Augustan age of cultural growth and stability, namely the ***Complaint of Peace Ejected from All Countries.*** Finally, from a rather disillusioned neo-Stoic viewpoint, he launched a number of satirical attacks upon the irrational follies of his age, including war, in the popular ***Colloquia,*** such as **"Charon,"** which appeared between 1518 and 1528.

Of all these humanistic plans for a rational society, however, *Utopia* is not only the most famous but by far the most logical, systematic, and artfully unified. More's aim in the satire was explicitly stated, so that the frequency with which it has been misunderstood is an oddity of scholarship: the satire revealed, now directly, now humorously, a good society in which the ruling authority was only natural reason, unaided by any divine revelation. Thus the edge of the satire was whetted finely by the manifold implications of the fact that, for all their felicity, the Utopians remained, from a European Catholic viewpoint, graceless creatures who could only endure their pagan destiny, devoid of Christian teaching. It is of course notable that the Utopians became converted to Christianity generally as soon as they learned of it. In effect More invited his European readers to contemplate the wonders of the superb civilization which men could build when the powers of pure reason in everyday life were completed by a true Christian renaissance.

Since space-limits of course preclude a full exposition of the philosophic unity of *Utopia*—a matter incidentally upon which few critics have ever been able to agree—may I suggest briefly that this unity appears best when every aspect of Utopian life is seen as a logical, internally consistent development of one basic idea:—that all uncorrupted men must "by nature" (i.e. by the natural laws of their being, or human nature) prefer to live strictly "according to reason," for the common good of all. It is notable that Utopian citizens (as distinct from the bondmen) *must* absolutely believe only two ideas: that man's soul is immortal, and that after death every man will be rewarded or punished in proportion to his merits or wrong-doing in life. Within the bounds of these sole limitations More then proceeded, wittily as well as realistically, to sketch the outlines and to suggest the details of a good society in which pure reason, or man's best "nature," rules all free men, a society in which the natural causes of such general European social evils as poverty, crime, and war are attacked at their roots in irrational and vicious custom. In every respect the Utopian conceptions of value,—religious, political, economic, esthetic,—are those approved both by pure reason and the test of experience during the seventeen centuries in which this new civilization was constructed out of the disordered society of the actual early sixteenth century.

Nevertheless, even those who agree that Utopian society consistently "realizes" in everyday life the whole Utopian philosophy are bound to admit an odd, even an astounding paradox in that philosophy. For More represented the Utopians as pursuing at one and the same time two kinds of "highest good" which appear to be clearly and irreconcilably opposed, to be indeed mutually exclusive. Like the Stoics the Utopians are devoted to virtue, justice, and the common welfare; yet also, like the Epicureans, they consider pleasure to be the main desire of man. May we then have the ethical joys of being wise sages (with or without passion) while we revel as porkers in Epicurus' sty? Perhaps, as some editors have perplexedly insisted, when More wrote this part of the satire he was simply daydreaming,—or merely joking in his grave way. A more acute study of Utopian philosophy will reveal that More was strictly logical, according to his premises, when he described the Utopians as pursuing both virtue and pleasure without conflict.

In explanation, consider that More quoted the accepted Stoical definition of virtue—a definition all Utopian citizens accept—from Cicero's *De finibus,* which is cited to that effect in the margin of the earliest editions. More was certainly well aware therefore of Cicero's attack in *De finibus* upon the Epicureans as anti-social men who refused to be governed by "natural law" or virtue. For instance, in his criticism of Epicureanism from the Stoic viewpoint, Cicero even flatly asserted that devotion to sensual pleasure was incompatible with moral rectitude. If Cicero's refutation of Epicureanism were not enough, More had available the *Morals* of Plutarch, with the essay in which Plutarch argued in Stoical terms "That a man cannot live pleasantly according to the doctrine of Epicurus." Indeed Plutarch derided the Epicureans as anti-intellectuals who foolishly deprived themselves of the highest human pleasure of all,—and that which the Utopians most enjoy,—full use of the natural gift of reason. Furthermore, Seneca's onslaught upon Epicureanism in the fourth book of *De beneficiis* was probably as familiar to More as to any other well-educated man who knew the common-place books of philosophy. If then we assume that in all probability More had his wits about him when he wrote *Utopia,* is it possible to frame a satisfactory explanation of the paradox, that the Utopians follow pleasure and virtue together?

On the one hand, More admired the philosophical ethics of the later Roman Stoicism as closest to the original Christian ethics. Nevertheless, he observed shrewdly that, in everyday life as well as in recorded history, most men everywhere actually sought pleasure before virtue, justice, and the common welfare. In short, he saw that while the Stoic social values were the finer, the Epicurean theory of social motivation was more practical. Wittily, therefore, More provided in Utopian society a restraint which enabled the citizens to be, as it were, simultaneously Stoics as well as Epicureans. In Utopia all *anti-social* pleasures—that is, all pleasures which the lessons of history have shown are destructive of the bond of nature between men—are absolutely forbidden to all citizens, under the terrible penalty of loss of citizenship as the punishment for a major breach of "taste." For instance, no Utopian may take pleasure in avarice, waste, hunting, or war. Thus, while all healthy pleasures are encouraged, a sound state of the public mind is *forcibly* maintained. Since obviously the only pleasures which remain are either innocent and harmless or are adjudged to be socially beneficial to the commonwealth (like the pleasures of marriage, or of natural science), it follows that the Utopians can consistently pursue both pleasure and virtue at the same time, ancient critics to the contrary notwithstanding. Toleration among the Utopians does not extend to those "attractive vices" which tend to destroy the commonwealth.

In conclusion, *Utopia,* like the ***Praise of Folly,*** is best seen as a work of literary art which belongs, not only to the English, but also to the continental renaissance. Both satires range over the broad reaches of European civilization; both hold up the life of reason as a model for the age. True—Utopia itself is an island state; but then the new age of culture, of which More, Erasmus, and Colet dreamed in 1509, was to begin in England. How these humanists conceived the classics should be used in the culture of their own time also emerges more clearly, as it appears that they commonly thought of the new order, not as a rebirth of ancient civilization, but as a new and original creation, potentially as different from the age which preceded it as Utopian culture was from the culture of contemporary Europe. Surely the vision of More and Erasmus of a new and rationalized good society leaps far beyond the intellectual confines of the tight little isle and embodies an international and cosmopolitan conception of the renaissance. (pp. 140-45)

Robert P. Adams, "Designs by More and Erasmus for a New Social Order," in Studies in Philology, *Vol. XLII, No. 2, April, 1945, pp. 131-45.*

Leonard F. Dean (essay date 1946)

[*In the following excerpt, Dean traces the development of Erasmus's thought, citing examples from several of the humanist's works.*]

From the beginning of his formal education, Erasmus was concerned with the proper relation of learning and piety. Upon entering the monastic school at Steyn in 1487, he composed ***De contemptu mundi,*** and other conventional religious exercises, but he very soon began to rebel against a curriculum that seemed to him excessively narrow and theological. This rebellion appears as a fine youthful enthusiasm for the classics and for the elegancies of Latin style. He conceived of himself, somewhat melodramatically, as living in the midst of barbarians. "It is certain," he wrote in 1489, "that in early ages the study of eloquence, as of other arts, was most flourishing, and afterwards, as the obstinacy of the barbarians increases, it disappeared . . . Our Thalia was well nigh extinct when our Laurentius and Philelphus by their admirable erudition saved her from perishing. The books of the former, which are called *Elegentiae,* will show you with what zeal he exerted himself both to expose the absurdities of the barbarians and to bring back into use the observances of orators and poets long covered with the dust of oblivion." At about this time Erasmus made an epitome of Valla's *Elegantiae* for school use; it was published in 1529, and followed in 1531 by a revised, authorized version, which became a standard textbook, nearly forty editions appearing within twenty years. Before he left Steyn in 1492, Erasmus attempted a written defense and clarification of his rebellious attitude by composing the ***Antibarbari*** or ***Book Against the Barbarians.*** It was to be an attack on the barbarians and a eulogy of classical literature, but only the first part has survived. (pp. 3-4)

The ***Antibarbari*** is a dialogue in which the subject under discussion is analyzed through speakers with different points of view. A physician, Jodocus, suggests that the stars are responsible for the deplorable state of humane learning; William Herman, a friend of the author, attributes it to the general decay of the world; and James Batt, another friend with humanistic leanings, lays the blame on ignorant monks and scholastic theologians, who have corrupted the purity of the early Christian faith and have deliberately kept the people in ignorance of the classics under the pretext of protecting religion. It follows that reform is possible and can be effected by getting rid of benighted school teachers and impoverished medieval textbooks. William Conrad, a practical and conservative mayor, wonders if it is wise to replace the standard texts with untried classics, which, furthermore, may be an immoral influence on young minds. Batt answers by denouncing bigots who attack literature in the name of religion. They write and teach a barbarous Latin style and assert that a knowledge of Greek is heresy. It may be also suspected, continues Batt, that classical poetry is less harmful than the immoral influence of monastic life. Actually, the split between religion and secular learning is needless and unreal: the Church Fathers knew and used the classics; they were pious and critical-minded at the same time. The discussion is extended at this point to include the belief of the mystics that the pure in heart, rather than the learned, will inherit heaven. Did not Christ Himself preach humility and simplicity? What of the ordinary people who are ignorant of syllogisms and fine rhetoric? The first reply is a facetious suggestion that those who wish to enter heaven with the innocent, dumb animals may do so. It is then argued more seriously that there is a distinction between simplicity of heart and simplemindedness, and that Christ was talking about character rather than intellect. The illiterate and licentious monks are a sufficient illustration of the confusion. Furthermore, the influence of piety is extended by means of learning; a good man who is also educated and eloquent can do more than an untutored person, even a martyr, to spread Christ's word. The argument that Christianity was founded by uneducated fishermen, the Apostles, is also suspect since it is usually no more than an excuse for people nowadays to continue in their own ignorance. The truth is that the Apostles were carefully instructed by Christ, the real father of philosophy; they needed no further secular training. Besides, not all of the Apostles were ignorant to begin with: witness Paul, Peter, John, and James. Our aim should be to combine the religious fervor of Peter, the foremost Apostle, and the learning of Jerome, the foremost Church Father. Here, the mayor interrupts with the objection that the issue has been confused. No one denies that the Apostles possessed divine learning; the subject in question is secular learning acquired through human discipline, and the piety of the Apostles was not the product of study, but of heavenly grace. True, grants Batt rather lamely in conclusion, and all our books are useless without the Holy Spirit, but an occasional visitation, when we are preaching or writing, is preferable to a complete and overwhelming revelation.

The issues presented somewhat crudely in the ***Antibarbari*** were sharpened for Erasmus by his experiences at the University of Paris, where he entered the College of Montaigu in August of 1495 and took a degree of Bachelor in Theology about two years later. Here, at first hand, he saw grown men arguing with the greatest energy and acuteness about words alone. Could Christ have appeared in the form of a gourd? If so, how could He have preached, performed miracles, and been crucified? Which is the greater crime: to kill a thousand men or to work on Sunday? The sight of this remarkable waste of human abilities helped Erasmus to distinguish more exactly between nominalism and a true, realistic theology. He writes about his experience in a wryly humorous letter to an English friend, Thomas Grey, sometime in 1497.

> I, who have always been a primitive Theologian, have begun of late to be a Scotist. . . . We are so immersed in the dreams of your compatriot,—for Scotus, who, like Homer of old, has been adopted by diverse competing countries, is especially claimed by the English as their own,—that we seem as if we should hardly wake up at the voice of Stentor. Then you will say, you are writing this in your sleep. Hush, profane one! thou knowest nothing of theological slumber. There are many that in their sleep not only write, but slander and get drunk, and commit other indiscretions. . . . What if you saw Erasmus sit gaping among those blessed Scotists, while Gryllard is lecturing from his lofty chair? If you observed his contracted brow, his staring eyes, his anxious face, you would say he was another man. They assert that the mysteries of this science cannot be comprehended by one who has any commerce at all with the Muses or with the Graces. If you have touched good letters, you must unlearn what you have learnt; if you have drunk of Helicon, you must get rid of the draught. I do my best to speak nothing in true Latin, nothing elegant or witty, and I seem to make some progress. There is hope that they will acknowledge Erasmus some time or other. . . . Sweet Grey, do not mistake me. I would not have you construe this as directed against theology itself, which, as you know, I have always regarded with special reverance. I have only amused myself in making game of some pseudo-

> theologians of our time, whose brains are rotten, their language barbarous, their intellects dull, their learning a bed of thorns, their manners rough, their life hypocritical, their talk full of venom, and their hearts as black as ink.

What it meant to be a "primitive theologian" was made clearer to Erasmus by John Colet, whom he met at Oxford in October of 1499, during his first visit to England. The two men, both about thirty years old, agreed in condemning scholastic theology. "In your dislike of that sort of neoteric divines, who grow old in mere subtleties and sophistical cavillings, your opinion is entirely my own," Erasmus writes. "In our day, theology, which ought to be at the head of all literature, is mainly studied by persons who from their dulness and lack of sense are scarcely fit for any literature at all. This I say not of learned and honest professors of theology, however. . . ." Colet exemplified the fruitful union of classical and biblical learning that Erasmus had advocated all along. Colet was as eager as the professors at the College of Montaigu to discuss theology, but his aim, unlike theirs, was to explain the essential meanings of the teaching of Christ and the Apostles. A conversation between the two men about the cause of Christ's agony in the garden illustrates the Englishman's point of view and method. Erasmus proposed the conventional scholastic explanation that the agony was a reflection of the natural fear of torment and death felt by Christ the man. Colet, following Jerome, urged that such a view was inconsistent with the principle of Christ the redeemer, who, far from fearing death, sought to die because of His infinite love for all mankind. His prayer that the cup might pass from Him, and the drops of bloody sweat wrung from Him in the garden, were not expressions of fear, but of compassion and sorrow at the thought of the crime which was to be committed. It was in a continuation of the same mood that He prayed, "Father, forgive them, for they know not what they do." It became evident, as the discussion was continued by letter, that Colet was directly opposed to the scholastic tendency to extract more than one literal sense from biblical texts. He did not deny that some passages should be interpreted allegorically, but he did believe that it was uncritical to read into the Scriptures a variety of literal meanings, for the purpose of argument, that were not consistent with the total meaning of the whole context. The critic must first absorb and comprehend the essential spirit of the Bible; in its light he might then proceed to explicate individual passages, much as one might attempt to master a secular classic. To the argument that manifold interpretations are justified in the case of the Bible because its author was God, who comprehends and expresses all meanings at one and the same time, Colet tended to oppose the point of view of historical scholarship. His "method," as Allen observes, "raised the question of the Tradition." The questions to be asked were "not how mankind would have been born if our first parents had not fallen, nor whether the wicked continue to sin in hell, but what were the words of Christ, and by what means these had been preserved to posterity. If the Scriptures were to be treated historically, they must be studied in their original form, or in the nearest form to that, which critical scholarship could discover."

The association with Colet seems to have strengthened and guided Erasmus in several ways. The ***Enchiridion Militis Christiani,*** or ***Manual of the Christian Knight,*** which Erasmus composed in 1501 on his return to the Continent, and published in 1503, reflects the Englishman's essential piety and justifies the author's characterization of the essay as a "straightforward description of the Christian way of life." ***The Praise of Folly*** picks up and expands the basic argument of the ***Enchiridion,*** which distinguishes between real and superficial piety. Religious ceremonies, particularly the worship of the saints, are condemned when they do not symbolize sincere righteousness; the only true worship is virtuous behavior. "***The Enchiridion,***" Erasmus explained to Colet in 1504, "was not composed from any display of genius or eloquence, but only for the purpose of correcting the common error of those who make religion consist of ceremonies and an almost Jewish observance of corporeal matters, while they are singularly careless of things that belong to piety." Piety was not to be confused, however, with ignorant mysticism. Erasmus still desired to unite learning and religion, as is indicated by the concluding sentences of the ***Enchiridion:*** "I hope to disarm some critics who think it is the highest religion to know nothing of good learning. It was not for empty fame or childish pleasure that in my youth I grasped at the polite literature of the ancients, and by late hours gained some slight mastery of Greek and Latin. It has long been my cherished wish to cleanse the Lord's temple of barbarous ignorance, and to adorn it with treasures brought from afar, such as may kindle in generous hearts a warm love for the Scriptures."

There is other evidence from this period that Erasmus had begun to outgrow his youthful delight in the mere elegancies of Latin style. Before leaving England, he had refused Colet's invitation to lecture at Oxford, on the ground that he was unprepared to treat theology. "Neither again," he adds, "did I come here to teach Poetry or Rhetoric. These studies ceased to be agreeable to me when they ceased to be necessary." They were no longer necessary, that is, in the sense that they had been mastered so as to become a part of his unconscious equipment as a writer. There, properly subordinated, they helped to increase the effectiveness of his message, as ***The Praise of Folly*** most clearly demonstrates. A further sign of his growing maturity in this respect and of his surer sense of direction as a scholar, is his turning from Latin to Greek, which he began to study seriously at about this time. "Latin erudition, however ample, is crippled and imperfect without Greek," he

Autograph signature from a letter written in 1522 to Duke George of Saxony.

wrote in 1501, and he saw that this was particularly true for one who wished as he now did to edit, translate, and interpret the Scriptures and the Church Fathers. "I see that it is mere madness to touch with a finger that principal part of theology, which treats of divine mysteries, without being furnished with the apparatus of Greek, when those who translated the sacred books have, with all their scrupulosity, so rendered the Greek figures of speech that not even the primary sense, which our theologians call 'the literal,' can be perceived by those who do not know Greek." Still clearer and more forceful are the arguments by Erasmus in his preface to Valla's *Notes on the New Testament.* Erasmus had found a manuscript of this unpublished textual criticism of the Vulgate and had printed it in 1505. He is well aware, he writes, that it will shock many people, and especially the conservative theologians who most need to profit by it. They will assert that a grammarian has no right to meddle with theology. But when theologians argue about the language of the Scriptures—as they always do, are they not for the moment grammarians? If the problem is grammatical, let it be called by its right name, and treated openly and in a scholarly fashion. "What crime is it in Valla, if after collating some ancient and correct Greek copies, he has noted in the New Testament, which is derived from the Greek, some passages which either differ from our version or seem to be ineptly rendered owing to a passing want of vigilance in the translator, or are expressed more significantly in the Greek; or finally if it appears that some thing in our text is corrupt?" Perhaps it will be answered that it is improper and dangerous to alter the Holy Scriptures, wherein even the smallest points possess hidden meanings. "This only shows how wrong it is to corrupt them, and how diligently what has been altered by ignorance ought to be corrected by the learned." To the further objection "that the old interpreters, skilled in three tongues, have already unfolded the matter as far as is necessary," I answer, first, that "I had rather see with my own eyes than with those of others; and in the next place, much as they have said, they have left much to be said by posterity . . . " Stimulated by Valla's essay and by a second visit to Colet, Erasmus began a Latin version of the New Testament, which he completed in manuscript form, except for Acts and Revalations, by 1506. Ten years later, after many revisions, it was printed with a Greek edition and notes, and thereafter re-edited four times. At the same time he began his editorial work on the writings of the Church Fathers which occupied him for the rest of his life. Jerome, in nine folio volumes, appeared in 1515, Cyprian in 1520, Ambrose in 1527, and Augustine in 1529. These were frequently revised and were accompanied by smaller undertakings.

It would be a mistake to conclude, however, that Erasmus resolved the conflict between piety and learning by becoming a biblical editor. His interests and methods were not altogether those of a modern scientific scholar, and he was never the dry-as-dust type. "Erasmus' was not the temper of a scholar as we understand it today," observes Allen. "Not for him was the slow labour of digging foundations and laying brick to brick to build up an edifice. His work was always done in heat, under the passion of his demand for knowledge. He read, he wrote, 'tumultuarie,' 'praecipitanter.' When he had formed a design, he liked to carry it out 'uno impetu'." Equally significant is the fact that he never went so far as to regard a knowledge of classical literature and rhetoric as simply an instrument for the establishment and preparation of the text of the Scriptures. Despite his assertions that he has outgrown his early naive delight in mere matters of style and that he longs to be at work on the New Testament and to throw aside all worldly tasks, he continued to value, or at least to enjoy, rhetorical skill and the content of the pagan classics for their own sakes. This is evident in the ***Adagia,*** in his translations from the Greek, especially Lucian, and in the theoretical description of a proper secondary school curriculum which he prepared for Colet. The latter, entitled ***De Ratione Studii,*** was begun perhaps as early as 1497, and was first published without authorization in 1511 from a manuscript that Erasmus had apparently completed while in Italy in 1508. He was doubtless planning its revision and enlargement in the following year, at the same time that he was writing ***The Praise of Folly.*** It describes, presumably, the kind of education that Erasmus had desired in his own youth and which he had been obliged to acquire through private study. It was introduced into practice at Colet's new school, St. Paul's, and became "the fundamental philosophy of the grammar school in England." It is chiefly concerned, as Erasmus explains at the beginning, with "the knowledge of words" rather than with "the knowledge of truths," for "if the latter is first in importance the former is acquired first in order of time." The student was to be thoroughly grounded, largely by inductive methods, in Greek and Latin grammar, in the technique of reading analytically for both content and style, and in composition and declamation. As he read, the student was to "pick out any unusual word, archaism, or innovation, anything reasoned or invented unusually well, or aptly turned, any outstanding ornament of speech, any adage, exemplum, *sententia*. . . . " He should have at the tip of his "tongue a *summa* of rhetoric; that is, propositions, the 'places' of proofs, exornations, amplifications, formulas of transitions." To aid the student, Erasmus had written two textbooks, ***Copia*** and ***Parabolae,*** which showed how to develop and amplify a theme by means of logical analysis, examples, figures of speech, and exornation or the "gorgious beautifying of the tongue with borrowed wordes, and change of sentence or speech with much varietie." At the climax of the course came the formal declamation, which the student studied part by part, "from exordium to narration, from narration to division, from division to reasoning, from proposition to proposition, from reason to reason, from the argument to the epilogue or peroration." The student developed facility by treating the same subject in a variety of ways, by essaying the "suasory, dissuasory, hortatory, dehortatory, narrative, gratulatory, expostulatory, commendatory, consolatory." He would be asked "to vituperate Julius Caesar, or praise Socrates in the demonstrative type." Although the assigned readings were obviously meant to "improve" the student and were therefore somewhat moralistic, Baldwin is probably right in concluding "that Erasmus had a genuine literary interest, and that he thought these works should be taught first as literature, only secondly as morality, even though the works should be selected and taught so that morality would not suffer." "Indeed we may say,"

Erasmus asserts strongly, "that a genuine student ought to grasp the meaning and force of every fact or idea that he meets with in his reading, otherwise their treatment through epithet, metaphor, or simile will be to him obscure and confused." It is clear that Erasmus had a lively interest in stylistic techniques and devices, and in fact the training which he advocates in such matters may seem excessively thorough, but sentences like the one that has just been quoted suggest that he understood the organic relationship of style and content.

This impression is supported by the course of his translations from the Greek. His immediate purpose was to increase his knowledge of the language; he also provided himself with the literary gifts that were required under the system of patronage that then prevailed. His first translation was a declamation by the Greek sophist, Libanius, the subject of which was Menelaus demanding of the Trojans the restoration of Helen. "The whole thing is of little importance," he wrote in 1503; nor did he have a much higher regard for his versions of Euripides' *Hecuba* and *Iphigenia.* He had selected the plays because of their rhetoric rather than because of their poetic power. Euripides is interesting, he wrote in 1507, for "the closeness of his arguments and a sort of declamatory power of persuading and dissuading. . . . " Not until he translated Lucian did Erasmus become, in his own words, "a genuine student" of Greek. (pp. 4-15)

Leonard F. Dean, in an introduction to The Praise of Folly, *by Desiderius Erasmus, translated by Leonard F. Dean, Hendricks House, 1946, pp. 1-30.*

Margaret Mann Phillips (essay date 1949)

[Phillips was an English educator who wrote widely on Erasmus. In the following excerpt, she explores how Erasmus reflected the social and political currents of his day in The Praise of Folly *and the* Colloquies.]

The book [Erasmus produced in Thomas More's Bucklersbury home] must have been somewhat of a surprise to himself. It was one of those trifles tossed off in a short time which reveal better than anything else the character and intentions of the writer.

The ***Moria*** falls into three sections, very unequal in length, and quite different in intention, though they are linked together by skilful transitions and the prevalence of the same bantering tone. Roughly they may be classed as follows:

(*a*) Folly introduces herself; a light-hearted attribution of all good things in life to Folly;

(*b*) A satiric attack on current abuses, and especially on the people and activities that Erasmus most disliked;

(*c*) A few mysterious pages in which the intention is apparently neither comic nor satirical, but with a much deeper sense.

The first two sections are easy to understand; it was the last which produced adverse comment and puzzled Erasmus's contemporaries.

The opening part of Folly's speech is really masterly fooling. It is gay and carefree, a scholar's joke in impeccable classical style, and as such it no doubt pleased everybody and made no enemies. Folly turns out to be quite well-read, and knows how authors in the past have written panegyrics of agues, flies, baldness and such other pests of nature; therefore why should she not extol herself? Nothing could be more in character, and the way in which she disclaims any intention of behaving like a rhetorician and opening her speech with a definition, then goes on to describe her origins with a closeness that equals any definition ever made, is charmingly in keeping with herself. Folly in this part of her discourse is really much more than mere foolishness: she is unquenchable animal spirits, the gaiety of youth, the irrational element in mankind, which makes us fall in love, have children, be merry in our childhood and youth; even the classical gods came under her spell, and Folly paints a merry picture, rather like a turbulent painted ceiling of the Renaissance, depicting all the gods of Olympus giving way to Folly. It is clear from this that Folly here represents all the qualities and all the activities of life which are outside the pale of reason. She finds it easy to prove that the motives which bring about great deeds, such as courage in war and the love of glory, are folly rather than wisdom, that a mob which will not listen to wise counsel will be moved by a childish fable, that Folly laid the foundation of cities, and that by her "Empire, Authority, Policy and publique Actions are preserved; neither is there anything in Human Life that is not a kind of pastime of Folly."

The whole of this argument mounts up to a profound conclusion closely related to the thought of Montaigne and of Pascal: namely, that human society largely depends for its existence on the accepting by a large number of people of certain appearances or conventions, which are seen as Folly by the truly wise man, but " 'tis the part of a truly Prudent man not to be wise beyond his condition." These conventions are essential for the conduct of life.

This part of Folly's sermon concludes with a sketch of the origins of happiness, (which is according to her, mainly delusion), and a rough classification of the different types of fools who enjoy her consoling bounty; thus she passes from the general to the particular, and embarks on the ironical review of the world's foolishness which constitutes the second section of the book.

And here the character of the speaker begins to change. An element of criticism comes in, and Folly is no longer the genial source of life's brightness, but something much nearer the general acceptation of her name. At the beginning of the list of fools, she merely makes people ridiculous, but at the end she makes them criminal. Naturally the most severe criticism falls on Erasmus's own pet aversions, worthless monks, vain Schoolmen and warring Popes, and such is his hatred of their unlikeness to their Christian profession that Folly nearly drops her bantering tone to turn on them with fury. This serious nature of the book is clear in these pages, and one understands why Erasmus could say that in the ***Moria*** he was doing exactly the same thing as in the ***Enchiridion,*** though in a different way: he was indeed broadcasting the same message, that we should look to realities rather than to names, to a man's life rather than to his words, to the spirit rather than to the letter of the law. But he had more confidence and more experience now than when he wrote the ***Enchiridion;*** and no serious book could ever have the sting or the brilliant satire of the ***Moria.*** The shafts went home in quite a different way.

It is the fate of all satirical writing to change in interest as the years go by, as different facets of the irony are caught by the light of rising and setting suns. To us the general picture is interesting, painted with merry humour rather than with a pen dipped in gall. We are amused to know that in the early sixteenth century it was the English who prided themselves on their music, their beauty and their banquets, the Scotch who vaunted their high descent and their subtle Schoolmen, the Parisians who thought themselves unique as students of divinity, the Italians, not unnaturally, who claimed to be the only masters of learning and eloquence and despised all other nations as barbarous. There are innumerable touches in ***The Praise of Folly*** which either illustrate amusingly the foibles of a bygone age, or shed a passing light on a permanent weakness which we recognise as of our world of today. But to Erasmus's contemporaries the parts of deepest interest in Folly's utterances must have been those which threw into relief the specific abuses of their own time—the pages in which Erasmus took his long-desired fling at the successors of the Schoolmen, and by his comical selection of their "Magisterial Definitions, Conclusions, Corollaries, Propositions Explicit and Implicit," dealt the dying science such a blow that it constitutes a *coup de grâce;* or those where the long procession of ignorant and conceited monks winds in front of our mental vision, with their meticulous observance of tiny rules concerning dress, as to the number of knots in shoe-strings or girdle, width of cowl or colour of habit, and their utter disregard of purity of life or the example of the Apostles. Erasmus really enjoyed himself here. He was fervently working for the reform of Christendom, and he was also avenging years of humiliation in which he had been forced to watch what he describes, and ostensibly to identify himself with it. This perhaps accounts for the specially bitter tone in which he always speaks of the trivialities of the monastic life. (pp. 101-04)

Folly has something to say of princes and court lords, but she warms up again when it comes to reviewing her share in the lives of Bishops, Cardinals and Popes. It is in her condemnation of the unapostolic activities of warlike Popes, such as Erasmus had observed with passionate indignation in Italy, that his eloquence rises to its height. The Papal court, with its pomp and trappings, its crowd of hangers-on, guards, clerks, notaries, muleteers, bankers, comes vividly back before his mind, and in the centre of this luxury the soldierly figure of Julius II. He makes Folly dare to say that through her alone, Popes live more voluptuously and with less trouble than almost any other kind of men, thinking that Christ will be well enough pleased if they act as bishops in title and ceremony only. (p. 105)

And here the character of Folly begins to change again. Under the influence of the texts of Scripture, such as "the preaching of the Cross is to them that perish foolishness," a different aspect of Folly comes into sight; she has already changed from something which amounted to a life-force into the blind self-love of deluded mankind, and now her Protean character melts into yet another shape, the self-forgetfulness of the mystics and the saints. The link between all three aspects is that they are all outside the pale of Reason; but as we have already seen, Erasmus was only up to a point an admirer of Reason. Only a reader who took him to be a whole-hearted rationalist could imagine that in these last pages he was mocking at sacred things, when he allows Folly to speak of the preference shown by Jesus for simple people, children and women and fishermen, or when she paints the mystic trance as a foretaste of Heaven. These pages did indeed alarm certain sober-minded contemporaries, and to a later taste they may be unexpected and doubtful, mingling as they do sacred things with profane. But to those who understood Erasmus's character and drift, as More, for instance, must have done, there could have been no ambiguity.

Two considerations may help here to come to an understanding of Erasmus's purpose. One is that the sixteenth-century writer did sometimes employ this technique, which was useful to him because it acted both as a disguise and a challenge. A good example is found in the chapters of the *Quart Livre* of *Pantagruel* (LVII-LXII), in which Rabelais describes the visit of Pantagruel and his friends, in the course of their wanderings, to the territory of Messer Gaster and his subjects the Gastolatres; Gaster appears to symbolise at one point human greed, at another economic necessity. Erasmus's Folly perhaps gave Rabelais a model for his swift change and counterchange in tone. An insubstantial goddess, she switches insidiously from one character to another; whatever she may say can immediately be excused because it proceeds out of the mouth of Folly, and her irrational behaviour in now forgetting and now remembering who she is, is distractingly in keeping with her personality.

Secondly, Erasmus's other writings illuminate his purpose here. As we have seen, the irony of the second part of the ***Moria*** need not lead us to suppose that when he allowed his Folly to describe the raptures of the mystics, Erasmus was either satirising them or cracking a bad joke. On the contrary, the meaning of this "true word spoken in jest" seems to be strictly in accordance with the message of the ***Enchiridion*** and the ***Paraclesis,*** in fact, with that side of Erasmus's outlook which we have partly traced back to the teaching of the Brethren of the Common Life: the distrust of the intellect, and the condemnation of intellectual pride. The propositions of Folly are inconsequent, as becomes her, but beneath the manner, which is preserved to the end, there is a serious respect for the supra-rational, the wisdom which has nothing to do with reasoning or calculation and, therefore, may be akin to Folly, the unworldliness which takes its models from children, lilies, sparrows and mustard-seed, for it belongs to the kingdom of Heaven. The behaviour of the Christian is utter foolishness in the eyes of Mr. Worldly Wiseman: and the saint in contemplation is lost to the world of common sense. He is ravished in soul like a lover, and the more complete his self-forgetfulness, the greater his foretaste of Heaven. (pp. 105-07)

And so ends ***The Praise of Folly,*** with perfect symmetry, making the unreason of the mystic at the end respond to the unreason of the lover or the child at the beginning. And here it may be remarked in passing that there is a curious resemblance between these three phases of ***The Praise of Folly*** and the three Orders whose discovery as a law of the universe so haunted Pascal. The point of similarity is that for Pascal the natural ignorance of the common people, constituting the first Order, and the inspired comprehension of the saint, constituting the third, often touch, especially in their attitude to worldly things. What then? Are we to conclude that Erasmus forestalled Pascal, or that Pascal was inspired by Erasmus? Manifestly neither is true. But we can conclude two things from this unexpected conjunction: that the influence of one spirit on another in the European tradition of thought (as of Erasmus on Montaigne and Montaigne on Pascal) is closer and more far-reaching than appears at first; and secondly, that for Erasmus to be dubbed a sceptic and a rationalist, on the score of ***The Praise of Folly,*** was a strange misreading of the facts, since he comes here into close sympathy with the greatest exponent of the relationship between reason and the intuition of the mystic.

THE COLLOQUIES

The ***Colloquies*** of Erasmus are one of the great books of the Renaissance. As one of their most devoted friends has said: "If literary theft be, like imitation, one of the sincerest forms of flattery, the ***Colloquies*** of Erasmus occupy the proud position of one of the most pillaged works in existence." They not only rejoiced the heart of their own generation, they were read throughout the sixteenth century and far beyond, and have acted as a quarry of humorous anecdote and local colour for fiction and drama up to our own time. In the sixteenth century, the list of borrowers from them includes such names as Shakespeare and Ben Jonson, Montaigne and Cervantes, Rabelais, Clément Marot, Marguerite de Navarre. Later, Molière and possibly even Pascal remembered them, and in the nineteenth century it was not surprising that Sir Walter Scott should turn to them in his search for descriptive detail of the past. The use made of them by Charles Reade in *The Cloister and the Hearth* is well known, but it is strange to find among their debtors Victorien Sardou. Probably many other traces of their influence could be found by a determined search, for they must have been one of the most widely read books ever written.

It is particularly in reading the ***Colloquies*** that we allow ourselves to regret Erasmus's fidelity to Latin: his easy fluency and witty conciseness are so apt to vanish under a translator's hand, and humour, like Vouvray, suffers in transit. And yet not only did the ***Colloquies'*** Latin dress allow them to have a wider influence in their day than would otherwise have been possible, but they owe their very inception to the interest of their author in the correct teaching of Latin. When Erasmus was a poor student in Paris, obliged to take a few pupils for the sake of earning his bread, he wrote a number of dialogues for them, to illustrate forms of speech and address and to familiarise them with the use of Latin as the language of everyday life. Through these first dialogues recur the names of his Paris friends and the students whom he taught there: Christian Northoff, Peter Gilles, Thomas Grey, James Maurice of Gouda, Francis Theodoric, Cornelius Gerard, Richard Arnold, Fausto Andrelini. One of them was an acquaintance whose activity in the bookselling line was useful to Erasmus, but for whom as a person he never cared: Augustine Vincent Caminade. This man appears to have given readings of new books in booksellers' shops (the contemporary form of advertisement) and was entrusted by Erasmus with some literary business. Long afterwards, in 1518, Augustine Caminade collected the Latin dialogues by Erasmus he possessed, and published them without the author's knowledge. This was often a transparent literary device, but in this case Erasmus's anger was quite genuine, and he hurried into print an authentic and more correct version (1519). This was the ***Familiorum Colloquiorum Formulae.*** In 1522, he brought out a much enlarged edition printed by Froben, and dedicated to Froben's little son Erasmius. This was the basis for the many subsequent editions, enlarged each time by the addition of new Colloquies, until three years before the author's death in 1536. The book which began as a few practical hints and "formulae," ended as the ***Colloquiorum Opus,*** containing over sixty Colloquies, many of them complete stories or one-act dramas and full of incident, personal opinions, acute psychological observation, detail and colour.

The book which was thus nearly forty years in the making can be compared in some ways to Montaigne's *Essais.* Like them, it grew from a short and formal exercise, in which the author acted more as a collector of material than as a creator, and it expanded into a highly original form of literature which expressed the author's deepest preoccupations and interests. But there the resemblance ends, for while the originality of Montaigne lay in his investigation of his own personality by favour of his retirement from the world, Erasmus's thought was continually directed outwards, in perpetual contact with the events of his time, commenting, criticising, attempting to influence by ridicule or by protest, exposing abuses or building up an ideal. The personality of the author is never absent, but it is involved in the active dramatic life of the speakers and their friends.

The ***Colloquies*** are an all-purpose book. Apart from their initial pedagogic intention (which assured their use as a schoolbook for many years, in spite of various attempts to ban them as unorthodox), they were a running commentary on current events, in which Erasmus could indulge his learning towards journalism; they belong in a way to the broadsheet class of literature which preceded the newspaper. In them, under cover of fictitious names and an apparently impersonal form, he could express his own ideas, follow the course of political or religious quarrels, discuss burning topics of the day at Bâle, recommend ways of living, from ethics to hygiene, attack his enemies and the enemies of sound learning, defend his friends and on occasion himself. Like both Montaigne and Rabelais, Erasmus realised in the course of writing what varied purposes could be served by the apparently simple form of literature he had embarked upon, and raised it to the status of a classic.

All these purposes were utilitarian. But Erasmus was not only a Latin scholar and a corrector of morals. He was a most human person, with an incurably frivolous side; he had a delight in the ridiculous, an acute eye, a knowledge of character and a sympathy with natural ways of living. The ***Colloquies*** are the only work of his (except his letters) in which all these qualities can find their full expression. They make the book into one of the richest and most crowded canvases depicting the life of the Renaissance.

On the whole the picture shown us is of the 1520's. As we have seen, some of the ***Colloquies*** were in existence long before, and some were still being added in 1533, but the great bulk of them appeared during 1523-8. They date from a period of maximum activity in Erasmus's life, when he was recognised as the greatest scholar in Europe, and as having a voice of authority; but also when he was resolutely avoiding the dangers of entanglement in the Lutheran controversy, which was sweeping Europe into war; and when he was beginning to fend off the attacks of critics and enemies which were to pursue him to the end of his life. The ***Colloquies*** can thus be roughly divided into three types, though some of the greatest partake of all three characters: there are the stylistic ones, directed to literary uses; the polemical ones, holding up to ridicule and scorn the abuses of the day, and defending the author; and those which illustrate some characteristic attitude of the Renaissance, or describe graphically what it was like to be alive in 1526, or tell entertaining stories, or paint an ideal picture such as always lingered at the back of Erasmus's mind.

Even the purely stylistic exercises have a flavour of their time. Not for nothing did Erasmus write ***De Copia.*** Some of the early conversations such as the one between Pamphagus and Cocles, discussing the varied uses that could be made of Cocles' nose, are in the exuberant vein which was carried to such lengths by Rabelais. Style, to the men of the early Renaissance, meant not only finding the right word, but rejoicing in a torrent of words, playing with them and tossing them in the air. It is said that Erasmus, so cautious in his letters and most of his writings, was highly indiscreet in his talk, and in the ***Colloquies*** we have an echo of his readiness of tongue as well as his biting wit. Other stylistic exercises include a classical imitation in which a young man holds a conversation with an echo, the last syllables of his question always being contrived to form an answer, sometimes in Greek; and a short conversation between friends, when one plays on the other a trick which Erasmus played on More—speaking verses to him as if they were prose. One Colloquy, the **"Poetical Banquet,"** seems to be an account of a real occasion, when Erasmus and his friends discussed classical texts and false quantities over a dinner of herbs provided grudgingly by Erasmus's crabbed housekeeper Margaret, who sends in beet-root-tops instead of lettuces to see if the poets will know the difference.

The contemporary abuses passed under review in the ***Colloquies*** cover a wide range. Foremost among them—and this, no doubt, contributed to put the ***Colloquies*** on the Index—are the habits and customs censured by Luther: the pushing of young people into monasteries and convents, the exaggerated praise of celibacy, superstitious reliance on indulgences and pilgrimages, rash vows, fasting, and the like, and the doubtful lives of the worst type of monk and friar. It is noticeable that all this criticism which rose to a crescendo about 1526—was written and published at a time when Erasmus was publicly disavowing Luther, and insisting on the differences of opinion which separated them. Yet he did not hesitate to add his weight to all the reformer's censures of the superstitions of his time. Erasmus had chosen his standpoint and he never deserted it; he had no intention of parting from the Church of Rome, but he endorsed all efforts to bring about a saner and healthier condition within it.

For this campaign, the dialogue form was a preeminent weapon. It allowed instant penetration of the barbed shaft, with the least ambiguity and circumvention. The dramatic force of the dialogues is tremendous, and they speak for themselves with no need of commentary. They are the voice of the people, as well as the admonition of the scholar from his study.

Why did Erasmus choose a girl, to represent the victim of a type of persuasion which he held in horror, the attempt to stock the monasteries and convents with deluded adolescents? Probably because he wished to show pressure being applied through emotional and imaginative channels on a docile subject, and also because the question was much debated at Bâle, where there was a movement against forcing girls into nunneries, just about the time when the ***Colloquies*** in question were being written (1523). In that year Erasmus published five new Colloquies dealing with women, and two of them on this subject. It is remarkable how gentle Erasmus was when women or girls were in question, how sympathetically he states their case, treating them entirely as equals with men. In this he was joining forces with an existing movement among humanists; educated women were to be found in Renaissance Italy, and whenever the breath of the Renaissance touched a society, some women were to be found who flowered into cultivated and intellectual maturity. They were not always great ladies like Marguerite de Navarre or Lady Jane Grey; Erasmus had known bourgeois families where the girls were as highly educated as the boys, like Pirkheimer's sisters or More's daughters, and he who had long ago declared that he wished women to be able to read the Scriptures, now added the powerful illustration of a gallery of portraits, collecting together sprightly and subtle and intelligent, and sometimes learned women. (pp. 107-13)

[Three] Colloquies between a lover and his lass are designed to combat the idea that celibacy is necessarily more holy than marriage, as well as to stigmatise the practice of deceiving young people into lightly embracing the monastic life. The first, **"The Lover and the Maiden,"** is a charming and delicate sketch of a courtship, in which the arguments put into the young man's mouth are all in favour of family life, and a marriage based on compatibility of origins and temperament. The girl is deliciously quick and subtle in her teasing vein, and reminds one a little of Rosalind, or the delicate crayon portraits of girls by the Clouets. The other two dialogues, **"The Virgin Averse to Marriage"** and **"The Virgin Repentant"** are more openly propagandist, and Erasmus when writing them must have thought of his own youth, remembering the impression he carried away of the proselytising activities of the Brethren of the Common Life.

Some of the other Colloquies are on the subject of the religious orders and their abuse of power, such as **"The Funeral,"** with its vivid picture of a deathbed swarming round with greedy and quarrelling monks and friars, contrasted with the quiet, trustful passing of a Christian philosopher free from subservience—one might compare the latter picture with the death of La Boëtie, as described by Montaigne. Superstitious insistence on fasting is the initial topic of the long Colloquy **"Ichthyophagia,"** with its famous description of the Collège de Montaigu, the most unsavoury recollection of Erasmus's student days. But by far the most celebrated of these Colloquies on the externals of religion are **"The Religious Pilgrimage"** and **"The Shipwreck."** Both rang through Europe, and are still among the best worth reading today, especially **"The Shipwreck,"** with its vivid and masterly description of a storm at sea. . . . The polemical part of the dialogue is, of course, concerned with the desperate vows and petitions to the saints put up by the passengers in peril of their lives; some vow to become Carthusians, another to go on a pilgrimage to St. James of Compostella barefoot and bareheaded, in a coat of mail and begging his bread all the way, another promises to the figure of St. Christopher on the top of a church in Paris, "rather a mountain than a statue," a wax taper as big as itself. When a more cautious friend reminds the last petitioner that he could never keep his word, he answers in a low voice "lest St. Christopher should hear him"—"You fool, do you think I mean what I say? If I once got safe to shore, I would not give him so much as a tallow candle." This famous incident is one of Erasmus's rare borrowings; it comes from the *Facetiae* of Poggio, an author whom Erasmus usually disliked as obscene, but one who came in opportunely here. And it reappears in Rabelais, where Panurge in his fright during the storm at sea promises a chapel to "Monsieur St. Nicolas," but when the sea is calm again admits that it is all a fiction, *une chapelle d'eau rose.* The robust old priest named Adam who exhorts the passengers in the Colloquy and then plunges half-naked into the sea, has a certain family likeness to Rabelais' Frère Jean.

A good example of Erasmus's modernity of thought can be seen in this Colloquy, where he points out that in antiquity Venus was said to protect sailors, because she was believed to be born of the sea, and the sailors' custom of calling on the Virgin, *stella maris,* was a Christian substitution for the pagan tradition.

"The Religious Pilgrimage" has a special attraction for English readers, because of its close description of two famous shrines, that of Our Lady of Walsingham and that of St. Thomas at Canterbury. Here Erasmus is drawing entirely from his own recollections, and very clear and vivid they were. He had gone to Walsingham with young Robert Aldridge to act as interpreter, and had even written some Greek verses to hang up in the shrine. But he was not pleased with what he saw. He could not help commenting on the amount of the blessed Virgin's milk which seemed to have been preserved, much as the relics of the true cross would make a ship-load of wood if they were all gathered together; and the transparency of the deceptions practised on every hand on the simple and guileless faithful, are mercilessly revealed. As for the shrine of St. Thomas, the account of the visit there is even more interesting, for he went there with a friend now recognised as no less than John Colet, here called Gratianus Pullus (Pullus=a colt). Under the mighty fabric of the minister, whose great towers welcome pilgrims from afar, they find first the place of Thomas à Becket's martyrdom and the multitude of relics which are brought out, and which they are expected to kiss (Colet draws back and the relics are all shut up again); and then they come to the shrine itself, covered with gold and immense jewels. Here ensues the memorable conversation between Colet and the shower of relics: "Good father," says Colet, "is it true that while he lived, Thomas was very charitable to the poor?" "Very true," says the keeper of the shrine. "And I expect that good inclination in him is not changed, except for the better?" "Undoubtedly." "Then don't you think he would be glad, now that he needs nothing, to relieve the miseries of the poor with all this wealth?" The troublesome visitors are nearly turned out of the cathedral for imagining such a question. Erasmus had had the same thought on looking at the great Chartreuse of Pavia.

The Colloquies on the false trappings of religion are perhaps the most brilliant and the most scathing. But Erasmus had plenty of other bones to pick with his own time. He brings before us a gallery of rogues: the trickster who sells a lame horse and is paid out in his own kind, the "alchemist" who hides the silver in the cinders before discovering it with great triumph in his crucible, the pretended knight who wins respect and a wife through his cheating braggadocio, the soldier of fortune selling his services to the highest bidder and bringing home from the wars poverty, disablement and disease. Two things Erasmus hated with special fervour, as the scourges of his day; war, and the new epidemic which was devastating Europe—syphilis. In his ideas on hygiene he seems to have been in advance of his time; he insisted by instinct on a standard of cleanliness which has only become generally accepted as a result of a greater knowledge of the transmission of disease. Things were tolerated in the sixteenth century which shocked him to the core, and one of the most hideous of them is described in **"The Marriage that was no Marriage"**—the forcible handing over of a beautiful girl to the embraces of a diseased old rake. The danger to the family of the soldier who comes home riddled with venereal disease is plainly spoken of in the dialogue between the soldier and the Carthusian. And Erasmus has general suggestions to makc: that barbers should not be surgeons, which was then the universal practice, that no two people should drink out of the same cup, or sleep in the same bed unless they were husband and wife, that inns should give each traveller clean sheets, that the custom of saluting all and sundry with a kiss should be discontinued.

It is in Cervicorn's edition of 1528 that we meet the best

of Erasmus's Colloquies on war, and perhaps one of the most artistically perfect in the whole book, **"Charon."** In the form of a discussion in the underworld between the ferryman of the "infernal lake" and the Genius Alastor, the messenger, who brings tidings of the state of affairs on earth, it is a comprehensive picture of the turbulent state of Europe and an impartial censure of all sides in the struggle. Erasmus was writing not long after the captivity of Francis I in Madrid as prisoner of the Emperor, at a time when all the nations of Europe appeared likely to fly at each other's throats: "The three monarchs of the world were bent upon each other's destruction with a mortal hatred, and there was no part of Christendom free from the rage of war; for these three have drawn all the rest in to be engaged in the war with them." So Charon is off to buy a new boat which will carry all the ghosts who are coming to him, weighed down by the dreams of the vain things they trusted in on earth, and urged on by the haranguing of the "certain sort of animals in black and white vestments, ash-coloured coats, and various other dresses" who are always hanging about the courts of princes and instilling into them the love of war. According to these people it is a holy war on both sides, for in France they say that: "God is on the French side and they can never be overcome that have God for their protector; in England and Spain the cry is, the war is not the King's but God's."

Two of the Colloquies were written in self-defence: **"The Sermon,"** a scathing reply to the criticisms of the Franciscan Medardus in a sermon preached in the Cathedral at Augsburg, where he accused Erasmus of presuming to correct the Magnificat and make the blessed Virgin call herself "vile." Erasmus enjoys replying, and corrects the Franciscan's name to a version which would still be appreciated in France (Merdardus). In **"Miserly Riches"** he replies to accusations of gluttony and insobriety during his stay in Venice: and his defence is perhaps regrettable, since it is based on the most acid description of the parsimony of his host, Andrea da Asola, Aldus's father-in-law. True, it makes amusing reading, and at the end Erasmus admits that different climates require different types of food, but most of his biographers have wriggled uncomfortably when faced with this breach of the etiquette of hospitality. Perhaps he should not have conjured up his picture of the dinner-table in Venice, with seven or eight learned men sitting round a dish where "seven small lettuce leaves swam in vinegar," or faring little better on soup made from boiled cheese, and stale tripe. But Erasmus could not resist a little embroidery, and it was more than twenty years ago.

In two Colloquies Erasmus was perfectly serious: an early one called **"The Boy's Piety,"** written for Erasmius Froben, and the discussion of Christian doctrine entitled **"An Enquiry Concerning Faith" ("Inquisitio de Fide").** The latter holds an important place, for in it one of the speakers (Barbatus) represents Luther, the other (Aulus) an orthodox man such as Erasmus considered himself. It was written before Erasmus had decided to write against Luther, but he never saw reason to disown it; and when at the end Aulus asks: "Well then, since you agree with us (the orthodox) in so many and weighty points, what hinders that you are not wholly on our side?" Barbatus replies, "I have a mind to hear that of you . . . "

But the ***Colloquies*** would never have enjoyed their lasting fame if they had been merely a weapon of controversy. Even the barbed ones owe their charm less to their incisive attack than to their wit and psychological insight: all are alive, and conjure up pleasant pictures of Renaissance interiors and their inhabitants. A good example of this is the delightful dialogue between the **"Abbot and the Learned Lady,"** in which the Abbot censures the Lady for the reprehensible habit of leaving classical books lying about everywhere, and she corners him by her skilful arguments in favour of humanistic learning. (pp. 114-19)

In these Colloquies a subject that is familiar to us from other sources comes to the fore: the ***Philosophia Christi.*** The last Colloquy is in its way a *tour de force,* proving that if virtue is pleasure then the greatest Epicurean is Christ himself, whose service is perfect freedom. A fitting end for a book of Erasmus's. But the **"Religious Banquet"** enshrines some of his deepest and most treasured convictions and ideals. It has often been observed how much the Renaissance writers loved picturing friendly talk in a garden: instances are the setting of the *Decameron,* or the idyllic resort of the Florentine philosophers at Careggi. The fact is, of course, that their minds were penetrated by the Platonic vision. Erasmus was haunted by it; one of his earliest extant works, the ***Antibarbari,*** opened in Platonic style with a description of the speakers sitting under the apple trees, and he wrote no fewer than six Colloquies with the theme of a Banquet or Symposium. The idea of the interweaving of natural beauty and intellectual pleasure, derived from the Platonic dialogues, runs through much of the finest literature of the Renaissance, and gives us not only the exquisite vignettes of Ronsard, losing himself deep in the woods of Vendôme *parlant avec un livre,* but the philosophising of the Forest of Arden and the haunted island of Prospero. (p. 121)

What is it that marks the ***Colloquies*** as essentially a work of the Renaissance? It is not the subjects of attack, near as they may be to the ideas of the Reformation, for satire on monks and clergy was common during the Middle Ages, and cheats and liars can be found in any age. It is not the dialogue form, though this is culled from the ancients and beloved by the Renaissance; but something like it had existed before, in drama and in the *jeu-parti,* and in such discussions as Alain Chartier's *Quadrilogue Invectif,* or in lighter vein, the delicious dialogues of Froissart. It is not the wide sweep of observation, marshalling all sorts and conditions of men, for as we have seen in reference to ***The Praise of Folly,*** earlier ages loved doing this; there are some strong similarities, for instance, between the ***Colloquies*** and the Prologue to the *Canterbury Tales.*

A full comparison between the picture of society given by Chaucer and that given by Erasmus has enticing possibilities, but it is outside the scope of this study. To notice a few of the similarities and differences may serve, however, to relate the ***Colloquies*** to their day and generation. If Erasmus could have known the Prologue—which is unlikely, his command of English being small—he would thoroughly have enjoyed the treatment of the hangers-on of the monastic system: the portraits of the Monk and Friar, the Summoner and Pardoner, would have been entirely after his own heart. For in Chaucer's view of society as well as in Erasmus's, these constitute the defective element. (Curiously enough, where Chaucer draws an endearing portrait of the secular clergy in the "poor Parson of a town," Erasmus's one allusion to them in the Colloquy **"Rich Beggars,"** is as uncomplimentary as any to the monastic tribe.) The sins of which they are accused are much the same in the two writers, though Chaucer has a genius for physical description which Erasmus lacks, and Erasmus proceeds more through reference to actions committed and words spoken—this is in part due to the choice of the dialogue form. But when we pass to the other members of the party, we are struck by a great difference; in Erasmus's world there is no "parfit gentil Knight." He is dealing not with the accepted gradation of medieval society, but with a much more fluid situation; groups are being modified and merging into each other, money is all-important. If there is any aristocracy in the ***Colloquies,*** it is an aristocracy of intellect, flowering out of a comfortable middle-class environment like that of the burghers of Bâle.

In Chaucer each portrait is carefully drawn, but there is little said of the effect on the community of the individuals named, except in the case of the Parson and his flock. What marks the ***Colloquies*** as of a later age is their strong concentration on social reform. In fact, Erasmus was in advance of his age in this. His sense of the debt of each individual to society, and of the extent to which society holds in its own hands the key to its improvement, foreshadowed the eighteenth century. His concern with the ethics of the individual nearly always relates them to the ethics of the group, especially when he is concerned with hygiene, motherhood, or such practical matters. And yet interacting with his interest in social improvement is his passionate desire for individual freedom, for liberty of conscience, which is clogged and fettered by superstition and custom and traditional subservience. Those two complementary urges, to free and expand the mental life of the individual, and to become more and more conscious of his human environment and its malleability, mark the ***Colloquies*** as speaking with the authentic voice of the Renaissance. (pp. 122-24)

Margaret Mann Phillips, in her Erasmus and the Northern Renaissance, *Macmillan, New York, 1950, 236 p.*

Eugene F. Rice, Jr. (essay date 1950)

[*Rice is an American historian and educator who has written extensively on the Renaissance. In the excerpt below, he traces the development and presentation of Erasmus's religious thought as revealed in his treatises and letters.*]

The writings of Erasmus in the years 1495-1499 reveal the gradual emergence, within a framework of conventional thought and practice, of a new synthesis of the Christian and antique. It arose, organically and largely unconsciously, from the interpenetration of a subtle but pervasive secularism, refined and formalized in terms of the humanely terrestrial ideals of Roman literature, and the traditional content of his religious thought and feeling. A naive secularism was innate in the young Erasmus. He delighted in Robert Gaguin's dinners at the Mathurin convent; the banquets with his pupils so circumstantially described in the ***Profane Feast;*** free and animated literary discussion, preferably in a quiet and shaded rural retreat; a jest shared with the witty and scandalous Faustus Andrelini or the aristocratic Lord Mountjoy. These predilections enabled him to penetrate deeply into the spirit of classical literature and made him singularly receptive to its secular bias. It, in turn, moulded the formal expression of his own thought and its ideals became in time an organic part of his own structure of values.

Erasmus, however, was an Augustinian Canon on leave from his monastery to study theology at the University of Paris, and this excessive commitment to the temporal posed difficult problems in his relation to the traditional patterns of religious thought and practice. An equal reverence for the human and divine is difficult to maintain; and *uti non frui* is a principle the young Erasmus could have grasped only intellectually. On the other hand, a moralized secularism and a Christianity drained of its mysticism may meet comfortably on the common ground of ethics. For the finest achievement of secularism is an ethic: the living of an ideal rather than its contemplation, a hope in the present rather than an expectation for the future; while the imitation of Christ can always be recommended as an ethical injunction by the least mystical. Yet ethical secularism, when embodied in a revealed religion whose principal aim is salvation, remains viable only so long as the contradictions between the ethic, essentially worldly, and the metaphysic, essentially supernatural, do not become explicit. Erasmus, however, never allowed this to happen. He, therefore, enjoyed a comfortable religion during his Paris years: a sincere acceptance of the old, of tradition and of centuries of accumulated doctrine; but beneath this a view of man and of life which drained that doctrine of its supernatural and apocalyptic visions. An examination of his religious thought and practice during these years will reveal the ambiguities in Erasmus' relation to his religious inheritance and perhaps throw further light on the general problem of the interplay of innovation and tradition in the thought and activities of the Northern humanists of the late Fifteenth Century.

At no time during these years did Erasmus seriously question either orthodox theological doctrine or the conventional religious practices of his age. Indeed the little we know of his own religious life reveals a conformity with such practices which appears to have been more than purely formal. He gave public commentaries on the Scriptures at Montaigu and delivered sermons "in praise of the saints," perhaps at St. Genevieve, whose loss he was to regret in later years. He not only praised the saints, he prayed to them and testified to the efficacy of their aid. In the spring of 1496 he fell ill "from the bad eggs and infected bed chamber" at Montaigu. William Cop, later court physician to Francis I, attended him and, apparently feeling there was little hope for his recovery, tried to console his patient, which, Erasmus later wrote, "made me as happy as if he had told me I should be hanging from the gibbet in four days." Despairing, therefore, of medicine, he turned to more spiritual remedies and prayed to St. Genevieve, promising her a poem if he recovered. His prayer was answered, and he lost no time in reporting the miracle to the Prior of Steyn. . . . (pp. 387-89)

Yet Erasmus treated his infirmities in a very different manner in the ***Lament on his Fates, Written in Illness,*** a poem dedicated to Gaguin and first printed in William Herman's *Sylva Odarum.* A Stoic elegy with astrological embellishments, it is wholly pagan in tone. The stars are now responsible for his misfortune. . . . Jupiter, Venus and Mercury rule our lives; and those are happy, consequently, who not only endure present evils, but are also capable of looking forward with renewed anticipation to a future no better than the past. He asks Heaven, nevertheless, to bring good fortune to Gaguin; but it is the Fates which are petitioned, not St. Genevieve.

The contrast between Erasmus' report of his illness to Nicholas Werner and this more generalized comment on what is probably the same misfortune is striking. The discrepancy arises less from the respect paid to astrological causation, however, than from the ethical attitude recommended to combat it. The significant contrast lies in Erasmus' varying responses to his illness; and, while recognizing in the former a partial attempt to impress a pious ecclesiastic and in the latter elements of a conventional classical imitation, the two points of view reveal more than verbal contradictions: on the one hand, an uncritical and apparently emotional attachment to a traditional religious practice; on the other, an ethical rationalization of misfortune which can logically exclude such irrational appeals as that to St. Genevieve. A sincere, if perhaps shallow, belief in the miracle co-exists with a resignation typically antique. Deep in Erasmus' emotional nature remained the feeling that St. Genevieve could, and would, cure him; and the shock of serious illness was enough to make this faith explicit. The danger removed, he was able to rationalize the experience in non-supernatural terms. In this context the appeal to the saint and the earlier sermons *de laudibus deorum* appear curiously arid, the sincere but mechanical acts of a man whose faith in them has been unconsciously vitiated by the secular ethics of Stoicism.

As in his religious practice there was no break with conventional behavior, so also there was little in his theological beliefs which could have troubled the most demanding Doctor. Indeed he takes pains to emphasize his orthodoxy. "Sweet Grey," he writes at the end of a long attack on the barrenness of scholasticism, "do not mistake me. I would not have you construe this as directed against theology itself, which, as you know, I have always regarded with special reverence." His general conformity, if not necessarily his reverence, is both negatively and positively apparent: in the absence of any serious attack on what was commonly held to be orthodox doctrine and in the generally traditional character of his own views. (pp. 389-91)

Such is the partial intellectual rationalization of the traditional apparatus of doctrinal beliefs which Erasmus comfortably accepted. The paradoxical co-existence of this acceptance in fact and of an intellectual attitude which obscured the spiritual significance of such acceptance (almost without transforming the thing itself) by emphasizing the ethic at the expense of the mystery, is even more striking in his views on monasticism.

Erasmus had been in intimate contact with monasticism for many years prior to his arrival in Paris. From 1486 to 1492 he was an Augustinian Canon at Steyn, and even after his departure he remained in close connection with his monastery through correspondence and by frequent return visits. In Paris he spent his first academic year in Montaigu College, a foundation whose austerity, vigorously maintained by the extraordinary personality of the reformer John Standonck, was considerably less tarnished than that of Steyn. Its atmosphere of religious virtuosity put Erasmus in daily contact with one of the last and finest flowerings of the hermit temper; and although he left it in the spring of 1496, he remained in contact both with Standonck and with the reform movement he initiated late in the same year by introducing six Windesheim monks into the monastery of Château-Landon near Fontainbleau. (p. 394)

Erasmus was, therefore, in close contact with monasticism both before and during his stay in Paris. In the ***De contemptu mundi,*** written at Steyn, he praised monasticism, but "as a dispassionate critic who employed his reason far more than his feelings." In the works of his Paris years, while his attitude is not often one of explicit praise, there is nowhere an attack on monasticism as an institution or as a principle. Indeed, as in his devotion to St. Genevieve, a crisis could lay bare his emotional involvement with the traditional forms. For example, on leaving Montaigu after the same illness which provoked the appeal to the saint, he returned to Holland with the intention of remaining at Steyn, strange behavior after his efforts to get away. A more serious illness in April and May, 1498, from which he barely recovered provoked an even more passionate reaction:

> What is man's life, and with how much sorrow it is mingled! I have been almost killed by a slight fever, but one that recurs daily. I have now no liking for the world, and despise all those hopes of mine; I desire that life of holy rest, in which I may have leisure for myself and God alone, may meditate on the holy Scriptures, and wash out with tears my former errors.

That this was more than a pious effusion to please the Prior of Steyn is clear from a letter to Arnold Bostius, a Carmelite of humanistic inclinations, with whom Erasmus had a less official connection:

> Take this for one thing; the world has long lost its attraction for me. I pass sentence on all my hopes. I wish for nothing but that leisure may be given me, in which I may live wholly to God, bewail the sins of my thoughtless age, busy myself with the holy Scriptures, and read or write something.

These are perhaps the most fervent lines Erasmus ever wrote on monasticism. Discouraged and weakened by illness, he thinks with longing of Steyn and of a holy and secluded life. One is curiously reminded that, after all, Erasmus was himself a monk.

This state of mind was not maintained for long. Indeed, even in the last letter he has recovered sufficiently to want to "read and write something" as well as bewail his sins. A more characteristic point of view was soon regained. This consisted in a full and sincere acceptance, qualified by a personal reservation, of monasticism as a principle and as an institution. Monasticism, he felt, was a perfectly acceptable life for some; he himself was unsuited for it. Consciously, he justified his lack of rapport with the cloister in terms of the fragility of his health:

> I cannot do this [lead a pious life] in a college or retreat, as I am in extremely delicate health. My constitution, even when at its best, cannot bear vigils or fastings or any discomforts. I fall ill from time to time even here, where I live so luxuriously; what should I do among the hardships of conventional life?

This is no criticism of monasticism *per se,* but merely the expression of an intensely personal desire to avoid physical hardship. (pp. 395-96)

Unlike monasticism, prayers to saints, or the corpus of orthodox doctrine, scholasticism was an aspect of the religious tradition Erasmus never wholly accepted. In this he merely reflects a mean position between the extremes of mysticism and scepticism which gradually grew out of the disintegration of the Thomistic synthesis. Like Gaguin, and indeed like Standonck, he had only contempt for the disputes of Realists and Nominalists, the subtleties of Terminist logic, and the cumbrous complexities of a Biblical exegesis whose pedantry was too often realized. His opinion of scholasticism as a method is pungently satirical. He ridiculed the "Catos" of the Sorbonne and derided their logical preoccupations in a contemporary colloquy:

> CHRISTIAN: Chrysippus is reported to have been so intent upon his logical subtleties, that he would have been starved at table, unless his maid Melissa had put the meat into his mouth.
>
> AUGUSTINE: He did not deserve to have his life saved.

Familiarized by four years of study in the theological faculty with the customary four-fold exegesis of Scripture and the *Sentences* of Peter Lombard, he mockingly applies it to wine:

> But there are some persons that are mighty deeply read in table philosophy, who deny that wine can be good, unless it pleases the four senses: the eye, with its color; the nose, with its smell; the palate, with its taste; the ears, by its fame and name.

Such a reaction against the methodological subtleties of scholastic theology was commonplace by the end of the Fifteenth Century. The attacks on the scholastic method found in the Paris ***Colloquies*** stand directly in the tradition of those in the *Imitatio Christi* and in the *De ignorantia* of Petrarch.

Toward scholasticism as a philosophic system, on the other hand, his reaction was more complex. Generally speaking, he showed little positive interest in it. As Huizinga has pointed out with customary insight, the cause lay partially in "the qualities of his own mind, which, in spite of all its breadth and acuteness, did not tend to penetrate deeply into philosophical or dogmatic speculation." For neither the rejuvenated Aristotelianism of Lefèvre d'Étaples nor the Florentine Platonism which was beginning to be known in France seems to have attracted him more than scholastic philosophy. His attitude to philosophy in general is curiously similar to his practice of invoking St. Genevieve:

> The philosophers of our time are wiser, who are content to dispute like Stoicks, but in living outdo even Epicurus himself. And yet for all that, I look upon Philosophy to be one of the most excellent things in Nature, if used moderately. I don't approve of philosophising too much, for it is a very jejune, barren, and melancholy thing. When I fall into any calamity or sickness, then I betake myself to Philosophy, as to a physician; but when I am well again, I bid it farewell.

This is typical Erasmus. As in his appeals to the saints or his views on monastic bachelorship, he combines an antique respect for the moderate with a Rabelaisian appreciation of the here and now. The metaphysical speculations of the Florentine Neo-Platonists and of the Scholastics had, if nothing else, a high degree of otherworldliness in common, and one suspects that Erasmus felt that they were only playing with words, a matter of "quiddities," "instances," and "formalities" having little or no relation to reality.

This is confirmed by the "Epimenides" letter to Thomas Grey which provides an insight into the more positive aspects of Erasmus' philosophical and religious views. The tone of the letter is bantering and lightly satirical. Its substance is an attack on scholasticism from two points of view: that of the classical scholar on the one hand and that of the moralist on the other. The former was fully developed as early as the ***Antibarbari;*** and when Gaguin, commenting on this work, supported Erasmus' views, he was only echoing a feeling shared by most humanists. The criticism was in terms of purely classical learning: the barbarous Latin of the schoolmen and the arid gracelessness of their style. (pp. 400-02)

In religious terms such an attack on the theologians for their lack of enthusiasm for the style and polish of classical rhetoric is superficial; but when the *point d'appui* for criticism becomes moralized, Erasmus is more penetrating. At its lowest level it takes the form of a denunciation of hypocrisy. For example, in the ***Profane Feast*** Christian is made to ask:

> CHRISTIAN: Pray what sect are you of, a Stoic or an Epicure?
>
> AUGUSTINE: I recommend Zeno's rules, but I follow Epicurus' practice.
>
> CHRISTIAN: Austin, what you speak in jest, a great many do in earnest, and are only philosophers by their cloaks and beards.

> AUGUSTINE: Nay, indeed they out-live the Asots in luxury.

Philosophy is felt to be a veil of pretense over an unethical reality. The theologians pretend to sleep piously, but "thou knowest not theological slumber. There are many that in their sleep not only write, but slander and get drunk, and commit other indiscretions. I find many things are done in reality, which the inexperienced could in no wise be made to believe." In short, pious disquisitions cannot excuse immorality.

The reference to "theological slumber," however, and the whole Epimenides allegory of which it is a part, has a more profound significance in terms of Erasmus' concept of reality. The philosopher Epimenides, so the story goes, was once meditating in a cave, and while "he was biting his nails there, and making many discoveries about *instances* and *quiddities* and *formalities,* he was overcome by sleep." He slept for forty-seven years, and on awakening found the world changed beyond recognition. His slumber was theoretical, and Erasmus precisely relates it to the speculations of scholastic philosophy:

> But look now, my Thomas, what do you suppose Epimenides dreamed of, all those years? What else but those subtlest of subtleties of which the Scotists now make boast? For I am ready to swear that Epimenides came to life again in Scotus.

The explicit opposition is thus between theology and philosophy on the one hand and the external world, natural and human, on the other. The implicit assumption is that the one is unreal, the other real. Philosophical speculation is a dream with no relation to the real world which lives and changes while Epimenides sleeps. This is a concept of reality, unsystematic as it is, basically opposed to philosophical idealism. Reality is in the here and now, in man in his relation to man and to nature. In a very real sense, Erasmus, by equating reality and the physical world, has transferred the ideal from heaven to earth.

This concept of reality is the philosophic basis of Erasmus' emphasis on ethics and utility at the expense of the supernatural. It is from this basis that he goes on to attack theological speculation as an obscurantist cult which hides the religious mysteries from the people. Epimenides' skin, with letters on it, is guarded at the Sorbonne, and interpreted by a sacerdotal caste. Only the initiate may approach it for "if any other person ventures to direct his profane glances toward it, he straightway becomes blind as a mole." For Erasmus a secluded contemplative religion is essentially no religion at all. It is simply unreal. A theology existing in a vacuum, away from the people and from the real world, is pure folly. Conversely, theology if it is to be more than a dream, must be *lived,* and this requires a primary emphasis on its ethic. The sacred books must not be sealed away like an old skin, but must be given to men that they may lead better lives. This, in turn, tends to imply that Scripture is essentially didactic, and that its principal function is to provide an ethical code for man. That Scripture is also divine conveniently exempts the code from the scandal of relativism, enabling it to fulfill its function more usefully. And that function emphasizes life, the good life, of course. It is perhaps not insignificant that Erasmus first characterizes himself as a "primitive theologian" in this letter to Grey.

Yet it is equally significant that even yet Erasmus did not attack scholastic philosophy in philosophic terms. When he said that he looked "upon philosophy to be one of the most excellent things in Nature" he meant precisely that; and he was referring to scholasticism. It was part of the religious tradition, and he accepted it in the same way he accepted monasticism. That his own tendencies toward ethical secularism tended to undermine them both follows logically; but Erasmus' was not a logical mind in this systematic sense. It was his good fortune that he could compromise to the point where moderation became not only viable, but an ideal. Scholasticism was excellent "if used moderately"; monasticism acceptable "if out of a great number of children one virgin be offered to God." Thus his own ethical and secular emphasis was never systematized in opposition to scholasticism, but it is generally apparent only as an assumption underlying much of his thought. Most clearly stated in the letter to Grey, it even more completely, though more subtly, pervades the ***Praise of Matrimony.*** An ethical secularism is thus the reverse side of a religious belief which also included appeals to the saints, traditional doctrine, monasticism and which, despite the satire, did not really attack scholasticism in its own terms. Logical inconsistencies, though real enough, were hidden by the refusal of a moderate mind to make the opposition overt by explicit and precise formulation, or indeed to recognize the existence of that opposition itself.

A final ambiguity is apparent in Erasmus' views on the ethical character of the classics. Latin literature continued to be his first love and major occupation during his years in Paris. The humanistic bias apparent in the ***Antibarbari,*** and indeed even in the ***De contemptu mundi*** was perpetuated in the works and activities of these years. The titles ***De conscribendis Epistolis, De copia, De Ratione studii,*** the didactic beginnings of the ***Colloquia,*** perhaps the ***Paraphrase*** of Valla's *Elegantiae*—chart his interests almost statistically. His fondest aim remained the development of a flexible, harmonious style; his most conscious ideal, to be known as a poet and orator, and to live a leisured, comfortable life discussing literature with his friends.

His acceptance of the religious tradition, however, made it unlikely that this mild and touching hedonism should be without a pious and conventional rationale. This was found in a two-fold justification of the classics from a religious point of view; the desirability of clothing Christian ideas in elegant language and the value of the classics as a repository of moral precepts and examples. The former was not unfamiliar to Erasmus before his arrival in Paris, but it is not unlikely that the views of the more conservative Gaguin influenced his own on this subject. The substance of Gaguin's argument was that fluency of style is the best preservative of a work. Ideas, however virtuously orthodox, have little chance of survival if barbarously presented, for "the memory of those who have a rather old-womanish, hesitating and stuttering style will truly last only a few days." Conversely "only those who have combined eloquence and knowledge are respected and renowned among men of letters." It follows that no better service could be done for Christian learning than to bless it with classical eloquence. Such eloquence, of course, must be seemly as well as classical, "not that wanton and fawning variety forever seeking verbal effects, so insipidly jejune, so mechanically honeyed. . . . " In this context the classics have a purely derivative, utilitarian character. Their raison d'être consists in their service to religion.

Beyond this the classics have a positive ethical value as well. They are filled with moral precepts and with examples whose Christian meaning can always be disclosed by a sufficiently allegorical ingenuity. (pp. 402-06)

It is paradoxical that in his emphasis on the possibility of moralizing the classics by allegory Erasmus is perhaps most medieval. As early as the ninth century Theodolphus, Bishop of Orleans and Latin versifier, had found in this notion the excuse for a more comprehensive sampling of the poets. They were often frivolous, of course, but beneath this skin of levity lay profound ethical truths. Theodolphus was not the last to perceive this, and throughout the Middle Ages the possibility of allegorical interpretations justified the reading of the pagan authors. Erasmus in a sense perpetuates this tradition. Equally traditional was his occasionally emphasized contention that the moral nature of the contents should determine the choice of authors to be read. Like Gaguin he could advise his pupils to "follow and seek to imitate serious and circumspect authors from whose sagacity you may instruct your natural gift and mould your character." (pp. 406-07)

Deep in the religious tradition was another concept to which Erasmus at least paid lip service when he followed Gaguin in maintaining the utilitarian and auxiliary character of the classics *vis à vis* religion. The Middle Ages had always preserved, with varying degrees of success, the relation between Christian and secular knowledge outlined by Augustine. The classics held a definitely secondary position in this relationship. Their purpose, if they had any at all, was to enable one to achieve a more sophisticated appreciation of Revelation. They were, in short, to be used, not enjoyed. Erasmus, as has been noted, appreciated the distinction. In the same way as he often found it convenient to neglect Terence and castigate Catullus, so also he could delegate the classics to the service of religion, making it "shine more brightly" with their aid.

Thus Erasmus accepted the views of traditional religion even on the humanistic studies. But as so much of the rest of what he had accepted from that source was either vitiated or transformed by his secular spirit, so too was this. The metamorphosis took place in different ways: on the one hand, by emphasizing the classics as an ethical source to such an unlimited degree that he passed far beyond the Medieval view, almost completely negating it by placing the classics on an ethical par with Scripture; on the other, by breaking, in practice, with the Augustinian dictum on the ends of classical study, a break which involved the virtual abandonment of the principle of *uti non frui.*

The former is evident in the ***De ratione studii,*** a little educational pamphlet detailing the proper course of studies for young students. Language claims the first place in the order of studies, and from the outset should include both Greek and Latin, for "within these two literatures is contained everything which we consider worth knowing." After a discussion of the best authors to read in order to acquire the necessary linguistic mechanics, he makes more precise remarks on authors who should be studied primarily for their content as opposed to ones previously read "for the purposes of vocabulary, ornament and style." He lays out the following rule of thumb: "Almost all factual knowledge [*rerum cognitio*] must be drawn from the Greek authors. For where else can one drink more profitably than from these very springs?" Furthermore, one finds here ethical insights as well. Among the Greeks four are preëminent in this respect: Plato, Aristotle, Theophrastus, and Plotinus; among the Latins: Pliny, Macrobius, and Aulus Gellius. The Fathers, so carefully mentioned in Erasmus' letter to his ecclesiastical patron, are markedly absent; and this absence here, in the work as written in Paris, is emphasized by their presence in later editions. For example, by 1514, the date of the first authorized edition, the passage on the moral authors has become:

> Indeed, to lay in a store of ancient wisdom the studious master must go straight to the Greeks; to Plato, Aristotle, Theophrastus and Plotinus; to Origen, Chrysostom, Basil. Of the Latin Fathers, Ambrose will be found most fertile in classical allusions. Jerome has the greatest command of Holy Scripture.

The implication of the original version is apparently that the classic moralists are an ethical source as valuable, and indeed, as authoritative, as the Fathers; while the absence of all mention of Scripture leaves even its position in some ambiguity. The Medieval practice of using the moral lessons embedded in the classics as a justification for reading them has been far transcended here. Indeed, the ethical validity of the classics is so completely taken for granted that the notion of justification itself has largely disappeared. Peers of the Fathers, they can stand on their own merits. Theodolphus' opening wedge has been carried to the point of contradiction.

The method of ethical allegory has been carried to a similar extreme. There is really nothing, however obscene or lacking in Christian virtues, which cannot be beneficially interpreted by allegory. The clearest example is, of course, Terence. Although Erasmus could omit him in the letter to Thomas Grey, elsewhere he not only defends, but recommends him. (pp. 407-09)

More significant is Erasmus' virtual abandonment in practice, despite this echoing of Gaguin's contrary opinion, of the traditional religious view on the relation of the classics to Christian learning. His humanism was more radical than Gaguin's, and went far beyond a love of the classics which limited itself to imputing an ethical relevance to style, the only field "where a man is enabled to surpass another without injustice." Its more revolutionary character, like that of the Italians, lay precisely in the fact that it was enjoyed for its own sake. Erasmus might love a Terence comedy or a dialogue of Lucian for its wit, its stylistic fluency, or its content. But more significantly, he brought to it a point of view and an imaginative grasp which enabled him to appreciate and enjoy it as a work of art, in its own terms. Such an absolute, non-hierarchical frame of reference is possible only to a mind essentially secular. Its spirit is joyful and needs no justification for its aesthetic pleasure and love of life.

Erasmus has given us a glimpse of this spirit in a letter written for one of his pupils to send to his brother in Germany, a pupil of former years:

> On the first of August, which was to me the brightest of days, when we had had a cheerful, and quite luxurious supper,—but who and how many? you will ask. I answer, three as good men and true as ever trod the ground; Erasmus, now indeed our own, Augustine the common friend of all. . . and thirdly myself, while you were not altogether absent. Delightful companions, the time suitable, the place well-chosen, the proper arrangements not neglected. How often did we drink Christian's health, how often did we long for his company! . . . After the second course we took a stroll in the very place among the vineyards, where, as Erasmus told us, he had more than once sauntered with you after finishing a bottle, when he recalled you by his eloquent exhortations from sordid cares, and ravished your whole soul with love of Letters. Do you recognise the spot? There Erasmus fed us with lettered speech, more delicate fare than the supper we had eaten.

In view of this peroration it is not surprising that the justification entailed by his acceptance of the religious tradition should be unconvincing. It may be splendid to clothe Christian ideas in a classical style, but one wonders whether it is to the ideas or the style that primary allegiance has been given. And when what is in Terence a joyful, gay, and even witty seduction is reputed to be, at the worst, a frivolous parable, a distinction between authors in terms of traditional Christian morality tends to have little significance. Similarly, when Lycurgus and Moses are equated; when Jonathan and David share allegorical honors with Orestes and Pylades; and when it is implied that most, if not all, moral learning is derived from selected Greek and Roman authors, the source of moral authority and example becomes ambiguous indeed.

Yet it was precisely in such ambiguities that Erasmus achieved an intellectual *modus vivendi* with the religious tradition. By emphasizing common ends, diversity of allegiance became less harrowing; while secularism and a supranatural religious inheritance might be drained of practical antagonism if aims foreign to neither could be found and emphasized. Ethics was the area most suitable for such adjustments. The ethical aspects of Christianity were consequently emphasized at the expense of its less worldly elements. At the same time, nothing was rejected, nothing formally altered. Erasmus' very appreciation of worldly charms denied fanaticism. There is merely a shift in emphasis, a shift which nevertheless reflects a profound spiritual transformation. For in Erasmus one sees the emergence of a new ideal, the good life, the result of a synthesis of the Christian and antique differing in character from that accomplished by the Middle Ages. Its formulation is classical, yet it is meaningless outside the context of Christian ethics. The "good" is secularly joyful and optimistic; but it is also morally seemly. "Life" implies the world, but it further implies an archetype in the life of Christ.

The emergence of this ideal in Erasmus' thought and life was singularly organic, rather like a snake preparing to shed portions of its skin and finding the replacement already at hand. The process was almost wholly unconscious, whether in discarding the old or assuming the new. The vitiation of the supranatural in Christianity was consequently not premeditated, nor sought, nor even recognized in those terms. Yet the very fact that this aspect was neglected and not deeply felt encouraged atrophy. Unwilling and unable to deny its inheritance, Erasmus' secularism chose for emphasis those elements most suitable to its temper. The result was a new synthesis lying beneath an accepted tradition, rarely explicit or consciously recognized, but imbuing that tradition with its own point of view and its own meanings. (pp. 409-11)

Eugene F. Rice, Jr., "Erasmus and the Religious Tradition, 1495-1499," in Journal of the History of Ideas, *Vol. XI, No. 4, October, 1950, pp. 387-411.*

Wallace K. Ferguson (essay date 1953)

[Ferguson was a Canadian educator who wrote widely on the Renaissance and Reformation. In the following excerpt from a paper read before the New England Renaissance Conference in 1953, he examines the Enchiridion *and the prefatory materials to Erasmus's first editions of the New Testament as evidence of the humanist's enlightened religious thought.]*

To define Renaissance tendencies in religious thought may seem a rash undertaking, as hazardous as the attempt to define the Renaissance itself, for in that transitional age the most varied tendencies were manifest on every hand. There can be no general formula for the piety or theology of a period that contained such exponents of the worldly authority of the Church as were the majority of the popes from John XXII to Julius II, such orthodox reformers as Gerson and Cusa, such heretical reformers as Wyclif and Huss, such sceptical critics as Lorenzo Valla, such humanists in the Vatican as Pius II, such practical mystics as the Brethren of the Common Life, and, in the generation immediately preceding the Reformation, such diverse religious types as Savonarola, Pico della Mirandola, John Colet, Noel Beda and Cardinal Ximenes. Yet, within this mixture of the medieval and the modern, there are, I think, certain tendencies that were peculiar to the age itself, however firmly their roots might be fixed in the past and however far their branches might reach into the future. And these were to a remarkable degree gathered together and welded into a coherent, if unsystematic, synthesis in the thought of Erasmus. In the words of Imbart de la Tour: "If it is true that in all the great epochs of thought there arises a man who summarizes the tendencies of his age, such a man was Erasmus."

So many tendencies, indeed, entered into the religious

thought of Erasmus that it seems at times fraught with inconsistencies, especially to those who regard it retroactively from the viewpoint of either Wittenberg or Trent. He was, in fact, the most unsystematic of philosophers, both by natural inclination and by conscious design. (p. 499)

The difficulties inherent in analyzing the thought of so unsystematic a thinker as Erasmus are rendered more acute by the fact that it was expressed most commonly in isolated *obiter dicta* or in little gems of satire scattered throughout works ostensibly designed for other purposes. Moreover, he trusted to wit rather than to logical exposition to make his points, and his constitutional inability to reject a good phrase once it had occurred to him sometimes drove him to make comments that a sober second thought might have suppressed. In two places only, with the possible exception of the ***Praise of Folly,*** did he attempt a formal and reasonably systematic presentation of his religious thought. In the ***Enchiridion Militis Christiani*** (first published in 1503 and reissued with a notable prefatory epistle in 1518) he offered a comprehensive guide to Christian piety. And in the prefatory materials published in 1516 and 1519 with the first two editions of the Greek New Testament, he presented the clearest statement of his conception of the nature of Christian theology. These included a ***Paraclesis ad Lectorem Pium,*** the ***Methodus*** which in the second edition was expanded into a lengthy essay significantly entitled ***Ratio seu Methodus compendio perveniendi ad veram theologiam,*** and finally an ***Apologia*** defending his presentation of a critical edition of the New Testament in its original tongue together with a new Latin translation. We may take these works as the principal evidence for the positive religious thought and emotion which formed the solid kernel of Erasmus' philosophy, but which elsewhere was usually expressed in the more negative form of criticism of the abuses and absurdities that he saw about him in the Church, the theological faculties and the society of his day.

There is actually very little in these works that can be regarded as original, except as the whole bears the unmistakable imprint of an original mind. Innumerable scholars have traced the intellectual antecedents of almost all of his most characteristic ideas, finding them in varying degree in the influence of Colet and his other English friends, of the Belgian theologian Jean Vitrier, of Lorenzo Valla, of Pico and the other Florentine Platonists, of Thomas à Kempis and the Brethren of the Common Life or simply in the teaching of Jesus Christ. It is not, however, my intention to reassess once more the intellectual sources of Erasmus' piety and theology, though the fact that parallels to his ideas may be found in so many diverse places is in itself significant, whether the parallelism was the result of direct borrowing or of independent progress toward similar conclusions. Rather I should like to note the correspondence of certain dominant tendencies in his religious thought to certain basic tendencies in the social and cultural evolution of the Renaissance period, and to suggest that it is in noting these that we will approach most closely to an understanding of the degree to which Erasmus was the representative figure of his age. For Erasmus, though incurably literate, was a man who learned not only from books. Throughout his adult life he wandered constantly over the face of the earth, observing and talking to men everywhere, drawing his own independent and frequently caustic conclusions, but also absorbing ideas and attitudes from the social atmosphere he breathed.

As a basis for this discussion. . . . I would say that the Renaissance was in essence a transitional age, one of the basic characteristics of which was that the economic, social and cultural balance was in process of shifting from the clerical and feudal elements that had dominated the Middle Ages to the lay and urban elements that have so largely dominated the modern world. And in that process one of the decisive factors was the increasing participation of laymen, and especially of urban laymen, in intellectual, religious and other forms of cultural activity. From this resulted an irreparable breach in the clerical monopoly of learning, a more questioning attitude toward ecclesiastical authority and a gradual laicization of religion and culture. From the growing complexities and expanding opportunities of this age of social dislocation, there also emerged a stronger awareness of individual personality and the rights of the individual. And this individualism found expression in equal degree in the religious and cultural life of the age.

A 1535 Holbein woodcut depicting Erasmus and the image of Terminus, the figure Erasmus adopted as his personal emblem.

For the religious life of the Renaissance it was of primary importance that the preponderant mass of the middle and upper classes was learning to read and was no longer solely dependent on the clergy for religious instruction and inspiration. This of course was to become increasingly true in the following centuries. What was peculiar to the Renaissance was the coincidence of this new phenomenon with a crisis in the history of the Church, as the medieval Church strove to adjust to the new forces of money economy and nationalism, while still retaining all its accustomed claims to secular power. Within the Church the administrative authority of the papacy was strengthened during the fourteenth and fifteenth centuries by increasing centralization of government, but the preoccupation with fiscal concerns that was a necessary concomitant to this development seriously weakened the moral authority of the clergy and bred a tendency to place a more materialistic emphasis upon the mere mechanics of salvation. And in reaction to these tendencies there grew throughout Europe, but especially in the northern countries, a specifically lay piety, orthodox in the main, but tending to shift the emphasis from the means of salvation to the individual's direct relation to God, and from theological dogma to the Christian conduct of daily life. It is this specifically lay piety that found its clearest expression in the ***Enchiridion Militis Christiani.***

This guide to Christian living was addressed to a layman, we are told, a courtier friend of the author, who was apparently much in need of it. It was obviously written for laymen and written, moreover, by one who in his manner of life and point of view was as nearly a layman as was possible at that time for anyone who had once entered a monastic order. The lay quality of its piety is as notable in what is omitted as in what is included. There is almost no reference to dogma save for those basic Christian doctrines that Erasmus loved to call the Philosophy of Christ; and such incidental references as there are to the services of the Church place them in a category of secondary importance.

Four major themes run through the entire work. The first is a persistent emphasis on the inner life of the spirit in contrast to all external observances, ceremonies and what were technically termed good works. This theme is founded upon a lengthy discussion of the distinction between soul and body, the inner and the outer man, and an identification of the former with things invisible, the latter with things visible, that might have been inspired as much by Neoplatonism as by Christianity. Without making the connection quite clear, he seems to make this distinction one of the bases for his perpetual contention that all external acts and visible symbols are of secondary importance and may degenerate into superstition.

> Consider perfect piety to be constituted in this one thing only, [he writes] that thou attemptest always to progress from things visible, which are for the most part imperfect or indifferent, toward things invisible, according to the division of man already discussed. This precept, indeed, pertains to the matter, since through neglect or ignorance of it most Christians are superstitious rather than pious and, except for the name of Christian, are not far removed from the superstitions of the gentiles.

True, he asserts repeatedly that he does not condemn formal observances as harmful, provided they are merely adjuncts to the Christian life. They may even be very helpful to those who are immature and infirm of spirit, and they should be practised by the more perfect lest they cause their weaker brethren to offend. . . . He does make it clear, however, that if pursued as an end in themselves, or regarded as the whole duty of a Christian man, formal observances may become pernicious.

The kernel of Erasmus' thought is an abiding faith that piety is a matter of the spirit, and all else is secondary. "It is the spirit that quickeneth; the flesh profiteth nothing." And he illustrates this theme with some pointed observations on the inadequacy of such practices as being buried in a religious garb, fasting, pilgrimages, veneration of relics, indulgences and even confession without full participation of the spirit. (pp. 500-03)

This is the first theme. The second is like unto it. True piety consists in the application to daily life of Christian virtues and the spirit of Christ. The obligation so to live, moreover, is laid upon all men, not only upon the professionally religious. . . . It is a call to the pious layman to practise his religion in practical deeds, not in external observances. "The uses of the spiritual life lie not in ceremonies, but in charity to thy neighbor."

It is also in essence an appeal to the individual conscience. That is where the emphasis lies. This is, indeed, a third theme, which runs throughout the book, but is developed especially in the early chapters where he enlarges on the theme: "know thyself," and stresses the need for constant examination of one's motives. The battle of the Christian knight is an inward and personal one, a matter primarily concerning the individual man. There is a distinct Renaissance note, too, in his suggestion that an efficacious remedy against falling into sin may be found in contemplating how unworthy it is of the dignity of man, as there is also in his confident assertion of the freedom of man's will. "The human mind never willed anything vehemently that it could not accomplish. The great part of Christianity is to will with the whole heart to be a Christian."

A fourth theme that runs implicitly or explicitly throughout the ***Enchiridion*** is that the only pure source of the Christian religion is to be found in antiquity, in the teaching of Christ and the apostles as set forth in the New Testament, interpreted when necessary by the earliest Fathers who were themselves close to the ancient sources, and supported by the wisdom of the ancient pagans, especially Plato and the Stoics, whose philosophy he found in many ways conformable to that of Christ. But this brings us to consideration of another of the major tendencies which we have noted in Renaissance culture: the laicization of learning, the most characteristic aspect of which was classical humanism. In their passionate desire to recover the literary treasures of antiquity, a desire inspired, as I have suggested elsewhere, by the needs of a rising class of educated urban laymen, the humanists developed a science of their own, that of philology. It was, as distinguished from the clerically dominated learning of the medieval universities, a layman's science, and what they drew from the philosophy of the ancients was essentially a layman's philosophy, dealing largely with moral problems rather than with metaphysics, unsystematic, and expressed in cultivated prose rather than in syllogisms or the technical jargon of the schoolmen. Whether actually a layman or technically a cleric, the typical humanist was a professional scholar and man-of-letters but an amateur philosopher and theologian. And it was thus that Erasmus, with a depth of religious feeling drawn from the contemporary currents of lay piety, undertook to place the fruits of classical scholarship at the service of Christian theology.

The Greek New Testament and the critical editions of the Fathers are the measure of his practical contribution to that end. And in the ***Ratio seu methodus*** he outlined his conception of how a theologian should be trained and by what methods he could attain to true theology. In the first place, the theologian should have a competent knowledge of the three ancient languages—Latin, Greek and Hebrew. This should be a first consideration: "citra controversiam prima cura debetur." There is no possibility of knowing what is written if you do not understand the language in which it is written. Next he argues the desirability of a general education, from which—and he mentions especially historical books—one may acquire a useful knowledge of the words and things mentioned in the Bible as well as the geography of the places and the history, manners and institutions of the people referred to there. The youth destined for theology should also be trained in the rules of grammar and rhetoric. The methods of dialectic and sophistical disputations, on the other hand, merely chill comprehension of the sacred Scriptures. Paul and the early Fathers did not despise poetry, rhetoric or profane learning. "But where," he asks, "in these is there any mention of first and second intentions, syllogistic forms, or formalities or quiddities or even haecceities?" And again: "What could be more different from the style of the prophets, Christ and the Apostles than that in which those who follow Thomas and Scotus now dispute about sacred matters?" This is the deeply-rooted prejudice of the humanist man-of-letters against the rigid logic and barbarous jargon of the schools, the amateur theologian's protest against the willful obscurities propagated by the professionals. But this is merely the negative side of his program. The positive side appears again in his insistence that the budding theologian should draw his knowledge of Christian doctrine as far as possible directly from the evangelical sources. These he should study with the utmost care, giving due consideration to the time, place and circumstance of each saying, collecting and comparing passages on all subjects, and learning to cite the Scriptures appositely, not distorted out of context. If he follows this method he will need no commentaries, for those who first wrote commentaries had none to follow, and others can do the same. Nor will he need the learning of the schools. At any rate, "It is better to be ignorant of the dogmas of Aristotle than not to know the decrees of Christ. . . . He is an abundantly great doctor who teaches Christ purely. If it is shameful not to know what Scotus defines, it is more shameful not to know what Christ has ordained."

This layman's declaration of independence is characteristic of Erasmus' whole approach to theology, for what he thought most essential in it were those simple doctrines and ethical teachings set forth by Christ and the Apostles in the New Testament so plainly that the wayfaring man though a fool might not err therein. True, he was not always consistent in this, for there was an inherent conflict between what might be called the democratic tendency of lay piety and the aristocratic tendency of lay learning as represented by the humanists. But it was a conflict that, like other inconsistencies in his thought, did not seriously trouble Erasmus, for the conflict was more apparent than real. As a classical scholar and serious student he could assert that a knowledge of Latin, Greek and Hebrew was essential to the understanding of sacred Scriptures. As an exponent of lay piety he could assert with equal conviction that nothing was needed but "a pious and alert mind, provided above all with simple and pure faith." In both instances he echoes the layman's protest against dependence on the clergy for religious instruction and against the clerical monopoly of the interpretation of the Bible. The essential matter was to get at the words of Christ directly, not through glosses and commentaries, and it was to this end that he devoted his philological labors. If he railed against the ignorance of those who did not know the biblical languages, it was the ignorance of the theologians—those ancient parrots—rather than that of the laymen that he had in mind. The theologian should read the Bible only in its original tongue, but the Scriptures should also be available to laymen who could not even read Latin. Nowhere is the right of every layman to independent access to the Scriptures more clearly stated than in Erasmus' preface to the Greek New Testament.

> I dissent most vehemently from those who would not have the divine Scriptures read by the unlearned, translated into the vulgar tongue, as though Christ taught in such an involved fashion that he would be but barely understood by a few theologians, as though the safeguard of the Christian religion lay only in its being unknown. . . . I would desire that all little women (*omnes mulierculae*) should read the Evangel, should read the Pauline epistles. And would that these might be translated in all languages so that they might be read and known, not only by Scots and Irishmen, but even by Turks and Saracens. . . . Would that from these the ploughman might sing at his plow, and that with something from these the weaver might keep time to his loom; would that with stories from these the traveller should while away the tedium of his voyage."

Just as in the ***Enchiridion*** he maintained that the religious life is not limited to the formally religious, but is open to all, so here he argues that "since baptism and the other sacraments and finally the reward of immortality are equally common to all Christians, it is not to be tolerated that dogma alone should be relegated to the few who are known today as theologians or monks." On the contrary, he who teaches the simple piety of Christ and exhorts and inspires thereto, "he, indeed, is a true theologian though he be a digger or a weaver." I will add one final quotation that sums up Erasmus' approach to both theology and Christian piety.

> This kind of philosophy [*i.e.*, the philosophy of Christ], which lies in the state of mind more truly than in syllogisms, is a way of life rather than a disputation, inspiration rather than erudition, *transformation magis quam ratio.* To be learned falls to the lot of but few, but there is no one who cannot be a Christian, no one who cannot be pious; I may add this boldly: no one who cannot be a theologian.
>
> (pp. 504-08)

Wallace K. Ferguson, "Renaissance Tendencies in the Religious Thought of Erasmus," in Journal of the History of Ideas, *Vol. XV, No. 4, October, 1954, pp. 499-508.*

Louis Bouyer (essay date 1955)

[*In the following excerpt from a work originally published in France in 1955, Bouyer discusses* The Praise of Folly, *claiming that too much meaning has been read into the work: that it was simply a lighthearted diversion written by Erasmus during a bout of illness.*]

With Erasmus we reach the maturity of the entirely new type of Christian personality and thought that we have seen in preparation under teachers such as Vittorino da Feltre, and flowering in that youthful prodigy, Pico della Mirandola. Erasmus was only three years younger than Pico, but his career continued until 1536, and humanist theology, in the sense in which we understand it here, was able, in his hands, to cast off the impetuosity and exuberance of youth. It is noteworthy that a man from the Low Countries was unquestionably the chief representative of this phase of humanism. With the end of the fifteenth century Italian humanism may be said to have ended. Its development seems to have been arrested. After a period of quiet, which might give an illusion of stability, though decay could already be detected, it withered and straightway collapsed. (p. 95)

Since we are concerned not with a study of the enormous output of Erasmus, but with an understanding of his spirit and general trend, the years at Basel—when 'Erasmianism' showed itself clearly as lying between an ultra-conservative Catholicism and the Protestant innovators—are the really significant ones. The close scrutiny to which Renaudet has subjected them in his *Etudes érasmiennes,* together with the synthesis he has formed so judiciously, make him the obvious guide to follow; though we reserve the right to criticise him after he has introduced us to the heart of the problems involved. But we must, first of all, dispose of the one question which stands in the way of anyone desirous of interpreting the work and the thought of Erasmus, and that will complete our introduction to the finest example of humanist theology.

The problem is that raised by Erasmus' ***The Praise of Folly.*** The great majority of authors who have spoken of Erasmus seem for the most part to have read nothing else of his than this slight volume, or else to have read (or perused) the rest of his works in the light of this lively but sibylline pamphlet. In addition, the most surprising errors are often committed by not paying attention to the literary genre which it represents. This results in interpretations which, seemingly literal, are yet completely misleading. These have to be weeded out; for, if they were admitted, there would be no point in proceeding further. It would be as profitable to examine the theology of Lucan or of Voltaire, as to attempt to elucidate that of Erasmus.

At first sight, indeed ***The Praise of Folly*** might pass for an extravagant mockery of Catholic theology or the Church itself, not to speak of other institutions whose connection with the latter made them all a part of what was still called Christendom.

But first it must be said that the literary genre of ***The Praise of Folly*** is of its very nature highly misleading. It is akin to those verbal pleasantries which grow and expand in a small select group, and then, one fine day, are given shape and published to the outside world. They begin as a game, the kind of thing indulged in by a group of students or artists. In becoming the object of continual allusions, apparently in all seriousness to those outside the group, but to the initiate merely flippant, the game is completely baffling to one who only reads about it. And no key can ever quite give the exact meaning of the text in question. To understand it, and particularly to judge of its importance, one must have been a participant in the common elaboration of the burlesque. In other words, publication of this kind of thing inevitably leads to misunderstanding; it is a psychological error. If it interests anyone outside the group, it is only because he is one of the targets of abuse, and such are not likely to learn from it. That is the case with the ***Encomium Moriae.***

Written down in one sitting by Erasmus, after a long and intimate talk with Thomas More, it is strongly redolent of that atmosphere *sui generis* which this very unusual saint always produced. In all justice to Erasmus it must be said that he did everything to warn the reader, beginning with a pun in the very title: ***Encomium Moriae.*** (The Praise of Folly . . . or of More.)

There are few men in all English history of whom humour is so characteristic as Thomas More. It is a quality almost incomprehensible to the Latin or the German. It belongs to the mind which loves to utter fantastic statements with complete imperturbability, but implying thereby, though in extremely paradoxical fashion, all sorts of common-sense truths. That was the very spirit of Thomas More. It is also precisely the spirit of ***The Praise of Folly;*** only that this has the inevitable drawback that parts of it cannot possibly be grasped by the uninitiated however intelligent, without becoming more or less falsified in the process.

It goes without saying then that this little book can only be understood in relation to the personality and works of More. Erasmus insisted on this continually, but unfortunately, practically no one has ever attempted it. There is not a single work of More's, whether of religious controversy, or even of edification, however serious, which does not contain page after page written in the same vein as ***The Praise of Folly.*** On the other hand Erasmus never tried his hand again at that sort of thing. We will shortly see how different is the style of the ***Colloquies,*** which are certainly the work of Erasmus. Consequently, we are bound to attribute the ***Folly*** to a wholesale appropriation or, perhaps, a momentary intoxication of Erasmus by More's humour.

The calmness and remorseless logic with which the most outrageous explanations of human life, and particularly of religion, are upheld in the book must not mislead us. This pseudo-nihilism is perfectly compatible with a robust faith. In fact, he is simply laughing at humbug, that is at people who confuse their personal insignificance with the importance of their function.

Such an interpretation is clearly indicated when we look at the ***Folly*** in conjunction with another cast of mind, prevalent in the Middle Ages, and more particularly in mediaeval Germany, whence came the humanism of Erasmus.

If there is one traditional theme not only in our fables, but especially in those basically religious productions such as the *danses macabres* of the fifteenth century, it is the pretended damnation of popes, princes and monks. To attribute to these satires a tendency analogous to our modern anticlericalism is to forget that those who perpetrated these things were more often than not the very persons who were being ridiculed. (In our own day, perhaps the most pungent stories about the clergy are those current among the clergy themselves).

We should, then, be in no hurry to see in the ***Encomium*** an attack on the papacy, or its ally the civil power, still less a bomb hurled at the Church; nor should we forget that Erasmus was a counsellor of the Empire, as well as a priest. It is simply a bitter satire against the identification by mediocre individuals of themselves and the causes they claim to be serving. Actually these causes come out quite unharmed inasmuch as they are never touched upon in the whole work. This is what Erasmus always asserted. Hence nothing justifies the attribution to him by the great majority of historians of a Machiavellian plan, the opposite of what he professed. All becomes clear if the ***Encomium*** is viewed in its proper setting and compared to other pieces of its kind. As he himself has said, the ***Encomium*** only took on a different meaning when long after its composition and publication, this satire on persons was gratuitously interpreted as a satire on institutions. The blame for this rests on Hutten and Luther. The prudence, or otherwise, of publishing such an enigmatic work is a totally different matter. But again it must be remembered that in 1515 it was difficult to foresee what the heretics, who were at that time still considered irreproachable Catholics, would make of it ten years later.

One thing is certain, and it is all that concerns us here, namely, that ***The Praise of Folly*** must be allowed the same latitude that all competent historians today grant to More's *Utopia.* Both are deliberately paradoxical works written in leisure moments, and in such cases the most literal interpretations are the most fallacious. All the more reason then, for not allowing such works—mere youthful amusements—to influence our judgement of other far more extensive ones, written in extremely critical circumstances. Written as it was in a lighthearted frame of mind when there was nothing serious to engage the attention, the book must not be allowed to influence our study of the longer works written at the height of the storm, and still less be held to dispense us from it. The way is now clear for the work in hand. (pp. 95-102)

Louis Bouyer, "Erasmus, More and 'The Praise of Folly'," in his Erasmus and the Humanist Experiment, *translated by Francis X. Murphy, Geoffrey Chapman, 1959, pp. 95-102.*

Craig R. Thompson (essay date 1957)

[*Thompson is an American educator who has written widely on Renaissance literature. In the excerpt below, he examines the composition, purpose, and history of the* Colloquies.]

In approaching the work of Erasmus, it may be better to keep before us the dates 1495-1536—those years in which virtually all his writings were produced—than to rely overmuch on conventional tags or generalizations about him and his epoch. Generalizations we must have, but they are more likely to be profitable if they develop from our reflections after we have read the texts than if they come to us ready-made. "Greatest humanist of the Renaissance," or some similar phrase, is the label usually attached to the name of Erasmus in encyclopedias or introductions. The label is correct but not precise. It is familiar; it tells us something at a glance, as a label should; but it begs the large, complex question of just what "Renaissance" and "humanist" mean. Try to define these words closely, and the difficulties quickly appear.

Fortunately, our reading of Erasmus or other sixteenth-century authors does not depend on agreement concerning the concept of "Renaissance" or the question of the relationship of the Renaissance to the Middle Ages. These are, of course, genuine and important problems, to which historians have found an impressive variety of solutions. There was a Renaissance, to be sure. We could argue that there have been many renaissances, in different lands, different ages, different activities. "Humanism" is equally ambiguous in common usage. It identifies modes of thought and art and education, yet some so-called humanistic doctrines are irreconcilable with others described by the same word. "Human," "humanistic," "humane," "humanitarian" all have distinctive meanings of their own in addition to common basic meanings. Erasmus the humanist was a Christian supernaturalist; but in certain modern writings on religion we often find "humanism" contrasted with "supernaturalism," as though the phrase "Christian humanist" were a contradiction in terms. Yet "Christian humanist" (why not "humanist Christian"?) continues to be used as a stock term in books about the Renaissance. "The" Renaissance? Even if we were to settle on "the" Renaissance and agree on the date of its occurrence, we should have to decide whether we meant renaissance generally (whatever that would be) or a renaissance in painting, literature, music, science, or some other department of human culture. We should discover that although there is sense in talking about "a renaissance" or "the Renaissance" in one field of activity, for example in Italian painting during a certain period, we must qualify the word "Renaissance" or readjust it as we move on to, say, seventeenth-century English poetry. Milton the Puritan was a Renaissance writer. So were Aretino, Calvin, Rabelais, Leonardo, More, Donne, Loyola. How much have they in common except that they all wrote in the sixteenth or seventeenth century?

Whatever the answer to this question, we may be sure that the more we investigated the history of the terms "Renaissance" and "humanism" or "humanist," the more complicated we should find them. Like "medieval," like that irrepressible pair "classical" and "romantic," the words "Renaissance" and "humanism" have both historical and critical associations, and as a result they bear so many meanings that indiscriminate use of the terms may confuse rather than clarify thought. Any attempt to use them consistently would undoubtedly compel us to make distinctions between other renaissances and "the" Renaissance in an art or a branch of learning or a region, and between "the" Renaissance in one century and "the" Renaissance in other centuries.

This much by way of caution only, not of prohibition, for labels so well established are unlikely to be discarded; nor need they be shunned if they are used with proper care. Erasmus himself used the concepts of "Renaissance" and "humanities" or "humane letters," although his terms for them did not always have the same reference that comparable terms have in modern English. To him, as to some other writers of the fifteenth and sixteenth centuries, "Renaissance" denoted first of all the recovery of sound (classical, they believed) Latin style, of literature and literary taste, after a long night of barbarism; that is, after the period that recent centuries have been pleased to look upon as the "Dark Ages" or "Middle Ages." Now this kind of Renaissance—which Erasmus, writing in 1518, dates from "about eighty years ago"—extended to certain other arts and studies also, yet the basis of it all was philological. The revival of philology opened the door to a new and improved understanding of ancient texts, sacred and secular. Philology, plus printing, made textual and historical criticism possible. Better understanding and teaching of sacred and patristic texts could lead to what, in the judgment of Erasmus, would be the greatest blessing of all those offered by the "Renaissance": the restoration of biblical theology, a theology liberated from Scholastic accretions and centered once more on what he constantly calls "the sources." (pp. vii-ix)

To infer that [Erasmus] wanted only to exhibit [the sixteenth century] world, or to record its ways for the sake of amusement, would be a serious error. He wanted to instruct it. But the writings by which he is best known to most modern readers are not those which he himself regarded as the most instructive or significant ones. He set more store by many others of his books than his ***Colloquies.*** In one colloquy, **"Cyclops,"** a character who is enumerating the calamities of the times says: "Kings make war, priests are zealous to increase their wealth, theologians invent syllogisms, monks roam through the world, the commons riot, Erasmus writes colloquies." The ironic anticlimax of this sentence is typical of the depreciatory tone Erasmus sometimes adopted in referring to his dialogues. On certain occasions he took them very seriously, as did his critics; on others, especially when it was advantageous to do so, he dismissed them as minor, lighter compositions. Probably both attitudes were sincere, despite apparent inconsistency. The attention he gave to the steadily expanding volume of colloquies, his concern for its reputation, and the trouble he took to defend it against attack are sufficient proof of his sensitivity about the book. On the other hand, if we examine his repeated affirmations of purpose as a writer, we can understand why the ***Colloquies*** could not, in his estimation, be counted among his most important works. He became fond of these dialogues; he came to take them far more seriously than he had at first; but many of them were essentially diversions, to be classed, like the ***Praise of Folly,*** among the writings described by his best editor as "trifles which he threw off to amuse himself, and of which he never ventured to be proud."

That Erasmus could change his mind from time to time regarding the ***Colloquies*** need not surprise us, then, provided we remember the main purpose of his lifework. This purpose was the advancement of learning and of the Christian religion. It was by his efforts in this direction that he wished to be judged. It was to this end that he produced, with prodigious toil, dozens of books, some of which remained useful to men for many generations: editions of the Fathers of the Church (Jerome, Cyprian, Hilary, Irenaeus, Ambrose, Augustine, Origen); editions and paraphrases of the Greek New Testament; commentaries and homilies; moral, religious, and political essays (e.g., ***Enchiridion, Ratio Verae Theologiae, Paraclesis, Modus Orandi Deum, Christiani Matrimonii Institutio, De Praeparatione ad Mortem, Ecclesiastes, Institutio Principis Christiani, Querela Pacis,*** to name only some of the best-known ones); works on education (***De Ratione Studii, De Copia, De Civilitate***); editions and translations of classical authors; a huge dictionary of proverbs, the ***Adagia.***

These, like everything else Erasmus wrote, were in Latin, the international language of educated men. Latin was the best way, indeed the only way, of reaching the readers he most desired to influence. He assumed, as did his public, that Latin should be the basis of education. For to understand the world, we must understand the past. And this obviously requires knowledge of the enduring human achievements in art, literature, law, philosophy. Since so many of these achievements were Greek and Roman, we must study Greek and Roman civilization; which means that first we must learn their languages. "Almost everything worth knowing has been set forth in these two tongues." (pp. xiii-xiv)

Few great books had more modest beginnings than the ***Colloquies.*** The earliest parts date from the closing years of the fifteenth century, when Erasmus was living in Paris. There he helped to support himself by tutoring. He prepared for his pupils some simple exercises designed to teach correct conversational and written Latin. These phrases and sentences, many of them in dialogue form, are the oldest material in our collection of ***Colloquies.*** They are of this sort:

> CHRISTIAN. I thank you. I commend you. So I invite you to dinner tomorrow. I beg you, then,

> to dine with me tomorrow. So I beg you to have lunch with me tomorrow. So I want you for my guest tomorrow.
>
> AUGUSTINE. But I fear I won't be free. I'm afraid I can't. I'll come if I'm free. But I'm afraid I won't be able to.
>
> CHRISTIAN. Why won't you be free? How come? Why so? What's the reason? On what ground? What cause? What's to hinder you? . . .
>
> AUGUSTINE. I can't promise. I can't assure you of it. I'm unable to promise for certain. I'll come when it's most convenient for both of us.
>
> CHRISTIAN. Then I wish you'd name the day on which you'll dine with me. Then you'll have to name the day. Then you must promise a day.
>
> AUGUSTINE. I wouldn't want you to know in advance. I don't want you to know in advance. I'll take you by surprise. . . .
>
> (pp. xviii-xix)

What the 1522 and 1523 editions made clear was that colloquies offered Erasmus an admirable medium for expressing, freely but informally, his observations on current issues, institutions, ideas, customs, and even individuals. The ten dialogues selected for translation in this book are typical Erasmian treatments of favorite topics, but the variety in the collection is greater than this group shows. Debates on moral and religious questions; lively arguments on war, government, and other social problems; advice on how to train wives, husbands, or children; discussion of innkeepers, beggars, and horse thieves, of methods of study or of sleep, of diet, funerals, and sermons; literary criticism; even a colloquy composed of puns—all this and much more is in the complete ***Colloquies.*** Dialogue was one of the oldest of literary modes in prose, to be sure, and in the sixteenth century one of the most popular, but nowhere in that period do we find it used with more brilliance or more assurance than in Erasmus' book. The ***Colloquies*** were journalism of a sort, but many of them journalism so superior, so artistic, so far from ephemeral that they became literature. Those added from 1522 on had plot and structure; some had impressive characterization as well. They were incipient dramas or novelettes. As such, they may have contributed more than we suspect to the development of drama and prose fiction during the sixteenth and seventeenth centuries.

Not all the colloquies are equally readable nowadays. Nor should we expect them to be, for in any large collection of writings there are bound to be inequalities. What matters is the large number of colloquies that can still give pleasure, still make the sixteenth century vivid to us. For all their sixteenth-century character and setting, these are no more out of date than the books of Rabelais or Cervantes. Sir Walter Raleigh's odd definition of great literature as that body of books which has been found useful in circumstances never contemplated by their authors fits the ***Colloquies*** neatly. True, they may have to be read in a different key as well as a different tongue. And they can be read profitably for purposes never considered by their sixteenth-century public; for instance, as an introduction to the social and intellectual environment of the sixteenth century itself. They take us by another route, through a different medium, into the milieu made familiar to us by Brueghel the Elder, Holbein the Younger, and Dürer, whose pictures are the best companions to the ***Colloquies*** a reader could wish.

To their author's natural dramatic talent were joined the moral purpose of a satirist and the temper of an ironist. Style is the man, we often hear. This man was shrewd, ironic, uncommonly observant, witty; at times able to suffer fools gladly. The irony was ingrained, a part of his character. We find it operative both in his serious and in his lighter works, but controlled by theme and purpose. In one composition, the ***Praise of Folly,*** it does more than affect the meaning. There theme and tone blend: the irony *becomes* the meaning. In the ***Colloquies*** irony is less pervasive and less profound, but still very important.

Less evident to some readers, but of interest to students of his thought, is the fact that the ***Colloquies*** often present in dramatic, informal dress the ideas Erasmus had already published, or was later to publish, in his more formal writings. Thus it is wise to check his essays and even commentaries against colloquies on the same or related themes. If we find that he writes an *ars moriendi* (***De Praeparatione ad Mortem,*** 1534), we shall do well to compare it with what he wrote on death and dying in the colloquy **"The Funeral"** . . . eight or nine years earlier. Half a dozen colloquies in the 1523 and the March, 1529, editions comprise a "marriage group" illustrating pointedly and entertainingly many of the admonitions set forth—with the customary positiveness of a moralist who is also a bachelor—in ***Christiani Matrimonii Institutio*** (1526). After reading **"Charon"** (1529), turn back to ***Institutio Principis Christiani*** (1516) and the famous ***Querela Pacis*** (1517). To understand better the position of Erasmus in the controversies over Luther and Lutheranism, read not only ***De Libero Arbitrio*** of September, 1524, but the little-known colloquy **"Inquisitio de Fide"** of March, 1524.

In appraising the ***Colloquies*** we have to remember that although this was a book which began as one thing and became something more, it did not forfeit its original purpose. It began as a school text, a short book of formulas, question-and-answer sentences, brief paragraphs of statement. Then it was enlarged; the dialogues grew longer, had plots, and could be read for their own sakes as much as for correct Latin forms. "It is the darling and delight of those who cultivate the Muses," Erasmus allowed himself to boast when dedicating the edition of August-September, 1524, to little Erasmius Froben. "This book makes better Latinists and better persons." It provided practice in learning Latin by the time-honored method of varying a phrase or sentence in order to show what different ways there are of expressing a meaning, and what the shades of difference signify. Like all successful texts, it made the examples relevant to the pupils' interests. It taught them how to express themselves *Latine* on matters of home, friends, parents, games, school, holidays, and the like.

The book "caught on" from the first. It became a standard textbook for schools, and continued to be used for three centuries. It was not the only book of Latin dialogues for schools, of course, nor the only popular one, but it outlasted its competitors; even in our own century one of the great university presses published adaptations of it for beginners in Latin. To many persons it must have been the book most commonly associated with the name of Erasmus, far better known than his formal tractates on education. We find it studied and imitated; we even hear of colloquies being acted out by pupils. To trace its fortunes in schools would require a survey of humanistic education for several centuries, and in the New World as well as the Old. The ***Colloquies*** came to America with the Puritans. Every Harvard student in the seventeenth century, we are told, "must have been familiar with the ***Colloquies*** of Erasmus," a familiarity gained, no doubt, in school rather than in college. A report on learning from modern Harvard gravely recommends putting "Renaissance Europe on the screen with the aid of Erasmus' ***Colloquies***" as an "immense educational eye opener." If this could be done without artistic damage to them, the ***Colloquies*** might prove as helpful in the teaching of history as they once were in linguistic and rhetorical training.

A student of literary history will notice in the ***Colloquies*** dozens of scenes or passages reminding him of themes, situations, and dialogues in vernacular literatures. Many a writer who had read the book, whether in school or out, must have remembered it. We know that Rabelais borrowed freely from it. Jonson knew it. Scott and Reade used whole colloquies for scenes in historical novels. It would be pleasant to be able to affirm that Shakespeare read and used it. We have no absolute proof that he did so, but there are a few phrases and lines in the plays that very probably came from Erasmus' book. Shakespeare's acquaintance with so popular a book is much more likely than unlikely.

The indebtedness of later writers to the ***Colloquies*** is a subject that deserves more attention than it has received. A comprehensive, critical account would not be easy to write. To list the obvious borrowings would be simple enough; to demonstrate indebtedness more subtle or elusive, though equally important, would not. Nevertheless the circulation of the ***Colloquies,*** and the impression we know it made on some sixteenth-century and later writers, justify us in thinking that there is much more to be found out and recorded about its influence on literature.

It was not popular with all readers. On the contrary, it was harshly condemned in some quarters. From the appearance of the 1522 editions until his death, Erasmus was compelled to defend it many times. He could—and did—protest that his too literal-minded opponents lost sight of the fact that sentiments expressed in a dialogue are those appropriate to the characters and to the dramatic situations, and are not necessarily the author's opinions. This was a perfectly plain, proper, and at times sincere defense. But it did not convince his stubborn critics, who suspected mere evasiveness in such replies.

Critics of the ***Colloquies*** made two major complaints. The first alleged that certain passages were indecent. This charge was not altogether surprising, for the book has a few passages that would probably be regarded as offensively coarse or as obscene by some readers today, as they were by some earlier readers. Erasmus attempted to brush the charge aside by retorting that the ***Colloquies*** was a book for boys, an answer that only made matters worse. He insisted that his dialogues were morally suitable as well as grammatically and rhetorically instructive for youth, scoffing at those who, he said, allowed boys to read the bawdy stories of Poggio but carped at the ***Colloquies.*** It is fair to say that whatever coarseness or obscenity there may be in the ***Colloquies*** is confined to a few pages.

The second complaint was more serious, and more troublesome to answer. It charged that many scenes of religious life and many utterances on religion were impious or heretical. Both Erasmus' words and the tone of those words were resented. His lively pages on the failings of monks and friars, his barbs at superstition and ignorance were bound to anger his persistent critics in the religious orders. Satire is sometimes a very effective social weapon, but the satirist must be prepared for counterattacks from those whose sensibilities he wounds or whose interests he endangers. As early as 1522, one of Erasmus' bitterest opponents, Nicholas Baechem (known as Egmondanus), Prior of the Carmelites at Louvain and also Inquisitor, wanted to burn the ***Colloquies,*** in which he believed he detected Lutheran heresies. More damaging than the opposition of a single official was that of the Sorbonne (the theological faculty of the University of Paris), the most celebrated and influential body of academic theologians in Europe. In May, 1526, the faculty censured the ***Colloquies,*** denouncing sixty-nine passages as questionable or heretical, and describing their author as a "pagan" who "mocked at the Christian religion and its sacred rites and customs." The book should be forbidden to all, especially to youth, said the faculty, lest under the pretext of instructing them it corrupt their morals. When rumors of the Sorbonne's intentions reached him, Erasmus added to the June, 1526, edition of the ***Colloquies*** a letter to the reader, ***De Utilitate Colloquiorum.*** This defense of his book denies accusations of indecency; on the contrary, says Erasmus, he has improved his young readers by inculcating piety and good manners along with good Latin, and he has condemned only the abuses of religion.

At times his pages disturbed patrons or friends also. While they might approve of the purposes of his satire, they thought his language went too far, or that he was unfair and thus likely to do more harm than good. In April, 1526, shortly before the action of the Sorbonne, he took care to assure Cardinal Wolsey that the ***Colloquies*** contained nothing unclean, irreverent, or seditious. A few years later Bishop Tunstall of London, a prelate who had long been favorably disposed toward Erasmus, objected to certain remarks on fasting, ceremonies, pilgrimages, and the invocation of saints.

Censure of the book continued as long as Erasmus lived, and long afterwards. In 1538, the *Consilium . . . de Emendanda Ecclesia,* a scheme of reform drawn up by cardinals appointed by Pope Paul III, recommended that the ***Colloquies*** "and any other books of this sort" be prohibited. When the Roman *Index Librorum Prohibitorum* was established, the ***Colloquies*** were in it, as they had been in earlier lists made by certain inquisitors, theological faculties, or synods. The Council of Trent condemned the entire ***Colloquies*** (1564). An *Index* of Paul IV (1559) had condemned all of Erasmus' commentaries, annotations, and translations as well as his ***Colloquies.***

A book enjoyed by so many, and yet offensive to others, must be valuable to any student of sixteenth-century thought and society. But it is not to be treated merely as a "source" for the information of historians. It is literature, and ought to be read and judged as literature. (pp. xxi-xxviii)

In the hands of Erasmus, Latin is no "dead" language but an instrument of thought and expression that is very much alive. The Latinity of the ***Colloquies*** is remarkably flexible in structure and tone, equally adaptable to dialogue, narrative, description; to sarcasm, banter, eloquence, or pathos. The difficulty of doing justice to this language in translation—that supreme risk for all literature—need not be pointed out to anyone who knows the original. So much felicity of style vanishes; so much of the wit goes lame. Yet a translator must hope to convey something of the spirit along with the sense of his author. If he fails, let him console himself with repeating what Erasmus says in the preface to his ***Paraphrase of Hebrews:*** "If you can't praise my wit and learning, at least give me credit for hard work." Or the translator may echo the apology of one of his sixteenth-century predecessors, Nicholas Leigh: "Because I have changed his eloquent style into our English phrase, and thereby altered his livery, and embased the perfect grace of his Muse, I am compelled to crave pardon of this my doings. Consider, I beseech thee (learned reader), that if it had still rested in that noble language wherein he left it, although thy knowledge had yielded thee greater felicity than this my travail can, yet thousands, which by this mine endeavor may draw out some sweet sap of these his pleasant and fruitful doings, might (through ignorance) have wanted this piece of delight. Therefore the offense (if any be) is made to Erasmus, a man of that patience in his life as I assure myself that this my bold dealing with him cannot a whit disquiet his ghost." (pp. xxviii-xxix)

Craig R. Thompson, in an introduction to Ten Colloquies of Erasmus, *by Desiderius Erasmus, translated by Craig R. Thompson, The Liberal Arts Press, 1957, pp. vii-xxix.*

Robert P. Adams (essay date 1962)

[*In the following excerpt, Adams examines the satiric element in several of Erasmus's works.*]

It is time to examine the antiwar satire in Erasmus' ***Praise of Folly.*** Should one not first ask, however, why Erasmus of Rotterdam holds so prominent a place in a study of *English* humanist social criticism? As the ferments of nationalism grew, many countries laid their claims to notable scholars, most of all to the widely traveled Erasmus. Was he not a Netherlander at heart, as say those who would minimize the importance of his English relationships? The "purest incarnation" of the Low Countries' genius in the arts of peace and civilization during the period just before the Wars of Religion exploded over Europe? Or none of these but instead above all a cosmopolitan and internationalist—"symbol of the bond that links men of learning across parochial, national, and ideological boundaries"? Something can be said—has been said—for all these views. I choose to side with those who, like A. L. Rowse, emphasize how much of Erasmus' greatest literary work grew out of the time between 1499 and 1517, when his life and work were so closely bound up with Colet and especially with More, with England. "Of this greatest of Europeans, it might almost be claimed that he was half an Englishman," just as Anglo-Saxon countries best appreciate "his humanitarianism, his love of peace and liberty, his lifelong service to international ideals, his spirit of moderation and tolerance in religion." Moreover, Erasmus' criticism of war is an integral part of the humanist thought on social reform which he developed together with Colet and More. And in the 1520's, Erasmus and More helped Vives to come to England as one (said Erasmus) by whom his own name would be overshadowed.

Erasmus' ***Praise of Folly,*** famous throughout the Europe of its day, is still well enough known to need little introduction. Perhaps its gaiety and verve can be best enjoyed, however, when it is squarely set at the dawn of what the humanists in England hoped was to be a new Golden Age of peaceful social reconstruction. The whole tone of the piece is bracing, optimistic, and constructive. Like all first-rate satire, it seeks to expose and explode accumulations of human asininities; idiot structures must be blown down (preferably by laughter) to clear the ground—and the air—for new ones better suited to decent human aspiration. Satiric laughter of Erasmus' kind seeks also to clear out pockets of decay, to repair what is worth saving. "Folly," in Erasmus' sense, means, comprehensively, human fatuity—but fundamentally of the curable kinds. Such a satire is possible only at one of those historic moments when the writer, at least, really believes that, if reason is brought rightly to bear, the human animal can yet be brought to live wisely and well, in harmony with his kind and the world around him. Satire grows despairing and suicidal when—as with the older Swift—pessimism overwhelms perhaps writer and readers alike, when man's age-old fatuities have taken on the sinister aspect of massive insanities, and hope for achievement of a rational and humane social order flickers very low. T. S. Eliot's *The Waste Land,* Franz Kafka's *The Trial,* Aldous Huxley's *Brave New World,* Arthur Koestler's *Darkness at Noon,* George Orwell's *Animal Farm* and *1984* suggest this bleak and terrible temper for western Europe in the mid-twentieth century.

It is important to remember the obvious—that in 1509 the London Reformers did *not* know that, just over the horizon, were to come the Lutheran turmoils, the terrifyingly swift collapse of the old medieval order (or what remained of it), and the explosion of Europe into the wars of religion. In the bright England of 1509, almost any good thing seemed possible to achieve, given wit, hard work, and the requisite royal leadership of a nobly Christian prince—Henry VIII. The ***Praise of Folly*** breathes an air of hope, of toleration, and of critical intelligence eager to be at work creating a peacefully reformed way of life. Whatever one may think of Erasmus as prophet in 1509, no one has ever been able to subject his satire to the fate of *Gulliver's*

Travels, which has been turned into an innocently droll fairy tale for children. Like Swift and Thomas More—perhaps like all great humorists and ironists—Erasmus, beneath the mask of laughter, is quite serious.

For our story, the ***Praise of Folly*** is most fascinating for its trenchant and central satire on war and warmakers, past and present. Within the whole work this forms a structure of relentlessly ironic social criticism, both destructive and constructive. Erasmus was addressing himself to an audience which, if schooled in the quite usual medieval patterns of thought, customarily regarded war (like the plague) as caused by man's sin and God's answering justice, yet at the same time (since St. Augustine) as an action approvable as just and Christian. The accretions of chivalrous romance, moreover, had dressed war in a heroic glamour suitable for one of nobility's most glorious occupations. In startling contrast, Erasmus presented a Christian-humanist image of war and warmakers as beastly, hellish, corruptive of human society, unjust, and unchristian. War is not treated as an incurable form of human folly; it is not in the nature of things inevitable and necessary; it is corrupted men who make it so. The satire was designed progressively to amuse, surprise, shock, appall, and, finally, prompt pensive men to re-examine time-hallowed medieval values and authorities, then—as necessary—to modify and reform them through the right use of reason and the Scriptures.

Erasmus' general method used the personification of Folly as a mouthpiece through which to deliver a witty monologue and commentary upon a wide range of human affairs. Sustained ironic praise is skillfully applied to the manifold absurdities or traditionally established (but potentially alterable and curable) follies of human life. Common patterns of thought and feeling are amusedly held up for inspection in an uncommonly bright humorous light. The opening viewpoint is much like that echoed by Ben Jonson in the prologue to *Every Man in His Humour,* ninety years later. Presented are:

> . . . deeds . . . / And persons, such as Comedy would choose,
> When she would shew an image of the times,
> And sport with human follies, not with crimes.
> Except we make them such, by loving still
> Our popular errors, when we know they're ill.
> I mean such errors as you'll all confess,
> By laughing at them, they deserve no less:
> Which when you heartily do, there's hope left then,
> You, that have so grac'd monsters, may like men.

The theme of war in the ***Praise of Folly*** is handled in three main divisions. First, mankind's martial and related proclivities (such as hunting) are ironically lauded as forming part of the general lunacy characteristic of civilization. Next—the attacks growing more specific and coming closer to home—the warmakings of popes and churchmen are treated. Finally, in the criticism of theologians who falsify Christ and the Scriptures to justify war, the whole movement rises to its climax, the grasp tightens, the mood becomes formidable, and that this Christian folly is, in Erasmus' view, "the most important thing he has to say, one cannot well doubt."

To begin with, the satire against war is fairly general, as Folly laughs with amused sympathy at choice varieties of whimsical prejudice and national *amour-propre.* She represents herself to us as the greatest of all inventors, creator of "all noble acts and arts" which cultural historians praise. But of all these noble inventions the first, the greatest, the maddest, and the most profitless to man, was war: " . . . is not war the seed-plot and fountain of renowned actions? Yet what is more foolish than to enter upon a conflict for I know not what causes, wherein each side reaps more of loss than of gain?" How can the carcasses left on the battlefield receive any glory? "As for those who fall, as was said of the Megarians, 'no particulars.' " But is it not always said that wise men are essential for military planning? Call it what it is—"military, not philosophical, wisdom." Of little use would be true philosophy—i.e., concerned with knowing the truth, including how to live well. "Far otherwise: this famous game of war is played by parasites, panders, bandits, assassins, peasants, sots, bankrupts, and such other dregs of mankind." Having thus begun with the semiparadox that wisdom is useless in war, Folly—with droll illustration—concludes that so-called wise men of peace are useless for all practical affairs.

From foolishness in general we move toward certain classes of folly large enough to take in the greater part of mankind—for instance, the custom of hunting, in which men everywhere find such joy. Erasmus' satire against hunting is an organic part of the mockery of war. In fact the theme of hunting is bound up with an apparently neo-Stoic theory devised to explain how primitive man may have fallen from the total peace which he enjoyed in the mythical golden age.

As Folly sees such activities as hunting, their general characteristic is that sheer custom has gradually so befuddled mankind that what is, to an objective observer (like Folly!), naturally hideous in itself has become transmuted into sheer joy. In their mutual delights, madmen laugh together. (pp. 43-6)

Already linked in Erasmus' thought on war are evidently at least three elements. One is that, earlier in history, man's inventive talents were misused by the invention of war itself—with its weapons, technologies, and ceremonies. Second, he observed the pleasure which contemporary men took in that miniature war, hunting. Third, he advanced the idea that, although the hunters are apparently happily unaware of it, what they have accomplished through habitual use of butchery is their own degeneration from the distinctively human toward the bestial. Evidently this reasoning process involves several simple presuppositions: that once upon a time man lived without war and without hunting; that in this earlier condition he lived in a fashion more admirably human, more perfect, than at present (when he unthinkingly enjoys butchery); that man is quite capable of so changing—from an earlier, uncorrupted state—until he is no longer consciously aware either that his tastes and habits are vile, or how vile they are ("the dung of the dogs smells like cinnamon to them").

What we have here seems to be a sketch toward a theory of history and of what might be termed progress. But Folly, through Erasmus' irony, attacks the entire process and holds it up to our view as one of degeneration. It was the ancient Prometheus myth which carried with it admiration for inventors; apparently Erasmus is not (here, at least) impressed unreservedly with the beauties of man's technological progress, including his invention of the art of war. Erasmus will return to the entire theory of history in his greatest piece of war criticism, the ***Bellum Erasmi*** (1515). Here perhaps it is sufficient to mention only that his efforts, in the ***Praise of Folly,*** to work out what I have termed a theory of history represent a striking example of his humanism. For he not only absorbed favorite classics (Lucretius, Ovid, Cicero, but above all Seneca and Plutarch), but transmuted them so that they furnished power and light for the English as well as European situation in 1509.

The tone of the satire becomes grimmer when the attack centers upon the warmaking of a degenerate papal hierarchy. The chief target becomes easily recognizable when he devises "an undoubtedly serious criticism of the Church as he had seen it in Italy under Julius II." As he warms to this theme, the irony becomes more brutal and the tension so great that the work almost breaks into outright denunciation. The result suggests the intensity and hard realism which mark the London Reformers' analysis of evil conditions whose reform became daily more vital to Christendom. To the historical method in criticism, Erasmus couples Lucianic irony and his own special form of wit: the result is work distinctive of the Christian humanism then emerging in England.

After a glancing cut at sycophantic courtiers and at kings who ignored the duties of kingship, Folly's satirical eye rested on the great princes of the Church. In general, contemporary cardinals compare badly with the ancient apostles. Why cannot these cardinals muster up enough purity and charity to work for the primitive Christian ends: "teaching, exhorting, chastising, admonishing, ending wars, resisting wicked princes, and freely spending blood—not money alone—for the flock of Christ?" But what can one expect when, as of late, "popes, cardinals, and bishops," after sedulous imitation, have almost beaten the secular princes at their own games? Besides, if they were actually to lead lives of Christian humility and poverty, think of the unemployment that would result! What would become of "all those advocates, promoters, secretaries, muleteers, grooms, bankers, and pimps" who now have steady employment?

The satire in the ***Praise of Folly*** grows still more intense and destructive when Folly considers the papacy. It would appear from her critique that it was no use looking now for St. Peter's apostolic virtues in the popes. Christian labor?—that "they hand over to Peter and Paul, who have leisure for it. But the splendor and the pleasure they take care of personally." They live in the grossest luxury and, worst of all, are devoted to the vice of war. Indeed their wars to gain and extend ill-gotten wealth have demoralized the Church, whose worst enemies such popes actually are. From them the name of Christ receives scant lip service, but the papal hand is always ready to whip out a sword and "stick it into the guts of his brother." The means which made the primitive Church grow strong—peace and self-sacrifice—are out of date. Nowadays the Pope's main business is to destroy anyone who (doubtless devilishly inspired) would reduce the "patrimony of Peter"—i.e., the vast wealth of the Church. And so they hurry to war: "On behalf of these things . . . they fight with fire and sword, not without shedding of Christian blood; and then they believe they have defended the bride of Christ in apostolic fashion." To war rush these "most holy fathers . . . and vicars of Christ"! No matter if war is more bestial than human, if it is hellish, if it blights morals like a plague, if it is unjust and the work of criminals, if it is truly unchristian:

> . . . nowadays they carry on Christ's cause by the sword. . . . And although war is so cruel a business that it befits beasts and not men, so frantic [*insana*] that poets feign it is sent with evil purpose by the Furies, so pestilential that it brings with it a general blight upon morals, so iniquitous that it is usually conducted by the worst bandits [*pessimis latronibus*], so impious that it has no accord with Christ, yet our popes, neglecting all their other concerns, make it their only task.
>
> (pp. 47-9)

Thus did Erasmus' ***Praise of Folly*** represent the old Pope Julius who, in Ranke's words, "from the tumults of a general war . . . hoped to extract the fulfillment of his purposes . . . to be the lord and master of the game of the world." Winding up this savage indictment, Erasmus has Folly at once ironically disclaim the slightest intention to "rattle up the vices" of any living Churchman. And of course Folly only praises bad men, whom she likes to eulogize, but she had better say so lest someone think the ***Praise of Folly*** to be satiric!

The last target of the satire that matters here is Erasmus' treatment of the traditional scholastic interpretation of Scripture by which, since St. Augustine's day, war had been justified. Unmistakably in this work he carried on what Colet had begun in his 1496 lectures on St. Paul at Oxford, using the same historical method in criticism but using it with superior flexibility, insight, and wit. This was deeply serious to Erasmus, and while the irony deepens toward the tragic, the passage tends to abandon the light and jocund tone with which he initiated his highspirited, humorous mock eulogy of human fatuity.

The literary climax of Erasmus' lifework was to be his edition of the New Testament—the ***Novum instrumentum*** of 1516—work largely done in England and doubtless in his plans when in 1509 he came to England to live, with every apparent intention of making it his permanent home. In 1496 Colet had searched for the original, primitive meaning of the Scriptures, largely bypassing the scholastic commentators. This whole vital question of biblical interpretation could not very long be separated from the question of a text whose editing would include the latest advances in scholarship.

When in the ***Praise of Folly,*** therefore, Folly began to cite

Scripture to bolster her authority in the world of deluded men, the satire rapidly came to a focus sharply on the question of the biblical authority for terming war to be just. Potentially there were few more explosive subjects for critical investigation; for when this is followed far enough, inevitably one is led to re-examine the basis and justice of power, monarchic or ecclesiastic.

At first Folly seems very pleased; ironically she affects to feel quite at home with these subtle scholastics, so clever and ingenious in reading meaning into the Scriptures. It's no less than "magistral"! Why, these days the "sons of theologues" can prove anything to their own purpose. The secret of their method, it seems, is to pluck out four or five little words "from here and there, even depraving the sense of them, if need be; although the words which precede and follow these are nothing at all to the point or even go against it." In short, by these critical devices (Folly applauds), scriptural precepts are mutilated and abridged, wrenched from their context, and so in the end readily found to mean something quite contrary to the example of Christ's own life. By such methods, indeed, "I pray you . . . tell me, what thing may be too hard for these doctors to bring about?"

For her part, Folly, using the example of Christ's conduct shortly before his death, admits to such stupidity that, to her, it seems Christ meant Christians to shun weapons and violence. Knowing the end to be near, Christ told his apostles to provide themselves with swords as needed in their mission of spreading the gospel. What did this counsel mean? To Folly (who resorts to historical criticism of a simple kind) the meaning is clear enough, in the context of Christ's whole life and teaching. The apostles were to secure and employ "not the sword with which bandits and murderers attack, but the sword of the spirit. . . . " Ah! but not so, says the scholastic expositor. To him (says Folly with some of Erasmus' bitterest irony) it is all quite different. It seems that Christ's injunctions of nonviolence really mean that his apostles should be armed to the teeth with all the latest military weapons. (Updating, Erasmus supplies "muskets.") Similarly the small knapsack of supplies that Christ had in mind is metamorphosed into a whole baggage train of fine food. Nor is such a critic at all disturbed "that He who thus earnestly bade that a sword be purchased, soon after with a rebuke ordered the same weapon to be sheathed; or that no one has ever heard it told that the apostles used swords or shield against the violence of the heathen . . . " though presumably they would have done so had Christ so intended.

The satire ends on a note of serious humor. Is it possible that Christianity itself has some deep "kinship with some sort of folly"? Just ponder the huge discrepancy between Christ's life and those lived by many of his professed modern followers! Many? A majority! And naturally, by majority vote, the minority (who seek to use Christ's whole life as their guide) can easily be declared quite mad. As for Folly, she always agrees with the majority. Why not? They are her faithful devotees. Encouraging readers to "applaud . . . live . . . drink," Erasmus' figure of Folly bids a fond farewell to a world crammed with fascinating lunacies.

The ***Praise of Folly*** (like More's *Utopia*) has often been termed a *jeu d'espirit,* and so it is. But it is much more than that, for it marks a tremendous forward step in social criticism. This is no shaft politely released from some Renaissance ivory tower. It belongs to world literature, true, but the satire's roots run deep into its own time. As critic Erasmus now permanently took his place as a man committed to aiding humanist reforms, not as one outside, a genial spectator, but as a fighter in the midst of a fateful struggle for a better social order, and as one passionately engaged in the great movement of the age.

As criticism, moreover, the work marks an immense growth in the structure of ideas. Summing up, Erasmus put forward five major points about war, points which link his attack to the search for vital reforms of Christendom. First, he argues that war is beastly, that is, more befitting the true, uncorrupted nature of beasts than of men. Here he revives and gives new impetus to the classical beast-man comparisons and analyses. But he is not content merely to echo certain classics, giving the satire a neo-Stoic cast. What he opens out, tentatively, is a critical inquiry into what may be a tragic dichotomy in human nature. Why is man, a creature of such wondrous natural and divine endowments, potentially "a little lower than the angels," seemingly (at least) capable of life ruled by reason and love, prone (as in war) to actions so vile? Why is this creature at times worse than any animal? "A beast without reason," Hamlet will mourn (confronted with another fall from ideal humanity) "would have mourned longer." The whole idea is central in English Renaissance tragedy. But, in the ***Praise of Folly,*** Erasmus is not content to offer the standard medieval answer, that the cause of this tragic fall is man's sin. Rather, as humanist, he examines intensely man's capacities for irrational and anti-human behavior. Clearly all this involves an implicit theory of what man's capacities for a good life actually are, as well as of means for its realization. This whole complex of thought will be more fully explored in the London Reformers' later social criticism, most fully by More and Vives.

The idea that war is bestial, however, may be a libel on the beasts. Secondly, Erasmus raises the view that war is hellish—"so frantic [*insana*] that poets feign it is sent with evil purpose by the Furies." This carries us toward a tragic perspective exceeding the first. Erasmus, nevertheless, again puts the idea in a humanistic and poetic rather than simply some traditional theological frame. The "devil theory" of historical causation has, to be sure, long had its advocates. Erasmus' way of raising the question invites deep reflection upon the interaction of reason and unreason (or sheer passion and overwhelming compulsions able to topple reason, as when men go berserk with mass-murderous fury) within the nature of man. Shakespeare's plebeians, listening with respect to Brutus' explanation of why he slew Caesar for the good of Rome, seem to be reasonable men. Mark Antony knows the potential vileness of human nature better than the too uncritically stoical Brutus, knows what these same Romans will do in frenzy when he has worked upon them, what unspeakable horrors will be commonplace when this hellish element is released (as perhaps periodically—we might say subconsciously—many men hope it may sometime be) when "Caesar's spirit, ranging for revenge, / With Ate by his side, come hot from hell," is given free play at the most fearful of all Renaissance military commands: "Havoc!" In the ***Praise of Folly*** Erasmus marks the line of insight which points toward Shakespeare's *Julius Caesar.*

Third, Erasmus advances the idea that war is "so pestilential that it brings with it a general blight upon morals." Thus he suggests the analogy of war and disease. The analogy invites the critical mind to search for causes, prompts again a search into the "nature" of man and the forces at work in his natural environment, an inquiry most imaginatively to be carried out by More in his *Utopia* and by Vives in his latest works.

The fourth and fifth points are closely related in the ***Praise of Folly***—that war is unjust and unchristian. Pursuit of both these themes leads toward sharp re-examination, not only of orthodox medieval doctrines of the Church, but of the uses (and abuses) of monarchic and papal powers. Every one of these ideas was potentially dynamite.

To be sure, in the ***Praise of Folly,*** while these five ideas are all present, some remain in a germinal state. Very probably, at this stage, Erasmus himself had not fully worked out his thought on war and social reform. Nevertheless, as humanist criticism of life, the ***Praise of Folly*** marks a substantial advance. Barely twenty-five years earlier, in Caxton's work, we moved in a medieval landscape; but now in Erasmus the scene, the very air—the ideas and their attached emotions—all are predominantly distinguished by a changed and Renaissance outlook. The ***Praise of Folly,*** moreover, appeals for both reflection and action. During the decade to follow, More, Erasmus, Colet, and their friends will (as voyagers of the mind) on the one hand follow out these five ideas and others, discovering many curious ramifications. On the other, being humanists concerned with the search for a good life in both practice and theory, they will be found busy in practical efforts to help design and construct a new social order in England. (pp. 49-53)

Robert P. Adams, "Approach to a Golden Age (1500-1509)," in his The Better Part of Valor: More, Erasmus, Colet, and Vives, on Humanism, War, and Peace, 1496-1535, *University of Washington Press, 1962, pp. 29-54.*

Werner L. Gundersheimer (essay date 1963)

[*In the following excerpt, Gundersheimer explores anti-Cabalistic and anti-Semitic attitudes revealed in Erasmus's letters.*]

Perhaps the most interesting and complicated examples of a prominent humanist's coolness towards Christian study of Cabala may be found in the letters of Erasmus. Recent historians of Christian cabalism have generally given the attitudes of Erasmus short shrift, since he was not a cabalist. Yet to his contemporaries, the views of Erasmus on any religious or scholarly question were of considerable importance. One could agree or disagree with them, but one could scarcely ignore them altogether. Thus, an examination of Erasmus's position towards the Christian study of the Cabala and towards the problems which such study raised in the early sixteenth century will be useful in presenting at least a major (if not the dominant) Christian position towards it. Moreover, such an investigation may shed some light on the complexity and differentiation of Erasmus's responses to the serious problems which cabalistic studies had indirectly brought about in Germany in the second decade of the century. Finally, this study should provide the basis for a more precise assessment of the importance of cabalistic study as an aspect of Renaissance humanism.

Erasmus first uses the word "Cabala" in a short letter to Wolfgang Koepfel, or Capito, dated March 13, 1518. The burden of his message to the noted Hebrew and Greek scholar is unmistakable:

> I should wish that you had a greater propensity toward Greek than to those Hebrew matters, though I do not censure them. I see that nation filled with the most frigid fables, casting forth nothing but various smokes; Talmud, Cabala, Tetragrammaton, 'Gates of Light', inane names. I would prefer that Christ be infected by Scotus than by such dirges. Italy has many Jews, Spain scarcely any Christians. I am afraid that by this opportunity the head of the plague formerly stifled may rise up. And would that the church of the Christians did not give so much preference to the Old Testament. Since it was given for a finite time it stands in shadows, yet it almost placed before Christian letters: meanwhile we are somehow turning away from Christ, who alone used to satisfy us thoroughly.

Erasmus's statement that he does not censure "ista Hebraica" is contradicted by the very next sentence, which is very doctrinaire indeed. By his listing of Cabala with a number of other "inania nomina" which have in common only the fact that they represent Jewish learning, Erasmus obfuscates the generic distinction between Jewish mysticism and the rationalistic Rabbinic tradition of the Talmudists.

Was Erasmus aware of such a distinction? Did he know what he was talking about when he used these Hebrew names? It seems highly possible that he did and that he was consciously and intentionally obliterating distinctions with which he was thoroughly familiar. Over a decade earlier he had been in Italy at a time when the lectures, treatises, and translations of the converted cabalist Paul Ricius were attracting considerable attention. He had probably read Reuchlin's early cabalistical dialogue *De Verbo Mirifico* (1494) and by 1518 was very probably familiar with the dialogue *De Arte Cabalistica* (1517), in which the German scholar defended his interests by demonstrating again the possibilities of cabalistical exegesis in establishing Christian truth. Here, then, in spite of what was probably a keen awareness of the basic distinctions between Talmud and Cabala, Erasmus conjoins them, regarding both as vanities to which even the detested writings of the schoolmen are preferable.

Thus Erasmus had for at least a decade been aware of the attempt to use Jewish writings for Christian, and especially Christological, purposes. Yet in all the time he knew about these efforts (and his meeting with Ricius in Pavia in 1506 may be considered a very late *terminus ad quem*) he never once encouraged or supported them. By 1515, then, when the battle of the Jewish books had been increasing in intensity in Germany for six years and the first volume of the *Epistolae Obscurorum Virorum* had already been published, Erasmus's unwillingness to commit himself in favour of such studies was perhaps nearly tantamount to a rejection of them, in a world wherein his support of a scholarly enterprise often augured well for its success. But as has been shown, Erasmus felt a deep-seated hostility towards Cabala, and thus implicitly rejected the idea of its usefulness to Christians. Though he did not mention "Cabala" until 1518, his fundamental position towards it had been formed many years earlier.

Indeed, Erasmus's attitude followed from a keen anti-Semitism, which was conventional for his times, and which he fully shared. "Italy has many Jews, Spain scarcely any Christians": Erasmus regarded Talmud and Cabala as the property of Jews, an accursed breed, the study of whose secrets could only deflect men from Christ, "who alone used to satisfy us thoroughly". But what did it mean to Erasmus to say that a book, or man, or idea was "Jewish"? An early instance of his meaning occurs in a letter to Colet in December 1504. Here he states that the purpose of his ***Enchiridion*** (1504) is to show that, at the expense of a neglect of true piety, religion is turning to a ceremonialism of even more than *Jewish* corporeality. This conception of Judaism as a religion of elaborate and meaningless rites recurs in Erasmus's letters. Indeed "Jewish" was to become a stock term of opprobrium toward Rome by humanists and reformers alike. *Res Iudaeorum* connoted for Erasmus all of the pretentious shams of vulgar religion which he satirized with devastating success in ***The Praise of Folly*** (1511) and ***The Colloquies.***

His traditional and conventional position towards Jewish matters within and without Christianity, combined with the widespread interest in the Hebrew language as a tool for right knowledge of Scripture which he had done much to support, had by 1517 led Erasmus to dread the possibility of a "Jewish renaissance". This, he felt, could ironically arise from the Christian use of *Hebraica pura,* which should be directed solely towards textual clarification and emendation of Scripture, preferably within the well-regulated community of the trilingual colleges. During the period of controversy over Hebrew learning, he made several allusions to his fear of Judaism. Writing to Capito on February 26, 1517, he formulated a statement which in context is particularly forceful. Erasmus first elaborated at great length his vision of a rapidly approaching Golden Age, wherein through the new learning in religion, jurisprudence, government, and the schools, that condition may exist in which "a simple and pure Christ be implanted deep within the hearts of men." But there is *one* real and present danger:

> One anxiety still claims my attention, lest under the protection of a rebirth of ancient literature, paganism may try to raise its head . . . and I am afraid that by the reborn letters of the Hebrews Judaism may consider a revival through the occasion; nothing more adverse and nothing more inimical to the teaching of Christ can be found than this plague. For so goes the nature of human affairs that there has never been so great a felicity but that under cover of it some evil tried to steal in at the same time. I should wish that those cold subtleties either be cut away absolutely or certainly not be the sole concern of theology, and that the simple and pure Christ be implanted deep within the minds of men.

Here again, Jewish subtleties are presented as precisely antithetical to the *philosophia Christi.* Erasmus actually uses the language of the obscurantist, and rejects Jewish learning not by considered arguments, but in emotive terms. The distinction, for him, is black and white. Erasmus validates his attack by means of what we may justly consider an anti-Jewish historiography:

> Lately there have gone forth among the masses some little books savouring of unadulterated Judaism. I see how much our Paul laboured strenuously to emancipate Christ from Judaism, and I feel that some are privately backsliding in that direction.

Judaism emerges as a recurrent stumbling-block to the spreading of Christ's Word in all ages. Now more than ever, when Hebrew is being revived, men must beware of such a snare. (pp. 39-42)

What could have made Erasmus think that Judaism might hold seductive powers over the minds of Christian scholars?

First, one must take into account Erasmus's conception of the historical rôle of Judaism, mentioned previously. He neither gives nor implies any other reasons for his fear, and was himself surely never attracted to the mysteries of Jewish language or doctrines. His early experiments in Hebrew were quickly abandoned, and his own interests gravitated strongly towards the New Testament. He tells Capito that the Old Testament stands in shadows, compared to the documents of Christian revelation, and his repeated condemnations of Hebrew texts in letters to a Hebraist whom he seems to have admired and trusted may be considered an index of his increasing concern for such matters between 1515 and 1518. Since he had obviously known of Cabala for many years, and since acquaintances of his had been concerned with its interpretation during those years, this sudden concern must be explained on other grounds than those of entirely new information about such matters.

It seems plausible that Erasmus's attacks result from the sudden prominence of the problem of "right learning" raised by the Dominican attacks on Reuchlin, the German Hebraist and humanist who, as Erasmus believed, had "first aroused a love of Greek and Hebrew literature" in his native land, for which "all Germany is indebted to him". The prolonged and complicated literary and judicial battle between the "Reuchlinists" and the supporters of Jacob Hochstraten, inquisitor of Cologne, became a *cause célèbre* of the humanists throughout Western Europe. Erasmus's responses to the participants of the controversy, and to the problems with which it threatened Christendom may suggest another line of explanation for his emphatic rejection of Jewish learning.

It could perhaps be argued with some justification that in refusing to commit himself openly and publicly in favour of the course of the beleaguered German humanists, Erasmus revealed his great personal weakness, that of the cowardly scholar, who buried his head in the sands of past times and tomes. However, a close examination of his own statements of his feelings as they developed between 1515 and 1520 tends to reveal the complexity of Erasmus's motives and the delicate and coherent logic of his position.

One obvious motive is the Dutch humanist's respect and sympathy for his German colleague, Reuchlin. Their surviving correspondence begins with a letter from Reuchlin, dated April 1514, but there is evidence that they had exchanged messages as early as 1510. Their only meeting took place in March or April 1515, and was characterized, according to Erasmus, by "civilis amicitia". In speaking of this meeting in a letter to Wolsey, he remarks that neither Talmud nor Cabala have ever been pleasing to him, and that in his meeting with Reuchlin in Frankfurt, nothing transpired but that amity which exists among all learned men. He goes on to say that this professional courtesy, as it were, does not involve any close alliance between himself and Reuchlin.

Yet Erasmus had interested himself in the case earlier. He had, for example, taken pains to suppress Ulrich von Hutten's satirical poem, "Triumphus Capnionis," in 1514. In August of the same year he wrote to Reuchlin from Basle, in a tone which suggests high esteem. He tells of how his friends in England had been amused by Reuchlin's spirited response to Dominican charges in his pamphlet *Augenspiegel.* Among his supporters are John Fisher, Bishop of Rochester, and John Colet, Dean of St. Paul's. Erasmus adds that while he could not help laughing, he feels some scruple lest Reuchlin may have written incautiously, but that he had satisfied himself as to Reuchlin's justification. (pp. 43-4)

Holbein portrait of English humanist John Colet, a friend of Erasmus.

Erasmus never renounced his opinion that Reuchlin was the victim of unjustified censure, although he never wished to be publicly associated with Reuchlin's cause. Perhaps the most striking feature of Erasmus's statements regarding Reuchlin is that they support him on purely personal grounds. Erasmus did not publicly concern himself with the substantive questions over which Reuchlin became a kind of symbol. That Reuchlin was a Cabalist, and was asserting the utility of Christian cabalism and therefore the need to save rather than burn Hebrew books, does not seem to have made the slightest difference to Erasmus in 1514 and 1515. He seems to have felt that a lay scholar of proven ability and great integrity was being used as the whipping boy of obscurantist monks, over what was basically a rather trivial question. No scholar of Reuchlin's stature and achievement should be subjected to such indignities. (p. 45)

Thus Erasmus's attitudes followed logically from a complex system of values, crowned by the vision of a modern Golden Age of Christendom, based on the *philosophia Christi.* This system of values is nowhere more evident than in a letter to Hochstraten, dated August 11, 1519. By this time several areas of contention between the two had already developed. As early as May 1517, the inquisitor had threatened "persecution" of Erasmus for his ***Novum Instrumentum,*** and in his *Destructio Cabale* had attacked Erasmus's views on divorce. In August 1518, Erasmus wrote to Pirckheimer that he would want to appeal to Hochstraten regarding his treatment of Reuchlin, were he not *plus quam alienissimus* to the whole matter. In August 1519, he determined to approach Hochstraten in what he later described as "a very friendly way". He discussed the controversy at some length, pointing out the undignified behaviour of both sides, and suggested to Hochstraten that the power of his office could be used constructively—"Inquisitio tibi mandata est, non ius pronunciandi". If Hochstraten will answer that he simply does his duty, then his duty must be re-assessed, in terms of a moderate, judicious policy, directed towards Christ. Erasmus defined Hochstraten's official responsibility at length, and concluded firmly:

> It is not necessary for you to confound heaven and earth, and to excite such great tragedies.

Erasmus goes on to ask what is to be gained by stirring up such agitation over the Jews.

> Who is there among us that does not sufficiently detest that race of men? If it is Christian to hate the Jews, we are all Christian enough in this regard.

Surely it is senseless to persecute the already hated Jews at the expense of Christendom. Erasmus finds it strange that Hochstraten has implicated him in the matter of the Cabala, "a quo sum alienissimus". He seems to commend Hochstraten's "very great hatred" of Cabala by this acknowledgement, and by exclaiming

> Would that Christ be closer to me than I am close to Cabala!

Erasmus goes on to discuss the case for some 355 lines, and concludes with a prayer that Hochstraten may find him worthy of commendation to Christ in his devotions, and that Christ will, in his most gentle spirit, always cause Hochstraten's mind to be kept within bounds. The letter is a good example of Erasmus's *philosophia Christi,* practically applied.

Erasmus, then, wished to remain above, or at least outside, the controversy, for a variety of reasons. In the first place, according to his Christian calculus, the battle could only injure Christendom. Moreover, he himself could not serve Christendom through partisan participation in the battle, regardless of his sympathies. As to those sympathies, they were not absolutely clear-cut, in a situation in which neither side seemed willing to respect the dignity of its opponents, or to consider the dangers of their somewhat irresponsible litigations. His disengagement increased as the theological issues became less relevant to the degraded discussion. No one—not even Erasmus—seemed to care that Reuchlin had never wished to save Hebrew and Jewish learning merely for its own sake, or for that of the Jews. No one seemed to respect the fact that Reuchlin's argument was based on one of the pillars of Christian *traditio,* the rule of thumb *uti non frui.*

As a result of the very effective work of the German humanist propagandists, the public image of the controversy (at least in international humanist circles) came to be polarized in terms of the forces of light and learning against the forces of darkness and superstition. The case thus provided a dramatic example of the increasingly powerful national and religious consciousness among learned lay circles in Germany. The original question of the utility or danger of Jewish texts became politicized, and transformed into larger issues of competing loyalties and ideologies within Christendom.

Erasmus alone seems to have kept the various issues distinct. He gives evidence of having understood them with perfect clarity, at the time when they were most perplexing. It is perhaps particularly signigicant that Erasmus, though disposed against Christian cabalism for reasons discussed earlier, never closed his mind to a demonstration of its usefulness. A letter to Paulus Ricius dated November 1520 refers to Ricius's defence of Reuchlin as a cabalist, the *Apologetica in allegorisantium seu Cabaleorum dogma Oratio,* which Erasmus may have seen in manuscript in 1519. Erasmus tells Ricius that his little book makes him feel a little more at ease about cabalistical business, and that there may indeed be some validity to it which he had not known about before. He goes on to say that Ricius's perpetual erudition is no new thing to him, but that his candour and perspicacity in the present instance places the matter before the eyes in such a way that it would be clear to a blind man. Erasmus also approves Ricius's manner of presenting the subject; he considers it a worthy moderation. He shows great respect for the learned apostate Jew, whom he calls "most consummate philosopher", "most erudite" and "most learned".

Erasmus had never strongly *and* publicly opposed the study of Cabala, but his new understanding of it probably tended to make him less disturbed about its possible dangers. But by 1520, much more serious tendencies towards disunity had appeared in Germany. The Cabala had been forgotten as the Lutheran schism came to command every man's attention. But even at its most benevolent, Erasmus's attitude can never have been stronger than John Colet's interested scepticism. Having read through Reuchlin's *De arte cabalistica,* the Dean of St. Paul's wrote to Erasmus:

> I do not dare to make a judgement about the book. I am aware of my own lack of knowledge, and of how blind I may be in matters so remote and in the works of so great a man. But sometimes the miracles seemed to me to be more verbal than real. For (as he shows) I know not what divine mysteries the Hebrew words may have in their characters and combinations.

And Erasmus would certainly at all times have agreed with Colet's conclusions from his "uncertainty":

> The Reuchlinists put forth those Pythagorean and Cabalistic things; but in my judgement we may follow no path other than by the burning love and imitation of Jesus. Whereby, having left roundabout ways behind, we may move toward truth by a short way. I wish it with all my strength.

For Pico, the builder of a universal system based on a Platonic naturalism, Cabala offered the sanction of a continuous tradition of Platonic doctrines within the Judaeo-Christian world. Since it was generally thought to be the written record of a second, oral revelation to Moses, Cabala could be used to defend Renaissance Platonism against charges of paganism. Moreover for Pico, and especially for Reuchlin, Cabala contained what might be called *vestigia Christi,* significant in themselves to Christians, and useful as well, as a demonstration to Jews of their own unreasonable archaism. For others, such as Agrippa, Cabala seemed to hold out hopes for a kind of certainty which could not be gained from terrestrial knowledge. For any Christian scholar of Hebrew, Cabala might provide nothing more than an absorbing side-line to a dominant interest in Biblical interpretation.

Yet for the "Christian humanist" of the north—the man who based a complete ethical philosophy on a learned conception of the life and teachings of Christ and his love—the Cabala appeared to be a kind of aberration. He could not understand that within Judaism it played the rôle of a reaction to Jewish scholasticism just as Renaissance mysticism (and in an important sense humanism itself) were reactions to the Aristotelian rationalism of the schoolmen. He could not see the need for establishing far-fetched relationships with Christ when the world itself offered so many direct approaches.

Yet even the northern humanist recognized that cabalism fell within the *letter* of the humanist ideology. Erasmus never denied that its antiquity within the Hebraic *corpus* made it a legitimate subject for scholarly investigation under ordinary circumstances. He observed repeatedly that it never captured his interest, and his general suspicion of Jewish mysticism can be considered natural for a devout Christian. This apprehension was augmented, as has been shown, by a distrust of the methods of cabalism and, one might suppose, by a kind of aesthetic, or at least emotive, revulsion at the subtleness of the cabalists' methods of exegesis. Such a revulsion would have been closely akin to that which was so frequently expressed towards scholasticism. It is indeed ironical, then, that Erasmus viewed Cabala, i.e. Jewish anti-scholasticism, as more dangerous to Christendom than Scotism. That is to say, while the northern humanist did not deny that cabalism had a well-established claim for scholarly attention, within the *letter* of humanism, he nonetheless felt that it was altogether antithetical to the *spirit* of his approach to learning.

Erasmus, as Professor Rice has shown [in "Erasmus and the Religious Tradition" (1950)] effected a thorough rethinking of the Christian universe in ethical terms. Even the ***Praise of Folly*** may be regarded as the statement of an ethical conception of Christian piety, for that is all that is left standing when Stultitia's speech has ended. And in his statements on Cabala and on the Reuchlin controversy, Erasmus's ideal of human reason informed by piety, though informally elaborated, is as clear as in any of his satirical writings. There is in these statements a deep-seated distrust of the passions of religious fanaticism on the one hand, and mystical exuberance on the other. Erasmus did not have the mystic's particular kind of confidence that man could somehow ascend to an immediate contemplation of God, or to some beatific vision. Instead he was glad to acknowledge the imperfect state of man's knowledge, and to rest on the assumption that the finite creature, while incapable of knowing *all,* could by his own striving know enough on earth to think and behave in a way befitting one for whom Christ had died. The other-worldly speculations of a cabalist could have little to offer to a critical sanity so engaged in affirming human possibilities in the world.

It is precisely this kind of Erasmian critical sanity, and not the "scientific systems of Copernicus, Kepler and Bruno", that is primarily responsible for the limited appeal of Cabala to humanist scholars. After Reuchlin, few men who could properly be regarded as humanists participated in Christian cabalism. Yet throughout the entire sixteenth century speculative Cabala was studied and practised by scholars, apologists, erudites, and missionaries. Later still, it would become the province of religious occultists and in its "practical" or "applied" forms would be taken up by some of the "scientists" of the late sixteenth century—astrologers, necromancers, demonologists, and divinators. (pp. 48-52)

Werner L. Gundersheimer, "Erasmus, Humanism, and the Christian Cabala," in Journal of the Warburg and Courtauld Institutes, *Vol. 26, 1963, pp. 38-52.*

Walter Kaiser (essay date 1963)

[*Kaiser is an American educator and literary scholar. In the excerpt below, he discusses the dedicatory letter to* The Praise of Folly, *highlighting the information it provides regarding the composition and nature of the work.*]

It was in More's house that the ***Moriae encomium*** was written; it was at his suggestion that it was expanded; and it is to him that it is dedicated. Like most Renaissance epistles dedicatory, Erasmus' letter to More is not only encomiastic of the recipient but programmatic of the work as well, and in it we are told when, why, and how the ***Encomium*** was composed. Any examination of Stultitia's oration ought therefore to begin with a consideration of this dedication. Because it is a letter to More, Erasmus' closest friend, some scholars have used it as important evidence about the composition and nature of the ***Encomium,*** assuming that if Erasmus were direct and accurate with anyone it would be with More. Read on the basis of this assumption, the epistle has been considered particularly valuable; for if, as some have assumed, Erasmus is here speaking without a mask, this would then be a far more "trustworthy" statement than anything he says after he dons the persona of Stultitia. Yet such an assumption fails to take into account the public nature of this epistle, which was, after all, specifically written to be printed at the head of the ***Encomium;*** and just as an autobiography is not the same thing as a private journal, so an epistle dedicatory and a letter represent two quite different genres. The epistle does indeed contain important evidence about the composition and nature of the ***Encomium,*** but much of that evidence lies between the lines; and this letter is not so ingenuous, nor its author so unmasked, as either would wish to seem.

In the epistle, the basic paradoxical device of the ***Encomium,*** the confusion of wisdom and ignorance, is set up. "I have called my book," says Erasmus to More, "***The Praise of 'Moria'*** because of your name, which comes as near to the word for folly as you are far from the meaning of it." The Ciceronian juxtaposition is a neat one—and yet not quite so neat as it appears thus isolated from context, for it follows hard upon a sentence in which Erasmus had deliberately confused similar concepts of nearness and farness. Nonetheless, the irony of the title is at once made plain: it can be translated either as "The Praise of Folly" or "The Praise of More," and if Folly is rude and stupid, More is "wholly learned and wholly gracious." From the outset, the names of More and Moria and the concepts of wisdom and folly, like those of absence and presence, are intentionally confused. Setting out from this ambiguity and traveling via the well-worn Horatian road of "aut prodesse . . . aut delectare," Erasmus arrives at a position from which he can claim both frivolity and gravity for his little treatise. Others may judge me as they will, he says, but, unless self-love deceives me badly, I have praised folly in a way not wholly foolish. It is upon this premise, of course, that the entire ***Encomium*** is based, and the possible seriousness of the joking to follow is hinted at several times in this prefatory epistle. Trifles may lead to serious things; fooleries may give profit; and while nothing is sillier than to treat serious things triflingly, nothing is more graceful than to treat trifling things in such a way that you seem to be less than trifling. This playing with words is, like the constant use of the double (or triple) negative, a characteristic of the style Erasmus employs in the ***Encomium;*** and the style itself becomes in this way a reflection of the ironic paradoxes of the argument.

The position established with regard to trifles and serious things is a commonplace in Renaissance defenses of secular and "light" literature and was inevitably brought forth to meet objections against works deemed "more frivolous (*leviores*) than befit a theologian." Yet when it appears, however briefly or tentatively, before the paradoxical title ***Moriae encomium,*** it also serves to warn the reader that he should look below the surface of the joking that is to follow. Chaloner, who unlike many Renaissance translators seems to have understood the work he rendered, comprehended this fact and the verbal device, and to drive their implications home to his English readers he reiterated them in his own introduction:

> A Folie it maie be thought in me to have spent tyme in englisshyng of this boke, entitled ***the praise of Folie,*** whereas the name it selfe semeth to set foorth no wisedome, or matter of gravitee: unlesse perhappes Erasmus, the autour therof, delited to mocke men, in callyng it one thyng, and meanyng an other.

Despite these allusions, however, the esoteric aspects of the ***Encomium*** are little more than hinted at. Not only was it dangerous to be more explicit, but Erasmus was concerned with defending himself against the attacks he could foresee. The defensive arguments he employs here are those he was to return to and expand in such utterances as the famous letter to Martin Dorp and, later, after the attacks had in fact begun, in the adage **"Ollas ostentare."** His defense begins, in the best humanistic tradition, with a citation of classical precedents, and the catalogue he supplies is the usual one, such as we find, for example, in Nashe's *Praise of the Red Herring.* Though Erasmus' list is, happily, briefer than Nashe's, it includes the most famous mock panegyrics—the pseudo-Homeric *Batrachomyomachia,* the pseudo-Virgilian *Culex,* Ovid's *Nux,* and that favorite of Renaissance authors from Spenser to Gelli to Montaigne, Plutarch's *Gryllus.*

This argument from precedent is buttressed by several moral arguments, all of them traditional and all of them repeated and elaborated in the letter to Dorp. I have, says Erasmus, censured only the general manners of men (*communem bomimum vitam*) and have mentioned no one by name, thus attempting to teach rather than to "bite." What is more, he claims that by attacking all classes of men he has shown that he was angry at no individual, but rather at all vices. Finally, with a characteristic side-swipe at Juvenal, he points out that he has deliberately avoided moving through "that occult sewer of vices". . . . The moral tone of the ***Encomium*** is thus demonstrated to be a high one, and Erasmus later even boasted that some had thought the book more edifying than Aristotle's *Ethics* or *Politics*—a "modernist" claim in defense of imaginative literature that one meets often in Renaissance authors, as in the celebrated passage where Milton asserts that Spenser is a better teacher than Scotus or Aquinas. Erasmus' final argument is his insistence—from one point of view quite proper, from another quite specious—that the reader remember that the oration is pronounced by Stultitia, not Erasmus, and that the decorum of the persona had to be maintained. This was perhaps his best defense, and he reiterated it for the rest of his life whenever the subject of the ***Encomium*** came up; in the edition of 1515 he emphasized the point often in the notes added to the ***Encomium*** by means of his amanuensis, Gerard Listrius.

These, then, are the main points in the epistle dedicatory that any casual reader comes away with. What is more, they are the points that Erasmus wished him to come away with. Yet if we examine the epistle with a more penetrating eye, certain questions present themselves, the answers to which bring us closer to Erasmus' intentions in writing it and lead us directly into the techniques of the ***Encomium*** itself. One may, for example, wonder why Erasmus should have felt it necessary to repeat the familiar clichés in defense of satiric and "frivolous" literature to More, of all people. Not only was More *doctissimus,* but it was he himself who had led Erasmus to Lucian. And it was Lucian who had fished the murex up for both of them. Erasmus' epistle dedicatory to his translation of Lucian's *Gallus,* written two years before, had been quite explicit about the nature of the game. Certainly Erasmus knew—he says in the epistle that he knows—how much More enjoyed this kind of joke which the two of them had found in Lucian. Presumably, therefore, no one less needed a justification of the ***Moriae encomium,*** nor would anyone have been more familiar than More with the traditional defenses. Why, Erasmus asks at the end of his epistle, should I say these things to you? The answer, of course, is that More did not need the epistle, that, as I have already suggested, it was not written for More but for the ***Encomium,*** because Erasmus intended that the reader should be led into that work by way of this epistle.

Evident though these facts are, their corollary has not always been so easily perceived: that Erasmus is not here talking privately and frankly to a friend, but publicly to his readers and future critics. He is, therefore, wearing as much of a mask as he is in the encomium itself, though not quite the same mask.

It is to this mask that we may attribute the lie Erasmus tells in the very first sentence of the epistle. For the ***Encomium,*** as we know very well, was not composed by Erasmus as he traveled from Italy to England, but rather in More's own house after he had arrived there. Some scholars, confronted with what Erasmus says in the epistle and what he acknowledges in another letter, have attempted to explain the discrepancy by claiming that, though he wrote his book in Chelsea, he thought it up while traveling. Such an explanation is by no means implausible, but it is unnecessary. It also misses the point. What we must seek is not the explanation of the contradiction, but rather the reasons why Erasmus perpetrated the inaccuracy that his book was written on the journey. Equally unnecessary and misguided has been the long discussion of the dateline, "Ex Rure, quinto Idus Iunias, An. M.D. VIII," which Erasmus placed at the end of the epistle. Scholars have often debated what Erasmus meant by *rus,* and P. S. Allen has conjectured that it does not necessarily mean

Chelsea, as most have thought (why write to More from his own house?), but possibly St. Germain-des-Prés. Yet surely what Erasmus means by the dateline is that the ***Encomium*** was written in the country rather than the city; and the point he is emphasizing is the same one Nashe is making when he writes at the beginning of his *Praise of the Red Herring,* "of my note-books and all books else here in the country I am bereaued." All these devices, the *ex rure,* the trip on horseback, its parody later in the epistle as a hobbyhorse ride, and Erasmus' subsequent descriptions of how he wrote the ***Encomium*** in only a week, while ill, and without any books at his disposal, are scholarly disclaimers. He protests too much, and we may be forgiven for wondering if there were no books in More's house that he could have borrowed. Erasmus is simply using these excuses to remove his book from the battleground of scholarship on which it could more easily be attacked. Thus, whenever an adversary might attempt to riposte Stultitia's thrusts, Erasmus could always explain that his sword was only a wooden toy, that he was only joking, that it was all simply a game. It is a trick that Falstaff, with his dagger of lath, also knew.

Of the many disclaimers which Erasmus proffers, the *en voyage* excuse is particularly interesting, since it helps us to locate the ***Encomium*** within a certain tradition. Perhaps the earliest Renaissance use of this particular antischolastic device is Petrarch's in his own book on folly. In the *De sui ipsius et multorum ignorantia* he is at pains to make the reader believe that his tract was written *en voyage*—specifically, while sitting in a boat going down the Po. Thus, he carefully explains that his book could not possibly be scholarly (*non denique grauitatem* [*habet*]) and that it is no wonder if the hand and speech of the writer float a bit (*fluctuat*): for lucubration requires a lamp, scholarship a study. The theme of the *hortus conclusus* that we find in Boccaccio and others is, in its insistence upon removal from the world of hard fact and moral codes, an analogous device to disclaim a certain type of responsibility; and Marguerite de Navarre, in her imitation of Boccaccio, removes her characters from any scholarly responsibility as well by specifically excluding from the group "those who had studied and were men of letters." Similarly, More's *Utopia* was not only put down on paper in spare moments ("onelye that tyme, whyche I steale from slepe and meate"), but it also claimed to be nothing more than a recounting of what he had been told, thus supposedly freeing him "of all the labour and study belonging to the invention of this work." Finally, Petrarch's description of writing in a boat may remind us that Cusanus also claimed that his philosophy of learned ignorance came to him "at sea while returning from Greece," while at the same time Petrarch's verb *fluctuat* anticipates Montaigne's explanation that he wrote down whatever came into his head, "divers et ondoyant," as he was attempting to describe his own ignorance.

Just as Erasmus claims that he wrote her speech under the most casual conditions, so Stultitia will repeatedly point out that she is speaking extempore and that her author is a man who writes down whatever enters his head or falls from his pen, "dum nulla lucubratione." Those nine Horatian years of study and revision during which, as he tells Arbuthnot, Pope urged writers to "keep your piece" are simply ridiculed by the unscholarly fool. Erasmus' insistence upon the unscholarly conditions under which the ***Encomium*** was composed is matched by his equal insistence upon the lusory character of the book; and the verb *ludere* and its derivatives (not to mention words with analogous connotations such as *jocus, nugae, festivus, ridere, delectare*) appear eleven times in this brief epistle to establish the ***Encomium*** as a "game of wit" (*hunc ingenii nostri lusum*). Let my readers, says Erasmus, think that I have been playing a game of checkers for fun or riding a hobbyhorse. For it is only a game, this little treatise—though, to be sure, Erasmus hints that such trifles may, as they do in Lucian, have serious implications (*maxime si nugae seria ducant*).

Now one of the defining characteristics of play is its formality, its established sequence of events and the accepted rules that govern those events. One cannot play the game unless one knows the rules, and neither can one watch the game with any comprehension unless one is aware of the formal pattern and the strict laws that control and define it. Like all games, the ***Encomium*** also has its patterns and its rules, and one must know them in order to comprehend Stultitia's speech. Thus the "serious matters" at which Erasmus hints can be accurately apprehended only after the nature and function of the "trifles" have been comprehended. In the game that is Stultitia's speech, the formal pattern is that of classical oratory, the rules are those of Erasmian irony. We must know something of both before we can accurately interpret the message of the first fool. (pp. 27-34)

Walter Kaiser, "Erasmus' Stultitia," in his Praisers of Folly: Erasmus, Rabelais, Shakespeare, *Harvard University Press, 1963, pp. 19-102.*

A. L. Rowse (essay date 1966)

[*Rowse is an English poet, biographer, and historian who has written extensively on Elizabethan literature. In the excerpt below, he provides a brief sketch of Erasmus's personality and its revelation through works such as* The Praise of Folly *and the* Julius exclusus.]

Erasmus is one of the great names of Europe; but it is doubtful whether he is much more than a name to us today. There upon the library shelves stand the dozen or more tall folios of the Louvain edition of his works; there are the ten volumes of his ***Letters;*** in addition, his texts of the Fathers, Chrysostom, Cyprian, Jerome, Ambrose, Augustine, together with his life's crowning glory, the edition of the New Testament. Is it any wonder that the man should be buried under such a mountain of Latin and Greek?

In spite of all this, he comes through to us as a singularly modern personality: a sensitive, queasy, thin-skinned, human being, self-conscious and self-aware like a modern man, no medieval. His problems were very much ours; he was agonised by similar issues, extraordinarily contemporary in character; living as he did in that sickening period when the Renaissance passed over into the Reformation and the Wars of Religion, he was caught at a dangerous turning of the ways in Europe. It is fitting that we should call him to mind: he was the first of modern writers, and his life holds a special significance for our age. (p. 100)

He was first and foremost the scholar, prince among the scholars of the Renaissance. He won this position after an apprenticeship over years, at school at Gouda and Deventer, at the Augustinian monastery of Steyn of which he was a canon, in Paris teaching himself Greek, at Oxford where Colet inspired him with a sense of his vocation, at Cambridge where he lectured and taught and studied. It was not until he was a man of thirty that he began to reap the rewards of his industry in a growing fame. In addition to his scholarship he was a brilliant original writer. Few had handled the Latin language as he since the Dark Ages closed down upon Europe, a resuscitation of the classical Latin of Cicero. If less of a living language than medieval Latin, at least it was living to Erasmus, who took pains not to speak his native Dutch and as far as possible to converse in Latin only, so as not to spoil his natural style.

No-one had more arresting things to say: he was a preternaturally sharp observer of events and persons, an acute commentator upon opinions, essentially moralist and critic, with a biting wit. He belongs to the small, well-defined class of writers to which Voltaire and Swift belong. But not even Voltaire's European reputation equalled Erasmus' recognised position in his lifetime. He was the admired of scholars, churchmen and princes, sought after by Charles V, Francis I, Henry VIII and successive Popes, the friend of Sir Thomas More and Fisher, since promoted saints; different countries competed for the honour of his presence, their leading men loaded him with presents and kindnesses.

Of the works that went to justify this immense reputation, we cannot here deal with those of pure scholarship; let us take his own original writings. I suppose the ***Moriae Encomium*** **(*The Praise of Folly*)** to be his most characteristic work, that one which best speaks for the man. The idea of the book occurred to him while journeying over the mountains from Italy to Northern Europe, on his way to England in 1509; arrived in London, he wrote it in the space of a few days in More's house in Bucklersbury—a characteristic play upon More's name gives it its title. The subject of the book is the foolery of mankind, the tragic condition that lies at the root of human nature. Why is it that man, the one animal gifted with reason, should choose the irrational, the foolish, the obviously absurd course? One sees that the book belongs to the same class as *Gulliver's Travels,* Voltaire's *Candide,* and Grimmelshausen's *Simplicissimus.* Why the Renaissance should have been so much concerned with the subject of human folly is an interesting, and perhaps profitable, speculation; there is a large Fool-literature of the time, of which the *Ship of Fools* and Rabelais's works are examples. The perfect expression of all that literature is, however, Erasmus's ***Praise of Folly.***

The treatment of the subject is appropriately ironical, and indeed at times one can hardly distinguish between what is seriously and what is frivolously intended. There is scarcely any form of human folly that is not touched upon, sometimes with a mock serious approval, sometimes with open castigation. The latter is employed for the abuses of the Church, the attention to forms instead of to things of the spirit, the concern with property and pomp instead of preaching the gospel, the character of secular priests who justify their name by being so much better acquainted with the affairs of this world than of the next. Let us take an example from the book:

> To work miracles is old and antiquated, and not in fashion now; to instruct the people, troublesome; to interpret the Scripture, pedantic; to pray, a sign one has little else to do; to shed tears, silly and womanish; to be poor, base; to be defeated, dishonourable and little becoming him that scarce admits even kings to kiss his slipper [*i.e.* the Pope]; and lastly, to die, uncouth; and to be stretched on a Cross, infamous.

The desire for practical reform is constantly in evidence, but more philosophical, or even anthropological, is such a thought as this:

> In a word, this Folly is that that laid the foundation of Cities; and by it, Empire, Authority, Religion, Policy and public Actions are preserved: neither is there any thing in Human Life that is not a kind of pastime of Folly.

Nothing could be more far-reaching than the scepticism implied by that: human folly is the foundation of all politics, and provides the necessity for authority, religion, the state: if only men were reasonable there would be no need for empires, states, authority. These two tendencies in Erasmus, the reforming and evangelistic ardour, and a profound scepticism regarding life and men, were held together in a delicate equipoise which gives the whole character to his mind. The equipoise was broken by the irruption of Luther into the European scene. The conflict between these two sides to Erasmus' nature was tragically revealed in the conflict with Luther over the Reformation.

Up to 1518-19 all had gone well with Erasmus: he stood at the apex of his European reputation. As both humanist and reformer, he appeared at the head of the movement for Reform within the Church; all men looked to him as such, yet he retained the favour of kings, Emperor and Pope. The revolutionary upheaval which Luther set in train destroyed all this. The confident Victorian age considered that Luther showed up Erasmus' weakness as but a Laodicean, as certainly he confessed that he was not the stuff that martyrs are made of. But the tragedy went deeper: it was that the sensible, moderate course of reasonable reform, within the framework of the universal Church, became impossible in the mad onrush of events with men's passions unleashed, their hatreds aroused.

The essential point of Erasmus' position was that he was a rationalist, he wanted men to be guided by reason. He had been not unsympathetic to Luther in the beginnings of his movement for reform; but he foresaw as Luther went farther and farther in his challenge to the Church, that new dogmas were being set up against the old and that this would lead to disastrous conflicts and wars, leaving the world in a worse state than before, Europe riven in two. Erasmus was right, but could do nothing; his own views about the folly of men were being only too precisely justified in the destruction they were bringing on themselves and in the ruin of all his hopes of agreed reform in a spirit of moderation and forbearance. Erasmus was caught by the whirlwind out of the interior depths of barbaric Germany, in much the same way as the Girondins were caught by the French Revolution, or the Mensheviks by the Russian. The contemporary parallel is obvious. It is regrettable that human beings are unable to bring about obvious and necessary reforms without pulling the house down about their ears. There is a discerning phrase of Froude's in his book on Erasmus, to the effect that two centuries of religious wars were to vindicate the rightness of his judgment [see Further Reading].

Similarly with his views on internationalism and peace. He had a horror of war and killing which went with his shrinking, unmasculine temperament and civilised preferences. A modern German scholar has called him 'the first of pacifists'; and some of his finest writings are denunciations of war and war-mongers. The fiercest exposure of all, the ***Julius Exclusus,*** is reserved for the most eminent offender, the war-like Pope Julius II, author of a general European war, whom Erasmus had seen entering Bologna in triumph and never forgot the spectacle. He is depicted clamouring for admission at the gate of Heaven: to be rejected.

Erasmus was a citizen of Europe, equally at home in the Netherlands, France, Italy, Germany or England, in Paris or London, Antwerp, Venice or Basel. Perhaps in the end equally homeless, for the city of the mind in which he dwelt was that Europe of which he was such a good citizen, but which has not even yet come to be. (pp. 101-04)

A. L. Rowse, "Erasmus and England," in his The English Spirit: Essays in Literature and History, *revised edition, Funk & Wagnalls, 1966, pp. 93-104.*

Roland H. Bainton (essay date 1969)

[Bainton was an English educator who wrote many works on the Renaissance and Reformation. In the excerpt below, he examines the content and various interpretations of The Praise of Folly.]

[In the ***Praise of Folly***] Folly herself enters and like a professor mounts the rostrum to deliver a discourse to a classroom of scholars. She declares that she will speak extempore without regard to rules and then constructs her discourse with all the divisions and subdivisions of the rhetoricians. Since Aristotle declares that an encomium should commence with a genealogy, she begins her laudation of herself by announcing that she is the daughter of Pluto and the goddess of youth, born in the Fortunate Isles, and nursed by drunkenness and ignorance. But this is not at all the genealogy of Erasmus' ***Stultitia.*** Among her ancestors was the court fool, sometimes an imbecile, who instead of being placed in an institution, was cared for in the household of a prince, while the courtiers, half with malice, half with compassion, derived amusement from his infantilism. But then again, he was sometimes a clever rogue who lodged barbed darts of irony and wit with impunity because he wore the cap and bells. Yet again the fools of Erasmus were those pilloried by the medieval preachers and moralists such as Geiler of Keyersburg and Sebastian Brandt, who filled his *Ship of Fools* with all those whom he meant to berate. The anomaly of Erasmus' Folly is that she herself berates the fools. Then at last she turns out to be the fool in Christ, who appears to be a fool to all those who in their folly esteem themselves as wise.

Our Folly is a very disconcerting dame. She is like mankind, whom Erasmus, following Lucian and anticipating Shakespeare, describes as actors on the stage of life wearing as in the ancient drama now one mask and now another. But the Erasmian Folly does not go behind the wings to change her masks, but by sleight of hand effects the shifts and thus tricks the reader into thinking she is still in the same role. Is he regarding her as a sot? Then of a sudden she becomes a sage, and when he gives credulity to her sagacity she turns into a satyr or a sot. The change occurs again and again for Folly prestidigitates from role to role.

She announces that it is she who keeps the human race extant. "For what man would ever put his neck into the halter of matrimony if, like the sages, he weighed the inconveniences, or what woman would ever give herself to a man if she took account of the perilous pangs of childbirth and the trouble of bringing up children? Or having done so once, would ever think of doing so again unless attended by Lethe, the goddess of forgetfulness?" Folly is spontaneity, a certain recklessness, an uncalculating readiness to take risks. She overrides prudence, yet is the highest prudence. For she delivers men alike from fear and shame and thus frees them to embark on great enterprises. Without her what cities, what empires would ever have been built?

Again Folly is the inhibition of that brutal candor which makes social intercourse insufferable. A little humbug is the lubricant of life. One can never get along with folk by utter truthfulness. A measure of dissembling, a touch of flattery smooths the path of friendship. All men are actors, deceived by their own masks, thinking themselves to be the very characters they impersonate. Shall we then pluck off the masks? Nay, rather let men play their parts, and happier perchance are we, too, if we do not perceive their masks. Illusion is the balm of life and a worse calamity than to be deceived is not to be deceived. If a man sincerely thinks his commonplace wife is a Penelope, all the better for their wedded bliss. Happier they who sit in Plato's cave, viewing the shadows, than those who come out into the light and see things as they really are.

The ignorance of the simple is a boon. How blessed were those pristine men of the golden age, who lived in accord with nature, knowing nothing of grammar, rhetoric, or law, nor bothering their heads as to what lay beyond the sky! How happy flies and birds! And look at morons. They play, sing, and laugh and bring others pleasure with their childishness. Compare the moron with the scholar "who squanders his youth in mastering the disciplines, wastes the sweetest of his years in worry, sweat, and vigils, always frugal, poor, lugubrious, gloomy, unjust, and harsh to himself, grating and grievous to others, lean, frail, bleary-eyed, old before his time."

The reader asks himself at this point just which mask Folly now is wearing. Erasmus himself was dedicated to his scholarly vigils and continued his indefatigable labors to the very end. Is Folly now really foolishness, who in her blindness is asking the scholar what good will come of it all? Or is she that prudent imprudence which drives a man to go on, even if he cannot foresee whether any fruit will come from his sowing? She is ambiguous because [she is] changing again her role. Speedily she becomes unmistakably the foolishness which Erasmus derides—the foolishness of those who leave slaughtering to the lower classes, but consider carving up a beast felled in the hunt to be fit work for gentlemen, the foolishness of inordinate builders, of gamblers, of those who call upon the saints to cure the toothache, of the thief who, saved from the gallows by the intervention of a saint, feels himself commissioned to relieve men again of their wealth, the foolishness of those who mock him who tells them the way to die well is to live well. Again the foolishness of those who at a funeral act as if the dead would be embarrassed to return and find a paucity of candles and hired pallbearers, the foolishness of chauvinists whether French, English, Scottish, Italian, Turkish, or whatever you please.

Then again Erasmus excoriates the folly of merchants who impose on the public by a display of gold rings, of grammarians who deem it the highest achievement of twenty years' labor to be able to distinguish eight parts of speech, of lawyers who roll the stone of Sisyphus by emitting six hundred laws in one breath, of theologians who debate how in the Eucharist accidents can subsist without substance and who conjure up sophisticated inanities about quidities and entities. Why not send the brawling Scotists, the adamant Occamists, the invincible Albertists to fight the Turks? And the monks, who will not touch money but are not so fastidious as to wine and women. At the judgment day one of them will boast that in sixty years he has never handled money save with gloves. Another will present himself with a cowl so dirty and greasy that no sailor would put it on. Another will display a voice grown hoarse with chanting. Christ will interrupt them saying, "Whence this new race of Jews?" [that is, of legalists].

Opprobrium is thrown on kings who leave the care of their subjects to the gods, fleece their people, and squander their substance on feeding fine horses; ladies who think the longer the trains they trail the nearer they are to the gods; popes and cardinals who delegate to Christ the care of their sheep; supreme pontiffs who, if there is any work to be done, turn it over to Peter and Paul; popes who think miracles outdated, instruction of the people irksome, explanations of Scripture pedantry, prayer a waste of time, who consider poverty to be sordid, defeat in war dishonorable, and to die on the cross a disgrace. They send men to hell with their excommunications and shed Christian blood to defend the papal patrimony. Whereas the Christian Church was founded on blood, strengthened by blood, increased by blood, Christ's cause today is advanced by war too cruel to befit men or beasts.

Then comes a jibe at scholars who throw a smog of annotations over the works of others, "like that Erasmus." What an incredibly trivial conclusion to such a catalog of enormities! By including himself was Erasmus throwing a sop to those whose gorge was rising?

After this startling interjection he takes one more fling at theologians who stretch Scripture like a sheepskin to justify the wars of Christians on the ground that Christ said "Let him who has no sword sell his mantle and buy one." (Luke 22:36). "As if Christ, who taught nothing but patience and meekness, meant the sword used by bandits and murderers rather than the sword of the Spirit. Our exegete thinks that Christ equipped the apostles with lances, crossbows, slings, and muskets."

At this point Dame Folly makes her final metamorphosis. Now she becomes the foolishness of the cross. For:

> no morons so play the fool as those who are obsessed with the ardor of Christian piety to the point that they distribute their goods, overlook injuries, suffer themselves to be deceived, make no distinction between friends and enemies, eschew pleasure, glut themselves with hunger, vigils, tears, toils, and reproaches, who disdain life, who crave only death, who seem utterly to contemn all common sense, as if the soul lived elsewhere and not in the body. What is this if not insanity? No wonder that the apostles appeared to be drunk with new wine and Paul seemed to Festus to be mad. Christ himself became a fool when he was found in fashion as a man that he might bring healing by the foolishness of the cross. 'For God has chosen the foolish things of the world to confound the wise, and the weak things of the world to confound the mighty.'

The ***Moria*** like the ***Enchiridion*** ends with the Platonic madness of ecstatic rapture, when the spirit rises above the things of sense and man is utterly beside himself, not knowing whether he is in the body or out of the body, for he experiences that which "eye hath not seen and ear hath not heard and neither hath it entered into the heart of man." He has already known a foretaste and a glow of that ineffable blessedness which shall be his when this mortal shall have put on immortality.

Then Folly leaves the rostrum saying, "Adieu, clap, live, drink, you celebrated devotees of *Moria*." And now once more she is the goddess of the cap and bells.

One interpreter has suggested that the ***Praise of Folly*** is the final attempt of the Renaissance to reduce all life to rational order, art to perspective, business to bookkeeping, war to strategy, statecraft to diplomacy. Now by Erasmus the irrational is shown to be the rational. Yes, but the irrational is shown to be the rational only because the rational is shown to be the irrational and all those disciplines so neatly reduced by men to order are but striving after wind.

Another interpreter also suggests an influence of the Renaissance, the Italian Renaissance, for in Italy Erasmus had tasted of the amenities of gracious living, and had come to distrust the fevered fury of those who inhabit the northern lands. But Erasmus had long since tasted the amenities of life in the north while kissing nymphs at Mountjoy's estate, whereas in Italy's sunny clime he had labored like a veritable Hercules. The point of the ***Moria*** is not to bask in the *dolce far niente.* It is not a moralistic denunciation as in Brandt's *Ship of Fools.* It is not buffoonery. It is not the *gaudeamus igitur* of the goliards. Erasmus himself said that the point was precisely the same as that of the ***Enchiridion.*** What there he had said seriously he said now in the guise of jest.

One may the better understand both the ***Enchiridion*** and the ***Moria*** by comparing them with another passage where Erasmus was commenting on the text, "All is vanity."

> Whence comes such vanity in the lives of Christians who enjoy the truth of the Gospel? With what tumults everywhere our lives are filled! We do business, we sail the seas, we engage in wars, we make treaties and we break them, we beget children, enroll heirs, buy fields and sell, cement friendships, erect buildings and tear them down. We are tonsured, anointed, vestured in cowls. We are exercised in various arts, sweat and become doctors of laws and theology. Some prefer the mitre and the crozier. With such cares we torture ourselves. In this we wax old. In this we let slip so many years and lose that precious treasure which alone is of worth. Then will come the last tribunal where only truth can stand. Too late we shall perceive that all these vanities were but shadows and we have squandered our lives in the delusion of a dream. Some one will say "Shall a Christian, then, have nothing to do with all of these vanities?" No, not that, but we shall participate only with detachment, being ready to forsake all for the sake of the one thing needful, as Paul said, "Having a wife as if not having," weeping as if not weeping, rejoicing as if not rejoicing, selling as possessing nothing, using the world as if not using, for the fashion of this world passes away. Use then the world but delight not in it.

Observe that the list of vanities here enumerated corresponds to those pilloried in the ***Praise of Folly,*** which, in the light of such similarity, may be described as an ironic version of the *contemptus mundi,* the contempt of the world. To say that it is ironic means, however, that it is not the medieval contempt of the world. Erasmus would not be willing, like Jerome and Colet, to see propagation cease that earth might be emptied and heaven filled. A more significant difference is the blending, everywhere to be found in Erasmus, of the Christian and classical themes. The Stoics distinguished the wise men and the fools, who because not governed by reason were both sots and knaves. The Neoplatonists deplored the servitude of man to the carnal. The first stage toward emancipation and self-mastery was self-knowledge—"Know thyself." The fool in the period of the Renaissance is consequently often portrayed eyeing himself quizzically in a mirror. He thus perceives that "everyman" is a fool including himself. His very existence depends on that *élan vital* which is not amenable to reason. This insight enables him to smile at himself as Erasmus does on more than one occasion. The smile is not a laugh of scorn so much as of pity and of hope. For man, enthralled by the senses and spending himself for ephemeral goals, can be emancipated by Folly of another sort, that divine rapture of Plato transcending reason, and the divine self-emptying of the Christian, who pursues his earthly pilgrimage with fidelity and detachment, following in the footsteps of him who trod the *via dolorosa.* (pp. 91-7)

Roland H. Bainton, in his Erasmus of Christendom, *Charles Scribner's Sons, 1969, 308 p.*

The Times Literary Supplement (essay date 1970)

[*In the following excerpt from an unsigned essay, the critic gives a concise survey of Erasmus's major works and themes.*]

In 1511, Erasmus issued the ***Praise of Folly.*** He was at least forty-three years old. Generations have applauded this biting satire of ecclesiastical worldliness and medieval monasticism. Scholars have analysed its send-up of the classical paradigms for encomia. Editors have puzzled over its text and commentators have assiduously identified most of the allusions. No one has yet mentioned that it must be a work of melancholy whimsy, the biting self-parody of a man whose intellectual assurance is betrayed by emotional uncertainty, and whose disappointed experience of post-Renaissance Italy had driven him into the momentary retreat of the security afforded by his close friendship with Thomas More.

In 1511, Erasmus had published very little. The ***Enchiridion*** of 1503-04 had allied apologetic with exhortation; but it was a hasty work, supporting interior, evangelical piety with a crassly Neo-Platonist psychology, important only in the light of what was to come, and too clearly indebted to Pico della Mirandola to bear the weight which has been put on it. The ***Adages*** had grown from the 818 proverbs in the ***Collectanea*** of 1500 to 3,260 in the Aldine ***Chiliades*** of 1508. But the fusion of biblical and classical worlds, of which Margaret Mann Phillips has written so perceptively in her study of the ***Adages,*** was not yet fully accomplished.

For all the virtuoso brilliance of its satirical techniques, its controlled ambivalence, and the steadfastness with which it attacks superstition, ecclesiastical abuse and clerical worldliness, the ***Praise of Folly*** is astonishingly tentative. Its failure to establish any tonic key by which Folly's voice might be related to that of Erasmus reveals real uncertainty. Folly speaks with at least four voices. The first represents youth, vitality, freedom from care, and praises all that is subversive of hierarchy and authority. The second, more astringent, strips the illusions from the pitiful and the grotesque to praise the ignorant and the mad. The consciousness of paradox begins to weigh down the text. Banter turns to acid as, without any change of tone or style, Folly throws in the long list of pious superstitions. The third voice is still harsher, as Folly turns to the theologians, monks and prelates; but the fourth voice is the most paradoxical of all. It turns the mock encomium into a real one with its moving and totally serious panegyric of the Pauline Folly of the cross, expressed in terms which deliberately excluded the learned if evangelical humanism to which, by 1511, Erasmus had dedicated his life.

After the Froben ***Adages*** of 1515, the Jerome letters and the prefactory material for the ***Novum Instrumentum*** of 1516, the note of intellectual uncertainty diminishes. There is no more nostalgia for the secure, unlettered piety of Erasmus's youth. Only the subtlety, the control of nuance, the unending checks and balances remain to remind us how tentative and exploratory so many of his views and attitudes were.

Erasmus's intellectual position and programme achieved definition only slowly, as he groped tentatively and at times erratically, with waspish arrogance and painful diffidence, towards the connexion he felt to exist between evangelical reform, the personal and social values of Neo-Platonist humanism, the restoration of classical rhetoric, textual criticism and educational reform. His achievement was to establish this connexion and to anchor the advanced values of an earlier Neo-Platonist humanism firmly in the text of the Church's own revelation. But the pole of his attitudes was the belief that human perfection was something intrinsic to human moral achievement. Against the scholastics who defended the strenuous and apparently arbitrarily prescribed "works" of late medieval religion, Erasmus held that even religious perfection was intrinsic to the highest moral development of which human nature was capable. Against Luther's anti-Pelagian denial of free will, Erasmus upheld man's autonomous power of self-determining moral choice.

Luther thought Erasmus's position Pelagian, and although Erasmus never made a directly Pelagian statement, it is true that the early sixteenth century knew no way of reconciling an autonomous human power of self-determination to good with a non-Pelagian theory of grace. Molina was to solve the dilemma in 1585, but only at the cost of re-importing the quasi-chronological distinction between divine acts rejected by the whole nominalist tradition. The obliqueness of so many of Erasmus's theological statements is due to his consciousness of the dilemma, finally to be solved by regarding nature itself as redeemed, and therefore as capable of accepting grace in virtue not of its own powers but of its redeemed aspirations.

Erasmus came astonishingly close to this solution, in spite of his awareness that it meant allowing grace to the Pagans, a view too radical in its dissociation of faith from justification to be more than cautiously explored by anyone who valued his orthodoxy. Marsilio Ficino had come very near to affirming the sanctity of Socrates in a famous letter from which Erasmus took the reference to "Saint Socrates" in the 1522 ***Convivium religiosum,*** and Lefèvre d'Etaples had defended the evangelical humanist view that religious perfection was intrinsic to moral achievement by suggesting in his 1512 commentary on the Pauline epistles that the unevangelized Americans might be saved by observing the natural moral law. Erasmus went farther than either in the preface to his 1523 edition of the ***Tusculan Disputations.*** But the delicate theological status of pagan virtue even more than the apparently Pelagian implications of his concept of free will accounts for the peculiarly elliptical nature of his theological thought and the enduring uncertainty of his tone.

"Erasmus the Cautious Humanist," in The Times Literary Supplement, *No. 3557, April 30, 1970, p. 483.*

A. E. Douglas (essay date 1970)

[*In the excerpt below, Douglas evaluates the effectiveness and use of satire in several of Erasmus's works, especially* The Praise of Folly, *which he finds "a brilliant but artless and uneven improvization."*]

Satire, unless it be defined as the works which their authors have at any time called satires (which is of no help for the present purpose), occupies a territory with ill-defined frontiers between serious moral discourse or homily on the one hand, and on the other invective or lampoon, direct verbal assault on named or easily identifiable individual persons. The former overlaps with satire when it makes ridicule its weapon, the latter when a general moral purpose and again the element of ridicule (but not ridicule alone: exaggeration and fantasy seem to be proper to satirical invective) can be detected. Of satirical invective against individuals Erasmus is hardly to be counted a practitioner. Even if only out of nervousness he eschewed such attacks, preferring to keep in reserve the satirist's escape-hatch 'If the cap fits. . . . ' Of the one possible example of personal invective, the ***Julius Exclusus,*** he would, in modern official phrase, neither confirm nor deny his authorship. But across the other border-zone, where solemn homily meets satire, Erasmus moves freely and frequently. Indeed while ***Julius Exclusus*** is doubtful in authorship and in taste, Erasmus' one certain contribution to sustained satirical writing, the ***Praise of Folly,*** is, we shall see, but partially successful; it is in the short aside or digression or the brief commentary, that is generally on a small scale and often in a non-satirical context, that his satirical gifts are best seen. (p. 31)

When Erasmus' satire is good, it is when it is used as but one weapon among many, to achieve a clear moral or intellectual end, and not as an end in itself, a literary form to be played with. With him, as he claimed, the satirical manner is subservient to the moral purpose. He does not merely set himself to write satire, come what may: he writes satirically when satire is the right weapon. Erasmus knows on the one hand that moral deficiencies may be too grave to be merely ridiculous; on the other hand he has an acute sense of what *is* merely ridiculous. Mankind is guilty of crimes as well as follies, and his crimes may outstrip the range of even the most mordant ridicule; yet the grimmest of human offences may include as subordinate elements absurdities and incongruities which can be proper objects of satire. But Erasmus is seldom concerned with confining himself to one or other aspect of human behaviour, his eye is on the situation in all its aspects; hence his frequent changes of tone and mood. (p. 32)

Erasmus' satire gains much by being written on a basis of firm conviction. Though he is sometimes lacking in the literary arts of the greatest satirists, he is preserved from their two besetting sins. One is the common ambivalence of being half in love with what one professes to hate, by which the satirist defeats his own ends, if these really are moral censure and not the expression of a general disgust with human life, or literary gymnastics. However unconvincing the surrounding context, Erasmus in his preface to the ***Praise of Folly*** strikes this nail on the head in saying that, unlike Juvenal, he will describe the *ridenda* rather than the *foeda,* the laughable rather than the filthy; or again in the ***Adages* (*Ollas ostentare*)**, he writes in defence of the ***Praise of Folly*** that from Juvenal readers learn how to criticize . . .

> the vices of rulers, priests, businessmen, and especially women . . . which they often so depict as to instruct in obscenity.

Sexual excess and perversion had been a stock subject for satirists from ancient times, but the most we have from Erasmus is a little gentle mockery of feminine foibles in a mood very different from that of Juvenal's sixth satire, to say nothing of his second. In an age like the present, which already shows signs of finding comic its own freedom in discussion and behaviour, one should hesitate to attribute Erasmus' restraint to mere prudery.

The other fault is of course indiscriminate destructiveness. While the satirist's method is necessarily critical—if he explicitly advances moral teaching to a significant extent, he becomes a preacher—*épater les bourgeois* is not really a very subtle or satisfying aim; nor is the 'professional' satirist's pose that everything human is merely ridiculous or contemptible, nothing sublime or satanic, less self-defeating than the trap of ambivalence. Indeed the strength of Erasmus' satire lies precisely in the lack of that pose. That he appealed even in satirical moments (we are not yet dealing with mere light-hearted banter of satirical quality: Erasmus' achievement in this field we shall consider later) to a firm moral centre, and a particular moral centre, helps to explain the hostility that his works aroused—and still arouse. His sheer efficiency as a writer, his enormous learning and fluency, provide, of course, part of the explanation of the bitterness he provoked: no one likes to feel helpless under a hail of ridicule. But more serious offence was given precisely by his persistent probing of what seemed to him the incongruity between Christian practices of his day and the teaching of the Gospel. The objects of his bitterest attacks could not retort with a *tu quoque* as Horace's victims had done ('Have you no faults'?), nor with a generalized, 'That's the way of the world'. Any satire implies some assumption of moral or intellectual superiority: yet the fact that Erasmus' implied claim is only to a clearer vision of the meaning of Christianity both lessens the arrogance and adds sharpness. Most of us would rather be by implication involved in general criticisms of the standards of society at large than constantly reminded of failure to live up to those standards which we actually profess. Even when assaulting intellectual excesses, of scholasticism in its decadence or extravagant Ciceronianism, his intention is to contrast pedantries with Christian simplicity and seriousness. His most consistently powerful satire is directed in fact not at those acknowledged by everyday standards as vicious—too easy targets—nor at groups he fortuitously disliked (though he can be amusing about these), but on those he saw as at best misunderstanding, at worst wilfully hypocritical about, the standards demanded by Christianity.

A further illustration. The rich and avaricious, the birth-proud, were derided by satirists long before Erasmus, partly because satirists have often been poor men, and more seriously because these targets can be shown to have misunderstood the true sources and values of human well-being. Erasmus satirizes them too, greed and hauteur being ridiculous rather than (in themselves) wicked. . . . But again Erasmus appeals to a moral centre which, as is not the case with many satirists, can easily be identified as the simplicity of Christ and the Gospel: . . .

> What was the point of the acquisition of these things which are attended by so many disadvantages? Can you be afraid that Christ will be too weak in his own strength unless a secular despot bestows something of his power? Do you think him insufficiently adorned unless a profane man of war grants him gold, and a goldsmith, gleaming carriage-horses and a retinue, that is, a share of his own luxury and pride?
>
> (pp. 33-6)

Just as, from our initial point of view, satire occupies a zone contiguous and partly overlapping with homily and invective, so in intensity it may vary from (i) passages of light-hearted criticism through (ii) passages of satirical manner but clearly serious intent, to (iii) passages in grave contexts where one reader may detect a flash of irony and ridicule, and another (or even that same reader in a different mood) only indignation and passion. We have been considering why Erasmus is particularly liable to offer passages of this third type, so presenting a certain problem to a contributor to a symposium who may feel an obligation not to stray too far beyond his assignment.

In this last category (we shall consider the three in reverse order) one may put much of what Erasmus wrote at length about war, notably the adage ***Dulce bellum inexpertis*** and the ***Querimonia Pacis.*** Is there a curl of the lip or pure anger in such passages as the following onslaught on Christian involvement in war? . . .

> Lastly, what I think more appalling than all this, the Christian (fights) with his fellow-man: I must add reluctantly the most appalling thing of all, Christian with fellow-Christian: and such is the blindness of the human mind, nobody is surprised at this, nobody execrates it. There are people who applaud, who extol, who call 'holy' this worse than hellish business, and who spur on princes who need no incitement to insanity, adding, as they say, 'oil to the flames'. One man from the holy pulpit promises forgiveness of all sins to those who fight under the standards of that Prince. Another cries, O most invincible Prince, do you but preserve your devotion to religion, and God will fight on your side.

Erasmus goes on to say that some distort Biblical quotations in the interests of the combatants, but then any hint of satire gives way, most characteristically, to tremendous solemn anger: . . .

> The battle-lines clash, both sides bearing before them the sign of the Cross, which of itself should suffice to show in what fashion Christians should gain their victories. From that heavenly rite in which is shown forth the perfect and ineffable unity of Christians they rush to mutual slaughter.

In the ***Complaint of Peace*** irony can be clearly heard in the passage where Erasmus contrasts the shame of submitting to a neighbouring ruler with the real shame of supporting one's self against him by alien alliances: . . .

> But how much lower you degrade your majesty when you are compelled to do obeisance to the troops of the barbarians and the lowest criminal dregs who can never be sated with gold, when you send envoys with smooth supplications to the Carians, the most worthless and withal most villainous of men, when you entrust your very life and the fortunes of your kindred to the good faith of those who hold nothing in respect, nothing holy.
>
> (pp. 36-7)

Perhaps the best known of Erasmus' exercises in bitter comedy is the colloquy ***Naufragium*** **(*The Shipwreck*).** The behaviour of the despairing crew and passengers is the vehicle for an attack on Mariolatry, the localization of the worship of the Virgin and the Saints, and other features of late medieval piety which were favourite targets of the Reformers. (p. 39)

It would have been a pity to leave aside the effective lighthearted ridicule in which Erasmus sometimes indulged. But it was of course the first two types of satire that gave Erasmus a reputation as a biting and dangerous critic of contemporary ecclesiastical doctrines and practices. To those mentioned already could be added from the ***Colloquia*** alone criticisms of pilgrimages, indulgences, and the prohibition of meat-eating on Fridays and other fasts.

Naturally the orthodox were suspicious and hostile, the Reformers impatient at his refusal to identify himself openly with their cause. Where Erasmus actually stood and whether on any particular matter he was right or wrong are questions which, in so far as this is a literary study, do not concern us here. Just as there is clearly a sense (though idealists like Cicero and some moralists since his time have denied it) in which a bad man can be a 'good' orator, so a bad or misguided man can be in a technical sense a good, that is to say, effective satirist. However greatly cherished or revered were the beliefs, practices and institutions that he attacks, we may still ask whether he writes well or ill. The extent to which he shocks and hurts is indeed one (not the only) measure of his effectiveness. Yet in Erasmus' case the matter cannot quite be left here. We have seen that we are not dealing with literary exercises. If a satirist is plainly as serious as Erasmus usually is, the question of whether he is right or wrong may be of some importance. It is worth considering why in Erasmus' case it has come to seem peculiarly important.

Erasmus' satire at the expense of Pope, clergy and the Church generally, is naturally associated in most minds with the tremendous upheavals of the Reformation period. Yet there was a long tradition of such criticism, sometimes more savage than Erasmus and even by modern standards blasphemous, something which (for reasons we need not reiterate) Erasmus never was. Criticism of the Roman Church as an institution, above all the Roman Curia for its greed, and of monks and friars, is a recurrent theme of medieval satire. Not of course did secular authority escape satirical censure on similar grounds. Even now that vigorous side of medieval writing is not perhaps as familiar as it might be: but many will have encountered (not, probably, without a sense of shock) the 'Gospel of the Marks of Silver', a cento of scriptural phraseology scandalously devised as a weapon to assail the greed of the Papal officials; and the world of the Archpoet and the other 'followers of Golias' is not distinguished by respect for the forms and institutions of established religion. There is much too in less deliberately outrageous vein. Bernard of Cluny's *De contemptu mundi,* a metrical *tour de force* in pure dactylic rhyming hexameters, attacks the worldliness of the clergy, the violence of soldiers, the greed and dishonesty of farmers, and with references to ancient Roman satirists, the avaricious and rich in general. To the same vigorously satirical age, the twelfth century, belongs Nigel Wireker's *Speculum Stultorum,* the tale of the disillusioning travels of Brunellus the ass: the work assaults all the monastic orders one by one, and kings, bishops, and laity. Gilles de Corbeil in his diffuse but often lively work and Jordan of Osnabrück are others who somewhat later carried on the tradition of satirizing the dignitaries of the Church.

We cannot now look in detail at the whole field of satire in the developing European vernaculars, which culminated in Erasmus' own day in Brant's *Ship of Fools.* But it is worth recalling that G. R. Owst explored and expounded the literary sub-world of the late medieval (vernacular English) sermon. He showed that in those sermons many ideas and moods found expression for which students of the period had been too willing to trace high literary pedigrees but which in fact were simply in the late medieval air for anyone to encounter and exploit: among those ideas and moods the satirical play no small part. Among the victims of these attacks by clergy are (above all) the Church and clergy themselves. (In Owst's view the Church's prestige was thus greatly weakened from within, long before the emergence of the Reformation movement in the usual sense of the term.)

Yet when all this is said, Erasmus cannot easily be separated from his time as a figure of Renaissance and Reformation. He is a Renaissance figure in that while he shows the influence of Renaissance writers like Poggio and Valla, his debt to medieval satirists is scarcely traceable, nor would he at all have countenanced association with the more scurrilous of the writers alluded to above. The brief dialogue of Barbaria and Thalia . . . shows what he thought of medieval Latin versification: and the major medieval satires are in verse. He owed much of course to the Roman satirists, Horace, Persius and Juvenal, and in this resembled his medieval predecessors from Adalbero of Laon in the tenth century and Egbert of Liège in the eleventh with their many reminiscences of the Roman writers, who were also well known to the twelfth-century writers of lyrics *cum auctoritate,* like Walter of Chatillon, to whom they frequently provided the borrowed tags that conclude their stanzas. But he owed more to a writer his forerunners did not know, the Greek prose-satirist Lucian, many of whose works Erasmus translated into Latin. His debt is evident in the crisp and vivid dialogue of some of the ***Colloquia:*** the Greek, one of the most entertaining of ancient writers, was a master of this form, and he too, unlike the Romans (except perhaps Juvenal in his tenth satire on the proper objects of prayer), attacked the intellectual and moral weaknesses of contemporary religion and its adherents as well as many other manifestations of the bogus, pretentious and hypocritical. If Erasmus has Christian models, he is in a tradition of Christian writing as old as St Jerome (if not St Paul), with his scathing denunciations of worldly Christianity.

Erasmus is a figure of the Reformation period not only in this appeal to the early Church. In his day not only the Church as an institution, but also the defects of its human representatives were, as so often before, under attack. Its religious practices and doctrines were under fire as never before, and though Erasmus was conservative about the Church's doctrine in the narrow sense, his other criticisms (on indulgences, auricular confession and so forth) certainly had theological implications. That is why it is still not easy to judge Erasmus as a satirist without taking into account whether one agrees with him or not.

It is time to turn from Erasmus' occasional use of satire within larger contexts to his purely satirical works, the ***Praise of Folly*** and ***Julius Exclusus.*** With these may be considered the ***Ciceronianus,*** for even though here as so often Erasmus' satirical criticisms give way to a serious and positive consideration of the issues involved and the procedures to be recommended, the work coheres as an attack on a single well-defined target.

The ***Praise of Folly*** was written very fast, within a week, though there is evidence that Erasmus, like Mozart, may have spent a good deal of time shaping his endlessly fertile ideas in his head before actually putting pen to paper—and it should perhaps be read fast too. For it scarcely bears close analysis. In it Folly delivers an oration on her own behalf, a fact which at once suggests a conflation of two forms anciently held distinct. Satire the work certainly is, and is intended to be, as Erasmus' preface and later defence (on ***Ollas ostentare*** *cf.* above) show. But it is also descended from a curious ancient form of *oratory* which may be called the paradoxical encomium (the Greco-Latin title of Erasmus' book is ***Encomium Moriae***), in which the writer exercised all his art and skill in defending the indefensible. It was originally intended as an exercise in ingenuity, which should demonstrate the powers of oratory even with an unpromising subject: it was not satirical, but rather paradoxical or ironical, and since Erasmus fails to observe this distinction, it is of some importance that we for the present purpose should.

It has often been pointed out that for all its brilliant passages and incidental flashes of wit, the ***Praise of Folly*** suffers from a fundamental incoherence, and this incoherence results precisely from the combination in it of everything that can paradoxically (i.e. untruthfully) be said on behalf of Folly, with everything that Folly can say by way of satirizing the real follies of mankind. This conflation of forms and approaches is perhaps more genuinely the source of the incoherence than the reason more commonly alleged: that Erasmus has entangled himself in the logical complexities of having Folly (who must not be believed) as the speaker. When Folly speaks of real human follies, she should defend them, and leave the reader to take the point, but too often Erasmus (not Folly) is clearly the speaker, and the half-hearted attempts to save the situation, which will be illustrated shortly, are altogether unconvincing, both aesthetically and as an attempt to save Erasmus from the odium which his (not Folly's) attacks—most of them were on familiar enough Erasmian themes—were bound to invite. It was also, of course, futile for Erasmus to try to defend himself by claiming that in so far as he was directly satirical he was *merely* writing in the ancient tradition of satire, of Greek Old Comedy and Lucian, and must therefore not be taken too seriously: did not his ancient models intend to be taken seriously?

To illustrate from the work itself: we are first told that all the pleasures of life, success and fame, are owed to one or another kind of folly, and in the world of the paradoxical encomium this is logically satisfactory. The standards of achievement accepted are those of the everyday world, and it is for the reader to decide how far amid arguments deliberately perverse or frivolous, he must acknowledge an element of truth in the attacks on intellectualism—reason is not the whole of a human being, philosophers are ineffective in public affairs, and much more effective are foolish stories like the fable of the interdependence of the parts of the body with which Menenius Agrippa allegedly quelled an insurrection of the Roman plebs. Fools take action instead of consulting antique tomes. Human life simply would not work without the element of 'folly' which makes so much of it just a theatrical performance. Thinking leads to suicide: I, Folly, make people love life—dirty old men and lecherous old women are here vividly depicted; surely it is better to be even like this than to hang oneself. The dilemma is of course false, and 'better' must be taken in a popular sense, but the point is a genuine one, as when within the same popular frame of reference, Folly contrasts the agonies of the intellectual with the cheerful vacuity of the fool and idiot.

But it is at this point that the *jeu d' esprit* gives way to satire on fools. Folly no longer utters her paradoxical half-truths. Without notice Erasmus takes over, and all the familiar targets of his scorn reappear—after cuckolds, those who build on an extravagant scale, alchemists, and gamblers, come foolish worshippers of saints and those who accepted doctrines of nicely calculated reliefs from Purgatory. At the close of this bitter passage Erasmus tries to reassert the ostensible mood of the piece: pride of birth is foolish, but it is in the context of praise of Folly, 'good'—people like it, and it makes them happy. Why bother to learn a skill? The inexpert man is more popular. Folly touches on other kinds of foolish pride, for example, sources of national pride. Then she turns to flattery: there is a valuable kind (a really valuable kind—Erasmus, not Folly, speaks). But again the focus shifts, and Folly tells us that opinions are more conducive to *felicitas,* 'happiness' as popularly understood, than is truth.

The same confusion appears in the criticisms of various social groups which begin at IV. 457 B. On the whole Erasmus speaks in the attacks on grammarians, poets, and rhetoricians, lawyers and theologians, and he can make good jokes: scholars wear bands round their heads because they are so full of rubbish that otherwise they would burst ('alioquin etiam plane dissilirent'). But again there is something unsatisfactory, though the wit is itself often good, about the sudden asides that remind us how it all began, as on monks: . . .

> In their own expectation they are happy, not without help from me.

Or on rulers and princes, who have tremendous responsibilities but 'thanks to me (Folly)' are not unduly worried by them; or in the savage attack on cardinals and prelates: men behave as they do because they misunderstand the truth, but they are happy because they misunderstand.

Perhaps the nearest we come to a clarification of objectives or reconciliation of aims is with the statement that Fortune favours the foolish and rash, but the wise are timid: wisdom is useless for *public* success. . . . But now, as often, Erasmus turns serious, neither satirical nor paradoxical. Many citations of the praise of folly from Classical and Biblical sources serve to introduce a new theme, the contrast of Christian folly with worldly wisdom. This folly is neither the anti-intellectualist folly that ensures worldly success nor the folly of fools as the satirist sees them at work in Church and society at large. The work approaches its end with a rhapsodical eulogy of Christian folly, though to be sure before we are done, the satirical note returns in a discourse on the folly—that is, now, the eccentricities—of the pious. And if we appear to be doing Erasmus less than justice, we must confess that he realized what he had been about. Just as at the end of the vast commentary on the adage ***Scarabaeus*** he turns the tables on the wilting reader by pointing to criticisms of his earlier commentaries as being too brief, so the last paragraph of the ***Praise of Folly*** is a brief acknowledgement of the chaos of the material: . . .

> I see you are awaiting a peroration but you are very silly if you think I can even remember what I have said, after pouring out such a hotch-potch.

It may not be coincidental that Erasmus here refers both to an *epilogus,* the technical term in antiquity for the peroration to a *speech,* and in the same breath to a *farrago,* famous as Juvenal's description of his own *satire.*

It will be clear that one reader at least finds it amazing that the ***Praise of Folly*** has ever been regarded as a literary masterpiece. It reads exactly like what it is, a brilliant but artless and uneven improvization by a man of great learning and fluency of style. Few at any time could have written this work in one week, but easy writing is notoriously liable to make hard reading. In this instance the difficulty is not in detail: no better example perhaps could be found of what the ancients called *volubilitas,* the style that rolls and rushes like a river. But unless the reader simply surrenders himself to the onrush of the invective, he must constantly ask himself which sort of folly, if indeed any, is now speaking. Erasmus' contemporaries of course knew when he was serious, and admired or resented his invective and wit; they were responsive to the appeal of a virtuoso's Latinity; and we can still appreciate these aspects of the ***Praise of Folly.*** But it is not being humourless to judge the work inadequate by higher critical standards. And it is no help to urge that this is a mere *jeu d' esprit,* and to accuse the judicious critic of heavy-handedness. The chief fault of the ***Praise of Folly*** is in fact precisely the same whether one takes it as a light-hearted trifle or as a serious piece of literature. Whichever way, the ***Praise of Folly*** is simply far too long. The joke, which began as a pedantic pun on Moria, the Greek for Folly, and the name of Erasmus' friend Sir Thomas More, to whom the work is addressed, will not last the distance, and desperate recourses are needed to keep the theme alive even in semblance. A joke seventy-five pages long (in the latest English translation) has to be a very good joke indeed.

One adage Erasmus as a writer seems not to have taken to heart was one of the most familiar of all: Do nothing in excess. Repeatedly his excessive fluency and extravagant parades of learning blunt the edge of his satire. There is a superfluity of matter and style alike. Too frequently we are reminded that Erasmus was the author of the ***Colloquia,*** which has provided us with some examples of satire, but which was after all a Latin phrase-book, beginning with around fifty courteous or insulting ways of saying 'Good morning' in Latin. (pp. 42-9)

Julius Exclusus is less famous than the ***Praise of Folly*** for two reasons, first, because of Erasmus' refusal to acknowledge authorship of this anonymously published work, and secondly, because this attack on the recently dead Pope Julius II—he is depicted as being refused admission to heaven by St Peter—has often seemed in poor taste. As to the first, we shall here assume the more probable of the two alternative authors suggested by contemporaries, 'Aut

Drawing by Hans Holbein of Folly speaking from the rostrum.

Erasmus aut Diabolus'. The second point cannot be belittled, yet the satire, though strong, is far less cruel than that in two lampoons on similar themes, Seneca's *Apocolocyntosis* on the lately dead Emperor Claudius, and Byron's *Vision of Judgment* where George III is the victim. Indeed the modern reader may well be struck by an almost *sympathetic* quality in the satire. It is a brilliant study in mutual incomprehension. St Peter simply cannot understand what has happened to the office which he was first to hold, and humbly asks to be instructed. Julius for his part is made to seem naïvely unaware of the enormity of his behaviour as he expounds it. . . . Much as Erasmus disliked in particular Julius' military ambitions and activities—it is his military aspect which first surprises Peter—he manages to make of him in this satire more than a victim of personal spite. Much of what Julius says condemns not only himself but aspects of the Church in general, and more than this, it is possible to ignore the ecclesiastical issue altogether, and to see Julius as any man in authority, *genuinely* concerned for the prestige of the institution he serves and of his own position within it, yet hopelessly superficial in outlook and blithely insensitive to any but material standards. Not only in Renaissance Popes do we find such objects for satire. The political, business, and academic worlds, as well as the ecclesiastical, are still able to produce examples.

Lastly, a glimpse of Erasmus as satirist in literary matters. A tiny early piece presents Thalia and Barbaria, symbols respectively of Classical and late Medieval Latinity, abusing each other like two (very literate) fishwives. Towards the end of his life, Erasmus gave much fuller attention to the extreme Classicists, or rather Ciceronians, those who, almost incomprehensibly to the modern mind (since they engaged in extravagant defence of, not attacks on, a tradition), rejected from their Latin every expression not found in the works of Cicero. The first part of Erasmus' dialogue ***Ciceronianus*** is among his liveliest writings. Bulephorus catches sight of an old friend Nosoponus, once jolly, red-faced, and inclined to portliness, but now almost wasted away by years devoted to the detailed study necessary to ensure no breach of strict Ciceronian principles. He has had of course to avoid the distractions of marriage and family life.

> BULEPHORUS: Very sensible of you, Nosoponus. My wife, if I prepared to study Cicero at night the way you do, would burst in through the door, tear up the indexes, and throw on the fire the sheets of Cicero-practice. Much worse than this, while I pay attention to Cicero, she would get a deputy to pay attention to her in my place. As a result, while I practise so as to resemble Cicero, she would produce someone not resembling Bulephorus.

Erasmus was not often as naughty as this. (pp. 51-4)

A. E. Douglas, "Erasmus as a Satirist," in Erasmus, *edited by T. A. Dorey, University of New Mexico Press, 1970, pp. 31-54.*

James D. Tracy (essay date 1971)

[*Tracy is an American historian. In the excerpt below, he examines the humanism of Erasmus, especially in regard to the latter's educational philosophy and humanistic theology.*]

Humanism is commonly thought to be the philosophy of the Renaissance, a new appreciation of human dignity and freedom in contrast to the medieval emphasis on authority and on the miseries of this earthly life. The humanism of Erasmus has sometimes been defined in this way. Gerhard Ritter finds the essence of Renaissance humanism in Erasmus's defense of free will: the famous controversy with Luther proves that the man-centered philosophy of humanism was not compatible with the God-centered theology of the Reformation. But Lorenzo Valla, a fifteenth-century Italian humanist whom Erasmus admired, wrote a treatise against the freedom of the will which was cited by Luther. Younger humanists in Germany during Erasmus's lifetime were not aware of any incompatibility between humanism and Reformation theology, for most of them became Protestants. (p. 29)

There was no single philosophical doctrine on which all humanists agreed. The one thing which almost all of them did have in common was a love of classical Latin. Their fascination with Latin style seems strange to modern readers; historians often ignore it and concentrate on other facets of humanism more interesting to the twentieth century. But Paul O. Kristeller, the leading contemporary student of humanism, rightly insists that a definition of humanism must begin with what humanists had most in common. They insisted that classical Latin style was useful as well as beautiful. In fourteenth-century Italy, where humanism arose, there was great demand for men who could speak and write Latin effectively. Francesco Petrarca, the father of humanism, popularized the idea that Cicero was the best model for a persuasive and eloquent style. Some humanists analyzed the techniques of persuasion employed by Cicero. Others studied the properties of vocabulary and syntax by which classical Latin differed from medieval Latin. Thus a preoccupation with classical style led to a cultivation of rhetoric and grammar. These two disciplines constituted the core of the intellectual interests shared by most humanists. It will be necessary to explore the implications of each before the humanism of Erasmus can be properly described.

Rhetoric in ancient Athens was the great rival of philosophy. Socrates the philosopher charged that students who went to the teachers of rhetoric learned only the art of winning arguments by trickery, not the art of reasoning in search of truth. Teachers of rhetoric retorted that students who went to Socrates wasted their time chewing over insoluble questions. The art of rhetoric, however, would be useful and profitable in the law courts and public assemblies. It would also promote virtuous habits, for no one could be a successful orator unless he were known to be a man of good character. Plato continued Socrates' criticisms of rhetoric. But as Greek culture was transmitted to the west the philosophers had no true successors among the practical-minded Romans. The two great Latin writers on education took over the theory and practice of Greek rhetoric. Quintilian's *Institutes of Oratory* laid down general principles of educational method as well as principles of effective speaking. Cicero suggested that the orator should gain a broad knowledge of human nature through what he called the *studia humanitatis* or the humanities: poetry, history, and moral philosophy. To be a successful orator one also had to be virtuous: for it was the orator's noble duty to persuade his fellow citizens to follow the path of reason, just as in past ages the power of eloquence had persuaded savage men to descend from their caves and dwell together in cities. In his treatises on philosophy Cicero was less interested in what might be true in theory than in what was conducive to morality. The purpose of education was not to indulge the mind in speculation but to train good citizens. Renaissance humanism was a revival of Cicero's educational program, just as medieval scholasticism had been a revival of Aristotelian philosophy. The main undergraduate subjects in medieval universities had been the logic and physics of Aristotle. Only in the fourteenth century did the subjects recommended by Cicero begin to be taught in Italian universities. A teacher of poetry was known in student slang as an *umanista*—a humanist. Humanists and teachers of logic sometimes debated the nature of education in terms that resembled the ancient debate between rhetoricians and philosophers. Thus [in his essay "The Humanist Movement" (1961)] Professor Kristeller concludes that humanism was a phase in the rhetorical tradition of Western culture. (pp. 30-1)

Renaissance humanists adopted the rationale of classical rhetoric as well as its techniques. [In his *Rhetoric and Philosophy in Renaissance Humanism* (1968)] Jerrold Seigel has shown that the Italian humanists of the fourteenth and fifteenth century sought to carry out Cicero's plan of subordinating philosophy to the practical needs of persuasion. Northern humanists developed a theory of consensus, according to which truth in ethics was founded not on logical arguments but on assumptions shared by all men, which the ancient rhetoricians had called "commonplaces." Humanist educators agreed with Cicero that men had a natural desire to learn. They recommended appealing to a pupil's sense of pride instead of using physical punishment. It may seem at this point that the discussion is returning to its beginning. The philosophical assumptions shared by humanists and rhetoricians sound like the emphasis on human freedom and dignity that was supposed to be an inadequate definition of humanism. The difference is a matter of context. During a certain period of history men who shared certain intellectual interests were called "humanists" by their contemporaries. If humanism becomes a naked idea, lifted from context, it becomes difficult to explain why the humanists were usually suspicious of speculative philosophy, or why Thomas Aquinas was not a humanist. Conversely, the context makes it easier to understand the aristocratic attitudes of the humanists. Cicero and Quintilian shared the common assumption of most ancient writers that the capacity for virtue was found primarily if not exclusively among members of the upper classes. The humanists, who often moved among the chief men of their society, had a higher opinion than ancient writers did of merchants but not of the lower classes. Finally, apart from the context it would be tempting to contrast humanist optimism about human nature with the pessimism of St. Augustine or Thomas Hobbes. In fact such a contrast would be misleading because the humanists, particularly in northern Europe, were primarily educators. Like their favorite classical authors they were concerned with moral ideals and not with the realities of power. They believed that an atmosphere of freedom was fitting for aristocrats and learned men. But no more than Hobbes or Augustine would they have welcomed the idea of extending such freedom to the common crowd of men. Rational persuasion was for the few and not for the masses.

The art of rhetoric alone was not sufficient to revive the eloquence of the ancients. The art of grammar was required to overcome the differences that separated the spoken Latin of the Church and the universities from the Latin of Cicero. Humanists were outraged that medieval writers had departed from the classical norm in vocabulary, sentence structure, and the rules of versification. Lorenzo Valla's *Elegantiae* or *Book of Elegances* sought to counteract ten centuries of linguistic change. The Latin tongue was "a great mystery, indeed a divine power." But the Gothic tribes who destroyed the empire of the Romans had also devastated their language. Classical purity was to be restored through Valla's collection of over three thousand "elegances" or illustrations of correct usage. Humanists divided the history of language into three stages of perfection, degeneration, and revival, thus anticipating the eighteenth-century division of European history into ancient, medieval, and renaissance periods. They themselves expanded their criticism of medieval Latin culture into other areas besides linguistic usage. Classical authors had to be reinterpreted because of misunderstandings that arose from the medieval emphasis on dialectic. The corpus of an author's works had to be purged not only of copyists' errors but also of spurious works that had been naively accepted by medieval readers. The science of philology or textual criticism became a vehicle for exposing the false historical basis of many cherished medieval beliefs. . . . Philology was to be humanism's most solid contribution to the intellectual heritage of Europe.

In order to imitate classical Latin the humanists cultivated the arts of rhetoric and grammar. Rhetoric implied a utilitarian attitude toward philosophy and an optimistic theory of education. Grammar led to the emergence of a new sense of the past. Long ago Richard McKeon suggested that the differences between humanism and scholasticism might be explained by the differing intellectual methods of grammar and rhetoric as opposed to logic or dialectic. This definition of humanism too is open to criticism but it does have the advantage that it fits Erasmus. Erasmus was not just a humanist. He learned much from the Fathers of the Church, and possibly also from the religious milieu in which he was raised, as well as from the classics. His ideas stem not just from reading but also from contemporary life, from friends, and from his own personality. . . . [Erasmus] was clearly a humanist in his love of classical Latin, his hopes for the moral improvement of mankind through education, and his great contribution to the science of philology. In his writings these humanist concerns merge into a new program for the reform of European society based on reforms in education and religion. Erasmus the humanist can best be understood as Erasmus the humanist reformer. The discussion will take up first his humanist philosophy of education and second his humanist theology. (pp. 32-4)

[Erasmus] attacked the primary or secondary education of his day on three familiar points: the teachers were brutal, the books were full of barbarisms, and the whole curriculum, even prior to entrance in the universities, was oriented around dialectic. . . . He followed Valla in his criticism of medieval Latin books. They were particularly bad because of farfetched etymologies and word associations. For example, part of the definition of the word "dog" was that a dog "adheres." This was so because of the gospel passage in which dogs are said to return to their own vomit. According to theologians the "dogs" in question were heretics who returned to their own false doctrines. The word "heretic" (which was actually Greek) was thought to derive from the Latin "adhaereo" or "adhere." Therefore dogs, like heretics, "adhere." After laboring through arguments of this kind one might better appreciate the sense of liberation that humanists experienced with classical Latin. Finally, Erasmus felt much harm had come from the permeation of lower schools by dialectic. As taught in the universities, dialectic produced more arrogance than learning. Its introduction into lower schools meant that Latin grammars, instead of simply describing usage, attempted to derive usage from a set of axioms. Schoolboys thus had to wrestle with logic before properly learning to read and write.

Thus far Erasmus's attack on medieval education contains nothing that cannot be found in humanists like Valla or, as regards the arrogance of dialecticians, in reform-minded churchmen as well. His expectation that men trained in scholasticism would be vain and quarrelsome was simply an application of the basic humanist belief that a man's character could be molded by education. He did, however, articulate the details of the argument more fully than others. Latin was learned by memorizing definitions and following strict rules. Teachers stood ready with a cane to ensure, for example, that a composition contained just so many lines and no more. At the university the same students learned in the study of dialectic to concentrate all their mental powers on each fine point of an opponent's argument. Unlike other humanists Erasmus saw little positive value in the study of dialectic. He seems to have felt that both dialectic and the rigid discipline of the schools constricted the energies of students within narrow channels and trained them to find their pleasure or satisfaction in attacking others; both would be illustrations of the humanist premise, found especially in Quintilian, that students are made bitter and rebellious by excessive constraint. Whatever his reasoning, he clearly did believe that the current system of education was responsible for producing theologians who spent their days hunting for heresies instead of studying the scriptures, and preachers who, instead of instructing the people, fulminated in righteous anger against married priests.

Erasmus's positive argument for classical education was likewise a new articulation of common humanist assumptions. Somewhat more than Cicero he identified "seeds of virtue" in human nature with the gentle instincts of peace and concord. These qualities would be fostered by the studies recommended by Cicero and the educational methods recommended by Quintilian. Erasmus believed that a humane character could be formed not only by the study of good literature but also by the imitation of classical style. A student who practiced speaking and writing in the clear, harmonious style of the ancients, and who steeped himself daily in the elegant wisdom of Cicero or Horace, could not fail to grow in dignity and compassion. . . . Erasmus was less interested in forensic language than in ordinary conversation. He knew that students of his day required special practice in order to converse freely in a language that was not their native tongue. He also had a theory about the connection between language habits and character formation. Thus he encouraged friends to practice writing extemporaneously on the grounds that it would train them to be more candid. Even more than Quintilian he believed in relaxing the rules and inhibitions of traditional education. The new education that he envisioned would be a mirror image of the prevailing system. An education which concentrated on dialectic and depended on the fear of punishment produced men of a violent and aggressive temperament. An education focussed on the humanities and depending on a free self-expression would produce men of a generous and peace-loving temperament. Thus Erasmus argued, as other humanists had before him, that reforms in the classroom would make students into better citizens. (pp. 35-7)

Among his contemporaries Erasmus was even more famous as a religious reformer. At some point which is difficult to date his main interest shifted from classical literature to theology. He went to Paris in 1495 to study scholastic theology but while there was obviously more interested in the classics. John Colet in England and Jean le Voirier in Flanders pointed the way to a new theology based more on personal conviction and a study of the Bible. After meeting Colet in 1499 Erasmus took up the arduous task of learning Greek in order to study the New Testament. But in 1503 he was apparently angling for a place at the court of Prince Philip of Burgundy. In 1504 he promised Colet he would devote himself to the New Testament. But his years in Italy were spent on the ***Adages*** and other classical projects. Finally, after a long and obscure stay in England from 1509 to 1514, he emerged with a vast store of learning in theology and church history. The fruition of these quiet years came in 1516 with the publication of his Greek New Testament and his edition of St. Jerome. In 1503, when he published a treatise called the ***Enchiridion*** or ***Handbook of the Militant Christian,*** it attracted little attention. But a new edition of the same work in the German city of Strassburg in 1515 was a great success. When it became known that the famous Erasmus had something to say about the reform of the church, the educated public, especially in Germany, was eager to listen. In theology as in education Erasmus developed humanist principles into an original program of reform. His theology was by no means entirely of humanist inspiration. But important humanist elements can be found first in his overwhelming emphasis on the moral or ethical dimension of religion, and second in his program for bringing about a reformation of morals.

Erasmus believed that religious reform was necessary because "the morals of Christians" at the present time "are worse than those of any age." Above all, the constant warfare among Christian states demonstrated that European society was not really Christian. Princes went to war for what Erasmus regarded as trivial and unnecessary reasons; men on either side marched off without hesitation to mutual slaughter. Part of the difficulty lay in the character of medieval religion. Christians paid too little attention to the ethical teachings of the Gospel because they paid too much attention to dogma. Like Cicero Erasmus was skeptical about the value of speculative philosophy or speculative theology; the real test of truth for any doctrine lay not in its logical coherence but in its practical effects in the lives of men. . . . He emphasized not the doctrines peculiar to Christianity but the universal teachings of peace and love. (pp. 39-40)

Erasmus was a humanist also in the structure of his program for the reformation of Christendom. His premises were that Christian people were made fearful and self-righteous by a false religion of external observances, that the words of the New Testament in its true meaning contained a marvelous power to change men's lives, and that the inner promptings of human nature itself were in sympathy with the message of the New Testament. He wrote the ***Enchiridion*** "in order to remedy the error of those who place all religion in the observance of certain more-than-Jewish ceremonies." "Ceremonies" included any external religious acts that Christians were commanded to perform under pain of sin. Ceremonies had originated among Christians with monastic observances, but, since monks were considered to be the most perfect Christians, various obligations, such as abstaining from meat on Friday or attending mass on holy days, were gradually made universal by the church. Thus ceremonies had become "the plague of all Christendom." . . . The fear of punishment made people scrupulous about ceremonies; the performance of these obligations made them secure in righteousness, so they could pursue their hatreds or indulge their passions in good conscience.

Erasmus believed that the words of the New Testament had power to heal the moral blindness of European society. Scripture was a great mystery, "a mere divine power." He who studied it with reverence would become a different man. In the words of the Gospels "Christ still lives, breathes and speaks, I almost said more efficaciously than when He walked among men." Erasmus's praise of Scripture echoes sentiments that can be found in the writings of the Fathers. It seems also to be a variant of the humanist belief in the magic of language: as Christ was far greater than Cicero, so his words must be the most efficacious of all. More clearly humanist was Erasmus's contention that the original meaning of the New Testament had become obscured by a tangle of inept commentaries. Dialecticians hunting through St. Paul for quotations failed to notice that the author of the Epistle to the Romans could not have written the Epistle to the Hebrews. Theologians looking for support for the religion of ceremonies referred the words of John the Baptist—"Do Penance!"—to the sacrament of confession. Erasmus was able to show that the Greek word *metanoiete* meant an interior change of heart and not an external rite. Thus critical scholarship could restore the original ethical or spiritual meaning of the text. Erasmus was greatly encouraged by a new emphasis on Greek and Hebrew at the universities. He also hoped that the Bible would be translated from the original into vernacular languages. At last the Word of God might be widely disseminated and clearly preached.

He was confident that the Gospel would take effect because he believed that human nature would be instinctively receptive to it. Again and again he returned to the words of Christ in the eleventh chapter of Matthew: "Come to me all you who labor . . . for my yoke is easy and my burden light." The yoke to which Christ referred was the law of charity; it was easy to bear because it corresponded to man's deep longing for peace and friendship. Thus the law of nature was the law of Christ. Just as Erasmus emphasized the gentle qualities of human nature, so he emphasized the mildness of Christ; in a moment of enthusiasm he even argued that Christ had never displayed anger. The Christ of Erasmus was meek and benevolent, like the Christ of contemporary Netherlands painters; perhaps he was more a product of Netherlands culture than he sometimes cared to admit. But he was a humanist in his belief in man's readiness to respond to the gentle Christ. Once men could hear the true Gospel, free from ceremonies, they would desire of their own accord to follow Christ; they did not need threats or coercion. This was what St. Paul meant by Christian liberty. True followers of Christ would do more of their own will than they were required to do by the law. Once the Gospel could be purely preached and freely accepted, there would be less greed, less violence, and fewer wars.

It can now be seen that Erasmus's critique of medieval religion has the same structure as his critique of contemporary education. In both cases coercion or constraint is an obstacle to virtue. Ceremonial obligations enforced by threats of eternal punishment, like lessons in logic enforced by threats of physical punishment, tended to produce bitter and violent men. In both cases Erasmus has great faith in the power of language—whether of Horace or of the Gospels—to bring about moral transformation. Finally, in both cases he believes that virtue can be achieved by encouraging instead of confining man's natural goodness—by an atmosphere of freedom instead of coercion. To make room for the natural eagerness of youth, schoolmasters must lay aside the book of rules; to make room for the promptings of natural piety, the church must change its laws so that ceremonies no longer bind under pain of sin. It should be said again that there were other influences on Erasmus besides the humanist tradition. But his critique of medieval religion and education would not be intelligible without premises that derive from the humanist preoccupation with rhetoric and grammar. His achievement was to fuse ideas and attitudes of his humanist predecessors into a comprehensive and original critique of late medieval culture, based, it is true, on the somewhat narrow assumption that a culture is the end product of its formal and explicit systems of training. In 1517, just after the publication of his Greek New Testament, he could see a new generation of teachers and preachers on the horizon. Others trained in the new learning were taking responsible positions at princely courts. Erasmus dreamed that his program for the moral reformation of European society might become a reality; for a moment he saw the birth of a new Golden Age. Perhaps no one has ever had greater faith in the power of education.

The dream of peaceful change was of course smashed to pieces in the tumult of the Protestant Reformation. Earlier in his career Erasmus had not been so hopeful as to demand that church laws be changed or relaxed. He asked only that educated Christians, who stood apart from the common herd, should have freedom to give a spiritual interpretation to ceremonial observances. But in the ***Praise of Folly*** (1511) he changed the significance of this conventional distinction between the common people and the intellectual elite: the philosophers, who cling to arid reason and despise ordinary emotions, are the real fools. In the great scholarly works that follow, riding the crest of his fame, he declared that church laws must be changed or abolished so as to free laymen from the "tyranny" of the clergy. The unspoken premise, however, was that the common people would still obey the authorities and would accept guidance from learned men. Hence the popular uprisings of the Reformation nudged Erasmus back toward the classical maxim that "the people is a great beast." In hopeful times he had written of the scholar's duty to proclaim the truth no matter what, especially in religion. But in 1522, two years before the terrible Peasants' War, he seemed willing to sacrifice part of the truth to preserve law and order. Even though the pope does not have all the powers that are claimed for him by some theologians, he suggested, it might be better if people were told that he did, for thus they would be more inclined to obey. No moral teaching was more classical than the Platonic lie. As many have said, the aristocratic character of Erasmus's humanist reform program helps to explain the fact that while the Reformation and the Counter-Reformation struck deep roots in popular culture, Erasmus was venerated only by a few intellectuals.

It is easy of course at a distance of four centuries to point out the naiveté of Erasmus's humanist optimism. One of the reasons why his name will survive this and probably subsequent commemorations is that he was indeed more than a humanist. He was able to discern some of the limitations of the humanist tradition even as he exploited its resources. This is clear, first, from the fact that he gradually overcame the conventional humanist prejudice against non-classical Latin. A disenchantment with the ideal of eloquence seems to have begun when certain Italian humanists in Venice suggested that he, a mere Dutchman, had not been able to master all the subtleties of a true classical style. Back in England he apparently took more seriously John Colet's view that preaching should be free of rhetorical devices. One of his prefaces to the New Testament praised the evangelists for writing simply, for it was not fitting for the Gospel to depend on human cleverness. In later writings he asserted, contrary to his own former opinions, that the Latin of medieval scholastic writers could be just as good as anybody else's, that people would be stirred "more by an unstructured sermon which comes from an ardent soul than by a sermon fitted out with all the devices of the rhetoricians but which comes from the lips and not the heart." Even his own Latin style seems to have become simpler as he grew older.

More significantly, he also advanced somewhat beyond the implications of his own naive optimism. His rosy vision of the future in 1517 was typically humanist insofar as humanists tended to believe in the moral improvement of mankind through a calm and peaceful process of education. He was puzzled and hurt by hostile reactions to his New Testament that arose later that same year. He could only surmise that there must be a conscious plot on the part of the friars to destroy his reforming ideas in order to preserve their own tyranny. . . . This reaction is a measure or index of his original naiveté. Like most northern humanists he had no experience of practical affairs. He had no sense of the intractableness of things, nor of the stormy, nonintellectual character of many of the forces which bring change. He was utterly unprepared for the violent outcry that greeted his own works, much less for the greater storm that soon gathered around Luther. Consequently he was driven to an explanation that fitted his own narrow understanding: the trouble must have been caused by evil men conspiring against him.

The magnitude of events soon forced him to realize that no mere personal explanations would suffice. In 1521, after his effort to prevent a rupture between Luther and Rome had proven futile, he began to speak less of conspiracy and more of tragedy. He had found in Homer and Euripides a literary clue that gave him some perspective. The *ate* or rage unleashed by the quarrel between Agamemnon and Achilles in the *Illiad* was a force stronger than reason. Similarly, the selfish rage of the friars had provoked Luther to respond with equal fury; preachers on both sides made inflammatory appeals and popular anger and resentment snapped the fragile bonds of restraint. In such circumstances no human power, much less the gentle persuasion of reason, could bring events under control. This tragedy was a punishment for the sins of Christians; it would end peacefully only if God himself somehow intervened, as in the *deus-ex-machina* endings of Euripides. In light of this view of things Erasmus became less confident about assigning blame. He still felt that the real trouble had been started by clergymen who were protecting their own vested interests. But he now saw that indulgences and other practices which he had attacked had been introduced originally for a reasonable purpose and not as instruments of clerical tyranny. Their evil consequences had simply not been foreseen. Thus human reason was mocked not only by tragic outbreaks of passion but also by the movement of time itself.

Erasmus was still not a fatalist. If ever passions could be calmed, he believed the doctrinal differences between Catholics and Lutherans could be resolved by discussions between carefully chosen men of learning. Those who might think he was hopelessly naive on this point as well should remember that Catholic and Lutheran spokesmen did agree on the doctrine of justification at the Regensburg Colloquy of 1541. But as time went on passions only intensified. Recognizing that his modulated tones would not be heard among the din of voices Erasmus fell silent. From his own day to the present many have accused him of cowardice for not committing himself to one side or the other. His dear friend Thomas More overlooked abuses in the Catholic Church in order to attack the Reformers with all possible vigor. Other friends, like John Oecolampadius in Basel, became pillars of the Protestant cause. But the humanism of Erasmus meant not merely that man is the measure of all things but that measure is the mark of man's humanity. Neither the doctrines of Luther nor the authority of the pope could justify religious hatred among the followers of Christ. Once the Reformation and the Counter-Reformation had become a part of history it was easy to look back on his growing isolation as the tragedy of Erasmus. But to Erasmus, who had the courage to remain alone in his convictions, the course of events could only be understood as the tragedy of Christendom. (pp. 41-7)

James D. Tracy, "Erasmus the Humanist," in Erasmus of Rotterdam: A Quincentennial Symposium, *edited by Richard L. DeMolen, Twayne Publishers, Inc., 1971, pp. 29-47.*

Sister Geraldine Thompson (essay date 1973)

[*Thompson is a Canadian educator. In the excerpt below, she examines the satiric technique employed in* The Praise of Folly.]

Only three full-length works of Erasmus are satiric: ***Encomium Moriae*** (which I shall continue to call ***The Praise of Folly***); ***Julius secundus exclusus,*** and ***Ciceronianus.*** Some of the colloquies are satirical, but not all; satire is incidental in the adages, but not continuous; the Lucianic translations though germinal to much of the satire, are Erasmian by adoption rather than birth . . . ; ***Querela pacis,*** or ***The Complaint of Peace,*** though it is censorious from start to finish, makes no use at all of the ridiculing devices and allows the figures which might have been surrogate for ridicule to dissolve before the work has proceeded far. Of the three properly satirical works, the ***Praise*** is the best and the earliest. (p. 51)

The Praise of Folly has been called learned parody, paradox, mock panegyric, an adoxigraphical essay; and rightly so, for it is indeed all that. But it is primarily satire, and the parody, eulogy, and paradox are geared to a serious moral purpose. It is no trifle, surely, to be shouldered easily into the group which Erasmus himself reviews, nor reduced to the level of its imitators.

Erasmus' list includes no work so complex as his own. Parody is not always panegyric, nor mock panegyric always parody; neither is necessarily satiric. Homer's *Battle* is parody but not mock praise; nor is there mock praise in Virgil's tale of the gnat; of the mock eulogies listed, only Lucian's two are parodies of rhetorical declamations; and of the fifteen works listed only five are satirical.

The ***Praise*** is unique in that it comprises all the qualities of all the works Erasmus lists. It is surely parody with the mocking Moria delivering such an oration as never before had followed the rules of rhetorical declamation. It is also an incisive and serious moral indictment of European society in all its aspects, an indictment that is sometimes eulogy, sometimes direct censure. It is, moreover, an oration that attempts, though awkwardly enough, to point in the end to that heavenly Jerusalem which sixteenth-century writers knew to be the end of any work of exhortation. Finally, and especially in comparison with contemporary works, it is a thoroughly human dramatic monologue, having as its satirical and allegorical device a woman. She is christened Moria because, like Europe, she is foolish, or perhaps because, like Thomas More, she is wise. Nonetheless she is no mere abstraction: she is a woman with a woman's varying moods, now confidential, now aloof, sometimes amused, often furious, ready to break her ironic vein to coax or plead, or to pursue some tangential thought; and she grows in folly or in wisdom as we listen to her diatribes and rhapsodies.

Although it is unlikely that Erasmus, who was not modest about his achievements, underestimated the worth of his work, it is surprising to find his Renaissance admirers failing to recognize its difference from other paradoxes. To some the ***Praise*** seems little more than a merry commendation of folly; others consider it a Jeremiad attacking immorality and ecclesiastical abuse. Sir John Harington, for instance, in *The Metamorphosis of Ajax,* mentions the ***Praise*** as one of many such pieces, serious treatments of light subjects, of which he cites seven. The ***Praise*** heads the list, although the other six are no more of its kind than is the *Metamorphosis* itself: 'an encomium on the Pox, a defense of usury, a commendation of Nero,' and so forth. John Grange, writing in 1577, does recognize that the ***Praise*** hides many profound reflections beneath a 'cloke of mery conceyte,' yet he couples Erasmus very easily with Skelton, whose good place in English letters is surely not in the Erasmian neighbourhood. Not long afterwards, Sir Philip Sidney points out that 'Agrippa will be as merry in shewing the vanitie of Science as Erasmus was in commending of follie'; and although Sidney's final comment (that both had 'another foundation than the superficiall part would promise') is sound, the casual juxtaposing of the mercurial Moria and Agrippa's sturdy denunciations is surprising.

In all these paradoxes there is, of course, some common denominator by which we recognize them as cognate to one another; but an examination of the paradoxes and false praises current in sixteenth-century England should, one thinks, justify the contention that Erasmus' ***Praise of Folly*** is not only superior to them, but, with one or two possible exceptions, quite different in scope and purpose. Its complexity is such that it seems to father two kinds of essay distinct from each other and germane only through this Erasmian progeniture. As mock eulogy and parody the ***Praise*** inspires some paradoxical essays delighting in clever urbane dialectic, little more than *jeux d' esprit;* as satire it is godmother to seriously didactic writing. Few of the works that follow in its train are similarly compounded of both toothless and biting wit.

Yet all the elements of form found in the 'trifles' he lists in his preface, mock rhetoric, parody, irony, and so on, Erasmus uses in the ***Praise;*** and the real achievement—a paradoxical one in another sense—is that he combines these forms and fuses them not only with each other, but with his critical purpose, so that they become satire. The mockery of his panegyric reduces the pomposity of serious rhetoric to absurdity, so the panegyric is parody, and the pretended seriousness is ironic; the subject of the eulogy is something about which the writer cares immensely, and the total effect is satirically ironic. The irony becomes doubly inverted, made both dramatic and satiric, because everything that Erasmus says he says through the person of a woman whom he calls a fool but who can grow to Christian wisdom and spirituality.

Perhaps there is more in a name than the poets think. If Sir Thomas' name had been other than 'More'—if it had been, say, Jones or Hopkins, and Erasmus had not been a learned philologist easily beguiled by puns, this praise might too have been a 'praise of injustice' (it is often that), or a 'praise of madness' (it is that too), or of cowardice or bravery or deception or love—for Folly is all of these and more. If so, the mood and tone and drive of the ***Praise*** would have been simple and single, as were the learned eulogies which were to follow. But folly is all things because wisdom is deeper than definition; and as wisdom shifts to new and richer levels, folly must be constantly reborn too, like the very cock Erasmus loves to mention, or the Silenus box with one self for the casual observer, and another for the percipient. (pp. 53-6)

The subject matter of the ***Praise*** has three broad divisions: the first part (roughly a third of the work) deals with the folly that is the natural concomitant of life, excusable, perhaps even unavoidable; the long middle section shows folly that is closer to vice, selfish, wilful, and deceitful; and the last part, less than a third, praises the folly of the cross. This division, of course, greatly oversimplifies the author's manipulation of complex moods and ironies, and is valuable only for surveying the substance of the work. But substance is important enough to warrant a few paragraphs of expansion.

Actually the ***Praise*** does begin as a mock declamation in the old classical style, a fairly simple affair, full of sound and fury and mock pomposity, finding absurdity in an inevitable condition and capitalizing on it in an oratorical style. There is nothing in the first few pages to suggest that vast intention of cataloguing all human folly, of finding fresher viewpoints and stronger wisdoms from which to view the frailties of men.

The tone of the mockery is light and graceful in this part, and it is interesting to remark that Moria will try to recapture this railing tone from time to time in the later parts of the declamation when she finds her gaiety becoming bitter and her irony turning to invective. She begins, then, by introducing herself, justifying her claim to speak by reason of her glorious birth, breeding, state, her usefulness in the economy of the world and the happiness of her devotees. As she states her case, we see that the folly she represents here is a constant of man's estate, a part of his nature, and not really folly at all, certainly not something crying out for rebuke or remedy. It is love's folly, she says, that effects procreation and so stands at the very fountainhead of life; the folly of innocence that makes childhood happy and lovable; the folly of forgetfulness that makes old age bearable; the folly of pleasant recreation and of the social give-and-take that makes life liveable. Folly promotes the arts too, and spurs man to build cities and defend them.

All of this is surely in the vein of the traditional paradox praise. This folly has in it no more of human choice than has quartan fever, or baldness, or the state of being a louse, and much less of obloquy. There are few overtones here and little irony. But it is more excellent than most of the paradoxes by reason of its vitality: Moria is even here a lively figure, and the emerging character of the speaker gives warmth and charm. Sometimes she is remote here, however, and the man she talks of remote too, for he tends to be natural man in a natural world (she herself speaks of the 'golden age'), and never has there been such a man really. In this slightly unreal world she could hardly come to asking, as later, puzzled beyond measure, she is to ask: 'What is the nature of man?'

She moves closer to reality when she begins to treat of man in his relation to others, first in friendship and marriage, then in the larger relations of society, where emulation, self-esteem, ambition become part of folly's composition and bring it closer to iniquity. Of the many images in this first round of Moria's oration, none is more significant for our understanding of its structure than that of the theatre. Moria has been reflecting, half-ironically, on the relation of prudence to wisdom. Prudence, she thinks, depends on experience of affairs; and it is the fool, unfettered by the wise man's restraint, that has tasted life to the full. In the theatre image that follows prudence and wisdom are again contrasted. On a stage the parts are often miscast, and Moria tries to picture what havoc would be wrought by a person who sees the miscasting and tries to interrupt the scene and strip the disguises from the players. But life, she goes on, presents an analogue; and 'suppose some wise man from the sky' should drop into the theatre of life and try to wrest from the characters the roles for which they are not suited. In this broader sense of theatre, the implication seems to be that the players are not miscast merely as a result of the producer's miscasting, but have connived and fought for position. Thus the intruder is not simply denouncing what cannot be helped, but the wilful folly of the masquers.

The significance of this passage . . . touches many aspects of this analysis and will be given more detailed study later; the character of Moria, for instance, becomes more complex here as she recognizes two faces to folly—or to wisdom; and the irony slithers between poles, now seeing right and choosing wrong, now seeing asquint but choosing well. In the second place, it is structurally important because, with the introduction of a more wilful and heinous folly, the new movement is heralded, though the lady moves back into her *jeu d' esprit* manner for a time. And the passage has a third importance: pattern is now beginning to emerge; we do not recognize it as such here, of course, and will not, until it begins to repeat itself in the later parts of the work. We do recognize, I think, that Moria is playing now with two kinds of folly, praising and damning both, for the 'wisdom' opposing the obvious folly is not entirely sound, and the succeeding pages show that Erasmus does not think it so, whatever Moria thinks; and in the next phase this pseudo-wisdom is to become the folly that is prime object of her praise. Against the new folly, Moria will oppose another wisdom, and this in turn, will become the folly of her predilection in the last part of her speech. Finally the human element is amplified in this theatre scene too, as fools, near-fools, wise men, and a woman orator gather before the reader. (pp. 56-60)

For all its teeming subject matter and rocketing moods, a structural pattern does emerge, cyclic rather than straightforward, but obvious enough. The first cycle begins with a survey of natural folly and swells into a picture of man in the golden age, happy in his natural world; as the movement comes to completion we have the man-fool elevated, foregathering with the gods whence he had emanated, and leaving Moria to eulogize herself. But somewhere in this part a counter-movement had been set up, a growing pre-occupation with the wise man who had been contrasted with the fool; and as the cycle of natural folly closes in, this counter-movement arches up to become a new cycle. Here the man who had been the wise man on the first pages has become the fool, the target of Moria's praise: in a particular and real civilization, far from the Arcady of the early part, he is deluded by Folly into thinking himself wise—and happy, though he is neither. The temporal sequence of the first part (one man from childhood to old age) has been discarded now for a spatial one (many men in various positions in life). The upswing of this cycle brings in tones of harsh and bitter reproach for man's worldly-wise ways, but as the movement rounds off, Moria tries once more to recapture the initial high-hearted tone and the earlier association with myths and gods.

But still another cycle had been in preparation: just as, in the first part, the worldly-wise man who was to be anatomized later had been faintly discernible in the shadows as foil to the natural fool, so throughout this long middle section, the truly wise man, the *philosophus Christi,* has been present by implication as the opposite to the pseudo-wise man. And this true wisdom now becomes the subject matter of Moria's third and last part. Thus the wisdom of one part is repeatedly made the folly of the next—or, if we use Moria's inversions, the follies of each part become the wisdoms of the next. In the last third of the book, the folly of the cross is to resolve the contradictions arraigned in the preceding cycles. Once again, too, Moria, in a sudden, whirling recollection of her original role, reaches for the old manner, tosses aside the need for a peroration, and as Folly, waves goodbye to her foolish audience.

It has been said that satire is not ageless, as is great literature, because its figures are unreal, that 'Gulliver cannot reach a happy hunting ground together with Robinson Crusoe, nor Pope's dunces hope to dance with Congreve's Millemant.' But Moria, we think, might aspire to flirting with Mirabell, and she does indeed wedge herself into a species of happy hunting ground. A complex figure, she rarely quite deviates into sense, yet never quite sinks to absurdity either. Because she is a woman, she can change her mood and tactics, can be now knowing, now unaware, can recognize folly and choose it, or fail to recognize it and so reject it, thinking it wisdom; she can even be wise at times and then pretend to an ignorance that is an obvious mask. Thus her irony can shift and turn and sometimes disappear, changing not only in intensity but in character.

Her simpliest irony, the one to which she keeps returning, after vehemence has led her to abandon it, is to recognize folly for what it is and yet to choose it for very love. This is not the usual kind of dramatic irony, for the ordinary satirist speaks through a dunce who lauds the folly because he thinks it wise. In the simple ironies of the early part of the oration, and intermittently throughout it, Moria's irony lies in choice, not recognition.

But Moria is rarely simple. Often she begins with a simple lauding of a folly, only to wriggle into an irony less characteristic of this kind of double-talk. For the most part she simply says: 'The combination of senility and sensuality is folly supreme' (seeing rightly); then 'In this folly is my delight' (choosing wrong). But now and then she dallies with some folk-sayings, and in them we find some provocative half-truth, and are seduced into thinking out the proposition for ourselves.

Moria's perception becomes flawed towards the end of this first part, in anticipation perhaps of the next section where percipience is often faulty; and in the passage on prudence she uses the tricks of witty paradox to set up a false syllogism. She has been speaking of folly as the mainspring of great exploits. The active life, she has said, depends on folly; and now it is a simple step to begin proving that folly is very like prudence. . . . (pp. 61-3)

The vexed question of prudence leads Moria into the imagery of the theatre and here the irony deepens considerably and becomes more complex. Long as it is, this passage warrants full quotation:

> If a person were to try stripping the disguises from actors while they play a scene upon the stage, showing to the audience their real looks and the faces they were born with, would not such a one spoil the whole play? And would not the spectators think he deserved to be driven out of the theatre with brickbats, as a drunken disturber? For at once a new order of things would be apparent. The actor who played a woman would now be seen a man; he who a moment ago appeared young is old; he who but now was a king, is suddenly a sorry little scrub. Destroy the illusion and any play is ruined. . . . Now what else is the whole life of mortals but a sort of comedy, in which the various actors, disguised by various costumes and masks walk on and play each one his part, until the manager waves them off . . .

Up to this point the folly has had about it some inevitability, the praise has been simply false praise, and the irony hardly more than recognition of the irony inherent in life. But as Moria goes on and makes of the theatre an analogue to life and its miscastings, new complexities arise:

> But suppose some wise man who has dropped down from the sky should suddenly confront me and cry out that the person whom the world has accepted as a god and master is not even a man, because he is driven sheeplike by his passions . . . or again, suppose the visitor should command someone mourning his father's

> death to laugh, because now his father has really begun to live—for in a sense our earthly life is but a kind of death. . . . Suppose . . . Suppose . . . As nothing is more foolish than wisdom out of place, so nothing is more imprudent than unseasonable prudence. And he is unseasonable who does not accommodate himself to things as they are, who is 'unwilling to follow the market,' who does not keep in mind at least that rule of conviviality 'Either drink or get out,' who demands in short, that the play should no longer be a play. The part of a truly prudent man . . . is not to aspire to wisdom beyond his station, and either, along with the rest of the crowd, pretend not to notice anything, or affably and companionably be deceived. But that, they tell us, is folly . . .

In assessing the irony of these paragraphs, surely we pause at the sentences beginning 'As nothing is more foolish . . . ' Here Moria seems to have dropped her ironic tone and to be speaking soberly, even as Erasmus would speak. And although the mocking tone has returned by the end of the paragraph, so that we are less than sure about the place and wisdom of moral intrusion, those perceptive sentences about unseasonable wisdom have prepared the reader for a new kind of folly to make its appearance, a folly masquerading as wisdom.

The transition is made through a shift in the irony, a shift that becomes more obvious if we oversimplify for a moment. Moria has been saying 'This is folly: and I love it,' with percipience right and choice wrong. Now she is going to present a pseudo-wisdom, and (except for that one revealing sentence) she is going to say 'This is wisdom: and such wisdom is not to be borne,' with recognition wrong (for the wisdoms she proceeds now to detail have small part with true wisdom), but judgement or choice right, for she wisely rejects this counterfeit wisdom. And this shift in ironic position allows Moria (or Erasmus) to use a more trenchant satire. Not that there are any hard and fast divisions: throughout this long middle portion the irony shifts from judgement to percipience and back again, as Moria now scorns the wise man and rejects him, and now takes his wisdom for folly and loves him.

Before we leave the theatre image, it might be well to notice that here the human and dramatic elements of the irony are enriched, for it gives us three sets of people all judging and choosing. The players on the stage have chosen not to see; this is folly of the intellect, though the will is hardly uninvolved: outwardly noble, inwardly inept, these players strut and fret their time upon the stage, quite unfit for their responsibilities. But Moria is hardly concerned with them (though she does come back to them later in the oration); she is preoccupied with the man of insight, whom she calls a 'wise man from the sky,' recognizing in him some illumination beyond that of the rest. He is a Lucianic figure, who might have graced the Dialogues of the Dead or the Menippean satires. He is similar too to More's Philosopher-councillor ironically proposed by Hythlodaye and repudiated in some measure by More. Moria's wise man has a difficult choice to make: he must either interrupt the play and so let loose the furies, perhaps doing more harm than good, or must compromise with injustice. Thirdly there is Moria herself, by now a human being caught in the web of her own argument, made to ponder and judge between two follies. (pp. 65-8)

Techniques other than irony also enrich the ***Praise,*** of course. The character of Moria gives body and dramatic rightness to the work; without her esprit the piece would never be so lively. Analogues and metaphors abound too, many of them bringing a new field of reference from classical writings; the Platonic image of the cave and its simulacra points up the darkness of self-delusion, and the double face of Janus and the Silenus box of Alcibiades do a like service for wilful deception; superstition is an ocean, and the theologians a Lake Camarina, a race apart, a field of noxious herbs, *anagyra foetida.* Sometimes metaphors are prolonged to make little scenes and so enrich the tapestry: the curtain goes up on some theatre folk, natural man foregathers with the gods in some heavenly bleachers to laugh at the human vaudeville act, Juvenal rakes into his 'occult cesspool,' scholars squint into their books by stingy candlelight, and the monarch listens to his court and his jester.

We have already noted too that the structural modes of classical oratory are followed, and thus the work becomes parody; and that the title is the best of literary jokes, with Moria doubling as two genitives, objective and subjective, and doubling too in allusion, as European folly and a wise Englishman.

Although the ironic inversions drop away from the ***Praise,*** and the satire fails to sustain the work to the end, it is not in any sense a failure. Indeed the sustaining of its satire might have been less satisfying. As an instrument of persuasion, satire is often unable to bring the work to completion; it is the expedient of a man aware of life's anomalies but unsure of how to resolve them. In many ways it is as tragic as comic, furtively concealing its tragic direction in a web of comic devices. Sometimes perhaps the perplexities find their resolution as the satirist's exasperation works itself out; and he is then ready to turn to his auditory with words of sweeter persuasion. The reader or listener may also respond to this catharsis—and the writer assumes he does, of course. Hence the satire, if it has prepared both speaker and listener for the exhortation, has been effective. The satiric parts of the ***Praise*** do just that. In the end, Moria's audience is readier to listen to her penultimate sober words than they would have been earlier, their minds prepared by the speaker's adroit tricks and tropes; they have been dislocated from accepted attitudes and made to see truth in new guises.

If the ***Praise,*** as a piece of cunning literature, is of high complexity, this is still more the case when it is considered on the level of instruction. For it is not assertive of a simple sustained rationale, but is rather a study in speculation about the nature of man. We can, of course, find and isolate certain of Erasmus' known preoccupations: monastic abuses, the prevalence of greed in high places and of superstition in low, worldly ambition among rulers and simony among ecclesiastics, the quarrelling, brawling, and fighting that destroys peace. But in this supposedly frivolous work, whether we concentrate on its survey of behaviour or its sometime excursions into the realm of the spirit, we are constantly aware of Erasmus prodding Moria to ask, 'What is the nature of man?' And if one is going to ask 'What is man?' instead of simply saying 'Don't be greedy, and don't talk in church,' one cannot expect to arrive at neat conclusions. As one commentator says, Moria 'undercuts and undermines her whole argument herself, to leave each reader alone with the unpleasant realization that Folly has been consistent to the last . . . she has abandoned the reader to make his own decisions about value.'

Erasmus' preoccupation with life's anomalies was well served by the genre of paradox, and he is ingenious in his use of *double entendre. Sapientia,* for instance, he interprets in a variety of ways, and the reader must be wary. The truly wise man is, for Erasmus, one supposes, the humanist devoted to the *philosophia Christi,* with all that title implies. But Moria, not quite percipient, though capable of choosing well, knows another wisdom, the proud perquisite of the Stoic, and wisely she rejects it. Here, as in many other instances, much that seems purely paradoxical and specious on first reading is worth a second. Moria, as we have seen, can use a tricky logic to lay claim to prudence, to show that prudence and wisdom are ambivalent terms, hardly laudable and mutually repellent, that shame and fear are not the qualities of the fool but of the man of experience. But this is more than clever dialectic, for Erasmus the moralist is very much behind Moria the wag as she advances her faulty syllogisms: *prudentia* and *sapientia* are just abstract terms to cover the ways in which silly man behaves and misbehaves. And if Erasmus hints that certain kinds of wise men are best left to scratch out their eyes in bramble bushes, he is in good company—with Horace, for instance, and Thomas More. And if the active life begets, with prudence, some modicum of shame and fear, are these not the brakes and disciplines of sober maturity? Whatever the answer, Moria turns soon to the man of thought, somewhat apart from the game of life. (pp. 70-3)

But what is the nature of man? In one of his educational works, under the direct influence of Quintilian and classical educational theory, Erasmus was to define it quite simply: it is the nature of man to be inclined towards 'honest things,' or again 'honest actions,' and 'philosophy'; man needs only proper direction and knowledge to fulfil his being. . . . But in the ***Enchiridion,*** which, he told Martin Dorp, was the companion piece of the ***Praise,*** saying directly what the ***Praise*** said inversely, he grants that man's nature knows conflicting elements. 'Man,' he says here, 'is . . . composed of two or three vastly unlike parts: a soul that is like something divine and a body like that of a dumb brute.' Although in mind he may excel the brute world and even aspire to rise above the angelic, in many ways he is no more than beast. To explain these contradictory elements in man, Erasmus here resorts to first causes: the Creator had meant the body to live in harmony with the soul, but the serpent had put them asunder so that now they can live neither together nor apart.

The ***Praise,*** however, raises questions and sees perplexities that the easy resolutions of the ***Enchiridion*** do not seem to cover. It may be true that 'nothing is unhappy if it fulfills its own nature'; but it may be man's nature to 'surmount . . . the nature of the angels,' or, as the ***Praise*** itself admits, to strive 'to go beyond the bounds proper to his station.' If man can desire eternal life, hankering after 'the life of the immortal gods,' leaving the now for dogs and apes, is 'nature' as slippery a term as 'wisdom'? And if man can long to be like those mighty giants who 'with arts and sciences as their engines . . . wage war on nature,' knowledge of the arts and sciences must help to fulfil his nature. But Moria will not have it so. It is the fool who is happy, she says, and only the logic-choppers who say that man is made for knowledge. To cap her point, she thinks again of man in the golden age, the innocent 'natural man' of the early part of the oration. He had had no need for sciences, and free of conscience, of shame and fear and envy, he is of course, free also of sin, though here Moria's eschatology leads us to Elysian fields, not a Christian heaven. Again, as in the larger pattern, the first few illustrations of delightful not-knowing are innocent enough, but soon become a kind of self-delusion that is a far cry from *honestae res,* and perhaps closer to not-thinking than to not-knowing. (pp. 75-6)

There is still a problem, and I do not think Erasmus solves it; perhaps no one ever does. For in the end, choice may depend on knowledge, or intelligence, or vision; and such vision as that wise fool has may compel his choice. What it is that makes one man seek integrity or holiness and another care nothing for it, one cannot perhaps say. In ***The Education of a Christian Prince*** Erasmus attributes the germ of all goodness or badness to the 'idea,' and so perhaps relieves man of much of his responsibility. For the teacher would teach according to his own idea, and the one taught would act on ideas partly his own and partly ingrafted by the teacher. Years later, when the Lutheran controversy forced Erasmus to take sides and formulate his principles, he was strongly on the side of man's freedom of will. In the ***Praise,*** where he has Moria's freedom of speech, he assumes man is responsible for the kind of vision he has and the kind of choice thereby compelled. And Moria does consider the question of vision and choice in the last few paragraphs of the book. One dominant image in this part is that of the cave of Plato's myth; and this time the shadows and substance do not concern indifferent things as they had done before—pictures, pearls, and kippered herrings had then been the mooted goods—but the things of eternal worth. Again, as before, those within think those outside are mad, while those outside (and they are few) know those inside to be deluded. It does seem here to be a question of vision, and so of the intellect (and grace) rather than the will. But the following paragraph throws the responsibility for holding one vision or another squarely on man's will to see.

> On particular points there are great degrees of difference between those two sorts of persons. In the first place, although all the senses have alliance with the body, certain of them are grosser, such as touch, hearing, sight, smell, taste, while certain ones are less closely tied up with the body, as the memory, intellect, and will. *To whichever one the soul applies itself, that one grows strong.* For as much as every energy of the devout soul strives towards objects which are at

farthest remove from the grosser senses, these grow numb, as it were, and stupefy; whence it comes that we hear about saints who have chanced to drink oil in place of wine. Among the passions and impulses of the mind, again, some have more connection with the physical body, as lust, love of food and sleep, anger, pride, envy. With these the pious are irreconcilably at war, while the multitude, on the other hand, consider that without them life does not exist. Then there are some feelings of the middle sort, merely natural, so to speak, such as love of one's father, affection for one's children, relatives, and friends; to these feelings the multitude pays considerable respect, but *the pious endeavour to pluck them too out of their minds,* except so far as, rising to the highest spiritual place, they love a parent not as a parent—for what did he beget but the body, and even that is owed to God as Father—but rather as a good man, one in whom is manifest the impress of that Supreme Mind, which they call the *summum bonum,* and beyond which, they assert, nothing is to be loved or sought for.

The satire in the ***Praise*** is not always so speculative and interrogatory. Many of the attacks strike at quite obvious wrongs. But we never get entirely away from Erasmus' interest in the part played by the well-informed intellect in the pursuit of virtue or vice. The Silenus box, for instance, shouldered aside just now for other interests, has great significance. It is one of Erasmus' favourite symbols, and stands for one of his constant preoccupations: the gap between what is and what should be, or (what is worse) between what is and what pretends to be. Sometimes this denotes simple deceit or hypocrisy, but more often it involves self-delusion, something in which intellect and will are interactive. (pp. 77-9)

Within this area of self-delusion are many follies which might be channelled under two headings: 1 / good things (or indifferent) pushed to extremes; and 2 / confusion in distinguishing between signs and things.

Erasmus' love of moderation is well-known. His peculiar list of Seven Deadlies is simply a series of violations of the golden mean, the reasonable. With the desirable middle way unexpressed but quite implicit, Moria scores monks who stay at home all the time and monks who never stay at home, miserly merchants and extravagant spendthrifts, reckless adventurers who hazard life needlessly, and men who vegetate for very caution, the over-prudent and the utterly indiscreet, the Stoics who care nothing for men's esteem, and the worldly who care too much.

The second channelling of folly is more interesting. If the foregoing is redolent of Aristotle and St Thomas, we come now to St Augustine. Of Erasmus' respect for Augustine we have already had occasion to speak. Augustine's *De doctrina* begins with a declaration that all teaching is concerned with things and signs. And it is thus that Erasmus too begins his ***De ratione studii*** (1513), written when his enthusiasm for Augustine was perhaps at its height. All knowledge, he says in this treatise, is concerned with things and words; and as late as 1518 he was still using these Augustinian distinctions and even phrasings in the ***Enchiridion,*** though in that same year, in a letter to Johann Eck, he admits that he rates Augustine below certain other Fathers, notably Jerome. It is not unlikely then that during the writing of the ***Praise,*** he was aware of Augustine's thought patterns. (pp. 79-80)

One could wish . . . that the conclusion of the ***Praise*** gave a glimpse of some great good wise man who is not an ecstatic. The perplexing tangles of the strongly satirical centre of the oration are hardly unravelled on their own rational level. It is right, of course, that all should be resolved in the life of faith and charity which the last part suggests. But one feels that Erasmus is making an awkward transition from the life of reason to that of faith in more than an artistic sense, that his answer to the problems that beset the stage of life is to retreat from them—a wise man returning to the skies.

Nevertheless the life of faith and hope and charity is warmly acclaimed in this last section, and we do find there a tranquillity that lifts the work to a transcendent level rarely found in Erasmian writing, and rarely found in satire. Erasmus was not a philosopher, nor even a theologian, if we take philosophy and theology to be speculative sciences. And we might look a long time to find his own definition of true wisdom. All thinking is behaviour to him; he is interested in ethical and practical wisdom primarily. But the converse is true too: if all thinking is behaviour, so too all behaviour is thinking in his estimation. The man who thinks well behaves well; and man can be taught to think. (pp. 84-5)

Sister Geraldine Thompson, "The Praise of Folly," in her Under Pretext of Praise: Satiric Mode in Erasmus' Fiction, *University of Toronto Press, 1973, pp. 51-85.*

John C. Olin (essay date 1975)

[*Olin is an American educator who has written extensively on humanism and the Reformation. In the excerpt below, he examines the* Enchiridion *as a handbook for Christian living and* The Praise of Folly *as a call for people to live "the folly of the Christian."*]

Erasmus composed the ***Enchiridion*** ostensibly for a soldier who he was afraid might fall among "the superstitious kind of religious" that would drive him into "a sort of Judaism, and teach him not to love but to fear." Developing the theme that life is a constant warfare against sin, he explains the weapons that the Christian must employ and the rules and precepts that must guide him in his unending struggle. Two fundamental and related ideas run throughout the book. One is that the great weapon of the Christian is the knowledge of Holy Scripture; the other is that religion consists primarily not of outward signs and devotions but of the inward love of God and neighbor. This latter idea is particularly emphasized—it will become Erasmus' master thought—and some of the most striking and characteristic passages of the ***Enchiridion*** express it:

You venerate saints; you are glad to touch their relics. But you contemn what good they have left, namely the example of a pure life. No worship of Mary is more gracious than if you imitate Mary's humility. No devotion to the saints is

> more acceptable and more proper than if you strive to express their virtue. You wish to deserve well of Peter and Paul? Imitate the faith of one, the charity of the other—and you will hereby do more than if you were to dash back and forth to Rome ten times. . . . And although an example of universal piety be sought most fittingly from Christ, yet if the worship of Christ in his saints delights you very much, imitate Christ in the saints, and to the honor of each one change one vice, or be zealous to embrace a particular virtue. If this happens, I will not disapprove those things which are now done in public.

Or again:

> Do not tell me therefore that charity consists in being frequently in church, in prostrating oneself before signs of the saints, in burning tapers, in repeating such and such a number of prayers. God has no need of this. Paul defines love as: to edify one's neighbor, to lead all to become members of the same body, to consider all one in Christ, to rejoice concerning a brother's good fortune in the Lord just as concerning your own, to heal his hurt just as your own.

This of course is a rule—*the* rule—for the Christian life which Erasmus draws from scripture, and he urges his friend to the zealous study of the Word of God. He suggests that some of the pagan authors may be read as a preliminary training, "for they are often good moral teachers," and he recommends the Platonists because "they approach as closely as possible the prophetic and Gospel pattern." However, Holy Scripture "divinely inspired and perfected by God its Author" is pre-eminent, and there is never a question in the ***Enchiridion*** (or any place else in Erasmus) of reducing Christianity to a level with paganism or of creating some kind of naturalistic religious synthesis. There is sometimes a misunderstanding of Erasmus on this score, but even a cursory reading of his works, it would seem, must dispel it. (pp. 7-9)

One other feature stands out most forcefully in reading the ***Enchiridion,*** and that is Erasmus' emphasis on the mystical body of Christ. He is constantly calling his reader's attention to the fact that he is a brother to his neighbor, a member of the same body whose Head is Christ:

> It is not the Christian's way to reason thus: "What have I to do with him? I know not whether he be white or black, he is unknown, he is a stranger, he never deserved anything well of me." . . . Consider this: he is your brother in the Lord, coheir with you in Christ, a member of the same body, redeemed by the same blood, a comrade in the common faith, called to the same grace and happiness in the future life.

This concept, which Erasmus roots firmly in the great Pauline texts, inspires most of his moral injunctions and forms the basis of what we may call, for want of a better term, his social outlook. He is led thereby to denounce the selfishness, the indifference, the greed that contribute to the ills and injustices of the world:

> Your brother needs your help, but you meanwhile mumble your little prayers to God, pretending not to see your brother's need.
>
> You gamble away a thousand pieces of gold in one night, while some poor girl, plunged into dire need, prostitutes her body and loses her soul, for which Christ poured out his soul. You say: "What has that to do with me? My own concerns take up all my thoughts." And afterwards will you see yourself a Christian with this mind, who may not even be a man? . . . The law punishes you if you take unto yourself what belongs to another. It does not punish you, if you take your possessions away from a needy brother. Yet even so Christ will punish you.

He is also led to deplore disunity and dissention among Christians and its most terrible manifestation—war. It remains for his later writings to express more fully the social application of the scriptural message, particularly on the subject of dissension and war, but there is no mistaking his realization of this application in the pages of the ***Enchiridion.*** In brief, Erasmus was already keenly aware of the relevance of Christianity to the problems of his day.

Erasmus thus emerges, as he begins those labors which thereafter will engage him, as a reformer—a reformer of theology, a reformer of morals, a reformer of society. The three spheres are intimately connected. The advance of humanist scholarship and the expansion of Christian knowledge are the means whereby the needed reforms will come. He is aware of the limitations of human learning, yet it is knowledge, not ignorance, that will reveal God's truth and God's way. His lifelong efforts are posited on that belief.

Practically the whole corpus of Erasmus' work can be interpreted in this light. . . . In this connection one cannot fail to speak of Erasmus' best known and most widely read book, ***The Praise of Folly.*** This little masterpiece, quite unlike anything else Erasmus ever wrote, was dashed off in 1509 at Thomas More's house in London, where Erasmus was recuperating after a long stay in Italy and an arduous journey back to England. It is a book which lends itself to varying interpretations, for it is a kind of seriocomic joke, expressing frequently the most outrageous things; yet, as its first English translator observed, in every sentence, "almost in every clause, is hidden, besides the mirth, some deeper sense and purpose." This deeper sense and purpose, in perfect accord with the spirit of the ***Enchiridion,*** are simply to reveal the sham and hypocrisy of human affairs and to recall men to that higher folly of which St. Paul speaks, the folly of the Christian. Erasmus does this, however, not in the straightforward way of the moral teacher, as in the ***Enchiridion,*** although there are passages that are straightforward enough in ***The Praise of Folly,*** but with the wit, the irony, and the guile of a mischievous jester. The book therefore is subject to certain confusions and misunderstandings, and readers have frequently been shocked at what they consider the rejection of sanity or the mockery of sacred things. Actually, as Bouyer has pointed out, Erasmus "is simply laughing at humbug."

Perhaps the most famous and remembered parts of ***The Praise of Folly*** are Erasmus' thrusts at religious superstitions and at the theologians, the monks, and the prelates who disfigure religion with their conceits and unchristian lives. These occupy a fair portion of the book, and it is here that it has its most cutting effect. The theologians, as we might expect, are given some rough treatment. They are in the vanguard of the followers of Folly, who is personified in the book and who speaks throughout, and, wrapped in their syllogisms and self-pride, they are far removed from the spirit of the Gospels or Epistles, which moreover "they have no time to open."

> Next to the theologians in happiness are those who commonly call themselves "the religious" and "monks." Both are complete misnomers, since most of them stay as far away from religion as possible, and no people are seen more often in public. . . . They are so detested that it is considered bad luck if one crosses your path, and yet they are highly pleased with themselves. They cannot read, and so they consider it the height of piety to have no contact with literature. . . . Most of them capitalize on their dirt and poverty by whining for food from door to door. They push into inns, ships, and public conveyances, to the great disadvantage of the regular beggars. These smooth fellows simply explain that by their very filth, ignorance, boorishness, and insolence they enact the lives of the apostles for us. . . . They forget that Christ will condemn all of this and will call for a reckoning of that which He has prescribed, namely, charity.

These are strong words, but Erasmus, speaking through the mouth of Folly, has reserved even stronger ones for unworthy popes. It is clear that he has in mind the pontiff then reigning, Julius II, the warrior pope whom he had recently seen in action in strife-torn Italy.

> They fight for these things [i.e., the possessions of the Church] with fire and sword, inflamed by Christian zeal, and not without shedding Christian blood. They look upon themselves as true apostles, defending the bride of Christ, and scattering what they are pleased to call her enemies. As if the church had more deadly enemies than impious popes who by their silence cause Christ to be forgotten, who use His laws to make money, who adulterate His word with forced interpretations, and who crucify Him with their corrupt life.

This piercing thrust at the pope who was then at the helm of the Church leads immediately into one of Erasmus' first great condemnations of war—a pursuit which he rejected as the very antithesis of the doctrine of Christ, who had called us all to be one:

> War is so monstrous a thing that it befits beasts and not men, so violently insane that poets represent it as an evil visitation of the Furies, so pestilential that it causes a general corruption of character, so criminal that it is best waged by the worst men, and so impious that it has no relation with Christ. Nevertheless, our popes neglect everything else to devote themselves to war. . . . I can't decide [he humorously concludes] whether the German bishops taught the popes all this, or whether it was the other way around.

The impact of ***The Praise of Folly*** was, and still is, considerable; but for its proper evaluation it must be read and understood in the light of certain facts. First, it is a particular and unusual kind of book, actually a fool's book—and fools, as Erasmus points out, can get away with murder. Then the general context of its composition must be borne in mind. It was written in 1509 in a Europe still Catholic though desperately in need of religious reform. Finally, Erasmus' deeper purpose must be grasped: this is, not simply to criticize the follies and evils of mankind but to amend a troubled world. Nowhere in ***The Praise of Folly*** does Erasmus actually attack the doctrines and institutions of the Church, but only those who, in his mind, have degraded and disfigured them. "Nor did I have any intentions in the ***Folly,***" he himself wrote to [Martin van] Dorp, "different from those in my other works, although the method may have differed." (pp. 10-14)

> *John C. Olin, in an introduction to* Christian Humanism and the Reformation: Selected Writings of Erasmus, with the Life of Erasmus by Beatus Rhenanus, *edited by John C. Olin, revised edition, Fordham University Press, 1975, pp. 1-21.*

Jesse Kelley Sowards (essay date 1975)

[*Sowards is an American educator and historian who has written widely on the Renaissance. In the excerpt below from his monograph on Erasmus, he provides an introductory survey of Erasmus's major satirical writings, including* The Praise of Folly, Julius exclusus, *and the* Colloquies.]

The ***Praise of Folly*** was not only Erasmus's most important work of satire: it was also the most popular of all his books. This was true in his own lifetime, despite the formidable reputation of his more weighty writings and his stature as the leading humanist scholar of his age. And it has remained true. The ***Moria*** went through more than forty editions by some twenty printers before the middle of the sixteenth century, and since that time it has been translated into nearly every language and published in literally thousands of editions.

And yet Erasmus . . . conceived the book as a diversion on his journey from Rome to London in the summer of 1509 and, as he tells us, actually wrote it in seven days. While this is probably not quite true, it is part of a carefully contrived literary pose, that the work is an improvisation, an impromptu occasional piece. The book takes the form of the classical oration of praise and becomes a verbal satire of its own rhetorical form. Folly uses the form badly—and reminds the reader that she is doing so! (p. 29)

The ***Praise of Folly*** is more specifically a further parody of the oration of praise, the praise of such abstractions as Philosophy, Truth, or Wisdom. But in this case it is Folly, making use of a pompous form to celebrate a ridiculous quality. "Yet," she says, "if it is foolish, it is certainly in character; for what is more fitting than that Folly should be the trumpeter of her praises? 'She blows her own horn.' " It is the ironic force of this *reductio ad absurdum* that makes the satire work.

In the best style of the classical oration Folly announces her lineage: her father is not Chaos, Saturn, or any of that "senile set of gods," but Plutus, the god of wealth and "the real father of men and gods"; and she was herself begotten on "Youth," "the best looking" and happiest of all the Nymphs.

With the stage thus set, the goddess proceeds to display her powers. To begin with, she claims power over life itself and the process of conception, for the wisest man "must send for me if he wants to be a father." "I ask, whether the head, the face, the breast, the hand, or the ear—each an honorable part—creates gods and men? I think not, but instead the job is done by that foolish, even ridiculous part which cannot be named without laughter. This is the sacred fountain from which all things rise." Moreover, she continues, what man would stick his head into the noose of marriage or what woman embrace her husband if either really weighed the consequences. She claims all the ages of man from the innocence and joy of childhood to the cheerful, babbling second childhood of senile old age. She claims men and women impartially, and every human relationship. What of the man who thinks his ugly mistress beautiful and "is charmed by the growth on her nose," or the father who believes his cross-eyed son's eyes twinkle.

She continues, "There are no great actions without my help, no important arts without my collaboration." She argues that war belongs to her and the arts of government, contending—contrary to Plato—that when philosophers are kings states suffer the most, not only because of the ineptitude of their rulers, but because, by holding resolutely to wisdom, they strip themselves of their common humanity. "I ask you, if it were put to a vote, what city would choose such a person as mayor?" Who would not prefer a fool to whom nothing human is alien?

She claims alchemists, gamblers, artists, noblemen, and all nations and cities. All classes and kinds of men are, in some way, fools and the "Followers of Folly." These include merchants with their "sordid business" and "corrupt methods;" grammarians, "a tormented, calamity-ridden God-forsaken body of men," and various other kinds of scholars and poets whose "empty reward is the praise of a handful [and that] obtained only at the cost of ceaseless study and sacrifice;" philosophers, and lawyers who "confuse tediousness with brilliance."

This long midsection of the book is the crest of its argument. There had been scattered references to religion and "the religious" throughout the earlier part, but from this point on attention is turned almost exclusively to these subjects. And there is a marked change of tone from bantering good humor to an increasingly savage irony. Folly claims first the theologians with their pride of learning, their reliance upon their "definitions, conclusions, corollaries, and explicit and implicit propositions," their ridiculous quarrels—"It is easier to escape from a maze than from the tangles of Realists, Nominalists, Thomists, Albertists, Occamists, and Scotists, to name the chief ones only"—and with their painfully obvious contrast to the simplicity of the apostles. "The apostles baptized many, although they were never taught the formal, material, efficient and final causes of baptism."

Folly next turns to the monks, who "would be very doleful if I did not relieve them in many ways." In addition to their filth, ignorance, and boorishness, she comments upon their punctilious observance of every detail of costume and every requirement of ceremony. "They forget that Christ will condemn all of this and will call for a reckoning of that which He has prescribed, namely, charity." And when the day of judgment comes and the monks present themselves—this one with a "peck of prayers," that one with "enough ceremonies to fill seven ships," and another with "a cowl so dirty and greasy that not even a sailor would wear it"—Christ will exclaim, "Whence come this new race of Jews? I acknowledge only one commandment as truly mine, and of that I hear nothing."

From the theologians and monks Folly next turns—after a brief proprietary nod once more in the direction of secular rulers, kings, and nobles—to the rulers of the church, the bishops, cardinals, and popes. And nowhere is she made to speak with such ferocious satiric bite. Her choicest venom, however, is reserved for the popes, the vicars of Christ, so unlike Him in every respect. This section of the book was obviously and profoundly affected by Erasmus's recent trip to Italy and by his observance at first hand of the Julian papacy.

It is from her tirade against the unworthy leaders of the church that Erasmus brings Folly to the conclusion of her address and to the concept of "the Christian Fool." The contrast is a stunning rhetorical coup. Indeed, in the opening passage of this section we see once more the rhetorical parody of the earlier Folly. But this time she is developing the argument that even scripture recognizes the universality, and more, the necessity, of Folly. (pp. 29-32)

It is rather easily observed that, in the course of the ***Moria,*** Erasmus progressively shifted the meaning of Folly. In the earlier part of the book he is really dealing with simple, relatively harmless self-deception—what today might even be called role-playing.

But Erasmus also includes in his definition of Folly the simplicity of the noble savage in the state of nature—the "golden age" when men "lived without the advantages of learning, being guided by instinct and nature alone . . . free from the insane desire to discover what may lie beyond the stars." And to these he adds those who, so to say, retain the innocence of the state of nature, "those we commonly call morons, fools, nitwits, and naturals," "whose cheerful confusion of mind frees the spirit from care."

Erasmus's own "confusion of mind" and confusion of terms is, of course, no confusion at all but the conscious employment of ambiguity: the very progression of the work depends upon the author's ability to move from one definition to another and ultimately to his concept of "the fool for Christ," for that is the purpose of the book. Both the device and the purpose were readily enough grasped by Erasmus's circle of humanist friends for whom he had originally conceived it. But its purpose was missed, or ignored, by most of the ***Moria's*** early critics.

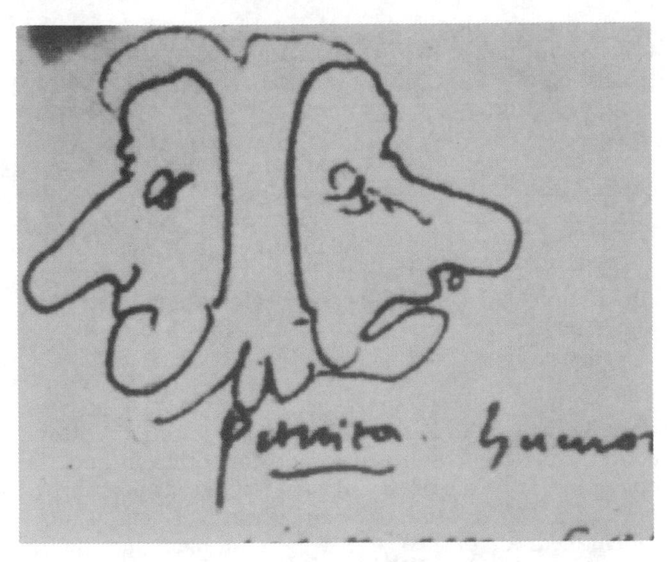

A Janus-faced caricature of Holbein and Erasmus, by the latter.

One of them was the conservative theologian Martin van Dorp whom Erasmus had known earlier in Louvain. Dorp wrote to him, complaining that the ***Moria*** "has excited a great disturbance" and suggesting that he "compose and publish in reply to Folly, a Defence of Wisdom." Dorp failed entirely to see that this is precisely what the ***Praise of Folly*** was, in the sense that Christian wisdom is the folly of the cross. But Erasmus took considerable pains to respond to Dorp in a lengthy letter not only to explain how he meant the work to be understood but the extent to which it was consistent with his other, more obviously serious writings. . . . (pp. 32-3)

Dorp was never truly convinced nor were most of ***Folly's*** other critics, despite the best efforts of Erasmus, his friends, and defenders. Not only was this true of the ***Praise of Folly*** but of many of Erasmus's other writings. For the ambiguity that baffled Dorp and was so strongly marked a characteristic of the ***Praise of Folly*** tended more and more to become a central feature of Erasmus's mind and style. It has also been called a taste for paradox, a tendency to present arguments "on the one hand" and "on the other."

The Erasmian taste for paradox owes much to the influence of the satirist Lucian. Erasmus's increasing preference for the pseudo-dramatic form of the dialogue as a vehicle of expression is probably, at least in part, owing to the influence of Lucian. His choice of the declamation—a dramatic monologue—as the form in which to write the ***Praise of Folly*** is a case in point: his use of the "theater of the world" figure is specifically taken from Lucian's *Icaromenippus.* But the ironic spirit of Lucian was even more congenial to Erasmus than the examples of his rhetorical usage, and it was more deeply influential. Erasmus has been aptly called the supreme Lucianist of the Renaissance.

The influence of Lucian in the ***Praise of Folly*** is only a part of the allusive richness of the book. This derives, of course, from Erasmus's general mastery of the classics, but it owes a good deal also to the fact that he had just completed the greatly expanded Aldine edition of the ***Adagia***—he makes specific reference to it in the ***Moria.*** Thus there is scarcely a line of the ***Praise of Folly*** that does not contain a reference or two to the Greek or Latin authors. Indeed, the very excess of classical allusion, Folly's tumbling out and heaping up of examples, is part of the verbal-formal parody to which we referred earlier. This is true also of the argumentation in which Folly pushes the absurdity of the rhetorical tradition of persuasion to its full limit, as when she proves that she has jurisdiction even over prudence, arguing from the figure of the classical Sileni that appearance and reality are really reversed, or when she argues "that the happiest creatures are those which are least artificial and most natural," that Gryllus (the companion of Ulysses who was changed by Circe into a pig) was considerably wiser than Ulysses and that the fool is to be preferred to be the wise man.

Erasmus was, however, not only a classical but a Christian scholar. And, as we have seen, the ultimate purpose of the ***Praise of Folly*** was the reform of Christian behavior and Christian institutions. That purpose could not be served without coming to grips with the Christian tradition. At the opening of the long final section on "The Christian Fool," Folly calls upon the testimony of Holy Scripture, as earlier she had called upon the authority of the classics. She calls also upon the tutelary spirit of Scotus "more thorny than a porcupine or hedgehog" and treats his followers, the traditional scholastic theologians, with withering contempt. But she makes an exception of "some of the more human divines" who "condemn as a kind of sacrilege . . . this tendency to speak with unclean lips about sacred things [and] to defile the majesty of divine theology with pedantic and wordy language." This was, of course, the theological reform party to which Erasmus himself belonged, along with his English friend John Colet and a handful of other theologians and biblical scholars. The last section of the ***Praise of Folly*** thus becomes a demonstration of the new, reformed theology and a forecast of the new Christian Humanism of which Erasmus would shortly be the greatest luminary.

The second most important single satiric work of Erasmus was the dialogue called ***Julius exclusus,*** closely related to the ***Praise of Folly*** and written some two years after the ***Folly*** was published. The occasion that prompted the work was almost certainly the news of the death of Pope Julius II in February of 1513. (pp. 33-5)

The ***Julius*** is a curious little book with an even more curious history. It was never published by Erasmus and not only never claimed by him but vigorously denied. Nevertheless, it was his. Several friends, including Thomas More, were aware of the existence of manuscript copies and one of these—we are not sure which—found its way to the printers and was published. Anonymous printed editions began to appear about 1517, part of the glut of pamphlet literature that was one of the staples of early sixteenth century printing. It proved to be extremely popular and was repeatedly reprinted by any number of publishers. The book caused a terrible furor, led by the same conservative theologians who disliked the ***Praise of Folly*** and distrusted the liberal theological views that Erasmus had already begun to express not only in his satiric writings but, as we shall see, also in his editorial works and biblical and patristic commentaries. Many of these critics were convinced that Erasmus had written the ***Julius,*** for, even though they were not aware of the external evidence for his authorship, the similarities of style and point of view between this work and others of Erasmus's, the ***Praise of Folly*** in particular, were simply too striking to be accidental. But Erasmus persisted in his denials, and his critics were never able to prove conclusively that he wrote it.

There are good reasons to believe that Erasmus never intended the book as anything more than a private document for a narrow circle of friends to see and that its publication was a genuine and serious embarrassment to him. It opened him to charges of the basest ingratitude, for he had received important favors from Pope Julius, as we have seen. He also needed the help of Julius's successor Leo X not only in the matter of a further dispensation but as patron and protector of Erasmus's Greek New Testament, which had just been published.

But there were serious reasons inherent in the ***Julius*** itself that made Erasmus reluctant to claim it. In one of his several letters denying its authorship, he wrote:

> It is true that I "played the fool" in the *Folly*—but bloodlessly! I have never injured the reputation of anyone by name. I have satirized the *mores* of men, not their reputations.

This he could no longer claim if he acknowledged the ***Julius.*** He saw clearly the difference between the ***Moria*** and the ***Julius exclusus.*** Folly had certainly attacked papal abuse, papal secularism, the popes' preoccupation with war. The figure of Julius II was recognizable enough when Folly spoke of "our popes [neglecting] everything else to devote themselves to war" or of "tired old men [acting] with youthful energy and [disregarding] all labor and expense, simply in order to overturn laws, religion, peace, and humane institutions." But the ***Julius*** was an extended personal attack upon the name, memory, and reputation of the pope himself. In the course of it Julius was accused of illegitimacy, drunkenness, lechery, and unnatural vice—and, incidentally, of suffering from syphilis—of simony, bribery, and assorted similar forms of personal corruption.

In more general terms, while both the ***Praise of Folly*** and the ***Julius exclusus*** attacked many of the same papal abuses, Folly had done it with graceful, if sometimes savage, irony. And, though the ***Julius*** has much of this same ironic spirit—indeed the whole work is a play upon the one simple and outrageous irony, that the pope cannot get into heaven!—still the result is not the irony of the ***Praise of Folly.*** It is rather the most malicious kind of invective satire. It is completely lacking in the ambiguity that Folly had so skillfully employed. This is due in part to the fact that the book, as we have seen, was never intended for publication, certainly not in the form in which it was published. In his reference to having seen a manuscript copy of it, Thomas More, for example, calls it a draft—his phrase is *tantum scriptio,* "only a scribble." Like the first version of the ***Praise of Folly*** it was a quickly written, fast-running piece for the amusement of Erasmus's English friends. But unlike the ***Praise of Folly,*** it was never completed, polished, or really prepared for the press. It thus remained rough and mean, filled with the "cruel and dirty words" that were part of the invective tradition, and much more direct about the abuses of papal power, much more explicit about church reform and ecclesiastical government than it was Erasmus's custom to be. On the other hand, it is of more than casual interest to have such a work in such a state of preparation. Even in draft form, truncated and unedited as it is, it is still a powerful piece of writing, surely made more so because Erasmus had no time to be evasive.

The central theme of the work is the contrast between Pope Julius and St. Peter, obviously suggesting the strong contrast between the historic apostolic church and the contemporary state of ecclesiastical affairs. It must be remembered that Erasmus was already at work on his monumental edition of the Greek New Testament and the letters of St. Jerome and that all his writings of these years, whether clearly serious or apparently trivial, are the documents of that inner purpose Erasmus called his Philosophy of Christ. The ***Julius*** no less than the ***Praise of Folly*** must be interpreted in terms of this emerging philosophy which endowed both these powerful satiric works with their purpose.

As in the ***Praise of Folly,*** literary form is made to serve satiric purpose in the ***Julius.*** Even more than the ***Moria*** it seems an improvisation, for the form of the dramatic dialogue permits the argument to flow back and forth in the apparently haphazard manner of conversation, with interruptions, repetitions, digressions. But it is only apparent: in reality Erasmus is employing a device to stress the point of the dialogue by repetition. (pp. 35-8)

In spite of the furor raised by the ***Julius exclusus*** and the great popularity of the ***Praise of Folly,*** by far the most often reprinted of Erasmus's books and the one with the greatest variety of editions was the ***Colloquies.*** It was also the most effective in spreading his ideas.

Unlike the ***Praise of Folly*** and the ***Julius,*** both of which were meant from the beginning as satires, the ***Colloquies*** were not. (pp. 39-40)

The popularity of the ***Colloquies*** is not hard to explain, even in the modest form of its earliest edition: it was an effective little manual of conversational style, the necessary beginning steps toward the Latin fluency that characterized anyone with the slightest pretention to education in the early sixteenth century. Most of the book was thus given over to simple sentences and conventional phrases—greetings to one's friends and family, "Greetings with good measure, my uncle," greetings of endearment, greetings of courtesy appropriate to various occupations and social estates, "Hail to your Holiness, Honor, Highness, Beatitude, Sublimity," forms of farewell, forms of inquiry on first meeting or to one in poor health, forms of typical domestic conversation, expressions of thanks, how to invite a friend to lunch. Despite the necessarily formulaic nature of such matter, this little book was clearly and refreshingly different from the many other similar manuals.

It owed nothing to them: it grew instead entirely out of Erasmus's own experience, out of his feeling for dialogue and his own mastery of Latin style, out of his genius for easy, lively, flowing conversation. Indeed, even the earliest colloquies may well recall bits of actual conversation, with their flashes of Erasmian wit and anecdote. (p. 40)

Even in the earliest editions there was an occasional instance of the satiric bite and reforming purpose that would come to characterize the later colloquies. In the conversation on the forms of inquiry to one in poor health, one of the speakers notes that some have recovered from an illness by putting on a Dominican or Franciscan cowl, to which another responds, "Perhaps the same thing would have happened had they put on a pimp's cloak."

This sort of thing—the timely, irreverent, or ironic comment on contemporary issues—enhanced the popularity of the ***Colloquies*** and caused the publication of more and more unauthorized editions, taking advantage of the demand with no advantage accruing to the author. For this reason, in part, Erasmus shortly adopted the practice of issuing new editions of the ***Colloquies,*** as he had done earlier, and continued to do, with editions of his popular ***Adagia.*** (p. 41)

It is clear that Erasmus's constant additions to the ***Colloquies*** were more than an attempt to protect the author's market. From the Froben edition of 1522 Erasmus had begun to take the book seriously, to add new and important material, and to go beyond the sketchy conversations of the original version to fully developed little microdramas in which he expressed his views on dozens of things—customs and fashions, the foibles of society, love and marriage and celibacy, literary tastes and practices, the church, and moral and religious questions. These substantial later colloquies owe as little to literary or formal antecedents as did the original version of the work. With only two or three fragmentary exceptions they are taken from the sights and sounds of the time, for which Erasmus had such a sharp eye and retentive ear and which he could depict so convincingly. There are bits of obviously real conversations. There are scenes thoroughly familiar to many of his readers—the steaming stench of the commonroom of a German inn and the meticulous description of the famous English shrines of the Virgin at Walsingham and of St. Thomas Becket at Canterbury. There are encounters with a prostitute, a lamed mercenary, a bogus nobleman, a cheating horse trader, a frightened little boy who can't get his pen sharpened or manage his ink well in a classroom where dictation has already started. There are a dozen scenes of dinner parties, one of them featuring Erasmus's sharp-tongued old housekeeper, Margaret. People bought the successive editions of the ***Colloquies*** certainly, in part, as much for the freshness and originality of the way in which Erasmus presented his ideas as for what he meant to convey by them. There is surely no other book in the western literary tradition quite like the ***Colloquies***. . . .

A number of the colloquies deal, directly or indirectly, with the education of women, a subject on which Erasmus had both strong and liberal views. The most substantial of these is **"The Abbot and the Learned Lady"** (1524). (p. 42)

In addition to those colloquies dealing with the education of women and with learned ladies there are a number dealing with other women's concerns. One of the most passionate is **"A Marriage in Name Only, or The Unequal Match"** (1529), the account of an arranged marriage between an innocent young girl and an old rake suffering from syphilis. In **"The Girl with No Interest in Marriage"** (1523) and **"The Repentant Girl"** (1523) he argues for a more equal role for women in deciding upon marriage, and in **"Courtship"** (1523) he creates a delightfully vivacious and strong-minded young woman who will not be rushed into an irrevocable choice.

These liberal feminist opinions were viewed with a special suspicion and hostility by many of the same religious conservatives who opposed Erasmus's liberal views on a broad range of topics. They saw his feminist views, quite correctly, as part of a larger argument Erasmus had developed from his first important devotional work, the ***Enchiridion*** (1501), through the ***Colloquies,*** and culminating in the ***Institutio Christiani Matrimonii*** (1526) and the ***Vidua Christiana*** (1529) that virtuous Christian marriage is not only parallel to clerical celibacy but is to be preferred to it. They saw, again correctly, that such opinions were corollary to his well-known hatred of monasticism.

Part of the hostility grew from the suspicious similarity between such Erasmian secularism and the growing Lutheran tumult of the 1520s. Luther had, after all, written his tract against the sacraments, *On the Babylonian Captivity of the Church,* in 1520. Clergy in Wittenberg and other places in Germany were already beginning to abandon their vows and take wives by 1521-22, and in 1525 Luther himself married. On these matters, as others, it made no difference to Erasmus's critics that he had expressed himself decisively twenty years before Luther was heard of.

All of this leads us into the largest and most important group of the colloquies, those devoted to religion, the church, and related objects of Erasmus's anger and ridicule. They were written mainly in the decade of the 1520s when Erasmus was in the midst of controversy with Luther, Zwingli, and other reformers on the one hand and a host of conservative Catholic apologists on the other. In spite of the increasing polarity of religious issues, in spite even of the fact that Erasmus himself was finally obliged to speak out publicly against Luther in 1524-25, as we shall see, he steadfastly maintained in the colloquies of the 1520s his advocacy of a middle position between the hostile factions. Even as he was at work on his tract against Luther, ***On Free Will,*** he wrote the colloquy **"An Examination Concerning Faith"** for the Froben edition of March, 1524. It is a straightforward, orthodox exposition of the Apostles' Creed. But he makes one of its speakers clearly represent himself and the other either Luther or a Lutheran spokesman. And the thrust of the dialogue is that in spite of hostility on some issues, there are many important things still held in common between Luther and the Catholic community, not least the Apostles' Creed itself, and that such areas of agreement can still be made the basis for peaceful compromise.

In most of this group of colloquies he takes the position

that the abuses, errors, excesses, and derelictions of the church are no less real and no less the continuing concern of orthodox Catholics for having been attacked by heretics.

As early as the March, 1522, Froben edition, in the colloquy **"In Pursuit of Benefices,"** he deplored the same scandalous pluralism that Luther had attacked in his *Address to the Christian Nobility of the German Nation.* In **"Rash Vows,"** prepared for the same edition, Erasmus dealt with the worthlessness of indulgences, although the condemnation of Luther, arising in part out of his attack upon indulgences, had just occurred at the Imperial Diet of Worms. But Erasmus's questioning of indulgences in **"Rash Vows"** grew out of his more direct attack in that colloquy upon the worthlessness of pilgrimages and the indulgence value attached to them.

His most famous attack on pilgrimages, however, was his colloquy **"A Pilgrimage for Religion's Sake"** (1526). It is based loosely upon personal experience, Erasmus's visit some years earlier to the Shrine of the Virgin at Walsingham and to that of St. Thomas Becket at Canterbury in the company of his austere English friend John Colet. But these two shrines are only examples of the general practice of the cult of saints and relics which had become so widespread and so abused as to be condemned by many serious-minded Catholics as well as by Luther and Lutheran sympathizers. Indeed, one of the speakers of the colloquy refers to "this new-fangled notion that pervades the whole world" and notes that it has cut seriously into the gifts given to the saints and may threaten the whole cult of saints. But it is not the purpose of Erasmus's satiric attack to second the views of Luther nor to attack basic doctrine. It is rather to reform corrupt practice and strengthen true Christian doctrine. Thus, the display of a vial of the Virgin's milk at Walsingham leads one of the speakers to doubt that she could have produced so much, displayed here and there at one shrine after another. His companion notes that there is so much wood of the true cross "which is exhibited publicly and privately in so many places that if the fragments were joined together they'd seem a full load for a freighter." (295)

"Exorcism, or The Specter" (1524) was directed at the ignorance and superstition of many clergy as well as, to some extent, at the concept of exorcism itself which Erasmus considered a questionable doctrine.

In **"A Fish Diet"** (1526), the obvious target of the satire is the conventional Christian prohibition against eating meat on holy days. To that end the chief speakers are a butcher and a fishmonger, themselves small masterpieces of comic invention. Again, as in the other colloquies of the same period, this one can be related to the din of controversy raised by the Lutherans, Zwingli, and other reformers over fasting and dietary laws in the early 1520s. But, as in so many other cases, Erasmus's concern with this question both predates the contemporary controversy, and goes beyond it to the larger matter, really, of Christian liberty. The colloquy is filled with satiric jibes at the ridiculous observance of trifles in religion. The butcher, for example, repeats a story about a pregnant nun who claims she was raped. But when asked why she didn't cry out, she answers, "I would have done so, but there's a strict rule against making noise in the dormitory." Erasmus makes the fishmonger speak for him recalling the savage asceticism he had endured in his own school days at the Collège de Montaigu in Paris, ending with the observation, "Who would deny that this was cruelty to a fellow human?"

"The Shipwreck" (1523) is one of the most enduringly popular of all the colloquies. Craig R. Thompson considers it among "the best satirical writing produced in the sixteenth century." Like most of Erasmus's satires its effectiveness is heightened by its literary quality and the tumultuous, breakneck pace of the narrative, vividly conveying the confusion of action and the terror of the events that form the nexus of the dialogue. Even the minor characters who are barely sketched in the narrative have life and character and substance. Adolph, the narrator, is telling his friend Antony of his narrow escape from a storm at sea and a shipwreck. While the precise choice of the setting may reflect a shipwreck that Erasmus actually heard of, it may also be either a literary borrowing or totally imaginary. It was chosen principally as a convincing crisis situation in which to depict faith under stress. The depiction reaches its point, as does the satire, when, as the fury of the storm mounts, the captain announces that the ship is about to sink and "warns each of us to commend himself to God and prepare for death." (pp. 43-6)

Conservative Catholic theologians—many of them already critical of Erasmus's Greek New Testament and his biblical commentaries and suspicious of the views expressed in many of his religious and devotional writings and of what they considered the mocking, "paganizing" tone of such books as the ***Praise of Folly***—were even more offended by the ***Colloquies.*** As early as 1522 the Inquisitor of Louvain objected to the book on the ground of its "Lutheran" tendencies. In 1526, Erasmus's enemies at the Sorbonne gained an official censure by that influential faculty against sixty-nine passages in the ***Colloquies*** and in others of his writings as "erroneous, scandalous, or impious," and it was forbidden to be used for instruction "lest under the pretext of instructing [students] it corrupt their morals."

This was a serious matter and for the next edition of the ***Colloquies***—within a month after the condemnation—Erasmus wrote a full-dress defence, **"The Usefulness of The *Colloquies.*"** He argued that the book was not a piece of systematic theology and should not be treated "as if the dogmas of the Christian creed were solemnly spelled out in [its] pages!" He argued further that he had done no more than to add to a harmless little book on the refinements of language," here and there, "some passages to direct the mind toward religion," and that far from being a pernicious book, the ***Colloquies*** was useful to Christian piety, that it promoted rather than undermined true religion.

In **"Rash Vows"** and **"A Pilgrimage for Religion's Sake"** he claimed only to have pointed out the abuses connected with the excessive zeal for pilgrimage which takes people from their proper vocations and uses religion "as a cover for superstition, faithlessness, foolishness, and recklessness." He reminds his critics that St. Jerome had said that to have visited Jerusalem was not as important as to have lived righteously. He defended both the doctrine and the method of the several colloquies dealing with marriage, pointing out that there are many ways in which men have tried to teach the precepts of Christianity and that there are always "those sour natures who are lacking in every grace, and to whom anything friendly and gay seems immodest." As to **"Exorcism,"** he was simply trying by "an amusing example" to expose ignorance and charlatanism. He argued further that he had not universally condemned the religious orders, pointing to his sympathetic portrayal of the monk in **"The Soldier and the Carthusian"** and that, moreover, if the orders are so sensitive to their honor, let them correct the practices of their worst members rather than slandering one who holds those practices up to ridicule.

In the same vein he claims that he has not everywhere disapproved of fasting or of the intercession of the Virgin and the saints any more than he universally condemned the orders. He adds, moreover, that, for example, in **"A Pilgrimage for Religion's Sake,"** "I reproach those who with much ado have thrown all images out of the churches." He defends himself by claiming that the offensive opinions sometimes expressed in the ***Colloquies*** cannot be uniformly attributed to him, that they rather belong to the characters speaking them, and that they serve dramatic effect as a foil for other opinions of other characters. If, as in **"Youthful Piety,"** a soldier or a drunkard is made to condemn fasting, "does that make Erasmus a condemner of fasts? I think not!"

Despite the ingenuity of his arguments, despite even the irenic note on which he ended his defence, an appeal to "the peacemaker among all men, the Holy Spirit, who employs his instruments in divers ways, [to] make us all united and of one accord in sound doctrine and godly living," Catholic conservative opinion continued to object to the ***Colloquies.*** The Sorbonne condemned it again in 1528, and in the following year the faculties of canon law and medicine of the University of Paris joined in the condemnation. There were condemnations and censures against the book in Louvain, Cologne, and various places in Spain. Individual church officials objected to all or part of it; even Erasmus's old friend Cuthbert Tunstall, now Bishop of London, joined in the censure of **"A Fish Diet"** in 1529. Reasons for this continuing opposition are not hard to find. For, despite Erasmus's disingenuous claims to the contrary, the main thrust of the ***Colloquies*** was indeed against monasticism, the mendicant orders, the ignorance and superstition of the clergy, the emptiness and worthlessness of the external practices of religion without their informing spirit. In more instances than not, his criticisms agreed with those of the increasingly vocal Protestant reformers at the very time orthodox Catholic apologists were calling for a closing of ranks. Erasmus's argument that he was not necessarily responsible for the opinions of speakers in his dialogues—the same argument he had used against the critics of the ***Praise of Folly***—only succeeded in further irritating his critics, especially as they often fancied they saw themselves held up to ridicule in the ***Colloquies,*** under one transparent guise or another. And, of course, they were even more enraged when their condemnations only succeeded in increasing the book's popularity, promoting its sales, and producing edition after edition. (pp. 47-9)

Jesse Kelley Sowards, in his Desiderius Erasmus, *Twayne Publishers, 1975, 152 p.*

Margaret Mann Phillips (essay date 1978)

[*In the following excerpt, Phillips traces the development of the* Adages *from a collection of "pagan trifles" to a major Erasmian opus.*]

The history of the ***Adagia,*** covering most of Erasmus's long working life, can be approached from two positions: the beginning and the end. We can ask ourselves the double question: what do we know of the inception of the book and is it possible to arrive at a definition of its final true character?

When and why did Erasmus develop the idea of a collection of proverbs? To date the answer is probably, very early. There is a proverb, later to be cited in the ***Adagia,*** in his first recorded letter, written apparently at the age of fourteen. And one of the few approachable people who inspired his boyhood, Rudolph Agricola, was associated for him with a proverb: *Quid canis et balneo?* as he wrote in the first ***Collectanea,*** and this memory was maintained in the ***Adagiorum Opus*** to the end. From the beginning he had a liking, which amounted to reverence, for the sayings consecrated by time. Not only were proverbs cherished by the authors he most admired—and the strongest influence here may have been Jerome—but they represented in tabloid form his deep urge to rediscover the wisdom of the past. (p. 51)

Perhaps Erasmus was attracted to proverbs because he was Dutch. The Dutch have always had a special facility for pithy sayings, and it was not hard to find in his own language what seemed like echoes of the ancient voices. But the ***Adagia*** seem to have been associated more particularly with England. The collection had been begun in Paris, but it was for an Englishman, Lord Mountjoy; and it was discussed in Oxford, where it had particular encouragement from the prior of the house of Austin Canons where Erasmus lodged, Richard Charnock. Charnock was a friend of Colet's and they spoke together about the brilliant stranger. But we may be sure that it was not Colet who wished Erasmus to go on with the ***Adages.*** Erasmus's letter of October 1499 shows clearly enough that Colet thought his friend had spent enough time on "the rocks of the Sirens." To him, as to mistaken critics of a later age, the ***Adages*** may have been merely pagan trifles. The developed Aldine ***Adagia*** must have made him change his mind.

It was the success of the slight and jejune performance of 1500 which launched Erasmus on the lifelong amusement and effort of construction which became the ***Adagiorum Opus.***

If one attempts to define the ultimate result, one thing at least is clear: it is not to be judged, like most books, by the author's purpose. In other cases it is often enough to ask, what was the author's objective and did he achieve it?

With the ***Adages,*** no; it is an organic growth. Erasmus certainly had a clear aim at the outset, which he describes in the preface-letter to Mountjoy, and it amounts to aids for the writer or speaker who wishes to embellish his prose; a pedagogical aim, parallel with the ***De copia*** and the ***De conscribendis epistolis,*** fruits of his teaching period, of which the first drafts date from about this time. There was the additional need to explain obscure allusions in the classical texts, as Erasmus points out, where ignorance of the meaning of a proverb may stand in the way of a correct reading. It was to be an exercise in comprehension and in the achievement of *copia.*

But as the book grew through nearly forty years, these humble aims became enclosed in the immense accretion like the grain of sand in an oyster. The book came to represent the author's mind in the same way as a long-built-up library can be a reflection of the owner's tastes and development. He said at first that it was a task without glamor or prestige, not allowing for flowers of rhetoric, dealing with things "so tiny, so humble, that not only do they not attract ornaments of speech and fluent writing but they repel everything of the sort." But that was near the beginning, when some of the uses of the ***Adagia*** were yet in the future, and it is amusing to see him at this time (1508) rejecting the reproach that he has not spent on his work the nine years recommended by Horace, with the typically Erasmian argument that you might spend nine years on a hundred items, but when it came to Thousands you would have to proceed more quickly. He was not then envisaging a process that would continue till he died; nor did he expect to live until nearly seventy. In 1524, however, he wrote: "A year ago the ***Adages*** came out augmented and corrected in many places. And a new edition is ready. I promise that I am going to do this as long as I live."

To arrive at any assessment of what is surely one of the most original books ever written, though compiled so largely from borrowed material, we must look at the result rather than the aim, and begin by deciding what it is not. A collection of proverbs, certainly, but obviously not merely that (Erasmus insisted from the beginning that he was not compiling a dictionary of proverbs). It is not systematic, nor is it haphazard; nor is it a book to be read straight through. It is not a sheaf of stories and anecdotes, though they form a large part of it; it is not, as the compilers of the *Index Librorum Probibitorum* seem to have thought, a subversive repertory of hidden topical allusions, though these are there. It is not the mouthpiece of any circle of humanists, nor a boosting platform for any individual or cause, though there are frequent, usually complimentary, mentions of contemporaries. It is decidedly one man's work, yet its structure is more severe than that of the usual commonplace book. It expresses one person's view of the world of his time, but linked continuously with a historical background and literary and ethical standards of a high order. His reader met not only Erasmus but the classics. We may attempt to follow the widening process that was the result of a lifelong *commerce des livres,* as one and another facet of Erasmus's reading struck him, and thus arrive at a definition of the book.

By 1508 the pedagogical aim had already been extended to teach the right attitude toward textual study and criticism. It was an age for waging war in the cause of clarification. Corrupt texts abounded, and the ***Adagia*** abounds in examples of Erasmus's campaign. He suggests emendations or variant readings, sometimes to be accepted by future generations of scholars, sometimes not. He discusses the views of others, usually with tact and respect (an exception is Apostolius). (pp. 51-3)

Some authors, like Andrea Alciati or Paolo Bombace, are mentioned with the highest praise. When a criticism is implied, great care is taken not to offend: giving a translation of a Greek epigram, he first transcribes the version of John Argyropoulos and then adds one of his own, giving his reasons, and adding: "I am not saying this to cast aspersions on a man whose scholarship deserves the thanks of liberal studies, but so that young readers may profit by the criticism; for this is mainly written for them." Similarly, he queries Domizio Calderini, but calls him *vir alioqui probe doctus.*

Two of the most revealing passages about his task as a textual critic are in ***Quis aberret a janua?*** and ***Amazonum cantilena.*** In the first it is a question of a misreading in Greek, θυδαδ for θηδαδ. "It often happens that an error in an archetype is carried on from one book to another. I am not saying this because I want to start a dispute, if anyone feels differently: that is beside our purpose, and also I know what a ticklish thing it is to alter anything in such important authors. However, I will bring out the conjectures I have made. If they seem likely to anyone, he can follow my opinion; if not, the old view will have all the more authority for having been called in question. On this point the learned will pronounce. I have done my duty as a commentator by exposing what I have found in the authors and what seems likely to me." On *Amazonum cantilena* he admits himself puzzled, and proposes the reading *mazonomon* (a dish in which food was brought into a banquet, denoting luxury). "But this is just a dream of mine, until something more certain is put forward by the learned. And no one need despair of that, since every day new authors are brought to light. After the fourth edition of this book, Caelius Rhodiginus's book came out, in which he suggests that this means not the Amazonian women, but the lower orders (*de tenuibus dicere*). As this comment is particularly feeble, how much more modest it is to do as I do, and say I don't know what I don't know!"

The book gave plenty of examples of Latin fluency, sometimes of contrived *copia,* of the tricks of style and diminutives Erasmus loved. But it was important not only to teach good Latin but to whet the appetite for Greek. The 1508 edition, emanating from the Aldine Academy, did not always offer Latin versions, but when Erasmus took the next edition to Froben he was conscious of the need to translate for the benefit of his northern audience, and he inserted many more Latin equivalents, and also turned the earlier Latin prose versions into verse. The Aldine edition had been so hurried, as he says in the letter already quoted of 1524, that there were bound to be roughnesses: "In the ***Adages*** I translated verse as rapidly as prose," while the presses worked. Greek is nearly always the key to the adage; sometimes a Greek word will illuminate the meaning, as when he gives the word λαβη for *ansa,* not only a "handle," but a "hand-hold" used by wrestlers in the palaestra. Surely such a shrewd psychologist as Erasmus would know that he only stimulated a schoolboy's curiosity when he said of a phrase in Aristophanes: "I would not hesitate to translate these lines if they were as decent as they are elegant!"

One of the most important functions of the ***Adagia*** was to supply an anthology of the Greek poets. (pp. 53-5)

Textual study could be dry, but not in the hands of a writer so conscious of the need for light relief. In the ***Adagia*** Erasmus put into practice the method he was advocating at much the same time in ***De pueris instituendis,*** written during his stay in Italy, 1506-09, though not published until many years afterwards. The most striking of his injunctions is to create pleasure in learning: study so arranged for the child that it seems not work but a game, *ut absit laboris imaginatio, sed puer existimet omnia per lusum agi.* Just so the education of Gargantua seemed "que mieulx ressembloit un passetemps de roy que l'estude d'un escholier." Erasmus's treatise is full of words like *blandimentum, dulcescere, blandae illecebrae*—pleasant inducements, as he suggests learning reading from letters made of biscuit or cut in ivory. Similarly, the ***Adagia*** is skillfully manipulated to rest the mind; learning must be lightened by pleasure or play. It may be the pleasure of fine writing or charming pictures, like the lines of Ennius quoted from Aulus Gellius describing the "friend for all hours," portrayed *eleganter simul et graphice;* the delight in words and especially in poetry, which he quotes at length for the same reason, one feels, as Montaigne—to lighten and give color to his prose.

Or it may be the simpler forms of entertainment, sheer play. He tells tales with evident relish, and when we read *non gravabor ipsius verba inscribere* we know that something has pleased him which he wishes to share with us: stories from Aesop or Pliny, or comic interludes like the illustration to *Oleum ac operam perdidi,* which reads like a folktale even if it is from Macrobius. . . . Illustrations from children's games abound: the poppy-leaf which girls rub between their fingers (if it crackles, he loves me; if it doesn't, he loves me not), the finger-game still played in Italy, the joke of softening an egg to make it pass through a ring. A learned explanation of *in simpulo,* involving Cicero, Faustus Pompeius, Varro, and Pliny, ends with the suggestion, apparently Erasmus's own, that it comes from a children's game, raising "a storm in a teacup" by blowing into a small receptacle through a straw.

More serious but no less entertaining are the many details of life in the past, calculated to awaken the curiosity of the Renaissance reader but also supplying a lively picture of the classical world: Greek coinage, calculation of time, status of slaves, military organization, clothes, baths, agriculture, music, painting, geographical identifications in Asia Minor—often linking mythology with fact. Even modern languages come into the picture, however remote from them Erasmus sometimes seems to be, but it is noticeable that he often hopes to link a vernacular with Greek; what he says about London is of some interest here:

> *Rhodii sacrificum* (2.6.43):
>
> Lindus is a town in Rhodes, from which London in Britain may be derived: Stephanus calls this Lindonium and quotes Martianus as his authority. Rhodes and Britain are both islands, and the ancient tongue of this people (which is now called Welsh, *Walica*) shows clearly enough that it comes from the Greeks, or is at least a mixture. Even in their way of life they are not far removed from that of Greece.

All through the ***Adagia*** we find the constant attempt to identify the classical proverbs with those of the present day. Phrases linger on: "They left with bag and baggage," "He carries water in one hand and fire in the other" (still said in Holland, according to Erasmus); if a silence falls on the feast, it is still an omen, even if nobody says "Mercury is passing"; *suum cuique pulchrum* has its modern counterpart, "No one ever found his sweetheart ugly." Not that there are not surprises: "to play ball" does not mean consent, but arguing for argument's sake, *velut Scotista respondet Scotistice;* and "to throw cold water" is a means "to stimulate to further effort." But on the whole, things change very little. Wedding parties are as silly as they were in ancient times, the barber's shop is a center of gossip as it always was, the great men chatter through divine service as they did in Greece, the astrologers have taken the place of the ancient augurs, and the soothsayers impose themselves not only on the mob but on kings and the rulers of the earth.

Are these lighter touches for the schoolboy or the scholar? No doubt they are often digressions to ease the tedium of learning. But they also have their serious purpose: to establish the continuity of history. The ***Adages*** were instrumental in changing the point of view toward the past, in introducing historical perspective, which is characteristic of their time. Tools for such a purpose were unperfected in Erasmus's day, and he may sometimes suggest untenable hypotheses. But the general tenor of the work was to make the past real and to see the present as an inheritance. Nowhere is this more plain than when there is a correlation to be noticed between biblical and Christian thought and the accepted notions of antiquity. For to Erasmus the study of the past was more than antiquarian speculation, it was an insight into the history of mankind which threw into prominence the coming of Christ.

These are, in a way, side issues in the ***Adagia,*** yet they form the essence of the book. Erasmus's whole lifework is adumbrated here, the classics are seen as a cultural force, as precursors yet on a different plane from the teaching of *Christus praeceptor noster*—from the unquestioned authority of the Lord. When the ***Adages*** speak of Christ, it is as a teacher—and how often this has been a grievance launched against Erasmus!—but this is because the field of the ***Adages*** is that of education and the proverb is hallowed by its use by the Master, "Christ the true Doctor of Divinity." It was not the place for preaching or doctrinal discussion, and Erasmus reserved these for other writings. But his tone makes it clear that the teaching of Christ is different, and to be taken differently, from the precepts of men. For example, in **"Lapides flere"** he says that to associate feeling with stone is a hyperbole, a poetic exaggeration. But when Christ used similar terms, when he said at the entry into Jerusalem, "If men were to keep silent these stones would cry out," and "God is able of these stones to raise up children unto Abraham," there is no hyperbole. For with him all is possible.

Perhaps the fact that the publication of the ***Adages*** and of the Greek New Testament jointly established Erasmus's fame has led critics to see him as dividing himself between the sacred and the secular and caused a critic of the calibre of Lucien Febvre to speak of "the pagan of the ***Adages.***" But this is quite misleading. The ***Adages*** are essentially a part of the whole Erasmian drive toward Christian humanism.

The most striking parts of the book, those for which contemporaries looked most eagerly, were the topical parts: the comic or biting criticisms of the current state of affairs, the mischievous vignettes of public or private life, the serious and eloquent arguments on pacifism and kingship, which have become the best-known parts of the ***Adagia.*** Side by side with these more spectacular passages are a host of quiet asides that would be particularly savored by many readers. Often these can only be guessed at today: the unexpectedly ferocious attack on pigs seems to recall other jokes like the appearance of Janotus de Bragmardo; the demure treatment of Pythagorean rules against fish-eating has a sober connection with the colloquy **"Ichthyophagia"**; the aspersions of Galen on the (philosophical) sects have quite a different ring in 1528. **"Artem quaevis alit terra"** produces a wry sentence about the traveling journeyman, "an honest fellow if his art be honest," but what of the people who make their traveling expenses by hawking dispensations? Or the man who buys a cardinal's hat so as to have the title engraved on his tombstone? Are mitres and cardinals' hats sometimes used, like "the magistrate's purple gown," to hide an ugly tumor? The punishment for adultery was severe among the Cumani; now we are almost at the stage of giving prizes to the man who seduces most wives. The priests who need a bribe before they will administer the sacraments, the hawkers of relics, had their counterparts in ancient Greece.

Considering all these different ingredients which go to make up the ***Adagia,*** it is clear that there are filiations connecting the book with all of Erasmus's other works. If it is not the keystone of the arch, it is at least the meeting-place of all the various elements which constitute his wide-ranging but consistent output. In this sense it is central to his work, and this is the definition we are seeking.

It is easy to see the connection between the ***Adagia*** and the treatises on style like the ***De copia,*** and the similarity of attitude with the ***De pueris.*** Textual criticism, so important a part of his contribution to learning, is represented here, as well as all the work on classical authors and the Fathers from which he gleaned his proverbs as the more fundamental work of editing went on. Long serious essays linked the ***Adagia*** with the ***Institutio principis*** (***Aut regem aut fatuum***), with his pacifist writings like the ***Querela pacis*** (***Dulce bellum inexpertis, Spartam nactus es***), and with the plea for a simplified Christianity in the ***Enchiridion militis christiani*** (***Sileni Alcibiadis***). Shorter comments chime with the ***Colloquies,*** on soldiers, on fish-eating, on pilgrimages, on banquets. The ***Praise of Folly*** is represented not only by a warm defense (**"Ollas ostentare"**) but by comedy (**"Scarabeus"**) and the very method of ***Sileni Alcibiadis,*** the paradox of holiness. Devotional works and biblical criticism have their discreet share. The ***Adagia*** was Erasmus's life-companion and necessarily became a running commentary on all he was doing and thinking.

If this is so, what are we to say about the construction of the book on which he spent so much care, as the renumbering of adages and switching of them around, the editing and corrections show? How did he see this centerpiece as a matter of arrangement? There is a sense of order in the ***Adagia,*** but it is hard to put a finger on the method used. The Greek collections supplied a certain order by marshaling similar proverbs; there is occasionally a brief spurt of alphabetical order; there is often an assimilation of subjects, but never so marked as to be wearisome or constitute a catalogue. Erasmus played with the order, shifting proverbs about until he was satisfied, making cross-references, noting "I shall mention this proverb in its place," *suo loco* or *alibi.* In the later sections, it is often the book he is reading which dictates a selection—Pindar, Homer, Plutarch. He takes care to open each thousand adages, often a hundred, with a long important essay. As in all his works, Erasmus is continually aware of his audience, careful to provide variety, to make the work readable in spite of its possibilities of ponderousness or diffusion, just as he left it to the last to add the touches of personal comment or homely wit which make the classical diet digestible (this we know from the manuscript of the last part of the ***Adagia***). This book, so long considered the most outdated of his works, was for his contemporaries the most up-to-date and topical.

Perhaps Erasmus's own metaphor in the 1500 preface is still the best description of his method: "I put aside my nightly labours over a more serious work and strolled through the gardens of the classics . . . and so plucked, and as it were arranged in garlands, like flowerets of every hue, all the most ancient and famous of the adages." The result was something like those Dutch flowerpieces, where flowers that could never have bloomed together are arranged with deceptive negligence, the superb and the humble in the same bouquet. (pp. 55-60)

Margaret Mann Phillips, "Ways with Adages," in Essays on the Works of Erasmus, *edited by Richard L. DeMolen, Yale University Press, 1978, pp. 51-60.*

E. Rummel (essay date 1981)

[*In the following excerpt, Rummel illustrates how Erasmus followed the rules for rhetoric he had previously set down in* De Copia *when composing his later work,* De Pueris.]

Erasmus' speech on the importance of early childhood education combines two literary genres: it serves both as a rhetorical exercise and as an educational treatise, an epideixis and a protreptic. Although the oration's double purpose has been recognized, its content has generally received more attention than its form. ***De Pueris*** has been studied many times for its pedagogical views, but rarely for its rhetorical character. . . . To establish suitable parallels between the rules set out in the second book of ***De Copia*** and their implementation in ***De Pueris*** is the subject of this article.

Erasmus suggests eleven methods of elaboration in his manual on style. Our purpose is best served by following his arrangement and pointing out how he applies the recommendations made in ***De Copia.*** Not all of the eleven methods need concern us here. Several of them contain overlapping ideas, present subordinate concepts, or concern elements that are so intricately woven into overall argumentation they cannot be documented separately. In this matter we let ourselves be guided by Erasmus who himself acknowledges that not all of the methods listed by him are of equal weight, and so treats individual sections accordingly.

The first method suggested in ***De Copia*** deals with procedures used in expanding the original "wrapped-up" statement by listing its constituent parts. As examples Erasmus uses the expression "comprehensive education," which he expands by listing the various fields of study, or the phrase "riotous living," which he enlarges by setting out a number of ways to waste money. ***De Pueris*** offers several examples of this method.

For instance, the statement "their own lives have served as [bad] examples" is detailed in the following manner:

> The youngster sees his father intoxicated and uttering streams of profanities, repeatedly witnesses banquets highlighted by extravagance and sensuality, constantly hears the house ringing with the din of mime-actors, flutists, lute-players and dancers.

Similarly, "parents crushed by unbearable shame" brought on them by their corrupted children is expanded by enumerating the ways their sons and daughters have compromised or grieved them: by committing criminal offences, prostituting themselves, contracting diseases or dying a disgraceful death as a consequence of their dissolute life. (pp. 127-28)

While Erasmus recommends the method of particularizing a general statement, he also cautions the student against heaping up arguments without discernible structure. He therefore suggests a division into organized parts. "He was a total monster" may be detailed by considering first the body, then the mind; "he was quite drenched" can be elaborated by proceeding to the various parts of the body, describing their condition in order, "from top to toe." We find the recommendation for organized particularization applied in ***De Pueris.*** Erasmus starts with a general accusation against people who allow their son's first years to pass without the benefits of education. He then subdivides this group into (a) parents who entirely neglect their children's education, (b) those who start too late and (c) those who provide an education that must be unlearned later on. The same pointedly organized approach is evident elsewhere. Discussing the idea of perfection, Erasmus divides the topic into three parts, dealing separately with each of the three contributing factors, nature, education and practice. A similar principle prevails in his discussion of the learning process. He starts with a statement of disposition—"The learning of a language depends mainly on two faculties: memory and imitation"—and then proceeds to discuss these elements in succession.

Methods Two, Three and Four involve elaboration by dwelling on results, causes and circumstances respectively. Erasmus treats these methods in passing since they may be viewed as special cases of Method One or as contributing factors to Method Five, which deals with *enargeia* or vividness. The examples given under this heading also involve listing details of a general proposition, but differ from Method One in accentuating description rather than analysis. The details related are designed to "bring an event before the eyes with all the colours filled in"—they have to be dramatic and involve not only the reader's mind, but also his eyes and ears. (pp. 128-29)

"Characterization" is another rhetorical device recommended in the ***Copia*** under the heading of *enargeia.* It involves describing characters or emotional states that have become stereotyped in comedy and rhetoric, such as boasters, sycophants, misers and gluttons. In ***De Pueris*** the description of the furious schoolteacher fits this category. He is described "with snake-like eyes and narrow, screwed-up mouth, a voice as shrill as that of a ghost, a ghastly visage and bobbing head . . . the image of a demon from hell."

Another method of producing vividness is the introduction of direct speech "in which we supply each person with appropriate utterances." Erasmus mentions the speeches inserted in their narratives by the historians Thucydides, Sallust and Livy, but also recommends, on a smaller scale, the introduction of striking sayings or vivid exclamations that can credibly be attributed to a story's main characters.

In ***De Pueris*** Erasmus highlights anecdotes by quoting directly. For instance, when relating an example of improper direction in studies, to emphasize the point that it is wrong to force a young person into studies that are distasteful to him, he switches to direct speech when describing the reaction of the victim: "I feel so strongly about this," the young man is made to exclaim, "that whenever I turn to my studies it is as if a sword were driven through my heart!" Similarly, Erasmus adds force to his rejection of punitive measures in education by quoting the *ipsissima verba* of a schoolmaster who has come to repent his actions: "I almost destroyed his character before I learned to understand it." Erasmus underlines the point of the example by letting the protagonist of the story pronounce the message in person, and so succeeds in presenting his argument more vividly.

A special mode of employing direct speech is "dramatization," introducing fictitious speakers of importance or gravity. Examples in the ***Copia*** include past leaders of a city, famous ancestors, the country speaking with parental authority or the laws personified. In the same sense Erasmus introduces Method as a speaker in ***De Pueris,*** crying out to the student: "If you do this you will bring ruin and disgrace upon yourself." (pp. 129-30)

Method Six is concerned with digression as means of elaboration Erasmus points out that commonplaces allow the speaker to dwell longer on a given proposition, listing as examples such topics as the fickleness of fortune, the inevitability of death, the power of money, etc. The device of digression is also used in ***De Pueris,*** where Erasmus dwells on the commonplace notion that "mankind has learned from animals many useful things" as part of the argument that a father should demonstrate as much responsibility as is shown by animals toward their offspring. Erasmus uses the commonplace to list all sorts of skills that man has acquired by imitating or observing animals. He mentions that we have learned the art of bloodletting from the hippopotamus, the use of the syringe from the ibis, the efficacy of various drugs from the practice of deers, lizards, swallows, turtles and bears. All this has no bearing on the argument, but allows the orator to display his skill and erudition, for a digression serves the purpose of pleasing the reader's literary tastes, creating a certain mood or, more generally, setting the stage for an argument.

In Method Seven Erasmus recommends the use of epithets, not only for description, but also for particularization and emphasis. The examples given in the ***Copia*** are closely paralleled in ***De Pueris.*** "Hercules, reducer of monsters" (used in ***De Copia***) is similar in kind to "Adam, the first man of the human race" in ***De Pueris***—both epithets are derived from the distinctive role played by each man. Similarly, the expression "history, the teacher of life" (found in ***De Copia***) is akin to the phrase "nature, the mother of all things," both appositions describing roles. Natural descriptive phrases are said in the ***Copia*** to belong to the realm of poetry, but the examples "liquid fonts, golden sun, rolling rivers" find their counterparts in phrases used in ***De Pueris,*** such as "sweetly smelling flowers" and "brightly verdant fields." Epithets may also add force to a statement. Examples cited in the ***Copia*** include "Plato, the most reliable authority" or "Aristarchus, the most learned of men," where epithets of praise are used to make the information conveyed sound more reliable. Similar expressions are found in ***De Pueris*** where Erasmus cites the authorities of "the great philosopher Aristotle" and the "supreme poet" Virgil. In both cases he employs laudatory terms to add gravity to his source and thereby lend authority to his own statements.

Method Eight concerns *peristasis,* the expansion of circumstances, but Erasmus contents himself with a definition of this method and goes on without giving an example because *peristasis* "pervades the whole speech and cannot be illustrated by a short example."

The ninth method deals with modes of amplification, one of the most important devices of epideictic speeches. Of those listed in the ***Copia, De Pueris*** employs most often the devices of "advancing by degrees," "comparing the lesser to the greater" and *synathroismos,* the accumulation of phrases, especially synonyms. As an example of the first mode, advancing by degrees, Erasmus quotes Cicero: "It is an offence to tie up a Roman citizen, a crime to flog him . . . what shall I call crucifying him?" This step-by-step escalation of an argument is also represented in ***De Pueris.*** In his accusation of parents who neglect their children's education, Erasmus proceeds from the basis that "infanticides only destroy the body, but these parents destroy the mind." From there he goes on to say that they "also cause harm to society . . . moreover, they sin against God." Thus the offence of negligent parents is gradually amplified from the basic statement, "murder is a crime, destruction of the mind is worse," to a more advanced one, "it is not only a crime against one person, but against society," to the most serious indictment, "a crime, not only against men, but also against God."

Amplification may also be achieved by arguing from the lesser to the greater. In the ***Copia*** Erasmus quotes Cicero as an example:

> Scipio, that distinguished figure, when holding public office, killed Tiberius Gracchus when he was causing a moderately serious political upheaval in Rome etc.

The comparison is between Rome and the world, a moderate upheaval and universal rioting, a private person and a man holding office—in each case the argument proceeds from the lesser to the greater. This type of reasoning is frequently found in ***De Pueris.*** Favourite comparisons are those between animals and humans, chattel and child (or more generally: inanimate and animate), body and soul, heathen and Christian. (pp. 130-32)

The heathen-Christian comparison is perhaps the most interesting variation as it is the logical development of the comparison between barbarian nations and their own native civilization used by ancient rhetoricians. Both the classical and the "modern" brand is represented in ***De Pueris:***

> If there existed a Thessalian witch who had the power and the desire to transform your son into a swine or a wolf would you not think that no punishment could be too severe for her? But what you find revolting in her you eagerly practise yourself.

Here are shades of Apuleius' *Golden Ass* and Homer's Circe. (p. 132)

In the context of expansion by amplification Erasmus also mentions *synathroismos,* accumulation of synonyms. . . . Accumulation is a device frequently employed in ***De Pueris*** although the expressions are more often related than strictly synonymic, as in the phrase "ravaged by gluttony, wine-bibbing, lack of sleep, brawling, duelling or, to crown them all, the disgraceful pox." A most impressive example because of its forcefulness is Erasmus' tirade against lack of self-control:

> Lust is a hideous brute; extravagance a devouring and insatiable monster, drunkenness a savage beast, anger a fearful creature, ambition a ghastly animal.

Similarly effective is the description of misanthropic teachers:

> their expression always forbidding, their speech

invariably morose; . . . they seem ill-tempered, are unable to say anything in a pleasant manner and can hardly manage to return a smile.

In each case the device used is *synathroismos,* a series of inter-related expressions that have a cumulative effect and therefore not only expand but also amplify the argument.

Method Ten concerns the invention of propositions, a skill that cannot be transmitted by rules, but requires imagination and practice. However, Erasmus points out some general guidelines: the student should take into consideration *staseis,* categories of arguments, appropriate to each type of speech. The "persuasive" type represented in ***De Pueris*** draws upon what is "proper and laudable, useful, safe and easy, necessary and pleasant."

Erasmus' propositions put forth in ***De Pueris*** rest on the following arguments:

—children are their parents' most precious possession and should therefore not be neglected;

—parents have an obligation (natural, social and religious) to educate their children;

—education is beneficial to the child because it leads him on the path of honesty, and to the parent because their child will be a credit and a source of comfort to them in their old age.

Possible objections are eliminated:

—objection: small children do not have the constitution to put up with the rigours of studying; answer: on the contrary, since knowledge is based on memory and imitation and children have a special ability for both, early childhood education is desirable;

—objection: very little is accomplished in the early years of training; it is therefore not worth the trouble and expense; answer: small contributions have a cumulative effect and add up to a great goal;

—objection: studies have a detrimental effect on the child's physical development; answer: licentious living has a more detrimental effect than studies; a good teacher will counteract any negative side-effects.

This last point is developed further: the ideal teacher is well-informed, of good character and gentle disposition, skilful and imaginative in his approach to education.

The various sources of argument are thus well represented in ***De Pueris.*** The topic of propriety is contained in the reference to the parents' obligation toward society and God; comparison with material goods and reminders that children are their parents' security and comfort in old age introduces the idea that education is useful and advantageous; mention of the children's receptiveness and good memory centres on the argument of facility and ease; the topic of pleasure is considered in the demand that the teacher be congenial and present his material in an attractive manner; nature supplies the topic of necessity.

Method Eleven deals with proofs by example. Erasmus discusses the various forms examples can take, such as stories, proverbs or well-known sayings, parallels or similes. This method is amply represented in ***De Pueris.*** Stories range from expanded quips to detailed scenes. An episode illustrating the usefulness of education provides a succinct example:

Aristippus once gave a witty answer to a wealthy but dull-witted citizen who had asked what benefits a young man would derive from education. 'Well, at least he will have this advantage that in the theatre he won't sit down as one lump of stone on another.'

Here only a bare outline of the circumstances is given. The story focuses on Aristippus' words and the audience is invited to draw their own conclusions. In another section Erasmus presents a more elaborate example illustrating the effects of brutality on a child's development. He outlines the victim's background, describes in detail the punishments inflicted, vividly pictures the tormentor and dwells on the consequences of the treatment, reiterating the point of the example.

Proverbs and maxims, recommended in the ***Copia*** as devices to establish the validity of a proposition, are also found in ***De Pueris.*** They range from popular sayings ("Seeing is better than hearing") to biblical wisdom ("Bad talk corrupts good manners") and classical *sententiae,* such as Senca's "No age is too old for learning," or Isocrates' "We learn best when we have a desire to learn."

In the ***Copia*** Erasmus acknowledges the usefulness of similes, metaphors and parallels as means of persuasion. Picturesque language is employed to good effect in ***De Pueris*** where Erasmus likens temptations to entanglement in brambles, the natural, uncivilized human being to a shapeless lump, or the educational process to pouring liquid into a vessel. More significant, however, is the use of such figures in proofs to illustrate a point made or to argue by analogy.

Modern textbooks may distinguish between examples and parallels, but Erasmus glosses over the difference:

The more pedantic may wish to distinguish the illustrative example from the parallel, taking the example as something definitely done by someone, the parallel as an analogous situation to be found in events in general . . . even so, the methods of expanding the parallel are exactly the same as those for the example.

We may therefore follow Erasmus' views in our arrangement by treating examples and parallels under one heading. (pp. 133-35)

In using comparisons, variety is important. The speaker should apply as many different illustrations as possible at each point. Erasmus recommends drawing from different sources, listing as possible suppliers of examples and parallels historians, philosophers, poets and theologians. Another way of achieving variety is to refer to different nations or to take examples from several periods in history or different walks of life. This recommendation is well heeded in ***De Pueris.*** Several of the illustrative examples are taken from Greek and Roman history using as models Alexander the Great, Aemilius Paulus, Pliny, the Gracchi and Cato. More frequently the heroes of anecdotes and sources of quotations are philosophers and orators, among them Demosthenes, Isocrates and Quintilian, Plato, Aristotle and Diogenes. St. Paul and Augustine represent the Christian tradition; among the poets Virgil and Hesiod are quoted more than once. Further variety is introduced by drawing not only on Greek and Roman tradition, but also by referring to other nations. For instance, Erasmus lists among the model families who surround their children with an atmosphere of learning, the Dutch Canter family, the court of Ferdinand and Isabella and the family of his friend Thomas More. He also draws examples from various professions, that of the farmer, sailor, soldier or athlete.

Even though most examples are classical and taken from ancient sources, contemporary history, and events are by no means neglected and are given weight by being represented as first-hand information and eye-witness reports. Thus we find among his examples references to contemporary initiation rites, teaching methods and school experiences. In this manner Erasmus encompasses all possibilities and appeals to a broad audience, true to his recommendation to include examples from a wide spectrum of illustrations, "ancient, splendid, national and domestic."

Throughout Erasmus' catalogue of methods in the ***Copia*** are sprinkled practical hints and professional tricks—special effects that will make the orator's speech more convincing and effective. He suggests using examples that "will make the hearer feel superior," which is to be done by introducing accounts about "women, children, slaves and barbarians." Another such trick is to inflate an example's source so as to make it the pronouncement of a great sage, an expert in the field or a proven counsellor. (p. 136)

Finally there is Erasmus' advice for clinching an argument: end it with *epiphonema,* a pungent remark or summary comment. Examples in the ***Copia*** are taken from Virgil ("Such toil it was to found the Roman race!") and Martial ("Shall I tell you what you are? A jack of all trades!"). These expressions are paralleled by Erasmian phrases in ***De Pueris:*** "Such is the mentality of most teachers!" or "[Such a father is] neither a man himself nor a son of man!" Remarks of this sort round off a paragraph and form an emphatic conclusion.

To examine an oration's rhetorical devices is like watching a play from the wings: it takes away the illusion of grandeur and lessens the special effects. Our examination can be justified, however, by the nature of ***De Pueris,*** which is labelled by Erasmus himself as an *epideixis,* "an example of a theme first handled concisely and then expanded and broadly treated." As the author of ***De Pueris,*** Erasmus assumes the rhetorician's role for the sake of his student audience; therefore we find his speech not just adequately but copiously illustrated, his examples not merely pleasing in variety but covering the whole range of sources, his style not only rich but occasionally cloying—we find in ***De Pueris*** the rules of rhetoric writ large for the benefit of the beginner.

The wealth of material exemplifying the methods recommended in ***De Copia*** makes ***De Pueris*** a fine example of rhetorical craftsmanship and indeed a suitable model to be set before the eyes of a young prince aspiring to letters or any other young man with rhetorical ambitions. The speech is a most useful example for readers of ***De Copia,*** which is itself amply supplied with illustrative material, but contains many rules that can only be fully explicated in context or on a larger scale. It is not surprising therefore that ***De Pueris*** gained instant popularity with Erasmus' contemporaries. Its success is no doubt also due to the fact that Erasmus combined a useful exercise with a literary composition, rhetorical form with moral content. (pp. 137-38)

E. Rummel, "Structure and Argumentation in Erasmus' 'De Pueris Instituendis'," in Renaissance and Reformation, *n.s. Vol. V, No. 3, 1981, pp. 127-40.*

Harry Berger, Jr. (essay date 1982)

[Berger is an American educator and literary critic. In the following excerpt from an essay originally published in English Literary Renaissance *in 1982, he examines misanthropic attitudes found within* The Praise of Folly.]

In their different ways both ***The Praise of Folly*** and *Utopia* dramatize the same vitiated attitude toward life and explore its consequences. Both undertake an analysis of what I shall call misanthropy and depict the structures this condition erects to protect itself from life. Erasmus's emphasis is primarily psychological, More's political. Erasmus shows how a cultural system may be mobilized to serve the interests of misanthropic self-deception. More imagines a society performing the same service. The two works may be distinguished, somewhat artificially, as enacting different phases of the pattern of withdrawal and return—withdrawal in the pastoral misanthropy envisaged by Erasmus, false return in the utopian misanthropy portrayed by More. The two versions of misanthropy are embodied in the characters of Folly and Hythloday. (p. 229)

Folly is the voice of that familiar schismatic illness in which the dream of life as golden ease is coupled with the nightmare of life as sheer misery. Her birth and parentage signify the moment when the golden fantasy so captivates the mind as to canker its prospect of mortal existence. The presence of plants like nepenthe, panacea, and lotus among the flora of the blessed isles implies that the birth of folly may be recurrent, a moment not merely of origins but also of return and escape from the cankered world. Folly is neither the fantasy nor the nightmare in itself but the obsessional dialectic between the two, the fantasy continually reanimated by contempt, the contempt exacerbated by fantasy. Her idyllism is a wax-winged flight. It arcs beyond the moon toward the fastness of the theologian's third heaven or the Olympian heights from which spectator gods look down and laugh, and thus, expecting too much, it generates its own Icarian plummet to the hard, cynical ground: "If you could look down from the moon, as Menippus once did, on the countless hordes of mortals, you'd think you saw a swarm of flies or gnats quarrelling amongst themselves, fighting, plotting, stealing, playing, making love, being born, growing old and dying. It's hard to believe how much trouble and tragedy this tiny creature can stir up, short-lived as he is, for sometimes a brief war or outbreak of plague can carry off and destroy many thousands at once."

The argument of Folly is that the examined life is not worth living, the examined self not worth knowing. In this gloomy cave of Trophonius the body is disgusting, the soul hateful, our fellow human beings to be neither trusted nor endured. The only glue that holds society together is the complicity whereby we deceive ourselves and each other. Folly is the sole alternative to anarchy. Her birth is the nepenthe that puts us to sleep or the dream that sustains us in our divine lethargy. She promises to restore the Golden Age by building a Babel of innocents, masking universal paranoia behind universal harmony. She offers us *Kolakia* and *Philautia* as guides. Following the first, we increasingly scorn those we flatter because of their gullibility. Following the second, we accept their flattery while remaining insensible of their scorn. Folly as a cultural system obviates the more painful and futile exercise of wisdom and virtue.

But Folly does not, cannot, simply persuade us to accept her remedy. Like one of Plato's sophists, she has first to persuade us that we need it—i.e., that the misanthropy she induces fits the facts of life. She does this by appropriating and misusing the powers of Momus. Her specific criticisms and analyses cannot easily be dismissed, not only because they flatter our sense of our worldly wisdom but also because they seem to hit their targets. Her targets may be easy, but this only leads us to agree all the more and to second her moral rebukes. And here lies the danger of her attitude and program: she speaks to our need for indignation and our capacity for self-deception but also, and more profoundly, to our underlying feelings of self-contempt and helplessness. Some examples will suggest the range of strategies by which she tries to establish her dominion and will lead us beyond her toward a glimpse of her creator.

Discussing insanity in chapter 38, Folly directs our attention to what is apparently an innocent dieretic exercise:

> The nature of insanity is surely twofold. One kind is sent from hell by the vengeful furies whenever they let loose their snakes and assail the hearts of men with lust for war, insatiable thirst for gold, the disgrace of forbidden love, parricide, incest, sacrilege, or some other sort of evil, or when they pursue the guilty, conscience-stricken soul with their avenging spirits and flaming brands of terror. The other is quite different, desirable above everything, and is known to come from me. It occurs whenever some happy mental aberration frees the soul from its anxious cares and at the same time restores it by the addition of manifold delights.

This is much more than a simple classification. The message of the first part is that we are neither responsible for the evil we think and do nor capable of dealing with the mental punishment that results from it; in both cases we are the victims of supernatural agencies whose powers we—with our meager spiritual resources—are unable to resist or fend off. No merely human ally can protect us from the furies, and the message of the second part is that we must throw ourselves on the mercy of our divine protectress, Folly. The second insanity is the only cure for the first.

Erasmus's readers may glimpse an alternative explanation in the devious redundancy of "pursue the guilty, conscience-stricken soul with their avenging spirits and flaming brands of terror": if we take the allegorical snakes and brands not as reifications but as metaphors of the soul's evil desires and guilt, we may ascribe both evil and guilt to an inner energy—the first to the energy of "that old earthly Adam" within us, the second to the ethical energy that stabs us with the pain of our willed betrayal of the Christ who died for us. Both Folly's analysis and her antidote evoke the message of the ***Enchiridion Militis Christiani,*** which they distort:

> Hence, therefore, the outcome . . . is not at all doubtful, for the reason that victory in no wise depends upon fortune, but all this lies in the hand of God, and, through Him, also in our hands. Here no one has failed to conquer unless he did not want to conquer. . . . He will fight for you . . . not without your own effort. For He who said, "Trust in me, for I have conquered the world," wishes you to be of a great, not a secure, mind. . . . Wherefore we ought to steer a middle course between Scylla and Charybdis, so that we neither act too securely because we rely on Divine Grace nor cast away our mind with our arms because we are dispirited by the difficulties of war.

Folly proposes eschewing the middle course and moving from the Charybdis of the furies to the Scylla of divine folly, for the human mind, lacking greatness, can only hope for the security of the happy aberration.

The same exclusion of the Christian middle informs her concluding meditation on the folly of the Cross. This section is generally taken straight as expressing Erasmus's—and not merely Folly's—view of Christian piety. In arguing for the integrity of the ***Praise,*** Wayne Rebhorn and Richard Sylvester have recently defended this view. Their account of the work's reflexive structure and movement is persuasive: Folly's "metamorphosis from ironist to satirist to Christian mystic," as Rebhorn puts it, articulates the three basic divisions of the ***Praise,*** and the final "vision of Christian folly" transcends

> the illusory hope of the first section and the horrifying "reality" of the second. Note that Folly no longer claims man's worship, for Christian folly clearly means worship of God. . . . Folly defines what she calls the doctrine of Christ and what elsewhere Erasmus labeled the "Philosophia Christi," insisting that it involves mildness, tolerance, charity, and most significantly, contempt for the life of this world.

But of course Folly's version of contempt in the previous section of the ***Praise*** is a misanthropic perversion of Christian contempt as Erasmus has discussed it, e.g., in the ***Enchiridion,*** while "mildness, tolerance, charity" are not her trump cards. The Rebhorn/Sylvester argument for the consistency of the work may possibly be extended to the consistency of the speaker's character, and I think a small change in their reading of the last section will strengthen their reading of the whole.

There is much in what the Penguin annotator calls "the praise of evangelical folly" which strikes a true chord—the themes of spiritual ignorance and simple piety associated with the *devotio moderna*—but this only adds to the strength, that is, the dangerousness, of Folly's argument. She pushes the power and virtue of ignorance through the middle course of the ***Enchiridion*** and toward the extreme of the foolish insanity discussed above. Her distortions of the handbook are subtle but significant. She notes of the "sword of the spirit" that it penetrates the bosom and "cuts out every passion with *a single stroke,* so that nothing remains in the heart but piety." But the idea of a one-battle victory, a once-and-for-all encounter is a mirage: the dagger, the handbook, is a way of life, and the battle must be fought until the very end. Folly interprets piety as an absolute rejection of intellectual effort and wisdom, a return to childhood and natural instinct; this is the way to be "free from care or purpose." But in the ***Enchiridion,*** Erasmus counsels the necessity of weaning ("to remain like an infant is unfortunate"), and although he criticizes modern theologians, he recommends reading the Fathers because "their very thoughts constitute a prayerful meditation."

Folly's praise of simplicity continues the praise of irresponsibility that dominated the first division of her speech. Like the bad interpreters she castigated in the second division, she marshals up texts from the Old and New Testaments to support a specious notion of divine mercy: "When men pray for forgiveness, though they may have sinned in full awareness, they make folly their excuse and defence. . . . What else is acting ignorantly but acting foolishly, with no evil intent?" By the end of the passage, the excuse has become the reality, while divine mercy has drawn closer to the folly of bad faith.

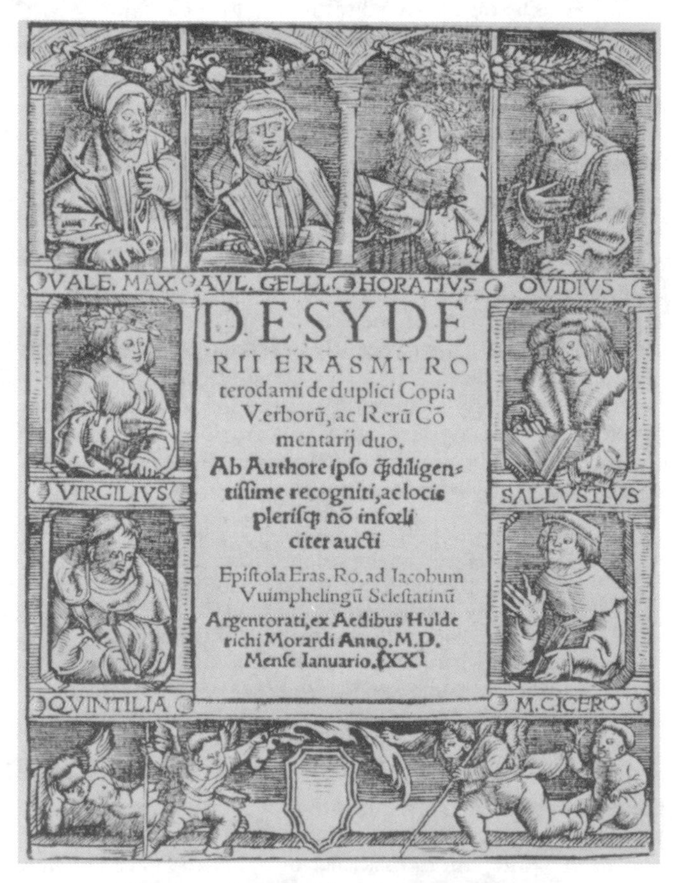
VALE. MAX. AVL. GELLI. HORATIVS OVIDIVS

D.ESYDE
RII ERASMI RO
terodami de duplici Copia
Verborũ, ac Rerũ Cõ
mentarij duo.
Ab Authore ipso q̃diligen-
tissime recogniti, ac locis
plerisq; nõ infœli
citer aucti

Epistola Eras. Ro. ad Iacobum
Vuimphelingũ Sclestatinũ
Argentorati, ex Aedibus Hulde
richi Morardi Anno. M.D.
Mense Ianuario. XXI

VIRGILIVS SALLVSTIVS
QVINTILIA M.CICERO

Title page of De duplici copia verborum (*1512*).

The uncompromising rejection of the body, its senses, and its affections is also suspect. It is a viewpoint which Folly shares with the Stoic censor she condemns, and the Christian critique of this viewpoint, deriving chiefly from St. Augustine, is familiar: since the body no less than the soul is God's creation, and since the soul is responsible for the body, it is both "angelic" presumption and ethical evasion to make the body the scapegoat for spiritual weakness; it is directly a slander of the body and indirectly a slander of the ethical will. Folly's hatred of creation, her contempt of ethical consciousness and effort, are still felt in the final section, which testifies not so much to a metamorphosis as to the ultimate *hybris,* the effort to use the Gospel message as a vehicle for the pastoral misanthropy which constitutes a perversion of the Gospel spirit. Thus, for example, the divine madness may be an even better antidote than *philautia* for the self-hatred which in Folly's eyes is inevitably conjoined to self-knowledge: "Anyone who loves intensely lives not in himself but in the object of his love, and the further he can move out of himself into his love, the happier he is," and a few sentences later Folly places the emphasis of this triumph not on union with God but on escape from self: "When the whole man will be outside himself, and be happy *for no reason except* that he is so outside himself, he will enjoy some ineffable share in the supreme good which draws everything into itself."

Folly promotes an ideal of piety which stands in direct contrast to Erasmian watchfulness, an ideal of self-forgetfulness which entails throwing away the Christian soldier's dagger or handbook. Those who try to achieve that ideal and return to the state of infancy will be precisely those least able to distinguish the Erasmian message of the ***Praise*** from its misanthropic inversion. As she describes the final rapture, it is not a refreshing of the spirit which renews the soldier's dedication to his earthly mission. Rather it is a repetition of the dialectic between fantasy and contempt that constitutes the anti-Christian condition of Folly. The ecstasy, which produces in pious fools the same symptoms as those displayed by theologians in scholastic disputes, sends them back to waking life freshly disgruntled: "All they know is that they were happiest when they were out of their senses in this way, and they lament their return to reason, for all they want is to be mad forever with this kind of madness." After this Folly resumes in her exordium the tone of flippant contempt for the audience that marked her "ironic" performance in the first section of the ***Praise:*** she can be as illogical and inconsistent as she pleases, for the fools who swallow her sophistries will believe anything that promises to dull their sense of the ugly truth about life and themselves.

The basis of the condition embodied as Folly, the source both of the golden-age fantasy and the *saeva indignatio* dialectically coupled with it, is hatred of self. Folly's contempt for her fools clearly displaces and relieves her contempt for herself. She operates on the principle that misery loves company. In flaying the grammarians, theologians, and ecclesiastics she practices the very abuses she condemns. The finest dramatic irony of this mirror relationship is not, however, to be located in the displacement of Folly's hatred from self to others. That irony lies in the underlying reversal of Folly's displacement, and it can be grasped only after we consider the fictive rhetorical situation of the work as a whole. It is only a partial truth, and a distracting one at that, to see Erasmus behind the mask of Folly. He shares his act of creation with others. For just as Folly creates fools, so fools create Folly. She does not appear before us with her hegemony already established. In fact, the occasion of her appearance is her effort to secure her regime. She comes to the podium knowing she is still in poor repute, an orator wearing an unaccustomed garb, a shadow in search of an embodiment and apotheosis long overdue. We ungrateful mortals do not yet appreciate her and have not yet granted her independent existence.

The point of her appearance, the reason for her oration, is that only her "subjects" can transfer to Folly the power she claims she already has. For she is our creation, our Daedalian puppet, at once our slave and our divinity. We alone can enthrone her over ourselves by persuading ourselves of our helplessness and passivity, by throwing away the Christian dagger and acknowledging our inability to confront life with mere ethical armor. Her being is in our hands. Her insistence that she is compact of nature and spontaneity reflects our desire to animate and reify our self-deception so that we can forget we are responsible for it. She has to encourage us to keep up the illusion, act out the farce, because her life depends on it. She is the voice within us asking to be released from our self-control. But her appearance gives us the chance to reject her. It testifies that the ultimate complicity is still unrealized. We are not yet fully confirmed in our bad faith. Recognizing that her true face is worn by each of us, we remain free to reach for a different enchiridion. (pp. 231-37)

Harry Berger, Jr., "Utopian Folly: Erasmus and More on the Perils of Misanthropy," in his Second World and Green World: Studies in Renaissance Fiction-Making, *edited by John Patrick Lynch, University of California Press, 1988, pp. 229-48.*

Eugene R. Hammond (essay date 1983)

[*In the following excerpt, Hammond argues that* The Praise of Folly *may have significantly influenced Jonathan Swift's* A Tale of a Tub, *and provides illustrative comparisons between the two satires.*]

An Erasmian spirit has long been observed in Jonathan Swift's *A Tale of a Tub*. . . . There is no better key to the ironic method, the mock encomium structure, and the thematic concerns of Swift's *A Tale of a Tub* than Erasmus' ***Praise of Folly.***

Although the ***Folly*** and the *Tale* are both works of religious controversy, both defending a unified Church against corruptions introduced by the temporal custodians of the Church, they share a spirit of scarcely bridled wit and exuberance. Both authors playfully disclose secrets of the authorial trade, like the usefulness of claiming to have dashed off one's manuscript in a day or two, or of prevailing on a friend to steal a copy of it. Each deliberately leaves parts of his text obscure, and then supplies a commentator who clears up obscurities in a voice as playful and ironic as that in the text. Each anticipates widespread criticism and attempts to disarm that criticism before it arises, Erasmus by entrusting the defense of the ***Folly*** to Thomas More, Swift by casting the *Tale* out as a diversion to occupy critics who might otherwise "pick Holes in the weak sides of Religion and Government." Erasmus and Swift were each roundly attacked by an orthodox clergyman for making light of religion—Erasmus by Martin Dorp and Swift by William Wotton. And each wrote a defense—Erasmus in a letter to Dorp, Swift in the *Tale*'s "Apology"—the arguments of which can hardly be distinguished (Swift's personal copy of the ***Praise of Folly,*** a 1668 Latin edition published at Oxford, included Erasmus' letter to Dorp).

Many of the satirical targets in the ***Folly*** reappear in the *Tale.* Swift's Aeolists closely resemble Erasmus' monks in their artificial and mechanical preaching and in their utter disregard for meaning. Folly's attendant Philautia (Self-love) may never find fuller embodiment than she does in the self-approving comments of the Swiftian narrator. What Erasmus finds true of the monastic orders—"nor is it so much their concern to be like Christ as to be unlike each other"—Swift sees in the antics of Peter and Jack. In addition, as Paulson has noted, both Erasmus and Swift make fun of the insensibility of satiric targets, and they share several image patterns, including clothing (to mask inner defects), asses and asses' ears (to signify stupidity and inability to discriminate), and raised platforms (from which preachers and mountebanks of all kinds can speak without interruption).

To effect their satire, both Swift and Erasmus choose the indirection of pretending to write panegyrics. Erasmus' academic-gowned Folly gets up on a speaker's platform to praise the folly extant in 1509; Swift's out-at-elbows "Hack" climbs up to his garret to praise the folly (he calls it great writing) he sees in 1697. With their fools at the lecterns, then, Erasmus and Swift, through their irony, conduct ethical critiques of the shallowness and the worldliness of rhetorical facility. In the spirit of Plato's *Phaedrus* and *Symposium,* they show that rhetoricians, by ignoring the truth about their subject matter, and by attending only to what will convince an audience, have rendered their art morally bankrupt. But the vices exposed in Folly and in the Hack are more universal than the vices of rhetoricians. What disturbs both Swift and Erasmus most is that rhetoricians and non-rhetoricians alike refuse to submit to the most obvious controls: they stubbornly place self-interest before any consideration of morality, meaning, or truth.

FOLLY AND "THE HACK" AS RHETORICIANS

Some time during the interval (c. 1694-6) between the

completion of his last ode and his commencement of the *Tale,* Jonathan Swift underwent "a startling transformation of literary personality." This transformation, in Ricardo Quintana's words, "was not a matter of development but, so far as we can judge, of sudden discovery." (pp. 253-55)

The remarkable similarities between Erasmus' Folly and Swift's Hack should lead us to suspect that Erasmus' ***Praise of Folly*** may have been Swift's "sudden discovery." Neither Erasmus' Folly nor Swift's Hack is a fully rounded character. Folly has at least two distinct forms, "Earthly Folly" (whose madness is ordinary) and "Christian Folly" (whose madness is divine). Swift's "Hack" is even more Protean. He is by turns a poet, a tailor-worshipper, a critic, an historian, an "Aeolist." In both works the personalities of these personae surge to the fore at times; at other times they fade away, and we clearly hear the voice of Erasmus or Swift. But the Hack's pronounced characteristics closely resemble those of Folly. Like Folly, the Hack is a virtuoso rhetorician with both a holiday exuberance and a holiday attitude that ignorance is the easiest and surest means to happiness. Like Folly, the Hack compensates for intellectual weakness by dazzling the reader with technique. Like her, he shows great wit and invention in amassing evidence, in making violent juxtapositions, and in slipping over abrupt transitions. Folly responds with Protean zest to every new challenge, proving herself (folly) to be literally everywhere on earth, even in worldly prudence. The Hack is also dazzlingly agile. His wit seems to burst the bounds of the book, filling up prefaces, flowing into digressions, deferring itself for later releases (in the list of books that he mentions as forthcoming), and even entertaining us in the final chapter while writing on "Nothing." But both pursue specious truths at these breakneck speeds, leaving the readers in their wakes to sort out dizzying moral complexities. Folly and the Hack share precisely the same strengths and the same weaknesses. Their strengths are their wit, their vigor, and their general high spirits. But both lack memory, both display an appalling lack of judgment, and the conclusions of both are vitiated by the assumption that man is merely mortal.

Like magicians so accomplished that they explain to the audience the techniques of their tricks as they perform them, Folly and the Hack display their command of the rhetorical trade by frequent yet casual remarks reminding the reader that they are in the process of creating a rhetorical work. Folly announces very early that she intends "to play the rhetorician." At one point she imitates the "rhetoricians of our time" by showing off her bilingual abilities. At another, she refuses to expound herself by definition or division "after the manner of these ordinary orators." After employing the rhetorical device of *congeries* (listing several disparate items), she calls attention to her having done so by commenting, "my breath is giving out." And she repeatedly tells us that she is going back to her "outline." The Hack lives in an age when print culture has largely replaced oral culture, yet he too writes as if he has "swallowed the rhetorical manual." Dedicating, prefacing, introducing, digressing, and even concluding ("I now go on to the Ceremonial Part of an accomplish'd Writer") with the utmost attention to his authorial duties, the Hack lets us know that he knows all the rules of his trade.

Both Folly and the Hack have mastered the art of leading on even a moderately lazy audience. Both use puns to make transitions, both fill logical gaps with logical jargon like "ergo" and "is it not clear," and above all both move along rapidly, doing all in their power to keep us from thinking. Folly openly tells us that she doesn't want listeners that are fully alert. She requests very early that we don the ears of Midas (and thus leave behind our powers of discrimination) as we listen to her. We tend, for a while, to grant Folly her wish, for her praise of ignorance is at first remarkably appealing. As she lectures to a group of stuffy academics, she helps them to relax. Contrasting her indulgence with the rigors of Stoicism, Folly claims for herself most of the joys of life—parties, feasts, childhood, laughter, sex, garrulity, friendship, sociability, and self-satisfaction. But as she continues, and begins to realize the power granted by her rostrum (the same power to speak without interruption which Swift satirizes in his account of oratorical machines), she begins to ignore both truth and morality as her rhetoric generates its own momentum. Soon she claims to govern hunters ("And what is so sweet as a beast being butchered?" and warriors ("is not war the seed plot and fountain of renowned actions? Yet what is more foolish than to enter upon a conflict for I know not what causes . . . "). War is indeed foolish, but it is also horrible; and yet the enthusiasm with which Folly claimed to govern old men or children is undiminished as she enlists the warriors in her ranks: "This famous game of war is played by parasites, panders, bandits, assassins, peasants, sots, bankrupts, and such other dregs of mankind; never by philosophers, with candles of wisdom." Ignoring the nefarious qualities of her allies, Folly is moved by the mere mention of "philosophers" to launch a new tirade: "How ineffective these philosophers are for the work of real life, the one and only Socrates . . . will serve for proof."

The war issue is gone forever. Folly has won a battle against her mortal enemy, wisdom, and she proceeds to new conquests, oblivious of any moral dimension in either her tactics or her allies. She is not troubled with a memory: "You are just too foolish if you suppose that after I have poured out a hodgepodge of words like this I can recall anything that I have said." Her mind travels forward by means of linear association rather than by the comprehension of a significant whole. Readers are all too inclined to follow, since Folly's language stirs with enthusiasm stemming from her seeming triumph. But Folly's indifference to the moral questions which should arise, to the brutality of the warriors and the hunters, creates a strange tension in the alert reader, and such a reader begins to realize that Erasmus could not possibly share the point of view of his persona.

Swift's Hack has not only more faces but more interests than Folly. At one point he is determined to prove the great advantages of digressions, at another the great mysteries concealed in modern works, at a third, the various uses of madness in a commonwealth. But in every case, he pursues his current interest with a single-mindedness and a moral oblivion precisely like that of Folly. He expresses his "philosophy of composition" succinctly in Section X: "since my *Vein* is once opened, I am content to exhaust it all at a Running." Like Folly, the Hack has an "unhappy shortness of . . . Memory." And like Folly, he relies on sheer speed to keep his readers from thinking. (pp. 256-59)

In the ***Praise of Folly*** and the *Tale,* Erasmus and Swift are carrying on the tradition of Plato's *Phaedrus* and *Symposium,* which also point up the ethical shortcomings of seemingly persuasive rhetoric. Some structural features of the *Symposium* proved useful to Erasmus, and possibly (perhaps through Erasmus) to Swift. The setting for the *Symposium* is a drinking party (no activity could be more pleasing to Folly). One guest, Eryximachus, begins by noting that heroes like Hercules are all too frequently praised, and then complaining that a subject as lowly as common salt had already been praised "in the most extravagant terms." It seems unaccountable to him that love, a great benefactor to man, has never been formally praised. So he and the rest of the company proceed to deliver extravagant encomia of Love (which, Socrates later complains, have little to do with the truth).

Folly begins like Eryximachus, by noting that the most common subjects for praise are heroes like Hercules, by complaining that trivial subjects have been given encomia, and by promising that her ensuing discourse will repay a long-standing debt of gratitude to a true benefactor of man—herself. She proceeds to repay the long-standing debt with usurious interest.

The *Tale* is not so obviously patterned on the *Symposium;* it purports, formally, to be an allegorical tale rather than an encomium. But its encomiastic center comes to dominate in spite of the tale form. From the Hack's perspective, the story of the three brothers is a restrictive framework which he proceeds to embellish with prefatory remarks and digressions that praise the subjects nearest his heart. Though the Hack is occasionally restrained by an historian's regard for the facts of his tale, he is as ambitious to promote modernism as Folly is to praise folly. Like Folly and Eryximachus, the Hack complains in his introduction that other writers (in this case, the Gresham College scientists and the Will's Coffee House wits) have not acknowledged their true debt to the subject of *his* encomium (the Grub Street Hacks). (pp. 260-61)

Both Folly and the Hack keep their audiences satisfied by amusing them with surfaces, with illusions, with dress, with the theatre. "How shrunk is every Thing," in the Hack's eyes, "as it appears in the Glass of Nature? So, that if it were not for the Assistance of Artificial *Mediums,* false Lights, refracted Angles, Varnish, and Tinsel; there would be a mighty Level in the Felicity and Enjoyments of Mortal Men." Folly too complains that it would be unreasonable, untimely, unfriendly, to strip away the masks which delight us "mortals": "If a person were to try stripping the disguises from actors while they play a scene upon the stage, showing to the audience their real looks and the faces they were born with, would not such a one spoil the whole play?" But neither Erasmus nor Swift allows the reader to be fully taken in by a love of theatre. Both hint that the worldly masks of the personae were thin.

Folly is overtly interrupted as she speaks by a "wise man who has dropped down from the sky," who confronts her and demands that the masks should be stripped from the actors, that the illusions be dispensed with, "that the play should no longer be a play." At the point of this wise man's appearance, Folly still seems quite attractive, and she has made Epicureanism seem attractive. As a result, many readers find the wise man a bit of a bore, and perhaps confuse him with the seeming-wise Stoics who are the usual butt for Folly's wit. But his "unseasonable" (*imprudentius*) warning that our earthly life is in fact a kind of death clearly foreshadows Erasmus' Christian message at the conclusion of the work. (p. 263)

To look beyond the surfaces that Folly and the Hack are content with requires a certain moral-intellectual courage which neither Folly nor the Hack is willing to aspire to. Both Folly and the Hack pepper their speech with the cliché "mortal men" (in Latin, *mortales*), and then take the term literally, so that they need not concern themselves with man's spiritual dimensions. Folly sees only trouble in the life of a wise man, and she appeals to our limitations as mortals as an excuse for giving up the effort to become wise: "The part of the truly prudent man . . . is (*since we are mortal*) not to aspire to wisdom beyond his station, and either, along with the rest of the crowd, pretend not to notice anything, or affably and companionably be deceived." The Hack, too, finds it easier to refrain from delving beyond the "best Furniture" of the mortal world. He seems almost to be quoting from Folly as he proceeds to his conclusion that "a Man truly wise" desires only "the sublime and refined Point of Felicity, called, *the Possession of being well deceived.*"

Early in Plato's *Phaedrus* Socrates imitates the sophist Lysias and delivers an eloquent speech arguing that a young boy should choose a nonlover rather than a lover for a companion. Phaedrus is pleased with the speech, but Socrates is ashamed and disturbed. The speech was "foolish, and somewhat blasphemous," he says, for it was based on a false assumption, the assumption that love is merely a physical passion. When Erasmus' Folly reaches her conclusion that man should not "aspire to wisdom beyond his station," or when Swift's Hack reaches his similar conclusion that "a Man truly wise" desires only *"the Possession of being well deceived,"* they have done so precisely in the manner of Socrates in his imitation of Lysias. They have not understood the term, wisdom, that they are making free with. They have ignored life's spiritual dimensions. Folly and the Hack both are limited by their assumptions, false in the eyes of their authors, that man is merely mortal, and that the utmost wisdom to which a man should aspire is the "wisdom" of this world. (pp. 264-65)

Eugene R. Hammond, "In Praise of Wisdom and the Will of God: Erasmus' 'Praise of Folly' and Swift's 'A Tale of a Tub'," in Studies in Philology, *Vol. LXXX, No. 3, Summer, 1983, pp. 253-76.*

FURTHER READING

Adams, Robert P. "Erasmus' Ideas of his Rôle as a Social Critic ca. 1480-1500." *Renaissance News* XI, No. 1 (Spring 1958): 11-16.

Considers possible influences upon Erasmus by John Colet, especially in regard to the development of the social theory revealed in such works as the *Adages.*

Allen, P. S. *The Age of Erasmus: Lectures Delivered in the Universities of Oxford and London.* Oxford: Clarendon Press, 1914, 303 p.

Critically acclaimed biographical work.

Bentley, Jerry H. "Biblical Philology and Christian Humanism: Lorenzo Valla and Erasmus as Scholars of the Gospels." *The Sixteenth Century Journal* 8, No. 2 (1977): 9-28.

Explores the scholarly relationship between Valla and Erasmus, determining that while "Erasmus owed a great deal to Valla's scholarly initiative," by 1516 "Erasmus had adopted an attitude remarkably independent of Valla."

Bishop, William S. "Erasmus." *The Sewanee Review* XIV, No. 2 (April 1906): 129-48.

General biographical sketch.

Brooks, Rev. Charles T. "Erasmus." *The Christian Examiner and Religious Miscellany* XLIX (July 1850): 80-100.

Brief biographical sketch with critical commentary on several of Erasmus's works.

Caspari, Fritz. "Erasmus on the Social Functions of Christian Humanism." *Journal of the History of Ideas* VIII, No. 1 (January 1947): 78-106.

Explores Erasmus's theory of humanism and humanistic education as the means to achieving world peace.

Froude, James Anthony. *Life and Letters of Erasmus.* New York: Charles Scribner's Sons, 1894, 433 p.

Essays, originally lectures, on many aspects of Erasmus's life and works.

Geraldine, Sister M. "Erasmus and the Tradition of Paradox." *Studies in Philology* LXI, No. 1 (January 1964): 41-63.

Examines the influence of paradoxical elements in *The Praise of Folly* on such contemporary works as Willibald Pirckheimer's *The Prayse of the Gout.*

Greenfield, Thelma N. "*A Midsummer Night's Dream* and *The Praise of Folly.*" *Comparative Literature* XX, No. 3 (Summer 1968): 236-44.

Notes several similarities between *The Praise of Folly* and *A Midsummer Night's Dream,* suggesting both that Shakespeare's drama should be considered more important than previously recognized and that Erasmus's literary influence was more pervasive than was earlier believed.

Hardin, Richard F. "The Literary Conventions of Erasmus' *Education of a Christian Prince:* Advice and Aphorism." *Renaissance Quarterly* XXXV, No. 2 (Summer 1982): 151-63.

Discusses the structure of the aphorisms in the *Education of a Christian Prince,* briefly touching upon their effect on both sixteenth-century and modern audiences.

Hudson, Hoyt Hopewell. "The Folly of Erasmus." In *The Praise of Folly,* by Desiderius Erasmus, translated by Hoyt Hopewell Hudson, pp. xi-xli. Princeton: Princeton University Press, 1941.

Examines Erasmus's satire and constructive techniques in *The Praise of Folly.*

Hyma, Albert. "Erasmus and the Oxford Reformers (1503-1519)." *Nederlands Archief voor Kerkgeschiedenis* XXXVIII, No. 2 (1951): 65-85.

Discusses Erasmus's contact with and possible influence upon the English reformers John Colet and Thomas More.

Kay, W. David. "Erasmus' Learned Joking: The Ironic Use of Classical Wisdom in *The Praise of Folly.*" *Texas Studies in Literature and Language* XIX, No. 3 (Fall 1977): 247-67.

Explores the use of classical allusions and their effectiveness within the satiric context of *The Praise of Folly.*

Kristeller, Paul Oskar. "Erasmus from an Italian Perspective." *Renaissance Quarterly* XXIII, No. 1 (Spring 1970): 1-14.

Examines "Erasmus' attitudes towards Italy and the Italians and the extent of his dependence on Italian sources."

MacDonald, William W. "Erasmus and the Protestant Reformation." *Illinois Quarterly* 34, No. 4 (April 1972): 54-62.

Surveys some of the influential twentieth-century studies of Erasmus.

Mackail, J. W. Introduction to *Erasmus Against War,* by Desiderius Erasmus, pp. ix-xxxiv. Boston: Merrymount Press, 1907.

Examines the socio-political climate surrounding and influencing Erasmus during the composition of *Dulce bellum inexpertis.*

Mangan, John Joseph. "Character and Influence." In his *Life, Character & Influence of Desiderius Erasmus of Rotterdam: Derived from a Study of His Works and Correspondence,* Vol. II, pp. 391-407. New York: Macmillan Co., 1927.

Analyzes the distribution and publication of Erasmus's works, attempting to determine which countries were most influenced by Erasmian thought.

Mansfield, Bruce. *Phoenix of His Age: Interpretations of Erasmus, c. 1550-1750.* Toronto: University of Toronto Press, 1979, 348 p.

Traces the rise and fall of Erasmus's scholarly and religious reputation, stating that "this is a history of the interpretations of Erasmus, not a history of his influence or Erasmianism."

Margetts, Michele. "Erasmus' *Colloquia*: Dramatic Elements Real and Metaphorical." *Renaissance and Reformation* VIII, No. 1 (February 1984): 1-18.

Examines dramatic elements in the *Colloquies* which "liven the presentation of the *Colloquia* for [its] readers."

Ogden, C. K. "Desiderius Erasmus and his Significance for the Reformation." *The Open Court* XXX, No. 718 (March 1916): 148-69.

Biographical essay with some discussion of Erasmus's influence on the Reformation and his "modernity."

Olin, John C. "The Pacifism of Erasmus." *THOUGHT: A*

Review of Culture and Idea L, No. 199 (December 1975): 418-31.

Traces the development of Erasmus's pacifism from *Dulce bellum inexpertis* to *Querela pacis.*

Payne, John B. "Erasmus and Lefèvre d' Étaples as Interpreters of Paul." *Archiv für Reformationsgeschichte* 65 (1974): 54-83.

Compares Lefèvre d' Étaples and Erasmus's interpretations of St. Paul's Epistles, determining that Erasmus favored a more spiritual and ethical view of Christianity, while d'Étaples utilized a mystical view of salvation.

Rebhorn, Wayne A. "The Metamorphoses of Moria: Structure and Meaning in *The Praise of Folly.*" *PMLA* 89, No. 3 (May 1974): 463-76.

Insightful reading of *The Praise of Folly,* arguing that the three sections comprise a unified structure which reflects the dynamism of Folly herself.

Reedijk, C., ed. *The Poems of Desiderius Erasmus.* By Desiderius Erasmus. Leiden, Netherlands: E. J. Brill, 1956, 424 p.

Provides the text to Erasmus's poetry along with background information regarding both the era and some of Erasmus's verse.

Reynolds, E. E. *Thomas More and Erasmus.* New York: Fordham University Press, 1965, 260 p.

A comparative study of the lives and literary careers of the two humanists.

Tracy, James D. "The Stupid and Tyrannical Fables of King Arthur." In his *The Politics of Erasmus: A Pacifist Intellectual and His Political Milieu,* pp. 49-69. Toronto: University of Toronto Press, 1978.

Places the *Querela pacis* and the *Institutio principis christiani* in relation to the political events of Erasmus's era.

Weiss, James Michael. "*Ecclesiastes* and Erasmus: The Mirror and the Image." *Archiv für Reformationsgeschichte* 65 (1974): 83-108.

Contends that rhetoric played a significant role in the organization of Erasmus's *Ecclesiastes.*

Whitney, J. P. "Erasmus." *The English Historical Review* XXXV, No. CXXXVII (January 1920): 1-25.

Biographical sketch containing some criticism of Erasmus's major works.

Ulrich von Hutten

1488-1523

German poet and essayist.

Hutten was an early sixteenth-century humanist whose literary career consists of bitter invectives against the Catholic Church and those scholars known as the Scholasticists. Perhaps his most famous critical assaults can be found in his contributions to the *Epistolae Obscurorum Virorum* (*Letters of Obscure Men*), two volumes of coarse letters satirizing these authorities. Hutten's writings generally emphasize the need for Germans to assert their nationalism by uniting to banish papal influence from their homeland. His radical works are considered a departure from those of contemporary reform leaders such as Desiderius Erasmus and Martin Luther; one of the most important distinctions being that though Hutten advocated religious autonomy from Rome, he viewed force of arms as a necessary means to achieve results. Hutten's provocative writings and actions against the conservative policies of the Scholasticists and the Church have earned him the reputation as an influential catalyst in bringing about the German Reformation.

Hutten was born in Steckelberg Castle, near Fulda, in 1488. Although his family belonged to a proud line of Franconian knights, Hutten's weak physical stature prevented him from becoming a effective courtier. Believing that the boy would make a better priest than a knight, his father ultimately enrolled him in a Benedictine monastery near Fulda in 1498. At the monastic order, Hutten established the foundation for his education, gaining particular expertise in the Latin language. He left the monastery in 1505, however, and enrolled himself in the University of Cologne where he became a disciple of the humanistic philosopher Rhagius Æsticampianus. Soon a staunch supporter of the humanist doctrine, he caused an enormous controversy by denouncing the conservative theories of the university's Scholasticist professors, an affair which ultimately led to his dismissal from the university. Following the dispute, Hutten matriculated at University of Frankfort-on-the-Main where he acquired his bachelor's degree. During the next three years, he became a traveler, journeying to such intellectual centers as Vienna and Wittenberg, serving as a foot soldier in Emperor Maximilian's army, allegedly working as a spy for the Swiss in the besieged city of Pavia, and surviving a shipwreck in the Baltic. Throughout his travels adventures, Hutten wrote numerous poems, letters, and essays attacking the proponents of Scholasticism as well as their supporters, the Church.

Hutten's reputation as a scholar and pamphleteer flourished at the universities, and he gained the patronage of Archbishop Albrecht of Mainz, who tolerated his liberal views of the Church. It was here that he met Erasmus, the renowned humanist who became his friend and correspondent. While serving as protegé of the archbishop, a tragic event occurred which amplified Hutten's literary career from the scholarly to a more prominent political level: the murder of his cousin, Hans von Hutten, at the hands of the Duke of Wurtemberg in 1515. The powerful German lord was never punished for the crime and actually flaunted the deed by retaining the victim's wife as his mistress. Outraged at the unjust circumstances surrounding his cousin's murder, Hutten wrote several letters, poems, and orations protesting and satirizing the duke's impunity. The most famous of these was *Phalarismus,* a dialogue depicting a fictional meeting between the duke and Phalaris in Hell, where the infamous Roman tyrant acknowledges the duke as his equal in cruelty. This and other works caused a great sensation throughout Germany and Europe, making the duke the object of universal scorn and transforming Hutten into a celebrated political figure.

The following year, Hutten became involved another controversy between the Scholasticists and the humanists; at issue was the question of whether to burn all Hebrew books except the Old Testament as heretical, as the Scholasticists desired. The affair was ultimately decided in favor of Johann Reuchlin, the leader of the humanists, by the Bishop of Speyer, who held the Scholasticists responsible for all legal expenses. The major literary response to this controversy was the *Letters of Obscure Men,* published in two parts from 1515 to 1517. Although the volumes were published anonymously, scholars have generally credited Hutten as a major collaborator to the work, along with Crotus Rubianus and Hermann Burchius. The letters were written in bad Latin to imitate the correspondence of monks, and they exposed the religious orders and the conservative scholars for their vices, indolence, ignorance, and their plots against Reuchlin and the humanists. At first, real-life monks relished the humorous letters, assuming that their fellow clerics had indeed composed the material; but upon learning that the epistles were in fact satires published for the general public, they furiously appealed to the pope to issue a bull warranting the burning of both the book and its authors. But Hutten and his friends were never prosecuted for writing the *Letters* because the Church was unable to successfully trace the authorship of the work.

With the success of this assault upon the authority of the Scholastics and the Church, Hutten became more bold in his critical attacks. His *Vadiscus, sive Trias Romana,* written in 1520, addressed not only the generally corrupt state of the Catholic church, but the injustices it had imposed upon Germany. In this work, he ultimately implored all Germans to unite in a revolution against the Church. Having witnessed the decadence of Rome firsthand in his travels, Hutten drew upon his impressions to compose the *Trias Romana,* which features a traveler named Vadiscus who describes the city to Hutten and a friend named Ehrenhold. These reflections appear in the form of triads;

for example, "Three things maintain the renown of Rome: the power of the Pope, relics, and indulgences. Three things are brought from Rome by those who go there: a bad conscience, a ruined stomach, an empty purse." Hutten's *Trias Romana* created a tremendous controversy in Germany, and it was a principal element that contributed to the growing popular opinion against the papacy in the early sixteenth century. This dialogue was by far Hutten's most provocative work to date, arousing the wrath of the pope and the episcopacy. In 1521 the pope issued a brief to the Archbishop of Mainz ordering him to punish Hutten for his offenses against the Church. Hutten escaped from the archbishop, however, and took refuge in the kingdom of Franz von Sickingen, a powerful German prince who sympathized with him.

In 1521 while Hutten was under Sickingen's protection, Luther was brought before the Diet of Worms to repudiate his anti-papist writings. Luther defended his works, claiming that his conscience was bound by the Word of God. The Diet ultimately passed the Edict of Worms, declaring Luther an outlaw and a heretic. Hutten was greatly interested in the proceedings at Worms, and wrote a series of passionate dialogues once again denouncing the corruption of Rome and appealing to all Germans to revolt against papal oppression. These issues are elucidated in *Bullicida, Inspicientes,* and *Praedones,* three of Hutten's best-known dialogues. Each of these essays caricatures the papacy as a degenerate force while depicting patriotic action in the face of this evil as a nobler expression of the Christian faith. By now Sickingen and Hutten considered the time right for an uprising, and they led the knights of the Rhine in a revolt against the German priests. The rebels failed to gain support from the other German princes, however, and they were soundly defeated by the forces of the Bishop of Treves. Sickingen was mortally wounded in the battle, and Hutten escaped only to find little overt support for his cause in the aftermath of the rebels' defeat. He fled to Switzerland, where he was initially welcomed by the town council in Basel. But the bishop there demanded that Hutten leave, and the council, fearful of incurring the Church's disfavor, entreated Hutten to depart. Further, Hutten was denounced by his old friend Erasmus, who was also staying in Switzerland; the aging humanist apparently realized the severity of Hutten's inflammatory deeds against the Church and elected to distance himself from his friend rather than face the wrath of the pope. Hutten eventually found refuge in Zurich where he was warmly received by Ulrich Zwingli. Consumed with syphilis, Hutten passed the final months before his death in 1523 writing an open letter to Erasmus. Entitled *Expostulatio cum Erasmo,* the essay is a bitter attack on the scholar's betrayal of the humanist cause.

Literary critics have generally agreed that of all Hutten's works, the *Letters of Obscure Men* is the satirist's most significant accomplishment. Johann Gottfried von Herder deemed it the national satire of Germany in the eighteenth century, and it is still recognized today as a milestone in German literature. Although there is little English criticism of Hutten's literary career, the available resources reflect the importance of the satirical work. Most nineteenth-century commentators observed the primarily historical significance of the work; for example, a critic writing for the *Cornhill Magazine* in 1867 declared that the *Letters* made "an epoch in the history of the Reformation." Further, the critic notes, the satire demonstrates how essential the concept of learning became during the Reformation: "Europe was, in fact, *deodorized* by the free dispersion of delightful essences long hidden in the buried caskets of classical literature." More recent critics have analyzed the satire's more technical aspects, particularly noting that the letters were so realistically written that they initially fooled the monks who were the objects of ridicule. Describing how the *Letters of Obscure Men* embarrassed both the Scholasticists and the Church, Hajo Holborn asserts that "[seldom] has human stupidity among scholars been so wittily depicted and a degenerate philosophy so cleverly held up to ridicule." Although critics today recognize the *Letters* as a great satirical work, it has nevertheless sustained a far greater reputation as a cornerstone for the German Reformation.

Hutten has generally been overshadowed by such contemporary reformers as Erasmus and Luther. Nevertheless he played a significant role in bringing about the German Reformation. Through his bitter invectives and satires against the conservative authorities of his day, Hutten probably contributed more to the rise of German Protestantism than any other author, arousing a strong sense of patriotism and injustice among the people who ultimately provided Luther with the necessary support to break away from Rome. According to Paul Herrmann, Hutten's writings "give us a clear conception of the dissatisfaction and conflicts, the vague dreams and aspirations, of the German people at the beginning of the sixteenth century."

PRINCIPAL WORKS

Nemo (poem) 1510
Querelae (elegies) 1510
De Arte Versificandi (poem) 1511
Epistolae Obscurorum Virorum (letters) 1515-17
[*Letters of Obscure Men,* 1909]
Phalarismus (dialogue) 1515
Aula (dialogue) 1517
De Falso Credita et Ementita Donatione Constantini Magni [editor] (treatise) 1517
Triumphus Capnionis (poem) 1517
Exhortation to the German Princes to Undertake War Against the Turks (letter) 1518
Febris Prima (dialogue) 1519
Febris II (dialogue) 1519
Fortuna (dialogue) 1519
De Schismate Extinguendo, et de Vera Ecclesiastica Liberate Adverenda (letters) 1520
De Unitate Ecclesiae Conservanda (treatise) 1520
Vadiscus, sive Trias Romana (1520) dialogue
Bullicida (dialogue) 1521
Ein Neu Lied (poem) 1521
Inspicientes (dialogue) 1521
Praedones (dialogue) 1521
Gesprächbüchlein (dialogues) 1522
Expostulatio cum Erasmo (essay) 1523

Fraser's Magazine for Town & Country **(essay date 1849)**

[*In the following excerpt, the critic comments upon some of Hutten's most significant works.*]

Ulrich Von Hutten—who may very fitly be selected as the representative of the lay portion of the struggle antecedent to the Reformation—was born of a noble family in Franconia, in the year 1488. Of a stormy and turbulent character, he was thrown into the world at one of its most stormy periods. All the elements of modern society were in a state of collision and ferment—a political and religious chaos waiting for the breath of life. Kings and princes were at war to establish the balance of power; learned men were launching folios at each other to establish what was true learning and what was not; the Church and the Empire alternately quarrelled and embraced; nothing was settled—everywhere lay scattered the materials which bold spirits use to achieve greatness. (p. 207)

[At] thirty years of age, [Hutten] had as yet assumed no distinct profession; he was apparently without any definite end. In all his writings up to this period, although many of them are equal in power and beauty to his after-productions, there is still an absence of a public purpose. The only continuous idea which we can recognize running through his works until now, is an intense nationality, a thorough German feeling, a desire that his country shall be once more a united German empire . . . . Events, however, were now approaching which were to determine his course, and bring him before the world as one who had a work to perform. He had long been 'nourishing a youth sublime,' the fruit was now to appear. . . . [It was] in the year 1513, when a converted Jew, named Pfefferkorn, in conjunction with some of the heads of the Church at Cologne, the most celebrated of whom was the grand inquisitor Hogstraten, had obtained, by misrepresenting the tendencies of the Hebrew literature, permission from the Emperor Maximilian to burn all books in the Jewish language, with the exception of the Old Testament. In pursuance of this object, Pfefferkorn went armed with the imperial mandate to Frankfort-on-the-Maine. The clergy and the magistrates assisted in the luminous proceeding, the houses of the Jews were searched in the name of the emperor, and an immense number of books seized and burnt. The patience of the Jews became exhausted, and they petitioned the emperor to appoint a commission to examine into the accuracy of the charges brought against their literature. The prayer of the petition was granted, and three commissioners were appointed, amongst whom was the celebrated Reuchlin, the most learned man of his day. He gave it as his opinion, in opposition to that of the other commissioners, that the charge against the literature, taken as a whole, was manifestly unjust, and that the imperial mandate ought to be put in force only against such books as were written against the Christian religion. This being a virtual nullification of the decree, the night-birds became frantic with rage, and a bitter paper-war ensued, in which Hutten assumed a leading position. In poems, satires, and letters—which latter were, in those days, a kind of public property, serving instead of newspapers amongst the learned—he scourged the unfortunate lovers of darkness in such a manner that they had not courage to prosecute their work; and Reuchlin not only obtained his ends, but succeeded in a lawsuit with Hogstraten (who was also on the commission), in which the latter was condemned to pay heavy costs. The most celebrated of the works to which this contest gave rise was written almost wholly by Hutten. This was the ***Literæ obscurorum Virorum*** (the **Letters of Obscure Men).** It purported to be a collection of letters written by the opponents of the higher literature. The barbarous monkish Latin in use amongst the parties satirized, their dense ignorance, their gross habits, were so admirably portrayed, that the monks themselves were deceived, and took the letters as genuine productions. The literary world was enchanted. Never had a work appeared which mounted so suddenly into popularity. When Erasmus read it, he was seized with such an uncontrollable fit of laughter that he burst an abscess in his face, which would otherwise have been laid open by the surgeon. This, observes Bayle, may be put down as one of the benefits produced by reading. By the time that the whole European literary community had become acquainted with the work, the monks discovered its meaning, and they howled with rage. They proclaimed the author to be a son of the devil, that the work was prompted by Satan himself, and that the writer would, without doubt, suffer the punishment of eternal fire in the life to come. Finally, they appealed to the Pope, and, by dint of perseverance and misrepresentation, prevailed upon him to issue a bull prohibiting not only the sale but the retention of the work.

The first proof which Hutten gave of his intention to direct his attacks against others of the clergy than the monks, was his publication of the excommunicated treatise of Laurentius Vallo, ***De falso credita et ementita Donatione Constantini Magni*** **(On the Pretended Donation of Constantine).** This treatise on the pretended gift of Rome and other territories to Pope Sylvester by Constantine had been long forgotten. Hutten not only reprinted it entire, but added to the effect of the writing itself by prefixing a dedication to Leo X. If the work had been before this deemed worthy of excommunication, it could scarcely be thought less so now. The preface begins with many flattering encomiums on the Pope, whether sincere or satirical it is impossible to say; the expressions are such as might be used by an Italian Liberal in a dedication to Pius IX. The age is congratulated which 'looks toward the new light of liberty, beholding Leo X. as the sun of freedom arising from lengthened darkness.' The author then draws a comparison between Leo and his predecessors, placing the latter in the most degrading light. At last, warming with his subject, he leaves Leo out of consideration; and, directing his attention to the Pope's predecessors, he loads them with a profusion of invective, to which there are few parallels to be found even in his own writings.

It is curious, that in this dedication Hutten, without any knowledge of Luther, and before the commencement of the war against indulgences, makes them the subject of attack. 'Your predecessors,' said he to Leo, 'introduced the custom of making a profit of the sins of other men, and even of the punishment of those sins after death.'

There is no evidence to shew that the work produced any other effect than that intended by the writer. It spread with astonishing rapidity throughout all Europe, its value was universally recognized, and its boldness, particularly by the Germans, admired. Even amongst the German clergy there were many who perceived clearly enough that the Papal system tended to destroy all nationality, and they willingly shut their eyes to Hutten's rebellious opposition to the claims of the Church in consideration of his powerful support of the national cause. (pp. 210-12)

At no period of his life had Hutten more reason to hope for the accomplishment of his heart's desire than in the period immediately succeeding the war in Wirtemberg. It appeared to him that the cause of sound learning was just on the point of triumphing over pedantic trifling,—that ignorance was giving way to knowledge. 'What a year for learning!' he writes to his friend Pirkheimer. 'Ancient barbarism, away!' And there certainly appeared to be some grounds for his exultation; he seemed to have infected half the world with his own enthusiasm. While at Mentz, to which place he retired at the close of the war, he was deluged with letters, not only from all parts of Germany, but even from France, Italy, Bohemia, and other lands, in which he was exhorted to continue his opposition to the Romish usurpations. The most learned men of all nations offered him their support. Kings and princes sent him their congratulations. Otto Brunfels, in his answer to Erasmus, states that he himself had seen as many as two thousand of these letters. Erasmus alone felt uneasy. The combat was becoming too fierce for his delicate nerves. As long as the weapons used were never more trenchant than his own elegant, but feeble satire, he was content; when the struggle began to assume a fiercer aspect, he trembled. 'I fear,' he says, 'that what has begun in jest will end in earnest; and that, as in Bohemia, we shall in the end have war declared against every one bearing the name of priest.' But Hutten had no misgivings; encouraged by the universal approbation bestowed on his labours, he again entered the field. The new attack was tremendous. All disguise was thrown off in the ***Vadiscus, sive Trias Romana,—Vadiscus, or the Roman Triad.*** It is in the form of a dialogue between the author and a friend. Hutten relates to this person the substance of a conversation between himself and Vadiscus, a traveller, who had lately arrived from Rome. The name 'Triad' is given to the work on account of the form which is employed to classify the abuses at Rome. The reader will observe that it is the same as that of the Welsh triads. For example,—

> Three things are brought back from Rome: a wounded conscience, a ruined digestion, and an empty purse. Three things are killed at Rome: a good conscience, genuine piety, and the sanctity of oaths. Three things are ridiculed in modern Rome: the examples and virtues of our ancestors, the priesthood of Peter, and the Judgment-day. Three things are not known in Rome: simplicity, moderation, and uprightness. Three things would at once liberate us from all Romish evils: freedom from superstition, the abolition of all Romish dignities, and an entire conversion of the Romish court. Three things are in the highest esteem in Rome: pretty women, fine horses, and papal bulls. Three things are quite common in Rome: arrogance, pride of dress, and lust of the flesh. Three things might improve Rome: the earnestness of the German princes, the despair of the German nation, and the weapons of the Turks. Three things are believed in Rome by very few men: the immortality of the soul, the communion of saints, and retribution after death.

Each of these triads is the subject of amplification in the dialogue. Many of them are illustrated from the history of the Popes, many from the current reports of the day. The object of the author seems to have been to heap together a mass of evidence against the Romish court, which should condemn its members, from the Pope downwards, to universal execration. The steady aim of Hutten to excite the *national* feeling against Rome is remarkable in this, as in most of his productions.

About this time Hutten published his treatise, ***De Unitate Ecclesia,*** a new edition of an old work, with a dedication to the Archduke Ferdinand, the bitterness of which was equal to that of the ***Trias Romana.*** He had now reached his culminating point. The renown he had acquired was universal. He was applied to by every one who espied some flaw in the edifice of the Church of Rome which might be made the subject of attack. He was looked upon as the head of the party of freedom. Who can wonder that he should have been a little deceived by the promise apparently visible in all these symptoms? He gave himself up to the most brilliant anticipations of the future. 'Our freedom,' says he, 'has long been bound in chains by the Popes; it shall be *my task* to break them. Truth was banished from our fatherland, *I* will bring her back again.'

It is evident that he meditated some great step in conjunction with [Franz Von] Sickingen, which was not yet fully matured. He seems to have had no doubt that he should be joined by every good man in Germany. He intimates as much in a letter to Melancthon, but does not give any hint as to the nature of the measure. But events were preparing which destroyed all his hopes. It was not possible that the Church of Rome could any longer remain quiescent under such repeated insults. The knowledge of the powerful protection afforded to Hutten may have had some effect in delaying the decisive step; but this hesitation could not last unless the Pope intended to yield up his authority. Leo X., therefore, sent a brief to the archbishop, in which he expresses his astonishment that he should have suffered such insolence to go so long unpunished, and charged him either to bring back those who had offended so long to a due sense of their allegiance to the Holy See, or else to punish them in such a manner that others should have no wish to imitate their evil doings. It is not improbable that Hutten saw the contents of this brief by the permission of the archbishop, for his conduct shortly after proves that he was little alarmed at its contents. He published a collection of old tracts, under the title, ***De Schismate extinguendo, et de vera Ecclesiastica Libertate adverenda,*** with one of his terrible prefaces, which he concluded with the words he had adopted for his motto, 'The die is cast—freedom for ever!' He had now, however, made a false step; he had depended too much on the justice of his cause, and the alliance of his friends and patrons. It was clear that he had now imprudently brought the affair to an issue before means were taken to ensure success. He had left the archbishop no other course to pursue but to choose between his own servant and the Pope, and there could be scarcely a doubt of the nature of the decision. (pp. 213-15)

Hutten acted with his usual decision in the case. Hitherto he had refrained from identifying himself with the adherents of Luther, inasmuch as the Reformer might be considered as the personal enemy of Hutten's patron, the Archbishop of Mentz; but there was no further need of restraint now, and he therefore appeared publicly as a supporter of Luther. Many have supposed that the cause of the Reformation would have been promoted by an earlier union between the two, but this is a mistake. The men were essentially different; they worked best each in his own sphere. Luther hated the Church of Rome because he found that *practically* it stood in the place of Christ, and trampled on Christ's doctrine: Hutten, because the Pope usurped the powers of the Emperor, and trampled upon the rights of the holy Roman empire. The object of the one was to purify Christ's religion from the traditions of men; that of the other to free Germany from the oppression of a foreign power. The one attacked Rome as a Church, the other as a State. Hutten saw the distinction clearly enough, but not until late in life. 'Thy work, O holy man!' he says, in one of his letters to Luther, 'thy work is of God, and will endure; mine is of man, and will perish.' (p. 215)

[Near the end of his life, Hutten is] unable to find a safe refuge in any town in Germany, he travels to Switzerland in company with his friends Œcolampadius and Bucer. On reaching Basle he is so well received by the magistrates and learned men that he determines to take up his abode there; but an obstacle arose in a quarter where he least expected one. It happened that Erasmus, wearied with the storm of literary warfare, and terrified at the still more terrible storm of religious warfare, had retired to the same place. The world had become too much in earnest for such as he: he was not fitted for the realities of life. His delight was to amuse himself with its history. The instant a necessity for action arose, he shrank in terror from the war of events. It was this feeling which prompted his retirement to Basle. He wished, like the spectator in Lucretius, to view the shipwrecked barks and the tumid ocean from a place of safety. The approach of Hutten filled him with dismay. He hesitated at first whether it would be more dangerous to welcome or to neglect the newcomer. He feared to compromise himself with the friends or the foes of the persecuted knight. He avoided seeing him under the shabbiest pretexts, and at last absolutely refused to hold any communication with a man whom but a short time before he had held up to admiration. Hutten's spirit always rose under oppression. Stricken with misfortune as he was, he yet found strength to avenge this insult. He published an ***Expostulation*** addressed to Erasmus, in which the conduct of the latter is exposed in a manner at once forcible and dignified. It does not enter into our plan to give in detail the account of the quarrel between Hutten and Erasmus, which only ended with the life of the former. As a piece of literary history it is curious enough, and is worthy of attention. Suffice it to say, that Erasmus, indignant at Hutten's remonstrance, employed his influence, which was all-powerful in Basle, in such a manner, that the latter was desired by the authorities to quit the city. Hutten complied with the requisition, but the vengeance of his enemy was not yet complete. He rested for a short time at Mulhausen, and then went on to Zurich, where he intended to remain for some time. Scarcely had he become settled in his new abode, when the authorities of Zurich received a letter from Erasmus, in which was pointed out in artful terms the danger of harbouring their new guest. Hutten wrote a letter in his own defence to the magistrates, intreating that he might not be condemned without knowing what charges were brought against him. This was his last effort; his infirmities had increased to such a degree, that he was incapable of further literary exertion. His friend Zuinglius, the Swiss Reformer, caused him to be removed to the small isle of Ufnau, not far from Zurich, in the hope that change of air and treatment might have some effect; but it was too late. Broken in spirit, mind, and body, persecuted by enemies, abandoned by friends, Ulrich von Hutten terminated, at the age of thirty-six, a life into which he had crowded more action than is to be found in the lives of thousands of those who number the three-score and ten of the Psalmist. (pp. 217-18)

"Ulrich Von Hutten and His Times," in Fraser's Magazine for Town & Country, *Vol. 40, No. CCXXXVI, August, 1849, pp. 207-18.*

J. Parkman (essay date 1863)

[In the excerpt below, Parkman studies both the anti-Catholic and nationalistic elements in the major literary works of Hutten, evaluating their effect upon the political developments of his time.]

The history of the Reformation has been written almost exclusively by those who saw in it a religious movement originated by Luther and his compeers. Influences not strictly religious, and the men who represented them, have usually been kept out of sight.

Among the persons of whom this is true stands pre-eminent Ulrich von Hutten; "the Reformation's man of wit and of the sword, who slew monkery with the wild laughter of his ***Epistolæ Obscurorum Virorum.***" Want of appreciation on the part of Church historians has not, however, prevented him from being a popular idol in Germany, and especially among those belonging to the party of "Young Germany." To these, he is the model knight about whom all the ideal virtues of the age of chivalry cluster; the accomplished scholar and poet; the man of rank and fortune, who left his lordly castle to take the people's side, to fight against oppression and for German liberty with pen and sword; the foe, too, of Romish usurpation, who anticipated Luther in denouncing indulgences, and who did more than Luther to bring about the Reformation.

Nor is this opinion limited to the more enthusiastic friends of German liberty and unity of our own day. Herder, who edited his poems, was his warm admirer. "Go, German youth," he exclaims, "to his grave, and say, Here lies the herald to the German nation of freedom and truth, and who was willing to be more than a herald." Camerarius compares him to Demosthenes, and says, "If his means had been on a par with his designs and enterprise, he would have revolutionized Europe." Melancthon writes of him, "Ut virum magni facere et admirari propter doctrinæ eruditionem et præstantiam ingenii." Even Erasmus, bitter as he was against him at one time, said, "The more I have loved the genius and talents of Hutten, the more concerned I am to lose him by these troubles." While Zimmerman, in whose apostrophe there is expressed, not a whit exaggerated, the popular estimate of his hero, speaks of him as

> the greatest man, the greatest writer, the greatest patriot, that Germany has produced. . . . Often he had nothing to cover himself with, he who gave up his fortune to regenerate his country. No monument tells where he lies, while mausoleums cover those who, compared with him, were pygmies. When Germany shall be what Sickingen and Hutten dreamed she might be, then will they have a monument glorious as their native land.

(pp. 339-40)

The controversy between the "Finsterlings" [i.e. the Scholasticists], on one side, and the liberal party, headed by Reuchlin and Albrecht, on the other, gave rise to the celebrated ***Literæ Obscurorum Virorum.*** The entire authorship of this work has been ascribed to Hutten, but without reason. He shared the honor with Reuchlin, and one or two others. The chief point of this ingenious and biting satire lies in making the monks themselves the assertors of their own stupidity while professedly attacking the new views. They complain, for example, that "some of the new-light men have said that the holy coat of Treves is nothing but a lousy old piece of cloth, and that the three kings of Cologne were honest peasants"; and how Hutten and other free spirits are spoiling the market for indulgences; and how "one had denied that the words of the priests were as authoritative as Christ's words." Another would not have the vices of Old Testament personages commented upon, thinks that priests especially should have a good deal of tenderness for Samson and Solomon, and more of like nature. It is said that many monks failed to see the joke, and quoted the defence as both genuine and admirable. Readers at large were not so dull. The satire passed through many editions, was scattered through Germany, and is rightly classed among the chief instrumentalities which worked in the same line with Luther's more passionate denunciations.

Spite of the honors and immunities now pressed upon him,—a laurel crown and ring from the Emperor's own hand, the diploma of poet-laureate, the privilege of lecturing in all the universities, the offer of a place at the imperial court,—Hutten now ventures upon more dangerous ground than any he has yet trodden. *Jacta est alea* was the motto on Hutten's signet-ring, and he is always prepared to stand the hazard of the die. So happening in an old library to meet with an ancient manuscript upon the donation of Constantine, he makes that the text for an attack on Leo's many short-comings, and with amazing audacity dedicates the book to the Pope himself. Professedly, its aim was to give a portraiture of the iniquities of the papacy during past ages, "which Leo indeed must regard with the same horror that he himself does." But every one knew—and no one knew better than Leo—who was meant. No better proof of the power of this work can be given than Luther's letter to Spalatin, (dated February 24, 1520,) in which he says that, "after reading it, he could not sufficiently wonder that such a shameless system of lies had been allowed to exist for so many centuries; and that he had now for the first time come to the conclusion that the Pope was Antichrist."

This work, though perhaps having something to do with the papal bull launched against its author subsequently, did not produce any immediate ill effects upon his fortunes. Stranger still, it did not forfeit the favor of Albrecht, at whose court he accepted a place, on the old footing of intimacy; the only drawback on his prosperity being constant illness, the scourge of a corrupt age, and (it must be confessed) of a licentious youth. His salary was liberal, his duties nominal, and the prince-bishop gratified his love of travel by sending him on confidential errands into Saxony, to the king of France, and elsewhere.

While thus engaged he writes to a friend, that "he has just heard that there is a party formed at Wittenberg against the Pope. He thinks, however, it is only a quarrel among the monks, and the more they are split up the better." An earnest appeal to the nation to take up arms against the Turks; the preparation of second editions of some of his works; a satire called "The Banished Pasquil," all in Latin, and all full of youth and life and vigor, while he was journeying from bath to bath in search of health,—were the chief employments of the two following years.

A letter to Pirkheimer of this period shows traces of an essentially generous and noble nature. This friend had advised him to devote himself to literature and the Muses.

> Would you advise me, . . . forgetful of duty to myself and friends, to confine all my energies within four walls? and if I did, of what shall I write or speak,—I who have so little experience of actual life? Hitherto, though I have seen and learned much, I have done little. I must begin to live in earnest. These twelve past years were only introductory, the prologue to the great life-tragedy. There must first lie behind me a rich and fruitful past, ere I can say, with the hero, 'The day will come when men will remember us.'

"The vainglorious Hutten," as a contemporary calls him, has also some modesty.

> Compared with Pirkheimer and Erasmus and Reuchlin, I am only a young beginner in literature. Don't think me so vain as to reckon myself among those who have enriched classic literature. . . . I have learned in the schools, as well as in my travels, to bear with patience and to seek definite ends.

Further on he adds:—

> I admit that I desire an honorable and high position, and I should like, too, to have a title of nobility. But woe to me if I count myself noble merely because I belong to a noble family, when I have not ennobled myself by honorable deeds. Don't reckon me among nobles who plume themselves on the deeds of ancestry. I will gather nobility from fresh sources, and transmit it to my descendants. Nor do I look down upon those who, whether they be tanners or weavers, or what not, have taken up and used the stuff which glory is made of, and which we have let lie idle. These men overcome obstacles which would have scared us. And why have the noble-born been forced to give place to such? Because they have spurned knowledge. It serves us right, that what we have thrown away, others have gathered up. All struggle savors of nobility, and that which has no master belongs to all.

As a sample of his ***Roman Triads,*** we give the following:—

> Three things in Rome are held in the highest honor,—the Pope's prerogative, the bones of the saints, and the sale of indulgences. Three things are banished from Rome,—simplicity, moderation, and piety. Three things are matters of traffic in Rome,—Christ, ecclesiastical benefices, and women. Three things are laughed at in Rome,—ancestral virtues, the priesthood of Peter, and the judgment-day. Three things pilgrims bring back from Rome,—a violated conscience, a ruined digestion, and an empty purse. Three things they don't want to hear about in Rome,—a general council, a reformation of the clergy, and an awakening of the German nation. Three things they fear much in Rome,—that the princes may unite together, the people open their eyes, and priestly rascality be unveiled. Three things might benefit Rome,—the earnestness of the German princes, the despair of the German people, and the arms of the Turks.

Each of these triads is amplified and illustrated by references to the history of the Popes and the common rumors of the day. The appeal to national feeling is observable in this as in most of Hutten's writings.

The effect produced by such a production was praise from some,—blame, warnings, threatenings, from others. Erasmus writes in the latter strain, and begs his young friend to moderate the freedom of his pen, and not to hazard his relations to the Bishop of Mayence. But the young friend was not impressed by such considerations. On the contrary, he immediately published another appeal in behalf of German liberty against the papal usurpations, which he dedicated to Ferdinand, viceroy of Charles V., now absent in Spain. (pp. 345-48)

[Under Franz von Sickingen's patronage] Hutten wrote many of his most celebrated compositions. Among them ***The Robbers,*** his Commentaries upon the papal bull, and ***The Monitor.*** These are all characterized by that fierce invective in which he was so skilful. There is in the style of them all a fiery impetuosity and rush which remind one of the knight charging, lance in rest, on the foe. His condensed, curt sentences strike on the monks like blows. He gives them no quarter or breathing-space, but returns again and again to the charge. His epistles to the Elector of Saxony and to the Emperor at this time are, on the contrary, not only respectful, but sober in tone. It is touching, indeed, to see how, in presenting to the Emperor the claims of Germany to freedom from papal rule, the loyal knight, in spite of occasional doubt, clings to the old traditionary reverence for the imperial house. He says, "He has nothing against the Bishop of Rome, if he will confine himself to his diocese, nor against other bishops, if they are good men and chosen by the people." He denies that he has fomented revolution, and refers to the fact that he has always written in Latin, and not in the language of the people. Elsewhere he says:—

> I have little of worldly riches. What I have, I am willing to lose; but my honor, with God's help, I will not lose. If I fail, I shall have the comfort that my aims were right, and that I have sown some seed which will one day, perhaps when I am dead, sprout. I do not think I have done wrong to any good man. I know I have sought glory and pursued the liberal arts in poverty, in many journeyings, and in sickness. Why, then, should good people rejoice if I meet misfortune? I should think they would feel kindly to me and pity me instead. I am sometimes asked why I, of all others, should concern myself about these matters. I can only say, that I have no more interest in them than others have,—yes, even less interest than many have; but God has given me, I sometimes think afflicted me with, a nature which makes public ills weigh more heavily on my heart than it does on the hearts of other men. I have waited a long time for one better fitted to the task than I; but as nobody came forward, and the evil grew, I have undertaken it in the name of God; and I hope that good men will at least bid me God speed.

Still, it must be admitted that all this is not in his usual vein, and that usually, when he sits down to write, he thinks less about good men's opinions than about bad men's misdeeds,—bad men whom he would like better to hew in pieces with his sword, than to attack pen in hand. His address to the Bishops at Worms is a good specimen of his usual manner. After suggesting that their persecution of Luther is simply owing to the fact that his life and doctrine shame theirs, he ends thus:—

> But the measure is full. Off with you from the pure stream, ye unclean swine; off with you from the temples which you have profaned by your teachings. What right have you to devote money set apart for charitable uses to your pomps and feastings and debaucheries,—and this while good men are hungry? The measure is full; see you not that the fresh breezes of freedom are beginning to blow, and that men are getting tired of the present state of things, and will have a change? As respects myself, my life you may take, but you cannot prevent any good deed of mine from living on. What is doing you may perhaps delay, and hinder what I had hoped to do, but what is already done you cannot undo. Life perishes, but not its memory. No! uncertain as I am about the issue of this affair, one thing I am sure of, those who come after me will recognize

> in me an honest purpose. That will be the best legacy of my life.

He warns his enemies further,—

> not to suppose that the good cause will be struck down, even if they should put him and Luther out of the way. Two men are of no great moment, but know that there are many Luthers, many Huttens, and, if anything should happen to us, you will only be in greater danger from these avengers of the innocent, who will unite with the fighters for freedom.

His comments on the papal bull are also in the same style. A few specimens will suffice. Leo having spoken of himself as the servant of the Lord, the commentator asks, "Why, then, talk as if you were the Lord himself?" "O Lord, arise!" says the Pope. "Yes, he will arise, and with a vengeance. Look out for yourself, Leo." "The progress of such heresy in Germany is particularly grievous to the Pope, since he has always borne the Germans in the very bowels of his love." Comment: "Yes, that he has, for he has devoured them; but now he has got to spit them out." "In former days, the Germans were the most zealous haters of heresy." "Ah," sighs Hutten, "if they only had been, then we should hear now nothing about a Pope." "If Luther had accepted my invitation, and had come to Rome, there would have been an end of his errors." "That's true," says the knight, "he never would have spoken again." The bull refers to the burning of Luther's writings. "Yes, they are burning now," is the commentary, "in the hearts of the people. They have kindled a fire for you, too; put it out if you can." (pp. 349-51)

On the 15th of April, 1521, Luther was summoned to Worms, and Ulric waited with intense anxiety the result. "Many," he writes to Luther, "are saying to me, O that he may remain steadfast! I always tell them Luther will be Luther." And when told by a letter from the Reformer's own hand that he is forbidden to preach, he bursts into tears, and feels for the time quite discouraged. It does not appear that he ever met Luther in person, but they frequently corresponded, and the young knight's letters, after he had conquered his first prejudice against the Augustine monk, were always full of respect and affection. The great Reformer professes also a friendly interest in his zealous young correspondent; still, the absence in him of religious earnestness, and his warlike views and his rash impulsiveness, readily explain why there is a certain degree of reticence on Luther's side. The two men differed widely in character and aim. Though now and then we find the man of the world quoting Scripture, when writing to the religious reformer, and expressing the hope "that Christ may bring us back to the light of his doctrine falsified by the Romish priests," it is quite clear that he wrote in a more accustomed, if not more honest vein, when in another letter he says: "Our paths are different; as for me, I am influenced by purely human considerations; while you, more perfect than I, place everything in the hand of God."

It is to be regretted that the correspondence of Hutten and Sickingen was burnt at the castle of Sickingen, and that the precise nature of their political plans and aims is not so clearly defined as we could wish. It is, however, sufficiently plain from various passages in Hutten's published writings still extant, that both wished to unite the lesser nobles and the burgesses of the cities against the papal power, and that subsidiary to this design was the hope of weakening at the same time the power of the princes and of giving to the imperial rule increased supremacy. The task was difficult. The nobles looked with aristocratic contempt on the citizens, and the citizens had not forgotten how these had often leagued with the princes, ecclesiastical and lay, against their liberties, nor how the robber knights had plundered their merchants and attacked their cities. That the attempt failed does not detract from the merit of those who initiated it.

Hutten is usually spoken of as the great champion of the common people. If by this phrase is meant the peasant classes of his time, the claim is an exaggerated one. Though it was only a year after his death that the great Suabian peasant war broke out, and though this was heralded during many previous years by various popular movements and commotions in the same direction, there is no evidence that he had any fellowship with their leaders. It may be that his relations with Sickingen, a large landed proprietor, prevented him. It may be that, like Luther, he feared the effect of rash appeal to the ignorant and rude; or it may be that, mindful of the jealousy and hatred existing not only between noble and citizen, but between citizen and peasant, he began with the more elevated classes, hoping one day to extend to the lowest their rights and privileges. Whatever its interpretation, the fact remains.

How far was he qualified to conduct the movement which his hopes and plans contemplated? He had great ability as a writer, and the temperament which makes men courageous, fearless, and hopeful, as well as earnest. He was of a generous nature, a hater of injustice, and a true lover of his country. In some respects he was more far-seeing than Luther or Melancthon. He took a larger view of the tendencies of the great intellectual movement of which the Reformation was only a part than did these great men. On the other hand,—to say nothing of his lack of religious earnestness and that irritable self-consciousness which made him fritter away energy, and in some cases reputation, in petty personal quarrels,—he lacked sound judgment, self-command, stability, and balance of character. Sickingen was in these respects better fitted than he to be a leader in the enterprise in which both were engaged. Hutten was one of that large class to which such men as Rienzi, Mirabeau, Rousseau, Lamartine, Mazzini, belong. Such men are unsuccessful, partly because their ideas are in advance of their age, and partly because circumstances are unpropitious; but partly, also, because the men themselves lack those personal qualities which invite confidence and cooperation. Like the great scholar of Rotterdam, "he outran his generation in thought," and, unlike him, did *not* "lag behind it in action"; nevertheless he resembles him in this also, that he was better fitted to lead the thought than to shape the action of men,—at least in his own time.

Ulric von Hutten was one of the heralds of the Reformation, and also an important ally of those whose aims were more exclusively religious than were his. His political ideas were not only in advance of those of his age, but of those of many centuries which followed, and they are now substantially the watchword of political progress in Germany. He shrank in their defence from no suffering or sacrifice, and died as he had lived, devoted to the great cause of German liberty. This is his chief honor. (pp. 352-54)

> *J. Parkman, in an unsigned review titled "Ulric Von Hutten," in* The Christian Examiner, *Vol. LXXV, No. III, November, 1863, pp. 339-56.*

The Cornhill Magazine (essay date 1867)

[*In the excerpt below, an anonymous critic surveys Hutten's* Letters of Obscure Men, *providing numerous excerpts from letters that appeared in the satirical work.*]

That Erasmus was the greatest of all the satirists of the Reformation, and the one who had most influence on Europe, no competent student of this branch of literature will deny. The place of honour next him belongs to another scion of the Teutonic race, the knightly wit, the daring adventurer, the free-living champion of the Gospel and of letters, Ulric von Hutten. (p.613)

[Half] soldier of fortune and half literary adventurer, and living, it would seem, much in the fashion of both classes, [Hutten] joined the Lutherans from a point of view of his own, and did essential service to their cause. He was a reformer, partly as a humanist, in the interest of letters; and partly as a German, who disdained to be governed in spiritual matters from the other side of the Alps. His talent was essentially a satirical one, ranging from pungent eloquence, in such works as his dialogue, ***Vadiscus or Trias Romana,*** to dramatic invention and rich ludicrous unctuous humour, in the famous ***Epistolæ Obscurorum Virorum,*** the appearance of which makes an epoch in the history of the Reformation.

The fate of this celebrated satire ("the great national satire of Germany," as Sir William Hamilton has called it) in our own literature has been curious. Whenever it has not been neglected, it has been the subject of the most singular blunders—the last, though perhaps the least surprising, being those of the bookmakers of our own day. When it was reprinted in Queen Anne's time, Steele made precisely the same mistake about it which had been made by British Dominicans and Franciscans, two centuries before, to the vast amusement of Sir Thomas More. He took the Epistles, in which the theologians of that age are made most inimitably to expose themselves, for genuine and serious; and laughed at the blockheads in perfect good faith. Our other English humorists seem generally to have passed them over; and it was reserved for Sir William Hamilton, whose mighty erudition embraced literature and philosophy indifferently, to do them full justice in the *Edinburgh Review* for March, 1831. Since then the Germans have bestirred themselves in the cause of Ulrich von Hutten's memory; an elaborate edition of his works has appeared at Leipsic; and the ***Epistolæ Obscurorum Virorum*** are easily accessible, in good forms, to all who wish to acquaint themselves with one of the memorable satires of that day. (pp. 613-14)

The plan of the satire is simple, but dramatic and effective. There had been recently published a collection of the letters of "illustrious" men to Reuchlin; and Ortuinus Gratius is supposed to publish those of his own friends, whom he modestly calls "obscure" men, in his turn. The obscure ones, accordingly, speak for themselves in all the freedom of confidential communication; and never did such a curious set of marionettes gambol before the world as those of which Ulric von Hutten and his colleagues in the task pull the strings. Now it is Magister Bernhardus Plumilegus writing from Leipsic; now it is Magister Petrus Hafenmusius writing from Nürenberg; or Magister Hiltbrandus Mammaceus from Tübingen; or Magister Gerhardus Schirruglius, from Mayence. But a family likeness runs through the whole of them. A stolid brutal ignorance, enlivened by the most unaffected self-conceit; a bigotry never modified by the shadow of a doubt; a sly, oily sensualism, to which the very hypocrisy accompanying it seems to lend additional piquancy—these are the common features of the race. Their mere Latin is delicious by its homely barbarism; and this is one chief charm of the letters to which no translation can do justice. (p. 615)

The perfect contentment of the crew at once with their dog-Latin and their ignorance of the humanities generally, is a favourite point with Hutten and his friends. "He writes Greek, too," says one of them about Erasmus, "which he ought not to do, because we are Latins and not Greeks. *If he wants to write what nobody can understand,* why does he not write Italian, and Bohemian, and Hungarian?" "These poets," another writer says, "are truly reprehensible; and when anybody writes anything, they say—'See there, see there, that is not good Latin!' and they come here with their new terms, and confound the ancient grammar." "Our masters ought to issue a mandate," observes Petrus Lapp, licentiate,

> that no jurist or poet shall write anything in theology, and shall not introduce *that new Latinity* into sacred theology, as John Reuchlin has done, and a certain person, as I hear, who is called the Proverbia Erasmi (!) . . If they say that they know Greek and Hebrew learning, you have the answer that such learning is not cared for by theologians, because Sacred Scripture is sufficiently translated, and we do not need other translations. The Greeks have gone away from the Church: therefore, also, they ought to be held as enemies, and their knowledge ought not to be practised (*practicari*) by Christians.

Another worthy, Magister Bartholomeus Kuckuck, confirms the erudite Lapp's view by insisting that "Greek is not of the essence of Sacred Scripture;" while Dominus Volwinius de Monteflascon remarks, for his part, that Paul having said that the Greeks were always liars, their literature was necessarily nothing but a lie. Virgil having been mentioned in the presence of one of the correspondents of Ortuinus Gratius, he tells, with much complacency, how he exclaimed—"What do I care for that pagan?" That so much of the fun of the ***Epistolæ*** should be derived from the illiterate character of the Popish theologians, shows how essential a part learning was of the whole movement of the Reformation. Europe was, in fact, *deodo-*

rised by the free dispersion of the delightful essences long hidden in the buried caskets of classical literature.

As may be supposed, the ***Epistolæ Obscurorum Virorum*** throw a good deal of light on the social habits of the clergy and monks of the old days. There seems to have been no little beer and wine swilling amongst them,—the Greek wine being held in an esteem which (as we have just seen) they did not by any means extend to the Greek language. In one of the letters occurs the famous ecclesiastical story of the divine who on first tasting "lachryma Christi," breathed a pious wish that our Lord had wept in his native land. With regard to the morality attributed to the body in other respects, it is as bad as bad can be; and it is exposed with the freedom of Rabelais, and with hardly less than his gross jolly humour. The satire of the ***Epistolæ*** is indeed perfectly unrestrained. That Ortuinus Gratius was the illegitimate son of a priest, and the nephew of a hangman, is evidently thought an excellent jest; while an intimate relation between him and the wife of the renegade Jew, Pfefferkorn, is assumed as a known fact, and made the subject of a score of playful allusions. Plainer speaking on all this side of life than that of the ***Epistolæ Obscurorum Virorum*** is not to be found in satirical literature from Aristophanes downwards; while Erasmus, though still too free for our modern tastes, is reserved, and even prudish in comparison. The exact amount of truth in all these charges of licentiousness cannot, we suppose, be determined; but they come from so many different countries, and such different men, that it is impossible to suppose them mere libels. The very fact that the ***Epistolæ*** were ever mistaken by the Romish party for a *bonâ fide* body of correspondence shows that the immortality which they assume in their writers did not necessarily prove their fictitious character in the eyes of the orthodox. Yet the orthodox were ready to admit their barbarism in point of style. "It is well worth seeing," Sir Thomas More writes to Erasmus, in October, 1516, "how much the ***Epistolæ Obscurorum Virorum*** please everybody,—the learned in sport, but the unlearned in earnest, who, while we laugh, think that we are laughing only at the style, which they do not defend, but say that it is compensated by the weight of the thoughts, and that a most beautiful sword lies hidden in the rude scabbard." Erasmus himself, in a letter to Martinus Lipsius, not only corroborates this, but adds an almost incredible anecdote about the delusion. "A Dominican prior in Brabant," he relates, "wishing to make himself known to the patricians, bought a heap of these books, and sent them to the chiefs of the order, never doubting that they were written in its honour."

"Yet these are they," adds Erasmus, "who are the Atlases, as they think themselves, of the tottering church, . . . these pronounce on the books of Erasmus, and according to their good will, we are Christians or heretics."

Erasmus, like the rest of the cultivated world, had been mightily amused by the fun of the ***Epistolæ;*** and there is an old story that he laughed so heartily in reading them as to break an imposthume from which he was suffering at the time. But Erasmus did not approve the famous satire, the scathing severity of which, its riotous freedom, and its daring liberties with living names, were quite out of keeping with the tone of his own Horatian and Addisonian pleasantry. He was particularly annoyed that his name should be used so freely in the second volume; and he must have winced at the pungent little sentence in one of the letters,—*Erasmus est homo pro se!* It is painful to remember that the gallant and brilliant Ulric von Hutten died his enemy; one of the latest pieces of work he did in the world having been to write an attack upon Erasmus. (pp. 616-17)

> *"The Satirists of the Reformation," in* The Cornhill Magazine, *November, 1867, pp. 609-28.*

David Friedrich Strauss (essay date 1871)

[*In the excerpt below, Strauss offers a detailed examination of the origin and contents of the* Letters of Obscure Men, *attempting to determine the extent of Hutten's own contributions to the satirical volumes.*]

A year before the date of this last letter, August, 1516, Hutten received news from home that a satire on Reuchlin's opponents had appeared under the title of ***Epistolæ Obscurorum Virorum,*** which had attracted a good deal of attention. He had not then received a copy, but a month later he wrote to Richard Crocus at Leipzig: "I have received the ***Obscure Men.*** Good gods! what a capital joke. The Sophists not only suspect, but say, that I am the author. Do take up the cause of your absent friend, and not let this dirt be cast at me. Tell me all about it, and let me know their designs."

The letters were already read and approved in England, and a second edition had appeared in Germany.

By the dirt which Hutten wished to avoid he did not mean the letters, but the attacks of the Obscure Men upon the supposed author. Not long afterwards he read letters in the same style to his countrymen at Bologna, who took him for the author, but he put them off with a jest.

To the third edition an appendix appeared, then a second part of the letters, to which also an appendix was afterwards added. The ***Epistolæ Obscurorum Virorum,*** therefore, as we now have them, consist, first, of the forty-one letters of the first and second editions of 1515 and 1516; secondly, of the seven letters forming the appendix to the third edition. Thirdly, of the second part, 1517, containing sixty-two letters, to the second edition of which an appendix of eight letters was added. The ninth, or rather first letter, is a repetition of one in Part I.; the eighth letter of the first appendix is a later interpolation; and the so-called third part of the ***Epistolæ,*** first printed in 1689, is a collection of additions of various periods, and has nothing whatever to do with the original work.

The title and idea of the work originated as a contrast to the *Epistolæ Clarorum Virorum* to Reuchlin, published by his party in 1514, by way of throwing a weight into the scale in his favour. The idea of producing a fictitious correspondence on the part of his opponents would readily suggest itself. Reuchlin had on his side illustrious and well-known men, but the other party consisted of obscure men, known to nobody. The first collection was intended to show what noble spirits, what praiseworthy efforts for culture and progress, had rallied round Reuchlin; this, to give a glimpse into the abyss of ignorance, stupidity, and vulgarity which was the element of his opponents. The letters were addressed, not to Pfefferkorn, he was too vulgar; not to Hochstraten or Tungern, they were too formidable; but to their Latin hodman and political shield-bearer, Ortuinus Gratius. Desirous of being a Humanist and polite scholar, and yet of serving old scholasticism, he always cut a comical figure; a man who employs the culture which he owes to modern progress in opposing progress in the service of the old school is sure to be looked upon as a traitor by, and to be a special object of dislike to the adherents of the new.

These letters also form a complement to the ***Triumphus Capnionis,*** in which the opponents of Reuchlin and Humanism were combated with seriousness, pathos, and contempt, while in the ***Epistolæ*** the weapons of satire come into play. It is not a third person who writes about the Obscurantists, but they themselves—the masters and bachelors of arts, Genselinus, Caprimulgius, Scherschleiferius, Dollenkopfius, Mistladerius, &c.; sometimes even Ortuinus, Hochstraten, and Tungern are the assumed correspondents, a plan which elevates satire into the region of pure comedy. Barbarism is, as Erasmus says, barbarously laughed at, for it exhibits itself unblushingly without a suspicion of its absurdity. To do this effectively it was necessary to collect together as in a focus the scattered elements of rudeness and imbecility. Satire involves caricature. But it is artistic only when so far tempered with reality as to produce the illusion that it deals with real persons. As is well known, these letters stood this test to such an extent, that when they first appeared the mendicant friars in England were delighted with a book in their favour and against Reuchlin, and in Brabant a prior of the Dominican Order bought a number of copies to present to his superiors. The last letter in the Appendix to Part II. exchanged irony for invective, and opened the good folks' eyes. (pp. 120-22)

It was a bitter satire upon scholasticism that [during Hutten's day] questions of the coarsest kind were discussed after the manner of the schools. Jests of this sort came naturally to the authors of the ***Epistolæ,*** from the custom of the age. There had been many comical parodies on the disputations at the universities, especially on the *Quodlibets,* so called, with the distinctions between *quæstiones principales* and *minus principales,* referring to the most gross and obscene topics. Several specimens of them have been preserved, and they help us to understand the letters better.

Through all these jests and improprieties there runs the scarlet thread of the Reuchlin trial, forming a solid background to the jocular foreground, and a connecting link for the letters, forming the whole almost into a romance. There are but few letters in which this theme is not touched upon. There is early mention made of Hochstraten's being at Rome, and we have the vacillating prospects of the cause, the hopes and fears as we know them from Hutten's and Mutian's letters, portrayed as from the other side. Now they send good news from Rome; Hochstraten has had remittances, and has given a banquet to the cardinals and auditors, and it is said that Reuchlin's means are exhausted. At another time it is reported that the Pope will confirm the sentence of Spire, and permit the *Augenspiegel* to be printed at Rome. They have not much confidence in Leo X., because he is a poet himself, and does not understand St. Thomas Contra Gentiles. The first part of the letters originally ended with the report that Reuchlin had conquered; in the enlarged edition there is a letter purporting to be from Hochstraten himself, in which he says that he wishes he had never undertaken the business, for things looked bad; he often had not bread to eat, and when he took a walk with Peter Meyer, of Frankfort, in the Campo Fiore, they were called after, "There go the two men who want to devour Reuchlin." Towards the end of Part II. the case is still pending, but it is known that the majority of the Commission are for Reuchlin, and all eyes are turned to the Reuchlinist conspiracy in Germany which is determined to gain his cause before the tribunal of public opinion.

So much has been said of Reuchlin that every one must be anxious to see him, and there is a letter in which a bachelor of arts describes a visit to him:—"When I entered his house, he said, 'Welcome, Mr. Bachelor; pray be seated!' He had a spectacle (unum brillum) on his nose and a book before him, which looked strange, and I saw at once that it was neither German, nor Bohemian, nor Latin. And I said to him, 'Excellent Mr. Doctor, what may the book be?' He answered, 'It is called the Greek Plutarch, and treats of philosophy.' Then I said, 'Read it then, in God's name,' and it made me think that he understands strange arts. Then I saw a little book, newly printed, under the bench, and said to him, 'Excellent Mr. Doctor, what is it lying there?' He said, 'It is an offensive book, which a friend at Cologne lately sent me; it is written against me by the Cologne theologians, and now they say that Johann Pfefferkorn wrote it.' Then said I, 'What are you doing in the matter? Will you not justify yourself?' Said he, 'Not I; I am justified enough already. I do not trouble myself any more with such nonsense; my eyes scarcely suffice to study what is useful to me.' "

Although we have honestly tried to give our readers an idea of the ***Epistolæ Obscurorum Virorum,*** we cannot escape from the humiliating conviction that we have attempted an impossible task. It is in the language that the difficulty lies. The Obscurantists of the early part of the sixteenth century are made to speak in their own tongue, in a Latin—if such it can be called—which had been formed in the course of the Middle Ages from a mixture of ecclesiastical and vernacular elements with the original stock. It is so comical, because though at every step it offends against the laws of classical Latinity, and, caricatured as it is, it is obviously a language that was actually in use. The writers, in spite of the absurdity of their doings, are as satisfied with themselves and each other as possible. But all these comical characteristics are bound up with the Latin; no skill of the translator into German or any other language can reproduce the impression of the original.

It evaporates the soonest in those parts where the ludicrousness lies not so much in the grammatical as in the logical construction, or when ignorance exhibits itself so naïvely as in the following letter to Ortuin from Rome:—

> You said when I took leave of you, 'Peter, when you get to Rome, see if there are any new books, and send me some!' Well, here is one for you, printed here, and as you are a poet, I think it will be of great use to you. For I heard from a notary, who is said to be perfect in this art, that this book is the well-spring of poetry, and that the author—named Homer—is the father of poets. And he said there was another Homer in Greek. And I said, 'What do I want with Greek? Latin is better; I will send it to Germany to Magister Ortuinus; he does not want Greek stuff.' And I asked what the book was about. And he said about certain people called Greeks, who went to war with some other people called Trojans. I have heard of them before, and these Trojans had a great city, and the Greeks besieged it and lay there ten years. And the Trojans sometimes came out and fought with them hand to hand, and they slew each other till the whole plain was filled with blood, and there was a river that was dyed red with blood; and some one threw a stone that twelve men could not lift, and there was a horse that spoke and prophesied; I don't believe that though, for it seems impossible, and the book does not appear to me to be very authentic. Please write and tell me what you think of it.

Some idea might be given of the Latin verses by translation, but the doggrel rhymes are by no means so ludicrous in the German as in the precise metre of the Latin. The full appreciation of the ***Epistolæ Obscurorum Virorum*** must be confined to those who can read them in the original.

It has been the custom to estimate them rather from their historical interest than as a work of art. But if our description has not quite failed in its purpose, the reader will agree with us in taking a different view. The work reminds us more than any other of the first of its kind, *Don Quixote;* that world-wide satire in which the contrast between a waning and dawning phase of life and thought was seized by the hand of genius and lifted out of the region of satire into that of humour. Just so with the ***Epistolæ.*** They have not the compact form of the romance, nor do they present actors on a stage; they may be compared rather to a group of figures in relief, in which asses, satyrs, and bacchantes are all jumbled together, and in which the value of the individual figures makes up for want of unity. But this unity is not altogether wanting, and all who note the impression left by the perusal of the book will allow that it soars into the region of poetic humour. It may be compared to that produced by a comedy of Aristophanes, or an episode with Sancho or Falstaff.

We should have had no right to go thus into detail about the ***Epistolæ*** if Hutten did not stand in the first rank of the conjectured authors. He was suspected on their very first appearance, and did not disclaim all share in it so decidedly as anxious friends desired. But it is only a question of a share in it. Erasmus thought he knew of three authors. The question then resolves itself into two: which part of the collection is Hutten's, and who were his coadjutors? It seems to have been the aim of the Reuchlinists in the championship of their master that these satirical shots should appear to proceed not from one person, but from a number who were combining against the Obscurantists. Individuals systematically kept in the background, that they might be more formidable as a masked army, more inconvenient as a nameless swarm of wasps.

In looking round the Humanist circle with a view of discovering whence the ***Epistolæ Obscurorum Virorum*** proceeded, many indications direct us to the Gotha-Erfurt circle. Crotus wrote in 1514 to Reuchlin, "You have on your side the whole Mutianic order; it comprises philosophers, poets, orators, and theologians, all ready to fight for you. You have only to give the word of command." Crotus enumerates, besides Mutian, Eoban Hesse and Hutten, and probably alludes to the ***Epistolæ,*** for he says that Hutten will crush the empty-headed Ortuin at a blow.

Crotus does not himself assume the position of a general in the enterprise in question, but there is irrefragable evidence that he was more than a subaltern officer. We have an anonymous letter addressed to Crotus Rubianus in 1532, formerly attributed to Justus Jonas, but now to Justus Menius. Crotus, once the bosom-friend of Hutten, Reuchlin's zealous champion, and later the admirer of Luther, had by this time deserted the cause which he had not a little advanced, joined himself to the party of the old Church, and acknowledged the change in an apology addressed to Archbishop Albert. The writer of the letter to Crotus tries to undermine his new position by disclosing his antecedents. He reminds him of his biting jests against the old Church system in the Mutianic circle at Gotha, of the anonymous lampoons which, even before Luther appeared, he and Hutten, at his instigation, had put forth against pope and cardinals, theologians and monks. The sharpest of all these was his ***Epistolæ Obsc. Vir.,*** which the writer justly calls "A not incomparable but immortal poem," a book which furnished those who had not so much wit at their command with new weapons against the papal supremacy, and which perhaps had been more effectual against it than any book of the age.

He writes as one who had belonged to the circle of which Crotus was one (Menius was at Erfurt from 1514-1516); he reminds him of their walks and confidential talks when Crotus had his work in hand, and used to read parts of it aloud; he would rather that the Iliad were lost than Crotus's immortal jokes over the papists.

The conception, then, of the ***Epist. Obsc. Vir.*** is attributed to Crotus by an obviously well-informed contemporary. A share in it is not denied to Hutten; one letter is expressly assigned to him, and it is remarked that in cutting up the cardinals and bishops, &c., Hutten was not equal to Crotus. But the writer had an interest in speaking thus, since all he could say in favour of the former Crotus sent the renegade up in the scale. He is so far right, that Hutten would hardly have hit upon his friend's peculiar style, but his versatile talents enabled him to adopt it. He was more inclined to pathos than Crotus. Hutten's writings, even his satires, spur his readers on to deeds; he never forgets that wrongs and stupidity must not only be laughed at, but fought with. The author of the ***Epistolæ*** forgets that the

Obscurantists are rogues, because they are such absurd fools; he would be sorry if they mended, for then he would not have them to laugh at; he forgets the practical in the æsthetical aspect of things.

And this answers to what we know of the character of Crotus. The humorous element in him did not exclude an interest in the struggles of the time, and his jests were weapons against stupidity; but his interest in these things was not so great as to induce him to incur danger, or to prevent him from making peace with the old state of things, rather than involve himself in tedious conflicts. He liked, therefore, to send forth his arrows from concealment; he never put his name to any of his writings, except to that last one which called forth this bitter anonymous rejoinder which silenced him for the rest of his life.

Ulrich Hutten had been since the autumn of 1515 in Italy. The rest of the year was taken up with the commotions which followed on the murder of his cousin. This will explain how it was that he took at first no active part in an undertaking, which afterwards awakened in him so lively an interest. His share in it must be assigned to the second part. The Cologners did not seem to have been sufficiently chastised. Pfefferkorn had published his *Defensio,* in which he took up his quarrel with Reuchlin from the beginning, and denounced the ***Epist. Obsc. Vir.*** to Pope and Emperor as a blasphemous, worse than Saracenic book. A rejoinder was therefore called for, and thus arose Part II.

It is quite equal to its elder brother. It stands in many respects in the same relation to Part I. as Part II. of *Don Quixote* to Part I. It is assumed that the writers of the letters have read Part I. The knowledge that many of the Obscurantists had taken the letters in earnest is turned to account. Still there are differences between the two parts. First, an external difference. The letters in Part I. are all from places in Germany, including the Netherlands. The first letter from Rome is in the appendix; and one-third of the seventy letters in Part II. is from Rome. There is often news from Rome in Part I., but not direct; in Part II. news comes direct from those who are studying or practising law there. Roman sights are mentioned—the Pope and his elephant; the Campo Fiore and the oranges; the intolerable heat; a route before mentioned from Germany to Rome, with its stations and objects of interest. It is certain that Crotus had never then been in Italy; and such little peculiarities as that there was no good chalk and no proper bootlaces to be had in Rome, point to a writer who had suffered from these little inconveniences himself.

There is also an internal difference. Jests, fun, and improprieties abound in Part II. as in Part I.; but serious discussions under the form of reported conversations are more often interwoven. Letters like that about the Würzburg preacher and the interpretation of a prophecy, do not occur in Part I. (we have quoted from both indiscriminately). Pathos more often appears beneath the irony. Böcking says that in Part I. a gimlet was used not less sharp than in Part II., but it made less noise and fewer chips. And he thinks he detects this more noisy gimlet, namely, Hutten as author, in the appendix to Part I. An interview with Erasmus is mentioned, and the author sometimes falls into good, Hutten-like Latin, as if he were not quite master of the jargon of the Obscurantists, and sometimes overdoes the caricature. The appendix to Part II. betrays a heavier hand, and it is altogether superfluous. The subject had been exhausted, and treated with all possible variations. The best joke must come to an end, or it produces satiety. All this favours the conjecture that Hutten was the chief author of Part II. and the appendix to Part I., as well as the fact that he is himself often mentioned and spoken ill of. As he spoke of comrades, and Erasmus mentions three authors of the ***Epistolæ,*** various conjectures have been rife as to who else had a share in them, but we need not go over this wide field, as all we have to answer for is our hero's share in it.

And even here we do not get beyond conjecture, though it has a high degree of probability. The most certain indication is the journey in rhyme by Magister Schlauraff, which Hutten read to his friends at Bologna. This *carmen rithmicale,* with its sparkling humour, its inexhaustible quips and cranks, and jumble of Latin and German in the rhymes, is unquestionably the gem of the whole collection. Then the time and route coincide with Hutten's second journey to Italy; in another letter there is a memorial to Ecbert Haarlem, Hutten's hospitable friend at Rostock; the servile offices accepted by the German benefice-hunters at Rome are spoken of in terms similar to those used by Hutten in a letter to Erasmus, and another assumed writer speaks of the perpetual darts of Hutten's polemical pen, and describes the preachers Peter Meyer, at Frankfort, and Bartholomew Zehender, at Mayence, quite in the style of the author of the *Triumphus Capnionis.*

One further remark only remains to be made, which marks the rapid progress of the times. The ***Epistolæ*** were very widely circulated, and found so many imitators, that Hutten was wearied with communications in the same style. Three editions of Part I. appeared before Part II. was printed, and two editions afterwards up to 1518. There is then no trace of any fresh edition till 1556. In October, 1517, Luther had put forth his theses; in 1519 the disputation with Eck occurred at Leipzig, and from that time the whole intellectual interests of the times were centred in the Reformation movement.

How this work, projected in his service and honour, was received by Reuchlin himself we do not precisely know. The letter in the *Lamentations* (of which presently), in which he deprecates them, is undoubtedly a fiction of his enemies. There is, however, a credible tradition that the worthy old gentleman, though he had written a satirical comedy in his youth, now thought the buffoonery of his young champions somewhat too extravagant. Erasmus tells us how much he was amused by some specimens sent him before the whole was printed; there is an old story that laughter over them cured him of a dangerous swelling by causing it to break. The first printed collection alarmed him; but when a new edition came out, with an appendix in the very first letter of which he himself was introduced, and, though mentioned with great respect, hit off exactly with his weak voice and his refined smile at the follies of men,—when a second part followed, in which he was represented as "one by himself," and yet as an ally of these turbulent young spirits,—the thing appeared to him to be fatal, and he was loud in his displeasure at a course which could only make the Humanistic tendencies hated. Just so Luther, at any rate at that period, wanted the humour to enable him to appreciate a work like the ***Epistolæ.*** He thought it impudent, and called the author a harlequin. Crotus could only laugh at the Obscurantists, Luther could only scold at and oppose them, Hutten could do both.

The objects of the attack turned, as was worthy of them, to the ecclesiastical authorities. They spent a great deal of money, and at length obtained a papal brief, which commanded all possessors of copies of the ***Epistolæ*** to burn them within three days, under pain of excommunication, and to report all who refused to do so to the parish priest. Armed with this weapon, Ortuin thought he could take the field in a literary sense against his enemies. He turned the appellation *Obscuri Viri* against the originators of the letters. They were the real Obscure Men, and he makes them lament over their, as he assumes, unsuccessful undertaking. The papal brief and the condemnatory letter of Erasmus were printed at the beginning. Another, assumed to be by Reuchlin, shows by its clumsiness that Ortuin was by no means a match for his adversaries. He makes the authors of the ***Epistolæ*** joined in a stupid *Pater Peccavi,* in flat and wearisome exclamations, *"Proh Jupiter!"* and *"Proh dii immortales!"* over their defeat and the victory of the theologians. The *Lamentations* are an absurdly stupid retort to so clever a production as the ***Epistolæ Obscurorum Virorum.*** Happily they are mostly very short, sometimes only a few lines, and it is plain that the powers of the writer could no further go. The worst piece is a list of the moral, that is immoral, principles ascribed to the Reuchlinists. The style was not intended to be bad, since the Humanists are assumed to be the writers, and Ortuin evidently does his best. It was often bad enough, yet not so as to be ridiculous. He wished to be thought moderate, and discriminates between good and bad Reuchlinists and poets, and for the sake of the latter he regrets that the ancient Church discipline of cutting off hands, tongues, &c., is at an end, and commends them as forerunners of Antichrist to the punishment of the secular arm. (pp. 129-40)

> *David Friedrich Strauss, in his* Ulrich Von Hutten: His Life and Times, *translated by Mrs. G. Sturge, Daldy, Isbister, & Co., 1874, 386 p.*

Kuno Francke (essay date 1915)

[*In the excerpt below from a lecture originally given in 1915, Francke explores how "Erasmian enlightenment turns into a revolutionary power" in Hutten's works, focusing particularly upon nationalistic implications in the dialogues* The Spectators, The Bull Killer, *and* The Robbers.]

Recent German criticism is inclined to undervalue the services rendered by Ulrich von Hutten to the cause of German culture. Friedrich Paulsen in his *History of Higher Education in Germany* calls Hutten's whole humanist propaganda a bombastic masquerade. Friedrich von Bezold in his *History of the Reformation* dismisses Hutten's plan for a reorganization of Church and State as fantastic dreams. And nearly every writer on Luther and his work contrasts with the deep and invincible faith of the Wittenberg monk and his irresistible pressing on from fight to fight the wayward, meteoric and fruitless career of the unbelieving and sceptical partisan of humanism.

It is my purpose to vindicate Hutten's activity, to show that his political ideals were by no means intrinsically unconstructive and that, if he failed in his work, if his cause was vanquished, there might be said of him what the ancient poet said of the unsuccessful opponent of Caesar: "Victrix causa Deis placuit, sed victa Catoni."

In Ulrich von Hutten's personality German humanism gains its most ravishing and irresistible expression; in him the Erasmian enlightenment turns into a revolutionary power, which shakes the foundations of existence. They misjudge Hutten's innermost being, who consider him above all as an ally of the Lutheran reformation. Hutten himself saw in Luther the ally and champion of his own humanist cause; he saw in him the destroyer of hierarchy, the deliverer of the German people from the Romish yoke. He would have been the last to submit to a new religious dogma as preached by the Wittenberg party. His aim was the political and intellectual reconstruction of Germany. Abolition of the monasteries, confiscation of church property, secularization of the schools and the higher institutions of learning, safe-guarding of free thought and free inquiry, centralization of the empire, limitation of the power of the territorial princes, utilization of the knighthood and the citizen class for the formation of a powerful German army—these were the practical ideals which fired his reformatory passion. Perhaps these thoughts were doomed from the beginning to remain unrealized. Perhaps the centrifugal development of Germany during the preceding centuries had made a radical reconstruction of the imperial power impossible. Perhaps the German masses were not yet ripe for the adoption of a rationalistic view of life, although Zwingli's reformatory activity in Switzerland has been a valid testimony to the capacity of humanism even for ecclesiastical organization. Perhaps the German knighthood was the least fitting instrument of national rejuvenation. And, surely, all these plans were wrecked by the fact that of the two German emperors of Hutten's time the fantastic Maximilian lacked the power, and the un-German Charles the Fifth the least disposition to carry them through. But are they on that account less remarkable or less worthy of the admiration of a posterity which has seen their fulfillment, not to be sure in the form which Hutten hoped for? Hutten remains in spite of all his errors and defects one of Germany's heroes. It remains a pathetic story how this man, thrust out a mere boy into a friendless world, tossed about in poverty, toil, and youthful excesses, early afflicted and tortured for years by a hideous disease, placed entirely upon his own resources, driven about in fruitless struggles and adventures,—steadfastly adheres to his ideals of country and liberty, preaches for them with flaming eloquence, works with restless activity for their realization, is never for a moment doubtful of himself, dedicates himself unreservedly to his cause, and finally at thirty-five years of age physically exhausted and politically annihilated, but inwardly unbroken, meets death in exile.

And it remains an honor to Zwingli that, while Erasmus as well as Luther finally shook off the impetuous and uncompromising fighter, the Swiss reformer was large-minded enough to offer him, as a soldier of freedom, a last refuge.

Hutten has expressed himself about his practical relations to life perhaps most emphatically in two letters to friends—the letter with which in 1514 he sends to Crotus Rubeanus, the principal author of the ***Epistolae Obscurorum Virorum,*** his humorous poem ***Nemo (The Nobody)***; and the letter of October, 1518, to the Nürnberg patrician and humanist, Willibald Pirkheimer, in which he justifies himself for his accepting a position at the court of the archbishop of Mainz.

In the former letter Hutten appears as the champion of a free, entirely unrestrained literary life. It had been the impulse for spiritual independence, for struggle with fate, for adventurous tests of power and for a full living out of himself, which had driven the sixteen-year old youth to flight from the cloister-school in Fulda, and then to vagrant journeyings from one German and Italian university to another, and finally into service in the imperial army in Italy. Without having brought his studies to a conclusion, without title and office, full of contempt for theological and legal pseudoscience, full of enthusiasm for the humanist ideals of life, he had, in 1514, returned home. Instead of being welcomed after so long an absence, he relates to Crotus, he was treated by his family as a degenerate, as a man who had wasted his time and not accomplished anything, as a "Nothing," a "Nobody." These mocking designations Hutten accepts as a title of honor.

> Yes . . . if to be something means to acquire a degree of master or doctor, if you are nothing until you stoop to take part in the farce of learned nonsense, if it is not a question what kind of a man you are but whether you have learned the tricks of rabulistic perverters of law, or the hair-splitting dialectics of hypocritical theologians, then I will rather not have learned anything, I will rather remain a "Nothing" and a "Nobody." For a man proves himself in the struggle with life and in the free service of the muses; and nothing shall induce me to swerve a hair's breadth from the striving after this genuine humanity, unfalsified by empty formulas and hollow names.

If this letter reveals the Faust-like craving of the Renaissance man for free individuality, we recognize in the letter to Pirkheimer the other side of Hutten: his passionate desire to accomplish something worthy, for humanity and above all for his country. In the meantime he had gained opportunity for activity on a larger scale as well as recognition from his sympathizers. Against the foreign enemies of the empire, especially Venice, France, and the Pope, he had sounded a call in his epigrams addressed to Emperor Maximilian. He had attacked in weighty philippics the Duke Ulrich of Wuertemberg, the murderer of his own cousin, Hans von Hutten, as a disturber of the inner peace, and had appealed especially to the knighthood to help in annihilating the "tyrant." He had contributed his share to Crotus' ***Epistolae Obscurorum Virorum,*** and here he had contrasted with monkish stupidity and sloth his ideals of free and enlightened humanism. By editing Lorenzo Valla's ***Constantine Donation,*** and by its ironical dedication to Leo X, he had, in 1517, struck his first great blow against the papacy. He himself had in the same year at Augsburg been crowned *poet laureate* by Emperor Maximilian, had then entered the service of the liberal-minded archbishop of Mainz and had prepared for the Augsburg diet of 1518 a flaming address in which he exhorted the German princes to unity and to the granting of means for a war against the Turks. All these things re-echo in the letter to his friend Pirkheimer of October, 1518, in which he justifies himself for his entering politics and court life. It is clear from this letter: Hutten now feels himself a public leader, a representative of Germany, a champion of national culture, honor, and freedom. He recalls to mind Pirkheimer's own example, his many-sided public activity, the highly developed public life of his native town, Nürnberg, which, Hutten says, had led not only to the highest development of industry and commerce, but had also offered room for the scientific and literary endeavors of a Regiomontanus and Celtes and for the brilliant creations of the German Apelles as he called him: Albrecht Dürer. What Pirkheimer and his like had done for the cities he, Hutten,—so he answers Pirkheimer—was trying to do for his own class, the knighthood. The knighthood, he tells us, unfortunately, still lacked the consciousness of its high, spiritual tasks, it was entirely absorbed in economic struggles and petty feuds. Therefore, it was his ambition to make clear to his class that true nobility must be acquired by service, and to give them in himself an example of genuine class honor and of knightly championship of national affairs. "May it fare ill with me, Willibald, if I think myself a noble unless I have made myself so by work. And let me not be contented with what I have inherited from my ancestors, but let me add something to it which by me will be bequeathed to posterity." The time is ripe, he thinks; not a few of the princes are inclined to further the new culture. Through entering their services, the nobility might again become a power for progress. For him personally such a practical participation in the affairs of public life is an inner necessity. He has not yet tamed himself, not yet calmed his youthful fire, not yet done enough to give himself over to scholarly leisure. But even in the unrest and the distractions of court life he will never cease to belong to himself. "I shall always be Hutten and never be found a traitor to myself." Never will he allow fate the control of his soul, always will he consider the struggle for humanism as the sacred concern of the time and call himself happy that he has been chosen to take part in the struggle. "O century, O arts, it is a joy to live and not to rest, my Willibald. The studies are flourishing, the spirit is awake. Barbarism, accept the yoke and submit to exile!"

Since the days of Walther von der Vogelweide no German had proclaimed as emphatically as Hutten did in these two letters, the union of spiritual independence with unselfish devotion to the cause of country as the ideal of manly activity. During the five years which now were left to him he endeavored with restless energy and with heroic exertion of his whole personality to realize this ideal and to make it, as far as lay in his power, a means of destruction of medieval theocracy and to found on it a new German public consciousness. These five years from 1519 to 1523 contain the writings of Hutten which show him at his height and associate him with the greatest German publicists of all times. (pp. 184-92)

In the ***Lament and Exhortation against the excessive un-Christian Power of the Bishop of Rome and the unministerial Ministers,*** he calls upon his countrymen to take to arms. He translates his Latin dialogues into German and adds to them pithy and stirring prefatory verses; and at the same time he publishes a new series of warlike dialogues, in spite of their Latin form of truly popular power. He follows from Sickingen's castle the Diet of Worms with feverish interest, he sends to Luther words of unreserved admiration and assurances of unqualified faith ("My affairs are human, you dwell entirely in the divine,"); he hurls invectives against the papal delegates, against the cardinals, bishops and abbots assembled in Worms, and addresses patriotic exhortations to the Emperor. And finally, when the imperial edict against Luther has been issued, he seeks a last means for saving the country in an offensive alliance of the knighthood and the cities. In the fatal campaign of Sickingen's against the Archbishop of Treves, which in 1522 leads to the breakdown of all of Hutten's hopes and plans, we lose trace of him, until he reappears as a fugitive in Switzerland. But even the hunted and exhausted fugitive rallies, in the controversy with Erasmus, to a last passage at arms for the Lutheran cause, and the dying one gives to his people in the resuscitated figure of Arminius, the destroyer of the Roman legions in the Teutoburg Forest, a new national hero.

The keynote of all these war manifestoes is a boundless, imperturbable trust in the cause of truth, and the unbending will to carry it to victory or to die for it. It was no mere phrase when from the Ebernburg he writes to the Elector of Saxony:

> Would to God that either you (the princes) who have the power had the will, or I had the power, as I have the will. But if I cannot move you nor elsewhere stir a fire, I shall at least do what I can accomplish alone. I shall do nothing unworthy of a brave knight, I shall never, as long as I have my senses, swerve one step from my undertaking; you, however, if I should see you deviate from manly firmness, I shall pity. I can die, but I cannot be a slave, nor can I see Germany enslaved. I hope the best from you; therefore I have written to you a freeman to a freeman. Farewell and be a man.

His own ideal of a man he has expressed in the ***New Year's Wishes*** with which he sends his German dialogues to Franz von Sickingen:

> And I wish you, not as we often wish our friends, an agreeable and enjoyable leisure, but plenty of serious, hard, and strenuous work, by which, for the benefit of the many, you may exercise and test your own proud and heroic mind.

And from his innermost heart there came the thrilling words with which he introduces these dialogues to the reader: glorying in the rebirth of truth; consecrating himself to its defence; defying all the powers of darkness, papal excommunication and imperial proscription; asking God's blessing for his pious mother in her care and anxiety for his fate; and winding up with the exultant "Ich habs gewagt!"

Hutten's was not a deep or a speculative nature. All mysticism, all religious fervor were foreign to him. Not like the great medieval mystics, not like Luther, did he want to serve the cause of God; but, like the ancients, he wished to accomplish great things and thereby leave his name to posterity. But that he was thoroughly in earnest in his attempt to make rationalism the basis of life, that he hoped from the victory of humanism the dawn of a new era of national culture for his fatherland, and longed for it with the whole glow of his passionate soul, words like those quoted are a sufficient proof, even apart from his whole life entirely devoted to this one idea.

And must we not admit that Hutten was indeed the representative of a higher culture? Apart from Crotus' ***Epistolae,*** Erasmus' *Colloquies* and Luther's manifestoes and hymns, what has German literature produced in those first hopeful years of the Reformation that reveals such inner strength and truthfulness, such a wide horizon, such a free sweep of artistic form as Hutten's Dialogues? Among the whole mass of polemics called forth through Luther's first stand against Rome nothing comes near them. To be sure, a fresh breath of wholesome life goes through the polemic dramas of a Pamphilus Gengenbach and Niklas Manuel. Certainly, the flood of peasant and bourgeois pasquils and satire let loose by the struggle against Rome has something overpowering in its elementary fury and recklessness. And even the principal leaders of the Romish party, such as Thomas Murner or Hieronymus Emser, did by no means lack power of persuasion and honesty of conviction. But how crude and uncouth on the one hand, how limited and reactionary on the other does all this appear when we contrast it with the sharply chiselled form and the free grand spirit of Hutten's Dialogues. Here, indeed, there is a man who, like Erasmus, has assimilated the best of ancient culture, the high conception of human dignity, but who is not, like Erasmus, content to cultivate and spread this spiritual refinement but is driven by the impulse to rejuvenate and reconstruct thereby the whole order of society. Justly David Friedrich Strauss has pointed out [in his *Ulrich von Hutten: His Life and Times*] that it is this youthful impulse of reform which so emphatically distinguishes Hutten's Dialogues from their formal prototype, the dialogues of the brilliant, but cool and blasé Lucian. At the same time, in spite of all his zeal for the common cause, Hutten remains a brilliant artist, a proclaimer of individual genius, and just hereby he lifts himself above the limitations of his subject and above the time to which he speaks; just hereby, he associates himself, like Erasmus, with the few of his age who speak to us also.

If Hutten had not written anything except ***The Spectators, The Bull Killer*** and ***The Robbers,*** these three dialogues would be sufficient to secure him a name among the classics of German literature. Who could read these little masterpieces of dialogue without feeling transported by them to the heights of free humanity, and lifted above all meanness, pettiness and artificial distortion? Who will not admit that here polemics against what is evil and doomed to destruction turns at the same time into a serene picture of the world and of a wholesome and hopeful life?

Delightful is the free and unconcerned manner with which, in ***The Spectators,*** the two divine aviators Sol and Phaethon, who from the height of their day's journey through the heavens look down upon earth, converse with each other about the struggles and joys of the small world of men that swarms far beneath them. It is the time of the Augsburg Diet of 1518, and the divine charioteers have just arrived over the old imperial town. How they crowd and jostle down below, how they push back and forth, draw hither and thither! What a noise, what a carousing, what a prattling and prancing! Sol instructs his inquisitive son: "It is the Germans; they cannot carry on politics or any public business without banquets and drinking bouts. To be sure, there are some sober people among them (Hutten means himself and his followers); men who hold themselves in control, drink water, cultivate their minds, and take serious things seriously; may they succeed in making themselves felt, for their country's good; but the mass, princes as well as knights and populace, are unfortunately still in the fetters of their inherited and besetting sin, of which Tacitus related long ago—'Excess in eating and drinking;' and just the best and freest among them, the Saxons, are the worst topers of all. But otherwise the Germans are a splendid people, true, brave, honest and joyous." "But what is the cause of the concourse below in Augsburg?" Phaethon asks. "They are conducting the papal legate, Cardinal Cajetan, in solemn procession to the city hall. He has been sent across the Alps to fool the Germans, has all his sacks full of indulgences, and hopes to bring them back to Rome filled with German gold." "How long is the Pope going to carry on this shameful game?" "Until the Germans who till now he has led by the nose have come to their senses." "Is the time near when the Germans will have come to their senses?" "Very near; for this Cardinal will be the first one who comes home with empty sacks, to the great terror of the Holy City, where they never would have believed that the barbarians would have been so bold." "Are the Germans then barbarians?" "According to the judgment of the Romans, yes. But if you look upon good manners and friendly intercourse, upon zeal in all virtues, upon constancy and honesty of mind, then the Germans are the most cultivated of all people and the Romans the most hopeless of barbarians. For they have been corrupted by luxury and debauchery and you find with them faithlessness, more than feminine fickleness, deceit and villainy as nowhere else." "I like what you say of the Germans, if they only were not such topers." The further course of the dialogue, which now goes on to enlarge on the political and social conditions of Germany, is interrupted by the Cardinal Cajetan himself, who in great excitement and full of wrath shouts up to them from the procession. He calls upon Sol, who thus far had only glanced through the clouds, that he should scatter the clouds and at last once more, as in Italy, shine from a clear sky; furthermore, he should bring heat and contagious diseases, so that more church livings fall vacant by deaths and thereby new revenues accrue to the Holy See. When Sol with proud calm rejects these requests of the "hot-headed little man," and Phaethon in youthful indignation calls down to him some pithy and bald truths, then the Cardinal in pompous rage pronounces the excommunication against the two heavenly travellers, but in return is delivered by them to the contempt of the world. Phaethon: "I give you over to the ridicule of the Germans, whom you are plundering, that they may chase you away in scorn." Sol: "Leave the wretch alone. It is time to turn our chariot downward and to give room to the evening star. Let the villain down below lie, cheat, steal, rob and pillage at his own risk." Phaethon: "Yes, and go to the devil, too. So then I spur the horses on our downward course and follow westward."

The second of the above mentioned dialogues, ***The Bull Killer*** reminds one of the clownish brawls of a medieval farce. But it is a farce imbued with mighty passion and moral pathos; and, as in Holbein's *Dance of Death,* here also medieval conceptions are made the vehicles of a thoroughly modern feeling. The bull of excommunication issued by Leo X against Luther appears here in person, as a fat, bloated monster, that attacks with threats and blows a beautiful woman, German Freedom. Freedom is too delicate for this passage at arms; she can oppose to the maltreatment by the fiend nothing but laments and calls for help. But finally upon her call: "Does no one dare to succor me, is there no true freeman, no one who strives for virtue, loves the good, hates deceit, honors justice, abhors sin—in a word, is no German there"—upon this call there appears, like a knight of Saint George, Ulrich von Hutten himself. "This call, from whomsoever it may come, concerns me"—with these words he presses upon the brute, which now, first cursing, then whining, tries to defend itself. But in vain, for Hutten comes from that "shelter of justice," the Ebernburg, "where the men are true men, where one keeps one's covenant, preserves faith, worships the divine, and protects innocence," while in Rome, whence the bull comes, the contrary of all this is the case. "If it were only a question of Luther," he exclaims, "I would let you go, but you attack not only his life, but that of her here, German Freedom; and therefore you must be deprived of your own life." Now there ensues the climax of the action. The bull, writhing under Hutten's merciless strokes, left in the lurch by all his superstitious German adherents ("For Germany now sees with her own eyes"), beseeching his victorious opponent on his knees for mercy, finally in greatest distress makes a last deceitful attempt to save himself. He offers indulgence and papal absolution to perjurers and murderers, robbers and desecrators of churches, adulterers, fornicators and blasphemers, if they only will help him—and, lo, first it seems like an army of fleas, then of ants, then of cats that moves on from the distance; it is the Roman courtiers and mercenaries pressing over the Alps. And now Hutten summons his warriors.

> Come, ye freemen; our common concern, the common weal is at stake. Here the tyrants will be crushed; here the servitude will be broken. Where are the freemen, where are the illustrious ones, the men of great names, where are ye, heads of nations?—They have heard me—a hundred thousand I see, at their head my friend, Sickingen. The gods be thanked! Germany has come to herself; even Emperor Charles is here,

> and all the princes about him. How, now, creature of Leo?

The Roman courtiers and their army flee; and Franz von Sickingen, who now comes forward, in a mighty speech of triumph once more sounds all the patriotic feelings and hopes with which Hutten's own soul was filled.

> The gates of freedom are opened, let us press on. God has unjustly destroyed the people of Sodom and Gomorrah, if he spares the people of Rome, in comparison with whose godlessness they were innocent babes. Let us at last fulfill what thus far seemed impossible. But I make the vow: if Christ will help me to do that which I have in mind, I will spare no labor, and will not give up, until the accursed courtiers, the godless Romans, find no more game in Germany.

With a last desperate exertion, the bull turns to the Emperor. Rejected by him also, the wrathful beast bursts in two, and from his belly there proceeds a vapor of poisonous vices. The dragon is dead.

The last of these three dialogues, ***The Robbers,*** is not the equal of ***The Bull Killer*** and ***The Spectators*** in concentrated power and dramatic weight. But we are compensated for this by the impressive, free and human manner in which the fundamental thought of this dialogue, the necessity of an alliance between the knighthood and the cities for common warfare, is brought out. At the beginning of the colloquy such an alliance seems far off. Hutten, the Hotspur, has got into a squabble with a merchant, a business manager of the great banking house of the Fuggers, on account of the latter's thesis that the knights were the true disturbers of peace in Germany, that they were highwaymen and robbers, and that the Emperor could not do anything better for the country than to stop their trade. Hutten is on the point of breaking the ribs of the business man, whom he contemptuously addresses as a "Peppersack," when Franz von Sickingen enters and with disinterested composure exhorts the hotheaded Hutten to moderation, and then himself undertakes the defense of the knighthood against the merchant. He does not deny that there are some knights who live from pillage and robbery, but, he thinks, they are disavowed by their own class. The nobility as a class consider it their highest duty to guard the public peace, to help the weak and to protect the innocent. But the worst robbers in Germany are not those occasional highwaymen and bushwhackers; they could easily be subdued; the worst are—"The monks," interrupts the irascible Hutten. "Wait," says Sickingen with superior calm, "I leave them to you for later treatment. First I must speak of the merchants themselves." And now there follows a discussion, resting largely on stoic principles, about the destructiveness of the greed for money, of the overcultivated city life, of luxury, of the consumption of nerve-exhausting stimulants; and popular invectives against usury, against foreign fashions, but above all against the extortion of the common people by the monopoly of the great corporations like those of the Medici and the Fuggers. "They are worse robbers than the robber-knights," says Sickingen, "but still worse are the scribes and lawyers; for they are the people who at the courts of the princes and in the councils and court-rooms of the cities, instead of the cause of the people, follow only their own private gain. They had Emperor Maximilian entirely in their power, so that nothing came of all his plans of reform. Now they begin the same intrigues with Emperor Charles. They pervert the law, they conceal truth, they deceive the people by sham trials, out of which they alone make money. A court fool is better company for a prince than such a sneaking scribbler and quibbler. And it would be better, if these doctors of law with their red caps, who make the greatest difficulties over the most insignificant trifles, and out of their mountains of books bring nothing but confusion of law, had never come into the country, and if the people, according to our ancestral traditions, were their own lawmakers and judges." The merchant listens with ever growing interest, and finally assents with full conviction to Hutten's wish that this vicious brood of law perverters be exterminated root and branch. But now Hutten cannot be restrained any longer. Together with Sickingen he falls with tempestuous fury upon the worst and most wicked of all robbers, the monks, the bishops, the cardinals, the pope and his courtiers.—Against all these robbers, all these exploiters of the common man and of the German Empire (this is the end of the dialogue) the people must make a common cause; to that pledge the merchant and the two knights give one another the hand. And Hutten closes with the solemn words of consecration: "May Christ, the Lord and Saviour confirm this covenant, and may He grant that our example find a mighty following throughout the land."

Did Hutten, apart from his incessant endeavors to unite the emperor, the princes, the knights and the cities into a great alliance for freedom, think of drawing the peasants also into this formidable union for progress? It almost seems so. For in the dialogue *The New Karsthans* which, although not written by Hutten, unquestionably reflects his thought, such plans are mentioned. But be this as it may, so much is certain: no writer of his time has looked at German national conditions from so high and broad a point of view as Hutten. None has contemplated so radical a national regeneration as he.

It is difficult to do justice to this man so prematurely snatched from life, to this restless spirit who conceived so much, and began so many things. He himself once said that it was the fate of Germany to be unhappy. If one understands by happiness above all the consciousness of success, then this was the fate of his own life; for the feeling of the goal attained was denied him. But if to be a man means to be a fighter, and if endeavor is the true measure of the greatness of character, then Hutten is one of the greatest and most human characters in German literature. How much in him seems to anticipate the great spirits of a later time! With Lessing he shares the restless striving for truth and the indomitable courage of truth. He is akin to Heinrich von Kleist in his contempt of compromise and his unconditional surrender to a cause. Something of Ernst Moritz Arndt one seems to feel in his romantic enthusiasm for German nationality and his defiance of foreign fashion. His historically unfair and yet historically justified hatred of the clergy reminds one of the excessive superciliousness of Nietzsche. His delight in cavalier-like sport, his pleasure in country life, his *Junker*-like hatred of cities, and his fervent passion for Germany's unity and greatness associate him with the greatest German *Junker* of the nineteenth century, Bismarck. Nay, one of the very most recent social tendencies, the temperance movement, finds energetic expression in his eager invectives against the German national vice of intemperance. What could this man not have accomplished, what might he not have become for Germany, if there had been more men like him, if his age had been more friendly to him, if he had succeeded in carrying public opinion.

That he by no means was a mere enthusiast or a mere destroyer, but also a man of constructive thought, our whole survey of his activity must have shown. But that with a successful carrying out of his thoughts he would also have learned moderation, is made probable by two of his last dialogues, ***The Warners.*** In one of them Luther appears, in the other Franz von Sickingen, both, in order to justify themselves to a friend for their attitude in the great concern of the times, the reformation of the church, and both do this with the greatest objectivity and restraint, although with entire decision and complete trust in their cause. Luther sees his task in leading the church back to the simplicity and inwardness of oldest Christian times; and Sickingen also refutes the accusation of his being an innovator, for him also the main question is the restitution of the true faith in place of superstition, of the religion of Christ in place of that of his Vicar at Rome.

What a view is opened by the thought of the possibility that it might have been granted to Hutten to carry through the war for this cause at the side of Luther, as he had hoped! If the aristocrat and the man of the people, the knight and the son of the miner had really understood each other, if the religious Reformation could have assimilated the ideal of humanity and the rational culture of humanism, if Hutten's thought of an alliance of all classes for the foundation of a free united Germany had been realized, what an age of national greatness and power would then have dawned for Germany! Hutten's own writings, so full of hope, stirred by such mighty thoughts, so perfect in form, even in their foreign garb so nobly popular, give us at least a foretaste of what might have been. That Hutten himself, vanquished, deserted, cast out, as a fugitive beyond the German boundaries, sank into his grave, is an impressive symbol of the tragic turn which the fate of Germany took from that moment when the Reformation shook off humanism and thereby, instead of a universally human movement came to be a question of church orthodoxy and theological zeal. But Hutten's figure stands before us transfigured by eternal youthfulness, as the earliest champion of an ideal to which after him many of the best sons of Germany have devoted themselves and which at last, in a more enlightened age, has been at least partially realized: the independence of secular life from the encroachments of clerical authority and the function of the State as the legitimate upholder of liberal culture and spiritual progress. (pp. 194-212)

Kuno Francke, "The Humanist Revolt: Ulrich Von Hutten," in his Personality in German Literature Before Luther, *Cambridge, Mass.: Harvard University Press, 1916, pp. 184-216.*

R. E. E. Harkness (essay date 1938)

[In the following excerpt from a review of Hajo Holborn's Ulrich von Hutten and the German Reformation *(1937), Harkness discusses the influence of Hutten upon the Reformation and his relationship with Erasmus and Luther.]*

Through the years not long gone by, Luther's was the only name attached to the German Reformation. Indeed he *was* the Reformation. It had its origin, motive and strength in him. It began when the doughty "little monk" nailed his theses to the cathedral door of Wittenberg and it reached its high point of majesty and heroism at Worms and in his declaration of resolute steadfastness, casting himself wholly upon the mercy and protection of the Almighty: "Here I stand, I can do no other, so help me God." True, it was understood that the people had suffered and so there were social causes for this movement. The ancient church had deceived them by its sale of indulgences; they were as sheep without a shepherd and the authorities of state, powerful and conscienceless princes, had held them in deep serfdom. Luther alone had been their champion.

Further unbiased study had changed this picture somewhat, or had given a new perspective. Luther still remained at the center but many associates were grouped about him. Their greatness, however, was the reflected light of his glory. (p. 275)

For three decades preceding the rise of Luther in 1517, many voices had been raised demanding reformation. Unable to enforce the verdicts of its own diets because of internal strife, menaced by the Turks in the east and plagued by France in the west, the empire had disintegrated. Among those many voices demanding action none was more eloquent and insistent than that of Ulrich von Hutten.

Born April 21, 1488, of noble family Hutten never forgot he was a knight. His attitude toward the problems of the times was always that of the warrior ready to take up arms in the conflict. Perhaps the very insecurity and disturbances of his own social order made him all the more belligerent. For the days were far past since "knighthood was in flower." Thus he was always more nationalistic than religious in his concern for the reformation. It was a new, free, independent Germany he sought, strong to strike forth in her own right.

His father in his impecunious station placed him in the convent of Fulda, thinking that thereby he would be assured a benefice. But the young knight fled the hated restraint and became an itinerant mendicant scholar, studying a few months at one or other of the many universities and finding a growing interest in humanism. It was in the days of Maximilian who "drew German humanism out of the schoolroom into the world arena and breathed into it something of the active joy of his own nature." It was of the joyous nature of Hutten as well.

Humanism's relentless attack upon scholasticism was to his liking and his associate authorship of the ***Letters of Obscure Men*** shows him perhaps at his best. He delighted in this mocking of Reuchlin's opponents. But here also Hutten is seen in clear contrast with his fellow writers.

Where Crotus reveals the scholar, keen and charming in satire, Hutten is heavy, bitter in his invective.

Perhaps . . . this explains his attachment to such a man as Erasmus, whom he regarded as the greatest teacher of the philosophy of life and whom he called the German Socrates. Yet he could not follow his teacher fully. The latter's ideal was the restoration of Western Christianity through the spread of a new or renewed culture. The study of the classics and early Christian authors was the way by which men were to be led to the height. A knowledge of the Church Fathers, but especially of the Gospels and the Pauline letters would restore Christianity to the intent of its founders, namely, a popular philosophy, a wisdom free from overrefined speculation, simply to tame the world, despise the bad, and learn to do good. "The Cross meant to him the victory over all human passion."

All of which might be true for the restless knight. He didn't quite know because he didn't quite understand. He knew something was wrong in this world of men—distress, insecurity, a weak, inefficient government. The papacy was the enemy of Germany, a breaker of the peace—smite it!

Eventually these men must draw apart. Could there be spiritual fellowship between them? Yet when the Reformation is well advanced Erasmus could say of the fiery warrior: "Where shall we find such a genius if anything goes wrong?"

Somewhat similar was the relationship between Hutten and the reformer Luther. When the difficulty first arose in Wittenberg it appeared nothing other than a quarrel over indulgences, and Hutten hoped that the theologians would devour one another. But after the Leipsic disputation he became a staunch supporter of Luther. The fearlessness of the monk endeared him to his heart. On June 4, 1520, he wrote Luther declaring his support. "I will stand by you whatever comes."

Yet that which bound these men together was their courage. They were not comrades either in objective or in method. Hutten, the humanist, was concerned for justice. His cause was not so much God's cause as it was a just cause. Luther was deeply religious. He was fighting God's cause. He was concerned not so much for himself as for others. Each was aware of the difference and Hutten wrote Luther: "Here is the difference between us. I look to men. You, who are already more perfect, trust everything to God." Hutten remained the same man. Luther was a changed man. Yet humanism, which never took deep root in Germany, prepared the way for the Reformation and Luther was aware of it. His *Address to the German Nobility* appropriated the national aspirations of the humanists. They needed each other—these two systems and these two men. Neither one alone could set Germany free. And that accounts for the mistakes and failures of the Reformation. There were compromises.

But who shall lay the charge of blame? Those were stirring, dangerous days of powerful forces. A new world was being created. Great men were seeking to mold it. (pp. 275-76)

R. E. E. Harkness, "The Nationalist as Reformer," in The Christian Century, *Vol. LV, No. 9, March 2, 1938, pp. 275-76.*

Lewis W. Spitz (essay date 1963)

[*In the following excerpt, Spitz provides a comprehensive analysis of Hutten's literary career, focusing on his bitter satires against the Church and his relationships with Erasmus and Luther.*]

The year 1521 was tense with crisis. All eyes were turned toward the Diet at Worms where Luther made his courageous stand in what J. A. Froude described as "perhaps the finest scene in human history." Germany was alive with excitement. Above the tumult rose a persistent, strident voice, heard often before, but soon to be heard no more—the voice of Ulrich von Hutten, German knight. He had called to Luther: "Long live liberty!" Now the die was cast. Hutten would not turn back, though church and empire conspired to crush him. That year he penned these words:

> With open eyes I've dared it
> And do not feel regret.
> Though I should fail to conquer
> True faith is with me yet.

Here indeed was a romantic figure raised on the shoulders of Uhland, Herder, Wieland, and Goethe to the stature of a national hero! Freedom was all to this tempestuous, restless, daring young man—free learning, free Fatherland. The weapons he chose for battle were sword and pen. Mutian characterized him as "sharp and vehement and a great poet, but such that he can be irritated by the slightest word." (p. 110)

The first period of Hutten's brief life span was dedicated to poetics, the second to polemics. "Behold, posterity," he penned, "the songs of Hutten the poet, whom you are rightly able to call your own." His early poems were conventional pieces on morals, good virtue, and the transient nature of life done according to the rules of the profession which he laid down in his ***De Arte Versificandi*** in 1511. He did not compose a single true love poem like Celtis. He was often an angry young man and many of his polemics poured from the depths of his choleric soul like a libation from the vial of his wrath. Such were his ***Querelae,*** blistering attacks upon his former hosts, the Lötze family of Greifswald, and the savage assaults against Duke Ulrich of Württemberg, the murderer of Hutten's unfortunate uncle. He went through the motions of gathering and editing several classic manuscripts, but he was no scholar at all and had to leave such labors to men of greater patience. He successfully resisted the attempts of his family to make a lawyer of him and returned from Italy a foe of Roman law, academic degrees, papal rule, and all enemies of the Emperor. His literary efforts, which were really better than is commonly conceded, earned for him the laurel wreath, when he was crowned in Augsburg on July 12, 1517, poet laureate of the Empire. In a letter to Pirckheimer the next year, Hutten cited the growing strength of the humanists, men like Oecolampadius, Budé, Erasmus, Lefèvre, Cop, and Ruellius, and exclaimed: "Oh century! Oh letters! It is a joy to be alive! It is not yet time to lapse into repose, Willibald. Studies thrive and minds flourish! Woe to you, barbarism! Accept the noose, look forward to exile!"

Two major elements determined Hutten's personal outlook. As a knight he belonged to a class which was rapidly losing status and utility. Politically he looked back to the great days of imperial glory and longed for their restoration. With intensified patriotism he leveled his lance against foes of the empire within and without—the princes, the Venetians, the courtesans, the Turks, and the papacy. As a humanist he was devoted to the growth of good learning. The chief foes of letters were the hypocritical priests and superstitious monks. Behind them stood the real *bête noire,* but it was only gradually that Hutten made the Pope his major target. In the ***Trias Romana*** Hutten has Ernholdus articulate what really amounted to his own program: "Truly it is a great and excellent deed to bring it about by persuading, exhorting, inciting, driving, and impelling that the fatherland come to recognize its own debasement and arm itself to win back its ancient liberty." "Even if it cannot be attained," responds Hutten in the dialogue, "there is merit in having tried."

Conditions in Germany were aggravated precisely because ecclesiastical influence and control were more effective than in France and England. For decades a meeting of the Reichstag never passed without an airing of the grievances (*gravamina*) of the German nation. As a cavalryman, Hutten believed in the attack strategy. To the explosive compound of an aggressive personality and patriotic discontent was added a bitter satirical element developed under the strong influences of Lucian, who in his own dialogues made such radical thrusts at second-century religion. Hutten's strictures ran the gamut from the moral indignation worthy of a Geiler von Kaisersberg and the cunning folkish jibes reminiscent of Sebastian Brant to the clean cuts of Italianesque Renaissance wit. His catalogue of ecclesiastical ills including the usual abuses—simony, nepotism, benefice-hunting, immorality, neglect of duties—all candidly recognized already by those conciliarists who had called for a "reformation in head and members."

In a letter to Count Hermann von Newenar, Hutten decried the low spirituality of the clergy, lacking zeal for religion, preaching the gospel with no remembrance of piety, acting proudly, crudely, immoderately, and insolently. Before making war on the Turks, Germany should first find a remedy for her internal ills. It was this kind of abuse which led the Bohemian nation away from the church, he hinted darkly. In the dialogue ***Febris II (Fever the Second)*** Hutten called for the abolition of celibacy with its unfortunate results and the reform of the numerous and wealthy clergy in the interest of sincere vocation and pure conduct. The Emperor should take the initiative in such reforms for a harder working, better educated, more ethical clergy, he wrote in words reminiscent of Wycliffe's *De dominio civili.* Above all, greater poverty was necessary. The higher clergy came in for special belaboring, those courtesans and their unsavory dealing with the Fuggers. Hutten the nobleman turns to clergy and bourgeois to cry a plague on both their houses. In ***Febris Prima (Fever the First)*** and the ***Inspicientes (Spectators,)*** breathing the spirit of Lucian, Hutten caricatured Cardinal Cajetan as a dissolute papal lackey come to cheat the Germans of their money to provide the Romans with luxuries, while pretending to be collecting for defence against the Turks. He would go home empty-handed, for the Germans would grow wise to him. Similarly, it was the financial losses involved which stirred Hutten's ire against the sale of indulgences by those pardon-merchants, not the religious principle involved.

With the exploitation and hypocrisy of the priesthood Hutten coupled the ignorance of the monks. To him the greatest monument to monkish folly was the construction of the scholastic system. In the preface of his ***Nemo [Nobody]***, addressed to Crotus Rubeanus, written under the immediate influence of Italian humanism, he decried the centuries of darkness under scholastic domination:

> The Paris theologists have judged otherwise, to their own great shame and infamy. When I reflect on it, I realize how this theology has damaged the Christian religion for three hundred years. For when the old true theology was abandoned, then religion truly declined together with learned studies and the very worst of plagues broke out, superstition, which with its darkness so obscured the true worship of God that you could not know whether many things which you observed belonged to Christ or to some new god who will reserve for himself this last age of the world. Moreover, they have the greatest accumulation of the worst books, while they neglect those ancient and rightly learned authors.

Their syllogisms illustrated the frivolity of their concerns, for example, whether St. Paul snatched up into the third heaven could see something more clearly than in his own cell. Their power was so great that Alexander VI himself declared he would prefer to make war with the most powerful king or prince than with one of the mendicant orders. Hutten objected to the way in which these preposterous disciples of Christ, who knew mercy, treated heretics. Yet they feared the Bohemians. They were ferocious where there was no work to be done, but where there was peril they withdrew and alleged that religion requires peace and quiet. "Oh customs! Oh studies!," he cried, "Oh you leaders of this age! Why do we not drive away these clouds and once again contemplate truth!" In view of his assaults on scholasticism it is all the more amusing that in the ***Epistolae Obscurorum Virorum*** Hutten and his friends vote no-confidence in Pope Leo, because as a poet he is incapable of understanding Thomas Aquinas' *Summa Contra Gentiles.*

The ill-will between the humanists and scholastics, under control for two decades, rose suddenly to the boiling point in the dramatic Reuchlin controversy. This affair, often viewed as a dress-rehearsal for the Protestant revolt, meant to the poets a battle for culture against scholastic ignorance and monkish superstition. Hutten, of course, was in the thick of it. Through Crotus Rubeanus and Eobanus Hessus, a bright young poet whom he had known since his first visit to Erfurt in 1506, Hutten had established close contact with Mutian's circle which now rushed to the defense of Reuchlin. In 1517 Hutten published a long poem entitled ***Triumphus Capnionis*** proclaiming victory over the rustic, barbarous, sophistical, ignorant, envious, obscure theologists. In the preface addressed to Maximilian he cited the advance in learning already achieved: Jerome reborn, the New Testament brought to light, many things produced from Hebrew and Greek.

But the most telling blow was the immensely popular ***Epistolae Obscurorum Virorum.*** "What prevents us from speaking the truth with laughter?" asked Pirckheimer in the words of Horace. Hutten conceded that the jokes were not half bad. In the second part, for which he was largely responsible, he refers to himself as "an arrant brute" who declared that if the preaching friars insulted him as they had Reuchlin he would lop off the nose and ears of every monk he met.

Hutten's opinion of the papacy progressively degenerated. He at first viewed the Pope as an enemy of the Emperor, but in the end as a foe of Christ himself. He expressed in a poem on Germany some hostility to Rome because of the bad effect of the popes and Italian churchmen on German morals, a modern echo of Tacitus. To Maximilian he wrote that the Emperor is the head of Rome and the head of the world and urged him to assume leadership. The Emperor is the true shepherd who will feed the sheep and drive the robbers out of Latium. But it was on Italian soil that Hutten's antipapal animus came to full bloom. His epigrams addressed to Maximilian were for the most part written there. It was precisely on account of these epigrams that Dr. Eck denounced Hutten to the Curia, and with good reason.

Hutten's attack on the papacy took two forms: general ridicule and historical argumentation. The warrior pope Julius II was his primary target. This successor to Peter, in a long line far removed, never prays for the people. He bears arms and rejoices in blood. Paul had a beard and a sword, but there the similarity ends. Julius is known for his perfidy. Unlike Christ and Peter, his work is death, his delight luxury. A merchant, seizing the whole earth by fraud, he sells the heavens, though he himself does not possess them, writes Hutten in words reflecting the views of the amusing anonymous tract *Julius Exclusus.* Julius with the Giants will drive the gods from Olympus, and when Jupiter is no longer there he will sell the stars and heaven itself. "Give us, o ye gods, another Brutus," cries Hutten, "for as long as Julius is in Rome it will perish!" At last Hutten paid him his final respects with a saucy epitaph:

> A shepherd wolf lies here concealed by this rubble.
> He used to sell bulls, but was only a bubble.

In a series of epigrams addressed to Crotus Rubeanus from the city itself, Hutten mocked the rampant venality of Rome where God himself is sold for gold. Unlike other commercial cities, Rome traffics in holy things. How can it be that this city of orgies once had a Curius, a Pompey, and Metellus, he writes in the epigram ***De Statv Romano*** in words which parallel Celtis' poem to a Roman girl?

The climax to Hutten's caustic campaign came in his ***Vadiscus sive Trias Romana*** (Roman Trinity), which was published in February 1520. In it he plays spokesman for the Germans who have always been the most pious and godfearing people. He catalogues in threesomes the ills of the nation. The bishop must buy his pallium in Rome; the priests prevent the conversion of unbelievers; the beautiful golden church is like the body with the real Church of Peter and the Apostles but its shadow. Three things are always under way in Rome, but never completed: the saving of souls, the rebuilding of churches, and the war against the Turks. Three things very few people in Rome believe in: the immortality of the soul, the communion of saints, and punishment in hell. One may kiss the hands, altars, and cheeks, but the feet only of the Pope. Three things are most lamentable: the wicked clique of Florentines ruling Rome, the flatterers who hold the Pope as God, and the Pope's assuming too much power in granting indulgences and pronouncing anathemas. The guile of the Italians and the inertia of the Germans prevent reform. In the ***Vadiscus*** Hutten even came out for the elimination of compulsory celibacy as a way to eliminate immorality, for it is better to be married than to consort with whores and handle holy things with soiled hands. "I have dared it!," concluded Hutten with a flourish.

Hutten's imperial leanings determined the nature of his historical arguments against the temporal power of the papacy. The deepest cut in his surgical operation for papal health was his new edition of Valla's ***De donatione Constantini,*** 1517. In an unctious dedication to Leo X, the "restorer of peace," he expressed the hope that this age would move from the long darkness of tyranny to the light of liberty. The pontiffs who invented the Donation were not shepherds but devoured the sheep of Christ and dragged governments and nations under the yoke. Hutten reminds Leo, the "father of studies," that Valla was befriended by his pontifical predecessors, implicitly suggesting himself as a parallel case worthy of consideration. Hutten looked to a Medici pope for progress, but with grave misgivings.

Hutten drew also on the literature of the investiture controversy which was ready-made for his purposes. In the preface (addressed to Archduke Ferdinand of Austria) to his edition of the ***De unitate ecclesiae conservanda,*** 1520, he states expressly that he was not fighting the papacy in blind hate, but with the intention of improving its picture. He wishes to make a true pontiff out of a tyrant, a father of a king, a shepherd of a robber. He concluded a letter attacking the Pontiff, Leo X, in December 1520, with the phrase, "Let us break their chains asunder and cast their yoke from us."

At last the issue was clearly joined. There was, he now believed, such an unbridgeable chasm between the teachings of the Pope and Christ as to make of him an antichrist. To prove his point he composed a dialogue between Christ and the Pope, bringing out in sixty-four exchanges the discrepancy between their teachings and practice. The contrasts are mostly matters external, however, and show little basic understanding of the dogmatic development from the Gospels to the sacramentalism of the medieval period. Christ says that his kingdom is not of this world; the Pope replies that he is the lord of the empire. Christ says that he had no where to lay his head; the Pope answers that he has Rome, Sicily, Corsica, and other lands. Christ was crowned with thorns; the Pope with gold. Christ turned the other cheek; the Pope uses force. Christ says "drink ye all of it"; the Pope objects that his priests alone should drink the sacramental wine. Christ assures us that he died for man's sins; the Pope protests that indulgences must be purchased. This latter exchange is the nearest approach in the dialogue to the central issue of the evangelical controversy. The ***German Requiem for the Burnt Bulls and Papal Laws*** contains a prayer to God that He should let these papal instruments rest in peace lest some antichrist or antichrists reawaken them in a Pythagorean manner and allow the Germans no rest. In his ***Expostulatio*** against Erasmus, Hutten offered himself body and soul to the devil if Erasmus did not perceive as well as he the chasm between the Roman and Apostolic churches. Christ is the true head of the church, not the Pope. Then, under the spell of the Reformation, Hutten pushed to its logical conclusion the historical contrast first brought to his attention by Aesticampianus, a careful student of patristics. Aesticampianus ended his days in Wittenberg.

Could such a tempestuous and critical activist, devoid of deep religious consciousness, develop a constructive philosophy of his own? There are some suggestions of positive religious reform ideas analogous to the notions of Celtis, Mutian, and Erasmus. This clearly raises the question as to whether or not these were entirely derivative, faint reflections of pale Erasmus. Baptista Egnatius of the New Academy, who learned to know both Hutten and Erasmus in Venice, called Hutten a "disciple of Erasmus." Their early contacts led to mutual adulation in the best humanist style. In 1510, in the first edition of the ***Nemo,*** Hutten showed evidence of an acquaintance with some of Erasmus' works and in the new preface to the piece (1518), he praised him as a godly restorer of early Christian teaching, the "old theology." "What could be more Christian than the labors of Erasmus?" he asked. Their first direct contact dates from the time of Hutten's second Italian journey, when on October 24, 1515, Hutten wrote asking Erasmus to commend him to his Italian friends. Thereafter for five years they maintained friendly relations, though not without tensions. Hutten, the knight, called Erasmus "the theologian," the light of Germany, Hercules, and wrote Erasmus that he showed his *Adages* to all the learned men in Rome. Erasmus, in turn, in his *Annotations to I Thessalonians* of 1516 praised Hutten as a young man of illustrious ancestry. Hutten seems to have received his appointment at Mainz as a protégé of Erasmus. It was, in fact, on a mission in 1517 for the Elector to the French court that he broadened his associations to include such leading French humanists as Budé and Lefèvre.

Hutten and Erasmus were comrades in arms in the Reuchlin affair, Erasmus confiding to Hutten that he favored Reuchlin for the sake of learning. Yet as the controversy became more violent, Erasmus increasingly withdrew, while Hutten grew all the more virulent, a sign of things to come. For, when the acid test came through Luther's final challenge, Erasmus turned back, but Hutten charged ahead. Hutten saw the difference between Erasmus and himself with a clear eye. He knew that it was a matter of issues and not merely one of personalities. He saw the estrangement in the offing and on March 6, 1518, he predicted to Erasmus that there would be a great uproar in Germany shortly and that Erasmus would chide him for his audacity rather than praise him for his fortitude. In the same letter in which he denied reading Luther's works, Erasmus complained of Germany's many importunate young men. Then frictions increased. Hutten, while recognizing Erasmus' legitimate concern for the *Respublica christiana,* accused him of destroying the ***Epistolae Obscurorum Virorum*** and opposing Luther whom he once supported. Hutten charged Erasmus with greed for glory, fear, jealousy of Luther, and other outrages. "Flee from us," he urged.

For Hutten's uncomplicated mentality issues were always clear, decisions were easy. He could not appreciate Erasmus' equivocation regarding the Reformation. In the ***Expostulatio*** he reminded Erasmus that he had himself not long before helped to resurrect piety and brought the gospel back to the light of day and now he turns away, although no pious Christian is unwilling to see the Roman church destroyed, which would be good for all Christendom. Hutten believed that the courtesans opposed Martin, not because of his teachings on free will, the sacraments, and the like, but because he had hurt their greed and exposed their rascality. He urged Erasmus not to keep silence about Christ's teachings because of the uproar and not to abandon the Word of God. Erasmus has acted against conscience and has sat down between two stools. If Hutten's expostulation was uncalled for, Erasmus' *Spongia* was unworthy. Melanchthon tried to dissociate Luther and himself from Hutten's mania in attacking learned Erasmus. Luther regretted Erasmus' rejoinder, asking, "If this is to wipe away with a sponge, I wonder what it means to malign and revile?" Erasmus replied that Luther should not have expected moderation about such a robber as Hutten and accused him of grave crimes: debauchery, prostitution, hopeless corruptions, and fatuous boastings. Hutten, Erasmus complained, was tolerant of no one, however friendly and forbearing. He was guilty of bankruptcies, of extorting money from the Carthusians, of cutting the ears off two preachers, and of robbery. He had assaulted three abbots on the public way, on account of which evil deed he was cut off by the head of his family, and had committed other crimes of which he had not even noted a word in the *Spongia.* The friendship of Hutten and Erasmus was ruined beyond repair. These two humanists were so radically different in outlook that the influence of Erasmus on Hutten was necessarily more a matter of individual impressions from specific writings rather than of the impact of his total person on the younger man.

Hutten's criticisms of abuse in the church were clearly of the same genre as the jibes of Erasmus. It is easy to point to similarities even in detail between the *Praise of Folly* and the ***Fortuna*** or ***Febris Prima*** and ***Febris II,*** the strictures against the monks, hypocrisy, repetitious prayers, and the abuses of celibacy. But when Erasmus turned to the task of constructing his *philosophia Christi,* Hutten caught only an occasional glimmer of its import. Nevertheless, at the point where Hutten ceased merely attacking his opponents and pressed for reform in terms of an ethical ideal he entered the Erasmian humanist reform movement. These reform impulses of Hutten fell into two broad catgeories: the desire for the advance of true religious culture against ignorance and barbarism, and the desire for the reform of the church in administration and morals.

Already in ***Nemo*** Hutten had outlined his attack on obscurantism. In terms paralleling Sebastian Brant's *Ship of Fools* he scored the scholastics and theologists who subverted true religion for three hundred years. He opposed pomp and circumstance, the lawyers, academic titles, and ignorant monks who tried to suppress the new philosophy. He challenged the Inquisition which interfered with developing cultures in the foreword to all free men in Germany in his ***De schismate extinguendo.*** He called for freedom of studies in his preface to the ***De unitate ecclesiae conservanda.*** Similarly, in the ***Vadiscus*** he ridiculed Leo X's suppression of a Tacitus edition with a bull forbidding its publication in other lands as an illustration of the way in which the church maintained the ignorance of the German people. On July 21, 1517, Hutten wrote Erasmus that he had seen his New Testament. Thereafter, he cited the Scriptures more often in the Latin translation of Erasmus than in the Vulgate, a move against the *textus receptus* of the medieval theologians. But Hutten did not have the patience for a constructive program so comprehensive as Erasmus laid down in his *Enchiridion.*

Hutten called for the church to return to its basic spiritual function. In a letter to Charles V, September 1520, Hutten complained because he was persecuted for opposing the fables of the Pope and fights for Christian truths. "Finally," he wrote, "where is religion, where is piety, if it is not necessary to remember what Christ has taught and we think that human traditions are to be preferred to his immortal instruction?" Toward this end in the ***Vadiscus*** he urged the convening of a council and also republished a conciliarist tract which he had discovered written by a follower of Felix V dating from the period of the Council of Basel. The election of bishops should be returned to the people. He attacked Leo for calling an appeal to a council a crime and cried out against the bulls of Pius II and Julius II, "Oh fraud! Oh violence!" He hoped that as a result of effective reform the reunion of the Bohemians, Greeks, and Russians might come about, since they would no longer be offended by the Pope.

There is only a faint trace of criticism of the sacramental system or inner substance of Catholic dogma which he left basically intact. How little he appreciated the evangelical issue involved in the matter of indulgences is evident from Doctor Reiss's argument in the ***Epistolae Obscurorum Virorum:*** "Naught can be compared with the Gospel: and whoever does well will fare well. If someone receives those indulgences a hundred times and has not lived well, he will perish and the indulgences will not help him." Here was sheer moralism opposed to crass formalism.

Hutten's closest approximation to philosophical speculation was his reflection on the problem of providence and fate. He could never escape the notion that blind fortune spun the wheel of life and gave him many bad turns, a figure going back to Boethius and the classics. In ***Nemo*** fortune posed its problems, and the theme recurs constantly in his correspondence with such friends as Pirckheimer. The idea was common enough as portrayed in Dürer's famous woodcut of Fortuna striding over the globe. Hutten may have known Petrarch's *Fortuna,* as well as the notions of Lucian and Aeneas on the influence of Fortune on court life. In his own dialogue ***Fortuna*** of 1519 Hutten fails to come through with a clear-cut solution. He uses the device as a vehicle for his personal grievances against life. On the matter of providence and fortune, Hutten comments noncommittally that religion teaches something quite different. He concludes that, since Fortune cannot be held responsible for her gifts, he should hold to Jupiter. But Fortune tells that people are themselves much more to blame. He then compares human life with a ship voyage and shifts the theme to all the world's stage and all the men and women merely players. After much torment, at the end of his dialogue Hutten turns to the Christian chapel to beseech from Christ the Redeemer his desires. The woodcut of Fortune on the title page of his ***Dialogi,*** 1520 shows the hand of God reaching from the clouds to turn the wheel of blind Fortune, with the inscription: "It is terrible for God and fate to battle." That is where Hutten left the problem—on a speculative level. As an activist the challenge that really moved him was that he should have the *virtú* with which to oppose fortune, the major concern of his Italian contemporary Machiavelli.

It is clear that Hutten had not appropriated very fully the religious ideas of Erasmus. His constructive suggestions were only faintly reminiscent of the *philosophia Christi.* He was not at all affected by the speculative ideas of Florentine spiritualized piety. For the "Pythagorians" he had only ridicule and there is no indication that he remotely understood Reuchlin's real purposes in his studies of the Cabala. But nowhere did his lack of religious depth in thought and feeling so clearly stand out as in his relation to Luther and the Reformation.

Hutten's great historical role began in earnest in 1520 when he joined Luther in his battle against the papacy. It was, in fact, for many years in vogue for historians to write of the two great reformers, Hutten and Luther. When the Wittenberg affair first came to his attention, Hutten, like Leo X, thought it was a mere monks' quarrel like that over the immaculate conception. "Devour and be devoured in turn," he chortled. But he soon discovered Luther and addressed him as "You, my dear brother." He cheered Luther on: "They tell me that you have been excommunicated. How great, o Luther, how great you are, if this is true!" He followed up this encouragement by announcing to Luther that he was ready to attack the priestly tyranny with letters and with arms. Hutten was as good as his word and the writing in defence of Luther poured from his inkwell as from a fountain. His ***Febris Prima*** and ***Inspicientes*** seared Cardinal Cajetan, Luther's interrogator and judge. In his glosses on the ***Bulla Decimi Leonis, contra errores Martini Lutheri*** Hutten began by citing the New Testament on the antichrist who sits in the temple and shows himself as if he were God. He praised Luther for preaching Christ's evangel, attacked the cupidity of the Pope, the papal arrogance of forbidding any appeal to a council. He charged the papacy with associating the church with force and terror, not with love as Christ had done. Therefore, Hutten responded with Tertullian: "When we are condemned by you, we are absolved by God."

Hutten followed this with a whole series of dialogues. The most dramatic among them was the ***Bulla*** or ***Bullicida,*** a conversation between the Bull, German liberty, Hutten, Franz, and other Germans. The bull called for aid from the canons, decrees, and excellent decretals. His ***Monitor I*** and ***Praedones*** (Robbers) are a prize example of how Hutten could appropriate the form of Luther's ideas without really understanding their meaning. In the ***Monitor*** he has Luther speak of the liberty given by Christ, the ministry of brethren as opposed to the pretensions of the Petrine succession, the primitive simplicity of the church which lacked triumphal splendors. Hutten shows that he has missed the precise center of Luther's theology when he has him say: "I truly marvel at men who place the protection of salvation in gifts, which induce the cessation of good works, when they know that faith without works is dead." Again he has Luther announce that "to give to the poor: this is the true, living, and everlasting church of Christ." In the ***Praedones*** Hutten reflected Luther's conception of the priesthood of all believers, arguing that Christ was the head of the church on earth, which had no need for a second head. But he advanced this notion as a cure for the frauds and superstition of the clergy, not as a concomitant of Luther's emphasis on personal faith which justifies.

Hutten had not been without influence on Luther himself. On February 23, 1520, Luther wrote Spalatin that in reading Hutten's edition of Valla's ***De Donatione,*** he was angered, surprised at God's patience, and was nearly convinced that the Pope was the antichrist. Now Luther repaid his debt in full. Hutten swam along with the torrent of his words. Under the impact of his popular appeal, Hutten lost his humanist inhibitions and turned to the people in their own language:

> For Latin penned I up to now,
> Which everybody did not know,
> Now cry I to the Fatherland,
> The German nation in its tongue,
> Vengeance to bring for every wrong.

His first German tract was ***A Remonstrance and a Warning against the Presumptuous, Unchristian Power of the Bishop of Rome and the Unspiritual Spiritual Estate.***

In the reform program which Hutten addressed to Frederick the Wise, he spoke like a Lutheran of his efforts in behalf of evangelical doctrine. But the tone quickly changed and he reverted to the old familiar themes of the curial greed for profit and the servile state of the Fatherland which of all nations loves liberty most. With an apocalyptic flourish he predicted the early fall of Babylon, the mother of whoredom and abomination, which has corrupted the earth with its prostitution. God will set things right, but through the hands of the princes, who would drive the antichrists from the land. Like Luther he made an ***Address to All the Estates of the German Nation.*** In December of that critical year Hutten composed in German some of his most telling lines in the ***Gesprächbüchlein;***

> The truth is born with a new chance;
> Deceit has lost appearance.
> Let all give God due praise and honor
> And heed the fearsome lies no longer.
> Yes, I say, truth which was suppressed
> Is hereby once again redressed.

The theme of Hutten's apologetic writings is always the same. In the ***Invective against Aleander,*** the ***Invective against the Luther-chewing Priests,*** the ***Exhortation to Emperor Charles V,*** and the ***Litany to the Germans,*** Hutten's thought conforms to the same pattern. The papal tyrant and his minions are trying to suppress Luther, the most faithful preacher of true evangelical doctrine and champion of German liberty, therefore the Germans should rally around the Emperor and break the tyrannous yoke. Hutten was committed emotionally to Luther's cause without ever really understanding its essence. On April 17, 1521, Hutten wrote to "the most invincible friend of the gospel" to fight strenuously for Christ, and not to give way to evils, but to go against them more daringly. Luther thanked him for the letter, and on April 20, Hutten wrote a second letter declaring his faith that Luther would remain Luther. Hutten wrote to Pirckheimer describing the unfairness of the trial at Worms, where Luther was given only one choice. But for all his enthusiasm for the reformer, Hutten remained vaguely aware of the difference between them.

In the first of the letters which Hutten wrote to Luther during the opening session of the Diet of Worms, he gave the classic expression to this difference: "We have, to be sure, different thoughts, for mine are human, but you, more perfect, already live entirely for things divine." Hutten felt that in a certain sense he never was a Lutheran at all. In the ***Expostulatio*** Hutten explained that, though he considered himself an independent, free of party affiliation, he allowed himself to be called a Lutheran on the strength of the fact that he fought the Roman tyranny. "I admire Luther's spirit," he wrote, "and his incomparable power in interpreting the secrets of Scripture, but Luther has been neither my teacher nor my comrade." It was symbolic that Hutten rode off to join Sickingen and not Luther in his war against tyranny.

Luther appreciated Hutten's writings in his behalf and his poems which were not calculated to please Babylon. But Luther could not condone Hutten's appeal to the sword as the final argument. On January 16, 1521, Luther wrote to Spalatin: "You see what Hutten wishes. But I do not desire to do battle for the gospel with violence and murder and I wrote him as much. Through the power of the Word the world is conquered, through the power of the Word the church has been created—and through the Word it will also be restored." Erasmus was all too right when in his *Spongia* he sneered that some Lutherans, like Hutten, had nothing of Luther about them except that they maligned the Roman pontiff. Hutten stood primarily for the outward freedom of the German man rather than like Luther for the inner liberty of the Christian man. His was the liberty for which Arminius fought, freedom from the new Roman imperium. Yet to his final days Hutten acclaimed Luther a hero of the Word, a prophet who gathers a following of the best men, a priest who is one with the Word he preaches. From his sickbed at Ebernburg not far from Worms, Hutten had written: "Not much depends upon two men. There are many Luthers and many Huttens here. Should either of us be destroyed, a still greater hazard confronts you. For then the avengers of innocence and punishers of injustice will make common cause with the men who are fighting for freedom! . . . Do you not see that the wind of freedom is blowing?"

Hutten remained essentially a medieval Catholic in the inner core of his religious life. These evidences of a medieval religious mentality are more than vestigial remains. They reveal that his understanding of sacerdotalism, sacramentalism, and popular medieval practices remained basically unchanged. Hutten denied vociferously that he was opposed to priests as such, but claimed that he had always been favorable to the true and honorable priesthood, citing his own poems to prove his point. He had attacked only the abuses and the evils, not the clergy itself. Hutten maintained intact the medieval-estate system in his social thought. He held to the distinction within the church of the two estates which Christ ordained, the clergy and the laity. The clergy should follow the counsels of perfection, while the laity could keep to this better way. The great offense for Hutten was the interference of the clergy in the affairs of the secular authority. He wished the return of the papacy to spiritual concerns, not its destruction. Like Cellini in his autobiography, he pictures the warring popes, Julius the bloodhound and Leo the man of force, last in a line of popes who for several hundred years had warred against the German emperors. What Hutten really desired was not the abolition of the papacy, but the elimination of false practices.

The very same conventional attitude is evident also with respect to the sacraments. His criticism of church practice at no point led him to strictures against medieval sacramentalism. There is no hint in Hutten of either rejection of the *ex opere operato* feature or an attempt to spiritualize the sacraments through a Neoplatonic mystique. Even though his own radical ***Vadiscus*** appeared at about the same time as Luther's *Babylonian Captivity,* Hutten took offence at this rejection of the traditional sacramental system.

Moreover, for all his satire in the ***Letters of Obscure Men,*** Hutten preserved intact many practices typical of medieval religiosity. In the last year of his life he still wrote in the ***Expostulatio*** of the saints, churches, and altars with all the deference of folk piety. In the German translation of the dialogues he baptized many antique references replacing pagan names with Christian substitutes. He wished Michael von Sensheim well on his pilgrimage to Jerusalem in 1515. What is more, if Crotus Rubeanus had not ridiculed the notion, he might at one point have gone on a pilgrimage to the Holy Land himself. His ***Exhortation to the German Princes to Undertake War against the Turks,*** 1518, was strictly in the medieval tradition. The princes would be called the active, brave, and pious liberators of the Christian world. Here again he had occasion to complain of Leo's interference in the affairs of state, collecting a tax for war against the Turks instead of devoting himself to prayer. But the most damaging treatise of all, reflecting the very worst side of medieval superstition and prejudice, was his blast at an unfortunate Jew with the same name as Reuchlin's opponent, Johannes Pfefferkorn. He accused this miserable fellow of a whole catalogue of crimes and scandals, including desecration of the host, murder of Christian children, maligning a saint, defacing an icon, and worse. He congratulated the Elector for having eliminated such a monster from the world.

D. F. Strauss in his day cheerfully depicted Hutten as the songbird of a new rosy dawn [in his *Ulrich von Hutten: His Life and Times*]. It was even possible for one liberal writer to describe him as a rationalist in things religious. Nothing could be further from the truth. Hutten was basically not at all philosophical. Like the Italians in the first phase of the humanist movement, he was essentially critical from the formal point of view without the philosophical substance to discuss the basic questions of metaphysics. Hutten's was the philosophy of the activist. "And lest you think I propose anything unreasonable, listen to this," he wrote: "all we who philosophize in the shade and do not in some way proceed to do things, what we know we do not really know!" His philosophic and religious capacity was very narrowly circumscribed. Nor did his program require an intellectual effort of the first magnitude. Precisely because he was merely anticlerical and not antisacerdotal, antischolastic and not antireligious, pro-Lutheran and not anti-Catholic, he could satisfy his acerbity by surface criticisms without encountering the deeper issues at stake. This lack of a third dimension, real religious and philosophical depth, spared him the agonies of a dichotomy in his spiritual personality such as plagued so many of his fellow humanists. It has always been difficult for any man in any age to combine successfully criticism and satire with constructive philosophy—witness Rabelais, Montaigne, Voltaire, or Nietzsche. For Hutten it was impossible.

Hutten was basically a romantic, imperialist, political propagandist, not a rationalistic liberal humanist. His social thinking was contained entirely with traditional concepts of the *corpus christianum,* and his basic criticisms of the church stemmed from his belief that the Curia and its minions had encroached on the Emperor's prerogatives and those of his imperial knights and had violated the ancient liberties of the empire. He conceived his historical mission to be the restoration of the right order of things. Seeing Hutten in this light resolves many perplexing problems with regard to his ambiguous relation to humanism and the Reformation.

For Hutten the belles-lettres even of the classic authors were not an end in themselves. Rather they were an instrument for the cultural and political rejuvenation of the empire. But Hutten could not expose himself to the radiating brilliance of antiquity without experiencing some inner change. This is the secret of those rays of the *philosophia Christi* shining here and there from his religious thought, analogous to the ideas of Erasmus and in part derived directly from him. But he was never altogether committed to this middle way with mind and heart.

As a militant critic Hutten was a pioneer and ally of the Reformation. If the now-dated view of the Reformation as primarily an attack on ecclesiastical abuses still prevailed, Hutten would rightly be considered one of the reformers. But Hutten did not understand the basic religious impulse of Luther's movement. To him the Reformation was but an ally in a program dictated by his own class status and personal bent. This is why he did not view with alarm the overshadowing of the renaissance of learning by the revival in religion. For him both movements served the same end. A controversial figure in a polemical age, he demonstrated to perfection that the conservative and traditionalist when he assumes the offensive may upset the world more than the self-conscious radical. (pp. 111-28)

Lewis W. Spitz, "Hutten: Militant Critic," in his The Religious Renaissance of the German Humanists, *Cambridge, Mass.: Harvard University Press, 1963, pp. 110-29.*

Hajo Holborn (essay date 1964)

[*Holborn is the author of the biography* Ulrich von Hutten and the German Reformation *(originally published in German in 1929). In the following excerpt from his introduction to an edition of* Letters of Obscure Men, *he traces the historical background and examines the content of the work. He also discusses Hutten's involvement in composing the volumes, concluding that "to him the Reuchlin affair became the first test in the struggle for German freedom."*]

The ***Letters of Obscure Men*** are the contribution of sixteenth-century German humanism to the great satires of world literature. While few of the scholarly and poetic works of the German humanists will arouse more than a historical interest among modern readers, the ***Letters of Obscure Men*** can still be enjoyed as humorous literature. Seldom has human stupidity among scholars been so wittily depicted and a degenerate philosophy so cleverly held up to ridicule. . . . (p. vii)

German humanism was predominantly a movement in the universities and schools. The humanist poets, as they were called, often migratory students and teachers, invaded the faculties of liberal arts and presented their new poetry and eloquence as the ideal education. They clearly challenged the traditional forms of teaching and study, although they were careful not to dispute the substance of the old faith. A free thinker, such as Mutianus Rufus, who cultivated a Platonic pantheism, while inviting friends and students to his home, avoided the academic halls.

It was only the Reuchlin feud that saw the schoolmen on one side and the poets on the other close ranks and begin a common battle. In 1507-8 a Jewish convert, Johannes Pfefferkorn, had denounced in four books the usurious practices of the Jews and their hatred of the Christians. He had demanded that the Hebrew books, particularly the "mendacious, fraudulent, and false" Talmud, which inculcated this spirit, should be taken from the Jews. The four books by Pfefferkorn soon appeared in Latin, at least two of them translated by the Cologne scholar, Ortvinus Gratius. In August 1509 Pfefferkorn succeeded in getting a mandate from Emperor Maximilian authorizing him to collect the Jewish books in the presence of local officials. The archbishop of Mainz objected to this procedure, whereupon the Emperor turned the matter over to the archbishop and directed him to call for the opinions of the universities of Mainz, Cologne, Erfurt, and Heidelberg, as well as of special experts. . . . (pp. vii-viii)

[One] of the experts spoke out clearly and firmly against the suppression of the Hebrew books. It was Johannes Reuchlin, a prominent lawyer in Württemberg, who had won general renown as the foremost Hebrew scholar and had written the books that made a systematic study of the Hebrew language and literature for the first time possible. Reuchlin recommended that whereas patently slanderous books should be taken away from the Jews, all others should be left in their hands. Unfortunately, Reuchlin attempted to make his statement more effective by questioning the motives of Pfefferkorn's conversion to the Christian faith. Pfefferkorn replied rudely with his *Hand Mirror,* which appeared in the spring of 1511 and was dedicated to Arnold von Tungern, one of the heads of the theological faculty in Cologne. In this pamphlet it was asserted that Reuchlin was not the true author of his own books and had been bribed by the Jews.

Highly agitated, Reuchlin, in August 1511, issued his *Eye Mirror,* in which he hotly inveighed not only against Pfefferkorn but also against the theological faculty of Cologne. The latter thereupon openly attacked Reuchlin. In September 1512 Arnold von Tungern published a pamphlet in which he pilloried a number of "articles and propositions" from the *Eye Mirror* as heretical. Moreover in the following month the theological faculty of Cologne secured an imperial order prohibiting the sale and print of the *Eye Mirror.* Shortly thereafter Pfefferkorn issued still another highly venomous pamphlet against the Jews and Reuchlin, entitled the *Brand Mirror.* But Reuchlin answered with his equally slanderous *Defense,* presented to the Emperor. . . . (pp. viii-ix)

Incensed, the Cologne theologians used their powerful influence to have Reuchlin's *Defense* suppressed by imperial mandate. In addition they requested their own theological faculty and the faculties of Louvain, Mainz, and Erfurt to pass judgment on the *Eye Mirror.* All four faculties condemned the work, although Erfurt at least pleaded the author's good intentions. Jakob von Hochstraten boldly moved to defeat Reuchlin by citing him before his court of inquisition in Mainz, where the Dominican intended to act both as prosecutor and judge. Thanks to the intervention of the archbishop of Mainz, who declared the proceedings of the court improper, Reuchlin was allowed to appeal to Pope Leo X. The Roman curia then commissioned the bishop of Speyer to adjudicate the case. The young bishop, Count Palatine George, after lengthy argument, passed judgment wholly favorable to Reuchlin. On March 29, 1514 he pronounced all accusations directed against the *Eye Mirror,* on account of heresy, disrespect of the Church and its doctrine or illicit favoritism toward the Jews, undeserved, unjust, and untruthful. He imposed "eternal silence" on Hochstraten and his followers and charged him with the cost of the Mainz and Speyer trials. . . . (pp. ix-x)

At the time of the Speyer judgment Reuchlin published a collection of letters written by prominent humanists in support of his scholarship. He had called the volume *Epistolae Clarorum Virorum.* About one-and-a-half years later a seemingly similar collection, containing forty-one letters addressed to Ortvinus Gratius, was published under the title ***Epistolae Obscurorum Virorum.*** This edition of October 1515 was followed a year later by a new edition that contained an appendix of seven additional letters. In the spring of 1517 a further augmented edition appeared, in which a second section of sixty-two letters had been added. All letters were fictitious, while their writers and publishers remained anonymous.

The documentary evidence strengthened by literary criteria leaves no doubt that the idea of lampooning the Cologne theologians originated with Crotus Rubeanus and Ulrich von Hutten. . . . (p. xi)

In 1509 Crotus Rubeanus went to Fulda as principal of the monastery's school and stayed there till the summer of 1516. In 1512 he was for a while in Cologne, where incidentally he met Pfefferkorn. The wish to help Reuchlin by the public disparagement of his enemies was expressed by Crotus Rubeanus as early as January 1514. Probably the conception of the ***Letters of Obscure Men*** came to him almost immediately after the appearance of Reuchlin's *Letters of Distinguished Men* in March 1514, and he must have started work soon thereafter. Whether his friend Ulrich von Hutten was from the outset a partner we do not know, but he undoubtedly approved the plan and promised cooperation.

Ulrich von Hutten, scion of a family of imperial knights, who had chosen the career of a "poet," had left Erfurt as early as 1506 and led the life of an itinerant scholar with all the insecurities and adversities it entailed. In 1513 Hutten gained a position at the court of the Elector and Archbishop Albert of Mainz. Since his new lord and his own relatives wanted him to finish his law studies, Hutten spent the period from the end of 1515 to the summer of 1517 in Italy. But his law study did not keep him from humanistic pursuits, particularly his involvement in the Reuchlin feud. He was able to show Erasmus of Rotterdam, whom he met in the summer of 1515, some of the pieces of the first part of the ***Letters of Obscure Men,*** among them his own contribution, the first letter that opened the collection. In all likelihood he wrote some more letters before he received rather belatedly, in August 1516, a copy of the first edition of the ***Letters of Obscure Men.*** The edition with the appendix of seven new letters was already distributed in early October 1516, and it is improbable that Hutten wrote all seven letters in such a brief time.

The appendix shows a shift in the tone of the letters. Crotus in his letters had attempted to draw satirical pictures of schoolmen and monks and make merry with their moral frailty, their self-deceit, and their intellectual ineptitude. Though not without biting sarcasm, Crotus's letters were intended as literary badinage, and the author himself so familiar with this world seems to smile at least at some of the characters on the stage. The writer of the appendix, in contrast, mixes polemics with satire and relates the academic controversy to the acute political problems of the day. He presents letters supposedly written by Jakob von Hochstraten and Arnold von Tungern instead merely by unknown people. He draws in Erasmus as a supporter of the humanistic cause. And in the second part of the ***Letters of Obscure Men*** this belligerency has been further enhanced.

Ulrich von Hutten, the knight among the German humanists, lived in a political arena. His national pride made him judge the conflict between scholasticism and humanism as a struggle for the future greatness of Germany. For half a year he followed with burning interest the activities of Hochstraten in Rome, and this prompted him to write the letters, or at least most of the letters, which were to form the second part of the ***Obscure Men.*** This humanist in armor did not merely wish to rise in laughter above his literary adversaries, as Crotus Rubeanus did, but wanted to smash the public enemies.

Six letters of the second part—11, 13, 17, 29, 42, 61, 62—do not clearly show the imprint of Hutten's mind. Some of them may be contributions of a German humanist who, together with Hutten, attended the university of Bologna, while the two last letters were probably added by a friend of Crotus and Hutten, Hermann von dem Busche, who looked after the publication of the second part of the ***Letters of Obscure Men*** and managed to do so right in Cologne.

Nobody ought to look in the ***Letters*** for a truthful likeness of the persons portrayed. The assertions of an immoral conduct of Arnold von Tungern and Ortvinus Gratius, for example, are outright slanders. But it is true that the German clergy at the beginning of the sixteenth century had fallen rather low, and although men of devotion and unimpeachable character were found in its ranks, it had lost the leadership of the people. In an atmosphere of popular criticism of the religious, moral, and intellectual state of the church the ***Letters of Obscure Men,*** which were widely read in spite of their immediate ban by the Church, intensified the clamor for a reform of the Church. In this respect they belong to the events which were instrumental in preparing the ground if not for the Lutheran reformation at least for the popular response to Luther's revolt against the politico-ecclesiastical order. However, it needed a new religious faith to shake the foundations of the medieval Church.

Luther called the author of the ***Letters,*** who was unknown to him, a "clown." Erasmus, though greatly amused by some early samples of the ***Letters,*** was unpleasantly surprised by the licentiousness of the whole book. Reuchlin, far from being happy about the ***Letters*** written to support him, seems to have been fearful that they were rather harmful to his cause. Crotus Rubeanus, originally a follower of Luther, ultimately made his peace with the old Church. Hutten, however, saw in Luther the liberator of the Germans not only from scholasticism but also from the yoke that Rome had imposed on Germany. To him the Reuchlin affair became the first test in the struggle for German freedom. (pp. xi-xiv)

Hajo Holborn, in an introduction to On the Eve of the Reformation: "Letters of Obscure Men," *by Ulrich Von Hutten, edited and translated by Francis Griffin Stokes, Harper Torchbooks, 1964, pp. vii-xiv.*

Thomas W. Best (essay date 1969)

[*In the excerpt below, Best analyzes the use of caricature in several of Hutten's poems and dialogues.*]

[We] are now to give some attention to [Hutten's] principal type of satire, caricature. The material that we will examine in this section is divided into two groups. The first and larger is caricature of others; the second, of the author himself.

Taking the first group, let us consider two examples of Hutten's epigrams caricaturing the nations and people involved in the wars in Italy during his first sojourn there, 1512-1513. In one of these he ridicules, though not without qualification, his own homeland for the national vice of overindulgence in alcohol, while also taking France and Venice to task for failings which are exaggerated to the point of being, along with the German fondness for wine, identifying characteristics:

> Venetians, French, and Germans covet Latium;
> Deceitful one, one proud, one steeped in wine—
> All odious. "Apollo, grant the lightest yoke,"
> Prays Italy, and Phoebus says, "The French
> Are always proud; Venetians, always full of guile;
> The Germans, though, not always drunk—choose one!"

In a number of these epigrams the caricature is more obvious, insofar as France is portrayed as a cock (*gallus*) and Venice, as a toad in the manner of ***Marcus,*** but in any case the satire is rather crude and tends to justify the common opinion on Hutten's sense of humor. More amusing, perhaps, is this light travesty of the Venetian commander Bartolomeo d'Alviano:

> If good the fight, you swear; if not so good, you swear.
> At rest you do the same, Bartholomew.
> In victory you swear; you swear when slipping up.
> In camp you swear, at market, and at court.
> You swear when you're in service, swear when banqueting;
> You swear shipwrecked upon the open sea.
> In arms you swear; you swear togated and at peace.
> You swear with jokes as well as earnest things.
> By day you swear, and night brings shadows while you swear,
> As Cynthia is borne by dusky steeds.
> Since everywhere you swear, by swearing tell me this:
> What don't you do, Bartholomew, by swearing?

Here we find Hutten surprisingly playful. If he wrote this burlesque in anger, there is at any rate no viciousness apparent. In it we have a piece of satire less typical of him than the longer caricatures on the Venetians, ***Marcus*** and ***De piscatura Venetorum.***

The title ***Marcus,*** while taken from the patron saint of Venice, is in Hutten's lampoon the name given to a megalomaniacal toad that is evidently the embodiment of Venetian spirit. It emerges from the Adriatic swollen with proud ambition and pulls on a lion's pelt. After summoning the people of the region, the toad proclaims that the Fate of Rome ("Sors Romana") has appeared to it, declaring that the Empire of the Caesars will be transferred to its power. Therewith the Venetians crown the toad King Marcus and embark on wars of conquest. All the world defers to them, except Germany. When Marcus attempts to reach the heavens, Jupiter dispatches the German eagle to humble the upstart. Such is this modest heroicomic beast epic. Its full title, it might be added, reveals an ironic touch: ***Marcus heroicum.*** Böcking notes in regard to the ***De piscatura Venetorum heroicum*** that Hutten was being satiric in calling these works "heroics" [*Opera quae reperiri potuerunt omnia*]. They definitely are written in heroic verse, yet we may assume that the author was artful enough to want his form, and consequently his title, to add a touch of the ludicrous. If he had not overworked his ***Marcus*** idea in the epigrams, we might enjoy its humor more.

The ***De piscatura Venetorum*** is similar to ***Marcus*** in subject matter but inferior as satire. Here the Venetians are caricatured as poor fishermen, who, joined by the scum of the earth, gradually grow in wealth until they have the power to conquer. Eventually the German eagle becomes impatient with their usurpation and reduces them to their original abject state. The work is hardly amusing. It is, in fact, to some extent similar to part of Hutten's ***Ad Caesarem Maximilianum ut bellum in Venetos coeptum prosequatur exhortatorium.*** As the title indicates, it was not written as satire but as an oratorical effort to urge the fickle emperor into further war. The two works are rather close in their treatment of the rise of the Venetians, as a comparison of the first 58 lines of the ***Piscatura*** with lines 77-201 *passim* from the ***Exhortatorium*** would show.

No superior to the ***Piscatura*** as satire but rather even more virulent is the ***Triumphus Capnionis,*** which fairly foams with rabid hatred, while we the onlookers gape more amazed than amused at the spectacle. It is the most blatant instance of satire reduced to ire in all of Hutten's works and justifies like nothing else the charge of grimness and austerity. (pp. 44-7)

As for caricature in the work, we find that it gives way to a procession of horrors, chief of which is the atrocity committed on the apostate Jew Pfefferkorn, who caused all of Reuchlin's trouble. He is maimed with loving detail and used as a bloody broom on the streets of Pforzheim, the scene of the liberals' triumph (Gerbel's and Reuchlin's home town), dragged on a hook, while thousands cheer the ebbing of his life in agony. Even Böcking, Hutten's staunchest admirer, cries out in protest at this outrage: "I wonder how such repulsive and odious things could please anyone but a hangman and how the poet failed to see that Pfefferkorn would win favor with humane readers because of the boundless cruelty."

The piece does have light, even happy, passages—those expressing joy at Reuchlin's accomplishments and his success over his enemies (actually never quite realized)—but they are not humorous. In the treatment of the theologians who comprise part of the procession there is some sarcasm, as,

> They're all convinced that they're the only ones who know
> What's true, what's false, what isn't right.
> They're more informed
> Than Phoebus's tripod, Delos, and Dodona's birds.
> If hornèd Hammon spoke to broiling Africans
> In Libyan sands, his words were not so true . . .

and these theologians are caricatured by means of their gods and weapons, carried on display.

Caricature becomes overdrawn grotesquerie with at least two more of the principal figures, though. Hochstraten, the Cologne inquisitor, is made a fiery demon obsessed with his own element:

> . . . he'll call for flames, shout "To the fire!"
> If something's judged correct, "The fire!" if wrong, "The fire!"
> If what you do is right, "The fire!" if not, "The fire!"
> He's fiery head to foot; he eats and swallows fire.
> His lung is fiery; through his throat he breathes out flames.
> His maw and liver glow with fire; he burns all things.
> The words he speaks are flames, and flames are what he writes.
> He always utters "Fire," his first and final word.
> His nose is fiery; fiery are his eyes; his heart
> Is made of charcoal. Scarcely he refrains in chains
> From shouting "Fire!" He wants this triumph, too, to burn, etc.

Ortvinus Gratius becomes a wretched poetaster with hellish, bewitching orbs: "Come, lictor, bind his eyes, lest all be hypnotized." What a contrast to ***Phalarismus,*** where, as we shall see, a monster is made laughable! Here some obscurantists are only made monstrous. Others are merely berated: Arnold von Tungern is tongue-lashed for inordinate ambition, while Bertram von Naumburg is called a glutton, Bartholomäus Zehender, a viper, and Peter Meyer, a vain, ignorant hypocrite.

To pass now from the ***Triumphus*** and Hutten's caricature in verse to that in his dialogues, we discover in ***Aula*** another example of attack more through denunciation and bizarrerie than clever burlesque. A strange composition, it reads like an expression of heartfelt animosity but was evidently composed as a rhetorical exercise, since Hutten repeatedly assures us that he wrote it merely as a joke. Though he complained about being at court, he admired Archbishop Albrecht and cannot have been as miserable as the dialogue implies.

Otto Flake calls the ***Aula*** a "Hofsatire," but its vituperative tone is rarely raised to the level of humor. What actual satire it contains, moreover, is, apart from some sarcasm, caricature that has become bitter and contemptuous. Describing the kind of person who is successful at court, Misaulus ("Hater-of-Court") says in part:

> Furthermore, princes are most foolish about choosing their attendants. Courtiers are selected not for their virtues but for their size—for broad shoulders, long legs, and high neck. It helps to have a terrifying beard or hair treated with the curling iron and to swagger on entering the court, throwing one's arms and legs about as though demanding those Virgilian boxing-gloves for a match with Entellus. Courtiers should also wear varicolored clothes decorated all over, gaudier than a cock with thirty hens, even though such Thrasos aren't up to satisfying one woman's desire.

Hyper-naturalistic descriptions of the filthiness at court reach the exaggerated proportions of caricature but nauseate rather than titillate. . . . (pp. 50-4)

Since Hutten calls ***Aula*** a joke, he may have intended for this Grobianism and crassness to be read as caricature; and since Erasmus's friend Johann Froben refers to the work as "a most charming dialogue," Hutten's contemporaries may in fact have been amused by this hyperbolic coarseness, however much his modern readers turn away with loathing. At the same time, it was perhaps only a negative reaction that Hutten wanted to elicit at all. We cannot definitely say that Misaulus's censorious speech is an instance of the author's humor. Here, certainly, as in the whole of ***Aula,*** anger is the moving force, even though in the employ of rhetoric.

In the dialogue ***Bulla*** Hutten chooses a representative of the Church as an object of his wrath. Whereas in ***Inspicientes*** we are to find a papal legate caricatured, here the victim is a haughty papal bull, a bull which is . . . also a bubble and which ends by bursting after Hutten beats her, as she has belabored Liberty. Such lowbrow fisticuffs, the approach of an army of *Curtisanen* who are quickly routed by the arrival of Sickingen and the emperor with an escort, plus the explosion of Bulla make the dialogue action-packed but do not improve the caricature. At one point, however, the author does lift his satire to a more intelligent level. From the standpoint of humor the climax of the work comes when Bulla unwittingly burlesques the Church's trade in religious liberties by proclaiming exaggerated rewards for anyone who comes to her aid. Her appeal reads partly in this manner:

> Is anyone willing to protect Leo's daughter, oh pious folk, oh Christians, and slay this wretch [Hutten] with impunity? You'll get as your reward from Leo X five-thousand ducats paid in full by the Camera and a sinecure Benefice amounting to three-hundred gulden annually. In addition you'll get complete remission of all sins, and indulgences for two-thousand years, plus fifty-six carenes, and will be a Protonotary with the power to legitimatize bastards and create Counts Palatine. Also you can mortally sin once every day, be free from confession for the next seven years, and thereafter need confess but once every seven years. I take that back. You'll only have to confess once as long as you live, except on the point of death. If you're not interested in benefices, you can marry your step-daughter, grand-daughter, or cousin, and if you make an oath, regardless of what it is, you don't have to

> keep it. If you make a deal, you can renege whenever you want. Whoever's been excommunicated, whether by law, canon, or individual decree, for whatever reason, because of whatever deed however heinous, whoever has committed incest or adultery, has raped virgins or matrons, whoever has perjured himself, murdered, or apostatized—repeatedly, even—whoever has killed a priest, whoever has transgressed against all law human and divine, be absolved and innocent. Whoever has taken sacred objects or plundered temples can enjoy the spoils forever and won't be forced to return them. Hear ye, wherever you are, you haters of God and you who're devoid of humanity, for a small job here you can cleanse yourselves of the filthiest sins—just by killing this fellow, as anyone can do with impunity etc.

This one passage contrasts starkly with the general want of sophistication in what Paul Kalkoff calls "jener ergötzliche Ringkampf."

With these dialogues ***Aula*** and ***Bulla,*** along with the ***Triumphus*** and the caricatures of the Venetians, we have surveyed Hutten's poorer productions in the genre. ***Phalarismus,*** by contrast, shows that he could be a master of ridicule through exaggeration. For a proper appreciation of this work it is necessary to have in mind the historical facts on which it is based. As in all good caricature, there is enough verisimilitude here to convince us that the satire is justified, with enough distortion to make the subject of it risible. In this work we find Hutten's most successful balance of fact with fiction.

Covetous of his young *Stallmeister*'s wife, Ulrich, duke of Württemberg, murdered her unsuspecting husband in May 1515. The victim, Hutten's cousin Hans, had served Ulrich well. His father Ludwig, furthermore, had loaned the duke 10,000 gulden interest-free (which had not been repaid) and had sent troops to help quell a peasant revolt. The murder was Ulrich's requital for all the service of Ludwig and his son. As though Hans had died in disgrace, the duke put a noose around the neck of the corpse. Adding further insult to injury, he refused to let his victim's family have the body. Hans's wife stayed on at court, while the duke's wife Sabine, Emperor Maximilian's niece, fled to her brothers in Bavaria. Ulrich agreed to the mildly punitive stipulations of the Treaty of Augsburg of October 1516 but soon afterwards broke his word. Such are the elements of this sordid tale important for ***Phalarismus.***

The situation in the dialogue is this: The duke, having been approached by the ancient tyrant Phalaris in a dream, is led to Hades by Mercury, in order to converse with the Sicilian and learn some fine points of fiendishness. The work opens at the edge of Acheron, where Charon is about to ferry across the messenger god and his charge, called simply "Tyrannus." Mercury explains how Phalaris is concerned that Germany finally get a tyrant like other nations. Charon is amazed: "In Germany a tyrant?" He orders his fare to grab an oar, provoking haughty indignation. When Charon repeats the order, Tyrannus snarls, "You would never say that in Germany, and how I wish you would!" Charon threatens to smash him over the head with a pole if he refuses to cooperate. Because he is not an airy shade, Tyrannus has to pay more for the trip. "He won't mind," says Mercury. "He's a lavish squanderer." Having passed over the river and found the abode of Phalaris, Mercury leaves Tyrannus in the arms of his proud preceptor, to return for him later.

Tyrannus relates the incidents of Hans von Hutten's death, and Phalaris replies that he never thought of doing anything so beastly himself. He killed only suspected enemies. "In this I have to yield to you," he says, "a veteran tyrant to a novice." Tyrannus adds that because the victim had no mother to mourn for him, he (Tyrannus) was afraid that a full measure of satisfaction would be denied him. "But the father's mourning was tremendous," he exclaims. He goes on to mention further events connected with the murder, such as his refusal to let Hans's family give the corpse a proper burial and the Treaty of Augsburg, which he says he is flaunting. "Splendid!" declares the tutor. "A tyrant must be perfidious."

The conversation shifts to Tyrannus's wife. "I hated her passionately. I don't know why. She was lovely and charming, as well as highborn, and my family had no greater asset. Still, I despised her," he confesses. "It's common for tyrants to want, fear, and hate much without knowing why," Phalaris sagely notes. "So I decided to murder her as soon as I finished some other business," continues Tyrannus. "She got away, though." Phalaris observes that his pupil would thus be a ravenous wolf. "As you say," replies Tyrannus.

After the latter relates how he has suborned a number of knights, including Franks ("everything's for sale in Germany now"), has put them under his henchmen, and plans to make war, he asks Phalaris to give him some pointers on how to continue. The master suggests a number of exquisite tortures, at mention of which Tyrannus becomes enraptured. "Especially," warns Phalaris, "don't believe in any gods, hold tyranny to be the greatest good, and cultivate cruelty." "That's in my blood," Tyrannus responds. "For that I don't need a teacher." At the close of the conversation Phalaris admonishes Tyrannus to be more prudent in the future in disposing of paramours' husbands: "You botched the job on that Frank, you know," and the apprentice replies, "Yes, I was carried away. Voluptuousness got the best of me. . . . "

After being introduced to the other tyrants and told to brand the cheek of Hans von Hutten's father-in-law for prostituting his daughter, Ulrich is shown to his uncle, who, it is explained, has wayward ways of entertaining himself. Mercury returns, and the dialogue ends.

Hutten stops at nothing in this vicious lampoon—nothing, that is, short of outright invective. In happy contrast to the ***Triumphus, Phalarismus*** is devastating without being denunciatory. Neither the author nor any of his characters attacks the duke. Ulrich, instead, is made to demolish himself. Needless to say, the best caricature is always of this kind. In ***Phalarismus*** Hutten's artistry, moreover, fails him no more than his wit. Well constructed, and with the usual lively and fluent dialogue, this work deserves to be recognized as a masterful piece of satire, despite the less favorable view expressed by several earlier critics.

Almost as effective as the caricature of Ulrich is that of Cajetan in ***Inspicientes.*** In the last eight pages of the work he appears as an arrogant little tyrant, shouting up at Sol that he ordered sunshine for the duration of his stay in the frigid North, and that for ten days he has had no ray of warmth. When Sol remarks that he was not aware of needing to obey the whims of mere mortals, Cajetan informs the god that as legate he has all the power of the pope to bind or loose on earth or in heaven. Sol replies that he has never believed papal claims. For that Cajetan threatens to send him straight to the devil unless he begs for forgiveness and does penance. This means, he explains, that Sol would have to fast several days, do some kind of labor, make a pilgrimage, give alms, or even be flogged. Sol remarks that the fellow must be insane. For that blasphemy he is excommunicated, *de facto.*

Cajetan renews his order for sunshine, and this time Sol says that he would have complied, but he thought it better not to shed any light on the shady dealings of the legate. Cajetan sees the wisdom of this policy and orders Sol to keep Germany in the dark. Furthermore, he wants it fogged up so that pestilence will vacate some prebends and bring more money into the papal coffers. After mutual reviling Sol rides away with Phaethon.

By treating a god in such a highhanded manner Cajetan becomes an absurd buffoon. While we laugh, however, we are bothered by one small point. We know that in reality the cardinal was not so overweening as to justify Hutten's burlesque. Caricature, as has been observed in the case of ***Phalarismus,*** should have verisimilitude. Basically it should be true to life; otherwise it is not appropriate to the subject. With the duke of Württemberg Hutten's caricature is highly pertinent, and enough fact is included to remind us that Ulrich was indeed an unprincipled reprobate. We laugh with satisfaction to see his depravity exaggerated to the point of absurdity. With Cajetan, on the other hand, we feel that Hutten is being unfair. We should perhaps see in this caricature, as in earlier description of the legate in ***Inspicientes,*** not the man himself, however, but the attitude of the institution which he represented. It may not have been that individual whom Hutten despised so much as the Church in general, for which Cajetan stood and for which he served as a scapegoat.

Before moving to our second group of Hutten's caricatures—those of himself—we might do well to take stock quickly of what we have found in this first assortment. While all satire is combative to some extent, part of what we have seen so far in this section tends to become impatient with the rapier of ridicule and to abandon it for the bludgeon of billingsgate. The epigrams included are rather light satire, to be sure. Heavier and more spiteful are ***Marcus*** and, especially, ***De piscatura Venetorum.*** As for ***Phalarismus*** and the caricature of Cajetan, while they are successfully comic, they are certainly vengeful. The ***Triumphus, Aula,*** and ***Bulla*** fully support the negative implications of the critical comments cited in the Introduction. When we examine Hutten's caricature of himself, however, we find again that those remarks become less than adequate. With this expression of his humor we re-enter a more jovial atmosphere. Anger and vindictiveness are again gone. The vicious tiger is once more a playful kitten.

In his biography of Konrad Celtis [*Conrad Celtis: The German Arch-Humanist*], Lewis Spitz writes, "Most of the humanists lacked real humor. They mocked a great many things human and divine. They seldom laughed at themselves." Spitz does not say whether Hutten should be included in this group, but if the ability to laugh at one's self is the mark of "real humor," then Hutten possessed it. He seems to have been well aware of his own potential as a comic figure, and he uses himself for a laugh in a surprising number of instances, a few of which we have already seen. To mention two or three more before we consider the caricatures in ***Fortuna*** and ***Febris II,*** Hutten makes himself comical in the dialogue ***Praedones*** with his hot-footed impatience to have the Romanists reprehended. When Sickingen observes that there are four classes of robbers in Germany, Hutten leaps into the conversation with his exclamation, "Of which, host, the first and most pernicious is that of the Priests." When Sickingen has begun denouncing the second class of robbers, the merchants, Hutten protests, "You're not leaving anything, host, to say afterwards against my *Curtisanen!*" In the dialogue ***Monitor II*** he has himself characterized as a *persona non grata:* Monitor remarks to Sickingen, " . . . they say you're one of Luther's faction and are fostering that Hutten at home, who's going to be the cause some day of the greatest evils." Otto Harnack may be right [in *Im Morgenrot der Reformation,* ed. Julius von Pflugk-Harrtung] in suspecting that Hutten is meant in ***Phalarismus*** when, in reference to the torture by which a roasted man is given water to sprinkle on himself, only to aggravate his pain, Tyrannus says, "That's certainly exquisite, and I'll remember it. I've got somebody that punishment would suit." (pp. 56-65)

Throughout the dialogue ***Fortuna*** he casts himself in the role of a veritable fool. This work, being one of Hutten's most enjoyable, has provoked considerable comment, but little if any attention has been given to the fact that in it the author makes great sport of himself. Critics have been more interested in Hutten as a philosopher here than as a good-natured comedian who does not shrink from displaying himself on a pillory. (pp. 65-6)

[***Fortuna***] opens *in medias res.* Hutten has come to the goddess to beg for special treatment. He wants first of all a comfortable salary—something which the rich can spare. Fortuna explains that the rich need all that they can get and have nothing left over for anyone else. Hutten wants, though, just enough for a life of leisure. This, he explains, consists of wife, home, gardens, villas with fish ponds, hunting dogs, and a few horses, so that one can go out occasionally; then servants, custodians, livestock, and at home, besides furniture, a portico, a library, dining rooms, sweating rooms, and baths; for the lady of the house clothes and jewelry. Finally, enough to provide for the children abundantly. All of this is to be used with splendor but not extravagantly. Such would be modest comfort, he thinks. Fortuna explains that the Fuggers are clamoring for a great deal more, and that if she were to start heeding demands for special favors, they would come first.

The conversation then turns to Fortuna herself, who says that she is blind because she used to reward the good but that they were being corrupted by her kindness. Jove, in taking the simplest corrective measures, put out her eyes. She goes on to say that Hutten should not look to the gods for favors but should strive on his own to build the life that he wants. As far as Jove is concerned, the only prayer worth praying is for a sound mind in a sound body.

After the discussion of Providence Fortuna instructs Hutten in the virtue of hard work. She also advises him to stay poor, since riches would distract him from study and would greatly increase his cares. Has he ever seen anyone with great wealth live in tranquillity, she asks. "Priests," says Hutten, whereupon Fortuna explains that Jove punishes them with gout, fevers, rheumatism, dissension, envy, and concubines. "And you want wealth," she adds, "the clear path to that kind of life. . . . " Hutten repeats that he wants only enough to live comfortably.

At his request the goddess dispenses some vicissitudes from her cornucopia. Charles becomes emperor, at which news the papal legate nearly hangs himself. Eager to find a wife, Hutten peeps into the horn, espying the girl of his dreams. She is scintillating with charms and has a tremendous dowry. What is more, she smiles at him. "At you, pretty as you are?" Fortuna asks sarcastically. "She's not the kind to care for looks," says Hutten. "She's admiring something else." Fortuna bids him stand back, gives the lass a toss from the wheel, and—oh, horrors! She lands in the lap of a pompous fop. What is even worse, the crops of the Huttens have been destroyed concomitantly. On the Steckelberg—the Huttens' fortress—fare will be scanty.

At this double calamity our hero becomes exasperated and loses all hope of succeeding with Fortuna. In the nearest chapel he will beg Christ for a sound mind in a sound body. "So, you've come to your senses at last," the goddess observes in her superior fashion. "To my great loss," moans Hutten, showing his disappointment. But Fortuna, far from being sympathetic, mocks him: "What are you waiting for? Is there another pretty girl smiling at you from my horn?" With her raillery ringing in his ears, Hutten departs in disgust.

That the theme of this dialogue is taken principally from [*The Tenth Satire* of] Juvenal seems very likely. Hutten comes to Fortuna with foolish requests, and she warns him away from them, recommending that satirist's simple prayer and hard work. Throughout the dialogue she has the part of Juvenal's wisdom and Hutten, that of the folly which Juvenal derides.

Hutten's intention of making himself a laughing-stock becomes further evident from the fact that he asks only for enough to live on in quiet comfort, which he then explains to be something far exceeding the bounds of modest retirement. He asks for an income of a thousand gulden per year, and he is ecstatic to discover that the girl in the cornucopia is wealthy. . . . Fortuna's scorn of both his looks and his disappointment shows also that he was not above letting himself be made the butt of a joke.

While ***Fortuna*** is a satire on the author, he is not the only object of ridicule in it. There are some slurs on representatives of the Church, including the pope, and the Fuggers are not spared, either; yet sharp satire and invective constitute but a relatively small part of this work.

In ***Febris secunda*** the reverse is true. We have already seen that Hutten makes use of irony and open censure here for one of his more extended sallies against the clergy. The caricature of himself dwindles proportionately, though it derives again in part from his desire for a wife (who Fever, like Fortuna, says would distract the scholar from his studies). As a matter of fact, Fever candidly states that Hutten is salacious. His desire keeps him from being prudent. She, however, can solve his problem: "I extinguish lust." A little later she adds, after he has asked whether he should let her in and be sick for six months, as he was once from her visit: "You should give me twelve, a whole year, so that I might make you completely wise by taking away this concupiscence, which has hampered serious learning on your part for so long." Fever tells Hutten that she will make him pale and scholarly looking. He declines. "You used to want to be that way, so your teachers would call you studious; now you want to look healthy, so you won't displease the ladies," she says. "But you're mistaken. . . . " She notes that he has put on a little excess weight. She can take care of that problem, too, as well as give him a serious mien. Since he laughs and jokes so much, someone might suspect him of being fatuous.

In other words, Hutten portrays himself again as something of a fool, this time a silly, fat, libidinous one. He does not deny the faults which Fever indicates. He protests merely that he does not want her "cure." Especially significant for us is the point that he laughed and joked a great deal. Through Fever, thus, Hutten pleads his own defense against charges of austerity. His self-caricature in ***Fortuna*** and in ***Febris II*** confirm the capacity for joviality. . . .

We have seen that he was a versatile, as well as erratic, caricaturist, producing quantities of crude burlesque but also some that is quite effective, and creating on occasion, especially where he himself is the subject, light, pleasant caricature along with the bitter travesties. As his irony is varied, so is his caricature, showing great range in tone and change in quality. Judging merely by the latter, we perceive that his humor is not so stereotyped as earlier critics would lead us to believe in their few brief remarks. (pp. 68-73)

Thomas W. Best, in his The Humanist Ulrich Von Hutten: A Reappraisal of His Humor, *The University of North Carolina Press, 1969, 104 p.*

Sam Wheelis (essay date 1977)

[*In the following excerpt, Wheelis surveys the literary canon of Hutten, focusing upon his patriotic and humanistic writings while placing them within the context of pre-Reformation German history.*]

The best introduction to Ulrich von Hutten is found in his great German poem ***Ein neu Lied (A New Song)***, his most accessible and familiar work to students of German literature. Written in 1521, at the outset of the feud Hutten declared on the clerical orders in Germany, the poem is both a self-justification and a challenge to his enemies. Even if we know little of its background, the poem reveals much about its author. In fact, in the long period of German literature between the death of Walther von der Vogelweide and the emergence of the young Goethe, there is scarcely a single poem that can offer a more vivid and telling picture of its author and his concerns. Even a prose rendering into English conveys a measure of its force.

> I dared it as I planned it and I still do not regret it, and though I may gain nothing from it, still you must grant my steadfastness. I did it, if you want to know, not for myself but for the country, although people simply call me anticlerical.
>
> Let them all lie and speak what they will: had I not disclosed the truth, I would have had supporters enough. But now I've spoken out and I've been banished. This I lament to all worthy men, although I'm not going to flee farther, indeed I may come back.
>
> I will not ask for mercy, because I am without guilt. I would have submitted myself to the law, had not impatience been so obstinate as to deny me my ancient rights to a hearing. Perhaps God wills it, perhaps fate forces it, that they have acted this way.
>
> Now this sort of thing has also happened before, that one of the mighty has wagered and lost. A large flame has often grown from a small spark. Who knows, if I can avenge myself? Things are already in motion, and I'm part of it, do or die.
>
> Incidentally, my conscience is good, for none of the evil ones can damage my honor, or say that I have ever by any means acted other than honorably. I started this affair in the right.
>
> If you won't tell this country to rid itself of its ruin, as I have warned, then I'm sorry. I will cut and shuffle the cards better. I am undismayed, I dared to do it, and look forward to the result.
>
> And though the wiles of the courtiers are plotting against me, a heart that knows it's right is not hurt. I know that many others want to join the game as well, even if it costs them their lives. Arise, ye yeomen and ye chivalry. Do not let Hutten perish.

Hutten's contemporaries would have been quick to recognize the first line, "ich habs gewagt," as a translation of Caesar's "jacta est alea," i.e., "the die is cast," as Hutten's own repeatedly expressed motto, and as the signature he invariably put on his works. Many editors have gone so far as to substitute "The Die Is Cast" for the proper title of the poem. Indeed, at the time of this poem's publication, Hutten had crossed his own Rubicon, and even to this day the poem emits the light of the burning bridge he left behind.

Defying excommunication and risking far worse, Hutten was the first to invoke the cause of freedom by raising arms against the property and might of the Roman church itself. This action alienated him from the good will of most of his erstwhile supporters, including Martin Luther. While Luther and Hutten were perceived for a time as equal threats by Rome, Luther had stood for caution, and in his tract *On the Freedom of a Christian Man* he had accordingly severely limited his definition of freedom to his followers. It was perhaps to Hutten, more than anyone else, that Luther addressed this warning. But Hutten ignored the warning of the reformer.

Hutten's poem expresses the character of a restless and reckless spirit, of an earnest gambler in a game for high stakes. Here we meet a man entirely convinced of the rectitude of his position, a man righteously free of any troubling shadow of personal doubt. The character that stands revealed in this poem is one of profound personal ideals—loyalty, selflessness, truth, justice, honor, conscience, and righteous confidence—ideals that derive more from chivalry than from humanism, to be sure, and to which Hutten characteristically added one further element, the ideal of nationhood, of patriotism. Hutten's humanism was dominated more by his poetry than by his scholarship, and less by detachment than by engagement. Of his time, Hutten was, without equal, *l'homme de lettres engagé.*

Hutten has been called a muddle-headed thinker by the prominent historian Johan Huizinga. It appears to this observer that if anything muddled Hutten's mind it was his chivalry. Yet the call for political union and spiritual freedom that Hutten sounded in this poem and in his other works has echoed through the years of German history. That he made the call with both pen and sword in hand makes Hutten a significant mover and shaker in Western history.

The spectre of Hutten's activism haunted his enemies for generations. Here Hutten may appear in a negative light, for the harshness of the later Counter Reformation derived in part from fears such as those Hutten kindled. Even a cursory reading of his works reveals that Hutten identified humanism and patriotism (and ultimately the nascent movement that came to be called Protestantism) as a single cause. He was not unique in this, but his exceptional energies and talents as a publicist marked him as the most important proponent of German national interest in his time; indeed, it is to Hutten that one must turn if one seeks to locate the beginnings of modern national feeling in Germany. The idea that nationalism traces its roots to the very heart of the humanist movement may be startling, but it is supported by the weight of historical evidence offered by Hutten's short, but brilliant, controversial, and often violent life.

That northern humanism is generally viewed as cosmopolitan is the legacy of Erasmus of Rotterdam. Hutten's sometime friend and mentor, with whom Hutten entered his final and perhaps bitterest conflict, an inevitable conflict, that continued even after Hutten's death and embittered the declining years of the aging Erasmus to an extraordinary degree. That in the popular view European humanism as a whole continued to be seen as a cosmopolitan, supranational movement hostile to any sort of nationalism is also largely due to Erasmus's dominance. Yet this view ignores the strongly local character of the beginnings of Italian humanism. Humanism was a movement characterized by a return to the past for a sanction of the canons of taste, beauty, style, and truth, and in Italy the sources to which the humanists returned were local and Italian. In a real sense, the Italian humanists were but rediscovering their own lost *national* tradition. This gave Italian humanism a distinctly different flavor from that of its northern counterpart.

The northern humanists, having no direct claim as heirs of the classical Roman tradition, tended toward views generally more cosmopolitan than those of their southern predecessors and contemporaries. But when other German humanists—although a minority, including Celtis, Wimpheling, Vadianus, and Bebel—began to explore the German past with a zeal that matched that with which the Italians had explored their own past, it became clear that Hutten was not alone in his interests. Beyond their delight in the flattering picture of barbarian Germany found in the newly rediscovered writings of the Roman historian Tacitus, the German humanists were pleased with the discovery of something resembling greatness in the Carolingian and Ottonian periods of their own empire. Celtis's discovery of the Ottonian Hrotswitha von Gandersheim's Latin plays (derived from Terence) charmed the German humanists, who had had to live with their barbarian heritage in the face of Italy's previous (and continuing) grandeur. The empire was, in fact, the Renaissance German's soundest claim to antique credibility, for the Holy Roman Empire was the legitimate, historically validated heir to the Augustan Empire. Yet even this claim was flawed, and long before Voltaire remarked that the Holy Roman Empire was neither holy, nor Roman, nor, in fact, an empire, Hutten came to recognize that the empire was an empire in name only. It was the aim of Hutten's reform to make the empire live up to its lofty name.

In equating patriotism with humanism, Hutten merely carried to an extreme a tendency already rather well established within the framework of the general European humanistic movement. Thus this equation had the all-important sanction of the past, so necessary to the humanist mentality. What set Hutten apart from the school of Erasmus was Hutten's belief that beyond its generally ennobling effects, humanistic learning was something to be put to overt political use; it was to be consequential.

While Hutten expressed understanding for the detached, scholarly quietude of an Erasmus, his own temper was overactive and he spent his life exhorting people to act for the cause of truth as he saw it. Hutten's activism contrasts vividly with Erasmus's tolerant, apolitical cosmopolitanism. Hutten invoked the German imperial tradition against the tradition of papal supremacy. While this imperial tradition was not entirely an historical fiction, its continuity was in Hutten's time certainly not unbroken, and the pulse of its vitality was decidedly weak. Hutten wanted to renew the struggle of the Hohenstaufen emperors of the High Middle Ages. The cornerstone of his political thought and the basis for his activities both scholarly and political was Hutten's belief in the empire's superiority in all temporal and some ecclesiastical affairs.

Prior to the Reformation, the empire had lagged far behind France and England in the governance of local church affairs and the accompanying control of fiscal matters. Rome exacted heavy tithes of assorted annates and tributes to the papacy from Germany, which both England and France had long ceased to pay. The disunity of Germany, whose emperor nominally presided over an independent collection of often jealous and conflicting principalities, made it easy for the papacy to exploit the empire. It is an apparent paradox that this political disunity could foster a successful religious reform, yet leave the political structure of Germany unchanged. The seven powerful elector princes had no interest in *political* reform; they were unwilling to cede to the emperor anything that might diminish their own position.

Yet from Hutten's point of view the time doubtless seemed ripe for reform. There were in Hutten's own lifetime a larger number of Reichstag meetings than at any prior (or, as it turned out, later) period in the history of the empire. Reform was in the air, but it was hampered by the intransigence of the territorial princes. It is easy to see why the later Hapsburg princes turned their efforts toward building a dynasty outside the empire, in Spain, where their control was more direct, their power more secure. Where Hutten gambled and lost was in staking his faith on the ability, or the inclination, of either Maximilian, or his successor Charles, or his fellow humanists and Protestants to interpret the imperial role as he did. Hutten's political failure seems in retrospect to have been foredoomed, because, for all his talents, his political and social views seem scarcely to have extended beyond the limits and prejudices of the aristocratic class into which he was born. (pp. 111-16)

Hutten's aristocratic background served to hinder both his intellectual and his political judgment. For this very class, which Hutten would endow with a new claim to old authority, was essentially moribund. We can now see clearly that the feuding robber barons of the late Middle Ages, from whom Hutten was himself scarcely one generation removed, were being pushed off the historical stage by forces beyond their control or their understanding. Feuding had been outlawed in Hutten's youth, though Hutten and Franz von Sickingen were later to ignore this legal nicety outrageously *in the name of honor.* Indeed, both came to be counted as nothing more than outlawed robber barons themselves prior to Sickingen's death during a successful, and portentously unchivalric, artillery siege against him.

While Hutten became humanist enough to give something more than a passing nod to the idea of an aristocracy of merit (most notably in his famous letter of October, 1518 to the Nürnberg patrician, Willibald Pirckheimer), and while many of his closest friends (Eobanus Hessus, for one) were of humble origin, Hutten retained the aloofness of his class toward the prosperity and concomitant growing dominance of the mercantile-banking class, already quite evident in his time. A poor man himself, in spite of his knightly birth, Hutten believed that a society dominated by money was entirely repulsive. His visceral rejection of the corrupt market place is reflected in his antipapal pamphleteering. He saw Rome as ruled by gold, and the thrust of his criticism of the relationship between Rome and the empire tends to be economic.

In 1505 Hutten forsook monastic life against his parents' wishes. He was to spend the next dozen years in penurious wandering and scholarly errantry. Hutten, unlike Luther, never spoke ill of his six years in the cloister. During his years of wandering, Hutten perfected his skills as a poet, gaining a fluid and graceful Latin style. He received a baccalaureate at Frankfurt on the Oder in 1506. And it is during this time that he fell prey to the syphilis that eventually was to kill him.

Hutten later developed friendships with a number of prominent humanists, such as Crotus Rubianus, Eobanus Hessus, Rhagius Aesticampianius, and Mutianus Rufus. Of the Neoplatonic theism derived from the Italian humanists Marsilio Ficino and Pico della Mirandola, which Mutianus taught and fostered in Germany, there is, however, no trace in Hutten. He was no speculative thinker. What he did perhaps draw from Mutianus was rather a general skepticism concerning both the sacramental system and the Scholastics in general. Mutianus, who prudently chose not to publish his heresies, appears to have made the church almost superfluous in terms of human salvation. The implications for Hutten's own development are clear. Hutten moved in a bohemian, satirically oriented circle whose view of life approached the pagan. His schooling was, in a word, radical.

In the summer of 1510 Hutten published his first major poem, ***Nemo (Nobody)***, which he was later to amplify with extensive borrowings from Erasmus's *The Praise of Folly.* The work has a rather fetchingly elegant and clever wit. While Hutten was no prude, he seems to have shown more general discretion than was the rule in the letters of his time. There is in Hutten, with the exception of his later contributions to the ***Letters of Obscure Men,*** none of the pornography or scatology seen in other writers of the period.

Details of Hutten's days as a student are sketchy at best, yet even as a student Hutten began to betray character traits that remained evident throughout his life. Stung by the stinginess of his erstwhile benefactors in Rostock, Hutten published a tract against the Lötze family, vicious in tone, critical in content, personal in stimulus. Hutten *was* combative. The issues with which he concerned himself in his writing tended to be personal. This is seen in the anti-Lötze tract, in his polemics against the Duke of Württemberg (***Phalarismus***), in his essay on syphilis (which he called the French disease), and elsewhere. (pp. 117-18)

Hutten wrote a pamphlet exhorting Emperor Maximilian to continue his war against Venice and a poem in hexameters on "Why the Germans are not degenerate in comparison with former times." Evidence of contemporary German brilliance he saw in the inventions of gunpowder and the printing press, a brilliance that to him rivaled the glory of Germany's heroic (pagan) past. Hutten saw great promise for the political future of the empire in the coming generation. Actual events were to show this optimism as wishful thinking. Derived from Aesticampanius's lectures on Tacitus, Hutten's view of Germany is that of Tacitus, who in his *Germania* had held up a primitive, agrarian culture as preferable to the overripe culture of classical Rome. Hutten's class prejudice limited his understanding of his contemporary society, and he was at constant odds with the realities of the shopkeeping economy of his time—it was the perfidy of the Venetian shopkeepers that Hutten castigated in his exhortation to Maximilian. (p. 119)

Hutten and Erasmus developed a mutual fondness, the younger man playing Alcibiades to the older man's Socrates. They corresponded regularly, and though in retrospect it appears that even at the time of their initial acquaintanceship their paths were going in different and conflicting directions, neither of them seems to have paid heed to this, and their relationship was to remain amicable for the next half-decade at least. Erasmus apparently recognized a powerful publicist in Hutten, while Hutten saw in Erasmus the restorer of primitive Christianity. In the conflict with Duke Ulrich, Hutten wrote a series of speeches patterned on Cicero's *Catalinian Orations,* but more importantly, he produced a dialogue of the dead in the style of Lucian, his ***Phalarismus.*** The dialogue became Hutten's favorite genre, and that it became the most popular literary form of the day as well is largely due to Hutten. The struggle against Duke Ulrich culminated in 1519 in a military action of the Swabian League that deposed the tyrant. Hutten took part in this effort and met Franz von Sickingen. At this time Hutten also adopted the Caesarian "jacta est alea" as his personal motto.

Again Hutten turned to Italy, a not all-too-willing student of Roman law. He seems to have shared with Wimpheling a feeling that the Roman law had no justifiable role in the affairs of the German empire, and he seems to have pursued his purely humanistic inclinations further at the expense of the study of law. Hutten turned up in humanist circles in Rome, Bologna, Ferrara, and Venice, driven from both Rome and Bologna in a rush of controversy. In Rome he killed a French soldier in a brawl and in Bologna played a leading role in a student revolt. His interest in the Reuchlin affair, already awakened in Germany, came to fruition in his contributions to the ***Letters of Obscure Men.*** Hutten may have received more credit than was his due for the composition of these letters, which hold both the literary and the life styles of the Scholastic opponents of Reuchlin up to bitter and telling scorn. Yet, though anonymous, these letters gained for Hutten a notoriety in the Western world and many enemies both in and outside the Roman curia.

Intellectually and politically Hutten was impressed with his reading of the *Annals* of Tacitus and with the picture of the great German hero, Arminius, that they portray. In ***Arminius,*** a dialogue of uncertain date, Hutten pictured his subject as the ideal German prince, the proper model for Emperor Maximilian. This dialogue started the Arminius cult in Germany. In Italy, too, Hutten came across Lorenzo Valla's previously unpublished essay that revealed the fraud of the ***Constantine Donation.*** This alleged "donation" was a chief document used by the papacy to justify the Holy See's claim to temporal power. Hutten edited and published this essay immediately on his return to Germany in 1517, ironically dedicating it to the new Pope

Leo X! The significance of Hutten's publication of Valla's essay rests primarily on the profound effect it had on its most important reader, Martin Luther. Stung by his rather unsuccessful debate with Johann Eck, Luther seized upon this work like a godsend when it came into his hands in 1520. To Luther it seemed clear, after reading this document, that the Pope was the Antichrist. This was not a point of view that lent itself to compromise.

We see that Hutten's humanism was by no means antiquarian in its orientation. Hutten's studies and efforts were all in the direction of what is now popularly called relevance. Not knowledge for its own sake, but knowledge for the sake of action was always his guide. He might even be called an "applied" humanist, though this would by no means imply that his humanism was actually practical in the real world of Renaissance politics and Reformation conflict. What impressed Hutten most in Italy was not the local esthetic and antiquarian delights, but the political machinations of the church apparatus, the abuses of clerical power, the simony, bribery, immorality, licentiousness, and general venality in human affairs. These he portrayed and castigated in a series of epigrams, many of which reemerge later in his antipapal, pro-Lutheran polemics. His dialogue ***On The Roman Trinity*** (or, ***Vadiscus***) of 1520 catalogues his perceptions of Roman evil in excruciating detail.

Returning to Germany, Hutten found himself lionized, and in July, 1517, Maximilian crowned him poet laureate. He was even in good favor, for a change, with his family; the poet's laurel atoned in part for his failure to secure the desired law degree. Hutten now entered the life of a courtier, composing a work on court life (***Aula***) that he sent to Pirckheimer for criticism. It is Hutten's response to the Nürnberger's critique that we find in his previously mentioned letter castigating the mercantile class.

At this time Hutten also involved himself in political affairs. Having entered the service of Archbishop Albrecht von Brandenburg, the powerful Imperial Elector, Hutten lent his talents to propagandistic efforts to promote a Christian crusade against the Turkish menace. Hutten, like Maximilian, saw in this an opportunity for the empire to prove its claim to leadership of Christendom as the military savior of Western values. What stamps Hutten's exhortation to the German princes with his own mark is his bitter criticism of both the selfishness of the territorial princes (such as Duke Ulrich) and the trickery of Rome. The Lutheran indulgence controversy was coming into full swing at this time, and Hutten turned his pen in two dialogues (***Fever, the First; Fever, the Second***) against Cardinal Cajetan, who had been sent to Germany to straighten out the entire Lutheran controversy. These works Hutten imbued with great invective and defamation, and in this he was the child of his time. (pp. 119-22)

Hutten's humanism now came completely into the service of imperial reform. The shape this reform was to take remained something of a muddle, yet it was clear to Hutten that Rome's economic plundering of Germany, in which the sale of indulgences represented an important but not, for Hutten, overriding part, had to stop. Unlike Luther, the primary thrust of Hutten's reform was more political than religious, and the emperor was to have taken the lead in freeing the bonds shackling Germany. The monetary savings to the empire would serve to support a stronger standing army, which would in turn allow the emperor to play a more powerful role in world affairs. Hutten's reform would aim at restoring both the primitive piety of the early Christians and the primitive virtue of the early Germans. What Hutten had in mind was to reestablish the austerely moral, and independent, Germany pictured by Tacitus. Hutten's Germany would become an agrarian society ruled over by a benevolent and humanistically educated aristocracy. Men such as Hutten, of course, would play leading roles in public affairs.

While Luther used Hutten's support, he does not seem to have been attracted by Hutten's dream. The two men were, however, drawn together, and from 1520 both were closely identified by their enemies, and both were, from Rome's point of view, outlaws. They both needed and received the protection of the mighty. Hutten was threatened with delivery to Rome without a legal hearing, and he now came to identify his personal cause as the cause of all Germans. Hutten quickly penned a number of complaints addressed to the emperor, to the Elector of Saxony (Luther's protector), to Archbishop Albrecht, and to the estates of Germany demanding their defense of him as a matter of national interest. He turned the burning of Lutheran works in Mainz into the subject of another antipapal poem. And finally, in 1520 he wrote an indictment (***Anzoig***) against the papacy, in which he tried to show, by quite selective historical argumentation, that papal policy from the time of Otto I (d. 973) onward had meant only ruin for the empire.

Early in 1521 Hutten wrote furiously, hoping to influence public opinion both lay and clerical prior to the Diet at Worms. The four Latin dialogues resulting from this activity (***Bullicida*** [The Bullkiller]; ***Monitor I, Monitor II,*** and ***Praedones*** [The Robbers]) show Hutten's gifts and limitations as a propagandist most clearly. Hutten himself appears in the dialogues, as do Luther, Sickingen, a personification of a papal Bull, the allegorical figure of German Freedom, cowardly papal supporters, indecisive Germans, and a merchant. The merchant appears in ***The Robbers,*** along with Hutten and Sickingen, a dialogue that shows how class-bound Hutten really was. The purpose of the dialogue was to convince the free German cities to support the knights in the upcoming conflict with the Church. But here again, Hutten expressed a contempt for mercantile wealth, and for the very merchant class whose support any rebellion would sorely need. Hutten's overt expression of class prejudice destroyed any possible chance of a positive response to his plea by the merchants of his time. And this dialogue appeared at the time when Hutten was at the very apex of his polemical career!

The Diet at Worms disappointed Hutten's hopes for a reform to be led by Emperor Charles. Hutten was in the service of the emperor at this time, and he and Sickingen had been assured by the imperial emissary, Clampion, that Charles supported reform. Yet when it became obvious that the imperial promises had been broken, when Luther was treated as an already adjudged heretic, Hutten let

Charles know in no uncertain terms of the depth of his dismay at the Hapsburg duplicity—the emperor stood revealed as the tool of Rome. Luther appeared before the imperial body on April 17-18, 1521; by June, Hutten had terminated his imperial service. From this point Hutten's position, and Sickingen's, deteriorated rapidly. Hutten came to declare a feud against the entire priestly class. He meant to strike at the allies of those forces dominant in the Roman curia who were opposed to him, to Luther, to Reuchlin and to any and all forces of change in the empire. In October, 1521, Hutten drew on the support of Sickingen to demand 10,000 gulden from the Carthusian order in Strassburg.

While Erasmus had once demanded heroism from those who would fight the significant battles of Christian warfare, it is unlikely that he had in mind the flagrant sort of action Hutten was promoting. Yet Hutten was at war with all priests dependent upon Rome. He expected many of his fellow knights to follow his example. We note in stanza four of ***Ein neu Lied*** his confident assertion that great flames may grow from small sparks. The Carthusians of Strassburg were to be merely the first group attacked, the first sparks in a great conflagration. They were Romanists of the first order, prominent, wealthy, and vulnerable. There is reason to believe that the strategic choice was Sickingen's. Hutten contented himself with the payment of 2,000 gulden and counted the enterprise a success. Further success did not appear. By 1522 the church had gained the support of the cities, particularly Strassburg and Frankfurt, and the combined efforts of Sickingen and Hutten rapidly degenerated into what most people saw as highway robbery. A series of propagandistic pleas from Hutten to the cities of Germany for support came to nothing. Sickingen's campaign against the powerful Archbishop of Trier met a series of military defeats, culminating in Sickingen's death in his beleaguered Landstuhl in May, 1523. This also marked the end of Germany's Free Knights as a power in Germany.

Now Hutten was alone. He himself had less than six months to live. Rejected by Erasmus at Basel, Hutten turned on his erstwhile mentor and charged him with betraying Germany, Luther, Hutten, and the cause of reform. Erasmus responded in kind after Hutten's death, charging Hutten with betraying his humanistic calling. Expelled from Basel, Hutten turned to the only available refuge, Ulrich Zwingli. The Swiss reformer put Hutten, who was forced to conceal his name from the local population, on the Isle of Ufenau in the Zurichsee. By the end of the summer of 1523 Hutten was dead.

In two letters written in 1518 Hutten expressed most succinctly his attitude toward his enemies. "Let them hate us," he wrote, "as long as they fear us at the same time." Perhaps even more than his ***Ein neu Lied,*** these words illustrate the reckless, gambling nature of the man. The formula, which Hutten employed on other occasions as well—in his dialogue ***Inspicientes (The Onlookers)*** he put the words into the mouth of an opponent, Cardinal Cajetan (here the "us" was Rome, the "them" the Germans)—is a rather chilling statement. It was, in fact, not original with Hutten, for he had borrowed it from a classical source, the late-Greek tragedian Accius, who had given the line to Caligula. One suspects that those among Hutten's contemporaries whose erudition matched his own reacted with various and mixed degrees of amusement or embarrassment, pleasure or chagrin, when they realized Hutten's appropriation of the Roman tyrant's extraordinarily cruel formula. Hutten's repeated use of this let-them-hate-us statement suggests that it became a sort of magical formula for him, not unlike his famous motto, *"ich habs gewagt."* Apparently fearless himself, Hutten seems not to have understood the power of fear to move men to action. What he expressed as a defiant challenge became instead his own inadvertent curse. The fears that he set loose did not, as he had hoped, immobilize his enemies.

Yet for all Hutten's feelings, his hopes for a finer *humanitas* within a framework of natural unity and spiritual freedom remained a worthy inspiration to generations of German thinkers, even in our time. Hutten's role as a pivotal figure in the age that separated the medieval from the modern world is secure. Hutten's contemporaries, friend and foe alike, conceded him this position, and our judgment must follow theirs. (pp. 122-26)

Sam Wheelis, "Ulrich Von Hutten: Representative of Patriotic Humanism," in The Renaissance and Reformation in Germany: An Introduction, *edited by Gerhart Hoffmeister, Frederick Ungar Publishing Co., 1977, pp. 111-27.*

FURTHER READING

"Ulrich von Hutten: The Second Luther of Germany." *The Eclectic Magazine* 45, No. 1 (September 1858): 89-98.

Studies Hutten's literary achievements in the context of the nascent German Reformation movement.

Goethe, J. W. von. "Part IV. Book XVII." In *Poetry and Truth: From My Own Life,* revised and translated by Minna Steele Smith, pp. 221-43. London: G. Bell & Sons, 1911.

Quotes at length a letter written by Hutten concerning his desire to attain the "nobility" of unassailable artistic greatness. Goethe, recalling his own life in 1775, notes that at that time as in Hutten's day, "[it] had become a creed, that everyone must earn for himself a personal nobility. . . . "

Herrman, Paul. "Ulrich von Hutten." In *The World Unveiled: The Story of Exploration from Columbus to Livingstone,* translated by Arnold Pomerans, pp. 75-7. London: Hamish Hamilton, 1958.

Briefly describes Hutten's role in bringing about the German Reformation.

Holborn, Hajo. *Ulrich von Hutten and the German Reformation.* Translated by Roland H. Bainton. New Haven: Yale University Press, 1937, 214 p.

Biography of Hutten, first published in Germany in 1929. Translator Bainton's introduction describes Hutten as the first of his countrymen to strive for free expression in the early stages of the Reformation.

"The Life and Writings of Ulrich von Hutten." *The London Quarterly Review* 28, No. 55 (April 1867): 65-87.
Comments upon Hutten's major works and his relationship with Martin Luther, noting differences in the respective philosophies of the two men.

Münch, Ernest. "Strauss's Life of Ulrich von Hutten." *The National Review* 6, No. 7 (April 1858): 280-310.
Sketches Hutten's historical background and literary accomplishments, in a review of David Friedrich Strauss's *Ulrich von Hutten.*

Justus Lipsius

1547-1606

(Also known as Joest Lips) Flemish-born Dutch philologist, essayist, critic, epistler, historian, and lexicographer.

Recognized as one of the most gifted textual critics of all time, Lipsius elucidated classical Latin prose during the late sixteenth century and established himself as a leading editor of Latin prose texts. His editions of the writings of Tacitus and of Seneca were long renowned as models of their kind and are still respected today. His lifelong interest in Seneca's thought led to the writing of his influential treatise *De Constantia libri duo* [*Two Bookes of Constancie*], while his familiarity with Tacitus's works inspired the political theory of *Politicorum sive civilis doctrinae libri sex* [*Sixe Bookes of politickes or civil doctrine*]. By the influence of his translations and treatises, Lipsius helped foster the Stoic orientation of the baroque era and profoundly influenced humanistic literature in the Low Countries.

Lipsius was born to Catholic parents in 1547 in Overijse, a village between Brussels and Louvain in what is now Belgium. His education progressed rapidly, and he continually astonished his masters with his precocity. In 1563 Lipsius entered the University of Louvain, where he distinguished himself as a student of Roman law as well as classical literature and history. Four years later, Lipsius accompanied Cardinal Granvelle to Italy as his Latin secretary. He remained there for two years, exploring Italy's great libraries and closely examining the ancient manuscripts and inscriptions he found. In 1572 the Duke of Saxe-Weimar offered him the chair of eloquence and history at the University of Jena in Protestant Germany, and Lipsius accepted. Although reared and educated as a Catholic, Lipsius converted to Lutheranism, but his associates at the university doubted the sincerity of his conversion and chose not to accept him as a colleague. Lipsius resigned and journeyed to Cologne. Renouncing Protestantism in 1574, he returned to the Catholic faith in order to marry Ann Calstria, a Catholic widow. That same year he also completed his famous edition of Tacitus, *C. C. Taciti historiarum et annaliem libri qui exstant.*

In 1576 Lipsius returned to the University of Louvain, where he remained for two years. When offered a chair at the Protestant University of Leiden in 1579, he accepted and converted to Calvinism. Lipsius and his wife settled in Leiden for twelve years, during which time he wrote his *Commentaries* on Tacitus, *Two Bookes of Constancie,* and *Sixe Bookes of Politickes.* These scholarly works enhanced Lipsius's international reputation, attracting other scholars from abroad and significantly contributing to the university's renown. In 1591 he reconverted to the Catholic faith, a decision which resulted in his dismissal from the University of Leiden. By then, however, Lipsius's fame was such that he was vigorously sought after by academics, ecclesiastics, and several royal households from throughout Europe. He chose to accept the chair of literature and history at the University of Louvain, where he lectured for the remaining fourteen years of his life. At Louvain he wrote religious tracts, completed his edition of Seneca, and published *Manuductio ad Philosophiam Stoicam* and *Physiologia Stoicorum.* He died in April 1606.

Lipsius was a prolific writer whose main strength lay in textual criticism and exegesis of classical Latin prose works. His masterwork in this respect was his edition of Tacitus's writings. Indeed, he was so familiar with the texts of Tacitus that he was reputed to have offered to recite any passage with a dagger at his chest—to be used against him if he erred. His *Two Bookes of Constancie,* perhaps his best-known work, advocates a Christianized Stoicism. Commentators agree that this work grew out of his personal agony over the civil wars which ravaged the Low Countries during his lifetime. He wrote in the preface: "I have written many other things for others; but this book chiefly for my self; the former for fame, but this for [spiritual] profit." Another work, the *Sixe Bookes of Politickes,* is an influential treatise which ultimately shaped some aspects of seventeenth-century European politics. In the *Six Bookes,* Lipsius discusses the proper conduct of civil governments, subscribing to the belief that rebellious subjects should be persecuted by "fire and sword." Of lesser importance are Lipsius's later works on Stoicism. His *Manuductio ad Philosophiam Stoicam,* an essay which defines the main points of Stoicism, appeared with his completed edition of Seneca's writings. Another work, *Physiologia Stoicorum,* explains Stoic natural philosophy.

Critics have long acknowledged Lipsius's significant influence upon the intellectual climate and literary tone of the late sixteenth and seventeenth centuries. According to Morris W. Croll, Lipsius "has now come to be known as the 'founder of seventeenth-century Neo-Stoicism' and the writer who must finally take an almost equal place with Montaigne and Bacon among the founders of the prose-style of the seventeenth century." Most commentators agree that Lipsius popularized the pointed Senecan prose style which seventeenth-century writers frequently imitated. Lipsius's philological work—most notably his editions of Tacitus and Seneca—has been generally esteemed by critics since the sixteenth century. In 1987, Anthony Grafton noted that "[Lipsius's] edition of Tacitus . . . marked a radical improvement in a notoriously difficult text . . . [and] that of Seneca . . . won him preferment in the academic centers of Lutheran Europe (Jena), Calvinist Europe (Leiden), and Catholic Europe (Louvain)." Despite the wide influence of Lipsius's works, only his highly personal *Two Bookes of Constancie* received widespread popular and critical acclaim; it ran through more than eighty editions over three centuries and has been translated into all the principal European languages. Even so, as P. H. Schrijvers has noted, sixteenth-century critics raised five objections against Lipsius's *Constancie:* "[They argued that] his tract showed too little Christian spirit; they protested especially against his glorification of right reasoning, against his views on fate and free will, against the idea that the ungodly are punished 'for their own good' and against denouncing emotions." Nevertheless, it is today perhaps his best-known work among scholars. They note that Lipsius's *Sixe Bookes of Politickes* exerted considerable influence among late sixteenth-century statesmen, most notably the Spanish. Theodore G. Corbett wrote that "many Spanish statesmen were first drawn to Lipsius as a source of classical letters or universal knowledge, and only indirectly discovered his value in the field of statecraft." Lipsius believed that this work would last as long as Latin letters themselves, and twentieth century critics suggest he may have been correct. Indeed most of his works have never been translated into contemporary vernacular, thus his literary reputation has suffered since the early eighteenth century. Grafton has claimed that "Justus Lipsius survives, barely, as a fading figure on the periphery of our mental panorama of Renaissance culture."

Thus, though his name and many writings are recognized by relatively few readers of world literature, Lipsius is widely regarded as one of the outstanding literary and intellectual figures of his time. He has been praised by Robert J. Hill as "undoubtedly one of the most erudite men in all Europe." And Désiré Nisard, in his *Le Triumvirat Littéraire au XVIe siècle,* has concluded that "any nation might be proud of having such a man as Lipsius for its compatriot; any nation might think itself honoured in rendering him some conspicuous homage to perpetuate the *scholar's* glory and the *nation's* gratitude."

PRINCIPAL WORKS

Variarum lectionum libri IIII. 4 vols. (criticism) 1569
Antiquarum lectionum commentarius, tributus in libros quinque. 5 vols. (philology) 1574
C. C. Taciti historiarum et annaliem libri qui exstant, J. Lipsii studio emendati et illustrati (philology) 1574
Ad annales Corn. Taciti liber commentarius, sive notae (criticism) 1581
Saturnalium sermonum libri duo, qui de gladiatoribus. 2 vols. (essay) 1582
De constantia libri duo. 2 vols. (essay) 1584
[*Two Bookes of Constancie,* 1595]
Opera omnia quae ad criticam proprie spectant (philology) 1585
Variarum lectionum III. 3 vols. (criticism) 1585
De recta pronunciatione latinae linguae dialogus (dictionary) 1586
Epistolarum selectarum, centuria prima (letters) 1586
Politicorum sive civilis doctrinae libri sex, qui ad principatum maxime spectant. 6 vols. (essay) 1589
[*Sixe Bookes of politickes or civil doctrine, . . . which doe especially concerne principalitie,* 1594]
Adversus diologistam liber de una religione (essay) 1590
Epistolarum centuriae duae: quarum prior innouata alter noua (letters) 1590
De cruce libri tres. 3 vols. (essay) 1592
De magistratibus veteris populi romani (history) 1592
De bibliothecis syntagma (history) 1595
De militia romana libri quinque. 5 vols. (history) 1595-96
Admiranda, sive de magnitudine romana libri quattuor. 4 vols. (essay) 1598
Epistolarum selectarum III. centuriae (letters) 1601
Epistolarum selectarum centuria singularis ad Italos & Hispanos (letters) 1601
Monita et exempla politica. 2 vols. (history) 1601
Epistolarum selectarum centuria miscellanea (letters) 1602
Epistolarum selectarum centuria prima . . . secunda . . . tertia . . . ad Belgas. 3 vols. (letters) 1602
Epistolarum selectarum centuria singularis ad Germanos & Gallos (letters) 1602
Epistolarum selectarum centuriae VIII (letters) 1603
Diva Virgo Hallensis (criticism) 1604
Manuductionis ad philosophiam stoicam libri tres. 3 vols. (essay) 1604
L. Annaei Senecae Philosophi Opera, quae exstant, omnia; a Justo Lipsio emendata et scholiis illustrata (philology) 1605
Louvanium: sive opidi et academiae eius descriptio. 3 vols. (essay) 1605
Epistolarum selectarum centuria prima miscellanea . . . secunda . . . tertia . . . quarta . . . quinta miscellanea postuma. 5 vols. (letters) 1605-07
De vetere scriptura Latinorum (criticism) 1607

Opera, quae velut in partes ante sparsa, nunc in certas classes digesta. 2 vols. (criticism, letters, essays, histories, dictionary, philology) 1613

Opera omnia. 4 vols. (criticism, letters, essays, histories, dictionary, philology) 1675

Iustus Lipsius (essay date 1584)

[*In the following excerpt from a work first published in Latin in 1584, Lipsius remarks on the intent of his* Two Bookes of Constancie, *noting that "this book [was written] chiefly for my self."*]

I am not ignorant of those new iudgments and censures I am likely to undergo in this new way of writing: Partly, from such as will be surprized with the unexpected profession of wisdom from him, whom they believed had only been conversant in the more pleasing and delightful studies; and partly from such as will despise and undervalue all that can be said in these matters, after what the ancients have written. To both these; it is for my concern, and no less for thine, that I should briefly reply. The first sort of persons seem to me to miscarry in two most different respects: in their care, and their carelessness. In the former that they assume to themselves a liberty of enquiring into the actions and studies of others: In the latter, that their enquiries are yet so overly and superficial. For (that I may give them an account of me) the Hills and Springs of the Muses did never so intirely possess me; as that I should not find frequent opportunities to turn back my Eyes and Mind upon that severer deity: I mean Philosophy. The studies of which (even from my Childhood) were so pleasing to me, that in this youthful kind of ardour I seemed to offend, and to stand in need of the bridle of restraint. My Tutors at *Ubich* know how all those kind of books were as it were forced out of my hands together with those writings and commentaries which I had laboriously composed out of all the best ranks of interpreters. Nor certainly did I afterward degenerate; for I know that in all the course of my studies; if not in an exact and straight line, yet as least in the flexure, I have tended towards this mark of wisdom. Not after the rate of most here that deal in Philosophy: who doting upon some thorny subtilties, or snares of questions, do nothing else but weave and unweave them with a kind of subtile thread of disputations. They rest in words, and some little fallacies; and wear away their dayes in the Porch of Philosophy, but never visit its more retired apartments. They use it as a divertisement, not as a remedy, and turn the most serious instrument of life, into a sportage with trifles: who amongst them seeks after the improvement of his manners, the moderation of his affections; or designs a just end and measure for his fears or hopes. Yes, they suppose that wisdome is so little concerned in these things, that they think they do nothing, or nothing to the purpose that look after them, And therefore if you consider of their life, and sentiments, amongst the vulgar themselves you shall find nothing more foul than the one, nor more foolish than the other. For as wine (though nothing is more wholsome) is yet to some no better than poyson: So is Phylosophy to them that abuse it. But my Mind was otherwise; who alwayes steering my Ship, from these quick sands of subtilties, have directed all my endeavours to attain that one Haven of a peaceable and quiet mind. Of which study of mine; I mean these books as the first and undeceivable instance. But say some others, these things have been more fully and better treated of by the ancients. As to some of them I confess it: As to all I deny it. Should I write any thing of manners or the affections after *Seneca* and the divine *Epictetus:* I should have (my self being judge) as little discretion as modesty: But if such things as they have not so much as touched upon, nor any other of the ancients (for I dare confidently affirm it) then why do they despise it, or why do they carp at it? I have sought out consolations against publick evils: Who has done it before me? Whether they look upon the matter, or the method; they must confess they are indebted to me for both: And for the words themselves (let me say it) we have no such penury, as to oblige us to become suppliants to any Man. To conclude, let them understand I have written many other things for others; but this book chiefly for my self; the former for fame, but this for profit. That which one heretofore said bravely and acutely; the same I now truly proclaim. To me a few Readers are enough, one is enough, none is enough. All that I desire is, that whosoever opens this book, may bring with him a disposition to profit, and also to pardon. That if possibly I have any where slipt (especially when I endeavour to climb those steep places of providence, Justice and Fate) they would pardon me. For certainly, I have no where erred out of malice and obstinacy: But rather through humane ignorance and infirmity. To conclude, I desire to be informed by them, and I promise that no Man shall be so ready to convince; as I to correct. The other frailties of my nature, I neither dissemble nor extenuate; but obstinacy and the study of contention, I do heartily pray I may never be guilty of, and I do detest it. God send thee good health, my Reader; which I wish may be in part to thee through this book. (pp. 205-08)

Iustus Lipsius, "Appendix: To the Reader Touching the Design and End of This Treatise," in his Two Bookes of Constancie, *translated by Sir John Stradling, edited by Rudolf Kirk, Rutgers University Press, 1939, pp. 205-08.*

William Jones (essay date 1594)

[*In the following excerpt, Jones describes the content of Lipsius's* Sixe Bookes of politickes, *highlighting obstacles he encountered while translating the text.*]

Touching the substance of the booke [***Sixe Bookes of Politickes or Civil Doctrine***], it containeth matter of pollicie, and especially concerneth the establishment of Principalitie. It is deuided into sixe seuerall books, in the foure former, he [Lipsius] sheweth what the Prince should be, what vertues he is especially to be endued withall, how he should make cheife of good Counsellers, and officers: and to be short, after what sort he should behaue, and establish himselfe in time of peace.

The fifth booke setteth downe, in what maner he should begin, vndertake, and execute, for aine warre: how that same should be finished, and peace established thereby, which is the true ende of warre. A worke so necessarie for Captains, and those that serue their prince in the field, that in many things it surpasseth all those discourses of warre, I could yet come to the sight of. In the sixth booke, he treateth of ciuill warre. (pp. v-vi)

And wheras I was perswaded by some, to leaue out the quotacion of the immorall Authors, and the notes of the margent; I agreed not to their perswasion for two respects. The one, that therby it might be thought, I had bene a corrupt, and faithlesse translator, and that I durst not set my worke to the touch. The other, that the said marginall notes, do giue great light to the worke, & serue to explaine many matters therein: besides they haue this singularitie in them (which I haue not seene in any other) that they do entertaine one another, as if they were a continued speech: which if you reade them by themselues, you shall soone finde out. Moreover, if any be pleased to confer, some one sentence of mine, or more, with the orginall, by the quotacion of the Authors, the same may be more easily found, and he the better satisfied, of my paines, and diligence in this labour, or what fault I haue committed therein.

Lastly, whereas I haue sometimes changed the tense, otherwhiles the person: I say, the discourse could not else be well knit together: and herein I haue especially in the whole worke auoyded the pluralitie of Gods (which all Christians detest) and the Author could not but mention, his sentences being taken altogether from prophane writers. And as concerning something left out in the third Chapter of the second Booke, it was a thing done of set purpose; for some important cause, which I meane not here to vtter.

Thus I haue (gentle Reader) giuen thee some taste of this notable discourse; which I desire may be well disgested by thee, the which I do leaue to thy fauourable perusing. . . . (pp. vi-vii)

William Jones, "To the Courteous Reader," in Sixe Books of Politickes or Civil Doctrine, *by Justus Lipsius, translated by William Jones, William Ponsonby, 1594, pp. vi-vii.*

Sir John Stradling (essay date 1594)

[*A well-respected scholar, Stradling was an English poet, epigrammatist, and translator. Beside his translations of several of Lipsius's writings, his best-known work is* Divine Poems: in seven severall Classes, written to his Most Excellent Maiestie, Charles (the First) *(1625). In the following excerpt, he defends Lipsius's arguments as presented in the* Two Bookes of Constancie, *noting that "he writeth so highly . . . although som times with the words of the Auncients."*]

After I had translated this treatise [***De Constantia***] (frendly reader) and presented it to him for whose priuate vse I intended it, being moued thereunto vpon occasion in the former epistle declared: it seemed not amisse to the patron to haue the same published for the benefit of many. Whose judgement I could not but very wel approue in respect of the matter, being both comfortable and pleasant to be red, and withall very orderly laid down, and handled after an vnaccustomed (yet most familiar) manner.

Vnderstand, that I haue for breuities sake purposely omitted the epistles before the booke, which are three: (being loath to pesterre thee with a packet of letters at the first). Onely I do here alleadge out of them a few things written by my Author [Lipsius] in his owne defence. And first whereas some men pretend he hath not handled this argument deuoutly enough in that hee applieth not places of holy scripture to his purpose: As he accepteth well of their admonition, so his answere is that seeing he profeseth himselfe herein no diuine, but a philosopher, (yet a Christian philosopher) they ought to beare with him. Hee acknowledgeth the only direct path-way to saluation to be comprised in those sacred bookes: but that good letters withal, and the writings of philosophers are both an ease and help for vs to attain vnto the vnderstanding of them, and do further vs in the way of vertue and godlines, howsoeuer som new Domitians maintaine the contrary, seeking to abolish all good arts & knowledge in humanity. That he writeth so highly in commendation of RIGHT REASON, although som times with the words of the Auncients: yet he accompteth no reason pure or right except it be directed by God & illuminated by faith. If in writing of destiny & other lik profound matters his tongue (through an ardente and earnest intente of a good meaning mind) hapned any wher to trip or his pen to slide; Be not thou too rigorus towards him for it, he yealdeth to amend whatsoeuer shalbe proued amisse. He professeth himselfe of the nomber of those that haue godlinesse rather in hearte, then in their mouth; And liketh not the time that is fruitefull of religious, and fruitelesse impietie. Finally he is none of those subtle sophisticall ianglers, that place philosophie in the quirks and quiddities of crabbed questions. But he directeth his studie to the forming of good manners, and moderating of affections, (especially feare, and sorrow in aduersitie) whereby hee may at length be safely harbored in the hauen of a contented mind. A notable testimonie whereof hee hath left vs in these two bookes, to the singular comforte of all that list to reade them. (pp. 67-8)

If thou reape any pleasure or profit by this discourse, giue thanks (next vnto God) to my Author; then to the patron, for whom onely and by whome the same was both englished and published. For mine owne part I desire no more but curteous acceptation of my trauaill, I hope I deserue no lesse. A little good-will and a few good wordes for many daies work, is no vnreasonable rewarde: And he that grudgeth to giue such bare wages, as I would be loth to be his man, so if himselfe were bound to serue a bad master seuen yeeres after the same rate, I wot well he would mislike his penny-worths before that prentiship were expired, and euer after looke on other mens labours with a more fauorable eie. But for thee (curteous reader) at whose hands I doubt not to receaue better entertainment, I beg hartely of him which giueth euery good gift, that by reading & meditating vpon this little treatise, it will please him to worke in thy mind such a firme impression of CONSTANCIE, as neither the violent flouds of common calamities may be able to wash away, nor the firie flame of priuate afflictions to consume the same: But that as a plant set in good ground, watred with the fruitfull streames flowing in (a) goulden and siluer cesterns from the sweete fountaine of *Lipsius,* and conueighed to thee through these clayie conduite-pipes of my tempering, thou maist take deepe roote, and stand immoueable against all the blastes of fortune, neither terrified with feare of future mishappe, nor dismaied for any perilles present or past. Which victory though it seeme full of difficulty, yet if thou take vnto thee the armour and wepons here offered, hauing an indifferent courage of thine owne, thou shalt assuredly remaine a conquerour of those selfe affections, which do tirannize ouer the greatest tyrants, holding their minds in more seruile subiection, then they do the bodies of their vilest captiues. (pp. 69-70)

Sir John Stradling, "The Epistle to the Reader," in Two Bookes of Constancie, *by Iustus Lipsius, edited by Rudolf Kirk, translated by Sir John Stradling, Rutgers University Press, 1939, pp. 67-70.*

Pierre Bayle (essay date 1697)

[*A French scholar and philosopher, Bayle was described by Voltaire as "one of the greatest men that France has produced." His* Dictionnaire historique et critique *(1697;* An Historical and Critical Dictionary, *1710), a vast compendium of biographical and critical portraits of biblical, classical, and modern figures, is notable for careful scholarship and for thoughtful consideration of philosophical and religious issues, often expressed in lengthy, digressive footnotes to the text. In the following excerpt, from the* Dictionary, *Bayle provides insight into contemporary appraisals of some of Lipsius's writings.*]

Lipsius (Justus) was one of the learnedest critics that flourished in the XVIth century. I could relate a great many curious things concerning him; but as others have already collected them, and have not even forgot what relates to his education, and early attainments, I think my self obliged to speak only of their omissions. One of the greatest faults Lipsius is reproached with, is his inconstancy in point of religion. [In a footnote, Bayle adds: "Dr. Schlusselburg's account will not stand amiss in this page, which teaches us, that Lipsius reckoned it the same thing to be Lutheran, Calvinist, or Papist. . . .

'Of this unsettled Pelargic way of thinking in religion was that other Lucian, the subtle Epicurean Philosopher, Justus Lipsius, formerly my colleague, and professor of Rhetoric in the university of Iëna, in Thuringia, where he pretended to be very fond of the Lutheran religion, and swore that he looked upon the doctrine of Luther to the one, eternal and, divine truth, and condemned the idolatry and blasphemy of the Romish Antichrist. But, coming to Leyden, he apostatized, like Pelargus, and denied the truth he had acknowledged and approved; tho' this he disowned, saying that he was a Christian, and had neither forsaken, nor denied Christ. This I can with truth say and affirm of this man. For, when, in the year 1582, in the summer season, upon my return from Antwerp, I paid him a visit in the university of Leyden, where he was professor, and asked him what account he could give of his apostacy from the true religion, which he had confessed at Iëna, in 1572, and from Christ, whom he had denied and forsaken; he answered me in his own house, and in the presence of Henry Latomus, formerly preacher at Antwerp; my friend Schlusselburg, once my colleague, I have not denied nor forsaken Christ, tho' here I do not profess the Lutheran doctrine, but follow the Calvinists. *For all religion and no religion are alike to me: and with me the Lutheran and Calvinist doctrines walk an equal pace.* Being shocked at this declaration, I said: my friend Lipsius, if you continue in this opinion, it will go ill with you; and I easily believe, since you are indifferent to both religions, that you will at last be a Papist, as you was at first. To which he replied, it was equal to him. And so it happened; witness his book concerning the invocation of the Virgin Mary of [Joseph] Hall.'

Observe, by the way, in these words, the extravagant zeal of a rigid Lutheran. Schlusselburg calls the change from a Lutheran to a Calvinist, apostacy, and the denying of Jesus Christ. I might cite a great many writers, who, upon the chapter of religion, look upon Lipsius as a weathercock; but let it suffice to produce here the judgment of Boeclerus, and the advice he gives young students. . . .

'It would not be worth while to examine particulars, when young students are rather to be admonished in the general, *not to study such questions under the instruction of Lipsius,* who is every where consistent with himself, that is, *in matters of Divinity, or any way relating to religion doubtful, wandring, and ready to take any shape:* who now consents, now retracts; which must necessarily be the case of a man who never thought seriously about the true religion, and quite ignorant of the holy writings.' "]

They ground that reproach on this, that being born a Catholic, he embraced Lutheranism, whilst he was professor at Iëna. Afterwards, being returned into Brabant, he lived there as a Catholic, and then having accepted a professorship in the university of Leyden, made profession of what they call Calvinism. At last he quitted Leyden, and returned into the Spanish Netherlands, where he not only lived in the Roman communion, but even fell into an effeminate bigotry; which he discovered in his printed books. [In a footnote, Bayle adds: "One of these books is intituled, ***Justi Lipsii Diva Virgo Hallensis: beneficia ejus & miracula fide atque ordine descripta.*** Another is intituled, ***Justi Lipsii Diva Sichemiensis sive Aspricollis: nova ejus beneficia & admiranda.*** He adopts the most trifling stories, and the most uncertain traditions that can possibly be found upon this subject. Some of his friends dissuaded him from this attempt, alledging the uncertainty of these traditions, and the injury he would do himself; but all their counsels could not divert him from his enterprize. . . . The verses he made, when he consecrated his silver pen to our Lady of Hall, are strangely singular, as well on account of the praises he gives himself, as the excessive homage he pays to the holy Virgin. . . . He hung up with his own hands a silver pen (the most valuable gift he had) in the church, before the altar of the Virgin, and wrote under these pious verses:

> 'GODDESS, this PEN, my mind's interpreter,
> Which bent it's flight o'er earth, and seas, and skies,
> Ever employ'd on science, prudence, wisdom,
> Which dar'd describe, and publish CONSTANCY;
> Which treated both the arts of WAR and PEACE;
> Which aggradiz'd thy GREATNESS, ROME; and spread
> A various light o'er works of ages past:
> This PEN, I, LIPSIUS, consecrate to thee,
> And justly, since thy influence first inspired,
> And to perfection brought, thy Vot'ry's works.
> O! ever smile propitious on the same,
> This PEN produc'd, and on thy LIPSIUS, GODDESS,
> Bestow long life, and never-ceasing joy.'

He left by his will his furred gown to the same, our Lady; which gave occasion to say, that he made her this present, because the miracles he had so much celebrated, were ready to die of cold. Some Protestants writ with great force against him; he let them talk on, and only answered one of them in a few words: See his ***Rejectiuncula,*** at the end of his ***Virgo Aspricollis.*** He desired to defend himself against the author of the treatise *De Idolo Hallensi,* and against Thomson, who confuted him among other things about the ***Virgo Sichemiensis:*** but he refused to engage in these disputes, and acted wisely. . . . (pp. 840-42)

"It must not be forgot, that Lipsius was said to have composed such books only to convince the world, that he was not lukewarm and indifferent in religion, as many suspected he was. It was also believed, that these works were pure injunctions, and that the Jesuits extorted them from him. . . .

> 'The artful Loyalites (Jesuits) either extorted this work form Lipsius, by intreaties, which with him carry the force of a command, or wheedled him into it; or perhaps both; for as he is entirely devoted to them, he can decently deny them nothing.'

If this was his case, he might be compared, to hired mourners, who cried more bitterly than the relations of the dead. The Poet Lucilius takes notice of these . . .

> 'As women, who for hire
> Mourn at the funeral of one unknown,
> And greater marks of grief in public shew.'

"And Horace says little less: . . .

> 'As hired mourners, at a funeral, speak,
> And act, with more extravagance of grief,
> Than those, whose hearts a real sorrow know,
> So flatt'ring sycophants more zeal betray,
> Than real friends.' "]

The strangest thing of all in his conduct, and which has not been pardoned him, is, that living at Leyden in the external profession of the Reformed Religion, he publickly approved the principles of persecution, at that time exercised all over Europe against this very religion. He was strangely confounded, when he was shewn the consequences of his doctrine. [In a footnote, Bayle adds: "Koornhert is not the only person, who treated him roughly on this subject. For the Jesuit Petra Sancta, having made complaints against the author of the ***Stricturae Politicae,*** the answer returned him was this: . . .

> 'You complain of the author of the *notes* or *strictures* on the deceitful letter of *Justus Lipsius,* who, after having resided in Holland, and been a pensioner of the States, and having left his benefactors without taking leave, turned his pen against them, and underhand gave advice against the interest of their republic. Who was the author of those *strictures* or *notes,* I confess I am ignorant, but, whoever he was, he was a great patriot, and saw thro' Lipsius's frauds. I know not whether you, who are so fond of Lipsius's works, and seem to take a pleasure in Poetry, will be willing to read those verses, which, in the year 1579, he prefixed to a book against a certain obscure person. They were then published at Leyden for *Andrew Schouten,* and shew what disposition he either was, or pretended to be of. Hear him:
>
> "The western Tyrant's double chains are broke:
> By arms your country bravely ye assert;
> Religion too with vigour ye defend:
> But the fierce Spaniard breaks your land's repose;
> And lo! this wretch religion would disturb.
> Let other arms your country's battles fight;
> This thine, Feugraeus, to defend the faith,
> And by your pen detect its latent foes;
> This task thy office, and thy genius suits."
>
> 'You see what Lipsius then thought of the king of Spain, of the Romish faith, and of religion; who afterwards became *a defender of religion, faithlessly, and thro' a wavering, uncertain, disposition,* as Montague expresses it.'

"These verses of Lipsius dishonour his memory, when we compare them with his own confession, that he was only a Protestant in appearance at Leyden, and that his heart was Catholic. . . . Let him have done and said what he pleased; he and all his apologists were unable to elude the proofs alledged, to shew that this stile answered his external profession, as long as he passed for a Protestant. The author of the *Idolum Hallense* proves, that Lipsius, having protested, at Iëna before Tilemannus Hoshusius, who was then, rector of the university, that he sincerely embraced the Lutheran religion, communicated publickly, and in a funeral oration of his, which has been printed, declared, that God had given to his church the house of Saxony, to ruin the pest of the Papacy. . . . It is owned that he never communicated while he was at Leyden; but it is proved, by several extracts of his letter, that, whilst he lived there, he looked on the cause of the Spaniards as unjust, and wished the ruin of it, and that many expressions fell from him, which bespoke him a Protestant.

"Here are some farther circumstances of his controversy with Theodore Koornhert. When his treatise of politics [***Sixe Bookes of Politickes***], wherein he approved persecution on the account of religion, came out in 1589, Koornhert, a great stickler for toleration, writ him his opinion of this book, and replied to the answers he received, and at last published a book, with the title of *Prodessus contra hereticiaium & coactionem conscientiarum.* He dedicated it to the magistrates of Leyden, sent copies of it to the magistrates of other towns, and exhorted them to take great care of this writer's opinions. The publishing of this book vexed Lipsius; but, as he was a great ornament to the university of Leyden, he obtained of the magistrates an act of complaisance, which might have comforted him. They published at the town house, that they did not accept of Koornhert's epistle dedicatory, and that this author, by dedicating his book to them, did them neither service, nor honour, nor friendship; that they did not however prohibit his book, but permitted the inhabitants to read it, and at the same time advised them to read Lipsius's excellent answer. They declared, they had a very particular esteem for this professor. This act did not fully satisfy him, nor was he at all pleased at hearing, that Koornhert, being recovered from a long indisposition, was preparing a reply. It is said too, that by favour of some towns, he endeavoured to get the States of Holland to forbid the answering his political writings; but that Gerhard de Lange, Burgomaster of Tergou, opposed it with this reason.

> 'If what Lipsius has written to be true, he can be but weakly answered, and we shall be confirmed in the truth, by the very weakness of the writings that are published against him; but if any one discovers in them, what we do not now perceive, any falsity prejudicial to the country, what harm can there be to correct them?'

"Lipsius quitted Holland soon after, under pretence of taking a turn to the Spaw-waters, for the sake of his health. Nor did he ever come back thither more, but returned to Popery, and protested in a letter, which he writ from Mayence, that he had always been of the antient religion, though he had professed another, when he was in places, where the antient was not received. This made many believe him a hypocrite. Some were of opinion, that the discontent which Koornhert gave him, and the apprehension he had, that the Hollanders, might be worsted in the war against Spain, made him change sides. However it be, Koornhert, detained in his bed, and seized with a distemper, of which he soon after died, failed not to go on with his reply, and to finish it. His executors got it translated out of Flemish into Latin, and published it.

"It must be observed, that Lipsius had let fall some works against the Spanish inquisition in the first editions, but struck them out of the following. Boeclerus had told him his own upon this, in the chapter *De naevis Lipsiani operis,* which is the fifth of his treatise *De Politicis Justi Lipsii.*"] [This] was doubtless one of the reasons, which obliged him to quit Holland. He was offered a professorship at Pisa, with the promise of enjoying his liberty of conscience, but refused that employment. He settled at Louvain, where he taught the *Belles Lettres* in a way that was much to his reputation; and he died there, the 23d of March, 1606, in his fifty ninth year. There were those among the Protestants, who never would second the passion of some of their brethren, in defaming this learned man. He married a widow at Cologne about the year 1574, but had no children by her. Some say, she was a very ill woman; but he affirms, he lived quietly with her. I know not whether I ought to take notice, that he wrote a very bad hand. [In a footnote, Bayle adds: He confesses it himself, and thereby confutes those, who pretended to have printed from the original the oration *de duplici concordia;* from the original, I say, very fairly written. . . . This is confirmed by a passage of Gabriel Naudé:

> "This worthy scholar of our Muretus M. Antonius Bonciarius of Perugia once complained, that he could read but two or three of the first lines of the letters of Lipsius wrote to him; all the rest was so horribly scrauled. Nancelius said as much of Ramus's writing."]

[Lipsius's] conversation and aspect answered not the idea, the world had conceived of him. [In a footnote, Bayle adds: "Here is Aubertus Miræus's testimony in this point:

> 'His behaviour, dress, and conversation were mean: insomuch that many who are wont to estimate great men by the standard of ambition, when they saw Lipsius, were disappointed in their expectations: few formed a just idea of him. It is certain, that foreigners, who came, we know, from farthest Sarmatia, for the sake of seeing and hearing him (as formerly happened to the great Livy) found their ideas of him not answered.' "]

His friends did not abandon him, after his death, to the censures of his adversaries. [In a footnote, Bayle adds: "The Jesuit Scribanius, as Lipsius always expected, appeared in his defence.

> 'Let me tell you (you, who vainly attack him, departing, and meditating greater and more serious things) if occasion shall be, there will not be wanting some friendly hand (he pointed at Charles Scribanius) which will not suffer Lipsius to go unrevenged.'

"I speak not of those, who have attacked or defended him upon the subject of learning. Vincent Contarini, successor to Sigonius in the chair of Padua, criticized him learnedly enough in 1609. . . .

> 'In relation to the largess of corn among the Romans, and their military pay.'

"Garasse, who gave him two bites, was sturdily repulsed. He pretended, that Lipsius's doctrine about fate *is a mere chimera without the least foundation,* and blamed him for *having erected Mausolaeum monuments to his three little dogs, the first whereof was called* Mopsus, *the second,* Saphirus, *the third* Christiani orbis. I cannot, he continues, approve all these ridiculous and prophane inventions, forasmuch as this is plainly to declare, though the intention of authors may be very different. . . . Men and beasts die alike, and the condition of both is the same. The censurer of this Jesuit's *Doctrine Curieuse* strenuously maintains, that the destiny, taught by Lipsius, is conformable to Thomas Aquinas's notion. He says, that

> 'Aubertus Miraeus . . . did not forget the love that Lipsius had for dogs, even the names of the three, which he cherished above the rest. . . . He had caused them to be painted in a piece,

with the names, age, colour, and shag, of each, with some verses underneath, wherein he had no less ingeniously, than pleasantly, hit upon verses and inscriptions mentioned in the book called *Selectae Christiani orbis deliciae.* This is what Garasse takes for a mausoleum and an epitaph; so that whoever has his parrot painted, his dog, his cat, his wife, &c. with an inscription or verse, erects an epitaph, a mausoleum to them. . . . As for the epitaph of Sapphirus alone, which is found in the said book, *Selectae deliciae,* &c. It is a supposititious piece, which even the compiler, F. Swertius, durst not place with the three inscriptions, which are found under the title *Lovanensia,* and which doubtless some one might easily have composed by Lipsius's inscription on his dog Sapphirus, to excite his wit, as plainly appears from the bare reading.'

"The censurer adds, that the pretended prophaneness, which Garasse findes in it, is a chimera: he is pretty large upon this, and shews the impertinence of the reason, founded on the *unus est interitus,* &c. Mr des Marets, who thought this criticiser of Garasse to be an anonymous doctor of the Sorbonne, is mistaken. . . ."] [But] it was difficult in many things to make his apology. I do not reckon in this class what Father Garasse thought himself obliged to censure. Lipsius found himself accused more than once of plagiarism, but never would acknowledge, that he was justly accused. A fit of sickness he got at a feast, has been reckoned one of the greatest dangers, he was ever exposed to. It is strange, that a Latin style, so bad as his should found a new sect in the republic of letters. [In a footnote, Bayle adds:

'Lipsius has put Cicero out of fashion. When he was in request, there were greater matters in eloquence, than there are at present.'

"Scaliger says this: an evident proof, that the sect of the Lipsians was very much increased. But here we ought to cry out; . . .

'Ye imitators, slavish herd, how oft
The stir ye make excites my spleen! how oft
Provokes my laughter!'

"People must dote upon ill models, when they can prefer Lipsius's stile before that of Paul Manutius, or Muretus; a stile, which proceeds by starts and bounces, and is full of points and ellipses, before a stile smooth and flowing, and which unfolds every thought. Lipsius is the less excusable, because he changed from a good taste to an ill one. He wrote well in his youth; as appears by a book he dedicated to cardinal de Granvelle, and by the funeral oration of the duke of Saxony. He degenerated as he grew old. "His third century of Epistles," said Scaliger, "is good for nothing; he has forgot to speak, I know not what Latin it is." A learned humanist thought he did his father, who was a famous divine, some honour, by shewing he expressed a contempt for the stile, which Lipsius had brought into fashion.

'But he was particularly disgusted at that new way of writing, which Justus Lipsius, otherwise a great man, forced upon our age, and which many have servilely imitated, but not with the same success.'

"He relates the judgment, which James, Pontanus, and Marc Velserus made of the same stile. . . .

'I applaud the great wit and learning of Justus Lipsius, and think no man deserved better of the learned. But I shun and abhor, for many, and I think just, reasons, his peculiarity of stile, and new manner of writing. I have myself heard Marcus Velserus, a great friend of Justus Lipsius, declare, that he had rather imitate Muretus, than Lipsius; blaming his novel and affected stile, at the same time that he highly applauded his wit and learning.'

"He afterwards shews how Scaliger, being ready to give up the ghost, declared his abhorrence of that affectedness in stile. He must needs take it much to heart, since in that condition, in which his attention ought to have been fixed on objects infinitely more important, he would let the company know how much it troubled him. . . . Upon his death-bed (as Daniel Heinsius informs us, in a letter to Isaac Casaubon) he expressed his abhorrence of that itch of writing in a new stile: for thus Heinsius writes concerning him:

'He greatly disliked Justus Lipsius's affected stile; in those pieces especially, which he wrote in his old age; and he sometimes read his letters with indignation: I know you judge of him in the same manner.'

"Henry Stephens published a book of five hundred and sixty pages against Lipsius's Latin; but this book is so full of digressions, that the author seldom comes to his point. However he gives us to understand, that he extremely disapproved Lipsius's stile.

'Lipsius allured many by his eloquence; for nature having formed him for a florid, copious, stile, he chose another way of writing, viz. the concise, yet not without wit, but quite new; which when writers of inferior wit and judgment imitated, they fell into every thing vitious in writing.'

"There is no fear, that such an affectation in French would ever make a sect, though the president of Novion should return to the world."] (pp. 842-46)

Pierre Bayle, in an entry in, The Dictionary Historical and Critical of Mr. Peter Bayle, Vol. III, *1736. Reprint by Garland Publishing, Inc., 1984, pp. 840-47.*

Henry Hallam (essay date 1853)

[*Hallam was an influential English historian who promulgated a decided Whig bias in his works, including* A View of the State of Europe during the Middle Ages *(1818),* Constitutional History of England *(1827), and* An Introduction to the Literature of Europe during the Fifteenth, Sixteenth, and Seventeenth Centuries *(1837-39). In the following excerpt from an 1853 revision of the last-named work, Hallam briefly comments on Lip-*

sius's literary style, concentrating on his edition of Tacitus's works and De militia romana.]

The ***Tacitus*** of Lipsius is his best work, in the opinion of Scaliger, and in his own. So great a master was he of this favorite author, that he offered to repeat any passage with a dagger at his breast, to be used against him on a failure of memory. Lipsius, after residing several years at Leyden, in the profession of the reformed religion, went to Louvain, and discredited himself by writing in favor of the legendary miracles of that country, losing sight of all his critical sagacity. The Protestants treated his desertion, and these later writings, with a contempt which has perhaps sometimes been extended to his productions of a superior character. The article on Lipsius, in Bayle, betrays some of this spirit; and it appears in other Protestants, especially Dutch critics. Hence they undervalue his Greek learning, as if he had not been able to read the language, and impute plagiarism, when there seems to be little ground for the charge. Casaubon admits that Lipsius has translated Polybius better than his predecessors, though he does not rate his Greek knowledge very high. (pp. 21-2)

. . . . .

[In a short production by [Henry] Stephens, *De Latinitate Lipsii Palæstra,* he turns into ridicule the affected style of that author [Lipsius], who ransacked all his stores of learning to perplex the reader. A much later writer, Scioppius, in his *Judicium de Stylo Historico,* points out several of the affected and erroneous expressions of Lipsius. But he was the founder of a school of bad writers, which lasted for some time, especially in Germany. Seneca and Tacitus were the authors of antiquity whom Lipsius strove to emulate. "Lipsius," says Scaliger, "is the cause that men have now little respect for Cicero, whose style he esteems about as much as I do his own. He once wrote well; but his third century of epistles is good for nothing." But a style of point and affected conciseness will always have its admirers, till the excess of vicious imitation disgusts the world. (p. 37)

. . . . .

Francis Patrizzi was the first who unfolded the military system of Rome. He wrote in Italian a treatise *Della Milizia Romana,* 1583, of which a translation will be found in the tenth volume of Grævius. It is divided into fifteen parts, which seem to comprehend the whole subject: each of these again is divided into sections; and each section explains a text from the sixth book of Polybius, or from Livy. But he comes down no lower in history than those writers extend, and is consequently not aware of, or but slightly alludes to, the great military changes that ensued in later times. On Polybius he comments sentence by sentence. He had been preceded by Robortellus, and by Francis, Duke of Urbino, in endeavoring to explain the Roman castrametation from Polybius. Their plans differ a little from his own. Lipsius, who some years afterwards wrote on the same subject [***De militia romana***] resembles Patrizzi in his method of a running commentary on Polybius. Scaliger, who disliked Lipsius very much, imputes to him plagiarism from the Italian antiquary. But I do not perceive, on a comparison of the two treatises, much pretence for this insinuation. The text of Polybius was surely common ground; and I think it possible that the work of Patrizzi, which was written in Italian, might not be known to Lipsius. But, whether this were so or not, he is much more full and satisfactory than his predecessor, who, I would venture to hint, may have been a little over-praised. Lipsius, however, seems to have fallen into the same error of supposing that the whole history of the Roman militia could be explained from Polybius. (pp. 59-60)

Henry Hallam, "History of Ancient Literature in Europe from 1550 to 1600," in his Introduction to the Literature of Europe in the Fifteenth, Sixteenth, and Seventeenth Centuries, Vols. I and II, *A. C. Armstrong and Son, 1891, pp. 13-65.*

Basil Anderton (essay date 1914)

[*Anderton was an English librarian and author whose best known work is perhaps* Sketches from a Library Window *(1922). In the following excerpt from a paper originally delivered in 1914 and later published in* Sketches, *Anderton outlines Lipsius's* Manuductionis ad philosophiam stoicam *and appraises the author's attitude toward Seneca and Stoic philosophy.*]

Though several books on Stoicism have been published of late years, yet a work on the subject written by a bygone scholar does not lose its attractiveness or its lasting qualities. The old may well contain somewhat that is lacking in the new. Such a treatise, for example, as Justus Lipsius issued in 1604 [***Manuductio ad Stoicam philosophiam***] may afford no small delight to one who spares time to read it through. The book is now, it would seem, tolerably rare—in England at all events. My own copy is the 1644 edition. It is a volume small in size, but containing a good deal of matter, since there are in it over 750 closely-printed pages. It is a guide or handbook to Stoic Philosophy and Physics, for illustrating Seneca and other writers. Lipsius had, in fact, a great admiration for Seneca, both as a man and as a writer. (p. 10)

Lipsius was the restorer of Stoicism to the Renaissance—or, rather, to be exact, the founder of Neo-Stoicism. Lipsius appears, then, as a sage, but as a very human sage. Of the antique virtue of the first Stoics, he preserved the moderation and not the courage. He endured Fate's vicissitudes rather than braved them. He suffered from them, yet would willingly have found a remedy so as not to suffer from them. That is the sentiment which inspired his ***De Constantia.*** The special form of his Stoicism is attributable to three things—temperament, practical conviction, and the education given him by the Jesuits, who were, be it remembered, excellent humanists. Of weak health, he was by temperament not a fighter; he lacked the strength. He would rather circumvent difficulties than meet them face to face. Life had taught him, moreover, how often great sacrifices were futile. If he had no taste for extreme poverty, for Epictetus' "pallet and earthenware lamp," on the other hand he set no store by riches and honours. He accepted duties which enabled him to live. He refused conspicuous offices, such as that of State Counsellor, which the Archduke Albert offered him, knowing the envy they aroused. His Stoicism took practical form first in his ***De Constantia.*** "This book," he said, comparing it with his other works, "I wrote chiefly for myself, for my own well-being; the others I wrote for my reputation." In it he assimilated Stoicism according to his needs, making a first practical selection of the dogmas which seemed salutary for him as a Christian humanist, a friend of letters, a scholar driven from his native land by a devastating civil war. Thus the definitive choice of Stoicism was prepared which he made later, in a period which may be called that of his dogmatic Stoicism. In this second period he studied point by point, in his ***Manuductio*** and ***Physiologia,*** the Stoicism whose whole history he traced with the manifest aim of comparing it with the Christianity of the Bible and the Fathers of the Church.

Such, then, is Zanta's summary. (pp. 17-18)

As to Lipsius' general reputation and high standing, the *Grande Encyclopédie* says: "The services rendered by J. Lipsius to philology and history are immense; there is hardly a problem relating to Roman antiquities on which his criticism has not thrown lasting light, and most of his treatises are models of depth and erudition. We resort to them even at the present day, and cannot deny him the glory of having given to literary and historical studies a fruitful and enduring impulse."

Much has often been said about Lipsius' religious changes and hesitations. It should perhaps be borne in mind, however, that he was primarily a humanist (as the long record of his publications shows) rather than a theologian. In matters of philosophy, as he himself says in effect in his book on Stoicism, "neither a Plato nor an Aristotle should be exclusively followed, nor even one school only. If we call ourselves anything, it might be Eclectics." He was quick to recognise the good points in the various sects he studied. Doubtless the same breadth of view characterised his attitude towards Christian creeds. Valuing the good in each, the minuter network of their dogmas may well have failed to appeal to him, or even have seemed to him a matter of some indifference. When it became somewhat urgent, however, to make a definite choice, he sided finally with his old friends and teachers the Jesuits.

What with his teaching, his controversies, and the long list of books that he published, Lipsius was a very busy man. From incidental distractions, too, he was no more immune than other learned men are wont to be. At one place in his book on ***Stoic Philosophy,*** where his pupil, coming to see him very early, finds him already busy, he describes the interruptions to which he is constantly liable; for his own pursuits and for serious matters he seems only to have broken oddments of time.

> "I could almost aver, with Livius Drusus," he says, " 'that to me alone no holiday has fallen, from boyhood up.' I get up in the morning. 'Here are letters; answer them.' That done, I turn to other things. My servant comes to say that some nobleman has called, or a youth from France, or Germany, or Sarmatia; they wish to pay their respects. The one and the other want some token of my friendship inscribed in their albums. I have hardly recovered breath when one of my Belgian friends appears: 'So sorry to disturb you, but I've written a poem—or a pamphlet—and I want you to read it.' 'Anything further?' 'Criticise it and correct it.' 'What else?' 'Just write some preliminary verses or commendation.' Then I think I'm really free; but someone else turns up and wants an epitaph, either for himself or his brother or his father or a friend, or else an inscription for a house or a citadel or an altar. Then what about my students—like yourself? You know how readily they have access to me, and how I listen to them, answer them, direct them, and set them in what I believe to be the right way of study. This is the one sort of work that I least regret amongst all the others. It makes little difference whether I help them by talking or by writing, except that in one case perhaps more hear me, whilst in the other, although fewer receive what I say, yet perhaps the result is more effective and fruitful. So my life is spent, and I learn to put up with it; patience lightens the burden which our shoulders must needs bear. . . . Still, from time to time I return to myself, and can turn over in my mind something healthful and profitable to myself—a little superficially perhaps, and incidentally; yet I do turn it over."

This account of Lipsius' life, and of his outlook on life, may perhaps suffice. (pp. 18-20)

In his own day, there was the eagerness with which many Universities and great rulers sought to win him to their own precincts or their own courts; but there were also the bitter attacks that were made upon him. Opinions about him, in fact, have been conflicting; he has had keen partisans and equally keen depreciators. Among his contemporaries, whilst many admired him greatly, others, such as H. Stephanus and Joseph Scaliger, roughly assailed and belittled him; apparently scholars' rivalry and *odium theologicum* influenced them. Sagittarius, too, was another foe. That Lipsius was a force to reckon with, that he was one of the outstanding figures of his time, seems proved by the very bitterness of their attacks. Then in recent days the view of Nisard, in the work already cited, is noteworthy. His general estimate is high, though he does not fail to draw attention to what he regards as defects in character and taste. Perhaps, indeed, he over-emphasizes them: they were partly the manners of the age; and in any case it is given to few men to live for sixty years *sans peur et sans reproche.* He thinks his character, whilst sweet and amiable, often showed an undue facility and a lack of strength. The following passage will show how he places Lipsius historically. It is taken from the first chapter of his *Triumvirat Littéraire.* After referring to an earlier triumvirate of the sixteenth century—Erasmus, Melanchthon, Joachim Camerarius—he says: "These three illustrious men had hardly concluded the first fifty or sixty years of the sixteenth century, when three others equally illustrious—viz., Joseph Scaliger, Justus Lipsius, and Isaac Casaubon—were born, and in the second half of the century came to occupy the glorious place which their predecessors had held in the first half. The juxtaposition which I make of this double triumvirate is not arbitrary; it is neither the result of caprice nor of a personal taste for analogies; it is sufficiently indicated by the facts. Erasmus, Melanchthon, and Camerarius, have all three exercised, by their writings, an equal and simultaneous influence on the study of Letters, properly so called, in Germany; and if they did not obtain from their contemporaries the *title* of a triumvirate, they nevertheless exercised its *authority.* But Lipsius, Scaliger, and Casaubon, had alike, its power and its name. In their time Learning, as it grew more refined, grew also more pedantic; therefore, in submitting to the laws of the three critics who were then its own highest expression, it scrupulously gave them, in the Republic of Letters, a title which proudly voiced their authority and their number. Thus it was that Justus Lipsius, Joseph Scaliger, and Isaac Casaubon, had the designation of *Literary Triumvirate* conferred upon them."

Nisard concludes his work on Lipsius thus: "Any nation might be proud of having such a man as Lipsius for its compatriot; any nation might think itself honoured in rendering him some conspicuous homage to perpetuate the *scholar's* glory and the *nation's* gratitude. Nevertheless, while the *place publique* of Rotterdam proudly exhibits the statue of Erasmus, the *place publique* of Louvain is still waiting for the statue of Lipsius."

Let us now turn to Lipsius' book on Stoicism, which was published, as I have said, in 1604. In my own edition (that of 1644) the whole title-page is engraved, and its illustration shows the interior of a stone building, with doorways and pillars, and seven grown men. The central figure is probably Lipsius himself (at least, it bears some resemblance to his likeness), and he is speaking, possibly on Stoicism, to some of the others. In the book itself, however, he has only one interlocutor—a youth.

Expressed in outline, the first part is as follows: After a general exhortation to the study of philosophy in preference to that simply of elegant, or entertaining, or practical arts (which, however, form a useful preliminary training of the mind), Lipsius comes to the question, From whom should we seek our philosophy? Neither a Plato nor an Aristotle should be exclusively followed, nor even one school only. If we call ourselves anything, it might be Eclectics. In order to exhibit what is the field of selection, Lipsius runs over the main schools that have existed—the Barbarian, the Italian, and more especially the Greek.

Having thus cleared the ground, he shows the origin and succession of the Stoic school, from the Cynics down to Seneca. To the founder of Stoicism, Zeno of Citium, and to his life, he of course gives prominence, and then passes on to Cleanthes, Chrysippus, Zeno of Sidon, Diogenes called the Babylonian, Antipater of Sidon, Panætius, Posidonius, etc. To the Cynics, at their best, and in essentials, he gives high praise; and he records some of their views, on which certain Stoic doctrines and paradoxes were founded. He then states, and answers, several customary objections to Stoicism, and *per contra* sings its praise, showing in what parts of philosophy Stoics have excelled, and naming as examples certain great Stoics, among the rest Seneca and Epictetus.

What are the parts and definitions of philosophy? One broad division is into Contemplative and Active. Another is that of Seneca—viz., into Moral, Natural, and Rational. The meanings assigned to these terms and divisions are discussed, and also their several importance and value, Ethics being ranked as the foremost in fruitfulness. Coming then to the distinction between Philosophy and Wisdom, Lipsius shows that it is similar to that between the end and the means; or to that between the perfect good of the human mind, and the love and pursuit of that good. The perfect Wise Man of the Stoics is not found, but is an ideal only; the man, however, who is in a *state of progress* towards Wisdom does exist. Wisdom, in the Stoic view, may be taught; and Lipsius gives the Stoic theory of Knowledge. The mind receives appearances (*phantasiæ* or *visa*), and is impressed or affected by them (whence the τυπωσισ of Zeno, the αλλοιωσισ or ετεροιωσισ of Chrysippus). The more lasting of these perceptions give rise to memory; repeated acts of memory to experience. Hence arise conceptions of things. Then come reason and ratiocination, and so at last knowledge and wisdom. The Object or End that is pursued is, for Stoics, the living according to Nature. This has been understood in somewhat different fashions, and the views of Zeno, Cleanthes, and Chrysippus, are shown in their gradual development from vagueness into clearness. Living according to Nature came to mean living according to right reason, or according to Virtue, and hence to mean seeking after God, who becomes the all-important Object or End. Hence Virtue alone is sufficient for happiness, and no outward goods or gifts of fortune are needful. If it is suggested that external goods (like health, strength, etc.), being in accordance with Nature, conduce to the practice of Virtue, the stricter Stoics would reply that they recognise no good things, and no evil things, save those of the mind. The Stoic division and classification of things that are good are next given, and are followed by the Stoic account of things neutral (or indifferent).

By way of introduction to the next division, Lipsius urges that we should arm ourselves against the anxieties of the world—its fears and hopes—by studying philosophy, and by having always in mind the Stoic Decrees (or Ordinances or Axioms). These *Decreta* are like the root, the trunk, and the branches, of a tree. The first of them (or the root) was the recognition of the Object or End described above. The second (or trunk) was the understanding of the nature of the Good, also defined and classified. The third (or ramification) comprises those decrees that are common to most schools of philosophy, as well as those that are special to the Stoics—viz., the Paradoxes. It is with these that Lipsius is now concerned, and he treats a number of them separately,—e.g. The Wise man is of constant and equable mind, and is always happy; The Wise man is happy even when in torments; The Wise man is imperturbable and free from excessive passions (this is the famous απαθεια); etc.

In the second part of the book we come to the Stoic *Physiologia,* or Physics. It comprises things above, around, and below us—the whole universe, in fact, and all that it contains—God, Genii, Men. The two main divisions of the subject are the Corporeal and the Incorporeal. The Corporeal comprises *Principia* (or the things which produce or make), and *Elementa* (or things that are produced, and what springs therefrom). The Incorporeals are space, time, etc. Following Seneca, Lipsius begins with the *Principia.* These are twofold—God (the active), and Matter (the passive). These two principia are called "Natures." The word "Nature," then, to the Stoic includes God and Divine Reason permeating the whole world and its parts; and they define Nature as a fire. This fire is generative and constructive and preservative, and its work is that of a reasoning artificer. God, according to the Stoics, is also the world itself; He is One, Good, Provident. This unity, this goodness, and this watchful providence (both for the universe and for individuals), are next discussed. In providence or foresight the idea of Fate is involved, this Fate being described as the reason, or method, according to which the world is administered. Chrysippus interprets Fate as the truth, the nature, and the necessity, of things.

Various objections are then considered against God's providence and goodness, and the inquiry, *Whence come natural or external evils?* is examined first. By natural evils are understood monsters and prodigies, poisons and evil beasts. Then a second inquiry, *Whence come internal evils, or sin?* is examined. Here the Stoic view is that, although God has given man powers and faculties which, by certain applications, may be employed to commit sin, yet it is by our own act and will that they are actually so applied. If our natural constitution provokes this wrong choice, then the first defect lies in nature, or the material of which we are made. The origin of evil, in fact, both internal and external, is placed, not in God, but in Matter (which is coeval with Him and eternal). Of course, too, many so-called evils, such as poverty, pain, etc., are in the Stoic view not evils at all. With regard to God's toleration of our wrongdoing, He may foresee or see things, without foreordaining or causing them. Man's choice must be left free if he is to approach perfection or be more than an automaton.

The next division is begun after a break of six months, during which Lipsius has had a dangerous illness. He comes now to the other Stoic division of the Principia—viz., Matter. It is twofold—Universal and Particular. The Universal neither waxes nor wanes; the Particular both waxes and wanes. Matter is eternal, and is corporeal. It can suffer change, since it can take different forms (in the Particular) and can be infinitely subdivided. All things that exist are to the Stoics bodies: God, Matter, Virtues, Vices, Passions, Qualities, and so on—all are bodies. Lipsius then comes to the World (Mundus), which is the greatest and noblest of the Bodies. In Stoic phrase it includes the heavens, the earth, and God, and is the equivalent of Rerum Natura or Communis Natura. It may consist of either formed or unformed material. It differs from the Universe, which includes empty space (vacuum); whereas the World does not include empty space, but is contained in it. It was made by God, who changed all existence first into air, then into water (or moisture), and so into the mingled elements—fire, water, air, and earth. The World is animate, a living thing, endowed with sense and reason. The elements of which it is built up having been treated separately (Fire, Air, Water, and Earth), Lipsius considers the world (Mundus) as a whole. It is spoken of in two senses—either as consisting of all Nature (in which sense it is eternal), or as the ordered World (in which sense it is periodically destroyed and renewed, and is not eternal). In the latter sense it is liable to destruction both by water—the cataclysm—and by fire—the conflagration. That by water affects only the earth with all its life; but life will thereafter begin again, and the old order be renewed. The greater destruction (or rather change) by fire is, however, universal. It occurs when the Great Year (magnus annus) arrives, and thereafter a redintegration of all things is made. The time, the manner, and the purpose, of this destruction and renovation are discussed. A chapter is added in which the Incorporeals—Motion, Space, and Time—are touched upon.

Lipsius' next subject is the knowledge of man's nature and mind. On the physical side, he gives the Stoic view of man's first origin and subsequent reproduction. A body having been produced, the soul itself is insinuated from without, after birth. The soul comes from the eternal fire, from God Himself, and is thus part of the universal soul that is diffused throughout the world. As to its immortality, Stoics speak doubtfully. On the whole they regard it as enduring for a long time, though not to eternity. At the great conflagration all souls are reabsorbed into the ethereal fire. Some held—e.g. Chrysippus—that only the wise endured so long; the evil perished sooner.

The various divisions of the soul are then indicated; and finally Lipsius discusses the principal part of the soul (ηγεμονικον, the Principale of Seneca, the Principatus of Cicero). It is that which imagines, assents, perceives, desires. With a few final words on the dignity of the soul, Lipsius closes his book.

Such, then, is the subject-matter of this book on Stoicism. In the course of his work Lipsius quotes from a great number of authors, partly for the purpose of direct exposition, partly for illustration and embellishment. As is indicated by the title-page, Seneca's writings are of especial value to him. Among these, the Epistles and the Dialogues stand out conspicuous, though the *Quæstiones Naturales* and other writings are freely used. Quotations from Cicero, also, as one would expect, are abundant, especially from the *De Officiis,* Tusculan Disputations, *De Finibus, De Natura Deorum, Quæstiones Academicæ.* Diogenes Laertius, of course, makes his appearance everywhere. After these, perhaps Plato and Plutarch are cited the most; nor is Aristotle neglected. Of Plutarch's works, the most frequently quoted are, perhaps, *De Placitis Philosophorum, Adversus Stoicos,* and *De Communibus Notionibus.* Others, however (such as *Quæstiones Conviviales, Quæstiones Platonicæ*), are also often requisitioned. Naturally, Epictetus is much in evidence; but Marcus Aurelius is found less often than one might have expected. The Scriptures are frequently quoted, so also are many of the Fathers of the Church. But the list is too long and too varied to give here. Suffice it to say that, besides the names mentioned, I have noted thirty-four others, and there still remain those not noted. That he gathered his materials from such diverse sources has been made a reproach to Lipsius; and Nisard is among his critics. Into certain writers, indeed, apart from his use of them for happy illustration, he does read Stoicism unnecessarily. Views which are the common property of mankind, and which, therefore, are also found in Stoicism, he sometimes quotes as showing that one man or another has Stoic leanings. Yet even the expansiveness of his methods, and the wide field he covered in seeking his materials, have their interest to those who for the nonce are not hurried in their reading, but can afford to go leisurably. It is a method that at least helps to remind one how close is often the relation between different schools of thought, and how many of the world's ideas are a possession held by all the schools.

The general contents of his book on Stoicism having been given, certain characteristics that illustrate Lipsius' tastes and style may now be touched upon. The Latin in which the work is written is often eloquent; it is free from superfluity, and, though here and there compact to the verge of obscurity, it is for the most part clear. Nisard gives on this subject some valuable pages, in which he speaks of Lipsius' departure from Ciceronian canons, and his delight in a more piquant Atticism; his power of subtle brevity, and yet of full eloquence; his use, and perhaps his abuse, of old words. He gives also an account of the disordered and broken style into which his scholars and imitators (the Lipsians) fell, through copying mannerisms which they, lacking the needful genius and learning, could not use with success. Hence Lipsius advised them, instead of imitating himself, to take Cicero's more natural style as their model. The passage is well worth perusal, and perhaps explains the disrepute into which the adjective "Lipsian," as applied to compositions, seems to have fallen before it became obsolete (as Webster now describes it). Looking at another aspect of Lipsius, one recognises the care of the scholar in the innumerable references he gives in the margin of the text; one finds it, too, in his frequent critical emendations of obscure or corrupt passages. As to his interlocutor (a pupil), one would not say much; he is a lay figure, a "man of straw," who, while giving a certain variety to the composition, and expressing opinions which Lipsius may combat and demolish, is in himself not personally interesting, and has but small dramatic value. It is Lipsius' own exposition that chiefly attracts one; and in it one relishes the ample and leisurely progress with which the argument is carried forward, and the fulness with which the points that arise are illustrated. His frequent little perorations, too, as he reaches stage after stage, are welcome and enjoyable. The whole work reveals in Lipsius wide reading, scholarly aims, and love of virtue. If at times, in his dealing with pagan writings and creeds and philosophies, he appears at curious pains to avow his Christianity, one remembers, after all, that he lived, as regards matters of religion, in a most restless and censorious age. Though he himself was quick to recognise moral excellence in many of the old ways of thought, yet he knew from experience how bitter the men of his own generation could be.

In Seneca, as is already apparent, Lipsius found perpetual delight; his innumerable quotations, and, indeed, the very title-page of the work, attest the enthusiasm he felt. He admired his literary style, and conceived his personal character to be of rare nobility and charm. In some eloquent pages he summarises the notable features of the one, and gives an *apologia* and a defence of the other. (pp. 20-8)

A valuable clue to a man's own ideals and aspirations is obtained by observing the things and the qualities which he spontaneously praises. They show "which way the wind blows," just as an artist's special bent is revealed by the kind of pictures he paints of his own free choice. To the view of Lipsius' character, therefore, which we have already formed, confirmation may be added by considering the high-minded Seneca whom he presents to us—whether that character is in part an ideal creation, or is indeed the veritable Seneca of history. We shall think of Lipsius, then, as a man of lofty aims, of broad and generous judgment, zealous for the welfare of those with whom he is associated, free from avarice and ostentation, devoted to learning, fain of a simple and virtuous life. As to Seneca himself, it is true that Lipsius ranked both his life and character higher than a good many scholars rank them now. Yet even if, in his eulogy and vindication, he fails to carry all modern readers the whole way with him, his judgment and his attitude, which are interesting in themselves, may at least give one pause. They are the views of a close student of Seneca, and of a famous scholar and teacher, who left his mark on a great University. The outward glory of that University, alas! is departed: its buildings are shattered, its library of priceless books and manuscripts charred to shreds and fragments, its portraits—Lipsius, Erasmus, Jansen (Bishop of Ypres), Vesalius (the anatomist), Puteanus (pupil and successor of Lipsius at Louvain)—all are hopelessly gone. Yet the history of that University's thought can be still kept in remembrance. The body indeed is dead, but the spirit may still live. (pp. 28-9)

Basil Anderton, "A Stoic of Louvain: Justus Lipsius," in his Sketches from a Library Window, *D. Appleton and Company, 1923, pp. 10-30.*

Morris W. Croll (essay date 1923)

[Croll was an American educator and essayist who regularly contributed articles about sixteenth- and seventeenth-century English prose style to various scholarly journals. In the following excerpt, he discusses the formative influence of Lipsius's writings and thought on the burgeoning Anti-Ciceronian, or "Attic," movement of the late sixteenth century.]

The decade beginning just before 1570 is clearly indicated as the time at which the Anti-Ciceronian, or "Attic," movement first arrived at a program and became conscious of its connection with a general change of intellectual interests that was coming over the world. It was the beginning of a century in which, in spite of many oppositions, at first from a dying generation, and later from a generation just coming to birth, it was to dictate the prevailing form of prose style in all the countries of Europe. In the career of [Marc-Antoine] Muret, for instance, we are able to mark with definiteness the late sixties and the early seventies as the time when he first arrived at a complete sense of his own meaning and mission; the succeeding years of his life were spent in working out the philosophical implications of the Anti-Ciceronian rhetoric in moral and political science.

It was not only Muret's conversion, however, that made this the decisive moment in the history of the movement. Muret was then too old to make the world clearly aware of his changed intentions: his record was confusing. Moreover, other men of his generation, almost equally authoritative, had taken the opposite direction to his. In the North particularly, whence it seemed that new impulses must come, in the great Protestant countries of Germany and England, the leading humanists, Ascham and Car, Sturm, Melanchthon, and Camerarius were all Ciceronian, mildly and moderately so, it is true, since Erasmus had spoken, but still definitely in the tradition of rhetorical education and eminently puristic in their theory of style. The situation was not clear and the world might be going in either direction for all one could tell. It all depended on what the *young* men would say, what formulas they would adopt, what challenges they would respond to; and it is chiefly because of what was thought and said by two men who were both comparatively young at that time that we are able to date the beginning of the Anti-Ciceronian period at approximately 1570. (pp. 117-18)

There is no scholar of the Renaissance concerning whom the opinion of scholars has undergone so radical a change in recent years as Justus Lipsius, of Leyden and Louvain. His association, from 1586 onward, with the Jesuits of Louvain won him the hatred and abuse of Protestant partisans in the Northern countries; on the other hand, the more orthodox of his own party regarded him with constant suspicion and refrained from acknowledging their real intellectual indebtedness to him because it was believed that he had imbibed from his Stoic masters in antiquity doctrines dangerous to the faith of a Christian; and, finally, the shadow of academic disapproval always rested upon his literary doctrines, even during the period when they were enjoying almost unrivaled success in the actual practice of the world. For these and other reasons his name appears much oftener in the seventeenth century in hostile than in friendly allusion, though it was recognized that he deserved his place beside Scaliger and Casaubon in the intellectual triumvirate of his time; and modern scholars were content until a few years ago to accept the judgment of his contemporary foes at their face value. It was sometimes recalled, with facile humor, that there was a Lepidus in the Roman triumvirate; and it was the custom to hold him up to scorn as a typical linguistic pedant insensible to the philosophy and literature of the ancient authors whom he edited. These were strange judgments to be passed on the philosopher who has now come to be known as "the founder of seventeenth-century Neo-Stoicism" and the writer who must finally take an almost equal place with Montaigne and Bacon among the founders of the prose-style of the seventeenth century.

The stages in Lipsius' development as a philosopher can be clearly discerned. His history properly began, when he was twenty-one years old, with his visit to Muret at Rome in 1568, though at that time he had already won considerable reputation as a linguist and rhetorician. The first result of this encounter was his quick,—if we may believe him, his *instantaneous,*—conversion from a purely literary and rhetorical learning to a realistic—or, as we should say, a positivistic—study of politics. He began at once the intense and rapid labors which bore fruit, after only seven years, in his famous edition of Tacitus (1575), and a little later in the important compilation known as ***Six Books of Politics.*** These works won him a reputation as a "politician," or student of *prudentia,* which was never equaled or corrected, at least in Italy, by the fame of his later work. The ***Politics*** unfortunately won him also the hatred of most scholars of the North by its advocacy of the policy of "fire and sword" in dealing with heresy, though a careful student of his mind will be convinced that his ruthlessness, like the orthodoxy of Montaigne and Browne, was founded in skepticism and not in bigotry.

These first works do not, however, represent his matured interests. They reflect directly the influence of Muret, just as we may discover in all the first part of his career the mobility of mind, the physical restlessness, the extravagance of wit veiling an inward dissatisfaction, which are observable in his master. The time of his full self-discovery may be fixed with some certainty at the point of his career when he severed his connection with the Protestant University at Leyden and deliberately chose a life of quiet and retirement as teacher in his own Louvain college. There was an interval in which he was received as an honored guest at several German courts and universities, and was offered more than one brilliant and conspicuous position of public activity. He deliberately chose to retire to the house on a quiet side street of Louvain not far from the college, where he spent the rest of his life in the placid orderliness that he describes in his letters, teaching a small number of chosen students, walking in the country with his Scotch dog Mops, and cultivating his tulips.

In the ***De Constantia,*** his first work of Stoic philosophy, he attributes his choice of retirement and his study of "apathy" to the trouble of his time, and the varied spectacle of human suffering that he has witnessed in the devastated towns and country regions of the Netherlands. But the roots of seventeenth-century Stoicism lie much deeper than the events of a generation. Once started by Muret in the way of a naturalistic study of public and private morality, Lipsius could never have rested until he had attained the formula of spiritual recollection and cure which his age required. Having found this, he had found himself at last, and the rest of his life was devoted to Seneca and the doctrines of Stoic *sapientia.*

The progress of his literary ideas was like that of his philosophy, and seems always to have kept a step in advance of it. Like Muret, he blundered into the wrong track at the beginning of his career—the back-track of Ciceronianism. In 1567, having scarcely finished his studies at Louvain, he published a volume of precocious learning containing three books of ***Variæ Lectiones.*** It is dedicated to the mighty Cardinal Granvelle—so high does he dare to aspire already—in copious Ciceronian periods, indistinguishable from many other examples of the same style produced by the rhetorical humanists of the sixteenth century. But his conversion was early, instantaneous, and thorough. Muret had gradually divined the new program of studies, had worked out their relations one to another, had discovered their appropriate rhetorical medium; Lipsius' task was merely to understand the meaning of his message, to develop the implications in it which Muret himself had not dared to reveal, and to devote the energy and fire of his youth to its propagation. It was in 1568, only a year after his Ciceronian début, that he met Muret in Cardinal Hippolito d'Este's palace at Tivoli, and a few days later wrote to him as a disciple to a master. Muret has found the true way of study: nothing more *Attic* has ever met Lipsius' eyes than the letter he has just received from him. A year later Muret wrote, admitting him, as it were, to the mysteries. At Tivoli, he said, it is true that we live in all the delights of the senses—a truly Phæacian life—but there are none who delight in the same studies that you and I enjoy. There is something of the strange secrecy and sense of danger in this correspondence that is often to be noted as characteristic of the Anti-Ciceronian movement; and it is not unlikely that Muret's description of the sensual life of Tivoli alludes in a veiled style to the rhetorical, purely literary tastes of the patrons whom he was serving, contrasting them with his own enthusiasm for the virile and "modern" studies which he did not dare to profess openly.

Lipsius' resolve is taken at once. Political and moral science, not rhetoric; Attic style, not Ciceronian, shall be the objects of his effort. And he begins to work on an edition of Tacitus. But how shall he make the transition decently from the opinions that the public still thinks he holds to those he has actually espoused? It was an embarrassing situation for a young man who had already attained reputation as a stylist; and we can follow—not without enlightenment—the steps of his cautious preparation. First he publishes nothing of any import for seven years after the date of his first work; and then he comes out, in a new preface, in 1574, with the astonishing statement that Plautus' old style has more savor for him than Cicero's. The quaint and ancient words, the piquant realism of this author made him a favorite of Anti-Ciceronians from Cujas to Gui Patin; he was tonic to minds suffering from the lassitude of a long season of purism. But Lipsius is careful to give the air of a whimsical and ingenuous weakness to his preference; and in the same tone he continues to speak of the style he uses in this new work, the ***Quæstiones Epistolicæ.*** While he professes that his subject compels him here to employ a style more pointed and significant than he has heretofore employed, he seeks a justification for his new manner in the *Letters* of Cicero.

The disingenuousness of all this is apparent when we consider that his Tacitus must already have been in the press when these words were written. The true account of the style he employs in the ***Quæstiones*** is contained in a letter to a friend, and the words are worth quoting as one of the best descriptions of the new Attic. "I am afraid," he says, "of what you will think of this work (the ***Quæstiones***). For this is a different kind of writing from my earlier style, without showiness, without luxuriance, without the Tullian concinnities; condensed everywhere, and I know not whether of too studied a brevity. But this is what captivates me now. They celebrate Timanthes the painter because there was always something more to be understood in his works than was actually painted. I should like this in my style." Both the terms of criticism in this passage and the style in which it is written come from Seneca.

Of course the air of mystery could not long be maintained after the appearance of his Tacitus in 1575. It is true that he continued to write to his literary intimates, even to Montaigne, as if he and they had been initiated into an esoteric cult, a secret order of taste and ideas, which involved them in opinions contrary to those they were bound to profess in public and odious to vulgar and orthodox intelligences. But this curious attitude continued to be characteristic of certain phases of the Anti-Ciceronian movement during at least two generations. The world soon became aware, through his voluminous and international correspondence, that Lipsius was a man with a philosophical and literary mission. Almost immediately after the appearance of the Tacitus he let it be known that he would devote the rest of his life to preparing an edition of Seneca. This resolve he faithfully carried out, and the great work did not appear until 1605, the year before his death. It was then already world-famous, however, and almost immediately attained a currency such as few works of learning have enjoyed. It was the chief instrument of the extraordinary diffusion of Seneca's influence throughout the seventeenth century, and was so closely identified with the study of the Stoic philosopher that people sometimes spoke of "Lipsius" when they meant the works of Seneca. There seems to have been doubt during the years following his death whether his influence was to be of more use to the imitators of Tacitus or to the imitators of Seneca. But there can be none in the mind of a modern student who studies the works of the many writers who derive from him. He and Montaigne are the chief sources of the Senecan literary mode, and his own style is obviously formed by a slight exaggeration of Seneca's point and brevity, and unfortunately a great exaggeration of his play upon words.

In the course of twenty-five years of preparation for his Seneca, Lipsius' program of studies gradually enlarged and at the same time defined itself. He found himself involved, like Muret, in the enterprise of rehabilitating the Latin masters of the silver age, but with the difference that his interests were almost wholly limited to prose writers—he is like Bacon, Browne, Balzac, Pascal, and many other literary masters of the seventeenth century in this respect—and that he was much clearer in his literary purposes than Muret. What these purposes were is described in a passage from a Latin eulogy composed by a Mechlin judge, a literary disciple of Lipsius, immediately after his death. The reader will perhaps be rewarded for his patience in enduring Rivius' style for a few sentences,—somewhat mitigated in translation, it is true,—for the sake of the information he conveys, and also because the passage will show that a certain kind of Asianism arises, as Cicero observed, from an exaggeration of the very qualities called Attic. Rivius is plainly one of those disciples of Lipsius, often mentioned in contemporary criticism, who imitated only the faults of his master.

> Declaring, Rivius says, that he existed for the good of the State, not the State for *his* good, he (Lipsius) decided at the beginning to save the lives of his own kind by his labors, to recover health to the sick by his ministrations, to restore their original possessions to those who had been unjustly despoiled, and to liberate them from their chains. It was for this purpose that he visit-

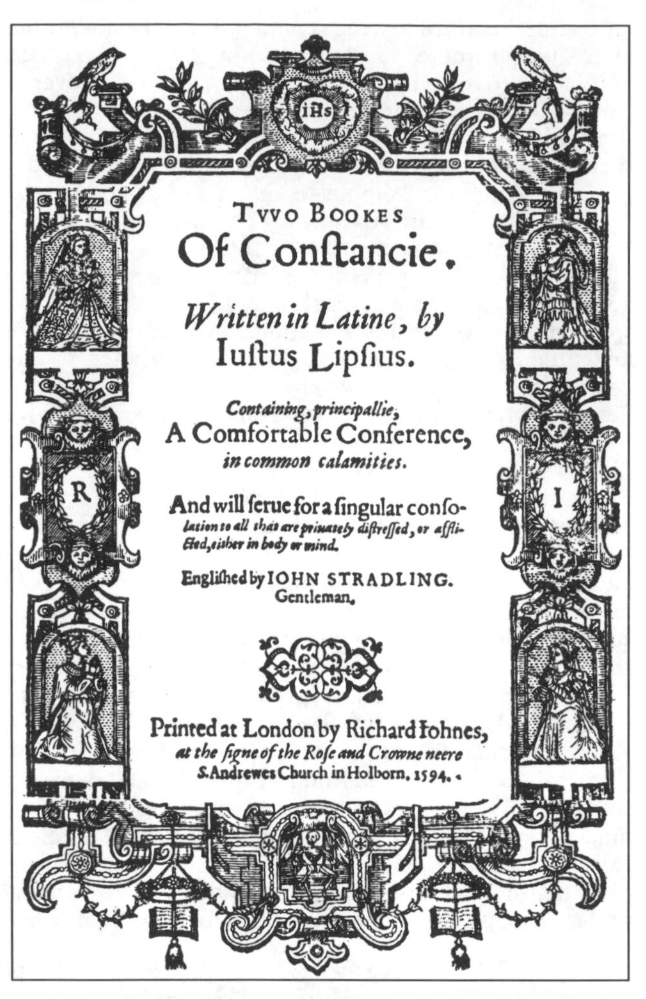

Tvvo Bookes
Of Conſtancie.
Written in Latine, by
Iuſtus Lipſius.
Containing, principallie,
A Comfortable Conference,
in common calamities.
And will ſerue for a ſingular conſo-
*lation to all that are priuately diſtreſſed, or affli-
cted, either in body or mind.*
Engliſhed by IOHN STRADLING.
Gentleman.
Printed at London by Richard Iohnes,
at the ſigne of the Roſe and Crowne neere
S. Andrewes Church in Holborn. 1594.

Title page of Stradling's translation of Two Bookes of Constancie (*1594*).

> ed all the prisons and took note of Seneca, the tragic poet, Velleius Paterculus, the famous Pliny, that once-celebrated panegyrist of Trajan, and many others besides, wearing the chains and the dress of prisoners, living there in mud and ordure, branded with the red-hot iron, shaven, half-dead. In the same wretched gang he saw also Valerius Maximus, so unlike himself, so unlike his name.
>
> . . . And two prisoners were particularly noteworthy as having been unjustly condemned—L. A. Seneca and G. Cornelius Tacitus. These men, who had held consular rank, he beheld crawling out of I know not what *barathrum,* what cave of Polyphemus, or rather what cavern peopled with tigers and panthers. . . . To Lipsius, who took pity on them and demanded to know why men who had served the public good as citizens had been thrown into chains, why they were bound who had attached all humanity in bonds to themselves by their services, and ought to be held in the hands and in the hearts of princes; why they lay darkened in filth who had cast a light beyond the limits of the world, beyond nature—the dazzling light of *prudentia* and *sapientia;* to Lipsius, inquiring thus. . . . (The period continues to much greater length.)

Rivius' words are valuable as indicating the full scope and deliberateness of Lipsius' innovations. They help us to understand, for instance, why several minor contemporaries of Tacitus and Seneca enjoyed so much more favor in the seventeenth century than they have done since: why Valerius Maximus is so often quoted by Montaigne, Jonson, and Browne, Velleius Paterculus by the concettisti in prose, and the younger Pliny by panegyrists and students of "point." But they also reveal the fact that Lipsius limited his charity to authors of this school and century. Though his classicism is deliberately not Augustan, it is a true classicism, and he carefully avoids the dangerous mistake which Muret did not sufficiently guard his followers against, and which the "libertine" prosaists of the seventeenth century were frequently to make, of frolicking anew in the semi-barbarism of the "low Latin" style.

Of course Lipsius was not the sole founder of the stoical philosophy of the seventeenth century or even of the Senecan imitation which accompanied it in prose literature. Du Vair, Montaigne, and Charron had all discovered the path of renunciation and self-dependent morals before him or without his aid. But the clearness and exclusiveness of his program, his international authority as a humanist, and his use of the new prose-model in the authoritative Latin language gave the impetus to the Stoic philosophy and style which carried them into every part of Europe and almost every lettered circle of society. He soon had many followers among professed scholars at the universities who dared to brave the imputation of heterodoxy. But the greatest success of his program (though he himself always wrote in the ancient tongue) was won in the more open fields of the vernacular languages and the popular philosophy of laymen. Most conspicuous among his professed disciples was Francisco Quevedo, the young Spanish nobleman who had already won a brilliant reputation in burlesque fiction. There was a correspondence between the two men during Lipsius' last years in which Quevedo hailed Lipsius as the hierophant of a new mystery in terms that recall the letter that Lipsius had written to Muret forty years before. To Lipsius he owes the discovery of the way that he will henceforth follow throughout his life. His writings soon showed what he meant; for he became the consistent and enthusiastic exponent of Christian Stoicism in many works of philosophy in Spanish and Latin, in which Job, Socrates, Cato, and Seneca appear as the saints and heroes of one dispensation. When one reads the bold and extravagant pages in which he equalizes pagan and Hebraic models of morality one easily understands why Lipsius himself narrowly escaped the Index, and why he felt it necessary to destroy his dissertation called ***Thraseas*** in defense of the right of suicide, which had won, even though unpublished, a dangerous notoriety. Quevedo's discipleship was complete; for he adopted not only Lipsius' philosophy, but also his literary style and his devotion to the masters of silver-age Latinity. "Mi Seneca, mi Lucano, mi Juvenali," he exclaims, in a kind of rapture. It was a literary program which gained peculiar plausibility in Spain from the fact that Seneca and Lucan had been natives of that country. The somber dignity of the Spanish character was believed to be as friendly to Stoic ideals of conduct as the Spanish love of "emphasis" was to the significant rhetoric of the first century.

The impression made by Lipsius upon England was almost as great, however. His dialogue ***Of Constancy*** was translated and published in 1593 by Sir John Stradling, a minor author who had a part also in disseminating the taste for Martial and the epigram in this decade. Jonson studied the political, the rhetorical, and the Stoic writings of Lipsius, and may have learned from them some of the admiration for the two Senecas which is displayed in his prose and poetry alike, and some of the Stoic philosophy which he expounds—or translates—so admirably in many a passage of his verse. A Senecanism more obsequious to Jacobean defects of taste is revealed in Bishop Hall's *Epistles* and *Meditations.* It is hard to believe that these works have not been directly influenced by the Belgian scholar, whom Hall met in person, encountered in sectarian controversy, and mentioned frequently in his writings. Lipsius' influence at least appears far and wide in many other English moral writings of the century; and it is recorded that his letters were sometimes used as Latin texts in English schools.

These are remarkable instances of Lipsius' authority, yet the knowledge of its range and power must chiefly be won, for reasons that have been explained, from the vigorous opposition it aroused. The attacks made by his opponents during his lifetime are of little value to the historian, because of the religious prejudices that mingle with and obscure their literary purposes. Henri Estienne, who was himself an Anti-Ciceronian,—though more nearly akin to Montaigne than to Lipsius,—published in his old age a long and fantastic book *De Lipsii Latinitate.* But he has so entangled the literary doctrines of Lipsius with the intrigues of Spain and the Ligue and the supposed alliance of the Catholic powers with the Turk that no modern reader can hope or care to discover his exact meanings. Scaliger is a better critic, and has left the first intelligent description of the new Senecan style by an opponent. But he was the official voice of Protestant literary orthodoxy, and his appointment to the chair of rhetoric at Leyden vacated by Lipsius was probably meant to have both sectarian and rhetorical significance.

Two decades later the cause of correct classicism in style rests in different hands, the hands of the Jesuit rhetoricians who have taken charge of the literary education of the French court and society. To rally the taste of their time to pure Augustanism is the task of Father Caussin and Father Vavasseur, and the tendencies they are hopelessly struggling against are chiefly those that were set going by Lipsius and his school. It is still so in the middle of the century, when Balzac is the arbiter of taste; Montaigne and Lipsius are the protagonists of the tradition from which he seeks—in vain—to disengage himself. And even a generation later, Bouhours attributes both good and bad elements in the prevailing modes of style to Lipsius' teaching. It is remarkable that a model set in Latin writing by a philologist should have had so much power in determining the form of prose-style in several of the living languages. But the explanation is clear: Lipsius provided the model of a *Stoic* style. (pp. 118-27)

Morris W. Croll, "Attic Prose: Lipsius, Montaigne, Bacon," in Schelling Anniversary Papers, *by Arthur Hobson Quinn and others, The Century Co., 1923, pp. 117-50.*

Theodore G. Corbett (essay date 1975)

[In the following excerpt, Corbett discusses the impact of Lipsius's writings upon the conduct of Spanish state affairs during the late sixteenth and early seventeenth centuries, asserting that his works "were responsible for the triumph and tribulations of Spanish statecraft."]

Studies of Justus Lipsius have emphasized his position as the Erasmus of his age: a shy, retiring humanist, whose intellectual endeavors dominated the literary and religious circles of the late sixteenth and early seventeenth centuries. By comparison few studies have noted that a great portion of the work of Lipsius concerned the molding of individuals for public life by teaching them the most sophisticated statecraft. The basic reason modern scholars have ignored the political aspect of Lipsius' writings is that he was not inclined like Machiavelli to center life around the preservation of the state. Instead, Lipsius still appealed to the more conservative values of Renaissance scholarship and Reformation religious conviction as a basis for statecraft. However, to say that Lipsius' writings had not improved upon earlier political works would not be fair; his concern for blunt realism, his efforts to penetrate to the inner motivations of men and states, his acceptance of dissimulation, carried his studies far beyond previous "mirror-of-the-prince" literature. In fact, among statesmen of Spain, the most powerful state of this period, Lipsius' combination of scholarship, religious piety, and sophisticated statecraft made him far more popular than any *politique,* including Niccolò Machiavelli. Thus, during the late sixteenth and early seventeenth centuries, Lipsius' writings more than those of any other figure were responsible for the triumphs and tribulations of Spanish statecraft.

Since he was not a practicing statesman, Lipsius' influence over the Spanish statecraft was based upon his writings and correspondence rather than his personal political accomplishments. The books that made his reputation among Spanish statesmen were his translation of ***Tacitus*** (1575), his study of moral conduct, ***De Constantia*** (1583), his insights into public life, ***Politicorum libri sex*** (1589), and his work on the Roman military establishment, ***De militia Romana*** (1595). An avid correspondent, Lipsius also wrote numerous letters to Spanish diplomats, *letrados,* and humanists. Moreover, he offered a prodigious output of literary and religious works which were popular among Spaniards, but which this study will not cover because they devoted little space to the subjects of politics, history, and military affairs—the essential ingredients of early modern statecraft. In all these writings, Lipsius' popularity was not totally based upon his own talents or the originality of his work. Like so many writers of his period, Lipsius was an eclectic whose ideas were based upon the gleaning of concepts from a host of classical authors. It is thus quite possible that many Spanish statesmen were first drawn to Lipsius as a source of classical letters or universal knowledge, and only indirectly discovered his value in the field of statecraft.

One of the ties between Lipsius and Spanish statesmen may be explained by his Flemish citizenship. Lipsius was born on October 18, 1547, in Isque, near Brussels, where his family was Catholic, stable, and typically bourgeois. A retiring scholar and amiable teacher, he spent most of his career in the seclusion of a university or his own garden. Still there was a streak of vanity in him, and as a subject of the Hapsburg Empire, he did seek rewards at the courts of Brussels and Madrid. But his ideas were not accepted by these courts before 1591 because of Lipsius' convictions. In the 1570's and 1580's Lipsius had difficulty in deciding upon firm religious and political beliefs. Whereas Spaniards demanded an unswerving commitment to the Counter-Reformation faith and the Spanish Empire, Lipsius vacillated on the subject, angering Spaniards by tutoring the Protestant general, Maurice of Nassau, and teaching history at the Protestant University of Jena. No doubt, Lipsius conceived of himself as the focal point of a republic of letters, above the turmoil of religious and political strife, advocating religious toleration and peace rather than adherence to any faith or state. But the Spanish courts would not recognize him until 1591, when he at last came over to the Catholic cause, was reconciled with the Roman Church, and received a political pardon and benefice from Philip II. Only after this accommodation did Lipsius' person and ideas become acceptable at the courts of Brussels and Madrid.

Another tie between Lipsius' thought and that of Spanish statesmen can be explained by the compatibility of his attitudes with those of Spanish traditions. The medieval *Reconquista* and constant exposure to the Moslem world had created in Spanish Catholicism an intense militancy which was further extended into the Counter-Reformation. This tendency to solve religious problems through political and military action, when combined with a respect for religion as a social and political unifier, made it impossible for Spaniards to accept statecraft that did not make religious piety fundamental to the well-being of the state. Spanish statesmen were thus obliged to perform the most aggressive and sophisticated statecraft in the service of their religious faith. Their problem became one of harmonizing the pagan and Machiavellian origins of such statecraft with Catholic religious values. It was here that Lipsius was most useful, for his works showed a Spanish statesman how he could learn from pagan and Machiavellian statecraft, and still maintain confidence in the moral and religious righteousness of his actions.

To obtain pagan and Machiavellian statecraft, Spanish statesmen turned to Machiavelli's sources, namely Tacitus and Seneca. Hence the need for the works of and commentaries upon Tacitus and Seneca led to another tie between Lipsius and Spanish statesmen. Spanish statesmen were as sophisticated as *politiques* in the development of statecraft. During the sixteenth century, Spaniards had come to accept the study of history as a source of political experience from which maxims of statecraft could be formed. At first, their historical examples were obtained from the reading of Livy, Plutarch, or their own imitations, such as Pulgar's *Claros Varones.* However, these works were not realistic enough for the practicalities of political life. Their idealized (and in the case of Pulgar, Christianized) portrayal of political life as a means of obtaining individual fame, did little to improve the techniques of statecraft. What was needed were historical studies which delved into the hidden motivations of statesmen so that the able practitioner of statecraft might discern the intentions of spokesmen for rival states. For this Tacitus soon became recognized as the unmatched source. Spanish translations of Tacitus' various histories appeared first in 1613, 1614, 1615, and 1629. In the introductions to nearly all of these translations there was praise of Lipsius' Latin translation of Tacitus. The 1614 Spanish translation also provided aphorisms and maxims which appeared in ***Politicorum*** and ***De Constantia.*** In the area of conduct, Seneca was even more valuable than Tacitus. Seneca showed how one could control one's own motivations in the face of political dangers, so that one could practice Tacitus' subtle arts and still maintain one's morality. Seneca appeared as early as 1491 in Spanish, but suffered a decline in published translations after the middle of the sixteenth century, only to undergo a revival of publication early in the seventeenth century. ***De Constantia*** served as a prime inspiration for these translations. The Senecan revival thus paralleled the first great interest in Tacitus and it was Lipsius who was considered the chief interpreter of both figures.

Looking at Lipsius' ideas in more detail, we can see how subtle he was in blending the realistic and pagan statecraft of Tacitus and Seneca with traditional Christian values. The merging of these beliefs had the effect of producing a system of practical ethics—if by no means a full-fledged philosophy—which has been generally referred to as "Neostoicism." Lipsius was so successful in showing the compatibility between Stoic and Christian ethics that his Spanish followers soon began to assert that Seneca, a pagan by any standard, was in fact a secret Christian. There were definite similarities: Stoics emphasized the virtues of constancy, goodness, modesty, prudence, and justice—the historical roots of much Christian ethics. Stoics also disdained the passions, pride, and excesses of pleasure and wealth, fundamental tenets of Christian ethic. Certain Stoics, like Tacitus and Seneca, supported religious belief and pious conduct as a stable foundation on which to rest the state. True there were some thorny problems in bringing together the two ideals: e.g., certain Stoics conceived of a world governed by the blind course of fate, not divine providence, and Stoic fortitude allowed for suicide, something which Christian teaching positively forbade. Another problem involved the mixing of Stoic beliefs with those of similar ethical systems. Lipsius himself had great respect for controlling the passions by practicing the Epicurean ideal of withdrawal from the world in order to contemplate. Stoics were not above such an ideal of withdrawal, but they emphasized its practice only occasionally to renew constancy and instead advocated participation in worldly endeavors. This confusion enhanced the Christian aspect of Lipsius' ethic from one viewpoint for it justified the monastic concept of retreat from society, though at a time when the Counter-Reformation had put the Church's greater emphasis on social participation.

This Neostoic ethic left a considerable amount of room for the practice of pagan and Machiavellian statecraft. For the Spanish statesman, Lipsius recommended the concept of prudence as a guide to carry him through the pitfalls and dangers of public life. The ultimate aims of prudence were found not in politics, but in constancy and piety in order that an individual or a state might flourish as a virtuous entity. Yet, for all the reference to the high ethical aims of prudent conduct, a statesman might use dissimulation, naked force, or the most underhanded statecraft to maintain his own virtue or that of the state. The single limitation was that only a few possessed the demanding qualities needed to practice prudent statecraft. One first had to examine the teachings of experience and history in a disciplined, rational manner which emphasized total detachment from worldly confusion and conflict. A statesman was thus called upon to be trained in the ways of the world and yet remain steadfast and aloof from them in making decisions which had to respect piety and morality. The key to this process was the firmness and constancy of one's conscience, the point at which secular decision making was tied to the influence of divine providence.

Perhaps a final way of synthesizing Lipsius' moral and political beliefs is to examine the political position that might have lured him from his secluded life. The office of Roman censor figured prominently in Lipsius' works. For example, in giving advice on the reform of government, Lipsius urged the creation of two censors on the Roman model as purveyors of Stoic morality to the masses. The elected censors were to regulate taxes and markets, restore faith in religion, and in particular prevent all forms of excesses in wealth, lust, drunkenness, quarrels, banquets, apparel, and other finery. Here was an office which combined respect for the moral virtue of the holder with the political acts of reform and preservation of the state. Even Spanish statesmen who did not share Lipsius' respect for the position of Roman censor, were inspired by such a figure, whose moral as well as political superiority gave him leadership over men.

The earliest Spanish appreciation of the political talents of Lipsius was expressed in intellectual centers at the Madrid court and in the cosmopolitan metropolis of Seville. In these humanist circles Lipsius was first known for his terse Latin and religious piety. But humanists were also *letrados* and courtiers who readily found Lipsius' works as valuable for their administrative duties as for their literary pleasure. Soon Lipsius' insights into the affairs of men were regarded by certain Spaniards as "unique and singular on earth" and his ability at piercing analysis earned him the honorable title of the "lynx-eyed." From the intellectual centers Lipsius' influence spread to the interior of Spain, as disgruntled and unemployed *letrados* used his ideas to criticize the corruption of the Madrid court and of Spanish social conditions. The peak of Lipsius' political influence was reached in the area of foreign affairs, by the conversion of three Spanish diplomats: Juan de Vera, Bernardino de Mendoza, and Baltasar Zúñiga. Their brilliant political accomplishments in every corner of the Hapsburg Empire were based upon Lipsius' teachings. As a consequence of Lipsius' growing influence, by 1612 the "cult of Lipsius" was acknowledged as one of Spain's foremost schools of political prudence and statecraft.

Lipsius' combination of morality and practical politics first made an impression upon the court in Madrid. The group was led by Spain's leading humanist and Philip II's own chaplain, Benito Arias Montano, and after his retirement this mantle fell to García de Figueroa, a prominent courtier. Although Arias had ignored Lipsius on a visit to Flanders and refused to correspond with him, the 1591 conversion changed this aloofness and the Spanish humanist now welcomed Lipsius as one of the "ornaments of the patria and republic," offering him residence in his own home where he was to be treated as a son. But Lipsius made excuses concerning the impossibility of coming to Spain; instead he sought further favor by bombarding the young Prince Philip (the future Philip III of Spain) with letters on military prowess and a dedication to the prince of his ***De Militia Romana.*** Prince Philip ignored these tributes and when Arias retired from the court, Lipsius' welfare was left to García de Figueroa. One of Arias' cohorts, Figueroa was a gentleman of the bedchamber of Philip II and Prince Philip, and a member of the Order of Santiago. At the same time, he also claimed literary pretension as the author of a history of the crucifixion scene. Though Figueroa had based his history on Lipsius' spiritual works, most of their correspondence was in the mundane terms of perennial pleas by Lipsius for recognition from the Spanish crown. In 1597, Figueroa did secure for Lipsius the appointment of royal chronicler with a worthy salary and a medal from Philip II. However, this security was more apparent than real; Lipsius never received the medal and his pay was continually in arrears. The entire relationship with the Madrid court does not show Lipsius in the most favorable light. He used Arias and Figueroa to obtain favor at court, an unfortunate, but not untypical situation for a humanist of this period.

A second and more successful center of Lipsius' influence was Seville, Spain's bustling commercial center, which served as a magnet for scholars from the rural areas of Andalusia and Extremadura. Arias brought the writings of Lipsius to Seville when he retired from the Madrid court. This area was Arias' homeland before coming to the University of Seville for his education, for he had been born in Fregenal de la Sierra, north of Seville in Extremadura. He spent the last seven years of his life in retirement, alternating between Seville, a country house near the metropolis, and La Peña, a small hermitage located in the cool, green Sierra Aracena Mountains. It was this home that Arias offered to Lipsius, as well as to the company of scholars like Pedro de Valencia, a devoted pupil of Arias from nearby Zafra. Valencia's concern with the economic problems of the area would later make him one of the leading reformers of the early seventeenth century. The culmination of Lipsius' influence in the south of Spain came in 1616 when a Spanish translation of ***De Constantia*** was published in Seville. It was attributed to Juan Bautista de Mesa, a poet and notary from the Andalusian municipality of Antequera. In this way the cult of Lipsius was established in the south of Spain.

The most prominent political figure of Lipsius' Sevillian adherents was Juan de Vera y Figueroa. Like other scholars of "the cult," Vera was a native of a provincial town, Mérida in Extremadura. The Vera y Figueroas belonged to the leading nobility of Mérida and after sending Juan to Seville for some educational refinement, he was pushed in the direction of a military and diplomatic career. As a young man he served as a soldier in Flanders and on embassies to Venice and Savoy; later he became a protégé of the Count-Duke of Olivares, who made him ambassador to Rome, a member of the Councils of State, War, and the Indies, and consequently, as a reward, the Count of Roca. During his career in the royal service Vera's pen was as active as his sword. His literary interest, inspired by his early studies in Seville, was directed toward historical and political subjects, his most extensive work being a biography of the Count-Duke. However, Vera's greatest claim to fame was a guide-book for ambassadors, appropriately entitled *El Embajador,* published at Seville in 1620. An ecletic work, Vera borrowed so liberally from ***De Constantia*** and ***Politicorum*** that a rival accused him of plagiarism. As in ***De Constantia,*** Vera's guidebook was set in a secluded garden, where a dialogue on the nature of public life took place between two imaginary scholars, Julio and Ludovico. The qualities the participants most admired in an ambassador were identical with Lipsius' belief in the harmony between prudence and piety, his determination to control the passions, and his fear of the dangers of excessive wealth. ***Politicorum*** provided Vera with justification of degrees of dissimulation in public life, while maintaining morality in one's private life. It appears that Vera's schooling in Seville and his reading of the 1616 translation of ***De Constantia*** provided an important basis for his *El Embajador,* indirectly spreading Lipsius' ideas among the diplomats of the period.

Vera was one of Olivares' most favored and successful protégés, a diplomat who was able to use Lipsius' statecraft against the enemies of the Spanish Empire. But other councilors and courtiers used Lipsius' techniques not so much to preserve the Spanish Empire as to maintain their own perilous careers at court. By the beginning of the seventeenth century, the Madrid court was taking on the characteristics of a parasitic Renaissance court: it was a magnet for unemployed office seekers from all Spain, who came to Madrid, adding to an already over-crowded urban population, and whose only chance for office was through bribery and petty intrigue. Moreover, since the court was the collection point for taxes and dues from the rest of the empire, it was a center of wealth that was lavished on ostentatious display, which seemed more of a waste of resources than a symbol of majesty. Lipsius was aware of the above dangers associated with Renaissance courts. His own example, supported by selections from his writings, comforted those who failed to secure a position at court and provided material for Spanish reformers by pointing to the court as a potential source of decadence. Lipsius had carefully side-stepped becoming a councilor at either the court in Brussels or Madrid. He condemned bureaucrats involved with the court, such as lawyers and tax collectors, and directed attention to urban dwellers, with their luxuries and frivolities, as the greatest obstacles to stability within a state. In contrast, Lipsius found one of the most virtuous portions of society to be the common husbandman, who made the best citizen-soldier and was consequently the backbone of the state. Lipsius' respect for rural life combined with his devotion to intellectual contemplation provided statesmen with an ideal vision of a society of industrious peasants and secluded scholars. Such a vision had a strong appeal to Spaniards who were rejected by the Madrid court and retired to isolated, less populous places in the peninsula.

At least two of Lipsius' Spanish correspondents, Leonardo de Argensola and Francisco de Quevedo, turned to Lipsius for solace, having failed to obtain a position at the Madrid court. Argensola's story is typical of the disgruntled courtier. An able humanist who had studied under Lipsius' teacher, Andrés Schott, Argensola had made a name for himself at the Madrid court late in the 1590's as secretary to the widowed Empress Maria. When she died in 1603 Argensola was left without a position or patron. In consequence, he was forced to retire to a modest country home at Monzalbarba, a suburb of Zaragoza. Here he read Seneca and Tacitus while continuing a correspondence he had begun with Lipsius in 1602, which centered upon the court's corruption and the excessive wealth and luxury of Spain. Lipsius was sympathetic to such sentiments, hinting that his own sufferings in the civil war which was devastating the Low Countries were caused by the aggressive military policy of the Madrid court. The case of Quevedo is similar: though his father had served as secretary to Queen Anne of Austria and his own academic career at the University of Alcalá was brilliant, Quevedo in his twenties found himself without a position, as a hanger-on at the Vallaloid court. Bitter and cynical about his failure to obtain a post and the corrupt state of the court, Quevedo began to pen satires against these conditions, which eventually were expanded into his famous *Sueños.* In a letter to Lipsius in 1604, Quevedo lauded him for the scholarship of a keen-sighted lynx, which he contrasted with the superficiality of short-sighted Spaniards. Eventually, after brief success at court, Quevedo followed Argensola's example and retreated to his mother's humble estate in the village of Torre de Juan Abad, in bleak La Mancha. In this seclusion Quevedo studied Lipsius, among other works on Stoicism, Epicureanism, Cynicism, and his favorite Biblical book, *Job.* The need for retreat and contemplation among rejected courtiers was great enough to carry Lipsius' works to the most rural areas of Spain.

Not all statesmen who followed Lipsius had *letrado* or impoverished *hidalgo* backgrounds. Like Vera, a substantial portion belonged to the ranking families of the nobility. In the fifteenth century this would have been unusual; the code of chivalry defined the nobility as a warrior class, limiting their respect for learning, so that they were neither inclined nor well enough educated to become statesmen. In the sixteenth century this attitude changed as nobles began to take important positions in the royal administration, particularly those posts concerned with diplomacy. The code of chivalry was modified so that prowess in the study of letters became as respected as strength in the practice of arms. Combining skill in both arms and letters became an ideal for segments of the nobility. For example, Don Quixote, the personification of chivalric virtue, justified the need for mental as well as physical capabilities in the exercise of military affairs; for "to know and to guess at the intent of the enemy, the designs, the stratagems, the traps, the avoidance of dangers, are all activities of the mind, in which the body plays no part." Lipsius' works were particularly useful for the development of such mental techniques. They were most valuable to those nobles with respect for classical letters, who were also called upon to pursue active military and political careers.

One of the most eminent nobles who practiced the arts of arms and letters was Don Bernardino de Mendoza. After a distinguished career in the service of Spain as a soldier, diplomat, and scholar, Mendoza indirectly revealed to his numerous enemies the secret of his success: his life had not been guided by Machiavellian maxims, as was thought, but rather by the teachings of Lipsius. This was made public in 1604, only a few months after Mendoza's death, when the labor of love of his last years, a Spanish translation of ***Politicorum,*** was published in Madrid. Until this time, Mendoza's aggressive activities had won him a reputation which enemy statesmen attributed to teachings of a Machiavellian nature. For one, in the 1560's, Mendoza had been a cavalry officer in the Low Countries of the type highly respected by the ruthless Duke of Alba. Later, as Ambassador to England, Mendoza had been a leading inspiration behind the Throckmorton and Babbington Plots against Queen Elizabeth. As Ambassador to France Mendoza's support of the Duke of Guise and the League had immobilized the second most powerful monarchy in Europe. This well-deserved reputation as a vigorous statesman, combined with Mendoza's dedication of his ***Politicorum*** translation to the Spanish aristocracy who could not read Latin, opened Lipsius' ideas to the unlettered but more practically involved Spanish soldier-statesman.

It should be recognized, however, that not all Mendoza's political accomplishments gained Lipsius' approval. Lipsius praised Mendoza's translation of ***Politicorum*** posthumously, but the two never corresponded. We do know that one of Lipsius' most cherished beliefs was to bring an end to hostilities in the Low Countries. Lipsius' own experience with Spanish efforts to crush the Dutch Revolt had left him a firm advocate of peace negotiations to terminate what he considered to be an evil civil war. Caught up in the hostilities Lipsius had been exposed to his own share of abuse: in 1570, Spanish troops sacked his patrimony in Louvain forcing him to flee to the Protestants at Jena. Even when he returned to Louvain in 1591, the University was still in ruins. His war-time experiences, combined with his respect for secluded contemplation, led Lipsius to urge the need for peace in the Low Countries with several of his Spanish correspondents, including Argensola and Quevedo.

Besides these two there were more important Spanish statesmen who were directly involved with the imperial war policy in the Low Countries. Lipsius' most daring effort to convince Spanish statesmen of the need for peace was aimed at the foremost Spanish negotiator for a settlement with England, Don Baltaser Zúñiga. Like Mendoza, Zúñiga was a statesman of universal accomplishments, who had been a soldier with the Armada and an administrator in Milan before he arrived in Flanders in 1599 to negotiate peace with the English as the representative of the Madrid Council of State. Brought together in Flanders by common scholarly interests, Lipsius and Zúñiga corresponded about Cicero and Seneca, exchanged books, and their friendship became firm enough for Lipsius to dedicate his ***Centura prima ad Belgas*** to the Spaniard rather than to a Belgian.

Yet the friendship was aimed at more than scholarly pursuits. In a letter to Zúñiga in 1600, Lipsius praised rumors of the diplomat's involvement in secret peace negotiations with the English. A year later, when Zúñiga asked for comment on the revival of Spanish efforts to reduce the Dutch stronghold of Ostend, Lipsius was critical. He pointed out the strengths of the Dutch defenders and hoped for other than military remedies to end the siege, falling back on the need for the guidance of divine providence. Unfortunately for Lipsius' effort Zúñiga did not display his full convictions in the correspondence. From other letters to the Madrid Council of State it is obvious that Zúñiga did not see eye to eye with Lipsius on the situation in the Low Countries. Whereas Lipsius conceived of Zúñiga's peace negotiations with the English as a step toward the end of hostilities in the Low Countries, Zúñiga saw peace with England as separating the Dutch rebels from their most valuable ally, so that the Dutch would be ripe prey for Spanish arms. While Zúñiga negotiated with the English, he was also urging the most militant proposals against the Dutch, including isolating them from all trade and strengthening the Spanish army in the Low Countries. Lipsius' efforts to further peace in the Low Countries through Zúñiga came to naught, and their friendship ended in 1603 when Zúñiga went to London to continue peace negotiations. A year later, Zúñiga was successful in concluding peace between Spain and England, but only to intensify the war with the Dutch, not to bring it to an end as Lipsius had hoped.

After achieving peace with England, Zúñiga went on to even greater enterprises which did much to spread Lipsius' ideas throughout the Spanish Empire. From 1603 to 1608 Zúñiga was Ambassador to France and from 1608 to 1617 he served in Prague as Ambassador to the Emperor. After this splendid diplomatic career, Zúñiga returned to Madrid to become a permanent member of the Council of State. From this position, Zúñiga introduced his nephew, Gaspar de Guzmán, the future favorite and Count-Duke of Olivares, to the court and together they dominated the first years of the government of Philip IV. Zúñiga's later career is significant in tracing Lipsius' influence in the Spanish Empire because Lipsius' works have appeared in the libraries of Zúñiga's political associates. For example, in Prague, Zúñiga became a firm friend of the Chancellor of Bohemia, Zdeněk Vojtěch Lobkovic, whose library possessed, probably through Zúñiga's influence, Latin editions of both ***Politicorum*** and ***De Constantia.*** In Madrid, Zúñiga left a legacy for the young Olivares: in the Olivares' family library could be found an almost complete Latin set of Lipsius' works, including two copies of his edition of ***Tacitus*** and single copies of his ***De militia Romana, Politicorum,*** and ***De Cruce.*** There is a good chance that these works were presented to Olivares' father by Zúñiga, for—with a single exception—the works in the family library were all printed by the same Antwerp publishing house, between 1599 and 1602, the years of Zúñiga's mission to Flanders. Thus the cult of Lipsius became extensive, reaching from Flanders to Prague and then to Madrid, influencing statesmen of every caliber, from the famous Olivares to the most obscure secretary.

One last problem remains to be examined. Imperial statesmen like Zúñiga, Mendoza, and Vera found Lipsius' works superb guides to statecraft, yet found little in his books to support patriotic ideas or a sense of civic duty. Lipsius was unusually ambiguous on the subject of participation in public life and it is surprising that his haziness did not have an adverse effect upon civic-minded Spanish statesmen. A major instance of this ambiguity can be found in ***De Constantia,*** where Lipsius appears to have been lured into an Epicurean garden, reluctant to emerge into the pitfalls of public life. In the dialogue of ***De Constantia,*** a rather feeble Lipsius seems to have been overwhelmed by the persuasive arguments of an Epicurean, Charles Langius. Langius submits that constancy of spirit and mind is incompatible with civic and patriotic duty; this, he contends, is because constancy demands the type of self-control and patience which ignores the sociopolitical conditions that are the basis of devotion to one's country. To Langius, patriotic bonds were "merely external and accidental," so that patriotic spirit went against man's own nature. Consequently most men enjoyed the safety of watching a battle from a protected mountain top, rather than participating in the combat. It was left to government, the law, and the armed forces to protect individuals and their property, as opposed to concerning themselves with measures for the well-being of the public. As a final argument, Langius warned that patriotic duty led one to conflict with the will of divine providence, whose authority overran man's in the punishing of tyrants, the cleansing of corruption, and the determining of future security. Such arguments in ***De Constantia*** showed how firmly Lipsius believed in his own maxims: to "be at rest in time of troubles" and "to be at peace in time of war."

In spite of Lipsius' negative attitude toward patriotism and civic service, there was limited material in his works to inspire civic service on the part of the statesman. Even sentiments similar to those of Langius on the dangers of public careers did not preclude the duty of certain individuals to serve in public life. Looking through Lipsius' political writings, three basic ideas stand out as reasons for civic service. For one, even Langius admitted that a few exceptional nobles or rich men might stand above their environment and provide order through government. This appeal to aristocratic duty (to which the chivalric ideal could easily have been added) was recognized by Lipsius. Secondly, following Counter-Reformation theology, Lipsius not only taught a statesman how to be pious, but urged him to lead an active life in furthering the ideal of piety. To Lipsius, man possessed free will and consequently was able to frame his own fortune, regardless of his inability to fathom the workings of divine providence. Here was justification of an active and even militant public life as a duty of religious and moral fulfillment.

Lastly, Lipsius' negative attitude concerning patriotic service had a practical, if indirect, advantage to the statesmen who devoted their energies to the well-being of the Spanish Empire. The Spanish Empire was a political unit in name only, for it embraced various nationalities, with divergent interests, languages, and customs. As such only the above appeals to aristocratic duty and to the cause of the Counter-Reformation faith, rather than to love of the motherland, could bind imperial statesmen together. In sum, Lipsius' ideals provided for a select few to practice civic service, while at the same time justifying their militant support of the Catholic faith, and ignoring the thorny problem of devotion to one's country in favor of an imperial concept.

The Spanish statesmen examined here were satisfied with Lipsius' statecraft and never desired to narrow themselves to the rigid political realm that led Machiavelli and other *politiques* to support the ideal of "reason of state." Spanish statesmen seemed to have been attracted to more individual, less idealistic aims. They conceived of civic service as a means of ornamenting their own virtue, rather than the virtue of the state. In a sense, civic service, like perfection in arms and letters, simply became a means of augmenting one's virtue or in more worldly terms, one's fame. This concept allowed for a confidence in the morality of personal conduct which could not be easily transferred to the idea of the state, where utility and success, not morality, were the measures of virtue. In the last analysis, Spanish statesmen were portrayed by their enemies as fanatical in their devotion to the Catholic cause, but it was a fanaticism of self-control and temperance, not irrationality. No doubt they were, for Spanish statesmen did not think of themselves as mere servants of the state, but rather as Roman censors or senators, personages whose rationality and moral righteousness destined them to govern above the normal run of mankind. Such an ideal came from the humanist in Flanders, not from the secretary in Florence, and it inspired a generation of Spanish statesmen to preserve the Spanish Empire. (pp. 139-52)

Theodore G. Corbett, "The Cult of Lipsius: A Leading Source of Early Modern Spanish Statecraft," in Journal of the History of Ideas, *Vol. XXXVI, No. 1, January-March, 1975, pp. 139-52.*

P. H. Schrijvers (essay date 1982)

[*In the following excerpt from a paper originally delivered in 1982, Schrijvers treats the philosophical and literary aspects of Lipsius's* De Constantia in Publicis Malis.]

The celebrated Lipsius dialogue ***De Constantia in Publicis Malis*** (1584) could be called a dialogue of conversion for two reasons. Lipsius describes his transition to the doctrine of steadfastness as well as his "conversion" from philology and letters to philosophy in general.

The first twelve chapters on travel, adversity, hypocrisy, patriotism and pity are of a more literary character in general, as is the introduction on gardening and the garden in Book II and the final section on adversity in the past.

This more light-hearted matter forms the framework of two principal sections on dogma, that is on providence, fate and free will and on God's goodness and the evil in this world. In these two central sections in particular Lipsius tries to combine stoic and Christian doctrines.

Up to now it is mainly the relationship between Lipsius and Seneca that has been examined in great detail. But as to form and content of this dialogue another author of late Antiquity has been of equal importance (at least), although he is hardly ever mentioned as a source of inspiration for Lipsius. This is Boethius, who wrote *De Consolatione Philosophiae.* In the central sections of ***De Constantia*** Lipsius was sometimes inspired by Books 4 and 5 of Boethius's *Consolatio* in great detail. In his comparisons too borrowed from for instance medicine, navigation, battle, light and darkness Lipsius often followed Boethius. In *De Consolatione Philosophiae* the philosophical observations are interspersed with poems by Boethius himself for the sake of variety. Fortunately Lipsius had sufficient self-knowledge in literature to restrict himself to one poem of his own included at the very end, which has no literary value and seems to serve mainly to illustrate his own religious devotion. Moreover we may conclude from this poem that Lipsius tended to consider his bad health as a *publicum malum.* With Lipsius the many poetic quotations, striking comparisons and the prose hymns inserted have the same function of varying the philosophical discourse. The introductory passages of both dialogues very clearly echo each other: when Boethius sits down, in low spirits and not knowing what to say, his interlocutor in this conversation, Lady Philosophy, softly lays her hand on his breast to console him; when Lipsius has arrived at Liège greatly confused and despondent, Langius, who embodies stoic philosophy, encouragingly pats him on the breast. Lipsius seems to have deliberately concealed Boethius's influence in his dialogue in order to make his originality stand out the more. In his letters to Coornhert he advances in defense of his doctrine of fate his conviction that he does not give new insights but only reflects the views that had been accepted long ago by the most learned theologians and scholastics (read Boethius and Thomas Aquinas). Also the wording of "relative necessity" occurring in these letters comes straight from the fifth book of Boethius's *Consolatio.*

Although Lipsius's journey to Vienna is historical fact, the dialogue itself in the form here presented has certainly been invented. It has been chosen for didactic, literary as well as strategic reasons. This manner of presentation enabled the author to put his possibly offensive opinions in the mouth of canon Langius, who had died in 1573 and was thus out of reach of the Inquisition—on earth that is. The biographical data about the interlocutor Langius does not in any way suggest that he had been such an enthusiastic follower of the Stoa. If the actual journey to Vienna took place in the autumn or winter of 1571, the dialogue contains as a matter of fact some references to historical events which took place in 1572 (the Massacre of St Bartholomew). Lipsius's personal interest in the Stoa and the shift of his attention from matters of philology and textual criticism towards practical philosophy seems to stem from the early eighties. Thus in his commentaries on Tacitus's *Annals* and *Histories* of 1581 and 1585 respectively we find highly personal panegyrics on the Roman stoics Thrasea Paetus and Helvidius Priscus, two symbols of *constantia;* their fate is also mentioned in the final section of his dialogue. Also in those years Lipsius writes a satire on philologists. In the argument put in the mouth of Langius about patriotism and punishment we meet with motives which return in more elaborate form in Lipsius's ***Politica*** of 1589. In other words, autobiographical data and personal aspects of the author have been introduced in both interlocutors (young Lipsius and canon Langius).

In his ***Praescriptio*** added to the second edition of ***De Constantia*** of 1585 Lipsius speaks of some five objections which are said to be made by the critics. Generally his tract showed too little Christian spirit; they protested especially against his glorification of right reasoning (*recta ratio*), against his views on fate and free will, against the idea that the ungodly are punished "for their own good" and against denouncing the emotions. Before discussing these five objections briefly I must point out that the publishing history of ***De Constantia*** knows two major stages. In the second edition of 1585 Lipsius has been conciliatory towards objections from Christian critics by a few additions to his text and by writing an apology in the preface, (the so-called ***Praescriptio***). These additions are lacking in the late sixteenth-century translations and their modern reprints. In the last edition, prepared by the author himself in 1599, a limited number of passages in the dialogue is again deleted; or changed (that is: mitigated). The edition of 1599 forms the basis of the text that is printed in the seventeenth-century ***Opera Omnia*** editions. Modern critical studies on Lipsius and the Neo-Stoa generally start from the ***Opera Omnia*** edition within reach, that is to say from a text of ***De Constantia*** which has been mitigated somewhat in philosophical, theological and political respects as compared to the first and second edition.

The dialogue's reception was dominated by the question whether a synthesis of the Stoa and Christianity was possible. Lipsius passes over differences of principle and dogma, which had been mentioned by Erasmus for instance in the preface to his second edition of Seneca's works (1529), by either smoothing them over or being quiet about them or by defining them as theological problems outside the domain of philosophy and by warning continually against man's dangerous curiosity as to divine matters. Only in his discussion of pity and of fate does he sum up some differences between Christian views and the Stoa's.

Concerning attempts in the sixteenth and seventeenth centuries to combine stoic and Christian ethics into a synthesis, we are to start with the question: which ranked first in the presentation, paganism or Christianity? The difference in emphasis is clearly illustrated when we compare Lipsius's dialogue with the tract of the Leyden family doctor Petrus Geesteranus (Pieter van der Geest) entitled *De Constantia Christiana* which appeared posthumously in 1679 and one copy of which is kept in the Amsterdam University Library. Lipsius's dialogue, especially in his first unchristianised edition is clearly marked by antique paganism. The Scriptures are not quoted; the reference to

Adam's Fall is worded so vaguely that the sixteenth-century translator Sir John Stradling (1594) seems not to have understood what the text was about. The author will have shocked some of his readers especially by everything he did not include: in his dialogue there was no mention of the Bible, faith, grace and the figure of Christ. Illustrating his doctrines Lipsius moreover referred to classical heroes, such as Cato, Brutus, Regulus and others; Job and Christian saints and martyrs were not mentioned. But the family doctor Petrus Geesteranus does refer continually to the gospels, the Pauline epistles, biblical examples. There follow in his case some stoic texts at the end taken from Seneca, Epictetus and Lipsius himself. Not until 1679 did *De Constantia Christiana* appear, more than forty years after the Leyden family doctor had died. This posthumous publication at a remarkably late date may be explained by the fact that in 1675 a new Dutch translation of Lipsius's dialogue appeared done by François van Hoogstraeten at Rotterdam. It seems possible that the Christian camp reacted by wanting to have a *constantia christiana* published.

The second objection Lipsius had to defend himself against was that he was excessive in his praise of right reasoning, just like classical authors. His defence in the second edition of the dialogue was limited to a few smoothing words in his ***Praescriptio*** and the addition of "and God" in some places where he mentions right reasoning as his starting point. When I consulted Lipsius's own copy of the first edition of ***De Constantia*** at the Leyden University Library, it was rather exciting to note how the author scribbled *ac Deus* next to the word *ratio,* as he had unfortunately forgotten to do in the first edition. At the time he seems to have preferred changing the pagan plural *Superi* (the gods) into a dogmatically more correct singular *deus.*

The Index of books prohibited for Spanish Catholics of 1667 orders Lipsius to be read with great caution in everything he tells us on fate (*caute legendus!*). Especially chapter 20 of Book I (Lipsius's own so-called doctrine of fate) was severely criticised. Because of this the author tinkered

Typographical device of Christopher Plantin, publisher of Saturnalium sermonum libri duo *(1582) and many other works by Lipsius.*

with the text in the various reprints that have been found. In his discussion of true fate, which he also calls moderate or pious fate, Lipsius wants to hold on to the Latin word *fatum* following Boethius in order to be able to distinguish between each man's individual fate and God's universal providence. In keeping to the word *fatum* he counters the views of among others Augustine, Thomas Aquinas (as well as Calvin), who all preferred to avoid the term considering its pagan (stoic) associations.

To maintain man's free will as opposed to universal divine providence, Lipsius derives the idea of "secondary causes" (place, time, order) from the Stoa (Chrysippus), which man can realize according to his wishes. More important for him is that man acts from necessity from the divine point of view, but in freedom from the human point of view. This conception leads to the phrase highly criticised by Coornhert: "man necessarily sins in full freedom." In this theory of divine and human perspectives Lipsius follows Boethius and Thomas Aquinas, as he reluctantly admits in his letters. After his death some defenders also referred to Thomas Aquinas in this respect.

Whereas Lipsius's exposition on fate and human will evoked much criticism towards the end of the sixteenth century, there is as far as I know hardly any contemporary criticism in reaction to his attempts to reconcile God's goodness and providence with the existence of evil in this world in Book II of ***De Constantia.*** The Index was not critical either. This reticence illustrates in how far his views on adversity as punishment for sin or as natural necessity were shared at the end of the sixteenth and for the greater part of the seventeenth centuries. To defend the idea of God's goodness and to justify his involvement in evil Lipsius often uses stoic concepts which greatly influenced Christian views as to the theodicy as well of among others Augustine, Boethius and Thomas Aquinas. Lipsius follows Seneca for instance who emphasized that physical harm is a means for Divinity to educate human beings. Aside from that he also introduces the cosmological arguments which the Stoa and Christianity used in their theodicy: the world forms one organic whole and complete order is often achieved only at the cost of several parts; the world is a beautiful work of art and there is no beauty without variety, no light without shadow. Such totalitarian concepts lead to a denial of the value of the individual, also characteristic of Lipsius. The problem of Albert Camus's *Les Justes* our Justus never posed.

Lipsius's justification of God's goodness in Book II of ***De Constantia*** can be considered a precursor of the theodicy discussions that broke out in Western Europe especially in the eighteenth century. It is to be regretted that in twentieth century surveys "on the problem of evil in West European philosophy" Lipsius's contribution has completely passed into oblivion. His "theodicy" resembles to a certain degree the famous *Théodicée* by the German philosopher Leibniz, especially the more ethical and pragmatic parts which in their turn have been strongly influenced by stoic and Thomist views. As we know, the optimism of philosophers like Leibniz and the Englishman Shaftesbury made Voltaire write his satiric novel *Candide ou l'Optimisme.* The character of doctor Pangloss in this novel is a caricature of Leibniz, but as a type he is in some ways also a second Lipsius. Voltaire's satire on optimism characterized by Candide as "the folly of maintaining that everything goes well when everything is going wrong" also presents us with the best indirect answer to Lipsius's concepts as to the theodicy. The cosmological and totalitarian views which are characteristic of this so-called optimism are being exposed by Voltaire. It is remarkable that the notorious concept of "man sinning necessarily in freedom" is parodied by Voltaire also.

The difference between Lipsius and Voltaire is also illustrated by the way in which both philosophers have used the favourite symbol of the garden to give expression to their world view and to their ideal of "The Happy Man." Lipsius (II.3) sees the garden as the ideal microcosm, to which he retires for rest and seclusion to think, to read and to write; what happens in the wide world outside is of no concern to him: "I sojourn inside myself." On the other hand Lipsius draws us a picture in ***De Constantia*** II.11 of the wide world as a garden, "as a plantation where God is the most accomplished planter; here he snaps off a few top-heavy twigs of some families, there he picks some leaves, some people. This helps the trunk." As we know, Voltaire's novel ends with a scene in the garden and shows those who live there working without reasoning in order to make life bearable. When doctor Pangloss starts again about this "best of all possible worlds," Candide answers: "This is excellently put but let us work in our garden."

The last objection that Lipsius quotes in his ***Praescriptio*** was that he wanted to restrain the emotions too much. Throughout the ages protest was heard against the stoic ideal of the superhuman Sage without emotions. I need only mention Erasmus's criticism of Seneca in *In Praise of Folly* and Pascal's criticism of the diabolical pride shown by the philosopher Epictetus. Pascal as well as our Leyden family doctor Petrus Geesteranus points out that the stoic ideal of απαθεια is incompatible with Christ's anguish and grief in the Garden of Gethsemane. I like to think that in his ***De Constantia*** edition of 1599 Lipsius has actually toned down his views on the emotions.

His ideas on the stoic Sage as Übermensch are also expressed in the dialogue itself. In Book II (chapter 3) Langius describes how in philosophical ecstasy he seems to shed everything that is human and to ascend to heaven on the fiery chariot of Wisdom. Irresistibly and paradoxically the image suggests the prophet Elia. Lipsius answers to this (II.4): "How happy you are in peaceful as in troubled times! Your life is one that is hardly human." In his commentary of Tacitus, Lipsius uses the same phrase to praise the Roman stoic Thrasea Paetus. In Book II, chapter 20 Lipsius describes himself as a man among men and asks for medicine that is somewhat more human. To our (modern) surprise this seems to consist of a series of terrifying disasters from the past, the so-called honey of historical examples. Never does Lipsius state explicitly that the stoic Sage is God's equal, but he suggests a divine dimension by the religious imagery he uses in connection with Constantia, called "a goddess" (II.5) and Langius's study, called "a temple with an altar" (II.5). Their conversations were called "a mystery ritual" (end of the dialogue). Highly characteristic is the final scene in which Langius imagines himself leading his pupil to the summit of Mount Olympus to show him the past, present and future of this world. A Christian reader might be reminded of the temptation scene between Christ and the devil on top of a high mountain!

These short remarks on literary and philosophical aspects of ***De Constantia*** take me to two desiderata: a new edition of the Latin text of ***De Constantia*** with variant readings; a comprehensive and profound commentary on this dialogue, that collects many earlier beams and itself has known a wide emanation. The historical value of the dialogue is not under discussion, but it has been variously judged and this will probably remain so. (pp. 275-80)

P. H. Schrijvers, "Literary and Philosophical Aspects of Lipsius's 'De Constantia in Publicis Malis'," in Acta Conventus Neo-Latini Santandreani, *edited by I. D. McFarlane, Medieval & Renaissance Texts & Studies, 1986, pp. 275-82.*

Anthony Grafton (essay date 1987)

[*Grafton is an American educator, historian, and author of several studies on classical scholarship and the history of fifteenth-, sixteenth-, and seventeenth-century education. In the following excerpt, he attempts to reconcile the image of Lipsius as stoic philosopher with that of Lipsius as "one of the most puzzling and unnerving intellectual celebrities" of his day.*]

Justus Lipsius survives, barely, as a fading figure on the periphery of our mental panorama of Renaissance culture. We are amused at his famous offer to recite the text of Tacitus while his listener held a dagger to his belly—and to allow the listener to plunge the dagger in if Lipsius stumbled on a word. We are amazed by his early career as a prodigy, one that made him the proverbial perfect schoolboy as late as the nineteenth century, when King, the classical master in Kipling's *Stalky & Co.,* still plagued his boys with anecdotes about "the learned Lipsius, who at the age of. . . ." We have admired the public image that he wished to leave behind him, as projected in his friend Rubens's *Four Philosophers:* a quiet, contemplative gentleman, one who is happiest when reading books or cultivating his legendary tulip garden while his dog Mops barked at his heels. We have even heard his voice. Lipsius, as Morris Croll showed many years ago, did more than anyone else to popularize the Senecan, pointed prose style that so delighted the strong wits of seventeenth-century Europe. When we read the epigrams of Quevedo or the essays of Bacon, we can detect many echoes of that pointed Latin prose, poor in verbs but rich in inkhorn terms, that enchanted students in Leiden and Louvain, inspired the great scholar-printer Henri Estienne to write a whole book *About Lipsius's Latinity*—and provoked Lipsius's Leiden successor Joseph Scaliger to cry, "Je ne sçay quel Latin c'est."

Yet recent scholarship has revealed another Lipsius as well, a figure both more flamboyant and more alienated than the stately icon that Rubens created and many later historians have helped to gild. Lipsius was no retiring academic who wrote for his colleagues in the "community of the competent." In fact, he was a best-seller. He took an active and often unattractive part in the great debates of his day about civil war and religious liberty. More dramatic still, he was a plagiarist, a liar, and a heretic. He changed churches in pursuit of sanctity—or safety—almost as easily as he changed jobs in the course of his dazzling academic career. His contemporaries knew him not as *Lipsius philosophus,* the Stoic unmoved by pain or fear, but as *Lipsius Proteus,* one of the most puzzling and unnerving intellectual celebrities of a time that included such rivals as Giordano Bruno and Tommaso Campanella. And we must come to terms with this second Lipsius, as well as with the first—and, finally, with the full range of paradoxes and enigmas that we are posed by the existence in one man of these two personae—before we can leave Lipsius in his garden and conclude with some reflections on the larger meaning of his case.

First, Rubens's Lipsius, the sage and scholar. There is no doubt that Lipsius ranked with the most learned and creative members of his generation—itself, perhaps, the most learned generation in European history, that of Joseph Scaliger and Isaac Casaubon. His first book, a miscellany of short essays on technical points of textual criticism, written in phosphorescent Ciceronian Latin, he finished in 1566, when he was all of nineteen years old. His edition of ***Tacitus,*** which marked a radical improvement in a notoriously difficult text, appeared in 1574, when he was not yet thirty. And throughout his life (which extended from 1547 to 1606), he issued a powerful stream of editions, commentaries, and monographs. These culminated in 1605 in a second magnificent edition, that of ***Seneca,*** and won him preferment in the academic centers of Lutheran Europe (Jena), Calvinist Europe (Leiden), and Catholic Europe (Louvain).

How can we judge Lipsius's achievement in the technical and rebarbative fields he liked to cultivate? We can turn for some enlightenment to modern classical scholars who have replowed his furrows. Elaine Fantham, for example, has recently confirmed the excellence of Lipsius's critical judgment as applied to Seneca. Presented with a late and not completely accurate manuscript descended from the famous *codex Etruscus* of the *Tragedies,* Lipsius realized that he was dealing not just with scribal errors but with a previously unused branch of the textual tradition. Accordingly he made so many valid changes in the text then standard that the discoverer of *Etruscus* itself, Gronovius, had little to do save confirm from the original source the justness of Lipsius's choices and emendations. J. Ruysschaert and C. O. Brink have subjected Lipsius's corrections of the text of Tacitus's *Annales* to even more searching scrutiny. The results are striking. In *Annales* I, modern texts contain some 130 emendations of the text transmitted by the *codex Mediceus.* Eighty of these, many obvious, were made by the first editor, the younger Beroaldo, who prepared the manuscript for the press in 1505 with great skill and tact. Lipsius comes next, with twenty to his credit. The competition lags far behind; indeed, the combined efforts of nineteenth- and early twentieth-century scholars have resulted in two emendations generally accepted. Statistics, admittedly, tend to glaze the reader's eye; but these few numbers do suggest just how gigantic an effort Lipsius made to improve the texts he worked on, and how secure his mastery was of the historical background and the historian's language. Most impressive, perhaps, are the fairly numerous passages that Lipsius left unchanged, that later scholars emended, and that modern scholars—catching up with their sixteenth-century predecessor—now take as Tacitean rather than corrupt.

Yet numbers tell an austere and limited story. To grasp a scholar's characteristic working methods, we must catch him in his study (or his garden), applying his favorite tools to his chosen raw materials. And we must compare his work systematically not to that of his modern successors but to that of his predecessors and contemporaries. We can spy on Lipsius as he attacks one of the many attractive complex problems posed by one of his favorite authors: the perennial question of which Seneca wrote what. In the Middle Ages, more or less everything that circulated under the name Seneca was attributed to the philosopher who suffered under Nero. But the fourteenth century saw the awakening of a new historical curiosity and a new stylistic sensitivity. In many cases, Renaissance humanism appeared and all was light; it took only one scholar of the new brand to read the younger Pliny's letters and notice that this Pliny could not very well be the author of the *Natural History,* since he vividly described that other Pliny's death. But in Seneca's case the humanist confronted a pullulating mass of disparate materials: letters, essays, tragedies, rhetorical exercises, works on natural philosophy, and a correspondence with Saint Paul. He also knew, from ancient testimony, that two writers named Seneca had flourished under the early Roman Empire. And he saw that no single man could have written this entire discordant corpus. No wonder, given this range of evidence and problems, that the new Senecan scholarship served to transmute the simple assumptions of the medieval scribe into an unbearable cacophony of contradictory hypotheses.

We can begin by following a learned man of the early fifteenth century, Sicco Polenton, as he worked at these problems in his pioneering history of Latin literature. Sicco knew from the play *Octavia,* so he thought, that the author of Seneca's tragedies had outlived Nero and described his death. But he also knew that Seneca the moral philosopher had died before Nero. He knew that Seneca the creator of rhetorical exercises had had three sons, one of whom was also named Seneca. And he tied all of this information together with a neat philologist's clove hitch. One Seneca had written the rhetorical and philosophical works and died a Christian; his son Seneca had written the tragedies. Naturally, this solution not only solved problems but raised them. But Sicco was equal to the challenge. When (unnamed) detractors suggested that the *Octavia,* the keystone of his argumentative arch, was not by the author of the other plays, he buried them under a flood of smug rebuttal of a kind unhappily still to be found in philological argument:

> Any expert can see that these tragedies reveal no variety, but that all of them have one and the same tenor of style, eloquence, dignity; thus all

> of them, as they are, seem the product of one source, one parent, one mind.

No one with insight, he concluded, could deny the plays' unity of authorship. This argument, which makes the one play all modern scholars have thought spurious the companion and even the touchstone of the rest, seems strange enough. But it is not half so curious as Sicco's other daring hypothesis. In the rhetorical work, Seneca mentions that he could have heard Cicero speak had the civil wars not made it impracticable. Accordingly, he must have been fairly mature—Sicco suggests fourteen years old at least—before Cicero died in 43 B.C. Yet Seneca the philosopher died in A.D. 65, and some humanists denied that he could have heard Cicero at all. Sicco, however, cut this knot as elegantly as he had tied the other. His opponents, he asserted, simply failed to see the obvious truth—Seneca must have lived to be 118 years old. Anyone who failed to accept this view "would rather quarrel than accept the obvious truth."

Erasmus, a hundred years later, saw far more sharply than Sicco had that not everything that glittered with Seneca's name was Senecan gold. For the correspondence of Seneca with Saint Paul he had only contempt, and he disproved its authenticity with an elegant piece of historical reasoning:

> There is nothing in the letters from Paul worthy of Paul's spirit. One hardly hears the name of Christ, which normally pervades Paul's discourse. [The author] makes that powerful defender of the Gospel cowardly and timorous. . . . And it's the mark of really monumental stupidity when he makes Seneca send Paul a book *De copia verborum* [On building vocabulary] so that he will be able to write better Latin. If Paul didn't know Latin he could have written in Greek. Seneca did know Greek.

But Erasmus made little effort to separate the rest of the Senecan corpus into its original components. He did doubt that one man could have written all of the tragedies. But of Cicero's contemporary, Seneca the rhetorician who died under Nero, Erasmus said only that he wished that his *Declamationes* had survived in their entirety, "for they would have been a great help in [learning rhetorical] invention and judgement."

With these efforts of earlier humanists we may now compare what Lipsius had to say in the set-piece chapter, sharp and concise, with which his ***Electa*** of 1580 begins:

> The *vulgus* holds that books entitled *Controversiae* and *Suasoriae* were written by the Seneca known as the philosopher, who was Nero's tutor. The *vulgus* holds this, and therefore it errs. That opinion is refuted by Seneca's period, his life, his style. I explain the problem of period in detail. Whoever wrote these books lived in the time of Augustus and Tiberius, not that of Claudius and Nero. I infer this from a number of passages where he speaks about himself. He says at one point that he knew Cestius Pius, Portius Latro, Valerius Messalla [minor rhetoricians who lived under Augustus]; at another that he heard the poet Ovid declaim; and that he knew Asinius Pollio [d. A.D. 5] both as a robust man and as an old one. I know that all these lights illuminated the middle of the principate of Augustus. But Seneca [the philosopher] flourished in the time of Claudius and Nero.

Lipsius easily disposes of his predecessor's effort to make Seneca the classical prototype of the two-thousand-year-old man. After all, he points out, Tacitus treats Seneca's last years and death in detail, and describes him as a fairly vigorous old man. He could hardly have applied such terms to a slippered pantaloon of 118. After dispelling this and other errors, the result of which had been to confuse the two Senecas as thoroughly as the two Menaechmi in Plautus's play, Lipsius sets out his own lucid hypothesis. Two writers named Seneca must be distinguished. The elder lived in the days of Augustus and wrote the rhetorical works; the younger, his son, lived under Claudius and Nero and wrote philosophy and tragedy.

Clearly Lipsius's philology was dramatically different from that of Sicco or Erasmus. What strikes the reader most sharply is not that Lipsius's solution is basically the modern one, but that his methods are so professional. He does not examine isolated passages or data as though a few bits of evidence could decide the case. Rather, he pulls from the rhetorical works every passage that mentions a contemporary, lines them up, and then draws from them a plausible and coherent theory. He does not refute his adversaries by claiming a superior sensibility, as though the ability to date a text were something as ineffable as a sense of smell. Rather, he gives all the relevant evidence and shows that no hypothesis but his can be reconciled with it. Above all, he establishes his point simply because he knows the history of Rome, civil and literary, year by year and almost day by day, and can thus make what had been mere names to his predecessors into unbreakable links in the chain of his arguments. This combination of learning and precision marks Lipsius off as a member of that great generation that set the history of the ancient world itself, as well as that of ancient literature, into its proper order.

Lipsius's virtuosity as a scholar enabled him not only to restore texts but also to reconstruct lost customs and institutions. His works on such topics have more virtues than a sample can reveal. He had the imaginative ability to see in disparate and difficult texts the traces of what he liked to describe as an ancient custom "fleeing into oblivion." He had a detective writer's gift for charging obscure subjects with excitement, so that the reader too becomes eager to know how long you had to serve in the Roman army before you could become a *veteranus,* or who the *iuvenes* were who made trouble at games and chariot races. And he had a dedicated scholar's willingness to work through any text, however unattractive; to nail down every detail, however obscure; and to use every possible device—including elaborate illustrations—to clarify his descriptions. His profusely illustrated and elaborately documented books marked a new stage in the development of historical research.

In one respect, to be sure, Lipsius tried to spoil the gleaming perfection of his own achievements. He stole emendations of the texts he worked on from any book and any person that could provide them. He gave little or no acknowledgment of his debts. And when these surfaced—as when his former friend Claude Chifflet protested that his own proposals to emend passages in Tacitus's *Annales* were presented as Lipsius's in the latter's commentary—he held his peace, ignored the fuss, and carefully effaced from his working copy of Tacitus—which still survives in Leiden—the references to Chifflet's name that he had neatly entered by Chifflet's proposals in his notes. Yet plagiarism of this kind, though ugly, was not unusual. Both Scaliger and Casaubon played down the merits of their predecessors and claimed others' achievements as their own. As Brink points out, in an age when few scholars fully identified the sources of the texts they printed, it was only natural for conjectures, too, to be passed on from hand to hand without full identification. Given the peculiar nature of conjectural emendations—which, like some sorts of scientific discovery, become private property only when they are published for the first time—it is not hard to see why even a brilliant and learned man might steal a few extra jewels to add to the vast piles that he had excavated, cut, and polished on his own.

Yet—and yet—this story is not the whole one. Lipsius's attitude toward the technical skills he deployed in editions and monographs is unexpectedly complex and ambivalent. On the one hand, he repeatedly mocked the scholars of his time for their perverse obsession with the details of scholarly problems. In an influential little dialogue dedicated to Scaliger, for example, Lipsius portrays himself attending, in a dream, a meeting of the senate of Roman writers. One after another, Cicero, Sallust, and Ovid, Tribonian and Pliny denounce the critics who have mutilated their texts and call for extreme punishments: "Have we no Cornelian law to deal with assassins? And are these men not assassins? How often have they been caught, pen and sword in hand, as they set out to kill a word?" Lipsius trembles in terror, and escapes punishment only when Varro, the greatest Roman scholar, persuades his colleagues that they owe some debt to modern printers and critics. And though the whole exercise ends with a set of rules—not very penetrating ones—for proper textual criticism, it leaves the reader with the impression that critics are intrinsically absurd creatures, who inflict wounds on the very texts they seek to heal. No wonder that Lipsius's ***Dream*** became the model for a whole subspecies of Latin satires of scholars and scholarship.

Yet Lipsius went further still. In his scholarly works, as well, he repeatedly expressed reservations about the ultimate value of philology. His first edition of the commentary on Tacitus, the greatest of his scholarly feats, carries a stern warning against excessive indulgence in conjectural emendation: "I have confirmed some old emendations and added new ones, but have not done either with great zeal. For this is the sin that besets us Critics, and Tacitus nowadays suffers as much from remedies as he once did from errors." Elsewhere he put the point more cogently: *non ad ista sed per ista,* textual criticism is a means not an end. And he added an extensive treatment of this theme to the unannotated edition of ***Caesar's Commentaries*** that he prepared for use by gentlemen in schools—and that remained standard long after his death.

Lipsius's ambivalence, moreover, is the direct result of a characteristic of his work that is as important as its solid basis of learning. Lipsius saw the real end of scholarship not as scientific but as practical. He chose the texts he edited and the issues he studied with his attention fixed above all on the needs of his own time. He concentrated on Tacitus and Seneca not simply because he esteemed their prose but because he felt that they had lived in, analyzed, and could help the careful modern scholar to put up with an age of despotism and rebellion. In Tacitus, he told his readers, they would find not useless stories about the austere early days of the Roman republic but cold and practical analysis of a world in which power was concentrated in the hands of a small group:

> Tacitus doesn't present you with showy wars or triumphs, which serve no purpose except the reader's pleasure; with rebellions or speeches of the tribunes, with agrarian or frumentary laws, which are quite irrelevant to our time. Behold instead kings and rulers and, so to speak, a theater of our modern life. I see a ruler rising up against the laws in one passage, subjects rising up against a ruler elsewhere. I find the devices that make the destruction of liberty possible and the unsuccessful effort to regain it. I read of tyrants overthrown in their turn, and of power, ever unfaithful to those who abuse it. And there are also the evils that accompany liberty regained: chaos, rivalry between equals, greed, looting, wealth pursued from, not on behalf of, the community. Good God, he is a great and useful writer! And those who govern should certainly have him at hand at all times.

If Tacitus cast the most searching light on the chiaroscuro political scene of the late sixteenth century, Seneca taught those caught up in such events how to survive them with their dignity intact. In the philosophy of later Stoicism, in fact, Lipsius found a simple guide to life, one that would enable the young aristocrat to purge himself of fear and anger, to master his passions, and then to instill discipline in himself and in his soldiers. This was the message that Lipsius made popular in his brief and vivid dialogues ***On Constancy,*** in which, as he said, he taught subjects their duty: that of suffering what their lords inflicted on them. This was the message, on a grander scale, of the Senecan commentary and the two great manuals of Stoic philosophy that occupied Lipsius during the last decade of his life, and that remained standard works until the nineteenth century.

Antiquarianism, finally, proved to be the most practical of all Lipsius's studies—a conclusion that may seem surprising, given the pejorative sense in which we nowadays use the term in English. In the detailed study of Roman institutions, Lipsius found solutions to the most pressing problems of military and political organization. For example, in the detailed accounts of Roman military organization and tactics given by Polybius and others, Lipsius thought that he could find the model for a military machine more effective than anything in existence. He reconstructed and recommended Roman soldiers' customs: their Spartan habit of living on bread and water in the field, their acceptance of a stern code of discipline enforced by condign punishment, their willingness to dig ditches and build palisades. He praised their weapons, their formations, their uniforms, and their chains of command. And though he admitted that some modern weapons, like the pike, had their place in the military order, he urged the commanders of his time to combine these with "ancient arms and the ancient order and line of battle"—and promised that if they would do so, their armies would give them a monopoly of violence in their states and enable them to create vast empires.

Lipsius, in other words, created a brand of philology that was entirely relevant to current and practical problems. No wonder, then, that his studies attracted the attention of his rivals—like Joseph Scaliger, who was still making sketches of the Roman *pilum* on his deathbed in order to show where Lipsius had gone wrong. No wonder, either, that his works reached generals as well as scholars. Maurice of Nassau, the most competent commander the Dutch had, studied with Lipsius at Leiden and put his lecture notes into practice afterward. In 1595 a friend reported to Lipsius that

> Count Maurice, while encamped at the Hague, has taught his soldiers to fight like Romans. There were 60 footsoldiers with spears on the one side, 40 on the other armed by ancient custom with the Roman shield. The fight took place, and the men with shields stood firm for a long time despite the opposition of those with spears, which had no effect. In the end, the men with shields were driven off thanks to the violence and agility of a few of the others—yet in such a way that they retained much dignity and praise.

It is bemusing to see scholarship so firmly in possession of the role that science enjoys now, the source of the powerful knowledge that statesmen most need. Yet the spectacle helps us to understand why Lipsius's work found a market. It shows that military leaders were predisposed to follow ancient precedents and models. And it shows that Lipsius really could interpret these far more subtly than professional soldiers. In this case Lipsius wrote back to explain that Maurice had chosen the wrong way to imitate the Romans:

> The experiment is a good one, but in my opinion should be carried out differently. One should not set one company, that is, 60 soldiers, against another 60, but several companies at once. It is that conjoining and mutual help which give strength, as beams do in buildings. The Roman legions always beat the phalanx—but together. Had you set a few Roman soldiers against a few Macedonians, things might have gone quite differently.

The cloistered scholar had to teach the general, then, that the shape of Roman shields mattered less than the cohesion of Roman armies as a whole. Lipsius, as G. Oestreich and W. Hahlweg have shown, provided Maurice and other influential military thinkers with the basic ideas from which they created the seventeenth-century Military Revolution, with its disciplined professional armies and elaborate chains of command. No wonder that Maurice seemed "to fall in love" with Lipsius's book on Roman arms, the ***De militia Romana.*** This great book not only brought lost aspects of antiquity back to life but reshaped the face of battle.

Lipsius did not only study war. In fact, he tried to distill the wisdom of the ancients on all political and military subjects into a single, accessible whole, and did so in a book that reached a public even larger than that of the ***De militia Romana.*** Lipsius's ***Six Books of Politics,*** published in 1589, guided the early modern monarch through the whole grim array of tasks and duties that confronted him. It told him how to raise an army, how to quell dissent, how to impose discipline. It told him which tricks against enemies were licit and which (those that involved the breaking of oaths) were not. And it did all of this in a couple of hundred uniquely pithy pages. For in the ***Politica,*** as Lipsius pointed out in the preface, he brilliantly mixed entirely traditional, even classical, ingredients in such a way that they made an ultra-modern concoction. One sample will give a taste of Lipsius's creation. Should a state, he asks, tolerate religious dissent? To begin with, one must distinguish between public and private dissent. Then one can lay out the opinions of the ancients in a coherent and useful way:

> I say that they sin publicly, who both entertain wrong opinions about God and the traditional rites and induce others to do so by making disturbances. Privately, who entertain the same wrong opinions, but keep them to themselves. As to the first, the question is, should such men get off scot free? No! "Let them be punished by you lest you be punished in their place." (Cyprian)
>
> Especially if they create disturbances. "Better that one perish than that unity perish." (Augustine)
>
> "The penalty for profanation of religions varies from place to place, but there always is one." (Seneca)
>
> There is no room for clemency here. "Burn, cut, so that a member perish rather than the whole body." (Cicero)
>
> "For crimes against holy religion amount to crimes against everyone." (Justinian)

Lipsius, in other words, created not a smooth fresco of his own devising but a brilliant mosaic of classical sentiments, astutely chosen and arranged. In this case, his assemblage of authoritarian *sententiae* draws on pagan and Christian, legal and oratorical texts. Nothing could seem clearer than that all wise men, at all times and places, have called for the suppression of public religious dissent. And Lipsius, drawing heavily on his wonderfully stocked memory, found and assembled quotations of equal brevity and pith on every subject from the need of real soldiers to dig their own ditches to the need of real tyrants to be punished.

This recipe for political discourse tickled even more palates than Lipsius's military cookbook. The ***Politics*** went through a staggering fifty-four editions in Latin and twenty-two more in vernacular translations. Statesmen read the book as eagerly as professors. Even a hard-bitten professional like Bernardino de Mendoza, a cavalryman under Alba in the 1560s and the Spanish ambassador to France in the days of the Holy League, took time off between efforts to assassinate Queen Elizabeth to translate the ***Politics*** into Spanish. Lipsius's new way of teaching politics induced thousands of foreign students to come to Leiden, which became for a time the largest university in Europe. His grim political maxims became the staple of political thought in much of Europe. They were vulgarized by the writers on state secrets, *arcana rerumpublicarum.* They were cannibalized by commentators on Tacitus and students writing dissertations. They were even satirized by the great opponent of centralized monarchy and religious repression, Traiano Boccalini, in his bitterly comic *Newsletters from Parnassus.*

It is not hard to account for the success of *Politica à la mode de Lipse.* Humanists of the generation before his had also seen philology as the one tool that could deal constructively with civil and religious war. But the great jurists of mid-sixteenth-century France, François Baudouin and Jean Bodin, had envisioned a philology very different from Lipsius's. They held that the young leader must begin by reading all significant historians (Bodin provided a helpful list of several hundred titles to be getting on with). He must next study each historian in the light of his original situation and assumptions. He must then study the events the historian recorded in the light of his nation's experience as a whole—in the light, in fact, of every available fact about the physical setting, climatic conditions, and political institutions that had shaped the individuals and the nation. Bodin knew that peoples migrated, and thus insisted that his future leader not only study the nations as the historians described them, but also pursue them back to their origins, however distant. In order to locate these he made magnificent use of etymology—arguing, for example, that the Belgian term for the Gauls, Walloon, was most informative; in its Latin form, *Ouallones,* it revealed that they were a French tribe that had wandered about saying "Où allons-nous?" Only after every battle and every institution had been set like a jewel into a context fully reconstructed by up-to-date scholarship could one hope to assess its value and write beside it, in one's notebook, CTV (*consilium turpe sed utile*—a vile plan, but a useful one) or CH (*consilium honestum*).

In theory this program realized the highest ideals of humanism. In practice it resulted in utter intellectual chaos. No one could hope to find straight answers to practical questions in Bodin's mistitled masterpiece, the *Method for the Easy Comprehension of History.* Bodin himself abandoned historicism and philology and found in conversion to Judaism and the persecution of witches an intellectual and emotional security that his scholarship had not afforded him. By contrast, Lipsius's ***Politica*** offered authoritative maxims stripped of context and complication. No wonder that these won the day, and held the high ground until they were replaced around 1650 by the new theories of Hermann Conring and William Petty, with their emphasis on economic and demographic problems. To be sure, Lipsius's synthesis was not his own invention. He owed his basic assumptions, at least, to the teacher he encountered in his early years in Rome, Marc-Antoine Muret. But Muret's Roman superiors never let him develop his views at any length—and at first would not let him lecture on an author so hostile to Jews and Christians and Tacitus. The details and the literary form at any rate were Lipsius's own.

It is just here, in Lipsius's most successful works, that the paradoxes seem most glaring. Lipsius was a professional student of the ancient world. He based his claim to provide modern rulers with powerful knowledge on his supreme ability to interpret ancient texts. And yet, to make his texts useful in the age of Philip II, Lipsius constantly had to interpret them not as his sense of their authors' views suggested but as his own requirements dictated. To re-create the Roman military order as a whole he had to use texts from many different periods as if they described the same institution—a practice that provoked Scaliger to enter many critical marginalia in his copy of the ***De militia Romana.*** To construct a Stoic ethics for the modern warrior, Lipsius had to pretend, far more strongly than the evidence warranted, that the writings of Epictetus and Seneca "secretly lead one to Christian doctrine and to piety"—and to support this view not with the evidence of the texts but with an anecdote about how useful Epictetus had been to the pious Cardinal Cesare Baronio. To construct his politics for the modern governor, finally, Lipsius had to banish all thought of literary or historical context from his mind. He himself compared his enterprise to the making of a poetic cento, and argued that in that genre one was not only free but obliged to twist lines from their original senses. This comparison is eloquent. The poetic cento Lipsius's readers knew best was perhaps the nuptial one by Ausonius, in which innocent lines and half-lines from Virgil are twisted into a splendidly obscene epithalamium complete with a section on the taking of virginity. In comparing his ***Politica*** to such works, Lipsius made clear that he saw himself less as a scholar collecting data than as a writer continuing—and reshaping—a literary tradition.

By the end of his life Lipsius readily admitted that his chief aim had been not to interpret the ancient world but to exploit it. He described the ***Politica*** and ***Constantia*** as the natural culmination of his life's work. And he described that as an effort to make philology useful: "I was the first or the only one in my time to make literature serve true wisdom. I made philology into philosophy." In this comment, as Renaissance readers knew, Lipsius was appropriating one of his favorite ancient texts, the 108th letter of Seneca. This described the reverse of the process Lipsius claimed to have brought about. It complained, that is, that in Seneca's time philosophy had degenerated into philology. Everyone was disputing about details and ignoring the main points. Future scholars were reading Virgil for merely scholarly ends:

> The future grammarian studying Virgil does not read that incomparable phrase, *fugit inreparabile tempus,* in order to reflect that "We must be on our guard; swift time drives us onward, and is driven; . . ." but to observe that whenever Virgil describes the speed of time's passage he uses the verb *fugio.*

Seneca and Lipsius prefer the productive, "philosophical" interpreter who appropriates his text to some moral end to the passive, "grammatical" interpreter who merely wants to know how and what his author meant. We must admire the ancient and the Renaissance writer's prescient insight into the methods readers use to construct meanings from their texts. But we must also be depressed by Lipsius's willingness to abandon the core of the humanistic enterprise, the effort to understand the past on its own terms, in his desire to make ancient experience accessible. Here, as well as in his thoughts on religious dissent, we see a humanist at his most inhumane. Lipsius was willing to crush the individuality of Tacitus or Cicero as ruthlessly as that of an Anabaptist; and it is hard to find his posture in either case an attractive one.

How then do we come to terms with Lipsius? Recent scholarship has provided two powerful and exciting ways of doing so. In the first place, Bernard Rekers and others have shown that Lipsius belonged to the Family of Love—that strange sect of spiritual reformers that stretched like a shadowy wheel across mid-sixteenth-century Europe, its hub in Christopher Plantin's printing shop in Antwerp and its spokes reaching London, Prague, and even Madrid (where a small group of disciples in the Escorial itself eagerly awaited each new batch of commentaries on the Apocalypse in code). The members of this group saw all formal religions as equally valuable for instilling discipline in ordinary folk and as equally irrelevant to themselves. Thanks to their prophets and their inward voices, they enjoyed a direct access to religious truth. They were independent of the organized churches, which they joined only out of prudence, and of the Scriptures, which they allegorized very freely. And they considered themselves free to conform to the ruling faith of any land they might settle in. At the same time, though, they laid great stress on the need for peace and order, and urged political authorities to enforce religious unity on the many-headed mob. Knowing that Lipsius belonged to this group, we can understand his willingness to play the Lutheran in Jena, the Catholic in Italy, the Calvinist fellow traveler in Leiden, and the Catholic once again in Louvain. Such changes in external practice and allegiance affected only the outward and visible husk of what was to Lipsius an inward and spiritual experience.

In the second place, Dutch and German scholars like W. Kühlmann and H. Wansink have found the key to Lipsius in his profession. He was a rhetorician by trade. He used the rhetorician's normal methods to determine the topics of political discourse, to find its verbal and argumentative content, and to adorn it. And he made his ***Politica*** as much a treasury of sentences to be quoted by other rhetoricians—rather like Erasmus's *Adages*—as a work of analysis. Rhetoricians, of course, seek to persuade their listeners rather than to provide absolutely valid proofs. They can do without convictions. And Lipsius, accordingly, could happily aim all his life not at knowledge of the true and the good but at his own immediate advantage. This body of literature represents Lipsius as a man with little individuality but great will to succeed—a young upwardly mobile philologist, one might say, who sold his matchless skills to a succession of higher bidders.

These two theories, unfortunately, are hard to reconcile with one another, and neither can account for all the facts. If Lipsius was above all a spiritual reformer, he did not have to become an enthusiastic Lutheran pamphleteer at Jena (where he praised the Dukes of Saxony as the race chosen by God to chastise the papacy) or an enthusiastic Catholic pamphleteer in his last years at Louvain (where he applied his philological skills to proving that Flemish shrines of the Virgin had produced miraculous cures for blindness, running sores, and diabolic possession, to the distress of his Catholic as well as his Protestant friends). If he was a pure pragmatist, on the other hand, he did not need to write a provocative argument for centralized monarchy and religious repression while teaching in decentralized and tolerant Holland.

Moreover, neither of these theories helps us to understand Lipsius the interpreter of texts; yet interpretation was the center of his intellectual life. In this area, what strikes the modern student most forcibly are the paradoxes we have already identified. Admittedly, humanists had always had to separate philology from pedagogy. Erasmus the scholar knew a great deal about Greek and Roman homosexuality. But Erasmus the teacher, as Jacques Chomarat has recently reminded us, gave instructions on how to teach the first line of Virgil's second *Eclogue* ("Corydon the shepherd was hot for pretty Alexis") in such a way as to distract the student from realizing what the poem was about. And Erasmus the translator, as Erika Rummel has shown, carefully fudged references to pederasty and homosexuality when rendering decently obscure Greek into worrisomely accessible Latin.

But by the end of the sixteenth century, the paganness of the pagans, their historical and cultural distance from modern Europeans, had become impossible to ignore. Montaigne had proclaimed the bankruptcy of any branch of thought that assumed—as humanism must assume—clear resemblances between ancient examples and modern imitations. And Lipsius can perhaps best be seen as the last serious scholar who tried to rebut these objections and to prove that the ancients still could offer detailed models and instructions for modern actions. The price he paid for splitting scholarship from practice, for insisting that the student keep separate notebooks for political and historical learning, was a high one. He had to transform humanism itself from a device for criticizing the world as it is by comparing it to an ideal past into a device for leaving the world unchanged while learning from the past how to cope with its defects. Where earlier humanists like Erasmus and More had criticized the militarism and greed of the fledgling New Monarchies, Lipsius joyfully collaborated in the creation of the far more powerful and less humane states of the seventeenth century. Yet no other solution could have preserved the apparent utility of classical studies for so long against the corrosive attacks of skepticism and the New Philosophy. And no gentler doctrine could have met the needs of that cruel age, when even Hugo Grotius would defend as legal the destruction of civilian property and the execution of hostages.

In the end, though, explanations like this operate on too general a level to satisfy. Lipsius's achievements can be described and his historical situation can be analyzed. But his personal motives and emotions remain obscure. And perhaps we should be willing to leave them so. It somehow seems appropriate that the man who unveiled the secrets of generals and emperors should preserve his own more modest—but more complex—philologist's secrets intact. (pp. 382-90)

Anthony Grafton, "Portrait of Justus Lipsius," in The American Scholar, *Vol. 56, No. 3, Summer, 1987, pp. 382-90.*

FURTHER READING

Boughner, Daniel. "Jonson's Use of Lipsius in *Sejanus.*" *Modern Language Notes* LXXIII, No. 4 (April 1958): 247-55.

Demonstrates that Ben Jonson relied on Lipsius's edition of Tacitus while composing his play *Sejanus.* Boughner focuses upon sharp contrasts between Jonson's and Lipsius's depictions of Caesar and the Roman Republic.

Grisé, Catherine. "Jean-Baptiste Chassignet and Justus Lipsius." *Vivarium* XIII, No. 2 (November 1975): 153-64.

Examines the texts of Lipsius's *De Constantia* and Chassignet's *Le Mespris de la vie et consolation contre la mort* (1594), investigating the latter's indebtedness to the former's Neo-Stoic philosophy.

Heesakkers, C. L. "Two Leiden Neo-Latin Menippean Satires: Justus Lipsius' *Somnium* (1581) and Petrus Cunaeus' *Sardi Venales* (1612)." In *Acta Conventus Neo-Latini Bononiensis: Proceedings of the Fourth International Congress of Neo-Latin Studies,* edited by R. J. Schoeck, pp. 500-09. Binghamton, N.Y.: Medieval & Renaissance Texts & Studies, 1985.

Considers general seventeenth-century appreciation of the two texts, basing observations on the "peculiar" order of the texts in the book *Elegantiores Praestantium Virorum Satyrae* (1655), a collection "of the most elegant satires."

Hill, Robert H. "The Great Galleon." *Blackwood's Edinburgh Magazine* CCXXXIX, No. 1445 (March 1936): 384-98.

Biographical anecdotes of Lipsius's academic career and scholarly accomplishments.

Kent, H. W. Introduction to *A Brief Outline of the History of Libraries,* by Justus Lipsius, translated by John Cotton Dana, pp. 9-20. Chicago: A. C. McClurg & Co., 1907.

Notes that "just as Lipsius's name is closely linked with one of the great epochs of printing, it has also a part in the history of the development of the library idea."

Kirk, Rudolf. Introduction to *Two Bookes of Constancie,* by Justus Lipsius, translated by Sir John Stradling, edited by Rudolf Kirk, pp. 3-62. New Brunswick, N.J.: Rutgers University Press, 1939.

A detailed introduction to Lipsius's English edition of *De Constantia.*

Oestreich, Gerhard. "The Main Political Work of Lipsius." In his *Neostoicism and the Early Modern State,* edited by Brigitta Oestreich and H. G. Koenigsberger, translated by David McLintock, pp. 39-56. Cambridge: Cambridge University Press, 1982.

Demonstrates how Lipsius's writings, particularly *Politicorum sive civilis doctrinae libri sex* and *De militia romana,* stimulated the development of modern political science and the theory of the state.

Pickering, F. P. "Justus Lipsius' *De Cruce Libri Tres* (1593), or the Historian's Dilemma." In his *Essays on Medieval German Literature and Iconography,* pp. 59-74. Cambridge: Cambridge University Press, 1980.

Debates whether Lipsius's *De Cruce* is a work "on Antiquity" or a devout Christian work. Pickering provides a detailed chapter-by-chapter description of the book's contents.

Sandys, John Edwin. "The Netherlands from the Foundation of the University of Leyden (1575) to 1700." In his *A History of Classical Scholarship,* Vol. II, pp. 300-32. New York: Hafner Publishing, 1958.

Brief biography and criticism of Lipsius's principal works.

Saunders, Jason Lewis. *Justus Lipsius: The Philosophy of Renaissance Stoicism.* Las Colinas, Tex.: Liberal Arts Press, 1955, 228p.

Examines Lipsius's principal works and their relationship to the growth of Neo-Stoicism.

Northern Humanism

The term "humanism" denotes a revival of classical letters that originated in Italy during the fourteenth and fifteenth centuries and later spread throughout Europe. This revival was accompanied by renewed emphasis upon the individual and a growing insistence upon secular values, with subjective thought seen as the proper starting point for determining truth. In Italy, humanism permeated nearly every facet of life, informing a cultural movement widely considered one of the most significant in world history: the Renaissance. It was not until the fifteenth and sixteenth centuries that humanism manifested itself in northern Europe, assuming a character similar to its Italian forerunner, and yet tailored to the limits and needs of northern society. Humanism, in this respect, arose concurrently with the Protestant Reformation and provided the Protestants with some of their movement's most influential spokesmen and writers.

Humanism is only one aspect of the Renaissance, but the two terms are often misunderstood to be synonymous. Historian Albert Hyma relates the two expressions in his seminal Erasmian study, *The Youth of Erasmus:* "It is of course well known that the word Renaissance is French, and that it literally means re-birth. When the term Renaissance is taken in its widest connotation, it implies the revival of all forms of learning and comprises an intellectual movement which resulted in . . . the downfall of sholastic philosophy, the spread of classical Latin, the renewed study of Greek and of Plato, the invention of printing—in short, the conquest of humanism. . . . " Primarily a literary and educational movement, humanism is defined by leading Renaissance scholar Paul Oskar Kristeller as "a movement that stressed the study of 'grammar, rhetoric, poetry, history and moral philosophy' but excluded the study of natural philosophy, metaphysics, and jurisprudence." The humanism of the north placed more importance on the literary and philological than did the movement in Italy. Humanistic expression in the north was dominated by a small number of schools and universities, and by such intellectuals as Desiderius Erasmus, Justus Lipsius, and Rudolf Agricola; while the south supported humanistic culture through its royal courts and public life. As a result, humanism in the Low Countries was never the all-encompassing way of life that it was in Italy; though Protestant thought, influenced by key humanists, spread worldwide during the centuries that followed.

An important aspect of northern humanism is the emphasis placed upon philology and education. As historian George Faludy notes, "The humanism of the Renaissance had been born of a preoccupation with the poets, writers and philosophers of antiquity. . . . In the eyes of the humanists antique society had been in every way superior to that of the Middle Ages; and classical writers were held to be the only competent thinkers and stylists, as opposed to the 'scholastic muddleheads and stammerers'." Dismissing medieval Latin as barbaric, the humanists sought to reinstitute the vocabulary, syntax, and therefore the eloquence, of the Latin of the ancients. Stimulated by the atmosphere of academic revival, scholars throughout the north sought lost manuscripts of the Latin classics. Recognizing the importance of both Greek and Hebrew in textual studies and clarifications, the humanists eagerly gained proficiency in the language to assist in their work. These three conditions converged and blossomed into a new awareness and appreciation of philology.

In addition to linguistics, the humanists were also concerned with education and its role of orienting the individual. Faludy asserts that humanism "never lost sight of its original aims: philology, which would elucidate the writings of the ancients, and pedagogy, which would disseminate their ideas." Educational reform became one of the important goals of the humanists, and they were assisted in this effort by the Brethren of the Common Life. The Brethren were a group of Christian men who lived monastic lives without taking the binding vows of a particular order. Thomas à Kempis, author of *The Imitation of Christ,* was one of the Brethren. Running schools that supported humanistic education to some extent, the Brethren instructed many boys in both rudimentary academic skills and such advanced studies as Greek and rhetoric, emphasizing the importance of piety and the ordering of the soul. Differing immensely from their scholasticist counterparts, humanistic teachers accentuated the active, tangible aspects of education by, as one critic stated, "arousing enthusiasm, explaining and illuminating their subjects during informal lectures which were really dialogues at times, and by taking the students out of the classroom to teach such things as botany and astronomy." Perhaps their greatest contribution is seen in the fact that, as historian Preserved Smith remarked, "though there was no radical reform in [European] education during the century between Erasmus and Shakespeare, two strong tendencies may be discerned at work, one looking towards a milder method, the other towards the extension of elementary instruction to large classes hitherto left illiterate."

The Brethren and other educators were assisted in their work by the increasing availability of affordable books as a result of great advancements in printing. The invention of movable type by Johann Gutenberg allowed greater quantities of books to be produced in less time and at less cost, thus bringing the price of books more affordable to a much greater portion of society than had purchased previously. Dissemination of ideas to the common man, not just clerics and other scholars, was thereby made possible. Because of this, the writings of Martin Luther and other Reformers were widely disseminated and had a lasting effect upon Christianity throughout Europe and the world. Prior to Gutenberg's innovation, manuscripts were copied out by hand by monks and other clerics. This time-consuming method permitted a great many copying errors to be introduced, resulting in inaccurate manuscripts. The invention of movable type and its effect upon printing is therefore recognized by scholars to be one of the most important events in Western history. A sixteenth-century essayist commented that printing "seems miraculously to have been discovered in order to bring back to life more easily literature which seemed dead." Elizabeth Eisenstein, a leading authority on Renaissance printing history, agrees that "the advent of printing was, quite literally, an epoch-making event. The shift from script to print revolutionized Western culture. It altered the way things changed and the way they stayed the same. It affected all forms of survival and revival. In particular, it affected a revival of learning that had got under way in quattrocento Italy."

The Renaissance was arguably one of the single most important eras in Western history, and humanism is an integral aspect of that age. Manifesting itself at different times and in different places, the humanism of Europe's northern countries possessed characteristics separating it from that of Italy, humanism's birthplace. Philology, education, and printing are three aspects of humanism that played a more substantial role in the north than in Italy. Jozef IJsewijn remarks in a study of humanism in the Low Countries that "the age of Renaissance and Baroque humanism was a great one in the cultural history of the Low Countries. . . . Situated at the crossroads of important political, cultural, and economic highways of early modern times, literary and artistic life flourished in its many prospering towns, in its schools and universities, its courts and abbeys, not rarely among the cruelties of brutal war or of ideological persecution. . . . The generalized use of Latin allowed writers, whose native Frisian, Dutch, or even French would have been of little or no use outside their own region, to speak to the entire Western world from Sicily to Iceland. Without this Latin Erasmus, Lipsius, [Daniel] Heinsius, and [Hugo] Grotius never would have had the worldwide audience they had then and still have now. And because of them and many of their less important colleagues the Low Countries are next to Italy a vital part of the European scene of humanism, a part that largely exceeds the narrow boundaries of that little corner of Europe."

BACKGROUND

Leonard Elliott Binns

[In the following excerpt, Binns examines the intellectual, political, and ecclesiastical aspects of life during the Renaissance.]

Regarded in its totality the period [of the Renaissance] stands revealed as one of unrest and expansion; in every department of man's life a new creative energy is seen to be at work; some peculiar manifestation of "a general excitement and enlightening of the human mind" which recalls the sun-swept days of an older civilization. For our present purposes it will be necessary to elaborate this statement and to trace its applicability to the various spheres of man's activity; for the sake of clearness we will arrange them under five heads: the intellectual, . . . the political, and the ecclesiastical. In days gone by it was commonly taken for granted that the Renaissance was the product almost solely of a revival of Greek thought, of a renewed study of the literature of Hellas. I cannot help thinking that such an assumption is not entirely justified; and that it would be more accurate to say that men found in Greek culture a ready-made form of expression for hopes and ideals which had arisen almost spontaneously in their own bosoms, that it was a moulding rather than an originating force. . . . But whatever may be the office which we assign to Greek culture in regard to the Renaissance the true inwardness of the movement cannot really be understood unless it be conceived of primarily as "the blossoming and unfolding of the mind of the Italian people."

What, it may be asked, was the immediate effect of the Renaissance upon religion, and what attitude did the leaders of thought adopt towards the Church? The New Learning was by no means opposed to the old religious system which had come down from the Middle Ages; many of its exponents were, in name at least, orthodox Catholics, and a strong sympathy with humanistic ideas was not unknown even in occupants of the throne of St. Peter himself. But eventually it proved to be an element of disruption and the faith of Italy was gradually weakened by a process which was almost imperceptible. Of direct attacks there were practically none; the revived paganism of the so-called Roman Academy was but the whim of an offended scholar, and even the exposure of the Donation of Constantine by Lorenzo Valla was not considered a bar to his employment at the Papal court. But the rigidity of the older system was bound to be abhorrent to the freedom-loving scholars of the Renaissance, and men who had come to despise the present and all connected with it made no exception in favour of religion; their eyes were so dazzled by the newly discovered glories of the world around them that they forgot the eternal splendours of the world to come. Christianity in the eyes of many of them only became respectable when forced into the mould of classical and pagan forms of expression.

One great department of knowledge, that of Natural Science, did not during the lifetime of Erasmus reveal any notable sign of its future eminence and usefulness. The main influence of the Renaissance be it remembered was Latin culture, and Latin culture, as distinguished from Greek, is rhetorical rather than scientific; hence "the science of that age was all clairvoyance, divination, unsubjected to our exact modern formulas, seeking in an instant of vision to concentrate a thousand experiences." Astronomy, it is true, was a subject upon which there was much practical knowledge diffused amongst the multitude, more even than in our own day; it could hardly be otherwise when the rising and setting of constellations marked the passage of time. The new era, however, which dates from Copernicus had not yet arisen.

Before leaving the subject of the New Learning some attention ought to be devoted to that art which was its ready handmaid. When printing first arose the humanists despised it as barbarous and unworthy of a scholar's attention; even to this day, as Lord Morley recently pointed out, it has never received its due meed of praise. Its importance for the spread of the new ideas, both of culture and of religion, cannot be exaggerated. Erasmus himself was one of the first who perceived its value, and in a well-known epigram he paid his tribute: "The library of Ptolemy," he says, "was contained within the walls of a house, but Aldus is constructing a library which shall have no limits but those of the world." One effect of printing upon letters was to give to the scholar an independent position and in part to do away with the necessity of patronage. There is a striking contrast between the early life of Erasmus with its continual series of degrading appeals to the great and wealthy for doles, and the later period when the sale of his books enabled him to exist in greater security; though even then it has to be confessed he still continued to receive large pensions from private patrons. (pp. 4-8)

Turning now to the world of politics we have to notice the beginnings of two great features of the modern world; the growth of nationality, and the recognition of the rights and the value of individuals.

During the Middle Ages the separate nations of Europe regarded themselves as parts of a single political and ecclesiastical organization (*einen einzigen weltlichgeistlichen Staat*), a condition of affairs which Ranke held to be essential to the naturalization of Christianity in the West. At the beginning of the Renaissance the decay of the feudal system announced the coming break-up of this vast organization. Its decay was especially rapid in Italy, which became in consequence a favourite experimenting ground for new forms of government. But Italy was entirely wanting in any real national feeling—even the invasion of Charles VIII had failed to unite its separate factions—and was moreover divided up into a number of small rival powers no one of which was strong enough to subdue the rest. In Spain, in England, and in France, the ruling dynasty, especially when the great feudatories had been exterminated or reduced, became the centre of the nation's life and the organ of its protest against all external interference whether political or ecclessiastical.

But this decentralizing tendency was further exemplified by the growing realization of the existence not merely of separate nations, but also of individual men. In the Middle Ages "man was conscious of himself only as a member of a race, people, party, family, or corporation," but that was all to be changed, henceforward his rights and value as a person were to be increasingly respected and acknowledged.

These changes in political organization and thought reacted appreciably on religion. The growing realization of national feeling, for example, with its resulting jealousies had been perhaps the most potent factor in wrecking the Conciliar Movement; so, too, the break-up of the Holy Roman Empire undoubtedly prepared men's minds for the break-up of the Holy Roman Church, more especially in Germany where an awakening national consciousness greatly helped the Reformers.

From the political we now turn to the ecclesiastical sphere. By the time of Erasmus the papacy had become almost completely secularized, and it might seem that the only just way of estimating or judging the various Popes themselves is by the standard of contemporary Italian despots. Their persistence, however, in claiming to be the successors of St. Peter, a simple fisherman, gave those who disapproved of their luxury and dissipation, a ready weapon against them. Erasmus, for example, in commenting on the statement in Acts ix. 43 that Peter lodged with one Simon a tanner, remarks that his successors would not be contented with less than three royal palaces.

So far had the spiritual responsibilities of the office been forgotten that on more than one occasion the papacy was actually sold to the highest bidder; and the Emperor Maximilian could actually conceive and nourish the idea of amalgamating it with the empire in his own person, thus making himself Pontifex Maximus as well as Cæsar.

The papacy, then, was to all intents and purposes a secular state; and its organization was that of an autocracy dependent upon a crowd of officials. The weakness of this form of administration lies in the difficulty of limiting either the number of the officials or the power which they exercise. Many of the papal servants received no salary at all, some had even paid for the privilege of holding office; vested rights had thus been allowed to multiply which were a burden on any reforming pope, since he would have to choose between performing an act of injustice by abolishing the offices without compensation, or repaying the invested capital, an impossible task.

Even those offices which were distinctively religious were held by quite unsuitable persons; "princes and nobles . . . though destitute of piety, learning, and vocation" were found masquerading as bishops. Pluralism was so common as to be taken as a matter of course; and the work of ministering to the flock which Christ purchased with His own blood was deputed to the inferior clergy, stage by stage, until it was actually performed by those who were too poor or too conscientious to hire a substitute. Such clergy as did make the endeavour, for one reason or another, to carry out the Church's system found their efforts constantly thwarted, especially in the matter of discipline, by the authorities at Rome, where dispensations and pardons for almost any conceivable crime could be bought at a fixed price.

In one important respect the papacy was at a disadvantage when compared with surrounding states; the succession being elective and not hereditary was uncertain. To remedy this weakness the popes of the later Middle Ages endeavoured to found principalities for their relations, and from the "time of Sixtus IV nepotism (was) elevated into a political principle."

Such were some of the abuses which disgraced the Church's administration; and yet good and pious men were not lacking to defend even such abuses, simply on the ground that as they formed part of the papal system to abolish them would seem to be a sign of weakness. If I mistake not similar arguments are advanced to-day against proposed changes in the Roman Church.

But a corrupt administration was not the worst feature of the Church of that period, and in the unworthy and sinful lives of her servants, from the popes downwards, men saw an even graver proof of desperate failure. The chief offenders, after the popes themselves, were the religious orders who spread everywhere "like the veins of the body," and everywhere they carried corruption and death where once they had been the bearers of life and peace. Those of the clergy who avoided bad moral lapses were often worldly and self-seeking, more interested in secular pursuits and their own advancement than in the cultivation of virtue and holiness. At so low an estimate did men hold the highest of all callings that to term anyone a clerk or a monk was the refinement of abuse. Machiavelli had no very high standard of moral rectitude, his condemnation is therefore the more damaging: "We Italians," he says, "are more irreligious and corrupt than others . . . because the Church and her representatives set us the worst example."

Yet widespread as the evil undoubtedly was there were still, as in our own Church in the eighteenth century, simple, God-fearing men going quietly about their duty. To produce such characters has always been a mark of the Church of Christ even in the times of her deepest degradation; hence, perhaps, her continued and almost miraculous survival.

The age was one of superstition, and the clergy were as much affected by it as were their neighbours; indeed they did not a little to foster this failing and to discover new forms for its exercise. One of the most popular superstitions was a belief in astrology; even so masculine a mind as Julius II was apparently under its influence and could delay his coronation as pope until a day which promised a fortunate conjunction of stars.

Amongst the vulgar multitude an accumulation of amazing beliefs was current; some of these were directly connected with the historic faith, some were mere pagan accretions which the Church had either deliberately adopted or had not chosen to condemn. Such were the habits of venerating relics and of making pilgrimages to famous shrines, habits which gave the people and their spiritual guides ample opportunity for indulging the prevailing weakness. Sometimes relics were of so great a value as to be purchased by a state, or to be presented by one ruler to another in return for some notable concession. An instance of the latter transaction was the presentation by the Sultan to Innocent VIII, whose friendship he greatly desired, of the veritable lance with which our Saviour's side was pierced. The proffered gift was at first regarded with suspicion, and since two other holy lances already existed—one at Paris, the other at Nuremberg—it was thought to be an act of derision. The pope, however, was equal to the occasion, and the Sultan's gift was received with appropriate ceremonies.

The whole tone of mind has been vividly preserved for us by Erasmus in the Colloquy entitled "The Shipwreck." The dialogue begins by describing the outbreak of a storm and the various precautions which were taken to meet the danger. At last all hope of safety having been abandoned, the mariners betook themselves to prayer. They pleaded with a being whom, in language coming down from remote times, they named the Star of the Sea, the Queen of Heaven, the Haven of Safety; terms which their heathen forefathers had used of Venus the sea-begotten, but which did not so readily apply to one who never took a voyage in her life. The passengers meanwhile were not slow to offer vows, each to his chosen protector. One man drew especial notice to himself by bawling out at the top of his voice the most generous promises to St. Christopher, pledging himself to give him a wax taper as big as his monument in Paris. An acquaintance reminding him of his inability to fulfil the contract received the whispered and ingenious reply; "Shut up, you fool, if once I get safe to shore, I won't give him a tallow dip."

The knowledge of abuses and corruptions such as these in the mother Church of Western Christendom cannot but distress us; as lovers of sound learning, however, we have the consolation of knowing that if the Church had not lost the respect of mankind, the substitution of the New Learning for the degraded and degenerate form of Scholasticism to which the Church was pledged would have been considerably delayed, perhaps for several generations. (pp. 11-19)

Leonard Elliott Binns, in his Erasmus The Reformer: A Study in Restatement, *Methuen & Co., Ltd., 1923, 138 p.*

Albert Hyma

[Hyma was a Dutch-born American educator who wrote widely on the Renaissance and Reformation. In the excerpt below, he relates some of the highlights of northern humanism.]

The period between 1465 and 1535—a most eventful period of "three score and ten years"—was above all a time of flux and change. It was in this period that the Middle Ages gave way to modern civilization, that human society in Europe underwent a combination of remarkable changes. Feudalism and serfdom now received a deathblow in several countries of western Europe; humanism spread beyond the Alps, and Italy ceased to be the one superior focus of higher civilization in Europe; scholastic philosophy was finally vanquished by humanists, mystics, and religious reformers; and the invention of printing made possible a vastly increased circulation of books. In this period great "national states" were reaching maturity, such as Spain, Portugal, France, and England; the Turks occupied practically the whole of the Balkan Peninsula and Hungary, but were halted before the gates of Vienna; they also failed to extend their power into the East Indian Archipelago, thus enabling the Portuguese to build a colonial empire east of Africa; America was discovered and the principal routes of sea-borne commerce shifted from the Mediterranean to the Atlantic, thus hastening the decline of Venice and Genoa and the rise of Antwerp, Amsterdam, and London.

This period also marked the end of the political weakness and the beginning of the expansion of Europe, now on a much grander scale than in the days of Alexander the Great and of Emperor Augustus. Europe was at last to reap the fruits of the advantages which its physical geography had kept in reserve for the age of Columbus, Da Gama, Drake, Cartier, Gutenberg, Erasmus, Copernicus, Bruno, Da Vinci, Luther, Calvin, and Loyola. When Erasmus passed away in 1536, the master minds of Europe had definitely embarked upon the policy of conquest in the realms of politics, economics, learning, art, and religion. Asia and Africa had lost the contest with Europe, while America merely formed a field for exploitation and colonization. The day seemed indeed very far distant when the latter continent would compete successfully with Europe in any phase of human enterprise. (pp. 3-4)

There is a tendency today in many places to underestimate the importance of the Christian Church and of religion at the end of the Middle Ages, because in our age men's minds appear to be drifting away from religious observances. One frequently hears the assertion that, although the great writers of the fifteenth century generally paid very little attention to political, social, and economic developments, the people as a whole were nearly as strongly subjected to the influence of these developments as they are today. Chroniclers in the fifteenth century recorded only those things in which they were interested, and therefore they presented a very one-sided picture of medieval civilization. Sound though this argument appears, the fact remains that the Christian Church was by far the mightiest institution of the Middle Ages and that the simple reason why Erasmus and Luther were the most celebrated figures during the first four decades of the sixteenth century is because they happened to discuss matters which aroused the greatest interest in the minds of thinking people.

Wherever Erasmus turned before he was forty he knew that everybody was born into the Church, just as today everybody is born a member of the State. There was in fact a great difference between the churches of his time and those of the present era. Shortly after the fall of the Roman Empire, when most European countries were being ravaged by hordes of barbarians, the Church had held out its hand of peace and order to millions of distracted Christians. It was the Church which restored order in Italy. It had assisted Charlemagne in building up his great empire. Its monasteries had preserved precious books, among others the Bible, the works of Aristotle, and of the Church Fathers. Its schools in almost all localities had been the only centers of learning. Thus it had richly deserved the privileges it enjoyed during the first five centuries of the Middle Ages.

Gradually the Church had grown exceedingly wealthy. Many a nobleman upon his death-bed had bequeathed part or all of his possessions to the Church. Not a few princes and rich nobles had deemed it expedient for the welfare of their souls to enter the ranks of the monastic orders. The monks had also found other ways of enriching the Church. They had secured immense tracts of land which had appeared of little value to the ignorant laymen, but which yielded bountiful crops, when once the swamps had been drained and the forests cleared. Around Rome the Papal States had grown up, controlled directly by the pope. In the twelfth and thirteenth centuries, the papacy had carried on a terrific contest for temporal supremacy with no lesser men than the emperors of the Holy Roman Empire, who in theory held all the countries of western and central Europe as their fiefs.

At the close of the thirteenth century, however, the power of the papacy began to wane. Most humiliating for the popes was the so-called Babylonian Captivity (1309-77) at Avignon, in France, where they were dominated by the French king. Equally distressing was the great schism (1378-1418), when there were two popes, one in Rome and one in Avignon. Then followed a period of twenty years in which the power of the papacy within the Church was contested by church councils, notably the Council of Basel (1431-33); but at the Council of Ferrara-Florence (1438-42), the pope was able to reassert successfully the claims of his greatest predecessors. His temporal power, however, continued to decline, particularly in France and England. Even in the Holy Roman Empire, where no great monarch stood ready to defend the national interests of the people, there was much discontent, and signs were not lacking that here too the pope could no longer strike terror into the hearts of princes, as had been the case in former days. In Russia and the Balkan Peninsula his authority had entirely disappeared since the middle of the eleventh century, because of differences in doctrine and church rites between the leaders in Rome and Constantinople. Europe possessed no longer one great Catholic Church, but two distinct branches, one called the Roman Catholic, the other the Greek, or Orthodox Catholic Church.

Nevertheless the Roman Catholic Church was exceedingly powerful, as almost every person believed that outside the Church nobody could be saved. For every individual in the Middle Ages the burning issue of his whole life was understood to be the possible salvation of his soul from eternal damnation. The only mediation between man and God was the Church. Such was the belief of the vast majority of people. Life on earth was comparatively short, and eternity had no end. Terrible was the prospect of the trembling sinner, if the Church should fail to save him. Hence the influence of the clergy and the importance of the seven sacraments.

There was much divergence of opinion concerning the efficacy of these sacraments. The Church as an institution had undergone many changes. Its creeds and its sacraments naturally had been subject to a great deal of criticism. Within the ranks of the hierarchy there had been intense rivalry. Church councils had sought to limit the power of the pope, and even some of the greatest cardinals had openly questioned several doctrines taught by the popes and their followers. Heretics had risen in various countries, some of whom had been put to death, while others had merely been silenced or persuaded to modify their criticism. Abuses had crept into the institution as a whole. National governments had begun to restrict the power of the papacy. Finally, a number of mystics had sought to secure salvation without the aid of the clergy. The whole structure of the Church seemed to totter as the fifteenth century drew to a close. Fifty years later it was felt by thousands of observers that it would actually crumble to pieces.

The attacks on the papal power by humanists had been far-reaching. The Emperor Constantine, who lived in the fourth century, and who had moved his capital from Italy to Constantinople, was supposed to have presented the bishop of Rome with the western half of his empire, in return for the assistance rendered by the bishop in saving his life. Lorenzo Valla had proved that this "Donation of Constantine" was simply a forged document. Valla and many other Italian scholars further hurt the papal cause by instilling into the minds of their numerous followers an attitude of skepticism and disrespect for authority. A great number of humanists made light of monastic discipline and the efficacy of the sacraments. They belittled the value of the soul and the importance of life after physical death, and consequently taught that people were foolish to be so intent on the salvation of the soul. They were opposed to asceticism, and some of them were even inclined favorably toward paganism. Not all of their views and deeds led up to the Reformation, but they certainly helped to prepare the way for several phases of this movement.

The humanists were supported in their attacks on the power of the Church as an institution by many theologians and mystics who believed that the Church had become too materialistic, and that there was in the Church too much empty formalism, with too little emphasis laid on personal piety. The mystics, in particular, strove to warn their pupils against the reliance on what they called "outward deeds," as contrasted with inner faith, feelings, and emotions. Books like the *Imitation of Christ* emphasized the need of love and faith rather than "works." The mystics tended to weaken the power of the clergy by laying stress on the relation between the individual soul and God, in which relation the sacraments play a comparatively insignificant part. The influence exerted by the mystics is very difficult to measure, but it was great.

Almost all classes of people agreed that the Church needed a reformation. Conservative minds would be content with a small number of changes; radical thinkers naturally wanted more. Some were interested chiefly in political and financial issues, while others were almost solely concerned with spiritual problems. There was scarcely a thinking person to be found anywhere in Europe at the end of the Middle Ages who felt that the Church was a perfect institution.

Some of the abuses which in the opinion of every honest reformer needed correction were simony and nepotism. Both were widespread at the time, and they were openly practiced by the higher clergy in Rome and elsewhere. The papacy itself was in need of reform. For at least a century the popes had not been the type of men who could be considered proper representatives of Christ on earth. They were all subject to criticism, for they did not try to be spiritual guides for the people. One pope would lead an army to battle, another would spend most of his time in studying art and literature, while still another would do little more than indulge in selfish pleasures. To many people it seemed that Rome was about the last place where one should look for the center of Christianity.

Then there were a number of practices and doctrines which were considered faulty by certain reformers. As early as the thirteenth and fourteenth centuries the question had often been raised whether it was right to have so many feast days, whether pilgrimages, relics, "good works" in general, were as efficacious as some claimed. The sale of indulgences was prohibited in Spain by Cardinal Ximenez. Cusa, the German cardinal, had taught the Augustinian doctrine of justification by faith and the depravity of human nature. Some of the Brethren of the Common Life in the Netherlands had preached the doctrine of the priesthood of all believers, which was taught later by the early Protestants. They, in common with other loyal church members, had bewailed the indolence, ignorance, and immorality of certain classes of monks, priests, and bishops.

Far more radical were those reformers, or so-called reformers, who were condemned as heretics by the Church. Notable among these were the Waldenses, the followers of Peter Waldo of Lyons, who lived in southern France at the close of the twelfth century. They not only attacked existing abuses, but rejected several of the doctrines regarding the sacraments, and insisted on the reading of the New Testament in the vernacular. They resembled the Puritans of a later age in that they wished to simplify rites in the Church and to elevate morals generally. (pp. 5-9)

What did the northern countries possess with which to emulate the Vatican and the basilicas at Rome, and the palaces and cathedrals at Florence, Pisa, Bologna, Milan, and Venice? In all the Low Countries there was only one university, namely at Louvain, and even that institution had not yet attained much eminence. Whereas in Italy the Greek and Roman writers were worshiped almost as saints, in countries north of the Alps but little progress had been made in reviving classical learning. Throughout the fifteenth century, nearly all scholars in transalpine countries frankly admitted the superiority of Italian schools and of Italian art.

It is of course well known that the word Renaissance is French, and that it literally means re-birth. When the term Renaissance is taken in its widest connotation, it implies the revival of all forms of learning and comprises an intellectual movement which resulted in the discovery of America and India, in the exploration of vast continents and of the starry firmament, in the rise of modern science, the downfall of scholastic philosophy, the spread of classical Latin, the renewed study of Greek and of Plato, the invention of printing—in short, the conquest of humanism, or the revival of interest in human and physical and material things, as contrasted with the realm of the soul or spirit.

The humanists stressed what contemporaries called *humanitas,* or humanity—something neglected and even despised by the medieval scribes. The humanists taught that man has a perfect right to enjoy himself in this world, that human nature is not fundamentally bad and that human beings have great innate power, for which reason they need not be so self-depreciating. They exalted human nature, but were less interested in pure theology. They were opposed to asceticism, which is a system of thought directed toward the suppression of physical enjoyment. The ascetic loathes human nature and believes that the flesh is the ally of the devil. The humanist entertains a very different opinion concerning human nature. It should be observed, however, that the word humanist may be defined in different ways, just as is the case with the terms Renaissance and Christianity. Some men were named humanists simply because they devoted themselves to the study of classical literature, while others received the appellation because they broke with scholastic philosophy or with the old grammars. (pp. 10-11)

Albert Hyma, "The Age of Erasmus," in his The Youth of Erasmus, *University of Michigan Press, 1930, pp. 3-12.*

Albert Hyma

[*In the following excerpt, Hyma provides a concise introduction to the concept of Transalpine humanism.*]

Transalpine humanism, unlike such movements as Italian humanism and the Reformation, is rarely presented as a well-defined entity. Although it has often enough been pointed out that the humanists who flourished north of the Alps differed from their kinsmen in Italy, the attempt is seldom made to regard the Transalpine Renaissance as a distinct force with an individuality of its own. One usually speaks of the Renaissance and the Reformation as if the former were simply a compact unit rather than a vast complex of widely different organs. In the present work, however, only one phase of the Renaissance will be depicted and analyzed, namely, Transalpine humanism; and this phase will be differentiated from both Italian humanism and the Reformation.

Those who look upon Transalpine humanism as a relatively independent force instead of a mere sub-division of a larger movement, can readily understand the rôle played by such leaders as Reuchlin, Lefèvre, Colet, and Erasmus,—men who simply cannot be classified among the champions of Protestantism or counter-reformation. It should be admitted that there was room in the age of Erasmus for a group of independent thinkers who refused to identify themselves with either Luther's cause or the plans of Loyola. In making such admission, however, one need not defend the viewpoint of Erasmus and his followers. For a student of history it will be sufficient to comprehend what thousands of well-meaning Protestants and Roman Catholics could never fathom,—namely, the desire on the part of the prince of the humanists to follow a course of his own and to view both Protestantism and the counter-reformation as unworthy of martyrdom.

The relation between Transalpine humanism and Italian humanism on the one hand and between Transalpine humanism and the Reformation on the other hand is one of the most fascinating problems in the history of modern civilization. This problem in its entirety has never been solved for the obvious reason that scholars are not yet fully acquainted with the process by which ideas spread from individual to individual and from country to country.

It is both customary and proper to point to Italian humanism as the chief source of Transalpine Humanism, particularly if the term humanism is defined in a narrower sense. All historians agree that the word humanism is closely related to the Latin noun *humanitas,* and also to the English noun humanity. Again, it is agreed that all humanists were especially interested in the study of classical literature. The Italian humanists were noted as a rule for their aim to exalt human nature, to exult in physical power and pleasure, to attack scholastic philosophy and ecclesiastical tyranny, and to magnify the importance of the world of the physical man as compared with life hereafter, where the soul or spirit will reign supreme. Hence the name humanism, which is often contrasted with asceticism.

It should be noted, however, that many of the Transalpine humanists were deeply religious, while some of them were actually ascetics. The name humanists was applied to them merely because of their interest in classical literature, and not because of their disapproval of asceticism or even of scholastic philosophy. That is the reason why one should be very careful in defining the term humanism. That is also the reason why it is futile to describe Transalpine humanism as little more than a transplanted Italian humanism. Those humanists north of the Alps, who like Peter Luder, resembled the Italian humanists the most nearly, were men of inferior caliber and lacking in national or international influence and prestige. The great leaders in Germany, the Low Countries, France, Spain, and England were all men of great moral and religious power. Although every one of them was greatly indebted to Italian humanism, they all showed a considerable degree of individual and national independence.

Much the same could be said about the relation between the Transalpine humanists and such men as Luther, Calvin, Loyola, and their numerous adherents. Superficial research would impel one to assert that Erasmus was changeable in that he first supported Luther and afterwards turned against him. It has too often been believed that Erasmus had no definite policy and cherished no firm convictions. A careful analysis of his life and work, on the other hand, will reveal a multitude of facts which disqualify such assertions. Since Erasmus in a large measure personified Transalpine humanism, his conduct and his writings are the most convincing proof of the integrity of this movement. (pp. 1-3)

Albert Hyma, in an introduction to his Erasmus and the Humanists, *F. S. Crofts & Co., 1930, pp. 1-11.*

Myron P. Gilmore

[*Gilmore was an American educator and essayist. In the excerpt below, he briefly surveys the underlying assumptions of Christian humanism.*]

The movements for the reform of the church and society at the end of the fifteenth century were diverse in origin and character. Yet, viewed as a whole, they can be conveniently divided into two main types. There was in the first place the pietistic and mystic approach to the problem of ecclesiastical reform, inherited from the Middle Ages.

This tradition emphasized the reliance on immediate divine guidance, the role of inspiration and the importance of the sanctified individual, whose extra-ordinary piety made manifest the operation of grace. In a corrupt society secular remedies were of no avail, only the indirect attack could be successful; the purification of society would be accomplished more by example than by precept, especially where the example was understood as the direct and immediate revelation of the divine plan, though exhortation and the imposition of discipline were not excluded. This conception of the nature of reform drew on the background of Franciscan and Dominican mysticism, on the piety of the Brotherhood of the Common Life, and in its more extreme aspects on the apocalyptic hopes of those heretics and prophets who had appeared outside the framework of orthodoxy in the late medieval church. The tradition was broad enough to include the mystic who withdrew from the world and the activist who applied his inspiration to a direct program for reforming abuses. From the point of view of their essential belief in the nature of man and his relation to God, individuals as various as Thomas à Kempis, Standonck and Savonarola can be grouped together.

The other principal category of reformers were inspired by the new scholarship and the new philosophy. They were above all distinguished by a belief in the power of the human intellect to bring about institutional and moral improvement. The new Greek and Hebrew learning, they held, could be productive only of good, even when it seemed at first glance farthest removed from the Christian tradition. The program of Christian humanism was built on a conviction of the importance of the rational faculties of man and it exalted the role of an intellectual aristocracy. It emphasized nature rather than grace, ethics rather than theology and action rather than contemplation.

The distinction between these two traditions does not imply that the European reform movement was sharply divided into two opposing camps which had no common meeting ground. If the contrast between an Erasmus and a Savonarola seems to reveal in a heightened form the differences between two approaches to the contemporary crisis in church and state, yet there were many in every European country who occupied an intermediate position. The reality behind the term "Christian humanist" covers a wide range of accommodation between Christian and classical ideals, but even the broadest interpretation of the humanist position cannot obscure the basic assumption which distinguished the generation of which Erasmus was the leader.

Among these intellectual reformers the results of assimilating the new learning had not yet reached the point of leading any to a conscious rejection of the Christian tradition. Much of what is commonly written and repeated about the paganism of even the Italian fifteenth-century humanists is misleading. There were some who moved in the direction of a theory of natural religion, and many who made a distinction between the observances of the uneducated and the beliefs of the intellectual aristocracy. But in an atmosphere still saturated with the forms, the thought and the daily ritual of Christianity it was impossible either to revive ancient paganism completely or to anticipate modern agnosticism. In whatever proportions the Christian, the classical and the Hebrew traditions were combined, the humanist of the age of Erasmus had as his most basic hope the more complete realization of the form of Christianity in which he believed.

The philosophical and theological position of this group rested on the acceptance of the natural world. In this respect their thought was not very different from the Thomistic solution of the problem of the relation between nature and grace. But if the compromise was fundamentally the same as that of the scholastics, the philosopher who inspired it was no longer Aristotle but Plato. Neo-Platonism was to the humanists what Aristotelianism had been to St. Thomas and his followers. It provided Christian humanism with a philosophy the influence of which was subtly and pervasively felt in many forms of thought and expression, including those far removed from metaphysical speculation.

Among the important implications of this disposition to come to terms with the natural world outside the boundaries defined by revelation was the more complete acceptance of the corpus of classical literature as containing nothing that was incompatible with Christianity. Greater learning could not corrupt; it would only purify. Erasmus, in a letter to the young Adolph of Veere, justified the study of even the most profane of classical authors, and in his edition of the works of St. Jerome discounted the story of the saint's dream about being beaten before the gates of Heaven for being a Ciceronian and not a Christian. If these arguments contained echoes of patristic and medieval justifications for the study of classical literature, yet they were now given a new emphasis and contained perhaps unconscious admissions of the growth of secular tastes.

All these assumptions found concrete expression in the theories of education of the Christian humanists. The nature of man, fundamentally good although corrupted by original sin, was capable of improvement by an intellectual discipline. Learning, whether sacred or profane, would increase piety. Indeed, this belief in the potentialities of educational reform was perhaps the most distinguishing characteristic of this school of reformers, marking them off most clearly from those whose hopes were committed to more revolutionary and more mystical ways of activity. In the minds of many of the humanists a new program of education was not only necessary; it was all that was necessary. Hence the multiplicity of treatises on the education of children, and the collections of precepts for those who were to occupy important positions in life. Today it may seem naïve to have held that peace, harmony and the fuller realization of a Christian society could be achieved by offering a new system of education. Yet these were the objectives in the mind of Erasmus when he wrote in the preface to the New Testament that he wanted every plowboy to be whistling the Psalms as he plowed his furrow. This was perhaps the first significant appearance of a hope which has recurred again and again in western thought and has remained one of the outstanding characteristics of the evolution of European civilization. It appeared in the early sixteenth century, in the Age of Enlightenment and again among those liberal utilitarians and devotees of progress in the nineteenth century who were the heirs of the Enlightenment. Each of these occasions was marked by an increasing broadening of the educational base; the humanist hopes were successively democratized.

So far these hopes have been disappointed in every age, but earlier deceptions have not prevented their recurrence in a new set of circumstances. For the humanists at the beginning of the sixteenth century there was, however, a particular brightness in the prospect for European civilization because there was no past history of disillusionment. Even a John Stuart Mill did not envisage that when the plowboy had learned to read he was more likely to read the Hearst papers than the Psalms, but the liberals of the nineteenth century had at least historical perspective on the experience of humanism and the enlightenment. The generation of Erasmus, on the other hand, could not have anticipated that their expectations would go down to disappointment in the wars of religion, as those of a later age were doomed by the wars of nationalism. There was thus a kind of innocence in this otherwise sophisticated group who represented an aristocracy of intellect, the first apostles of the salvation of society by the use of human reason.

This mood and these assumptions were shared in different ways and different degrees in all countries of European Christendom at the beginning of the sixteenth century. In spite of great differences in emphasis and divergent theological and philosophical interests, their common bond was an acceptance of the new learning and an attempt to apply it to the reform of the church and state. In the short run their very willingness to build on and even to compromise with the results of humanism gave them a greater degree of success than was achieved by a Savonarola, but in the long run the Lutheran revolution was to prove that this kind of rationalism was not enough. (pp. 204-07)

Myron P. Gilmore, "The Program of Christian Humanism," in his The World of Humanism, 1453-1517, *Harper & Brothers Publishers, 1952, pp. 204-28.*

Stefan Zweig

[*Zweig was an Austrian biographer and historian. In the excerpt below, he discusses some characteristics of humanism and Erasmus's role in promoting and developing them.*]

There is nothing imperialistic in humanism; in its domain there are neither foes nor thralls. He who refuses to belong to the select circle can remain outside if he prefers; no one compels him; he is not pressed forcibly to accept the new ideal. Every form of intolerance—and intolerance invariably implies misunderstanding—was alien to the doctrine of universal understanding. On the other hand, none were denied an entry into this spiritual guild. Anybody was eligible to become a humanist if he desired education and culture. Men of any class, and women too, nobles and priests, kings and merchants, the laity and the clergy, all had free access to this free community; none were asked whence they came and to what race or class they belonged, no inquiries were made to discover what was their native speech or the nation to which they owed fealty. Thus an unheard-of concept came to freshen European thought: the idea of supranationalism. Languages, which had hitherto formed an impenetrable wall between nation and nation, must no longer separate the peoples. A bridge would be built by means of a universal tongue, the Latin of the humanists. At the same time the concept of a fatherland for each nation would have to be proved untenable because it formed too narrow an ideal. It should be replaced by the European, the supranational ideal. "The entire world is one common fatherland," declared Erasmus in his *Querela pacis (Complaint of Peace),* and from this commanding position he looked down upon the senseless quarrels between the nations, the hatred between English, Germans, and French, to exclaim: "Why do such foolish names still exist to keep us sundered, since we are united in the name of Christ?" Disputes between Europeans seemed to the humanists to be the outcome of misunderstandings arising from too narrow-minded an outlook, too faulty an education; the duty of coming generations of Europeans would be to replace the vainglorious claims of petty princelings, of fanatical sectarians, and of national egoists, by sympathetic co-operation, by emphasizing that which could lead to harmony, by raising the European spirit to preside over the national spirit, to change Christianity as a simple religious congregation into a universal and all-embracing Christliness, where love of mankind and a desire to serve meekly and devotedly should prevail. Erasmus, we see, aimed higher than merely achieving a cosmopolitan community. What he showed was a resolute will to create a new spiritual form of unity in the West. Before his day, there had been men to promote the notion of a united Europe: the Roman Cæsars, for example, with their idea of the *pax Romana,* Charlemagne, as, at a later date, Napoleon. But these autocrats worked with fire and sword, endeavouring to compel the nations to unite under the threat of violence; and the fist of the conqueror weighed heavily on the weaker in order to bind them the tighter to the strong. The great difference between their ideas and those of Erasmus was that to him European unity seemed to be a moral aim, utterly unselfish, a spiritual demand. With him began to be postulated the concept (which many are still advocating to-day) of a United States of Europe under the ægis of a common culture and a common civilization. (pp. 72-4)

The humanistically educated, the humanely minded man in the Erasmian sense, can never pledge himself unreservedly to any kind of ideology, for every idea strives in its own fashion to achieve hegemony; nor may he bind himself to any party, since every member of a party must of necessity be a partisan, and see himself and feel himself and think of himself as adhering to that party. A man must at all costs guard his freedom of thought and of action, for in the absence of this freedom no justice is possible—and yet justice is the one idea which all mankind should share in common. To think in the Erasmian way is to think independently; to act in the Erasmian way is to work for mutual understanding. The Erasmian creed, which is equivalent to a belief in mankind, demands that the faithful shall never promote dissension, but unity; never encourage the partisanship of the biased, but, rather, shall broaden the bases of mutual understanding and shall initiate further understandings; the more fanatical the epoch, the more above party should the true humanist be, gazing upon human errors and perplexities with indulgence and compassion, acting as the incorruptible champion of intellectual freedom and of justice here below. Erasmus, therefore, considered that every idea had a right to existence, and none could make an exclusive claim to being correct; and he who had tried to understand even folly and to sing its praises, could not feel antagonistic to any theory or thesis unless it endeavoured to do violence to others. A humanist, knowing so much, loves the world precisely because of its variegated manifestations, and its contrasts do not alarm him. Nothing is farther from his mind than to endeavour to abolish these contrasts after the manner of the fanatic and the system-monger who would like to see all values reduced to a common integer and every flower constrained to take one shape and one colour. This is the sign-manual of the humanist: never to look upon contrasts with an inimical eye; always to work with a view to bringing about unity even where unity seems impossible to achieve; invariably to seek out what is human in everything. . . . This ultimate and universal understanding—spiritual understanding among all the peoples of Europe—is, as a matter of fact, the only sort of religious creed which the level-headed and rationalistic humanists were trying to establish; and they worked for this end as ardently as their contemporaries did for a belief in God, proclaiming their message of a belief in man, declaring that upon this idea the meaning, the goal, and the future of the world depended. Instead of one-sidedness there must be unanimity, and thereby an ever humaner world of men.

The humanists recognized one single road whereby to achieve this training towards humanism: Education. Erasmus and those who shared his views, maintained that man would become more human by means of education through the printed book, for only the uneducated, only the unlettered yielded irreflectively to his passions. An educated man, a civilized man—and herein we see the tragical failure in their reasoning—was no longer capable of resorting to gory violence, and when once the educated, cultivated, and civilized got the upper hand, chaos and brute force would inevitably disappear, and war and persecution of opinions would become anachronisms. In their overvaluation of the effects of civilization, the humanists failed to take account of the basic impulses and their untameable strength; in their facile optimism, they overlooked the terrible and wellnigh insoluble problem of mass-hatred and the vast and passionate psychoses of mankind. Their view was too simple. For them there existed two layers, an upper and a lower: in the latter were to be found the uncivilized, rough, and passion-ridden masses; in the former lived the educated, the penetrating, the humanistic, the civilized. They fancied that the main business was accomplished when increasingly large portions of the lower layer were transferred satisfactorily to the upper. Just as in Europe an ever-increasing area of land was reclaimed and brought under the plough, whereas previously these lands had been the haunts of savage beasts, so also must it be with mankind. Gradually ignorance and roughness among the peoples of Europe would be extirpated, to be substituted by cleared and fruitful zones of humanity. Thus religious thought would be replaced by the ideal of an uninterrupted ascent of man. The concept of a progressive evolution (at a later date to be converted into a scientific method by Darwin) became under the ægis of the humanists an ethical ideal towards which the men of eighteenth and nineteenth century Europe strove. Even in our modern scheme, Erasmian ideas play an important part. Nevertheless it would be erroneous to believe that humanistic culture and Erasmus's teaching were in any way democratic, and heralds of liberalism. Never for a moment did it enter Erasmus's head, never did it occur to his followers, that even the most insignificant rights should be granted to the folk, to the uneducated, to those who were still under age—for them, all the uneducated were "under age"; and although in the abstract they loved the whole of mankind, they were careful to eschew the company of the *vulgus profanum.* If we examine their theories more closely, we shall see how the ancient arrogance of the nobly born has been replaced by another kind of arrogance, by the pride of intellect which was to hold sway for three hundred years to come, and which maintained that only the man who was sure of his Latinity, who had passed through a university, had a right to judge what was right and what was wrong, what was moral and what was immoral. The humanists, in the name of reason, were as determined to govern the world as were the princes in the name of authority and the Church in the name of Christ. They aimed at establishing an oligarchy, at inaugurating the dominion of an educated aristocracy; the best, the most cultured, οι αριστοι, were, in the Greek sense of the term, to take over the leadership of the "polis," the State. Thanks to their erudition, their clear and humanistic outlook, they felt that they had been singled out to act as mediators and leaders, to come to the rescue when the nations were waging war or quarrelling; nevertheless the improvement they looked for was not to be brought about with the aid of the people at large, but over the heads of the masses. At bottom, humanism was, therefore, far from being a denial of the knightly order; it was a renewal of this order along intellectualist lines. The humanists hoped to conquer the world by means of the pen just as those others had conquered with the sword; and, like those others, all unconsciously, they created a social convention adapted to their needs, a convention which should set them apart from "barbarians," a convention with a kind of courtly ceremonial of its own. They raised themselves to a novel kind of nobility by translating their names into Latin or Greek equivalents so as to dissemble the fact of their plebeian origins: Schwarzerd became Melanchthon, Geisshüssler became Myconius, Oelschläger became Olearius, Kochhase became Chytraeus, Dobnick became Cochläus, and so forth. They were careful to array themselves in black clothing with ample folds, to differentiate themselves even outwardly from their fellow-citizens. It was considered to be beneath their dignity to write a book or a letter in the mother tongue, just as a knight would have been scandalized had he been asked to march forth to battle on foot amid the troops instead of mounted on horseback. Each felt it incumbent upon him to deport himself with special seemliness when mixing with the herd of those who had not entered the sacred precincts; they avoided hasty speech, cultivated decorous and courtly ways, while their contemporaries were rude and boisterous in behaviour. In writing and in style, in speech and in conduct, these aristocrats of the intellect aimed at dignity of expression and of thought, so that in the humanists the last faint rays of the epoch of chivalry fluttered up anew, after having been dimmed and laid to rest along with Emperor Maximilian's bones. This was an order of the mind whose insignium was the book in place of the Cross. And, since the order of knighthood had had recourse to the uncouth violence of the cannon in order to maintain itself in power, this noble company of idealists would fight against the boorish impacts of the folk revolutionaries, Luther and Zwingli, with the no less effective weapon of beauty.

But such deliberate ignoring of the masses, such studied indifference towards the world of reality, rendered it impossible to give durability to the kingdom Erasmus hoped to establish, and sapped the vital energy from his ideas. The fundamental mistake of the humanists was that they wished to teach the people from the heights of their idealism, instead of going down among the masses and endeavouring to understand them and to learn from them. The academic idealists fancied that they were already in power, because their kingdom spread over all lands, because in every country, at every court, in the universities, monasteries, churches, everywhere, they had those that served the cause, they had their envoys and in the name of authority and the Church in the name of Christ. They aimed at establishing an oligarchy, at inaugurating the dominion of an educated aristocracy; the best, the most cultured, were, in the Greek sense of the term, to take over the leadership of the legates, who proudly furthered the progress of *eruditio* and *eloquentia* in the regions where barbarism held sway. But, though their realm was extensive, its roots did not go deep; it only influenced the most superficial layers, having but feeble relations with reality. When enthusiastic messages reached Erasmus almost daily from Poland, Bohemia, Hungary, or Portugal; when emperors, kings, and popes sought the philosopher's favour, how could he fail at times, alone in the seclusion of his study, to give himself up to the sweet delusion that the reign of reason had truly begun? But behind this huge accumulation of Latin epistles, he surely could not have been unaware of the complete unresponsiveness of the masses? Surely he could not have failed to hear the growing rumble of discontent arising from the depths? The "people" simply did not exist so far as Erasmus was concerned; he considered the masses were unworthy the attention of a refined and educated man, and it would be beneath his dignity to woo the favours of "barbarians."

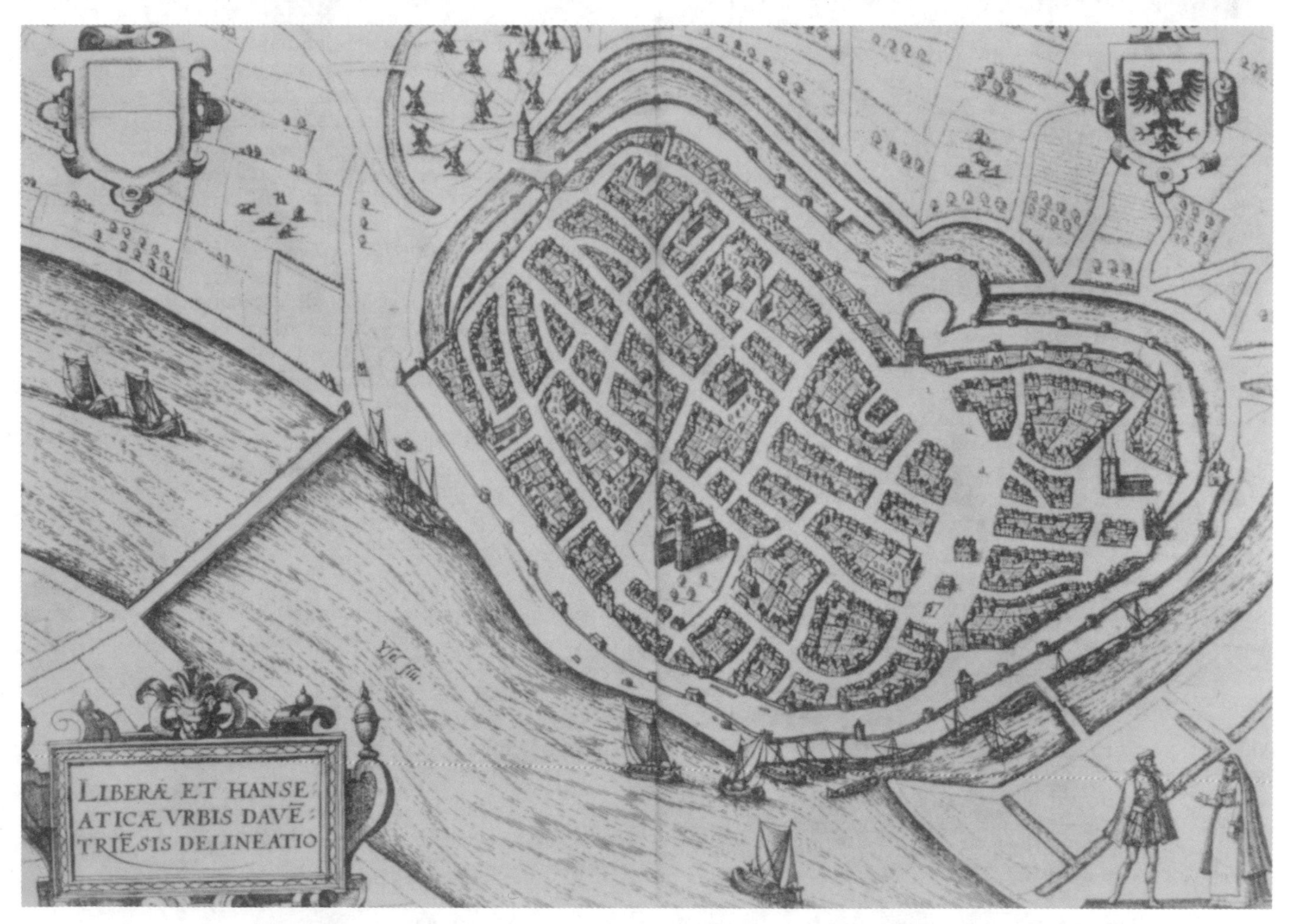

Map of sixteenth-century Deventer. Gerhard Groote founded the Brethren of the Common Life here in the fourteenth century.

Thus, humanism was for the happy few, not for the broad multitude; it was never anything better than a kingdom set amid the clouds, lighting up for one moment the whole world, beautiful to contemplate, a pure picture painted by a creative mind looking down serenely from its unattainable heights upon the tenebrous world below. Such an airy and artificial structure could make no stand against a genuine storm; it was doomed to perish unresistingly, and to fall into oblivion.

The tragical side of the humanistic movement, and, indeed, the cause of its decline, was that though the ideas which animated it were great, the men who were its prophets proved inadequate. As always with armchair philosophies, there was a tincture of the ludicrous in these well-meaning efforts to better the world. Thoroughly earnest and honest, wearing their Latinized names as if they were intellectual masks, the protagonists suffered from a dash of pedantry and vanity, so that their loveliest theories were thinly coated with these two far from attractive qualities. Erasmus's pygmy followers are touching in their professorial and academic naivety, having much in common with the excellent persons we meet in philanthropic and universal improvement societies; theoretical idealists whose religion consists in a belief in the inevitability of human progress, jejune dreamers constructing moral universes while sitting at their desks and writing down thesis after thesis on the subject of everlasting peace—while in the world of reality one war follows upon the heels of another, and the very same popes, emperors, and kings who have enthusiastically acceded to these ideas of conciliation, are simultaneously agreeing and running counter to one another and setting the world aflame. Were a new Ciceronian manuscript discovered, the humanist clan went wild with excitement, fancying the whole world would reecho with the joyful tidings; every sympathetic pamphlet, be it never so unpretentious, roused their most ardent and passionate approval. But that which moved the man in the street, that which stirred the masses to the depths, all those things were outside the pale; they did not even wish to know about them; and, since they continued shut up in their studies, the words they uttered lacked resonance, and could find no echo in the world of reality. It was owing to this disastrous seclusion, this absence of popularity, that the humanists were never able to produce harvest out of their fecund ideas. The immense optimism which inspired the whole of their work could not grow into a healthy and fruitful plant and develop adequately, because among these theoretical pedagogues of the idea of human progress there was not one who possessed the power of speaking to and being understood by the people. Thus a great and sacred thought was doomed to rot away for several hundred years because the man did not exist who could convey it to the masses.

And yet that historic hour, in which the sun of human trust shone with gentle effulgence down upon our European earth, was a beautiful moment in time; and if the delusion that the people were already at peace and united was premature, still we must respect it, and return grateful thanks that it ever existed. Men have always been needed who would be bold enough to believe that history is not a dull and monotonous repetition, the same game played over and over again under different disguises, but have had an invincible confidence that moral progress is a reality, that mankind is slowly climbing an invisible ladder to better things, leaving behind its bestiality and attaining to godliness, abandoning the use of brute force in favour of the rule of a well-ordered mind, and that the highest, the final rung where full understanding will be achieved is no longer so very far aloft. The Renaissance and the humanistic movement combined to create a moment of intense optimism throughout the western world. We cannot do otherwise than love this epoch and admire its wonderful illusion, since then, for the first time, mutual confidence arose among the peoples of Europe, inspiring them with the idea that a higher, more knowledgeable, and wiser humanity would be created, outstripping in accomplishment even the civilizations of Greece and Rome.

And at the outset it seemed as if these optimists were right, for were not wonders and portents rife in those days, marvels superseding all that had hitherto gone to the making of the human story? Would it not seem that Dürer and Leonardo were Zeuxis and Apelles reborn, that Michelangelo was a new Phidias? Did not science set order among the stars, and promulgate new laws for the terrestrial globe? Gold, streaming from freshly discovered continents, created fabulous wealth, and this wealth begot new arts. Gutenberg's invention made the production of books so easy that the word of enlightenment could spread over the whole surface of the earth. Ah, it could not be long now, cried Erasmus and his disciples gleefully, before mankind, so lavishly endowed by the products of its own energies, would recognize its mission, its ethical purpose here below—to live in fraternal concord, to act uprightly, and to extirpate every vestige of the bestiality handed down from its animal ancestry. Ulrich von Hutten's cry sounded like a trumpet call over the land: "It is a joy to be alive!" From the pinnacles of the Erasmian temple the citizens of a new world looked down upon a new Europe, and saw the sun rising on the horizon of the future, a light announcing that at long last, after a weary eternity of spiritual darkness, the day of universal peace was at hand.

But they were mistaken. The dawn was not the holy one they expected to shine over a gloomy earth: on the contrary, the light came from the brand which was to destroy with incendiary force the ideal world so confidently expected by the humanists. As the Germanic hordes of old swept down upon the world of classical Rome, so Luther, the fanatical man of action, backed by the irresistible force of a mass movement, sallied forth to swamp and to destroy this supranational dream. Ere ever the humanists had properly set about inaugurating their schemes for world unity, the Reformation disrupted the intellectual harmony of Europe, destroyed the *ecclesia universalis,* shattering the whole fancied structure as with the blows of a Titan's hammer. (pp. 79-88)

Stefan Zweig, "Greatness and Limitations of Humanism," in his Erasmus: The Right to Heresy, *translated by Eden Paul and Cedar Paul, Cassell and Company Limited, 1951, pp. 67-88.*

Jozef IJsewijn

[*In the following excerpt, IJsewijn studies the essential characteristics and literary expression of humanism in the Low Countries.*]

The Low Countries or Netherlands of the Middle Ages and Renaissance period do not correspond to any modern country. The Burgundian and later Habsburg or Spanish or independent territories called "Germania Inferior," "Belgium" (or "Belgia" by the poets), "XVII Provinciae (belgicae)," comprise the modern kingdoms of the Netherlands (or Holland) and Belgium, the Grand Duchy of Luxembourg, some border areas in western Germany belonging to Niedersachsen and Rhineland as well as a substantial part of northern France. . . . (p. 156)

The Low Countries, being a small nook of Europe without natural boundaries except the sea in the west and the north (though the sea more often served as a highway than as a barrier), are open in all respects to foreign influences and exchanges. Humanism came to it from Italy through the Rhine valley, or by way of Paris, or in the luggage of Italians establishing themselves at Louvain, Brussels, Bruges or elsewhere in the country. At the same time, native students and scholars went abroad for education or for a whole career. One cannot study the humanism of the Low Countries without carefully taking into account that continuous exchange of learning and learned men. In the course of the (late) fifteenth century several Italians were at work at Louvain (Raimundus Marlianus, Antonius Gratiadei, Cornelius Vitellius, Stephanus Surigonius, Lodovicus Brunus), but at the same time Rudolf Agricola, the first northern humanist, was in Italy (Pavia and Ferrara), Jacob Canter from Groningen in Augsburg and Bohemia, Matthaeus Herbenus from Maastricht (not a Walloon as was believed until recently) at Rome in the households of Niccolò Perotti and Cardinal Bessarion and later in Venice. This exchange of learning and learned men, facilitated by the universal use of Latin, intensified during the sixteenth and seventeenth centuries, and not rarely the most brilliant scholars in the Low Countries were foreigners, whereas our outstanding humanists often went abroad. The cause of these expatriations could be scholarly (as when courts, printing houses, or universities invited the best authors or teachers available), but very often the reason was a search for spiritual liberty or even a flight from death or imprisonment. Tolerance was hardly known in those days. (pp. 159-60)

The history of humanism and humanist learning in the Low Countries extends over about two centuries, from the middle of the fifteenth to the middle of the seventeenth century. In 1450 culture in the Low Countries was still by and large scholastic and late medieval, but a few individuals were aware of the new humanist currents in Italy. (p. 161)

The rather late development or acceptance of humanistic learning and literature in the Low Countries and elsewhere in transalpine Europe is certainly not due to ignorance of it. Cultural relations between Italy and the Netherlands are as old as the Roman Empire, and northern scholars always had gone south: Bishop Ratherius of Verona (tenth century), a native of Hainaut and the only known reader of Catullus in the Middle Ages; the Fleming William of Moerbeke, the most famous translator of Aristotle; and his compatriot Dominicus of Flanders (ca. 1425-1479), a scholastic professor at Bologna, Pisa, and Florence, are only a few outstanding names. And conversely Petrarch himself had visited Liège and the Ardennes, discovering there Cicero's speech *Pro Archia.* (p. 162)

Humanism outside Italy possibly never would have gone as far as it did but for the invention of the printing press and its rapid expansion in Italy. As a result the classics and the new humanist textbooks of Gasparino Barzizza, Valla, Giovanni Tortelli, Filelfo, and others now became available in ever larger quantities. One wonders how many of these texts men such as Erasmus never would have seen at school if only manuscripts had been there and how different a course their intellectual development might have taken! In any case, Erasmus himself never would have been as universally read as in fact he was: Who would ever have written the 2.5 million copies of his works that we know were printed from 1500 to 1925? Therefore the date of the establishment of the first printing presses in the Netherlands—1473—has an outstanding importance in the history of humanism, even if its first publications were mainly patristic and medieval works. The first printers were Nicolaas Ketelaer and Gerrit van Leempt at Utrecht in the North, Dirk Martens and Johann of Westphalia at Aalst (Alost, Alostum) in Flanders. (p. 163)

Another incentive and a landmark in the history of humanism was the foundation in 1517 of the Louvain Collegium Trilingue, one of the very first of such institutions in Europe. It followed less than ten years after the Collegio de San Ildefonso (1508), the heart of the newly founded Spanish University of Alcalà de Henares (Complutum), but it preceded by almost fifteen years the Collège des Lecteurs Royaux (Paris 1530) of François I. It is of course sheer coincidence, but nevertheless a kind of symbol of a changing generation, that about the same time two major teachers and grammarians of the previous generation died: Johannes Murmellius of Roermond (d. 1517 at Deventer) and Johannes Despauterius of Ninove (d. 1520 at Komen/Comines in southern Flanders). The first Trilingue generation, to which belong Erasmus, Vives, Hadrianus Barlandus, Rutgerus Rescius, Conrad Goclenius, Nicolaus Clenardus, and its printer Martens, dominated the humanist scene until about 1540.

By that time the religious conflicts had developed to such an extent that they threatened to suffocate any other intellectual concern. (pp. 163-64)

Humanism did not escape the storm of religious fanaticism and the unhappy wars it unchained. In the end even the Trilingue was closed down for many years (1590-1606), and Lipsius in his well-known description of the town and the University of Louvain (*Lovanium,* Antwerp 1605) sighed his melancholy in the words: "At nunc iacent ibi omnia et silent" (and now all things there lie silent). Other fine and important humanist undertakings collapsed in those years, such as the Officina Goltziana in Bruges (1562-76), the printing office that the famous engraver Hubert Goltz (Goltzius) (1526-1583) set up with the financial help of the humanist-minded Lord Marcus Lauweryns (Marcus Laurinus, 1530-1581).

More and more writers in both camps had to produce works acceptable to their intolerant theological supervisors. Censorship began its devastating work, Erasmus being one of their privileged victims, especially so because he had dared to apply the new philological criticism to the text of the New Testament. Here again one notices the multiplying and intensifying effect of the printing press. Giannozzo Manetti and Valla had done much the same before this invention, but their work remained hidden in a few manuscripts until the moment Erasmus discovered a version of Valla's *Adnotationes in Novum Testamentum* in the abbey library of Park just outside the walls of Louvain and brought it to Bade in Paris, or even until modern scholars unearthed Manetti's translation of the Psalms directly from the Hebrew.

The consequences of these changes for the development of humanist activities are clearly discernible. Many scholars withdrew into the neutral and safer work of the purely classical philological kind. Yet even there the censor's eye could find objectionable pages, as the case of Lipsius abundantly testifies. Poetry and drama, except for the pious and moralizing kinds, withered almost completely in the South, to a lesser degree (at least for some time) in the North. It is also true, however, that from the very beginnings of humanism all branches of literature in the Low Countries were deeply impregnated by Christian piety and morals. In this respect the overwhelming success of the Italian Carmelite poet Baptista of Mantua—the Christian Vergil—north of the Alps, almost generally ignored in Italian humanist circles, is quite typical. (pp. 164-65)

I shall now proceed to examine briefly the principal contributions of the humanists of the Low Countries in the fields essential to Renaissance humanism, namely, grammar, rhetoric, poetry, history, and moral philosophy. These areas I shall consider in as broad a perspective as possible so as to include most of the humanists' achievements or aspects of intellectual life influenced by humanism. The impact of humanism on scholarship and sciences in general will be the subject of a further and last section.

The teaching and knowledge of pure (classical) Latin was the cornerstone on which every humanist activity was built. It divided the "barbari" and "obscuri viri" from the "docti" and the "eloquentes," who alone could be real "oratores et poetae," as the humanists presented themselves. This point is stressed over and again by Erasmus (see his *Antibarbari* and other works), his predecessors, his friends and followers: "Grammar especially," says Dorpius in his *Praise of Every Art,* "by its own law, can take pride that it is the parent and nurse of all learning." This formula is central to humanist thinking, and turns up in many similar expressions: sound scholarship (be it theology, or law, or philology for that matter) is impossible without the use of a pure and clear language, which in its turn directly depends on a good grammatical foundation. Otherwise one becomes one of those "pseudodialectici" or teachers of the "Scoticae tenebrae," which the humanists held responsible for the decay of schools and culture in their time.

Many humanists of the old Netherlands contributed significantly to renovating grammatical instruction in their time, and some of them wrote books used far beyond their small country and as late as the nineteenth century or, in derived versions, even to the present day. The history of humanist Latin grammar in the Seventeen Provinces can be formulated as a gradual transition from the old Alexander of Villedieu and his *Doctrinale* to Despauterius and, ultimately, to Gerardus Vossius. If Alexander was the quintessential symbol of late medieval Latin (versified) grammar, so the Fleming Despauterius is for humanist grammar (in a later stage together with the Portuguese Emmanuel Alvares, 1526-1582): more than four hundred editions and adaptations are the manifest proof of its wide and lasting success, which even the Jesuit Alvares could not obliterate. (pp. 167-68)

An offspring of humanist interest in ancient languages is the study of Hebrew, the third sacred language. A first course in the Netherlands was organized in 1518 in the recently founded Trilingue, which hired an itinerant Jew named Matthaeus Adrianus. More famous, however, became professor Jan van Campen (Johannes Campensis, 1521-31), author of a short grammar. His work was very rapidly outshone by the *Tabula in grammaticam Hebraeam* (1529) of Clenardus, who was teaching the language privately. A *Dictionarium Hebraicum* was prepared by the printer Dirk Martens as early as 1520 for use in the Trilingue. Later the study of Hebrew languished at Louvain, but it throve in the North, especially at Leiden. (p. 175)

In conclusion one can say that next to the brilliant achievements of the Quattrocento Italian humanists, their colleagues and successors in the Low Countries made fundamental contributions in the field of the study and teaching of the classical languages on a scale that surpasses most of the other European countries. Erasmus and Vives, Despauterius and Clenardus, Lipsius and Vossius have indeed a European importance and impact, not just a local one. They are in many respects on the same level with Valla and Perotti, Budé and Philipp Melanchthon, Antonio de Nebrija or Alvares in the history of humanist language studies.

Humanists never felt themselves satisfied with a purely grammatical knowledge. They knew from Quintilian: "aliud est grammatice, aliud est Latine scribere" (it is one thing to write grammatically correct Latin, another to write good Latin). Their ideal was eloquence, and grammar only laid the foundations for it. The building itself is the work of the *ars rhetorica* and, in poetry, of the *ars poetica.* Rhetorical theory and the practice of eloquence in elegant orations are essential features of the humanist world. How important it was to be an eloquent orator even at the end of the humanist age is proved by Puteanus's initiative in organizing a "Palaestra bonae mentis" within the Louvain Collegium Trilingue and by its counterpart in Leiden: in 1620, at the request of students who wanted a more thorough training in eloquence, the university charged professor Petrus Cunaeus to organize a "Collegium oratorium privato-publicum." It was inaugurated on

10 November with a solemn speech by Cunaeus himself. (pp. 175-76)

Oratorical theory in the Renaissance was not only important within the walls of the school. Latin still had an undeniable importance in public life and, on certain occasions, it was vital to be able to deliver an elegant speech in the old Romans' tongue. First of all, academic life in the universities was entirely latinized. At the opening of every academic year a solemn Latin oration was delivered by one of the professors (or another member of the Universitas Magistrorum et Studiosorum), usually on the theme of a praise of the arts. . . . To a large extent Latin also was the language of the Roman church and of international diplomacy. As a consequence, stately visits of princes, bishops, and ambassadors were given added luster by means of official welcome orations, often prepared and even pronounced by professional humanists. In the fifteenth century the University of Louvain sometimes hired an Italian orator for that job, undoubtedly because the local latinists were not yet enough master of the new style. (pp. 178-79)

Next to eloquence, poetry in its classical forms was the most genuine expression of the humanist mind. Every major and minor event in private, public, or social life—birth and death, marriage and appointments, the publication of a book or a memorable visit—was "immortalized" in Latin poems, sometimes also in Greek or even Hebrew verses. In the course of the sixteenth century multilingualism, including both the ancient and the modern vernacular languages, began to develop and soon became widely popular. After 1550 most humanists were writing verses in several languages, often including Italian.

For a humanist any conceivable subject could be treated in verse, even mathematics or a chapter of Roman civil law, as the poems of Hugo Grotius eloquently demonstrate. This point is less surprising than it may seem to be to a modern or Romantic reader. In fact, if an intellectual movement attaches paramount importance to a refined linguistic expression of its thoughts in every situation and if, in addition, it considers the *oratio ligata* or verse as the summit of linguistic elegance, it necessarily follows that nothing can be more attractive and beautiful than a versified elaboration, whatever the subject. Well-turned verses are always a joy for a true humanist, even if their contents are as dry as dust.

Even if a Latin adage says that "poeta nascitur," most humanists sincerely believed that writing poetry as well as writing prose could be learned. As a matter of fact it is not very difficult to learn to write correct, fluent, and even elegant verses in classical Latin. Moreover, most of the rules formulated in the *artes rhetoricae* could be applied as well in prose as in poetry, which explains in part why specific *artes poeticae* were written more rarely, especially in the Low Countries. No fundamental contribution in this field seems to have been made in the old Netherlands before the very end of the sixteenth century, that is, many years after Scaliger's influential *Poetica* (1561) or the even earlier and equally widely read *Ars poetica* of Marco Girolamo Vida, not to mention several early Jesuit *Institutiones poeticae.* (pp. 181-82)

As I said at the beginning of this section, poetry was an integral part of cultural and social life of the Renaissance and the Baroque ages. Instead of sending a telegram of congratulations or filling in application forms, the men of those ages wrote a nice poem in Latin. Until far into the seventeenth century the educated classes in the Netherlands were perfectly bilingual, the other language being Latin. Even the so-called "Muiderkring," those writers and artists who met in the Amsterdam home and in the castle at Muiden of their common friend, the historian and poet Pieter C. Hooft, counted many expert latinists among its members. . . . The history of humanist Latin poetry began in the late fifteenth century with the verses of men such as Rudolf Agricola (trained in Italy) and the young Deventer students around Erasmus; its full flowering extended over more than a century, from the second quarter of the sixteenth century to far into the seventeenth. In fact, Latin poetry in the humanist tradition did not die completely until the nineteenth century in the southern and the early twentieth century in the northern Netherlands. . . . As was to be expected in the context of the northern Christian world, pious and moralizing verse predominates in quantity, from Agricola's early poem to St. Ann or Murmellius's *Elegiae morales* to the elegiac cycle on the "Cursus vitae humanae" of the Jesuit Sidronius Hosschius, the eclogues of his confrère Gulielmus Becanus, or the innumerable poems in honor of the Holy Virgin. Even if they are written in perfect Ovidian or Vergilian style, which is often the case, most of these poems will not be easily palatable to a modern and lay taste; but one cannot deny their immense success in their own time and, in cases such as Hosschius and Becanus, until the early nineteenth century. Fundamentally, these northern humanist poems very often are only humanist in their Latin words and style. Underneath lies a purely Christian and often medieval content.

There is, of course, also a profane strand, which originated for the most part in the South, but finally survived almost exclusively in the northern provinces, from which it had been chased at the outset. Young Erasmus and some of his fellow students at Deventer and at Gouda had been strongly enticed by classical poetry: Erasmus's first attempt in Latin verse was an eclogue on loving shepherds. But very soon his friend and poet Cornelius Aurelius had convinced him to prefer the Christian lyre. Not many years later another young man, the Walloon Remacle d'Ardenne (Remaclus Arduenna), who was not locked into a monastery, decided to imitate the amorous poetry of the Italian Fausto Andrelini, royal professor in Paris and a great man in those days of the budding northern humanism. By his decision and his own *Amores* Remacle paved the way for the next generation and especially for the unequaled Everaerts brothers, Janus Secundus, Nicolaus Grudius, and Hadrianus Marius. "The Kisses for Neaera" and the "Elegies for Julia" of the first are among the most famous and influential works in Neolatin poetry. (pp. 185-87)

It goes without saying that all genres of classical poetry were practiced by authors of the Low Countries: long-winded epics (for example the *Borbonias* of Louis Des Masures [Masurius] from Tournai), didactic and philosophical poems ("De contemptu mortis" of Daniel Heinsius or "De ventis" of the Jesuit Charles Malapert [Carolus Malapertius] from Mons/Bergen), elegies, eclogues, satires (from the early ones by Petrus Montanus from 's Heerenberg or Kempo Thessaliensis from Texel to the Antwerp Juvenal of the seventeenth century, Pieter Scholier [Petrus Scholirius]) and epigrams (such as Grotius's *Instrumentum domesticum,* a congenial imitation and adaptation to Holland of Martial's *Apophoreta*). There is no point in extending this list much longer, but I want to mention a last genre, because it is particularly typical for later humanism: I mean the *emblemata,* a special kind of epigrammatic illustration of moralistic or erotic images, which were cherished by the reading public from the time of Andrea Alciati's epoch-making *Emblematum libellus* of 1531. (p. 187)

Before taking leave of the humanist poets, I must not forget to present another outstanding accomplishment due to scholars from the Netherlands, namely, the collection of some huge anthologies, which preserve large quantities of texts otherwise lost or hard to find. First of all there was Janus Gruterus from Antwerp, a poet himself, who as a librarian at Heidelberg published under the anagram of Ranutius Gherus his famous collections of *Delitiae poetarum,* divided into *Gallorum, Germanorum, Italorum,* and *Belgicorum* (1608-14), which were imitated for other countries by other collectors. A few years earlier his Dutch contemporary Damasus Blijenburgius from Dordrecht had planned five volumes of poetry dealing with ethics, love, household affairs, politics, and wisdom. Only two of them ever appeared, the *Cento ethicus ex variis poetis hinc inde contextus . . . iuventutis maxime institutioni accommodatus* (1599), a perfectly humanistic topic, and the better-known *Veneres Blijenburgicae sive Amorum hortus* (1600), divided into five "flowerbeds" (*areolae*) planted with poems on all kinds of themes concerning love. Not only is the argument typically humanistic, but its almost pedantic completeness is also characteristic of the development of later humanism, which excelled in cataloguing rather than in creative power. (p. 188)

Not less important than poetry are the humanist dramas of the Netherlands, which in this field of humanist activity occupy a foremost position. Latin theater was an excellent means of language training and moral education in the humanist schools. The school therefore was its natural milieu, its authors the professors of the old Roman tongue, its performers the young students. This background must be kept in mind when proffering a judgment on their literary value. In the Low Countries the main center of humanist theater were the Colleges of the Arts Faculty at Louvain; the Latin schools in such towns as Bruges, Ghent, Liège, Gouda, Haarlem, Amsterdam, Utrecht, 's Hertogenbosch, and the like; and at a later stage also the University of Leiden and the colleges of religious orders such as Jesuits, Benedictines, Augustinians, and Oratorians. Apart from an isolated Dutch forerunner in Bologna at the end of the fifteenth century (H. Knuit van Slyterhoven), humanist theater appears to have been nascent in the first years of the sixteenth century and to have come into full growth in the following decades, maintaining itself on a high level until the mid-seventeenth century, in the time of Vondel and Hooft. Texts were written for the purpose or borrowed from Italian, French, and German colleagues, a good example being the Latin school of the Zandberg at Ghent under master Eligius Eucharius in the second decade of the sixteenth century. (pp. 188-89)

Apart from comedy and tragedy there were several other kinds of plays: *dialogismi* (Nannius's *Dialogismi heroinarum*), *dialogi ioculares* (Arnoldus Madirius's *Pisander Bombylicus,* 1540), tragicomedies, which appear in the Low Countries only fifty years after the first experiments by the Verardis in Rome at the end of the fifteenth century; and even an *amphitragoedia* (Franciscus Eutrachelus's *Edessa sive Hester,* 1559 in Ghent), the precise meaning of which remains unclear because the author does not explain himself and the piece has not been studied so far. It may be a pedantic variant of tragicomedy, perhaps with some inept reminiscence of amphitheater.

The theme of all those plays is predominantly Christian. The heroes are figures borrowed from the Bible or church history (saints, martyrs, persecutors), a few from classical history (Pompeius) or mythology (Hercules). The latter sometimes will be christianized, as in the allegorical play *Andromeda belgica dicta* by Jan Baptist Gramaye (Gramaius), with which the students of Louvain in 1600 bade welcome to Archdukes Albert and Isabella as the liberators of the Netherlands from the heretic (Protestant) Beggars. Popular life was sometimes the source of comical plays such as Macropedius's village farces (*Aluta, Andrisca, Bassarus*), Gabriel Jansenius's *Fabellae* (1600), Madirius, or the *Vitulus* of Cornelius Schonaeus, but they are on the whole exceptional, as are the students' life plays. Equally rare are translations or adaptations from the vernacular. The most typical case is Eucharius's *Grisellis,* taken from Boccaccio (but through Petrarch's Latin version) and the adaptation of the Elckerlyc (Everyman) theme by Macropedius, Christianus Ischyrius, and a few more.

The high quality of humanist drama from the Low Countries is demonstrated by its international success. Compared to other countries, such as Italy or Germany, so much larger than the Low Countries, the number of plays and authors who found their way far outside their own school or country is strikingly high. I mention, without pretending to completeness, Macropedius, Gulielmus Gnaphaeus (*Acolastus*), Petrus Papaeus, and Jacobus Zovitius in the first half of the sixteenth century, and Cornelius Crocus (*Iosephus*) and Livinus Brechtus, whose *Euripus* (1549), another variant of the Everyman theme, acquired a seminal importance in the development of Jesuit theater from Germany to Spain. In the second half of the century a schoolmaster from Haarlem, Cornelius Schonaeus, the "Terentius Christianus," who achieved a worldwide fame for about two centuries in scores of editions, enjoyed unrivaled success. Finally Daniel Heinsius, Hugo Grotius, Nicolaus Vernulaeus (at Louvain), or even Jacob Cornelius Lummenaeus a Marca (in Italy and in Ghent) close the rich harvest of Neolatin tragedy with works of considerable or even great quality.

Two more areas remain that are within the inner core of humanist concern: history and moral philosophy. In both fields the Low Countries have a fair share in the general output of humanist writings. Let us first have a look at history and let us begin with a warning. The Latin word *historia* can have such different meanings as "history," "historiography," and "story." If one is not aware of this very simple fact, the interpretation of humanist Latin texts will suffer heavily and modern students will be led (and already have been led) into very serious errors. Let me also point out here that (auto)biography, according to most classical and humanist authors, is not a part of historiographical literature, but a kind of portrait painting with words, which can be practiced in widely different literary genres (letter, oration, elegy, and so on), in prose as well as in verse. (pp. 189-91)

Many humanists wrote historical works. Some of them also devoted attention to the question how to be a good historian, a theme already discussed by the ancient Greek Lucian, a favorite author of the humanist world. Vives included history in his search into the causes of the decay of the arts, the first part of his major work *De disciplinis.* One of Nannius's inaugural lectures at the Louvain Trilingue deserves particular mention, his *In T. Livium de laudibus historiae* (printed in his *Orationes tres,* Louvain 1541). The praise of history was a theme that attracted many humanists before and after. (p. 191)

Philosophy never was a direct concern of the humanists in general, at least not its speculative branches, and certainly not the late scholastic terministic subtleties of the dialecticians against whom Vives launched his *In pseudodialecticos.* This statement is true in principle, yet historical facts sometimes can be different. The famous Deventer schoolman Alexander Hegius, considered one of the greatest humanist pedagogues, is also the author of epistemological and other speculative opuscules such as *De scientia et eo quod scitur contra Academicos, De tribus animae generibus,* and *De sensu et sensili.*

More generally speaking, philosophy was an integral part of the arts curriculum at the universities; therefore, most humanists had attended these courses in their youth, and many had taught them as senior students (or *legentes* in the late medieval academic jargon). Martinus Dorpius at Louvain offers us a typical case. There can be no doubt as to his profound humanist inclinations. As a *legens* he taught Latin, even taking the initiative—quite new at Louvain at that time—of performing Plautus with his junior students; but at the same time he was a teacher of philosophy, and as such he wrote a handbook *Introductio facilis . . .ad Aristotelis libros logice intelligendos,* which was published at Paris in 1512. And the same Dorpius at a certain moment went so far as to scold Lorenzo Valla in a public speech, because he had read the latter's criticism of Aristotle in his *Dialectics.* In fact, logic or dialectic often became a meeting place or a battlefield between scholastics and early humanists. Valla's work is a perfect example of the point, along with Vives's attack on the Sorbonne dialecticians. But Gerardus Listrius not only wrote a commentary on Erasmus's *Praise of Folly,* but also on Peter of Spain's *Summulae logicales,* the universal textbook of the time.

Yet it is true and certainly not a happenstance that during the two centuries of humanism in the Low Countries no important name in philosophy can be found, except perhaps the Spaniard Vives, who became a forerunner of modern psychology in one of his major works, *De anima,* and who used to introduce himself as a "philosophus," not as a "poeta et orator." But apart from him, all forces either were drawn to the humanist-literary field or became involved in the endless theological conflicts. (pp. 195-96)

Practical philosophy had a stronger appeal to the humanist mind. Ethics, educational theory, and political thought always attracted many pens. This state of affairs is quite normal for men who revered Cicero and Quintilian as their great masters, to say nothing of Seneca and Plutarch. And no work of Petrarch was more popular among our early humanists than his *De remediis utriusque fortunae,* which was copied, read, or abbreviated over and over again. Its theme still returns in Lipsius's most successful *De constantia.* To a modern reader this dialogue may seem downright naïve and hardly fitted to offer consolation in hard times, but that feeling was not shared by Lipsius's contemporaries, who definitely liked very much this rather strange mixture of Christian and Stoic reflections on the troubles of human life.

Equally popular were discourses on the respective values of the *vita activa* and the *vita contemplativa* and the possibility of their combination, questions that one finds in both early and late humanists. Such is Jacob Canter's dialogue *De solitudine* (ca. 1491), in which the contrast is represented by life in town versus life on the land, perhaps a reflection on Horace's famous fable of the town and country mice. . . . In fact, it is a theme that had already occupied the early Florentine humanists of the Quattrocento, and it may even be thought about today by political or academic authorities.

The humanists' traditional concern with moral problems could find a fertile soil in the North, where the medieval Christian way of life easily could be amalgamated with the precepts of the classical thinkers, or at least could be adorned by classical flowers of speech or various mythological images. A good example of such a mixture is the supplement to Sebastian Brant's *Narrenschiff: Stultiferae navis additamentum de quinque virginibus* by Josse Bade (Jodocus Badius). The image of the five unwise virgins is biblical; the theme is a traditional Christian warning against the sins of the human senses, but large parts of the text and its *ornatus* are purely classical-humanistic. (pp. 196-97)

As can be expected from students and teachers of the *humaniores litterae,* the humanists very frequently concentrated their efforts on questions concerning the education of children and young people. In the Netherlands several interesting pamphlets were written. They begin very early with Alexander Hegius's *Contra modos significandi invectiva* (first draft, ca. 1480), which already stresses the necessity of adapting teaching methods to the children, and Rudolf Agricola's letter *De formando studio* (1484). Next come the important contributions of Erasmus and Vives, and finally, at the end of the sixteenth century, two more remarkable treatises: the Catholic teacher and grammarian Simon Verepaeus (1522-1598) wrote the most complete treatise of humanist Christian paedagogy "ad mentem Concilii Tridentini" ever written in the Netherlands, namely, his *Institutionum scholasticarum libri tres* (Antwerp 1573), whereas the Calvinist Lord Philips van Marnix van Sint-Aldegonde is the author of an extremely interesting *Ratio instituendae inventutis* (1583), about which I shall say more presently.

All those treatises have one basic concern in common: the religious, moral, and intellectual education of youth, or, to say it with the words of Verepaeus in his dedication letter (par. 3): "In scholis . . . una cum litterarum institutione etiam pietatis et virtutum praecepta proponuntur" (in schools the precepts of piety and virtue are put forth together with the teaching of letters). (pp. 197-98)

Another topic, which is omnipresent in humanistic literature, is peace, or rather complaints for the loss of peace. Erasmus not only made Folly speak out, but with an equally loud voice he made Peace lament publicly in the *Querela Pacis* "undique gentium eiectae profligataeque" (which is cast out and overthrown everywhere). In vain she appealed to the European princes: "I call upon you, princes. . . . Acknowledge the voice of your King [Christ] calling you to peace!" Many indeed were the causes of war and conflict, political as well as religious, and with Erasmus many others, such as Vives, wrote pamphlets on behalf of peace and concord in the Christian world, addressing themselves to the pope, the emperor, kings, or other authorities. Their voices were joined by those of scores of poets who also lamented the loss of peace or, occasionally, exulted with joy when it seemed to be restored. The Luxemburger Nicolaus Mameranus and Cornelis de Schrijver (Cornelius Grapheus) at Antwerp are only two examples out of many during the reign of Charles V (1519-55).

Political thought was also the subject of more systematic works (Plato, Aristotle, and Cicero were the bright examples to imitate). They could be of a more speculative and general kind, or they could search its practical application in old or modern state systems. Most influential were Lipsius's *Politicorum sive civilis doctrinae libri sex* (1589), in which his own ideas were hidden under the cover of a massive collection of excerpts from ancient authorities. This caution not only was a measure of prudence in an intolerant age; it also was a well-tried humanistic scholarly method, the efficaciousness of which had been amply demonstrated by such works as Erasmus's *Parabolae.* Basically, it was a public application of a most common method of humanist education: every pupil in his school time had to collect well-turned sentences, adages, and the like on specific themes, as an aide-mémoire for life. (p. 202)

As we have seen, the humanists' efforts first and foremost focused on the improvement of the study of Latin, the care for an elegant Latin style as a means to better learning, and a renewed contact with an exemplary ancient civilization through a better knowledge of its authors, now directly read in improved editions. Latin being the universal language of instruction in grammar schools and universities, sooner or later repercussions of the humanistic ideas must be felt in all fields of scholarship and science. As a matter of fact scholars and scientists in the course of the sixteenth century more and more adapted their language to the new principles and began to write a more classical and stylistically more polished idiom. This does not mean that all became Ciceronians. Ciceronianism was always a trend of the strictly literary prose, and it influenced technical languages much less in their vocabulary than in their style. There it did no harm; on the contrary, the humanists were quite right in positing that a clear and pure style reveals orderly thinking and that an obscure jargon by no means contributes to a better quality of learning.

Also, humanist studies had unearthed scores of forgotten ancient sources, which now helped to advance modern scholarship in many fields: philosophy, history, the natural sciences, medicine, and more. This enrichment of knowledge, together with many new discoveries, laid the foundation for the development of modern science from the seventeenth century onward. During the period of humanism the progress was still modest, albeit real, and the Netherlands can boast a long series of first-class philologists, scientists, and doctors. . . . Naturally, in some cases humanism and modern science met each other to the profit of both. Such was the case in law, when a famous but not profoundly humanist scholar such as the Frisian Viglius van Aytta published the first edition of the Greek translation of Justinian's Institutes: *Institutiones iuris civilis in Graecam linguam per Theophilum traductae* (Basel, 1533); or when the Antwerp geographer Abraham Ortelius added maps of the ancient world to his modern atlas *Theatrum orbis terrarum parergon sive Veteris geographiae tabulae* (1624), which thus became the humanists' contribution to the genre of historical atlases hardly known before. (p. 203)

Not only scholarship and sciences ultimately felt the impact of humanism. Something similar happened to the fine arts, when humanism in the course of the sixteenth century caused a break with the Gothic Middle Ages and fostered a return to classical norms and models. In this process the princely courts, such as those in Mechlin, Brussels, and Liège, often played a decisive role. Princes, bishops, and courtiers underwent a double influence: contact with Italy and its new art through the reciprocal visits of diplomats, bankers, artists, or the rulers themselves; then, local humanism at work through secretaries, counselors, preceptors, and the like, who often were at the same time poets (Remaclus Arduenna) or scholars (Erasmus, Vives) in the first ranks of humanism. The father of Janus Secundus (Everaerts) and his brothers was a prominent officer of the high court in Mechlin, of which he was the chairman during the last years of his life. Another member was Frans Craneveldt (Franciscus Craneveldius), who even in his later years passed his time in Mechlin translating the Greek poet Theognis. These princes and courtiers began to order works of art in the new style, began to build or adorn palaces and churches according to classical principles, and at times even sent their artists to Italy. The porch of St. Jacques at Liège (1552-58) was created by Lambert Lombard, who had been sent to Rome in 1538 by his bishop and had seen there the Septizonium near the Palatine. Nevertheless, the renewal of architecture and the visual arts went much slower than the renewal of language and literature. Only in 1606 did *Den eerste boeck van architecture* appear, being a translation of Sebastiano Serlio's *Regole generali di architettura* (1549), made by Pieter Coecke of Aalst, an important mediator between Italy and the Low Countries in matters of art. But slow as it was, the change was real. It makes the difference between two such important monuments as the town hall of Louvain, a most splendid example of Gothic art, finished by Matthias de Layens about the time Erasmus came into this world, and the town hall of Antwerp, one of the first Renaissance buildings in the old Netherlands. It was erected in 1560-65 by Cornelis Floris de Vriendt, a man who had seen Italy. At that time Lipsius was a student, and literary humanism was already moving to its last and learned stage. One could also compare from the humanist point of view the great artists of the Low Countries in painting or sculpture. Compare, for example, Erasmus's elder contemporary Jeroen Bosch (ca. 1450-1516) and his late medieval allegories, with Pieter Bruegel the Elder (ca. 1528-1569), who had visited Rome and married Coeck's daughter, yet remained largely attached to local popular traditions, and finally with Peter Paul Rubens (1577-1640), who lived in Rome for many years, whose brother Philip was a minor humanist philologist and whose works after his return to Antwerp in 1608 perfectly reflect many of the ideals of humanism in its last stage. At that moment the broad gap between literary and visual arts had been covered, and one understands that many humanist publications of the early seventeenth century were illustrated by Rubens and his workshop: they spoke the same language and met harmoniously in the engravings and the texts of the same books.

The age of Renaissance and Baroque humanism was a great one in the cultural history of the Low Countries, the old "Belgium." Situated at the crossroads of important political, cultural, and economic highways of early modern times, literary and artistic life flourished in its many prospering towns, in its schools and universities, its courts and abbeys, not rarely among the cruelties of brutal war or of ideological persecution. But in that respect the Low Countries' humanism did not really differ from that in Tuscany or other Italian states, where often enough war and bloodshed were daily experiences. The generalized use of Latin allowed writers, whose native Frisian, Dutch, or even French would have been of little or no use outside their own region, to speak to the entire Western world from Sicily to Iceland. Without this Latin Erasmus, Lipsius, Heinsius, and Grotius never would have had the worldwide audience they had then and still have now. And because of them and many of their less important colleagues the Low Countries are next to Italy a vital part of the European scene of humanism, a part that largely exceeds the narrow boundaries of that little corner of Europe. (pp. 206-07)

Jozef IJsewijn, "Humanism in the Low Countries," in Renaissance Humanism: Foundations, Forms, and Legacy, Vol. 2, *edited by Albert Rabil, Jr., University of Pennsylvania Press, 1988, pp. 156-215.*

James K. Cameron

[*In the following excerpt, Cameron discusses the characteristics and impact of humanism in the Low Countries.*]

In the Low Countries, classical and biblical scholars, academics, diplomats, public administrators, men of letters, of the arts, and of commerce, all united in their devotion to antiquity, worked together to establish in their country a golden age of humanist achievement that enriched the western world.

It was from Italy that humanism reached this region, initially through personal contacts brought about by diplomatic, ecclesiastical, scholarly and cultural exchange. Its successful development, which extended over several generations, was largely accomplished by the enlightened application by a patriotic people of some of the country's increasing economic and commercial prosperity. This is all the more remarkable in that the political conditions generally supposed to be necessary for nurturing the seeds of a great cultural flowering were in the Netherlands of the fifteenth and early sixteenth centuries at best precariously balanced and at times decidedly lacking.

The nearest universities, Cologne (founded in 1388) and Louvain (founded in 1425), were bastions of scholasticism and were largely to remain so. The centres of learning were the monasteries, and the contemporaries of the poets and literary men of the Italian Trecento were the mystics Ruysbroek (1293-1381) and Groote (1340-84). Further, the future of literature seemed to be in the vernacular. The fortunes for Latin and ultimately for humanism changed only at the end of the fifteenth century with the strengthening of Latin studies at the schools of some of the chief cities, among them Bruges, Ghent, Deventer, Zwolle, 's Hertogenbosch and Groningen. For this advancement credit has usually been assigned to the Brethren of the Common Life, but it is now generally agreed that their importance as educators has been exaggerated. Although their founder, Gerhard Groote, showed an interest in books and learning, his example was not always followed by his associates and successors. 'The city school, with its Latin and logic, was enough for them! Philosophy was unnecessary, not to mention theology, law, or medicine.' However, as humanism began to make itself felt towards the end of the fifteenth century in the schools of the cities where the Brethren had their houses, and where they maintained hostels for young boys, they began to take an interest in it and in developing closer relations with the rectors and teachers. Humanist influences were not imposed by the Brethren of the Common Life, yet they helped to put into effect what was being advocated by others. In the history of humanist education in the Low Countries, pride of place must be given to the city schools in which the 'new Latin' was fostered by generations of learned rectors, many of whom were or were to become significant humanists. The school at Deventer, for example, where Alexander Hegius (c. 1433-1498) was rector from 1483 to 1498, reached unparalleled fame, and is regarded as the first school north of the Alps to provide for its pupils instruction in Greek. Such schools were for the greater part public institutions in which local civic leaders took considerable interest, and they undoubtedly benefited from the developing economic prosperity, and they in turn served their communities by providing them with well educated merchants and administrators.

The origins of the teaching of the 'new Latin', the solid foundation of Northern humanism, had been prepared in the mid-fifteenth century at Louvain by Antonius Hameron (d. 1490), whose aim was 'to teach Latin from the ancient sources and on a level adapted to the capacities of the young students' minds', and by Rudolph Agricola (1444-85) who had 'thoroughly assimilated humanism in its Italian form'. He stressed the study of the Bible and the moral reformation of Christendom as did the group of scholars associated with him and Wessel Gansfort (1419-1484) and known as the Adwerth (Aduard) Academy. Following the practice of John Pupper of Goch and Gansfort of adopting humanist linguistic dress in their religious writings, Agricola attained an unrivalled pre-eminence in the early history of humanism in the Netherlands. Strenuously advocating the study of Greek, he aroused the enthusiasm for that study in Alexander Hegius through whom the torch of learning was passed on to the generation of Erasmus and Vives. (pp. 137-39)

The next stage in this development centres on the foundation of the *Collegium Trilingue* in Louvain in 1517. The way had been prepared by the establishment of a lectureship in Latin literature held by Italian scholars in the last quarter of the previous century—with the happy result that the young Erasmus found there 'a busy centre of humanistic studies in full flourish'. The founding of the College was the direct outcome of an intense but locally confined interest created by the two-way intellectual traffic between Italy and the Netherlands that had followed in the wake of trade and diplomatic relations. It was made possible by the generosity of one of those who had taken part in this exchange, Jerome Busleyden (1470-1517), and the untiring efforts of Erasmus. Busleyden's travels in France and Italy provided him with an intimate knowledge of the Renaissance in many of its varied forms and inspired in him the plan, fostered by Erasmus, to set aside from the considerable fortune which he had amassed (largely from ecclesiastical benefices held subsequent to his ordination) sufficient funds for the founding of the Trilingual College. Shortly before his death in 1517 he bequeathed much of his wealth, together with the fine collection of classical manuscripts which he had brought together at his Renaissance residence in Mechlin, for establishing in Louvain a college with adequate provision for both professors and students of the great languages and literatures of antiquity: Latin, Greek, and Hebrew.

The initial stages proved difficult despite the fact that the university numbered among its professors some who were more than anxious to further the new cause. Nevertheless such was the determination of the college's promoters that professors were appointed and the nascent institution had entered on its career even before arrangements could be made for housing it. Rapidly, thereafter, and with its recognition as part of the university, it succeeded in becoming not only the chief centre of humanist learning in the Netherlands, but also one of the most effective means of diffusing it throughout Northern Europe. As described by its historian, its aim was to set forward the reform plan of Erasmus, to bring back 'Theology from the muddy marshes of the *Sententiae* and *Summae* to the limpid fountain of Holy Scripture and the teaching of the Fathers'. Much attention was, however, given to Latin literature, particularly to Cicero and to Greek authors, as texts became increasingly more available through the endeavours of Dierk Martens, the father of Greek printing in the Low Countries. The study of Hebrew moved forward at a slower pace. As interest in the new foundation and in the new learning developed, student numbers increased year by year and began to include not only those with a professional interest in scholarship, but also young noblemen, the sons of aristocrats from many countries, and the sons of the merchant classes rising to prominence with the country's economic prosperity. But perhaps for the impact of humanism in the Netherlands the college initially rendered its finest service by providing an ever increasing number of teachers for the city Latin schools in most of which humanism was to secure a dominant place, thereby encouraging in the future members of civic society a love of learning and of classical literature, along with the desire to become proficient in its and to contribute to its propagation. (pp. 140-41)

Humanistic studies could not, however, have flourished without the outstanding efforts and pioneering work of the developing printing industry. Indeed, 'the history of humanism in the Netherlands is inseparably connected' with that of its great printing houses which both shared in and contributed to the region's commercial prosperity. Before 1500 significant presses were in operation at Utrecht, Delft, Gouda, Deventer, Zwolle, Nijmegen, Leiden, Louvain, and Antwerp. The most prolific of the Northern printers, Richard Pafraet and De Breda at Deventer together printed 71 per cent of all Dutch classical editions, some 114 works in all. In addition and indicative of the stress upon Latin in the schools there was an extensive printing of grammars. The presses of Deventer appear to have worked in close association with the schools as they were responsible for nearly half of all Dutch fifteenth-century school grammars. Painter, in his bibliographical study, estimated that the proportion of editions of the classics, grammars, and humanist texts, no less than 48 per cent of all Dutch printing, was probably higher than that in any other country. Printing in the Southern Provinces was, however, no less significant. Between 1477 and 1495 Johannes van Westphalen, along with his associates in Louvain, published translations of Aristotle and Plato as well as editions of classical and humanist writers. He has in addition been credited as the first to use Hebrew type in a book in the Netherlands in order to demonstrate the unreliability of the Vulgate. Some of his classical texts were printed to meet the needs of students attending lectures on Latin literature, but others, beautifully executed, were destined for wider circulation, thus giving proof of an ever-increasing interest in the new learning. (pp. 143-44)

The rise of Antwerp as a humanist centre lagged behind that of Louvain, Deventer, and Zwolle. Its development as an educational centre coincided with its emergence as a city of extraordinary commercial prosperity and was inseparably connected with it, thereby enabling it to play a leading role in the outstanding development of the art of printing that had already taken place throughout the Low Countries. With the aid of the Antwerp printers, scholars were enabled to take 'an extremely important part in the development of Western thought'. (pp. 144-45)

The printing of editions of the Bible, in the original languages and in the vernacular, forms a significant element in the history of humanism in the Netherlands. Erasmus, whose epoch-making Greek text of the New Testament was published in Basel in 1516, had imbued in northern humanists a keen desire to study the original languages. However, scholars in the Low Countries initially did not play a leading part in working on the text of the Scriptures, probably because of the association of such study with the rise of heterodoxy. Nevertheless the Low Countries were to benefit from the earlier achievements of biblical humanists and scholar printers, and in particular the city of Antwerp in an outstanding endeavour which has been described as 'a later flowering of the earlier sowing in the Complutensian Polyglot'. Antwerp had been in the early days of printing an important centre for the diffusion of the printed Bible; between 1500 and 1540 at least seventy editions of the Scriptures or of Biblical extracts were published in the city. Johannes Hentenius (1500-66), a Dominican of Louvain and biblical scholar of some repute, prepared a highly regarded version of the Vulgate, which was printed by Gravius in 1547. In its preparation he had used earlier printed versions, those of Estienne and of Colines and Kerver, as well as some thirty manuscripts. Published by Plantin in 1559, it proved a resounding success. An edition of the Hebrew bible followed in 1566. The impelling objective of biblical humanists to arrive at an authentic text behind that of the Vulgate had, however, to be met, and to that end Plantin, encouraged by his success, proposed to issue a revised version of the Complutensian Polyglot. A project of such colossal dimensions required and was given careful preparation. The entire work was to be officially sponsored by Philip II, king of Spain, and was to be under the expert supervision of the erudite and indefatigable Benedictus Arias Montanus (1527-98) who settled in Antwerp in 1568. The collaboration of the finest scholars was secured, including Joannes Isaac Levita who was given responsibility for revising Sante Pagini's Hebrew Lexicon, and Guy Lefevre de la Boderie, whose expertise in the Syriac version of the New Testament brought this valuable text within the reach of all European scholars. Plantin also enlisted the help of several scholars in collating texts and in the arduous work of correcting proofs, among them the Hellenist Guilielmus Canterus, the Syriac specialist Andreas Masius, and Franciscus Raphelengius, his son-in-law and subsequently Professor of Hebrew at Leiden. No effort was spared in making use of contemporary scholarship, Jewish, Protestant, and Catholic. Begun in August 1568, the entire work in eight magnificent volumes was completed in May 1572. It represents the cumulative endeavours of some of the outstanding humanists of the day, and not just in the Low Countries, and remains a lasting monument to contemporary biblical scholarship that concentrated on the text and its historical understanding. To assist in the study of the text the Polyglot provided much ancillary humanist material. Its *Apparatus Sacer* included Hebrew, Aramaic, Syriac, and Greek dictionaries, and a vast amount of miscellaneous information in a series of treatises on the geography of the Holy Land and the antiquities of the Jewish people.

The publication of the Royal Polyglot marked Antwerp's heyday in the history of humanism in the southern region of the Low Countries. A new phase began after the reconquest in 1585. Thereafter humanism in Antwerp was to take on a different colour. It was still 'the principal cultural centre of the Southern Netherlands', but its scholarship became more narrowly defined, serving primarily the Counter-Reformation. (pp. 146-47)

In the first half of the seventeenth century humanism in the northern Netherlands flourished almost as never before at the hands of a large number of scholars from virtually every section of educated society, political and administrative as well as professional. Of the academic scholars who succeeded Lipsius and Scaliger, three deserve special attention: G. L. Vossius (1577-1649), Daniel Heinsius (1581-1655) and Hugo Grotius (1583-1645). Not involving themselves too closely in the dogmatic and confessional controversies that darkened so much of the seventeenth century, they persevered in prosecuting that northern Christian humanism which had been so distinctive a feature of its early development in the Low Countries. At a time when understanding of the past had deepened enormously, when vast new areas of human activity especially in the empirical sciences were being opened up and ever widening man's horizons, and when confessional attitudes were hardening and relations between Christians were becoming more embittered, humanists in the Low Countries were advocating a tolerance and unity of which Vossius, and to a much greater extent, Grotius, were the leading figures. By their vast erudition and enormous literary output they bring to its culmination humanism in the Netherlands.

In the face of Protestant theological scholasticism which began to dominate the academic and religious scene in Leiden, the humanism that had brought about the foundation of the university still held good. The study of Latin and Greek and of ancient history continued the essential basis of scholarship, and to these subjects Vossius contributed significantly. Particularly noteworthy are his dictionaries of Greek- and Latin-writing historians of both antiquity and the Renaissance. The all pervasive influence of humanism in education, fostered by the humanistically-trained in both government and education, found noteworthy expression in the attempt to consolidate past achievements and to transmit them to posterity by legally requiring a uniform national curriculum cast in the humanist mould with ordered progression based on instruction in prescribed classical texts. In the Holland School Act of 1625 the ideal of the humanists 'was elevated to the level of law'.

Endeavours to further humanist education, which as we have seen had gone hand in hand with commercial and economic prosperity, were given significant expression in Amsterdam. In the seventeenth century Amsterdam was becoming 'more and more the focus of cultural life within the Northern Netherlands', and not surprisingly took steps to provide for its citizens a centre for a broadly based cultural education which led to the foundation of the *Athenaeum Illustre.* Not intended to be a university and not permitted to rival its near neighbour, Leiden, it was nevertheless intended that it should by the lectures of its public professors provide for the cultural needs of any of the citizens who cared to take advantage of them. Ambitious from the outset, Amsterdam succeeded in securing the services of Vossius to head the *Athenaeum.* According to the wishes of the founders, he gave lectures on history which they considered as an essential study. In Amsterdam he completed his works on the art of poetry which 'had great influence on dramatic art in the Netherlands as well as abroad'.

The widespread impact of humanism in the Low Countries is given one of its finest expressions in the contribution of the Netherlands to the contemporary art of neo-Latin poetry. Indeed the composing of Latin verse was one of the significant features of sixteenth- and early seventeenth-century humanism. Why this was so need not detain us here. To that literary corpus the contribution of the Low Countries was not only substantial in quantity, but much of it was of very high quality. Mention has already been made of Joannes Secundus who was the major literary influence. Yet virtually every scholar of any note seems to have felt compelled to express himself in Latin verse. Not surprisingly many in public life, such as Janus Dousa and Jan van Hout, were well practised in the Muses' art. Indeed there developed something of a 'Leiden school' in the years immediately following the foundation of the University. Amongst its galaxy of professors, some of whom have already been mentioned, Daniel Heinsius (1580-1655) is regarded as the one who in his day 'made Leiden a European centre of literary scholarship'. (pp. 156-58)

Humanism in the Netherlands from the days of Gerhard Groote and the Brethren of the Common Life to those of Vossius, Heinsius and Grotius was essentially Christian humanism—an amalgam of the values of classical antiquity, biblical, particularly New Testament, ethics, and patristic theology. From that combined inheritance had come into being the unity and harmony of the ancient Christian world which sixteenth- and especially seventeenth-century northern humanist scholars wished to restore and for which there had been brought into being a *Respublica Litterarium* that transcended national boundaries, that sought both to rise above man-made political and religious barriers, and to unite mankind in respect for human dignity, love of human liberty, and the maintenance of harmony. It was the belief of practically every individual who has briefly figured in this survey, a belief shared by the large number of schoolmasters, scholars, statesmen, churchmen, administrators, printers, and philanthropic citizens of the Netherlands who were its unstinting propagators, that a life of scholarship dedicated to those ideals was not only 'the highest form of humanity', but also the essential expression of their faith for their day. This all-embracing devotion to humanism was expressed paramountly in literary production. Nevertheless its inspiration, its impact, was felt throughout the whole of society. (p. 163)

James K. Cameron, "Humanism in the Low Countries," in The Impact of Humanism on Western Europe, *edited by Anthony Goodman and Angus MacKay, Longman, 1990, pp. 137-63.*

Margaret E. Aston

[Aston is an English educator. In the following excerpt, she studies the spread of humanism throughout Europe.]

At the same time that humanist interests beyond the Alps grew, in certain places, with the help of Italians or native-speaking Greeks, many more individuals were finding their way to Italy. The earliest indigenous exponents of humanism in the north were those who—whether or not they had gone there expressly for this purpose—had experienced Italian culture firsthand. The mission which took Guillaume Fichet to Milan in 1469-70 played a part in the beginnings of the first Paris printing press which he and Jean Heynlin, prior to the Sorbonne, established in the college that year. Itself a humanist undertaking—its first book was the model letters of the Italian Gasparino Barzizza and in 1471 appeared Lorenzo Valla's *On the Elegances of the Latin Language*—the press marked the real arrival of humanism in Paris. Among those who rejoiced with Fichet (and urged him on to publish his own *Rhetoric*), was his friend Robert Gaguin—another who had direct experience of Italy.

Veteran students from German universities enlarged their capacities, and sometimes their vision, by pursuing their studies into Italy. Wessel Gansfort (c. 1419-89) had studied at Cologne, Heidelberg, and Louvain, and already begun to learn Greek and Hebrew, before his visit to Italy in 1470-71, where he met both Cardinal Bessarion and the future pope Sixtus IV. Gansfort's interest helped to promote linguistic studies, particularly through the stimulus he gave to two younger men, both of whose fame surpassed his: Agricola and Reuchlin. (pp. 75-6)

Not for nothing did [Thomas] Linacre, on his way home to England at the turn of the fifteenth century, erect an altar at the top of an Alpine pass which he dedicated to Italy as the "holy mother of studies." The debts owed to Italy are too numerous to count, and contemporaries were all too aware of them. On both sides of the Alps there was plenty of talk—defensive on one side, proud or arrogant on the other—about Italian superiority and transalpine barbarism. "The Italians," wrote Erasmus in England in 1509, "value themselves for learning and eloquence; and, like the Grecians of old, account all the world barbarians in respect of themselves; to which piece of vanity the inhabitants of Rome are more especially addicted, pretending themselves to be owners of all those heroic virtues, which their city so many ages since was deservedly famous for." . . .

Yet, in fact, by about 1500 the balance of learning was significantly changing. The hope which Agricola had expressed thirty years earlier was already being realized: "that we shall one day wrest from proud Italy the reputation for classical expression which it has nearly monopolized . . . and free ourselves from the reproach of ignorance and being called unlearned and inarticulate barbarians." Jibes about barbarians might long continue, but the need to travel south for the civilizing influence of Italy became progressively less impelling. (p. 77)

Erasmus did not need Italy for his humanist outlook or his humanist training. He had found in England, as he wrote soon after this visit, so much good learning, "exact and ancient, Latin and Greek, that now I hardly want to go to Italy, except for the sake of seeing it." And it was in Paris that he learned his Greek. Admittedly the going was not always easy. "My Greek studies," he wrote in March 1500 to his friend James Batt, "are almost exhausting my powers, while I have neither the time nor the means of procuring books or the help of a teacher." Yet despite repeated complaints about such deficiencies he stuck to his purpose, and by the time he at last reached Italy in 1506 it seemed to do little for him. "I knew more Greek and Latin when I went to Italy than I do now," he wrote with the confidence of retrospect in 1531. "My literary education owes nothing to Italy—I wish it owed a great deal. There were people there from whom I could have learnt, but so there were in England, in France, in Germany. In Italy there was really no opportunity, since I had gone there simply for the sake of seeing the place." This is not to say, of course, that Erasmus's scholarship, and perhaps his style—as opposed to his education—did not benefit considerably from what Italy had to offer. The greatly enlarged edition of the *Adages* brought out by Aldus in 1508 bears witness to the enrichment provided by manuscripts which the author was able to consult in Venice, while the Platonic influences evident in both the *Praise of Folly* and the *Enchiridion* show how Erasmus followed the studies of Italian humanists. But it remains true that he had found his humanist training and sense ofvalues before he ever went to Italy.

A number of other famous humanists of the north who were contemporaries of Erasmus reflect this diminished dependence on Italy. Sir Thomas More, unlike Colet, Linacre, and Grocyn—all of whose achievements he surpassed—was educated entirely in England, and learned his Greek with Grocyn and Linacre, as well as with William Lily (who had acquired his in Rhodes). Lefèvre d'Etaples, though impressed by his Italian meetings with Pico della Mirandola and Ermolao Barbaro, does not seem to have learned Greek in Italy, but in Paris after his return. Meanwhile in Germany Conrad Celtis (1459-1508) was the first leading humanist of the empire to have received a humanist education at home before setting foot in Italy—and others of his generation distinguished themselves in humanist letters without ever going there at all.

Humanist learning can therefore be said to have arrived in northern Europe by the earlier years of the sixteenth century. If we judge it in this way, taking the continuous availability and fluency of Greek as an important criterion, it seems that the north took almost a century to catch up with Italy. How is one to explain this time-lag? It is not as if the north had not been in close contact with the best of Italian efforts since the days when Petrarch met Richard of Bury in Avignon and there made discoveries which

Fifteenth-century Basel, Switzerland. In the sixteenth century, this city became an important center of humanistic and Reformation activity.

greatly helped his textual restoration of Livy. In the fifteenth century there were individuals who became polished stylists, with claims to genuine humanist distinction, in many parts of Europe. In France, Nicolas de Clémanges (c. 1360-1437) explored the resources of monastic libraries and found a complete text of Quintilian twenty years before Poggio Bracciolini, whose discovery of a copy of this work at St. Gallen in 1417 had much greater repercussions. Poggio himself, learning in 1451 of a dean of Utrecht who had collected several manuscripts of Cicero, was astonished to find a man so devoted to eloquence and good letters "so far from Italy." Yet currents of humanism flowed—almost underground—in places where the opportunities existed. (pp. 78-9)

It takes more, however, than the enthusiasm of individuals to change long-established outlooks and institutions. It needs continuity of support—or revolutionary technology. Such promising humanist beginnings as there were in Parisian circles, or in England around Duke Humphrey, did not succeed in creating lasting new patterns of study in the north. To account for this failure it is not sufficient to point to the effects of the Hundred Years' War in France, or the Wars of the Roses in England. There was, after all, plenty of dislocation in the sixteenth century—and yet these studies survived. One obvious contrast between Italy and the rest of Europe in this formative period is the range of available patronage. In the fifteenth century the north could boast nothing to compare with the brilliant rivalry of Italian courtly society in Florence, Milan, Ferrara, Urbino, Rome, and Naples. Individuals such as the duke of Gloucester or John Tiptoft, earl of Worcester, or Matthias Corvinus of Hungary were exceptional and isolated, incapable of effecting a permanent change in the course of studies. In the "gothic" north, patrons themselves needed educating, and for fashions to change many people have to become aware of changes of fashion. From the end of the fifteenth century, royal actions did a great deal—if largely indirectly—to increase northern awareness of the exuberant world beyond the Alps. (p. 79)

When humanist learning finally became established in the north it had the advantage not only of royal patrons like Francis I and Henry VIII, but also of tools which made it possible to bypass or overtake established institutions and traditional modes of study. The arrival of printing made the teaching and learning of humanists—and others—less dependent upon formal institutional methods.

What Aldus did for Greek grammar Reuchlin later did for Hebrew, and the strides forward which northerners were able to make in both languages in the early sixteenth century were closely linked with the availability of printed texts. Erasmus, deservedly famous as the first man of letters who earned his living by his pen, and who has left a vivid description of himself working against the clatter of Aldus's press, was only one of the increasing numbers whose living and learning revolved around printers' offices.

Northern and southern scholars shared many of the same desires and objectives. They wanted to recover the ancient world in order to recreate the new. For both, skill in Greek was an indispensable prerequisite. Yet there were age-old differences in the worlds north and south of the Alps, differences of outlook and education, which affected this transference of learning. In the north, where university teaching had always been more clerical than it was in Italy (with its tradition of secular learning), the study of theology held the place of honor which was given to law and rhetoric in the south. Theology, as we shall see, had its place in Italy, but the schools and scholars to which it owed its fame belonged elsewhere. These differences affected the transposition of humanist interests to the world beyond the Alps. (p. 80)

Northern humanists produced works of rhetoric, poetry, history, and epigraphy comparable to those of their Italian predecessors and contemporaries. It was, however, the field of theology which gave northern studies their leading and most significant direction and which produced in the work of Erasmus the peak of their achievement. In him we can see the tools, methods, and wisdom of the *studia humanitatis* of the south grafted onto the Christian piety of the north to reach a new growth. It was a change of emphasis, not a break. Italian humanist learning, taken home and transplanted in the north, grew into a rather different tree. Or should one say that northerners cultivated a graft which Italians had tried but failed? (p. 82)

Margaret E. Aston, "The Northern Renaissance," in The Meaning of the Renaissance and Reformation, *edited by Richard L. DeMolen, Houghton Mifflin Company, 1973, pp. 71-130.*

Albert Hyma

[*In the following excerpt, Hyma briefly compares the Italian and northern Renaissances.*]

One of the most interesting problems in the history of modern civilization is the relation between the Renaissance in Italy and the Transalpine Renaissance. Although a great many books and articles have dealt with various phases of this problem, no serious attempt has ever been made to treat it as a whole and on a comprehensive scale. The problem may forever remain unsolved, for nothing seems so difficult to trace as the course of ideas. One is too likely to ignore the possibilities of telepathy, intuition, and inspiration, and one usually jumps at conclusions too quickly. It must baffle a casual reader to peruse a multitude of conflicting opinions concerning the humanists in Italy; it certainly is bewildering to note that the moment one seeks the truth beneath dogmatic statements he becomes more and more confused until he has read practically every production of all the Italian humanists as well as those composed beyond the Alps. And who can ever say that he has done that?

Many historians have pointed out that the humanists in Italy were irreligious, that the scholars north of the Alps were naturally more religious, and that humanism gradually adopted a more serious and pious aspect as it traveled northward. But are the Germans by nature more religious than the Italians? Perhaps they are at times, but a historian takes a great deal for granted when he uses this theory as an infallible hypothesis. No one has yet answered the question why the Transalpine Renaissance differed so greatly from its parent in Italy, because a considerable number of monographs are required before the larger problem can be solved in its entirety.

Since Erasmus in a large measure personifies the Transalpine Renaissance, it will be impossible at the present time to say conclusively where he got his humanistic principles. Long before he first saw Italy he had absorbed much of the spirit of the Italian Renaissance, but just how he happened to do this is by no means clear. The same thing is true of the Brethren of the Common Life in Deventer and elsewhere. It will not do to say that the Devotio Moderna remained unaltered from generation to generation. Right in the citadel of the movement, so to speak, in the brethren-house at Deventer, some very pious souls became greatly affected by the teachings of the humanists. When Alexander Hegius wrote to his friend Rudolph Agricola that he had read Valla's dialogue *On the True Good,* he seemed not a bit shocked, although Gerard Groote would have exhorted his friends never even to touch it. Can we say then that Alexander Hegius was not true to the spirit of the Devotio Moderna, although he was intimately associated with the Brethren of the Common Life at Deventer? We may or we may not do so, according to the definition we give of the Devotio Moderna.

It is also possible to define the terms humanism and Italian Renaissance in various ways, as was indicated above. Fortunately a number of satisfactory accounts of the Italian Renaissance have been produced, of which the contributions by Burckhardt and Symonds still remain standard references. Symonds has unquestionably given a more comprehensive survey than Burckhardt; the latter's work is disappointing because of its high reputation. Especially valuable for the present study is the ninth chapter of Symonds' volume which is entitled *The Revival of Learning.* It presents an admirable summary of the character of humanism in Italy during the fifteenth century, upon which the following discussion is partly based. (pp. 36-8)

Another fact which needs emphasis at the present time is the hostility of the lower clergy in Italy to humanism. Savonarola was but one among thousands of preachers who warned their flocks against the vanity, mockery, and deceit of the wandering scholars. The latter did make a great deal of noise, but were vastly outnumbered by the members of the lower clergy who opposed them and survived them. The humanists, living as they did in an isolated world of their own, did not voice the spirit of the Italian people. They did even frame a workable school system, but catered almost exclusively to sons of princes and aristocrats. What did it matter if the pope himself sponsored humanism, except that the head of the Roman Catholic Church ceased to function as the representative of Jesus the Christ? He was so far removed from the common people that his actions were scarcely noticed by them, for they remained illiterate, neglected alike by prelates and scholars. If they were pious and the humanists irreligious, they owed their piety very largely to their pastors, while the latter cared not what the humanists declared fashionable in manners and speech. Even if the Italian people had been the most religious in Europe, as they probably were at one time, the humanists need not have felt duty-bound to drop their sophistry and imitate the early Christians.

That the majority of the humanists were grossly immoral cannot be gainsaid. Gyraldus, a distinguished professor at Ferrara, did not exaggerate when he described the general run of humanists in the following manner: "No class of human beings are more subject to anger, more puffed up with vanity, more arrogant, more insolent, more conceited, idle-minded, inconsequent, opionated, changeable, obstinate; some of them ready to believe the most incredible nonsense, others skeptical about notorious truths, some full of doubt and suspicion, others void of reasonable circumspection." The humanists, as Symonds indicates, recognized no laws except those of their own taste and inclination; they accepted no authority superior to their own judgment. Their passionate admiration for pagan antiquity "undermined their Christianity without substituting the religion or the ethics of the old world. They ceased to fear God; but they did not acquire either the self-restraint of the Greek or the patriotic virtues of the Roman. It is not, therefore, a marvel that, while professing stoicism, they wallowed in sensuality, openly affected the worst habits of pagan society, and devoted their ingenuity to the explanation of foulness that might have been passed by in silence. Licentiousness became a special branch of humanistic literature. Under the thin mask of humane refinement leered the untamed savage; and an age that boasted not unreasonably of its mental progress, was at the same time notorious for the vices that disgrace mankind. These disorders of the scholars, hidden for a time beneath a learned language, ended by contaminating the genius of the nation."

It is safe to say that Erasmus and most of the other humanists in transalpine Europe differed widely from the typical humanists just described by Symonds; and it is equally true that there were in Italy at all times a number of scholars who by their integrity, modesty, honesty, and generosity distinguished themselves from the less worthy members of their class. When Agricola, Hegius, and Erasmus extolled the virtues and the characters of the great scholars in Italy, they unquestionably referred to such men as Traversari, Guarino, Petrarch, Ficino, and Pico. The latter exerted more influence beyond the Alps, and it is therefore desirable to study in detail the views of these men if one wishes to trace the spread of humanism from Italy into the northern countries. (pp. 39-41)

It is extremely difficult to say how much of the thought of Valla, Ficino, and Pico was absorbed by the leading humanists north of the Alps. Some scholars became personally acquainted with Italian humanists, as did Colet; others read their works and had to be content with the reports of friends and acquaintances, as did Erasmus for a time. A halo of almost supernatural learning seemed to surround those favored beings who told with rapture how they had actually heard the voice of the great Ficino or of the famous Pico. When ambitious boys of twelve or thirteen saw such a scholar, freshly arrived from the land of intellectual giants, they were nearly struck dumb with awe. This happened one day to Erasmus when he beheld the beaming features of Rudolph Agricola, "who was one of the first to bring a breath of the new learning from Italy." (p. 48)

Albert Hyma, "The Humanists," in his The Youth of Erasmus, *University of Michigan Press, 1930, pp. 36-48.*

PRECURSOR OF THE REFORMATION

Preserved Smith

[Smith was an American historian who wrote extensively on the Renaissance and the figures associated with it. In the excerpt below, he identifies and discusses several causes of the Reformation.]

In the eyes of the early Protestants the Reformation was a return to primitive Christianity and its principal cause was the corruption of the church. That there was great depravity in the church as elsewhere cannot be doubted, but there are several reasons for thinking that it could not have been an important cause for the loss of so many of her sons. In the first place there is no good ground for believing that the moral condition of the priesthood was worse in 1500 than it had been for a long time; indeed, there is good evidence to the contrary, that things were tending to improve, if not at Rome yet in many parts of Christendom. If objectionable practices of the priest had been a sufficient cause for the secession of whole nations, the Reformation would have come long before it actually did. Again, there is good reason to doubt that the mere abuse of an institution has ever led to its complete overthrow; as long as the institution is regarded as necessary, it is rather mended than ended. Thirdly, many of the acts that seem corrupt to us, gave little offence to contemporaries, for they were universal. If the church sold offices and justice, so did the civil governments. If the clergy lived impure lives, so did the laity. Probably the standard of the church (save in special circumstances) was no worse than that of civil life, and in some respects it was rather more decent. Finally, there is some reason to suspect of exaggeration the charges preferred by the innovators. Like all reformers they made the most of their enemy's faults. Invective like theirs is common to every generation and to all spheres of life. It is true that the denunciation of the priesthood comes not only from Protestants and satirists, but from popes and councils and canonized saints, and that it bulks large in medieval literature. Nevertheless, it is both *a priori* probable and to some extent historically verifiable that the evil was more noisy, not more potent, than the good. But though the corruptions of the church were not a main cause of the Protestant secession, they furnished good excuses for attack; the Reformers were scandalized by the divergence of the practice and the pretensions of the official representatives of Christianity, and their attack was envenomed and the break made easier thereby. It is therefore necessary to say a few words about those abuses at which public opinion then took most offence.

Many of these were connected with money. The common man's conscience was wounded by the smart in his purse. The wealth of the church was enormous, though exaggerated by those contemporaries who estimated it at one-third of the total real estate of Western Europe. In addition to revenues from her own land the church collected tithes and taxes, including "Peter's pence" in England, Scandinavia and Poland. The clergy paid dues to the curia, among them the *servitia* charged on the bishops and the annates levied on the income of the first year for each appointee to high ecclesiastical office, and the price for the archbishop's pall. The priests recouped themselves by charging high fees for their ministrations. At a time when the Christian ideal was one of "apostolic poverty" the riches of the clergy were often felt as a scandal to the pious.

Though the normal method of appointment to civil office was sale, it was felt as a special abuse in the church and was branded by the name of simony. Leo X made no less than 500,000 ducats annually from the sale of more than 2000 offices, most of which, being sinecures, eventually came to be regarded as annuities, with a salary amounting to about 10 per cent. of the purchase price.

Justice was also venal, in the church no less than in the state. Pardon was obtainable for all crimes for, as a papal vice-chamberlain phrased it, "The Lord wishes not the death of a sinner but that he should pay and live." Dispensations from the laws against marriage within the prohibited degrees were sold. Thus an ordinary man had to pay 16 grossi for dispensation to marry a woman who stood in "spiritual relationship" to him; a noble had to pay 20 grossi for the same privilege, and a prince or duke 30 grossi. . . . Dispensations from vows and from the requirements of ecclesiastical law, as for example those relating to fasting, were also to be obtained at a price.

One of the richest sources of ecclesiastical revenue was the sale of indulgences, or the remission by the pope of the temporal penalties of sin, both penance in this life and the pains of purgatory. The practice of giving these pardons first arose as a means of assuring heaven to those warriors who fell fighting the infidel. . . . In the fourteenth century the pardons were extended to all who contributed a sum of money to a pious purpose, whether they came to Rome or not, and, as the agents who were sent out to distribute these pardons were also given power to confess and absolve, the papal letters were naturally regarded as no less than tickets of admission to heaven. In the thirteenth century the theologians had discovered that there was at the disposal of the church and her head an abundant "treasury of the merits of Christ and the saints," which might be applied vicariously to anyone by the pope. In the fifteenth century the claimed power to free living men from purgatory was extended to the dead, and this soon became one of the most profitable branches of the "holy trade."

The means of obtaining indulgences varied. Sometimes they were granted to those who made a pilgrimage or who would read a pious book. Sometimes they were used to raise money for some public work, a hospital or a bridge. But more and more they became an ordinary means for raising revenue for the curia. How thoroughly commercialized the business of selling grace and remission of the penalties of sin had become is shown by the fact that the agents of the pope were often bankers who organized the sales on purely business lines in return for a percentage of the net receipts plus the indirect profits accruing to those who handle large sums. (pp. 20-4)

It is natural that public opinion should have come to regard indulgences with aversion. Their bad moral effect was too obvious to be disregarded, the compounding with sin for a payment destined to satisfy the greed of unscrupulous prelates. Their economic effects were also noticed, the draining of the country of money with which further to enrich a corrupt Italian city. Many rulers forbade their sale in their territories, because, as Duke George of Saxony, a good Catholic, expressed it, before Luther was heard of, "they cheated the simple layman of his soul." (p. 24)

Much is said in the literature of the latter Middle Ages about the immorality of the clergy. This class has always been severely judged because of its high pretensions. Moreover the vow of celibacy was too hard to keep for most men and for some women; that many priests, monks and nuns broke it cannot be doubted. And yet there was a sprinkling of saintly parsons like him of whom Chancer said

> Who Christes lore and his apostles twelve
> He taught, but first he folwed it himselve,

and there were many others who kept up at least the appearance of decency. But here, as always, the bad attracted more attention than the good.

The most reliable data on the subject are found in the records of church visitations, both those undertaken by the Reformers and those occasionally attempted by the Catholic prelates of the earlier period. Everywhere it was proved that a large proportion of the clergy were both woefully ignorant and morally unworthy. Besides the priests who had concubines, there were many given to drink and some who kept taverns, gaming rooms and worse places. Plunged in gross ignorance and superstition, those blind leaders of the blind, who won great reputations as exorcists or as wizards, were unable to understand the Latin service, and sometimes to repeat even the Lord's prayer or creed in any language.

The Reformation, like most other revolutions, came not at the lowest ebb of abuse, but at a time when the tide had already begun to run, and to run strongly, in the direction of improvement. One can hardly find a sweeter, more spiritual religion anywhere than that set forth in Erasmus's *Enchiridion,* or in More's *Utopia,* or than that lived by Vitrier and Colet. Many men, who had not attained to this conception of the true beauty of the gospel, were yet thoroughly disgusted with things as they were and quite ready to substitute a new and purer conception and practice for the old, mechanical one.

Evidence for this is the popularity of the Bible and other devotional books. Before 1500 there were nearly a hundred editions of the Latin Vulgate, and a number of translations into German and French. There were also nearly a hundred editions, in Latin and various vernaculars, of *The Imitation of Christ.* There was so flourishing a crop of devotional handbooks that no others could compete with them in popularity. For those who could not read there were the *Biblia Pauperum,* picture-books with a minimum of text, and there were sermons by popular preachers. If some of these tracts and homilies were crude and superstitious, others were filled with a spirit of love and honesty. Whereas the passion for pilgrimages and relics seemed to increase, there were men of clear vision to denounce the attendant evils. A new feature was the foundation of lay brotherhoods, like that of the Common Life, with the purpose of cultivating a good character in the world, and of rendering social service. The number of these brotherhoods was great and their popularity general.

Had the forces already at work within the church been allowed to operate, probably much of the moral reform desired by the best Catholics would have been accomplished quietly without the violent rending of Christian unity that actually took place. But the fact is, that such reforms never would or could have satisfied the spirit of the age. Men were not only shocked by the abuses in the church, but they had outgrown some of her ideals. Not all of her teaching, nor most of it, had become repugnant to them, for it has often been pointed out that the Reformers kept more of the doctrines of Catholicism than they threw away, but in certain respects they repudiated, not the abuse but the very principle on which the church acted. In four respects, particularly, the ideals of the new age were incompatible with those of the Roman communion.

The first of these was the sacramental theory of salvation and its corollary, the sacerdotal power. According to Catholic doctrine grace is imparted to the believer by means of certain rites: baptism, confirmation, the eucharist, penance, extreme unction, holy orders, and matrimony. Baptism is the necessary prerequisite to the enjoyment of the others, for without it the unwashed soul, whether heathen or child of Christian parents, would go to eternal fire; but the "most excellent of the sacraments" is the eucharist, in which Christ is mysteriously sacrificed by the priest to the Father and his body and blood eaten and drunk by the worshippers. Without these rites there was no salvation, and they acted automatically (*ex opere operato*) on the soul of the faithful who put no active hindrance in their way. Save baptism, they could be administered only by priests, a special caste with "an indelible character" marking them off from the laity. Needless to remark the immense power that this doctrine gave the clergy in a believing age. They were made the arbiters of each man's eternal destiny, and their moral character had no more to do with their binding and loosing sentence than does the moral character of a secular officer affect his official acts. Add to this that the priests were unbound by ties of family, that by confession they entered into everyone's private life, that they were not amenable to civil justice—and their position as a privileged order was secure. The growing self-assurance and enlightenment of a nascent individualism found this distinction intolerable.

Another element of medieval Catholicism to clash with the developing powers of the new age was its pessimistic and ascetic other-worldliness. The ideal of the church was monastic; all the pleasures of this world, all its pomps and learning and art were but snares to seduce men from salvation. Reason was called a barren tree but faith was held to blossom like the rose. Wealth was shunned as dangerous, marriage deprecated as a necessary evil. Fasting, scourging, celibacy, solitude, were cultivated as the surest roads to heaven. If a good layman might barely shoulder his way through the strait and narrow gate, the highest graces and heavenly rewards were vouch-safed to the faithful monk. All this grated harshly on the minds of the generations that began to find life glorious and happy, not evil but good.

Third, the worship of the saints, which had once been a stepping-stone to higher things, was now widely regarded as a stumbling-block. Though far from a scientific conception of natural law, many men had become sufficiently monistic in their philosophy to see in the current hagiolatry a sort of polytheism. Erasmus freely drew the parallel between the saints and the heathen deities, and he and others scourged the grossly materialistic form which this worship often took. If we may believe him, fugitive nuns prayed for help in hiding their sin; merchants for a rich haul; gamblers for luck; and prostitutes for generous patrons. Margaret of Navarre tells as an actual fact of a man who prayed for help in seducing his neighbor's wife, and similar instances of perverted piety are not wanting. The passion for the relics of the saints led to an enormous traffic in spurious articles. There appeared to be enough of the wood of the true cross, said Erasmus, to make a ship; there were exhibited five shin-bones of the ass on which Christ rode, whole bottles of the Virgin's milk, and several complete bits of skin saved from the circumcision of Jesus.

Finally, patriots were no longer inclined to tolerate the claims of the popes to temporal power. The church had become, in fact, an international state, with its monarch, its representative legislative assemblies, its laws and its code. It was not a voluntary society, for if citizens were not born into it they were baptized into it before they could exercise any choice. It kept prisons and passed sentence (virtually if not nominally) of death; it treated with other governments as one power with another; it took principalities and kingdoms in fief. It was supported by involuntary contributions.

The expanding world had burst the bands of the old church. It needed a new spiritual frame, and this frame was largely supplied by the Reformation. Prior to that revolution there had been several distinct efforts to transcend or to revolt from the limitations imposed by the Catholic faith; this was done by the mystics, by the pre-reformers, by the patriots and by the humanists. (p. 25-9)

Preserved Smith, "The Old and the New," in his The Age of the Reformation, *1920. Reprint by Henry Holt and Company, 1936, pp. 3-61.*

Eckhard Bernstein

[*Bernstein is a German scholar who specializes in comparative literature. In the excerpt below, he explores the nature of the relationship between humanism and the Reformation.*]

In 1521, four years after Martin Luther had nailed his ninety-five theses on the door of the Schlosskirche in Wittenberg, setting off the epoch-making event of the Reformation, there appeared a short illustrated pamphlet called *Die göttliche Mühle* [The divine mill]. The woodcut on the title page shows God in the clouds as the owner of the mill; Christ is pouring the grain (i.e., Saint Paul and the Gospels) into the hopper; Erasmus as the miller's man is bagging the flour (strength, faith, hope, and love), and behind him Luther can be seen as the baker who is kneading bread into dough. The text explains the picture:

Erasmus of Rotterdam
has shown to us the proper way
so that we firmly go, we pray,
to the Good Book, the evangel,
which does all other things excell . . .

Erasmus of his own will
at once proceeded to the mill,
so that he may not be behind
to see about the flour's grind.
The Holy Gospel's miller man,
to bag the flour he teaches everyman,
with his writings does explain,
so that the flour's sweet taste will remain . . .

Doctor Luther, an herald of the doctrine true
has taken it upon himself to bake
the bread, mixing the flour for our sake.

What is suggested here is that the word of God treated and purified by Erasmus has become the basis of the new Protestant faith. The picture thus expresses what contemporaries took for granted, namely, that there was a causal relationship between the work of Erasmus and that of Luther, or, to express it in more general terms, between Humanism and the Reformation.

The problem of the relationship between these movements is, of course, more complicated than this pamphlet from the beginning of the Reformation implies, and has been a controversial topic among scholars for a long time. Avoiding simplifications, one must ask oneself two sets of questions: First, in what way, if at all, did Humanism prepare the ground for the Reformation? What are the common elements and what are the differences between these two cultural forces? Second, what happened to Humanism after religious struggles had begun to dominate life in Germany? Was it stifled by the Reformation, as some scholars argue, or modified and integrated to serve confessional ends, as other critics maintain? Drawing partially on the material presented in the previous biographical sketches and partially on some new material, we can attempt to answer these questions, although clear-cut answers are virtually impossible to find.

It is not difficult to see why Pirckheimer, Erasmus, Reuchlin, and Hutten were perceived by their contemporaries as forerunners of the Reformation. Each had done his share in exposing abuses of the Church, such as benefice-hunting, misuse of temporal power, as well as the alleged ignorance and immorality of the monks and clergy. Most had also criticized the externalization of piety, demanding a return to an inner religiosity freed from the whole apparatus of institutionalized religion. In addition to criticism of the established Church, Humanists and Reformers shared strong anti-Roman sentiments, albeit for different reasons. The former resented the pretended superiority of the Italians out of national pride, while the latter were outraged by the sameless exploitation of Germany by the Roman Curia. In Hutten these two elements merged.

Historically speaking, both Humanists and Reformers rejected the immediately preceding historical developments as a wrong path, going back instead to a previous period as the true source of inspiration. The Humanists turned to the literature of the Greeks, Romans, and Church fathers; Luther and his followers turned to the Bible. Thus, just as for the champions of the *studia humanitatis* classical antiquity became a norm to be followed, the Holy Scriptures assumed normative character for the Protestants.

In light of these affinities it is not surprising that, at least initially, almost all Humanists enthusiastically supported Luther, often considering his fight against the old ecclesiastical authorities as a continuation of Reuchlin's struggle against the theologians of Cologne.

This was, of course, a profound misunderstanding of Luther's real concerns, which could only last for a limited time. Soon the significant differences between the two movements were bound to emerge. What were these differences?

As a literary and pedagogical movement, Humanism was essentially the achievement of a small number of men who regarded themselves as an élite, an aristocracy not of birth but of the mind, and who used as their medium of communication Latin, the international language of scholarship and learning. The Reformers, on the other hand, increasingly employed the vernacular in order to mobilize the masses for their cause. Hutten's switch from Latin to German exemplifies this tendency most clearly. Moreover, primarily interested in poetry, rhetoric, and philology, the Humanists regarded literature as an autonomous genre, while the Protestants, concerned with the essential question of man's relationship to God, considered its function the dissemination of their religious beliefs.

A decisive rift between Humanists and Reformers occurred when the Reformation threatened to degenerate into open rebellion. Riots in Wittenberg and other cities in 1521/22, the destruction of religious statues and pictures, the open harassment of nuns and monks, and finally the Peasants' War of 1525/26 seemed to demonstrate the disastrous social and political consequences of the Reformation. Afraid that it would destroy not only the social order but also the cultural accomplishments, many Humanists turned away from Luther. As early as 1519 Erasmus had recommended to Luther *civilis modestia* ("civilian modesty") and Mutianus had dryly remarked, "Ego phanaticos lapidatores non amo" ("I don't like these fanatical stone-throwers"). Realizing that the Reformation would only succeed in conjunction with a worldly power, Luther thereupon formed an alliance with the princes, a policy which entailed the virtual elimination of the more radical wing of the Reformation. But even after Luther had come down solidly on the side of the civil authorities with a number of pamphlets including his unequivocal publication "Against the Murderous and Plundering Peasants" (1526) and after the "plundering peasants," who had tried to improve their wretched conditions in a desperate uprising, as well as the "fanatical stone-throwers" had been defeated in a number of brutally one-sided battles, many Humanists remained skeptical because the differences concerning the essential theological truths remained.

According to Luther, man could only hope to be saved by God's grace through his own faith while good works as a way to salvation were rejected. This belief in the redemption *sola fide,* through faith alone, was not a minor theological squabble but the cornerstone of the Lutheran theology. Yet by repudiating the traditional doctrine of salvation through good works, Luther also rejected Humanist ideas which stressed man's part in his own redemption. Thus the very idea of man's perfectibility through the study of ancient literature and culture contrasted sharply with the Reformer's view of man's essentially sinful nature. Whereas the Humanists had set out to humanize religion and to make the path to God easier rather than difficult, Luther deemphasized man's part in the redemptive process. There is no doubt, then, that in the last analysis, Humanism in its essence and the evangelical message were incompatible and that there was no inner affinity "between Luther's religious experience and the efforts of Humanism." The theological differences between the Protestant Reformation and Humanism are personified most dramatically by Luther and Erasmus and their exchange of essays on the free and enslaved will. "You are not pious," Luther wrote on the margin of his personal copy of the Dutch Humanist's edition of the New Testament. "You don't have any civility," was the latter's opinion of the religious Reformer.

The realization of the basic differences between Humanism and the Reformation, however, does not answer the second question posed at the beginning of this chapter: What happened to Humanism after the religious strife had begun to dominate intellectual life in German lands? Various theses concerning this problem have been advanced. According to a widely held opinion, for instance, the success of the Reformation actually marked the end of Humanism. The Germans became so much absorbed by religious issues, so the theory goes, that typically Humanist concerns like literature and poetry became irrelevant. One literary historian characterized the situation as follows: "The muses became silent, theology alone had the floor." Another critic, coining the phrase of the "Lutheran pause" argued: "For a generation the German was willing to forego artistic life because he was completely spellbound by religious matters. The young Humanist buds and sprouts were either nipped completely by the Lutheran movement or had to be bent into the same direction as the Church." This notion of the end of the Humanist movement through the Reformation has been challenged recently by a number of scholars who argue that, far from being stifled by the Reformation, Humanism was integrated into it. To support their theory, they can point not only to the many Humanist works that appeared in the very center of the Reformation, in Wittenberg, during the most active decades of the Reformation, but also to the many dramas, poems, and historical works written by Protestant Humanists in other cities. These Humanists achieved something like a synthesis between the two movements. (pp. 129-33)

Eckhard Bernstein, "Humanism and the Reformation," in his German Humanism, *Twayne Publishers, 1983, pp. 129-40.*

Alister E. McGrath

[In the following excerpt, McGrath examines the concept of northern European humanism and briefly examines its influence upon the Swiss and Wittenberg reformations.]

When the word 'humanism' is used by a twentieth-century writer, we are usually meant to understand an anti-religious philosophy which affirms the dignity of humanity without any reference to God. 'Humanism' has acquired very strongly secularist, perhaps even atheist, overtones. It is perhaps inevitable that many students approach the theme 'Humanism and the Reformation' on the basis of this twentieth-century understanding of the word 'humanist'. The scene seems set for the confrontation of religion and atheism. Yet that confrontation never materializes. As we shall see, however, remarkably few—if any—humanists of the fourteenth, fifteenth or sixteenth centuries correspond to our modern understanding of 'humanism'. Indeed, they were remarkably religious, if anything concerned with the *renewal* rather than the *abolition* of the Christian church. The word 'humanist' had a meaning in the sixteenth century which is quite different from the twentieth-century meaning of the word, as we shall see shortly. To anticipate a little, it is now clear that humanism was generally theologically neutral in the Renaissance. The reader is asked to set aside the modern sense of the word 'humanism', as we prepare to meet this phenomenon in its late Renaissance setting. (p. 27)

The term 'humanism' was first used in 1808, to refer to a form of education which placed emphasis upon the Greek and Latin classics. The term was not used at the time of the Renaissance itself, although we find frequent use of the Italian word *umanista.* This word refers to a university teacher of *studia humanitatis*—'human studies', or 'liberal arts', such as poetry, grammar and rhetoric. Although some early studies suggested that humanism originated outside a university context, the evidence available unquestionably points to a close link between humanism and the universities of northern Italy.

This present section is chiefly concerned with the problem of defining humanism. The term is still used widely in Renaissance and Reformation studies, often with an irritating degree of fluidity. What is meant by the term 'humanism'? In the recent past, two major lines of interpretation of the movement were predominant. First, humanism was viewed as a movement devoted to classical scholarship and philology. Second, humanism was the new philosophy of the Renaissance. As will become clear, both these interpretations of humanism have serious shortcomings. (p. 29)

In fact, it is clear that the Italian Renaissance is so multifaceted that just about every generalization concerning its 'characteristic ideas' tends to distort the phenomenon. It is for this reason that the view of humanism developed by Paul Oskar Kristeller is of decisive importance. Kristeller's view of humanism has gained wide acceptance within North America and European scholarship, and has yet to be discredited.

Kristeller envisages humanism as a cultural and educational movement, primarily concerned with the promotion of eloquence in its various forms. Its concerns with matters of morals, philosophy and politics are of secondary importance. To be a humanist is to be concerned with eloquence first and foremost, and with other matters incidentally. Humanism was essentially a cultural programme, laying emphasis upon the promotion of eloquence, which appealed to classical antiquity as a model of that eloquence. In art and architecture, as in the written and spoken word, antiquity was seen as a cultural resource, which could be appropriated by the Renaissance. Petrarch referred to Cicero as his father, and Virgil as his brother. The architects of the *Quattrocento* studiously ignored the Gothic style of northern Europe, in order to return to the classical styles of antiquity. Cicero was studied as an orator, rather than as a political or moral writer.

In short: humanism was concerned with *how ideas were obtained and expressed,* rather than with *the actual substance of those ideas.* A humanist might be a Platonist or an Aristotelian—but in both cases, the ideas involved derived from antiquity. A humanist might be a sceptic or a believer—but both attitudes could be defended from antiquity. The enormous attractiveness of Kristeller's view of humanism derives from the fact that it accounts brilliantly for the remarkable diversity of the Renaissance. Where Baron identifies one set of ideas as central, and Burckhardt another, Kristeller points to the way in which ideas are generated and handled as being central. The diversity of *ideas* which is so characteristic of Renaissance humanism is based upon a general consensus concerning *how to derive and express those ideas.*

It will be obvious that any discussion of the relation of humanism and the Reformation will be totally dependent upon the definition of humanism employed. Kristeller's definition of humanism allows the most reliable assessment of the relation of these two movements now available. (pp. 31-2)

At this point, we must pause to clarify one important point. The 'humanism' which affected the Reformation is primarily *northern European humanism,* rather than *Italian* humanism. We must therefore consider what form this northern European movement took.

It is becoming increasingly clear that northern European humanism was decisively influenced by Italian humanism at every stage of its development. If there were indigenous humanist movements in northern Europe which originated independently of their Italian counterpart (which, it has to be stressed, is very much open to doubt), the evidence unambiguously points to those movements having subsequently been decisively influenced by Italian humanism. Three main channels for the northern European diffusion of the methods and ideals of the Italian Renaissance have been identified.

> 1 Through northern European scholars moving south to Italy, perhaps to study at an Italian university or as part of a diplomatic mission. On returning to their homeland, they brought the spirit of the Renaissance back with them.
>
> 2 Through the foreign correspondence of the Italian humanists. Humanism was concerned with the promotion of written eloquence, and the writing of letters was seen as a means of embodying and spreading the ideals of the Renaissance. The full extent of the foreign correspondence of Italian humanists was considerable, extending to most parts of northern Europe.
>
> 3 Through printed books, originating from sources such as the Aldine Press in Venice. These works were often reprinted by northern European presses, particularly those at Basle in Switzerland. Italian humanists often dedicated their works to northern European patrons, thus ensuring that they were taken notice of in the right quarters.

Three main themes dominate northern European humanism. First, we find the same concern for *bonae litterae*—written and spoken eloquence, after the fashion of the classical period—as in the Italian Reformation. Second, we find a religious programme directed towards the corporate revival of the Christian church. The Latin slogan *Christianismus renascens,* 'Christianity being born again', summarizes the aims of this programme, and indicates its relation with the 'rebirth' of letters associated with the Renaissance. Although Burckhardt is unquestionably right to state that the Renaissance led to a new emphasis upon the subjective consciousness of the individual, northern European humanists supplemented this new emphasis upon the individual with a recognition of the need to reform the communities (both church and state) to which the individual belonged. It is worth noting at this point that the Renaissance emphasis upon the subjective consciousness of the individual is particularly linked with the doctrine of justification by faith. . . . Third, northern European humanism was strongly pacifist during the early sixteenth century, largely in reaction to the tragedy of the Franco-Italian war. The quest for international peace and mutual understanding was espoused by most humanists at the time, particularly in Switzerland, which was caught up in the disastrous Franco-Italian war. Distaste for papal political manoeuvring was an important element in the background to the Swiss Reformation. (pp. 34-5)

Erasmus is often presented as reflecting northern European humanism at its best. While there is much that could be said in support of this suggestion, certain tensions within northern European humanism must be recognized. Two are of particular interest.

> 1 The question of national languages. Erasmus regarded himself as a 'citizen of the world', and Ciceronian Latin as the language of that world. National languages were an obstacle to his vision of a cosmopolitan Europe united by the Latin language. To other humanists, especially in Germany and Switzerland, national languages were to be encouraged as promoting a sense of national identity. Erasmus, however, regarded any sense of national identity as an obstacle to a culturally united Europe—which explains his negative attitude to national boundaries.
>
> 2 The question of national boundaries. For Erasmus, the vision of a cosmopolitan Europe was threatened by nationalism. The adoption of Latin as the cosmopolitan language would remove outdated concepts such as a 'sense of national identity', and associated ideas such as national boundaries. Other humanists, however, saw themselves as engaged in a struggle to *promote* national identity. Thus the Swiss humanists Glarean, Myconius and Xylotectus saw themselves as having a sacred duty to defend Swiss national identity and culture by literary means—where Erasmus would much have preferred to concentrate upon *eliminating* such nationalist ideas.

This tension between the 'cosmopolitan' and 'nationalist' humanist visions, between *abolishing* and *consolidating* national identities, indicates both the variety of views current within humanism: it also demonstrates that Erasmus cannot be regarded as a totally representative spokesman for humanism, as some scholars appear to suggest. (p. 36)

What impact did humanism have upon the Reformation? In order to give a reliable answer to this perennial question, it is necessary to draw a distinction between two wings of the Reformation: the Reformation as it developed at Wittenberg, under Martin Luther; and the Reformation as it developed at Zurich, under Huldrych Zwingli. These two wings of the Reformation had very different characters, and generalizations about 'the Reformation' tend to confuse them. As we emphasized earlier, the Wittenberg and Swiss reformations—which ultimately led to the establishment of the Lutheran and Reformed churches—were very different in character. Even though they appealed to much the same theological sources (scripture and the fathers) as the basis of their reforming programmes, they did so using very different methods and with correspondingly different results. One of the most striking differences between these wings of the Reformation concerns their very different relation to humanism. We shall consider them individually, before returning to some more general points.

Humanism and the Swiss Reformation

The origins of the Swiss Reformation may be traced back to the rise of humanist groups (usually known as 'sodalities') at the universities of Vienna and Basle in the early 1500s. Swiss students, who in the fifteenth century had tended to study at universities noted for their links with scholastic theology, now demonstrated a marked preference for universities with strongly humanist associations. Switzerland was geographically close to Italy, and appears to have become a clearinghouse for the northern European dissemination of the ideas of the Renaissance by the beginning of the sixteenth century. Many of the leading printing houses of Europe—for example, Froschauer in Zurich, and Froben and Cratander in Basle—were Swiss. At a time when Swiss national identity appeared to be threatened by the Franco-Italian war, many Swiss humanists appear to have been inspired by the vision of establishing the literary and cultural identity of Switzerland.

The overall impression gained of early sixteenth-century Swiss intellectual life is that of groups of intellectuals based in the Swiss university cities, beginning to develop the vision of *Christianismus renascens.* The turning point for this movement came when one member of a humanist sodality, Huldrych Zwingli, was called to Zurich as a preacher in January 1519. Exploiting his position, Zwingli initiated a programme of reform based on broadly humanist principles, especially the vision of the corporate renewal of church and society on the basis of scripture and the fathers.

Zwingli had earlier studied at the humanist universities of Vienna (1498-1502) and Basle (1502-6), and his early works reflect the particular concerns of Swiss humanism. Zwingli had met Erasmus, however, while the latter was at Basle in 1516, seeing his Greek New Testament through Froben's presses, and was deeply influenced by his ideas and methods. The following points illustrate Erasmus' influence upon Zwingli:

> 1 Religion is seen as something spiritual and internal; external matters (e.g., the precise ordering of church services, or the form of church government adopted) are of no fundamental importance.
>
> 2 Considerable emphasis is placed upon moral and ethical regeneration and reform. To many scholars, the early Swiss Reformation appears to be primarily a *moral* reformation, with emphasis upon the need to regenerate both individual and society.
>
> 3 The relevance of Jesus Christ to the Christian is primarily as a moral example. Erasmus developed the idea of Christian faith as an *imitatio Christi,* an 'imitation of Christ', and Zwingli follows him in this respect.
>
> 4 Certain of the early church fathers are singled out as being of particular importance. For both Erasmus and Zwingli, Jerome and Origen are to be particularly valued. Although Zwingli would

later begin to recognize the importance of Augustine, this development dates from the 1520s: the *origins* of Zwingli's reforming programme seem to owe nothing to Augustine.

5 Reformation concerns primarily the life and morals of the church, rather than its doctrine. For most humanists, 'philosophy' was about the process of living, rather than a set of philosophical doctrines (see, for example, Erasmus' concept of the *philosophia Christi,* the 'philosophy of Christ', which is essentially a code of life). Initially, Zwingli does not seem to have regarded reformation of the church as extending to its doctrine—merely to its life. Thus Zwingli's initial reforming actions concerned the practices of the Zurich church—such as the way in which services were ordered, or the manner in which churches were decorated.

6 Reformation is viewed as a pedagogical or educational process. It is an essentially human process, based upon the insights contained in the New Testament and the early church fathers. It was only in the early 1520s that we find Zwingli breaking away from this idea, to embrace the idea of Reformation as a divine action overruling human weakness.

To summarize, then: the Swiss Reformation was dominated by humanism, which was the only intellectual force of any significance in the region at the time. Zwingli's early programme of reform is thoroughly humanist, drawing both on the characteristic insights of Swiss humanism, and on those of Erasmus. The influence of humanism upon the Swiss Reformation was nothing less than decisive. This makes the contrast with the Reformation at Wittenberg, to which we now turn, all the more obvious.

Humanism and the Wittenberg Reformation

Although humanism was a fairly important intellectual force in Germany by the early 1500s, its impact upon Martin Luther appears to have been limited. Luther was an academic theologian, whose world was dominated by the thought-patterns of scholastic theology. Through a careful reading of the writings of Augustine, Luther became convinced that the form of scholastic theology he was familiar with was wrong. It failed to do justice to the grace of God, and tended to suggest that the individual could earn his or her own salvation. His task now was to oppose this theology. Where Zwingli regarded the *morals* of the church as requiring reform, Luther saw that it was her theology which was in need of reform. Luther's reforming theology is thus set in an academic context (the University of Wittenberg), and aimed at an academic target (the theology of 'nominalism', or the *via moderna* . . . . Furthermore, Luther's controversy with scholastic theology concerned the doctrine of justification—a concern which finds no echo in the Swiss Reformation.

Equally, Luther's concern with *doctrine* as such finds no echo in either humanism or the early Swiss Reformation. As we noted above, humanism saw reformation as concerning the *life and morals* of the church—but not doctrine. Indeed, most humanists seem to have regarded an interest in doctrine as equivalent to an obsession with scholastic theology! With Luther, however, we find a determination to inquire into the teaching of the church, with a view to reforming it in the light of scripture. This interest in doctrine in general distinguishes Luther sharply from humanism in general, and the early Swiss Reformation in particular. It is, of course, true that the later Swiss Reformation—especially under the leadership of Bullinger and Calvin—would become much more concerned with matters of doctrine. But at this early stage, under Zwingli's leadership, doctrine was marginalized.

In order to combat scholasticism, Luther drew heavily upon scripture and the fathers, supremely Augustine. In doing so, of course, he used the new editions of the Greek New Testament and the writings of Augustine which had been prepared by humanist editors. Luther regarded it as nothing less than providential that these new sources were available to support his programme of reform. There is, however, no real evidence that Luther had any interest in humanism as such—he simply exploited its products for his own ends. Both Luther and the humanists were strongly opposed to scholasticism (although for different reasons, as we shall see below)—and many humanists seem to have thought that Luther's strongly antischolastic attitude at the Leipzig Disputation (1519) demonstrated that he was one of their number. The Leipzig Disputation might have remained an obscure academic debate, had not humanists taken up Luther's cause with enthusiasm.

The overall impression which emerges of the relation between the Wittenberg Reformation and humanism is that Luther exploited the resources of humanism for his own ends. The origins of Luther's reforming theology owe nothing to humanism, except indirectly through its providing him with the tools he needed to carry out his programme of reform. His knowledge of Hebrew; his editions of Augustine; his Greek text of the New Testament—all were provided by humanist editors and educationalists. In many ways, the theological programme developed by Luther and Karlstadt at Wittenberg, which can be summed up in the slogan 'back to the Bible and Augustine!', could be seen as humanist. Yet the superficial similarities between the two programmes mask profound differences. Luther and his colleagues used only the textual and philological skills of humanism, while remaining hostile to humanist attitudes. (pp. 41-5)

Tensions between Reformation and Humanism

It will be obvious that humanism had a decisive contribution to make to the Reformation. Humanist and Reformer alike rejected scholastic theology, in favour of a more simple theology based upon scripture and the fathers. We have already seen how humanism made decisive contributions to the development of the Reformation, through making available reliable editions of the New Testament and the fathers. Yet tensions remained between humanism and both wings of the Reformation. Five areas may be singled out for comment.

1 *Their attitude to scholastic theology.* The humanists, the Swiss Reformers and the Wittenberg Reformers had no hesitation in rejecting scholasticism. In this respect, there is a strong degree of affinity between the three movements.

The humanists, however, rejected scholasticism because of its unintelligibility and inelegance of expression: a simpler and more eloquent theology was required. Similar attitudes are evident within the Swiss Reformation, indicating strong affinity with humanism at this point. The Wittenberg Reformers however (especially Luther and Karlstadt), had no difficulty in understanding scholastic theology: their rejection of scholasticism was based on their conviction that its theology was fundamentally wrong. Where the humanists and Zwingli dismissed scholasticism as an irrelevance, the Wittenberg Reformers regarded it as the most important obstacle in the path of a reforming theology.

2 *Their attitude to scripture.* All three groups held that scripture held the key to reform of the church, in that it bore witness to Christian belief and practice in its original form. For the humanists, the authority of scripture rested in its eloquence, simplicity and antiquity. The Swiss and Wittenberg Reformers, however, grounded the authority of scripture in the concept of the 'word of God'. Scripture was seen as embodying the commands and promises of God, thus giving it a status over and above any purely human document. The phrase *sola scriptura,* 'by scripture alone', expresses the basic Reformation belief that no source other than scripture need be consulted in matters of Christian faith and practice. A further tension exists between the Swiss and Wittenberg Reformers: the former regarded scripture primarily as a source of moral guidance, whereas the latter regarded it primarily as a record of God's gracious promises of salvation to those who believed.

3 *Their attitudes to the fathers.* For the humanists the writers of the patristic period represented a simple and comprehensible form of Christianity, lent authority by their antiquity and eloquence. In general, humanists appear to have regarded the fathers as being of more or less equal value, in that all dated from roughly the same period of antiquity. Erasmus, however, regarded certain fathers as being of particular importance: in the early 1500s, he singled out Origen (a Greek father from the third century, noted as much for the unorthodoxy as for the elegance of his writings) for special mention, while by 1515 he had decided to opt for Jerome. His new preference for Jerome is to be explained on the basis of Erasmus' textual studies in the New Testament, leading to the publication of the Greek edition of the New Testament in 1516. Jerome had earlier undertaken extensive work on the scriptural texts, and Erasmus appears to have regarded Jerome with new interest for this reason. This Erasmian attitude towards the fathers is also evident within the Swiss Reformation.

The Wittenberg Reformers Luther and Karlstadt, however, regarded Augustine as pre-eminent among the fathers. The humanists employed two criteria in evaluating the fathers: antiquity and eloquence. Thus Erasmus' preference for both Origen and Jerome is justified by the elegance of their writings, in addition to their antiquity, in common with the other patristic writings. The Wittenberg Reformers, however, used an explicitly *theological* criterion in evaluating the fathers: how reliable were they as interpreters of the New Testament? On the basis of this criterion, Augustine was to be preferred, and Origen to be treated with some suspicion. The humanists were not prepared to use such an explicitly theological criterion in evaluating the relative merits of the fathers, thus heightening the tension between these two movements.

4 *Their attitudes to education.* In that the Reformation witnessed the birth of a series of new religious ideas (or, at least, ideas which were new to most people in the sixteenth century), it was essential to both the Wittenberg and Swiss reformations that a major programme of religious education be undertaken. Humanism was essentially an educational and cultural movement based upon reform of the liberal arts, with the result that most early sixteenth-century humanists were professional educators. It is therefore interesting to note that most northern European humanists joined the cause of the Reformation, not necessarily because they approved of its *religious* ideas, but because they were attracted strongly by its *educational* ideals. The tension is obvious: the Reformers were concerned with the religious ideas being taught, viewing the educational methods as the means to that end—whereas the professional humanist educators were primarily concerned with the development of educational techniques, rather than the ideas being taught.

5 *Their attitude to rhetoric.* As we have seen, humanism was concerned with eloquence, both written and spoken. Rhetoric was thus studied as a means to this end. The Reformers, in both Germany and Switzerland, were concerned with the promotion of their religious ideas through the written word (e.g., as in Calvin's famous *Institutes of the Christian Religion*) and the spoken word in sermons (Luther and Calvin both being, by all accounts, superb preachers). Rhetoric was therefore the means to the end of the propagation of the ideas of the Reformation. Recent studies, for example, have emphasized how Calvin's style is heavily influenced by rhetoric. Both humanist and Reformer, therefore, regarded rhetoric highly—but for different reasons. For the humanists, rhetoric promoted eloquence; for the Reformers, it promoted the Reformation. Once more, we encounter superficial similarities between the two groups, which mask profound differences.

On the basis of our discussion so far, it will be clear that the Swiss wing of the Reformation was influenced to a far greater extent by humanism than its counterpart at Wittenberg. Even at Wittenberg, however, the new programme of study of the Bible and Augustine appeared to many to be thoroughly humanist in inspiration. With the benefit of hindsight, it is very easy for us to distinguish Luther and Karlstadt from the humanists—yet *at the time,* this distinction was virtually impossible to make. To most observers, Luther and Erasmus were engaged in precisely the same struggle. We have one very famous illustration of this misunderstanding of Luther by humanists. In 1518 Luther delivered the famous Heidelberg Disputation, in which he developed a radically antihumanist and antischolastic theology. One of his audience was the young humanist Martin Bucer, later to become a leading Reformer in the city of Strasbourg. Bucer wrote with enthusiasm to his humanist correspondent Beatus Rhenanus, declaring that Luther merely stated Erasmus' views, but did so more forcefully. As a close examination of that letter indicates, Bucer seems to have misunderstood Luther on virtually every point!

The full extent of the tension between humanism and the Reformation only became fully apparent in 1525. In this year, both Zwingli and Luther composed attacks on Erasmus, both concentrating their attention on the concept of the 'freedom of the will'. For both Reformers, Erasmus' teaching of the total freedom of the human will led to a grossly overoptimistic conception of human nature. With the publication of Zwingli's *Commentary on True and False Religion* and Luther's *On the Bondage of the Will,* the tensions that had always been in existence between humanism and the Reformation were made obvious to all. (pp. 45-8)

Alister E. McGrath, "Humanism and the Reformation," in his Reformation Thought: An Introduction, *Basil Blackwell, 1988, pp. 27-49.*

THE BRETHREN OF THE COMMON LIFE, THE DEVOTIO MODERNA, AND EDUCATION

Albert Hyma

[*In the excerpt below, Hyma outlines the history of the Brethren of the Common Life, providing a synopsis of the daily practices followed by the Brethren.*]

On the 21st of September, 1374, [Gerard] Groote ceded the use of his house to some poor women. Five years later he drew up a constitution for the little society, in which he clearly set forth the reason why he had asked these women to live in his house. Not to found a new monastic order, he wrote, had they come to live here, or a beguinage, but simply to find a place where they might worship God in peace. Only those could secure admittance who were not bound by monastic vows; nor were they expected to take such vows on entering the house. They should all be free to leave if they chose, though they could not reenter, after once having taken their departure. All the inmates of the house would remain members of the local parish church, just as all other laymen. Their clothes should in no respect be different from those of the other women in the city, for they were neither nuns nor beguines. One might even be a member of the society without living in the *"Meester-Geertshuis,"* or Master Gerard's house, at all. At first they had one matron, later two. The matrons were to act as treasurers of the house, and would have authority to make all the members perform manual labor. Their orders were expected to be promptly obeyed. In case of ill-behavior the matrons would consult with two other sisters as to the form of punishment for breach of discipline. The offender would in most cases lose her share in the common savings. But if more serious offences were committed, such as theft, stubbornness, or too great a familiarity with men, the guilty person would have to be expelled. After Groote's death the city council of Deventer would be asked to deal with such cases. During the first few years, when the new society counted but a limited number of members, the two matrons took care of all the business transactions, such as buying supplies, matters of discipline, and supervision of the sisters' daily tasks. Later a division of labor was created. A provisor was chosen, and in 1383 Groote appointed John van den Gronde as the first rector. A procurator was appointed in 1435 and the various tasks of the sisters were also supervised after Groote's death by members specifically directed by the superiors.

The constitution of the "House of Master Gerard" further stated that the members were to live soberly, wear simple clothes, avoid familiar intercourse with men, and restrict their visits to a limit of eight days and a distance of not more than ten miles. No one would be expected to cede her property, on entering the house; the sisters would all work in common and share the expenses together, while the income would be equally divided. Every member of the house who was able to work would be expected to contribute her share of manual labor, for Groote did not want the sisters to beg under any circumstances. Each member, however, was to perform those tasks for which she was specially fitted by nature. Soon the sisters became great adepts in agricultural pursuits; they had a flourishing dairy business, and many of them earned neat little sums through their skill in sewing, knitting, weaving, spinning, and similar purely feminine employments.

In composing this constitution for the Sisters of the Common Life, Groote prepared the way for a mightier organization, known later as the Brethren of the Common Life. Shortly after he left the Carthusian monastery of Monnikhuizen near Arnhem, he had succeeded in recruiting a number of devout followers. In 1380 a man joined them who was destined to become the leader of the Devotio Moderna. This man was called Florentius Radewijns. Born at Leerdam in the year 1350, he had gone to Prague in 1374, and received a master's degree in 1378. Thereupon he had gone home to Gorinchem, where he lived with his parents till the news of Groote's fame as preacher reached him. This must have happened in the year 1380, for Groote had not yet left the Yssel valley. So much impressed was he by Groote's imposing personality that he decided to imitate him in all things. One of the first things he did was to give up his prebend at Utrecht, in order to be nearer to Groote. At Deventer he became vicar of the altar of St. Paul in St. Lebwin's Church. (pp. 49-51)

The sources, however, show plainly that Groote, shortly after his return from the monastery of Monnikhuizen near Arnhem, began to preach in the cities along the Yssel. Among his numerous followers there were twelve who clung quite faithfully to the master, except one of them, called a backslider, and traitor. Groote advised some of them to live together in one house, where they could exhort each other, work and pray together—in short, serve God with greater chance of success. We also read that Groote had several boys and young men copy books for him. The boys were often invited to his house. He purposely paid them a little each time so that they would have to come quite often and have a talk with him. It was not these boys whom Groote urged to live together in one house. And not only Groote invited school boys to his house, but also some of his followers at Zwolle and Deventer, most of whom were soon to become known as Brethren of the Common Life. Hence the founders of the new organization were not those school boys who were asked to Groote's house from time to time. The fact is, there were also girls among the young people entertained by Groote's friends. Moreover, the sources do not at all tell us that these boys and girls who were given financial or other assistance by Groote and his followers founded the congregation or brotherhood, called Brethren of the Common Life. It is only some modern critics who make that assertion, and wrongly so.

Among the twelve disciples at Deventer there were several copyists, who made their living by copying books, and some of them, we saw, were living in Radewijns' vicarage. Now these copyists wanted to join their funds. Accordingly, Radewijns came to Groote one day and said to him: "Master, what harm should there be in our uniting our weekly earnings, and living the common life"? "Unite your funds"? Groote exclaimed in surprise. "Impossible, for the mendicant monks would surely attack us for trying to found a new monastic order". But as Radewijns would not give up his plan so readily, Groote finally answered that in case they would in the near future lead the common life, he would gladly be their leader and instructor.

Should one call Florentius Radewijns then the founder of the Brethren of the Common Life? For did not he suggest to Groote the idea of uniting the funds? It should be remembered, however, that Groote had composed the constitution for the Sisters of the Common Life before

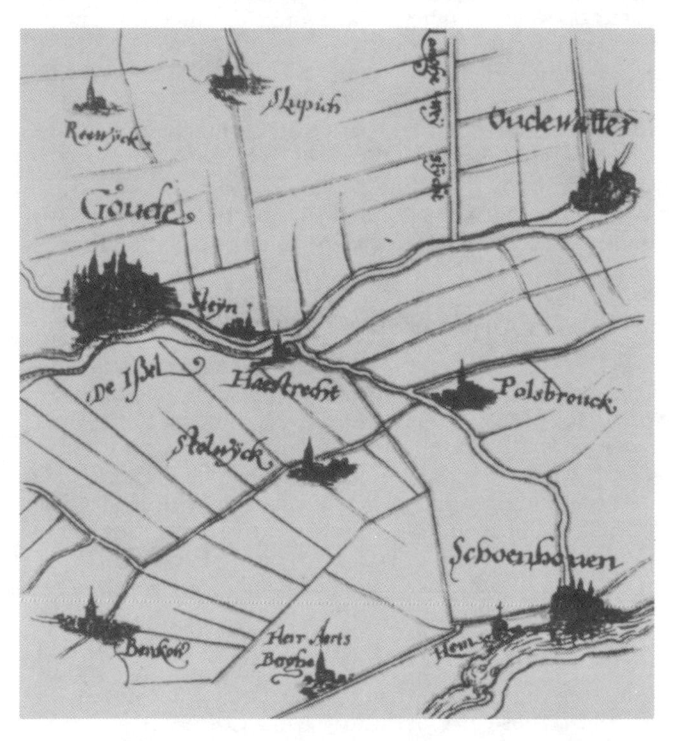

Map depicting the region of Gouda and Steyn, where northern humanist leader Erasmus lived early in his life.

Radewijns had ever heard of him. And it was Groote himself who had stipulated that the sisters should combine their wages and share the common expenses. For this reason the mendicants had already attacked him.

He had even found it necessary to defend them in a sermon at Deventer, together with the beguines, who also united their earnings. When the men in Radewijns' house wanted to lead a life similar to that of the Sisters of the Common Life, he naturally hesitated, and pointed out to them the great danger of attack from his enemies, the mendicant monks, who were living a life of indolence and hated Groote for his love of poverty and manual labor. But his hesitation did not last long, for he knew well that the Canon Law would protect them. He mapped out their future mode of life, drew up a schedule for their daily tasks and their religious exercises, and would undoubtedly have made further arrangements, if the hand of death had not suddenly intervened, as it did on the twentieth of August, 1384. Groote was indeed the founder of the new brotherhood, though his plans were only materialized after his death.

On the afternoon of the twentieth of August, 1384, a pathetic scene was enacted at Deventer. In one of the houses on the Bagynestraat a group of men were standing around Groote's bed. Their beloved master was dying. They saw his life ebbing fast and trembled. And he himself was conscious of their dismay. There was a long silence. But at last he opened his eyes and spoke: "My friends," he said, "do not fear, and let not your hearts be troubled. You will not have to give up your present mode of life. In order that you may protect your temporal possessions I advise you to build a monastery, where those among you best fit for the monastic life may find shelter and perform their work in peace, while at the same time it will protect the others who prefer to remain in the world." "But which order shall we join"? they asked. "The Augustinian," he answered, "for their rules are not so harsh as those of the Carthusians and Cistercians."

Groote also gave a last message to the Sisters of the Common Life. He had regretted the fact that only middle-aged women were willing to join the little society. But better times would come, he thought. "When I shall have departed hence," was his final remark, "I shall send some little flowers from above, benignant spirits, which will swell your numbers."

Thus we are told by John Busch and Thomas à Kempis, the two most reliable historians of the Windesheim circle. Their narratives do in no respect contradict each other, as some writers have thought, who failed to read Thomas à Kempis carefully. On the contrary, they are supported by other trustworthy sources. It was not John Busch, for seven years the pupil and assistant of John Cele at Zwolle, who indulged in flights of the imagination, but those modern scholars who insist on overthrowing the best sources we have. Groote, it appears, had openly attacked Bartholomew of Dordrecht, a mendicant monk, and the clergy at Utrecht besides. They were furious. Moreover, Groote, as founder of the Sisters of the Common Life, had instituted a semimonastic organization which was looked upon by mendicant monks as a hostile rival of their order. He was also translating parts of the Bible into the vernacular, preached against indolence, abhorred all forms of begging, and bitterly denounced those monks and priests who failed to perform their duty. Last but not least, he had a group of disciples who were holding regular meetings in the vicarage of Radewijns. One half of these disciples were actually living with the vicar. They copied books for Groote and for others, and were surely going to live the common life. Perhaps they had already given up their private property. At any rate, they were founding a monastic order, it seemed, without taking the customary vows, or asking the pope for his sanction.

Whenever these copyists were seen on the streets, they were addressed as Beghards and Lollards, hooted at, and commended to burn in hell, or some other suitable place of torture. The common people, and those among the lower classes who frequented inns or lounged about the streets all day, were instigated by some monks to slander Groote's disciples. These monks composed songs in which Groote was mocked and ridiculed. Then there were many laymen as well as clergymen who had attended Groote's sermons, and had felt some compunction about their evil ways, but finally had decided to ignore Groote's appeals. They gradually moved away farther and farther from the path so persistently pointed out to them by Groote. Finally the clergy resented his attacks. For it seemed to some as if he had singled them out for reproval. Groote had advised them to give a large share of their possessions to the poor, to visit the sick and afflicted, to take care of the homeless, and to shun all forms of indolence, intemperance, and immorality. The man was insane, they said to each other. And look at those copyists: always writing books on religion, and never ready to visit us in the tavern and the dance-hall. Do you think we would lead such miserable lives as those wretched copyists are doing? Thus they argued, glad to find support among other members of the clergy, both secular and regular.

Groote was aware of these things. He had already told Radewijns to act with caution. As the people grew bolder each day, and the mendicants increased their attacks, the situation began to look serious. The brethren, not being protected by monastic vows, were uneasy and held daily consultations in Radewijns' vicarage. Finally they came to the conclusion that a monastery should be built where a part of them could live and by their example lead and protect the others. They were to join the Augustinian Canons Regular.

But Groote's end was near, as we have seen. Though he must be considered the founder both of the Brethren of the Common Life and the Windesheim Congregation, he left his work unfinished. Would he also leave his disciples without a leader? Great was their affliction in having to lose so kind and so learned a master. But as he looked up for the last time at his faithful followers, now only eleven in number, his eyes rested upon the one he loved best. "I will not leave you defenseless," he said, "I appoint Florentius as your new leader. He will instruct you, and help you, as I have tried to do." And then he departed. (pp. 51-5)

In the year of Groote's death the religious revival inaugurated by him gained a foothold in those places where he himself had preached, or where his followers had begun to continue his work, namely at Deventer, Zwolle, Doesburg, Zutphen, Kampen, Almelo, Utrecht, Amsterdam, Haarlem, Leiden, etc. But among all these cities and villages only those situated nearest to the Yssel valley succeeded in retaining the master's best thoughts. Naturally there were Deventer and Zwolle which at once assumed a leading position in the history of the Devotio Moderna, and kept the fires of religious zeal burning, when all the others gradually lost their first ardor.

During Groote's lifetime the question of the common life had been brought up for discussion. Groote had assured his followers that he would gladly become their leader and protector, in case they should decide to follow the mode of life practised by the women in his own house at Deventer. Some of them were to build a monastery, he had said, while the others would remain at Deventer. The monastery was not built at once, however. Two years elapsed before the brethren felt the need of seeking protection there. For they had not yet begun to lead the common life, wherefore the mendicant monks left them comparatively at ease, seeing that their society did not resemble a monastic organization. The brethren used to meet in a very informal way. Some of them were living with Radewijns in the vicarage, but not a few merely came to visit at stated times. Not long after Groote's death an important event took place. Radewijns had been accustomed to keep charge of the money earned by the men living in his house. When he noticed their indifference to merely temporal advantages, such as wealth, fame, and honor, he decided to unite their wages, and make of them one common fund. From that day they were Brethren of the Common Life. The exact date of this is not clear; it naturally must have happened between Groote's death and the foundation of the new monastery. For they built that monastery because they had offended their rivals, the mendicant monks, by founding a semi-monastic oranization, having united their funds and shared their expenses in common. It had now become a vital necessity for them to build the monastery, where some could live and all would find protection. Since Groote died on August 20, 1384, and the monastery was founded in 1386, we may assume that the common life was begun before 1387, and probably during the fall of 1384 or the year 1385, inasmuch as Groote had drawn up definite rules in August or July, 1384. (pp. 63-4)

The next event of importance took place in the year 1391, when the "House of Florentius" was founded, the first real house of the Brethren of the Common Life, and named after the first rector, Florentius Radewijns. Till 1391 the brethren had been living in the vicarage with Radewijns. As their number increased from year to year, they finally decided to move to more comfortable quarters. There was a devout lady, called Zwedera of Runen, the wife of a nobleman, who had heard of their plight. She offered them a house and lot, situated in the Pontsteeg, in exchange for two small buildings in the Enghe Straat. This house in the Pontsteeg was torn down and replaced by a fine new building, the "House of Florentius." Most of the brethren now moved from the vicarage to the "House of Florentius," taking their books and furniture with them.

Still another house was founded during the life of Radewijns: the *"Nova Domus," "Domus Pauperum,"* or the new house for poor clerks. It was built in 1398, and intended for the poorer class of pupils attending the school. For the Brethren of the Common Life faithfully continued Groote's policy in helping poor boys and girls to get an education. Radewijns and his followers often invited them to their house, providing them with material and spiritual sustenance. "Behold," Radewijns wrote in 1398, "we take these youths into our house, inexperienced as they are, changeable, having as yet no definite aims or exerting much will power, but they are tractable and pliable. Oh what would happen, if one, or two, or three of us would persuade these boys to work, and teach them discipline, and humility"? Many devout burghers at Deventer would take an interest in the younger boys, due to Radewijns' influence. One Lambert van Galen always had eight of them in his house, and a certain Bye van Dunen also took care of eight boys. These boys were all consigned to the people by the brethren in the "House of Florentius." For only after 1400 did the Brethren of the Common Life take in boys who had not yet finished their work at the cathedral school.

Upon the whole we may say that the brethren during the rectorate of Florentius Radewijns conscientiously tried to imitate the lives of Apostles as set forth in the New Testament. It was the simple life they led, a life of work and devotional exercises. (pp. 64-5)

When Thomas à Kempis lived in the house of Radewijns (1398-1399) there were about twenty inmates, three of whom were laymen. And in a document of the year 1396 we read that there should be at least four priests and eight clerics, that is, twelve members belonging to the clergy; the number of laymen was not specified. Gradually their number increased for their fame soon spread even into distant countries. Many priests, says one biographer attracted by the rumor of Radewijns' virtues and those of his followers, came to Deventer and submitted themselves to Radewijns' rule, laying open to him their hearts. Particularly from Westphalia they came in great numbers. It was not long before the mendicant monks and their friends heard of the growing repute of the Brethren of the Common Life. Groote's fear had not been ill-founded. In spite of the new monastery they had built, the men at Deventer who now remained behind, were not sufficiently protected, having taken no monastic vows. One of their friends and protectors, named John ter Poorten, a prominent member of the city council, was publicly attacked as "Pope of the Lollards."

Not satisfied with instigating the people and inventing sundry unofficial attacks, the Dominicans began to look for other ways of harming the brethren. They carefully studied the Canon Law and its commentaries, thereby hoping to prove that the Brethren of the Common Life had no right of existence. To live the common life without taking monastic vows was a crime, they said. No one had a right to found a new religious order without the pope's consent. And here were those upstarts at Deventer who had never asked for the pope's consent. They had a rector whom they had decided to obey, yet they took no vows of obedience. They earned their daily bread with their own hands, had definite rules and regulations, read sacred writings in the vernacular, and even held addresses to the people in their own language. All this they did without waiting for any one's permission. Surely, so strange and newfangled an institution was an offense to the Church!

The attacks grew fiercer, as time went on, for the jealousy of the mendicant and other monks increased in correspondence with the rising power of the new brotherhood. The Augustinian Canons Regular of Windesheim heard of these attacks. In 1395 they drew up a document in which they defended their friends at Deventer. The Brethren of the Common Life were virtuous men, they wrote. They taught no heresy of any kind, represented no secret societies or lodges, did not preach outside of the churches, had assumed no rules, no new monastic garments, had taken no new vows, and their whole mode of life had been approved by Gregory XI.

This document was not sufficient, however, to stop the enemy's assaults. What was worse, in 1398 another enemy appeared in the form of a terrible pestilence. William of Vianen first caught the disease. Ten brothers were infected and died. They were nursed by John Ketel, their pious cook, but he also passed away in 1398. Then the remaining brethren, led by Radewijns, decided to leave the city and go to Amersfoort across the Veluwe, leaving a few members behind to take care of their property at Deventer. At Amersfoort the brethren continued their work with new energy. They had take several school boys with them, for whom they found suitable quarters among Groote's disciples at Amersfoort, where the first brethren-house west of the Yssel had been founded in 1395. Here the men from Deventer copied books, and preached to the people in the vernacular, especially on holidays, "instructing them by example and doctrine." But it was not a happy time for them. They were now staying far away from the home they had built with their own hands and means. The attacks of their enemies continued, and the pestilence was sweeping one after another to the grave in Deventer. True, they were living with friends who were hospitable and kind, but still these friends were comparative strangers to them.

A spirit of sadness pervades the letters written by the fugitives at Amersfoort to the men at Deventer. "Let us go and die with them," says Gerard Zerbolt of Zutphen, one of the brethren who had gone to Amersfoort, "or else let them come and die with us, though we are able to die here and you to live there. What will life be worth to me, after they have passed away?" And when they were told that one of their beloved friends at home had followed the others to the grave in their absence, they were almost overwhelmed with grief. Their next three letters also breathe anguish. The brethren appeared to have lost all interest in life, so down-cast they were. But in their last letter the dawn of a new hope breaks. They are expecting to return to Deventer soon! "Just as the members of one body all suffer together and console each other," they now write, "so do they also exult in each other's good fortune. The expectation of our return home is a great source of joy to us. Florentius is going to Amsterdam soon and when he returns, we hope to go back home to you."

And what of their other enemies, the mendicant monks? Suddenly their attacks were rendered forceless by a scholar, who came to their aid at the right moment. This new defender of the brethren was Gerard Zerbolt of Zutphen, a man of considerable learning and sharp insight into all questions pertaining to law and tradition. A much greater scholar than Radewijns himself, he was more successful in affairs. With a sort of prophetic vision he perceived the dangers encircling the new brotherhood on all sides, when the brothers themselves were scarcely aware of impending trouble. They had written a great deal about the sorrows of separation, but the dangers from without they could not perceive.

The crisis came in 1398. Radewijns had been at Utrecht and at Amsterdam. The brethren at Deventer and Amersfoort were sure of his success in obtaining privileges from Frederick van Blankenheim, Bishop of Utrecht. But Radewijns had to write home from Amersfoort: "The business of the Lord has made no progress; wherever we turn we meet with obstacles." That was all he could say. He now was homesick. He had resolved to leave Amersfoort for Deventer in secret. His first attempt was a failure, but finally he succeeded in fleeing. Strange though it seems, Radewijns, the first rector of the Brethren of the Common Life, forsook his followers in the thick of the fight. He had been unequal to his task. (pp. 66-9)

How did the Brethren of the Common Life usually pass their time, and what were the most characteristic features of their organization? Their constitutions which were practically uniform in Germany, and nearly so in the Low Countries, together with a number of chronicles, treatises, and biographies, enable us to gain a fairly accurate knowledge of their daily work, habits, and ideals.

[The brethren of Deventer and Zwolle wrote:]

> Our house was founded . . . with the intention that priests and clerics might live there, supported by their own manual labor, namely, the copying of books, and the returns from certain estates; attend church with devotion, obey the prelates, wear simple clothing, preserve the canons and decrees of the saints, practise religious exercises, and lead not only irreproachable, but exemplary lives, in order that they may serve God and perchance induce others to seek salvation. Since the final end of religion consists in purity of heart, without which we shall see perfection in vain, let it be our daily aim to purge our poisoned hearts from sin, so that in the first place we may learn to know ourselves, pass judgment upon the vices and passions of our minds, and endeavor with all our strength to eradicate them; despise temporal gain, crush selfish desires, aid others in overcoming sin, and concentrate our energy on the acquisition of true virtues, such as humility, love, chastity, patience, and obedience. Toward this end we must direct all our spiritual exercises: prayer, meditation, reading, manual labor, watching, fasting—in short, the harmonious development of our internal and external powers.
>
> Whereas the fear of the Lord is necessary to those who wish to overcome evil, it is expedient for each of us to meditate on such subjects as induce man to fear the Lord, like sin, death, judgment, and hell. But lest continued fear might engender dejection and despair, we shall have to add more hopeful subject matter for meditation, such as the kingdom of heaven, the blessings of God, the life of Jesus Christ, and his passion. These subjects we shall arrange in such a way that on Saturdays we shall meditate on sin, Sundays on the kingdom of heaven, Mondays on death, Tuesdays on the blessings of God, Wednesdays on the final judgment, Thursdays on the pains of hell, and Fridays on the passion of Christ.

The constitutions further state that the brethren were to rise between three and four o'clock in the morning (later shortly before five), preparing themselves at once for prayer and the reading of certain prescribed selections. All the members of the house were expected to attend the daily mass, and were exhorted to free their mind from all distractions, "thus preparing themselves, as it were, for a spiritual communion."

Since it was considered most beneficial for all men to perform some manual labor every day, the brethren would be expected to spend several hours a day in copying religious books, or else in performing other tasks. But lest the spirit suffer from neglect, they should occasionally utter short prayers, called "ejaculations." The brethren were to consume their meals in silence, in order that they might pay proper attention to the reading of a selection from the Bible. After supper they could do as they pleased in their own rooms till eight o'clock. At eight all guests would have to leave the house. The doors were shut fast, and silence was observed till half past eight, when they went to bed.

On Sundays and holidays certain passages in the Scriptures were read and explained; and in this connection there was opportunity for general discussion, when each member of the house could freely express his opinions, as long as he did not indulge in impractical disputes and argumentations. The school boys and other people were invited to attend the discussions which were held in the vernacular. The influence thus exerted upon the common people by the brethren is incalculable. For not only were there a great many among them whose fame as orators brought people long distances to hear them, but it was their combined, their continued efforts, which must have brought tangible results, considering the great number of holy days they observed. Not one of them was as famous as a Brugman, Wycliff, Hus, or Savonarola, but they formed a vast organization. Their voices were seldom heard on the streets, for they wished to avoid publicity. Nevertheless, their influence, though not always manifested visibly, reached the minds of thousands, while the books they circulated reached still larger numbers. They continued their labors in an orderly way. Like the persistent drops of water, which in the course of time even form impressions on the most solid rocks, so did the efforts of the Brethren of the Common Life affect the most perverse sinners. One could always rely on their addresses. The brethren were always ready to help the sick and comfort the afflicted. And the school boys could always get a room in their dormitories, no matter whether they were able to pay for them or not. By avoiding notoriety and scandal, by preaching reform to all men and women without stressing unduly the faults of the clergy, the brethren labored—unnoticed by those historians who record only the interruptions against the course of nature, against peaceful reform and bloodless revolution, thereby ignoring the great movement which throughout the fifteenth and sixteenth centuries helped to change the medieval mind into the modern mind.

The most interesting feature about the brethren's labors as preachers was their informal addresses. On Sundays and holy days the people were accustomed to assemble in the room designated for this purpose. A chapter of the Bible was read in the people's language which contained some practical advice or instruction. Those passages in particular were selected which in very plain words taught the people how to "extinguish vice, acquire virtue, despise worldly things, and fear the Lord." Thereupon all members of the house, in so far as they were gifted by nature to act as spiritual guides of the masses, would be expected to exhort the people, either separately in their respective rooms, or in addressing the whole assembly in turns. But they were not to preach, the constitutions state—merely to exhort and instruct. Confession of sins, and mutual correction were looked upon by the brethren as very helpful means of combatting evil.

As time went on the Brethren of the Common Life found it necessary to appoint rectors, procurators, librarians, and several other office-holders. In the constitutions of the houses at Deventer and Zwolle the duties of the rector, procurator, librarian, tailor, and nurse were carefully outlined; several other offices were treated together in one chapter, though later they were more elaborately discussed in the constitutions used by the German houses, belonging to the "Colloquium of Münster."

The houses of the Brethren of the Common Life in the Low Countries used to send representatives to their annual meeting, called "Colloquium Zwollense." Another means of preserving discipline and unity were the annual visitations by two rectors, preferably those of Zwolle and Deventer. The houses in Germany, of which the one at Münster was the chief, also were visited in the same manner. There also were held monthly meetings in each house, where divers matters relating to discipline, religious exercises, or manual labor could be discussed.

Each house should, if possible, have four priests and some other members of the clergy. If somebody applied for admission, the brethren were required to examine his physical condition, and his mental equipment; he should be asked from which country he had come. He would be asked, also, whether he could write, and loved to read books. In case he was found to be in good health and of sound mind and habits, he would be allowed to remain in the house for two or three months, whereupon he might be promoted to a further trial of ten or twelve months. After this lapse of time he might become a Brother of the Common Life, having first sworn before a notary public and in the presence of some witnesses that he renounced all claim to any property of his own. Members could be expelled in case of ill-behavior. The brethren were exhorted to preserve mutual love, peace, and harmony, and although none of them would be expected to take the vows of chastity and obedience, nevertheless they all should strive to cultivate these virtues. The virtue of humility in particular was highly extolled by the brethren at Deventer and Zwolle. No member of the brotherhood was to have any property of his own, as it had been ceded by him to the house on being admitted as a member there. They were to spend a part of their income to meet current expenses, and the remainder for the relief of the poor. As for the other regulations found in the various constitutions, they need not be commented upon here.

The Brethren and Sisters of the Common Life may well be called practical mystics, in distinction from such men as John Ruysbroeck. Love for their neighbor impelled them to work among the people in the cities. Their highest aim was the reformation of the Church, which could most effectively be done, they thought, by educating the youths of the land, and by instructing the common people in the essentials of the Christian religion. They paid much attention to their "spiritual natures," or their "inner selves." Formed in the image of God, as they believed, and assured by Christ that the kingdom of heaven is found within the human heart, they continually strove to explore their inner lives, to unite their inner selves with God or Christ, and thus regain their lost heritage. They were also much given to meditation.

As Christian mystics they constantly aimed to imitate the lives of Christ, and the apostles. They loved to seek parallels between Christ's life and their own, for their religion was one of action, of deeds. Groote had instructed them to read the Gospels and the lives of the Church Fathers in preference to other books, as the former contained biographies. Paul's Epistles and the various books of the Old Testament were by no means neglected by them, however. As they read the Acts of the Apostles, the thought must often have struck them that it was not at all necessary for a good Christian to seek refuge in a monastery. At any rate, their desire to win ever more souls for Christ kept them in the cities. "We have decided," the Brethren of the Common Life at Zwolle wrote 1415, "to live in cities, in order that we may be able to give advice and instruction to clerics and other persons who wish to serve the Lord." One of the most successful ways by which the brothers at Deventer won the hearts of young men, was the church drama. Theodore Herxen, as we saw above, devoted several treatises to the "art of drawing boys to God." Both the Brethren and the Sisters of the Common Life were particularly fond of finding practical lessons in the selections read from the Scriptures at their meals. These lessons they tried to remember for the purpose of applying them on specific occasions, and for the sake of mutual exhortation. Another feature of their practical mysticism was the collection of excerpts from writings perused by them. These were called "good points" or "rapiaria." Special notebooks or slips of paper were at all times kept in readiness in order to improve their knowledge.

The Brethren and Sisters of the Common Life, in conscientiously following Christ, gloried in self-denial, poverty, humility, and obedience, but if we bear in mind the circumstances under which they had founded and sought to develop their institution, we may say that their outlook upon life was quite free from excessive asceticism. True, they lived very soberly: their meals were extremely simple, their clothing at first scarcely respectable. But whatever may have been their worst form of mortifying the flesh, their asceticism was of a mild nature. And as time went on, experience taught them that stinting the body does in no way enhance the beauty of the soul, or the dignity of the spirit. Consequently, we find that after the year 1400, they dressed more properly, used more wholesome meals, reduced the number of hours devoted to copying books, took more exercises in the open air, lived less estranged from "worldly" people, and also acquired more respect for learning as a final end.

It has often been asserted by scholars of late that the Brethren of the Common Life paid little or no attention to education. On the other hand one also frequently reads statements to the effect that they even made their living by teaching. Once again the sources should be consulted, rather than the conflicting opinions of modern scholars. In the first place, then, let it be understood that the brothers at Deventer never had a real school of their own there, nor did any of their members teach in the cathedral school of that city until several years after the death of Radewijns. There were two schools at Deventer during the days of Groote and Radewijns. From 1378 till 1381, they were both supervised by William Vroede, Groote's friend, who upon Groote's advice brought about certain reforms in these two schools. As rector of the cathedral school he was succeeded by John Lubberts (1381-1385), and not by Florentius Radewijns, as some writers believe.

At Zwolle John Cele was rector of the city school from 1375 1417. His educational labors, which were imitated at Deventer, together with the assistance freely accorded to the school boys by the Brethren of the Common Life and the other disciples of Groote at Deventer and Zwolle, were causes which made the schools of Zwolle and Deventer famous long before the days of Hegius. It will be remembered that under the administration of Cele the attendance at the school at Zwolle rose to 1200. The hearty welcome extended by those pious matrons and the kind-hearted brethren must have acted as a very powerful magnet for the boys who had come from Poland, the interior of Germany, the upper Rhine valley, and the distant shores of Flanders, where on their return they extended the influence of the school. The brothers themselves received their interest in education from Groote and Cele. Groote had always laid stress on the importance of offering a better education to future pastors. Hence his friendship with the teachers at Deventer and Zwolle. The brethren, in inheriting most of Groote's ideals, soon shared his views on the need of a better education, particularly for those boys who intended some day to join the ranks of the clergy. Groote's chief aim had been the reform of the Church; the surest and quickest way to reach that happy end in his opinion was the training of young men. This training should by no means exclude the study of literature, pagan or classic as well as Christian; while grammar, rhetoric, logic, mathematics, and philosophy were to retain their places in the curriculum. Cele materialized Groote's plans at Zwolle, aided as he was by the brethren in that city. Not long after his death the reform inaugurated by him spread to Deventer and many other places where Groote's disciples had founded brethren-houses. (pp. 109-16)

The most important schools were found at Deventer, Zwolle, and Münster, where also the most influential brethren-houses had been established. A complete proof of the excellence of these schools was given by John Sturm, the celebrated rector at Strasbourg, when he outlined the plans of his "gymnasium" to the magistrates of the Alsatian metropolis. He did not recommend the schools of Cologne, of Louvain, and of Trier, and preferred Deventer to Utrecht. Nor was Sturm the only teacher who acknowledged the debt he owed to Cele's followers, as will be seen later. (p. 117)

It is no wonder that among all those boys at least a few great minds were found. And where Groote's ideas were acted upon with so much tender devotion, where so much love was lavished upon responsive hearts, and such ideals were expounded as the *Imitation of Christ* contained, the school at Zwolle could not fail to send out once more a host of religious youths. The names of most of these boys have been lost to memory, and of the others only a few can be mentioned here. Naturally one turns first to him who became the most famous educator in Transapline Europe—to Alexander Hegius.

Hegius was born near the village of Heek in Westphalia in 1433. He was teacher at Wesel in 1474, and from 1475-1483, taught school at Emmerich, no doubt supported in the usual way by Brethren of the Common Life, who had a house in each of these two places, while at Emmerich they had founded two dormitories for the pupils of the local school. In 1483, Hegius was appointed rector of the school attached to St. Lebwin's at Deventer, where he remained until his death in 1498. When teaching school at Emmerich he had become acquainted with Agricola, of whom he learned Greek. Gansfort also was an intimate friend of his, as appears from one of his letters. Anxious to promote the study of the classics, he encouraged his pupils to learn both Latin and Greek. He himself had been taught Greek too late to master that language so well as some of his contemporaries. But he was always eager to learn more, and diligently read the classics and the Fathers.

Alexander Hegius, though he may be called one of the leading humanists of the late fifteenth century, as he showed a great interest in the study of the Ancients, was nevertheless too closely associated with the Brethren of the Common Life to despise the use of the vernacular, as so many scholars of his time were doing. As poet, he became the forerunner of the "younger humanists," and, although he lacked real poetic enthusiasm, his labors in this direction are nevertheless of historical significance.

His school at Deventer grew to 2200 pupils. This was due in part to the assistance given him by the brethren. At Zwolle he had been instructed in what might be called the rudiments of Christian education. The ideals of the Christian Renaissance were never opposed to art or learning, as many a manuscript will show us today, written and illuminated as they were by the Augustinian Canons Regular and the Brethren of the Common Life. Before Hegius began the study of Greek, he had managed to attract fifteen hundred pupils to his school at Emmerich. In 1475, he was not yet a humanist in the proper sense of the word. Still his fame had reached the cities of Trier, Cologne, Strasbourg, Liége, Magdeburg, and other centres of learning. His love of poetry, of the Greek language, and of ancient letters in general were not the causes of his early fame. The secret of his success lay deeper than that. It was the favorable circumstances attending the presence of the brothers at Wesel and Emmerich, Hegius' early instruction at Zwolle, and the peculiar bent of his nature which enabled him to become Cele's truest successor. Hegius was not a Petrarch nor a wandering humanist like Agricola or Hermann von dem Busche, to name some of the best types of the true humanists, but he was the greatest educator of Transalpine Europe in the fifteenth century, and the marvelous success he enjoyed as teacher from 1474 till 1498 he owed mainly to the work of two men: Gerard Groote, founder of the Brethren of the Common Life, and John Cele, who inaugurated, upon Groote's advice, the reform which assisted the revival of learning in Northern Europe. This revival till 1455, developed largely independently of the Italian Renaissance and later added the best thoughts of the classics, in so far as they were discovered by Italian humanists, to its great store-house of medieval learning. Hegius, in continuing Cele's work, advocated a reform in the text-books. The *Medulla* was not worth being read any longer, he said. On the last page of his *Invectiva* he gives a list of grammars which should be altered. Throughout this whole essay, in fact, he indicates the need of better text-books. As for style, he asserted in his *Farrago* that one should appropriate the diction of Cicero, Virgil, and Sallust, and imitate the Italian humanists. The *Disciplina Scholarium,* the *Gemma Gemmarum,* and the Lexica of Hugutio Brito and John Januensis, should be cast aside as no longer worthy of study. Here he does not speak as a true medievalist, but appears to have absorbed some of the ideas of the Italian Renaissance. (pp. 118-20)

It was easy enough for the wandering Bohemians of learning in the early sixteenth century to poke fun at existing conditions. A negative criticism is easy. When it came to actual reform, however, it was the school at Deventer which furnished the required missionaries. Thus it had been in the early years of the fifteenth century, and so it remained throughout the whole life-time of Hegius. The priors were always glad to get recruits from Deventer. While certain contemporaries of his, like the celebrated Anton Vrye, or Liber, were soon forgotten after their death, Hegius continued to be a living force in the hamlets and cities of the Yssel valley and beyond.

During the rectorate of Hegius, then, Deventer was one of the chief centers of the movement usually referred to as the German Renaissance. The best thoughts of the Italian Renaissance were absorbed at Deventer and Zwolle, and from there some entered Germany, now transformed by the Devotio Moderna, which had become an intellectual movement, though its chief aim remained the restoration of the Church in all its members. An index of how strong an intellectual movement this was, is the fact that many classics were issued from the presses at Deventer before 1500: more than four hundred and fifty works. (pp. 120-21)

Much might be written about other pupils of the Brethren of the Common Life, some of whom taught school while they were members of the celebrated brotherhood. Thus the schools at Deventer and Zwolle not only served as a means of improving intellectual standards among the clergy, but offered preparatory courses for students intending to enter the universities, and also sent out a great number of teachers to other cities. So great was their number that in the Netherlands scarcely a school could be found during the opening years of the sixteenth century, where there was not felt at least some connection with the Yssel valley "gymnasia." In Germany at that time, and throughout the preceding century, if one were to study the origins of each of the early secondary schools throughout the North and West, he would undoubtedly be able to trace the influence of Deventer and Zwolle. Mention can only be made here of the two chief centers of the German Renaissance, that is, the two schools which contributed most largely to the dissemination of learning in Germany from 1450 till 1520—the schools of Schlettstadt and Münster.

For several centuries Strasbourg had been the ecclesiastical and intellectual metropolis of Alsace. With Trier, Cologne, Liége, Aachen, and Utrecht it had possessed a sort of educational monopoly in the regions which once had separated Germany from France. But conditions did not always remain thus. Cologne and Trier began to send their most promising sons to little Zwolle, which was only an insignificant parish in the diocese of Utrecht, but the town of Cele's school. It was not long before Alsace developed a similar situation.

A Westphalian teacher, named Louis Dringenberg, who had been trained at Deventer, came to Schlettstadt in 1441. Here for a period of 36 years, he was rector of the public or town school. There were no Brethren of the Common Life in Schlettstadt, which may account for the fact that he was unable to draw such vast numbers of pupils to his school as Cele had done to Zwolle, but this school at Schlettstadt eventually surpassed that at Strasbourg. The reason was given by a learned author: "While thus Strasbourg and most other cities lagged behind, Schlettstadt already possessed a flourishing school. Founded about the middle of the fifteenth century and supervised by the magistrates, its rector was the Westphalian Louis Dringenberg, who had carried hither the spirit and method of the Brethren of the Common Life." More to the point is the following statement by G. C. Knod, another Alsatian scholar of note: "This spirit of pedagogical skill and pious wisdom, as it prevailed in the schools of the Brethren of the Common Life, had also asserted itself in the town school of Schlettstadt. It was the first school conducted by laymen in South-German regions which, in conscious deviation from the clerical institutions, outlined its scope and method after the humanistic fashion." (pp. 121-22)

The fact is, Münster and Deventer sent out so vast a host of really great scholars and teachers that it is quite impossible to enumerate them. Under their leadership practically all the larger schools in Western Germany were organized and reformed. Through them the benevolent influence of Cele's work found its way into many a city where no Brethren of the Common Life were found, such as Attendorn, Dortmund, Düsseldorf, Eisleben, Essen, Lübeck, Luneburg, and Minden. And as the pupils of these teachers in their turn continued Cele's work, the literary productions and the educational reforms of Groote's followers were diffused throughout the land, entering shop and farm-house, chapel and monastery, kitchen and workshop, appealing to the hearts of high and low, of rich and poor, of old and young. Who can calculate or describe the influence which thus radiated from the Yssel valley schools in all directions? Such influence never dies, and readers must have been impressed by the fact that modern education perpetuates the best features of the reformed education of Groote, and Cele, and the Brethren of the Common Life. (pp. 125-26)

Albert Hyma, "The Rise of the Devotio Moderna" and "The Brethren and Sisters of the Common Life," in his The Brethren of the Common Life, *Wm. B. Eerdmans Publishing Company, 1950, pp. 49-95, 96-126.*

R. R. Post

[*In the excerpt below from his book* The Modern Devotion: Confrontation with Reformation and Humanism *(1968), Post summarizes several main points of William Spoelhof's unpublished 1946 thesis,* Concepts of Religious Nonconformity and Religious Toleration as Developed by the Brethren of the Common Life in the Netherlands, 1374-1489, *including the organization and mysticism of the Brethren. In an unexcerpted portion, Post notes that "the writer, who sent me this typed book of 306 pages, has really broken new ground."*]

[William Spoelhof] clearly described a factor often considered as one of the qualities of the Devotio Moderna, yet seldom expressly qualified or proved. This is the influence of the Brethren upon the rise and spread of Humanism and the Reformation. Those who support this thesis, being compelled to abandon their propositions one by one so far as concerns the Brethren's teaching, academic training and practice, entrench themselves on this domain, and it is very difficult to dislodge them. The thesis is vague and offers little grounds for certainty. This embarrasses both the supporters and the opponents of the theory. Spoelhof, on the contrary, is not vague. He says exactly what he means and tries to find support for his opinion in the writings of [various northern humanists].

His view is clearly stated in the introduction. The Brethren of the Common Life did not strive definitely for complete tolerance, nor did they purposely hold themselves aloof from existing faith and rites. They adopted rather an attitude of deliberate and conscious indifference (not scepticism) towards the externals of institutionalized Christianity and by their practical mysticism they placed more emphasis upon personal piety than on the objective expression of religious feeling. The more they cultivated their religious ardour, the less importance they attached to formal ceremonies and the Roman Catholic articles of faith.

Their toleration and non-conformity reveal themselves in their attitude towards the external standards of institutionalized Christianity whereby conformity was prescribed. This does not mean that they fiercely defend the ideas of non-conformity and toleration, since these are in fact never goals in themselves, but always means to the goal. The goal of the Brethren was personal piety and immediate communion with God, which is the same thing. Spoelhof deals only with the Dutch Brethren and covers the period up to the death of Wessel Gansfort (1489). In actual fact this marks the end of the history of the Brethren. They then lose their independent entity. In the last part of the fifteenth and the first quarter of the sixteenth centuries, the Brotherhood was absorbed into the intellectual and religious currents to which Humanism and the Reformation gave rise.

On the basis of this, Spoelhof's main interest in the Brethren is to describe:

1. The organizational aspect of the movement, characterized, in the case of the Brethren of the Common Life, by anti-institutionalism.

2. The mysticism of the Brethren of the Common Life, with its emphasis on practical ethics, the return to the first primitive Christianity and anti-intellectualism.

The first point is fairly quickly dealt with. The organization of the Brethren and Sisters of the Common Life who form the heart of the Devotio Moderna was never so strictly institutionalized as the congregation of Windesheim. The fraternity retained always the independent, democratic spirit intended from the beginning. There were no vows, they were free to come and go as they wished. Although Spoelhof admits that this anti-institutional character was more passive than active he none the less thinks that from the very beginning this trait constituted a real power in the fraternity. They held that religion was a personal matter between a man's conscience and God and not a question of an institution to be practised only within the cloister. It might be seen as a return to the communal life of apostolic christianity. The fact that the Brethren adopted a completely monastic pattern of life and even founded and filled several monasteries and set themselves to train and fit young men for the monastic state does not detract from this anti-institutional character. The retention of the democratic character of their congregation was enough to save their independence. Spoelhof concludes from this that the Brethren of the Common Life indicated a reaction against the idea that a religious life could only develop within the walls of a monastery. This reaction, their lay character and their democratic government preserved the fraternity from absorption by the Windesheimers, whose institution led as we saw to intolerant regulations. It was different with the Brethren. There, individualism formed part of their teachings. Theirs was not, however, a purely personal religion; this was discouraged. But they learned that in their form of communal life, each individual was of more account than if he lived and acted alone. "This is true democratic individualism." Although this idea is not completely clear, Spoelhof appears to be referring to the rejection of the forbidden extreme individualism. The individualism of the Brethren also led to their being condemned and harrassed by the Dominicans. The fraternity clearly displays a diminishing respect for the externals of religion and a greater emphasis upon the internal. In other words, it favoured personalism and individualism at the expense of institutionalism. In this deviation from the normal path lay the seeds of indifference to institutional Christianity and of non-conformity and freedom. This also springs from their mysticism, which differs from that of the 14th century German mystics and is unique of its sort. It knows no extasy, with the exception perhaps of Henry Mande, but is entirely practical, ethical and social. It was, moreover, inspired by the example of the apostles (not only as regards community of possessions) and the imitation of Christ, described in the famous book of Thomas a Kempis which comprises the essence of the teaching of the Brethren of the Common Life. It is, in addition, anti-intellectual. This is revealed, not in an aversion to education and knowledge, but in a mistrust of formal scholastics, and emerges in a certain letter of Groote's and in the writings of Florens Radewijns, Gerard Zerbolt and especially in Thomas's *Imitation.*

Before demonstrating all this, Spoelhof deals with the thesis: mysticism produces religious individualism and thus is opposed to ecclesiastical conformism and unity. Or, to put it more positively, mysticism, by its very nature, leads to non-conformity and demands toleration. In all religions objective and subjective aspects must be distinguished. Among the objective must be numbered the externals, the rites, practices, decisive dogma and ecclesiastical organization and authority. The subjective, on the other hand, comprise the free inward life. Objective unity deprives subjectivity of inner freedom. It is thus with medieval Catholicism, in which the objective side is greatly stressed. The mystic strives for union with God and disregards the Church and the hierarchy. They are thus always opposed. Several writers like Jones, Preger, R. Bainton and J. Havelaar are even of the opinion that mysticism always leads to freedom and toleration. Spoelhof contests this, however. St. Augustine and St. Bernard were both great mystics, yet recommended persecution. One must agree with Harnack in dividing the mystics according to their degree, way and energy. It is precisely in these three points that the mysticism of the Brethren differs from that of the German mystics. They are not so absorbed in God that their individuality is neutralized or deified. According to Gilson they desire a practical Christian life and nothing more. For the rest, in the text quoted, Gilson says that this attitude is not mystic. Under the influence of the *Via Moderna,* the mysticism of the Devotionalists stresses the will more than the intellect. According to de Beer, Groote was anti-intellectual. Mysticism among the Brethren and according to the Imitation of Christ, which proceeds from the heart of the fraternity, had the qualities indicated in the beginning. These repose notably in the question of religious non-conformity. Dogma was not considered important, except for its consequences in the domain of morals. In this connection Spoelhof refers to a few texts from the first chapter of the first book of the Imitation. The Imitation is completely devoid of specific references to theological dogmas. The essential thing is the personal, virtuous life. Groote's sermon *sermo contra focaristas* has the same quality. This anti-dogmatic attitude was passive. They took it for granted and did not devote much thought to it. The Brethren thus tended towards a spirit of indifference. Such personal piety could not be contested by the Church or state. This Christian primitivism is revealed by the propaganda for the Imitation of Christ. The *fides simplex* of the Deventer circle was an indirect criticism, a drawing away from the ecclesiastical and the dogmatic, a putting into practice of medieval catholicism. This attitude also gave rise to a Biblicism which differs from that of the Humanists.

"The Brethren of the Common Life were not deliberate champions of religious toleration and religious non-conformity. They were not iconoclasts . . . However, in spite of a conscientious effort at ecclesiastical conformity there emanated from the Brotherhouses an equally strong inclination toward toleration of personal forms of religious life and faith". Despite their pietistic forms of life, their tendencies towards mysticism and their orthodoxy with regard to the dogmatic churches, they were considered in their time as liberals.

Spoelhof must naturally still give his argumentation for these theses: that their practical mysticism led the Brothers of the Common Life to contrast their personal religious life with that of the church and inner piety with its outward manifestations and, secondly, that their contempt for the dogma led to tolerance. These theses are, however, deceptive and it is understandable that they should attract supporters. They do, indeed, offer the possibility of maintaining the theory of the Brethren's influence which many have rated highly for over a century. . . . First, however, a few general considerations. Spoelhof is here employing the ambiguous meaning of mystic or mysticism. The fact that some of the German mystics, and Eckhart especially, during the conflict of Ludwig of Bavaria with the Avignon Popes and during the interdict imposed at that time, may have sought union with God along mystical channels alone, (perhaps even to the extent of displaying indifference towards the Church), has nothing to do with the Brethren of the Common Life. They were devout men who tried, by meditation and "rumination" to keep always before their minds the life and Passion of Christ and who directed their lives to this end. Their piety and the practice of virtues like humility, obedience, chastity and diligence demanded no aversion to the external cult and other usages or ceremonies. The external serves rather to define the inward life. The liturgy is in the first place a worship of God, but is intended also to associate the faithful inwardly with the prayers and acts and thus arouse inner piety. The contrast assumed by Spoelhof and others would imply that no inner piety existed in Christianity before the coming of the Devotio Moderna. It would even mean that one could scarcely speak of religiosity at all in the Eastern Churches, notably in the monasteries. Spoelhof's opinion assumes too that all who did not belong to the Brethren of the Common Life and who recognized the value of the external ceremony with which all churches and monasteries were filled, possessed no inner piety at all. It cannot be denied that the inner significance escaped very many and that too much emphasis was placed on outward devoation and on pilgrimage. Still less can one deny that the performance of the outward ceremonies left much to be desired. This is common to every period. One can safely assume that not all the Brethren imitated the ideals of inward piety, nor were they perpetually conscious of these ideals. Complaints of negligence at the outward ceremonies and of absentmindedness or wool-gathering at meditation are indeed means to improvement, like the repeated collation, the examination of conscience and fraternal admonition. A remarkable fact is that neither Spoelhof nor Hyma mentions that the Brethren of the Common Life began the day with the communal praying (or singing) of Matins; that they heard Mass daily and also prayed the other Hours every day, not to mention that for the canons of Windesheim, to whom H. Mande, G. Peters and Thomas a Kempis belonged, the choir prayer formed one of their principal duties. One sees how important it was for Spoelhof to associate these three as much as possible with the Brethren. And even if what he thinks of them is true, the fact remains that all three wrote their works as canons. It is thus a difficult undertaking to deduce from these particular works the assumed essential contrast between external and internal, between subjective and objective, between Brethren and Windesheimers. Besides, the nonmention of dogma is not necessarily a sign of contempt or indifference. The aim of the Imitation was the fostering of virtue, the intensification of spirituality, and not catechization. It assumes that the reader or hearer was already acquainted with the dogma as the basis of Christianity.

I shall be content, for the present, with these general considerations and refrain from taking issue on all points, for example that the organization of the Brethren and Sisters of the Common Life implies a reaction against the idea that a "religious life" can only be lived within the limits of a monastic order. 'Religious Life' in this context is an ambiguous expression. *Religio* in the Middle Ages can be synonymous with the monastic life which can, naturally, only be experienced in a monastic order. But it can also have the general meaning of a life lived in the service of God. This could formerly also be led outside the monasteries. We have, for example, the third order of Franciscans and Dominicans, and the hermits and saints who never lived in a monastery like kings Stephen and Louis. Moreover, one must be careful with the statutes of the Master Geertshuis of which we possess two versions. They were drawn up not by Geert Groote, but by the city magistrates. That the Sisters were free to leave the house as they wished and that the mistress was elected yearly, refers to a time when the house was still an "almshouse" and not a convent. As a proof of the democratic organization of the Sisters and Brethren it is valueless. The same can be said of the lay character of the Brethren. (pp. 23-8)

R. R. Post, in an introduction to The Modern Devotion: Confrontation with Reformation and Humanism, *E. J. Brill, 1968, pp. 1-49.*

Julia S. Henkel-Hobbs

[Henkel-Hobbs is an American educator and essayist. In the excerpt below, she examines the establishment, organization, and expansion of the schools run by the Brethren of the Common Life.]

The Netherlands—with its windmills and wooden shoes, its dikes and tulips—is a traditionally spirited and proud little country. It was in this picturesque land that a great religious and educational reform movement was born through the Brethren of the Common Life. Gerard Groote (1340-1384) of Deventer was the founder.

When Groote dreamed of educational reform, he envisioned it as a means of effecting religious revival. Quite naturally, then, the training of youth in a good religious way of life became the first aim in the Brethren's educational program. Other important aims were to develop in the pupils a keen intellectual life, a sound physical and moral life, and a democratic social life.

Quite obviously, these lofty objectives called for implementation. How were the Brethren to bring their goals to practical fruition? The curious mind poses questions about supervisory problems, financial arrangements, and instructional developments. It is evident that in some of these matters the Brethren educators were very much like their predecessors and contemporaries; in other ways they were unique and contributed new insights into educational organization.

We first notice the supervisory problems. When news of the remarkable achievements of the pioneer Brethren in Deventer and Zwolle was noised about and Groote's dream began to snowball into reality, the resulting growth produced for the Brotherhood an ever-increasing mass of problems concerning both buildings and pupils.

Where, for example, could schools be conducted? To this question the Brethren found an answer by utilizing various facilities. Sometimes they taught in homes, sometimes in courts, sometimes in churches, and sometimes in specially constructed educational buildings. Their situation was much like that in schools of their predecessors. Earlier, the "catechumenal" schools had met in the portico or some special portion of the church. Later, the "episcopal" or "bishop's" schools were held in church buildings.

The Brethren owed their success, in part, to their consistency in providing dormitories and Christian homes for their pupils. They built these dormitories and made certain that the Brethren in charge of them would be effective spiritual, moral, and intellectual guides. Brethren in the dormitories helped the boys with their lessons and invited them to join in the religious exercises and discussions. When existing buildings were used for instruction, alterations had to be made in order to provide for organizational divisions. Besides individual rooms for classes, there was commonly a large meeting room where the whole school could assemble for certain activities.

Often, students were housed in separate buildings according to their means; but, whenever possible, students at similar levels of learning were taught under one roof. (The Brethren's significant plan of grade division will be discussed later.) Several references can be found which indicate separate buildings or dormitories. For example, the dormitories listed for Zwolle were as follows: the "House of St. Gregory" (the building in which the Brothers themselves lived); "Domus divitum scolarium" (house for rich boys); "Domus vicina" (house next door), or "Parva domus" (smaller house); "Domus pro mediocribus" (house for boys of moderate means); and "Domus pauperum scolarium" (house for poorer boys).

Gradually, the Brethren gained control of many schools which they had not themselves organized. Frequently, city councils which observed the success and fame of the Brethren as teachers gave them control of all teaching in their schools. This was the case, for example, in Utrecht, where the Brethren had the monopoly in schools where pupils were twelve years of age or older. In 1555, the Brethren in Amersfoort also obtained control of the secondary school work—a fact not well known. Recent Dutch scholars fail to note the power exercised by the Amersfoort Brethren, assuming incorrectly that when these Brothers left their House in 1529 and joined the Augustinian Canons Regular, their school came to an end. On the contrary, their educational work continued. They had always taken care of the boys living in their dormitory, paid the rector's salary, and performed teaching duties. The Augustinian Canons in the House of St. John had no interest in this work, so the Brethren kept it up.

In many cases, the Brethren did not wait for an invitation from a city council to institute one of their schools, but went ahead, as it were, with their own "missionary work." This happened in Nijmegen, Delft, and many other cities.

It should not be assumed from the foregoing discussion that Brethren schools were simply a case of grafting new teachers and ideas upon already existing church schools or city schools. The Brethren frequently built and controlled their own buildings, and continued to do so as their educational work expanded. They had schools of their own in such cities as Ghent, Liège, Utrecht, and Rostock. Though they had no desire for personal wealth, power, or fame, they exerted great influence over the educational program in the cities they served.

Before long, the Brethren saw the wisdom of forming controlling organizations larger than simply the local House or school. This development came about quite naturally. After all, in most instances, new Houses and schools were usually "children" of already existing Brethren institutions. For example, when Zwolle became the parent of a new institution like Hulsbergen, the Zwolle Brethren felt a strong responsibility for oversight. This developed very easily into a larger organization called the Zwolle Colloquium. Such an organization also existed in Germany. The Münster Brethren were instrumental in the formation of new Houses such as those in Cologne and Rostock. (pp. 323-26)

Another supervisory problem of the Brethren involved the matter of control of the pupils themselves. The Brethren system of education was indeed organized in a way that allowed regulation of the lives of their students. In the first place, the Brethren teachers very frequently induced pupils to wear garb similar to their own. John Cele, rector at Zwolle, evidently set the example. Of him, John Busch observes that "in clothing, external manners, and conversation, he conformed in all details to Groote, Florentius [Radewijns] and the fathers of all the congregations, except in his outer garment he wore white instead of black. He induced his students to do the same." And when Nicholas of Cusa's donation of 4800 Gulden was turned over to the Brethren in Deventer in 1469, it was stated that students living in the new institution were to wear gray clothes in imitation of the Brethren. Furthermore, such practice evidently still prevailed in 1532, for in that year Martin Luther wrote a letter to the Brethren of the Common Life at Herford, praising them and stating that their dress did not injure the Gospel. (p. 326)

The Brethren were deeply concerned with the moral conduct of their pupils. Though the question of discipline will not be discussed at this point, it should here be stated that the Brethren influenced their communities to such an extent that their regulation of pupils' lives was frequently supported by civil authorities. An instance was the Amersfoort city council's prohibition, in 1562, of "clercken" (secondary school pupils of the Brethren) from lounging in places where liquor was sold.

An organizational innovation in pupil control was the Brethren's radical departure from the customary school-hour plan. Most of the elementary and secondary schools in transalpine Europe kept their pupils in school from six in the morning until four in the afternoon, with an hour for dinner. The Brethren scorned this plan and cut the school hours in half. They realized that a child's mind is dulled by weariness. Rather than spend hours on rehearsal of lessons that had never been explained, they used teaching methods designed to bring better and faster results.

The second major question to which we address ourselves concerns the financial structure of the Brethren schools. The problem of finance has always seemed to plague school administrators, and the Brethren administrators were no exception. Prior to the appearance of the schools of the Brethren of the Common Life, the cathedral schools were usually endowed by wealthy benefactors: sometimes kings, sometimes well-to-do magnates and bishops. Occasionally, even humble citizens endowed grammar schools. The Brethren, as a result of their piety, devotion, and reputation for success in teaching, were also usually able to induce benefactors to support their cause. The wealthy Henry von Ahaus was one such benefactor, and the eminent Nicholas Cardinal Cusa was another. (pp. 326-27)

In those days poor pupils often begged for their sustenance. It was against the principles of the Brethren to turn away a student because of his lack of funds, and the question now arises, did they allow such students to beg? On this point the sources disagree. Groote himself certainly disapproved of the practice. Even when some Sisters of the Common Life at Deventer lapsed into begging after Groote's death, a new rector arrived and reprimanded them severely, reminding them that it was Master Groote's express command that they should work for their sustenance and not beg. The Sisters immediately resumed their practice of industry, plus piety. But in spite of the general principle, Busch records that some of Cele's poor pupils begged for their sustenance. It is difficult to imagine how this practice could have escaped the notice of Cele and Groote. Was it, perhaps, another case in which the pupils did a commonly accepted thing and were later halted and instructed in a more excellent way by their leaders? Busch also records, it should be noted, that the master himself taught free of charge in Zwolle and even gave the students money for paper and other things for their school work.

The Brethren used a sliding tuition scale. Pupils of rich parents paid a handsome fee. Others paid less, while some did not have to pay anything. The situation was the same in the dormitories. Some paid much for their room, board, and spiritual supervision; others paid little or nothing at all.

According to the 1555 Amersfoort city council minutes, the Brethren had a tuition scale which increased with the development of the pupil. The Nullani (lowest grade) were to pay an annual tuition of twelve "stuivers" (five cents, Dutch currency); the Octani (second grade), sixteen; and those in the third grade and up, twenty-one (the highest grade was called the first, the lowest grade the ninth).

Salaries of teachers in some Amersfoort schools came partially from the municipal council, but even that stipend was supplemented by tuition. The rector decided the amount each teacher in his school would receive, based upon the teacher's ability, education, and experience. In instances where advanced pupils assisted in teaching the children of the lower grades, they usually received either small stipends or "tips," or nothing at all. Sometimes, when city control was exerted, a satisfactory salary arrangement was reached through a discussion with the prospective teacher and the municipal council. The *Quarta* grade in the Amersfoort school was to be taught by John van Nuys, and his salary was to be fifty Carolingian florins (gulden), which amount was to come from city council funds. A number of other teachers' salaries were also mentioned in the minutes, all cared for from a total amount set aside by the council.

The cost of buildings was handled in various ways. Sometimes, as we have seen, Brethren taught in buildings which existed before their arrival upon the scene. Even in these instances, however, new buildings were added as the schools grew. These were usually financed by either a wealthy patron or community help. When Brethren started schools of their own without an invitation or offer of help from people in a given community, the Brethren themselves worked to bring the buildings into existence. Sources reveal cases of extreme poverty and self-sacrifice—even to the point of death in certain cases. As a rule, however, Brethren schools and Brethren teachers were not destitute. Cele, for example, made a great deal of money through his school. To amass wealth for himself was against his principles, though, so with this money he built an excellent library in the church of St. Michael at Zwolle.

Our third general area of consideration is the crucial matter of instructional developments. Our treatment of these developments will include discussion of equipment, levels of instruction, and organization for instruction.

Portrait by Holbein of Johan Froben, an important Renaissance publisher who printed several of Erasmus's works.

At first, the Brethren and their pupils made extensive use of traditional equipment such as writing boards, pens, and paper. The students amassed great quantities of personal notes from their lectures and studies, and the notes were, in turn, organized into books called *rapiaria.* The use of visual aids furnishes an interesting subject in this area of equipment. A fact seldom mentioned is Erasmus' early understanding of the value of such aids. It is known that the Brethren utilized maps and illustrations, but the extent to which they employed Erasmus' suggestion for visual aids in their later years has never been fully explored.

Instruction not only on the elementary level but also on the secondary was fairly widespread in the period of developed medieval culture. Hence, it is not unusual to find that the Brethren of the Common Life were interested in both levels. Because of the development of their eight-grade plan, the impression could be gained that all of the educational work of the Brethren was centered upon what we today call the elementary school. However, sources indicate clearly that secondary-school education was indeed a concern of theirs. In fact, before 1500 the Brethren provided middle or secondary training in a number of places. Their schools in Zwolle and Liège were particularly large establishments. And in the best of these schools, the upper forms did work quite comparable to that of the faculty of arts in a contemporary university.

The notices in the minutes of the city council of Amersfoort also indicate the Brethren's serious interest in secondary school education. The word "clercken," as distinguished from "school-kinderen" (school children) refers to those students in the higher grades who were associated with the Brethren. The Brothers provided room and board for about 200 high-school students in Amersfoort.

It should also be remembered that in Utrecht the city council gave the Brethren the monopoly of all teaching in schools where pupils of twelve or older attended. In fact, a study of the school of Jerome in Utrecht indicates that the Brotherhood became a tremendous force in the field of secondary education. (pp. 327-30)

Perhaps the Brethren's most important innovation in the field of education was their organizational plan for grade division. This idea apparently originated with John Cele at Zwolle, though it probably will never be known if this concept was part of the educational reform vision committed to Cele by Groote. The grade-division concept practiced in schools today frequently is attributed to John Sturm. Later in the chapter, we will show that Sturm himself claimed no originality, but simply stated that his idea was that of the Brethren of the Common Life. (pp. 330-31)

Cele divided the Zwolle school into eight grades. He appointed the best students in the first class (eighth grade) to assist in teaching the lowest six grades and to conduct examinations in those grades. Specialists—university men with Master's degrees—were in charge of the two highest grades. This plan became a pattern and was carried out in Deventer and successive schools operated by Brethren teachers. The development had an added feature in that it made possible the inclusion of the quadrivium as well as the trivium in the curriculum. Moreover, it also made possible the incorporation of more advanced studies for the two highest grades. Sources indicate that in Deventer during Hegius' time, Latin, Greek, and simple elements of Hebrew were part of the program.

The extreme size of some of the schools resulted in exceptionally large numbers of pupils in each grade. Busch, who was in charge of the fifth class (fourth grade) in Cele's school, had sixty to eighty pupils and taught them grammar and logic.

It has been conjectured that students in a particular grade were sometimes divided into smaller study groups. The main type of evidence which points in this direction is the fact that more teachers than grades are recorded for certain schools. For example, Cele and three university men with Master's degrees taught in the two highest grades in Zwolle. Records of other schools also bear out this same probability. The small study-group idea may be a forerunner of the famous "Lancaster Plan."

An attempt to trace the spread of this organizational plan provides an exciting venture. A first path to follow is the one which leads to the famous German educator, John Sturm. Earlier, we made mention of the nine-grade system in the school at Amersfoort. This was exactly the plan which Sturm introduced in the city of Strasbourg. His work "involved the amalgamation of five previously existing schools and their reduction to one." He borrowed his organizational plan from the Brethren of the Common Life in Liège. The Liège teachers, in turn, had received their instruction from the 's-Hertogenbosch Brethren, who were the founders of the House in Liège.

When Sturm outlined the plan for his gymnasium to the city magistrates, he acknowledged it as being that of the Brethren of Deventer and Zwolle which he had observed in Liège. The innovation was the eight-grade system with a well-defined curriculum for each grade. The ninth grade was a sort of appendix. This system spread all over Germany, and later the idea was carried to American schools.

Sturm's assistant in Strasburg from 1539 to 1541 was John Calvin, who returned once again to that city in 1556, to study the development of the secondary school there. Calvin, in the school he founded in Geneva in 1559, imitated Sturm, but reduced the amount of classical literature and increased the amount of Biblical instruction. In this regard, he more closely approximated the method of the Brothers in Liège. Calvin also decided to have seven grades, whereas Sturm had nine and Cele had had eight. (pp. 331-33)

It is also possible to trace some links between the Brethren of the Common Life and the schools of the Jesuits. When John Sturm visited a Jesuit school in Dillingen in the lower Rhine valley some 22 years after the founding of his own gymnasium in Strasbourg, he was amazed at the similarities it bore to his school. He decided that the Jesuits must have copied from him—an opinion which has often been expressed by later educators, though the theory has never been proved. It must be remembered that Ignatius Loyola and his successors worked for many years to perfect their educational plan. It must also be remembered that Loyola, like Erasmus, was at one time a student at the College of Montaigu in Paris, where both men were influenced by the work of Jean Standonck, a disciple of the Brethren of the Common Life at Gouda. It is true that when Ignatius compared Thomas à Kempis' *Imitation* with Erasmus' *Enchiridion,* he greatly preferred the *Imitation;* but it must, nevertheless, be borne in mind that both books owed their origin to the Brethren of the Common Life.

In 1584 six Jesuits were called to Rome by Aquaviva, the fifth general of the Order. These men studied everything they could find on methods and administration of education. Then, in the light of their experiences in the Society of Jesus and the insights gained from their special study, they presented the first draft of the *Ratio atque institutio studiorum Societatis Jesu* in August, 1585. Revisions followed and the final plan of studies was published in 1599.

The Jesuits never claimed great originality, but they firmly believed that their plan represented the best educational practice of the day. And on one occasion, Miraeus, a Belgian Jesuit, wrote, "For does not the Society of Jesus, in imitation of the Brethren, open schools throughout the whole world?"

This relationship between the educational work of the

Brethren of the Common Life and that of the Jesuits is not a new concept. [In his *History of Education* (1929)] Paul Monroe, for example, after considering the work of the Brethren, states that "the work and the constitution of this order furnished the chief source of suggestion for the organization of the Jesuit schools, which by the latter half of the sixteenth century superseded those of the 'scholarly brethren,' as the Hieronymians were called." (pp. 333-34)

This inquiry into the organizational patterns of the schools of the Brethren of the Common Life has indicated that although the Brethren were like their predecessors and contemporaries in many ways, they also contributed new ideas to educational work. They recognized that dormitory supervisors could give educational, moral, and religious help to students. They decided to shorten the school day by explaining lessons before drilling, a procedure which reduced student weariness, heightened interest, and capitalized upon learning efficiency. They saw value in teaching students at their own levels and in smaller groups. And lastly, in this same connection, the Brethren developed a grade plan which caught fire and which continued to spread long after their own movement died out. (pp. 336-37)

Julia S. Henkel-Hobbs, "School Organizational Patterns of the Brethren of the Common Life," in The Dawn of Modern Civilization: Studies in Renaissance Reformation and Other Topics Presented to Honor Albert Hyma, *edited by Kenneth A. Strand, Ann Arbor Publishers, 1962, pp. 323-38.*

R. R. Post

[In the excerpt below, Post traces the history of the humanistic educational reform carried out by the Brethren of the Common Life, focusing on the school at Liège.]

During [the mid-fifteenth century] the Devotionalists, and notably the Brethren, were confronted with new and considerable problems. In the first place there was the effect of the art of printing, invented and practised by John Gutenberg in Mainz, between 1450 and 1465. Printing works sprang up in various towns, principally those in which there was a flourishing school, and thus logically, where the Brethren had their houses and hostels. In the early days these printers, who were at the same time publishers, concentrated on school books and religious literature, for which there was evidently considerable demand. It is unlikely that the Brethren and canons were immediately aware of the possible threat to their own work of copying. In the first place they usually worked to order, their main output being fine editions. Moreover, the demand for books probably kept pace with production. But competition did exist and increase and it must soon have been obvious to the Brethren that they stood to lose a great deal of their income from the copying of books. Specialization and change were indicated, not only in order to maintain their income level, but also in order to find suitable hand work for the Brethren, for this was considered essential if the balance of their religious life was to be preserved. It is therefore not surprising that they too set up printing works and began to print books. They were, in this, merely continuing their original work in a new form. Their activity in this field, however, was not impressive. So far as I can judge, only the Brothers of Brussels, Gouda, and 's-Hertogenbosch in the Netherlands, and Marienthal and Rostock in Germany, seized upon this method of circulating books. The most important printing office set up by the Brothers was undoubtedly the Brotherhouse of Brussels, which began in 1475 already with a small work in the Dutch language and in 1476 produced a legend of Henry II and Kunigund. They also published breviaries, letters of indulgence, homilies and exegetic and apologetic works, besides the letters and sermons of St. Bernard, the *collationes* of Cassian, and the *Vitae Patrum.* This printing office, however, seems only to have survived for about ten years. (pp. 551-52)

From the scarce data available, which might perhaps be supplemented by experts, it appears that the Brothers laboured modestly, but to good purpose, in this new branch, which may be considered as a continuation of their copying work. However, in comparison with the extensive production of the great printing works in Deventer, Antwerp, Louvain, Zwolle and Gouda, which were in lay hands, the production of the Brethren appears quite insignificant. These lay printers also published ecclesiastical, pious, theological and patristic works but in addition produced numerous classics, school books, commentaries on the classics and *humanistica.*

In this field too, the *fraters* revealed themselves as anything but pioneers, and remained far behind the lay printers. The old and famous houses of Deventer and Zwolle and very many others did not venture into printing at all. Another remarkable fact is that the Brothers printed nothing of the authors of the Modern Devotion. Two works by the Zwolle rector Dirk of Herxen appeared very early, but not with the Brothers. The *Devota exercitia* was published by Richard Paffroet in Deventer and the *Speculum juvenum* by John Vollenhove in Zwolle. The sermons of Thomas a Kempis were printed by Nicolas Ketelaar in Utrecht. On the other hand, the printing of the Bible of Emser at Rostock showed courage, conviction and a spirit of enterprise.

A more important enterprise, from our point of view, was the Brothers' attempt to extend their teaching activities among the school-boys either by setting up schools themselves, replacing the purely supervisory work in their hostels by formal school teaching, or by allowing the Brethren to teach in the city schools. Their good relations with various rectors seemed to offer them fair prospects. However, they already knew from experience that those who held the school rights, usually the city magistrate but sometimes the *scholaster,* clung firmly to these rights, mostly on behalf of the city school and for the benefit of the school rector. They were above all anxious that the school fees should be reserved for the rector and teachers. There were already some indications that the Brothers wished to branch out in this direction. We shall now attempt to discover in how far they succeeded. The sporadic activities of the *fraters* in the preceding period, up to around 1485, were without significance.

Now too the Modern Devotionalists and in particular the *fraters* were confronted with the new cultural trend, Humanism, which towards the end of the preceding period, around 1480, reached those places in which the Brothers had their houses, both in the Netherlands and in the towns situated deeper within the German Empire. Although this new culture manifested itself in various fields, political, ecclesiastical and religious, during this first period it was chiefly active in the domain of the school, advocating better teaching and education in the city and parochial schools as well as in the universities. . . . [Several present day critics] argue that several of the first Humanists in Germany and the Netherlands attended schools run by the Brethren of the Common Life where they acquired the first principles of this new way of thinking. It is hence of considerable interest to determine the position of the Brethren in the culture of the time, especially with regard to teaching.

Finally, in the 16th century, the Devotionalists were also faced with the Reformation, which from 1517 onwards spread over the entire region where they had their houses and monasteries. The Reformation period was virtually the end of the Modern Devotion, although a few monasteries and some of the Brotherhouses survived this difficult time. They lost their driving force, their desire for expansion, their propagandist spirit, and, to a certain extent, their original character. Did they, or many of them, adopt the ideas of the Reformation? Were they obliged to bow to superior forces? Or were their ideals no longer suited to the changing state of affairs. An answer to these questions must be sought in the facts which will be dealt with in this [discussion].

One of the main difficulties, however, is the absence of the house chronicles which provided some insight into the life of the Brothers during the preceding period. Those of the Brother houses at Zwolle, Deventer, Gouda, Emmerich and Hildesheim covered the period up to about 1485, 1490. The Hildesheim annals went a little further, but the reports of the years 1493 to 1505 are very brief. Only 1546 is covered in detail. Fortunately, the still unpublished chronicle of Doesburg covers the middle of the 16th century and provides important information concerning the attitude of the Brethren towards the Reformation. This loss of documentation on the abovementioned houses, however, is counterbalanced by the gain of certain annalistic notes from the house of Wolf on the Moselle, which, as we saw, was founded at the end of the preceding period. Valuable documents, such as charters, have been preserved from other houses, and these inform us whether any change took place in the aims and methods of the Brethren, and if so, what these changes were. None the less there remain several Brotherhouses of which we know little or nothing. The religious, usually ascetic, treatises of the *fraters* came to an end even earlier than the historical works, with the exception of the sermons of people like John Veghe. In their place we have a number of 16th century publications of a completely different nature, and characteristic of the change, in two houses at least. Before going any deeper into the history of the Brethren and the Brotherhouses in the sixteenth century, we must bear in mind that several of the Brotherhouses had developed into canon-chapters, in other words, colleges which served a so-called collegiate or chapter church. In consequence the Brothers of these houses had become canons with communal possession. So far as we can judge, this transformation took place in the majority of the houses, not perhaps the house at Amersfoort, but probably in those of 's-Hertogenbosch, Brussels, Ghent, Geraardsbergen, Cassel and Magdeburg, and certainly in Hildesheim, Münster, Cologne, Herford, Wesel, Marienthal, Königstein, Butzbach, Wolf, Urach, Herrenberg, Dettingen, Einsiedel and Marburg. Yet if, as we saw, the results of this change were chiefly juridical, it cannot be denied that the choir prayers which the Brothers already had, now received particular emphasis. This facilitated any future transformation of such canons into secular vicars or canons enjoying their own income. And, although men like Gabriel Biel praised such foundations and recommended them, from the Brothers' point of view this change appeared to signal a decline of the old spirit, a fading of the old ideal.

One sign of this weakening towards the beginning of this period is that there was no longer such an urge to expand. During this time only two new houses were founded, and one of these, that of Liège, really belonged to the transitional period. The second house, in Trèves, also displayed a distinctive character. The foundation in Liège, however, was a great success, and showed signs of being in tune with the times. The plan to found the house was conceived by bishop John of Hoorn and the city magistrate. They contacted the Brothers in 's-Hertogenbosch and invited them to begin a new Brotherhouse in Liège. It was an attractive offer, since the *fraters* were able to find immediate lodgings in the existing priory of Mary Magdalen, while the magistrate proposed to build the Brothers a church with hostel on the island in the Maas. Since this was situated in the middle of the city, the Brothers could use it as a centre to practise their normal pastoral duties. The *fraters* from 's-Hertogenbosch accordingly sent four of their Brothers to Liège and these took up residence in the priory of Mary Magdalen on June 26th 1496. The first stone for the church was laid on May 27th, 1497, but it was not consecrated until January 21st 1509. The new house was ready for occupation by rector and *fraters* in 1497. They began by taking the boys into their own house, but later placed them in a separate hostel which is mentioned in 1501. It was intended for the poor boys who attended the school. They had already received permission for this from the chapter in 1499. The school situation in Liège, where not only the parish, but also the chapter churches, had their own school, allowed more instruction to be given in this hostel than in those of other cities. Elsewhere, the one school enjoyed sole rights in teaching Latin, and this privilege was jealously preserved by the municipality, by force of law where necessary. Private schools were sometimes tolerated on condition that the pupils also paid school fees to the rector of the big school. In towns like Utrecht, Maastricht, and even Amsterdam and Groningen, where there was more than one parish church, the suppression of the private schools was rendered more difficult, or even impossible. It was thus easier for the Liège *fraters,* like those in Utrecht and Groningen, to give more instruction in their hostels than in Deventer or Zwolle, where the one old city school (or chapter school) carefully preserved its ancient rights. However, the fact that several Latin schools existed in one city, as for example in Utrecht and Liège, had the fatal effect of limiting the development of all the schools equally. The number of pupils was too small to attract several teachers, so that one man was usually responsible for the entire educational programme. This seems to have been tolerated in the Middle Ages, but it was scarcely feasible in the sixteenth century when the Humanists were advocating better and broader education. In actual fact the city authorities did take steps to achieve one large Latin school, either by amalgamating the existing schools or by forbidding the other schools to take Latin any further than the first principles and exercises. The real teaching of the classical language was to be reserved for one particular school. (pp. 553-57)

[In Liège], around 1500, the *fratres* began a school, probably in the hostel. In describing the history of the Brethren in Liège one must always take into account the three foundations for which they were responsible: their own dwelling house and chapel under the direction of the *pater,* also known as the rector; the *domus pauperum* under its own rector, sometimes called procurator, and on occasion also coming directly under the jurisdiction of the rector of the dwelling house; and finally the school, run by another person who also bore the title of rector. Naturally enough this school took time to gain a reputation. It had to compete against the various chapter and parish schools, and was of no great significance before 1515. In 1515, however, this school possessed a brilliant teacher in the secular priest Nicolas Nickman. Through his influence perhaps, and in any case before September 9th, 1515, an important change must have taken place. This is revealed by a decree of this date, whereby Liège was proposed as model for the suggested plans of Maastricht described above. This change amounted to the *fraters'* school being recognized henceforth as the one main school in Liège, and as such being supported by the municipality. This meant that the Latin schools of the Liège chapters and parishes were curtailed in some way or another, as would happen in Maastricht. This is made clear by John Sturm, who went to school in Liège from 1521 to 1524. When, twenty years later, he was called upon to organize the educational system in Strasbourg, he took as his model the school position in Liège as he had known it in his youth. This we know from a document dated February 24th 1538. It was necessary, in his opinion, to decide on having only one Latin school in the city. He based his opinion on the experiences in Liège, Deventer, Zwolle and Wesel. As he remarked in a marginal note this should succeed well in Strasbourg, since the city was smaller than Liège. This limiting of the number of schools to one must have been introduced before Sturm's arrival in Liège since, as he says, a reaction began during his stay there. Some of the teachers of the school began to give lessons on their own account. If this initiative had succeeded, it would have meant the end of the "Hieronymitanum Gymnasium". "For if each teacher attempts to acquire pupils, they learn not what is useful but what is pleasant, and adapt themselves more to the demand than to the understanding of their audience." This statement is also important since it makes clear that not all the teachers of this one new school were members of the Fraternity. No one *frater* could have started a school entirely at his own risk. Fortunately, this difference of opinion was settled so that the school was able to go forward. Sturm reviews the subjects taught in the eight classes. These do not differ essentially from what we know of other schools. With a few exceptions the curriculum is the same as in the medieval schools. The most important difference is that the boys learn reading and writing in the lowest class, with the declension of nouns and the conjugation of verbs. There were several other places in which the boys could learn these subjects at school—the so-called writing schools—so that the gymnasium really began with the seventh class and then consisted of five classes, like the five which Erasmus completed in Deventer. Then came the two top classes, which were rare, but which did exist in Zwolle and Deventer. As we shall see, these classes offered different subjects. Two new subjects—Greek and rhetoric—were added to the normal curriculum of the medieval school. The Humanists were responsible for this innovation. The introduction of these new subjects meant that the teaching of dialectic suffered—it was relegated from the fifth to the fourth class—but Sturm adds that this subject and rhetoric were only touched upon in the fifth class (*indicabantur*). Greek and rhetoric continue to form part of the curriculum up to and including the second class (the first of the two top classes) together with philosophy (Aristotle, Plato), Geometry (Euclid) and even law. Some theology was given in Liège in the first (or highest) class, but this is found nowhere else. Each class has a separate teacher, who sometimes has to cope with 200 pupils, but this is not uncommon in the Middle Ages. What is new is that the second and first classes were required to have more than one teacher—the introduction of specialization. The pupils of the two classes were combined for some subjects—which again promoted specialization. (pp. 558-59)

Two questions arise in this connection. Were the *fratres* themselves responsible for enlarging the curriculum by the addition of Greek and rhetoric, for cutting down on dialectics, for the reading of certain classical authors and for the introduction of the two top classes? Or was the influence of the Humanist school requirements already so great around 1515 that the Brothers simply adopted what had already been introduced in several places? Sturm unfortunately only mentions those authors read in the two top classes, and these were either philosophers or mathematicians, who offer little material for comparison. Nor do we know anything about the kind of Latin taught, about the grammars and other school books or even about the method of teaching.

The second question is: Did the *fraters* take the classes, or at least the majority of them, in their own school themselves, or did they leave the teaching to assistants from outside, while continuing to run the school as their fellow Brethren in Brussels had done, and as the Brothers in Utrecht later did with the Hieronymus-school. Did they find their rector and teachers inside or outside their community? If they taught themselves, had they received the necessary training? Had they received their Master's degree from the Arts faculty of a university, as had most of the other teachers, at least those of the top classes?

It is plain that the Liège *fraters* were not the first or the only ones to aim at an educational reform, employing such means as the addition of Greek and *eloquentia* to the curriculum. This movement towards reform had been in progress for some time now in the south of Europe, and had already achieved results in certain city schools. From around 1485 onwards some of the Dutch Humanists passed themselves off as reformers in the world of education, or, if they were not actually concerned with teaching, as the champions of new ideas in this field. Even before the Liège school reform, that is, before 1517, Rudolf Agricola, Desiderius Erasmus and Alexander Hegius were writing treatises and schoolbooks, as were others throughout the German Empire. Their main theme was the reform of instruction in the Latin language, by improving and simplifying the grammar and by reading classical authors in order to imitate their style. In addition several advocated the introduction of what they called *eloquentia,* by which they understood facility of language in conversation, correspondence and delivery. The first Humanists saw in the use of elegant language and a polished style (*eloquentia*) a means of improving both Church and society. Unfortunately there is nothing to confirm that this *eloquentia* was introduced as a separate subject in Dutch schools before 1517. Nor does this appear necessary, for as Paulsen says: "Eloquenz und zwar zunächst in lateinischer Sprache, ist das erste Ziel der gelehrten Unterrichts, die Nachahnung der alten Schriftsteller das wesentliche Mittel." Greek, however, was an entirely new subject in these parts and at the outset a knowledge of this language was not very common among the teaching personnel. . . . The programme with which J. Sturm was personally familiar from his school years 1521-24 is exactly appropriate to the period. It is not an invention on the part of the Brothers but an adaptation of the ideas prevalent at that time in the world of education, which many desired to see put into practice. It was an important step to take and one which did credit to Liège, but it was not the realization of a creative spirit. The *fraters* were merely practising what the Humanists had been preaching for the past thirty or forty years. Their work may still have been considered progressive around 1520, but they were certainly not pioneers. (pp. 560-62)

R. R. Post, "The Brethren of the Common Life after ca. 1485," in his The Modern Devotion: Confrontation with Reformation and Humanism, *E. J. Brill, 1968, pp. 551-631.*

Richard L. DeMolen

[*DeMolen is an American educator and scholar who has written widely on the Middle Ages, the Reformation, and Erasmus. In the excerpt below, he introduces the Renaissance concept of the* Devotio Moderna *and examines the impact of humanism on the beginning of the Reformation.*]

Transalpine Europe's union of two apparently immiscible currents, humanism and the *Devotio Moderna,* began the development of Christian humanism, an intellectual movement which became the salient characteristic of the Northern Renaissance. Typified by Erasmus of Rotterdam, Christian humanists were literate, scholarly optimists who foresaw human perfection as man's ultimate earthly reward for following their simple set of recommendations. Beneath the aura of humanist optimism, however, lay pockets of pessimism. Religious unrest was widespread. It became increasingly intense in the second decade of the sixteenth century when, having found in Martin Luther its eloquent leader, it burst forth in full fury as the Reformation. Significantly, the cause of irritation was the same species of church corruption which had predicated the *Devotio Moderna.*

The *Devotio Moderna* was "spontaneously" generated by Christianity's predilection for self-purification. Beginning with the life's work of Gerard Groote, it grew into a multifaceted religious reform which sought to cast off the church's corruption through a return to primitive simplicity. Geographically centered on the River Yssel, the movement's influence spread throughout the Low Countries and Germany. Groote's "present day devotion" derived broad but simple principles from the Bible, early Christian manuscripts, and the teachings of selected medieval theologians. After Groote's death the work of the *Devotio Moderna* was continued by his protégé, Florentius Radewijns, and was embraced by three religious orders, the most notable of which was the Brethren of the Common Life.

The Brethren, a semimonastic brotherhood, strove to inspire clerical and church reform through the practice of virtue. Their "imitation of Christ" entailed a life of sacrifice, study, and labor. The Brothers lived primarily in the cities, where they supported themselves and simultaneously spread Christ's word by transcribing manuscripts, counseling, and teaching.

Humanism and the *Devotio Moderna* shared many ideas. Both emphasized simplicity and attempted to educate the young. The limited disdain with which the *Devotio Moderna* viewed the papal court and scholastic theologians was in keeping with humanist standards. Where they were not in full agreement, their divergent beliefs were often complementary. The humanist ideal of moral perfection was especially well-suited to adaptation by men who believed in free will.

The actual union of these two currents can be seen best in the work of Desiderius Erasmus, the foremost representative of Christian humanism. Erasmus was educated in the *Devotio Moderna* and early in life became a monk. He seemed destined for the cloistered cell. While pursuing his priestly studies, however, Erasmus read classical Latin texts which, through their tone and beautiful language, stimulated a life-long interest in the ancients. Ultimately, he exchanged the cowl for the laurel.

Christian humanism remained the demesne of the literate few. To the majority of Europeans, the ideal of human perfectibility must have sounded absurd. Nevertheless, the problems that humanism identified in the church were thought by many people to be signs of intrinsic corruption, requiring a fundamental change in church structure. When Martin Luther, who was in many ways thoroughly orthodox in outlook, began to articulate the feelings of dissatisfied people, a following developed. The protest movement that started with Luther would soon reach such intensity that it would fragment the church and destroy that hallowed concept of a one, holy, catholic, and apostolic church.

When humanism and the *Devotio Moderna* combined in northern Europe, they built a façade of optimism atop an unsound foundation of corrupt Christianity. The Christian humanism which grew out of the union of these two movements held forth perfection as a goal and simplicity as its panacea. Thus the Northern Renaissance, in a brief celebration of anticipated triumph, was played out in the shadow of the impending catastrophe of the Reformation. Indeed, the movement was so premature that a conservative reaction seemed inevitable. When the reaction came, it was passionate, violent, and tragic. (pp. 14-16)

The Protestant Reformation of the early sixteenth century was a reaction against the inconsistency in the ideals of Christianity and in the actual organization of the church and the practices of its members. Dissatisfaction with Catholicism was rooted in the court and the printing press. Political and economic conditions also facilitated the emergence of new Christian sects by predisposing countries to accepting religious change. The major reform movements—Lutheranism, Zwinglianism, Calvinism, and Anglicanism—enacted desired changes by revising the elements of Catholic doctrine that were subject to criticism. The Protestant movement, given direction by Martin Luther, was thus both a cause and an effect in the long chain of events which determined Europe's development during the sixteenth and seventeenth centuries, and the roots of that movement could be discerned in embryonic form long before the advent of Lutheranism.

The background of the Protestant Reformation involves religious, intellectual and political-economic trends which stimulated its development. For instance, there were many religious movements predating the Reformation spirit, including the Lollards, the Waldensians, and the Hussites—all heretical sects which preached "protestant" ideas. As early as the fourteenth century, the structure of the church was weakened by the Great Schism and the Babylonian Captivity. Without an effectively united papacy, abuses crept easily into church organization. Anti-clericalism derived from antagonism to the worldliness and immorality of the clergy, to their having lost contact with church members, and to the degrading educational status of rural priests. Two severely criticized abuses were the sale of spiritual offices (simony) and the sale of indulgences. Another source of dissatisfaction was the intervention of canon law in state issues: the church made a practice of selling religious dispensations for marriage or for the holding of benefices, and these dispensations exempted the buyer from certain civil laws. Heterodox feelings ultimately emerged from the specious practices of clergy and the questionable ethical and theological basis of papal prerogatives.

Many intellectual influences that incited religious discontent originated during the Renaissance. The critical spirit of humanism encouraged a return to first-century Christianity and to Christian idealism. Textual criticism was another facet of the critical spirit that anticipated Protestant thought. For instance, Lorenzo Valla, by uncovering as a forgery the Donation of Constantine, which sanctioned the Papal States of Italy with the pope as secular head, indirectly undermined papal supremacy. The techniques of the critical spirit provided an awareness of the need for reform by articulating inconsistencies within the church.

Advanced communications media, as by-products of the Renaissance spirit, were also instrumental in the development of the Reformation movements. Printing, implemented by engravings, had a profound importance as a vehicle of communication. By advertising their beliefs in the vernacular, religious movements made these beliefs accessible to both the aristocracy and the common people. Universities, often the centers of radical thought, became important catalysts, in that they furnished a sympathetic climate for the introduction of religious change.

The critical spirit of humanism, the development of printing techniques, and the university atmosphere provided a foundation for reform movements. Political and economic trends further precipitated the imminence of the Reformation. By encouraging national and secular loyalties, European monarchs were in effect exploiting reform movements as a way of diverting allegiances and of strengthening their own power. They were jealous of the income which was derived from papal taxation and naturally sought this revenue for their own purposes.

Discontent with a deteriorating church and a confused political-economic situation, operating within the framework of humanistic awareness, served as the breeding ground for vanguard reform movements: Lutheranism flourished in Germany and Scandinavia; Zwinglianism affected religious thought in Switzerland; Calvinism, more internationally appealing, was significant not only in Switzerland, but in France, Scotland, Poland, and Hungary as well; and Anglicanism developed its own brand of Protestantism in England. By 1520, Western Europe was ripe for reform, and a measure of its success, in succeeding decades, lay in the premature efforts of the past.

The Middle Ages and the Renaissance had bequeathed to the Age of Reformation such compelling influences as the Hussites in Bohemia and Moravia, the Lollards in England, and the Waldensians in Savoy and Piedmont; the mysticism of the *Devotio Moderna,* which culminated in Thomas à Kempis' *Imitation of Christ* and necessarily affected religious thinkers; France and England's anti-papal and Erastian reactions against the inordinate power and wealth wielded by churchmen; a divided Germany, politically helpless before the excessive clerical extortions levied upon the German peoples; a new biblical theology based on humanist scholarship which was replacing philosophical theology and supplying a new intellectual framework for the coming Reformation; Sigur de Brabant's double standard of truth that disputed philosophy's ability to confirm or deny the data of revealed religion and sharply divided reason from faith; a holy Roman See busily using church funds for its own self-aggrandizement and selling indulgences like a "salvation assurance company"; an increasingly impersonal ecclesiastical authority spiritually separated from the clergy and people; Erasmian rejection of the pomp and circumstance of the Catholic Church and Erasmus' desire to return to early Christianity and its simple affirmation of faith; new secular allegiances fostered by the economic and cultural vitality of growing towns and cities, the founding of new universities, and the rapid rise of book production. In view of this turbulent political, social, and intellectual background, the Reformation easily explains itself. (pp. 16-18)

Richard L. DeMolen, "The Age of Renaissance and Reformation," in The Meaning of the Renaissance and Reformation, *edited by Richard L. DeMolen, Houghton Mifflin Company, 1973, pp. 1-25.*

Margaret E. Aston

[*In the excerpt below, Aston considers the educational and spiritual influence of the* Devotio Moderna *and the Brothers of the Common Life.*]

The spiritual, as opposed to the intellectual, beginnings of the movement we are considering must take us back to the late fourteenth century. At this time when, after long years of papal absence from Rome, the contested election of 1378 opened a lengthy period of schism, the voices of nothern Christians—admonitory, heretical, quietistic, or simply pious—seemed to take on an independent note of their own, as they called their spiritual leaders to task or sought for other means of religious regeneration. The same critical period that saw St. Catherine of Siena multiplying her appeals for reform, John Wycliffe moving towards a more extreme doctrinal position, and John Gerson formulating his views of conciliar authority, produced the beginnings of a movement which drew upon and replenished the springs of piety in northern Europe for many years to come. This is the movement already known in the fifteenth century as the *Devotio Moderna,* the most famous branch of which is the Brothers of the Common Life.

The two starting-points of the *Devotio Moderna* indicate the two directions in which, in the following century, it was to extend its influence. In 1374 Gerard Groote (1340-84), who had abandoned an academic career in Paris to take up a life of evangelical preaching, turned his house in Deventer into a hostel for a group of pious women. According to the constitution he drew up five years later, they were to live a communal life, sharing work and expenses, bound by no obligations of vows, and free to depart as they wished. After Groote's death, his friend and disciple Florence Radewijns (c.1350-1400) brought to completion in 1387 the foundation at Windesheim of a monastery which Groote had inspired and which was, according to his wish, placed under the rule of the Augustinian canons.

From these simple but inspiring beginnings flowed two currents of vitalizing influence upon contemporary religion. One, more conventional but answering a widely-felt need of the time, was a response to the problem—which became more urgent as the fifteenth century proceeded—of how existing institutions could be made to answer the ancient Christian call to an ascetic monastic life. Groote and his followers were far from alone in recognizing this need, but the foundation at Windesheim proved particularly capable of meeting it, and grew into a congregation of houses, linked with the first in spiritual observance and a dedicated monastic life. Although there are signs that by the end of the fifteenth century the movement had lost some of the freshness of its first years and was succumbing to some of the less worthy aspects of contemporary monasticism, the Windesheim Congregation was still a regenerating source. In the 1490s, when French reformers were anxious to improve the houses of Château-Landon in the diocese of Sens and Saint Victor in Paris, it was to Windesheim that they looked for help. A prominent part in these moves was taken by Jean Standonck, whose dietetic stringencies were criticized as well as suffered by some of those (including Erasmus) who experienced the harshness of the reformed regime he had introduced at the Collège de Montaigu in Paris. Standonck was deeply affected by the spirit of the *Devotio Moderna.* It was he who went to Windesheim to seek help for Chàteau-Landon, as the result of which a mission of six men was sent to France. They included Jean Mombaer (c. 1460-1501), whose *Rosary of Spiritual Exercises* influenced Ignatius Loyola.

The other, related part of Groote's movement, keeping to the pattern of his first house of sisters and the groups of his immediate followers at Deventer and Zwolle, remained unattached to any existing order. These Brothers and Sisters of the Common Life joined together in the pursuit of a common devotional life which participated in the monastic ideal but imitated it without the formalities of vows or religious habits, and without any life-commitment to their profession. Like the first women who came together in Groote's house, they were at liberty to return to ordinary secular life. In these ways they were clearly distinguished from the established orders, with whom, however, they were linked through the Windesheim foundation, and to which they contributed members.

The Brothers of the Common Life also concentrated their activities toward specific ends, notably educational ones. Their common labor before the days of printing was, in particular, the copying of books, and they were also—though here their achievement has been exaggerated—closely associated with the great expansion of education which took place in Germany and the Low Countries in the fifteenth century. They became influential, and affected the lives of many devout and perhaps disillusioned people, because they answered a great need of the period. They helped to provide for the growing educational demands—of laymen, as well as those who intended to enter the church—in the greater urban centers. And, in times of religious uncertainty and ecclesiastical dislocation, they offered methods of spiritual consolation, islands of contemplative security accessible to any reader who would take as his spiritual weapon a book. The aims were not grandiose, but the results were very impressive. The achievement of the *Devotio Moderna* was not that of a network of schools and teachers—as it has sometimes been made to appear—but that of a less easily definable geneaology of spiritual inspiration, which was carried by individuals and books as well as through continuing institutions.

It is necessary to make clear this distinction between the educational and spiritual influence of the Brothers of the Common Life, since their work in the former sphere seems to have been misunderstood. The Brothers were undoubtedly much concerned with the educational needs of their time, but it is a mistake to think of them as having had a revolutionary impact upon contemporary education. The extent of their teaching was less far-reaching, and the methods they employed less innovative, than has often been supposed. The Brothers were not in the first instance, or ever primarily, schoolmasters, and several of the more celebrated schools with which their name has been linked (such as the chapter school at Deventer, or the city school at Zwolle) cannot be said to have belonged to them or been under their direction. These schools existed before the Brothers were founded, and though John Cele (1350-1417), the famous rector of Zwolle, was in close communication with Groote, he was not a member of the Brotherhood. The Brothers' calling was neither scholarship nor teaching, and indeed both these activities might have been felt to conflict with their pious preoccupations.

From the outset, however, members of the movement devoted themselves to the needs, both material and spiritual, of the increasing numbers of boys who came to be schooled in the towns and cities of the Low Countries. The hostels which they founded to board these schoolboys were in some cases able to provide tuition or guidance for individual pupils, as for instance 's Hertogenbosch did for the youthful Erasmus, who by the time he got there had probably completed all the classes of the school at Deventer. In general, however, what the Brothers offered was spiritual guidance rather than teaching; they were spiritual mentors and confessors more than they were ever schoolmasters. Only in a relatively few and late cases do they seem themselves to have taken up teaching, and founded or assumed the direction of schools. Among such exceptions was the small grammar school at Louvain which, after it came under the control of the Brothers in 1433, they enlarged in 1470 into a regular boarding school which enjoyed a century's existence. And at Liège, where they had given instruction in their hostel, the Brothers started a school at the turn of the fifteenth century in which Greek and rhetoric were taught in the advanced classes. Such cases were exceptional. The work which the Brothers did in this sphere reflected their concerns as a whole; the objectives were devotional, not pedagogical, and focused upon the cities where pastoral needs were most pressing. "We have decided," wrote the Brothers in Zwolle in 1415, "to live in cities, in order that we may be able to give advice and instruction to clerics and other persons who wish to serve the Lord."

While recognizing this limitation, it would be a mistake to underestimate the influence of the *Devotio Moderna.* As spiritual directors, the Brothers were able to inspire many, not all of whom subsequently adopted a religious vocation, with the intensity of the inner religious life. Among those who respected the values of the movement, without ever formally belonging to it, were Wessel Gansfort and Erasmus's teacher Hegius. And Erasmus himself retained throughout his life the impressions of those early years he had spent in school at Deventer, at the Brothers' hostel in 's Hertogenbosch, and in the Augustinian house of Steyn where he was professed. He might in retrospect be critical—especially of unfair pressures to get him into a monastic order—but he took to heart and made his own the characteristics of the circles in which he received his education.

We should not, therefore, look to the Brothers of the Common Life for an enthusiasm for classical scholarship or humanist learning. If some of the schools with which they were associated did occasionally provide such teaching, they stand out from the traditional methods perpetuated by the others. And rarely did the Brothers produce, as opposed to influencing, men of learning. Gabriel Biel, who combined a professorship of theology at Tübingen (1484) with the office of prior of the Brothers at Urach, was unique in his double position. Such lack of intellectual leadership can scarcely be surprising given the constant tendency—which stemmed from the movement's founder—to turn aside from academic disputes and deadening scholastic controversy. "Why should we," asked Groote, "indulge in those endless disputes, such as are held at the universities, and that about subjects of no moral value whatsoever?" He had himself shown the way by his rejection of the University of Paris. It was a recipe for devotion more than a criticism. And the devout exercises which Groote and Radewijns bequeathed to their successors, and which influenced among others Thomas à Kempis, included the advice: "Resolve to avoid and abhor all public disputations which are but wranglings for success in argument, or the appearance thereof (such as the disputations of graduates in theology at Paris), and take no part therein."

This outlook, based upon the belief that there were higher truths to which scholastic argument rendered no useful service, was still a vital force in the *Devotio Moderna* in the later fifteenth century. It resembles an important strain of humanist thought—though Gansfort wrote, having witnessed the achievements of the humanists of Florence, that while the capacities of the Florentines exceeded those of the men of Zwolle, "Yet I prefer the incapacity of these to the subtlety of those." He found St. Paul's accomplishments in "barbarous" Thessaly and Corinth, as compared with learned Athens, to be a weighty argument against universities; "It goes to show that liberal studies are not very pleasing to God." Through the *Imitation of Christ,* the mystical ideal of *docta ignorantia,* learned ignorance, about which Nicholas of Cusa had written, became familiar to the devotional exercises of many who were not bothered by the limitations and defects of university methods. "Of what value are lengthy controversies on deep and obscure matters, when it is not by our knowledge of such things that we shall at length be judged? . . . Truly, 'we have eyes and see not': for what concern to us are such things as *genera* and *species?*" Through Christ, "the teacher of teachers and lord of angels," the lowly mind could "understand more of the ways of the everlasting truth in a single moment than ten years of study in the schools." "Non alta sapere, sed bene agere," right acting rather than high learning, was the theme of the *Imitation.*

The Brothers of the Common Life did not belittle books or studies; they stressed that learning should be of the right sort. The mind of the reader must be devoutly, not inquisitively or acquisitively, directed; learning is the tool and servant of piety; intellectual subtlety has no independent value. From Groote's time onwards, their meditation focused upon the life of Christ and their learning upon the Gospel, the Scriptures, and the Church Fathers. The labor to which they were especially committed was the work of "holy writing" and, though the "good books" they copied were by no means limited to scriptural texts, it was the Bible which was the center of their daily readings and meditation. *Sacra scriptura* was their daily bread in more senses than one: both as the written labors which earned their living and as the day's learning in holy writ. The books which were copied for Groote (who was very well-read in the Scriptures, and who himself employed several scribes and added to his collection of books after he had taken up an evangelical career) were mostly Gospel commentaries and texts of the Fathers. And, as the four books which we know as the *Imitation of Christ* show, studded as they are with Biblical quotations, it was Bible-reading above all which enriched the mind of the Augustinian canon Thomas à Kempis.

The scriptural preoccupations of the *Devotio Moderna* took two directions which were significant as a foreshadowing of later developments. During the later fourteenth century, at a time when the Bible was being translated into various vernaculars, the Brothers participated in the effort to give the laity direct knowledge of Holy Writ. Their own Biblical studies—which differed markedly from contemporary university practice in approaching the scriptural text without years of preparatory training—were open to laymen. At Zwolle, where an hour each day was devoted to the study of scripture, after services on Sundays and feast days the Brothers held a lecture or instruction intended for schoolboys, but open to interested comers, at which a Biblical passage was read in the vernacular and followed by a talk. Gerard Zerbolt (1367-98) defended the right of laymen to read the Bible in their own language, though he admitted that some of its books, such as Revelation, needed explanation. How much better, he thought, for them to read scripture than the frivolous romances that commonly held their interest.

It was a natural outcome of such beliefs for the Brothers to turn to Biblical translation. Some of the translations into Dutch which were made in the later fourteenth century can be attributed to Groote himself, including versions of the Psalms and other passages in his Dutch *Book of Hours.* This dates from 1383 and was later often printed, as well as being translated into Low German. Another Dutch Biblical translation which appeared before the end of the century, and which evidently stems from the same circles, includes more books of both testaments and prefaces arguing the case for vernacular scriptures. It seems clear that the followers of the *Devotio Moderna* acted on their belief that laymen should have Biblical texts in languages they understood; when, in the last decade of the fourteenth century, two lawyers put up a justificatory case for the Brothers of the Common Life (whose lawfulness had been called in question), they defended such vernacular scriptures, provided the translations were not distorted. One of them, Everard Foec, also argued the usefulness of schools equipped to teach Hebrew, Arabic, and Chaldean—a suggestion which was not new but which had to wait many years to become even remotely practicable.

In another instance as well the Biblical work of the *Devotio Moderna* was suggestive of future directions. This was not a work of translation but of textual scholarship. John Busch, the chronicler of Windesheim, relates how the Brothers "attempted to reduce all the original books of the Old and New Testaments to the text as translated by St. Jerome from Hebrew into Latin, using the best models obtainable." For this purpose they had to undertake manuscript research, collecting codices from different libraries in order to collate and correct textual variants. Both the objective and the work were remarkable, and to realize their aim of reconstituting Jerome's original text the Brothers gave the highest respect to the oldest texts and corrected a number of Hebrew expressions. They succeeded in producing an improved version of both books of the Vulgate, corrected throughout according to the oldest variants to which they had access, carefully punctuated and revised. It might seem that in this work we have a notable anticipation of sixteenth-century scholarship. There were, however, important differences which make it impossible to describe this labor as humanistic. First, although the Brothers had recourse to the oldest available texts, their aim was not to get back, with a fresh and truer grasp, to the textual context. Their concern was uniformity, not understanding. They wanted a single purified text for liturgical reasons, so that the different houses of their observance should not be using conflicting versions; the choir books in all their monasteries were to employ the one corrected Bible. Given the problems of manuscript diffusion, this was a remarkable enough aim. Also, unlike the humanists' textual studies, the Windesheimers' work on the Bible was static and finite; their investigation ended when they had arrived at their corrected version; it was not extended by the discovery and discussion of further variants. Once they had made their corrected Vulgate it was forbidden to make any textual alterations.

Like all reforming movements the *Devotio Moderna* had its limitations, but the inspiration of its first followers continued to feed subsequent spiritual streams. It was never simply or predominantly a spirituality of laymen, but there was a novelty about the way in which it answered the spiritual needs of seculars—men, women, and boys—in the growing urban centers of the later Middle Ages. It provided help, in ways which were more informal, less rigid, and more adaptable than the institutions of existing orders, for those who lived in the world of affairs while responding to an ancient aesthetic summons—the most venerable of all Christian callings—the imitation of Christ. Perhaps the best way of approaching this far-reaching spiritual heritage, which influenced far more people than ever formally became members of the Brothers of the Common Life or the Windesheim Congregation, is through books.

Most celebrated of all the works produced in the circles of the *Devotio Moderna* is the *Imitation of Christ.* More properly described as four treatises joined together under the later title of "Admonitions useful for the spiritual life. Concerning the Imitation of Christ and the contempt of all the vanities of the world," this small work, long attributed to Jean Gerson, is now generally ascribed to Thomas Hemerken of Kempen, or à Kempis, who died in 1471 having spent most of his long and uneventful life as an Augustinian canon in the house of St. Agnetenburg near Zwolle, which was a member of the Windesheim chapter. À Kempis went to school at Deventer, and among his various writings left a testimonial to his awed respect for the "holy man" Florence Radewijns, of whom he wrote a biography. One of the most striking aspects of the enormous influence of the *Imitation* (of which there were many manuscript copies, as well as early translations and editions) is the way in which spiritual admonitions composed within and addressed to monastic circles could be welcomed and taken to heart by individuals of differing faith living in a variety of worldly circumstances. This reflects not only upon the author—and what he took for granted—but also upon that search for a pruned and simplified piety which characterized some of the strongest spirituality of the time. It turned away from outward ceremonial to concentrate upon exploring and strengthening inner spiritual resources through quiet reading and meditation. So the *Imitation,* which addresses its reader as a confessor might advise a penitent or speaks as a soul communing alone with God, says little about church ceremonies or saints, and nothing in recommendation of pilgrimages, images, and relics. The emphasis throughout is upon the inner purification of the humble mind. "Some carry their devotion only in books, pictures, and other visible signs and representations," but they are mistaken, for while "Nature regards the outward characteristics of a man; grace considers his inner disposition." "God walks with the simple, reveals himself to the humble." It was an ancient message, but one of refreshing simplicity amidst the multiplying ceremonies of the late medieval church. (pp. 82-9)

Finally, it is not out of place to consider here Erasmus's *Enchiridion Militis Christiani.* This small book, written at St. Omer in 1501 at the request of a friend, and first published two years later, holds an important place in Erasmus's *oeuvre* and points the course of his future work. The name *Enchiridion* (already used by St. Augustine) indicates the character of the work: a pocketbook which should be ready to hand as a spiritual dagger. Erasmus, unlike Mombaer and à Kempis, was specifically addressing a layman, but the two weapons which he recommended for the soldiering Christian knight were not unlike the tools of piety they had offered. "Two weapons should especially be prepared for him who must fight . . . against the whole troop of vices, of which the seven capital sins are numbered most powerful. These two weapons are prayer and knowledge . . . prayer is indeed the more powerful, making it possible to converse with God, yet knowledge is no less necessary." Erasmus was here concerned with practical piety—the needs of an ordinary layman for ordered procedures of devotion—and the rules he set down reflect some of the emphases of the *Devotio Moderna.* The essential armoury for the layman's mind was the Bible; he should be equipped by "an eager study of the Scriptures." "Bread is not as much the food of the body as the word of God is the food of the soul." For one fortified with this nourishment, no assaults by inner enemies need be feared. "Therefore if you will dedicate yourself wholly to the study of the Scriptures, if you will meditate on the law of the Lord day and night, you will not be afraid of the terror of the night or of the day." Erasmus, true to his own beliefs, also carefully allowed for the role of secular learning, classical poetry and philosophy, and brought Platonic theories of the spiritual ascent of the soul to serve Christian thinking. He laid great stress on the need to put invisible values above attendance to the visible ceremonies of worship. To honor the bones of saints, to pilgrimage to the Holy Sepulcher, or to make offerings before images were ritualistic acts involving many dangers to true worship of Christ. Invisible piety was what was pleasing to God. The truly Christian knight would "hear the word of God within." He had spiritual wings with which to lift himself up, "from the body to the spirit, from the visible world to the invisible, from letter to mystery . . . as if by the rungs of Jacob's ladder." Erasmus, with his ample reading and amplifying aims, added several rungs to the spiritual step-ladder of the *Devotio Moderna.* (pp. 89-90)

Margaret E. Aston, "The Northern Renaissance," in The Meaning of the Renaissance and Reformation, *edited by Richard L. DeMolen, Houghton Mifflin Company, 1973, pp. 71-130.*

Preserved Smith

[*In the following excerpt, Smith analyzes the type of education received by European scholars during the sixteenth century.*]

[Let us] turn to the noblest, most inspiring and most important work of humanity. With each generation the process of handing on to posterity the full heritage of the race has become longer and more complex.

It was, therefore, upon a very definite and highly developed course of instruction that the contemporary of Erasmus entered. There were a few great endowed schools, like Eton and Winchester and Deventer, in which the small boy might begin to learn his "grammar"—Latin, of course. . . . Each of these two English schools had, at this time, less than 150 pupils, and but two masters, but the great Dutch school, Deventer, under the renowned tuition of Hegius, boasted 2200 scholars, divided into eight forms. Many an old woodcut shows us the pupils gathered around the master as thick as flies, sitting cross-legged on the floor, some intent on their books and others playing pranks, while there seldom fails to be one undergoing the chastisement so highly recommended by Solomon. These great schools did not suffice for all would-be scholars. In many villages there was some poor priest or master who would teach the boys what he knew and prepare them thus for higher things. In some places there were tiny schoolhouses, much like those now seen in rural America. . . .

When the boys left home they lived more as they do now at college, being given a good deal of freedom out of hours. The poorer scholars used their free times to beg, for as many were supported in this way then as now are given scholarships and other charitable aids in our universities.

Though there were a good many exceptions, most of the teachers were brutes. The profession was despised as a menial one and indeed, even so, many a gentleman took more care in the selection of grooms and gamekeepers than he did in choosing the men with whom to entrust his children. Of many of the tutors the manners and morals were alike outrageous. They used filthy language to the boys, whipped them cruelly and habitually drank too much. They made the examinations, says one unfortunate pupil of such a master, like a trial for murder. The monitor employed to spy on the boys was known by the significant name of "the wolf." Public opinion then approved of harsh methods. (pp. 661-63)

The principal study—after the rudiments of reading and writing the mother tongue were learned—was Latin. As, at the opening of the century, there were usually not enough books to go around, the pedagogue would dictate declensions and conjugations, with appropriate exercises, to his pupils. The books used were such as *Donatus on the Parts of Speech,* a poem called the *Facetus* by John of Garland, intended to give moral, theological and grammatical information all in one, and selecting as the proper vehicle rhymed couplets. Other manuals were the *Floretus,* a sort of abstruse catechism, the *Cornutus,* a treatise on synonyms, and a dictionary in which the words were arranged not alphabetically but according to their supposed etymology—thus *hirundo* (swallow) from *aer* (air). One had to know the meaning of the word before one searched for it! The grammars were written in a barbarous Latin of inconceivably difficult style. Can any man now readily understand the following definition of "pronoun," taken from a book intended for beginners, published in 1499? "Pronomen . . . significant substantiam seu entitatem sub modo conceptus intrinseco permanentis seu habitus et quietis sub determinatae apprehensionis formalitate."

That with all these handicaps boys learned Latin at all, and some boys learned it extremely well, must be attributed to the amount of time spent on the subject. For years it was practically all that was studied—for the medieval trivium of grammar, rhetoric and logic reduced itself to this—and they not only read a great deal but wrote and spoke Latin. Finally, it became as easy and fluent to them as their own tongue. Many instances that sound like infant prodigies are known to us; boys who spoke Latin at seven and wrote eloquent orations in it at fourteen, were not uncommon. It is true that the average boy spoke then rather a translation of his own language into Latin than the best idiom of Rome. (pp. 663-64)

Though there was no radical reform in education during the century between Erasmus and Shakespeare, two strong tendencies may be discerned at work, one looking towards a milder method, the other towards the extension of elementary instruction to large classes hitherto left illiterate. The Reformation, which was rather poor in original thought, was at any rate a tremendous vulgarizer of the current culture. It was a popular movement in that it passed around to the people the ideas that had hitherto been the possession of the few. Its first effect, indeed, together with that of the tumults that accompanied it, was for the moment unfavorable to all sorts of learning. Not only wars and rebellions frightened the youth from school, but men arose, both in England and Germany, who taught that if God had vouchsafed his secrets to babes and sucklings, ignorance must be better than wisdom and that it was therefore folly to be learned.

Luther not only turned the tide, but started it flowing in that great wave that has finally given civilized lands free and compulsory education for all. In a *Letter to the Alderman and Cities of Germany on the Erection and Maintenance of Christian Schools* he urged strongly the advantages of learning. "Good schools [he maintained] are the tree from which grow all good conduct in life, and if they decay great blindness must follow in religion and in all useful arts. . . . Therefore, all wise rulers have thought schools a great light in civil life." Even the heathen had seen that their children should be instructed in all liberal arts and sciences both to fit them for war and government and to give them personal culture. Luther several times suggested that "the civil authorities ought to compel people to send their children to school. If the government can

Title page of Martin Luther's tract De captivitate Babylonica ecclesiae praeludium *(1520).*

compel men to bear spear and arquebus, to man ramparts and perform other martial duties, how much more has it the right to compel them to send their children to school?" Repeatedly he urged upon the many princes and burgomasters with whom he corresponded the duty of providing schools in every town and village. A portion of the ecclesiastical revenues confiscated by the German states was in fact applied to this end. Many other new schools were founded by princes and were known as "Fürstenschulen" or gymnasia.

The same course was run in England. Colet's foundation of St. Paul's School in London, for 153 boys, has perhaps won an undue fame, for it was backward in method and not important in any special way, but it is a sign that people at that time were turning their thoughts to the education of the young. (pp. 664-66)

In Catholic countries, too, there was a passion for founding new schools. Especially to be mentioned are the Jesuit "colleges," "of which," Bacon confesses, "I must say, *Talis cum sis utinam noster esses.*" How well frequented they were is shown by the following figures. The Jesuit school at Vienna had, in 1558, 500 pupils, in Cologne, about the same time, 517, in Trèves 500, in Mayence 400, in Spires 453, in Munich 300. The method of the Jesuits became famous for its combined gentleness and art. They developed consummate skill in allowing their pupils as much of history, science and philosophy as they could imbibe without jeoparding their faith. From this point of view their instruction was an inoculation against free thought. But it must be allowed that their teaching of the classics was excellent. They followed the humanists' methods, but they adapted them to the purpose of the church.

All this flood of new scholars had little that was new to study. Neither Reformers nor humanists had any searching or thorough revision to propose; all that they asked was that the old be taught better: the humanities more humanely. Erasmus wrote much on education, and, following him Vives and Budé and Melanchthon and Sir Thomas Elyot and Roger Ascham; their programs, covering the whole period from the cradle to the highest degree, seem thorough, but what does it all amount to, in the end, but Latin and Greek? Possibly a little arithmetic and geometry and even astronomy were admitted, but all was supposed to be imbibed as a by-product of literature, history from Livy, for example, and natural science from Pliny. Indeed, it often seems as if the knowledge of things was valued chiefly for the sake of literary comprehension and allusion.

The educational reformers differed little from one another save in such details as the best authors to read. Colet preferred Christian authors, such as Lactantius, Prudentius and Baptista Mantuan. Erasmus thought it well to begin with the verses of Dionysius Cato, and to proceed through the standard authors of Greece and Rome. For the sake of making instruction easy and pleasant he wrote his *Colloquies*—in many respects his *chef d'oeuvre* if not the best Latin produced by anyone during the century. In this justly famous work, which was adopted and used by all parties immediately, he conveyed a considerable amount of liberal religious and moral instruction with enough wit to make it palatable. Luther, on Melanchthon's advice, notwithstanding his hatred for the author, urged the use of the *Colloquies* in Protestant schools, and they were likewise among the books permitted by the Imperial mandate issued at Louvain.

The method of learning language was for the instructor to interpret a passage to the class which they were expected to be able to translate the next day. Ascham recommended that, when the child had written a translation he should, after a suitable interval, be required to retranslate his own English into Latin. Writing, particularly of letters, was taught. The real advance over the medieval curriculum was in the teaching of Greek—to which the exceptionally ambitious school at Geneva added, after 1538, Hebrew. Save for this and the banishment of scholastic barbarism, there was no attempt to bring in the new sciences and arts. For nearly four hundred years the curriculum of Erasmus has remained the foundation of our education. Only in our own times are Latin and Greek giving way, as the staples of mental training, to modern languages and science. (pp. 666-68)

When the youth went to the university he found little change in either his manner of life or in his studies. A number of boys matriculated at the age of thirteen or fourteen; on the other hand there was a sprinkling of mature students. The extreme youth of many scholars made it natural that they should be under somewhat stricter discipline than is now the case. . . . At colleges like Montaigu, if one may believe Erasmus, the path of learning was indeed thorny. What between the wretched diet, the filth, the cold, the crowding, "the short-winged hawks" that the students combined from their hair or shook from their shirts, it is no wonder that many of them fell ill. Gaming, fighting, drinking and wenching were common.

Nominally, the university was then under the entire control of the faculty, who elected one of themselves "rector" (president) for a single year, who appointed their own members and who had complete charge of studies and discipline, save that the students occasionally asserted their ancient rights. In fact, the corporation was pretty well under the thumb of the government, which compelled elections and dismissals when it saw fit, and occasionally appointed commissions to visit and reform the faculties.

Instruction was still carried on by the old method of lectures and debates. These latter were sometimes on important questions of the day, theological or political, but were often, also, nothing but displays of ingenuity. There was a great lack of laboratories, a need that just began to be felt at the end of the century when Bacon wrote: "Unto the deep, fruitful and operative study of many sciences, specially natural philosophy and physics, books be not only the instrumentals." Bacon's further complaint that, "among so many great foundations of colleges in Europe, I find it strange that they are all dedicated to professions, and none left free to arts and sciences at large," is an early hint of the need of the endowment of research. The degrees in liberal arts, B.A. and M.A., were then more strictly than now licences either to teach or to pursue higher professional studies in divinity, law, or medicine. Fees for graduation were heavy. . . . (pp. 668-70)

Germany then held the primacy that she has ever since had in Europe both in the number of her universities and in the aggregate of her students. The new universities founded by the Protestants were: Marburg 1527, Königsberg 1544, Jena 1548 and again 1558, Helmstadt 1575, Altdorf 1578, Paderborn 1584. In addition to these the Catholics founded four or five new universities, though not important ones. They concentrated their efforts on the endeavor to found new "colleges" at the old institutions.

In general the universities lost during the first years of the Reformation, but more than made up their numbers by the middle of the century. Wittenberg had 245 matriculations in 1521; in 1526 the matriculations had fallen to 175, but by 1550, notwithstanding the recent Schmalkaldic War, the total numbers had risen to 2000, and this number was well maintained throughout the century.

Erfurt, remaining Catholic in a Protestant region, declined more rapidly and permanently. In the year 1520-21 there were 311 matriculations, in the following year 120, in the next year 72, and five years later only 14. Between 1521 to 1530 the number of students fell at Rostock from 123 to 33, at Frankfort-on-the-Oder from 73 to 32. Rostock, however, recovered after a reorganization in 1532. The number of students at Greifswald declined so that no lectures were given during the period 1527-39, after which it again began to pick up. Königsberg, starting with 314 students later fell off. Cologne declined in numbers, and so did Mayence until the Jesuits founded their college in 1561, which, by 1568, had 500 pupils recognized as members of the university. Vienna, also, having sunk to the number of 12 students in 1532, kept at a very low ebb until 1554, when the effects of the Jesuit revival were felt. Whereas, during the fifteen years 1508-22 there were 6485 matriculations at Leipzig, during the next fifteen years there were only 1935. By the end of the century, however, Leipzig had again become, under Protestant leadership, a large institution.

Two new universities were founded in the British Isles during the century, Edinburgh in 1582 and Trinity College, Dublin, in 1591. In England a number of colleges were added to those already existing at Oxford and Cambridge, namely Christ Church (first known, after its founder, Wolsey, as Cardinal's College, then as King's College), Brasenose, and Corpus Christi at Oxford and St. John's, Magdalen, and Trinity at Cambridge. Notwithstanding these new foundations the number of students sank. During the years 1542-8, only 191 degrees of B.A. were given at Cambridge and only 172 at Oxford. Ascham is authority for the statement that things were still worse under Mary, when "the wild boar of the wood" either "cut up by the root or trod down to the ground" the institutions of learning. The revenues of the universities reached their low-water mark about 1547, when the total income of Oxford from land was reckoned at £5 and that of Cambridge at £50, per annum. Under Elizabeth, the universities rose in numbers, while better Latin and Greek were taught. It was at this time that a college education became fashionable for young gentlemen instead of being exclusively patronized by "learned clerks." The foundation of the College of Physicians in London deserves to be mentioned.

A university was founded at Zurich under the influence of Zwingli. Geneva's University opened in 1559 with Beza as rector. Connected with it was a preparatory school of seven forms, with a rigidly prescribed course in the classics. When the boy was admitted to the university proper by examination, he took what he chose; there was not even a division into classes. The courses offered to him included Greek, Hebrew, theology, dialectic, rhetoric, physics and mathematics.

The foundation of the Collège de France by Francis I represented an attempt to bring new life and vigor into learning by a free association of learned men. It was planned to emancipate science from the tutelage of theology. Erasmus was invited but, on his refusal to accept, Budé was given the leading position. Chairs of Greek, Hebrew, mathematics and Latin were founded by the king in 1530. Other institutions of learning founded in France were Rheims 1547, Douai 1562, Besançon 1564, none of them now in existence. Paris continued to be the largest university in the world, with an average number of students of about 6000.

Louvain, in the Netherlands, had 3000 students in 1500 and 1521; in 1550 the number rose to 5000. It was divided into colleges on the plan still found in England. Each college had a president, three professors and twelve fellows, entertained gratis, in addition to a larger number of paying scholars. The most popular classes often reached the number of 300. The foundation of the Collegium Trilingue by Erasmus's friend Jerome Busleiden in 1517 was an attempt, as its name indicates, to give instruction in Greek and Hebrew as well as in the Latin classics. A blight fell upon the noble institution during the wars of religion. Under the supervision of Alva it founded professorships of catechetics and substituted the decrees of the Council of Trent for the *Decretum* of Gratian in the law school. Exhausted by the hemorrhages caused by the Religious War and starved by the Lenten diet of Spanish Catholicism, it gradually decayed, while its place was taken in the eyes of Europe by the Protestant University of Leyden. A second Protestant foundation, Franeker, for a time flourished, but finally withered away.

Spanish universities were crowded with new numbers. The maximum student body was reached by Salamanca in 1584 with 6778 men, while Alcalá passed in zenith in 1547 with the respectable enrollment of 1949. The foundation of no less than nine new universities in Spain bears witness to the interest of the Iberian Peninsula in education.

Four new universities opened their doors in Italy during the year 1540-1565. The Sapienza at Rome, in addition to these, was revived temporarily by Leo X in 1513, and, after a relapse to the dormant state, again awoke to its full power under Paul III, when chairs of Greek and Hebrew were established.

The services of all these universities cannot be computed on any statistical method. Notwithstanding all their faults, their dogmatic narrowness and their academic arrogance, they contributed more to progress than any other institutions. Each academy became the center of scientific research and of intellectual life. Their influence was enormous. How much did it mean to that age to see its contending hosts marshalled under two professors, Luther and Adrian VI! And how many other leaders taught in universities:—Erasmus, Melanchthon, Reuchlin, Lefèvre, to mention only a few. Pontiffs and kings sought for support in academic pronouncements, nor could they always force the doctors to give the decision they wished. In fact, each university stood like an Acropolis in the republic of letters, at once a temple and a fortress for those who loved truth and ensued it. (pp. 670-73)

Preserved Smith, "The Temper of the Times," in his The Age of the Reformation, *1920. Reprint by Henry Holt and Company, 1936, pp. 641-98.*

THE IMPACT OF PRINTING

Kenneth A. Strand

[Strand is an American educator and literary scholar. In the following excerpt, he presents a historical overview of the achievements in printing accomplished by the Brethren of the Common Life.]

Not least among the contributions of [the fifteenth] century was the second invention of movable type. The first, which had occurred in China some 400 years earlier, remained almost completely unknown in Europe before the end of the Middle Ages. But this new, European invention was from the beginning readily recognized and diligently exploited, as evidenced by the veritable "mushrooming" of printing establishments during the last half of the century. Not only did printers set up their shops in the large centers of Germany and Italy, but craftsmen of the new art began to ply their trade in even some of the smaller towns and remoter sections of western Europe.

Among those people who took a most active interest in printing was the Brotherhood of the Common Life, that deeply religious semi-monastic order of the Low Countries and Germany, for enlightenment on whose history we are so heavily indebted to Professor Albert Hyma. This group not only gave support to the printing activities of others but also established four of the earliest presses working in Europe, three of which were the first presses operating in their particular cities or localities. (p. 341-42)

The Brethren seem to have been somewhat of an unusual lot in their literary pursuits. They were not only exceptionally eager to disseminate knowledge, but they also frequently struck a rather uncommon median by revealing interest in both theological works and the classics and by using both Latin and the vernacular. Thus they overcame certain failures on the part of the humanists, on one hand, and of the more conservative and traditional circles, on the other. Indeed, Alois Bömer in his study of the literary life in Münster has seemed much impressed with the fact that the Brethren of the Common Life honored and respected the language and the literature of the peoples among whom they labored. And as he has so aptly stated, the Brethren "zealously promoted the cause of literature and actively spread better education, for which they rightfully earned the gratitude of posterity."

The literary interests of the Brethren of the Common Life were in evidence from the very first. The early followers of Groote earned their living largely by copying manuscripts, this pursuit being specifically mentioned in the constitutions of the early Brethren houses at Deventer and Zwolle. In each of these constitutions we find a statement indicating the purpose of these houses to be that "priests and clerics" might live there, supported by "their own labor, namely the copying of books, and by the returns of certain estates." (pp. 342-43)

The attitude of the Brethren of the Common Life toward the spread of knowledge was quite constant. The invention of movable type produced, however, rather strange implications and complications for them. On the one hand, this new development made manuscript production an unprofitable business, causing the Brethren to turn in greater degree to other pursuits, such as teaching school. On the other hand, it inevitably led the Brethren into a deep interest in the new art itself. Just how extensive was their influence upon early printing in the Low Countries and Germany is not clear, but there can be no doubt that in a number of places where they established houses, they took an especially profound and active interest.

In Deventer and Zwolle, the heartland of the Devotio Moderna and an area which saw the establishment of more Brethren and Sister houses than any other like-sized area anywhere, there was outstanding achievement along both educational and printing lines. A definite link has been seen between the existence of Brethren houses in those cities and the remarkable educational accomplishments there. It seems likely that a similar link may have existed between that same presence of the Brethren and the printing achievements of such presses as those of Richard Paffraet, Jacob de Breda, and Peter Os. In fact, Ludwig Schulze made mention years ago of the Brethren's support of Paffraet. And in this connection, it might be of interest to notice also an item called to attention by Alfred Pollard; namely, that during a temporary interruption of Paffraet's activity, his fonts of type were used by De Breda for printing a number of small quartos for students, and that this was a class of book to which Paffraet devoted himself exclusively and voluminously when he resumed his publishing activity. In any event, the kinds of works coming from the presses at Deventer and Zwolle—including textbooks—were precisely such as we would expect under the influence of the Brethren.

Let us now take a brief closer look at the printing achievements of those fifteenth-century presses in Deventer and Zwolle. A study of recent work in the field of cataloguing reveals that in incunabula, Deventer exceeded every other city of the Low Countries, including Zwolle, by having printed some 500 to 600 editions. This total compares favorably with totals from even much larger centers outside as well as inside the Low Countries. The fifteenth-century publication record of Zwolle, though also impressive, is by no means so striking as that at Deventer. Zwolle's output of well over 100 editions, when added to that at Deventer, helps, nevertheless, to produce a result which other like-sized areas were indeed hard-put to match or exceed.

But not only is the quantitative aspect of the printing work at Deventer and Zwolle of interest. The type of publications also merits attention. Though many of the works were of a practical religious nature, a remarkably large percentage represented classical works. There were also humanistic productions, as well as grammar texts and the like.

At this point, some further statistics, called to attention a few years ago by Professor Hyma is his article "Erasmus and the Reformation in Germany" may be of interest: In the Low Countries the large centers of Antwerp and Louvain ranked below Deventer in the output of incunabula, the former with some 350, the latter with some 250 editions. Even Zwolle well outstripped Utrecht's approximately 70 editions and Brussels' approximately 40. The grand total from all presses in the Low Countries as given by Hyma is 1705 works, 177 of which were classics. And of the classics, well over two-thirds came from the presses at *Devotio Moderna* and Zwolle. By way of contrast, the grand total for all England was 364 editions of incunabula, 29 of which represented classical works. The output for England, thus, was only approximately one-fifth of that for the Low Countries and but two-thirds of that of Deventer alone. In classical works, it was only about one-third of that of Deventer. As for France and French-speaking Switzerland, one listing of incunabula gives approximately 1050 to 1100 publications as coming from this area, some 100 of them being classics. For Spain and Portugal the grand total is 833 works, 41 of which are classics. As Professor Hyma has stated, "The number of classical books printed in Paris is probably smaller than that for the little town of Deventer, while Salamanca in Spain, in spite of its great fame as a university center, could boast of only 5 classical books."

In view of all this, is not the achivement of Deventer and Zwolle most striking! But what can we say with regard to areas where houses of the Devotio Moderna were not so concentrated; or more specifically, what can we say with regard to the Brethren of the Common Life themselves in such areas? In some places the Brethren apparently worked in close relationship with printers, as, for example, in Cologne. And in several places they established, as we have already indicated, their own printing operations. It is to these presses of their own that we must now turn our attention.

In what is modern Belgium, the Brethren instituted a printing press at Brussels, which press was the earliest printing establishment working in that city. The period of its active production lasted from approximately 1475 to 1487, but during that time it issued some 40 or more editions. The relative importance of this early press in Brussels can perhaps be better realized by considering the fact that the next major printer to begin work there, Thomas van der Noot, did not do so until 1507 and even at that late date had hardly a more glorious or long-lived career than did the pioneer press of the Brethren. Van der Noot's last publication appeared in the year 1520.

In Gouda, within the boundaries of what is South Holland in the modern Netherlands, the situation was somewhat different from that at Brussels. Here the Brethren seem to have taken up their printing activity rather late in the fifteenth century—but in any event by 1496, inasmuch as they issued the *Getijden vanden seven bliscappen onser liever vrouwen* and several other works during that year. Moreover, in Gouda no less than eight or nine other printers seem to have been active during the fifteenth century. (pp. 343-46)

Some 80 to 90 incunabula seem to have come from Gouda. The vast majority of these—58, according to M.F.A.G. Campbell's original listing—were from the press of Leeu. The Brethren, however, appear to have ranked second highest in output of incunabula in that city, by their publication of some ten or twelve editions. This was not necessarily a small accomplishment on their part, especially in view of the late beginning of their printing activity there. They continued operation, moreover, well into the sixteenth century.

Neither Brussels nor Gouda was outstanding for production of classical works. In those cities the interest apparently lay more with religious books for practical use. Such books were not, however, strictly in Latin, as certain titles will indicate; for example, the *Getijden vanden seven bliscappen onser liever vrouwen,* already mentioned as coming from the Brethren's press at Gouda. This press and that of Leeu at Gouda revealed, in fact, a decided preference for the vernacular, with some two-thirds of their incunabula bearing Dutch titles. At Brussels, on the other hand, the Latin was used quite consistently.

In Germany, the first press established by the Brethren of the Common Life was at Marienthal, some fifteen miles south of Mainz. Apparently this press was in operation as early as 1468—little more than a decade after the appearance of the famed "Gutenberg Bible"—, for it seems that an indulgence letter was issued from it during that year. The second publication bearing a date was the two-part quarto-edition *Mainz Breviary and Psalter* of 1474. (pp. 346-47)

Another location at which the Brethren of the Common Life established an early printing operation in Germany was the north-German city of Rostock. The press there was undoubtedly the Brethren's printing establishment *par excellence* with regard both to output and duration of life. It was instituted about 1475, its first dated work being Lactantius' *Opera* issued in April of the following year. It closed its career as a press of the Brethren about 1531 or 1532 when work on a Low-German Emserian New Testament was forcefully restrained by the city council.

The press at the "House at the Green Garden"—as thc Rostock house of the Brethren came to be known—was one of the earliest in all northern Germany. Only that of Lucas Brandis in Lübeck preceded it, and that by only a few months at most.

Rostock was important both as a commercial city and as

an educational center, and the Brethren's press must surely have held a position of unique significance there. This press was, in fact, the main one operating in that city until those established by Herman Barkhusen in 1507 and Ludwig Dietz in 1509, the former of which continued operation until 1512 and the latter until about 1559. (pp. 347-48)

Turning to the incunabula, our chief interest here, we find that the Rostock Brethren published materials of some variety. There are, for example, works of medieval scholstics and mystics, on the one hand, and works of a Roman classical writer as well as later humanists, on the other. And then there are publications, too, containing materials of practical nature for church administration and for liturgical use.

Among the works of medieval scholastics and mystics we may mention the *Sententia determinativa, Soliloquium jubilaeum,* and *Stimulus amoris* of Anselm of Canterbury, an extreme realist whose life span fell between 1033 and 1109 A.D.; the *Sermones super Cantica canticorum* of Bernard of Clairvaux, the Cistercian monk who in 1115 founded the monastery of Clairvaux; and the *De praparatione ad missam* of Saint Bonaventura, the mystic John Fidanza, who became general of the Franciscans in 1256 and in 1273 was made bishop of Albano and a cardinal. The productions of the classical writer are Ovid's *Fasti* and *Metamorphoses.* Among works of more practical intent for the life of the church may be listed such publications as missals and indulgence letters. And then there is also Lactantius' *Opera* already mentioned. This perhaps belongs in a class by itself, inasmuch as it represents a work by a writer in the ancient church. Lactantius was rector at Nicomedia at the time of Emperor Constantine the Great and is known for his hostility to classical civilization and religion.

The Rostock Brethren's incunabula reveal some use of the vernacular, at least five of the 23 editions bearing German titles. The proportion increases most strikingly, however, as we enter the sixteenth century, with Low German being used for some 24 of the 33 works dating from that century, and with another five works being in Danish.

The forced termination of the activity of this Rostock printing establishment as a press of the Brethren, an item we have already mentioned, marked also the close of the general printing work carried on by the Brethren of the Common Life under their own auspices at their own foundations. Four presses, as we have seen, had been instituted by this Brotherhood during the fifteenth century. One of these—at Marienthal—was evidently introduced little more than a decade after Gutenberg's earliest publication from movable type; two others—at Brussels and Rostock—were in operation within about two decades after that important event; and the final one—at Gouda—began its work shortly before the end of the century. These presses were not necessarily the most voluminous producers among the many which were established in western Europe during the fifteenth century. But that they nevertheless deserve to hold a significant place in the history of printing, especially as pertains to their own localities, is quite clear.

Furthermore, the work done at the Brethren's own presses is, as we have seen, only part of the story. The Brethren's general interest in literature and education laid the foundation for a diligent interest on their part in printed works and in printing itself, even at places where the Brethren were not able to institute presses of their own. In this connection, the outstanding printing record of Deventer and Zwolle certainly merits attention, as we have already indicated.

Precisely how extensive the influence of the Brotherhood of the Common Life really was with regard to the printing activities of the fifteenth century is, however, a question for which we will probably never have an absolutely clear and adequate answer. The Brotherhood itself was at no time exceptionally large numerically; but it did, nonetheless, have an impressive array of foundations scattered rather widely throughout the Low Countries and Germany, and it made its influence felt in other places as well. For its size, its impact upon such fields as religion and education was truly phenomenal. And were our source materials more complete, so that the whole story could be told, perhaps we would find the same to hold true with regard to this further important aspect of the "dawn of modern civilization"—the accelerated dissemination of knowledge through the new art of printing. (pp. 348-50)

Kenneth A. Strand, "The Brethren of the Common Life and Fifteenth-Century Printing: A Brief Survey," in The Dawn of Modern Civilization: Studies in Renaissance, Reformation and Other Topics Presented to Honor Albert Hyma, *edited by Kenneth A. Strand, Ann Arbor Publishers, 1962, pp. 341-55.*

John Rothwell Slater

[*In the following excerpt, Slater gives a concise history of publishing and book-selling during the Renaissance.*]

Printing did not make the Renaissance; the Renaissance made printing. Printing did not begin the publication and dissemination of books. There were libraries of vast extent in ancient Babylon, Egypt, Greece, Rome. There were universities centuries before Gutenberg where the few instructed the many in the learning treasured up in books, and where both scholars and professional scribes multiplied copies of books both old and new. At the outset of any examination of the influence of printing on the Renaissance it is necessary to remind ourselves that the intellectual life of the ancient and the mediaeval world was built upon the written word. There is a naive view in which ancient literature is conceived as existing chiefly in the autograph manuscripts and original documents of a few great centers to which all ambitious students must have resort. A very little inquiry into the multiplication of books before printing shows us how erroneous is this view.

We must pass over entirely the history of publishing and book-selling in ancient times, a subject too vast for adequate summary in a preliminary survey of this sort. With the fall of Rome and the wholesale destruction that accompanied the barbarian invasions a new chapter begins in the history of the dissemination of literature. This [discussion] opens with the founding of the scriptorium, or monastic copying system, by Cassiodorus and Saint Benedict early in the sixth century. To these two men, Cassiodorus, the ex-chancellor of the Gothic king Theodoric, and Benedict, the founder of the Benedictine order, is due the gratitude of the modern world. It was through their foresight in setting the monks at work copying the scriptures and the secular literature of antiquity that we owe the preservation of most of the books that have survived the ruins of the ancient world. At the monastery of Monte Cassino, founded by Saint Benedict in the year 529, and at that of Viviers, founded by Cassiodorus in 531, the Benedictine rule required of every monk that a fixed portion of each day be spent in the scriptorium. There the more skilled scribes were entrusted with the copying of precious documents rescued from the chaos of the preceding century, while monks not yet sufficiently expert for this high duty were instructed by their superiors.

The example thus nobly set was imitated throughout all the centuries that followed, not only in the Benedictine monasteries of Italy, France, Germany, England, Scotland, Ireland, Iceland, but in religious houses of all orders. It is to the mediaeval Church, her conservatism in the true sense of the word, her industry, her patience, her disinterested guardianship alike of sacred and of pagan letters, that the world owes most of our knowledge of antiquity. Conceive how great would be our loss if to archaeology alone we could turn for the reconstruction of the civilization, the art, the philosophy, the public and private life of Greece and Rome. If the Church had done no more than this for civilization, it would still have earned some measure of tolerance from its most anti-clerical opponents. It is of course to the Eastern rather than to the Roman Church that we owe the preservation of classical Greek literature, copied during the dark ages in Greek monasteries and introduced into Italy after the fall of Constantinople.

A second stage in the multiplication and publication of manuscript books begins with the founding of the great mediaeval universities of Bologna, Paris, Padua, Oxford, and other centers of higher education. Inasmuch as the study of those days was almost entirely book study, the maintenance of a university library with one or two copies of each book studied was inadequate. There grew up in each university city an organized system of supplying the students with textbooks. The authorized book-dealers of a mediaeval university were called *stationarii,* or stationers, a term apparently derived from the fixed post or station assigned in or near the university buildings to each scribe permitted to supply books to the students and professors. . . . Another name for the university book-dealers was the classical Latin word *librarii,* which usually in mediaeval Latin meant not what we call a librarian but a vender of books, like the French *libraire.* These scribes were not allowed at first to sell their manuscripts, but rented them to the students at rates fixed by university statutes. A folded sheet of eight pages, sixteen columns of sixty-two lines each, was the unit on which the rental charges were based. Such a sheet at the beginning of the thirteenth century rented for about twenty cents a term; and since an ordinary textbook of philosophy or theology or canon law contained many sheets, these charges constituted no inconsiderable part of the cost of instruction. The books must be returned before the student left the university; sales were at first surreptitious and illegal, but became common early in the fourteenth century. Reasonable accuracy among the stationers was secured by a system of fines for errors, half of which went to the university, the other half being divided between the supervisor or head proof-reader and the informant who discovered the error.

The original regulation which forbade the stationers to sell books was intended to prevent students of a profiteering turn of mind from buying books for resale to their fellow-students at a higher price, thus cornering the market and holding up the work of an entire class. In course of time, however, the book-dealers were permitted not only to sell textbooks, at prices still controlled by official action, but also to buy and sell manuscripts of other books, both those produced by local scribes and those imported from other cities and countries.

This broadening of the activities of the university bookstores led naturally to the third and last stage which the publishing business underwent before the invention of printing. This stage was the establishment in Florence, Paris, and other intellectual centers, of bookshops selling manuscripts to the general public rather than to university students. These grew rapidly during the first half of the fifteenth century, receiving a marked impetus from the new interest in Greek studies. Some years before the fall of Constantinople in 1453 Italian book-sellers were accustomed to send their buyers to the centers of Byzantine learning in the near East in quest of manuscripts to be disposed of at fancy prices to the rich collectors and patrons of literature. There is evidence of similar methods in France and Germany during the earlier decades of the Renaissance.

This preliminary sketch of the book-publishing business before printing is intended to correct a rather common misapprehension. Manuscript books were indeed relatively costly, but they were not scarce. Any scholar who had not been through a university not only had access to public libraries of hundreds of volumes, but might also possess, at prices not beyond the reach of a moderate purse, his own five-foot shelf of the classics. The more elegant manuscripts, written by experts and adorned with rich illuminations and sumptuous bindings, were of course not for the humble student; but working copies, multiplied on a large scale by a roomful of scribes writing simultaneously from dictation, might always be had. (pp. 1-5)

When we consider the enormous number of manuscript books that must have existed in Europe in the middle ages, we may well wonder why they have become relatively rare in modern times. Several explanations account for this. In the first place, the practice of erasing old manuscripts and using the same vellum again for other works was extremely common. Secondly, vast numbers of manuscripts in the monasteries and other libraries of Europe were wantonly or accidentally destroyed by fire, especially in times of war and religious fanaticism. In the third place, the early binders, down through the sixteenth century and even later, used sheets of vellum from old manuscripts for the linings and the covers of printed books. Finally, after the inven-

Drawing by Hans Holbein the Younger of the More household, depicting Sir Thomas More seated at the center. Standing second from the left is More's daughter Margaret, who translated Erasmus's exposition of the Lord's Prayer.

tion of printing, as soon as a given work had been adequately and handsomely printed in a standard edition, all but the finest manuscripts of that book would naturally be looked upon as of little value, and would be subject to loss and decay if not to deliberate destruction. Owing to these and perhaps other causes it is almost entirely the religious manuscripts that have survived, except those preserved in royal libraries and museums from the finer collections of the middle ages.

The invention of printing was not the work of any one man. Not only were printed pages of text with accompanying pictures produced from woodcut blocks in Holland a quarter of a century before Gutenberg began his work at Mainz, but it is pretty well established that movable types were employed by Laurence Koster, of Haarlem, as early as 1430. But Koster, who died about 1440, did not carry his invention beyond the experimental stages, and produced no really fine printing. Moreover, his work had no immediate successor in Holland. Whether it be true, as sometimes alleged, that Gutenberg first learned of the new art from one of Koster's workmen, we have no means of knowing. At any rate, Gutenberg's contemporaries as well as his successors gave to him the credit of the invention. That he was not the first to conceive the idea of multiplying impressions of type-forms by the use of a screw press is evident; but he was the first to develop the invention to a point where it became capable of indefinite extension. He seems to have worked in secret for some years on the problems involved in type-founding and printing before the year 1450, when he set up his shop in Mainz.

The capital for the new business was furnished by a wealthy goldsmith named Johann Fust. Between 1450 and 1455 Gutenberg printed an edition of the Latin Bible, sometimes known as the Mazarin Bible, which is ordinarily regarded as the first printed book. It was a magnificently printed volume, exhibiting at the very foundation of the art a skill in presswork scarcely surpassed by any of Gutenberg's immediate successors. He was a great printer, but not a financially successful one. Fust sued his partner in 1455 for repayment of the loans advanced, and upon Gutenberg's failure to meet these obligations Fust foreclosed the mortgage and took over the printing plant. Although Gutenberg started another publishing house at Mainz, and continued it until his death in 1468, the main development of printing after 1455 was in the original plant as carried on by Fust and his son-in-law, Peter

Schoeffer. They printed in 1457 an edition of the Psalms in which for the first time two-color printing was employed, the large initial letters being printed in red and black. This innovation, designed to imitate the rubricated initials of the manuscripts, involved great technical difficulties in the presswork, and was not generally adopted. Most of the early printed books, even down to the end of the fifteenth century, left blanks for the large capitals at the beginnings of the chapters, to be filled in by hand by professional illuminators.

From the establishments of Gutenberg and of Fust and Schoeffer in Mainz knowledge of the new art spread rapidly into many German cities. In 1462 Mainz was captured and sacked by Adolph of Nassau in one of the local wars of the period, and printers from the Mainz shops made their way to other cities throughout the empire. Before 1470 there were printing establishments in almost every German city, and hundreds of works, mostly theological, had been issued from their presses. (pp. 6-8)

But the new invention was at first looked upon by some famous scholars and patrons of learning as a detriment rather than a help. The great Trithemius, abbot of Sponheim, wrote as late as 1494 in the following terms:

> A work written on parchment could be preserved for a thousand years, while it is probable that no volume printed on paper will last for more than two centuries. Many important works have not been printed, and the copies of these must be prepared by scribes. The scribe who ceases his work because of the invention of the printing-press can be no true lover of books, in that, regarding only the present, he gives no due thought to the intellectual cultivation of his successors. The printer has no care for the beauty and the artistic form of books, while with the scribe this is a labor of love.
>
> (p. 9)

John Rothwell Slater, in a speech in 1921, in his Printing and the Renaissance: A Paper Read Before the Fortnightly Club of Rochester, New York, *1921. Reprint by Battery Park Book Company, 1978, pp. 1-11.*

Pierce Butler

[*Butler was an American librarian and bibliographer. In the excerpt below, he provides a concise overview of the history of printing, from scribing to "true publication."*]

The origin of printing itself was but the first stage in the development of books as we know them. To understand the modern book one should know something of its history and comprehend the gradual process whereby it emerged from the penwritten medieval manuscript. There were four distinct phases in this metamorphosis.

The first was the origin of the mechanical process. In the beginning this was merely a device for performing a scribe's work more quickly, neatly, and cheaply than was possible by hand labor. The earliest printers, like the public to whom they sold their books, had learned to read in pen-written volumes and knew no other kind. The printer's problem was to devise a method for producing in quantity a ware already standardized. He was not free to turn out a new product which might serve the same purpose as the old one. He was limited psychologically as well as economically to established conventions. His goal was simply to reproduce the manuscript but to do this mechanically.

Thus his task was far more arduous than we usually regard it. Many features of the manuscript which were time-saving and labor-saving devices for the scribe were only additional impediments for the printer. But he could not at first perceive this. Indeed, until he had reproduced on his press every characteristic of the written volume he did not feel that he had succeeded. It is highly significant in this connection that the first printed volume to be signed by its craftsmen in their pride of accomplishment was essentially a manuscript. The Mainz Psalter of 1457 exhibits in print all the scribal ornamentations which were expected at that time in a finished volume—a letter text in black, embellished with intricate initials and capitals in color.

Only gradually did the early printers and their customers learn to accept the technical limitations of typography and to exploit its peculiarities. As they did this the books they made took on new forms and developed new cultural potentials. Calligraphic ornaments were supplanted by those of typographic style, and all sorts of new facilities were provided for the reader—title-pages, illustrations, maps, tables, indexes, etc. This was the second historical phase in the development of the modern book.

The third was the discovery of true publication. Under the manuscript economy a scribe merely responded to current demands. Usually he transcribed books to order, or, if he built up a stock in anticipation of sales, it was of the volumes most frequently asked for—school and university textbooks and standard works in theology, law, or medicine constantly used by professional students and practitioners. The printer, however, soon went beyond this and discovered the possibilities of publication. To extend his business he undertook to create new demands. He ransacked old libraries for whatever books he thought the public might buy if they were made available. To the same purpose he also printed new writings brought to him by living authors, and, finally he came to order on his own initiative journalistic accounts of recent happenings. In response to his enterprise the world learned to read books and not merely to study them. At the publishers' instigation reading for its own sake again became the normal habit of educated men—a practice forgotten since the collapse of Roman civilization.

And, finally, the printed book entered into the fourth phase of its metamorphosis—it became itself a determinative agent in history. Publishers discovered that the book could not only inform and entertain people but also affect their thoughts and actions. Henceforth, it was utilized to spread new beliefs, to sway men's judgments, to win their support, and to arouse their passions. Within the first century of printing the press became a potent instrument of public appeal and propaganda. During the Protestant Revolution this technique was perfected. Already in fact, although not yet in name, typography was the fourth estate of European society. (pp. xi-xiv)

Pierce Butler, in an introduction to his The Origin of Printing in Europe, *The University of Chicago Press, 1940, pp. xi-xv.*

Elizabeth L. Eisenstein

[*Eisenstein is an American educator and one of the leading scholars of Renaissance publishing history. In the excerpt below, she discusses the evolution, spread, and impact of printing in Europe during the Renaissance.*]

> Besides the restoration of learning, now almost complete, the invention of many fine new things . . . has been reserved to this age. Among these, printing deserves to be put first. . . . The invention has greatly aided the advancement of all disciplines. For it seems miraculously to have been discovered in order to bring back to life more easily literature which seemed dead.

These remarks were made in passing by a sixteenth-century scholar who was surveying the course of world history and, incidentally, recording what had happened in his own age. I have cited the passage in order to draw attention to a seemingly valid observation that has slipped out of sight. Among new things reserved to his age, Le Roy said, printing deserves to be put first. A large literature devoted to "the problem of the Renaissance" has somehow buried this insight. The purpose of this paper is to bring it back into view and to suggest why it is relevant to current historical debates.

My thesis, briefly stated, is that the advent of printing was, quite literally, an *epoch-making* event. The shift from script to print revolutionized Western culture. It altered the way things changed and the way they stayed the same. It affected all forms of survival and revival. In particular, it affected a revival of learning that had got under way in quattrocento Italy. Some puzzling features associated with this revival can best be explained by recognizing that it was initiated in the age of scribes and perpetuated in the age of printers. A similar approach may be usefully applied to the larger problem of periodization that is associated with the term "Renaissance". The so-called transitional era that lies between 1300 and 1600 may be regarded as a hybrid construct. The last century or so of scribal culture and the first century or so of typography have been grafted together. (p. 19)

First let me point out that most current accounts of Renaissance developments treat the advent of printing in an off-hand and casual manner. It is passed over altogether in many conventional surveys of Western civilization and in most histories of Western religion, art, literature, philosophy, political theory and the like. When noted at all, it is customarily presented as an incidental example: as a characteristic late medieval invention, as an instance of early capitalist enterprise, or as a by-product of the expansion of lay literacy. In keeping with conventions established by early chronicles the printing press is frequently coupled with other innovations, such as the compass and gunpowder, or mining and shipbuilding. It is placed between the university and the mechanical clock in one account; between the insurance contract and advances in metallurgy in another. It is apt to crop up almost anywhere in history books at present, except at the beginning of chapters introducing a new era. Indeed it usually appears as something of an afterthought, coming, as it does, after the Italian revival has got under way.

Not infrequently we must wait until chapters on the Renaissance are closed and those on the Reformation are opened, for authors to remember that Gutenberg's invention did play a significant historical rôle. A recent study, for example, sketches the "pre-history of the Enlightenment" by devoting one section to the Italian Renaissance and beginning the next one with a familiar grouping: the modern state system, the circumnavigation of the globe, the Copernican Revolution, and the Protestant revolt. Only after this does a paragraph on printing appear, and we learn that the *philosophes* hailed it "as a cultural revolution" while Condorcet placed it at the beginning of a new phase of human history. The author concurs: "Condorcet was right". . . . In theory, most historians agree that the invention and utilization of movable type was a revolutionary and an epoch-making event. In practice, they tell us a very different story.

At first glance, it seems odd that this should be so, that there is such a discrepancy between theory and practice. The advent of printing entailed a very large cluster of changes that came in a relatively short span of time. In four or five decades, printers' workshops were established in urban centres throughout Europe. The infant industry was rapidly emancipated from conventions that had prevailed in scriptoria. By 1500, various effects produced by the consumption of printed materials were already being registered. Compared with the three centuries that stretch from 1300 to 1600, the age of incunabula is short indeed.

Nor is it necessary to move from one region to another in order to find this large cluster of changes. One must leave Paris and its environs with its Gothic cathedrals and faculties of theology, cross over the Alps and journey into Italy to find an early Renaissance. When one considers what was happening elsewhere on the continent between 1350 and 1450, one may wonder if an encounter with peculiar local conditions has not been mistaken for the advent of a new age. But one may move freely across all sorts of European frontiers—from Mount Etna to regions north of Stockholm, from Atlantic coasts to the mountains of eastern Montenegro—during the last half of the fifteenth century and one will find that the same sort of new workshops in major urban centres are producing books in almost all the languages of Western Europe. New trades such as that of compositor or type-founder are being created; traditional skills developed by metal workers, merchants and scholars are being directed towards new ends. New occupational groups are, in all regions, being mobilized by lay entrepreneurs driving to tap new markets and extend new trade networks. By 1500, one may say with some assurance that the age of scribes has ended and the age of printers has begun. (p. 21-23)

The advent of printing completely transformed the conditions under which texts were produced, distributed and consumed. It changed the way the contents of books were arranged, illustrated and presented. It arrested textual corruption, fixed texts more permanently, and enabled them to accumulate at an accelerated rate. It made possible new forms of crosscultural interchange and systematic large-scale data collection. It extended the reach of authors through time and through space, introduced eponymous authorship and subverted traditional forms of collective authority. However all this (and much else) was accomplished in a most deceptive way—not by discarding the products of scribal culture but by reproducing them in greater quantities than ever before. The *ars artificialiter scribendi* was first and foremost a duplicating process. Even while the conditions of scribal culture were being outmoded, texts reflecting these conditions were becoming more abundant and different spirits from different times were being simultaneously released. (p. 24)

The most revolutionary impact of the new technology was initially exerted simply by increasing the output of extant texts—whatever their original provenance.

This point is worth stressing because it is often overlooked. Attention is usually centered on trying to determine whether early printers drew on scribal backlists or contemporary authors to furnish their main stock-in-trade. The somewhat naïve assumption is made that such evidence will show whether printers encouraged the circulation of new ideas or not. Upon this basis, judgements are formed concerning the contribution made by printing to cognitive advance. Since the evidence is itself ambiguous, since most "new" works in the fifteenth century consisted of epitomes of old works while many old texts yielded much that seemed new in this era, conflicting interpretations are bound to result. The conviction that printing made a definite impact on Western culture is weakened by this kind of argument. It conveys an impression of cultural change that is too blurred and confused to leave much of a mark in our historical accounts.

[Printers] initially contributed to "the advancement of disciplines" less by marketing so-called "new" works than by providing individual readers with access to *more* works. The sheer increase in the quantity of copies in circulation was actually of immense significance. Augmented book production altered patterns of consumption; increased output changed the nature of individual intake. The literary diet of a given sixteenth-century reader was qualitatively different from that of his fourteenth-century counterpart. His staple diet had been enriched and intellectual ferment had been encouraged whether he consulted living authors or dead ones, "new" books or "old" ones. But a twentieth-century observer, intent on tracing trends or shifts in styles of thought and expression, is poorly situated to see this. (pp. 25-6)

Let me begin then by considering an issue which seems to be of fundamental importance and which enters into all debates centreing on the "problem of the Renaissance". The issue I have in mind is that of permanence. Given a classical revival that was still under way when new preservative powers were brought into play, one might expect that this revival would pose peculiar problems. Since it was initiated under one set of circumstances and perpetuated under wholly different ones, it would probably begin by resembling previous revivals and yet take an increasingly divergent course. Among other differences that would become apparent with the passage of time one would expect this revival to be more permanent than previous ones.

"To put it briefly, the two medieval renascences were limited and transitory; the Renaissance was total and permanent". As Panofsky's now celebrated formulation suggests, the issue of permanence does figure prominently in current debates. However typographical fixity does not. To be sure, one scholar has suggested that "humanism may have owed the ultimate survival of its ideas to Gutenberg's invention". But this comes as a casual aside, qualifying the author's main argument that the distinctive features of the "Italian Renaissance, as such" owed nothing to the "novelties of the printing press". "The pattern of the movement had been clearly established", he contends, before printing began to exert an impact. Since he does not deal with the question of how printing affected the patterning of cultural movements, I find Bolgar's argument ambiguous and incomplete, but that is somewhat beside the point. My basic concern is that his casual remark about "ultimate survival" has not been followed up. The implications of typographical fixity do not often get brushed aside in Renaissance studies simply because they are usually left out of account altogether.

This unfortunate omission may be partly attributed to the somewhat subtle, intangible nature of typographical fixity itself. One is reminded of the fifteenth-century abbot who exhorted his scribes to copy printed books because inscriptions made by hand upon skin were destined to outlive impressions made by printers' ink upon paper. Although hindsight shows clearly that the abbot was mistaken, we are no less prone to be deceived by appearances and appearances have become increasingly deceptive. By and large, printing required the use of paper—a less durable material than parchment or vellum to begin with and one that became ever more perishable as the centuries wore on and rag content diminished. Whereas the scraping and reuse of skin does not obliterate letters completely, the scrapping or reconversion of discarded printed matter leaves no palimpsests behind. When written messages are duplicated in such great abundance that they can be consigned to trash bins or converted into pulp, they are not apt to prompt thoughts about prolonged preservation. Manuscripts guarded in treasure rooms, wills locked in vaults, diplomas framed behind glass do appear to be more indestructible than road maps, kitchen calendars or daily newspapers.

Such considerations may help to explain why the preservative powers of print are still concealed in historical studies and why the capacity to fix data in a permanent form is often erroneously attributed to the invention of writing. . . . [The] preservative powers of print affected *all* forms of survival and revival; their impact was by no means confined to the return of the muses in quattrocento Italy. Medieval as well as classical traditions, technological as well as aesthetic developments were also affected by typographical fixity in ways that need to be investigated.

The immense consequences of the preservative powers of print are at present, however, concealed by the problem of the Renaissance. Instead of being attributed to the new technology, or even recognized as a new cultural trait that needs to be accounted for, permanence currently serves as a debating point. As an inherent virtue, somehow exuded by Renaissance culture, it is invoked to save the appearances of a century-old theory that has been steadily undermined. No explanation is offered as to why medieval classical revivals were more transient than that which occurred in quattrocento Italy. The fact that the latter did prove more permanent and hence lent itself to continuous systematic development is taken to justify setting it apart from prior revivals and inaugurating a new epoch with its advent. (pp. 27-9)

This brings me to some familiar variations played on the theme of permanence, centreing on the rise of classical scholarship and the recovery of classical texts. Kristeller, who accepts Panofsky's thesis and wishes to apply it more widely, stresses the unprecedented range and scope of classical studies in the Renaissance. Instead of being subordinated to theology, he notes, these studies became more autonomous. At the same time the selection of texts known to medieval scholars was greatly enlarged, almost reaching present limits. In drawing these distinctions, the activity of copyists is not distinguished from that of printers. Instead, both are merged in a general consideration of the humanist movement. To be sure, we are informed in one sentence that "the wide diffusion and popularity of the Latin classics in the sixteenth century and afterwards would not have been possible without the printing press". But the point is virtually cancelled out by the next sentence: "The introduction of paper . . . and the organization of a regular trade in manuscript books had a similar effect". Emphasis is placed on "the tremendous activity of humanists as copyists and later as editors". That copyists and editors performed significantly different rôles and that editing copy was a revolutionary innovation go unnoted. The humanist movement in general is thus credited with presenting the Western world with all those ancient texts that are, even now, still regarded as standard classics.

> It would be wrong to maintain that classical Latin literature . . . was neglected during the Middle Ages. . . . It would be equally wrong to deny that as a result of humanist discoveries the available patrimony of Latin literature was extended almost to its present limits. . . .
>
> Almost the entire body of extant Greek literature was deposited in Western libraries and diffused through handwritten copies and printed editions.
>
> Thus . . . both in the Latin and Greek fields, the Middle Ages possessed a significant selection of classical sources but . . . Renaissance humanism extended its knowledge almost to the entire range of its extant remains, that is to the point where modern scholarship has made its further discoveries from palimpsests and papyri.

It is difficult to ascertain just how far short of "present limits" is covered by the term "almost", and just at what point modern scholarship took over to make possible "further discoveries". From the advent of printing on, one must deal with a continuous process of recovery and with a continuous development of techniques for investigating the past. Further discoveries have never ceased to be made (for example certain plays of Menander are still being retrieved in this century) and in this sense the Renaissance has never come to an end. But more recent discoveries have come too late to be inserted into an undergraduate curriculum that was fixed, in a more or less permanent form, in the course of the sixteenth century. Hence they are regarded as being somewhat peripheral to the central corpus of Greek and Latin texts. The fixing of this corpus in a permanent mould *was* unprecedented, but Renaissance copyists were no more capable of accomplishing this than medieval copyists had been. If "Renaissance humanism extended its knowledge" almost to present limits, this is surely because ancient texts recovered by the humanists were not again "lost", that is actually destroyed, progressively corrupted, transplanted or mislaid.

In fact, many of the manuscripts that Petrarch and his successors managed to track down and get copied *have* since been lost. Some of the libraries in which the "recovered" texts were found have also disappeared. The same fate awaited quattrocento transcriptions and the new collections that were made of them. One example may suffice to illustrate this point. "*De Rerum Naturae* had been practically unknown for centuries and for a time its survival seems to have depended on a single manuscript. Then Poggio found it late in 1417". This stereotyped version breaks off the story before the crucial event occurred. The manuscript of Lucretius's poem that Poggio found also got lost. Fortunately he had had one more copy made. How many scribes would thereafter be set to work to preserve Lucretius's poem? How many friars might ferret out and destroy all extant copies? Might a few be "discovered" again by later book-hunters?—these are questions that cannot be certainly answered. But surely the future of the text was still uncertain until 1473 when it reached a printer's workshop in Brescia. Possibly it *still* remained uncertain thereafter—but not for very long. By the end of the sixteenth century, thirty whole editions had been issued. A school of pagan philosophy, long frowned upon by many churchmen, intermittently revived and repeatedly extirpated, had secured a permanent position within Western culture for the first time. But it was a Brescian printer and not Poggio Bracciolini who transformed the ancient Epicurean into the author of a standard classic.

As this example suggests, the book-hunting of quattrocento humanists was of immense significance for the future development of Western culture because—unlike texts which had been retrieved previously only to be lost again—the texts which the humanists rescued were duplicated in print and permanently secured. (pp. 43-5)

The distinction between making discoveries and securing them may seem somewhat subtle. Nevertheless, troublesome questions can be handled more easily if it is drawn. Why, for example, should humanists be credited with "discovering" ancient works that were obviously known already to some medieval scholars since they were found in the form of medieval copies? Kristeller sidesteps the question and suggests that the "merit" of humanist discoveries is "unduly disparaged" by posing it. Yet unless it is posed, medieval contributions to the survival of ancient classics are apt to be concealed from view.

> If an ancient Latin text survived only in one or two Carolingian copies and if there are but scanty traces of its having been read during the subsequent centuries the fact that such a text was found by a humanist and made generally available through numerous copies does constitute a discovery . . . the fact that some classical Latin authors such as Virgil or Ovid or Seneca or Boethius were widely known throughout the Middle Ages does not refute the equally obvious fact that some other authors such as Lucretius or Tacitus or Manlius were discovered by the humanists.

What constitutes a "discovery" is not really a fact at all—let alone an obvious one. "Finding" a text and making it "generally available" are two distinctly different sorts of activities. (p. 46)

By prolonging a precarious lifeline that carried fragments of antiquity down to the age of print, Petrarch and his successors performed much the same function that had been performed long before by Carolingian scribes and court scholars. By importing Greek texts from Byzantium and working with Greek scholars to translate them, Renaissance humanists functioned in much the same way as had the twelfth-century schoolmen who reintroduced the works of Aristotle, Galen, Euclid and others into the West. Different cross-cultural routes were involved in the twelfth-century revival and the early Italian Renaissance. But both shared in common limitations imposed by the conditions of scribal culture. They were confined to restricted regions and to a limited selection of classical texts. They were also directed at regaining ground that had been lost in preceding eras. The ground that humanist book-hunters sought to regain and the manner in which it had been lost is, I think, particularly worth pausing over. In this way we may bring out more clearly the peculiar limitations imposed by scribal book production and, at the same time, also suggest a possible connection between the twelfth-century and quattrocento revivals. (pp. 47-8)

Until the advent of printing, classical revivals were necessarily limited in scope and transitory in effect; a sustained and permanent recovery of all portions of the antique heritage remained out of reach. The introduction of paper (temporarily in eleventh-century Spain and later in Italy) could not possibly have had a "similar effect". Cheaper writing material probably quickened the pace of commercial correspondence and encouraged the recording of more sermons, orations, adages and poems. Diaries, memoirs, copybooks and notebooks could become more abundant; men of letters would find it easier to become their own scribes. But paper could only enliven arts and letters on an ephemeral basis. It could do nothing to lighten the labours or increase the output of the professional copyist. The same number of scribes had to be recruited and trained, and the same number of man-hours had to be expended to keep in circulation the same number of books. As long as texts could be duplicated only by hand, perpetuation of the classical heritage rested precariously on the shifting requirements of local élites. Texts imported into one region depleted supplies in others; the enrichment of certain fields of study by an infusion of ancient learning impoverished other fields of study by diverting scribal labour. For a full century after the coronation of Petrarch, the revival of learning in Italy was subject to the same limitations as had been previous revivals. If we accept the distinction between several limited and transient renaissances on the one hand, a permanent Renaissance of unprecedented range and scope on the other, then we must wait for the "novelties of printing" to appear before we can say that a genuinely new pattern was established.

This point seems particularly relevant to Panofsky's remarks about the formation of new disciplines such as history, philology and archaeology, to Kristeller's assertion that the "humanist movement" was responsible for the "rise of classical scholarship", and to many recent interpretations of the "historical revolution" of early modern times. (pp. 50-1)

A similar line of analysis may be applied to conventional treatments of Renaissance scholarship and historiography. Otto of Friesing had shown that the Donation of Constantine was a forgery in the twelfth century. Three centuries later, Lorenzo Valla had to show the same thing all over again. It was not Valla's critique that was unprecedented but rather the possibility of building systematically upon it. Classical scholarship and historical research along with a variety of auxiliary disciplines became subject to continuous cognitive advance only after and not until the establishment of printing plants in the second half of the fifteenth century. Valla was no more capable than Otto of Friesing had been of introducing a permanent revolution in textual criticism. "Jerome emended, but what he emended has since been corrupted", noted Valla's disciple, Erasmus. Erasmus also emended, but what he emended—instead of being corrupted—was progressively purified, improved and corrected. The initial impetus for a *continuous* development of scholarly disciplines was not provided by any group of scribal scholars whether they were sponsored by Carolingian or Medici patrons. This impetus was provided instead by an occupational group that came into being only after a new mode of book production had been introduced in Western Europe.

Numerous precedents may be found for the functions performed by the poets and rhetoricians, pedagogues and civil servants, who shaped the humanist movement between the days of Petrarch and those of Valla. None may be found for the functions performed by early scholar-printers who processed old texts in new workshops (aptly described as laboratories of erudition) and who turned out grammars and dictionaries as well as translations and editions. Whether freshly uncovered or long since assimilated, whether preserved in the form of one copy or corrupted by numerous transcriptions, almost all the texts of antiquity that are now described as classics were fixed in a new format and permanently secured in the remarkably short span of five or six decades. "By 1520, the great work of printing the classics was for the most part complete". During the same interval, moreover, the translation into

Latin of "almost the entire body of Greek literature then known" was also brought to completion.

The unprecedented character of the scholarly revolution wrought by printing is well illustrated by the fate of Greek studies in the West. Ever since the division of the ancient Roman Empire, knowledge of Greek had been rare among Western scholars and had largely hinged on intermittent contacts with Byzantium. Although a regional revival based on collaboration with Greek churchmen, envoys and exiles had flourished in Rome and Florence during the mid-fifteenth century, "knowledge of Greek remained comparatively rare even during the Renaissance". By the early sixteenth century, contacts with Byzantium had been severed, Ottoman advances consolidated, refugee enclaves were dying out, and Italy itself was the scene of invasions from the North. Given this constellation of events and keeping in mind that all major Greek texts had been translated into Latin by 1520, one might expect that "the impulse given by the humanists to the study of Greek" would have died out. Instead it was the scribal phrase "Graeca sunt ergo non legenda" that disappeared from Western texts—never to reappear again. The study of Greek was permanently inserted into the curriculum of academic institutions throughout Europe and the reach of classical scholars was gradually extended to encompass earlier phases of Hellenic civilization. If old forms of collaboration had produced entirely novel results, this was surely because Greek type-founts had been cut, dictionaries and grammars had been compiled and printed and original texts had been made available in the form of whole editions.

In this regard it seems unwarranted to blur the difference between earlier groups of scribal scholars and copyists and later groups of editors and correctors when discussing the contribution made by Greek expatriates to Western scholarship during the Renaissance. It is useful to learn how much the remarkable output of the Aldine press between 1494 and 1515 owed to aid furnished by Cretans and other Greek exiles who became members of the printer's household, formed the nucleus of his academy, and served him in innumerable ways. It is worth noting that these scholars accomplished more during a quarter-century in Venice than had their predecessors in Florence during an interval four times that long. But the Greeks who aided Aldus in Venice did not merely perform more efficiently the same functions that similar enclaves had previously performed. Since they were employed by a printer and engaged in processing copy for the new presses, they were bound to perform entirely new functions as well. When presenting their activities as a "chapter in the transmission of Greco-Byzantine learning to the West" it is essential to underline the unusual nature of this particular chapter. It covers an interval that saw major changes in the way all forms of learning were transmitted. Intellectual trade routes were drastically reoriented in a manner that revolutionized traditional contacts between East and West—to the extent of outmoding previous reliance on personal intercourse and diminishing the impact of emigré movements. The Aldine editions drew on Greek aid. But they also emancipated Western scholars from their traditional reliance upon this kind of aid, so that Germans beyond the Alps, Englishmen across the Channel—ultimately Western colonists in the new world—could pursue Hellenic studies regardless of what happened to Greeks in Constantinople or Athens, in Crete, Venice, Florence or Rome. (pp. 52-4)

In view of the foregoing, it seems misleading to stop short with the humanist movement in Italy when trying to account for the so-called rise of classical scholarship and the development of auxiliary disciplines. Humanism spurred efforts to retrieve classical texts and artefacts, sharpened sensitivity to anachronism, and quickened curiosity about all aspects of antiquity, but it could not supply the new element of continuity that is implied by the use of the term "rise". Findings relating to lost texts and dead languages began to accumulate in an unprecedented fashion not because of some distinctive ethos shaped in quattrocento Italy but because a new technology had been placed at the disposal of a far-flung community of scholars. (p. 55)

Elizabeth L. Eisenstein, "The Advent of Printing and the Problem of the Renaissance," in Past and Present: A Journal of Historical Studies, *No. 45, November, 1969, pp. 19-89.*

Paul F. Grendler

[*Grendler is an American historian and educator. In the excerpt below, he examines the history and impact of printing and book distribution during the fifteenth and sixteenth centuries.*]

Printing had an enormous effect on all learning, but its impact was neither revolutionary nor sudden. Instead, over a period of fifty to one hundred years it so greatly facilitated the dissemination of the results of enquiry as to propel philosophy and all other branches of learning into a new era. (p. 25)

An earlier innovation helped make printing possible: paper came from China through the Near East into the West about 1100. It spread quickly throughout Europe until the majority of manuscript books were written on paper in the early fifteenth century. Paper suited printing far better than vellum (prepared animal skin): it was more pliable, absorbed ink better than vellum, and was considerably cheaper.

Johann Gutenberg at Strasburg and Mainz experimented for years before he and his associates were able to solve the technical problems necessary for printing. Their first major achievement was the beautiful forty-two-line Bible, probably begun in 1452 and certainly completed by 1455. But printing did not make a significant impact on learning until presses had multiplied, their production had diversified, and the reading public had become aroused. This led gradually to a broad system of distribution and marketing. This process began about 1470 and came to full fruition about 1500. By the end of the year 1470, some nineteen towns had printing presses; by 1500, about 255 towns did. By the end of the incunabular period, European presses had produced over 30,000 editions, a large majority of them in the 1480s and 1490s. Moreover, any count omits those books which disappeared without trace; that is, not a single copy of the press run survives to document its existence. Possibly 10 to 25 per cent of fifteenth-century editions may have been lost, and the figure may be higher in the sixteenth century. Printing expanded severalfold in the sixteenth century, but counting the editions is not yet possible because insufficient bibliographies of countries, places and individual printers have been compiled. A great number of towns of 2,000 or more inhabitants, and many smaller ones, had a press at one time or another between 1455 and 1600, some of them continuously. Compared with the production of manuscripts, printing multiplied the available stock of books by a factor that is difficult to estimate. But it never completely eliminated the scribe, partly because some readers and book collectors preferred manuscripts for their beauty and historicity.

The first printed books imitated manuscripts, and like them, lacked title pages in the modern sense. Instead, following the custom of manuscripts, the recto (front or righthand) side of the first leaf presented very brief information about the contents, perhaps with the author's name. It then launched into the text. Much of the information about the book frequently appeared at the end of the text in a colophon, which consisted of a few lines giving several or all of the following: title, author, name of printer, the person who commissioned the printing (i.e., paid the expenses), place of publication, and perhaps the day, month, and year of the completion of printing.

Gradually printers departed from the model of the handwritten book. Since books were usually shipped as unbound sheets, the recto of the first leaf became easily soiled; so printers in the 1460s and 1470s often kept it blank. Between 1470 and 1480 they began to create the title page by placing a word or two that indicated the contents on the otherwise blank page. Only after 1520 did almost all printed books provide title pages that listed most of all of the following: title, author, printer's mark, sometimes a comprehensive description of the contents, name of dedicatee, name of publisher, and year of publication. Indeed, the printer's emblem became a famous and striking feature of title pages. Few symbols anywhere match the beauty and simplicity of the Aldine dolphin and anchor. Title pages of the second half of the sixteenth-century became cluttered with too much of everything for modern tastes: information, decoration, several sizes and kinds of type. They reflected the growing variety of the tools at the printer's command and an almost baroque artistic standard.

Printed books evolved into better-designed packages of information. Since they cost less per copy than manuscripts, they could include certain 'extravagances', such as better spacing, clearer type, fewer abbreviations, illustrations, contents lists and indexes, if the publisher was confident of sufficient sales. Successful and clever printers adjusted their topography to meet the taste and requirements of the readership that they hoped to attract for given kinds of books. (pp. 25-7)

Most manuscripts had limited foliation and rarely pagination; contents lists and indexes were uncommon. Printers developed such aids to readers gradually and adopted them selectively. Gaining experience as producers and sellers, printers adjusted their output to meet the requirements of different readers, ranging from the schoolboy to the learned humanist, lawyer or university professor teaching Aristotle. In the sixteenth century especially, large comprehensive volumes such as the Bible, theological *summae,* and compilations like Erasmus' *Adagia* became festooned with indexes, contents lists, marginalia, lists of authorities and Greek terms.

Once well established, the printing press had the great advantage over the scriptorium of the ability to produce numerous identical copies in a comparatively short time. There is a tendency to contrast the error-filled single manuscript, each the unique product of a scribe's labours, with the hundreds and thousands of exact copies that streamed from the press. The contrast is overdrawn. At least some manuscript copying had developed safeguards against error, guaranteeing that copies were identical in essentials. Printed books, on the other hand, added printers' errors and editorial mistakes; if these were caught during the press run, ad hoc corrections were made in some copies. Errors and variants stemmed from lack of experience, poor craftsmanship and economic pressure. The preparation of copy (which might be a slovenly manuscript, a heavily annotated one or even an emended printed book), composition (setting of type in the forme), correction (running off a sample, reading it for errors, then correcting the type), presswork (the mechanical part of pressing the images on paper) and dispersing the type (taking it out of one forme in order to prepare the next sheet) went on more or less simultaneously. Renaissance printers generally lacked the equipment to set up the type for an entire book, to proofread and correct, then print from corrected type, in separate stages. Because paper was expensive, printers tried to use everything that was printed, making corrections as they went along. Printers might hire cheap labour; if so, numerous people might participate, helping to get the job done but increasing the possibility of error and variation. Given the far from ideal working conditions, it is remarkable that Renaissance printers produced relatively accurate copies.

How many copies? The number of copies in a press run (i.e., a single edition or printing) was modest at first but then rose. The estimates of the press run for the Gutenberg Bible range from 54 copies on paper and 16 on vellum to 240 on paper and 30 on vellum. Between 1465 and 1471, Sweynheym and Pannartz, the pioneer printing firm of Rome, apparently printed press runs of 275 copies of a varied group of Latin works, the majority classical and patristic titles, in different formats. Press runs of 400 copies were also common at this time, and ones of 1,000 had already appeared in the early 1470s. Press runs of about 1,000 became common perhaps as early as the 1480s and definitely by the close of the incunabular period. The figure of 1,000 remained the norm for Venetian imprints of titles of ordinary sales potential throughout the sixteenth century.

The Antwerp Press of Christophe Plantin (active 1555-89) printed average press runs of 1,250 or 1,500 copies because a single press in Plantin's shop could print 1,250 sheets of a normal edition in one day. But individual press runs in the sixteenth century varied a great deal, from as few as

Venice in the early sixteenth century, when the city stood at the height of its importance as a center of printing and trade.

100 copies for commissioned works intended for limited distribution to as many as 5,000 copies for books of great interest and anticipated high sales. Luther's *An den Christlichen Adel deutscher Nation* (Wittenberg 1520) had an initial press run of 4,000 copies plus numerous reprints. But the high number of copies and the circumstances were unusual. Books intended for a scholarly audience (legal, philosophical and scientific titles, for example) were likely to have press runs of up to 1,000 copies, and often considerably fewer. Works demanded by a wide audience or intended for an assured readership (bibles, liturgical manuals, school texts like Latin grammars, vernacular classics, such as Ariosto's chivalric epic poem *Orlando Furioso,* and works of controversy on contemporary issues) had larger press runs.

The number of reprints, if any, presents a truer measure of a book's diffusion. Publishers did not risk a large first edition, unless they had evidence of a considerable demand, because of the high cost of printing and the lack of legal protection (see below). But when a title sold well, a publisher or his competitor issued reprints. A popular title might go through numerous editions within a few years, both those issued by the first publisher and those issued by others. The press runs of reprints were probably the same size as first editions.

Practically all major publishers printed books in Latin and the regional vernacular language. Specialised publishers in important commercial centres also published in other European vernaculars and/or Greek, Hebrew, Arabic and so on. For example, Spanish titles were printed in Venice, and Italian titles in Elizabethan London.

Book distribution was remarkably international. Latin titles, which included most works in humanistic studies, and works on philosophy (although moral philosophy was a limited exception), theology, law, medicine and physical sciences were printed widely and sold across Europe. Although the majority of vernacular books were sold in one linguistic area, a few were distributed internationally. Regular and extensive commercial networks developed so that, for example, Venetian publishers shipped their books as far away as London, Madrid, Cracow and the Near East. Publishers stocked not only their own imprints but, acting as booksellers, those of other presses. Regional and international trade fairs played a key role in the international distribution of books. (pp. 27-9)

The Renaissance scholar had a new means of communicating with his public: the printing press. When an author finished his book, he took his text to a publisher, and the two joined forces. If the printer was willing, they entered into some kind of verbal or, rarely, written agreement to publish. Instead of a standard contract, authors and printers made a variety of ad hoc agreements. Renaissance men boasted that printing conferred immortality on authors, but few received direct financial reward for their books. The following arrangements are typical for both scholarly and popular books.

First, the printer might ask the author to bear all the printing costs. A wealthy author could pay them from his own pocket; if he had a patron, such as a prince, ecclesiastical lord or religious institution, the patron bore the cost. Author or patron subsidised publication either with an outright payment or by agreeing to purchase a large number of copies. Since printing might involve several hundred ducats or more, a substantial amount of money changed hands.

When the author partially subsidised publication—a more common accord—author and printer shared printing costs and finished volumes. The author might agree to purchase a substantial part of the press run (perhaps 300 of a press run of 600 copies), leaving the rest for the printer to sell. Third, the printer frequently published at his own risk and retained the entire press run except for a few—twenty-five or fifty—author's copies. The printer paid the author nothing; he bore the risk and earned a profit if his judgement was good.

The fourth arrangement, probably least common and a later development, was that the publisher paid the author a small sum for his manuscript. Obviously he would do that only when he felt certain that the book would be a commercial success. But payment did not depend on a fixed standard, such as royalties calculated as a percentage of sales: the publisher would give the author a lump sum and/or payment in kind depending on his eagerness to publish. Even Erasmus could not change the system. Between 1517 and 1520, he tried to persuade Johann Froben of Basle, his major publisher and good friend, to pay him on a regular fixed basis, but Froben remained evasive. Froben gave Erasmus occasional gifts and sums of money, and named his son Johannes Erasmius, but offered no contract. However, Froben did publish Erasmus' first editions of the Church Fathers, paraphrases of the New Testament, and Greek New Testament.

The author might gain indirect rewards by selling the copies he received. Indeed, printers sometimes promised to delay offering the book for sale for a short period, such as a month, in order to give the author a better opportunity to dispose of his copies.

The author also sent copies of his book, accompanied by flattering letters, to potential patrons. This was a variation on the common practice of prefacing a book with a dedicatory letter to a prince, noble or prelate. Indeed, some authors dedicated each section of a book to a new patron. Although these sycophantic letters make uncomfortable reading and might suggest that the author had sold his integrity, this was not necessarily the case. Authors viewed such letters as commercial ventures: they expected to receive favours for their praise. Patrons, in turn, liked to be 'honoured' and accepted it as an obligation to support learning. Moreover, flattering dedicatory letters burnished a prince's or cardinal's reputation. And if the patron did not send a gift, the author might hint at the patron's miserliness in his next book.

While authors received little or nothing for their books, the printer bore responsibilities and expenses that went beyond press work. The publisher might have to arrange and pay for the preparation of indexes and tables and for proofreading in the author's absence. If the author was present, he might live in the publisher's house and work closely with the printer and his staff. These happy circumstances produced the warm collaboration of author, editor, publisher and workmen seen in the house of Aldus Manutius in Venice and Johann Froben in Basle. Then publishing truly became an enterprise of common purpose and close bonds. More often, proofreading and indexing were done by an employee or a local collaborator, such as a schoolteacher, who worked for a small fee. Author and readers then complained bitterly about the numerous errors.

Behind the publisher's parsimony toward authors lay the lack of copyright protection. Publishers were loath to risk much of their own money on a new book because they would almost always see it quickly pirated. That is, another publisher would obtain a copy of the first edition and reprint it without compensating the original publisher. Since the original publisher had no effective means of stopping his rival, his own edition would have to compete with the pirated reprint, and he might be left with hundreds of unsold copies on his hands. So publishers demanded that authors should bear most of the financial risk of initial publication.

Printing began without any legal restrictions on the right of publication, and the concept won only limited acceptance in the sixteenth century. As early as the 1480s and 1490s, and with increasing frequency later, an author or more often the publisher might obtain a copyright (called a 'privilege') giving him exclusive publication rights for a limited period of time (typically ten years) to be enforced through threat of fines and confiscation of illegal editions. But the privilege was valid only within the political jurisdiction (city, princedom or similar) which granted it, and sometimes had limited efficacy there. International copyright did not exist, even though a volume might carry pompous and threatening privileges of king and pope. These were intended more for advertising purposes than copyright protection; printers hoped that the approval of authority would help to sell copies.

So, despite the privilege, a printer in another political jurisdiction, which might be a city only fifty miles away, could obtain a copy of the book and reprint it under his own name. For example, from 1509 to 1520, Erasmus' *Moriae encomium* appeared in at least thirty-five editions in nine different cities, printed by fourteen or more publishers. The places of publication were Antwerp, Basle (two publishers), Cologne, Florence, Mainz, Paris (four publishers), Sélestat, Strasburg and Venice (two publishers), plus editions lacking typographical information. Reprinting was almost routine at a time when the concept of literary property or binding commercial restrictions hardly existed. Only large and complicated books, such as those with technical illustrations, escaped unauthorised reprinting because they were too much trouble and expense to pirate.

Authors and printers complained about the lack of protection, but hastened to take advantage of the situation. A famous author like Erasmus could even turn the publishers' piracy to his advantage. After the first edition of a work of his appeared, rival publishers offered Erasmus money for a revised version. Erasmus obligingly made a few changes, wrote a new prefatory letter, and the publisher issued the work as a 'new edition revised by the author'. Readers then bought the new edition, leaving the original publisher and booksellers with unsold copies on their hands. (pp. 31-4)

The lack of copyright protection had serious financial disadvantages for author and publisher, and encouraged the sharp practices characteristic of the printing industry. But it aided the dissemination of ideas. Luther's views could not have spread so astonishingly quickly without the unrestricted reprinting of his tracts.

Books of less inflammatory subject-matter also enjoyed the same freedom of wide diffusion. A good edition of Cicero's *Epistulae ad familiares,* a text used in schools across Europe, could be reprinted at will. It meant that teachers and students everywhere could use the text at small cost, because unrestricted reprinting probably drove down the price. (p. 34)

Printing quickened the pace of intellectual discovery, communication, discourse, and learning. The Renaissance did not depend on the press for its birth or survival. The intellectual, civic, economic and political circumstances that nurtured the 'revival of learning' in Italy long preceded the date at which printing began to make an impact (not before *c.* 1470). Petrarch, Leonardo Bruni and other key figures lived and died before the advent of printing. Major discoveries of classical texts were made before printing. Above all, the *studia humanitatis* and the scholars and schools who perpetuated them were well established in Italy before printing. In like manner, the intellectual stirrings that produced the Renaissance in Northern Europe were under way by the time that printing came of age. Printing did facilitate the diffusion of ideas from Italy to the North, and their circulation there, thus compressing into a generation or two developments that had taken three to four generations in Italy.

Printing enhanced or altered the conditions of enquiry in great and small ways, most of which contemporaries judged to be beneficial. Some changes are self-evident, others are more subtle. A significant but sometimes overlooked contribution of early printing was to make quickly and widely available the corpus of medieval philosophy. Incunabular publishers printed the works of Albertus Magnus, Duns Scotus, William of Ockham and others in great number. For example, over 200 printings of the works of Thomas Aquinas appeared before 1501. Thereafter, the printing of medieval philosophical texts slowed considerably with the exception of those that retained their position in the curriculum. Peter of Spain's *Summule logicales* (1246) was printed over 150 times before 1600 because it continued to serve as a university text for logic. The massive printing of medieval philosophy during the first fifty years of printing ensured its survival and continuity; philosophers then accepted, modified or rejected the medieval traditions.

While printing perpetuated the old, it also ensured quick and wide diffusion of the new. Lorenzo Valla died in 1457, just at the appearance of the printing press. It spread his new views in *De voluptate, De libero arbitrio* and other works, in Italy and beyond long before 1500. The *Elegantiae linguae Latinae libri sex,* his linguistic and cultural manifesto that so influenced the humanistic perception of language and history, had numerous incunabular editions, and was printed again and again through the sixteenth century, either in its original form or in abridged versions. Printing also helped give birth to new philosophical doctrines by making available ancient sources. The emergence of a sceptical tradition was primarily the consequence of the recovery and printing of ancient collections of sceptical ideas, above all the publication in 1562 and 1569 of Latin editions of the works of Sextus Empiricus. While his works remained in manuscript, they were barely known; in print they had considerable influence.

The astonishing multiplicity of books produced by the printing press greatly facilitated the mastery of basic skills that were the prerequisites for learning. Incunabular presses printed more Latin grammars than any other kind of book; sixteenth-century presses probably followed suit, although the low survival rate of copies, even of whole printings of these books, makes the statement tentative. School-children and adult learners could own printed copies of Latin grammars, glossaries and elementary reading texts. The same was true for other kinds of textbooks: the classics studied in school, the books used in the university curriculum, arithmetics, technical manuals, vernacular self-help books and letter-writing manuals. Even writing could be taught more easily through printed texts. It is likely that printing helped broaden intellectual participation, because anyone with facility in Latin and a rudimentary knowledge of the pagan and Christian classics could join in the major scholarly, political and religious discussions of the age. This state of affairs lasted so long as the unity of knowledge persisted. After the sixteenth century, the centrifugal forces unleashed by the destruction of Christian unity, the growth of the vernaculars (which the press also encouraged) and the addition of new subjects of study fragmented the republic of letters.

For the scholar, the sheer quantity of available books broadened and deepened his scholarship. If the meaning of a passage in Aristotle baffled him, he could examine his own copies of other works of Aristotle, plus the commentaries, and the texts of other classical and medieval authors for clarification. He could also refer to the original Greek, if he read it. In similar fashion, scholarship became more cumulative and wide-ranging, because the Renaissance scholar could use a greater variety of authors and texts to make his point than could his medieval predecessor. Printing facilitated the eclecticism so typical of Renaissance philosophy; philosophers gloried in being able to use the numerous philosophical works now printed. And printing largely freed readers from geographical constraints: the London scholar could own books printed in Basle. Indeed, a sign of the geographical freeedom conferred by the press is that few university towns became large publishing centres, while commercial and population centres did.

In science, the printed book offered the great technical advantage of the means of duplicating the graphic arts (woodcuts and engravings) for scientific illustration. A manuscript drawing was unique; it required an artist of equal skill to copy it, and his copy would not necessarily be identical. Now printing could reproduce thousands of identical illustrations. The anatomical drawings in medical works, geometrical and trigonometrical diagrams in mathematical works, pictures of plants in botanical books, illustrations of animals in works of zoology, maps in geographies, and diagrams of mechanical contrivances in books of technology contributed greatly to these fields. Even inaccurate illustrations, such as the fanciful animals to be found in early zoological books, were useful, because they could be improved or rejected after the real thing had been seen.

Printing made possible the diffusion of knowledge through translation and popularisation to a degree unimaginable earlier. The press produced an immeasurable number of translations, especially in the sixteenth century. Practically all ancient Greek works were translated into Latin. There were also many translations from those languages into one or another vernacular, a smaller number from one vernacular to another, and relatively few from the vernacular into Latin. Translations of ancient works of history, literature and moral philosophy into vernacular languages were especially numerous. This suggests that those who lacked the opportunity to learn Latin and Greek had a great desire to acquire the wisdom of the ancients, and they succeeded. Popularisations of learned material achieved the same results. One example among many is the theory of love articulated by Marsilio Ficino from Plato and the later Neoplatonists. Ficino first synthesised his doctrine of 'Platonic love' in a learned Latin commentary on Plato's *Symposium*; Platonic love later had remarkable diffusion among writers of prose and poetry in many vernacular languages.

Printing certainly broadened and probably intensified controversy in an already contentious age. Before printing, two men engaged in a public disputation in an academic setting, or exchanged letters, and only a small audience heard or read their words initially; it took time for their views to spread. Not so after printing, for the press offered the opportunity to respond quickly and repeatedly to an ever-widening audience. Anyone with access to a press could join in as quickly as the author could write and the printer print. In extreme cases, this was a matter of days. Controversy carried on by means of inflammatory printed matter began in the early years of printing, but Savonarola's tracts printed in Florence in 1494-8 against those who opposed his reforms demonstrated the great polemical power of the press. (pp. 37-40)

Paul F. Grendler, "Printing and Censorship," in The Cambridge History of Renaissance Philosophy, *edited by Charles B. Schmitt, Quentin Skinner, Eckhard Kessler and Jill Kraye, Cambridge at the University Press, 1988, pp. 25-53.*

Stanley Morison and Holbrook Jackson

[*Morison was an English typographer, and Jackson was an English essayist and literary historian. In the excerpt below, they briefly examine the origins and impact of printing in Europe.*]

The form of the written book, the ancestor of the printed book, was the lineal descendant through many stages of the author's own personal copy. The scribes imitated the author and the printers imitated the scribes. Hence it is that the title page, the running headline, the chapter division, and the index are not to be found in early printed books. Progress in so revolutionary an invention as printing was necessarily slow. The scribes naturally hated its merciless rivalry, and the Church, though quick to seize upon the invention for the printing of indulgence-certificates, liturgical, legal, and theological works, took care to control the new craft. The State itself was suspicious of sedition. Schoolmasters, however, seem to have welcomed the craft with enthusiasm, and the favourite grammatical treatise, called the *Donatus* from its author's name, Aelius Donatus, enjoyed a considerable vogue. It was apparently the first book printed with movable types, and fragments of many early editions testify to its very considerable circulation. Gutenberg printed it in 1448 or so. Broadsheets and bibles, psalters, law books, and commentaries followed. Slowly but surely the scribe was superseded. At first the printer kindly left him a space at the chapter heads for a decorated initial, to be inserted at the scribe's leisure. Red and blue paragraphing was also jobbed out to the writers, but when two-colour printing became practicable the rubricators were out of work, and sought refuge in the establishments of bookbinders, where they filled in their time as rulers of the page, i.e., they squared the book with thin red rules. Finally this supererogatory work was taken from them and they disappeared altogether. It took the printers sixty years or more in which to emancipate the book from the manuscript tradition and to place their craft upon an independent basis. The title-page began as a mere two-line text printed high up on the page. The printer's trade-mark or device, a pictorial woodcut, subsequently became an integral part of the title-page, and, while the printer's name was to continue in its position at the end of the book, it became usual to foot the title-page with the name of the bookseller or publisher. In the sixteenth century the spread of learning, the heat of controversy, and the stimulus of commercial gain did much to develop the craft. The activity of the Aldi at Venice in the field of these plain reprints was a remarkable portent. From 1495 to 1597 they were prolific producers of editions of classic authors. Nor was the example lost. Their success created a number of imitators in all parts, notably in Lyons, where Sebastian Gryphius, an Italian, did a thriving business in pirated aldines. . . . Desire for quick and easy profit did its deadly work of lowering the standard of printing. Worn types, inferior ink, and bad paper destroyed by degrees the power to produce and the taste to appreciate good printing. From the later decades of the sixteenth century the story is one of increasing degradation. Books were never so popular. The great Leyden firm of Elzevir who issued a sort of Everyman Library of their day, inferior though their issues were to the best Italian and French work, kept alive in some sort the old tradition of Tory and Jenson. Their editions, more famous perhaps than they deserve, on the whole fail in their illustrations. At last it was the age of engraving. Book illustration from incised plates had been attempted by early printers in Italy and the Low Countries. In 1477 full-page engravings appeared in a devotional work printed at Florence. The printer was pleased enough, however, to equip the second edition (1491) with woodcuts. The experience of the other pioneers also pointed against the use of metal. Experiments by goldsmiths, craftsmen and others continued here and there, but it was not until 1551 that a really practical attempt was made at illustration by means of the copper plate. At this time one Jerome Cock, who was later to become a colleague of Christopher Plantin, the famous Antwerp printer, put forth a series of cuts of Roman antiquities. The elapse of ten years or so saw the invention by Plantin of the engraved title-page, and in 1568 the English Bishops' Bible appeared with an engraved frontispiece. In 1596 appeared the brilliant and delicate work of Theodor de Bry of Frankfort. The rest of Europe followed. In a few years the woodcut was no longer a thing of the present, and book-illustration in the seventeenth-century was completely in the hands of the engravers. In England, Hollar and Faithorne, in France François Chauveau, and the Luykens in Holland, produced an abundance of work of varying merit. (pp. 11-14)

Stanley Morison and Holbrook Jackson, "A Survey of Printing History," in their A Brief Survey of Printing: History and Practice, *Knopf, 1923, pp. 1-23.*

FURTHER READING

Bush, M. L. *Renaissance, Reformation, and the Outer World.* London: Blandford Press, 1967, 387 p.

Surveys the history of Europe from 1450 to 1660.

Chamberlin, E. R. *Everyday Life in Renaissance Times.* London: B. T. Batsford, 1965, 200 p.

Background information on everyday life among the courtly and the common during the Renaissance. Explores violent aspects of life common to the era such as the plague, witch-hunts, and the Inquisition.

Elton, G. R. "The Age." In his *Reformation Europe, 1517-1559,* pp. 274-325. New York: Harper Torchbooks, 1963.

Introduces social aspects of the Reformation era such as the religious revolution, art, literature, and learning, the nation-state, and the expansion of Europe.

Green, V. H. H. "The Renaissance." In his *Renaissance and Reformation: A Survey of European History between 1450 and 1660,* pp. 29-57. London: Edward Arnold (Publishers), 1964.

Provides a general background to the Renaissance, focusing on its manifestation in both Italy and northern Europe.

Hoar, George A. "Protestant Reformation—Tragedy or Triumph for Christian Humanism?" In *The Dawn of Modern Civilization: Studies in Renaissance, Reformation and Other Topics Presented to Honor Albert Hyma,* edited by Kenneth A. Strand, pp. 29-53. Ann Arbor, Mich.: Ann Arbor Publishers, 1962.

Examines the humanists' role during the Reformation.

King, Margaret. "Renaissance and Humanism." In *Humanism and the Renaissance,* by S. Dresden, translated by Margaret King, pp. 214-37. New York: World University Library, 1968.

Examines the relationship between the Renaissance era and humanism.

Kristeller, Paul Oskar. "Paganism and Christianity." In his *The Classics and Renaissance Thought: Martin Classical Lectures,* Vol. XV, pp. 70-91. Cambridge: Harvard University Press, 1955.

Explores the relationship of the Protestant and Catholic controversy to the Renaissance, concluding that "since the religious convictions of Christianity were either retained or transformed, but never really challenged, it seems . . . appropriate to call the Renaissance a fundamentally Christian age."

———. *Renaissance Thought II: Papers on Humanism and the Arts.* New York: Harper and Row, 1965, 234 p.

Compilation of previously published essays on Italian and European humanism.

Pigman, G. W., III. "Versions of Imitation in the Renaissance." *Renaissance Quarterly* XXXIII, No. 1 (Spring 1980): 1-32.

Examines the imitation of classical authors by some leading writers of the Renaissance, including Desiderius Erasmus.

Spitz, Lewis W. Introduction to *The Religious Renaissance of the German Humanists,* by Lewis W. Spitz, pp 1-19. Cambridge: Harvard University Press, 1963.

Explores several interpretations of and influences upon the development and significance of northern humanism.

Webster, David and Green, Louis, eds. *Documents in Renaissance and Reformation History.* North Melbourne, Australia: Cassell, 1969, 226 p.

Utilizes excerpts from extant documents to trace the development of European cultural attitudes during the Renaissance and Reformation.

James Thomson

1700-1748

Scottish poet and dramatist

Regarded as one of the leading poets in eighteenth-century European literature, Thomson is primarily known for *The Seasons,* a four-part poetic work about nature and its transformations during the course of the year. Considered Thomson's masterpiece, *The Seasons* immensely influenced eighteenth-century English and Continental literature, reflecting the period's fascination with nature and establishing a paradigm for pastoral poetry throughout Europe. Thomson is also known for his patriotic poem "Rule Britannia," from the masque *Alfred,* written with David Mallet and set to music by Thomas Augustine Arne. Since its debut in 1740, "Rule Britannia" has been perhaps the emblematic song of Great Britain.

Born the son of a clergyman in southern Scotland, Thomson was raised in the picturesque rural environment, depicted in his most famous poems and later studied for the ministry at Edinburgh University. In 1725, he went to London, wishing to pursue a literary career. While employed as a tutor, he worked on *The Seasons,* publishing *Winter* in 1726, *Summer* the following year, *Spring* in 1728, and *Autumn* in 1730. Even after publishing the collected cycle that same year, Thomson continued reworking and revising his masterpiece, introducing significant changes and additions and eventually publishing a revised edition in 1744. The poem was received enthusiastically, bestowing not only literary fame on Thomson but also the attractive position of travelling companion and tutor to Charles Talbot, son of the future Lord Chancellor. Thomson held this post, which provided him with the opportunity to visit France and Italy, until 1733, when he became Secretary of Briefs in the Court of Chancery. In 1737, he lost the secretarial appointment, owing to the death of the Lord Chancellor. The following year, upon the intervention of his friend George Lyttelton, the poet received an annual pension from the Prince of Wales. His financial situation became quite comfortable in 1744, when he was named Surveyor-General of the Leeward Islands. Highly esteemed by literary London, surrounded by loyal friends, and the recipient of sinecures, royalties, and a royal pension, Thomson spent the last years of his life quietly, in a fine house in Kew Lane, Richmond, not far from his friend Alexander Pope. As many commentators—including Thomson himself—have noted, his life, though closely bound to writing, was characterized by a certain quality of indolence, which is one of the themes of his poetic oeuvre, notably, the last poem completed before his death, *The Castle of Indolence.*

Characterized as a descriptive work lacking a narrative structure, *The Seasons,* with its stately blank verse construction and Latinate vocabulary, harks to the poetry of John Milton. Yet Thomson, while emulating Milton, superimposed his idiosyncratic diction onto an archaic poetic form, thus creating striking and highly suggestive images and harmonies. Thomson's descriptions are eminently pictorial, conjuring up the characteristic atmosphere encountered in the works of such landscape artists as Nicolas Poussin, Claude Lorrain, and Salvator Rosa. "Thomson and Dyer," wrote Mario Praz in *The Romantic Agony,* "with their descriptions which translate into terms of literature the pictorial manner of Claude Lorrain and Salvator Rosa, are the godfathers of the Picturesque." Influenced by artists, the author of *The Seasons* in turn inspired the English painter Joseph Mallord William Turner, who honored the Scottish poet in his 1811 picture *Thomson's Aeolian Harp.* However, as critics have argued, *The Seasons* is more than a purely descriptive poem, considering that Thomson extends his interest to include not only nature but the observer, as well as the gamut of feelings elicited by the contemplation of nature's majesty. Thomson's concern for feelings, as commentators remark, reflects the spirit of the time, pointing to the Romantic sensibility of later poets. As such, Thomson is considered a forerunner of such poets as William Cowper and William Wordsworth.

Described by some critics as a precursor of Romanticism,

Thomson is nevertheless firmly rooted in the traditions of Classicism and Rationalism, his world view being clearly defined by the paramount significance he accorded science. Thomson venerated the scientist and philosopher Sir Isaac Newton, whose philosophy of nature represented the dominant intellectual paradigm of the period. "Newton," as Douglas Bush points out, "sees everywhere in the universe the proofs not only of design, both majestic and minute, but of God's continuously active care." The Newtonian conception of God as architect and guardian of the universe constitutes the religious and philosophical foundation of *The Seasons.* Related to Newton's theology, and also incorporated into the intellectual framework of *The Seasons,* is the idea of the Great Chain of Being, ultimately traceable to Platonic idealism, which postulates a hierarchical gradation of beings, from the lowest to the highest. In addition Thomson, as did many other poets, turned to Newton for accurate poetic description; the seminal scientific work from which Thomson benefited was Newton's *Opticks,* a treatise explaining the nature of color and light. "With Newtonian eyes," Marjorie Hope Nicholson explained, "the poets discovered new beauties in the most familiar aspects of nature, which had always been the stuff of poetry: in individual colors seen through the prism, the rainbow, in sunrise and sunset, in the succession of colors throughout the day." But no poet of the mid-century, Nicholson asserted, "responded to Newtonian color and light more fully than did Thomson in *The Seasons,* and no other poet so well used the new techniques."

In *Liberty,* a five-part poetical panorama of various countries and their governments and mores, Thomson drew from the optimistic moralism of Anthony Ashley Cooper, Lord Shaftesbury, to extol the unrivalled virtues of Britain's political system. Indicative of Thomson's British patriotism, *Liberty,* as well as the poem *Britannia,* also reveals the poet's sympathies for the political opposition—headed by the Prince of Wales—to the Whig prime minister Sir Robert Walpole, known for his feuds with writers. *The Castle of Indolence,* a verse allegory detailing, in Spenserian diction, the ills of indolence and the blessings of industry, has been hailed by critics as a brilliant and highly suggestive recreation of an old poetic mode. Thomson's other writings include incidental poems, exemplified by gentle love lyrics, and five dramas, which seldom rise above rhetorical bombast, according to critics. Thomson did gain some measure of fame as a playwright, however, particularly with his 1745 tragedy *Tancred and Sigismonda,* which is based on an episode from Alain-René Lesage's popular picaresque novel *Gil Blas.*

Thomson's international reputation can be measured by the success of *The Seasons.* Accessible to readers in translation, the poem became immensely popular shortly upon publication in England, eliciting praise from both the reading public at large and litterateurs and exerting an extraordinary influence on writers. In the German-speaking world, Thomson's admirers included Albrecht von Haller, author of the poem *Die Alpen (The Alps),* Ewald von Kleist, who wrote *Frühling (Spring),* the lyric poet Johann Peter Uz, and Gotthold Ephraim Lessing. In an adaptation by Gottfried van Swieten, the poem served Franz Joseph Haydn as a text for his celebrated oratorio *Die Jahreszeiten.* In a conversation with Johan Peter Eckermann in 1832, Johann Wolfgang von Goethe said that the "English poet Thomson wrote a very good poem on the Seasons, but a very bad one on Liberty; and that not from want of poetry, but from want of poetry in the subject." In France, Thomson was praised by Voltaire and emulated by poets. His influence can also be seen in the pastoral poetry of the Spaniard Juan Melendez Valdés. Thomson's English critics appreciated his originality but also expressed certain technical concerns. For example, such eminent contemporaries as Alexander Pope and Samuel Johnson, while recognizing *The Seasons* as a remarkable literary accomplishment, noted its compositional weakness. William Hazlitt thought highly of Thomson, naming him the foremost descriptive poet. Anticipating a theme in later criticism, Wordsworth recognized Thomson's talent but complained about his "vicious style." Indeed, later nineteenth-century commentators, such as George Saintsbury and Edmund Gosse, focused on the formal structure of Thomson's poetry, identifying technical and stylistic faults and placing his diction under careful scrutiny. Twentieth-century critics have attempted to offer a balanced assessment of Thomson's poetry, noting that stylistic imperfections and dissonances in diction hardly diminish his poetic voice. "Despite the general and particular flaws," affirmed Douglas Grant in his acclaimed 1951 biography of Thomson, "*The Seasons* is a great if not a good poem, and it would be impossible to exaggerate its influence on English poetry." Commentators have also questioned earlier evaluations of Thomson's diction and style, arguing that some of his cadences may sound awkward because thay are heard outside the natural context of Scottish speech. Finally, as the work of a Scottish poet who spent his productive years in England, Thomson's poetry has inevitably attracted the attention of scholars interested in Anglo-Scottish literary relations.

Thomson's poetry may not elicit the popular enthusiasm it once commanded; however, it still speaks to humankind's universal and timeless fascination with the wonders of nature. "Thomson," wrote the distinguished French literary historian Louis Cazamian, "had given voice to deep aspirations, which many shared; he restored Nature to one of the first places among the subjects of poetry, and to a place from which she was never to be dislodged. He had immediately a following, and found imitators, while his diffuse action is felt everywhere."

PRINCIPAL WORKS

Winter. A Poem (poetry) 1726
Summer. A Poem (poetry) 1727
A Poem Sacred to the Memory of Sir Isaac Newton (poetry) 1727
Spring. A Poem (poetry) 1728
Britannia. A Poem (poetry) 1729
The Seasons. A Poem (poetry) 1730
The Tragedy of Sophonisba (drama) 1730
Antient and Modern Italy Compared: being the first Part of Liberty, a Poem (poetry) 1735
Greece: being the Second Part of Liberty, a Poem (poetry) 1735

Rome: being the Third Part of Liberty (poetry) 1735
Britain: being the Fourth Part of Liberty (poetry) 1736
The Prospect: being the Fifth Part of Liberty (poetry) 1736
Agamemnon. A tragedy (drama) 1738
The Works of Mr. Thomson (poetry, dramas) 1738
Edward and Eleonora. A Tragedy (drama) 1739
Alfred. A Masque (drama) 1740
Tancred and Sigismunda. A Tragedy (drama) 1745
The Castle of Indolence: an Allegorical Poem. Written in Imitation of Spenser (poetry) 1748
Coriolanus. A Tragedy (drama) 1749

John More (essay date 1777)

[*In the following excerpt, More praises Thomson's eloquent expression of sublime thoughts and feelings.*]

Notwithstanding the modern acquisitions of philosophy, the whole apparatus of mind is still extremely mysterious. The mechanism of thought, however, proceeds on laws and principles we apprehend not less invariable than those of matter. Our powers of conception uniformly imbibe the respective qualities of their objects, just as our bodies are affected by those of food and climate. We behold with conscious dignity whatever is great and elevated. It is impossible to take a steady view of the surrounding heavens, without feeling a growing capaciousness of soul and a placid swell of the heart. But impressions of simple grandeur are received only from objects of pure magnitude. The ocean, extensive desarts, and a range of enormous mountains, are all sources of great ideas. Height and depth, and breadth and length of any uncommon demensions, are likewise viewed with similar sensations. But the human soul brooks no sort of restraint, or at least possesses not capacity sufficient, to comprehend the scene she evidently pants to occupy. It is in the contemplations, especially of infinite space, omnipotent power, immense existence and eternal duration, where mind seems most at home and imagination most in character. Those objects indeed are peculiarly fitted to act on all the capital movements in our system. And every other energy is necessarily absorbed in theirs. (pp. 249-50)

Thunder, earthquakes, lightnings, and hurricanes, alarming and tremendous as they are, indicate something not unpleasing however awful! Outrageous as they seem to us, they are under a check which they cannot resist, and subject to a will that orders every thing for the best. By the same hand that launches the thunderbolt, our fleeting lives are sustained, and he who impregnates the clouds with sulphur and darts the impetuous fire-ball, perfumes the air we breath and tempers the light we see. Nor is he less conspicuous to the philosophic eye, in the murmuring brook than in the raging sea, in a gentle gale, than in a violant storm, in the glimmerings of a glow-worm, than in the blaze of the sun, in the shades of a rose than in the colours of the rainbow, in the shell of a snail than in the vaulted heavens, and in the web of a spider than in the general system of the universe!

Such are some of the various and affecting phenomena from which the *Muse* of Thomson culled her choicest flowers. To him nature, was happily familiar in all her fairest and sublimest forms. He saw nothing but beauty, heard nothing but music, and felt nothing from the objects around him but palpitations of joy and sentiments of gratitude! Nor is it easy to say whether he succeeds most as a sublime Writer, in delineating the wonders of external nature or disclosing the magnanimous sentiments of a worthy mind. We can only now afford the reader a short illustration of these two particulars.

The first of these involves in part at least, almost every description in the ***Seasons.*** But we mean to select for the reader's satisfaction and entertainment, only a few of the most striking instances, merely to give him an idea of that sublime majestic manner in which the muse of Thomson kept pace with his subject.

An idea of grotesque wildness involving much latitude, impresses the mind with sensations of astonishment and awe. In his descriptions of the tropical countries, how many objects formed on this capacious scale are flung together in the sublimest groups imaginable

> Majestic woods, of every vigorous green,
> Stage above stage, high waving o'er the hills;
> Or to the far horizon wide diffus'd,
> A boundless deep immensity of shade.

He adds in the same characteristic tone of unaffected grandeur; where by the way, the additional circumstance of shade, wonderfully deepens the solemnity of the scene

> Here lofty trees, to ancient song unknown,
> The noble sons of potent heat and floods
> Prone-rushing from the clouds, rear high to Heaven
> Their thorny stems, and broad around them throw
> *Meridian gloom.*———

What a moving and awful picture does he give us of the *pestilence,* that dreadful visitation of the Almighty, as it rages in full horror among the noxious climates of the east? In the lines that conclude the passage, we have an image of *despair,* singularly beautiful, picturesque and new.

> Thus o'er the prostrate city *black Despair*
> *Extends her raven-wing;* while, to complete
> The scence of desolation, stretch'd around,
> The grim guards stand, denying all retreat,
> And give the flying wretch a better death.

Nothing can possibly be more affecting, even in idea, than the ocean in one of those tremendous *blasts* which happen so frequently between the tropics. Here inevitable destruction impending from the heavens above, and yawning from the depths beneath, increasing darkness, conflicting elements, and mutual consternation and terror, combine to fill imagination with fear, and overwhelm the heart with sorrow.

> ———A faint deceitful calm,
> A fluttering gale, the dæmon sends before,
> To tempt the spreading sail. Then down at once,
> Precipitant, descends a mingled mass

Of roaring winds, and flame, and rushing floods.
In wild amazement fix'd the sailor stands.
Art is too slow: By rapid fate oppress'd,
His broad-wing'd vessel *drinks* the whelming tide,
Hid in the bosom of the black abyss.

Some of the circumstances that announce the awful approach of *thunder,* are narrated in terms that exhibit the object in all its natural importance and sublimity. Such as

A boding silence reigns,
Dread thro' the dun expanse; save the *dull sound*
That from the mountain, previous to the storm,
Rolls o'er the muttering earth, disturbs the flood,
And shakes the forest leaf without a breath.

And where the birds and herds are alarmed with the signs of the coming tempest, surely the canvas never exhibited any thing more real and affecting.

Prone, to the lowest vale, the aërial tribes
Descend: the *tempest-loving raven scarce*
Dares wing the *dubious dusk.* In *rueful gaze*
The *cattle* stand, and on the scowling heavens
Cast a deploring eye.

His description of thunder and lightening, is not only just and picturesque, but enriched with strokes of the deepest sublimity. The progress of that wonderful phenomenon is finely traced, and the natural grandeur that accompanies all its stages supported throughout.

At first, *heard solemn o'er, the verge of heaven,*
The *tempest* growls; but as it nearer comes,
And *rolls* its *awful burden on the wind,*
The lightnings flash a larger curve, and more
The noise astounds: till over head a sheet
Of livid flame *discloses wide;* then shuts,
And opens *wider;* shuts and opens still
Expansive wrapping *ether in a blaze.*
Follows the loosen'd aggravated roar,
Enlarging, deepening, mingling; peal on *peal*
Crush'd horrible, *convulsing* heaven and earth!

In the following scene, relenting nature may well be figured, weeping over the direful catastrophe, occasioned by the furious elements among the most harmless of her offspring and those of her walks, that are least accustomed to violence and outrage. He introduces it with one of the fairest spectacles of nature, perhaps that the eye of man can behold!

Wide-rent, the clouds
Pour a whole flood; and yet, its flame unquench'd,
Th' unconquerable light'ning *struggles* through,
Ragged and *fierce,* or in *red whirling balls,*
And *fires* the *mountains* with redoubled *rage*
Black from the *stroke,* above, the smould'ring pine
Stands *a sad shatter'd trunk;* and, stretch'd below,
A lifeless group the *blasted cattle* lie:
Here the soft flocks, with that same *harmless look*
They *wore* alive, and *ruminating still*
In *fancy's eye;* and there the frowning bull,
And *ox half-rais'd.*

He has even made the approach of the autumnal fogs a subject of sublime description, by interweaving in his account of it the receding of a most majestic object from human view. A mountain is always great, but eminently sublime when thus surrounded with clouds

No more the mountain, *horrid, vast, sublime,*
Who pours a sweep of rivers from his sides,
And high between contending kingdoms rears
The rocky long division, *fills the view*
With great variety; but in *a night*
Of gathering vapour, from the baffled sense
Sinks *dark* and *dreary.*

His description of the moon, may perhaps be thought a little too severely wrought. For grandeur suffers essentially from the least want of simplicity. The truth is, Thomson generally explains at the same time that he describes. This unavoidably wears an air of obscurity, to such readers at least, as are not previously acquainted with the subject. Fortunately, the exceptionable lines may here be omitted, without injuring the rest, which apart from these, cannot but leave some pleasing impressions of sublimity on every susceptible heart.

———Mean-while the *moon*
Full orb'd and *breaking* thro' the *scatter'd cloulds,*
Shews her *broad visage* in the *crimson'd east.*
Now thro' the *passing cloud* she seems to *sleep,*
Now up the pure cerulean *rides sublime!*
Wide the pale deluge floods, and streaming mild
O'er the sky'd mountain to the shadowy vale,
While rocks and flood reflect the *quivering* gleam,
The whole air whitens with a boundless tide
Of silver radiance, *trembling* round the world.

It is the distinguishing province of all true poetry, to people the regions of imagination with such beings as are best adapted to the situation. This may be called the truth of fiction, and is just as essential to description as the strictest characteristical propriety, to dramatic composition. Every thing the muse addresses, has a genius suited to its nature, with whom, she establishes an immediate correspondence. Thus, the capital harbingers of a winter tempest, are pointed out in all their specific colouring and qualities. The whole passage is replete with shades of the deepest solemnity and grandeur; but the lines subjoined deserve peculiar attention, for the sake of a circumstance uncommonly picturesque and original.

Along the woods, along the moorish fens,
Sighs the sad *Genius* of the *coming storm;*
And *up* among the *loose disjointed* cliffs,
And *fractur'd* mountains *wild,* the brawling brook
And *cave,* presageful, send a *hollow moan,*
Resounding long in listening Fancy's ear.

The terror inspired by the scence, thus presaged even in a situation of the greatest security, and some of its most alarming accompaniments, are finely marked in the subsequent verses. It is moreover an instance of familiar ideas, being wrought up into sentiments, not less sublime than picturesque.

Sleep frighted flies; and round the *rocking* dome

For entrance *eager, bowls* the *savage* blast.
Then too, they say, thro' all the *burden'd air,*
Long groans are heard, *shrill sounds,* and *distant sighs,*
That, utter'd by the *demon* of the *night*
Warn the devoted *wretch* of *woe* and *death.*

From the same passage, I add one of the grandest images perhaps that ever swelled the human mind. Nor do I just now recollect an instance from any Author, ancient or modern, in which simplicity and sublimity are more happily and completely united.

Meantime the *mountain-billows,* to the clouds
In dreadful *tumult* swell'd surge above surge,
Surst into chaos with tremendous *roar,*
And *anchor'd navies* from their stations *drive,*
Wild as the winds across the howling waste
Of mighty waters:

Here follows a very striking example of greatness, or force without sublimity. It is needless to say why. Let us but examine the sensations which these words produce in our minds the moment we read them. The principles to which criticism refers, in this case, are as obvious and incontestible as axioms of geometry. We are all moved in a similar manner by similar objects. Perhaps the sudden and unexpected exertion of extraordinary force, startles or shakes, but may not leave imagination leisure enough, to feel any sublimer emotions. Such at least are seldom coincident to the first impression.

If some sharp rock,
Or shoal insidious break not their career,
And in loose fragments fling them floating round.

A circumstance not improbable from the natural history of the most noble and magnanimous of animals, intitles these three lines to a place, among the many examples of sublimity to be found in the ***Seasons.*** The contrast between the savage indescriminating cruelty of the *Wolf,* and the well known generosity of the *Lion,* in this instance, is not only strictly characteristical but equally interesting and sublime!

Even beauty, force divine! at whose bright glance
The generous Lion *stands* in *soften'd gaze*
Here bleeds a hapless undistinguish'd prey!

We shall but trouble the reader with one quotation more, in which the object loses nothing of its natural sublimity from the description. It is where a thaw takes place, in some large capacious river, while vessels, barks and barges, are unhappily expossed to all the accumulated dangers and horrors of floating piles of ice, tumbling down with vast rapidity and threatening immediate destruction to whatever comes in their way.

And hark! the lengthening *roar continuous* runs
Athwart the *rifted* deep: at once it *bursts,*
And *piles* a thousand *mountains* to the clouds.
Ill fares the bark with trembling wretches charg'd,
That, toss'd amid the *floating fragments* moors
Beneath the shelter of an icy isle,
While night o'erwhelms the sea, and *horror* looks
More *horrible.* Can human force endure
Th' assembled mischiefs that besiege them round?
Heart-gnawing hunger, fainting weariness,
The *roar* of *winds* and *waves,* the *crush* of ice,
Now-*ceasing,* now *renew'd* with louder *rage,*
And in dire echoes *bellowing* round the *main.*
More to embroil the deep, Leviathan
And his *unwieldy* train, in dreadful sport,
Tempest the loosen'd brine, while *thro' the gloom,*
Far, from the *bleak inhospitable shore,*
Loading the winds, is heard the *hungry howl*
Of *famish'd monsters!*

But it is not among the inanimate parts of nature only or chiefly, that our bard displays the sublimity of his genius. Many zoological descriptions in the ***Seasons*** are equally simple and exalted. The graceful impetuosity of the *Steed,* and rampant fury of the *Bull,* are both delineated with dignity and truth. His strictures on the *Lion,* the *Elephant,* the *Hippopotamos* and the *Eagle,* are still however touched with a bolder pencil. He seizes indeed, with inimitable dexterity and ease every thing great and majestic in nature! And his poem contains more sublime images perhaps, in proportion to its size, than any other purely descriptive one we have.

It is now high time, however, to examine a little that sentimental sublimity of which also he is no inferior master. (pp. 251-61)

[How] concise and emphatical his account of those illustrious characters, whose useful science and active virtue adorned the earlier periods of society. Indeed there is no reading this sublime roll of heroes without emotions of emulation. Such are the powerful attractions of superior worth, and so much more congenial to the inmost affections of the heart is good than bad example! The calm majestic invincible fortitude of *Socrates* embracing the sternest fate in the mildest composure—the dispassionate and disinterested patriotism and intrepidity of *Leonidas* in sacrificing himself for the good of his country, . . . [etc.]. (p. 262)

[Thomson] has certainly very few equals, in . . . delineating the various energies and effects of a good heart. According to his philosophy, which is that of nature and experience, how vastly superior the private abodes of humble fortitude to all the troublous scenes of tumultuous pride and tormenting impatience! Think on this, ye bustling factious petulant and aspiring spirits, to whom, all the forms of decency and moderation are equally contemptible, who mistake the punctillios of a frivolous for the dictates of an elegant mind, affectation for dignity, and temerity for ardour; and who consume your fortune and constitutions in grasping at phantoms, that never can be realized. What an eloquent and emphatical picture does the poet here set before you, of the infinite mortifications, disasters, and agonies that so frequently chequer such lives as yours. Who would not pity, from the bottom of their hearts, those poor giddy frantic wretches, who can read such a passage as this, with a wanton or a listless indifference, without imbibing the most settled convictions of the reality and importance of virtue to human welfare, without instantly, and for ever renouncing every vicious prepossession, and every worthless habit, and without resolutely adhering to the positive injunctions of truth and nature, in spite of all the criminal influence and address of art. Consider the man of hidden worth and unaffected delicacy. . . . In giving way to many incumbent evils, he only prepares himself for overcoming them. . . . How temperate his appetites, how orderly his passions, how meek his dispositions, how placid his life! The beautiful serenity of his mind, communicates a certain air of composure to every thing around him. His house is the mansion of purity, the temple of virtue, and the asylum of the destitute. There, dwell social concord, domestic comfort, holy friendship, unbroken health, blooming beauty, youthful innocence, and age matured by experience, and rather softened than soured, with infirmity and years.

> Let such as deem it *glory* to *destroy,*
> Rush into *blood,* the *sack* of *cities* seek;
> *Unpierc'd,* exulting in the *widow's wail,*
> The *virgin's shriek,* and *infant's trembling cry.*
> Let some, far-distant from their native foil,
> Urg'd or by want, or harden'd avarice,
> Find other lands beneath another fun.
> Let *this* through cities work his eager way,
> By *legal outrage* and *establish'd guile,*
> The social sense extinct; and *that* ferment
> Mad into tumult the *seditious herd,*
> Or *melt* them down to *slavery.* Let these
> Insnare the wretched in the *toils* of law,
> *Fomenting* discord, and *perplexing* right,
> An iron-race! and those of *fairer front,*
> But *equal inhumanity,* in courts,
> *Delusive pomp,* and *dark cabals,* delight;
> Wreathe the *deep bow,* diffuse the *lying smile,*
> And tread the weary labyrinth of slate.
> While *he,* from all the stormy passions *free*
> That restless men involve, *hears,* and but *hears,*
> At distance *safe,* the *human tempest* roar,
> Wrapt close in *conscious peace.*
>
> (pp. 263-65)

Whatever is great and amiable in the creatures and objects around us, naturally awakens our admiration and attracts our esteem. Magnificence expands the mind, and Beauty captivates the heart. But these qualities, however diversified, are the native expressions of power and goodness. Mind can only be affected by mind. Nor can any form or modification of matter produce either mental or moral emotion, but as it points to an invisible Agency. So that raising our hearts to heaven is not transferring them from nature, but from the imperfect image to the all-perfect Original. For all that charms our senses, enlarges our conceptions or exalts our expectations among the complicated wonders of the universe, are but the temporary shadows of his excellence, whose being is uncreated, whose perfections are infinite, and whose nature is eternal. (pp. 266-67)

[What] body is to *mind,* that the visible creation is to its *Author,* a mere *Sensorium;* to use an expression of some late philosophers, by means of which, he discovers himself to his rational offspring in all that greatness which fills them with veneration, in all that effusion of goodness that warms them with gratitude, in all those lovely assemblages of beauty, that ravish them with delight, and in all those indications of the tenderest attentions to their best interest, that dispose them to a cordial acquiescence in every appointment of Providence!

This fine idea, that does more honour to the spirit of ancient philosophy, than all her other discoveries put together, unites and completes the universal plan of things. (p. 269)

Such are some of the sublime dictates which the genius of universal Nature inspires, and with which the Muse of Thomson is still in the happiest unison. On this glorious and propitious system he reconciles his heart to all those apparent contradictions, which, in the moral government of the world, embroil the present scene and darken that of futurity. That this is only the seed-time of immortality, that our harvest is reserved for a purer period, and that the ***Seasons*** figuratively as well as literally, depend on a destination which nothing can frustrate, are some of the leading convictions he would imprint on the minds of men. And he rejoices in full concert with the whole world of the *Virtuous,* that when this unaccountable and confounding jumble of things; when all the present strange mysterious schemes of Providence are unravelled, *human happiness shall appear the necessary consequence of human worth,* as well as the ultimate determination of Heaven. Hence the following passage is not more inimitably simple and sublime than pathetic and consolatory. And often as it has been quoted from motives of taste, perchance in company to improve the conversation, or of pedantry in publick to embellish the tawdry common place of pulpit declamation, it still possesses charms enow, to affect the serious, and melt the feeling heart.

> Ye good distress'd!
> Ye noble few! who here *unbending stand*
> *Beneath life's pressure,* yet *bear up a while,*
> And what your *bounded view,* which only saw
> A *little part,* deem'd *Evil,* is no more:
> The *storms* of WINTRY TIME will *quickly* pass,
> And one *unbounded* SPRING incircle *all.*
>
> (pp. 273-74)

[The piety of the ***Seasons*** can be illustrated by] the sublime Hymn that concludes them. Never surely was human composition more sweetly stored with the sentiments of gratitude or richly adorned with the graces of poetry. Simplicity of numbers, elevation of diction, sublimity of thought and ardour of conception, are its general characteristics. . . . Thomson meant it as an epitome of the whole poem. (p. 274)

John More, "On the Sublimity of the Seasons," in his Strictures, Critical and Sentimental, on Thomson's "Seasons," *1777. Reprint by Garland Publishing, Inc., pp. 247-79.*

Samuel Johnson (essay date 1781)

[*A prolific and influential lexicographer, essayist, poet, and critic, Johnson was one of the dominant figures in eighteenth-century English literature. His works include the lucid and extensively illustrated* Dictionary of the English Language *(1755) and* Prefaces, Biographical and Critical, to the Works of the English Poets *(10 volumes, 1779-81; reissued in 1783 as* The Lives of the

Most Eminent English Poets). *Relying on common sense and empirical knowledge, Johnson was an acute and perceptive judge of literary works, exerting a great influence on his contemporaries. In the following excerpt from the second-named work, he lauds* The Seasons *as an impressive poetic accomplishment, remarking nevertheless that the poem, lacking method, "is too exuberant, and sometimes may be charged with filling the ear more than the mind."*]

As a writer [Thomson] is entitled to one praise of the highest kind: his mode of thinking, and of expressing his thoughts, is original. His blank verse is no more than blank verse of Milton, or of any other poet, than the rhymes of Prior are the rhymes of Cowley. His numbers, his pauses, his diction, are of his own growth, without transcription, without imitation. He thinks in a peculiar train, and he thinks always as a man of genius; he looks round on Nature and on Life, with the eye which Nature bestows only on a poet; the eye that distinguishes, in every thing presented to its view, whatever there is on which imagination can delight to be detained, and with a mind that at once comprehends the vast, and attends to the minute. The reader of the ***Seasons*** wonders that he never saw before what Thomson shews him, and that he never yet has felt what Thomson impresses.

His is one of the works in which blank verse seems properly used; Thomson's wide expansion of general views, and his enumeration of circumstantial varieties, would have been obstructed and embarrassed by the frequent intersection of the sense, which are the necessary effects of rhyme.

His descriptions of extended scenes and general effects bring before us the whole magnificence of Nature, whether pleasing or dreadful. The gaiety of ***Spring,*** the splendour of ***Summer,*** the tranquillity of ***Autumn,*** and the horror of ***Winter,*** take in their turns possession of the mind. The poet leads us through the appearances of things as they are successively varied by the vicissitudes of the year, and imparts to us so much of his own enthusiasm, that our thoughts expand with his imagery, and kindle with his sentiments. Nor is the naturalist without his part in the entertainment; for he is assisted to recollect and to combine, to arrange his discoveries, and to amplify the sphere of his contemplation.

The great defect of the ***Seasons*** is want of method; but for this I know not that there was any remedy. Of many appearances subsisting all at once, no rule can be given why one should be mentioned before another; yet the memory wants the help of order, and the curiosity is not excited by suspense or expectation.

His diction is in the highest degree florid and luxuriant, such as may be said to be to his images and thoughts *both their lustre and their shade;* such as invest them with splendour, through which perhaps they are not always easily discerned. It is too exuberant, and sometimes may be charged with filling the ear more than the mind.

These Poems, with which I was acquainted at their first appearance, I have since found altered and enlarged by subsequent revisals, as the author supposed his judgement to grow more exact, and as books or conversation extended his knowledge and opened his prospects. They are, I think, improved in general; yet I know not whether they have not lost part of what Temple calls their *race;* a word which, applied to wines, in its primitive sense, means the flavour of the soil.

Liberty, when it first appeared, I tried to read, and soon desisted. I have never tried again, and therefore will not hazard either praise or censure.

The highest praise which he has received ought not to be suppressed; it is said by Lord Lyttelton in the Prologue to his posthumous play, that his works contained

> No line which, dying, he could wish to blot.

(pp. 358-59)

Samuel Johnson, "Thomson," in his Lives of the Poets, Vol. II, *1906. Reprint by Oxford University Press, 1955-56, pp. 348-59.*

Joseph Warton (essay date 1782)

[*An English critic and poet, Warton is known for* An Essay on the Writings and Genius of Pope *(1782), in which he proposes a typology of poetry. In the following excerpt from that work, he identifies Thomson as a descriptive poet of genius.*]

THOMSON was blessed with a strong and copious fancy; he hath enriched poetry with a variety of new and original images, which he painted from nature itself, and from his own actual observations: his descriptions have therefore a distinctness and truth, which are utterly wanting to those, of poets who have only copied from each other, and have never looked abroad on the objects themselves. Thomson was accustomed to wander away into the country for days and for weeks, attentive to "each rural sight, each rural sound;" while many a poet who has dwelt for years in the Strand, has attempted to describe fields and rivers, and generally succeeded accordingly. Hence that nauseous repetition of the same circumstances; hence that disgusting impropriety of introducing what may be called a set of hereditary images, without proper regard to the age, or climate, or occasion in which they were formerly used. Though the diction of the ***SEASONS*** is sometimes harsh and inharmonious, and sometimes turgid and obscure, and though in many instances, the numbers are not sufficiently diversified by different pauses, yet is this poem on the whole, from the numberless strokes of nature in which it abounds, one of the most captivating and amusing in our language, and which, as its beauties are not of a transitory kind, as depending on particular customs and manners, will ever be perused with delight. The scenes of Thomson are frequently as wild and romantic as those of Salvator Rosa, varied with precipices and torrents, and "castled cliffs," and deep vallies, with piny mountains, and the gloomiest caverns. Innumerable are the little circumstances in his descriptions, totally unobserved by all his predecessors. What poet hath ever taken notice of the leaf, that towards the end of autumn,

> Incessant ruffles from the mournful grove,
> Oft startling such as, studious, walk below,
> And slowly circles through the waving air?

Or who, in speaking of a summer evening hath ever mentioned,

> The quail that clamours for his running mate?

Or the following natural image at the same time of the year?

> Wide o'er the thistly lawn, as swells the breeze,
> A whitening shower of vegetable down
> Amusive floats.———

In what other poet, do we find the silence and expectation that precedes an April shower insisted on, as in ver. 165 of ***Spring?*** Or where,

> The stealing shower is scarce to patter heard,
> By such as wander through the forest walks,
> Beneath th' umbrageous multitude of leaves

How full, particular and picturesque is this assemblage of circumstances that attend a very keen frost in a night of winter!

> Loud rings the frozen earth, and hard reflects
> A double noise; while at his evening watch
> The village dog deters the nightly thief;
> The heifer lows; the distant water-fall
> Swells in the breeze; and with the hasty tread
> Of traveller, the hollow-sounding plain
> Shakes from afar.———

In no one subject are common writers more confused and unmeaning, than in their descriptions of rivers, which are generally said only to wind and to murmur, while their qualities and courses are seldom accurately marked. Examine the exactness of the ensuing description [in ***Summer***], and consider what a perfect idea it communicates to the mind.

> Around th' adjoining brook, that purls along
> The vocal grove, now fretting o'er a rock,
> Now scarcely moving through a reedy pool,
> Now starting to a sudden stream, and now
> Gently diffus'd into a limpid plain;
> A various groupe the herds and flocks compose,
> Rural confusion!———

A groupe worthy the pencil of Giacomo da Bassano, and so minutely delineated, that he might have worked from this sketch;

> ———On the grassy bank
> Some ruminating lie; while others stand
> Half in the flood, and often bending sip
> The circling surface.———

He adds, that the ox in the middle of them,

> ———From his sides
> The troublous insects lashes, to his sides
> Returning still.———

A natural circumstance, that to the best of my remembrance hath escaped even the natural Theocritus. Nor do I recollect that any poet hath been struck with the murmurs of the numberless insects, that swarm abroad at the noon of a summer's day: as attendants of the evening indeed, they have been mentioned;

> Resounds the living surface of the ground:
> Nor undelightful is the ceaseless hum
> To him who muses through the woods at noon;
> Or drowsy shepherd, as he lies reclin'd
> With half-shut eyes.———

But the novelty and nature we admire in the descriptions of Thomson are by no means his only excellencies; he is equally to be praised, for impressing on our minds the effects, which the scene delineated would have on the present spectator or hearer. Thus having spoken of the roaring of the savages in a wilderness of Africa, he introduces a captive, who though just escaped from prison and slavery under the tyrant of Morocco, is so terrified and astonished at the dreadful uproar, that

> The wretch half wishes for his bonds again.

Thus also having described a caravan lost and overwhelmed in one of those whirlwinds that so frequently agitate and lift up the whole sands of the desart, he finishes his picture by adding that,

> ———In Cairo's crouded streets,
> Th' impatient merchant, wondering waits in vain,
> And Mecca saddens at the long delay.

And thus, lastly, in describing the pestilence that destroyed the British troops at the siege of Carthagena, he has used a circumstance inimitably lively, picturesque, and striking to the imagination; for he says that the admiral not only heard the groans of the sick that echoed from ship to ship, but that he also pensively stood, and listened at midnight to the dashing of the waters, occasioned by throwing the dead bodies into the sea;

> Heard, nightly, plung'd into the sullen waves,
> The frequent corse.

A minute and particular enumeration of circumstances judiciously selected, is what chiefly discriminates poetry from history, and renders the former, for that reason, a more close and faithful representation of nature than the latter. (pp. 42-8)

These observations on Thomson . . . might be still augmented by an examination and developement of the beauties in the Loves of the birds, in ***Spring,*** verse 580. A view of the torrid zone in ***Summer,*** verse 626. The rise of fountains and rivers in ***Autumn,*** verse 781. A man perishing in the snows, in ***Winter,*** verse 277. The wolves descending from the Alps, and a view of winter within the polar circle, verse 809, which are all of them highly-finished originals. . . . ***Winter*** is in my apprehension the most valuable of these four poems; the scenes of it, like those of *Il Penseroso* of Milton, being of that awful, solemn, and pensive kind, on which a great genius best delights to dwell. (pp. 49-50)

Joseph Warton, "Essay on the Genius," in his An Essay on the Genius and Writings of Pope, Vol. I, *1782. Reprint by Garland Publishing, Inc., 1970, pp. 41-51.*

J. Aikin (essay date 1791)

[Aikin was a physician and author whose books include

the work for children Evenings at Home *(1792-96), written with his sister Anna Laetitia Barbauld, as well as memoirs and biographical works. In the following excerpt, he lauds* The Seasons *as a multi-faceted poetic work, declaring that it "is as eminently a religious as it is a descriptive poem."*]

The extent of knowledge, as well as the powers of description, which THOMSON has exhibited in [his ***Seasons***], is, on the whole, truly admirable; and though, with the present advanced taste for accurate observation in Natural History, some improvements might be suggested, yet he certainly remains unrivalled in the list of descriptive poets.

But the rural landscape is not solely made up of land, and water, and trees, and birds, and beasts; *man* is a distinguished fire in it; his multiplied occupations and concerns introduce themselves into every part of it; he intermixes even in the wildest and rudest scenes, and throws a life and interest upon every surrounding object. *Manners* and *character* therefore constitute a part even of a descriptive poem; and in a plan so extensive as the history of the year, they must enter under various forms, and upon numerous occasions.

The most obvious and appropriated use of human figures in pictures of the Seasons, is the introduction of them to assist in marking out the succession of annual changes by their various labours and amusements. In common with other animals, man is directed in the diversified employment of earning a toilsome subsistence by an attention to the vicissitudes of the seasons; and all his diversions in the simple state of rustic society are also regulated by the same circumstance. Thus a series of moving figures enlivens the landscape, and contributes to stamp on each scene its peculiar character. The shepherd, the husbandman, the hunter, appear in their turns; and may be considered as natural concomitants of that portion of the yearly round which prompts their several occupations.

But it is not only the bodily pursuits of man which are affected by these changes; the sensations and affections of his mind are almost equally under their influence: and the result of the whole, as forming the enamoured votary of Nature to a peculiar cast of character and manners, is not less conspicuous. Thus the Poet of the ***SEASONS*** is at liberty, without deviating from his plan, to descant on the varieties of moral constitution, and the powers which external causes are found to possess over the temper of the soul. He may draw pictures of the pastoral life in all its genuine simplicity; and, assuming the tone of a moral instructor, may contrast the peace and felicity of innocent retirement with the turbulent agitations of ambition and avarice.

The various incidents too, upon which the simple tale of rural events is founded, are very much modeled by the difference of seasons. The catastrophes of Winter differ from those of Summer; the sports of Spring from those of Autumn. Thus, little history pieces and adventures, whether pathetic or amusing, will suggest themselves to the Poet; which, when properly adapted to the scenery and circumstances, may very happily coincide with the main design of the composition.

The bare enumeration of these several occasions of introducing draughts of human life and manners, will be sufficient to call to mind the admirable use which THOMSON throughout his whole poem has made of them. He, in fact, never appears more truly inspired with his subject, than when giving birth to those sentiments of tenderness and beneficence, which seem to have occupied his whole heart. An universal benevolence, extending to every part of the animal creation, manifests itself in almost every scene he draws; and the rural character, as delineated in his feelings, contains all the softness, purity, and simplicity that are feigned of the golden age. Yet, excellent as the moral and sentimental part of his work must appear to every congenial mind, it is, perhaps, that in which he may the most easily be rivalled. A refined and feeling heart may derive from its own proper sources a store of corresponding sentiment, which will naturally clothe itself in the form of expression best suited to the occasion. Nor does the invention of those simple incidents which are most adapted to excite the sympathetic emotions, require any great stretch of fancy. The nearer they approach to common life, the more certainly will they produce their effect. Wonder and surprise are affections of so different a kind, and so distract the attention, that they never fail to diminish the force of the pathetic. On these accounts, writers much inferior in respect to the powers of description and imagery, have equalled our poet in elegant and benevolent sentiment, and perhaps excelled him in interesting narration. Of these, it will be sufficient to mention the ingenious author of a French poem on the Seasons; who, though a mere copyist in the descriptive parts, has made many pleasing additions to the manners and incidents proper for such a composition.

But there is a strain of sentiment of a higher and more digressive nature, with which THOMSON has occupied a considerable portion of his poem. The fundamental principles of Moral Philosophy, ideas concerning the origin and progress of government and civilization, historical sketches, and reviews of the characters most famous in ancient and modern history, are interspersed through the various parts of the ***SEASONS.*** The manly, liberal, and enlightened spirit which this writer breathes in all his works, must ever endear him to the friends of truth and virtue; and, in particular, his genuine patriotism and zeal in the cause of liberty will render his writings always estimable to the British reader. But, just and important as his thoughts on these topics may be, there may remain a doubt in the breast of the critic, whether their introduction in a piece like this do not, in some instances, break in upon that unity of character which every work of art should support. We have seen, from the general plan and tenor of the poem, that it is professedly of the rural cast. The objects it is chiefly conversant with are those presented by the hand of Nature, not the products of human art; and when man himself is introduced as a part of the groupe, it would seem that, in conformity to the rest, he ought to be represented in such a state only, as the simplest forms of society, and most unconstrained situations in it, exhibit. Courts and cities, camps and senates, do not well accord with silvan scenery. From the principle of congruity, therefore, a critic might be induced to reject some of these digressive ornaments, though intrinsically beautiful, and doubtless contributing to the elevation and variety of the piece. His judgment in this respect would be a good deal influenced by the manner of their introduction. In some instances this is so easy and natural, that the mind is scarcely sensible of the deviation; in others it is more abrupt and unartful. As examples of both, we may refer to the passages in which various characters from English, and from Grecian and Roman history, are displayed. The former, by a happy gradation, is introduced at the close of a delightful piece, containing the praises of Britain; which is itself a kind of digression, though a very apt and seasonable one. The latter has no other connexion with the part at which it is inserted, than the very forced and distant one, that, as reading may be reckoned among the amusements appropriated to Winter, such subjects as these will naturally offer themselves to the studious mind.

There is another source of sentiment to the Poet of the ***Seasons,*** which, while it is superior to the last in real elevation, is also strictly connected with the nature of his work. The genuine philosopher, while he surveys the grand and beautiful objects every where surrounding him, will be prompted to lift his eye to the great cause of all these wonders; the planner and architect of this mighty fabric, every minute part of which so much awakens his curiosity and admiration. The laws by which this Being acts, the ends which he seems to have pursued, must excite his humble researches; and in proportion as he discovers infinite power in the means, directed by infinite goodness in the intention, his soul must be wrapt in astonishment, and expanded with gratitude. The economy of Nature will, to such an observer, be the perfect scheme of an all-wise and beneficent mind; and every part of the wide creation will appear to proclaim the praise of its great Author. Thus a new connexion will manifest itself between the several parts of the universe; and a new order and design will be traced through the progress of its various revolutions.

Thomson's ***Seasons*** is as eminently a religious, as it is a descriptive poem. Thoroughly impressed with sentiments of beneration for the Author of that assemblage of order and beauty which it was his province to paint, he takes every proper occasion to excite similar emotions in the breasts of his readers. Entirely free from the gloom of superstition and the narrowness of bigotry, he every where represents the Deity as the kind and beneficent parent of all his works, always watchful over their best interests, and from seeming evil still educing the greatest possible good to all his creatures. In every appearance of nature he beholds the operation of a divine hand; and regards, according to his own emphatical phrase, each change throughout the revolving year as but the "varied God." This spirit, which breaks forth at intervals in each division of his poem, shines full and concentred in that noble Hymn which crowns the work. This piece, the sublimest production of its kind since the days of Milton, should be considered as the winding up of all the variety of matter and design contained in the preceding parts; and thus is not only admirable as a separate composition, but is contrived with masterly skill to strengthen the unity and connexion of the great whole.

Thus is planned and constructed a Poem, which, founded as it is upon the unfading beauties of Nature, will live as long as the language in which it is written shall be read. (pp. lv-lxiii)

J. Aikin, "An Essay on the Plan and Character of Thomson's "Seasons'," in The Seasons, *by James Thomson, 1791. Reprint by G. G. & J. Robinson and others, 1799, pp. xxxiii-lxiii.*

William Wordsworth (essay date 1815)

[*A leading ninteenth-century poet and critic, Wordsworth believed that poetry should provide pleasure while illuminating the mystery of human nature and its relation to the world. Wordsworth's poetry, which reflects the spirit of Romanticism, addresses humankind's perennial spiritual questions. His writings include* Lyrical Ballads *(with Samuel Taylor Coleridge, 1798) and* The Prelude, *an autobiographical poem in blank verse, published posthumously in 1850. In the excerpt below, from his "Essay, Supplementary to the Preface [of the* Lyrical Ballads] *(1815)," he characterizes Thomson as an inspired poet who notwithstanding his high power "writes a vicious style."*]

Something less than sixty years after the publication of the *Paradise Lost* appeared Thomson's ***Winter;*** which was speedily followed by his other Seasons. It is a work of inspiration; much of it is written from himself, and nobly from himself. How was it received?

> "It was no sooner read," says one of his contemporary biographers, "than universally admired: those only excepted who had not been used to feel, or to look for anything in poetry, beyond a *point* of satirical or epigrammatic wit, a smart *antithesis* richly trimmed with rhyme, or the softness of an *elegiac* complaint. To such his manly classical spirit could not readily commend itself; till, after a more attentive perusal, they had got the better of their prejudices, and either acquired or affected a truer taste. A few others stood aloof, merely because they had long before fixed the articles of their poetical creed, and resigned themselves to an absolute despair of ever seeing anything new and original. These were somewhat mortified to find their notions disturbed by the appearance of a poet, who seemed to owe nothing but to nature and his own genius. But, in a short time, the applause became unanimous; every one wondering how so many pictures, and pictures so familiar, should have moved them but faintly to what they felt in his descriptions. His digressions too, the overflowings of a tender benevolent heart, charmed the reader no less; leaving him in doubt, whether he should more admire the Poet or love the Man."
>
> (p. 419)

[We] must distinguish between wonder and legitimate admiration. The subject of the work is the changes produced in the appearances of nature by the revolution of the year: and, by undertaking to write in verse, Thomson pledged himself to treat his subject as became a Poet. Now, it is remarkable that, excepting the nocturnal "Reverie" of Lady Winchilsea, and a passage or two in the "Windsor Forest of Pope, the poetry of the period intervening between the publication of the *Paradise Lost* and the ***Seasons*** does not contain a single new image of external nature; and scarcely presents a familiar one from which it can be inferred that the eye of the Poet had been steadily fixed upon his object, much less that his feelings had urged him to work upon it in the spirit of genuine imagination. To what a low state knowledge of the most obvious and important phenomena had sunk, is evident from the style in which Dryden has executed a description of Night in one of his Tragedies, and Pope his translation of the celebrated moonlight scene in the Iliad. A blind man, in the habit of attending accurately to descriptions casually dropped from the lips of those around him, might easily depict these appearances with more truth. Dryden's lines are vague, bombastic, and senseless; those of Pope, though he had Homer to guide him, are throughout false and contradictory. . . . If these two distinguished writers could habitually think that the visible universe was of so little consequence to a poet, that it was scarcely necessary for him to cast his eyes upon it, we may be assured that those passages of the elder poets which faithfully and poetically describe the phenomena of nature, were not at that time holden in much estimation, and that there was little accurate attention paid to those appearances.

Wonder is the natural product of Ignorance; and as the soil was *in such good condition* at the time of the publication of the ***Seasons,*** the crop was doubtless abundant. Neither individuals nor nations become corrupt all at once, nor are they enlightened in a moment. Thomson was an inspired poet, but he could not work miracles; in cases where the art of seeing had in some degree been learned, the teacher would further the proficiency of his pupils, but he could do little *more;* though so far does vanity assist men in acts of self-deception, that many would often fancy they recognized a likeness when they knew nothing of the original. Having shown that much of what his biographer deemed genuine admiration must in fact have been blind wonderment—how is the rest to be accounted for?

Thomson was fortunate in the very title of his poem, which seemed to bring it home to the prepared sympathies of every one: in the next place, notwithstanding his high powers, he writes a vicious style; and his false ornaments are exactly of that kind which would be most likely to strike the undiscerning. He likewise abounds with sentimental common-places, that, from the manner in which they were brought forward, bore an imposing air of novelty. In any well-used copy of the ***Seasons*** the book generally opens of itself with the rhapsody on love, or with one of the stories (perhaps Damon and Musidora); these also are prominent in our collections of Extracts, and are the parts of his Work which, after all, were probably most efficient in first recommending the author to general notice. Pope, repaying praises which he had received, and wishing to extol him to the highest, only styles him "an elegant and philosophical Poet;" nor are we able to collect any unquestionable proofs that the true characteristics of Thomson's genius as an imaginative poet were perceived, till the elder Warton, almost forty years after the publication of the ***Seasons,*** pointed them out by a note in his *Essay on the Life and Writings of Pope* [see excerpt dated 1782]. In the ***Castle of Indolence*** (of which Gray speaks so coldly) these characteristics were almost as conspicuously displayed, and in verse more harmonious, and diction more pure. Yet that fine poem was neglected on its appearance, and is at this day the delight only of a few! (pp. 419-21)

William Wordsworth, "Essay Supplementary to the Preface (1815)," in his The Poetical Works of William Wordsworth, *edited by E. de Selincourt, 1944. Reprint by Oxford at the Clarendon Press, 1952, 548 p.*

William Hazlitt (essay date 1818)

[An influential English critic and essayist, Hazlitt is known for his significant contribution to historical criticism. His writings include Lectures on English Philosophy *(1812),* Lectures on the English Poets *(1818), and* The Spirit of the Age *(1825). In the following excerpt from the second-named work, Hazlitt discusses several aspects of Thomson's oeuvre, asserting that, despite certain faults of style, Thomson is a remarkably imaginative and expressive poet who "makes all his descriptions teem with life and vivifying soul."]*

Thomson, the kind-hearted Thomson, was the most indolent of mortals and of poets. But he was also one of the best both of mortals and of poets. Dr. Johnson makes it his praise that he wrote 'no line which dying he would wish to blot' [see excerpt dated 1781]. Perhaps a better proof of his honest simplicity, and inoffensive goodness of disposition, would be that he wrote no line which any other person living would wish that he should blot. (p. 130)

As critics, however, not as moralists, we might say on the other hand—'Would he had blotted a thousand!'—The same suavity of temper and sanguine warmth of feeling which threw such a natural grace and genial spirit of enthusiasm over his poetry, was also the cause of its inherent vices and defects. He is affected through carelessness: pompous from unsuspecting simplicity of character. He is frequently pedantic and ostentatious in his style, because he had no consciousness of these vices in himself. He mounts upon stilts, not out of vanity, but indolence. He seldom writes a good line, but he makes up for it by a bad one. He takes advantage of all the most trite and mechanical commonplaces of imagery and diction as a kindly relief to his Muse, and as if he thought them quite as good, and likely to be quite as acceptable to the reader, as his own poetry. He did not think the difference worth putting himself to the trouble of accomplishing. He had too little art to conceal his art: or did not even seem to know that there was any occasion for it. His art is as naked and undisguised as his nature; the one is as pure and genuine as the other is gross, gaudy, and meretricious.—All that is admirable in the ***Seasons,*** is the emanation of a fine natural genius, and sincere love of his subject, unforced, unstudied, that comes uncalled for, and departs unbidden. But he takes no pains, uses no self-correction; or if he seems to labour, it is worse than labour lost. His genius 'cannot be constrained by mastery'. The feeling of nature, of the changes of the seasons, was in his mind; and he could not help conveying this feeling to the reader, by the mere force of spontaneous expression; but if the expression did not come of itself, he left the whole business to chance; or, willing to evade instead of encountering the difficulties of his subject, fills up the intervals of true inspiration with the most vapid and worthless materials, pieces out a beautiful half line with a bombastic allusion, or overloads an exquisitely natural sentiment or image with a cloud of painted, pompous, cumbrous phrases, like the shower of roses, in which he represents the Spring, his own lovely, fresh, and innocent Spring, as descending to the earth.

> Come, gentle Spring! ethereal Mildness! come,
> And from the bosom of yon dropping cloud,
> While music wakes around, veil'd in a shower
> Of shadowing roses, on our plains descend.

Who, from such a flimsy, round-about, unmeaning commencement as this, would expect the delightful, unexaggerated, home-felt descriptions of natural scenery, which are scattered in such unconscious profusion through this and the following cantos? For instance, the very next passage is crowded with a set of striking images.

> And see where surly Winter passes off
> Far to the north, and calls his ruffian blasts:
> His blasts obey, and quit the howling hill,
> The shatter'd forest, and the ravag'd vale;
> While softer gales succeed, at whose kind touch
> Dissolving snows in livid torrents lost,
> The mountains lift their green heads to the sky.
> As yet the trembling year is unconfirmed,
> And Winter oft at eve resumes the breeze,
> Chills the pale morn, and bids his driving sleets
> Deform the day delightless; so that scarce
> The bittern knows his time with bill ingulpht
> To shake the sounding marsh, or from the shore
> The plovers when to scatter o'er the heath,
> And sing their wild notes to the list'ning waste.

Thomson is the best of our descriptive poets: for he gives most of the poetry of natural description. Others have been quite equal to him, or have surpassed him, as Cowper for instance, in the picturesque part of his art, in marking the peculiar features and curious details of objects;—no one has yet come up to him in giving the sum total of their effects, their varying influences on the mind. He does not go into the *minutiae* of a landscape, but describes the vivid impression which the whole makes upon his own imagination; and thus transfers the same unbroken, unimpaired impression to the imagination of his readers. The colours with which he paints seem yet wet and breathing, like those of the living statue in the *Winter's Tale.* Nature in his descriptions is seen growing around us, fresh and lusty as in itself. We feel the effect of the atmosphere, its humidity or clearness, its heat or cold, the glow of summer, the gloom of winter, the tender promise of the spring, the full overshadowing foliage, the declining pomp and deepening tints of autumn. He transports us to the scorching heat of vertical suns, or plunges us into the chilling horrors and desolation of the frozen zone. We hear the snow drifting against the broken casement without, and see the fire blazing on the hearth within. The first scattered drops of a vernal shower patter on the leaves above our heads, or the coming storm resounds through the leafless groves. In a word, he describes not to the eye alone, but to the other senses, and to the whole man. He puts his heart into his subject, writes as he feels, and humanizes whatever he touches. He makes all his descriptions teem with life and vivifying soul. His faults were those of his style—of the author and the man; but the original genius of the poet, the pith and marrow of his imagination, the fine natural mould in which his feelings were bedded, were too much for him to counteract by neglect, or affectation, or false ornaments. It is for this reason that he is, perhaps, the most popular of all our poets, treating of a subject that all can understand, and in a way that is interesting to all alike, to the ignorant or the refined, because he gives back the impression which the things themselves make upon us in nature. 'That', said a man of genius, seeing a little shabby soiled copy of Thomson's ***Seasons*** lying on the window-seat of an obscure country ale-house—'That is true fame!'

It has been supposed by some, that the ***Castle of Indolence*** is Thomson's best poem; but that is not the case. He has in it, indeed, poured out the whole soul of indolence, diffuse, relaxed, supine, dissolved into a voluptuous dream; and surrounded himself with a set of objects and companions, in entire unison with the listlessness of his own temper. Nothing can well go beyond the descriptions of these inmates of the place, and their luxurious pampered way of life—of him who came among them like 'a burnished fly in month of June', but soon left them on his heedless way; and him,

> For whom the merry bells had rung, I ween,
> If in this nook of quiet, bells had ever been.

The indoor quiet and cushioned ease, where 'all was one full-swelling bed'; the out-of-door stillness, broken only by 'the stock-dove's plaint amid the forest deep',

> That drowsy rustled to the sighing gale—

are in the most perfect and delightful keeping. But still there are no passages in this exquisite little production of sportive ease and fancy, equal to the best of those in the ***Seasons.*** Warton, in his *Essay on Pope* [see excerpt dated 1782], was the first to point out and do justice to some of these; for instance, to the description of the effects of the contagion among our ships at Carthagena—'of the frequent corse heard nightly plunged amid the sullen waves', and to the description of the pilgrims lost in the deserts of Arabia. This last passage, profound and striking as it is, is not free from those faults of style which I have already noticed.

> ———Breath'd hot
> From all the boundless furnace of the sky,
> And the wide-glitt'ring waste of burning sand,
> A suffocating wind the pilgrim smites
> With instant death. Patient of thirst and toil,
> Son of the desert, ev'n the camel feels
> Shot through his wither'd heart the fiery blast.
> Or from the black-red ether, bursting broad,
> Sallies the sudden whirlwind. Straight the sands,
> Commov'd around, in gath'ring eddies play;
> Nearer and nearer still they dark'ning come,
> Till with the gen'ral all-involving storm
> Swept up, the whole continuous wilds arise,
> And by their noon-day fount dejected thrown,
> Or sunk at night in sad disastrous sleep,
> Beneath descending hills the caravan
> Is buried deep. In Cairo's crowded streets,

Th' impatient merchant, wond'ring, waits in vain;
And Mecca saddens at the long delay.

There are other passages of equal beauty with these; such as that of the hunted stag, followed by 'the inhuman rout',

———That from the shady depth
Expel him, circling through his ev'ry shift.
He sweeps the forest oft, and sobbing sees
The glades mild op'ning to the golden day,
Where in kind contest with his butting friends
He wont to struggle, or his loves enjoy.

The whole of the description of the frozen zone, in the ***Winter,*** is perhaps even finer and more thoroughly felt, as being done from early associations, than that of the torrid zone in his ***Summer.*** Anything more beautiful than the following account of the Siberian exiles is, I think, hardly to be found in the whole range of poetry.

There through the prison of unbounded wilds,
Barr'd by the hand of nature from escape,
Wide roams the Russian exile. Nought around
Strikes his sad eye but deserts lost in snow,
And heavy-loaded groves, and solid floods,
That stretch athwart the solitary vast
Their icy horrors to the frozen main;
And cheerless towns far distant, never bless'd,
Save when its annual course the caravan
Bends to the golden coast of rich Cathay,
With news of human kind.

The feeling of loneliness, of distance, of lingering, slow-revolving years of pining expectation, of desolation within and without the heart, was never more finely expressed than it is here.

The account which follows of the employments of the Polar night—of the journeys of the natives by moonlight, drawn by reindeer, and of the return of spring in Lapland—

Where pure Niemi's fairy mountains rise,
And fring'd with roses Tenglio rolls his stream,

is equally picturesque and striking in a different way. The traveller lost in the snow, is a well-known and admirable dramatic episode. I prefer, however, giving one example of our author's skill in painting common domestic scenery, as it will bear a more immediate comparison with the style of some later writers on such subjects. It is of little consequence what passage we take. The following description of the first setting in of winter is, perhaps, as pleasing as any.

Through the hush'd air the whitening shower descends,
At first thin wav'ring, till at last the flakes
Fall broad and wide, and fast, dimming the day
With a continual flow. The cherish'd fields
Put on their winter-robe of purest white:
'Tis brightness all, save where the new snow melts
Along the mazy current. Low the woods
Bow their hoar head; and ere the languid Sun,
Faint, from the West emits his ev'ning ray,
Earth's universal face, deep hid, and chill,
Is one wide dazzling waste, that buries wide
The works of man. Drooping, the lab'rer-ox
Stands cover'd o'er with snow, and then demands
The fruit of all his toil. The fowls of heav'n,
Tam'd by the cruel season, crowd around
The winnowing store, and claim the little boon
Which Providence assigns them. One alone,
The red-breast, sacred to the household Gods,
Wisely regardful of the embroiling sky,
In joyless fields and thorny thickets leaves
His shivering mates, and pays to trusted man
His annual visit. Half-afraid, he first
Against the window beats; then, brisk, alights
On the warm hearth; then hopping o'er the floor,
Eyes all the smiling family askance,
And pecks, and starts, and wonders where he is:
Till more familiar grown, the table-crumbs
Attract his slender feet. The foodless wilds
Pour forth their brown inhabitants. The hare,
Though timorous of heart, and hard beset
By death in various forms, dark snares and dogs,
And more unpitying men, the garden seeks,
Urg'd on by fearless want. The bleating kind
Eye the bleak heav'n, and next, the glist'ning earth,
With looks of dumb despair; then, said dispers'd,
Dig for the wither'd herb through heaps of snow.

It is thus that Thomson always gives a *moral sense* to nature.

Thomson's blank verse is not harsh, or utterly untuneable; but it is heavy and monotonous; it seems always labouring uphill. . . . [However the] moral descriptions and reflections in the ***Seasons*** are in an admirable spirit, and written with great force and fervour.

His poem on ***Liberty*** is not equally good: his Muse was too easy and good-natured for the subject, which required as much indignation against unjust and arbitrary power, as complacency in the constitutional monarchy, under which, just after the expulsion of the Stuarts and the establishment of the House of Hanover, in contempt of the claims of hereditary pretenders to the throne, Thomson lived. Thomson was but an indifferent hater; and the most indispensable part of the love of liberty has unfortunately hitherto been the hatred of tyranny. Spleen is the soul of patriotism, and of public good: but you would not expect a man who has been seen eating peaches off a tree with both hands in his waistcoat pockets, to be 'overrun with the spleen', or to heat himself needlessly about an abstract proposition.

His plays are liable to the same objection. They are never acted, and seldom read. The author could not, or would not, put himself out of his way, to enter into the situations and passions of others, particularly of a tragic kind. The subject of ***Tancred and Sigismunda,*** which is taken from a serious episode in *Gil Blas,* is an admirable one, but poorly handled: the ground may be considered as still unoccupied. (pp. 130-39)

William Hazlitt, "On Thomson and Cowper," in his Lectures on the English Poets, *Humphrey Milford, 1924, pp. 130-59.*

Thomas Campbell (essay date 1819)

[*Campbell was a Scottish poet whose works include* The Pleasure of Hope *(1799),* Gertrude of Wyoming *(1809), and* The Pilgrim of Glencoe and Other Poems *(1842). In the excerpt below, from a work first published in 1819, he comments on Thomson's poetry, comparing it with that of William Cowper, and observing that Thomson's poetic voice remains persuasive as "long as he dwells in the pure contemplation of nature, and appeals to the universal poetry of the human heart."*]

It is singular that a subject of such beautiful unity, divisibility, and progressive interest as the description of the year should not have been appropriated by any poet before Thomson. Mr. Twining, the translator of Aristotle's *Poetics,* attributes the absence of poetry devoted to pure rural and picturesque description among the ancients, to the absence or imperfections of the art of landscape painting. The Greeks, he observes, had no Thomsons because they had no Claudes. Undoubtedly they were not blind to the beauties of natural scenery; but their descriptions of rural objects are almost always what may be called sensual descriptions, exhibiting circumstances of corporeal delight . . . rather than objects of contemplative pleasure to the eye and imagination. From the time of Augustus, when, according to Pliny, landscape painting was first cultivated, picturesque images and descriptions of prospects seem to have become much more common. But on the whole there is much more studied and detailed description in modern than in ancient poetry. There is besides in Thomson a pure theism, and a spirit of philanthropy, which, though not unknown to classical antiquity, was not familiar to its popular breast. The religion of the ancients was beautiful in fiction, but not in sentiment. It had revealed the most voluptuous and terrific agencies to poetry, but had not taught her to contemplate nature as one great image of Divine benignity, or her creatures as the objects of comprehensive human sympathy. Before popular poetry could assume this character, Christianity, philosophy, and freedom, must have civilized the human mind.

Habits of early admiration teach us all to look back upon this poet as the favourite companion of our solitary walks, and as the author who has first or chiefly reflected back to our minds a heightened and refined sensation of the delight which rural scenery affords us. The judgment of cooler years may somewhat abate our estimation of him, though it will still leave us the essential features of his poetical character to abide the test of reflection. The unvaried pomp of his diction suggests a most unfavourable comparison with the manly and idiomatic simplicity of Cowper; at the same time the pervading spirit and feeling of his poetry is in general more bland and delightful than that of his great rival in rural description. Thomson seems to contemplate the creation with an eye of unqualified pleasure and ecstasy, and to love its inhabitants with a lofty and hallowed feeling of religious happiness; Cowper has also his philanthropy, but it is dashed with religious terrors, and with themes of satire, regret, and reprehension. Cowper's image of nature is more curiously distinct and familiar. Thomson carries our associations through a wider circuit of speculation and sympathy. His touches cannot be more faithful than Cowper's, but they are more soft and select, and less disturbed by the intrusion of homely objects. Cowper was certainly much indebted to him; and though he elevates his style with more reserve and judgment than his predecessor, yet in his highest moments he seems to retain an imitative remembrance of him. It is almost stale to remark the beauties of a poem so universally felt; the truth and genial interest with which he carries us through the life of the year; the harmony of succession which he gives to the casual phenomena of nature; his pleasing transition from native to foreign scenery; and the soul of exalted and unfeigned benevolence which accompanies his prospects of the creation. It is but equal justice to say, that amidst the feeling and fancy of the ***Seasons,*** we meet with interruptions of declamation, heavy narrative, and unhappy digression—with a parhelion eloquence that throws a counterfeit glow of expression on common-place ideas—as when he treats us to the solemnly ridiculous bathing of Musidora; or draws from the classics instead of nature; or, after invoking Inspiration from her hermit-seat, makes his dedicatory bow to a patronizing Countess, or Speaker of the House of Commons. As long as he dwells in the pure contemplation of nature, and appeals to the univeral poetry of the human breast, his redundant style comes to us as something venial and adventitious—it is the flowing gesture of the druid; and perhaps to the general experience is rather imposing; but when he returns to the familiar narrations or courtesies of life, the same diction ceases to seem the mantle of inspiration, and only strikes us by its unwieldy difference from the common costume of expression. Between the period of his composing the ***Seasons*** and the ***Castle of Indolence,*** he wrote several works, which seem hardly to accord with the improvement and maturity of his taste exhibited in the latter production. To the ***Castle of Indolence*** he brought not only the full nature, but the perfect art, of a poet. The materials of that exquisite poem are derived originally from Tasso; but he was more immediately indebted for them to the *Fairy Queen;* and in meeting with the paternal spirit of Spenser he seems as if he were admitted more intimately to the home of inspiration. There he redeemed the jejune ambition of his style, and retained all its wealth and luxury without the accompaniment of ostentation. Every stanza of that charming allegory, at least of the first part of it, gives out a group of images from which the mind is reluctant to part, and a flow of harmony which the ear wishes to hear repeated. (pp. 449-50)

Thomas Campbell, "James Thomson," in Specimens of the British Poets: With Biographical and Critical Notices and an Essay on English Poetry, *edited by Thomas Campbell, Henry Carey Baird, 1853, pp. 449-57.*

Hippolyte Taine (essay date 1863)

[*Taine was a French philosopher, critic, and historian who viewed heredity and environment as crucial factors in the development of human character. In his well-known work,* Histoire de la littérature anglaise *(1863-64;* History of English Literature, *1871), he analyzed literature in the context of race and milieu. In the following excerpt from that work, Taine identifies Thomson as a precursor of Jean-Jacques Rousseau, affirming that, like Rousseau, the Scottish poet "praised gravity, patriotism, liberty, virtue; rose from the spectacle of nature to the contemplation of God, and showed to man glimpses of immortal life beyond the tomb."*]

[Thomson] saw and loved the country in its smallest details, not outwardly only, as Saint Lambert, his imitator; he made it his joy, his amusement, his habitual occupation; a gardener at heart, delighted to see the spring arrive, happy to be able to add another field to his garden. He paints all the little things, without being ashamed, for they interest him, and takes pleasure in "the smell of the dairy." We hear him speak of the "insect armies," and "when the envenomed leaf begins to curl," and of the birds which, foreseeing the approaching rain, "streak their wings with oil, to throw the lucid moisture trickling off." He perceives objects so clearly that he makes them visible: we recognise the English landscape, green and moist, half drowned in floating vapours, blotted here and there by violet clouds, which burst in showers at the horizon, which they darken, but where the light is delicately dimmed by the fog, and the clear heavens show at intervals very bright and pure:

> Th' effusive South
> Warms the wide air, and o'er the void of heaven
> Breathes the big clouds with vernal showers distent.
> Thus all day long the full-distended clouds
> Indulge their genial stores, and well-showered earth
> Is deep enriched with vegetable life;
> Till in the western sky, the downward sun
> Looks out, effulgent, from amid the flush
> Of broken clouds, gay-shifting to his beam.
> The rapid radiance instantaneous strikes
> The illumined mountain; through the forest streams;
> Shakes on the floods; and in a yellow mist,
> Far smoking o'er the interminable plain,
> In twinkling myriads lights the dewy gems.
> Moist, bright, and green, the landscape laughs around.

This is emphatic, but it is also opulent. In this air and this vegetation, in this imagination and this style, there is a heaping up, and, as it were, an impasto of effaced or sparkling tints; they are here the glistening and lustrous robe of nature and art. We must see them in Rubens—he is the painter and poet of the teeming and humid clime; but we discover it also in others; and in this magnificence of Thomson, in this exaggerated, luxuriant, grand colouring, we find occasionally the rich palette of Rubens.

All this suits ill the classical embroidery. Thomson's visible imitations of Virgil, his episodes inserted to fill up space, his invocations to spring, to the muse, to philosophy, all these pedantic relics and conventionalisms, produce incongruity. But the contrast is much more marked in another way. The worldly artificial life such as Louis XIV. had made fashionable, began to weary Europe. It was found meagre and hollow; people grew tired of always acting, submitting to etiquette. They felt that gallantry is not love, nor madrigals poetry, nor amusement happiness. They perceived that man is not an elegant doll, or a dandy the masterpiece of nature, and that there is a world beyond the drawing-room. A Genevese plebeian (J. J. Rousseau), a Protestant and a recluse, whom religion, education, poverty, and genius had led more quickly and further than others, spoke out the public secret aloud; and it was thought that he had discovered or rediscovered the country, conscience, religion, the rights of man, and natural sentiments. Then appeared a new personality, the idol and model of his time, the man of feeling, who, by his grave character and liking for nature, contrasted with the man at court. Doubtless the man of feeling has not escaped the influence of the places he has frequented. He is refined and insipid, melting at the sight of the young lambs nibbling the newly grown grass, blessing the little birds, who give a concert to celebrate their happiness. He is emphatic and wordy, writes tirades about sentiment, inveighs against the age, apostrophises virtue, reason, truth, and the abstract divinities, which are engraved in delicate outline on frontispieces. In spite of himself, he continues a man of the drawing-room and the academy; after uttering sweet things to the ladies, he utters them to nature, and declaims in polished periods about the Deity. But after all, it is through him that the revolt against classical customs begins; and in this respect, he is more advanced in Germanic England than in Latin France. Thirty years before Rousseau, Thomson had expressed all Rousseau's sentiments, almost in the same style. Like him, he painted the country with sympathy and enthusiasm. Like him, he contrasted the golden age of primitive simplicity with modern miseries and corruption. Like him, he exalted deep love, conjugal tenderness, the union of souls and perfect esteem animated by desire, paternal affection, and all domestic joys. Like him, he combated contemporary frivolity, and compared the ancient republics with modern States:

> Proofs of a people, whose heroic aims
> Soared far above the little selfish sphere
> Of doubting modern life.

Like Rousseau, he praised gravity, patriotism, liberty, virtue; rose from the spectacle of nature to the contemplation of God, and showed to man glimpses of immortal life beyond the tomb. Like him, in short, he marred the sincerity of his emotion and the truth of his poetry by sentimental vapidities, by pastoral billing and cooing, and by such an abundance of epithets, personified abstractions, pompous invocations and oratorical tirades, that we perceive in him before hand the false and ornamental style of Thomas, David, and the first French Revolution. (pp. 371-74)

H. A. Taine, "The Poets," in his History of English Literature, Vol. 3, *translated by H. Van Laun, Edmonston and Douglas, 1873-74.*

William Bayne (essay date 1898)

[*In the excerpt below, Bayne provides an interpretation of* The Seasons *and* The Castle of Indolence. *While commenting on the "pictorial power" of* The Seasons, *he extols the latter poem as a work whose exquisite musicality and grace anticipated the poetry of Romanticism.*]

Thomson, when he wrote ***The Seasons,*** was remarkable as the founder of a new literary era. This was less felt when he composed his great work than it is to-day, strongly supported as his deliberate study of Nature has been by such writers of our own century as Wordsworth, Byron, and Shelley. . . . The modern love of Nature in its beauty and in its invigorating purpose reaches much beyond any previous idea of its qualities alike in variety and range. This intensity of regard came notably into English literature, and it might be safely concluded, into all European literature through Thomson. It was no new thing to touch, it might be, with deft and subtle allusiveness on the charm and sweetness of Nature; but he it was who first emphasized beyond all modern writers the 'living activities and operant magic of the earth.' After him philosophy and art alike found a new field in which to work. Nature in the poetry of Thomson was pointed to as a fresh and abiding source of wonder, of attractiveness, of solace. He was the veritable discoverer of a new world of æsthetic and spiritual perceptions.

Wordsworth, forgetful of the more mature growth of the feeling for Nature in his own day, and also of the different artistic conditions in which the poetry of Nature was written, passed an exaggerated condemnation on the state of thought as the subject in the eighteenth century, and on the character of the poetical work of the kind produced by the contemporaries of Thomson [see essay dated 1815]. . . . Professor Wilson in one of his *Blackwood* essays brought Wordsworth promptly to book for this mistaken idea [see Further Reading]. . . . The 'blind wonderment' of the reading public of Thomson's day, Wilson affirms warmly to be beside the mark; contemporary admiration for the work of Thomson, if not so expansive as in Wordsworth's day (or, as Wordsworth hoped it was) was candidly and thoroughly appreciative. The critic of Wordsworth was in the right. Precisely the same criticism as Wordsworth here offered, would have applied in the case of Rousseau; the artificial society of his day, however, had nothing but cordial approval for the graphic and powerful delineations of Nature in the *New Heloïse.* The delightful descriptions of rural life round Montmorency, caused singular and reciprocated pleasure to the readers of the French sentimentalist. The severity of Wordsworth's judgment distinctly called for such refutation. He reduced Thomson's popularity to a wholly specious one, ascribing much of it to his 'false ornaments' and 'sentimental commonplaces.' Professor Wilson proceeded in his review to give weight to the fact that the merit of Thomson lay not in the positive novelty of his work, but in its sincerity and variety. The author of ***The Seasons,*** he said, outdid his contemporaries in noting Nature more truly and on a wider scale; and this, no slight commendation, may be readily granted as the criterion of his rank as a poet.

The plan of ***The Seasons*** is exceedingly uniform. ***Autumn,*** the last to be composed, differs in no important point of form from ***Winter,*** the original of the series. The plan adopted was that of the natural development of each of the year's divisions. Considerable objection has sometimes been taken as to the introduction of the didactic passages which appear in all. These, it is true, embody the poet's philosophy of Nature, but are by no means of the best illustrations of his art. But apart from their philosophical bearing they have in their place a distinct literary utility, creating as they do an appropriate sequence of pauses in the general narrative. The same may be said on behalf of his idyllic stories. None of them, with the exception of that on Lavinia, can count for more than a necessary variation in the treatment of the subject at large. Without these endeavours at diversity, the purely descriptive discourse would have incurred undoubted risk of monotony; and, howsoever serious their faults, the discretion that originated their introduction was a sound one. The usage, in short, is not more than an ordinary necessity of any continued literary composition. Any teller of a story who wishes his narrative to be engrossing must do the same. The most obvious instance occurs in that of the writer of tragic drama, wherein departure from a regular line of development is enforced by the clearest mandate. The true literary artist must accommodate himself to the needs of his reader or auditor.

Hazlitt called Thomson 'the best of our descriptive poets,' and the title, in its exact sense, will not with justice be denied him [see excerpt dated 1818]. His claim springs first from the completeness of his devotion to the treatment of external nature; no British poet rivals him in absolute absorption in this subject. No work in the range of British literature approaches ***The Seasons*** in dealing with Nature in a manner so apt and strenuous. Again, he excels in the expansiveness of his power in transcribing from Nature; his imagination ranges afar, while it depicts with precision; he can treat broad and striking areas with force as well as picturesqueness. A third eminent characteristic is the freshness with which he invests his portrayal. In this he is second to none of the most original of his Scottish precursors.

In all essentials of his art he compares favourably with Wordsworth and Cowper, his greatest rivals in poetical description. Wordsworth, it is true, concerned himself with the imaginative statement of a natural theodicy rather than with the special interpretation of Nature; Cowper, also, was not an avowedly descriptive poet. But the works of both are shot through with passages of natural description of the finest texture. Alike in actual extent and consistency of his study of Nature, Thomson is superior to both. Moreover, in the inherent descriptive qualities that signalise the work of all, Thomson claims corresponding if not greater praise. His reach and vividness counterbalance Wordsworth's intensity, Cowper's pleasing and sedulous exactness of detail. No passage of ***The Seasons*** equals in dazzling grandeur the cloud scene and other too rare passages of *The Excursion;* but there are not a few as naturally clear and striking. Cowper's *Morning Walk,* it must be allowed, exhausts with wonderful nearness of review almost every object of note that enters into his landscape; yet Thomson succeeds with a few bold and vigorous strokes in setting forth a similar scene with an effect quite as just. As far as the 'unbought grace' of poetry is considered, Thomson brooks no assertion of surpassing quality on the side of either Wordsworth or Cowper. The stumbling-block to his equal authority of claim consists in his crudity of style. Bombastic, cumbrous, vapid, all these epithets forcibly apply to the language of not a few passages, lines, and phrases of ***The Seasons;*** here Thomson, in all other respects to be praised, must be assigned an inferior position; in this artistic part of his work he greatly fails beside the studied, and yet satisfying ease of Wordsworth, and the polished grace of Cowper.

Most conspicuous of the gifts of the poet of ***The Seasons*** is his pictorial power. ***The Seasons*** has a wealth of clearly-limned and finished pictures. They stand out as truthfully and effectively as if drawn upon canvas. Concerned in the main with still life, there are included also figure pieces of the deftest workmanship. Thomson is not only the Claude of British poetry, he may also with fairness be called the Teniers or the Wilkie. Background, colour, and careful technique distinguish his transcripts derived from the world of external nature; spirit, verisimilitude, humour, his efforts in figure pieces. This class of picture scenes is met with least frequently in ***Winter,*** due perhaps to the less advanced power of the author's art. In ***Winter*** the poet is above all the *raconteur.* His effects there as elsewhere are skilfully managed; but the artistic result is less firm, less delicate. Only one or two of these delightful vignettes decorate the pages of ***Winter.*** We have the Snowstorm in the one class of pictorial representations; the Hall Sports in the other. They certainly challenge comparison with the best of the poet's similar achievements. But ***Winter,*** altogether, does not cohere so truly as do its companion studies. Description, episode, moralising, are intermixed in a way that disappears in the rest of the ***Seasons.*** When once, however, Thomson found the measure of his power, he carried out his design without hesitation or flaw. To place beside the solitary ***Winter*** sketch from still life, there are in ***Spring*** the well-defined transcripts of Meadow and Forest, the Sunset, the Dawn, the Valley, and the Garden. Here, however, no figure pieces find a place. ***Summer*** has a large number of descriptive feats in both classes of work. Unsatisfactory to the author in its first draft, the scrupulous revision bestowed upon this book justifies itself fully in this particular line of description. A beautiful picture of Dawn holds the leading place; then in close array comes a varied series of well-felt landscapes and rustic scenes. First is that of Haymaking, followed closely by one of Sheep-shearing, and others—the Pasturing Horse, the Waterfall, the Hill, the Desert Storm, the Thunderstorm, and the Shepherd's Courtship. ***Autumn,*** too, contains not a few of these brightly defined drawings. Chief among them are the Fall of the Leaf, the Hunted Stag, the Revelling Fox-hunters, (one of the most successful of all, though Lyttelton in his edition excised it, from a fancied idea of its coarseness), the Orchard, Moonlight, and the Village Dance. Two examples of Thomson's rare power of presentation in this respect are subjoined; that of 'Moonlight' from ***Autumn*** being an outstanding example of his gift as a painter of still life.

> Meanwhile the moon,
> Full-orbed and breaking through the scattered clouds
> Shows her broad image in the crimsoned East.
> Turned to the sun direct her spotted disk,
> Where mountains rise, umbrageous vales descend
> And caverns deep, as optic tube descries,
> A smaller earth, gives all his blaze again,
> Void of its flame, and sheds a softer day.
> Now through the passing cloud she seems to stoop,
> Now up the pure cerulean rides sublime.
> Wide the pale deluge floats, and streaming mild
> O'er the skied mountain to the shadowy vale,
> While rocks and floods reflect the quivering gleam,
> The whole air whitens with a boundless tide
> Of silver radiance, breaking round the world.

'Haymaking' in ***Summer*** forms a rustic picture of the fullest exactness and verve. After introducing as leading figures

> The rustic youth, brown with meridian toil
> Healthful and strong; full as the summer rose
> Blown by prevailing suns, the ruddy maid,

the picture is charmingly developed thus:—

> Even stooping age is here; and infant hands
> Trail the long rake, or with the fragrant load
> O'ercharged, amid the kind oppression roll.
> Wide flies the tedded grain; all in a row
> Advancing broad, or wheeling round the field,
> They spread the breathing harvest to the sun
> That throws refreshful round a rural smell:
> Or, as they rake the green-appearing ground,
> And drive the dusky wave along the mead,
> The russet hay-cock rises thick behind
> In order gay; while, heard from dale to dale,
> Waking the breeze, resounds the blended voice
> Of happy labour, love, and social glee.

The style in ***The Seasons*** with the undeniable pomposity that grievously culminates at times in such phraseology as 'plumy people,' 'opponent bank,' and 'afflictive noon,' exhibits no inconsiderable number of felicitous lines. There is displayed none of the pre-eminence of expression shown by the great masters in poetical art, no line that impinges on the memory by the very mellifluous beauty of its accent. Never does it reach the haunting resonance of

> Perilous seas in faery lands forlorn,

or,

> Tall oaks branch-charmed by the earnest stars,

or,

> With the moon's beauty and the moon's soft pace.

Yet Thomson, as well as Keats and Wordsworth, owned the same gift of melody, not only in lines, but in passages. Had it not been that the verbose diction of his day held him so closely in its grasp, and irrevocably impelled him to the employment of its jarring chords, there might have been little to complain of in his work in this respect. Some of his verses sustain with unmistakable force the plea on behalf of his real power of expressiveness. Take, for instance,

> The thunder holds his black tremendous throne,

or,

> And Mecca saddens at the long delay,

or,

> Sighs the sad genius of the coming storm.

These, and other lines, are touched with the finest illuminating art, and could have been written only by a poet whose judgment in regard to diction was, at its best, of unusual discernment.

The originality of Thomson's genius declared itself as markedly in the literary method by which he chose to express himself as in the choice of material to which he dedicated his poetical insight. The heroic couplet, so overwhelmingly fashionable in his day, had no attraction for him. In ***Autumn*** he speaks with undisguised admiration of John Philips as the second

> Who nobly durst, in rhyme-unfettered verse
> With British freedom, sing the British song.

He evidently felt that the somewhat metallic form in which Dryden and Pope enshrined their reflections, was equally open to criticism with their conception of the sphere of poetical thought. The success of his attempt at a new style of verse says much for his artistic penetration. For it was undoubtedly from his appreciation of Milton that he boldly essayed this revolution in the art of verse. The conviction dated from an early period. In more than one of his juvenile productions this idea of the superiority of blank verse influenced him. The pity is that his genius was not strong enough to go further, and to assert itself against the accepted rotund and unnatural diction with which he laboured, and which, indeed, was but a kind of meaningless echo of Miltonic language. Keats, with a finer intuition, but also, it must be remembered, with fuller literary advantages, faced the same problem, and solved it. In one of his letters, he speaks of the difficulties that beset him in seeking to conjure with the harmonies of the 'organ-voice of England.' Keats wrote:—

> The *Paradise Lost,* though so fine in itself, is a corruption of our language. It should be left as it is—unique, a curiosity, a beautiful and grand curiosity—the most remarkable of the world; a Northern dialect accommodating itself to Greek and Latin inversions and intonations. The purest English, I think—or what ought to be purest—is Chatterton's. The language had existed long enough to be entirely uncorrupted of Chaucer's Gallicisms, and still the old words are used. I prefer the native music of it to Milton's cut by feet. I have but lately stood on my guard against Milton. Life to him would be death to me. Miltonic verse cannot be written, but is the verse of art. I wish to devote myself to another verse alone.

Not only was Thomson unable to perceive that for him Miltonic verse was an impossible vehicle; he attempted to adapt it as far as in him lay. Alike in rhythm and in language he modelled his chief work upon it. Not a perfect success—this was in the nature of the case impossible—it was yet far removed from failure. The blank verse of Thomson moves with spirit and a fair amount of musicalness, and often with a certain graceful dignity. But the rich notes of Milton's verse were due both to the nobility of his theme and the unrivalled insight which he had into the rhythmical capability of the language used, and his extraordinary gift of melodious composition. Thomson fell altogether short in the two last qualities. Especially was his ear dull in the matter of verbal cadences. The general movement in the music of a passage he could perfectly understand and practise; but the subordinate touches proper to the elaboration of the whole escaped him. But success as well as defect must be acknowledged in the character of his verse. The merit of expansiveness that belongs to him in rendering landscape applies under different conditions to his rhythmical skill. He is deficient, in short, in the production of harmony. His blank verse is informed only with melody; but it is melody that, if sometimes overweighted, is, as a rule, clear, buoyant, and tuneful.

The general embodiment of opinion throughout ***The Seasons*** comprehends subjects of a varied characater. Though it was not the primary object of the poet to set forth opinion in the work, he had well-marked views on social and political matters, and on religion, which he was able to introduce with perfect aptness into his pages. So clearly-defined, indeed, is his religious philosophy of Nature that consideration of this is of distinctive moment. But, apart from the religious attitude of Thomson, other topics of importance, seriously handled, arrest attention. Following closely upon his frank and ardent love of the external world comes his insistence on a tender regard for the lower creation, in which he was so worthily succeeded by Cowper, Burns, and Blake, and which in the nineteenth century has assumed the terms of a pretty definite creed. He misses no opportunity of dwelling upon this subject to a practical purpose, and his picture for instance, of the hunted stag in ***Autumn*** might be found to profoundly appeal to one with a sense of feeling unusually blunted. It has been pertinently said that Burns's 'Wounded Hare' will live in men's memories when hares are no longer shot for sport. Thomson's feeling with respect to the humane treatment of the lower animals was evidently as deep as that of Burns; and, although he gave no expression to his conclusions in lines so memorable, his whole-hearted humanity appears to have had in this respect, as in others, a strong community with his great Scottish successor.

The patriotism of Thomson shines with no fickle light throughout ***The Seasons.*** As he showed, not only in ***Liberty*** and ***Rule Britannia,*** but in his general attitude in practical affairs, his convictions upon political matters were settled and pronounced. . . . He was . . . a Scot first, and then a loyal adherent of the British constitution. On more than one occasion he recalls the perfervid spirit and robust strain of his fellow-countrymen. One of the most compact and effective passages in ***The Seasons*** conveys an enthusiastic account of Scotland. He was fully cognisant, at the same time, of the many sterling qualities of the Anglo-Saxon and the Celt in other quarters of the kingdom. In a few lines of ***The Prospect*** he characterises each of the nations with much keenness of appreciation.

> She rears to freedom an undaunted race
> Compatriot zealous, hospitable kind,
> Hers the warm Cambrian: hers the lofty Scot,
> To hardship tamed, active in arts and arms,
> Fired with a restless, an impatient flame,
> That leads him raptured where ambition calls;
> And English merit hers, where meet combined,

Whate'er high fancy, sound judicious thought,
An ample, generous heart, undrooping soul,
And firm tenacious valour can bestow.

This enlightened feeling of patriotism prevails throughout ***The Seasons.*** A united and prosperous Britain forms ever the poet's warmest political aspiration. In one phase of his constitutional opinions he maintained a certain individuality of outlook; like Burns, who, however, did not approve himself the unswerving constitutionalist we know Thomson to have been, he was at heart something of a democrat. As truly as did Burns, he realised the mighty safeguard of the 'wall of fire' that was set round a country by a hardy and contented peasantry. A man of the people, Burns's earnest advocacy of popular right admits of no manner of difficulty; the position of Thomson was somewhat different. True, he was born in a sufficiently humble rank of life; but during most of his career he mingled only in a society of culture, refinement, and, it might be, exclusiveness. Notwithstanding the circumstances in which he thus was placed, he preserved from first to last a true and deeply rooted esteem for the 'rustic' and other sons of toil. The sheep-shearing scene in ***Summer*** is followed by a number of reflective lines in which the poet urges the vital dependence of British greatness upon the industrial activities of the common people:—

Hence Britannia sees
Her solid grandeur rise; hence she commands
The exalted stores of every brighter clime;
The treasures of the sun without his rage;
Hence, fervent all, with culture, toil, and arts,
Wide glows her land; her dreadful thunder hence
Rides o'er the waves sublime, and now, even now,
Impending hangs o'er Gallia's humbled coast,
Hence rules the circling deep and awes the world.

He returns to the subject in the same poem, comparing favourably the condition of the British people with that of foreign nations. The contemplation leads him to dwell upon the general happiness of the peasant and the mechanic; the heroic capability of the soldier and the sailor; and the characteristic generosity of the British nobility. This is succeeded by a long and eloquent passage on past leaders in British greatness, celebrating the deeds of the Edwards and the Henries, of Drake, Raleigh, Hampden, Algernon Sidney, and Lord William Russell. Then comes a final stirring piece of writing, in which the poet recites the glories of British literature.

Is not wild Shakespear thine and Nature's boast?
Is not each great, each amiable Muse
Of classic ages in thy Milton met?
A genius universal as his theme,
Astonishing as chaos, as the bloom
Of blowing Eden fair, as heaven sublime.
Nor shall my verse that elder bard forget
The gentle Spenser, fancy's pleasing son
Who, like a copious river, poured his song
O'er all the mazes of enchanted ground;
Or thee, his ancient master, laughing sage;
Chaucer, whose native manners-painting verse
Well-moralised, shines through the gothic cloud
Of time and language o'er thy genius thrown.

It has been discriminatingly pointed out by Mr Logie Robertson that Thomson's patriotism was inspired from a peculiar external source; that he primarily loved his country, and Scotland, principally, as viewed 'rather in its geographical than its historical aspects.' As far as Scotland was concerned, this national pride had much to nourish it. . . . ***Britannia,*** too, he wrote upon one occasion, in language that bespeaks a note of this affectionate memory, 'includes our native kingdom of Scotland.' But, withal, his affection for England also was at length firmly planted; the scenes at Richmond and at Hagley drew out his friendly zeal as well. (pp. 111-26)

The religious philosophy of Nature presented in ***The Seasons*** does not, as a rule, attract the closest regard. This absence of concern as to the speculative character of the poem has some defence in the positive character of the work itself; for it was not the chief aim of the poet to expound a philosophy. But, along with the graphic and subtle interpretation of Nature in ***The Seasons,*** there exists a carefully-balanced and systematic religious philosophy, with a meaning and a force of its own. The choric passages of reflection that are introduced in each division of ***The Seasons*** exhibit it with distinctness, while it burns with a steady and effulgent light in the ideas of the culminating **"Hymn."** Criticism has been wont to content itself with the assurance that Thomson in these philosophical passages did no more than give ready and unconsidered utterance to the ordinary, and often superficial, philosophical beliefs of his day. There is some truth in this. Both philosophical thought and language in the eighteenth century were of a stereotyped order, and only a writer of the greatest originality could have been expected to throw aside their encompassing bonds. Further vindication of the concessions paid to received intellectual fashions in ***The Seasons*** proceeds from the fact that the writer was an artist first and then a philosopher. But there is sufficient reason to suppose that Thomson also thought and wrote with an independent outlook; the passage on *Creative Wisdom* in ***Summer,*** the concluding passage of the same poem, and the **"Hymn"** fully warrant such a decision.

Thomson's creed regarding Nature was an impersonal one, and here, perhaps, he comes nearer to man's attitude to Nature to-day than do the highly-wrought philosophies of nature intervening between his date and the present. Modern science, which has dispelled to some extent the enchantment of the splendid pantheistic systems of Wordsworth and Shelley, has not been able to pierce beyond the inscrutable veil in the presence of which the poet of ***The Seasons*** reverently worked. Nor has it, with its relentless connotation of the evil as well as of the brightness that exists in Nature, succeeded in sapping the foundation of that earnest optimism on which his spirit was stayed against all reck of shock. The cardinal terms of his creed of Nature—its sanity, its calm, its self-centred strength—remain a powerful faith to-day. One great voice of our century proclaims this:—

From the intense, clear, star-sown vault of heaven,
Over the lit sea's unquiet way,

In the rustling night-air came the answer,
Wouldst thou *be* as these are? *live* as they.

Unaffrighted by the silence round them,
Undistracted by the sights they see,
These demand not that the things without them
Yield them love, amusement, sympathy.

And with joy the stars perform their shining,
And the sea its long moon-silver'd roll;
For alone they live, nor pine with noting
All the fever of some differing soul.

Bounded by themselves, and unobservant
In what state God's other works may be,
In their own tasks all their powers pouring,
These attain the mighty life you see.

The joy of the earlier poet in the glory of Nature sounded a more jubilant and more thrilling note than this. And yet by implication both might, with perfect sincerity, have been attuned to the more inspiring strain. The radiant hopefulness of the **"Hymn"** has not been silenced:—

I cannot go
Where Universal Love not smiles around,
Sustaining all yon orbs, and all their sons;
From seeming evil still educing good,
And better thence again, and better still,
In infinite progression.

(pp. 126-28)

Spenser was a long-established favourite of Thomson's, and he therefore took up a very congenial piece of work when he began his ***Castle of Indolence,*** avowedly based upon the great epic narrative of the 'poet's poet.' The poem was begun, according to his own words, as early as 1733, and engaged his attention at intervals of more or less duration till its publication in 1748. It formed another 'departure' in his poetry. The intention of the writer obviously was that the work should be a reflection of his ideas and capabilities as an artist—as an artist especially of the effects of poetical cadence, and of the literary grace of language. The result fully justified his aim. No imitation of a similar kind ever made has attained so near a rank of excellence to the original as do certain passages of ***The Castle of Indolence*** to *The Faery Queen*. . . . (p. 129)

A professed and successful imitation of Spenser, [***The Castle of Indolence***] is also much more: a quite spontaneous and living poem.

The comparison in method between ***The Seasons*** and ***The Castle of Indolence*** is fraught with suggestive interest. In ***The Seasons*** we have the poet, in his most representative character, dealing with the intrinsic imaginative elements of his art, with the conception, vividness, and lively comprehension of his ideas; in ***The Castle of Indolence*** he seeks to emphasise the power of expression of his thought, the aptness and felicity of his language, the beauty and tunefulness of phrase and rhythm. In ***The Seasons*** we recognise chiefly the hand of the poet; in ***The Castle of Indolence*** the hand of the artist. In the one he achieves distinction beside those whose special office it has been to grasp and vivify some poetic truth; in the other he enters the select ranks of the formal stylists of our literature. Here he belongs of right to the school of Coleridge and Keats. In deft and curious arrangement of topic, and in the exercise of subtle peculiarities of form and diction, ***The Castle of Indolence*** bears adequate consideration beside the masterpieces of the great romanticists of our own century. Nor does this excellence in point of outward form remain its simple recommendation. The poet's imagination asserts its capacity to answer to the particular demands made upon it by the conditions of the form upon which he works; and the result is something of that ethereal temper which characterises alone the best products in rare and delicate romance. Realistic, in a sense, in ***The Seasons,*** Thomson now becomes the exponent of an idealism in poetry. The region of ***The Castle of Indolence*** has no locality or name. It is a region of dream, of entrancing vision and enticing sound, of sun-flushed skies and radiant air, of bright sward and purple hill, of murmurous forest and melodious river, but where there lurks, moreover, depth of horror, and where landscape not far removed shines fair beneath a temperate day. It is a region consecrated indeed by the 'light that never was on sea or land.'

No work of poetry between the time of Spenser and Thomson is so marked by this absolutely delicate idealising tendency; nothing like it appears again till the time of Keats. We do not hear much about the significance of Thomson's part in setting forth anew the 'sweet-slipping movement' and charm of the Spenserian manner as a model for the poets of the nineteenth century literary renaissance; but there can be no doubt about the validity of his right in this matter. In the romantic method, so excellently represented by Thomson, Keats may be taken as the most direct successor who understood the extraordinary richness of the note that was struck in ***The Castle of Indolence;*** for though there is its mystic glamour in the poetry of Coleridge, Keats, in his work, combines in a more general way, the main aims in the literary design of Thomson. The supreme greatness of Coleridge and of Keats has tended to dim the less splendid glory of their distinguished predecessor; but the claim of his accomplishment in this direction demands acknowledgment. The matter is valuable if only as an item in the historical development of our literature. Mr. Theodore Watts-Dunton, in an admirable essay on *Chatterton,* contributed to Ward's *English Poets,* points out with conclusive force that the gracefully light and flexible octosyllabic rhythms, which became so great a power in the hands of Colerdige and Scott, had already received efficient illustration from the bright genius of Chatterton. The brilliancy of conception, the wealth of imagery, the ample command of the musical resources of language displayed in ***The Castle of Indolence,*** certainly seem to constrain the like recognition of a strong claim on the part of its author as a master of style in which worked some of the greatest who came after him.

The Faery Queen was not only the model upon which Thomson based his ***Castle of Indolence,*** but it supplied him with a definite hint as to the very scene in which he should set his narrative. This was the House of Sleep, whence the wizard Archimago sent for a dream by which to cast a spell over the Red Cross Knight:

And more to tell him in his slumber soft,
A trickling stream from high rock tumbling
down,

And ever-drizzling rain upon the loft,
Mix'd with a murmuring wind, much like the
sound
Of swarming bees, did cast him in a swound.
No other noise, no people's troublous cries,
That still are wont t'annoy the walled town,
Might there be heard; but careless Quiet lies
Wrapt in eternal silence, far from enemies.

But this hint given him, Thomson owed nothing more with respect to the actual evolution of his story. With the playful picture of the little society at North Haw as a nucleus, he wove his own fascinating romance, original, picturesque, and stored with new and strange allusions. The figures who act in the drama, if not altogether novel, are freshly and decisively drawn; while the circumstances by which they are surrounded, and the light in which their activity is made clear and captivating, take their origin from no source but that of the moulding imagination of the poet himself. The difference in the matter of allusiveness between Spenser and Thomson is emphatic enough. The bounteous fields from which Spenser chiefly garnered his imposing array of literary allusions were medieval legend and classical mythology. In *The Faery Queen* no surprise attends the reader should he now and again even meet the co-existence of persons and events from these sources so widely separated by time and space; when perhaps Venus and the Graces are introduced side by side with historic personages of a new era,

Knights of Logres and of Lyonesse,
Tristrem, and Pelleas, and Pellenore.

In ***The Castle of Indolence,*** a totally different fund of illustration is utilised. Now it is Oriental story that lends its personages and its incidents as enriching factors; the literary treasures of Chaldea and Arabia and their neighbouring kingdoms, and these almost solely, afford the material wherewith the poet of ***The Castle of Indolence*** adorns his story.

Although the art, rather than the subject-matter, of the allegory may be fairly premised—indubitably so from the superiority of the art to the story with which it deals—to have given the poet most concern, the theme which he strove to elaborate is important enough. This designates the old and perennial story of the conflict between Pleasure and Duty. The poetical literature of the eighteenth century evinced a special leaning to this subject. This bias, ultimately borrowed from the supremely ethical tone which pervaded the religious discussion of the day, affected alike all and sundry in the busy class of poetical writers. No doubt Thomson's choice was also considerably guided by the precise nature associated with allegory in the pages of Spenser. But the didactic spirit was abroad in the eighteenth century with a power of exceeding energy. It did not, however, enter into poetical art with very satisfactory result. The doctrine that poetry is a criticism of life has much to commend it; but, as far as it is pertinent, there must be the admission that the poetical outcome should be conditioned by laws of beauty as well as of truth. . . . The poetical transition made in passing from the perusal of [Edward Young's *Night Thoughts*], to the allegorical method of Thomson, is of the most significant character. Both works alike inculcate momentous truth; both works are alike sound and decisive in what they aim to enforce. But in the entire legitimate appeal of the argument of each, how far does the one outvie the other! Inasmuch as both are to be judged as poetry, the predominant merit of the one stands out with singular clearness. The morality of the one cannot be dissevered from that of the formal tractate; that of the other partakes in a very great degree of the transforming and heightening power of imagination.

The two parts of ***The Castle of Indolence*** have a kind of antithetical relation. The first canto, describing the abode and circumstances of the wizard Indolence, teems with rich and resplendent imagery; the vein in which the narrative is conveyed is of the most delicately-wrought sweetness. The more restrained gift of the poet is revealed in the second canto. Now, the pictures are less finely-drawn and less gorgeous; the music of the verse is touched with less aerial tone; the diction has not so much subtlety and skilful refinement of workmanship. The allegory, in short, assumes conditions that do not so readily kindle in the glow of the poet's imagination. The story of the triumph of Industry brings him back to the concrete affairs of the everyday world, and to the necessity of emphasising the value and character of its normal activities. The didactic element more decidedly prevails, and though to Thomson as well as to Spenser it was vouchsafed to inspire brightness into the didactic note of poetry, it was scarcely given to either to form it, 'musical as is Apollo's lute.'

Interesting alike from their biographical interest and their nice elaboration is the group of portraits that are introduced in the first canto, and that formed the first suggestive draft of the whole poem. The least distinct is the first, which may be a composite presentment. Were it not that the author speaks of Paterson, to whose personality it answers with considerable faithfulness, the resemblance might be as aptly referred to Collins. Perhaps the original idea was taken from the character of Paterson, to be afterwards developed and coloured with various hints from that of Collins, who was no infrequent dweller in the society of Thomson in his last years. The second portrait also bears some slight divergence from the original of Armstrong, to whom tradition has generally applied it. Thomson, indeed, averred that Armstrong was the victim of a 'certain kind of spleen that is both humane and agreeable, like Jacques in the play;' but another report speaks of Armstrong's ready share in London social affairs, and makes it plain that 'pensiveness' was certainly not a prominent feature of his character. Welby, who is said to have been the third of the group, did not belong to the choice literary coterie at Richmond. He must have gained admittance to this poetical distinction from sheer merit of his personal characteristics, which receive such pointed and humorous setting in the poem. The fourth portrait was in all likelihood that of young Forbes of Culloden, but this, like the first two, is a somewhat generalised drawing. Any young man of sprightly and masculine character would answer equally well. The friendship of Thomson with Forbes, however, gives much reliableness to the conjecture that the description is one from life. Lyttelton's portrait is faithfully and gracefully done. The poet does not err, as he was so prone to do, on the side of exaggeration; but presents a clear and natural picture of the estimable friend of his later life. The last three portraits—those of Quin, the poet himself, and Murdoch—have the most piquant character, and are perhaps most felicitous of all. Quin is drawn with sympathetic firmness. Lyttelton has generally received the credit of writing the inimitable account of Thomson himself. If so, he accomplished a portraiture of rare spirit and exactness. Familiar enough in some of its particulars, the whole stanza may be cited as reflecting with quaintly humorous precision and effect the character of the poet.

> A bard here dwelt, more fat than bard beseems;
> Who void of envy, guile, and lust of gain,
> On virtue still, and Nature's pleasing themes,
> Poured forth his unpremeditated strain;
> The world forsaking with a calm disdain,
> Here laughed he careless in his easy seat;
> Here quaffed, encircled with his joyous train;
> Oft-moralizing sage! his ditty sweet
> He loathed much to write, ne cared to repeat.

The contrast between the artistic method of ***The Seasons*** and that of ***The Castle of Indolence*** is most definitely brought out in the first canto of the second poem. No approach is made in ***The Seasons,*** vivid and striking as are so many of its descriptive passages, to the superb imagery of the introductory part of ***The Castle of Indolence;*** and of the marvellously fine rhythmical cadences of the Spenserian imitation there may, indeed, be said to be no trace at all in the earlier poem. No better summary of this salient factor of ***The Castle of Indolence*** could be desired than that expressed in these words of Mr Logie Robertson:—"Now the style is serious, grave, and solemn; now it is cheerful, lively, and gay. It sometimes borders on burlesque, mostly of a brisk and airy character. There are, however, numerous descriptive passages of clear-ringing and exalted melody, sufficient in themselves to rank Thomson as a genuine singer of commanding rank." As a typical instance of these passages, where it may be added, the poet proves that he possessed the gift of harmonious movement, which is so lacking in the blank verse of ***The Seasons,*** there is here given the stanza which describes the music of the harp of Æolus. *Christabel* contains nothing better.

> Ah me! what hand can touch the string so fine?
> Who up the lofty diapason roll
> Such sweet, such sad, such solemn airs divine,
> Then let them down again into the soul:
> Now rising love they fanned; now pleasing dole
> They breathed, in tender musings, thro' the heart;
> And now a graver sacred strain they stole,
> As when seraphic hands a hymn impart:
> Wild warbling nature all; above the reach of art.

Nothing of this bewitching music is to be heard in the second canto, where the Knight of Industry and his energetic train are depicted. The solemnity of his position lends to the poet's verse something of its soberness. The epithets lack the brightness and lucidity of the first canto; the rhythm is more moderated and exact. But one or two passages, especially that in which appears the hortatory song of the bard, are written in well-compounded verse of great excellence—nervous, fluent, and graceful. This is, perhaps, best noticeable in the comparison made between the vigour belonging to Nature and its reflection in man. (pp. 130-39)

The realistic scene of horror with which the poem concludes, though terminating somewhat abruptly, is drawn with intense and masterly force. Slight as it is, and thrown into denser obscurity by the magnificence and extent of the scenes in which it is enclosed, it takes a noteworthy place in its own line of poetical art. It may not have suggested, but certainly deserves a place beside, the description of the final terrors that beset the path of Browning's 'Childe Roland.'

The apparent value of ***The Castle of Indolence*** as an example of the application of careful æsthetic conditions in poetry makes it less needful to dwell upon the character of the work as an allegory. Thomson himself, although he published the poem as an avowed effort in allegorical reflection, probably did not feel that this feature of the story was of paramount note. His preface, in truth, declares as much. It runs as follows:—

> This poem being writ in the manner of Spenser, the obsolete words, and a simplicity of diction in some of the lines which borders on the ludicrous, were necessary to make the imitation more perfect. And the style of that admirable poet, as well as the measure in which he wrote, are, as it were, appropriated by custom to all allegorical poems writ in our language; just as in French the style of Marot, who lived under Francis the First, has been used in tales and familiar epistles of the age of Louis the Fourteenth.

Clearly, the material and strain of the allegory do not bulk very largely in the consideration of the author. But in the matter of just evolution of the allegorical materials of the story, Thomson reached a requisite amount of success. The scene is perfectly realised; the characters are drawn with distinctiveness and breadth; the moral to be derived from the story does not thrust itself unpleasantly upon the attention. In respect of structural arrangement, indeed, the allegory of ***The Castle of Indolence*** is sufficiently praiseworthy. Especially has this to be said of the balance preserved throughout the development of the allegorical narrative. Though it were scarcely justifiable to bring an allegorical effort so much less ambitious into any sort of comparison with the great allegories of Spenser and Bunyan, yet the merit of adequate discrimination as to the respective places of allegory and romance in a narrative of the kind seems, at least, to be carried out with signal faithfulness by the author of ***The Castle of Indolence.*** The clear outlines of Bunyan's landscapes and the actuality of his personages save his work from the overpowering depression incidental to the general arrangement of his didactic narrative; while Spenser's gorgeous scenes and moving episodes fulfil a like virtue for his great epic. Both of these allegories are weighed down by unvitalised material, by ethical or theological doctrine, and other matters, that hardly come with perfect right into the natural progress of the story. There is good reason to think even from the slighter performance which Thomson achieved, that had he extended the plan of his work, built turret and pinnacle on the pleasing edifice which he raised, the result would have been a great and very convincing testimony to the genius of the designer and builder.

Tennyson, in the recent biography of the late laureate by his son, is reported to have declared that Thomson was his earliest model. The appreciation thus begun was not abandoned, we may infer, in the critical conclusions of his later years. He has, at any rate, signified his sincere approval of ***The Castle of Indolence*** in the imaginative beauty, rich colouring, and finished literary form of *The Lotos Eaters.* The imitation, though individual enough, plainly intimates the closeness and fulness with which the earlier artistic masterpiece had enlisted his regard. The sun-tinted sky, the soothing streams, the sombre pine, the 'joy of calm,' all point to one undoubted source. Tennyson's power of limpid and magical expression was all his own; and so too was his gift of intricate and delicious harmony; but it may be said with every truth that in this poem, at least, he was not forgetful of the unique picturesqueness and winning music of the art of ***The Castle of Indolence.*** (pp. 141-43)

William Bayne, in his James Thomson, *Oliphant Anderson & Ferrier, 1898, 160 p.*

Edmund Gosse (essay date 1906)

[*Gosse was an English critic, poet, biographer, and translator who gained prominence as an interpretor and proponent of foreign, particularly French and Scandinavian, writers. Viewed by some as a popularizer, he is nevertheless esteemed for his broad interest in and knowledge of foreign literatures. Gosse's writings include* A History of Eighteenth Century English Literature: 1660-1780 *(1889),* Northern Studies *(1890), and* Father and Son: A Study of Two Temperaments *(1907). In the following excerpt from an introduction to Henry D. Roberts's 1906 edition of* The Seasons, *he describes Thomson as an important poet who, despite stylistic excesses and imperfections, exerted an unparalleled influence "upon the epical and descriptive parts of subsequent English poetry."*]

There is not to be found, among the English poets, one who holds a more anomalous rank than the author of ***The Seasons,*** nor one to whom it is more difficult to be scrupulously just. It would not be decent to claim for him a place among the ten or twelve supreme masters whose magnitude quietly asserts itself more and more as each generation passes, and yet it is equally invidious to consign Thomson, with all his originality, his distinction, and his extended influence, to the class of secondary writers. The glory of innovation, the laurel due to the man who introduced, with definite success, a manner of writing which is still, after one hundred and seventy years, in the main approved, are clouded and flagged by the limitations to which he himself subjected the exercise of his gift, and by the languid way in which he soon abandoned his discoveries. From a great poet we expect an individual note, a novel and commanding outlook upon Nature, and an utterance which shall excite and yet defy imitation. These qualities we discover, to an eminent degree, in Thomson. But from the great poet we certainly do not expect, in comparatively early youth, a resignation of all these graces, a return to the vague and outworn symbols of language, nor reams of sterile verse that stultify the writer's pretensions. Yet this is what it is our misfortune to meet with from Thomson. He should have died in 1733, after drafting ***The Castle of Indolence***; unhappily, he lived until 1748, and thus forbade us to place him by the side of Marlowe or of Keats. Yet, had his career been as brief as were his years of genius, we should have had to insist upon many analogies between him and those 'inheritors of unfulfilled renown'.

But if Thomson is hardly among the great poets, he is not, for that reason, of less absorbing interest to the critic. His inherent originality, indeed, is probably more obvious to us than it was to his immediate contemporaries, and is certainly far more significant. Since Marvell in 1650 had written about birds and flowers in the garden at Nunappleton, the English poets seemed to have lost the power of observing external nature. Dryden, with all his noble qualities, remained absolutely blind to the aspect of phenomena. During the last decade of the seventeenth century, a single writer, Anne, Countess of Winchelsea, described natural objects exactly in her delicate verses, but she was rewarded by absolute neglect. We may search the poems of Addison, Garth, and Prior in vain for one solitary touch of genuine landscape. With the second decade of the eighteenth century, a certain attention to external nature once more came into fashion. Pope's *Windsor Forest,* in 1713, Gay's *Rural Sports* of the same year, and *Shepherd's Week,* of 1714, Croxall's *Vision,* in 1715, and the posthumous poems of Parnell in 1718, showed the tendency of public taste. All these poems appeared during Thomson's boyhood, and it is not improbable that each of them reached him in turn. He would find little to stimulate him, perhaps, in the gorgeousness of Croxall, or in Pope's Dutch *genre,* but it is not possible that Parnell's solemn sentiment should leave him unmoved, or that his heart should not leap within him when Gay described how

> Far in the deep the sun his glory hides,
> A streak of gold the sea and sky divides;
> The purple clouds their amber linings show,
> And edg'd with flame rolls every wave below.

Such large touches of landscape were, however, exceedingly rare, even with Gay, and they are found only in his earliest works. With him, as with Pope, coloured vignettes of still life make up the sum of what passes for scenery, and even these touches are put in without sentiment, for their local colour, and in obedience to an instinct like that of such painters as Hondecoeter or Ostade. In the case of Gay, especially, whose natural eye was very fresh and precise, a hint of burlesque scarcely ever fails to accompany the rural picture; he is Theocritus with a pipe of tobacco and a pot of beer. Even this little access of restricted landscape, moreover, proved too simple for the taste of the times; it flickered for a moment, and faded away. Thomson was destined to eclipse it altogether with his larger light.

These his predecessors had all written in rhyme, and, except Parnell, all in the heroic couplet. Thomson himself adopted this, the dominant form, in his earliest copies of verses. Those curious essays, dating from 1713 to 1720,

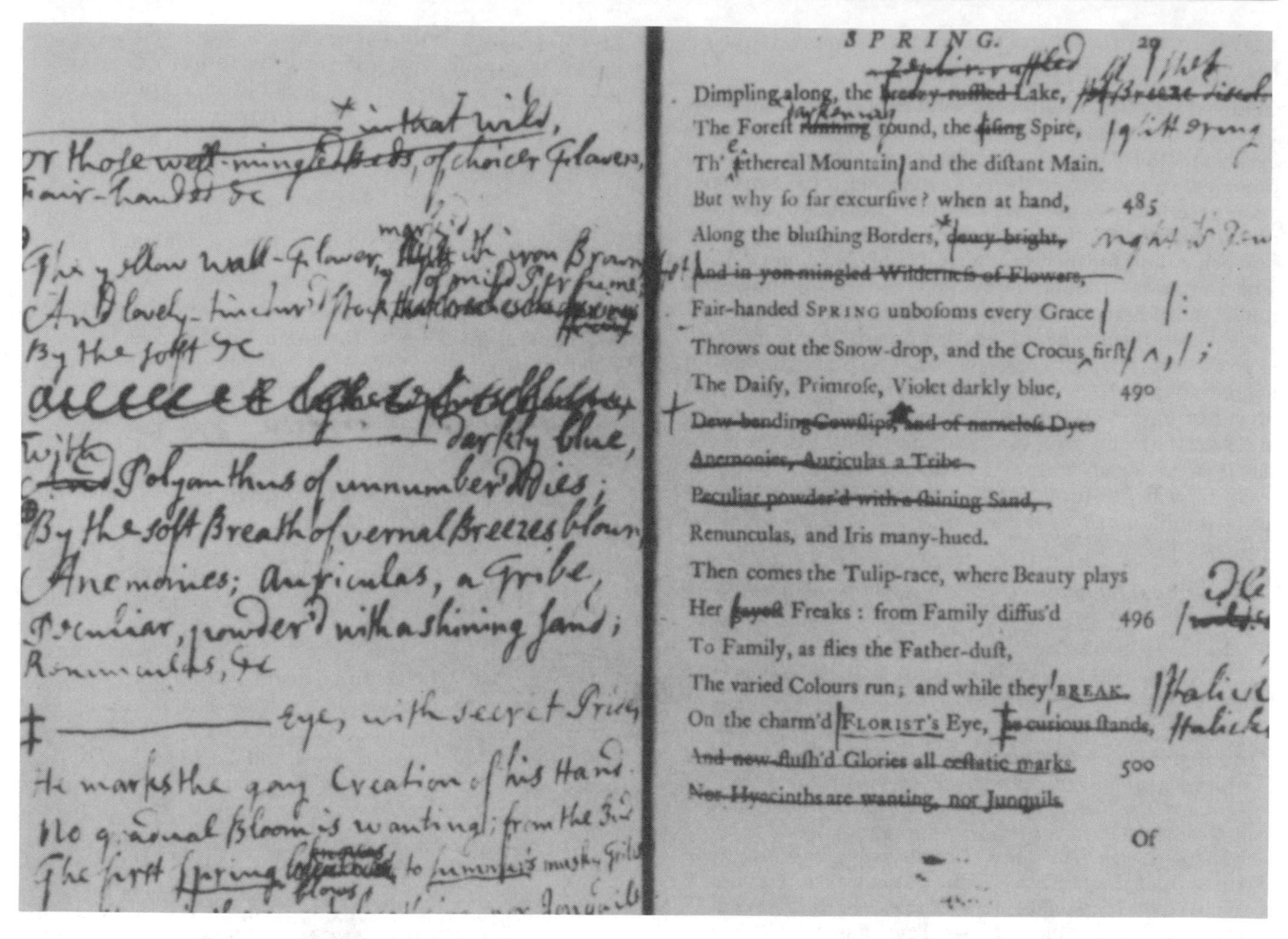

SPRING. 29

Dimpling along, the breezy-ruffled Lake,
The Forest running round, the rising Spire,
Th' æthereal Mountain, and the distant Main.
But why so far excursive? when at hand, 485
Along the blushing Borders, dewy bright,
And in yon mingled Wilderness of Flowers,
Fair-handed SPRING unbosoms every Grace;
Throws out the Snow-drop, and the Crocus first;
The Daisy, Primrose, Violet darkly blue, 490
Dew-bending Cowslips, and of nameless Dyes
Anemonies, Auriculas a Tribe
Peculiar powder'd with a shining Sand,
Renunculas, and Iris many-hued.
Then comes the Tulip-race, where Beauty plays
Her gayest Freaks: from Family diffus'd 496
To Family, as flies the Father-dust,
The varied Colours run; and while they BREAK
On the charm'd FLORIST'S Eye, he curious stands,
And new-flush'd Glories all ecstatic marks. 500
Nor Hyacinths are wanting, nor Junquils.
Of

Thomson's revisions to Spring *in a copy of* The Works of Mr. Thomson *(1738).*

which Sir H. Nicolas was the first to print, present us with a link between Thomson and his eminent contemporaries, which would otherwise be entirely missing. Until his twenty-first year it seems that Thomson had no idea of making any metrical innovation. For the next four or five years he disappears from our sight, and when we meet with him again, it is as the possessor of a finished system of blank verse, which, in future, he uses upon almost every serious occasion. The rare pieces which he composed in the heroic couplet in mature life are not only, without exception, valueless, but they have not even the crude merit of some of his childish effusions in the same form. It is plain that in discovering his native tendency to blank verse, he lost such imitative skill in couplet-making as he had acquired.

From a passage in ***Autumn*** it may be gathered that the idea of recording his impressions of nature in blank verse came to Thomson from a writer who is now scarcely remembered:

> Philips, Pomona's bard, the second thou
> Who nobly durst, in rhyme-unfettered verse,
> With British freedom sing the British song.

This was John Philips, author of *Blenheim, Cider,* and *The Splendid Shilling,* all of them exercises in blank verse and patent although homely imitations of Milton. The didactic poem of *Cider,* published in 1708, is, indeed, a curious and even anomalous production. It is difficult to believe that it belongs to the age of Queen Anne, so precisely is the style that of the disciples of Thomson. On every page we might think we recognized the hand of Armstrong, who was not born when it appeared. It was Philips, without a doubt, who started Thomson on his plan of recording the progress of natural phenomena in ponderous and highly Latinized rhymeless iambics, with literal accuracy, and with an eye on the object. It is even difficult to realise that such a passage as the following is not a rather poor specimen of the genuine Thomson:

> Lo, on auxiliary poles, the hops
> Ascending spiral, rang'd in meet array!
> Lo, how the arable with barley-grain
> Stands thick, o'ershadow'd, to the thirsty hind
> Transporting prospect! These, as modern use
> Ordains, transfus'd, an auburn drink compose,
> Wholesome, of deathless fame. Here, to the sight,
> Apples of price, and plenteous sheaves of corn
> Oft interlac'd occur, and both imbibe
> Fitting congenial juice; so rich the soil,
> So much does fructuous moisture o'er-abound,

Nor are the hills unamiable.

If, however, the value of John Philips as a manifest precursor of Thomson, and as the medium through which the Miltonic measure passed to him, is by no means to be overlooked, it would be an error to suggest that anything of the true sublime of Thomson, was anticipated by the author of *Cider.* Philips' accurate pictures of life under the apple-orchards, in a misty odour of pomace, have a certain pastoral charm, but are strictly confined to the foreground, and treat that from a business-like or a scientific point of view. There is scarcely a line here and there left to show that if Philips had been encouraged by the sympathy of his age he might have taken loftier and more romantic perspectives. The modern sentiment of landscape, however, was revealed to him no more than it was to Gay or to Pope. This was left to be the discovery of the author of ***The Seasons.***

Had there been anyone in the English literary coteries in 1727 capable of taking wide views in poetry, he would surely have felt, as he closed the episode of Damon and Musidora, and read of—

> Him who lonely loves
> To seek the distant hills, and there converse
> With nature, there to harmonise his heart
> And in pathetic song to breathe around
> The harmony to others,

that here was indeed a spirit unprecedented in English song, and a true originality. This is the real Thomson, and the invention of this peculiar philosophy of landscape, of which Wordsworth's entire system is but the development, claims for him a very high place in our regard. It is true that he has to share it in some measure with a poet of much smaller significance than himself, with John Dyer, the appearance of whose *Grongar Hill* was exactly simultaneous with that of *Winter.* Dyer, however, not merely never fulfilled the promise of his first very delicate and picturesque lyric, but even in that lyric itself, full as it is of contemplative imagination, he never rises to the conception of Thomson, who realised for the first time the power of

> the discerning intellect of man
> When wedded to this goodly universe
> In love and holy passion.

As was to be afterwards the case with Wordsworth, this new philosophy was not founded in the mind of Thomson upon mere nebulous enthusiasm for pretty prospects, or even upon the painter's generalisations. The author of ***The Seasons*** was distinguished, above any writer who had preceded him, at least for a hundred years, by his tireless habit of observation. After a century of romantic effort, it is not easy for us to appreciate the novelty and startling brightness of Thomson's touches. Addison, in his famous poem of *The Campaign,* was supposed to have depicted a storm with such moving, such horrific force as to have added a new masterpiece to descriptive literature. No one seems to have been dissatisfied to observe, no one, in fact, seems to have observed, that Addison in all his torrent of conventional couplets gives not one solitary touch which can aid us to realise what sort of storm it was, not one image or adjective which brings the scene before our eyes. But Thomson, among the first lines of his ***Winter,*** with a nonchalant air as though everybody knew what were the phenomena preceding storms, mentions that

> rising slow,
> Blank, in the leaden-coloured east, the moon
> Wears a wan circle round her blunted horns,

and we perceive that the cataract which concealed external nature from the eyes of Augustan Englishmen has been successfully couched.

It is not, however, in his earliest poem that Thomson ventures most freely upon these audacities. In ***Winter*** they occur but seldom, and are introduced in an apologetic manner, as by a poet obliged to say what it is he has seen, yet desirous not to be too unfashionable. The eminent beauties of this book are either of another order, or were introduced into the text after 1730. In ***Summer*** the touches drawn direct from the observation of Nature are far more abundant. Here we have

> While the quail clamours for his running mate,

the swimmer, bathing in 'the inverted landscape' of the lucent pool,

> While, from his polished sides, a dewy light
> Effuses on the pleased spectators round,

and those often-imitated lines,

> The house-dog, with the vacant greyhound, lies
> Outstretched and sleepy. In his slumbers one
> Attacks the nightly thief, and one exults
> O'er hill and dale; till, wakened by the wasp,
> They starting snap.

It is, however, in ***Spring,*** which appeared in 1728, that we find the greatest profusion of these novel beauties. Thomson was by this time convinced, by the warm reception of his two previous works, of the favour of the public. He threw off all restraint, and wrote with the full passion of his intellect. His brain teemed with bold images and surprising reminiscences, and he no longer shuddered at his own audacity. It is in ***Spring,*** accordingly, that we have the description of the hedge-rows in flower:—

> One boundless blush, one white-empurpled shower
> Of mingled blossoms,

the bouquet of garden-sweets,

> The yellow wall-flower, stained with iron brown;
> And lavish stock that scents the garden round;
> From the soft wing of vernal breezes shed
>
> Anemones; auriculas, enriched
> With shining meal o'er all their velvet leaves;
> And full ranunculus, of glowing red,

and the vignette of the angry swan, who

> with wary feet
> Beats forward fierce, and guards his osier-isle,
> Protective of his young.

In ***Autumn,*** finally, although this section of the work is full of passages of extraordinary beauty, there is a slackening of the profuse flow of images taken directly from the eye.

Here the nature-study is suffused into elaborate compositions, and in exchange for those brilliant adjectives and short groups of epithets which brought before our vision in a moment the object of the poet's recollection, we have rich scenes and compacted landscapes, true, indeed, and highly beautiful, but no longer realistic. ***The Seasons*** once closed, and ***Liberty*** undertaken, these bright strokes of naturalism disappear altogether, to return, in a certain measure, in the early stanzas of ***The Castle of Indolence.*** But, for the study of Thomson as a painter of vividly exact vignettes of wild life, it is ***Spring*** which offers most advantages to the reader.

On the other hand, if we desire to observe our poet as a landscape painter in the broader sense, we find no more delicate or complete examples of his art than those which meet us in ***Autumn.*** It is there, for instance, that we discover this passage:—

> But see the fading many-coloured woods,
> Shade deepening over shade, the country round
> Imbrown; a crowded umbrage, dusk and dun,
> Of every hue, from wan declining green
> To sooty dark.

This noble and judicious composition, so closely packed with colour, suggests to the mind a translation into verse of one of the most highly-finished canvases of Richard Wilson, some 'Wynnstay' or 'Tabley Park,' in which the classic school of British landscape has reached its culminating point. But when it was published Wilson was a child, the fashionable insipidities of [Francesco] Zuccarelli, which Wilson was to drive out of England, had not yet made their appearance amongst us, and Vernet himself was not heard of. Landscape painting was still absolutely primitive, if at all existent in this country, while landscape poetry, with a single bound, had reached this height of perfection. It is scarcely necessary to recall to readers the greatest of the composed landscapes with which Thomson has enriched ***The Seasons,***—the magnificent evening after harvest, in ***Autumn***; the storm of thunder and lightning, in ***Summer***; the trout-fishing scene introduced in the 1730 edition into ***Spring,***—these may be taken as examples of the poet's splendid gifts in this direction, gifts the more extraordinary because they had not in any way been led up to by the art or literature of his country. The only way in which it is possible to lessen the apparent miracle of Thomson's landscapes is to suppose that he was not unfamiliar with the paintings of Claude Lorraine and Gaspar Poussin. Yet it is extremely difficult to believe that the rustic lad can have seen a single example of these or of similar artists until he came up to London, and a letter to Dr Cranston gives evidence that his taste was already formed. The following passage, written in September, 1725, deserves the closest attention. Preceding as it does the publication of his earliest poem, it is really the first expression in the English language of the modern sentiment of landscape:—

> Now I imagine you seized with a fine, romantic kind of a melancholy on the fading of the year; now I figure you wandering, philosophical and pensive, amidst the brown, withered groves, while the leaves rustle under your feet, the sun gives a farewell, parting gleam, and the birds
>
> Stir the faint note, and but attempt to sing.
>
> Then again, when the heavens wear a more gloomy aspect, the winds whistle, and the waters spout, I see you in the well-known cleugh, beneath the solemn arch of tall, thick, embowering trees, listening to the amusing lull of the many steep, moss-grown cascades, while deep, divine Contemplation, the genius of the place, prompts each swelling, awful thought. . . . Nature delights me in every form.

It can scarcely have been that anyone in England was already attuned in 1725 to this language, yet it was rapidly responded to. The popularity of ***The Seasons*** cannot but have led to that eagerness with which, a year or two afterwards, the engravings of Chatelain and Vivares, after the Italian landscape-painters, began to be welcomed. But when this remarkable letter was written, it is interesting to note that Gray was a child of nine years old, and William Gilpin still in the cradle. (pp. xi-xxiii)

It was not a small difficulty connected with the composition of [***The Seasons***] poem, that the subject was necessarily of a desultory character. No thread of narrative runs through, it has no distinct evolution. The poet watches the year revolve, describes what he sees, and sums up his reflections in a hymn to the spirit which pervades the whole. A certain air of indecision hangs about the entire central plan of ***The Seasons,*** an air which we need not regret, since some of the most beautiful touches which the poem contains are due to this intellectual vacillation. The author is never certain whether to remain at home or to fly abroad. Now his reveries seem to be those of a man whose experience has never passed outside his mountain home at Southdean, who has scarcely crossed the ford of the sweeping Jed, and to whom all that lies beyond the scalp of Carter Fell is unknown ground. Now he writes as one to whom both hemispheres are familiar, from China to Peru. More inconsistently still, he sometimes languishes for the age of innocence to come again, for

> Those white unblemished minutes, whence
> The fabling poets took their golden age,

to free him from 'these iron times, these dregs of life', and then, immediately afterwards, he pities the barbarian, and congratulates himself on the regular march of modern civilisation, casting off the inexperience of infancy, 'and ever rising with the rising mind'.

This absence of coherency, in the execution no less than in the plot of ***The Seasons,*** is by no means such a disadvantage to it as we might be prepared to suppose. The existence of an iron framework, especially in the eighteenth century with its incurable habit of reposing on mechanical helps, might have injured the poem far more than it improved it. As it is, the individuality of Thomson has to come every instant to the aid of his conception; the poet is forced to carry on the thread of his languidly constructed poem by a repeated effort of character, and the consequence is that we are charmed and startled by the incessant interposition of a living mind, where we might have been abandoned to a system or a plot. The inconsistencies do not trouble us, for they are those of a natural man, and our sympathies are gratified even when we smile at the wavering judgment of our charming interlocutor. His didactic intentions, moreover, are not, in our eyes, his main claim to our respect. We hang upon his lips not to hear what he has to say about providence and civilisation, but to enjoy the rich stores of his observation, to look out at nature with his keen and brilliant vision.

A striking proof of Thomson's consciousness that ***The Seasons,*** though so successful in essence, were not without incoherencies in execution, is his treatment of their text during the quarter of a century by which he survived their commencement. Often as each portion of the poem was reprinted, he never permitted it to appear unaltered, and if he had lived to be eighty years of age, the entire texture of the work would probably have been unravelled and rewoven. No volume in English literature has been revised so frequently and so searchingly as ***The Seasons,*** and though editor after editor has proposed a variorum text, no one has yet been willing to give the needful time and care to the colossal task. (pp. xxv-xxvii)

Thomson took the advice. We seem to see him with the volumes for ever open before him in his study, and the poet altering an epithet here, adding a line there, and transposing two clauses a paragraph further on.

The corrections which he made are so numerous and so intricate that it requires not a little study to obtain any notion of their character. Dr Johnson thought that they were improvements in general; 'yet I know not', he continued, 'whether they have not lost part of what Temple called their *race*; a word which, applied to wines, in its primitive sense, means the flavour of the soil' [see excerpt dated 1781]. Perhaps the truth of this acute suggestion may be gathered from a few examples. The sunset scene in ***Summer*** now reads thus:

> Low walks the sun, and broadens by degrees,
> Just o'er the verge of day. The *shifting* clouds
> *Assembled gay, a richly glorious* train,
> *In all their pomp attend his setting throne;*
> *Air, earth and ocean smile immense. And now,*
> *As if his weary chariot sought the bowers*
> *Of Amphitrité and her tending nymphs*
> (*So Grecian fable sung*), he dips his orb;
> Now half immersed; and now a golden curve
> Gives one *bright glance,* then *total* disappears.

The words printed in italics are those not found in the original text, which now follows; it will be noticed that nearly two-thirds of the passage suffered revision:

> Low walks the sun, and broadens by degrees,
> Just o'er the verge of day. The rising clouds,
> That shift perpetual in his vivid train,
> Their watery mirrors, numberless, opposed,
> Unfold the hidden riches of his ray;
> And chase a change of colours round the sky.
> 'Tis all one blush from east to west! and now
> Behind the dusky earth, he dips his orb;
> Now half-immers'd; and now a golden curve
> Gives one faint glimmer, and then disappears.

On the whole, the alterations here are, as Johnson says, an improvement; we are glad to lose the clumsy pedantry about the cloud's 'watery mirrors'. But the sharp presentation of the scene is blunted with gorgeousness, and Amphitrité is a poor exchange for the 'one blush from east to west'.

Occasionally the changes are from a too-startling realism to what Thomson conceived to be a more decent moderation. Thus in ***Autumn*** the 'red North' became 'black', and in ***Spring*** the 'strip'd carnations and enamel'd pinks' were toned down to 'broad' and 'gay-spotted'. It is to be noticed, too, that as his revision of the work progressed, Thomson found courage to take things more and more upon his own responsibility; theories are put forward on their own merits which in earlier editions had been introduced with a timid 'perchance' or an apologetic 'men say'. Some of the most delightful personal passages, too, were the result of afterthought. The first edition of *Autumn* knows nothing of

> the Tweed, pure parent-stream,
> Whose pastoral banks first heard my Doric reed,
> With, sylvan Jed, thy tributary brook,

nor is the beautiful address to Lyttelton in any early text of ***Spring.*** The geographical and geological passages, by which the grandeur of Thomson's imagination are particularly illustrated, were mainly added when the poem was already before the public, and many favourite vignettes, from the sheep-shearing in ***Spring*** to the robin's visit in ***Winter,*** were unknown to those who only saw the first completed text of 1730. On the whole, the damage which Thomson did to his first sprightly fancy by his alterations was very small, while he greatly strengthened and clarified weak and turgid passages by his revisions, and enormously increased the debt of readers by the value of what he added. His conscientious treatment of his text deserves high praise; he was not always well inspired, perhaps, but he worked in the true spirit of the artist. On the other hand, it is matter for regret that he more and more fell under the sway of those Latinisms which were his peculiar snare.

Thomson's pompous and turgid language, which seems to deform his poetry whenever he turns from the direct record of observation to what he considers philosophy, is too marked a defect of style with him to be left unnoticed by his eulogists. Mr Saintsbury has, indeed, declared the Latinisms of Thomson to be neither a crutch nor a staff to him, but 'a mere clouded cane which, as he mistakenly thinks, is an appropriate ornament'. This is an acute apology, but hardly does justice to an inherent vice in Thomson. It is difficult not to believe that he was in reality afraid to trust to a simpler diction, and that, dealing, as he did, with rural subjects, a certain intellectual snobbishness led him to try to cover their rusticity with an excess of gentility in diction. The result is sometimes downright ludicrous, and at all times blurs or deadens the effect of the poetry. Fortunately it does not occur so frequently as it does in the verse of the minor Thomsonians, where it continually mars our pleasure, but it is prominent enough to be a tiresome element.

The blank verse of Thomson was founded, as has been said, on that of Milton studied through Philips. But while the author of *Cider* merely imitated, as best he could, the organ-harmonies of *Paradise Lost,* Thomson invented a new species of blank verse for himself. It was full, dignified and sonorous, exercised with less variety and much less masterly caprice than Milton's had been, but for that very reason more within the grasp of powers that were below the highest, and more suitable to ordinary themes. In the richness of his single lines, Thomson is perhaps less remarkable than Young, who was his metrical disciple, but he is often singularly happy. Such lines as

> Books are but formal dulness, tedious friends,

or

> The purple-streaming amethyst is thine,

or

> Sighs the sad genius of the coming storm

impress their music on the ear, and live for ever in the memory. But, as a rule, Thomson prefers the overflow, and is most happy when he employs it. His system of blank verse may be studied to most advantage on the small scale of the ***Hymn,*** which is, upon the whole, the most highly finished exercise in this form which the eighteenth century presents to us. It will be found that Thomson manipulates his blank verse very skilfully in the occasional narrative passages which were the delight of his own age and have a little gone down since in the esteem of his admirers. I am among those who still are delighted to learn that 'the lovely young Lavinia once had friends', and who can smile with indulgence at the indiscretions of Damon.

Thomson died in August 1748, and ***The Castle of Indolence*** had not made its first appearance until three months previously. This exquisite poem must not, however, be regarded as the work of Thomson's latest years. (pp. xxviii-xxxii)

A close examination of ***The Castle of Indolence*** reveals some interesting peculiarities which throw light on the manner of its composition. The first stanza is evidently an afterthought, written to tie together what is to follow. The next seven stanzas are of an enchanting melody and sweetness, in character like nothing else to be found between Spenser and Shelley. This I take to be the early germ of ***The Castle of Indolence,*** and I am prepared to suppose it written not long after 1730, in immediate succession to ***Autumn*** and the ***Hymn.*** The speech of Indolence, which then follows, is smooth and appropriate, but not splendid; it may be later. But with stanza 24, the poem wakes up again, and every cadence, every touch is redolent of Thomson's prime. It reaches a sort of climax in the magnificent lines about 'the shepherd of the Hebrid Isles', which seem to have been in the ears of Collins when he wrote his latest ode. In all this portion of Thomson's poem the mellifluousness of the versification is extraordinary, the voluptuous colour not to be paralleled till Keats wrote his *Eve of St Agnes.* (pp. xxxiii-xxxiv)

[The] whole of Canto I is excellently written, though of unequal merit, and it never quite sinks below a high average.

Canto II is not of a piece with its predecessor. The three opening stanzas of it, indeed, are written in the same vein and with no less art than what has preceded. The third presents us with an exquisite epitome of Thomson's sincere philosophic temper:

> I care not, Fortune, what you me deny;
> You cannot rob me of free nature's grace;
> You cannot shut the windows of the sky,
> Through which Aurora shows her brightening
> face;
> You cannot bar my constant feet to trace
> The woods and lawns, by living stream, at eve:
> Let health my nerves and finer fancies brace,
> And I their toys to the great children leave:
> Of fancy, reason, virtue, naught can me bereave.

Here, doubtless, the original draft of the poem came to an end, and was not resumed until shortly before Thomson's death. What follows is well written, but in a distinctly lower pitch. We should think Canto II charming, if we had never read Canto I. But the highest imagination, a 'sensuous, simple and passionate' strain of poetry, has given place to graceful and patriotic eloquence. The Knight of Arts, Sir Industry, is not very interesting, though exceedingly respectable. We feel that the poet had lost his early freshness, and now 'polished nature with' what he considered 'a finer hand'. What is most happy in Canto II is the description of Philomelus, 'the little Druid wight'.

This decline in freshness is still more marked when we arrive at ***Liberty,*** the didactic poem in five thin volumes published by Thomson from 1734 to 1736. Here are found all the disadvantages under which the scheme of ***The Seasons*** laboured, the want of cohesion, the tendency to rhetoric, the adoption of turgid Latinisms, with none, or very few, of the eminent beauties which enlivened that work. The difficulty of reading ***Liberty*** has been proverbial since it was first published; we need not be ashamed of finding that dull which scandalized by its prolixity even the faithful Lyttelton. Pictures drawn direct from nature are rare in ***Liberty***; there is a brilliant little vignette of a shower on the Alps,—

> an amphitheatre of hills,
> Whence, vapour-winged, the sudden tempest
> springs

in **"Britain,"** but it would be difficult to point to another in the whole poem that could rank with such lines as are to be found in almost every page of ***The Seasons.*** Thomson's journey to Italy might have been undertaken by a blind man, for any addition it made to the stores of his memory. Mellifluous blank verse, elevated sentiment, dignity in rhetoric, these are the only qualities for which ***Liberty*** can be praised. The minstrel had, surely, sunken low when the best he could say about Hymettus was that it 'spreads to botanic hand the stores of health'.

Nor are the remaining poems of Thomson eminently interesting or characteristic. None of them would ever be looked at if they were not his. **"Britannia",** which appeared as early as 1729, has the bad eminence of being the first piece which shows the blight of mere eloquence which was already invading his genius. The elegies on Congreve, 1729, and on Talbot, 1738, though inspired by genuine admiration in the one case, and real affection in the other, are quite valueless. It is otherwise with the poem **"To the**

Memory of Sir Isaac Newton", 1728, which has some very picturesque and brilliant astronomic landscapes, and a procession of 'the gorgeous train of parent colours' which is remarkably effective. Thomson's lyrics, few in number and exceedingly timid in form, are of an exasperating insipidity. He had none of the epigrammatic grace which inspired so many of his contemporaries, especially the younger men, and his songs are uniformly tame and soft. **"Rule, Britannia"** is the one evident exception, yet, even here, if the associations of the air and of the sentiment be removed, the value of the lyric itself does not seem to be very great. As to the four tragedies and half a masque which compose Thomson's dramatic works, subsequent criticism has found little to revise in Voltaire's remark that 'Mr Thomson's tragedies seem to me wisely intricated and elegantly writ; they want perhaps some fire, and it may be that his heroes are neither moving nor busy enough'. The most poetical is ***Agamemnon,*** in which some fine passages may be discovered. As a dramatist Thomson was a disciple of Nicholas Rowe.

It is now nearly one hundred and sixty years since Thomson died, and looking back over the history of our literature during that period, we may safely say that if other writers have exercised a more intense influence than he, none has left so broad a stamp upon the epical and descriptive parts of subsequent English poetry. Until the manner of Tennyson began to come into fashion, it may be said that no one wrote blank verse without being in some measure the imitator of Thomson. When he died, in 1748, he was already surrounded by a school of disciples. He had seen writers much older than himself adopt his prosody and something of his attitude to nature. The intelligent and ductile spirit of Pope, quick to disdain the feeble, but equally quick to welcome and applaud the strong, had early appreciated the genius of Thomson; and though Pope had been too long wedded to the heroic couplet to adopt another form of verse, yet the lesson of ***The Seasons*** was not thrown away on one who could produce, in advanced life, the fourth of the *Moral Epistles.* That Pope, had he chosen to do so, could have written exquisite blank verse, the additions to the episode of Lavinia prove. In Young we find another poet, much older than Thomson, who achieved excellence for the first time when he accepted, from the hand of his junior, the Miltonic manner of writing. But the veritable scholars of Thomson, such as Armstrong, Lyttelton and Glover, knew no other master than he, and by their practice spread and made general the imitation of his style.

Less completely under the denomination of Thomson was Akenside, whose icy talent has little in common with the warmth of the poet of *The Seasons.* Yet, even here, we find in *The Pleasures of the Imagination* a versification directly founded upon Thomson's. Down the eighteenth century, from *The Hop-Garden* of Smart to the *Edge-Hill* of Jago, we meet the prosody of Thomson, in all its mannerisms, accepted as the only possible vehicle for topographical and descriptive verse, in the hands of minor writers. Even the great poets were distinctly affected by it. The intimate passages in Goldsmith, the finer landscapes in Cowper, instinct as they are with the peculiar genius of those writers, would have been expressed quite otherwise if Thomson had never lived. Towards the close of the century, the worst parts of his style were selected and exaggerated. His artifice and grandiloquence, his occasional brassy eloquence, were taken as models to the exclusion of his natural beauties, and his influence in this way hastened the decline of the artificial school. When true romantic poetry began to assert itself, this side of Thomson went down in critical esteem, but the other, so long neglected, rose with equal promptitude. In his famous attack on the poetry of the eighteenth century, Wordsworth was careful to except Thomson's; ***'The Seasons',*** he said, 'is a work of inspiration' [see excerpt dated 1837], and he might have gone on to admit that not a few of its passages had inspired the movement of Wordsworth's own blank verse. Coleridge's *Hymn in the Valley of Chamouni* follows, so closely as only genius in its audacity can follow, the **"Hymn"** of Thomson. The blank verse, the mental attitude, of Campbell, of Rogers, of Southey, in descriptive passages, is often scarcely to be distinguished from that of Thomson. Finally, in the movement of his *Alastor,* Shelley paid his ancestor of ***The Seasons*** the splendid compliment of direct imitation. It was not until the manner of Tennyson in his blank verse became paramount, that the direct influence of Thomson ceased to be observed in English poetry. In an indirect form it is still to be found there, and will not soon disappear, since it is diffused through all that is written about landscape with sincerity and passion. (pp. xxxv-xl)

Edmund Gosse, "Critical Study of James Thomson," in The Seasons *by James Thomson, edited by Henry D. Roberts, George Routledge & Sons, Limited, 1906, pp. xi-x1.*

George Saintsbury (essay date 1906-10)

[*An influential English critic and literary historian of the late nineteenth and early twentieth centuries, Saintsbury represents the formalistic approach to literary criticism. His writings include* A Short History of French Literature *(1882),* A Short History of English Literature *(1898), and* The History of Criticism and Literary Taste in Europe *(1900-04). In the excerpt below, he discusses the formal aspects of Thomson's poetry, particularly the poet's use of blank verse, observing that Thomson's formal artificiality is often countervailed by inventive craftsmanship.*]

[Thomson's] ***Winter*** and its sister ***Seasons*** not merely established blank verse, as Prior and Swift had established the octosyllable, and as the first of these had at last established the anapæst, but did more. They practically introduced a new form of the metre that they established. Thomson's is not, as all previous blank verse since Milton had been, more or less direct *imitation* of Milton: new elements and features, some good, some not so good, make their appearance. In fact, Thomson deserves to rank in the genealogy of non-dramatic blank verse between Milton and Tennyson. Of course, he does not achieve, or attempt, any absolute independence of his great exemplar. He could not have achieved, and he was too wise to attempt. . . . Thomson's finer sense avoided, for the most part, excessive discarding of articles and particles, prodigal apposition, and even to some extent, though to a less, persistent inversion and "geometrical" disposition of phrase. But he kept, and even (though in a new fashion) exaggerated, the Miltonic buckram and affectation; while he had not the Miltonic fire to warm and lighten these things. But Thomson was really a person of prosodic genius—his double record with blank verse and the Spenserian proves this,—and he succeeded in new-moulding the measure in a way which Smith might have again called "very particular," and which nearly all eighteenth-century writers of it followed. In one very important respect he, indeed, comes short; and that is the management of the verse-paragraph. It is not that he wishes to neglect it: quite the contrary. Typographically, he is very careful of his paragraph; and, what is more, he has invented a peculiar mannerism of his own to distinguish and mark it off otherwise than typographically, in the shape of the curious end catchlines more or less identical in form, which every tolerably careful reader of the ***Seasons*** must have noticed. But he is not able, as Milton had been and as Tennyson was to be, to modulate the whole music of a paragraph into a perfect symphony, and to make the reader feel that its prosodic career ends exactly with the career of the thought.

Nor could he arrange these symphonies with the same gorgeous accompaniment of proper-name sound. But, on the other hand, he is a much more definitely pictorial poet than Milton; and he makes the structure of his paragraphs prosodically subservient to his pictures with no little skill. The lines are touches; they build up the subject to eye, if not to ear, and in order to do this, something more than the mere "brick-upon-brick" of the common blank verse was wanted. Thomson is particularly fond of that kind of enjambment which consists in multiplying full stops and colons in the middle of lines; and he has borrowed, from Spenser rather than from Milton, the device of linking one paragraph to another with a "turn of words." He likes to throw up his verse with a monosyllable of some weight and strength at the end; and he utilises prosodically the exacter nature-painting which in general poetic history is his glory, by putting the distinctive words for colour and shape in notable places of the verse, so as to give it character and quality. Even his rather too distinct "poetic diction," his fondness for the forms in *y,* for heavy Latinisms and the like, are definitely defensible as expedients to get blank verse out of the old reproach of being measured prose.

Johnson, therefore, was at least sufficiently justified—he usually was, save when some special disqualification was present—when he said, "His numbers, his pauses, his diction, are of his own growth"; and the reference to pauses shows, among a thousand other things, what a critic Johnson was when he would let himself be [see excerpt dated 1781]. There is nothing more characteristic of Thomson's blank verse than its peculiarly broken character. The breakages are not such as cause roughness, but such as hinder continuity. All good verse is serpentine; but Thomson's serpents are rather like those very excellent ones which are compounded (for the use of childhood) of a large number of sections artfully strung together. His lines and sections of lines are not interfluent, but conjoined: the resulting structure is a sort of mosaic. This, with his peculiar diction, is the source of the artificiality which for the last century or so has been charged against him; and there is a modicum of truth in the charge. But it is extremely probable that these brilliant bits of verse—these tesselations of marble of divers colours, if not of positive gem-substance—did a great deal to reconcile his readers to the absence of the rhyme-stroke and flash; while there is no doubt either, that the style also suited what his frank but friendly critic (who tried to read ***Liberty*** when it appeared, and never tried again) characteristically calls his "enumeration of circumstantial varieties." Yet even in ***Liberty***—false, frigid, hollow, pedantic, sciolist as it is—such passages as the well-known one on the Retreat of the Ten Thousand justify the unusual mercy which Johnson shows to this blank verse.

But, though undoubtedly Thomson's horsemanship, to vary the metaphor, savours for our modern taste rather too much of the *manège*—though he owes the bit more than is perhaps consistent with absolutely perfect riding,—this is not quite invariable with him. There are passages, and a good number of them, where, if he does not exactly throw rein on neck, he never makes the curb ostentatiously felt; and these constitute a very agreeable set-off to, and relaxation from, his more artificial style. Nay, more—and it is in this that his merit very largely consists,—he knows how to interpose fluent and unchecked lines in the very passages where break and check are generally prominent.

If it be said that even these reliefs from artificiality are not quite artless enough, the objection, though a little ungracious, cannot be met with a blank denial. It may, however, be demurred to as excessive, and it may be met, most successfully of all, by a consideration of the reasons and the circumstances. It must be remembered that it was Thomson's mission—a mission which, let it be also remembered, he achieved, though perhaps, as so often, unconsciously enough—to refashion blank verse so that it might assist, in the graver and severer regions of poetry, the efforts which the octosyllable and the anapæst were making against the inordinate and exclusive domination of the heroic couplet. For this purpose the pure Miltonic model, which had hitherto been followed, was clearly insufficient. To begin with, it required a Milton to manage it; and anybody who endeavoured to do so was but too likely, whether he meant it or not, to slip into a caricature of a Milton. Again, it was almost necessarily bound up with the Miltonic diction, which was by this time in parts obsolete. And for a third remark, it might not unjustly be pronounced, like the first project of Tennyson's *Princess,* too "grand, epic, homicidal" for the semi-pedestrian didactics and descriptions which the time wanted.

On the other hand, there was the danger, not only of the meanness and lowness which had long attached itself to the very idea of blank verse, but (not to adopt quite such derogatory language) of the flatness and prosaic quality which Roscommon, its first post-Miltonic practitioner, had actually displayed. On this side it was as much in need of raising, varying, decorating, as on the Miltonic side it was of humanising and adapting to miscellaneous needs.

And all this had to be done with due regard to eighteenth-century notions about poetic diction, dignity, decency, and the rest of it.

That Thomson was immensely assisted by his nature-studies, by the interest which his landscape-painting enabled him to offer to his readers so as to make them forget the absence of their usual douceur or bonus, rhyme, is undeniable. But this should not make us disregard the technical skill which he showed in beating out, and throwing into system, the peculiar music of his verse. His natural gift for this—a gift which in other times might have made him one of the greatest of verse-smiths—is, as has been said, shown in his Spenserians, which, of all the numerous imitations of Spenser which amused their writers and annoyed Johnson at this time, are simply the only ones that come near the motion and the music of that Pactolus-Mæander, the Spenserian river of song. The fingering of the stanza, in the First Part of the ***Castle of Indolence*** especially, is nearly faultless: it is the inferiority of the lexicon that, whenever the subject admits of it, prevents Thomson from coming quite close to his master. Nay, there are a few places where he is actually not far off. Other measures he hardly tried; and in his few lyrics the curse of the century . . . was much on him, especially in that matter of diction. Yet the opening verse of "Tell me, thou soul of her I love" could not easily be better in its own way, and approaches a way better than its own. His heroics are undistinguished; but a man can hardly be expected to distinguish himself in a style which he deliberately declines. And, in fact, he needs no ekings from these minor performances. The Spenserian imitation of the ***Castle of Indolence*** would have been a very great prosodic achievement had it stood alone, and it is still greater as showing up, and contrasting with, the more independent variation on Milton in the blank verse. But that blank verse itself, if it has not given us his very best poetry, is certainly his main prosodic title-deed. It is great in performance, and greater still in example. The colour-passage in the Newton poem in particular must have been, to every poet of that time and immediately afterwards, who read it with eyes to see, a casket of jewels much richer than itself, with the key in the lock. The somewhat too high stepping pace could easily be modulated; the somewhat formal and even rigid diction could in due time be suppled and simplified. But here once more was an important metre got ready for various poetic uses; and for this we say "O" to Jemmy Thomson, not in the manner of the scoffer at ***Sophonisba,*** but in that of Man Friday—who came into the world just seven years before ***Winter*** made its appearance. (pp. 478-84)

George Saintsbury, "Blank Verse After Milton," in his A History of English Prosody: From the Twelfth Century to the Present Day, Vol. II, *1906-10. Reprint by Russell & Russell, 1961, pp. 473-99.*

G. C. Macaulay (essay date 1908)

[*Macaulay was a scholar whose writings include* Francis Beaumont: A Critical Study *(1883) and* James Thomson *(1908), which is widely considered one of the best critical introductions to Thomson's works. In the following excerpt, he identifies Thomson as a seminal representative of the eighteenth-century poetry of nature, commenting on the suggestive power of his descriptive poetry.*]

Thomson, it cannot be denied, was an original poet, but he did not create the taste by which he was appreciated; and the very artificiality of the London literary society had been preparing the way for some such assertion as his of the claims of the country.

There was indeed nothing in the task which Thomson undertook, which was necessarily at variance with the principles of the so-called classical school. "Nature" was the watchword of that school, and there was no reason why the term should be restricted to the application made of it by Boileau or Pope. The idea of truth to nature in its widest sense is one which pervades the literary criticism of the age, and this idea suggests something quite definite and intelligible. It suggests primarily the representation of things as they really are, or rather as they naturally present themselves to the imagination, and the abandonment of what is fantastic, far-fetched, or allegorical. In this there was nothing which in the least precluded the new poetry of nature. Indeed, the very word "Nature," and the suggestion which it conveyed of the value of truth to nature in poetry, pleaded in favour of true and vivid representation of every kind. Some literary critics insist on regarding Thomson chiefly as a herald of the romantic revival; but this is wholly to misconceive his position. He was essentially a representative of his own age, and that was also the age of Pope. He was, in fact, in a certain sense the complement of Pope, applying to country scenes something of the same power of true observation and vivid portraiture which Pope used upon the town. It is hardly necessary to say that there is nothing necessarily "romantic" about the scenes and operations of external nature. No doubt, in the infinite variety of its forms and influences, and in the awful character of some of its aspects, there are suggestions of mystery and terror, which are congenial to the romantic temper. Thomson has distinct touches of true romance, . . . and he repeatedly uses the word "romantic" quite in the modern sense, as when he says of the lover,

> Sudden he starts,
> Shook from his tender trance, and restless runs
> To glimmering shades and sympathetic glooms;
> Where the dun umbrage o'er the falling stream
> Romantic hangs.

But for all that, Thomson is not on the whole a romantic poet; his representations are broadly objective, not lyrical or personal, and he does not by preference select for treatment that which is wild or awful in nature: he is led by the love of nature to a cheerful and practical religion, rather than to a sense of the inexplicable mystery of the universe. When he expresses the mood of pensive melancholy, which is suggested in the lines just quoted, he is dealing with what he regards as a morbid or exceptional state of mind. Every age has its share of the romantic as of the classical spirit, and the evidences of this which we find in Thomson (and it may be added in Pope also) are characteristic of that time and not of the next generation but one.

In imitating Milton he was following one who had been established as a model worthy of general imitation, and in the ***Castle of Indolence*** he was not endeavouring to revolutionise English poetry, but merely following a fashion of Spenserianism, which had by that time set in with considerable violence.

The philosophy and religion of Thomson, as it appears in his poetry, is an optimistic Deism, and this in effect was also the philosophy and religion of Pope. His optimism, however, was not, like that of Pope, a theory adopted for the purposes of poetical argument, but the result of a deep feeling of the perfection and beauty of the created world and of the adaptation of external nature to the needs of living creatures. He had exceptionally keen and delicate sense perceptions, and he was naturally disposed to enjoyment of the more refined pleasures which the exercise of his senses afforded. An essentially healthy and cheerful temperament produced in him a happy and hopeful view, both of this life and of the next. But the sentimental melancholy which was already a note of the times is also occasionally expressed in Thomson's work, and pity for the sufferings of the poor and of the lower animals was a feeling congenial to his kindly disposition.

With all this it is true, of course, . . . that Thomson's poetry represented something of a reaction against the one-sided view of life which had been presented in very much of the poetry of the age; and this reaction, like most movements of the kind, had itself a somewhat one-sided character. Thus, while Pope, for example, dealt almost exclusively with the interests of an artificial town society, Thomson is led by his enthusiasm to conceive of what he calls "the works of Nature," as almost the only subject worthy of poetical treatment. "Where can we meet with such variety, such beauty, such magnificence, all that enlarges and transports the soul?" By his genius indeed he was peculiarly qualified to supply the element which was, to some extent at least, wanting in the poetry of the period. But he does not really transcend the limits imposed by the artificial division between nature and man. It is true that there are numerous passages in his poetry, where the labour of man is represented as dependent upon or co-operating with the conditions of the seasons, or where the influences of nature upon the human spirit are in some measure represented. But the human element in ***The Seasons*** is to a great extent a matter of embroidery; it is not wrought into the fabric of the poem. These episodes and digressions do not really belong to the subject, but are a concession to the spirit of the age. The ***Castle of Indolence,*** again, in which the aspects of external nature are up to a certain point successfully harmonised with the theme, is partly spoilt by the author's determination to extract a conventional moral from his work. The important difference between Pope and Thomson in the matter of poetical development is that the former realised his own powers more completely. He did not long wander "in Fancy's maze," but early chose the path which was most suitable to his genius, and hardly left it except when he was decoyed by Bolingbroke into the mazes of philosophy. He seldom failed in perception of the bent of his own genius. Thomson, on the other hand, partly because he had a high ideal of the functions of poetry, and partly from the influence of the prevailing literary fashions, failed to estimate correctly the limits of his own powers, and was constantly attempting tasks for which he was unfitted. ***Liberty*** is an admitted failure, and the dramas, though admired at the time, must on the whole be given up. Apart from a few songs, for he had also a lyrical gift, which might with advantage have been more fully developed, his reputation must rest upon the poetry of natural description which is to be found in ***The Seasons*** and in ***The Castle of Indolence.*** To represent him as primarily a "philosophical poet" [as W. J. Courthope did in his *History of English Poetry* (1905); see Further Reading] is a strange aberration of criticism which has been reserved for our own times.

The question arises therefore more especially in the case of Thomson: What rank can properly be assigned to poetry of this kind? Landscape-painting has successfully asserted its right to a distinct and honourable place in modern art, and the question is whether the poetry of natural description can claim an analogous position as compared with other poetry. It is idle to maintain as a general maxim that, as regards poetry, "The proper study of mankind is man." The operations of Nature generally are as much a legitimate field of poetical study as the doings of man, and may properly be treated objectively, and not merely as subordinate to human actions and emotions. The artistic success or failure will depend upon the method of treatment, and in some degree Thomson justly illustrates by the treatment of his subjects the true principles of distinction between the methods of painting and poetry.

Lessing wrote the *Laokoon* chiefly as a criticism upon the "picturesque" school of poetry, a school which took its rise in Germany quite independently of Thomson, though it was afterwards profoundly influenced by him; indeed it may be said that descriptive poetry in Germany underwent a complete change of style owing to Thomson's influence. Haller's poem *Die Alpen,* which seems to be particularly the object of Lessing's attack, was published in 1729, and the author does not seem to have been acquainted at that time with Thomson's ***Seasons,*** of which three out of the four parts had then been published. Lessing himself had a great regard for Thomson as a poet, and speaks of him with an affectionate admiration. He must therefore have seen reason to distinguish him, to some extent at least, from those descriptive poets whose method he altogether condemns, and we can without difficulty perceive on what lines he might have justified Thomson, while still condemning the picturesque school.

He would have adopted the line of defence which he follows in dealing with Homer's descriptions of the chariot of Hera or of the shield of Achilles. In these cases what we have is not the mere description of an object with successive enumeration of characteristics which exist simultaneously, but an account of the successive acts of fitting together the parts of the chariot, the axle, the seat, the pole, the traces, the straps, or again of the successive operations of the divine craftsman, as he works one after another the figures which are the ornament of the shield. It would be hard if he could not have demonstrated that Thomson presents us not with landscape pictures, but with a succession of descriptive strokes, each representing a definite development of action or natural movement. We should have had another of those specimens of special pleading of which Lessing has given us so many masterly examples, and the descriptions which violate the rules, as for example those of the view from Richmond Hill or from Hagley Park, would have been dismissed as lightly as the wheels of the chariot of Hera. He has himself suggested the line that might have been taken, in his remarks upon Kleist's *Frühling*: "Had he lived longer, he would have thrown it into an entirely different form. He was intending to introduce a plan into the poem, and was devising a method by which the multitude of pictures which he had taken apparently at random, now here and now there, . . . might be made to appear before his eyes in a natural order and to follow one after another."

After all, in the case of Thomson this line of defence would not be altogether unreasonable. It is true that the poems of ***The Seasons*** are too diffuse and too loosely constructed; but if from criticism of the structure of the poems we turn our attention to the particular parts of which they are composed, we shall see that Thomson's method of description is by no means disorderly, and that it is, properly speaking, that of the poet and not of the painter: the points of his description arise in a certain natural order of succession; he describes, in fact, for the most part, not the several parts of a scene as it lies at rest before him, but the appearances which are successively developed, the changes caused by the action of the elements, of the lower animals, or of human beings. This is the character of Thomson's best work in description. Let us take for example the snow-storm:—

> Through the hush'd air the whitening shower descends,
> At first thin-wavering; till at last the flakes
> Fall broad and wide and fast, dimming the day
> With a continual flow. The cherish'd fields
> Put on their winter robe of purest white.
> 'Tis brightness all; save where the new snow melts
> Along the mazy current. Low the woods
> Bow their hoar head, (etc.)

Or again the delicately worked out *genre* picture of the redbreast, which follows shortly after:—

> Half-afraid, he first
> Against the window beats; then brisk alights
> On the warm hearth; then, hopping o'er the floor,
> Eyes all the smiling family askance,
> And pecks, and starts, and wonders where he is;
> Till, more familiar grown, the table-crumbs
> Attract his slender feet.

These passages give details in each case which serve to build up a picture, but under the form of a succession of events; and this will be found to be the usual character of Thomson's descriptions, and an essential part of their poetical effectiveness.

The second of the passages above quoted, however, is less characteristic of Thomson than the first, and in its delicate minuteness of detail reminds us rather of the style of Cowper. Thomson had a certain largeness of view, a power of presenting his scene in masses and in a generalised form, which Cowper does not attain to. He seems to have hesitated with regard to the propriety of this particular passage: it appeared first in the second edition of ***Winter,*** published in June, 1726, but it was omitted in the quarto of 1730, though it remained in the more popular octavo, and appeared again in 1738. It does, in fact, by its indoor details somewhat injure the general effect of the description, which in the first edition passed directly from—

> The fowls of heaven,
> Tam'd by the cruel season, crowd around
> The winnowing store, and claim the little boon
> That Providence assigns

to

> The foodless wilds
> Pour forth their brown inhabitants.

Probably he was persuaded, against his better judgment, that the passage was too good to be omitted. In any case, Thomson's effects depend usually upon the power of creating a vivid impression by a few rapid touches, while Cowper builds up his delicate and beautiful pictures by patiently adding one detail after another.

Neither Thomson nor Cowper can be said to have arrived at a quite satisfactory view of the relations of man with external nature; and a question naturally arises as to the value which such poetry as theirs may have with a view to the attainment of a more complete conception. That it gives pleasure is undoubted, but how far does it tend towards the highest poetical truth? The answer is, that such poetry represents a preliminary stage, which must necessarily be traversed before the ultimate synthesis can be reached. Wordsworth's descriptions have great beauty and truth to nature, yet Wordsworth is not properly a descriptive poet, because his imagination constantly transforms the sense perceptions into symbols of spiritual truth. Wordsworth, however, himself went through the preliminary stage of which we are speaking, and it was this to which he referred when he wrote of his earlier years:—

> The sounding cataract
> Haunted me like a passion: the tall rock,
> The mountain, and the deep and gloomy wood,
> Their colours and their forms, were then to me
> An appetite, a feeling, and a love,
> That had no need of a remoter charm
> Unborrow'd from the eye. That time is past.

Of that past time he has left memorials in his early poems. Nature indeed must first be deeply loved for herself alone, her sounds and her sights must haunt the poet like a passion, the colours and forms which she presents must be to him "An appetite, a feeling, and a love," before he can rise to the higher sense of spiritual harmony. Thomson possessed what we may perhaps call the representative imagination: he was able to select the elements of his description in such a manner as to bring before his readers an impression nearly resembling that which he had experienced, and to communicate to them, in some degree at least, the emotions which it excited in himself. If we are ultimately to transcend the phenomena, and to realise the harmony between the aspects of external Nature and the spiritual needs of Man, we must first pass through the stage of poetical observation. It is this which is especially represented by Thomson, and however incomplete his work may seem to be, it is undeniable that the poetry of the eighteenth century has an appreciable obligation to his genius.

Thomson had, it may be admitted, an essentially poetical temperament; he saw things always with the eye of a poet, but "notwithstanding his high powers, he writes a vicious style." Such is Wordsworth's verdict, and it must to some extent be accepted [see excerpt dated 1837]. In Wordsworth's celebrated attack upon the poetic diction of the eighteenth century, Gray was selected as the special object of criticism, being at the head of those who, by their reasonings, had attempted to widen the space of separation between prose and metrical composition, and being also "more than any other man curiously elaborate in his own poetic diction." If the main attack had been made upon Thomson, it would probably have been more successful; for unquestionably the poetic diction of Thomson may with good reason be criticised, while at the same time it is more truly representative of the tendencies against which Wordsworth really desired to protest, than that of Gray. Thomson, equally with Gray, thought it right to maintain a wide space of separation between the language of prose and that of "metrical composition"; and so far he is not to be blamed. His fault was, not that he wrote in poetical language, but that he adopted a highly artificial kind of poetical language. Not satisfied with the poetry of his own day, which he justly criticised as wanting in elevation both of subject and of style, he chose to adopt Milton as his principal model of diction as well as verse. The Miltonic diction is a form of speech which was suitable to the genius of its original author, and to a great extent in harmony with the subjects of which he treated; but it was the source of most of that conventional unreality which characterises the poetical language of the eighteenth century. Even in the hands of Milton the results are not always happy; and when applied by an imitator to ordinary subjects, this style of diction is apt to produce the effect either of pompous artificiality or of unpleasant mannerism.

Thomson, however, was not a mere imitator in the matter of style. He was moved by a genuine impulse to restore to the language some of the richness and poetical colour of which it had been deprived by the writers of his own age in their endeavours after lucidity and common-sense. He instinctively felt that, for the subjects which stirred his imagination, a more truly poetical diction was needed than that which was current in the poetry of the day. He naturally looked back to the last great example in English literature of exalted poetical expression; and besides borrowing the actual language of Milton, he endeavoured to advance further in the spirit of his exemplar, and ventured himself to make such additions to the poetical language as he felt to be needed for the expression of his own conceptions. He deserves the credit . . . of having made an adventurous endeavour to vary and enrich the forms of poetical expression in English, and of having partially succeeded in his enterprise. (pp. 92-103)

G. C. Macaulay, in his James Thomson, *Macmillan and Co., Limited, 1908, 259 p.*

Louis Cazamian (essay date 1924)

[*An eminent French educator and literary scholar, Cazamian is known for his contribution to English studies, particularly for the widely acclaimed* Histoire de la littérature anglaise *(1924;* A History of English Literature, *1926-27), written with Emile Legouis. His other writings include* Modern England *(1912) and* Criticism in the Making *(1929). In the following excerpt from the first-named work, he provides a concise overview of Thomson's oeuvre. Characterizing* The Seasons *as a pre-Romantic work, he remarks that Thomson "restored Nature to one of the first places among the subjects of poetry, and to a place from which she was never to be dislodged."*]

The growth of the poetry of sentiment proceeds by successive advances. Nothing is richer than emotion as a motive of poetry; in a sense, it constitutes the normal and necessary source of all rhythmic language. What is recommencing, therefore, is not a particular kind, but all the diversity of poetry itself.

No doubt, the eighteenth century will be far from exhausting this whole range. On account of the effect of social restraint, which has a retarding influence upon moral evolution, it will give as yet only a sober sketch of its possibilities. It will be left to the following century to allow sentimental effusion all its intensity and freedom, and to decisively harmonise form with a renewed inspiration. But already we are shown with sufficient clearness the main lines along which this inspiration will work. And the successive appearance of these lines, as revealed by exact chronology, enables us to perceive without too much artifice a coherent order of development.

The first element which comes into prominence is the emotional theme of Nature. The instinctive naturalism of the English mind was never completely neutralised by classical influences. The vigorous reviviscence of this tendency well before the middle of the century is therefore in itself nothing of a surprise. It must also be made clear that at its source this vein is less properly sentimental than it is sensitive. It represents more easily a continuation of classicism than will the purer emotions, freer from all material support, that will develop shortly after.

From a certain point of view, the feeling for Nature with Thomson springs from that realism of concrete description which is an essential element of classical art and which already, even with the masters of the school, was sometimes tinged by a fond affection for natural scenery. Thomson's inspiration is a realism that has blossomed out into a keen, coloured and glowing sensation. This ardour of sensuous perception is an undoubted originality in itself; besides, it is accompanied by a general tone of deeply moved sensibility. But we are here only in the rather exterior regions of the poetry of sentiment; and this exteriority might not be unconnected with the fact that form, with Thomson, is still very closely allied to the intentions and devices of classicism.

His features are therefore above all mixed. In the light of his work as of his life, we find two men in him. The one is an amiable epicurean, care-free, the friend of easy leisure, who through his mind, tastes and character was very readily won over to the cult of ancient beauty and of traditional literary models. The other bears the stamp of an ecclesiastic education, more severe and moralising; religiously inclined, and fond also of sentiment. Judged by certain traits, if the first Thomson is in many ways at one with Pope, the second is already in keeping with Richardson. And it is the second, no doubt, who is better in agreement with the social and psychological movement in which the line of literary progression is dimly outlined.

It seems temptingly simple to connect the classical elements in the work of Thomson with the first group of tendencies, and the elements of transition with the second. Such an interpretation would not be altogether wrong, but things are not so clear-cut. What we can distinguish as the most certain feature of Thomson's originality—the sense of the physical world, the rich perception of Nature—is at once made up of the two temperaments which he unites in himself, and the distinction of which is, to say the truth, wholly abstract.

The scenery of the seasons, as Thomson paints it, is made up of still general touches; a mind guided by literary memories, by time-consecrated models, constructs its main framework. It is the course of the sun through the signs of the zodiac which sets moving this changing sequence; the Muse presides over all the transitions; mythology is the background of the modern and real horizon in which the festivities or the sorrows of Heaven and Earth unfold themselves, in all their grandeur and brilliance. The scenes of country life irresistibly assume the style of typical and Vergilian episodes; the spirit of the *Georgics* puts them together and evolves them. This classical atmosphere is more distinctly felt in a language that is scholarly, strewn with Latinisms, where the epithet has often a character of conventional banality, and from which poetic diction is by no means absent. Thomson describes Nature by educing from the multiplicity of facts the forms to which they can be reduced, and which enable the mind to classify them. The seasons are the most general of these forms; the aspects of each season, the activities associated with them, are others. His inspiration of a generalising and didactic trend remains in so far intellectual; and the inner quality of his style appears in the constant employment of the definite article (not necessary for present use), which suggests the influence of French syntax, and gives to the poetry as to the prose of this epoch the colour of a literature written under the constant stimulus of a search after universality of statement.

But as against the abstraction of the central thought, we have the particular value of the images and sensations evoked. Built up on a need for truth, classicism contained within itself the very principle of realism; but the almost exclusive preoccupation of general truths kept its effort away from the wealth of reality. With Thomson, classical art opens itself broadly to the concrete; and immediately it receives a new vitality from this contact.

The reason is that the intelligence is no longer exclusively called upon to receive this inrush of sensations, to organise them, distribute them, despoil them of their characteristic element; the realism of Thomson is of a superior poetic fecundity, because it is the spontaneous exercise of a sensitive temperament, capable of strong and delicate impressions, trained from an early hour in the discriminations and enjoyments of the eye and ear and touch. The voluptuous epicurean whose instincts harmonise so well, in other respects, with a traditional culture and a humanistic inspiration, has been an unconscious innovator because he has not forgotten, as he wrote, that he had senses. By loading his verse with all their joys, he introduced into a rational and jejune art a complexity and a luxuriance foreign to its usual effects.

It is therefore difficult to believe that the coloured intensity of sensation, in the ***Seasons,*** would have developed with this tranquil audacity, had not other tendencies intervened to favour it. The wealth of concrete description is strengthened by a whole group of impulses of the emotional order. Here it is, to speak properly, that the feeling for Nature appears. It springs from the diffuse sentimentalism which, in the case of Thomson, is bound up with his moralising temperament, religious, patriotic, and in full sympathy with the instincts of the middle classes. Thus the minute attention with which the charm of the English countryside is appreciated and depicted appears as it were animated by an inner ardour, strong enough to become a dominant passion of the soul, and to gather all its desires around itself.

But it is a tempered passion, without anything violent or exalted; a sort of fond complacency, that includes many elements destined to develop with the progress of the century: the taste for pure and peaceful emotions, the calm rapture called forth by verdant sites, the relaxing of body and mind, the soothing sense reaped from the sight of innocent, idyllic simplicity; the half-sincere preference for a primitive, upright and pious life, far removed from the overheated artificiality of towns. Thomson's feeling for Nature has already something religious about it, just as it has something national; but while it is conscious of its social and philosophic prepossessions, it does not as yet uphold them with the uncompromising zeal of a Rousseau.

Its success is elsewhere, in the notation of what it sees and feels. To pass from the pastorals of Pope, or from *Windsor Forest,* to the ***Seasons,*** is to pass from too expert a flute, or from a pompously sylvan lyre, to an arranged but harmoniously sweet concert of all the voices of fields and woods and hills. No doubt, it will happen that the description is more conscientiously precise than poetic. But a decisive step has been taken towards the discovery of a sensible world then forgotten, if not unknown.

The episodes, anecdotes and moralising reflections fade from our memory; what remains is a series of visions, of a delightful freshness and penetrating charm. The poetry of nature is actually there in its blooming fullness, for the first time in many years. It springs, first and foremost, from exactitude. Its range is certainly not complete; it lacks its grandest, wildest, most mystical notes. However, it would be wrong to look upon Thomson as a Dutch painter of fat pastures and jolly farm-houses, whose outlook is limited by an ideal of comfortable sanity. The landscape he describes is indeed that which he could love and observe in the south of Scotland or in the neighbourhood of London; the sky and the ground in his pictures are familiar and reassuring; if he leaves this well-known domain for the high mountain, the pole or the desert, the effort is immediately perceptible. But within the limits of his experience, he was able to feel, and knew how to convey, a remarkable vivacity of character. The notes of vernal sweetness, and of pensive autumnal beauty, are those best suited to the tone of his temperament; and he expresses the rapture of the ones, as the melancholy of the others, with an intensity of feeling, a fullness of emotion, that will be surpassed only by Romanticism at the zenith of its power.

It is towards Romanticism, indeed, that this work is unwittingly verging, however immune it may be from all revolutionary intent. The hymn which closes the ***Seasons*** makes one think of Coleridge. Their form even is not entirely cast in the classical mould. Out of a desire to react against an oversummary opinion, one has perhaps, in the opposite sense, too much connected Thomson with the past. However artificial his language, it none the less obtains effects of light and sonority which restore to literature resources of art neglected for several generations. His search for imitative harmony is carried to a sort of impressionism. And to the cult of Pope, he has added that of Milton and Spenser.

It would be wrong to think that at the end of the seventeenth century, and in the beginning of the eighteenth, these masters were ignored. The broadest minds of the time preserved a veneration for them, which they reconciled very well with classical principles. But it was Thomson's desire to borrow from the strong solemn beauties of *Paradise Lost,* a religious, national and poetic classicism; he wanted to model his blank verse on that of Milton. His talent of a soft happy temper did not lend itself to the powerful austere orchestration of that writer; his attempt, however, was only half an error. He borrowed from Milton, over and above his Latinisms, something of his nobleness; and the versification of the ***Seasons*** is of a very creditable quality; its tones, in an age swayed by the imperious rule of the rhymed couplet, ring with a strength, a liberty, a suppleness, the tradition of which had been lost.

There are traces in the ***Seasons*** of the influence of Spenser; but it is in ***The Castle of Indolence*** that it displays its fecundity. This unequal poem, the edifying intention of which scarcely corresponds with its artistic truth, is perhaps the most successful imitation in English literature; and in certain respects it is better than an imitation. Here Thomson gives vent to all his somnolent epicurean tastes more than he himself wanted to, and symbolises with charming felicity the soul's succumbing to the pleasures of a care-free nature. The Spenserian stanza, which he strews with archaisms at times quite fanciful, but animates with a generally very correct movement, seems as if it had been made for the theme to which it is here applied; its richness, its ample musical unfolding, suit both the temperament of Thomson, and the subject. No more evocative poem was written in the eighteenth century.

Thomson had given voice to deep aspirations, which many shared; he restored Nature to one of the first places among the subjects of poetry, and to a place from which she was never to be dislodged. He had immediately a following, and found imitators, while his diffuse action is to be felt everywhere.

Louis Cazamian, "The Poetry of Sentiment," in his A History of English Literature: Modern Times (1660-1914), Vol. 2, *translated by W. D. MacInnes and Louis Cazamian, The Macmillan Company, 1927, pp. 147-63.*

Oliver Elton (essay date 1928)

[*Elton was a critic and literary historian whose books include* A Survey of English Literature 1780-1830 *(1912),* A Survey of English Literature 1830-80 *(1920), and* A Survey of English Literature 1730-1780 *(1928). In the following excerpt from the last-named work, he discusses Thomson's poetry and dramatic works. While praising* The Seasons *as a skillfully crafted poetic work, despite obvious technical flaws, he criticizes the dramas as formalistic and basically rhetorical exercises lacking true passion.*]

[Many features of the Miltonic tradition] can be traced in Thomson; yet the moment we name Thomson, we think not only of his poetical reading, but of that great phenomenon of the time, the renewal of the feeling for natural beauty and grandeur. As all know, he marks a great stage in this process, and his achievement is carried on by Gray and Collins, by Cunningham and Chatterton, and by many a lesser poet. . . . [And] it was not only the poets who were, literally, recovering their senses. The same awakening is found in the novels, the memoirs, the diaries, and the books of travel. The 'return to nature' is fitful, intermittent, and unconcerted: that is to say, it is seen in persons far apart, who know nothing of one another; there are flowery patches in unexpected spots. Even the philosophers are not exempt from the influence: there are the happy descriptions of scenery in Berkeley's *Alciphron.* And the philosophers actually furthered the sentiment for nature. It is now clear that the *Characteristics* of Shaftesbury, and even the theories of Hutcheson on the nature of beauty, told directly or obliquely on poets like Thomson and Akenside, and helped to exalt their actual sensations of things seen and heard into something like a cult, or half-mystical creed, which gives us many a foretaste of Wordsworth. The 'natural religion' of the deists, with its emphasis on the loveliness of creation as a proof of theism, wrought in the same direction; so that this derided and seemingly forgotten school after all left its legacy. A more immediate influence was that of the painters, whether of the tradition of Claude and Poussin, or of the early school of English water-colour. They shaped many a poetical description; and they also affected the new development of landscape gardening. This rested on the conception that nature herself has to be trained to be like a picture, and that there may be something wrong with her if it cannot be done—if she cannot bc *made* 'picturesque.' The experiments of Shenstone, and the theorising of writers like William Gilpin, attest this belief. But the root of the matter is the direct fresh unbookish apprehension of visible and audible beauty; of sky and water, of meadows and mountains, of ploughland and garden, of flowers and birds and insects. And, for the poets, the real problem was to get a *language* that would not misstate their impressions; nay, that would not fatally cloud and dull their very senses. This was to be a long struggle, which can be watched in writer after writer. . . . [There are] abundant traces of this great change in the English mind. The first example is the author of the ***Seasons.*** He was at once popular, for his good work and for his bad alike. He does not seem to have been one of the artists who know when they are writing well. His pages were to be strewn with barren wastes; and he was to be led away, by the most admirable motives, into producing ***Sophonisbas*** and ***Britannias.*** But he felt that in his descriptions of scenery he was doing something new, or rather was recovering a lost inspiration. As we all know, it had dwindled down; it had just been kept alive, in the shade, by Lady Winchelsea and Parnell; and more vividly, as will be seen, by Dyer. Thomson's own language is worth quoting; it is found in the second edition of ***Winter,*** published in June 1726, and is pleasantly flushed and youthful:

> Nothing can have a better influence towards the revival of poetry than the choosing of great, and serious, subjects; such as, at once, amuse the fancy, enlighten the head, and warm the heart. These give a weight, and dignity, to the poem. . . .
>
> And what are we commonly entertained with, on these occasions, save forced, unaffecting fancies; little, glittering prettinesses; mixed turns of wit, and expression; which are as widely different from native poetry, as buffoonery is from the perfection of human thinking? A genius fired with the charms of truth, and nature, is tuned to a sublimer pitch, and scorns to associate with such subjects. . . .

Thomson clearly thinks that true poetry, in the year 1726, is dead, and that he is destined to resuscitate it. Men have forgotten the scripture itself; and he speaks first of the *Book of Job* with its 'description of the grand works of nature,' and then quotes the *Georgics* (*Me vero primum,* etc.); and he breaks out:

> I know no subject more elevating, more amusing, more ready to awake the poetical enthusiasm, the philosophical reflection, and the moral sentiment, than the works of nature. Where can we meet such variety, such beauty, such magnificence? All that enlarges, and transports, the soul? What more inspiring than a calm, wide, survey of them? In every dress nature is greatly charming! whether she puts on the crimson robes of the morning! the strong effulgence of noon! the sober suit of the evening! or the deep sables of blackness and tempest!

We do not expect any writer in a didactic age to take the point of view of the pure artist, and simply to say that he wants to paint. But Thomson's exalted ideals, if they often diverted him from his true business, also impelled him to go about it. (pp. 353-55)

The ***Seasons*** are sometimes described as a scion of the old 'local poem,' of the type of *Cooper's Hill*; but they are not much like it, except in their discursiveness. They are a miscellany, and really consist of passages of poetry laced together by passages of verse. They might serve to point the paradox of Edgar Poe, that a *long* poem 'does not exist.' There are plenty of what one critic of Thomson calls his *hors d'œuvre*: protests against cruelty to animals; pathetic tales limpidly but rather insipidly told; sallies of political and humanitarian feeling; praises of Chesterfield, or of Wilmington, or of Dodington; reflections in the vein of the *Essay on Man*; and echoes of Virgilian pantheism. In these passages, it would be wrong to deny, poetry is sometimes present; but it is oftener round the corner. Thomson, unlike Pope, is always sincere. But it is the English landscapes and cloudscapes and the country scenes that hold the mind and give to the ***Seasons*** such unity as they have. Sometimes, indeed, Thomson triumphs when he describes that of which he has only read. Two of his most musical lines are inspired by the flowers that grow among the frosts of Lapland:

> Where pure Niemi's fairy mountains rise,
> And fringed with roses Tenglio rolls his stream.

He was the first English poet of any power who made the description of natural things the primary subject of a long work. For a parallel we must go back to Gavin Douglas and the *Prologues* to his *Æneid.* Landscape, though abundant in the poets, had usually been a background, or incidental; or, as in *L'Allegro,* had been so inwrought that we think first of the writer and his mood rather than of the object. Thomson's scenes are marked, first of all, by the resolution to observe nature exactly, and even literally; next, by his liking for wide spaces of land and water, and horizons of cloud; then, by his inclination to strong and even violent colouring, which does not exclude a subtlety in giving muffled, or subdued, effects of light and shadow, as of the sun striking through mist and rain; and lastly, by a steady endeavour to unite these pictorial effects with musical ones. And, in general, he succeeds in proportion as he can bring himself to be simple. Many of the changes and additions in his text show an inclination, and not always a happy one, to elaborate. The chorus of birds in ***Spring*** (1727) is much more birdlike—though the sophisticated element is already there—than in the 1744 version of ***Winter.*** In the first passage,

> Up-springs the lark,
> Shrill-voiced and loud, the messenger of morn;
> Ere yet the shadows fly, he mounted sings
> Amid the dawning clouds, and from their haunts
> Calls up the tuneful nations. Every copse
> Thick-wove, and tree irregular, and bush,
> Bending with dewy moisture o'er the heads
> Of the coy quiristers who lodge within,
> Are prodigal of harmony . . .
> The blackbird whistles from the thorny brake;
> The mellow bullfinch answers from the grove. . . .

In ***Winter*** comes the somewhat overloaded picture of the storm, which terrifies beast and bird:

> With broadened nostrils to the sky upturned,
> The conscious heifer snuffs the stormy gale . . .
>
> . . . but chief the plumy race,
> The tenants of the sky, its changes speak.

> Retiring from the downs, where all day long
> They picked their scanty fare, a blackening train
> Of clamorous rooks thick-urge their weary flights,
> And seek the closing shelter of the grove.
> Assiduous, in his bower, the wailing owl
> Plies his sad song. The cormorant on high
> Wheels from the deep, and screams along the land.

The observation is as precise as ever, but a frost is settling upon the language. Not that Thomson's toil was idle; there are touches added that make all the difference. In 1726 he wrote:

> . . . An icy gale, that, in its mid career,
> Arrests the bickering stream.

But in 1730 the wind becomes visible:

> An icy gale, oft shifting, o'er the pool
> Breathes a blue film, and in its mid career
> Arrests the bickering stream.

These are the things in Thomson that we remember: the 'blue film'; the 'yellow mist Far-smoking o'er the interminable plain'; the shepherd lying 'with half-shut eyes, beneath the floating shade Of willows grey'; and 'the pale, descending year, yet pleasing still.'

Thomson, when he is not describing, abounds in all sorts of high-minded declamation which comes short of poetry. Yet it would be untrue to say that he is a poet only when he is describing. He does not try, like Pope, to reason in verse; nor does he attempt 'metaphysical' verse in the stricter sense. But he has a 'religion of nature' of his own, which sometimes finds expression in his purest style; prophesying Wordsworth, and perhaps helping to inspire him, in passages that we might think were from the *Prelude.* Nature is not only a 'subject,' but a refuge and an inspirer. In any case, light is cast upon the 'history of a poet's mind.' One confession portrays Thomson's youth, and reveals the inner motive power of the ***Seasons***:

> With frequent foot,
> Pleased have I, in my cheerful morn of life,
> When nursed by careless solitude, I lived,
> And sung of nature with unceasing joy,
> Pleased have I wandered through your rough domain;
> Trod the pure virgin-snows, myself as pure;
> Heard the winds roar, and the big torrent burst;
> Or seen the deep fermenting tempest brewed,
> In the grim evening sky. Thus passed the time,
> Till through the lucid chambers of the South
> Looked out the joyous Spring, looked out, and smiled.

From what other source can Wordsworth have learnt the cadence of his autobiographic style? Lines like

> knowledge, sacred peace, and virtue pure,
> Sacred, substantial, never-fading bliss,

strengthen this impression; and so do the lines in ***Spring,*** which for some bad reason Thomson omitted after the edition of 1730:

> thus the glad skies,
> The wide-rejoicing earth, the woods, the streams,
> With every life they hold, down to the flower
> That paints the lowly vale, or insect-wing
> Waved o'er the shepherd's slumber, touch the mind
> To nature tuned, with a light-flying hand
> Invisible, quick-urging, through the nerves,
> The glittering spirits, in a flood of day.

There are phrases in these extracts which Wordsworth might not have let pass, as being 'poetic diction' of the wrong mint; but the strain, after all, is nearer to the *Tintern Abbey* of 1798 than it is to the *Descriptive Sketches* written in 1791. Thomson now and then attained at once the style towards which his successor had painfully to work his way. His own course, no doubt, was also a hindered one, and in the ***Seasons*** he is never quite sure how to write.

He aimed at nothing less than the grand style; he found it in Milton; and he sought to appropriate, chiefly for the description of scenery, Milton's verse and language. Scholars have dissected Thomson's imitative technique to the last fibre, and the results need only be glanced at. His Latinised vocabulary set a bad example; the 'conscious heifer' and the 'faint erroneous ray' tell their own tale, and so do Thomson's own inventions of the same kind. It is too late in the day to ridicule the 'sordid stream,' the 'gravid boughs,' and the 'fond sequacious herd,' or terms like 'effulged,' 'protended,' and 'constringent.' The circumlocutions, like the 'copious fry' and the 'bleating herd,' are in the same case. This last kind of ornament is found, of course, in many poets, and the only question is whether or no it is heated by the imagination. The Anglo-Saxons, and Pope, and Tennyson all use it in different ways; and Thomson was encouraged by Pope's practice, with the result that we are usually left cold. Another device, in its origin Latin, but suggested more immediately by Milton, hampers him yet more. This is the dislocation of the epithet, which comes to count as an adverb, or rather as the logical predicate of the sentence:

> See where the winding vale its lavish stores,
> Irriguous, spreads:

—an irritating trick, that often mars a good landscape like a smear.

In spite of these blemishes, Thomson's management of his form is interesting and beautiful. He felt to the full the supremacy of the instrument which he was learning to play. He tried, with fitful success, to reproduce, first of all, the variety and power of Milton's single lines; next, the modulations within the line, and, the overflow from line to line; and, lastly, the concerted music of the long Miltonic period, with its overture and swell and always triumphant close. And this close, now on a louder now on a softer note, Thomson was always trying to achieve; to seize, as it were, the ghost of a tune that haunted him. He usually fails; while seeking to end with a crash, he is apt to end with a kind of slam, like that of a banging door. This is the point at which most followers of Milton break down. They cannot gain the effect of

> Gorgons, and Hydras, and Chimeras dire,

nor yet the effect of

> And Eden raised in the waste wilderness.

One passage from the ***Seasons*** may illustrate Thomson's cadences. It has the fault described; and it certainly does not give us Milton's undulations within the line, or his melting of wave into wave as the new line begins; but it does show a true and splendid management of the individual lines, which belong to what has been well called the 'single-moulded' species: the Muse, he says, has passed through spring and summer:

> Then swept o'er Autumn with the shadowy gale;
> And now among the wintry clouds again,
> Rolled in the doubling storm, she tries to soar;
> To swell her note with all the rushing winds;
> To suit her sounding cadence to the floods,—
> As is her theme, her numbers wildly great.

The melody is true nearly up to the last, and then, before it has wrought itself out, it jerks to a stop. But we need not be too pedantic over all Thomson's drawbacks of language and versification. We get used to them, as to an old-fashioned costume. Still, it is clear that poetry had to get rid of them. Thomson himself abandoned them, and really found himself, in the ***Castle of Indolence.*** (pp. 357-61)

Some verses of the ***Castle of Indolence*** might go into the *Faerie Queene,* and would hardly be known for changelings. For nearly a hundred lines of the first canto the sleepy music is kept up without the dialect of the Georgian age intruding. The stanza is fully understood, and the charm remains, which never fails in the original, of the rhyme repeated at the fifth line, like the turning over of a wave. There is also the pomp of the closing alexandrine, sometimes varied by a pause after the light seventh syllable:

> Loose life, unruly passions, and diseases pale.

The old spell is laid at once on the dreaming vision and on the drowsy hearing. Then, unluckily waking up, the poet slips into another manner; there are 'soft gales of passion,' and the 'crimson-spotted fry,' namely trout, and, worse still, the 'social sense.' These two strands of diction remain interlaced, with an effect quaintly disconcerting; the poetry going out and coming in again, more or less in correspondence. In the best passages colour and sound unite, as in Spenser himself:

> as when, beneath the beam
> Of summer-moons, the distant woods among,
> Or by some flood, all silvered with the gleam,
> The soft-embodied fays through airy portal stream.

There are yet other virtues in the poem. Spenser has a subdued humour of his own and a power of gay or bitter invective. Thomson has humour too, and some passages in the ***Seasons*** belong to the poetry of manners. The drinking-bout in ***Autumn*** is in what was called the 'Dutch style'; and, as an afterthought, a Hogarthian figure was inserted:

> Perhaps some Doctor, of tremendous paunch,
> Awful and deep, a black abyss of drink,
> Outlives them all.

This is not like Spenser or Milton; but the same vein occurs in the ***Castle of Indolence,*** in the admirable figures of the page and the porter.

To all this there is a half-serious and somewhat ragged allegorical lining. To complete the tribute to the sage and serious poet, Indolence must be not only enjoyed but reproved. As with Spenser, we care more for the *right* side of the fabric than for the lining. The Morphean music of the Hall of Idleness is better than the lecture. Yet Thomson, like his master, can satirise well; and the picture of the Mirror of Vanity, with its sharp fling at the idler and the waster, shows another side of his power. He has yet a further resource when he falls to drawing playful sketches of his contemporaries. They are his own friends; and some of them would be forgotten but for their presence in the Castle. But they also include Lyttelton, Quin, and Armstrong, the poet of the 'art of preserving health'; who wrote one line, 'A bard there was, more fat than bard beseems,' in the picture of Thomson himself. The rest of this was by Lyttelton; and Armstrong added the medical, the too professional, verses at the end of the first canto.

In the second, the ingredients are much the same; but, alas, poetry and Spenser begin to recede. Thomson becomes didactic, patriotic, and British. Indolence is now a monster to be overthrown by the 'Knight of arts and industry,' who is in turn an athlete, an artist, a man of science, and a patron of agriculture. There is vigorous rhetoric, but we long for the intermitted music. Parts of this canto, which Byron may have studied, curiously resemble a harangue by Childe Harold. At the end is a startling burst of realism, when the swine, descendants of Spenser's Gryll, charge grunting through the town of Brentford. With all its disparities, the ***Castle of Indolence*** remains not only the best imitation of Spenser, but the most original poem amongst all the imitations. (pp. 363-64)

. . . . .

Thomson's five plays were all produced after the ***Seasons.*** They rest, it is to be feared, in much the same limbo as his ***Liberty*** and his **"Brittannia"**; and they often leave us wondering that he still had it in him to write the ***Castle of Indolence.*** Yet they have poetic, if little dramatic, interest; the fire is by no means dead. ***Sophonisba*** (1730) is avowedly a Racinian drama; and the preface states the rules of symmetry as clearly as anything in English: the subject is

> one, regular, and uniform; not charged with a multiplicity of incidents, and yet affording several revolutions of fortune; by which the passions may be excited, varied, and driven to their full tumult of emotion.

The passions, unluckily, are cooled by the high politics of Sophonisba, who gravely argues with her husband Syphax that it is for the good of Carthage that she should marry his captor Masinissa. Thomson, in his preface, is careful to say that 'by the laws of Rome and of Carthage, the captivity of the husband dissolved the marriage of course.' And the queen announces:

> All love but that of Carthage I despise.

> I formerly to Masinissa thee
> Preferred not, nor to thee now Masinissa;
> But Carthage to you both.

The amiable soul of Thomson lacked heat to animate the scenes in which Masinissa sends the queen poison and is then in despair upon finding that she has taken it. Unlike the turgid but really impassioned *Sophonisba* of Nathaniel Lee, the piece is cold; and the cold does not, like that in Milton's Hell, 'perform the effect of fire.' In ***Agamemnon*** (1738) there is much more poetry, and some scenery:

> But straight, as evening fell, the fluttering gale
> Encreasing gradual from the red north-east,
> Blew stiff and fierce.

But Thomson was rash enough to disfigure the heroine of Aeschylus. Egisthus is all too prominent, and in an immense speech persuades the *wavering* Clytemnestra to her crime. A timid Judith would be equally startling. And the classical canon, that blood may only be spilt in the wings, is half-defied; for

> the noise of Agamemnon's assassination is heard indistinctly and at a distance behind the scenes . . . the noise heard distinctly and nearer.

Thomson's Cassandra, although she is capable of saying

> O heavens and earth! you shock me to distraction!

can still talk poetry to the Chorus:

> *Chor.* O the yellow banks
> Of far Scamander, in whose silver stream
> We used to bathe, beneath the secret shade!
> *Cass.* O cheerful Ida's airy summits, where
> The Gods delight to dwell!
> *Chor.* O silent Troy,
> Whose seats have often echoed with our song!

The most pleasing of Thomson's dramas, ***Edward and Eleonora,*** is not a tragedy but a historical tragi-comedy. It was banned from the stage for political reasons, and printed in 1739. The features of Frederick Prince of Wales, endowed with a halo, were too clearly visible in those of the noble Edward, destined to deliver his country from corruption. Thomson, as we know, was a fervent supporter of the Opposition. But there is also a breath of romance and chivalry in ***Edward and Eleonora.*** It has been compared with the *Talisman*; and the likeness is plain, though probably an accident; Scott does not mention it amongst his sources. There is the English prince crusading before Jaffa; and the gallant sultan, Selim, who comes disguised as a dervish, partly to clear himself of the charge of having hired a ruffian to poison the king, and partly to cure Eleonora. She has sucked the wound and risked her life; but Selim reveals himself, and produces her in perfect health.

Thomson's most telling and popular tragedy, ***Tancred and Sigismunda*** (1745), had a long life on the boards and was translated into French and German; but it now seems a rhetorical and pseudo-passionate affair. It is adapted from a romance inserted in *Gil Blas,* and has at any rate a dramatic plot, too intricate to describe at length. Tancred, another 'patriot king' in the making, is tricked by the tortuous Siffredi, the father of his ladylove Sigismunda, into accepting, along with the throne of Sicily, a bride, Constantia, who never comes upon the stage. Siffredi also forces, or beguiles, Sigismunda into a marriage with his own accomplice Osmond. We may fancy what Ford, or even Shirley, might have made of the scene in which Tancred passionately urges Sigismunda to flee with him, learns too late that she is a wife, and is interrupted by Osmond. Blood flows; Tancred kills Osmond, who has stabbed Sigismunda mortally; and Tancred is left lamenting. Thomson's verse here approaches to poetry, and the episode is stirring even in the level prose of Lesage. After this, Thomson's ***Coriolanus*** hardly needs a mention. But in the masque ***Alfred*** (1740), which he wrote with David Mallet, another note is often heard:

> What time the glow-worm through the dewy path
> First shot his twinkling flame.

Here is also the first version of **"Rule, Britannia,"** which is now fully credited to Thomson. A poem by courtesy, it lives, like many an excellent hymn, by its rhythm and setting. Of the masque itself enough to say that it presents Alfred first chased by the Danes, and then beating them; receiving good advice from a hermit; and hearing a band of aerial spirits chant the future glories of England. (pp. 315-17)

Oliver Elton, "Followers of Pope, Milton, and Spenser" and "Tragedy," in his A Survey of English Literature: 1730-1780, Vol. I, *Edward Arnold (Publishers) Ltd., 1928, pp. 332-85, 309-31.*

David Nichol Smith (lecture 1937)

[*Smith was a literary scholar specializing in seventeenth- and eighteenth-century English literature; his writings include* John Dryden *(1950). In the following excerpt, he analyzes Thomson's diction, noting the importance of the poet's cultural background—exemplified by his typically Scottish Latinisms—for the understanding of his poetry.*]

[We know] that whereas there is general agreement about Elizabethan poetry and the poetry of the seventeenth century, there are at least two "schools of thought" about the poetry of the eighteenth. To one school the century is mainly of interest as being the seed-time of the poetry which blossomed in the days of Wordsworth and Coleridge. . . . [We] have at some stage been taught to picture the marches and the counter-marches which, about the middle of the century, began to disturb the Peace of the Augustans, and the final triumphal onslaught of *Lyrical Ballads.* The good verse, we were asked to believe, belonged to the future, and the poor verse or the indifferent verse was in its proper place. Good poets, like Gray, were said to be born out of their time. Somehow Nature had made a slip and dropped a poet in an age of prose.

Others prefer the modest alternative that when a poet seems to have got into the wrong place what is wrong is our idea of the place. Like every other century the eighteenth was an age of transition, but we need not therefore assume that its poets were engaged in one long campaign. The good poets of the eighteenth century spoke frankly about each other, as poets usually do; and though their aims might be divergent, they were always as ready as poets have ever been to acknowledge merit when they found it. (pp. 56-8)

[Thomson] has been hailed, rightly or wrongly, as introducing a new element into our poetry. The work of every good poet must be in some sense novel. No man, as Johnson said, was ever great by imitation; and whether or not this is invariably true, it is certainly true of the artist. But . . . [Thomson never] imagined himself to be a rebel.

Nor must we imagine that Pope, or Johnson, believed the empire of Wit to be limited and defined. They may have charted the portions of it with which they were familiar, but they knew that it was always expanding. Pope had maintained in the *Essay on Criticism* that anything is permissible provided it succeeds, but that the poet was less likely to succeed if he neglected what could be learned from his great predecessors. Should

> Some lucky licence answer to the full
> The intent proposed, that licence is a rule.

Thomson's ***Winter*** was a new kind of poem, but it fulfilled its purpose, and Pope welcomed it. He came to know Thomson and in the next edition of ***Winter*** Thomson inserted a glowing tribute to his friendship:

> Or from the muses' hill will *Pope* descend,
> To raise the sacred hour, to make it smile,
> And with the social spirit warm the heart:
> For tho' not sweeter his own *Homer* sings,
> Yet is his life the more endearing song.

(pp. 58-9)

Pope's very excellence . . . was an incentive to younger poets to seek new fields; and they had Pope's encouragement when they proved their competence. This side of Pope's relations with his contemporaries has not yet received the attention which it deserves. The best of all the poets whom he encouraged was Thomson.

With the Union of England and Scotland came the long and endless procession of Scots intent on finding their livelihood in London or elsewhere in the richer south, and among the early stragglers was James Thomson. He left Scotland at the age of twenty-five with "a poem in his pocket". It was his ***Winter.*** Within a few years it was to be one of the four parts of ***The Seasons.*** He had spent all his youth on the Scottish Border, where his father was a parish minister, or in Edinburgh, where he had himself studied for the ministry at the University.

The traveller who enters Scotland by the Cheviots finds a change in the prospect as he reaches the Border at Carter Bar. He has been passing through miles and miles of the moorland of Northumberland, but on a sudden he looks down, over a hilly foreground, to a richly wooded and cultivated country, with Jedburgh in the near distance, and further off Hawick and Kelso. This was Thomson's country. His early home lay between the rich district to the north and the rough hill country of the Cheviots to the south. The scenery which inspired ***The Seasons*** was the daily scenery of his youth, viewed through "a kind of glory". He may refer to many countries, but what he has experienced as a lad is behind what he tells us. When he writes of frost in winter, and frozen rills, and the death of the shepherd, he is thinking of the Cheviots. The fishing he describes was in the tributaries of the Tweed. His agricultural pictures are suggested by farming in the Merse, one of the richest agricultural districts of Scotland. When he speaks of the joys of bathing in summer, he is recollecting through the beautifying mists of memory the warm seasons by the burns of the Jed Water in the parish of Southdean. That ***The Seasons*** is in origin a poem of the Scottish Border is disguised by the absence of local references and the purposely general description of the great movements of Nature. Sooner than speak of the Border, Thomson will draw imaginary pictures of the Sahara, or Lapland, or the fate of Siberian exiles. Such passages were introduced when his poem became more ambitious, while he was living in the gentler climate of the south of England. But even in them we discover the recollected emotion as, amid the distractions of the great city, he cherishes the memory of his early home.

Nothing in ***The Seasons*** has given English readers more trouble than the diction. What Pope thought of it is not on record; evidently it did not obscure the merits of the poem from him. But Johnson could not praise it: "His diction is in the highest degree florid and luxuriant. . . . It is too exuberant, and sometimes may be charged with filling the ear more than the mind" [see excerpt dated 1781]. Wordsworth is less judicial, and says bluntly that "he writes a vicious style" [see excerpt dated 1837]. And I think that all English purists regard it as a vicious style, produced in the main by a forced imitation of Milton. But the English reader is here at a disadvantage. Thomson was a Scot, and to the educated Scot—who has always excelled in compiling dictionaries of the English language, but has not quite the Englishman's sense of the usage of the words which he is so proficient in collecting and defining—the language of ***The Seasons*** does not offer so great difficulties.

When Thomson was at the University of Edinburgh studying for the ministry, he was reprimanded by the Professor of Divinity for being too poetically splendid in an exercise on the 119th Psalm. He was told that "if he thought of being useful in the ministry he must keep a stricter rein upon his imagination, and express himself in language intelligible to an ordinary congregation". A wholesome censure no doubt, and a common censure in Scotland. The Scottish student has always been prone to rhetoric, and his tastes have been judiciously encouraged. The best English treatises on rhetoric were produced by Scottish professors in the eighteenth century. The English chair at Edinburgh is still called the chair of "Rhetoric and English Literature"; it used to be called the chair of "Rhetoric and Belles Lettres". To the present day the Scottish student dearly loves a well-rounded resounding sentence. . . . I believe it is still the experience of a large number of Scots who have followed Thomson and set up their rest in England that they become aware of the need of simplifying their style—of using shorter words now and again, and perhaps fewer words. (pp. 59-63)

We are apt to forget the large place occupied by Latin in vernacular Scots. Latin was at one time as familiar to the educated Scot as his mother-tongue, and was his means of communication with foreigners. The Scot abroad made his way with Latin. The Scottish authors who were known abroad wrote in Latin. Scots Law, which is founded on Roman Law, has a larger Latin element than English Law. Latin words were bound to creep into the vernacular. More than that, Latin words have come into English from Scottish usage. An instance is "narrate", which is thus defined by Johnson in his *Dictionary*—"to relate, to tell; a word only used in Scotland". Richardson in his *Clarissa* has "when I have least to narrate, to speak in the Scottish phrase, I am most diverting". Here we have the explanation why the Scottish historians and philosophers of the eighteenth century write in a style which seems to the English reader to be over-Latinized in vocabulary, and, as our school-masters know, is eminently suitable for conversion into Latin prose. (pp. 63-4)

On a style naturally rhetorical, and Latinized, Thomson superimposed a Miltonic element. He found in Milton a language after his heart. "Chimeras huge", "in endless mazes, intricate, perplexed",—such words and phrases as these made their way into ***The Seasons*** much more easily than we are apt to suppose. ***The Seasons*** is sometimes spoken of as if it were a long exercise in aureate diction; but it is too vital a poem for its language to be a continuous artifice. The style came easily to Thomson; it was natural to him. We can understand why Wordsworth called it vicious, for it is not a style which could have been cultivated by any good English poet. But I should be surprised if, even to-day, it is perplexing to the home-bred Scot. For myself, who may now have to be excluded from that category, I confess that I am attracted by it. Thomson always seems to me to succeed in conveying the impression which he means to convey.

Johnson detected a change of style in the revisions of ***The Seasons.*** "I know not whether they have not lost part of what Temple calls their *race*; a word which, applied to wines, in its primitive sense, means the flavour of the soil." His observation of the change is no less interesting than his admission of his regret. Thomson's way of writing, like that of other Scots who have left Scotland, was probably modified unconsciously. But after more than twenty years' residence by the banks of the Thames he preserved the Scottish vernacular in his talk. . . . Thomson's feelings were always easily moved. We should not be far wrong if we called him the first of the Scottish sentimentalists in English literature. It is sentiment which gives ***The Castle of Indolence*** its peculiar grace—sentiment which never gets out of control, which is never false or aggressive. Remembrance of Scotland inspires the most famous lines of that poem:

> As when a Shepherd of the *Hebrid-Isles,*
> Plac'd far amid the melancholy Main.

Thomson had seen no more of the Hebrides than of the Sahara or Lapland, but the Hebrides are in Scotland. The emotional element to be found in all his nature pictures in ***The Seasons*** is their most characteristic quality.

He begins his ***Winter*** by describing the delight which as a boy he took in wandering over the hilly country near his home in frost and snow:

> Pleas'd, have I, in my cheerful Morn of Life,
> When, nurs'd by careless *Solitude,* I liv'd,
> And sung of Nature with unceasing Joy,
> Pleas'd, have I wander'd thro' your rough Domains;
> Trod the pure, virgin, Snows, my self as pure:
> Heard the Winds roar, and the big Torrent burst:
> Or seen the deep, fermenting, Tempest brew'd,
> In the red, evening, Sky.—Thus pass'd the Time,
> Till, thro' the opening Chambers of the South,
> Look'd out the joyous *Spring,* look'd out, and smil'd.

He knows the

> sensations sweet
> Felt in the blood, and felt along the heart,

that are given by the "beauteous forms" of Nature; but that other gift "of aspect more sublime" which Wordsworth speaks of in *Tintern Abbey* Thomson does not reveal. He remains the observer and lover of nature. Her secrets have to be won from her; she is not an *active* teacher; we have to draw our own lessons from what she provides. "I know no subject more elevating, more amusing", he says, "more ready to awake the poetical enthusiasm, the philosophical reflection, and the moral sentiment, than the works of Nature." He will

> solitary court
> Th' inspiring Breeze; and meditate the Book
> Of Nature, ever open, aiming thence,
> Warm from the Heart, to learn the moral Song.

He meditates the book of Nature. His interests are partly intellectual, partly moral, and we shall agree that what he says comes "warm from the heart".

The emotional bearings of Nature on man are his true theme. The fault of Pope's early poems, his *Pastorals* and his *Windsor Forest,* was that they were too purely descriptive. . . . They do not give us the clue to his own mood. That was the great lesson which Thomson taught the nature poets of the eighteenth century. Johnson has put it in a memorable sentence: "The reader of *The Seasons* wonders that he never saw before what Thomson shews him, and that he never yet has felt what Thomson impresses" [see excerpt dated 1781]. But of all Thomson's critics I think that Hazlitt is still the best. Like other Englishmen he did not appreciate Thomson's language, but it could not hide from him the poet. "Thomson", he says,

> is the best of our descriptive poets, for he gives most of the poetry of natural description. Others have been quite equal to him, or have surpassed him, as Cowper for instance, in the picturesque part of his art, in marking the peculiar features and curious details of objects;—no one has yet come up to him in giving the sum total of their effects, their varying influences on the mind. . . . Nature in his descriptions is seen growing around us, fresh and lusty as in itself. . . . In a word, he describes not to the eye

alone, but to the other senses, and to the whole man. He puts his heart into his subject, writes as he feels, and humanises whatever he touches" [see excerpt dated 1818].

High praise, and the more remarkable as it was written when Hazlitt was familiar with the poetry of Wordsworth. But Wordsworth is not primarily a descriptive poet. He has an unsurpassed power of suggesting a scene in a few words, but he soon takes us far beyond it. The art of Thomson remains purposely pictorial; and this is true of the best nature poetry of the century.

Treating Nature pictorially, he presents it as a background to human activity, the scene on which man has his being. It was more than a background to Wordsworth. But I would suggest that it is not more than a background to most of us, and that even among Wordsworth's most ardent admirers there are few who can bring themselves to think of it habitually, or for any length of time, as he did. (pp. 64-9)

David Nichol Smith, "Thomson—Burns," in his Some Observations of Eighteenth Century Poetry, *1937. Reprint by University of Toronto Press, 1964, pp. 56-81.*

Marjorie Hope Nicolson (essay date 1946)

[*Nicholson is an American educator and literary scholar whose writings include* Newton Demands the Muse: Newton's Opticks and the Eighteenth Century Poets *(1946) and* Mountain Gloom and Mountain Glory: The Development of the Aesthetics of the Infinite *(1959). In the following excerpt from the first-named work, she identifies Thomson as the preeminent literary exponent of Sir Isaac Newton's theory of light, focusing upon the importance of color and light symbolism in* The Seasons.]

The profound symbolism which Milton felt in light is too familiar to be rehearsed at length. In part because of his philosophic and poetic heritage, in part because of his blindness, Light remained to him remote, godlike, awful. It was both the essence of divinity and the garment of Deity—"dark with excessive light Thy skirts appear." The "Author of all Being" was the

Fountain of Light, thyself invisible
Amidst the glorious brightness where thou sitt'st
Thron'd inaccessible.

No single passage from *Paradise Lost* was more familiar to the eighteenth century poets than the invocation in Book III:

Hail, holy Light, offspring of Heaven first-born!
Or of th' Eternal coeternal beam
May I express thee unblamed? since God is light,
And never but in unapproached light,
Dwelt from eternity, dwelt then in thee,
Bright effluence of bright essence increate!
Or hear'st thou rather pure ethereal stream,
Whose fountain who shall tell? before the Sun,
Before the Heavens, thou wert, and at the voice
Of God, as with a mantle didst invest
The rising world of waters dark and deep,
Won from the void and formless infinite!

Echoes of that invocation, with phrases from other prologues and from Satan's address to the Sun, recur constantly among the later poets. Yet the differences are as striking as the similarities. Thomson, Savage, Mallett, did not forget Milton but they also remembered Newton. They reminded their readers that the ultimate source of light is God, but they were even more aware that the immediate source of light is the sun, a physical body which, in spite of its pre-eminence in the solar system, is nevertheless responsive to laws of nature which man had come to comprehend. (pp. 20-1)

Newton might say that, thanks to his prism, the "Science of Colours" had become a truly mathematical speculation, but the interest of the descriptive poets in the *Opticks* had nothing to do with mathematics. It is no exaggeration to say that Newton gave color back to poetry from which it had almost fled during the period of Cartesianism. Like Galileo before him and Locke after him, Descartes had regarded the primary qualities of size, shape, figure as the only inherent properties of natural objects or of the ultimate atoms. Until Newton's experiments the geometrical conception of nature had not been extended to color. Although . . . the "Newtonian philosophy" came to be involved with the Cartesian and the Lockean, there is no question that the first effect of Newton's resolution of the colors and his careful analyses of their properties was to produce a new scientific grasp of a richer world of objective phenomena peculiarly sympathetic to poets.

To the descriptive poets of the Age of Newton, light was the source of beauty because it was the source of color. This is a persistent refrain in the period. While light was glorious in itself, it was most immediately and obviously beautiful when it was refracted into color, affording beauty, as Glover said, to Nature's otherwise "unadorned face":

whatever charms,
Whatever beauties bloom on Nature's face,
Proceed from thy all-influencing light.

(pp. 22-3)

With Newtonian eyes, the poets discovered new beauties in the most familiar aspects of nature, which had always been the stuff of poetry: in individual colors seen through the prism, in the rainbow, in sunrise and sunset, in the succession of colors throughout the day. There entered into eighteenth century descriptive poetry what might be called a "symbolism of the spectrum," which came to its height in Thomson, yet which was suggested by various poets. Sometimes the prismatic colors were described by and for themselves. . . . Immediately following the description of the "whitening undistinguished blaze" of light [in **"To the Memory of Sir Isaac Newton,"** Thomson] introduced the "gorgeous train Of parent colours":

First the flaming red
Sprung vivid forth; the tawny orange next;
And next delicious yellow; by whose side
Fell the kind beams of all-refreshing green.
Then the pure blue, that swells autumnal skies,
Ethereal played; and then, of sadder hue,
Emerged the deepened indigo, as when

The heavy-skirted evening droops with frost;
While the last gleamings of refracted light
Died in the fainting violet away.

Other poets called the roll of colors in connection with gems. . . . Carew's stones came to him from Exodus; their symbolism was as old as the language of flowers, drawn from astrology, physiology, legend, and superstition. William Thompson in the eighteenth century drew his heavenly gems from the Apocalypse, but combined Scripture with Newtonian science; the laws of refraction held in heaven as on earth. . . . (pp. 25-7)

No poet combined the Newtonian science with gems so deftly and charmingly as did James Thomson. In ***Summer,*** the light which streams from the central sun affects every part of nature, animate and inanimate. Diving beneath the "surface of the enlivened earth," into the "embowelled cavern . . . darting deep" it wakens the precious stones:

The unfruitful rock itself, impregned by thee,
In dark retirement forms the lucid stone.
The lively diamond drinks thy purest rays,
Collected light compact. . . .
At thee the ruby lights its deepening glow,
And with a waving radiance inward flames.
From thee the sapphire, solid ether, takes
Its hue cerulean; and, of evening tinct,
The purple-streaming amethyst is thine.
With thy own smile the yellow topaz burns;
Nor deeper verdure dyes the robe of Spring,
When first she gives it to the southern gale,
Than the green emerald shows. But, all combined,
Thick through the whitening opal play thy beams;
Or, flying from its surface, form
A trembling variance of revolving hues
As the site varies in the gazer's hand.

Here are the red, yellow, green, blue, violet of the spectrum, but here is also something much more subtle and charming—the resolution of light into colors, and the return of colors back to light. Thomson begins with the white light of the diamond, watches in the spectrum the ruby's red, the yellow of the topaz, the green of the emerald, the "hue cerulean" of the sapphire, and the purple of the amethyst, with its evening tint. All the colors come together in the "whitening opal," which dimly reflects each of them, and which begins to return them to the white light from which they were derived.

Sometimes the poets, instead of merely calling the catalogue of the colors, showed themselves pondering vari-

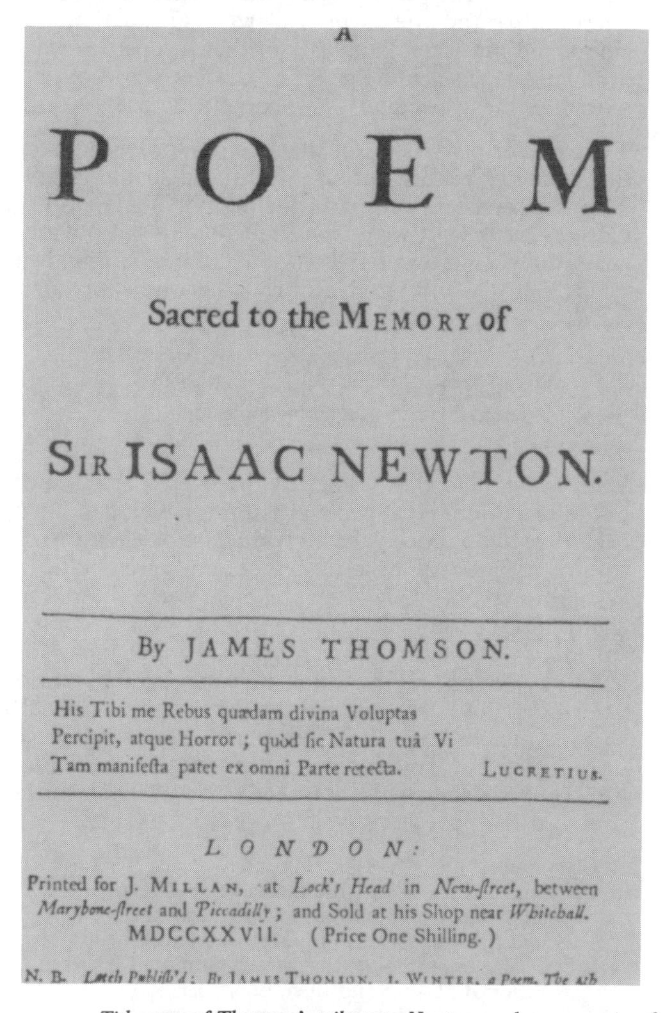

A

POEM

Sacred to the MEMORY of

SIR ISAAC NEWTON.

By JAMES THOMSON.

His Tibi me Rebus quædam divina Voluptas
Percipit, atque Horror; quòd sic Natura tuâ Vi
Tam manifesta patet ex omni Parte retecta. LUCRETIUS.

LONDON:

Printed for J. MILLAN, at *Lock's Head* in *New-street*, between *Marybone-street* and *Piccadilly*; and Sold at his Shop near *Whitehall*.
MDCCXXVII. (Price One Shilling.)

N. B. *Lately Publish'd*: By JAMES THOMSON. 1. WINTER, *a Poem. The 4th*

Title page of Thomson's tribute to Newton, and an engraving from The Seasons, *of Newton's monument in Westminster Abbey.*

ous associations of Newton's prismatic discoveries. (pp. 27-9)

Most obviously, of course, the prism was associated by poets with "Newton's rainbow," for in spite of Newton's own careful statement about his predecessors, the rainbow was and remained Newton's. To the eighteenth century poets, as to Keats, Newton alone had explained and unwoven it. Both Glover and Thomson introduced the rainbow into their tributes to Newton immediately after describing the prismatic colors. Glover wrote:

> and hence when vernal rains
> Descending swift have burst the low'ring clouds,
> Thy splendors through the dissipating mists
> In its fair vesture of unnumber'd hues
> Array the show'ry bow.

Thomson, too, had turned from the spectrum to the rainbow [in his poem **"To the Memory of Sir Isaac Newton"**]:

> These, when the clouds distil the rosy shower,
> Shine out distinct adown the watery bow;
> While o'er our heads the dewy vision bends
> Delightful, melting on the fields beneath.
> Myriads of mingling dyes from these result,
> And myriads still remain—infinite source
> Of beauty, ever flushing, ever new.

The poem on Newton was written in 1727; in the following year Thomson described the Newtonian rainbow in ***Spring***:

> Meantime, refracted from yon eastern cloud,
> Bestriding earth, the grand ethereal bow
> Shoots up immense; and every hue unfolds,
> In fair proportion running from the red
> To where the violet fades into the sky.
> Here, awful Newton, the dissolving clouds
> Form, fronting on the sun, thy showery prism;
> And to the sage-instructed eye unfold
> The various twine of light, by thee disclosed
> From the white mingling blaze.

In his description of the rainbow, as in his comet-passage in ***Summer,*** Thomson contrasted the attitude of the "fond sequacious herd" who feared the comet and the swain who "runs to catch the falling glory" of the rainbow with that of the "enlightened few Whose godlike minds philosophy exalts." The difference between Thomson and Keats is not entirely one of period, for Shelley would have agreed with Thomson. One adjective, used by both Thomson and Keats, is significant. Keats said in *Lamia*: "There was an *awful rainbow* once in heaven." Thomson used the same adjective with different connotation: "Here, *awful Newton* . . ." We are not yet ready to consider one implication which might be read into those passages—that the "awe" felt by the eighteenth century poets was less for a miracle of God than for the thinking mind of man which had come to comprehend laws of nature, whether in the rainbow or the "law of love" of the planets. To Keats glory and loveliness passed away when scientists attempted to strip Nature and leave her exposed and bare. In his mind the eighteenth century poets had "taken on the mysteries of things as if they were God's spies"; they, like Newton, had destroyed the poetry of the rainbow by reducing it to its prismatic form. Yet there is one glory of the moon, another of the sun—and the eighteenth century poets adored the greater luminary, symbol of Light, symbol of Reason, the "Newtonian Sun." The sun was never more beautiful to them than when it shone in full meridian splendor, its light streaming through ether in straight lines, refracted as little as possible by atmosphere, cloud, or mist. They delighted in their own intellectual maturity, feeling that they had outgrown the childlike attitude of the simple swain who seeks a pot of gold, or of Noah, to whom the rainbow was miracle. They did not believe that Newton had taken beauty from poetry; he had added new beauty, because he had added new truth. (pp. 30-2)

No poet of the mid-century . . . responded to Newtonian color and light more fully than did Thomson in ***The Seasons,*** and no other poet so well used the new techniques.

Standing upon Greenwich Hill, as he pondered Newton's discovery of the nature of color and light, James Thomson watched a sunset—as he had watched a rainbow—with Newtonian eyes:

> Even now the setting sun and shifting clouds,
> Seen, Greenwich, from thy lovely heights, declare
> How just, how beauteous the refractive law.

The "justice" and the "beauty" of Newtonian law is a recurrent motif in Thomson's poetry. As philosophical and as scientific as the professed "philosophical" and "scientific" poets we shall later consider, Thomson was nevertheless primarily a poet, with a poet's need for and response to beauty. He admired the surpassing intellectual attainments of "Newton . . . our philosophic sun," "Newton, pure intelligence, whom God To mortals lent to trace his boundless works"; he recognized the fact that Newton's scientific genius consisted in his formulation of "laws divinely simple":

> O unprofuse magnificence divine!
> O wisdom truly perfect! thus to call
> From a few causes such a scheme of things
> Effects so various, beautiful, and great.

But as poet, he never ceased to stress the fact that, while the "effects" were various and great, they were also poetically beautiful.

In ***The Seasons,*** because of the very subject he set himself, Thomson was almost equally concerned with color and light. While he used all the colors of the spectrum, some were more significant than others. Indigo appears only once or twice; orange is almost conspicuous by its absence, as indeed it is in English landscape, though we might expect to find it more often than we do in his exotic tropical scenes. Red is often used, usually associated with morning; "violet, darkly blue," with few exceptions, is an evening color. Green, of course, is persistent in the poem, as it is in nature; it was a color in which Thomson found special pleasure. While red and violet might be either beautiful or ominous, green—with a single exception—was a happy color. "Moist, bright, and green, the landscape laughs around"; in the Golden Age of the World, spring "greened all the year." "Gay green" was the chief color of the "vivid verdure" and the "various hues" of "vernant earth":

chiefly thee, gay green!
Thou smiling Nature's universal robe!
United light and shade! where the sight dwells
With growing strength and ever-new delight.

More important, from the point of view of the *Opticks,* is Thomson's treatment of azure and yellow. Rarely did Thomson use "azure" and "blue" interchangeably. "Azure" was associated correctly with the sky, and, like Newton, Thomson used it to describe the clarity of ethereal light in which there is a minimum of refraction by moisture:

The lessening cloud,
The kindling azure, and the mountain's brow,
Illumined with fluid gold, his near approach
Betoken glad.

After a summer storm:

As from the face of Heaven the shattered clouds
Tumultuous rove, the interminable sky
Sublimer swells, and o'er the world expands
A purer azure.

In ***Autumn,*** as the "fierce effulgence" of summer departs and mists begin to rise, azure imperceptibly changes to "a serener blue," which "with golden light enlivened wide invests the happy world."

Of all colors, the "golden light" of yellow was most beautiful to Thomson; it occurs most frequently in ***The Seasons,*** and seems to have possessed a kind of mystical significance. In Spring we see the "woods with yellow lustre bright," and

a yellow mist,
Far smoking o'er the interminable plain,
In twinkling myriads lights the dewy gems.

In ***Summer*** the "valleys float with golden waves"; the mountain brow is "illumined with fluid gold"; later, "Autumn's yellow lustre gilds the world." In the rainbow, the "glittering robe of joy" is "set off abundant by the yellow ray." Newton, too, in the *Opticks,* had frequently paused over yellow, calling attention to the facts that so-called "white light," is usually "yellow light," that homogeneal yellow, with its heterogeneal companion orange, is "the most luminous of the Prismatick Colours . . . in the Focus of those Rays which are in the middle of the orange and yellow; there where the Colour is most luminous and fulgent. . . . " In yellow Thomson felt the radiance of light: "With thine own smile the yellow topaz burns." On the one hand, yellow as a color was beautiful; on the other, in its effulgence it approached sublimity. But we are not yet ready to distinguish between the "Sublime" and the "Beautiful" in light and color.

More than any of the other poets, Thomson developed what has been called the "symbolism of the spectrum." We have already seen him following the colors through the spectrum: "flaming red," "tawny orange," "delicious yellow," "all-refreshing green," "pure blue," "and then, of sadder hue . . . the deepened indigo," associated with the "heavy-skirted evening" and with frost as "the last gleamings of refracted light Died in the fainting violet away." We have seen, too, that he played delightedly with the spectrum in his lines on gems and on the rainbow, in which the same general symbolism was implied. In his gem-passage, Thomson went still further, indicating not only the emergence of colors from pure light in the diamond, but their return to white light in the opal. Is it to consider too curiously to find the same symbolism in ***The Seasons*** as a whole? As spring emerges from the icy arms of winter, we are conscious that

Whate'er the Wintry frost
Nitrous prepared, the various-blossomed Spring.
Put in white promise forth.

Spring "lifts the white clouds sublime, and spreads them thin, Fleecy, and white." "Fair-handed Spring . . . throws out the snowdrop and the crocus first"; the "hawthorn whitens"; only as spring progresses do "the varied colours run." Throughout the rest of "Spring," and throughout ***The Seasons*** as a whole, we almost forget white in nature until in ***Winter*** the year dies away, as it began, in the whiteness of snow, glittering frost, and ice. But we need not overlabor this particular analogy, which, while it actually exists in nature in northern climes, may not have occurred to James Thomson. Certainly the "symbolism of the spectrum" appears often in Thomson's sequence of colors in an individual day from the reds of dawn through the spectrum to the "sad violet" of evening, when color vanishes into darkness in which all colors are temporarily lost. Thomson was too good an artist to labor his symbolism obviously, but in at least one "Season," he followed the device of breaking white light into color, and returning his colors again to white light. Morning in ***Summer*** begins:

The meek-eyed morn appears, mother of dews,
At first faint-gleaming in the dappled east;
Till far o'er ether spreads the widening glow,
And, from before the lustre of her face,
White break the clouds away.

After running the gamut of colors and the succession of lights, day ends; "low walks the sun . . . gives one bright glance, then total disappears":

sober Evening takes
Her wonted station in the middle air,
A thousand shadows at her beck. First this
She sends on earth; then that of deeper dye
Steals soft behind; and then a deeper still,
In circle following circle, gathers round
To close the face of things.

As in the morning we were first conscious of white, so for a moment before total darkness blots out nature, we momentarily see whiteness again:

Wide o'er the thistly lawn, as swells the breeze,
A whitening shower of vegetable down
Amusive floats.

Thomson was a poet of color, but he was still more a poet of light. Like his master Milton, whose influence is clear throughout his poetry, he was even more susceptible to light than to color and read into it deeper symbolic meaning. His apostrophe to Light in ***Summer,*** if taken from its context, seems only a paraphrase of Milton's invocations:

Prime cheerer, Light!
Of all material beings first and best!
Efflux divine. Nature's resplendent robe,
Without whose vesting beauty all were wrapt
In unessential gloom; and thou, O Sun!
Soul of surrounding worlds! in whom best seen
Shines out thy Maker! may I sing of thee? . . .
How shall I then attempt to sing of Him
Who, Light Himself, in uncreated light
Invested deep, dwells awfully retired
From mortal eye or angel's purer ken;
Whose single smile has, from the first of time,
Filled overflowing all those lamps of heaven
That beam forever through the boundless sky.

Yet as Thomson followed the progress of light throughout a day or watched it at night, he showed an exactness of expression and an accuracy of observation which marks him as a Newtonian poet. Sometimes the exactness lies in his careful employment of terms which, formerly vague in poets, had now become technical. A good example may be found in his use of the word "ether." Newton himself. . . had said [in his *Opticks*]: "I do not know what this Aether is," yet his long discussions of ether and its function in connection with the transmission of light made the intelligent layman self-conscious in the use of the word, particularly in discriminating between "ether" and "atmosphere" or "air." Milton's Attendant Spirit in *Comus* had descended from "regions mild of calm and serene *air*"; Satan upon his interplanetary journey "winds with ease Through the pure marble *air* his oblique way"; as he stood upon the sun, "the *air,* Nowhere so clear, sharpened his visual ray." To Thomson, Summer, "child of the Sun," came "from brightening fields of *ether* fair-disclosed"; his distinction between "ether" and "air" or "atmosphere" may be seen in many careful descriptions of the effect of clouds, mists, or fogs upon light. As a storm gathers in spring:

the effusive South
Warms the wide air, and o'er the void of heaven
Breathes the big clouds with vernal showers distent.
At first a dusky wreath they seem to rise,
Scarce staining ether; but by fast degrees,
In heaps on heaps the doubling vapour sails
Along the loaded sky, and mingling deep
Sits on the horizon round a settled gloom.

In ***Winter***:

Hung o'er the farthest verge of heaven, the sun
Scarce spreads o'er ether the dejected day.
Faint are his gleams, and ineffectual shoot
His struggling rays in horizontal lines
Through the thick air; as clothed in cloudy storm,
Weak, wan, and broad, he skirts the southern sky.

Even more exact is a description in ***Autumn***:

Meantime, light shadowing all, a sober calm
Fleeces unbounded ether; whose least wave
Stands tremulous, uncertain where to turn
The gentle current; while, illumined wide,
The dewy-skirted clouds imbibe the sun,
And through their lucid veil his softened force
Shed o'er the peaceful world.

Elsewhere in ***The Seasons*** a difference which we feel between Milton and Thomson in their treatment of light is the result of the fact that Thomson took for granted not only that light travels at incredible speed, but that it is everywhere diffused in the luminiferous ether. Satan, on his journey from world to world, believed that there were limits to light, as he found in the "dark illimitable ocean, without bound, Without dimension," that "hoary Deep" stretching beyond Hell, and in the "dark world" of Limbo, where he wandered long in gloom "till at least a gleam Of dawning light turned thitherward in haste His travelled steps." And for all Milton's interest in the Galilean astronomy, reflected in passing references in these very scenes, Satan on his visit to the sun harked back to such fictional hardy mariners as those of Lucian, who seemed as comfortable in the blazing sun as in the Hesperian isles. Nowhere did Satan indicate any discomfort as he stood in the full splendor of the "magnetic beam, that gently warms The universe"; yet this is the same Satan who so short a time before had used his tall spear "to support uneasy steps Over the burning marle," for "such resting found The sole of unblest feet"! Satan was child enough of the seventeenth century to show a keen intellectual interest in the light of the sun, which he could now observe empirically:

The place he found beyond expression bright,
Compared with aught on Earth, metal or stone—
Not all parts like, but all alike informed
With radiant light, as glowing iron with fire. . . .
Here matter new to gaze the Devil met
Undazzled.

But, in the eighteenth century, when the "soaring soul" of Newton sailed among the spheres and flew "through those endless worlds He here so well descried," he traveled among the "radiant tracts on high" with the speed of light itself, through a universe in which light was never-ceasing, until, at journey's end, he was greeted by the "sons of light":

Thy swift career is with the whirling orbs,
Comparing things with things, in rapture lost,
And grateful adoration for that light
So plenteous rayed into thy mind below
From Light Himself.

Summer is, of course, the book of ***The Seasons*** in which Thomson's descriptions of light and of the sun are most frequent, and in which reminiscences of the Newtonian theories most abound.

Yonder comes the powerful king of day. . . .
Aslant the dew-bright earth and coloured air,
He looks in boundless majesty abroad,
And sheds the shining day, that burnished plays. . . .

To the sun's light and heat all nature responds, but as day goes on, heat and light become excessive:

'Tis raging noon; and vertical, the sun
Darts on the head direct his forceful rays.
O'er heaven and earth, far as the ranging eye

Can sweep, a dazzling deluge reigns; and all
From pole to pole is undistinguished blaze.

Yet the light and heat of a northern climate are as nothing in comparison with the power of the sun in the torrid zone: "Climes unrelenting! with whose rage compared, Yon blaze is feeble and yon skies are cool," where

the bright effulgent sun,
Rising direct, swift chases from the sky
The short-lived twilight, and with ardent blaze
Looks gaily fierce o'er all the dazzling air.

In temperate zones, even on the hottest day of midsummer, late afternoon and evening bring relief from the excess of light and heat:

The Sun has lost his rage; his downward orb
Shoots nothing now but animating warmth
And vital lustre; that with various ray,
Lights up the clouds, those beauteous robes of heaven,
Incessant rolled into romantic shapes,
The dream of waking fancy. . . .
Low walks the sun, and broadens by degrees,
Just o'er the verge of day. The shifting clouds,
Assembled gay, a richly-gorgeous train,
In all their pomp attend his setting throne.
Air, earth, and ocean smile immense. And now
As if his weary chariot sought the bowers
Of Amphitrite and her tending nymphs,
(So Grecian fable sung) he dips his orb;
Now half-immersed; and now, a golden curve,
Gives one bright glance, then total disappears.

Thomson's observations of light gleaming through darkness are only less frequent than his descriptions of light during the day. Meteors, the "lambent lightning," a comet, the moon and the stars, even the glow-worm, are described with eighteenth century accuracy:

When from the pallid sky the Sun descends,
With many a spot, that o'er his glaring orb
Uncertain wanders, stained; red fiery streaks
Begin to flush around. The reeling clouds
Stagger with dizzy poise, as doubting yet
Which master to obey; while, rising slow,
Blank in the leaden-coloured east, the moon
Wears a wan circle round her blunted horns.
Seen through the turbid fluctuating air,
The stars obtuse emit a shivering ray;
Or frequent seem to shoot athwart the gloom,
And long behind them trail the whitening blaze.

Thomson's moon in ***Autumn*** was his heritage from a long line of scientific ancestors, beginning with Galileo, culminating in Newton; yet "oft, as if her head she bowed, stooping through a fleecy cloud," she is reminiscent too of Milton:

Meanwhile the moon,
Full-orbed and breaking through the scattered clouds,
Shows her broad visage in the crimsoned east.
Turned to the sun direct, her spotted disk
(Where mountains rise, umbrageous dales descend,
And caverns deep, as optic tube descries)
A smaller earth, gives all his blaze again,
Void of its flame, and sheds a softer day.
Now through the passing cloud she seems to stoop,
Now up the pale cerulean rides sublime.
Wide the pale deluge floats, and streaming mild
O'er the skied mountain to the shadowy vale,
While rocks and floods reflect the quivering gleam,
The whole air whitens with a boundless tide
Of silver radiance, trembling round the world.

Thomson, however, was not only a "Newtonian" descriptive poet. Like his contemporaries, he was upon occasion both a "scientific" and a "philosophic" poet. He pondered both the physics of light and the physics of sight; he was aware of aesthetic and metaphysical implications which he and others read into the *Opticks.* (pp. 42-54)

Marjorie Hope Nicolson, "Color and Light in the Descriptive Poets," in her Newton Demands the Muse: Newton's "Opticks" and the Eighteenth Century Poets, *Princeton University Press, 1946, pp. 20-54.*

George Sherburn and Donald F. Bond (essay date 1948)

[*Sherburn's critical writings include* The Early Popularity of Milton's Early Poems *(1920) and* The Early Career of Alexander Pope *(1934). In the following excerpt from a work first published in 1948, Sherburn and Bond provide an overview of Thomson's works, with reference to the historical, social, and philosophical background of English literature of the first half of the eighteenth century.*]

James Thomson (1700-1748) was much influenced by [the Miltonic] literary traditions, which reinforced a true love of natural scenery, acquired from the Scottish lowlands where he was born. . . . He had in David Mallet and others good friends who encouraged his bent to poetry, which he had manifested as early as 1720 by then publishing three poems in the *Edinburgh Miscellany.* One of these, *Of a Country Life* (in couplets), was prophetic of ***The Seasons.*** Mallet and Thomson exchanged manuscripts and criticized each other's verses during these years when Thomson was writing *The Seasons* and Mallet his *Excursion* (1728). They remained lifelong friends. ***The Seasons*** (1726-30) established Thomson's fame. . . . (p. 935)

The Seasons is both descriptive and philosophical in nature. Moral reflection was indispensable, but description was what gave novelty and charm. Even landscape painters of the time always placed somewhere in their canvases human figures: Aristotle had announced that men in action were the proper subjects of poetry. Mere description, with no attention to manners, was juvenile. In 1756, writing about Pope, Joseph Warton remarked "that description of the external beauties of nature, is usually the first effort of a young genius, before he hath studied manners and passions." Warton may here be laboring under the prejudice of Pope's opinion that youth was the time

When pure description held the place of sense;

but the opinion lasts on, and Gibbon, for example, in his *Essai sur l'Étude de la Littérature* (1761) thought "the external beauties of nature" were not advantageous if used as substance rather than ornament.

By enlarging ***The Seasons*** in successive revisions Thomson made them increasingly episodic. ***Winter*** first appeared, in 1726, as a poem of 405 lines; it went through several editions with augmentation: in the first collected edition of ***The Seasons*** (1730) it included 787 lines and in its final revised edition (1746) had 1069 lines. Similarly ***Summer,*** which in the first edition had 1146 lines, grew to 1805; ***Spring*** (1728) and ***Autumn,*** which, with the important ***Hymn to the Seasons,*** appeared first in the collected edition of 1730, each added about 100 lines. The evolution of the final text is complicated, but the essential structure, of which Thomson was perhaps more careful than most authors of his day who produced works of similar length, remained fairly fixed. ***Autumn*** and ***Winter*** are organized on a loose narrative pattern, following the progress of the season in time. ***Summer*** presents a typical day, with passages devoted to dawn, forenoon, noon, and so on through sunset to contemplation of the nightly stars and Serene Philosophy. ***Spring,*** finally, presents the effects of the season on the rising scale of being: "on inanimate matter, on vegetables, on brute animals, and last on Man; concluding with a dissuasive from the wild and irregular passion of Love, opposed to that of a pure and happy kind." There is, obviously, in all four poems an expository as well as a descriptive purpose, and these devices of organization are hardly more than strings upon which to hang episodes or individual landscapes. Even the episodes may be organized for expository purposes: in ***Winter*** the reflections on poverty (lines 322-388), appended to the brief death of the husbandman frozen in the snow, arouse sentiments of sympathy just as in the same poem the famous passage on the robin (lines 245-256) dramatizes the sympathy that should exist between man and the lower animate creation.

Thomson has doubtless favorite ideas that he wishes to express; but in his choice of materials for description it is hard to find favorite scenes. Forest, river, sky, sea, plains, mountains, meadows, valleys, flowers, and animals, are all presented with an equal eye in varying aspects: the mass of detail is most inclusive. It has been urged that his repeated use of the epithet "horrid" for mountains expresses a conventional dislike rather than a romantic love of the rougher aspects of landscape. But the truth seems to be that he felt sympathy for titanic as well as for intimate details. He ranges from "the repercussive roar" of thunder to a thoroughly sentimental treatment of the domestic animals: "rapturous terror" and "generous purpose" are both characteristic of his moods. Familiarity was no pedantic requisite: he gives us the wolves of the Alps and Apennines and the sand storms of the desert along with the British countryside. In general his descriptive passages are marked by motion and change and are not composed pictures of landscapes. There is a keen love of varying light and shade, of changing mood and shifting color. His colors are treated definitely in a kaleidoscopic fashion, as onc sees in his apostrophe to the sun in ***Summer:***

> At thee the ruby lights its deepening glow,
> And with a waving radiance inward flames.
> From thee the sapphire, solid ether, takes
> Its hue cerulean; and, of evening tinct,
> The purple-streaming amethyst is thine.
> With thy own smile the yellow topaz burns;
> Nor deeper verdure dyes the robe of Spring,
> When first she gives it to the southern gale,
> Than the green emerald shows.

Such lines are typical also of the large vague effects that he loves. He is seldom minutely particular, but he is capable both of massing specific detail and of a realistic observation unusual, and practically unknown, in his time:

> not a breath
> Is heard to quiver through the closing woods,
> Or rustling turn the many-twinkling leaves
> Of aspen tall.

Coupled with his love of motion is an exuberance in the presentation of his details that is highly significant: in Thomson it is the plenitude rather than the order of nature that arouses enthusiasm—though both principles are felt. His picture of man in the primitive state of the Golden Age "replete with bliss" as well as the benevolent aspect of nature itself is full of this mood:

> Clear shone the skies, cooled with eternal gales,
> And balmy spirit all. The youthful sun
> Shot his best rays, and still the gracious clouds
> Dropped fatness down; as o'er the swelling mead
> The herds and flocks commixing played secure.
> This when, emergent from the gloomy wood,
> The glaring lion saw, his horrid heart
> Was meekened, and he joined his sullen joy.
> For music held the whole in perfect peace:
> Soft sighed the flute; the tender voice was heard,
> Warbling the varied heart; the woodlands round
> Applied their quire; and winds and waters flowed
> In consonance. Such were those prime of days.

Many passages like this, better in feeling than in poetic expression, suggest reflective processes going on behind the descriptions. Thomson observes and loves details in external nature; he does not much depend on the nostalgic love of scenes once dear in childhood, such as Goldsmith later was to feel for "Sweet Auburn," and he has less of the mere sense of the picturesque in nature than had Dyer and perhaps others of his day. Fundamentally his love of nature is in a large sense philosophic. There is, to be sure, a religious aspect in it, seen in the appended **"Hymn to the Seasons"** and in various passages such as ***Summer,*** lines 185-191, in which he echoes the Psalmist's theme, "All Thy works praise Thee!" This idea, much used by deistical believers in natural religion, may perhaps be called the basic warrant for the mass of descriptive detail Thomson lovingly presents. There is, however, an added attitude, derived from the physico-theologists like John Ray and William Derham, the scientific theologians like Sir Isaac Newton, and such widely read works as Shaftesbury's *Moralists.* It is difficult to disentangle the various strands of influence here involved: Shaftesbury contributes the vague enthusiasm for contemplation of nature; the more scientific writers support a rational reflection upon the divine *teachings* of nature. Nature is a book to be reverentially studied:

> To me be Nature's volume broad displayed;
> And to peruse its all-instructing page,

Or, haply catching inspiration thence,
Some easy passage, raptured, to translate,
My sole delight.

Thomson has the curiosity of a scientist. The passage quoted about the sun and its gem-like diffractions is not merely a passage delighting in color: it has behind it notions as to the origin of precious stones. Many times Thomson insists that the study of nature frees us from the credulous superstition of the ignorant. He appended his **"Hymn to the Seasons"** as an important justification and explanation of the rational purpose that he fuses with enthusiastic delight in nature. It is this latter that now captures romantic critics: in his own day the philosophy was probably of equal importance.

Thomson's favorite ideas occur in poems other than ***The Seasons.*** While writing these four poems he had published some smaller pieces, two of which are notable. His **"Hymn on Solitude,"** published in James Ralph's *Miscellaneous Poems by Several Hands* (1729), is an evening piece contemplating nature somewhat more sedately than Theocles had done at dawn in *The Moralists.* Thomson here uses a simpler and more pleasing idiom than in ***The Seasons.*** So likewise in the other poem, **"To the Memory of Sir Isaac Newton"** (1727), the elegiac tone softens the blank verse, and enables the poet to pay dignified and worthy praise to the great scientist, to whom his mind owed so much stimulus.

It is, however, in ***Liberty,*** published in five parts in 1735-6, that Thomson most explicitly expresses ideas concerning society and government that had been incidental in ***The Seasons.*** The poem to Newton had been dedicated, apparently without due response, to Sir Robert Walpole, and though in sympathies a Whig, Thomson passed to the group of "Patriots" who under the guidance of Lyttelton were attacking the Walpole ministry. Thomson was an ardent nationalist and a sentimental benevolist: his political ideas followed somewhat the line of his Patriot group and somewhat that of his own contradictory personality. By nature indolent, he throughout his career praises industry perhaps more often than any poet has done. In ***Autumn*** there are several passages that enunciate the principle that

All is the gift of industry—whate'er
Exalts, embellishes, and renders life
Delightful.

And in the second part of his ***Castle of Indolence*** the Knight of Art and Industry is the rescuing hero. ***Liberty*** is in a sense a "progress piece," in which Thomson traces the development of civil liberty from Greece and Rome to Britain—and into the future prospects. His philosophy of history, like that of many of his contemporaries, involved a worship of primitive times and a belief, not so contradictory as it at first sight appears, in progress. The pristine days were the best man had known, but man could not retrace his steps: his best hope, then, was to "relume the ancient light" (as Pope phrased it) in some millennial day far ahead. With a divine origin behind him man could only work towards a heavenly city of the future. So Thomson repeatedly, in the best Whig fashion, condemns luxury, praises the simple virtues and the force of the arts, and, looking before and after, at times laments the decadence of man in the Walpole era and at times is optimistic concerning men, industry, and trade. Of course victims of an undue thirst for gold are, as he had shown in ***Summer,*** enemies of human progress:

Ill-fated race! the softening arts of peace,
Whate'er the humanizing muses teach,
The godlike wisdom of the tempered breast,
Progressive truth, the patient force of thought,
Investigation calm whose silent powers
Command the world, the light that leads to
Heaven,
Kind equal rule, the government of laws,
And all-protecting freedom which alone
Sustains the name and dignity of man—
These are not theirs.

Here and in many other passages speaks the spirit of Illumination. Thomson, like his patron Lord Talbot, was alive to the humanitarian movements of his day. As solicitor-general Lord Talbot had acted (1729) for the crown in the prosecution of Bambridge, the inhuman warden of Fleet prison, and thereafter Thomson more than once expressed enthusiasm for prison reform, and for the work of General Oglethorpe both in that respect and in regard to the colony of Georgia. Among other humane projects he praised, in the last, prophetic part of ***Liberty,*** the not yet realized project of Thomas Coram for a foundling hospital—

The dome resounding sweet with infant joy,
From famine saved, or cruel-handed shame.

After ***The Seasons*** Thomson wrote over a period of fifteen years five tragedies, which were staged with only moderate success. His final work of distinction was his ***Castle of Indolence,*** published a few weeks before his death in 1748. Somewhat deficient in action (it tells merely how the wizard Indolence enticed pilgrims into his castle, and how the Knight of Art and Industry liberated them), the poem is one of the best imitations of Spenserian melody and descriptive techniques in the language, and is by all odds metrically the most harmonious of Thomson's poems. It is rich in portraiture, and has fewer passages devoted to the prosaic topics treated in ***Liberty.*** The description of the castle and its environs at the opening of the poem is both admirable Spenser and admirable "atmosphere":

A pleasing land of drowsyhed it was:
Of dreams that wave before the half-shut eye;
And of gay castles in the clouds that pass,
For ever flushing round a summer sky:
There eke the soft delights, that witchingly
Instil a wanton sweetness through the breast,
And the calm pleasures always hovered nigh;
But whate'er smacked of noyance, or unrest,
Was far far off expelled from this delicious nest.

The life of the enchanted idle pilgrims is like a dream—

As when a shepherd of the Hebrid Isles,
Placed far amid the melancholy main,
(Whether it be lone fancy him beguiles,
Or that aerial beings sometimes deign
To stand embodied to our senses plain)
Sees on the naked hill, or valley low,
The whilst in ocean Phoebus dips his wain,
A vast assembly moving to and fro;

> Then all at once in air dissolves the wondrous
> show.

From this bit of supernaturalism the poet has some difficulty recalling himself without breaking the mood: he describes some of the rooms of the castle and with stanza lvi turns to sketching the characters of some of the idlers. These stanzas—very likely among the earliest to be written—sketch actual friends of the poet, and stanza lxviii (by a friend, except for the first line) portrays Thomson himself:

> A bard here dwelt, more fat than bard
> beseems. . . .

Obviously here we have left the abode of Indolence for some House of Good Fun, and the spell of "drowsyhed" is gone. Though lacking in substance, the poem is in many ways the author's most poetical effort.

The individuality and merit of Thomson's work can be easily grasped if one considers the moment at which ***The Seasons*** appeared. Their chief rivals in immediate vogue were the seven satires by Edward Young, called *Love of Fame,* and Pope's *Dunciad.* It was a moment when poets, animated by a desire to ennoble the poetic art, were "stooping to truth" and moralizing their songs; but while both Young and especially Pope were dealing with petty particularities, Thomson was dealing with more general and fundamentally moral subjects. If Pope was in part led to write satirical epistles because of the success of *Love of Fame,* it is conceivable that in writing his *Essay on Man,* which he began during the first vogue of ***The Seasons,*** he was influenced by Thomson. At least the two men are expressing very similar sets of ideas—the one in rather harsh and unmelodious "rhyme-unfetter'd verse," the other in smooth and polished couplets. But Thomson anticipated Pope in expressing the benevolism of Shaftesbury in verse, and he avoided some of Pope's difficulties by being vaguely optimistic and forbearing to attack head-on, so to speak, the problem of evil and of man's moral responsibility. Neither in blank verse nor in the Spenserian stanza was Thomson a pioneer, but his success helped to popularize these metres and to subvert the couplet. As description his work is vastly superior to *The Excursion* of his more ambitious and sensational friend Mallet. Thomson's excellence clearly lay in his sensitiveness to sense impressions and his confident use of such impressions: his blank verse is not smoothly rhythmed, and his diction is, like that of Young, greatly inferior to Pope's. Pope could never have passed a cacophonous line like

> Who nobly durst, in rhyme-unfetter'd verse;

and he would surely have pilloried (if ***Liberty*** had been written in time) the bathos of such another as

> And ventilated states renew their bloom.

Other oppressive artifices are his self-conscious compound epithets, which no page is without, and his love of polysyllabic monstrosities like *irriguous, contiguous, convolutions,* etc. Not Thomson's gifts of expression but rather his natural poetic sensitiveness that emerges in spite of the heavy-going style makes him a memorable part of the movement to reform poetry as the drama and prose style were being "reformed." In his preface to the second edition of ***Winter*** Thomson voices this objective:

> That there are frequent and notorious abuses of Poetry is as true as that the best things are most liable to that misfortune. . . . To insist no further on this head, let poetry once more be restored to her ancient truth and purity; let her be inspired from heaven, and in return her incense ascend thither; let her exchange her low, venal, trifling, subjects for such as are fair, useful and magnificent; and let her execute these so as at once to please, instruct, surprise, and astonish . . . and poets [shall] yet become the delight and wonder of mankind.

In certain aspects such ideals and Thomson's application of them to his work tend towards the romantic; they more clearly tend towards the quality that Matthew Arnold aptly called "high seriousness." (pp. 936-42)

George Sherburn and Donald F. Bond, "New Voices in Poetry," in their The Restoration and Eighteenth Century, 1660-1789, *Appleton-Century-Crofts, 1967, pp. 933-49.*

Patricia Meyer Spacks (essay date 1959)

[*Spacks is a literary scholar whose writings include* The Varied God: A Critical Study of Thomson's The Seasons *(1959),* The Insistence of Horror: Aspects of the Supernatural in Eighteenth-Century Poetry *(1962), and* The Poetry of Vision: Five Eighteenth-Century Poets (1967). *In the following excerpt from the first-named work, submitted for publication in 1958, she comments on Thomson's poetic diction, laying particular emphasis on his descriptive technique, and concluding that the description of nature "does not in* The Seasons *exist for its own sake, but as part of a larger scheme." In her opinion, Thomson is capable "of using natural description as part of his presentation of man and moral concerns."*]

There is no denying that Thomson used, in ***The Seasons,*** a thoroughly aureate style, one which sets up many barriers of communication for the modern reader. It is possible, however, to account for such a style, not only by tradition, but by a high poetic intention.

Tradition, to be sure, offers the most obvious explanations. The poet was influenced, first, by the general rhetorical tradition of his native Scotland. In his essay on Thomson [see excerpt dated 1937] David Nichol Smith points out that the educated man in Scotland has always been characterized by elaborate use of rhetoric; he strains for rhythm rather than wit. One element in this characteristically rhetorical style, and one most apparent in Thomson, is its predominantly Latin composition. This fact may be explained by reference to Scottish history:

> We are apt to forget the large place occupied by Latin in vernacular Scots. Latin was at one time as familiar to the educated Scot as his mother-tongue, and was his means of communication with foreigners. The Scot abroad made his way with Latin. The Scottish authors who were known abroad wrote in Latin . . . Latin words

> were bound to creep into the vernacular. More than that, Latin words have come into English from Scottish usage. . . . Here we have the explanation of why the Scottish historians and philosophers of the eighteenth century write in a style which seems to the English reader to be over-Latinized in vocabulary, and, as our school-masters know, is eminently suitable for conversion into Latin prose.

The same explanation accounts for many of the convolutions of Thomson's language.

The Latinate tradition, in its poetic aspects, had more important implications. The shadow of Virgil lay over the nature poets of the eighteenth century; the classic pastoral and georgic dominated many of their conceptions. Many words and phrases were borrowed or adapted from Virgil; by virtue of such words and phrases, Geoffrey Tillotson remarks [in *Essays in Criticism and Research* (1942)], "the nature-poems of the eighteenth century have a quality which is usually denied them, the quality of 'atmosphere.' The diction is coloured with Virgilian connotation." For the average modern reader, most of this connotation has vanished completely; the language seems dead, and its selection by writers presumably striving for poetic effect, virtually inexplicable. Yet a richness of allusion is inherent within the language of ***The Seasons;*** Thomson's choice of Virgil's language is not dissimilar in some respects to the tendency of such poets as Eliot and Pound today to enrich their works with excerpts from the literature of other lands and other generations. The difference between the two devices depends on expectation. The poets of the eighteenth century did not have to create the taste by which they were appreciated; the structure of Virgilian allusion was expected of anyone writing in the georgic or pastoral mode. This was an eighteenth-century tradition as well as a classic one, part of the structure of rules by which the successful poet must be governed. It is important to realize, however, that this structure had meaning: it was not a barren system constructed for its own sake. That its application of principles lacks universality may be a valid criticism, but the fact remains that the principle itself of extending the implications of poetry through the use of a system and vocabulary of proved value has also a certain validity.

An earlier English poet dominated by Latinate language patterns, whose model particularly appealed to Thomson in relation to his own poetic intention, was John Milton. The Miltonic elements in ***The Seasons*** have been frequently traced; Milton seems to have offered the clearest English standards of diction and verse for Thomson. The use of the Miltonic model, like many other aspects of the poet's diction, is closely related to the central purpose of glorifying God through attention to His works in nature. Milton had used exalted language for an exalted purpose in *Paradise Lost;* Thomson, with a different theme, had a similarly exalted purpose in ***The Seasons.*** He felt the need for a language of richness and color; perceiving in Milton the richness he desired, he transferred the Miltonic patterns as directly as possible to his own work. Lacking his master's genius, he frequently produced awkwardness rather than splendor, although he, too, sometimes succeeded in exploiting rolling syllables to their full value.

But the relation between Thomson's language and his theme is closer than that suggested by the somewhat vague concept of elevated diction for an elevated purpose. The vocabulary of stock words and phrases upon which he, like most of the poets of his time, drew heavily was for him in many ways especially appropriate. The early critics of Thomson condemn his diction for elaborateness, not for the emptiness that may seem apparent to modern readers. Doubtless they perceived no such emptiness. Much of what seems today simply figured language, with no value apart from that of custom, was then actually scientific and philosophic, a language of definition. ***The Seasons*** abounds in examples of such periphrases as "the scaly breed," "feathered race," "watery inhabitants." The modern critic is likely to feel that such phraseology, in place of the more forthright "birds" or "fish," shows the poet's inability to particularize, his inexplicable tendency toward broad and empty generalization. More accurately, however, it shows his deep interest in a particular sort of world view, and the extent to which his thought was dominated by one philosophic vision. John Arthos has documented his study of the language of natural description in the poetry of Thomson's age [*The Language of Natural Description in Eighteenth-Century Poetry* (1949)] with abundant examples of usage from scientists and philosophers as well as poets. Examination of his excerpts quickly shows the physico-theological justification for Thomson's "watery inhabitants," for example. Arthos quotes from several sources, including Derham's classic *Physico-Theology:* "The Watery, the Amphibious, the Airy Inhabitants, and those on the Dry-land, they all Live and Act with Pleasure." Or for the many periphrases such as Thomson's "glossy kind" or "fearful kind" for birds, Arthos lists numerous examples of the scientific usage of "kind" as a term of precise definition, concluding with this: *"Genuses* making an awkward plural, and *genera* not being English; I have often wished that we might be allowed to substitute *kind* for *genus,* and *sort* for *species."*

It would be foolish to multiply examples, since Arthos' detailed documentation is readily available. The important point is that recognition of the scientific and philosophic associations of much of Thomson's diction opens the possibility of new sorts of connotative richness in his description. His epithets are a means of extending the significant implications of his poetry; they illustrate that order of nature which is the poet's central concern. The terms which in their generality are likely to seem almost devoid of meaning today are most significant in their associations, used to establish an identity of reference with a specific scheme of the universe. The concept of natural order which afforded Thomson inspiration and subject matter also in many respects governed his choice of language; a rich linguistic structure of allusion to it underlies ***The Seasons.***

When the scientific implications of Thomson's poetic diction are understood, as well as the vast weight of literary tradition that such language also carries, the most conventional aspects of the poet's expression may be recognized as essential for conveying the total meaning of ***The Seasons.*** Tillotson observes that one important difference between the nature poetry of the eighteenth century and that of the nineteenth is that the nineteenth-century poet is interested in the freshness of his response to experience, whereas his predecessor was rather "interested in that response at a later stage: when the new has been welcomed by the old, when it has been accommodated to the existing harmony." The "old" element in Thomson's poetry is established to a large extent by his language, which owes so much to Virgilian tradition, and implies reference to the Virgilian outlook on nature in the *Georgics,* one of Thomson's important models.

The standards set up by Wordsworth are not the standards which govern James Thomson; Thomson's perceptions are communicated by a different frame of reference. Yet the standards implicit in *The Seasons* offer rich possibilities, and the diction which Wordsworth condemned [see excerpt dated 1837] is a partial reason for the poem's complexity. (pp. 23-7)

. . . . .

Wordsworth was not the first to notice Thomson's genius for close observation. A quarter of a century before the preface to *Lyrical Ballads,* a poetic commentator on Thomson's work implied that his genius lay in his ability to observe nature precisely and to record the results in his description. Thomson is characterized as the "curious bard" who

> examin'd every drop
> That glistens on the thorn; each leaf survey'd
> Which Autumn from the rustling forest shakes
> And mark'd its shape, and trac'd in the rude wind
> Its eddying motion.

But we have already seen abundant evidence that Thomson was more interested in the essential qualities and relationships of things than in their mere appearances. Although a sizable proportion of ***The Seasons*** consists of description, such passages (as our examination of ***The Seasons*** of 1746 and of the early ***Winter*** has already suggested) are closely related in method and emphasis to Thomson's deeper concerns. Consequently, a certain change is perceptible between the descriptions in the earliest parts of ***The Seasons*** and those in its later versions. Let us investigate some specific examples.

Elizabeth Manwaring was probably the first to point out an important difference between the ***Winter*** of 1726 and the Summer of 1727: that is, the slight use of pictorial landscape in the former compared with the greater emphasis on panoramic scenes in the latter. "The far more abundant later use of landscape," she remarks [in *Italian Landscape in Eighteenth Century England,* (1925)], "implies that Thomson had both grown more interested in making pictures, and had better learned the technique of the art, after that first venture." Ralph M. Williams, more than twenty years later [in *The Age of Johnson: Essays Presented to Chauncey Brewster Tinker* (1949)], agreeing with this exposition of the difference between ***Winter*** A and ***Summer*** A, suggested a possible reason for it in Thomson's association with John Dyer, primarily a painter, and just back from Italy with a large collection of prints. From Dyer, perhaps, Thomson first learned to admire and to imitate, in a different medium, the techniques of Claude Lorrain and Salvator Rosa, the two dominant influences on English landscape painting and landscape poetry during the eighteenth century.

In the 1727 ***Summer,*** the Claudian influence is more apparent in the descriptive emphasis on sunrises and sunsets, extended views, and pastoral scenes. A typical example of the Claudian technique occurs in the long discussion of noonday heat. After introducing the scene with stress on the sun's "dazzling Deluge", which turns all into "undistinguish'd Blaze", the poet proceeds to evoke vividly the atmosphere of summer heat and inactivity, touching on many members of the natural universe—men and streams suffer alike. Then he continues to present a fine rural scene:

> All in th'adjoining Brook, that shrills along
> The vocal Grove, now fretting o'er a Rock,
> Now scarcely moving thro' a reedy Pool,
> Now starting to a sudden Stream, and now
> Gently diffus'd into a limpid Plain,
> A various Groupe the Herds and Flocks compose,
> Rural Confusion! On the grassy Bank
> Some ruminating lie; while Others stand
> Half in the Flood, and, often bending, sip
> The circling Surface. In the Middle droops
> The strong, laborious Ox, of honest Front,
> Which, incompos'd, He shakes; and from his Sides
> The busy Insects lashes with his Tail,
> Returning still. Amid his subjects safe,
> Slumbers the Monarch-Swain; his careless Arm
> Thrown round his head on downy Moss sustain'd;
> Here laid his Scrip, with wholesome Viands fill'd;
> And there his Sceptre-Crook, and watchful Dog.

On the most obvious level, that of pictorial effectiveness, this description is thoroughly successful. Despite the fact that it is concerned in part with various sorts of motion (the moving stream, cattle drinking, the ox lashing his tail), its dominant effect is static; it is composed as a painting. The grouping is clearly visualized; the scene as a whole is conceived with a distinct sense of form which is more important than the details of any of its components. Except for the stress on the sound of the stream, it is based on exclusively visual imagery.

The success of the passage, however, does not rest simply on the manner of its visualization. The implications of its language are carefully controlled. In the weight of denotative and connotative meaning is realized the sort of richness that eighteenth-century diction is capable of achieving.

The diction of these lines reinforces the suggestion of their position in the poem, immediately following a welcome to the shades, which provide delicious shelter for the soul as the stream may offer physical shelter to the hunted hart. Man is thus once again brought into analogical relation with nature. As the succeeding description of the rural scene begins, with emphasis now turned to nature, the relation of nature to man—here important as part of a broad concept, rather than indicative of a narrowing of emphasis—is suggested by the diction of the first two lines. The brook *shrills* along; it sometimes *frets* over a rock; the grove is *vocal.* Shrillness suggests the human voice; fretting suggests the human personality; vocal ability reminds us, again, of the human, although it refers immediately to birds. The condensed and conventional phrase, "The vocal Grove," hints at a wide range of meaning: the physical reality of the grove, the presence in it of animate inhabitants, and—most important of all—the idea that the works of nature attest their Creator in tuneful or expressive terms. Thus, it suggests the order of the natural world, all parts of which are dominated by the Orderer, as the verbs used to describe the brook suggest a relation of the brook to man and, by extension, the kinship of all aspects of the creation in the pattern of the whole.

After these buried references to the natural order (which it seems hardly farfetched to find, in view of the poet's preceding explicit declarations), the phrase "Rural Confusion" in the seventh line of the passage acquires the complexity of paradox. It is only at first glance that the scene could be described as exemplifying confusion: the observer who found confusion would demonstrate his lack of awareness. Not only is the vista conceived pictorially in carefully grouped forms, but the whole acquires meaning from perception of an order in which all confusion must be only apparent. Most of its epithets relate more or less closely to a sense of order or form. The surface of the water is not dimpled or wavy, but "circling"—and the circle is the perfect geometric form. The ox is "laborious," an adjective suggesting his important function in the scheme of things. He shakes from his sides "busy Insects," and we are reminded of the attention the poet has previously given to these insects and their functional activity in the natural order.

Finally, the scene is resolved in relation to man, explicitly described as the "Monarch-Swain." His place is at the apex of the animal creation, although like the other animals he is subservient to greater forces. The lower forms of creation partly fulfill their purpose in serving him: his head is sustained by downy moss, and his watchful dog is the guardian of his slumbers. The fact that he, too, has a function and that the system of responsibility works both ways is emphasized, however, in the immediately following lines. If angry hornets should attack the herd, the man's slumbers must fly: he is responsible for the animals, as they are, in a sense, responsible to him.

The reason for dealing so extensively with a single passage of this sort is not simply the excellence of the individual section. It is rather that in such lines as these we may most clearly discern the precise way in which Thomson's world view raises the level of even his descriptive poetry above that of many of his contemporaries who deal with exactly the same sort of material. Matthew Green, for example, writes charming verse, excellent of its genre. But how much less weighty is his appealing description of a country scene than Thomson's:

> And may my humble dwelling stand
> Upon some chosen spot of land:
> A pond before full to the brim
> Where cows may cool, and geese may swim;
> Behind, a green like velvet neat,
> Soft to the eye, and to the feet;
> Where odorous plants in evening fair
> Breathe all around ambrosial air; . . .
> Fenced by a slope with bushes crowned,
> Fit dwelling for the feathered throng,
> Who pay their quit-rents with a song;
> With opening views of hill and dale,
> Which sense and fancy too regale.

The description contains the same sort of pictorial components as Thomson's: water, cows cooling themselves in it, a soft greensward corresponding to Thomson's downy moss. Green uses these components primarily for pictorial effect, creating a scene as delightful and as stiff as a primitive painting ("The Peaceable Kingdom," for example), a scene which exists solely for the sake of its pleasantness. Thomson's Claudian scene is pleasant, too, and a good deal less stiff. But the really important difference between the two is not a matter of artistic comparison: it is that Thomson's description does not provide a picture for its own sake; its meaning derives from and includes larger concepts. In this respect it is typical of most of the best description in the first edition of ***Summer.***

But the Claudian scene is not always in Thomson put to the same use, as the changes in his point of view exercised their subtle effects on his descriptive techniques. Miss Manwaring mentions specifically, as an elaborately composed landscape "with real Claudian distances," Thomson's description in the 1744 ***Spring*** of Lyttelton's country seat, Hagley Park. The new passage, significantly enough, replaces one on universal harmony: the emphasis of the fifty-nine new lines is very different indeed. Nature is there, to be sure, at the beginning, where Lyttelton and his wife are conceived as sitting in the shade "Of solemn Oaks, that tuft the swelling Mounts / Thrown graceful round by Nature's careless Hand", and at the end, where the last fifteen lines present the prospect that Miss Manwaring mentions. The couple reach the top of a hill, from which

> The bursting Prospect spreads immense around;
> And snatch'd o'er Hill and Dale, and Wood and Lawn,
> And verdant Field, and darkening Heath between,
> And Villages embosom'd soft in Trees,
> And spiry Towns by dusky Columns mark'd
> Of rising Smoak, your Eye excursive roams.

This is like the earlier pastoral description in its sense of form, of large forms and patterns this time. But here the consciousness of pattern has no particular meaning beyond the pictorial: the ideational foundation has vanished. There are, to be sure, ideas in this passage as a whole; they are even made explicit, not left to implication. But they are ideas which do not lend power to the description; indeed, they rather detract from the importance of the described scene. Lyttelton wanders through the countryside "Courting the Muse". When the first scene is described, its significance is immediately negated—"From these abstracted oft, / You wander through the Philosophic World"—and the passage moves into a panegyric on Lyttelton's political virtues, clearly more admirable than the beauties of nature. Lyttelton's wife joins him, and "Then Nature all / Wears to the Lover's Eye a Look of Love".

Man, in other words, has become the measure; his importance is far greater than that of nature. As natural description turns into a pretext for reflection on human qualities, it loses its more profound justification, the sense of significance with which it was earlier invested. The process had begun a good deal earlier than 1744; the year 1730 produced a comment on Dodington's country seat, "serene, and plain; / Where simple Nature reigns" (***Autumn*** A)—this despite the fact that the Dodington estate was notorious even in its own time for tasteless magnificence and ornateness. Pope, for example, commented sneeringly in his "Epistle IV," almost exactly contemporaneous with ***Autumn:***

> See! sportive fate, to punish awkward pride,
> Bids Bubo build, and sends him such a Guide:
> A standing sermon, at each year's expense,
> That never Coxcomb reach'd Magnificence!

Yet not only does Thomson confuse simple nature with complex human achievement, he professes to be fired *by thirst for Dodington's applause* to meditate the book of nature—nature, again, is no longer to be admired for its own sake. And his purpose in meditation is to learn the "moral song"—presumably such moral songs as the immediately following turgid description of vineyards, ending with praise of various wines.

Or, on still another country seat, the ***Autumn*** of 1744 deals with Stowe, Pitt's estate, praised by Thomson for

> such various Art
> By Genius fir'd, such ardent Genius tam'd
> By cool judicious Art; that, in the strife,
> All-beauteous Nature fears to be outdone.

The poet dreams of walking there with Pitt.

> While there with Thee th'inchanted Round I walk,
> The regulated Wild, gay Fancy then
> Will tread in Thought the Groves of Attic Land;
> Will from thy standard Taste refine her own,
> Correct her Pencil to the purest Truth
> Of Nature, or, the unimpassion'd Shades
> Forsaking, raise it to the human Mind.

The possibility of nature's being outdone by genius and art seems a very real one to the poet, despite his description of nature as "all-beauteous." The later lines make clear his delight in methodized nature, and his greater delight in man. Nature itself is not important in this passage; it is merely a stimulus to man. The description itself becomes so shadowy that it is impossible to visualize the scene. The approach, the relative emphasis, are characteristic of eighteenth-century poets who could by no stretch of the imagination be called nature poets. Take Robert Dodsley, for instance, whose major work belongs to the same georgic tradition as ***The Seasons:***

> There sweet prospects rise
> Of meadows smiling in their flow'ry pride,
> Green hills and dales, and cottages embower'd,
> The scenes of innocence and calm delight.
> There the wild melody of warbling birds,
> And cool refreshing groves, and murmuring springs,
> Invite to sacred thought, and lift the mind
> From low pursuits to meditate the God!

In a passage such as this, the references to nature—"green hills and dales," "warbling birds," "cool refreshing groves"—are not intended to evoke any pictorial reality; they are simply code words intended to suggest a certain well-established sort of response.

The function of nature in the passage from ***The Seasons*** is identical: it provides merely a starting point, an excuse. What Thomson is really interested in here is refining his taste by a standard, and it is only through that standard—a human standard—that he conceives it possible to correct his pencil to the purest truth of nature. Moreover, even the purest truth of nature is of lesser importance than the human mind—the woodland shades are, after all, unimpassioned. The poet had turned to writing tragedies, and tragedies now represented to him a higher form of art. He had forgotten the pure truth of nature which he earlier perceived—that truth which *included* the human mind.

The other primary pictorial model of the century, Salvator Rosa, encouraged description of a more somber kind. Cliffs, cascades, torrents, "delightful horrors," were his typical subject matter. Under his influence, a poet would be more likely to write "sublime" poetry. Addison, despite the fact that he finds "the Works of Nature still more pleasant, the more they resemble those of Art" (*Spectator,* No. 414), points out that those pleasures of the imagination derived from sight impressions arise from the sight of "what is *Great, Uncommon,* or *Beautiful.*" By greatness, he continues, he means the largeness of a whole view.

> Such are the Prospects of an open Champian Country, a vast uncultivated Desart, of huge Heaps of Mountains, high Rocks and Precipices, or a wide Expanse of Waters, where we are not struck with the Novelty or Beauty of the Sight, but with that rude kind of Magnificence which appears in many of these stupendous Works of Nature. Our Imagination loves to be filled with an Object, or to grasp at any thing that is too big for its Capacity. [*Spectator,* No. 412.]

[Kenneth MacLean, in *John Locke and English Literature of the Eighteenth Century* (1936)] has pointed out that a corollary of the Lockean view that the imagination is supplied by sensations from the outer world was the eighteenth-century notion that the larger the object contemplated, the greater the thought provoked—a notion which encouraged the connection of vastness with sublimity.

Whether the influences on Thomson were artistic or philosophic, however, he specialized in scenes of somber grandeur as well as in rural landscapes. The most vivid examples come from ***Autumn,*** where we find both sublime descriptions in his early and most successful manner, and description dealing with the same sort of theme, but obviously influenced by the poet's growing concern with the affairs of men and with narrow human morality.

One of the most successful pieces of description in all ***The Seasons*** is that in Autumn dealing with fog. At the beginning, we are told how "the mountain, horrid, vast, sublime" disappears from view, and are thus prepared for the atmosphere of grandeur and mystery which permeates the entire passage, reaching its climax in the suggestion that this is the same sort of atmosphere as that in which light originally forced its way through chaos. Between these two sections is some very vivid description, despite the fact that its emphasis is on vagueness.

> The huge dusk, gradual, swallows up the plain.
> Vanish the woods. The dim-seen river seems
> Sullen, and slow, to rowl the misty wave.
> Even in the height of noon opprest, the sun
> Sheds weak, and blunt, his wide-refracted ray;
> Whence glaring oft with many a broaden'd orb
> He frights the nations. Indistinct on earth,
> Seen thro' the turbid air, beyond the life,
> Objects appear; and, wilder'd, o'er the waste
> The shepherd stalks gigantick.

Wordsworth, too, has his gigantic shepherd:

> When up the lonely brooks on rainy days
> Angling I went, or trod the trackless hills
> By mists bewildered, suddenly mine eyes
> Have glanced upon him distant a few steps,
> In size a giant, stalking through thick fog,
> His sheep like Greenland bears. . . .
> Or him have I described in distant sky,
> A solitary object and sublime,
> Above all height! like an aerial cross
> Stationed alone upon a spiry rock
> Of the Chartreuse, for worship. Thus was man
> Ennobled outwardly before my sight,
> And thus my heart was early introduced
> To an unconscious love and reverence
> Of human nature.

The passage occurs in the eighth book of *The Prelude,* entitled, significantly, "Retrospect—Love of Nature Leading to Love of Man." For Thomson, the shepherd was merely one of several images suggesting the effect of the fog. For Wordsworth, he was an important symbol, a symbol to indicate the method of progressing from nature alone to man-in-nature. Human and physical nature were linked for Wordsworth, bound together in a mystically conceived whole. They acted upon each other: when the poet looked upon a flower, the human heart by which he lived was filled with thoughts too deep for tears. To be sure, Wordsworth lived in a time when individuality was valued; his private perceptions of experience, his personal reaction to a flower, might be of the greatest significance. Thomson, in contrast, was cut off from poetic expression of private experience by the values which dominated his age. He could hardly be expected to go so far as Wordsworth, although his interests in some respects lay in the same direction.

Both *The Prelude* and "Tintern Abbey" make it clear that Wordsworth considered the natural progression of human interest to be from nature to man. This is precisely the progression that took place in Thomson. The eighteenth-century poet, however, working within a less clearly defined poetic mode, found it virtually impossible to make of his love of man poetry as effective as that dominated by the love of nature. His greatest success comes when, as in the lines on fog, he uses man merely as one unit in a great whole. The fog passage shows a brilliant sense of the appropriate image for evocation of a specific atmosphere; the atmosphere is the most important element, and it is so dominant that it carries its own weight of implication, its sense of universal structure, heavily reinforced by the explicit reference to the coming of light—order—to chaos. The Wordsworthian personal emotion is lacking, but Thomson achieves, nevertheless, a rich emotional effect.

A strong sense of atmosphere dominates also the brief description in ***Autumn*** of birds on the northern islands, a true imaginative realization.

> Or where the northern ocean, in vast whirls,
> Boils round the naked, melancholy isles
> Of farthest Thule, and th'Atlantic surge
> Pours in among the stormy Hebrides;
> Who can recount what transmigrations there
> Are annual made? What nations come and go?
> And how the living clouds on clouds arise?
> Infinite wings! till all the plume-dark air,
> And white resounding shore are one wild cry.

The stormy Hebrides here, as in "Lycidas," convey a sense of remoteness, mystery, and grandeur, emphasized by the picture of the ocean boiling around the naked, melancholy islands of Thule and by the other details of the description. The poet is concerned with conveying a sense of the emotional impact of a certain sort of reality rather than a definite picture of that reality, and he does so admirably. The suggestions of paradox and confused sense impressions in the last two lines are especially effective. The "plume-dark air" suggests touch as well as sight; the "white resounding shore" mingles sight and hearing. The same birds darken the air and whiten the shore; their reality and all the different impressions are finally summed up aurally rather than visually—all in "one wild cry." Using this subtle method of description, Thomson achieves tremendous force; he produces an effect of sublimity from material which might have been altogether commonplace, from the kind of travelbook source which so often produces his weakest poetry.

A more usual subject for "sublime" writing is exploited in a brilliant descriptive addition to the ***Summer*** of 1744, in which Thomson makes effective use of the Miltonic technique of exploiting the sonorous values of proper names.

> Amid Carnarvon's Mountains rages loud
> The repercussive Roar: with mighty Crash,
> Into the flashing Deep, from the rude Rocks
> Of Penmanmour heap'd hideous to the Sky,
> Tumble the smitten Cliffs; and Snowden's Peak,
> Dissolving, instant yields his wintry Load.
> Far-seen, the Heights of heathy Cheviot blaze,
> And Thulè bellows thro' her utmost Isles.

The poet does not weaken his effect here, as he does often, with explanatory footnotes. He achieves a sense of scope and grandeur altogether appropriate to his subject. Most characteristically, Thomson writes best in short sentences; the brilliant passages of description in ***The Seasons*** are frequently marked by their short and simple constructions. This passage, however, exemplifies the skill with which he is sometimes able to handle more extended periods. The sentences move weightily and thus add to the consciousness of mass which the emphasis on mountains, rocks, cliffs, loads of snow, has evoked. This preliminary presentation of the vast effects of lightning on the most massive objects in inanimate nature heightens the impact of the story dealing with the effect of lightning on man, and aids the reader in achieving the proper broad perspective.

But Thomson's more typical use of description, even description of "sublime" scenes, as early as 1730, is found in connection with rather narrow purposes. Williams, in his essay on Thomson and Dyer, generalizes that Thomson typically uses his landscapes as preparation for moralizing, with a didactic purpose, and hints that the poet would have reversed Aikin's view that the business of ***The Seasons*** was to describe and the occupation of its leisure to teach. The generalization is dangerous; yet it is all too true that often in ***The Seasons*** description occupies a place subsidiary to that of the moralizing which it introduces.

So we find in ***Autumn*** yet another storm description. The tempest gathers force until the river floods, and before its rush

> Herds, flocks, and harvests, cottages, and swains,
> Roll mingled down, all that the winds had spar'd,
> In one wild moment ruin'd, the big hopes,
> And well-earn'd treasures of the painful year.

The husbandman observes all this, and his point of view is understandably narrow: he worries about the coming winter and about his children, for whom he has no provisions. The poet, however, makes no effort to suggest the possibility of a broader perspective. Instead, completely caught up by the vision of man as primarily important, he adjures the masters to remember the laborers and not

> cruelly demand what the deep rains,
> And all-involving winds have swept away.

His sentiments are unimpeachable, but this sort of emphasis is seriously weakening to a work originally conceived with a much broader perspective.

Unfortunately, the revisions that Thomson made in descriptive passages for the collected editions of 1730 and 1744 are typically in the direction of narrow moral emphasis. The passage in ***Autumn*** A, lines 897-998, corresponds roughly to ***Winter*** B (1726), lines 29-96; in its early form it was one of Thomson's successful achievements in depicting man as a part of nature—but not as it was changed for ***Autumn.*** The original version, for example, included the brilliant lines already noted, about the woodcocks which "mock / The nimble Fowler's Aim", an idea which suggests the participation of men with birds in a total natural pattern. There is no hint of destruction to ensure if the fowler's aim is accurate. In ***Autumn,*** however, the woodcocks have vanished altogether. Instead, there are some more of Thomson's moral adjurations to man:

> O let not, aim'd from some inhuman eye,
> The gun the music of the coming year
> Destroy; and harmless, unsuspecting harm,
> Lay the weak tribes, a miserable prey!
> In mingled murder, fluttering on the ground.

The division between the human world and that of other animals is emphasized, rather than the possibility of unity. The difference of attitude represented by the two passages points up vividly the different direction of Thomson's later interests.

Most of the changes emphasize the same change of interest. A section purely descriptive in ***Winter*** ends in ***Autumn*** with a line suggesting that the primary function of external nature is to please man: "The desolated prospect thrills the soul". The succeeding lines on melancholy, which occupied ten lines in ***Winter,*** in ***Autumn*** are given twenty-seven lines. In ***Winter,*** the initial emphasis of the passage had been on the progress of the year itself: the declining year breathes philosophic melancholy over the soul. In ***Autumn,*** however, Melancholy is personified; Melancholy itself comes to have various specific effects, dwelt on in loving detail, on the human soul. Nature is not even mentioned in the first seventeen lines of the passage, which are concerned with humanitarian sentiment. When nature does enter the scene, it is expressly subordinated to human values. Melancholy is to produce "The love of Nature unconfin'd, and *chief* (italics mine) / Of humankind". And as the passage continues, it is concerned entirely with the various worthy sentiments toward humankind that are to dominate the philosophic soul.

In the final section of this transferred passage, Thomson increases the descriptive emphasis on the moon. In doing so, he is unable to avoid referring parenthetically to the scientific achievements of man: the spotted disk of the moon shows

> (Where mountains rise, umbrageous dales descend,
> And oceans roll, as optic tube descries).

Moreover, the moon is, after all, only "A lesser earth"—the domain of man is temporarily of supreme importance in the universe. That the poet's purely descriptive skill has not deserted him, however, is indicated by the last two lines added to this passage:

> The whole air whitens with a boundless tide
> Of silver radiance, trembling round the world.

One typical manifestation of Thomson's descriptive efforts toward "sublimity" is his inclusion of several passages of description taken directly from travel books. These tend to emphasize the more terrifying aspects of foreign lands (as in the passage on wolves in the second edition of ***Winter***), and to demonstrate the poet's great interest in natural catastrophe, ranging from the ravages of wild animals to the terrors of tropic forest fires.

The effectiveness of such passages, all of which possess a certain spectacular richness, seems to depend largely on the degree to which they have been absorbed into the dominant philosophic scheme of the poem as a whole. When, for example, Thomson is recounting the "Treasures of the Sun" (Summer), a subject entirely appropriate to his general interest in the sun as the apex of creation, he captures a sense of naïve wonder which makes his description delightful:

> Rocks rich in Gems, and Mountains big with Mines,
> Whence, over Sands of Gold, the Niger rolls
> His amber Wave; while on his balmy Banks,
> Or in the Spicy, Abyssinian Vales,
> The Citron, Orange, and Pomegranate drink
> Intolerable Day, yet, in their Coats,
> A cooling Juice contain. Peaceful, beneath,
> Leans the huge Elephant, and, in his Shade,
> A Multitude of beauteous Creatures play;
> And Birds, of bolder Note, rejoice around.

The multitude of beauteous creatures playing in the shade of the leaning elephant have a quality of almost Renaissance charm, a manner which one does not tend to think of in connection with Thomson.

With his frequent sense of the ambiguity of natural forces, the poet is able to give strength, too, to his description of barren desert scenes

> where Heaven above,
> Glows like an Arch of Brass; and all below,
> The Earth a Mass of rusty Iron lies.

Similarly, his presentation of the wild animals of the tropics, conceived as a hierarchy headed by a "shaggy King", has the same forcefulness in idea and presentation. The beauty and power of the beasts are effectively emphasized, and the immense strength of wildness contrasted with the weakness of "th'ungarded Swain". Finally, the beasts' relation to man is suggested in a description of a shipwrecked man, vainly contemplating the ocean in search of a vessel, to whom the sun represents a power of salvation and the wild animals, heard in the distance, the forces of evil.

But this mode of writing presented too much of a temptation. Under the necessity of expanding and changing his poetry for the sake of sales, Thomson turned more and more readily to the use of secondhand material, and made less attempt really to absorb it into the fabric of ***The Seasons*** as a whole. The descriptions tend less and less to stand on their own—see, for example, what becomes of our elephant in the revisions of 1744.

> Peaceful, beneath primeval Trees . . .
> Leans the huge Elephant: wisest of Brutes!
> O truely wise! with gentle Might endow'd,
> Tho' powerful, not destructive! Here he sees
> Revolving Ages sweep the changeful Earth,
> And Empires rise and fall; regardless he
> Of what the never-resting Race of Men
> Project: thrice happy! could he 'scape their Guile . . .

And so on, for five lines more of moral reflection. Descriptive vividness—to say nothing of descriptive charm—has been altogether lost, and replaced by more intellectual, but less appealing, contemplation. Although the poet's obvious enjoyment of spectacular scenery sometimes communicates itself to the reader in his revisions, even those made as late as 1744, the effect is more often marred by heavy moralizing, perfunctory versification, and the frequent interpolation of lengthy scientific footnotes.

A third kind of natural description in which Thomson specialized, in addition to his presentations of pastoral panoramas and of terrifying and "sublime" scenes, is the description of natural scenes depending for its effect on precision of observed detail. The most extended examples of this sort of writing occur in the first edition of ***Spring*** (1728), in the long section on birds.

> The Black-bird whistles from the thorny Brake;
> The mellow Bull-finch answers from the Grove:
> Nor are the Linnets, o'er the flowering Furze,
> Pour'd out profusely, silent. Join'd to These,
> Thousands beside, thick as the cov'ring Leaves
> They warble under, or the nitid Hues
> Which speck them o'er, their Modulations mix
> Mellifluous.

Blackbird, bullfinch, linnets—the attention to specific varieties of birds here emphasizes the fact that when Thomson calls birds "tuneful Nations" or "feathery Folk" he does so for a purpose, and not simply because he is interested only in generalization. The specificity of this passage, however, extends further than the naming of individual sorts of birds. The blackbird *whistles;* the bullfinch is *mellow:* the variations in timbre between one bird and another are thus suggested. The environment of each bird is also different. There is the thorny brake—sharpness corresponding to the sharpness of the blackbird's whistle; the grove, of a dignity appropriate to the mellow tone of the bullfinch; the flowering furze, in which the profusion of the small linnets seems fitting. Moreover, the variety of physical environments suggests the other aspects of the natural order, the presence of variety and pattern in inanimate as well as animate nature, and the relatedness of the birds to the other members of the natural order.

The similes used to indicate the numbers of the birds also work in two directions, acting on both their members. The tremendous number of leaves, the wide variety of brilliant colors, as well as the presence of many birds, are emphasized. Leaves and colors thus vivify the picture in two ways; the leaves also reinforce the suggestions of *brake, grove,* and *furze* to remind the reader of the other parts of the natural order. Their richness suggests an underlying theme of lavishness, fecundity, the "fullness" of the Great Chain of Being.

The same attention to specific detail appears in the description of the birds building their nests, which, however, also shows a new tendency of Thomson's. The section on birds [in ***Spring***] is by no means all of a piece.

> Among the Roots
> Of Hazel, pendant o'er the plaintive Stream,
> They frame the first Foundation of their Domes,
> Dry Sprigs of Trees, in artful Manner laid,
> And bound with Clay together. Now 'tis nought
> But Hurry Hurry thro' the busy Air,
> Beat by unnumber'd Wings. The Swallow sweeps
> The slimy Pool, to build his hanging House
> Ingeniously intent. Oft from the Back
> Of Herds and Flocks a thousand tugging Bills
> Pluck Hair, and Wool, and oft when unobserv'd
> Steal from the Barn the Straw: till soft, and warm,
> Clean, and compleat, their Habitation grows.

Specificity is by no means rare in ***The Seasons:*** it is sufficient here to note its presence. Another aspect of the passage is more interesting. Elsewhere Thomson mentions the *nests* of birds; here, when he is actually dealing with them, there is no mention of the word. The birds are building domes (in the Latin sense of house), habitations, or houses—not nests. The language suggests the relation of the birds to man, a relation hinted also in other parts of the passage, although there is no explicit mention whatever of the presence or existence of man. The implications of the diction in the description of bird courtship offer another example of the same sort of subtle suggestion. Love teaches the tender arts of pleasing *even* to birds and beasts: the "even" indicates the presence of "higher" forms of life to which such arts might seem more naturally appropriate. Moreover, such lines as

> The cunning, conscious, half-averted Glance
> Of their regardless Charmer

indicate that the poet is conceiving the activities of the birds in relation to the maneuvers and emotions of their human counterparts.

The difference between the sort of use Thomson makes of his close observation, in lines such as those on nest-building, and the use a scientist would make of the same sort of observation, is striking. . . . Here, like the scientist, he is concerned mainly with the ingenuity of the birds. They *frame* the foundations of their nests; the verb suggests purposeful art. Dry sprigs of trees are laid in "artful Manner"; the swallow is "ingeniously intent" on building his hanging house. But the *fact* of ingenuity, not its explanation or definition, concerns Thomson. The dominant impression of the lines quoted is of ingenuity and activity, but he gives no scientifically accurate detail. The poet is not observing as a scientist, but as a thinker moving toward the view that the significance of the animal world is largely its usefulness in offering lessons or parables for man. His closest attention here is given to the birds' plucking hair and wool from the herds and flocks, and stealing straw from the barn: activities which imply certain ties between birds and men.

For the real logical connection between the section on the birds and the rest of ***Spring*** is in relation to the theme of man rather than that of natural order. Emotional emphasis throughout this long section is on the birds' capacity to love, the romantic love of the birds, and, toward the end, their love for their young. The total structure of ***Spring*** is largely based on the idea of the dominance of love, a theme resolved finally in human terms. Thomson's long consideration of the birds contains sections in which the theme of natural order is dominant, descriptive passages in the manner of ***Winter*** and ***Summer.*** But it also hints at the poet's movement toward greater stress on human values. As far as natural description is concerned, the tendency of ***Spring*** is toward a sort of description which places implied emphasis on man even when man is in no way a part of the described scene. Although this sort of description can, as we have seen, function to remind the reader of the natural order, in the context of ***Spring,*** with its general emphasis on man, it seems to corroborate the other evidence of a gradual change in the poet's interests.

As a matter of fact, ***Spring*** contains virtually no natural description for its own sake: descriptive passages are more frequently introductory to long discussions of science or morality than evocative of natural reality. Descriptive deftness remains, but it subserves new purposes. Yet even here, and in ***Autumn,*** which is still more dominated by strictly human concerns, brief sections stand out to reveal the poet's ability to capture the essential reality of a scene by a skillful use of specific detail. Thus, in the midst of the tedious discourse on hunting, in ***Autumn,*** we find a brilliant presentation of the hare in her natural habitat:

> Poor is the triumph o'er the timid Hare!
> Shook from the corn, and now to some lone seat
> Retir'd: the rushy fen; the ragged furz,
> Stretch'd o'er the stony heath; the stubble chapt;
> The thistly lawn; the thick, intangled broom:
> Of the same friendly hue, the wither'd fern;
> The fallow ground laid open to the sun,
> Concoctive; and the nodding sandy bank,
> Hung o'er the mazes of the mountain-brook.
> Vain is her best precaution; tho' she sits
> Conceal'd, with folded ears; unsleeping eyes,
> By Nature rais'd to take th'horizon in;
> And head couch'd close betwixt her hairy feet,
> In act to spring away.

The details are precise without being minute; the scene is conceived as a whole principally through suggestions of color—monotone brownish gray—but with explicit reference to its individual components. The hare is individualized solely as a part of nature, presented, in her fearful huddle, as simply another mass of brown in a brown landscape; and this very fact, of course, makes man's violation of the natural order in his attempt to destroy her the more horrifying.

Similar examples could be multiplied from all parts of ***The Seasons:*** the redbreast passage in ***Winter*** is but the most famous of many of its kind. In this sort of description, as in the other kinds that Thomson uses, however, the general tendencies are the same. Description does not in ***The Seasons*** exist for its own sake, but as part of a larger scheme. At its most brilliant, it is likely to be part of the pattern of consciousness of natural order: the turning toward man tends to lessen the emphasis on natural description in later part of ***The Seasons.*** But Thomson is capable, too, of using natural description as part of his presentation of man and moral concerns. (pp. 101-22)

Patricia Meyer Spacks, "The Achievement of 'the Seasons'" and "Description in 'The Seasons' (1727-1744)," in her The Varied God: A Critical Study of Thomson's "The Seasons", *University of California Press, 1959, pp. 8-28, 101-22.*

Bonamy Dobrée (essay date 1959)

[Dobrée was an English educator, writer, and editor whose works include Restoration Comedy 1660-1720 *(1924),* Modern Prose Style *(1934), and* Of Books and Human Kind *(1964). In the following excerpt, he offers a general assessment of Thomson's oeuvre, concluding that "it is unlikely that Thomson will ever again be a*

popular poet, though he will always be read by a circle considerably larger than that of student and historian."]

It was during the twenties that the poetry of [the 1700-40] period took definite shape, the expression of men living in the time that they did. It is to be valued as existing in its own right, not merely as faintly heralding the romantic movement. We might hazard a general description by saying that the poetry from about 1720—it had its forerunners, of course—was chiefly of the compendious kind—contemplative, philosophic, variously didactic, and intrepidly descriptive. In replacing the epic, it took all knowledge for its province and attempted a synthesis, so that we have presented to us what seems an inordinate number of poems about creation or the cosmos, sometimes in blank verse, but also in couplets and even in quatrains. These poems were necessarily objective, even when divagating on the human mind; never, we might think, was a period of poetry so little egocentric. It follows that, ignoring the individual soul it could not use emotion as its material; so it does not much move the post-romantic mind. In so far as it allowed itself to be emotive, the emotions it worked upon were such as might be derived from seeing the glory of the Divinity impelling the universe, or, to use the title of Ray's book, from grasping 'the wisdom of God manifested in the works of the creation'.

The poetry of the first two decades had to some extent been a fading echo of seventeenth-century thought and feeling, and had been largely occasional. That generation, working within an old sensibility, had passed; Prior, Parnell, Congreve, Lady Winchilsea had died; or they had faded from the poetic scene as did Tickell and Ambrose Philips; and though Gay went on writing, one feels that his *Fables* could have been written under Queen Anne as readily as under Queen Caroline. Pope, by far the most highly geared of his contemporaries, alone moved on. The change was gradual, though we now see it to have been radical. It is not only, as Mr. T. S. Eliot has said, that poetry ceased to be courtly, and came to seem as though it were all written by country parsons (as a good deal of it was), but that the poets with whom we now have to do were men daring to desert the individual in a narrow society as their usual subject, and follow Newton into strange seas of thought, or to venture into landscape painting. They were, in fact, consciously or not, reacting against Hobbes's dictum, hitherto complied with, that 'the subject of a poem is the manners of men, not natural causes'. We see them rapt with the mystery of colour and light as revealed to them in the *Opticks,* delighted with what geographers or botanists had to tell them, carried away by the excitement of mercantile expansion, loud in praise of liberty, moved by a sense of patriotism, and boldly declaring for domesticity. Naturally much of what they had to say had already been adumbrated by their forebears; but being less curious about the soul they gained a firmer grip of external nature, and a much firmer technique—surer though more crude—based on a freer mastery of Milton, and less funk of Spenser.

To the non-co-operative reader much of this poetry is dull, except for selected passages; he will skip with Thomson, yawn over Dyer apart from *Grongar Hill,* and—here quite rightly—touch Young's nocturnal vapourings very gingerly. Being largely didactic it can add little to the sensibility of the man of today, since, except with a major poet such as Pope, what is taught is always transient. We know about the rainbow and the comet, the springs and micro-organisms, and know it differently. The patriotism is often oddly stressed, too much inspired by faction; and the theme of commerce no longer warms our poetic fires. Nor does this poetry seek to reconcile opposites; the imagination, filled by what the mind discerned, is contemplative rather than creative; the symbols of the emotions are the things which themselves caused the emotions. 'There is a poetry', Goethe remarked, 'without figures of speech, which is a single figure of speech', and it is to this category that much of the poetry of this time belongs. Thus figurative imagery is largely out of place, and this poetry too lacks metaphysical tension. It reasons certainly, but the reason is treated, in Montesquieu's phrase, as 'le plus noble, le plus parfait, le plus exquis de nos sens'. Thus, for anyone prepared to take the trouble to apply the form of criticism that Mr. R. P. Blackmur has dubbed 'elucidation of scripture', it can give lively pleasure and acquire positive value; while to those who are delighted and enriched, or even entertained by understanding how a generation felt, and strove to express itself, the period can teach much, if only moderation, tolerance, and, yes, humility before so real an achievement.

Moreover there is here the interest of watching the new sensibility trying to find the medium in which to express itself. The Pindaric would not do—it was too clumsy; the eclogue, besides being of the wrong scale, had been laughed out of court, and so on; there seemed nothing for it but experiments with Milton, and bashful attempts to see if something could not be got out of that quaint old poet Spenser; as Thomson remarked prefacing ***The Castle of Indolence,*** 'the obsolete words, and simplicity of diction in some of the lines, which borders on the ludicrous, were necessary to make the imitation more perfect'. It was, of course, some time before imitation became unconscious, and thus modified become a valid instrument in the living tradition, which along that line of development had its end with Wordsworth. Yet it must be recognized that in accepting the older dictions as valid, the poets of the century may have denied themselves the full expression of what they had to say. Neither Spenserian nor Miltonic verse would seem the best expression for the complex of emotions, domestic, humanitarian, or contemplatively religious by which the century lived. It was an age of consolidation, using the terms of an age of exploration or of struggle. Abandoning the older tradition of which Pope was the last exponent, with its logico-dialectical inner structure, with its fierce, dramatic colloquialism, in attempting to universalize, the poets tended to stifle the more disturbing emotions of the domestic scene. . . . In substituting an externally organized style for one intellectually built up from within, they sacrificed the sense of tension. But if their poetry is low-toned, it repays attentive listening; it is not to be read in the same way as that of the preceding century; its wheels, to adopt Coleridge's phrase regarding the poetry of Donne and Dryden, do not grow hot with the rapidity of their motion. The sympathetic reader, however, will supply the warmth.

Dyer may serve as a vantage point from which to attack the vast array of poems; he is an interesting 'case', for though to begin with he corresponded technically to his contemporaries (he later fell well behind), he was not trying to say what, for example, Thomson or Savage or Glover were anxious to declare, though in some ways they come nearest him. His interest for us at this point lies in his technical innovation, and his example as a landscape poet. Finding that the Pindaric form would not convey what he wished of his painter's sensations when climbing Grongar Hill, he broke back to Miltonics of the *Allegro* sort, beautifully varying his cadences, and achieved a happy, successful poem of just the right verse density for what he felt. It is illuminating to read the three available versions, beginning with the Pindaric . . . , going on to the tetrameter version which, though written later, had been printed by Warner in 1725. . . . We can see what is happening. Dyer is ridding himself of stale forms, hereditary diction, and, what is more, inflated abstractions, all of which muffled his direct contact with what he wanted to enjoy, and thus prevented him from singing about it. A few lines from each form will illustrate the process; first the Pindaric:

I

Fancy! Nymph, that loves to lye
On the lonely Eminence;
Darting Notice thro' the Eye,
Forming Thought, and feasting Sense:
Thou! that must lend Imagination Wings,
And stamp Distinction, on all worldly Things!
Come, and with thy various Hues,
Paint and adorn thy Sister Muse.
Now, while the Sun's hot Coursers, bounding high;
Shake lustre on the Earth, and burn, along the Sky.

II

More than Olympus animates my Lays,
Aid me, o'er labour'd, in its wide surveys;
And crown its Summit with immortal praise:
Thou, aweful Grongar! in whose mossy cells
Sweetly-musing Quiet dwells . . .

which is making distinctly heavy weather of it; you hardly feel he is enjoying himself, as he so clearly is in the final version:

Silent Nymph, with curious Eye!
Who, the purple Ev'ning, lye
On the Mountain's lonely Van,
Beyond the Noise of busy Man,
Painting fair the form of Things,
While the yellow Linnet sings;
Or the tuneful Nightingale
Charms the Forest with her Tale;
Come with all thy various Hues,
Come and aid thy Sister Muse;
Now while *Phoebus* riding high
Gives lustre to the Land and Sky!
Grongar Hill invites my Song,
Draw the Landskip bright and strong;
Grongar, in whose Mossie cells
Sweetly-musing Quiet dwells . . .

the abstractions, it is true, have not quite gone, but they are homely and understandable, and are not compelled to carry ponderous philosophic conceptions: the hackneyed catchwords, as Saintsbury suggested, are *un*hackneyed into propriety and personality. If the main originality of the poem lies in its approach, the charm of the final version is the unifying swing of the whole, the pace getting faster, the excitement increasing, as Dyer walks higher and higher to get an ever more extended view. Something had been done in this poem to free country poetry, and it was done by the sheer exuberance of the metre married to the novelty of the vision.

We shall revert to Dyer later in another connexion, noting here what is most significant for us at the moment about the passage quoted, namely the appeal from the muse of poetry to her sister muse of painting to come and help her. The country poem is ceasing to be a Georgic, or a 'place', or 'estate' poem, or merely décor—and becoming a picture, a subject in its own right: the writers are going to try to convert to poetry

Whate'er *Lorrain* light-touch'd with softening hue,
Or savage *Rosa* dash'd, or learned *Poussin* drew,

and luckily at that very moment they discovered for their palettes the whole spectrum which Newton had revealed to them in his *Opticks.* As Professor Marjorie Nicolson has brilliantly shown, from about 1725 the *Opticks* and its implications became almost a major theme in poetry for some decades, or, as the first excitement lapsed, a structural-decorative part of much minor philosophical poetry [see excerpt dated 1946]. In the earlier years of the century the country had been taken for granted; it was part of everybody's life, the poets had no separate consciousness of it; thus most of the rural poetry written was rustically didactic. Now, however, that the landscape painters had drawn attention to a possible new visual treatment, and the scientists had added an inner vision of how nature worked in such a way as to produce a renascence of wonder, the poets felt that they had something exciting here to work with. The difficulty was to find an adequate vehicle in which to express this. In going back to Milton rather than attempting to continue the Pindaric tradition (the heroic couplet, one may remark parenthetically, had before the turn of the century ceased to exercise whatever 'tyranny' it may ever have been able to impose), their instinct was right—or so we say, judging after the event. But what they did not all notice, or forgot, was that to employ the whole battery of the Miltonic poetic implies that you have something as important to say as Milton had, and as strong a poetic pressure moving you. Some tried to supply a deficiency of ideas by using elevated language, the result often being to produce that sort of stupor to which the term 'academic' best applies, a devastating effect of the platitudinous. Here, for instance, is Thomson, no mere poetaster, telling us that it is nice to sit down in the shade on a hot summer's day:

Welcome, ye Shades! ye bowery Thickets, hail!
Ye lofty Pines! ye venerable Oaks!
Ye Ashes wild, resounding o'er the Steep!
Delicious is your Shelter to the Soul,
As to the hunted Hart the sallying Spring,
Or Stream full-flowing, that his swelling Sides

> Laves, as he floats along the herbag'd Brink.
> Cool, thro' the Nerves, your pleasing Comfort glides;
> The Heart beats glad; the fresh-expanded Eye
> And Ear resume their watch; the Sinews knit;
> And Life shoots swift thro' all the lighten'd Limbs.

A dire result, we may think, of trying to adapt a form evolved for the conveying of an old ethos to fit a new sensibility. A heavy price has to be paid by the generation that sets itself to undergo a necessary discipline. Here and there certainly, the innovating generation reaps the benefit as when Thomson is setting the scene for his tumultuous birds:

> Or, where the NORTHERN ocean, in vast whirls
> Boils round the naked, melancholy isles
> Of farthest THULE, and th' ATLANTIC surge
> Pours in among the stormy HEBRIDES.

The metric—together with the borrowing from *Lycidas*—we feel is justified. Thomson, moreover, had learnt to vary and develop the metres, as we can see in continuing the passage:

> Who can recount what transmigrations there
> Are annual made? what nations come and go?
> And how the living clouds on clouds arise?
> Infinite wings! till all the plume-dark air,
> And white resounding shore are one wild cry.

That superb iamb-spondee conclusion is certainly not Miltonic. Sometimes, in ***The Seasons,*** there is a complete break away from the master into a colloquialism which shows, at least momentarily, an unshackled freedom within the form.

In the main, however, the Miltonics of this time—oddly enough after the freedom attained earlier by John Philips—produce a dulling effect upon the mind; it is—tell it not in Gath—with some relief that we turn even to such obvious satiric material as Young's *Universal Passion* to enjoy the sureness and conciseness of the couplet, which did at least bound and circumscribe the often too conscientious fancy. We might say they were too involved (just as Keats was to be) when they went to Milton, though they could be 'artful' enough, detached enough, when playing with Spenser as Thomson did in ***The Castle of Indolence,*** and Shenstone in *The Schoolmistress.* They were, moreover, too plainly imitative, and laboured too much under the yoke of the 'sublime'—this last may account partly for the turgidity of the first quotation from Thomson—to do more than here and there reveal the authentic poet. Dyer is a case in point. Though *The Ruins of Rome* and *The Fleece* belong to the next phase, it is interesting to note that instead of adapting Miltonic verse to what he had to say, he more and more crushed his material under the weight of an inappropriate form, though indeed *Paradise Regain'd* does not serve the former poem badly. But it is no use to treat traffic on the high seas, as Dyer does in *The Fleece,* as sonorously as if it were the trafficking of the Archangels in the Miltonic cosmos. The passages of musical and imposing proper names fail to produce the sense of sublimity, and the line

> Woods, tow'rs, vales, caves, dells, cliffs, and torrent floods,

evokes, not the picture of the shepherd climbing Bredon after a kidling, but, with a smile, Satan skirting

> Rocks, caves, lakes, fens, bogs, dens, and shades of death,

while the stress on an important word beginning a line often becomes a reiterated thump. This is not to decry *The Fleece* as a whole; it is, in its way, an admirable construct, eruptive of poetry, sometimes in flashes attaining real vividness; it has here been unfairly treated to illustrate the kind of bondage from which Thomson at his best broke free.

For it is James Thomson who, Pope apart, is the outstanding poet of this phase; and since he transcends it less than Pope does, being more innocent, he is in some ways more representative. He belongs more surely to the eighteenth century, not only in its thraldom to Newtonian physics (seeking comfort in Derham and like thinkers with him), but also in its sentimentality: his Shaftesburian optimism does not feel the restraints that Pope imposed upon his own variant. Beginning with perfectly happy natural reactions to the enchanting countryside of Teviotdale in which he was brought up, he never had to struggle for his philosophy, any more than he had to probe deep for his symbolic subject-matter, as his **'Juvenilia'** make plain. That is where his weakness lies. There is no battling for his intellectual or moral position, and even his abandonment of a career in the Church seems to have caused no alarming qualms; while the solution of the problem of evil he took happily from current Physico- and Astro-Theology. (pp. 475-82)

[Thomson's] **'Juvenilia'** already exhibit the figure in his carpet, and it is interesting to have it pointed out, as it has been by Professor Herbert Drennon, that this execrably clumsy blank-verse poem, **'The Works and Wonders of Almighty Power'**, is almost a transcript of a passage in Shaftesbury's *Moralists,* while **'Upon Happiness'** derives from John Norris of Bemerton. Very much a harbinger too is a poem in quite neat couplets comparatively free of 'poetic diction', **'Of a Country Life'**, published in the *Edinburgh Miscellany* in 1720. This has some agreeably vivid description, born of participating enjoyment, of the sights and sounds of the countryside. In it Thomson applauds rural sports in a way he would later reject, but foreshadows what was to be his major life-work by a description of the seasons which clearly enough indicates his preferences, since he gives four lines each to Spring and Summer, two to Autumn, and no less than sixteen excitedly appreciative ones to Winter. Again, the **'Hymn on the Power of God'**, in common measure, though not so Deistic as the Hymn which was to conclude ***The Seasons*** in 1730, asks us to praise 'The God of Nature', and is an earnest of the religious colouring which was to be diffused over so much of Thomson's work.

Religious colouring rather than any deep religious sense, which it would be useless to demand from this amiable scientific-rationalist, moved to a sentimental Deism only a bigot need be annoyed by. He was all that is stated in Stanza 68 of the first Canto of ***The Castle of Indolence,*** engaging, easy-going, genial, soft-hearted, sensitive to the charms of nature, and interested, one might add, in any and every current philosophy without criticizing its sources or pursuing its implications. If his only completely successful works are the first ***Winter, To the Memory of Sir Isaac Newton,*** and ***A Hymn on the Seasons,*** there is no reason why the rest of his poetry should be put aside as flat or faded, spurious, or disgustingly didactic.

Evidently it is by that widely influential and for long immensely popular but chaotic poem ***The Seasons*** that Thomson must be judged. It is extremely uneven in performance because the impulse formative of the various parts springs from such different levels of awareness and response; and since it was so much a matter of patchwork and insertions no one can guess what incongruity is coming next. The purpose as it seems to have formulated itself gradually in Thomson's mind was to show the workings of Creative Nature: that, together with the framework of the progression of the year, is what holds the poem together at all, coherence being given by a certain inner rhythm of movement from, in each morsel, the material to the spiritual. To judge from the first 1726 version of ***Winter,*** Thomson seems to have begun as a landscape painter sensitive to light and 'feel', by the very act of creating the harmony necessary for a picture led into a sense of the Deity, a sense that all was well, which in turn drew him on to the somewhat oddly emergent and totally unconvincing solution of the problem of evil which concludes the poem. The earliest version is a charming spontaneous thing, not too long, and there is just the right modicum of 'philosophy' to give it substance. Then something disastrous happened, and the Scottish border poem became a didactic work, a kind of *Essay on Man.*

In the Preface which Thomson added to the second 1726 edition of ***Winter,*** after deploring the decay of poetry in his day, its triviality, he exalts nature as a great and serious subject; it contains 'all that enlarges and transports the soul'. Although this Preface is, amusingly enough, a close adaptation of Norris of Bemerton's address 'To the Reader' in his 1687 *Collection of Miscellanies,* it is the differences rather than the likenesses that are significant; for whereas Norris declares that he will raise poetry to its height by treating of 'Divine and Moral Subjects', Thomson is going to rely on 'wild romantic country' and 'the Works of Nature', though he will not reject the help of the *Georgics.* This, of course, is where the disaster which had overtaken Thomson becomes apparent. He is about to assume the mantle of the theosophic-rationalist preacher. Everything has to be 'philosophically', that is, scientifically solved. 'Frost or the moral order, it makes little difference which,' Professor Drennon remarks, 'he always feels it incumbent on him to give a rationalistic explanation.' The Preface indicates that he is to become—among other things—a lay Derham to whom many sorts of different knowledge were to be added. There was really no need for Thomson to justify himself; there was nothing startlingly new about the kind of poetry he had given the reading world, so that we can regard the Preface rather as the symptom of what had happened to him. He had become entangled with the intelligentsia, beginning with his Scotch friends Mallet (or Malloch) and Murdoch, going on to Aaron Hill, Thomas Rundle, and others, and being made at home among the rich intellectuals such as Lord Binning, whose son he tutored, and Bubb Dodington.

Thomson, to put it plainly, was no thinker, and he tried to do far too much. There is no driving force in the poem to give it direction such as informs Pope's at least equally complex *Essay on Man,* no brilliant mind, no formative energy as we can feel there fusing the incompatible elements. Pope is all the time selecting, criticizing, arguing; his poem is, of course, from first to last a moral argument, whereas Thomson simply imparts any piece of popular philosophy he thinks picturesque. It is the very lack of limitations that limits his vision, makes it less intense; thus nobody would quote ***The Seasons*** to describe the human situation today as Sir Winston Churchill in 1949 was able to quote the *Essay.*

Yet the poem has some delightful passages, often extensive, either where Thomson is intensely interested, as when he tries to describe the various qualities of light—then he becomes succinct; or when he lets the man of sentiment have unabashed play—then he is likeable; or when his Deistic fervour, however 'optimistic' it may be, carries him along with notable speed and intensity. If his Miltonism may now and again be tiresome (it is absurd to argue with Dr. Johnson that there is no tang of Milton in his versification), it often has about it much of the rude sweetness of a Scottish tune. It is harder, perhaps, to get over some of his craggy latinisms and his pet words—his diffusives, effusives, amusives, and so on—or again his too frequent use of adjectives in place of adverbs; but once you get used to the idiom the variations within it become attractive and, what is more, expressive, as do departures from his sometimes monotonous prosody such as the surprising and effective

> And shiver ev'ry Feather with Desire.

It becomes a positive value to go with him, to adventure with him to see how he makes his none too flexible medium begin to express the sensibility of his time, as in the domestic-love passage in **'Autumn',** or when he praises the social virtues; it is a positive value because it is; when embraced in this way, an exploration of reality. There are times when, stirred by his personal discovery of natural scenery, together with other people's discoveries of how nature works, he presents us with an object nobody else offers us in that sort of way, together with an invitation to share that particular sensibility. It would be nonsensical to claim this as a great poem: it is readable *in toto* only by the curious and the scholar; nevertheless, it need not be insisted, it contains a very great deal that should delight the reasonable reader.

Nobody can fail to admire the immense industry, not only in the rearranging and the rewriting that went to this poem, but in reading. It is a work of enormous erudition, a compendium of lore and learning; the literary and philosophic sources traced by Professor McKillop represent a library, and it is just to say that Thomson's description of the subjects he would like to spend evenings discussing with his friends very fairly describes the scope of the

A scene from Summer *painted by Benjamin West in 1795. Here, Damon (left, background) discovers Musidora and two companions bathing.*

poem. Not indeed, the original scope, but such as it appeared to Thomson to have been when he made the 1730 revision of ***Winter,*** where a pretty stiff conversational programme is suggested, covering metaphysics, science, ethics, history, and geography. To us, with our ideal of specialized knowledge for its own sake, it seems monstrous; but to Thomson's contemporaries our procedure, leading to an admirably segregated sterility, would, perhaps with some justice, have engendered scorn. For there was, after all, some object in all this labour:

> As thus we talk'd
> Our hearts would burn within us, would inhale
> That portion of divinity, that ray
> Of purest heaven, which lights the glorious flame
> Of patriots and of heroes. But if doom'd
> In powerless humble fortune, to repress
> These ardent risings of the kindling soul;
> Then, even superior to ambition, we
> Would learn the private virtues . . .

and if this should be thought too priggish or intense, wit, and humour, and laughter 'deep-shaking every nerve' is to act as relief.

The whole passage is calmly and happily serious. Thomson is talking; he has forgotten Milton, since there is no need to reach for the sublime. It is the statement of 'progressivism', evolutionary Deism we might call. . . . And it is time to ask ourselves how that passage taken with the whole theme of 'fittingness' differs in essentials from:

> How exquisitely the individual Mind
> (And the progressive powers perhaps no less
> Of the whole species) to the external World
> Is fitted:—and how exquisitely, too—
> Theme this but little heard of among men—
> The external World is fitted to the Mind;
> And the creation (by no lower name
> Can it be called) which they with blended might
> Accomplish:—this is our high argument.

One would say that in *The Recluse,* at any rate, Wordsworth's philosophy differs from Thomson's only in the sense—somewhat faint—of the creative capacity of the mind. But Wordsworth could not help feeling what he did; Thomson, had he lived in a different age, might, we think, have felt otherwise; but both began with much the same reaction towards nature. Thomson, however, never gets very near to describing the actual impact of the external things upon the nerves; the following is possibly as close as he ever does get:

'Tis *Harmony,* that World-attuning Power
By which all Beings are adjusted, each
To all around, impelling and impell'd
In endless Circulation, that inspires
This universal Smile. Thus the glad Skies,
The wide-rejoycing Earth, the Woods, the Streams
With every *Life* they hold, down to the Flower
That paints the lowly Vale, or Insect-Wing
Wav'd o'er the Shepherds' Slumber, touch the Mind
To Nature tun'd, with a light-flying Hand,
Invisible; quick-urging, thro' the Nerves,
The glittering Spirits, in a Flood of Day.

That passage, dropped in 1744, expresses the kind of sentiment later generations have wished he had explored and developed; but even had he felt impelled to do so, it is doubtful whether the prosody into which he had built his sensations, and the diction he had so whole-heartedly inherited, could have communicated it.

At the present day there are, it seems, two schools; those who regard Thomson primarily as a 'nature poet', and those who conceive his main interest to have been philosophical. But the argument is idle, because it is quite likely that Thomson, after the first flush of youthful reaction, found nature by herself not enough and wished to deepen his theme. The argument, moreover, is meaningless, since it was only through philosophy that nature could mean anything; nature and philosophy were the same. This was altogether in the line of thought of Ray and others, and had been long enough popularized by Steele and Addison. What the poets such as Thomson (who was one among many) were doing was to express the ethos of the time, its apprehension of the universe. So when we say that something disastrous happened to Thomson, that is only from our point of view; for him and his contemporaries the development was only right and proper. After all, the business of the poet was to instruct, and it was the new natural philosophy that his readers wished to be instructed in. . . . (pp. 483-89)

Thomson, it is evident, was profoundly stirred by the revelation afforded by Newton of how Creative Divinity works. In the poem ***To the Memory of Sir Isaac Newton*** he asks:

Did ever Poet image aught so fair,
Dreaming in whispering Groves by the hoarse Brook?
Or Prophet, to whose Rapture Heaven descends!

And it is hardly Thomson's fault that the occasion of this pæan, namely the justice and beauteousness of the refractive law, does not appeal to us in the same way as it did to him. The rainbow was lovely, as Thomson saw; but what was really marvellous was the way it happened. That was the stupendous thing. In due course people became accustomed to this, and wc can understand, though we need not excuse, the exuberance at Haydon's 'immortal' dinner, when he with Keats, Lamb, and Wordsworth drank confusion to mathematics, after Keats had declared that the prism had destroyed all the poetry in the rainbow. Naturally, if Keats had had the spectrum drummed into him at school he might well write

There was an awful rainbow once in heaven
We know her woof and texture; she is given:
In the dull catalogue of common things.
Philosophy will clip an angel's wings . . .

But Thomson and his generation would simply not have understood this attitude; they might, alas! have regarded it as immature, and have said with Coleridge: 'In wonder all philosophy began; in wonder it ends; but the first wonder is the offspring of ignorance, the last is the parent of adoration.' For what was happening in the poetry of the twenties was a renascence of the second kind of wonder, that of most of the Romantics would have seemed to the earlier poets like the gaping of country bumpkins. Yet wonder was not enough. The thinking man could go beyond this to a conception of the moral governance of the universe. Happy the man who can know the causes of things—the Virgilian tag echoes through much of ***The Seasons***—for then, to his contemplative mind, a great deal will be revealed. To such, endowed with an 'exalting eye',

a fairer World
Of which the Vulgar never had a Glimpse
Displays its Charms; whose Minds are richly fraught
With Philosophic Stores, superior Light.

To the philosopher, but not to the vulgar, it is evident that there is an analogy between the natural and moral world. And since to a man of Thomson's nature and real love of beauty the natural world declared benevolence as its principle, benevolence must be the ruling factor in the moral order. The essential goodness of God being granted, it followed that the happier man was, the better pleased God would be, a point of view based perhaps on what such divines as Barrow and Tillotson had said; there was at least that much orthodox support. The argument from analogy—not the same that would be developed by Butler, its opposite indeed—had been argued at least as early as Joseph Glanvill, who seems to be echoed at the end of ***Winter,*** where there intrudes another form of optimism, briefly stated perhaps as the belief that the justice of God corresponded with man's idea of justice. To some extent all this was derivable from Clarke's *Being and Attributes of God* (1705), for Clarke's second law of righteousness was benevolence, a benevolence manifested in the created world order. To the modern reader the argument at the end of ***Winter*** seems an amazing *non sequitur,* and therefore an unconvincing solution of the problem of evil. The argument, however, would seem to be mainly one for immortality; nature 'dies' in winter, but spring is not far behind; if this was not also true of man, nature would not be a reflection of the moral order. Also, since to be judged by only one life would be unjust, there must be a succession of lives (this also fits in with the rising scale of being), and it is an easy step from there to the Pythagoreanism which Thomson expressed more clearly in ***Liberty*** than in ***The Seasons.*** (pp. 489-91)

None of this much matters to us wishing to enjoy in the poem what Thomson alone has to give, but even so very light an 'elucidation of scripture' is necessary if we are to get unobstructed the enjoyment open to us; and it would seem clear that Thomson's own original enjoyment, which helped to produce his philosophy, was enormously sharpened, made more tense and exciting, by the philosophy itself. He had achieved, if not synthesis, or a unified vision, at least a syncretism; there was no split, no dualism such as Butler was to insist upon, and he could sail happily away, feeling that anything he put into his poem was appropriate, adding more and more 'as books or conversation extended his knowledge and opened his prospects'. So the modest 405 lines of the 1726 ***Winter*** became 1,069 lines in 1744, and the first ***Seasons*** of 1730 (where ***Winter*** was already nearly doubled), containing 4,464 lines, expanded some eleven hundred by the final revision of 1746, which was the last that Thomson attempted.

The present-day reader probably finds most exciting not the well-known set pieces such as the snowstorm, the thunderstorm, the sandstorm, and so on, nor even the landscapes, where Thomson sometimes fails to distinguish between description and cataloguing, nor the sentimental stories; but those occasional lines or short passages where by some kind of magic Thomson opens doors he himself does not seem to be aware of. Apparently he thinks he is describing; he is really lifting the shutter of intensely imaginative vision. The reader comes across these things with a shock of delighted surprise, as at the end of the Siberian passage in the 1730 editions of ***Winter.*** The passage first occurs in the second 1726 edition, where we see

> the *Bear*
> Rough *Tenant* of these Shades! shaggy with Ice
> And dangling Snow, stalks thro' the Woods, forlorn.

But in 1730, after the bear we have:

> While tempted vigorous o'er the marble waste,
> On sleds reclin'd, the furry Russian sits;
> And by his rain-deer drawn, behind him throws
> A shining kingdom in a winter's day,

a connotative glimpse which easily makes up for the bear shaggy with ice having become 'the shaggy bear with dangling ice all horrid'. But, and this is why we suspect his unawareness, in the 1744 version the bear becomes merely 'shapeless', and the furry Russian is extinguished, in the interests of 'accuracy'. Or take again the passage in ***Spring*** where Thomson, using Burnet's *Theory of the Earth,* gives a vision of the time when nature was deemed to have changed her course, a kind of terrene 'Fall' to correspond with the Fall of man:

> Hence in old time, they say, a deluge came;
> When the disparting orb of earth, which arch'd
> Th' imprisoned deep around, impetuous rush'd,
> With ruin inconceivable, at once
> Into the gulph, and o'er the highest hills
> Wide-dash'd the waves in undulation vast;

and so far the effect is a little laboured; but then we get a transition which brings us to a last line which is miraculous, even though it may be derived from Milton:

> Till, from the centre to the streaming clouds
> A shoreless ocean tumbled round the globe.

And here it was not science that captivated Thomson, for by then even popular opinion was beginning to reject Burnet; and, moreover, no optimist could accept him seeing that if the world had once been better than it now is, all cannot be for the best in the best of all possible worlds: Thomson himself referred to 'fabling Burnet'. What spurred him was the sudden vision, and here, perhaps, is the clearest example of Thomson exploring his imagination, and so releasing that of the reader.

Yet if we read Thomson with an eye for this sort of stimulus, we shall lose sight of the after all rather important fact that this is a poem about climate, and that what interests Thomson most about climate is light, and the effect of light, colour itself being light analysed. The obvious rotation of the seasons is of course illustrated, the flowers in woodland or garden change as do the crops; sheep need different attention; there is a time for work and a time for love, for labour and for feasting. Men endure the heat of the tropics or the rigours of Lapland, the birds migrate, avalanches wipe out brigades of unfortunate soldiers, and everything in due course lends itself to moralizing, especially when stories are told, such as the Lavinia variant of the Ruth story, or the one of the lover struck by lightning, or the paterfamilias meeting his death in the snow. And if these stories all come from traceable sources, they are none the less impressive for that, and equally well illustrate the weather. But although Thomson evidently likes all this well enough, and feels it to be good material for poetry, it is only when he is describing light that we feel he could not but write poetry; he is absorbed in watching its changes, filled with delight and wonder, sensing in its behaviour some revelation of the divine, something which puts him in touch with the inapprehensible. Already in the first ***Winter,*** although it is full of the noise of storm and tempest where 'Huge Uproar lords it wide', we feel Thomson's almost mystic sense of light, at this season of the year more particularly of light as whiteness. Throughout the poem we feel that Thomson is moved by

> the fair power
> Of light to kindle and create the whole

and it is in his rapt attention to the changes of light and colour, far more than in the apostrophes and invocations—a little too reminiscent of Milton—that we are immediately aware of the depth of his response, a depth it cannot offend anyone to call religious.

It is revealing to look for a moment at the sort of thing Thomson was doing in some of his revisions. To begin with there were enormous additions. Sometimes they were admirable, and in tone; when they stuck to the theme of the seasons, which is after all that of the poem, they were valuable contributions, as are the fishing scene, and the flower-pieces in ***Winter.*** Often the corrections of words or phrases are great improvements, as when in *Winter* he alters 'Is all one dazzling Waste' to 'Is one wild dazzling Waste'. But it is the larger alterations we must consider. What is happening? we ask. Abstraction, personification, metaphor, and classical reference have ousted objectivity and sensitiveness. It is all done, we imagine, in the interests of 'the sublime'. Can we blame Lyttelton, who had a finger in the later versions? Probably not; 'the age', it seems, was tending in that direction, or at least one part of it was, moving towards Gray's Odes and Burke *On the Sublime,* and more and more to that generalization which was not so much the expression of common experience, as the refusal with Imlac in *Rasselas* to number the streaks of the tulip, or with Sir Joshua Reynolds to notice 'particularities, and details of every kind'. Lyttelton, that perfect good boy of his time, was no doubt in part responsible; but his influence lay rather in the fields of religious or moral thinking, struggling as he used to do to convert Thomson to Christianity. Yet there does not seem to be much retrenchment of Deistic statement, or intrusion of a specifically Christian ethos. Lyttelton seems to have urged a higher degree of intensity, but his influence appears for the more part to have told in the direction of a prudery the mid-nineteenth century would have approved. In the closing passages of ***Winter,*** for example, 'Those Nights of secret Guilt' become 'Those gay-spent, festive Nights', which makes us wonder why Virtue should have been dragged in as a contrast a few lines later. Again, in ***Summer,*** the story of Damon, first introduced in 1730 as a healthy, happy story, is in 1744 made vulgar and even slightly salacious in the interests of 'morality'; it appears too from the manuscript corrections that Lyttelton would have expunged from ***Spring*** the line which states that beauty 'is when unadorn'd adorn'd the most'.

But it is not such revisions that make it difficult for us to grasp the poem as an entity; it is the extravagant amount and variety of material inserted. Thomson is a perfect jackdaw; he goes about making finds, and adding them to the treasures he hoards in his nest. He is so charmingly eager in his discoveries, from the *Psalms* to Maupertuis, that he has to tell us everything, and the man who tells everything becomes a bore. Thomson incurs the danger of being such, even to those naturalized in his idiom; for the organic sense is dissipated, as it is not in the *Essay on Man.* The fact is that he confused the 'kinds'; and 'the confusion of kinds', as Henry James remarked, 'is the inelegance of letters and the stultification of values'. And since the values in ***The Seasons*** from this very cause tend to become blurred, the bulk militates against our grasping the object whole. Try as we will the poem obstinately resolves itself into separate morsels, many of them indubitably fine, others touching; some, it would be foolish to deny, either emotionally or poetically unworthy. Here and there the work is intolerably slack; Dr. Johnson could read passages aloud omitting every other line, to the 'highest admiration' of Shiels, and G. C. Macaulay gave an example of how this might be done. Yet if it is not a poem of the first order, it is one that we would not do without; and, after all, a work which had so much effect on European poetry and which was praised by Goethe demands respect. It contains magnificences and felicities; it is above all a friendly poem, and to converse with it is not always to miss exaltation, and at least we often share the excitement of sharpened recognition. A good portion of what it has essentially to impart can be derived from the admirable poem ***To the Memory of Sir Isaac Newton,*** written in 1727, the year Newton died, after ***Winter*** had appeared and while ***Summer*** was being composed. We may think that scientific fact is incompletely absorbed, but a little sympathetic imagination can dissolve the particles foreign to poetry.

It succeeds then; and it is sad to note that in the same year Thomson perpetrated ***Britannia,*** which was not published until 1729. In our modern jargon we should call it a blatantly warmongering poem. It cannot be denied a certain vigour; it is not the work of a hack-poet, and contains such things as

> —where loud the Northern main
> Howls through the fractur'd *Caledonian* isles;

but indignation aroused by Walpole's refusal to make war did not bring forth first-rate verses in any quantity. And here we come upon the most disastrous part of Thomson's social milieu, for he had become absorbed in the gifted circle which formed the opposition. Again and again we meet laments for the decay of British virtue, morals, integrity, and valour. Even the later versions of ***The Seasons*** are infected. The prevailing atmosphere in that coterie led Pope himself into some absurdities, and the effect on Thomson was lamentable in that it induced him to waste a great deal of time and energy on the long elaborate poem ***Liberty,*** published at intervals in five parts during 1735 and 1736. It has not the narrative and epic interest of *Leonidas,* yet it is a far better poem than any others on that theme. Thomson, however, tried to do far too much in it. It is really a history of civilization, which can flourish only where freedom exists, as it did with such vigour in England until Walpole's fatal accession to power. Goethe found it bad because in it Thomson had given himself over to party feeling, and it is true that the worst portions are those devoted to 'corruption'. It is a pity that the pleasurable parts, which are those where Thomson praises the countryside and looks forward to a happy, prosperous, golden-age England, should be overlaid by so much tedious historical matter—though even that becomes livelier where Britain comes into view and the poet writes good Whig history. It is not altogether just that it should be relegated to the shelf where Dr. Johnson consigned it 'to harbour spiders and to gather dust', for it repays a first careful reading so that enjoyable lines may be marked. Here again we may think Thomson erred in confusing the kinds; for it is not a travel poem as is Addison's *Letter from Italy,* nor strictly historical, nor mainly political; it fails now as it did at its birth, because it has not the force to unify and give single direction to the emotional responses it was meant to call forth.

There is no such error either in the conception or the contrivance of ***The Castle of Indolence,*** at any rate as far as the first canto goes. Born of a mood of idleness and friendship, cast in a form chosen because it was fun to fool about with quaint old versification and diction, it has an ease and spontaneity, a freedom from rhetoric, in the bad sense, which makes it delightful; and delightfully easy reading, provided always that you will enter into the game. Half-hearted Spenserians may revolt at the flippancy, but true worshippers will no more mind this than the Dryden devotee objects to *The Rehearsal* or the Montague-Prior *jeu d'esprit;* the general reader may resent eftsoons, ne and moe, depainted and yblent, not to mention the occasional grotesqueness of phrase, until he realizes that he is not meant to take them seriously. And when, carried away by the theme, Thomson forgets all the frippery of imitation, he really exudes something of the original, a sensuous music, and a simple directness of expression, combined with a freedom from contemporary poetic diction, which are refreshing. It is possible to say that this is Thomson's best poem, though it is not his most important, if best means most immediately apprehensible and enjoyable, and one in which the kinds are not confused. Where he does not attempt any archaisms he speaks the language of his day, which is almost that of ours. A few of his happier favourite expressions remain; the streams bicker, the word serene is used as a verb, and he occasionally invents (enough has not been made of Thomson as an inventor in this sense), or adapts from Milton's prose as when he refers to 'the wretch who slugs his life away'. Exquisite? No; that is too high distinction. It is not too much to say that it provides a charming pleasaunce. (pp. 491-97)

[Soon] after the enchanter Indolence begins his seductive singing we are caught up in the atmosphere of the idle Abbaye de Thelème. Indolence is no fool; he knows that to offer sensuous joys is not enough for the intelligent man; some higher general principle must be appealed to:

> What, what is Virtue but Repose of Mind?
> A pure ethereal Calm! that knows no Storm,
> Above the Reach of wild Ambition's Wind,
> Above those Passions that this World deform,
> And torture Man, a proud malignant Worm!
> But here, instead, soft Gales of Passion play,
> And gently stir the Heart, thereby to form
> A quicker Sense of Joy; as Breezes stray
> Across th' enlivened Skies, and make them still
> more gay.

There is movement in the canto, a little light satire (we have momentary forebodings when we read of 'the patriot's noble rage, Dashing corruption down through every worthless age', but the danger soon passes), and throughout there is a general feeling of richness, of luxury, of a *fays-ce que voudras* life in which boredom is guarded against, though not, alas, hypochondria, gout, apoplexy, and other ailments of the rich not unusual in a society in which Addison plaintively complained, 'How can a man help his being fat who eats proper to his quality?' It is a good lotus-eating world, which it is pleasant to inhabit for a time. And the moral of it?

Well, the moral is round the corner, not so much in the hidden hospital for incurables, which is obviously worth risking, but in the second canto, where the Knight of Arts and Industry, somewhat oddly begotten by savagery on poverty, breaks up the sham paradise. It is often complained that Thomson spoilt the poem by forcing the moral forward in this way; but Thomson is not being puritanically moral. Canto II is not so much a set of moralizing stanzas as a poem on industry and commerce, one of the very many of that age; it was a theme Thomson could believe in. Poems of that family will be touched upon later; what is worth noticing here is a new note, a different pace, of which one would not have thought Thomson capable; the verse has forgotten sublimity but has a vigour and an ease, almost one would say a lordly Byronic assumption of careless power, not it is true sustained, but never far away. The third stanza, for example:

> I care not, Fortune, what you me deny:
> You cannot rob me of free Nature's Grace;
> You cannot shut the Windows of the Sky,
> Through which *Aurora* shows her brightening
> Face:
> You cannot bar my constant Feet to trace
> The Woods and Lawns, by living Stream, at Eve.
> Let health my nerves and finer Fibres brace,
> And I their toys to the *great children* leave:
> Of Fancy, Reason, Virtue, nought can me bereave.

But alas, only some four months after the poem was published, in May 1748, Thomson died, an event celebrated in Collins's famous tribute. Yet ***The Castle of Indolence*** happily rounds off a varied enough body of poetry—the plays have been treated in the section on drama—which any writer not of first rank might look upon with satisfaction. His smaller poems and occasional verses call for no especial comment; they are neat, they breathe a delicacy of feeling rather than any passion of love or fervour of friendship. It is worth noting that Thomson was adept enough in the quatrain or rhymed stanza, but his couplets, as instanced say by his humorous lines on Murdoch, 'the incomparable soporific doctor' (who seems to have been able to stand any amount of chaff), lack variety of movement or attack. Some of his shorter pieces should be better known, but it is unlikely that Thomson will ever again be a popular poet, though he will always be read by a circle considerably larger than that of student or historian. (pp. 497-99)

Bonamy Dobrée, "Poetry, 1720-1740," in his English Literature in the Early Eighteenth Century, 1700-1740, *1959. Reprint by Oxford at the Clarendon Press, 1964, pp. 475-99.*

David Daiches (essay date 1960)

[*Daiches is a scholar and writer whose books include* Two Worlds *(1957), an autobiographical work,* A Critical History of English Literature *(1960), and* Scotch Whisky *(1969). In the following excerpt, he places Thomson's works in the context of the literary and intellectual climate of eighteenth-century England, maintaining that Thomson "is emphatically an English rather than a Scottish poet."*]

Though the Augustan poets believed that the proper study of mankind was man, they were far from indifferent to the beauties of Nature, and throughout the eighteenth century is found a strain of descriptive and meditative poetry in which natural description prompts moral reflections on the human situation. The pioneer here was James Thomson, whose four long poems on the seasons—***Winter*** (1726), ***Summer*** (1727), ***Spring*** (1728), and ***Autumn,*** which appeared in 1730 in the collected volume—employ a quasi-Miltonic blank verse in describing the countryside at different times of the year and interlarding his descriptions with meditations on man. In his Preface to ***Winter*** Thomson expressed a view of his subject which was to become increasingly popular:

> I know of no subject more elevating, more amusing, more ready to awake the poetical enthusiasm, the philosophical reflection, and the moral sentiment, than the works of Nature. Where can

we meet with such variety, such beauty, such magnificence? All that enlarges and transports the soul? What more inspiring than a calm, wide survey of them? In every dress Nature is greatly charming—whether she puts on the crimson robes of the morning, the strong effulgence of noon, the sober suit of the evening, or the deep sables of blackness and tempest! How gay looks the spring! how glorious the summer! how pleasing the autumn! and how venerable the winter!—But there is no thinking of these things without breaking out into poetry; which is, by the bye, a plain and undeniable argument of their superior excellence.

For this reason the best, both ancient and modern, poets have been passionately fond of retirement and solitude. The wild romantic country was their delight. And they seem never to have been more happy than when, lost in unfrequented fields, far from the little busy world, they were at leisure to meditate, and sing the works of Nature.

Thomson was born in the Scottish Border country and came to seek literary fortune in London after studying at Edinburgh University; it may be that the country environment in which he grew up permanently affected his imagination. But he is emphatically an English rather than a Scottish poet; if he brought to Augustan poetry something if not altogether new yet somewhat different from what was most in favor with the literary men of the time, he absorbed from the climate of early eighteenth-century English opinion the view of an ordered universe directed by universal laws framed by the original designer, God, and discovered by Newton, and the phenomena of Nature which he describes are seen as parts of this ordered system. His **"Poem Sacred to the Memory of Sir Isaac Newton"** expresses this view clearly:

O unprofuse magnificence divine!
O wisdom truly perfect! thus to call
From a few causes such a scheme of things,
Effects so various, beautiful, and great,
A universe complete! And O beloved
Of Heaven! whose well purged penetrative eye
The mystic veil transpiercing, inly scanned
The rising, moving, wide-established frame.

And the Hymn with which he concluded ***The Seasons*** sees the phenomena of Nature as the result of the benevolent contrivance of God:

These, as they change, Almighty Father, these
Are but the varied God! The rolling year
Is full of Thee. Forth in the pleasing Spring
Thy beauty walks, Thy tenderness and love.
Wide flush the fields; the softening air is balm;
Echo the mountains round; the forest smiles;
And every sense, and every heart, is joy.
Then comes Thy glory in the Summer months,
With light and heat refulgent. . . .
Thy bounty shines in Autumn unconfined,
And spreads a common feast for all that lives.
In Winter awful Thou! with clouds and storms
Around Thee thrown, tempest o'er tempest rolled,
Majestic darkness! . . .
Mysterious round! what skill, what force divine,
Deep felt in these appear! a simple train,
Yet so delightful mixed, with such kind art,
Such beauty and beneficence combined,
Shade, unperceived, so softening into shade,
And all so forming an harmonious whole
That, as they still succeed, they ravish still.

The ideas expressed in ***The Seasons*** were not new, but the sensibility reflected in the poem was, at least in some degree. The age admired the kind of "local poetry" represented by Denham's "Cooper's Hill," but Denham and his imitators were content to embellish description—in Dr. Johnson's phrase—"by historical retrospection, or incidental meditation." Thomson's meditations went deeper, and the deliberate cultivation of pensiveness in the contemplation of Nature showed a quite different kind of sensibility:

Thus solitary, and in pensive guise,
Oft let me wander o'er the russet mead,
And through the saddened grove, where scarce is heard
One dying strain, to cheer the woodman's toil. . . .
He comes! he comes! in every breeze the Power
Of Philosophic Melancholy comes!
His near approach the sudden-starting tear,
The glowing cheek, the mild dejected air,
The softened feature, and the beating heart,
Pierced deep with many a virtuous pang, declare.
O'er all the soul his sacred influence breathes;
Inflames imagination, through the breast
Infuses every tenderness, and far
Beyond dim earth exalts the swelling thought. . . .
As fast the correspondent passions rise,
As varied, and as high: Devotion, raised
To rapture and divine astonishment;
The love of Nature unconfined, and, chief,
Of human race; the large ambitious wish
To make them blest; the sigh for suffering worth
Lost in obscurity; the noble scorn
Of tyrant-pride; the fearless great resolve; . . .
The sympathies of love and friendship dear,
With all the social offspring of the heart.
Oh, bear me then to vast embowering shades,
To twilight groves, and visionary vales,
To weeping grottoes and prophetic glooms,
Where angel-forms athwart the solemn dusk
Tremendous sweep, or seem to sweep, along;
And voices more than human, through the void
Deep-sounding, seize th' enthusiastic ear!

(***Autumn***)

The use of "enthusiastic" here, without any of the reservations or suspicions with which Shaftesbury or Pope or Johnson would have used the term is significant. Yet Thomson's optimistic Deism derives in large measure from Shaftesbury, who had also hailed Nature in rapturous terms, as one of the speakers in his dialogue entitled *The Moralists: A Rhapsody* (1709) illustrates:

Ye fields and woods, my refuge from the toilsome world of business, receive me in your quiet sanctuaries and favour my retreat and thoughtful solitude. Ye verdant plains, how gladly I salute ye. . . . O glorious Nature! supremely fair and sovereignly good! All-loving and all-lovely, all-divine! . . . To thee this solitude, this place, these rural meditations are sacred; whilst thus inspired with harmony of thought, though unconfined by words, and in loose numbers I sing of Nature's order in created beings, and celebrate the beauties which resolve in thee, the source and principle of all beauty and perfection.

And Dr. Johnson was to pay tribute to Thomson's ability to reveal things which, once revealed, were seen to be of universal application: "The reader of the ***Seasons*** wonders that he never saw before what Thomson shows him, and that he never yet has felt what Thomson impresses" [see excerpt dated 1781]. And Pope and his circle admired and encouraged Thomson. We must not therefore see Thomson as representing a pre-Romantic enthusiasm in his treatment of Nature which was opposed to the more sophisticated polite poetry of an age. Though in his feeling for the sights and sounds of the countryside and the affectionate detail with which he could describe them he displays a sensibility rather different from that which we readily associate with the spirit of the age, in his moralizing, his using natural description as a jumping-off place for generalizations about man, and his deistic view of order, he spoke with the voice of his age and pleased his contemporaries. Only Swift objected to the want of action in the poems: "I am not over fond of them, because they are all descriptions, and nothing is doing," he wrote to a friend in 1732; and Dr. Johnson, in his "Life of Thomson," was to combine admiration with the remark that "the great defect of the ***Seasons*** is want of method."

It is interesting that in Johnson's account of ***The Seasons*** he is so taken up with the attraction of Thomson's descriptions that he uses Thomson's word "enthusiasm" in Thomson's sense, not in the pejorative sense which he gives it in his own dictionary:

His descriptions of extended scenes and general effects bring before us the whole magnificence of Nature, whether pleasing or dreadful. The gaiety of ***Spring,*** the splendour of ***Summer,*** the tranquillity of ***Autumn,*** and the horror of ***Winter,*** take in their turns possession of the mind. The poet leads us through the appearances of things as they are successively varied by the vicissitudes of the year, and imparts to us so much of his own enthusiasm, that our thoughts expand with his imagery, and kindle with his sentiments. Nor is the naturalist without his part in the entertainment; for he is assisted to recollect and to combine, to arrange his discoveries, and to amplify the sphere of his contemplation.

This is interesting evidence of the way in which ***The Seasons*** struck the eighteenth-century reader. Johnson seems to be expressing with his usual cogency the common opinion of Thomson in his own time.

Thomson's diction is deliberately elevated, to give dignity to his descriptions. Johnson called it "florid and luxuriant" in the highest degree. Sometimes the pseudo-Miltonic Latinizations have an almost comic effect.

At last
The clouds consign their Treasures to the fields,
And, softly shaking on the dimpled pool
Prelusive drops, let all their moisture flow,
In large effusion, o'er the freshened world.
The stealing shower is scarce to patter heard,
By such as wander through the forest walks,
Beneath the umbrageous multitude of leaves.

His description of fishing in ***Spring*** has something of the half-burlesque quality of Gay's similar description in *Rural Sports,* though it is not intended:

Now when the first foul torrent of the brooks,
Swelled with the vernal rains, is ebbed away,
And, whitening, down their mossy tinctured stream
Descends the billowy foam; now is the time,
While yet the dark-brown water aids the guile,
To tempt the trout. The well-dissembled fly,
The rod fine-tapering with elastic spring,
Snatch'd from the hoary steed the floating line,
And all thy slender watery stores, prepare.
But let not on thy hook the tortured worm,
Convulsive, twist in agonising folds; . . .
When with his lively ray the potent sun
Has pierced the streams and roused the finny race,
Then, issuing cheerful, to thy sport repair; . . .

The tricks of diction and phrasing which Thomson got from Milton derive from the most superficial aspects of Milton's style: as Dr. Johnson put it, "His blank verse is no more the blank verse of Milton, or of any other poet, than the rhymes of Prior are the rhymes of Cowley." The use of dignified periphrasis in the description of homely or rustic things has, as we have seen, its burlesque element, and to tell the rural fisherman to "throw, nice-judging, the delusive fly" sounds somewhat absurd; but Thomson can use this diction to give real weight and feeling to his verse:

With broadened nostrils to the sky upturned,
The conscious heifer snuffs the stormy gale.
Even as the matron, at her nightly task,
With pensive labour draws the flaxen thread,
The wasted taper and the crackling flame
Foretell the blast. But chief the plumy race,
The tenants of the sky, its changes speak.
Retiring from the downs, where all day long
They picked their scanty fare, a blackening train
Of clamorous rooks thick-urge their weary flight,
And seek the closing shelter of the grove.
Assiduous in his bower, the wailing owl
Plies his sad song.

(***Winter***)

In his choice of descriptive detail to suggest a mood and in building up the mass of his verse to carry the weight of the mood, Thomson is at his best. In his frequent apostrophes, reflections, moralizings, invocations, and rhetorical questions his verse is at its most turgid and tedious.

Thomson's other important poem is ***The Castle of Indolence*** (1748), a descriptive-narrative poem in two cantos written in Spenserian stanzas and with an intermittent and half-hearted attempt at a Spenserian vocabulary. Thomson did however succeed in capturing something of Spenser's mood and movement:

A pleasing land of drowsy-head it was
Of dreams that wave before the half-shut eye;
And of gay castles in the clouds that pass,
For ever flushing round a summer sky.
There eke the soft delights, that witchingly
Instil a wanton sweetness through the breast,
And the calm pleasures, always hovered nigh;
But whate'er smackt of noyance or unrest
Was far, far off expelled from this delicious nest.

Thomson was aware of the half-humorous effect of using Spenser's language (or traces of it) in the eighteenth century. In the "Advertisement" prefixed to the poem he wrote: "This poem being writ in the manner of Spenser, the obsolete words, and a simplicity of diction in some of the lines which borders on the ludicrous, were necessary to make the imitation more perfect." Nevertheless, in spite of some deliberately humorous flickers in the handling of language and in portraits of his friends, the sleepy movement of the first canto of the poem—reminding us at times of Tennyson's "The Lotos-Eaters"—is intended as a serious poetic effect, and it is so. The second canto, where the knight Sir Industry overthrows the Castle of Indolence, shows Thomson turning to a favorite theme, the progress of the arts and industry in Britain (treated in his dull blank-verse poem, ***Liberty***); it is less successful than the first, lacking its music and sleepy movement and concentrating on an allegorical action of little subtlety and on Sir Industry's exhortation to the inhabitants of the castle to rouse themselves and *do* something. That Thomson should choose the Spenserian stanza and the form of the allegorical romance, however uncertainly serious his mood, is interesting testimony to the search for new models and wider poetic horizons that was going in the very heart of the Augustan Age. (pp. 652-58)

David Daiches, "Poetry from Thomson to Crabbe," in his A Critical History of English Literature, Vol. II, *The Ronald Press Company, 1960, pp. 652-58.*

R. R. Agrawal (essay date 1978)

[*In the following excerpt from a work completed in 1978, Agrawal discusses Thomson's lesser-known works, focusing on his love lyrics and elegiac poems.*]

Thomson's love lyrics and songs bring him in line with the Elizabethan and Caroline love poets on the one hand and the Romantic and Victorian love poets on the other. They are all essentially inspired by his deep love and devotion for Amanda. The sentiments in most of these lyrics have been expressed through beautiful Elizabethan figures and images. There is an inexplicable tenderness and beauty in his sentiments and expression that touch the chords of the reader's heart. This may be accounted for by the fact that Thomson's object of love was not merely a fancy beloved or a poetical abstraction but a real woman with a warm pulsating heart. Some of these lyrics, directly addressed to Amanda, show the depth of the poet's love for her. The poet finds no joy or beauty in life or in Nature without the warm and genial company of his beloved:

Awakened by the genial year,
In vain the birds around me sing;
In vain the freshening fields appear:
Without my love there is no Spring.

The happiest of these lyrics is the one addressed to Myra, in which the poet offers his adoration to his beloved:

O Thou whose tender serious eyes
Expressive speak the mind I love—
The gentle azure of the skies,
The pensive shadows of the grove—.

The enchanting effect of her superb beauty is described in the following lines through beautiful images and sentiments:

Ah, 'tis too much! I cannot bear
At once so soft, so keen a ray:
In pity then, my lovely fair,
O turn those killing eyes away!
But what avails it to conceal
One charm where nought but charms I see?
Their lustre then again reveal,
And let me, Myra, die of thee!

Love has two sides—union and separation, fruition and frustration. In intense love separation gives pain and disappointment in the same proportion as union gives joy and thrill. No situation is more painful or heart-breaking than the one in which the lover is forced to stifle his effusion of sentiments or in which adequate response does not come from the beloved:

Hard is the fate of him who loves
Yet dares not tell his trembling pain
But to the sympathetic groves,
But to the lonely listening plain.

The same 'plaintive strain' of love is heard in the stanzas **"To The Nightingale"**:

'Tis mine, alas! to mourn my wretched fate:
I love a maid who all my bosom charms,
Yet lose my days without this lovely mate;
Inhuman fortune keeps her from my arms.

. . . . .

And hence in vain I languish for my bride—
O mourn with me, sweet bird, my hapless flame.

The poet complains of the cruelty of the beloved in **"The Bashful Lover":**

Sweet tyrant Love, but hear me now!
And cure while young this pleasing smart;
Or rather, aid my trembling vow,
And teach me to reveal my heart.

The poignancy reaches its climax in lines like the following:

It is no common passion fires my breast—
I must be wretched, or I must be blest!
My woes all other remedy deny—
Or pitying give me hope, or bid me die!

In moments of pain and frustration such as these the lover finds fault with everything near and around him, but with fate and dispensation of God above all. Fate often works against a zealous lover:

For ever, Fortune, wilt thou prove

An unrelenting foe to love,
And, when we meet a mutual heart,
Come in between and bid us part;
Bid us sigh on from day to day,
And wish, and wish the soul away;
Till youth and genial years are flown,
And all the life of life is gone?

And from this malicious and sadistic fate the lover seeks but one boon:

For once, O Fortune! hear my prayer,
And I absolve thy future care—
All other blessings I resign;
Make but the dear Amanda mine!

But the sportive playfulness with the golden tresses, rosy cheeks and dreamy eyes of the beloved is not the goal of Thomson's love. His love is much deeper and higher than this physical ecstasy. In essence his love is Platonic. In the glow and ecstasy of love the beloved is transformed into a symbol of beauty and joy or even of divinity. True love is a transcendental force that deifies both the lover and the object of love. Not only in its fruition but sometimes even in frustration it illumines the human soul with a spiritual vision and glory. This is what characterizes the love of Thomson:

'Tis not for common charms I sigh,
For what the vulgar beauty call;
'Tis not a cheek, a lip, an eye;
But 'tis the soul that lights them all.

To such a lover the object of love becomes a symbol of divinity:

To love thee, Seraphina, sure
Is to be tender, happy, pure;
'Tis from low passions to escape,
And woo bright virtue's fairest shape;
'Tis ecstasy with wisdom joined,
And heaven infused into the mind.

It is this kind of sublime and divine love,

Which clears the mind and cleans the heart,
Is like the sacred queen of night
Who pours a lovely gentle light
Wide o'er the dark—by wanderers blest,
Conducting them to peace and rest.

These love lyrics are largely a study in the emotional autobiography of the poet. They express not only the glow and ecstasy of love but also a deep romantic longing and agony which impart to them a new lyrical charm and melody. Some of these lyrics recall to our mind the love lyrics of Shelley, Keats and Byron. While lacking the elusive delicacy of Shelley, the noble distinction of Wordsworth, and the lilting charm and melody of Byron, the lyrics of Thomson are none the less noted for a grace, melody and delicacy of feeling, and a simplicity and lucidity of expression not easy to find in the entire range of English lyric poetry. Their range of appeal is very wide. Their Elizabethan and Caroline thrill, sweetness and poignancy satisfy the aesthetic sense of the reader, while for the purely literary artist there is enough to interest both in their sentiment and in their verse-form.

Next may be considered Thomson's elegiac and memorial verses occasioned by the deaths of some of his friends, associates, benefactors and patrons. An intense emotion of grief and a grateful remembrance of the dead for their great qualities and achievements are the two distinguishing features of these poems. At least three of them—**"On the Death of His Mother," "On the Death of Mr. William Aikman, the Painter,"** and **"Epitaph on Miss Elizabeth Stanley"**— are an unaffected expression of personal grief and sincere feeling, while the other three, viz. **"To the Memory of Sir Isaac Newton," "To the Memory of the Right Honourable the Lord Talbot,"** and **"A Poem to the Memory of Mr. Congreve,"** are in the nature of poetic tributes to the rare talents of these great men.

Thomson's elegiac and memorial verses may best be seen in relation to a type of poetry which was coming into vogue in the first half of the eighteenth century. This poetic type was the funeral elegy, with which the litterateurs and sophisticated readers with a grounding in classical literature were well acquainted. The funeral elegy, commemorating the death of an individual, usually assumed the form of a pastoral elegy. This elegy usually followed a set plan, i.e. statement of the subject, lamentation, and consolation through philosophical and metaphysical reflections on death and immortality of the soul. These mixed elegies were largely inspired by Milton's *Lycidas,* the most famous of the formal pastoral funeral elegies in English.

Thomson's memorial verses conform to this eighteenth-century mixed type of elegy in sentiment and structure without, of course, adopting the pastoral garb. In each of them he commemorates the death of an individual and follows the set plan. Each first proposes or states the subject, then passes on to lamentation and finally ends in consolation and stoic resignation.

The most important thing about these elegiac poems is that they are all permeated with a melancholy spirit, tone and atmosphere that in the nineteenth-century poetry came to be known as 'Romantic gloom'. Further, since they do not take on the artificial garb of the pastoral elegy, the emotions of grief, as expressed in them, are genuine and sincere, making a direct appeal to the heart of the reader. The genuineness of grief and intensity of feeling are, for example, best seen in his moving poem **"On the Death of His Mother,"** Here the poet disclaims the aid of 'fabled muses' lest the sincere effusions of his heart may be brushed aside as mere poetical exercises:

Ye fabled muses, I your aid disclaim,
Your airy raptures, and your fancied flame:
True genuine woe my throbbing breast inspires,
Love prompts my lays, and filial duty fires;
The soul springs instant at the warm design,
And the heart dictates every flowing line.

The poet wistfully recalls the day on which, while embarking from Leith to London, he saw his mother last and bade her farewell, little knowing that it was destined to be his last farewell to her:

Why was I then, ye powers, reserved for this,
Nor sunk that moment in the vast abyss?
Devoured at once by the relentless wave,
And whelmed for ever in a watery grave?

These lines are marked with a lyric intensity and impassioned expression that cannot fail to impress the reader. Similarly, Thomson's lines on Aikman, the painter, are painfully wrung from his heart by real grief. The concluding lines of this poem are deeply moving:

> As those we love decay, we die in part,
> String after string is severed from the heart;
> This loosened life, at last but breathing clay,
> Without one pang is glad to fall away.
> Unhappy he who latest feels the blow,
> Whose eyes have wept o'er every friend laid low,
> Dragged lingering on from partial death to death,
> Till, dying, all he can resign is breath.

These elegiac poems are also notable for their consolatory message. They end on a note of philosophic consolation and stoic calm, so important a feature of the funeral elegy. The concluding lines of the poem **"On the Death of His Mother"**, for example, offer the typical consolation that comes to the heart of the mourner through metaphysical reflections:

> Down, ye wild wishes of unruly woe!
> I see her with immortal beauty glow;
> The early wrinkle, care-contracted, gone,
> Her tears all wiped, and all her sorrows flown;
> The exalting voice of Heaven I hear her breathe,
> To soothe her soul in agonies of death.
> I see her through the mansions blest above,
> And now she meets her dear expecting love.

This recalls to us the spirit of consolation and calm resignation so well expressed in Milton's *Lycidas,* Shelley's *Adonais* and Arnold's *Thyrsis.*

The memorial verses, however, are not all elegiac. Some of them are eulogistic and some fiercely satirical. The eulogistic pieces pay a glorious, even exaggerated, tribute to the benefactors and patrons of the poet. The poem written in memory of his patron, Lord Talbot, for example, is a panegyric on his numerous virtues and talents:

> What grand, what comely, and what tender sense,
> What talent, and what virtue was not his?
> All that can render man or great or good,
> Give useful worth, or amiable grace?

In at least one of these poems, **"To the Memory of Mr. Congreve,"** the poet is guilty of personal satire. In this poem Thomson, like Dryden and Pope, directs his poetic lash at Asper and Cenus—two 'ignoble names', as he calls them—who have not been properly identified. Mark how contemptuously the poet speaks of Asper:

> Not so the illiberal mind, where knowledge dwells,
> Uncouth and harsh, with her attendant, pride,
> Impatient of attention, prone to blame,
> Disdaining to be pleased; condemning all,
> By all condemned; for social joys unfit,
> In solitude self-cursed, the child of spleen.
> Obliged, ungrateful; unobliged, a foe,
> Poor, vicious, old; such fierce-eyed Asper was.

Here Thomson's satire is as pungent and offensive as that of Swift, as fiercely personal and bitter as that of Pope and Dryden. It is full of spleen and contempt, couched in a language unbecoming to a sober-minded and philanthropic poet like Thomson. (pp. 183-90)

R. R. Agrawal, " 'Liberty' and Other Miscellaneous Works," in his Tradition and Experiment in the Poetry of James Thomson (1700-1748), *Institut für Anglistik und Amerikanistik Universität Salzburg, 1981, pp. 166-95.*

Mary Jane W. Scott (essay date 1988)

[*Scott is an American scholar specializing in Scottish literature. In the following excerpt, she analyzes the language of* The Seasons, *noting that Thomson's upbringing as a "divinity student, like his education in the humanities and classical rhetoric, had considerable impact on his poetic style."*]

The Seasons, inspired as it was by such amazing diversity of purpose and plan, demanded stylistic and linguistic versatility far beyond the conventions of formal Augustan poetic English. Thomson recognized this as soon as he began to write ***Winter.*** As a Scots speaker, he also recognized the limits of his own language, yet, remarkably, he found the will to turn these formidable linguistic limitations into positive strengths and the distinctive language of ***The Seasons*** began to evolve.

Thomson had to find the appropriate verse form for his poem and, fortunately, for many good reasons, he chose to work in blank verse. Further, he had to create a more flexible, readily adaptable literary language for his eclectic poem, a poetic diction which would draw not only upon his familiarity with Latin, his Calvinist religion, and his knowledge of Newtonian science (all idioms of his Scottish background) but also, in more subtle ways, upon his vernacular Scots literary and linguistic heritage. Thomson's highly original language for ***The Seasons*** is eclectic, empirical, experimental, in the spirit of the Scottish Enlightenment. It speaks with an accent that is unmistakably Scottish.

James Thomson was a native Scots speaker, so his relative unfamiliarity with spoken English when he began ***The Seasons*** probably had much to do with his choice of the less-restrictive blank-verse form, which was not so heavily dependent on any standardized pronunciation as rhymed verse. (p. 182)

Along with his versatile blank-verse form, Thomson's poetic diction for ***The Seasons*** grew from his compulsion to portray in language the complex and transforming patterns of nature. Formal rules of Augustan English were simply not adequate to this task, as even the juvenilia had hinted; Thomson's poetic language in ***The Seasons*** is no more purely Augustan English than is the variety of themes and modes he employs in the poem. It is an eclectic yet decorous literary language, organically linked to the diverse ***Seasons*** genres and themes themselves: neoclassical-georgic, Scottish-descriptive, religious-philosophical and homiletic, and scientific. Thomson, for whom literary English was virtually a foreign language at first, certainly found formal English an uncomfortably restrictive vehicle for his miscellaneous descriptive poem and had thus to experiment with language to create a new poetic diction for his new sort of poetry. His incentive to develop a more versatile diction perhaps had its source in his Scottish naiveté about formal English usage, but ultimately his very Scottish freedom from English aesthetic and linguistic limits, motivated by his strong empirical impulse, came to produce an apt and unique poetic language. More immediately, Thomson's background as a Scots speaker actually influenced the words he chose and the sound patterns he composed. His language potential was not merely bilingual (Latin, English) but trilingual (Scots); in seeking accuracy and comprehensiveness, he succeeded in expanding English poetic diction through Latinate neo-aureation (much as his forebear Gavin Douglas had done), through exploitation of biblical and homiletic elements and scientific terms, and, most significantly, through use of Scots and northern vocabulary. (pp. 183-84)

His poetic language followed no ready-made poetic formula, Augustan or otherwise, and while he indeed borrowed from Milton, Philips, and many others, his poetic language could never simply be called derivative. Rather, it grew naturally from his miscellaneous subject matter and sources, as in an important sense the poet applied the empirical scientific method to the synthesis of his own literary language, observing, experimenting with, and discovering the dynamic means to convey the world-in-process and man's relationship to it. In so doing, the poet also exemplified the changing aesthetic principles of his time which encouraged more varied and original, as well as more realistic, descriptive diction and imagery. (pp. 184-85)

One element of Thomson's linguistic experimentation was his enthusiastic coinage of new words. Most notable are his compound epithets, condensing and intensifying description. These compounds were mostly used as adjectives, joining verb with participle; for example, "gay-shifting"; "mute-imploring" (***Spring***); "prone-descending" (***Summer***). He occasionally joined two nouns together, suggesting the archaic, periphrastic "kenning" (for example, "Summer-Ray," **"Hymn,"** with its compact connotative force; or "Forest-Walks," ***Spring***). He also tried unusual "unpoetic" or colloquial words, even alongside of Latin or formal English ones, if they could convey more precisely what he intended to describe. He freely exchanged parts of speech when expedient: participles function as nouns ("Bleatings," ***Spring***); intransitive verbs become transitive ("looking lively Gratitude," ***Spring***); and adjectives are often used with adverbial force (for example, "Man superior walks"; "Earth / Is deep enrich'd"; "Radiance instantaneous strikes"; "Sun / Looks out, *effulgent*"; "Shower is *scarce* to patter heard" ***(Spring)***. These unusual "quasi-adverbs" (as the *OED* labels them) set up a certain ambiguity as to whether they modify their nouns or whether they are simply contracted adverbs and thus refer to the verbs. In fact, while grammatically they are inverted adjectives, they also add a new dimension to the description through the tension they create, adding to the interpretation of the verb as well and drawing noun and verb into closer, active relationship. "Man superior walks," for instance, indicates that man is superior to the rest of earthly Creation and also describes his proud manner of walking and his active role as the world's overseer. "Shower is scarce to patter heard" suggests both the sparse quantity and the gentle, quiet aural quality of the falling rain. Thomson's deletion of the adverbial suffix *-ly* in many quasi-adverbs also calls to mind the typical Middle Scots contraction of certain adjectives, such as "contrair," "extraordinair," "necessair," which were likewise transposed, placed after their nouns; such variations of orthography and syntax in Thomson's poetic language give it further archaic, and Scots, flavor.

Another characteristic of Thomson's empirical adaptation of language is his use of abundant verbs and verb forms, particularly participles; he is fascinated with verbals and experiments freely with them, the better to describe in terms of action and transformation. He shares such descriptive energy with the ballads and also with the Middle Scots Makars. Thomson's Scottish trilingual heritage generally allowed for a greater flexibility of usage and syntax—since Scots and Latin syntaxes both differ from standard English—than his English contemporaries dared to attempt in poetry. Such traits as these represent what some critics have censured as "vague," indecorous, or incorrect characteristics of Thomson's diction; they should instead be recognized as examples of the subtlety, complexity, and native originality of the Scottish poet's descriptive language as he portrays the natural world-in-process. (pp. 185-86)

The most often remarked—and reproved—characteristic of Thomson's language in ***The Seasons*** is its pervasive Latinity. While this quality has been studied in some detail, there has been scant attention paid to its roots in the poet's Scottish culture and education. In formal Augustan English poetry, Latinisms are, of course, standard, but in invoking the Scoto-Roman ideal he so revered and directly drawing upon its classical vocabulary, Thomson added a further, Scottish dimension to the neoclassical linguistic convention of the age. Passages illustrating Thomson's Latinity abound in ***The Seasons;*** one such is the ***Spring*** shower, where many of the examples cited here occur. Much of Thomson's Latinate diction derives from Virgil, particularly in the more descriptive scenes adapted from the *Georgics;* some passages are virtually paraphrases of Virgil, while others blend Latinate with other types of language. Thomson adapted Virgilian rhetorical devices, notably periphrasis, to achieve control and precision of descriptive language. Despauter's textbook defines periphrasis as an indirect, circumlocutory way of saying something in few but meaningful words; it is based in logic and is one means of classifying or placing an element of a complicated scene into perspective. Thomson typically used the device to highlight a particular group, without describing its members individually, within the larger landscape; examples from ***Spring*** are "plumy People" (birds), "umbrageous Multitude of Leaves," and "milky Nutriment" (life-giving sap).

Use of strongly Latinate English was also a Miltonic trait; Thomson's Latinate language in ***The Seasons,*** however, surpasses even Milton's in density. Most significant is Thomson's frequent use of words in their original Latin sense to achieve precision; he seems at times actually to "think" in Latin, choosing words directly from that familiar language which had not yet been filtered through literary English. Examples are "Indulge" in the original sense of "yield, give up," and "Gems" (***Spring***) in the sense of "buds" as well as colorful jewels. Another instance is the revealing word "Cogenial" (***Winter***), as the poet hails the season's "Cogenial Horrors." Where one would have expected the poet to choose the standard Latinate-English "congenial," his unusual Latin "Cogenial" implies a more intimate, one-to-one relationship between himself and the well-known Scottish season; the distinction, though fine, is real. (pp. 186-87)

Latin had long been Scotland's second language, her formal diplomatic language; Latin had directly influenced Middle Scots, and while Scots had suffered a loss in status by the eighteenth century, Latin maintained its close kinship with Scottish literature as the ideal literary language. English as a literary medium ran a poor third until that time. After his native Scots, then, Latin was Thomson's second language at school and at university; he was less familiar even with colloquial English than he was with Latin. His classical education and cultural bias disposed him to choose words with a Latin root over Southern English words in seeking both descriptive accuracy and rich connotation. Thomson's Latinate language in ***The Seasons*** has occasioned problems for those of a different linguistic background than his own; numerous critics from his own day to the present have insensitively charged him with obscurity and pomposity due to the strong Latinate cast of his language. But Thomson's aureation was far from a pretentious attempt merely to elevate the formal tone of the poetry; the poet drew upon Latin consciously to strengthen the expressive, descriptive power and precision of literary English. He actually added to the stock of poetical diction in English in a process eminently comparable to Gavin Douglas's enrichment of literary Middle Scots. Far from being forced or stilted, Thomson's Latinate diction came naturally and easily to him as a Lowland Scot and usually succeeded in conveying exactly what he intended. So persistent has been the classical bias in Scottish schooling that the educated Scotsman even today would have little problem with Thomson's Latinate diction. The poet's Latinate linguistic facility contributes enormously to the economy and accuracy of his descriptions and constantly manifests, especially to the classically tuned reader, Thomson's Scottish humanistic heritage.

Thomson's rhetorical faults, like his strengths, are very much rooted in his Scottish formal education. These faults include his occasional tendency toward verbosity and his predilection for the grandiose rhetorical flourish or convoluted construction. Such lapses, where the sonorous effects of the words themselves obscure and overpower their sense and proportion, usually occurred in his more public and Augustan voice, where abstract ideas and bombastic pronouncements left little room for natural description. The art and science of rhetoric had become something of a Scottish preoccupation by the eighteenth century and would come into its own as a Scottish Enlightenment achievement. . . . In writing descriptive poetry, Thomson was working in the classical rhetorical mode of imitation—"setting forth the nature of a 'thing' in words"—with new, more realistic focus on those "things" themselves. He was seeking to describe as fully and accurately as he could, but his rhetorical discipline was liable to fail him when he left the concrete basis of *descriptio,* or when in his enthusiasm for comprehensive expression he simply said too much and lost perspective. Nonetheless, Thomson's training in rhetoric was most often an advantage in helping him to integrate and "improve" such diverse subjects and styles as his ambitious ***Seasons*** encompasses.

Thomson's upbringing as a son of the manse and divinity student, like his education in the humanities and classical rhetoric, had considerable impact on his poetic style. Language derived from Christian Neoplatonic philosophy and physicotheology and from the religious poetry of Milton is abundantly present in ***The Seasons;*** more directly, the very language of the Scriptures is there, along with the forceful rhetoric of the old-style Presbyterian pulpit. These influences were important even in the juvenilia. ***The Seasons'*** motivation being primarily a religious one, both devotional and didactic functions operate in the poem; the persuasive power of classical rhetoric is reinforced by the rhetoric of the Bible and the sermon. Both the rigorous homiletic tone and the "mystical" enthusiastic tone, demonstrating two sides of Thomson's deep-seated Scottish Calvinist emotional response, resound throughout ***The Seasons.*** Scriptural allusions in the poem are almost all from the *Old Testament* with few exceptions; most echo *Job, Genesis, Ruth, Ecclesiastes,* and the *Psalms.* Several passages in the poem show direct influence of the *Psalms,* such as the **"Hymn on the Seasons,"** closely based on *Psalm 148* in language and structure as well as theme; it is typical of several such enthusiastic, exuberant "praising" passages in the poem. Like other "religious" passages in ***The Seasons,*** the **"Hymn"** illustrates subtle linguistic blending, and Latinisms abound. Alliteration is strong, enhancing imitative sound effects and forward, intensifying movement; typically, verbs and verbals are plentiful and well chosen. Natural description is inherent in the religious and rhetorical purpose of this Psalm paraphrase, which shows Thomson in his happiest mode, portraying God's Creation in joyous process.

Even more significant is the influence of the traditional Scottish sermon, with its negative rhetoric of fear and trepidation. Thomson's stern religious-didactic "preaching" voice is heard in both manner and message of such passages as ***Summer*** on "CREATIVE WISDOM" and the vanity of those who disregard it ("LET no presuming impious Railer tax / CREATIVE WISDOM"). The passage concludes with a powerful parable, typical of the highly literal and concrete, image-laden Scottish sermon style:

> THICK in yon Stream of Light, a thousand Ways,
> Upward, and downward, thwarting, and convolv'd,
> The quivering Nations sport; till, Tempest-wing'd,
> Fierce Winter sweeps them from the Face of Day.
> Even so luxurious Men, unheeding, pass
> An idle Summer-Life in Fortune's Shine,
> A Season's Glitter! Thus they flutter on

From Toy to Toy, from Vanity to Vice;
Till, blown away by Death, Oblivion comes
Behind, and strikes them from the Book of Life.

Here Thomson blends Latinate language ("convolv'd," "luxurious," periphrastic "quivering Nations") and his own brand of concise descriptive epithet ("Tempest-wing'd") with increasingly intense homiletic language. Visual metaphors of men "fluttering" like insects in a realm of "Shine" and "Glitter," from "Toy to Toy," then "blown away" and struck from the "Book of Life" work more through cumulative force than descriptive precision: the comparison between vulnerable insects and men carries great emotional impact. The adverbial "Even so" falls heavy with didactic emphasis, clarifying the analogy and imitating the sudden, frightening force of death's ("Fierce Winter" 's) final blow; the conventional seasonal symbol of death as winter is apt and contrasts pointedly with the summer context of the parable. Parallelism, alliteration, and repetition ("from the Face of Day," "from Toy to Toy," "from Vanity to Vice," "from the Book of Life") reinforce the message of vain man's inexorable march to death and ultimate spiritual exile ("from") into "Oblivion." (pp. 187-91)

Along with these religious and classical influences on his language, Thomson also employs the language of science, more sparingly but to good effect, in ***The Seasons.*** While this general topic has been the subject of study elsewhere, it is important to recall that Thomson's scientific vocabulary was to a great extent based on Newtonian concepts acquired at Edinburgh University and also later in London; such diction contributes to the didactic function of the poem as well as its description. One example is the "rainbow" passage in ***Spring,*** where Thomson pays explicit tribute to Newton and uses such technical terms as "refracted" and "Prism," adding realism and demonstrating his own "sage-instructed Eye," his knowledge of the laws of nature first learned in Scotland. He simultaneously portrays the swain's wonder at the beautiful phenomenon, a delight he himself never lost, lending his description double the impact.

Classical, religious, and scientific influences on Thomson's diction, while Scottish in that they were the languages of the various disciplines to which he was educated in the Borders and Edinburgh, still cannot fully account for the extraordinary immediacy and vigor of the descriptions in ***The Seasons.*** Thomson required a still broader, more versatile and expressive literary language, and he set out to forge it. The poet's successful and original use of language in ***The Seasons*** comes in large measure from his background as a Scots speaker. He retained a Scots accent and Scots expressions all his life and certainly knew Scots literature and oral tradition. While this is not to say that Scotticisms and northern archaisms abound in ***The Seasons,*** some are there, and clearly Thomson's choice of descriptive diction owes a very great deal to his Scots habit of mind.

Perhaps the most striking stylistic quality about Thomson's poetic language coming from his Scots-speaking background is his close attention to sound effects. The poet himself, in a passage in ***Summer,*** placed "Music" before "Image," "Sentiment," and "Thought" in listing the chief characteristics of poetry, and his own "Music" sounds a pleasingly native note. Thomson's choice of descriptive language very often reflects those traits of written and spoken Scots which contribute to its acknowledged expressive power, such as abundant alliteration, which he uses especially strongly in passages describing action and process in nature, as well as assonance and consonance. He also shows a general tendency to choose onomatopoeic and imitative words, or more broadly words whose sounds enhance their meanings; Scots vocabulary itself claims a large proportion of imitative words whose very sounds evoke their sense. Such skillful use of "extended onomatopoeia" and imitative sound patterns was evident even in the juvenile poems; the poet's preoccupation with intricate and subtle sound effects can be compared in some points to Scottish Gaelic poetic modes which had, in turn, influenced the Lowland Scots literature and language he knew. Thomson was extraordinarily sensitive to the emotional connotations or suggestive values of certain sounds and wove in ***The Seasons*** delicate designs of "sound-symbolism"; his sound effects are not merely decorative but organic and help to convey his intellectual, emotional, and especially sensuous meanings in descriptive poetry.

Beyond indirect, aural influence on Thomson's use of sound effects, Scots language was a more immediate influence on his diction, as the poet employed a number of actual Scots or northern words and derivatives in ***The Seasons.*** Further, his Scots linguistic background predisposed him to choose certain English words with close similarity of sound and sense to Scots words and carrying their richer connotative value. Thomson's deliberate use of Scots vocabulary is perhaps the most relevant and convincing illustration in ***The Seasons*** of the poet's general, instinctive "etymological" curiosity, his informed interest in the origin and history of the meanings of words themselves. This sensitivity to the sources of language had also compelled him to choose Latin words in their original sense and would later influence his significant use of archaic language in ***The Castle.*** In ***The Seasons,*** Scottish linguistic influences are seen most clearly in the language of passages of most pure, energetic, and immediate natural description, often derived from first-hand Scottish experience, where the rare quality of race or native vitality which Dr. Johnson had praised is its strongest. Some brief passages will illustrate that race which is the happy result of Thomson's Scottish linguistic background.

This passage from ***Autumn,*** demonstrating Thomson's sympathy with animals and elaborating on a similar scene in **"Of a Country Life,"** describes the hunted hare's futile search for refuge from her predators:

POOR is the Triumph o'er the timid Hare!
Scar'd from the Corn, and now to some lone Seat
Retir'd: the rushy Fen; the ragged Furze,
Stretch'd o'er the stony Heath; the Stubble chapt;
The thistly Lawn; the thick entangled Broom;
Of the same friendly Hue, the wither'd Fern;
The fallow Ground laid open to the Sun,
Concoctive; and the nodding sandy Bank,
Hung o'er the Mazes of the Mountain-Brook.

Thick alliteration reinforces natural description here in Thomson's characteristic sound-sense patterning: "rushy Fen . . . ragged Furze," "friendly Hue . . . Fern . . . fallow" (Scots rolled *r* and fricative *f* alliteration imitate the rustling sounds of the hare's swift movement through the varied landscape); "Stretch'd . . . stony . . . Stubble," "thistly Lawn . . . thick" (repetition of *st* and *th* phonemes suggests friction as the hare forces its way through obstructions in the rugged terrain); "Mazes of the Mountain-Brook" (softer *m* mimics slow, gentle winding and murmur of the stream). In general, imitative alliteration facilitates the sense of rapid yet cautious forward movement of the hare's search for shelter. Thomson's individual word choices also typically enhance extended onomatopoeia ("Stubble," "ragged," "chapt," "thistly," "entangled") as their sounds contribute to the sense of difficult passage (abruptness suggested by double consonants *bb, gg, pp;* "thistly" 's fricative; multisyllabic "entangled"). Thomson further follows the practice, common in older Scottish poetry, of listing the elements of the varied landscape while simultaneously describing them with apt adjectives and effective alliteration; this concise cataloging, quickly shifting descriptive focus from point to point, also imitates the hare's frantic movements. The setting is probably Scottish: hints are "thistly" (the thistle is the Scottish national flower, though not exclusive to Scotland) and the Scotticism "chapt" ("having been dealt a blow, cut down—a variation of 'chopped,' " *Dictionary of the Older Scottish Tongue*). "O'er," which occurs frequently in the poem, is of course conventional poetical diction but also reflects current Scottish pronunciation of "over," according to James Beattie. The Latinism "Concoctive" stands out amid more colloquial descriptive language: "Sun / Concoctive" is one of Thomson's "quasi-adverbs" and conveys the sun's mysterious power as well as the complex process of natural chemistry happening within the "fallow Ground." (pp. 192-96)

The following passage [from the 1744 version of ***Winter,*** lines 94-105], describing a Scottish Border scene of a river in spate, has been compared to Burns's description in "Brigs of Ayr." It likewise illustrates Thomson's skill at dynamic natural description:

> WIDE o'er the Brim, with many a Torrent swell'd,
> And the mix'd Ruin of its Banks o'erspread,
> At last the rous'd-up River pours along:
> Resistless, roaring, dreadful, down it comes,
> From the rude Mountain, and the mossy Wild,
> Tumbling thro' Rocks abrupt, and sounding far;
> Then o'er the sanded Valley floating spreads,
> Calm, sluggish, silent; till again constrain'd,
> Between two meeting Hills it bursts a Way,
> Where Rocks and Woods o'erhang the turbid Stream;
> There gathering triple Force, rapid, and deep,
> It boils, and wheels, and foams, and thunders' thro'.

This scene was original to ***Winter*** (1726). The Scots adjective "chapt" appeared here in early versions (1726-1738) describing the bare, rugged mountain; it was altered with "loss of race" to "rude" (l. 98) in 1744. Otherwise, the passage seems to have lost little race in revision and even to have gained in descriptive impact. The passage opens with a quasi-adverb "WIDE," describing both the river itself and its spreading action (i.e., widely). Thomson retained the most effective alliterative line, "Resistless, roaring, dreadful, down it comes," with its strong caesuras and suggestion of the northern alliterative line. To this he prefixed "At last the rous'd-up River pours along": the added *r* alliteration enhances the sense of the river's motion and sound. The *d* alliteration, with its negative sound associations, suggests falling, colliding heavily, as does the *u* assonance of the phrase "Tumbling thro' Rocks abrupt." Even the rhythm of the phrase adds to its descriptive force, as the explosive, forward-moving participle "Tumbling," perhaps given the Scots pronunciation "tummling," contrasts with the contracted "abrupt," transposed to come at the end of the line, imitating the water's sudden impact with rocks. Thomson's characteristic coupling of participle with quasi-adverb ("abrupt") concisely conveys the river's action in addition to the position of the rocks themselves; "abrupt" is probably used in both the geological sense of "suddenly cropping out" (*OED*) and the original Latin sense of "breaking," that is, interrupting the river's flow. This is yet another example of Thomson's acute etymological awareness. As the river slows ("Then o'er the sanded Valley floating spreads, / Calm, sluggish, silent") sibilant *s* alliteration predominates, suggesting smoother, gentler motion and quietening; imitative words ("sluggish") also lend realism. The river regains momentum, having been "constrained" between two hills; the weighty Latinism "constrained" creates a concise image of the compacted, forceful water. Then the released river "boils, and wheels, and foams, and thunders' thro' "; this line repeats, with slight variation, the energetic caesura pattern of line 97. Thomson also catalogs the river's various actions here in verbs whose sounds reinforce their descriptive sense. Again, the poet has proven his consummate skill at describing, with a strong sense of dramatic pacing, the dynamic events of nature. (pp. 196-97)

Even though . . . many Scotticisms and racy English words bearing Scottish connotations had been excised from ***The Seasons,*** the fact that Thomson kept so many more proves that he had hardly abandoned his Scots linguistic heritage; on the contrary, he sensed that Scots words—their sounds and meanings—were a vital force in his poetic expression. Over years of revisions he made the effort to eliminate Scotticisms and northern or local usages which might not have been as clear or resonant to English as to Scottish readers, but he still allowed some to remain, as if he could not bear to part with such expressive, evocative, and, to him, accurate descriptive language, especially where Scots associations could enhance standard English definitions. With these, he still further expanded and enriched English poetic diction.

James Thomson's use of language in ***The Seasons*** was daring indeed for a Scottish poet in eighteenth-century England, as William Somerville had warned. But Thomson's bold Anglo-Scottish experimentation proved surprisingly successful. He discovered the natural flexibility and flow of blank verse for a poetry describing the processes of nature. Sensitivity to the sounds of words and their infinitely varied patterns, too, seemed to come naturally to him; he was already attuned to the descriptive possibilities of such northern sound effects as alliteration, which he used skillfully to compose subtle imitative patterns capturing the music and movement as well as the moods of the natural world. In the Enlightenment spirit of empiricism, Thomson tried new words and new usages for old words. He adapted Latinate English and even Latin words themselves to his comprehensive descriptive purpose. He borrowed both from the traditional language of the *Bible* and the Scottish sermon and from the fresh-minted language of contemporary philosophy and science. Most especially, he invoked the strength of his native Scots speech to intensify emotional response and at the same time to sharpen descriptive precision in his complex poem. Thomson accomplished the Virgilian ideal of progressive adaptation which inspires ***The Seasons*** generally by applying it to language, transforming conventional, formal literary English to meet his own descriptive needs and to "control" and ultimately improve nature through poetic art. Thus did Thomson create his highly original and genuinely Anglo-Scottish poetic idiom in the cause of natural description. (pp. 202-03)

Mary Jane W. Scott, in her James Thomson: Anglo-Scot, *The University of Georgia Press, 1988, 373 p.*

FURTHER READING

Aubin, Robert Arnold. *Topographical Poetry in XVIII-Century England.* New York: Modern Language Association of America, 1936, 419 p.

Identifies Thomson as a seminal representative of the genre of topographical poetry.

Barrell, John. *The Idea of Landscape and the Sense of Place, 1730-1840: An Approach to the Poetry of John Clare.* Cambridge: Cambridge University Press, 1972, 244 p.

Discusses the influence of Italian landscape painting on Thomson's poetic technique, as well as Thomson's impact on the poetry of John Clare.

Bush, Douglas. "Newtonianism, Rationalism, and Sentimentalism." In his *Science and English Poetry: A Historical Sketch, 1590-1950,* pp. 51-78. New York: Oxford University Press, 1950.

Includes comments on the Newtonian inspiration of Thomson's poetry of Nature. According to Bush, Thomson, like Newton, viewed God as immanent in all creation, and not merely, as the Deists believed, as a cosmic First Cause.

Campbell, Hilbert H. *James Thomson.* Boston: Twayne Publishers, 1979, 175 p.

Introductory biographical and critical study. Campbell traces the life and major works of Thomson, and examines his reputation and influence.

Chalker, John. "Thomson's *Seasons.*" In his *The English Georgic: A Study in the Development of a Form,* pp. 90-140. Baltimore: Johns Hopkins Press, 1969.

Chalker traces the sources of Thomson's pastoral motifs to Vergil's *Georgics.* Other classical influences are recognized, including Ovid and Lucretius, but Thomson's inspiration, Chalker maintains, is principally Vergilian.

Courthope, W. J. "Philosophical English Poetry in the Eighteenth Century: Influence of Deism, Nature-Worship, Liberty, and the Arts." In his *A History of English Poetry,* Vol. V, pp. 272-326. London: Macmillan, 1905.

Includes a concise overview of Thomson's life and works, with critical commentary on *The Seasons* and *The Castle of Indolence.*

Gosse, Edmund. "The Dawn of Naturalism in Poetry." In his *A History of Eighteenth Century Literature,* pp. 207-41. New York: Macmillan Co., 1924.

Chapter contains a succinct biographical and critical survey of Thomson's life and career.

Grant, Douglas, *James Thomson, Poet of "The Seasons."* London: Cresset Press, 1951, 308 p.

Considered the standard biography of Thomson. This richly documented work also includes lengthy commentaries on *The Seasons* and *The Castle of Indolence.*

Manwaring, Elizabeth Wheeler. *Italian Landscape in Eighteenth Century England,* pp. 101 ff. New York: Oxford University Press, 1925.

Argues that Thomson drew his inspiration and descriptive modes from landscape painters such as Salvator Rosa and Claude Lorraine.

McKillop, Alan D. *The Background of Thomson's Seasons.* Minneapolis: University of Minnesota Press, 1942, 191 p.

Provides the intellectual background of Thomson's poem, with reference to scientific and philosophical works which influenced the poet.

Nicoll, Allardyce. "Pseudo-Classic Tragedies." In his *A History of English Drama,* pp. 85-95. Cambridge: Cambridge University Press, 1969.

Includes a brief discussion of Thomson's tragedies.

Reynolds, Myra. *The Treatment of Nature in English Poetry between Pope and Wordsworth* pp. 83-111. Chicago: University of Chicago Press, 1896.

Includes a discussion of Thomson, defining him as a precursor of Romanticism.

Spacks, Patricia Meyer. "Vision and Meaning in James Thomson." *Studies in Romanticism* IV, No. 4 (Summer 1965): 206-19.

Argues that Thomson's descriptive technique was affected by his realization that description never faithfully reflects its object.

Spencer, Jeffry B. "James Thomson and Ideal Landscape: The Triumph of Pictorialism." In his *Heroic Nature: Ideal Landscape in English Poetry from Marvell to Thomson,* pp. 253-95. Evanston, Ill.: Northwestern University Press, 1973.

Examines the impact of landscape art on Thomson's descriptive technique. Arguing against the traditional view which connects Thomson to Claude Lorrain and Salvator Rosa, Spencer suggests Guido Reni, Annibale Carraci, and Nicolas Poussin as possible sources of inspiration.

Stephen, Sir Leslie. "Thomson." In his *History of English*

Thought in the Eighteenth Century, Vol. II, pp. 360-62. New York: G. P. Putnam's Sons, 1876.

Includes a discussion of the intellectual background of Thomson's poetry. Stephen posits that Thomson, despite his emotional response to nature, assumed an intellectual attitude, viewing it as the ultimate argument against atheism.

Strachey, Lytton. "The Poetry of Thomson." In his *Spectatorial Essays,* pp. 153-59. New York: Harcourt, Brace & World, 1964.

An unfavorable review of G. C. Macaulay's work on Thomson (see excerpt dated 1908). Taking Macaulay to task for his praise of Thomson, Strachey declares that Thomson "was not a landscape painter but a rhetorician."

Thompson, Francis. "James Thomson." *The Academy* n.s. 51, No. 1302 (17 April 1897): 417.

Denigrates Thomson as a poet whose name "stands for little or nothing." Thompson claims Thomson's name is preserved only because of its frequent association with the names of John Milton and William Wordsworth.

Wilson, John. "A Few Words on Thomson." In his *The Recreations of Christopher North,* pp. 260-67. Philadelphia: Carey & Hart, 1845.

Discusses and praises *The Seasons* at length.

Literature Criticism from 1400 to 1800

Cumulative Indexes

This Index Includes References to Entries in These Gale Series

Contemporary Literary Criticism Presents excerpts of criticism on the works of novelists, poets, dramatists, short story writers, scriptwriters, and other creative writers who are now living or who have died since 1960.

Twentieth-Century Literary Criticism Contains critical excerpts by the most significant commentators on poets, novelists, short story writers, dramatists, and philosophers who died between 1900 and 1960.

Nineteenth-Century Literature Criticism Offers significant passages from criticism on authors who died between 1800 and 1899.

Literature Criticism from 1400 to 1800 Compiles significant passages from the most noteworthy criticism on authors of the fifteenth through eighteenth centuries.

Classical and Medieval Literature Criticism Offers excerpts of criticism on the works of world authors from classical antiquity through the fourteenth century.

Short Story Criticism Compiles excerpts of criticism on short fiction by writers of all eras and nationalities.

Poetry Criticism Presents excerpts of criticism on the works of poets from all eras, movements, and nationalities.

Children's Literature Review Includes excerpts from reviews, criticism, and commentary on works of authors and illustrators who create books for children.

Contemporary Authors Series Encompasses five related series. *Contemporary Authors* provides biographical and bibliographical information on more than 97,000 writers of fiction, nonfiction, poetry, journalism, drama, motion pictures, and other fields. Each new volume contains sketches on authors not previously covered in the series. *Contemporary Authors New Revision Series* provides completely updated information on active authors covered in previously published volumes of *CA*. Only entries requiring significant change are revised for *CA New Revision Series. Contemporary Authors Permanent Series* consists of updated listings for deceased and inactive authors removed from the original volumes 9-36 when these volumes were revised. *Contemporary Authors Autobiography Series* presents specially commissioned autobiographies by leading contemporary writers. *Contemporary Authors Bibliographical Series* contains primary and secondary bibliographies as well as analytical bibliographical essays by authorities on major modern authors.

Dictionary of Literary Biography Encompasses three related series. *Dictionary of Literary Biography* furnishes illustrated overviews of authors' lives and works and places them in the larger perspective of literary history. *Dictionary of Literary Biography Documentary Series* illuminates the careers of major figures through a selection of literary documents, including letters, notebook and diary entries, interviews, book reviews, and photographs. *Dictionary of Literary Biography Yearbook* summarizes the past year's literary activity with articles on genres, major prizes, conferences, and other timely subjects and includes updated and new entries on individual authors.

Concise Dictionary of American Literary Biography A six-volume series that collects revised and updated sketches on major American authors that were originally presented in *Dictionary of Literary Biography.*

Something about the Author Series Encompasses three related series. *Something about the Author* contains well-illustrated biographical sketches on juvenile and young adult authors and illustrators from all eras. *Something about the Author Autobiography Series* presents specially commissioned autobiographies by prominent authors and illustrators of books for children and young adults.

Yesterday's Authors of Books for Children Contains heavily illustrated entries on children's writers who died before 1961. Complete in two volumes.

Literary Criticism Series Cumulative Author Index

This index lists all author entries in the Gale Literary Criticism Series and includes cross-references to other Gale sources. References in the index are identified as follows:

AAYA: *Authors & Artists for Young Adults,* Volumes 1-6
CAAS: *Contemporary Authors Autobiography Series,* Volumes 1-13
CA: *Contemporary Authors* (original series), Volumes 1-132
CABS: *Contemporary Authors Bibliographical Series,* Volumes 1-3
CANR: *Contemporary Authors New Revision Series,* Volumes 1-33
CAP: *Contemporary Authors Permanent Series,* Volumes 1-2
CA-R: *Contemporary Authors* (revised editions), Volumes 1-44
CDALB: *Concise Dictionary of American Literary Biography,* Volumes 1-6
CLC: *Contemporary Literary Criticism,* Volumes 1-65
CLR: *Children's Literature Review,* Volumes 1-24
CMLC: *Classical and Medieval Literature Criticism,* Volumes 1-6
DC: *Drama Criticism,* Volume 1
DLB: *Dictionary of Literary Biography,* Volumes 1-104
DLB-DS: *Dictionary of Literary Biography Documentary Series,* Volumes 1-8
DLB-Y: *Dictionary of Literary Biography Yearbook,* Volumes 1980-1988
LC: *Literature Criticism from 1400 to 1800,* Volumes 1-16
NCLC: *Nineteenth-Century Literature Criticism,* Volumes 1-30
PC: *Poetry Criticism,* Volumes 2-2
SAAS: *Something about the Author Autobiography Series,* Volumes 1-12
SATA: *Something about the Author,* Volumes 1-64
SSC: *Short Story Criticism,* Volumes 1-7
TCLC: *Twentieth-Century Literary Criticism,* Volumes 1-40
YABC: *Yesterday's Authors of Books for Children,* Volumes 1-2

Literary Criticism Series Cumulative Topic Index

Topic Index

This index lists all topic entries in the Gale Literary Criticism Series *Contemporary Literary Criticism, Literature Criticism from 1400 to 1800, Nineteenth-Century Literature Criticism,* and *Twentieth-Century Literary Criticism.*

LC Cumulative Nationality Index

LC Cumulative Title Index

Title Index

Title Index

Title Index

Title Index

Title Index

Title Index

Title Index

Title Index

Title Index

Title Index